Lecture Notes in Computer Science 13687

More information about this series at https://link.springer.com/bookseries/558

Shai Avidan · Gabriel Brostow ·
Moustapha Cissé · Giovanni Maria Farinella ·
Tal Hassner (Eds.)

Computer Vision – ECCV 2022

17th European Conference
Tel Aviv, Israel, October 23–27, 2022
Proceedings, Part XXVII

Editors
Shai Avidan
Tel Aviv University
Tel Aviv, Israel

Moustapha Cissé
Google AI
Accra, Ghana

Tal Hassner (iD)
Facebook (United States)
Menlo Park, CA, USA

Gabriel Brostow (iD)
University College London
London, UK

Giovanni Maria Farinella (iD)
University of Catania
Catania, Italy

ISSN 0302-9743   ISSN 1611-3349 (electronic)
Lecture Notes in Computer Science
ISBN 978-3-031-19811-3   ISBN 978-3-031-19812-0 (eBook)
https://doi.org/10.1007/978-3-031-19812-0

This Springer imprint is published by the registered company Springer Nature Switzerland AG
The registered company address is: Gewerbestrasse 11, 6330 Cham, Switzerland

Foreword

Organizing the European Conference on Computer Vision (ECCV 2022) in Tel-Aviv during a global pandemic was no easy feat. The uncertainty level was extremely high, and decisions had to be postponed to the last minute. Still, we managed to plan things just in time for ECCV 2022 to be held in person. Participation in physical events is crucial to stimulating collaborations and nurturing the culture of the Computer Vision community.

There were many people who worked hard to ensure attendees enjoyed the best science at the 16th edition of ECCV. We are grateful to the Program Chairs Gabriel Brostow and Tal Hassner, who went above and beyond to ensure the ECCV reviewing process ran smoothly. The scientific program includes dozens of workshops and tutorials in addition to the main conference and we would like to thank Leonid Karlinsky and Tomer Michaeli for their hard work. Finally, special thanks to the web chairs Lorenzo Baraldi and Kosta Derpanis, who put in extra hours to transfer information fast and efficiently to the ECCV community.

We would like to express gratitude to our generous sponsors and the Industry Chairs, Dimosthenis Karatzas and Chen Sagiv, who oversaw industry relations and proposed new ways for academia-industry collaboration and technology transfer. It's great to see so much industrial interest in what we're doing!

Authors' draft versions of the papers appeared online with open access on both the Computer Vision Foundation (CVF) and the European Computer Vision Association (ECVA) websites as with previous ECCVs. Springer, the publisher of the proceedings, has arranged for archival publication. The final version of the papers is hosted by SpringerLink, with active references and supplementary materials. It benefits all potential readers that we offer both a free and citeable version for all researchers, as well as an authoritative, citeable version for SpringerLink readers. Our thanks go to Ronan Nugent from Springer, who helped us negotiate this agreement. Last but not least, we wish to thank Eric Mortensen, our publication chair, whose expertise made the process smooth.

October 2022

Rita Cucchiara
Jiří Matas
Amnon Shashua
Lihi Zelnik-Manor

Preface

Welcome to the proceedings of the European Conference on Computer Vision (ECCV 2022). This was a hybrid edition of ECCV as we made our way out of the COVID-19 pandemic. The conference received 5804 valid paper submissions, compared to 5150 submissions to ECCV 2020 (a 12.7% increase) and 2439 in ECCV 2018. 1645 submissions were accepted for publication (28%) and, of those, 157 (2.7% overall) as orals.

846 of the submissions were desk-rejected for various reasons. Many of them because they revealed author identity, thus violating the double-blind policy. This violation came in many forms: some had author names with the title, others added acknowledgments to specific grants, yet others had links to their github account where their name was visible. Tampering with the LaTeX template was another reason for automatic desk rejection.

ECCV 2022 used the traditional CMT system to manage the entire double-blind reviewing process. Authors did not know the names of the reviewers and vice versa. Each paper received at least 3 reviews (except 6 papers that received only 2 reviews), totalling more than 15,000 reviews.

Handling the review process at this scale was a significant challenge. To ensure that each submission received as fair and high-quality reviews as possible, we recruited more than 4719 reviewers (in the end, 4719 reviewers did at least one review). Similarly we recruited more than 276 area chairs (eventually, only 276 area chairs handled a batch of papers). The area chairs were selected based on their technical expertise and reputation, largely among people who served as area chairs in previous top computer vision and machine learning conferences (ECCV, ICCV, CVPR, NeurIPS, etc.).

Reviewers were similarly invited from previous conferences, and also from the pool of authors. We also encouraged experienced area chairs to suggest additional chairs and reviewers in the initial phase of recruiting. The median reviewer load was five papers per reviewer, while the average load was about four papers, because of the emergency reviewers. The area chair load was 35 papers, on average.

Conflicts of interest between authors, area chairs, and reviewers were handled largely automatically by the CMT platform, with some manual help from the Program Chairs. Reviewers were allowed to describe themselves as senior reviewer (load of 8 papers to review) or junior reviewers (load of 4 papers). Papers were matched to area chairs based on a subject-area affinity score computed in CMT and an affinity score computed by the Toronto Paper Matching System (TPMS). TPMS is based on the paper's full text. An area chair handling each submission would bid for preferred expert reviewers, and we balanced load and prevented conflicts.

The assignment of submissions to area chairs was relatively smooth, as was the assignment of submissions to reviewers. A small percentage of reviewers were not happy with their assignments in terms of subjects and self-reported expertise. This is an area for improvement, although it's interesting that many of these cases were reviewers hand-picked by AC's. We made a later round of reviewer recruiting, targeted at the list of authors of papers submitted to the conference, and had an excellent response which helped provide enough emergency reviewers. In the end, all but six papers received at least 3 reviews.

The challenges of the reviewing process are in line with past experiences at ECCV 2020. As the community grows, and the number of submissions increases, it becomes ever more challenging to recruit enough reviewers and ensure a high enough quality of reviews. Enlisting authors by default as reviewers might be one step to address this challenge.

Authors were given a week to rebut the initial reviews, and address reviewers' concerns. Each rebuttal was limited to a single pdf page with a fixed template.

The Area Chairs then led discussions with the reviewers on the merits of each submission. The goal was to reach consensus, but, ultimately, it was up to the Area Chair to make a decision. The decision was then discussed with a buddy Area Chair to make sure decisions were fair and informative. The entire process was conducted virtually with no in-person meetings taking place.

The Program Chairs were informed in cases where the Area Chairs overturned a decisive consensus reached by the reviewers, and pushed for the meta-reviews to contain details that explained the reasoning for such decisions. Obviously these were the most contentious cases, where reviewer inexperience was the most common reported factor.

Once the list of accepted papers was finalized and released, we went through the laborious process of plagiarism (including self-plagiarism) detection. A total of 4 accepted papers were rejected because of that.

Finally, we would like to thank our Technical Program Chair, Pavel Lifshits, who did tremendous work behind the scenes, and we thank the tireless CMT team.

October 2022

Gabriel Brostow
Giovanni Maria Farinella
Moustapha Cissé
Shai Avidan
Tal Hassner

Organization

General Chairs

Rita Cucchiara	University of Modena and Reggio Emilia, Italy
Jiří Matas	Czech Technical University in Prague, Czech Republic
Amnon Shashua	Hebrew University of Jerusalem, Israel
Lihi Zelnik-Manor	Technion – Israel Institute of Technology, Israel

Program Chairs

Shai Avidan	Tel-Aviv University, Israel
Gabriel Brostow	University College London, UK
Moustapha Cissé	Google AI, Ghana
Giovanni Maria Farinella	University of Catania, Italy
Tal Hassner	Facebook AI, USA

Program Technical Chair

Pavel Lifshits	Technion – Israel Institute of Technology, Israel

Workshops Chairs

Leonid Karlinsky	IBM Research, Israel
Tomer Michaeli	Technion – Israel Institute of Technology, Israel
Ko Nishino	Kyoto University, Japan

Tutorial Chairs

Thomas Pock	Graz University of Technology, Austria
Natalia Neverova	Facebook AI Research, UK

Demo Chair

Bohyung Han	Seoul National University, Korea

Social and Student Activities Chairs

Tatiana Tommasi   Italian Institute of Technology, Italy
Sagie Benaim   University of Copenhagen, Denmark

Diversity and Inclusion Chairs

Xi Yin   Facebook AI Research, USA
Bryan Russell   Adobe, USA

Communications Chairs

Lorenzo Baraldi   University of Modena and Reggio Emilia, Italy
Kosta Derpanis   York University & Samsung AI Centre Toronto,
                                      Canada

Industrial Liaison Chairs

Dimosthenis Karatzas   Universitat Autònoma de Barcelona, Spain
Chen Sagiv   SagivTech, Israel

Finance Chair

Gerard Medioni   University of Southern California & Amazon,
                                      USA

Publication Chair

Eric Mortensen   MiCROTEC, USA

Area Chairs

Lourdes Agapito   University College London, UK
Zeynep Akata   University of Tübingen, Germany
Naveed Akhtar   University of Western Australia, Australia
Karteek Alahari   Inria Grenoble Rhône-Alpes, France
Alexandre Alahi   École polytechnique fédérale de Lausanne,
                                      Switzerland
Pablo Arbelaez   Universidad de Los Andes, Columbia
Antonis A. Argyros   University of Crete & Foundation for Research
                                      and Technology-Hellas, Crete
Yuki M. Asano   University of Amsterdam, The Netherlands
Kalle Åström   Lund University, Sweden
Hadar Averbuch-Elor   Cornell University, USA

Bohyung Han   Seoul National University, Korea
Tian Han   Stevens Institute of Technology, USA
Emily Hand   University of Nevada, Reno, USA
Bharath Hariharan   Cornell University, USA
Ran He   Institute of Automation, Chinese Academy of
                                Sciences, China
Otmar Hilliges   ETH Zurich, Switzerland
Adrian Hilton   University of Surrey, UK
Minh Hoai   Stony Brook University, USA
Yedid Hoshen   Hebrew University of Jerusalem, Israel
Timothy Hospedales   University of Edinburgh, UK
Gang Hua   Wormpex AI Research, USA
Di Huang   Beihang University, China
Jing Huang   Facebook, USA
Jia-Bin Huang   Facebook, USA
Nathan Jacobs   Washington University in St. Louis, USA
C.V. Jawahar   International Institute of Information Technology,
                                Hyderabad, India
Herve Jegou   Facebook AI Research, France
Neel Joshi   Microsoft Research, USA
Armand Joulin   Facebook AI Research, France
Frederic Jurie   University of Caen Normandie, France
Fredrik Kahl   Chalmers University of Technology, Sweden
Yannis Kalantidis   NAVER LABS Europe, France
Evangelos Kalogerakis   University of Massachusetts, Amherst, USA
Sing Bing Kang   Zillow Group, USA
Yosi Keller   Bar Ilan University, Israel
Margret Keuper   University of Mannheim, Germany
Tae-Kyun Kim   Imperial College London, UK
Benjamin Kimia   Brown University, USA
Alexander Kirillov   Facebook AI Research, USA
Kris Kitani   Carnegie Mellon University, USA
Iasonas Kokkinos   Snap Inc. & University College London, UK
Vladlen Koltun   Apple, USA
Nikos Komodakis   University of Crete, Crete
Piotr Koniusz   Australian National University, Australia
Philipp Kraehenbuehl   University of Texas at Austin, USA
Dilip Krishnan   Google, USA
Ajay Kumar   Hong Kong Polytechnic University, Hong Kong,
                                China
Junseok Kwon   Chung-Ang University, Korea
Jean-Francois Lalonde   Université Laval, Canada

Vittorio Murino   Istituto Italiano di Tecnologia, Italy
P. J. Narayanan   International Institute of Information Technology,
                                  Hyderabad, India
Ram Nevatia   University of Southern California, USA
Natalia Neverova   Facebook AI Research, UK
Richard Newcombe   Facebook, USA
Cuong V. Nguyen   Florida International University, USA
Bingbing Ni   Shanghai Jiao Tong University, China
Juan Carlos Niebles   Salesforce & Stanford University, USA
Ko Nishino   Kyoto University, Japan
Jean-Marc Odobez   Idiap Research Institute, École polytechnique
                                  fédérale de Lausanne, Switzerland
Francesca Odone   University of Genova, Italy
Takayuki Okatani   Tohoku University & RIKEN Center for
                                  Advanced Intelligence Project, Japan
Manohar Paluri   Facebook, USA
Guan Pang   Facebook, USA
Maja Pantic   Imperial College London, UK
Sylvain Paris   Adobe Research, USA
Jaesik Park   Pohang University of Science and Technology,
                                  Korea
Hyun Soo Park   The University of Minnesota, USA
Omkar M. Parkhi   Facebook, USA
Deepak Pathak   Carnegie Mellon University, USA
Georgios Pavlakos   University of California, Berkeley, USA
Marcello Pelillo   University of Venice, Italy
Marc Pollefeys   ETH Zurich & Microsoft, Switzerland
Jean Ponce   Inria, France
Gerard Pons-Moll   University of Tübingen, Germany
Fatih Porikli   Qualcomm, USA
Victor Adrian Prisacariu   University of Oxford, UK
Petia Radeva   University of Barcelona, Spain
Ravi Ramamoorthi   University of California, San Diego, USA
Deva Ramanan   Carnegie Mellon University, USA
Vignesh Ramanathan   Facebook, USA
Nalini Ratha   State University of New York at Buffalo, USA
Tammy Riklin Raviv   Ben-Gurion University, Israel
Tobias Ritschel   University College London, UK
Emanuele Rodola   Sapienza University of Rome, Italy
Amit K. Roy-Chowdhury   University of California, Riverside, USA
Michael Rubinstein   Google, USA
Olga Russakovsky   Princeton University, USA

Mathieu Salzmann	École polytechnique fédérale de Lausanne, Switzerland
Dimitris Samaras	Stony Brook University, USA
Aswin Sankaranarayanan	Carnegie Mellon University, USA
Imari Sato	National Institute of Informatics, Japan
Yoichi Sato	University of Tokyo, Japan
Shin'ichi Satoh	National Institute of Informatics, Japan
Walter Scheirer	University of Notre Dame, USA
Bernt Schiele	Max Planck Institute for Informatics, Germany
Konrad Schindler	ETH Zurich, Switzerland
Cordelia Schmid	Inria & Google, France
Alexander Schwing	University of Illinois at Urbana-Champaign, USA
Nicu Sebe	University of Trento, Italy
Greg Shakhnarovich	Toyota Technological Institute at Chicago, USA
Eli Shechtman	Adobe Research, USA
Humphrey Shi	University of Oregon & University of Illinois at Urbana-Champaign & Picsart AI Research, USA
Jianbo Shi	University of Pennsylvania, USA
Roy Shilkrot	Massachusetts Institute of Technology, USA
Mike Zheng Shou	National University of Singapore, Singapore
Kaleem Siddiqi	McGill University, Canada
Richa Singh	Indian Institute of Technology Jodhpur, India
Greg Slabaugh	Queen Mary University of London, UK
Cees Snoek	University of Amsterdam, The Netherlands
Yale Song	Facebook AI Research, USA
Yi-Zhe Song	University of Surrey, UK
Bjorn Stenger	Rakuten Institute of Technology
Abby Stylianou	Saint Louis University, USA
Akihiro Sugimoto	National Institute of Informatics, Japan
Chen Sun	Brown University, USA
Deqing Sun	Google, USA
Kalyan Sunkavalli	Adobe Research, USA
Ying Tai	Tencent YouTu Lab, China
Ayellet Tal	Technion – Israel Institute of Technology, Israel
Ping Tan	Simon Fraser University, Canada
Siyu Tang	ETH Zurich, Switzerland
Chi-Keung Tang	Hong Kong University of Science and Technology, Hong Kong, China
Radu Timofte	University of Würzburg, Germany & ETH Zurich, Switzerland
Federico Tombari	Google, Switzerland & Technical University of Munich, Germany

James Tompkin   Brown University, USA
Lorenzo Torresani   Dartmouth College, USA
Alexander Toshev   Apple, USA
Du Tran   Facebook AI Research, USA
Anh T. Tran   VinAI, Vietnam
Zhuowen Tu   University of California, San Diego, USA
Georgios Tzimiropoulos   Queen Mary University of London, UK
Jasper Uijlings   Google Research, Switzerland
Jan C. van Gemert   Delft University of Technology, The Netherlands
Gul Varol   Ecole des Ponts ParisTech, France
Nuno Vasconcelos   University of California, San Diego, USA
Mayank Vatsa   Indian Institute of Technology Jodhpur, India
Ashok Veeraraghavan   Rice University, USA
Jakob Verbeek   Facebook AI Research, France
Carl Vondrick   Columbia University, USA
Ruiping Wang   Institute of Computing Technology, Chinese
                             Academy of Sciences, China
Xinchao Wang   National University of Singapore, Singapore
Liwei Wang   The Chinese University of Hong Kong,
                             Hong Kong, China
Chaohui Wang   Université Paris-Est, France
Xiaolong Wang   University of California, San Diego, USA
Christian Wolf   NAVER LABS Europe, France
Tao Xiang   University of Surrey, UK
Saining Xie   Facebook AI Research, USA
Cihang Xie   University of California, Santa Cruz, USA
Zeki Yalniz   Facebook, USA
Ming-Hsuan Yang   University of California, Merced, USA
Angela Yao   National University of Singapore, Singapore
Shaodi You   University of Amsterdam, The Netherlands
Stella X. Yu   University of California, Berkeley, USA
Junsong Yuan   State University of New York at Buffalo, USA
Stefanos Zafeiriou   Imperial College London, UK
Amir Zamir   École polytechnique fédérale de Lausanne,
                             Switzerland
Lei Zhang   Alibaba & Hong Kong Polytechnic University,
                             Hong Kong, China
Lei Zhang   International Digital Economy Academy (IDEA),
                             China
Pengchuan Zhang   Meta AI, USA
Bolei Zhou   University of California, Los Angeles, USA
Yuke Zhu   University of Texas at Austin, USA

Technical Program Committee

Yang Bai
Yuanchao Bai
Ziqian Bai
Sungyong Baik
Kevin Bailly
Max Bain
Federico Baldassarre
Wele Gedara Chaminda
  Bandara
Biplab Banerjee
Pratyay Banerjee
Sandipan Banerjee
Jihwan Bang
Antyanta Bangunharcana
Aayush Bansal
Ankan Bansal
Siddhant Bansal
Wentao Bao
Zhipeng Bao
Amir Bar
Manel Baradad Jurjo
Lorenzo Baraldi
Danny Barash
Daniel Barath
Connelly Barnes
Ioan Andrei Bârsan
Steven Basart
Dina Bashkirova
Chaim Baskin
Peyman Bateni
Anil Batra
Sebastiano Battiato
Ardhendu Behera
Harkirat Behl
Jens Behley
Vasileios Belagiannis
Boulbaba Ben Amor
Emanuel Ben Baruch
Abdessamad Ben Hamza
Gil Ben-Artzi
Assia Benbihi
Fabian Benitez-Quiroz
Guy Ben-Yosef
Philipp Benz
Alexander W. Bergman

Urs Bergmann
Jesus Bermudez-Cameo
Stefano Berretti
Gedas Bertasius
Zachary Bessinger
Petra Bevandić
Matthew Beveridge
Lucas Beyer
Yash Bhalgat
Suvaansh Bhambri
Samarth Bharadwaj
Gaurav Bharaj
Aparna Bharati
Bharat Lal Bhatnagar
Uttaran Bhattacharya
Apratim Bhattacharyya
Brojeshwar Bhowmick
Ankan Kumar Bhunia
Ayan Kumar Bhunia
Qi Bi
Sai Bi
Michael Bi Mi
Gui-Bin Bian
Jia-Wang Bian
Shaojun Bian
Pia Bideau
Mario Bijelic
Hakan Bilen
Guillaume-Alexandre
  Bilodeau
Alexander Binder
Tolga Birdal
Vighnesh N. Birodkar
Sandika Biswas
Andreas Blattmann
Janusz Bobulski
Giuseppe Boccignone
Vishnu Boddeti
Navaneeth Bodla
Moritz Böhle
Aleksei Bokhovkin
Sam Bond-Taylor
Vivek Boominathan
Shubhankar Borse
Mark Boss

Andrea Bottino
Adnane Boukhayma
Fadi Boutros
Nicolas C. Boutry
Richard S. Bowen
Ivaylo Boyadzhiev
Aidan Boyd
Yuri Boykov
Aljaz Bozic
Behzad Bozorgtabar
Eric Brachmann
Samarth Brahmbhatt
Gustav Bredell
Francois Bremond
Joel Brogan
Andrew Brown
Thomas Brox
Marcus A. Brubaker
Robert-Jan Bruintjes
Yuqi Bu
Anders G. Buch
Himanshu Buckchash
Mateusz Buda
Ignas Budvytis
José M. Buenaposada
Marcel C. Bühler
Tu Bui
Adrian Bulat
Hannah Bull
Evgeny Burnaev
Andrei Bursuc
Benjamin Busam
Sergey N. Buzykanov
Wonmin Byeon
Fabian Caba
Martin Cadik
Guanyu Cai
Minjie Cai
Qing Cai
Zhongang Cai
Qi Cai
Yancheng Cai
Shen Cai
Han Cai
Jiarui Cai

Bowen Cai
Mu Cai
Qin Cai
Ruojin Cai
Weidong Cai
Weiwei Cai
Yi Cai
Yujun Cai
Zhiping Cai
Akin Caliskan
Lilian Calvet
Baris Can Cam
Necati Cihan Camgoz
Tommaso Campari
Dylan Campbell
Ziang Cao
Ang Cao
Xu Cao
Zhiwen Cao
Shengcao Cao
Song Cao
Weipeng Cao
Xiangyong Cao
Xiaochun Cao
Yue Cao
Yunhao Cao
Zhangjie Cao
Jiale Cao
Yang Cao
Jiajiong Cao
Jie Cao
Jinkun Cao
Lele Cao
Yulong Cao
Zhiguo Cao
Chen Cao
Razvan Caramalau
Marlène Careil
Gustavo Carneiro
Joao Carreira
Dan Casas
Paola Cascante-Bonilla
Angela Castillo
Francisco M. Castro
Pedro Castro

Luca Cavalli
George J. Cazenavette
Oya Celiktutan
Hakan Cevikalp
Sri Harsha C. H.
Sungmin Cha
Geonho Cha
Menglei Chai
Lucy Chai
Yuning Chai
Zenghao Chai
Anirban Chakraborty
Deep Chakraborty
Rudrasis Chakraborty
Souradeep Chakraborty
Kelvin C. K. Chan
Chee Seng Chan
Paramanand Chandramouli
Arjun Chandrasekaran
Kenneth Chaney
Dongliang Chang
Huiwen Chang
Peng Chang
Xiaojun Chang
Jia-Ren Chang
Hyung Jin Chang
Hyun Sung Chang
Ju Yong Chang
Li-Jen Chang
Qi Chang
Wei-Yi Chang
Yi Chang
Nadine Chang
Hanqing Chao
Pradyumna Chari
Dibyadip Chatterjee
Chiranjoy Chattopadhyay
Siddhartha Chaudhuri
Zhengping Che
Gal Chechik
Lianggangxu Chen
Qi Alfred Chen
Brian Chen
Bor-Chun Chen
Bo-Hao Chen

Bohong Chen
Bin Chen
Ziliang Chen
Cheng Chen
Chen Chen
Chaofeng Chen
Xi Chen
Haoyu Chen
Xuanhong Chen
Wei Chen
Qiang Chen
Shi Chen
Xianyu Chen
Chang Chen
Changhuai Chen
Hao Chen
Jie Chen
Jianbo Chen
Jingjing Chen
Jun Chen
Kejiang Chen
Mingcai Chen
Nenglun Chen
Qifeng Chen
Ruoyu Chen
Shu-Yu Chen
Weidong Chen
Weijie Chen
Weikai Chen
Xiang Chen
Xiuyi Chen
Xingyu Chen
Yaofo Chen
Yueting Chen
Yu Chen
Yunjin Chen
Yuntao Chen
Yun Chen
Zhenfang Chen
Zhuangzhuang Chen
Chu-Song Chen
Xiangyu Chen
Zhuo Chen
Chaoqi Chen
Shizhe Chen

Xiaotong Chen
Xiaozhi Chen
Dian Chen
Defang Chen
Dingfan Chen
Ding-Jie Chen
Ee Heng Chen
Tao Chen
Yixin Chen
Wei-Ting Chen
Lin Chen
Guang Chen
Guangyi Chen
Guanying Chen
Guangyao Chen
Hwann-Tzong Chen
Junwen Chen
Jiacheng Chen
Jianxu Chen
Hui Chen
Kai Chen
Kan Chen
Kevin Chen
Kuan-Wen Chen
Weihua Chen
Zhang Chen
Liang-Chieh Chen
Lele Chen
Liang Chen
Fanglin Chen
Zehui Chen
Minghui Chen
Minghao Chen
Xiaokang Chen
Qian Chen
Jun-Cheng Chen
Qi Chen
Qingcai Chen
Richard J. Chen
Runnan Chen
Rui Chen
Shuo Chen
Sentao Chen
Shaoyu Chen
Shixing Chen

Shuai Chen
Shuya Chen
Sizhe Chen
Simin Chen
Shaoxiang Chen
Zitian Chen
Tianlong Chen
Tianshui Chen
Min-Hung Chen
Xiangning Chen
Xin Chen
Xinghao Chen
Xuejin Chen
Xu Chen
Xuxi Chen
Yunlu Chen
Yanbei Chen
Yuxiao Chen
Yun-Chun Chen
Yi-Ting Chen
Yi-Wen Chen
Yinbo Chen
Yiran Chen
Yuanhong Chen
Yubei Chen
Yuefeng Chen
Yuhua Chen
Yukang Chen
Zerui Chen
Zhaoyu Chen
Zhen Chen
Zhenyu Chen
Zhi Chen
Zhiwei Chen
Zhixiang Chen
Long Chen
Bowen Cheng
Jun Cheng
Yi Cheng
Jingchun Cheng
Lechao Cheng
Xi Cheng
Yuan Cheng
Ho Kei Cheng
Kevin Ho Man Cheng

Jiacheng Cheng
Kelvin B. Cheng
Li Cheng
Mengjun Cheng
Zhen Cheng
Qingrong Cheng
Tianheng Cheng
Harry Cheng
Yihua Cheng
Yu Cheng
Ziheng Cheng
Soon Yau Cheong
Anoop Cherian
Manuela Chessa
Zhixiang Chi
Naoki Chiba
Julian Chibane
Kashyap Chitta
Tai-Yin Chiu
Hsu-kuang Chiu
Wei-Chen Chiu
Sungmin Cho
Donghyeon Cho
Hyeon Cho
Yooshin Cho
Gyusang Cho
Jang Hyun Cho
Seungju Cho
Nam Ik Cho
Sunghyun Cho
Hanbyel Cho
Jaesung Choe
Jooyoung Choi
Chiho Choi
Changwoon Choi
Jongwon Choi
Myungsub Choi
Dooseop Choi
Jonghyun Choi
Jinwoo Choi
Jun Won Choi
Min-Kook Choi
Hongsuk Choi
Janghoon Choi
Yoon-Ho Choi

Yukyung Choi
Jaegul Choo
Ayush Chopra
Siddharth Choudhary
Subhabrata Choudhury
Vasileios Choutas
Ka-Ho Chow
Pinaki Nath Chowdhury
Sammy Christen
Anders Christensen
Grigorios Chrysos
Hang Chu
Wen-Hsuan Chu
Peng Chu
Qi Chu
Ruihang Chu
Wei-Ta Chu
Yung-Yu Chuang
Sanghyuk Chun
Se Young Chun
Antonio Cinà
Ramazan Gokberk Cinbis
Javier Civera
Albert Clapés
Ronald Clark
Brian S. Clipp
Felipe Codevilla
Daniel Coelho de Castro
Niv Cohen
Forrester Cole
Maxwell D. Collins
Robert T. Collins
Marc Comino Trinidad
Runmin Cong
Wenyan Cong
Maxime Cordy
Marcella Cornia
Enric Corona
Huseyin Coskun
Luca Cosmo
Dragos Costea
Davide Cozzolino
Arun C. S. Kumar
Aiyu Cui
Qiongjie Cui

Quan Cui
Shuhao Cui
Yiming Cui
Ying Cui
Zijun Cui
Jiali Cui
Jiequan Cui
Yawen Cui
Zhen Cui
Zhaopeng Cui
Jack Culpepper
Xiaodong Cun
Ross Cutler
Adam Czajka
Ali Dabouei
Konstantinos M. Dafnis
Manuel Dahnert
Tao Dai
Yuchao Dai
Bo Dai
Mengyu Dai
Hang Dai
Haixing Dai
Peng Dai
Pingyang Dai
Qi Dai
Qiyu Dai
Yutong Dai
Naser Damer
Zhiyuan Dang
Mohamed Daoudi
Ayan Das
Abir Das
Debasmit Das
Deepayan Das
Partha Das
Sagnik Das
Soumi Das
Srijan Das
Swagatam Das
Avijit Dasgupta
Jim Davis
Adrian K. Davison
Homa Davoudi
Laura Daza

Matthias De Lange
Shalini De Mello
Marco De Nadai
Christophe De
  Vleeschouwer
Alp Dener
Boyang Deng
Congyue Deng
Bailin Deng
Yong Deng
Ye Deng
Zhuo Deng
Zhijie Deng
Xiaoming Deng
Jiankang Deng
Jinhong Deng
Jingjing Deng
Liang-Jian Deng
Siqi Deng
Xiang Deng
Xueqing Deng
Zhongying Deng
Karan Desai
Jean-Emmanuel Deschaud
Aniket Anand Deshmukh
Neel Dey
Helisa Dhamo
Prithviraj Dhar
Amaya Dharmasiri
Yan Di
Xing Di
Ousmane A. Dia
Haiwen Diao
Xiaolei Diao
Gonçalo José Dias Pais
Abdallah Dib
Anastasios Dimou
Changxing Ding
Henghui Ding
Guodong Ding
Yaqing Ding
Shuangrui Ding
Yuhang Ding
Yikang Ding
Shouhong Ding

Haisong Ding
Hui Ding
Jiahao Ding
Jian Ding
Jian-Jiun Ding
Shuxiao Ding
Tianyu Ding
Wenhao Ding
Yuqi Ding
Yi Ding
Yuzhen Ding
Zhengming Ding
Tan Minh Dinh
Vu Dinh
Christos Diou
Mandar Dixit
Bao Gia Doan
Khoa D. Doan
Dzung Anh Doan
Debi Prosad Dogra
Nehal Doiphode
Chengdong Dong
Bowen Dong
Zhenxing Dong
Hang Dong
Xiaoyi Dong
Haoye Dong
Jiangxin Dong
Shichao Dong
Xuan Dong
Zhen Dong
Shuting Dong
Jing Dong
Li Dong
Ming Dong
Nanqing Dong
Qiulei Dong
Runpei Dong
Siyan Dong
Tian Dong
Wei Dong
Xiaomeng Dong
Xin Dong
Xingbo Dong
Yuan Dong

Samuel Dooley
Gianfranco Doretto
Michael Dorkenwald
Keval Doshi
Zhaopeng Dou
Xiaotian Dou
Hazel Doughty
Ahmad Droby
Iddo Drori
Jie Du
Yong Du
Dawei Du
Dong Du
Ruoyi Du
Yuntao Du
Xuefeng Du
Yilun Du
Yuming Du
Radhika Dua
Haodong Duan
Jiafei Duan
Kaiwen Duan
Peiqi Duan
Ye Duan
Haoran Duan
Jiali Duan
Amanda Duarte
Abhimanyu Dubey
Shiv Ram Dubey
Florian Dubost
Lukasz Dudziak
Shivam Duggal
Justin M. Dulay
Matteo Dunnhofer
Chi Nhan Duong
Thibaut Durand
Mihai Dusmanu
Ujjal Kr Dutta
Debidatta Dwibedi
Isht Dwivedi
Sai Kumar Dwivedi
Takeharu Eda
Mark Edmonds
Alexei A. Efros
Thibaud Ehret

Max Ehrlich
Mahsa Ehsanpour
Iván Eichhardt
Farshad Einabadi
Marvin Eisenberger
Hazim Kemal Ekenel
Mohamed El Banani
Ismail Elezi
Moshe Eliasof
Alaa El-Nouby
Ian Endres
Francis Engelmann
Deniz Engin
Chanho Eom
Dave Epstein
Maria C. Escobar
Victor A. Escorcia
Carlos Esteves
Sungmin Eum
Bernard J. E. Evans
Ivan Evtimov
Fevziye Irem Eyiokur
    Yaman
Matteo Fabbri
Sébastien Fabbro
Gabriele Facciolo
Masud Fahim
Bin Fan
Hehe Fan
Deng-Ping Fan
Aoxiang Fan
Chen-Chen Fan
Qi Fan
Zhaoxin Fan
Haoqi Fan
Heng Fan
Hongyi Fan
Linxi Fan
Baojie Fan
Jiayuan Fan
Lei Fan
Quanfu Fan
Yonghui Fan
Yingruo Fan
Zhiwen Fan

Zicong Fan
Sean Fanello
Jiansheng Fang
Chaowei Fang
Yuming Fang
Jianwu Fang
Jin Fang
Qi Fang
Shancheng Fang
Tian Fang
Xianyong Fang
Gongfan Fang
Zhen Fang
Hui Fang
Jiemin Fang
Le Fang
Pengfei Fang
Xiaolin Fang
Yuxin Fang
Zhaoyuan Fang
Ammarah Farooq
Azade Farshad
Zhengcong Fei
Michael Felsberg
Wei Feng
Chen Feng
Fan Feng
Andrew Feng
Xin Feng
Zheyun Feng
Ruicheng Feng
Mingtao Feng
Qianyu Feng
Shangbin Feng
Chun-Mei Feng
Zunlei Feng
Zhiyong Feng
Martin Fergie
Mustansar Fiaz
Marco Fiorucci
Michael Firman
Hamed Firooz
Volker Fischer
Corneliu O. Florea
Georgios Floros

Wolfgang Foerstner
Gianni Franchi
Jean-Sebastien Franco
Simone Frintrop
Anna Fruehstueck
Changhong Fu
Chaoyou Fu
Cheng-Yang Fu
Chi-Wing Fu
Deqing Fu
Huan Fu
Jun Fu
Kexue Fu
Ying Fu
Jianlong Fu
Jingjing Fu
Qichen Fu
Tsu-Jui Fu
Xueyang Fu
Yang Fu
Yanwei Fu
Yonggan Fu
Wolfgang Fuhl
Yasuhisa Fujii
Kent Fujiwara
Marco Fumero
Takuya Funatomi
Isabel Funke
Dario Fuoli
Antonino Furnari
Matheus A. Gadelha
Akshay Gadi Patil
Adrian Galdran
Guillermo Gallego
Silvano Galliani
Orazio Gallo
Leonardo Galteri
Matteo Gamba
Yiming Gan
Sujoy Ganguly
Harald Ganster
Boyan Gao
Changxin Gao
Daiheng Gao
Difei Gao

Chen Gao
Fei Gao
Lin Gao
Wei Gao
Yiming Gao
Junyu Gao
Guangyu Ryan Gao
Haichang Gao
Hongchang Gao
Jialin Gao
Jin Gao
Jun Gao
Katelyn Gao
Mingchen Gao
Mingfei Gao
Pan Gao
Shangqian Gao
Shanghua Gao
Xitong Gao
Yunhe Gao
Zhanning Gao
Elena Garces
Nuno Cruz Garcia
Noa Garcia
Guillermo
    Garcia-Hernando
Isha Garg
Rahul Garg
Sourav Garg
Quentin Garrido
Stefano Gasperini
Kent Gauen
Chandan Gautam
Shivam Gautam
Paul Gay
Chunjiang Ge
Shiming Ge
Wenhang Ge
Yanhao Ge
Zheng Ge
Songwei Ge
Weifeng Ge
Yixiao Ge
Yuying Ge
Shijie Geng

Zhengyang Geng
Kyle A. Genova
Georgios Georgakis
Markos Georgopoulos
Marcel Geppert
Shabnam Ghadar
Mina Ghadimi Atigh
Deepti Ghadiyaram
Maani Ghaffari Jadidi
Sedigh Ghamari
Zahra Gharaee
Michaël Gharbi
Golnaz Ghiasi
Reza Ghoddoosian
Soumya Suvra Ghosal
Adhiraj Ghosh
Arthita Ghosh
Pallabi Ghosh
Soumyadeep Ghosh
Andrew Gilbert
Igor Gilitschenski
Jhony H. Giraldo
Andreu Girbau Xalabarder
Rohit Girdhar
Sharath Girish
Xavier Giro-i-Nieto
Raja Giryes
Thomas Gittings
Nikolaos Gkanatsios
Ioannis Gkioulekas
Abhiram
  Gnanasambandam
Aurele T. Gnanha
Clement L. J. C. Godard
Arushi Goel
Vidit Goel
Shubham Goel
Zan Gojcic
Aaron K. Gokaslan
Tejas Gokhale
S. Alireza Golestaneh
Thiago L. Gomes
Nuno Goncalves
Boqing Gong
Chen Gong

Yuanhao Gong
Guoqiang Gong
Jingyu Gong
Rui Gong
Yu Gong
Mingming Gong
Neil Zhenqiang Gong
Xun Gong
Yunye Gong
Yihong Gong
Cristina I. González
Nithin Gopalakrishnan
  Nair
Gaurav Goswami
Jianping Gou
Shreyank N. Gowda
Ankit Goyal
Helmut Grabner
Patrick L. Grady
Ben Graham
Eric Granger
Douglas R. Gray
Matej Grcić
David Griffiths
Jinjin Gu
Yun Gu
Shuyang Gu
Jianyang Gu
Fuqiang Gu
Jiatao Gu
Jindong Gu
Jiaqi Gu
Jinwei Gu
Jiaxin Gu
Geonmo Gu
Xiao Gu
Xinqian Gu
Xiuye Gu
Yuming Gu
Zhangxuan Gu
Dayan Guan
Junfeng Guan
Qingji Guan
Tianrui Guan
Shanyan Guan

Denis A. Gudovskiy
Ricardo Guerrero
Pierre-Louis Guhur
Jie Gui
Liangyan Gui
Liangke Gui
Benoit Guillard
Erhan Gundogdu
Manuel Günther
Jingcai Guo
Yuanfang Guo
Junfeng Guo
Chenqi Guo
Dan Guo
Hongji Guo
Jia Guo
Jie Guo
Minghao Guo
Shi Guo
Yanhui Guo
Yangyang Guo
Yuan-Chen Guo
Yilu Guo
Yiluan Guo
Yong Guo
Guangyu Guo
Haiyun Guo
Jinyang Guo
Jianyuan Guo
Pengsheng Guo
Pengfei Guo
Shuxuan Guo
Song Guo
Tianyu Guo
Qing Guo
Qiushan Guo
Wen Guo
Xiefan Guo
Xiaohu Guo
Xiaoqing Guo
Yufei Guo
Yuhui Guo
Yuliang Guo
Yunhui Guo
Yanwen Guo

Akshita Gupta
Ankush Gupta
Kamal Gupta
Kartik Gupta
Ritwik Gupta
Rohit Gupta
Siddharth Gururani
Fredrik K. Gustafsson
Abner Guzman Rivera
Vladimir Guzov
Matthew A. Gwilliam
Jung-Woo Ha
Marc Habermann
Isma Hadji
Christian Haene
Martin Hahner
Levente Hajder
Alexandros Haliassos
Emanuela Haller
Bumsub Ham
Abdullah J. Hamdi
Shreyas Hampali
Dongyoon Han
Chunrui Han
Dong-Jun Han
Dong-Sig Han
Guangxing Han
Zhizhong Han
Ruize Han
Jiaming Han
Jin Han
Ligong Han
Xian-Hua Han
Xiaoguang Han
Yizeng Han
Zhi Han
Zhenjun Han
Zhongyi Han
Jungong Han
Junlin Han
Kai Han
Kun Han
Sungwon Han
Songfang Han
Wei Han

Xiao Han
Xintong Han
Xinzhe Han
Yahong Han
Yan Han
Zongbo Han
Nicolai Hani
Rana Hanocka
Niklas Hanselmann
Nicklas A. Hansen
Hong Hanyu
Fusheng Hao
Yanbin Hao
Shijie Hao
Udith Haputhanthri
Mehrtash Harandi
Josh Harguess
Adam Harley
David M. Hart
Atsushi Hashimoto
Ali Hassani
Mohammed Hassanin
Yana Hasson
Joakim Bruslund Haurum
Bo He
Kun He
Chen He
Xin He
Fazhi He
Gaoqi He
Hao He
Haoyu He
Jiangpeng He
Hongliang He
Qian He
Xiangteng He
Xuming He
Yannan He
Yuhang He
Yang He
Xiangyu He
Nanjun He
Pan He
Sen He
Shengfeng He

Songtao He
Tao He
Tong He
Wei He
Xuehai He
Xiaoxiao He
Ying He
Yisheng He
Ziwen He
Peter Hedman
Felix Heide
Yacov Hel-Or
Paul Henderson
Philipp Henzler
Byeongho Heo
Jae-Pil Heo
Miran Heo
Sachini A. Herath
Stephane Herbin
Pedro Hermosilla Casajus
Monica Hernandez
Charles Herrmann
Roei Herzig
Mauricio Hess-Flores
Carlos Hinojosa
Tobias Hinz
Tsubasa Hirakawa
Chih-Hui Ho
Lam Si Tung Ho
Jennifer Hobbs
Derek Hoiem
Yannick Hold-Geoffroy
Aleksander Holynski
Cheeun Hong
Fa-Ting Hong
Hanbin Hong
Guan Zhe Hong
Danfeng Hong
Lanqing Hong
Xiaopeng Hong
Xin Hong
Jie Hong
Seungbum Hong
Cheng-Yao Hong
Seunghoon Hong

Yi Hong
Yuan Hong
Yuchen Hong
Anthony Hoogs
Maxwell C. Horton
Kazuhiro Hotta
Qibin Hou
Tingbo Hou
Junhui Hou
Ji Hou
Qiqi Hou
Rui Hou
Ruibing Hou
Zhi Hou
Henry Howard-Jenkins
Lukas Hoyer
Wei-Lin Hsiao
Chiou-Ting Hsu
Anthony Hu
Brian Hu
Yusong Hu
Hexiang Hu
Haoji Hu
Di Hu
Hengtong Hu
Haigen Hu
Lianyu Hu
Hanzhe Hu
Jie Hu
Junlin Hu
Shizhe Hu
Jian Hu
Zhiming Hu
Juhua Hu
Peng Hu
Ping Hu
Ronghang Hu
MengShun Hu
Tao Hu
Vincent Tao Hu
Xiaoling Hu
Xinting Hu
Xiaolin Hu
Xuefeng Hu
Xiaowei Hu

Yang Hu
Yueyu Hu
Zeyu Hu
Zhongyun Hu
Binh-Son Hua
Guoliang Hua
Yi Hua
Linzhi Huang
Qiusheng Huang
Bo Huang
Chen Huang
Hsin-Ping Huang
Ye Huang
Shuangping Huang
Zeng Huang
Buzhen Huang
Cong Huang
Heng Huang
Hao Huang
Qidong Huang
Huaibo Huang
Chaoqin Huang
Feihu Huang
Jiahui Huang
Jingjia Huang
Kun Huang
Lei Huang
Sheng Huang
Shuaiyi Huang
Siyu Huang
Xiaoshui Huang
Xiaoyang Huang
Yan Huang
Yihao Huang
Ying Huang
Ziling Huang
Xiaoke Huang
Yifei Huang
Haiyang Huang
Zhewei Huang
Jin Huang
Haibin Huang
Jiaxing Huang
Junjie Huang
Keli Huang

Lang Huang
Lin Huang
Luojie Huang
Mingzhen Huang
Shijia Huang
Shengyu Huang
Siyuan Huang
He Huang
Xiuyu Huang
Lianghua Huang
Yue Huang
Yaping Huang
Yuge Huang
Zehao Huang
Zeyi Huang
Zhiqi Huang
Zhongzhan Huang
Zilong Huang
Ziyuan Huang
Tianrui Hui
Zhuo Hui
Le Hui
Jing Huo
Junhwa Hur
Shehzeen S. Hussain
Chuong Minh Huynh
Seunghyun Hwang
Jaehui Hwang
Jyh-Jing Hwang
Sukjun Hwang
Soonmin Hwang
Wonjun Hwang
Rakib Hyder
Sangeek Hyun
Sarah Ibrahimi
Tomoki Ichikawa
Yerlan Idelbayev
A. S. M. Iftekhar
Masaaki Iiyama
Satoshi Ikehata
Sunghoon Im
Atul N. Ingle
Eldar Insafutdinov
Yani A. Ioannou
Radu Tudor Ionescu

Umar Iqbal
Go Irie
Muhammad Zubair Irshad
Ahmet Iscen
Berivan Isik
Ashraful Islam
Md Amirul Islam
Syed Islam
Mariko Isogawa
Vamsi Krishna K. Ithapu
Boris Ivanovic
Darshan Iyer
Sarah Jabbour
Ayush Jain
Nishant Jain
Samyak Jain
Vidit Jain
Vineet Jain
Priyank Jaini
Tomas Jakab
Mohammad A. A. K.
  Jalwana
Muhammad Abdullah
  Jamal
Hadi Jamali-Rad
Stuart James
Varun Jampani
Young Kyun Jang
YeongJun Jang
Yunseok Jang
Ronnachai Jaroensri
Bhavan Jasani
Krishna Murthy
  Jatavallabhula
Mojan Javaheripi
Syed A. Javed
Guillaume Jeanneret
Pranav Jeevan
Herve Jegou
Rohit Jena
Tomas Jenicek
Porter Jenkins
Simon Jenni
Hae-Gon Jeon
Sangryul Jeon

Boseung Jeong
Yoonwoo Jeong
Seong-Gyun Jeong
Jisoo Jeong
Allan D. Jepson
Ankit Jha
Sumit K. Jha
I-Hong Jhuo
Ge-Peng Ji
Chaonan Ji
Deyi Ji
Jingwei Ji
Wei Ji
Zhong Ji
Jiayi Ji
Pengliang Ji
Hui Ji
Mingi Ji
Xiaopeng Ji
Yuzhu Ji
Baoxiong Jia
Songhao Jia
Dan Jia
Shan Jia
Xiaojun Jia
Xiuyi Jia
Xu Jia
Menglin Jia
Wenqi Jia
Boyuan Jiang
Wenhao Jiang
Huaizu Jiang
Hanwen Jiang
Haiyong Jiang
Hao Jiang
Huajie Jiang
Huiqin Jiang
Haojun Jiang
Haobo Jiang
Junjun Jiang
Xingyu Jiang
Yangbangyan Jiang
Yu Jiang
Jianmin Jiang
Jiaxi Jiang

Jing Jiang
Kui Jiang
Li Jiang
Liming Jiang
Chiyu Jiang
Meirui Jiang
Chen Jiang
Peng Jiang
Tai-Xiang Jiang
Wen Jiang
Xinyang Jiang
Yifan Jiang
Yuming Jiang
Yingying Jiang
Zeren Jiang
ZhengKai Jiang
Zhenyu Jiang
Shuming Jiao
Jianbo Jiao
Licheng Jiao
Dongkwon Jin
Yeying Jin
Cheng Jin
Linyi Jin
Qing Jin
Taisong Jin
Xiao Jin
Xin Jin
Sheng Jin
Kyong Hwan Jin
Ruibing Jin
SouYoung Jin
Yueming Jin
Chenchen Jing
Longlong Jing
Taotao Jing
Yongcheng Jing
Younghyun Jo
Joakim Johnander
Jeff Johnson
Michael J. Jones
R. Kenny Jones
Rico Jonschkowski
Ameya Joshi
Sunghun Joung

Felix Juefei-Xu
Claudio R. Jung
Steffen Jung
Hari Chandana K.
Rahul Vigneswaran K.
Prajwal K. R.
Abhishek Kadian
Jhony Kaesemodel Pontes
Kumara Kahatapitiya
Anmol Kalia
Sinan Kalkan
Tarun Kalluri
Jaewon Kam
Sandesh Kamath
Meina Kan
Menelaos Kanakis
Takuhiro Kaneko
Di Kang
Guoliang Kang
Hao Kang
Jaeyeon Kang
Kyoungkook Kang
Li-Wei Kang
MinGuk Kang
Suk-Ju Kang
Zhao Kang
Yash Mukund Kant
Yueying Kao
Aupendu Kar
Konstantinos Karantzalos
Sezer Karaoglu
Navid Kardan
Sanjay Kariyappa
Leonid Karlinsky
Animesh Karnewar
Shyamgopal Karthik
Hirak J. Kashyap
Marc A. Kastner
Hirokatsu Kataoka
Angelos Katharopoulos
Hiroharu Kato
Kai Katsumata
Manuel Kaufmann
Chaitanya Kaul
Prakhar Kaushik

Yuki Kawana
Lei Ke
Lipeng Ke
Tsung-Wei Ke
Wei Ke
Petr Kellnhofer
Aniruddha Kembhavi
John Kender
Corentin Kervadec
Leonid Keselman
Daniel Keysers
Nima Khademi Kalantari
Taras Khakhulin
Samir Khaki
Muhammad Haris Khan
Qadeer Khan
Salman Khan
Subash Khanal
Vaishnavi M. Khindkar
Rawal Khirodkar
Saeed Khorram
Pirazh Khorramshahi
Kourosh Khoshelham
Ansh Khurana
Benjamin Kiefer
Jae Myung Kim
Junho Kim
Boah Kim
Hyeonseong Kim
Dong-Jin Kim
Dongwan Kim
Donghyun Kim
Doyeon Kim
Yonghyun Kim
Hyung-Il Kim
Hyunwoo Kim
Hyeongwoo Kim
Hyo Jin Kim
Hyunwoo J. Kim
Taehoon Kim
Jaeha Kim
Jiwon Kim
Jung Uk Kim
Kangyeol Kim
Eunji Kim

Daeha Kim
Dongwon Kim
Kunhee Kim
Kyungmin Kim
Junsik Kim
Min H. Kim
Namil Kim
Kookhoi Kim
Sanghyun Kim
Seongyeop Kim
Seungryong Kim
Saehoon Kim
Euyoung Kim
Guisik Kim
Sungyeon Kim
Sunnie S. Y. Kim
Taehun Kim
Tae Oh Kim
Won Hwa Kim
Seungwook Kim
YoungBin Kim
Youngeun Kim
Akisato Kimura
Furkan Osman Kınlı
Zsolt Kira
Hedvig Kjellström
Florian Kleber
Jan P. Klopp
Florian Kluger
Laurent Kneip
Byungsoo Ko
Muhammed Kocabas
A. Sophia Koepke
Kevin Koeser
Nick Kolkin
Nikos Kolotouros
Wai-Kin Adams Kong
Deying Kong
Caihua Kong
Youyong Kong
Shuyu Kong
Shu Kong
Tao Kong
Yajing Kong
Yu Kong

Zishang Kong
Theodora Kontogianni
Anton S. Konushin
Julian F. P. Kooij
Bruno Korbar
Giorgos Kordopatis-Zilos
Jari Korhonen
Adam Kortylewski
Denis Korzhenkov
Divya Kothandaraman
Suraj Kothawade
Iuliia Kotseruba
Satwik Kottur
Shashank Kotyan
Alexandros Kouris
Petros Koutras
Anna Kreshuk
Ranjay Krishna
Dilip Krishnan
Andrey Kuehlkamp
Hilde Kuehne
Jason Kuen
David Kügler
Arjan Kuijper
Anna Kukleva
Sumith Kulal
Viveka Kulharia
Akshay R. Kulkarni
Nilesh Kulkarni
Dominik Kulon
Abhinav Kumar
Akash Kumar
Suryansh Kumar
B. V. K. Vijaya Kumar
Pulkit Kumar
Ratnesh Kumar
Sateesh Kumar
Satish Kumar
Vijay Kumar B. G.
Nupur Kumari
Sudhakar Kumawat
Jogendra Nath Kundu
Hsien-Kai Kuo
Meng-Yu Jennifer Kuo
Vinod Kumar Kurmi

Yusuke Kurose
Keerthy Kusumam
Alina Kuznetsova
Henry Kvinge
Ho Man Kwan
Hyeokjun Kweon
Heeseung Kwon
Gihyun Kwon
Myung-Joon Kwon
Taesung Kwon
YoungJoong Kwon
Christos Kyrkou
Jorma Laaksonen
Yann Labbe
Zorah Laehner
Florent Lafarge
Hamid Laga
Manuel Lagunas
Shenqi Lai
Jian-Huang Lai
Zihang Lai
Mohamed I. Lakhal
Mohit Lamba
Meng Lan
Loic Landrieu
Zhiqiang Lang
Natalie Lang
Dong Lao
Yizhen Lao
Yingjie Lao
Issam Hadj Laradji
Gustav Larsson
Viktor Larsson
Zakaria Laskar
Stéphane Lathuilière
Chun Pong Lau
Rynson W. H. Lau
Hei Law
Justin Lazarow
Verica Lazova
Eric-Tuan Le
Hieu Le
Trung-Nghia Le
Mathias Lechner
Byeong-Uk Lee

Chen-Yu Lee
Che-Rung Lee
Chul Lee
Hong Joo Lee
Dongsoo Lee
Jiyoung Lee
Eugene Eu Tzuan Lee
Daeun Lee
Saehyung Lee
Jewook Lee
Hyungtae Lee
Hyunmin Lee
Jungbeom Lee
Joon-Young Lee
Jong-Seok Lee
Joonseok Lee
Junha Lee
Kibok Lee
Byung-Kwan Lee
Jangwon Lee
Jinho Lee
Jongmin Lee
Seunghyun Lee
Sohyun Lee
Minsik Lee
Dogyoon Lee
Seungmin Lee
Min Jun Lee
Sangho Lee
Sangmin Lee
Seungeun Lee
Seon-Ho Lee
Sungmin Lee
Sungho Lee
Sangyoun Lee
Vincent C. S. S. Lee
Jaeseong Lee
Yong Jae Lee
Chenyang Lei
Chenyi Lei
Jiahui Lei
Xinyu Lei
Yinjie Lei
Jiaxu Leng
Luziwei Leng

Jan E. Lenssen
Vincent Lepetit
Thomas Leung
María Leyva-Vallina
Xin Li
Yikang Li
Baoxin Li
Bin Li
Bing Li
Bowen Li
Changlin Li
Chao Li
Chongyi Li
Guanyue Li
Shuai Li
Jin Li
Dingquan Li
Dongxu Li
Yiting Li
Gang Li
Dian Li
Guohao Li
Haoang Li
Haoliang Li
Haoran Li
Hengduo Li
Huafeng Li
Xiaoming Li
Hanao Li
Hongwei Li
Ziqiang Li
Jisheng Li
Jiacheng Li
Jia Li
Jiachen Li
Jiahao Li
Jianwei Li
Jiazhi Li
Jie Li
Jing Li
Jingjing Li
Jingtao Li
Jun Li
Junxuan Li
Kai Li

Kailin Li
Kenneth Li
Kun Li
Kunpeng Li
Aoxue Li
Chenglong Li
Chenglin Li
Changsheng Li
Zhichao Li
Qiang Li
Yanyu Li
Zuoyue Li
Xiang Li
Xuelong Li
Fangda Li
Ailin Li
Liang Li
Chun-Guang Li
Daiqing Li
Dong Li
Guanbin Li
Guorong Li
Haifeng Li
Jianan Li
Jianing Li
Jiaxin Li
Ke Li
Lei Li
Lincheng Li
Liulei Li
Lujun Li
Linjie Li
Lin Li
Pengyu Li
Ping Li
Qiufu Li
Qingyong Li
Rui Li
Siyuan Li
Wei Li
Wenbin Li
Xiangyang Li
Xinyu Li
Xiujun Li
Xiu Li

Xu Li
Ya-Li Li
Yao Li
Yongjie Li
Yijun Li
Yiming Li
Yuezun Li
Yu Li
Yunheng Li
Yuqi Li
Zhe Li
Zeming Li
Zhen Li
Zhengqin Li
Zhimin Li
Jiefeng Li
Jinpeng Li
Chengze Li
Jianwu Li
Lerenhan Li
Shan Li
Suichan Li
Xiangtai Li
Yanjie Li
Yandong Li
Zhuoling Li
Zhenqiang Li
Manyi Li
Maosen Li
Ji Li
Minjun Li
Mingrui Li
Mengtian Li
Junyi Li
Nianyi Li
Bo Li
Xiao Li
Peihua Li
Peike Li
Peizhao Li
Peiliang Li
Qi Li
Ren Li
Runze Li
Shile Li

Sheng Li	Zhuowei Li	Che-Tsung Lin
Shigang Li	Zhuowan Li	Chung-Ching Lin
Shiyu Li	Zhuohang Li	Chen-Hsuan Lin
Shuang Li	Zizhang Li	Cheng Lin
Shasha Li	Chen Li	Chuming Lin
Shichao Li	Yuan-Fang Li	Chunyu Lin
Tianye Li	Dongze Lian	Dahua Lin
Yuexiang Li	Xiaochen Lian	Wei Lin
Wei-Hong Li	Zhouhui Lian	Zheng Lin
Wanhua Li	Long Lian	Huaijia Lin
Weihao Li	Qing Lian	Jason Lin
Weiming Li	Jin Lianbao	Jierui Lin
Weixin Li	Jinxiu S. Liang	Jiaying Lin
Wenbo Li	Dingkang Liang	Jie Lin
Wenshuo Li	Jiahao Liang	Kai-En Lin
Weijian Li	Jianming Liang	Kevin Lin
Yunan Li	Jingyun Liang	Guangfeng Lin
Xirong Li	Kevin J. Liang	Jiehong Lin
Xianhang Li	Kaizhao Liang	Feng Lin
Xiaoyu Li	Chen Liang	Hang Lin
Xueqian Li	Jie Liang	Kwan-Yee Lin
Xuanlin Li	Senwei Liang	Ke Lin
Xianzhi Li	Ding Liang	Luojun Lin
Yunqiang Li	Jiajun Liang	Qinghong Lin
Yanjing Li	Jian Liang	Xiangbo Lin
Yansheng Li	Kongming Liang	Yi Lin
Yawei Li	Siyuan Liang	Zudi Lin
Yi Li	Yuanzhi Liang	Shijie Lin
Yong Li	Zhengfa Liang	Yiqun Lin
Yong-Lu Li	Mingfu Liang	Tzu-Heng Lin
Yuhang Li	Xiaodan Liang	Ming Lin
Yu-Jhe Li	Xuefeng Liang	Shaohui Lin
Yuxi Li	Yuxuan Liang	SongNan Lin
Yunsheng Li	Kang Liao	Ji Lin
Yanwei Li	Liang Liao	Tsung-Yu Lin
Zechao Li	Hong-Yuan Mark Liao	Xudong Lin
Zejian Li	Wentong Liao	Yancong Lin
Zeju Li	Haofu Liao	Yen-Chen Lin
Zekun Li	Yue Liao	Yiming Lin
Zhaowen Li	Minghui Liao	Yuewei Lin
Zheng Li	Shengcai Liao	Zhiqiu Lin
Zhenyu Li	Ting-Hsuan Liao	Zinan Lin
Zhiheng Li	Xin Liao	Zhe Lin
Zhi Li	Yinghong Liao	David B. Lindell
Zhong Li	Teck Yian Lim	Zhixin Ling

Zhan Ling
Alexander Liniger
Venice Erin B. Liong
Joey Litalien
Or Litany
Roee Litman
Ron Litman
Jim Little
Dor Litvak
Shaoteng Liu
Shuaicheng Liu
Andrew Liu
Xian Liu
Shaohui Liu
Bei Liu
Bo Liu
Yong Liu
Ming Liu
Yanbin Liu
Chenxi Liu
Daqi Liu
Di Liu
Difan Liu
Dong Liu
Dongfang Liu
Daizong Liu
Xiao Liu
Fangyi Liu
Fengbei Liu
Fenglin Liu
Bin Liu
Yuang Liu
Ao Liu
Hong Liu
Hongfu Liu
Huidong Liu
Ziyi Liu
Feng Liu
Hao Liu
Jie Liu
Jialun Liu
Jiang Liu
Jing Liu
Jingya Liu
Jiaming Liu

Jun Liu
Juncheng Liu
Jiawei Liu
Hongyu Liu
Chuanbin Liu
Haotian Liu
Lingqiao Liu
Chang Liu
Han Liu
Liu Liu
Min Liu
Yingqi Liu
Aishan Liu
Bingyu Liu
Benlin Liu
Boxiao Liu
Chenchen Liu
Chuanjian Liu
Daqing Liu
Huan Liu
Haozhe Liu
Jiaheng Liu
Wei Liu
Jingzhou Liu
Jiyuan Liu
Lingbo Liu
Nian Liu
Peiye Liu
Qiankun Liu
Shenglan Liu
Shilong Liu
Wen Liu
Wenyu Liu
Weifeng Liu
Wu Liu
Xiaolong Liu
Yang Liu
Yanwei Liu
Yingcheng Liu
Yongfei Liu
Yihao Liu
Yu Liu
Yunze Liu
Ze Liu
Zhenhua Liu

Zhenguang Liu
Lin Liu
Lihao Liu
Pengju Liu
Xinhai Liu
Yunfei Liu
Meng Liu
Minghua Liu
Mingyuan Liu
Miao Liu
Peirong Liu
Ping Liu
Qingjie Liu
Ruoshi Liu
Risheng Liu
Songtao Liu
Xing Liu
Shikun Liu
Shuming Liu
Sheng Liu
Songhua Liu
Tongliang Liu
Weibo Liu
Weide Liu
Weizhe Liu
Wenxi Liu
Weiyang Liu
Xin Liu
Xiaobin Liu
Xudong Liu
Xiaoyi Liu
Xihui Liu
Xinchen Liu
Xingtong Liu
Xinpeng Liu
Xinyu Liu
Xianpeng Liu
Xu Liu
Xingyu Liu
Yongtuo Liu
Yahui Liu
Yangxin Liu
Yaoyao Liu
Yaojie Liu
Yuliang Liu

Yongcheng Liu
Yuan Liu
Yufan Liu
Yu-Lun Liu
Yun Liu
Yunfan Liu
Yuanzhong Liu
Zhuoran Liu
Zhen Liu
Zheng Liu
Zhijian Liu
Zhisong Liu
Ziquan Liu
Ziyu Liu
Zhihua Liu
Zechun Liu
Zhaoyang Liu
Zhengzhe Liu
Stephan Liwicki
Shao-Yuan Lo
Sylvain Lobry
Suhas Lohit
Vishnu Suresh Lokhande
Vincenzo Lomonaco
Chengjiang Long
Guodong Long
Fuchen Long
Shangbang Long
Yang Long
Zijun Long
Vasco Lopes
Antonio M. Lopez
Roberto Javier
   Lopez-Sastre
Tobias Lorenz
Javier Lorenzo-Navarro
Yujing Lou
Qian Lou
Xiankai Lu
Changsheng Lu
Huimin Lu
Yongxi Lu
Hao Lu
Hong Lu
Jiasen Lu

Juwei Lu
Fan Lu
Guangming Lu
Jiwen Lu
Shun Lu
Tao Lu
Xiaonan Lu
Yang Lu
Yao Lu
Yongchun Lu
Zhiwu Lu
Cheng Lu
Liying Lu
Guo Lu
Xuequan Lu
Yanye Lu
Yantao Lu
Yuhang Lu
Fujun Luan
Jonathon Luiten
Jovita Lukasik
Alan Lukezic
Jonathan Samuel Lumentut
Mayank Lunayach
Ao Luo
Canjie Luo
Chong Luo
Xu Luo
Grace Luo
Jun Luo
Katie Z. Luo
Tao Luo
Cheng Luo
Fangzhou Luo
Gen Luo
Lei Luo
Sihui Luo
Weixin Luo
Yan Luo
Xiaoyan Luo
Yong Luo
Yadan Luo
Hao Luo
Ruotian Luo
Mi Luo

Tiange Luo
Wenjie Luo
Wenhan Luo
Xiao Luo
Zhiming Luo
Zhipeng Luo
Zhengyi Luo
Diogo C. Luvizon
Zhaoyang Lv
Gengyu Lyu
Lingjuan Lyu
Jun Lyu
Yuanyuan Lyu
Youwei Lyu
Yueming Lyu
Bingpeng Ma
Chao Ma
Chongyang Ma
Congbo Ma
Chih-Yao Ma
Fan Ma
Lin Ma
Haoyu Ma
Hengbo Ma
Jianqi Ma
Jiawei Ma
Jiayi Ma
Kede Ma
Kai Ma
Lingni Ma
Lei Ma
Xu Ma
Ning Ma
Benteng Ma
Cheng Ma
Andy J. Ma
Long Ma
Zhanyu Ma
Zhiheng Ma
Qianli Ma
Shiqiang Ma
Sizhuo Ma
Shiqing Ma
Xiaolong Ma
Xinzhu Ma

Gautam B. Machiraju
Spandan Madan
Mathew Magimai-Doss
Luca Magri
Behrooz Mahasseni
Upal Mahbub
Siddharth Mahendran
Paridhi Maheshwari
Rishabh Maheshwary
Mohammed Mahmoud
Shishira R. R. Maiya
Sylwia Majchrowska
Arjun Majumdar
Puspita Majumdar
Orchid Majumder
Sagnik Majumder
Ilya Makarov
Farkhod F.
    Makhmudkhujaev
Yasushi Makihara
Ankur Mali
Mateusz Malinowski
Utkarsh Mall
Srikanth Malla
Clement Mallet
Dimitrios Mallis
Yunze Man
Dipu Manandhar
Massimiliano Mancini
Murari Mandal
Raunak Manekar
Karttikeya Mangalam
Puneet Mangla
Fabian Manhardt
Sivabalan Manivasagam
Fahim Mannan
Chengzhi Mao
Hanzi Mao
Jiayuan Mao
Junhua Mao
Zhiyuan Mao
Jiageng Mao
Yunyao Mao
Zhendong Mao
Alberto Marchisio

Diego Marcos
Riccardo Marin
Aram Markosyan
Renaud Marlet
Ricardo Marques
Miquel Martí i Rabadán
Diego Martin Arroyo
Niki Martinel
Brais Martinez
Julieta Martinez
Marc Masana
Tomohiro Mashita
Timothée Masquelier
Minesh Mathew
Tetsu Matsukawa
Marwan Mattar
Bruce A. Maxwell
Christoph Mayer
Mantas Mazeika
Pratik Mazumder
Scott McCloskey
Steven McDonagh
Ishit Mehta
Jie Mei
Kangfu Mei
Jieru Mei
Xiaoguang Mei
Givi Meishvili
Luke Melas-Kyriazi
Iaroslav Melekhov
Andres Mendez-Vazquez
Heydi Mendez-Vazquez
Matias Mendieta
Ricardo A. Mendoza-León
Chenlin Meng
Depu Meng
Rang Meng
Zibo Meng
Qingjie Meng
Qier Meng
Yanda Meng
Zihang Meng
Thomas Mensink
Fabian Mentzer
Christopher Metzler

Gregory P. Meyer
Vasileios Mezaris
Liang Mi
Lu Mi
Bo Miao
Changtao Miao
Zichen Miao
Qiguang Miao
Xin Miao
Zhongqi Miao
Frank Michel
Simone Milani
Ben Mildenhall
Roy V. Miles
Juhong Min
Kyle Min
Hyun-Seok Min
Weiqing Min
Yuecong Min
Zhixiang Min
Qi Ming
David Minnen
Aymen Mir
Deepak Mishra
Anand Mishra
Shlok K. Mishra
Niluthpol Mithun
Gaurav Mittal
Trisha Mittal
Daisuke Miyazaki
Kaichun Mo
Hong Mo
Zhipeng Mo
Davide Modolo
Abduallah A. Mohamed
Mohamed Afham
Mohamed Aflal
Ron Mokady
Pavlo Molchanov
Davide Moltisanti
Liliane Momeni
Gianluca Monaci
Pascal Monasse
Ajoy Mondal
Tom Monnier

Aron Monszpart
Gyeongsik Moon
Suhong Moon
Taesup Moon
Sean Moran
Daniel Moreira
Pietro Morerio
Alexandre Morgand
Lia Morra
Ali Mosleh
Inbar Mosseri
Sayed Mohammad
    Mostafavi Isfahani
Saman Motamed
Ramy A. Mounir
Fangzhou Mu
Jiteng Mu
Norman Mu
Yasuhiro Mukaigawa
Ryan Mukherjee
Tanmoy Mukherjee
Yusuke Mukuta
Ravi Teja Mullapudi
Lea Müller
Matthias Müller
Martin Mundt
Nils Murrugarra-Llerena
Damien Muselet
Armin Mustafa
Muhammad Ferjad Naeem
Sauradip Nag
Hajime Nagahara
Pravin Nagar
Rajendra Nagar
Naveen Shankar Nagaraja
Varun Nagaraja
Tushar Nagarajan
Seungjun Nah
Gaku Nakano
Yuta Nakashima
Giljoo Nam
Seonghyeon Nam
Liangliang Nan
Yuesong Nan
Yeshwanth Napolean

Dinesh Reddy
    Narapureddy
Medhini Narasimhan
Supreeth
    Narasimhaswamy
Sriram Narayanan
Erickson R. Nascimento
Varun Nasery
K. L. Navaneet
Pablo Navarrete Michelini
Shant Navasardyan
Shah Nawaz
Nihal Nayak
Farhood Negin
Lukáš Neumann
Alejandro Newell
Evonne Ng
Kam Woh Ng
Tony Ng
Anh Nguyen
Tuan Anh Nguyen
Cuong Cao Nguyen
Ngoc Cuong Nguyen
Thanh Nguyen
Khoi Nguyen
Phi Le Nguyen
Phong Ha Nguyen
Tam Nguyen
Truong Nguyen
Anh Tuan Nguyen
Rang Nguyen
Thao Thi Phuong Nguyen
Van Nguyen Nguyen
Zhen-Liang Ni
Yao Ni
Shijie Nie
Xuecheng Nie
Yongwei Nie
Weizhi Nie
Ying Nie
Yinyu Nie
Kshitij N. Nikhal
Simon Niklaus
Xuefei Ning
Jifeng Ning

Yotam Nitzan
Di Niu
Shuaicheng Niu
Li Niu
Wei Niu
Yulei Niu
Zhenxing Niu
Albert No
Shohei Nobuhara
Nicoletta Noceti
Junhyug Noh
Sotiris Nousias
Slawomir Nowaczyk
Ewa M. Nowara
Valsamis Ntouskos
Gilberto Ochoa-Ruiz
Ferda Ofli
Jihyong Oh
Sangyun Oh
Youngtaek Oh
Hiroki Ohashi
Takahiro Okabe
Kemal Oksuz
Fumio Okura
Daniel Olmeda Reino
Matthew Olson
Carl Olsson
Roy Or-El
Alessandro Ortis
Guillermo Ortiz-Jimenez
Magnus Oskarsson
Ahmed A. A. Osman
Martin R. Oswald
Mayu Otani
Naima Otberdout
Cheng Ouyang
Jiahong Ouyang
Wanli Ouyang
Andrew Owens
Poojan B. Oza
Mete Ozay
A. Cengiz Oztireli
Gautam Pai
Tomas Pajdla
Umapada Pal

Simone Palazzo
Luca Palmieri
Bowen Pan
Hao Pan
Lili Pan
Tai-Yu Pan
Liang Pan
Chengwei Pan
Yingwei Pan
Xuran Pan
Jinshan Pan
Xinyu Pan
Liyuan Pan
Xingang Pan
Xingjia Pan
Zhihong Pan
Zizheng Pan
Priyadarshini Panda
Rameswar Panda
Rohit Pandey
Kaiyue Pang
Bo Pang
Guansong Pang
Jiangmiao Pang
Meng Pang
Tianyu Pang
Ziqi Pang
Omiros Pantazis
Andreas Panteli
Maja Pantic
Marina Paolanti
Joao P. Papa
Samuele Papa
Mike Papadakis
Dim P. Papadopoulos
George Papandreou
Constantin Pape
Toufiq Parag
Chethan Parameshwara
Shaifali Parashar
Alejandro Pardo
Rishubh Parihar
Sarah Parisot
JaeYoo Park
Gyeong-Moon Park

Hyojin Park
Hyoungseob Park
Jongchan Park
Jae Sung Park
Kiru Park
Chunghyun Park
Kwanyong Park
Sunghyun Park
Sungrae Park
Seongsik Park
Sanghyun Park
Sungjune Park
Taesung Park
Gaurav Parmar
Paritosh Parmar
Alvaro Parra
Despoina Paschalidou
Or Patashnik
Shivansh Patel
Pushpak Pati
Prashant W. Patil
Vaishakh Patil
Suvam Patra
Jay Patravali
Badri Narayana Patro
Angshuman Paul
Sudipta Paul
Rémi Pautrat
Nick E. Pears
Adithya Pediredla
Wenjie Pei
Shmuel Peleg
Latha Pemula
Bo Peng
Houwen Peng
Yue Peng
Liangzu Peng
Baoyun Peng
Jun Peng
Pai Peng
Sida Peng
Xi Peng
Yuxin Peng
Songyou Peng
Wei Peng

Weiqi Peng
Wen-Hsiao Peng
Pramuditha Perera
Juan C. Perez
Eduardo Pérez Pellitero
Juan-Manuel Perez-Rua
Federico Pernici
Marco Pesavento
Stavros Petridis
Ilya A. Petrov
Vladan Petrovic
Mathis Petrovich
Suzanne Petryk
Hieu Pham
Quang Pham
Khoi Pham
Tung Pham
Huy Phan
Stephen Phillips
Cheng Perng Phoo
David Picard
Marco Piccirilli
Georg Pichler
A. J. Piergiovanni
Vipin Pillai
Silvia L. Pintea
Giovanni Pintore
Robinson Piramuthu
Fiora Pirri
Theodoros Pissas
Fabio Pizzati
Benjamin Planche
Bryan Plummer
Matteo Poggi
Ashwini Pokle
Georgy E. Ponimatkin
Adrian Popescu
Stefan Popov
Nikola Popović
Ronald Poppe
Angelo Porrello
Michael Potter
Charalambos Poullis
Hadi Pouransari
Omid Poursaeed

Shraman Pramanick
Mantini Pranav
Dilip K. Prasad
Meghshyam Prasad
B. H. Pawan Prasad
Shitala Prasad
Prateek Prasanna
Ekta Prashnani
Derek S. Prijatelj
Luke Y. Prince
Véronique Prinet
Victor Adrian Prisacariu
James Pritts
Thomas Probst
Sergey Prokudin
Rita Pucci
Chi-Man Pun
Matthew Purri
Haozhi Qi
Lu Qi
Lei Qi
Xianbiao Qi
Yonggang Qi
Yuankai Qi
Siyuan Qi
Guocheng Qian
Hangwei Qian
Qi Qian
Deheng Qian
Shengsheng Qian
Wen Qian
Rui Qian
Yiming Qian
Shengju Qian
Shengyi Qian
Xuelin Qian
Zhenxing Qian
Nan Qiao
Xiaotian Qiao
Jing Qin
Can Qin
Siyang Qin
Hongwei Qin
Jie Qin
Minghai Qin

Yipeng Qin
Yongqiang Qin
Wenda Qin
Xuebin Qin
Yuzhe Qin
Yao Qin
Zhenyue Qin
Zhiwu Qing
Heqian Qiu
Jiayan Qiu
Jielin Qiu
Yue Qiu
Jiaxiong Qiu
Zhongxi Qiu
Shi Qiu
Zhaofan Qiu
Zhongnan Qu
Yanyun Qu
Kha Gia Quach
Yuhui Quan
Ruijie Quan
Mike Rabbat
Rahul Shekhar Rade
Filip Radenovic
Gorjan Radevski
Bogdan Raducanu
Francesco Ragusa
Shafin Rahman
Md Mahfuzur Rahman
   Siddiquee
Hossein Rahmani
Kiran Raja
Sivaramakrishnan
   Rajaraman
Jathushan Rajasegaran
Adnan Siraj Rakin
Michaël Ramamonjisoa
Chirag A. Raman
Shanmuganathan Raman
Vignesh Ramanathan
Vasili Ramanishka
Vikram V. Ramaswamy
Merey Ramazanova
Jason Rambach
Sai Saketh Rambhatla

Clément Rambour
Ashwin Ramesh Babu
Adín Ramírez Rivera
Arianna Rampini
Haoxi Ran
Aakanksha Rana
Aayush Jung Bahadur
   Rana
Kanchana N. Ranasinghe
Aneesh Rangnekar
Samrudhdhi B. Rangrej
Harsh Rangwani
Viresh Ranjan
Anyi Rao
Yongming Rao
Carolina Raposo
Michalis Raptis
Amir Rasouli
Vivek Rathod
Adepu Ravi Sankar
Avinash Ravichandran
Bharadwaj Ravichandran
Dripta S. Raychaudhuri
Adria Recasens
Simon Reiß
Davis Rempe
Daxuan Ren
Jiawei Ren
Jimmy Ren
Sucheng Ren
Dayong Ren
Zhile Ren
Dongwei Ren
Qibing Ren
Pengfei Ren
Zhenwen Ren
Xuqian Ren
Yixuan Ren
Zhongzheng Ren
Ambareesh Revanur
Hamed Rezadegan
   Tavakoli
Rafael S. Rezende
Wonjong Rhee
Alexander Richard

Christian Richardt
Stephan R. Richter
Benjamin Riggan
Dominik Rivoir
Mamshad Nayeem Rizve
Joshua D. Robinson
Joseph Robinson
Chris Rockwell
Ranga Rodrigo
Andres C. Rodriguez
Carlos Rodriguez-Pardo
Marcus Rohrbach
Gemma Roig
Yu Rong
David A. Ross
Mohammad Rostami
Edward Rosten
Karsten Roth
Anirban Roy
Debaditya Roy
Shuvendu Roy
Ahana Roy Choudhury
Aruni Roy Chowdhury
Denys Rozumnyi
Shulan Ruan
Wenjie Ruan
Patrick Ruhkamp
Danila Rukhovich
Anian Ruoss
Chris Russell
Dan Ruta
Dawid Damian Rymarczyk
DongHun Ryu
Hyeonggon Ryu
Kwonyoung Ryu
Balasubramanian S.
Alexandre Sablayrolles
Mohammad Sabokrou
Arka Sadhu
Aniruddha Saha
Oindrila Saha
Pritish Sahu
Aneeshan Sain
Nirat Saini
Saurabh Saini

Takeshi Saitoh
Christos Sakaridis
Fumihiko Sakaue
Dimitrios Sakkos
Ken Sakurada
Parikshit V. Sakurikar
Rohit Saluja
Nermin Samet
Leo Sampaio Ferraz
    Ribeiro
Jorge Sanchez
Enrique Sanchez
Shengtian Sang
Anush Sankaran
Soubhik Sanyal
Nikolaos Sarafianos
Vishwanath Saragadam
István Sárándi
Saquib Sarfraz
Mert Bulent Sariyildiz
Anindya Sarkar
Pritam Sarkar
Paul-Edouard Sarlin
Hiroshi Sasaki
Takami Sato
Torsten Sattler
Ravi Kumar Satzoda
Axel Sauer
Stefano Savian
Artem Savkin
Manolis Savva
Gerald Schaefer
Simone Schaub-Meyer
Yoni Schirris
Samuel Schulter
Katja Schwarz
Jesse Scott
Sinisa Segvic
Constantin Marc Seibold
Lorenzo Seidenari
Matan Sela
Fadime Sener
Paul Hongsuck Seo
Kwanggyoon Seo
Hongje Seong

Dario Serez
Francesco Setti
Bryan Seybold
Mohamad Shahbazi
Shima Shahfar
Xinxin Shan
Caifeng Shan
Dandan Shan
Shawn Shan
Wei Shang
Jinghuan Shang
Jiaxiang Shang
Lei Shang
Sukrit Shankar
Ken Shao
Rui Shao
Jie Shao
Mingwen Shao
Aashish Sharma
Gaurav Sharma
Vivek Sharma
Abhishek Sharma
Yoli Shavit
Shashank Shekhar
Sumit Shekhar
Zhijie Shen
Fengyi Shen
Furao Shen
Jialie Shen
Jingjing Shen
Ziyi Shen
Linlin Shen
Guangyu Shen
Biluo Shen
Falong Shen
Jiajun Shen
Qiu Shen
Qiuhong Shen
Shuai Shen
Wang Shen
Yiqing Shen
Yunhang Shen
Siqi Shen
Bin Shen
Tianwei Shen

Xi Shen
Yilin Shen
Yuming Shen
Yucong Shen
Zhiqiang Shen
Lu Sheng
Yichen Sheng
Shivanand Venkanna
  Sheshappanavar
Shelly Sheynin
Baifeng Shi
Ruoxi Shi
Botian Shi
Hailin Shi
Jia Shi
Jing Shi
Shaoshuai Shi
Baoguang Shi
Boxin Shi
Hengcan Shi
Tianyang Shi
Xiaodan Shi
Yongjie Shi
Zhensheng Shi
Yinghuan Shi
Weiqi Shi
Wu Shi
Xuepeng Shi
Xiaoshuang Shi
Yujiao Shi
Zenglin Shi
Zhenmei Shi
Takashi Shibata
Meng-Li Shih
Yichang Shih
Hyunjung Shim
Dongseok Shim
Soshi Shimada
Inkyu Shin
Jinwoo Shin
Seungjoo Shin
Seungjae Shin
Koichi Shinoda
Suprosanna Shit

Palaiahnakote
  Shivakumara
Eli Shlizerman
Gaurav Shrivastava
Xiao Shu
Xiangbo Shu
Xiujun Shu
Yang Shu
Tianmin Shu
Jun Shu
Zhixin Shu
Bing Shuai
Maria Shugrina
Ivan Shugurov
Satya Narayan Shukla
Pranjay Shyam
Jianlou Si
Yawar Siddiqui
Alberto Signoroni
Pedro Silva
Jae-Young Sim
Oriane Siméoni
Martin Simon
Andrea Simonelli
Abhishek Singh
Ashish Singh
Dinesh Singh
Gurkirt Singh
Krishna Kumar Singh
Mannat Singh
Pravendra Singh
Rajat Vikram Singh
Utkarsh Singhal
Dipika Singhania
Vasu Singla
Harsh Sinha
Sudipta Sinha
Josef Sivic
Elena Sizikova
Geri Skenderi
Ivan Skorokhodov
Dmitriy Smirnov
Cameron Y. Smith
James S. Smith
Patrick Snape

Mattia Soldan
Hyeongseok Son
Sanghyun Son
Chuanbiao Song
Chen Song
Chunfeng Song
Dan Song
Dongjin Song
Hwanjun Song
Guoxian Song
Jiaming Song
Jie Song
Liangchen Song
Ran Song
Luchuan Song
Xibin Song
Li Song
Fenglong Song
Guoli Song
Guanglu Song
Zhenbo Song
Lin Song
Xinhang Song
Yang Song
Yibing Song
Rajiv Soundararajan
Hossein Souri
Cristovao Sousa
Riccardo Spezialetti
Leonidas Spinoulas
Michael W. Spratling
Deepak Sridhar
Srinath Sridhar
Gaurang Sriramanan
Vinkle Kumar Srivastav
Themos Stafylakis
Serban Stan
Anastasis Stathopoulos
Markus Steinberger
Jan Steinbrener
Sinisa Stekovic
Alexandros Stergiou
Gleb Sterkin
Rainer Stiefelhagen
Pierre Stock

Ombretta Strafforello
Julian Straub
Yannick Strümpler
Joerg Stueckler
Hang Su
Weijie Su
Jong-Chyi Su
Bing Su
Haisheng Su
Jinming Su
Yiyang Su
Yukun Su
Yuxin Su
Zhuo Su
Zhaoqi Su
Xiu Su
Yu-Chuan Su
Zhixun Su
Arulkumar Subramaniam
Akshayvarun Subramanya
A. Subramanyam
Swathikiran Sudhakaran
Yusuke Sugano
Masanori Suganuma
Yumin Suh
Yang Sui
Baochen Sun
Cheng Sun
Long Sun
Guolei Sun
Haoliang Sun
Haomiao Sun
He Sun
Hanqing Sun
Hao Sun
Lichao Sun
Jiachen Sun
Jiaming Sun
Jian Sun
Jin Sun
Jennifer J. Sun
Tiancheng Sun
Libo Sun
Peize Sun
Qianru Sun

Shanlin Sun
Yu Sun
Zhun Sun
Che Sun
Lin Sun
Tao Sun
Yiyou Sun
Chunyi Sun
Chong Sun
Weiwei Sun
Weixuan Sun
Xiuyu Sun
Yanan Sun
Zeren Sun
Zhaodong Sun
Zhiqing Sun
Minhyuk Sung
Jinli Suo
Simon Suo
Abhijit Suprem
Anshuman Suri
Saksham Suri
Joshua M. Susskind
Roman Suvorov
Gurumurthy Swaminathan
Robin Swanson
Paul Swoboda
Tabish A. Syed
Richard Szeliski
Fariborz Taherkhani
Yu-Wing Tai
Keita Takahashi
Walter Talbott
Gary Tam
Masato Tamura
Feitong Tan
Fuwen Tan
Shuhan Tan
Andong Tan
Bin Tan
Cheng Tan
Jianchao Tan
Lei Tan
Mingxing Tan
Xin Tan

Zichang Tan
Zhentao Tan
Kenichiro Tanaka
Masayuki Tanaka
Yushun Tang
Hao Tang
Jingqun Tang
Jinhui Tang
Kaihua Tang
Luming Tang
Lv Tang
Sheyang Tang
Shitao Tang
Siliang Tang
Shixiang Tang
Yansong Tang
Keke Tang
Chang Tang
Chenwei Tang
Jie Tang
Junshu Tang
Ming Tang
Peng Tang
Xu Tang
Yao Tang
Chen Tang
Fan Tang
Haoran Tang
Shengeng Tang
Yehui Tang
Zhipeng Tang
Ugo Tanielian
Chaofan Tao
Jiale Tao
Junli Tao
Renshuai Tao
An Tao
Guanhong Tao
Zhiqiang Tao
Makarand Tapaswi
Jean-Philippe G. Tarel
Juan J. Tarrio
Enzo Tartaglione
Keisuke Tateno
Zachary Teed

Ajinkya B. Tejankar
Bugra Tekin
Purva Tendulkar
Damien Teney
Minggui Teng
Chris Tensmeyer
Andrew Beng Jin Teoh
Philipp Terhörst
Kartik Thakral
Nupur Thakur
Kevin Thandiackal
Spyridon Thermos
Diego Thomas
William Thong
Yuesong Tian
Guanzhong Tian
Lin Tian
Shiqi Tian
Kai Tian
Meng Tian
Tai-Peng Tian
Zhuotao Tian
Shangxuan Tian
Tian Tian
Yapeng Tian
Yu Tian
Yuxin Tian
Leslie Ching Ow Tiong
Praveen Tirupattur
Garvita Tiwari
George Toderici
Antoine Toisoul
Aysim Toker
Tatiana Tommasi
Zhan Tong
Alessio Tonioni
Alessandro Torcinovich
Fabio Tosi
Matteo Toso
Hugo Touvron
Quan Hung Tran
Son Tran
Hung Tran
Ngoc-Trung Tran
Vinh Tran

Phong Tran
Giovanni Trappolini
Edith Tretschk
Subarna Tripathi
Shubhendu Trivedi
Eduard Trulls
Prune Truong
Thanh-Dat Truong
Tomasz Trzcinski
Sam Tsai
Yi-Hsuan Tsai
Ethan Tseng
Yu-Chee Tseng
Shahar Tsiper
Stavros Tsogkas
Shikui Tu
Zhigang Tu
Zhengzhong Tu
Richard Tucker
Sergey Tulyakov
Cigdem Turan
Daniyar Turmukhambetov
Victor G. Turrisi da Costa
Bartlomiej Twardowski
Christopher D. Twigg
Radim Tylecek
Mostofa Rafid Uddin
Md. Zasim Uddin
Kohei Uehara
Nicolas Ugrinovic
Youngjung Uh
Norimichi Ukita
Anwaar Ulhaq
Devesh Upadhyay
Paul Upchurch
Yoshitaka Ushiku
Yuzuko Utsumi
Mikaela Angelina Uy
Mohit Vaishnav
Pratik Vaishnavi
Jeya Maria Jose Valanarasu
Matias A. Valdenegro Toro
Diego Valsesia
Wouter Van Gansbeke
Nanne van Noord

Simon Vandenhende
Farshid Varno
Cristina Vasconcelos
Francisco Vasconcelos
Alex Vasilescu
Subeesh Vasu
Arun Balajee Vasudevan
Kanav Vats
Vaibhav S. Vavilala
Sagar Vaze
Javier Vazquez-Corral
Andrea Vedaldi
Olga Veksler
Andreas Velten
Sai H. Vemprala
Raviteja Vemulapalli
Shashanka
  Venkataramanan
Dor Verbin
Luisa Verdoliva
Manisha Verma
Yashaswi Verma
Constantin Vertan
Eli Verwimp
Deepak Vijaykeerthy
Pablo Villanueva
Ruben Villegas
Markus Vincze
Vibhav Vineet
Minh P. Vo
Huy V. Vo
Duc Minh Vo
Tomas Vojir
Igor Vozniak
Nicholas Vretos
Vibashan VS
Tuan-Anh Vu
Thang Vu
Mårten Wadenbäck
Neal Wadhwa
Aaron T. Walsman
Steven Walton
Jin Wan
Alvin Wan
Jia Wan

Jun Wan
Xiaoyue Wan
Fang Wan
Guowei Wan
Renjie Wan
Zhiqiang Wan
Ziyu Wan
Bastian Wandt
Dongdong Wang
Limin Wang
Haiyang Wang
Xiaobing Wang
Angtian Wang
Angelina Wang
Bing Wang
Bo Wang
Boyu Wang
Binghui Wang
Chen Wang
Chien-Yi Wang
Congli Wang
Qi Wang
Chengrui Wang
Rui Wang
Yiqun Wang
Cong Wang
Wenjing Wang
Dongkai Wang
Di Wang
Xiaogang Wang
Kai Wang
Zhizhong Wang
Fangjinhua Wang
Feng Wang
Hang Wang
Gaoang Wang
Guoqing Wang
Guangcong Wang
Guangzhi Wang
Hanqing Wang
Hao Wang
Haohan Wang
Haoran Wang
Hong Wang
Haotao Wang

Hu Wang
Huan Wang
Hua Wang
Hui-Po Wang
Hengli Wang
Hanyu Wang
Hongxing Wang
Jingwen Wang
Jialiang Wang
Jian Wang
Jianyi Wang
Jiashun Wang
Jiahao Wang
Tsun-Hsuan Wang
Xiaoqian Wang
Jinqiao Wang
Jun Wang
Jianzong Wang
Kaihong Wang
Ke Wang
Lei Wang
Lingjing Wang
Linnan Wang
Lin Wang
Liansheng Wang
Mengjiao Wang
Manning Wang
Nannan Wang
Peihao Wang
Jiayun Wang
Pu Wang
Qiang Wang
Qiufeng Wang
Qilong Wang
Qiangchang Wang
Qin Wang
Qing Wang
Ruocheng Wang
Ruibin Wang
Ruisheng Wang
Ruizhe Wang
Runqi Wang
Runzhong Wang
Wenxuan Wang
Sen Wang

Shangfei Wang
Shaofei Wang
Shijie Wang
Shiqi Wang
Zhibo Wang
Song Wang
Xinjiang Wang
Tai Wang
Tao Wang
Teng Wang
Xiang Wang
Tianren Wang
Tiantian Wang
Tianyi Wang
Fengjiao Wang
Wei Wang
Miaohui Wang
Suchen Wang
Siyue Wang
Yaoming Wang
Xiao Wang
Ze Wang
Biao Wang
Chaofei Wang
Dong Wang
Gu Wang
Guangrun Wang
Guangming Wang
Guo-Hua Wang
Haoqing Wang
Hesheng Wang
Huafeng Wang
Jinghua Wang
Jingdong Wang
Jingjing Wang
Jingya Wang
Jingkang Wang
Jiakai Wang
Junke Wang
Kuo Wang
Lichen Wang
Lizhi Wang
Longguang Wang
Mang Wang
Mei Wang

Min Wang
Peng-Shuai Wang
Run Wang
Shaoru Wang
Shuhui Wang
Tan Wang
Tiancai Wang
Tianqi Wang
Wenhai Wang
Wenzhe Wang
Xiaobo Wang
Xiudong Wang
Xu Wang
Yajie Wang
Yan Wang
Yuan-Gen Wang
Yingqian Wang
Yizhi Wang
Yulin Wang
Yu Wang
Yujie Wang
Yunhe Wang
Yuxi Wang
Yaowei Wang
Yiwei Wang
Zezheng Wang
Hongzhi Wang
Zhiqiang Wang
Ziteng Wang
Ziwei Wang
Zheng Wang
Zhenyu Wang
Binglu Wang
Zhongdao Wang
Ce Wang
Weining Wang
Weiyao Wang
Wenbin Wang
Wenguan Wang
Guangting Wang
Haolin Wang
Haiyan Wang
Huiyu Wang
Naiyan Wang
Jingbo Wang

Jinpeng Wang
Jiaqi Wang
Liyuan Wang
Lizhen Wang
Ning Wang
Wenqian Wang
Sheng-Yu Wang
Weimin Wang
Xiaohan Wang
Yifan Wang
Yi Wang
Yongtao Wang
Yizhou Wang
Zhuo Wang
Zhe Wang
Xudong Wang
Xiaofang Wang
Xinggang Wang
Xiaosen Wang
Xiaosong Wang
Xiaoyang Wang
Lijun Wang
Xinlong Wang
Xuan Wang
Xue Wang
Yangang Wang
Yaohui Wang
Yu-Chiang Frank Wang
Yida Wang
Yilin Wang
Yi Ru Wang
Yali Wang
Yinglong Wang
Yufu Wang
Yujiang Wang
Yuwang Wang
Yuting Wang
Yang Wang
Yu-Xiong Wang
Yixu Wang
Ziqi Wang
Zhicheng Wang
Zeyu Wang
Zhaowen Wang
Zhenyi Wang

Zhenzhi Wang
Zhijie Wang
Zhiyong Wang
Zhongling Wang
Zhuowei Wang
Zian Wang
Zifu Wang
Zihao Wang
Zirui Wang
Ziyan Wang
Wenxiao Wang
Zhen Wang
Zhepeng Wang
Zi Wang
Zihao W. Wang
Steven L. Waslander
Olivia Watkins
Daniel Watson
Silvan Weder
Dongyoon Wee
Dongming Wei
Tianyi Wei
Jia Wei
Dong Wei
Fangyun Wei
Longhui Wei
Mingqiang Wei
Xinyue Wei
Chen Wei
Donglai Wei
Pengxu Wei
Xing Wei
Xiu-Shen Wei
Wenqi Wei
Guoqiang Wei
Wei Wei
XingKui Wei
Xian Wei
Xingxing Wei
Yake Wei
Yuxiang Wei
Yi Wei
Luca Weihs
Michael Weinmann
Martin Weinmann

Congcong Wen
Chuan Wen
Jie Wen
Sijia Wen
Song Wen
Chao Wen
Xiang Wen
Zeyi Wen
Xin Wen
Yilin Wen
Yijia Weng
Shuchen Weng
Junwu Weng
Wenming Weng
Renliang Weng
Zhenyu Weng
Xinshuo Weng
Nicholas J. Westlake
Gordon Wetzstein
Lena M. Widin Klasén
Rick Wildes
Bryan M. Williams
Williem Williem
Ole Winther
Scott Wisdom
Alex Wong
Chau-Wai Wong
Kwan-Yee K. Wong
Yongkang Wong
Scott Workman
Marcel Worring
Michael Wray
Safwan Wshah
Xiang Wu
Aming Wu
Chongruo Wu
Cho-Ying Wu
Chunpeng Wu
Chenyan Wu
Ziyi Wu
Fuxiang Wu
Gang Wu
Haiping Wu
Huisi Wu
Jane Wu

Jialian Wu
Jing Wu
Jinjian Wu
Jianlong Wu
Xian Wu
Lifang Wu
Lifan Wu
Minye Wu
Qianyi Wu
Rongliang Wu
Rui Wu
Shiqian Wu
Shuzhe Wu
Shangzhe Wu
Tsung-Han Wu
Tz-Ying Wu
Ting-Wei Wu
Jiannan Wu
Zhiliang Wu
Yu Wu
Chenyun Wu
Dayan Wu
Dongxian Wu
Fei Wu
Hefeng Wu
Jianxin Wu
Weibin Wu
Wenxuan Wu
Wenhao Wu
Xiao Wu
Yicheng Wu
Yuanwei Wu
Yu-Huan Wu
Zhenxin Wu
Zhenyu Wu
Wei Wu
Peng Wu
Xiaohe Wu
Xindi Wu
Xinxing Wu
Xinyi Wu
Xingjiao Wu
Xiongwei Wu
Yangzheng Wu
Yanzhao Wu

Yawen Wu
Yong Wu
Yi Wu
Ying Nian Wu
Zhenyao Wu
Zhonghua Wu
Zongze Wu
Zuxuan Wu
Stefanie Wuhrer
Teng Xi
Jianing Xi
Fei Xia
Haifeng Xia
Menghan Xia
Yuanqing Xia
Zhihua Xia
Xiaobo Xia
Weihao Xia
Shihong Xia
Yan Xia
Yong Xia
Zhaoyang Xia
Zhihao Xia
Chuhua Xian
Yongqin Xian
Wangmeng Xiang
Fanbo Xiang
Tiange Xiang
Tao Xiang
Liuyu Xiang
Xiaoyu Xiang
Zhiyu Xiang
Aoran Xiao
Chunxia Xiao
Fanyi Xiao
Jimin Xiao
Jun Xiao
Taihong Xiao
Anqi Xiao
Junfei Xiao
Jing Xiao
Liang Xiao
Yang Xiao
Yuting Xiao
Yijun Xiao

Yao Xiao
Zeyu Xiao
Zhisheng Xiao
Zihao Xiao
Binhui Xie
Christopher Xie
Haozhe Xie
Jin Xie
Guo-Sen Xie
Hongtao Xie
Ming-Kun Xie
Tingting Xie
Chaohao Xie
Weicheng Xie
Xudong Xie
Jiyang Xie
Xiaohua Xie
Yuan Xie
Zhenyu Xie
Ning Xie
Xianghui Xie
Xiufeng Xie
You Xie
Yutong Xie
Fuyong Xing
Yifan Xing
Zhen Xing
Yuanjun Xiong
Jinhui Xiong
Weihua Xiong
Hongkai Xiong
Zhitong Xiong
Yuanhao Xiong
Yunyang Xiong
Yuwen Xiong
Zhiwei Xiong
Yuliang Xiu
An Xu
Chang Xu
Chenliang Xu
Chengming Xu
Chenshu Xu
Xiang Xu
Huijuan Xu
Zhe Xu

Jie Xu
Jingyi Xu
Jiarui Xu
Yinghao Xu
Kele Xu
Ke Xu
Li Xu
Linchuan Xu
Linning Xu
Mengde Xu
Mengmeng Frost Xu
Min Xu
Mingye Xu
Jun Xu
Ning Xu
Peng Xu
Runsheng Xu
Sheng Xu
Wenqiang Xu
Xiaogang Xu
Renzhe Xu
Kaidi Xu
Yi Xu
Chi Xu
Qiuling Xu
Baobei Xu
Feng Xu
Haohang Xu
Haofei Xu
Lan Xu
Mingze Xu
Songcen Xu
Weipeng Xu
Wenjia Xu
Wenju Xu
Xiangyu Xu
Xin Xu
Yinshuang Xu
Yixing Xu
Yuting Xu
Yanyu Xu
Zhenbo Xu
Zhiliang Xu
Zhiyuan Xu
Xiaohao Xu

Yanwu Xu
Yan Xu
Yiran Xu
Yifan Xu
Yufei Xu
Yong Xu
Zichuan Xu
Zenglin Xu
Zexiang Xu
Zhan Xu
Zheng Xu
Zhiwei Xu
Ziyue Xu
Shiyu Xuan
Hanyu Xuan
Fei Xue
Jianru Xue
Mingfu Xue
Qinghan Xue
Tianfan Xue
Chao Xue
Chuhui Xue
Nan Xue
Zhou Xue
Xiangyang Xue
Yuan Xue
Abhay Yadav
Ravindra Yadav
Kota Yamaguchi
Toshihiko Yamasaki
Kohei Yamashita
Chaochao Yan
Feng Yan
Kun Yan
Qingsen Yan
Qixin Yan
Rui Yan
Siming Yan
Xinchen Yan
Yaping Yan
Bin Yan
Qingan Yan
Shen Yan
Shipeng Yan
Xu Yan

Yan Yan
Yichao Yan
Zhaoyi Yan
Zike Yan
Zhiqiang Yan
Hongliang Yan
Zizheng Yan
Jiewen Yang
Anqi Joyce Yang
Shan Yang
Anqi Yang
Antoine Yang
Bo Yang
Baoyao Yang
Chenhongyi Yang
Dingkang Yang
De-Nian Yang
Dong Yang
David Yang
Fan Yang
Fengyu Yang
Fengting Yang
Fei Yang
Gengshan Yang
Heng Yang
Han Yang
Huan Yang
Yibo Yang
Jiancheng Yang
Jihan Yang
Jiawei Yang
Jiayu Yang
Jie Yang
Jinfa Yang
Jingkang Yang
Jinyu Yang
Cheng-Fu Yang
Ji Yang
Jianyu Yang
Kailun Yang
Tian Yang
Luyu Yang
Liang Yang
Li Yang
Michael Ying Yang

Yang Yang
Muli Yang
Le Yang
Qiushi Yang
Ren Yang
Ruihan Yang
Shuang Yang
Siyuan Yang
Su Yang
Shiqi Yang
Taojiannan Yang
Tianyu Yang
Lei Yang
Wanzhao Yang
Shuai Yang
William Yang
Wei Yang
Xiaofeng Yang
Xiaoshan Yang
Xin Yang
Xuan Yang
Xu Yang
Xingyi Yang
Xitong Yang
Jing Yang
Yanchao Yang
Wenming Yang
Yujiu Yang
Herb Yang
Jianfei Yang
Jinhui Yang
Chuanguang Yang
Guanglei Yang
Haitao Yang
Kewei Yang
Linlin Yang
Lijin Yang
Longrong Yang
Meng Yang
MingKun Yang
Sibei Yang
Shicai Yang
Tong Yang
Wen Yang
Xi Yang

Xiaolong Yang
Xue Yang
Yubin Yang
Ze Yang
Ziyi Yang
Yi Yang
Linjie Yang
Yuzhe Yang
Yiding Yang
Zhenpei Yang
Zhaohui Yang
Zhengyuan Yang
Zhibo Yang
Zongxin Yang
Hantao Yao
Mingde Yao
Rui Yao
Taiping Yao
Ting Yao
Cong Yao
Qingsong Yao
Quanming Yao
Xu Yao
Yuan Yao
Yao Yao
Yazhou Yao
Jiawen Yao
Shunyu Yao
Pew-Thian Yap
Sudhir Yarram
Rajeev Yasarla
Peng Ye
Botao Ye
Mao Ye
Fei Ye
Hanrong Ye
Jingwen Ye
Jinwei Ye
Jiarong Ye
Mang Ye
Meng Ye
Qi Ye
Qian Ye
Qixiang Ye
Junjie Ye

Sheng Ye
Nanyang Ye
Yufei Ye
Xiaoqing Ye
Ruolin Ye
Yousef Yeganeh
Chun-Hsiao Yeh
Raymond A. Yeh
Yu-Ying Yeh
Kai Yi
Chang Yi
Renjiao Yi
Xinping Yi
Peng Yi
Alper Yilmaz
Junho Yim
Hui Yin
Bangjie Yin
Jia-Li Yin
Miao Yin
Wenzhe Yin
Xuwang Yin
Ming Yin
Yu Yin
Aoxiong Yin
Kangxue Yin
Tianwei Yin
Wei Yin
Xianghua Ying
Rio Yokota
Tatsuya Yokota
Naoto Yokoya
Ryo Yonetani
Ki Yoon Yoo
Jinsu Yoo
Sunjae Yoon
Jae Shin Yoon
Jihun Yoon
Sung-Hoon Yoon
Ryota Yoshihashi
Yusuke Yoshiyasu
Chenyu You
Haoran You
Haoxuan You
Yang You

Quanzeng You
Tackgeun You
Kaichao You
Shan You
Xinge You
Yurong You
Baosheng Yu
Bei Yu
Haichao Yu
Hao Yu
Chaohui Yu
Fisher Yu
Jin-Gang Yu
Jiyang Yu
Jason J. Yu
Jiashuo Yu
Hong-Xing Yu
Lei Yu
Mulin Yu
Ning Yu
Peilin Yu
Qi Yu
Qian Yu
Rui Yu
Shuzhi Yu
Gang Yu
Tan Yu
Weijiang Yu
Xin Yu
Bingyao Yu
Ye Yu
Hanchao Yu
Yingchen Yu
Tao Yu
Xiaotian Yu
Qing Yu
Houjian Yu
Changqian Yu
Jing Yu
Jun Yu
Shujian Yu
Xiang Yu
Zhaofei Yu
Zhenbo Yu
Yinfeng Yu

Zhuoran Yu
Zitong Yu
Bo Yuan
Jiangbo Yuan
Liangzhe Yuan
Weihao Yuan
Jianbo Yuan
Xiaoyun Yuan
Ye Yuan
Li Yuan
Geng Yuan
Jialin Yuan
Maoxun Yuan
Peng Yuan
Xin Yuan
Yuan Yuan
Yuhui Yuan
Yixuan Yuan
Zheng Yuan
Mehmet Kerim Yücel
Kaiyu Yue
Haixiao Yue
Heeseung Yun
Sangdoo Yun
Tian Yun
Mahmut Yurt
Ekim Yurtsever
Ahmet Yüzügüler
Edouard Yvinec
Eloi Zablocki
Christopher Zach
Muhammad Zaigham
    Zaheer
Pierluigi Zama Ramirez
Yuhang Zang
Pietro Zanuttigh
Alexey Zaytsev
Bernhard Zeisl
Haitian Zeng
Pengpeng Zeng
Jiabei Zeng
Runhao Zeng
Wei Zeng
Yawen Zeng
Yi Zeng

Yiming Zeng
Tieyong Zeng
Huanqiang Zeng
Dan Zeng
Yu Zeng
Wei Zhai
Yuanhao Zhai
Fangneng Zhan
Kun Zhan
Xiong Zhang
Jingdong Zhang
Jiangning Zhang
Zhilu Zhang
Gengwei Zhang
Dongsu Zhang
Hui Zhang
Binjie Zhang
Bo Zhang
Tianhao Zhang
Cecilia Zhang
Jing Zhang
Chaoning Zhang
Chenxu Zhang
Chi Zhang
Chris Zhang
Yabin Zhang
Zhao Zhang
Rufeng Zhang
Chaoyi Zhang
Zheng Zhang
Da Zhang
Yi Zhang
Edward Zhang
Xin Zhang
Feifei Zhang
Feilong Zhang
Yuqi Zhang
GuiXuan Zhang
Hanlin Zhang
Hanwang Zhang
Hanzhen Zhang
Haotian Zhang
He Zhang
Haokui Zhang
Hongyuan Zhang

Hengrui Zhang
Hongming Zhang
Mingfang Zhang
Jianpeng Zhang
Jiaming Zhang
Jichao Zhang
Jie Zhang
Jingfeng Zhang
Jingyi Zhang
Jinnian Zhang
David Junhao Zhang
Junjie Zhang
Junzhe Zhang
Jiawan Zhang
Jingyang Zhang
Kai Zhang
Lei Zhang
Lihua Zhang
Lu Zhang
Miao Zhang
Minjia Zhang
Mingjin Zhang
Qi Zhang
Qian Zhang
Qilong Zhang
Qiming Zhang
Qiang Zhang
Richard Zhang
Ruimao Zhang
Ruisi Zhang
Ruixin Zhang
Runze Zhang
Qilin Zhang
Shan Zhang
Shanshan Zhang
Xi Sheryl Zhang
Song-Hai Zhang
Chongyang Zhang
Kaihao Zhang
Songyang Zhang
Shu Zhang
Siwei Zhang
Shujian Zhang
Tianyun Zhang
Tong Zhang

Tao Zhang
Wenwei Zhang
Wenqiang Zhang
Wen Zhang
Xiaolin Zhang
Xingchen Zhang
Xingxuan Zhang
Xiuming Zhang
Xiaoshuai Zhang
Xuanmeng Zhang
Xuanyang Zhang
Xucong Zhang
Xingxing Zhang
Xikun Zhang
Xiaohan Zhang
Yahui Zhang
Yunhua Zhang
Yan Zhang
Yanghao Zhang
Yifei Zhang
Yifan Zhang
Yi-Fan Zhang
Yihao Zhang
Yingliang Zhang
Youshan Zhang
Yulun Zhang
Yushu Zhang
Yixiao Zhang
Yide Zhang
Zhongwen Zhang
Bowen Zhang
Chen-Lin Zhang
Zehua Zhang
Zekun Zhang
Zeyu Zhang
Xiaowei Zhang
Yifeng Zhang
Cheng Zhang
Hongguang Zhang
Yuexi Zhang
Fa Zhang
Guofeng Zhang
Hao Zhang
Haofeng Zhang
Hongwen Zhang

Hua Zhang
Jiaxin Zhang
Zhenyu Zhang
Jian Zhang
Jianfeng Zhang
Jiao Zhang
Jiakai Zhang
Lefei Zhang
Le Zhang
Mi Zhang
Min Zhang
Ning Zhang
Pan Zhang
Pu Zhang
Qing Zhang
Renrui Zhang
Shifeng Zhang
Shuo Zhang
Shaoxiong Zhang
Weizhong Zhang
Xi Zhang
Xiaomei Zhang
Xinyu Zhang
Yin Zhang
Zicheng Zhang
Zihao Zhang
Ziqi Zhang
Zhaoxiang Zhang
Zhen Zhang
Zhipeng Zhang
Zhixing Zhang
Zhizheng Zhang
Jiawei Zhang
Zhong Zhang
Pingping Zhang
Yixin Zhang
Kui Zhang
Lingzhi Zhang
Huaiwen Zhang
Quanshi Zhang
Zhoutong Zhang
Yuhang Zhang
Yuting Zhang
Zhang Zhang
Ziming Zhang

Zhizhong Zhang
Qilong Zhangli
Bingyin Zhao
Bin Zhao
Chenglong Zhao
Lei Zhao
Feng Zhao
Gangming Zhao
Haiyan Zhao
Hao Zhao
Handong Zhao
Hengshuang Zhao
Yinan Zhao
Jiaojiao Zhao
Jiaqi Zhao
Jing Zhao
Kaili Zhao
Haojie Zhao
Yucheng Zhao
Longjiao Zhao
Long Zhao
Qingsong Zhao
Qingyu Zhao
Rui Zhao
Rui-Wei Zhao
Sicheng Zhao
Shuang Zhao
Siyan Zhao
Zelin Zhao
Shiyu Zhao
Wang Zhao
Tiesong Zhao
Qian Zhao
Wangbo Zhao
Xi-Le Zhao
Xu Zhao
Yajie Zhao
Yang Zhao
Ying Zhao
Yin Zhao
Yizhou Zhao
Yunhan Zhao
Yuyang Zhao
Yue Zhao
Yuzhi Zhao

Bowen Zhao
Pu Zhao
Bingchen Zhao
Borui Zhao
Fuqiang Zhao
Hanbin Zhao
Jian Zhao
Mingyang Zhao
Na Zhao
Rongchang Zhao
Ruiqi Zhao
Shuai Zhao
Wenda Zhao
Wenliang Zhao
Xiangyun Zhao
Yifan Zhao
Yaping Zhao
Zhou Zhao
He Zhao
Jie Zhao
Xibin Zhao
Xiaoqi Zhao
Zhengyu Zhao
Jin Zhe
Chuanxia Zheng
Huan Zheng
Hao Zheng
Jia Zheng
Jian-Qing Zheng
Shuai Zheng
Meng Zheng
Mingkai Zheng
Qian Zheng
Qi Zheng
Wu Zheng
Yinqiang Zheng
Yufeng Zheng
Yutong Zheng
Yalin Zheng
Yu Zheng
Feng Zheng
Zhaoheng Zheng
Haitian Zheng
Kang Zheng
Bolun Zheng

Haiyong Zheng
Mingwu Zheng
Sipeng Zheng
Tu Zheng
Wenzhao Zheng
Xiawu Zheng
Yinglin Zheng
Zhuo Zheng
Zilong Zheng
Kecheng Zheng
Zerong Zheng
Shuaifeng Zhi
Tiancheng Zhi
Jia-Xing Zhong
Yiwu Zhong
Fangwei Zhong
Zhihang Zhong
Yaoyao Zhong
Yiran Zhong
Zhun Zhong
Zichun Zhong
Bo Zhou
Boyao Zhou
Brady Zhou
Mo Zhou
Chunluan Zhou
Dingfu Zhou
Fan Zhou
Jingkai Zhou
Honglu Zhou
Jiaming Zhou
Jiahuan Zhou
Jun Zhou
Kaiyang Zhou
Keyang Zhou
Kuangqi Zhou
Lei Zhou
Lihua Zhou
Man Zhou
Mingyi Zhou
Mingyuan Zhou
Ning Zhou
Peng Zhou
Penghao Zhou
Qianyi Zhou

Shuigeng Zhou
Shangchen Zhou
Huayi Zhou
Zhize Zhou
Sanping Zhou
Qin Zhou
Tao Zhou
Wenbo Zhou
Xiangdong Zhou
Xiao-Yun Zhou
Xiao Zhou
Yang Zhou
Yipin Zhou
Zhenyu Zhou
Hao Zhou
Chu Zhou
Daquan Zhou
Da-Wei Zhou
Hang Zhou
Kang Zhou
Qianyu Zhou
Sheng Zhou
Wenhui Zhou
Xingyi Zhou
Yan-Jie Zhou
Yiyi Zhou
Yu Zhou
Yuan Zhou
Yuqian Zhou
Yuxuan Zhou
Zixiang Zhou
Wengang Zhou
Shuchang Zhou
Tianfei Zhou
Yichao Zhou
Alex Zhu
Chenchen Zhu
Deyao Zhu
Xiatian Zhu
Guibo Zhu
Haidong Zhu
Hao Zhu
Hongzi Zhu
Rui Zhu
Jing Zhu

Jianke Zhu
Junchen Zhu
Lei Zhu
Lingyu Zhu
Luyang Zhu
Menglong Zhu
Peihao Zhu
Hui Zhu
Xiaofeng Zhu
Tyler (Lixuan) Zhu
Wentao Zhu
Xiangyu Zhu
Xinqi Zhu
Xinxin Zhu
Xinliang Zhu
Yangguang Zhu
Yichen Zhu
Yixin Zhu
Yanjun Zhu
Yousong Zhu
Yuhao Zhu
Ye Zhu
Feng Zhu
Zhen Zhu
Fangrui Zhu
Jinjing Zhu
Linchao Zhu
Pengfei Zhu
Sijie Zhu
Xiaobin Zhu
Xiaoguang Zhu
Zezhou Zhu
Zhenyao Zhu
Kai Zhu
Pengkai Zhu
Bingbing Zhuang
Chengyuan Zhuang
Liansheng Zhuang
Peiye Zhuang
Yixin Zhuang
Yihong Zhuang
Junbao Zhuo
Andrea Ziani
Bartosz Zieliński
Primo Zingaretti

Nikolaos Zioulis
Andrew Zisserman
Yael Ziv
Liu Ziyin
Xingxing Zou
Danping Zou
Qi Zou

Shihao Zou
Xueyan Zou
Yang Zou
Yuliang Zou
Zihang Zou
Chuhang Zou
Dongqing Zou

Xu Zou
Zhiming Zou
Maria A. Zuluaga
Xinxin Zuo
Zhiwen Zuo
Reyer Zwiggelaar

Contents – Part XXVII

Relative Contrastive Loss for Unsupervised Representation Learning 1
 Shixiang Tang, Feng Zhu, Lei Bai, Rui Zhao, and Wanli Ouyang

Fine-Grained Fashion Representation Learning by Online Deep Clustering 19
 Yang Jiao, Ning Xie, Yan Gao, Chien-chih Wang, and Yi Sun

NashAE: Disentangling Representations Through Adversarial Covariance
Minimization 36
 Eric Yeats, Frank Liu, David Womble, and Hai Li

A Gyrovector Space Approach for Symmetric Positive Semi-definite
Matrix Learning 52
 Xuan Son Nguyen

Learning Visual Representation from Modality-Shared Contrastive
Language-Image Pre-training 69
 Haoxuan You, Luowei Zhou, Bin Xiao, Noel Codella, Yu Cheng,
 Ruochen Xu, Shih-Fu Chang, and Lu Yuan

Contrasting Quadratic Assignments for Set-Based Representation Learning 88
 Artem Moskalev, Ivan Sosnovik, Volker Fischer, and Arnold Smeulders

Class-Incremental Learning with Cross-Space Clustering and Controlled
Transfer 105
 Arjun Ashok, K. J. Joseph, and Vineeth N. Balasubramanian

Object Discovery and Representation Networks 123
 Olivier J. Hénaff, Skanda Koppula, Evan Shelhamer, Daniel Zoran,
 Andrew Jaegle, Andrew Zisserman, João Carreira, and Relja Arandjelović

Trading Positional Complexity vs Deepness in Coordinate Networks 144
 Jianqiao Zheng, Sameera Ramasinghe, Xueqian Li, and Simon Lucey

MVDG: A Unified Multi-view Framework for Domain Generalization 161
 Jian Zhang, Lei Qi, Yinghuan Shi, and Yang Gao

Panoptic Scene Graph Generation 178
 Jingkang Yang, Yi Zhe Ang, Zujin Guo, Kaiyang Zhou, Wayne Zhang,
 and Ziwei Liu

Object-Compositional Neural Implicit Surfaces 197
  Qianyi Wu, Xian Liu, Yuedong Chen, Kejie Li, Chuanxia Zheng,
  Jianfei Cai, and Jianmin Zheng

RigNet: Repetitive Image Guided Network for Depth Completion 214
  Zhiqiang Yan, Kun Wang, Xiang Li, Zhenyu Zhang, Jun Li, and Jian Yang

FADE: Fusing the Assets of Decoder and Encoder for Task-Agnostic
Upsampling 231
  Hao Lu, Wenze Liu, Hongtao Fu, and Zhiguo Cao

LiDAL: Inter-frame Uncertainty Based Active Learning for 3D LiDAR
Semantic Segmentation 248
  Zeyu Hu, Xuyang Bai, Runze Zhang, Xin Wang, Guangyuan Sun,
  Hongbo Fu, and Chiew-Lan Tai

Hierarchical Memory Learning for Fine-Grained Scene Graph Generation 266
  Youming Deng, Yansheng Li, Yongjun Zhang, Xiang Xiang, Jian Wang,
  Jingdong Chen, and Jiayi Ma

DODA: Data-Oriented Sim-to-Real Domain Adaptation for 3D Semantic
Segmentation 284
  Runyu Ding, Jihan Yang, Li Jiang, and Xiaojuan Qi

MTFormer: Multi-task Learning via Transformer and Cross-Task
Reasoning 304
  Xiaogang Xu, Hengshuang Zhao, Vibhav Vineet, Ser-Nam Lim,
  and Antonio Torralba

MonoPLFlowNet: Permutohedral Lattice FlowNet for Real-Scale 3D
Scene Flow Estimation with Monocular Images 322
  Runfa Li and Truong Nguyen

TO-Scene: A Large-Scale Dataset for Understanding 3D Tabletop Scenes 340
  Mutian Xu, Pei Chen, Haolin Liu, and Xiaoguang Han

Is It Necessary to Transfer Temporal Knowledge for Domain Adaptive
Video Semantic Segmentation? 357
  Xinyi Wu, Zhenyao Wu, Jin Wan, Lili Ju, and Song Wang

Meta Spatio-Temporal Debiasing for Video Scene Graph Generation 374
  Li Xu, Haoxuan Qu, Jason Kuen, Jiuxiang Gu, and Jun Liu

Improving the Reliability for Confidence Estimation 391
   Haoxuan Qu, Yanchao Li, Lin Geng Foo, Jason Kuen, Jiuxiang Gu,
   and Jun Liu

Fine-Grained Scene Graph Generation with Data Transfer 409
   Ao Zhang, Yuan Yao, Qianyu Chen, Wei Ji, Zhiyuan Liu, Maosong Sun,
   and Tat-Seng Chua

Pose2Room: Understanding 3D Scenes from Human Activities 425
   Yinyu Nie, Angela Dai, Xiaoguang Han, and Matthias Nießner

Towards Hard-Positive Query Mining for DETR-Based Human-Object
Interaction Detection 444
   Xubin Zhong, Changxing Ding, Zijian Li, and Shaoli Huang

Discovering Human-Object Interaction Concepts via Self-Compositional
Learning 461
   Zhi Hou, Baosheng Yu, and Dacheng Tao

Primitive-Based Shape Abstraction via Nonparametric Bayesian Inference 479
   Yuwei Wu, Weixiao Liu, Sipu Ruan, and Gregory S. Chirikjian

Stereo Depth Estimation with Echoes 496
   Chenghao Zhang, Kun Tian, Bolin Ni, Gaofeng Meng, Bin Fan,
   Zhaoxiang Zhang, and Chunhong Pan

Inverted Pyramid Multi-task Transformer for Dense Scene Understanding 514
   Hanrong Ye and Dan Xu

PETR: Position Embedding Transformation for Multi-view 3D Object
Detection 531
   Yingfei Liu, Tiancai Wang, Xiangyu Zhang, and Jian Sun

S2Net: Stochastic Sequential Pointcloud Forecasting 549
   Xinshuo Weng, Junyu Nan, Kuan-Hui Lee, Rowan McAllister,
   Adrien Gaidon, Nicholas Rhinehart, and Kris M. Kitani

RA-Depth: Resolution Adaptive Self-supervised Monocular Depth
Estimation 565
   Mu He, Le Hui, Yikai Bian, Jian Ren, Jin Xie, and Jian Yang

PolyphonicFormer: Unified Query Learning for Depth-Aware Video
Panoptic Segmentation 582
   Haobo Yuan, Xiangtai Li, Yibo Yang, Guangliang Cheng, Jing Zhang,
   Yunhai Tong, Lefei Zhang, and Dacheng Tao

SQN: Weakly-Supervised Semantic Segmentation of Large-Scale 3D
Point Clouds   600
    *Qingyong Hu, Bo Yang, Guangchi Fang, Yulan Guo, Aleš Leonardis,
    Niki Trigoni, and Andrew Markham*

PointMixer: MLP-Mixer for Point Cloud Understanding   620
    *Jaesung Choe, Chunghyun Park, Francois Rameau, Jaesik Park,
    and In So Kweon*

Initialization and Alignment for Adversarial Texture Optimization   641
    Xiaoming Zhao, Zhizhen Zhao, and Alexander G. Schwing

MOTR: End-to-End Multiple-Object Tracking with Transformer   659
    *Fangao Zeng, Bin Dong, Yuang Zhang, Tiancai Wang, Xiangyu Zhang,
    and Yichen Wei*

GALA: Toward Geometry-and-Lighting-Aware Object Search
for Compositing   676
    Sijie Zhu, Zhe Lin, Scott Cohen, Jason Kuen, Zhifei Zhang, and Chen Chen

LaLaLoc++: Global Floor Plan Comprehension for Layout Localisation
in Unvisited Environments   693
    Henry Howard-Jenkins and Victor Adrian Prisacariu

3D-PL: Domain Adaptive Depth Estimation with 3D-Aware
Pseudo-Labeling   710
    Yu-Ting Yen, Chia-Ni Lu, Wei-Chen Chiu, and Yi-Hsuan Tsai

Panoptic-PartFormer: Learning a Unified Model for Panoptic Part
Segmentation   729
    *Xiangtai Li, Shilin Xu, Yibo Yang, Guangliang Cheng, Yunhai Tong,
    and Dacheng Tao*

Author Index   749

Relative Contrastive Loss
for Unsupervised Representation
Learning

Shixiang Tang[1,3], Feng Zhu[3], Lei Bai[2(✉)], Rui Zhao[3,4], and Wanli Ouyang[1,2]

[1] University of Sydney, Camperdown, Australia
stan3906@uni.sydney.edu.au
[2] Shanghai AI Laboratory, Beijing, China
baisanshi@gmail.com
[3] Sensetime Research, Hong Kong, China
[4] Qing Yuan Research Institute, Shanghai Jiao Tong University, Shanghai, China

Abstract. Defining positive and negative samples is critical for learning visual variations of the semantic classes in an unsupervised manner. Previous methods either construct positive sample pairs as different data augmentations on the same image (i.e., single-instance-positive) or estimate a class prototype by clustering (i.e., prototype-positive), both ignoring the relative nature of positive/negative concepts in the real world. Motivated by the ability of humans in recognizing relatively positive/negative samples, we propose the Relative Contrastive Loss (RCL) to learn feature representation from relatively positive/negative pairs, which not only learns more real world semantic variations than the single-instance-positive methods but also respects positive-negative relativeness compared with absolute prototype-positive methods. The proposed RCL improves the linear evaluation for MoCo v3 by **+2.0%** on ImageNet.

1 Introduction

Recent progresses on visual representation learning [1,15,26,28,36,40,48,53] have shown the superior capability of unsupervised learning (also denoted as self-supervised learning in some works [7,21,46]) in learning visual representations without manual annotations. Contrastive learning [7,9–11,19,21,24,46,50,57], which is the cornerstone of recent unsupervised learning methods, optimizes the deep networks by reducing the distance between representations of positive pairs and increasing the distance between representations of negative pairs in the latent feature space simultaneously. As an amazing achievement, it is shown in [19,24,50] that the pretrained feature representation with recent contrastive learning methods is comparable with supervised learning in image classification.

Supplementary Information The online version contains supplementary material available at https://doi.org/10.1007/978-3-031-19812-0_1.

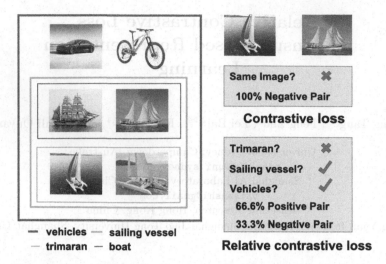

— vehicles — sailing vessel
— trimaran — boat

Same Image? ✖
100% Negative Pair

Contrastive loss

Trimaran? ✖
Sailing vessel? ✓
Vehicles? ✓
66.6% Positive Pair
33.3% Negative Pair

Relative contrastive loss

Fig. 1. Motivation of the Relative Contrastive Loss. *Left:* Blue, purple and, orange rectangles denote vehicles, sailing vessel, and trimaran, respectively. The concepts of vehicles, sailing vessels, and trimarans show that the concepts of two images belonging to the same category depend on the level of hyponymy, motivating us to conduct the relative contrastive learning in this paper. *Right:* Any image pair in relative contrastive loss are determined postive or negative by multiple criteria. (Color figure online)

One of the critical components for contrastive learning methods is constructing positive pairs and negative pairs. In particular, *single-instance-positive* methods, such as MoCo [9,21], SimCLR [7,8], and BYOL [19], apply random image augmentations (*e.g.,* random crops, color jittering, etc.) on the same sample (image) to obtain different views of the same sample as *positive* pairs and optionally take the augmentations of other samples as *negative* pairs. Though demonstrated effective, such augmentations are insufficient to provide positive pairs with natural intra-class variances such as different camera viewpoints, non-rigid deformations of the same object, or different instances of the same category. *Clustering-based* methods [3,5] and *neighborhood-based* methods [16,39] can handle the above problems in *single-instance-positive* methods by using the prototypes of pseudo-classes generated by clustering [2,3,5] or k nearest neighbors in the feature space [16,39] as the positive samples. Despite their great success, all these unsupervised learning methods define positive and negative pairs absolutely, ignoring the relative nature of positive and negative concepts in the real world.

Instead of constructing positive and negative pairs categorically in previous self-supervised learning methods, human beings have the relative recognition ability. In biotaxonomy, the Swedish botanist Carl Linnaeus described the relative similarity of biological organisms under seven hierarchies, *i.e.,* Kingdom, Phylum, Class, Order, Family, Genus, Species, forming the current system of Linnaean taxonomy [17]. Popular benchmarks in computer vision such as ImageNet [14], iNat21 [45], and Places365 [56], also respect the positive-negative relativeness and include hierarchical labels. For example, in ImageNet, trimaran and boats all belong to sailing vessels (more general concept) and vehicles (the most general concept in Fig. 1(left)). However, trimaran and boats are different classes when we aim to specify different sailing vessels.

In this paper, we respect the nature of relativeness in human recognition and propose a new *relative contrastive loss* by recognizing a given sample pair partially positive and negative based on a set of semantic criteria to capture real world instance variation of a class in a relative way (Fig. 1(*right*)). Given two images, *i.e.*, query and key, we feed them into the encoder and momentum encoder to get their features, respectively. Then, the relatively positive-negative relations among them are determined by a set of criteria, which are instantiated by hierarchical clustering. Each level in hierarchical clustering is considered as a specific criterion. The proposed relative contrastive loss leverages the query feature, the key feature and their relatively positive-negative relations to supervise the training process.

In summary, our main contributions are introducing the general idea of relative contrastive loss for self-supervised learning, and accordingly designing a framework incorporating the online hierarchical clustering to instantiate it. The effectiveness of our proposed method is demonstrated via extensive experiments. For instance, on ImageNet linear evaluation, our method well boosts the top-1 accuracy of ResNet-50 by **+2.0%** gain (73.8% → 75.8%) compared with MoCov3. Experimental results also validate the effectiveness of our method for semi-supervised classification, object detection, and instance segmentation.

2 Related Work

Single-Instance-Positive Methods. Instead of designing new pre-text tasks [3,15,33,34,54], recent unsupervised learning methods are developed upon contrastive learning, which tries to pull the representations of different augmented views of the same sample/instance close and push representations of different instances away [7,9,12,16,20,21,24,25]. Contrastive methods require to define positive pairs and negative pairs in an absolute way, which violates the relativeness of human recognition. This issue of previous contrastive methods strongly motivates the need for relative-contrastive approaches that can reflect the nature of relativeness when human recognize objects. We achieve this goal by introducing a new relative contrastive loss. Instead of defining positive and negative pairs according to one absolute criterion, we assign a sample pair positive or negative by a set of different criteria to mimic the relative distinguish ability.

Clustering-Based Methods. Instead of viewing each sample as an independent class, clustering-based methods group samples into clusters [3,5,52,57]. Along this line, DeepCluster [3] leverages k-means assignments of prior representations as pseudo-labels for the new representations. SwAV [5] learns the clusters online through the Sinkhorn-Knopp transform [6,27]. Our method is also related to these clustering-based methods in that we instantiate our relative contrastive loss with an online hierarchical clustering. [4] leverages the hierarchical clustering to tackle non-curated data [41], instead of tackling curated data, *i.e.*, ImageNet-1K, in our paper. However, these clustering-based methods define positive and negative pairs absolutely. In our method, a pair of samples can be partially positive, respecting the relativeness of similarity between a pair of samples.

Neighborhood-Based Methods. Neighborhood-based methods stand the recent states-of-the-art methods in unsupervised learning. NNCLR [16] replaces one of the views in single-instance-positive methods with its nearest neighbor in the feature space as the positive sample. MSF [39] makes a further step by using the k nearest neighbors in the feature space as the positive samples. Neighborhood-based methods perform better than single-instance-positive methods because they can capture more class-invariances that can not be defined by augmentations and better than clustering methods because the query and the positive samples are more likely to belong to the same class. Our work also consider neighbors, but in a relative way.

3   Background: Contrastive Learning

Given an input image $\mathbf{x}$, two different augmentation parameters are employed to get two different images/views: image $\mathbf{v}$ and image $\mathbf{v}'$ for the query and the key branch, which output $\mathbf{q} = \mathcal{P}(\mathcal{Q}(\mathbf{v}, \theta), \theta_p)$ and $\mathbf{z}' = \mathcal{K}(\mathbf{v}', \xi)$, respectively. Here, $\mathcal{Q}$ and $\mathcal{K}$ respectively denote feature transformations parameterized by θ and ξ. $\mathcal{P}$ is an optional prediction [10,19,36] of $\mathbf{z} = \mathcal{Q}(\mathbf{v}, \theta)$ implemented by MLP. The contrastive loss is presented in InfoNCE [23], *i.e.*,

$$\mathcal{L}_{ctr}(\mathbf{x}, \theta) = -\log \left[\frac{\exp\left(\mathbf{q}^\top \mathbf{z}'\right)/\tau}{\exp\left(\mathbf{q}^\top \mathbf{z}'/\tau\right) + \sum_{k=1}^{K} \exp\left(\mathbf{q}^\top \mathbf{s}_k/\tau\right)} \right], \qquad (1)$$

where $\mathcal{S} = \{\mathbf{s}_k | k \in [1, K]\}$ is a support queue storing negative features and $\tau = 0.1$ is the temperature. Contrastive loss pulls the features of the query-key pair $(\mathbf{q}, \mathbf{z}')$ together and pushes features of the query-negative pairs $(\mathbf{q}, \mathbf{s}_k)$ apart.

4   Relative Contrastive Learning

We are interested in defining a query-key pair $(\mathbf{q}, \mathbf{z}')$ positive or negative relatively. Therefore we propose a relative contrastive loss and present an instantiation by online hierarchical clustering method to achieve it. Specifically, we generate a set of semantic criteria $\mathcal{M} = \{\mathcal{M}_1, \mathcal{M}_2, ..., \mathcal{M}_H\}$ (H denotes the number of criteria) to define $(\mathbf{q}, \mathbf{z}')$ positive or negative by online hierarchical clustering (Sect. 4.3), and then compute our relative contrastive loss (Sect. 4.1). This loss (defined in Eq. 2) is obtained by aggregating the vanilla contrastive losses in Eq. 1 with $(\mathbf{q}, \mathbf{z}')$ defined as positive or negative by every semantic criterion $\mathcal{M}_i$ in $\mathcal{M}$.

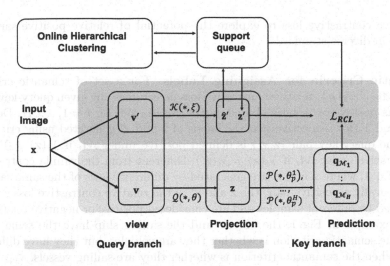

Fig. 2. The pipeline of relative contrastive learning. In the key branch, the feature $\hat{\mathbf{z}}'$ after projection is used to search the relative keys $\mathbf{z}'$ from the support queue by hierarchical clustering. For the feature $\mathbf{z}$ after projection in the query branch, we feed it into criterion-specific projectors to generate multiple predictions $\{\mathbf{q}_{\mathcal{M}_1}, \mathbf{q}_{\mathcal{M}_2}, ..., \mathbf{q}_{\mathcal{M}_H}\}$. Multiple predictions, $\mathbf{z}$ and $\mathbf{z}'$ are then fed into the relative contrastive loss $\mathcal{L}_{RCL}$.

Overview. As shown in Fig. 2, the relative contrastive learning has the following steps.

Step 1: Image $\mathbf{x}$ to features $\mathbf{z}$ and $\hat{\mathbf{z}}'$. Specifically, given two different views $(\mathbf{v}, \mathbf{v}')$ of an image $\mathbf{x}$, their projections can be computed by $\mathbf{z} = \mathcal{Q}(\mathbf{v}, \theta)$ and $\hat{\mathbf{z}}' = \mathcal{K}(\mathbf{v}', \xi)$. Following [19,21], the query branch $\mathcal{Q}(*, \theta)$ is a deep model updated by backward propagation, while the key branch $\mathcal{K}(*, \xi)$ is the same deep model as the query branch but with parameters obtained from the moving average of $\mathcal{Q}(*, \theta)$.

Step 2: Key-branch features $\hat{\mathbf{z}}'$ to retrieved features $\mathbf{z}'$. On the key branch, we retrieve key features $\mathbf{z}'$ from the support queue $\mathcal{S}$ with multiple criteria $\mathcal{M}$ implemented by hierarchical clustering (Sect. 4.3). On the query branch, similar to [10,19], we add criterion-specific predictors $\{\mathcal{P}_1, \mathcal{P}_2, ..., \mathcal{P}_H\}$ on $\mathbf{z}$ to get $\{\mathbf{q}_{\mathcal{M}_1}, \mathbf{q}_{\mathcal{M}_2}, ..., \mathbf{q}_{\mathcal{M}_H}\}$.

Step 3: Backpropagation using the relative contrastive loss. The retrieved feature $\mathbf{z}'$, multiple predictions $\{\mathbf{q}_{\mathcal{M}_1}, \mathbf{q}_{\mathcal{M}_2}, ..., \mathbf{q}_{\mathcal{M}_H}\}$, and whether $(\mathbf{z}, \mathbf{z}')$ is positive or negative according to semantic criteria $\mathcal{M}$ (designed by online hierarchical clustering in Sect. 4.3) are then fed into the relative contrastive loss (Eq. 2).

4.1   Relative Contrastive Loss

In the conventional contrastive learning, the positive-negative pairs are defined absolutely, *i.e.*, only augmentations of the same image are considered as positive pair. Motivated by the relative recognition ability of human beings, we introduce a relative contrastive loss to explore the potential of relative positive samples defined in diverse standards.

Semantic Criteria for Assigning Labels. For a set of semantic criteria $\{\mathcal{M}_1, \mathcal{M}_2, ..., \mathcal{M}_H\}$, relative contrastive loss determines any given query-key pair $(\mathbf{z}, \mathbf{z}')$ as positive or negative based on the criteria $\mathcal{M}_i$ for $i = 1, ..., H$. Denote $\mathcal{Y}_i(\mathbf{z})$ and $\mathcal{Y}_i(\mathbf{z}')$ respectively as the labels of $\mathbf{z}$ and $\mathbf{z}'$ generated using criterion $\mathcal{M}_i$. The query-key pair $(\mathbf{z}, \mathbf{z}')$ is defined positive under $\mathcal{M}_i$ if $\mathcal{Y}_i(\mathbf{z}) = \mathcal{Y}_i(\mathbf{z}')$, and negative under $\mathcal{M}_i$ if $\mathcal{Y}_i(\mathbf{z}) \neq \mathcal{Y}_i(\mathbf{z}')$. Different from the vanilla contrastive loss in Eq. 1, where $\mathbf{z}$ and $\mathbf{z}'$ are generated by different views of the same sample and naturally a positive pair, the $\mathbf{z}$ and $\mathbf{z}'$ in the relative contrastive loss can be generated by different samples and are considered positive or negative relatively. As an example in Fig. 1, the bicycle and the sailing ship have the same label when the semantic criterion is whether they are vehicles, but they have different labels when the semantic criterion is whether they are sailing vessels.

With the semantic criteria and their corresponding labels defined above, the relative contrastive loss is defined as

$$\mathcal{L}_{RCL}\left(\mathbf{z}, \mathbf{z}', \theta; \{\mathcal{M}_i\}_{i=1}^{H}\right) = \sum_{i=1}^{H} \alpha_i \mathcal{L}(\mathbf{z}, \mathbf{z}', \theta; \mathcal{M}_i), \qquad (2)$$

where α_i is trade-off parameter among different criteria. $\alpha_i = 1/H$ in our implementation. Loss $\mathcal{L}(\mathbf{z}, \mathbf{z}', \theta; \mathcal{M}_i)$ in Eq. 2 for criterion $\mathcal{M}_i$ can be defined as

$$\mathcal{L}(\mathbf{z}, \mathbf{z}', \theta; \mathcal{M}_i)$$
$$= -\log\left[\frac{\mathbb{I}\left[\mathcal{Y}_i(\mathbf{z}) = \mathcal{Y}_i(\mathbf{z}')\right] \cdot \exp\left(\mathbf{q}_{\mathcal{M}_i}^\top \mathbf{z}'/\tau\right) + \mathbb{I}\left[\mathcal{Y}_i(\mathbf{z}) \neq \mathcal{Y}_i(\mathbf{z}')\right]}{\exp\left(\mathbf{q}_{\mathcal{M}_i}^\top \mathbf{z}'/\tau\right) + \sum_{k=1}^{K} \exp\left(\mathbf{q}_{\mathcal{M}_i}^\top \mathbf{s}_k/\tau\right)}\right], \qquad (3)$$

where $\mathbf{z} = \mathcal{Q}(\mathbf{v}, \theta)$, $\mathbf{z}' = \mathcal{K}(\mathbf{v}', \xi)$, $\mathbf{s}_k$ is the feature in the support queue $\mathcal{S}$, K is the size of $\mathcal{S}$ and $\mathbb{I}(x)$ is an indication function, $\mathbb{I}(x) = 1$ when x is true, while $\mathbb{I}(x) = 0$ when x is false. $\mathbf{q}_{\mathcal{M}_i} = \mathcal{P}(\mathbf{z}, \theta_p^i)$ is the output of the criterion-specific predictor $\mathcal{P}(*, \theta_p^i)$ for the query projection $\mathbf{z}$, which is explained in the following.

Criterion-Specific Predictor. Inspired by BYOL [19] and Simsiam [10], the predictor layer aims to predict the expectation of the projection $\mathbf{z}$ under a specific transformation. Therefore, we propose to use the multiple criterion-specific predictors, each of which is to estimate the expectation of $\mathbf{z}$ under its corresponding semantic criterion. Specifically, we add H MLPs, forming predictors $\{\mathcal{P}(*, \theta_p^1), \mathcal{P}(*, \theta_p^2), ..., \mathcal{P}(*, \theta_p^H)\}$ after the projectors in the query branch.

4.2   Analysis of Relative Contrastive Loss

In this section, we mathematically illustrate how relative contrastive loss supervises the feature distance between a query-key sample pair. We will show the feature distance of a image pair with higher possibility of being positive should be smaller than that with lower possibility of being positive.

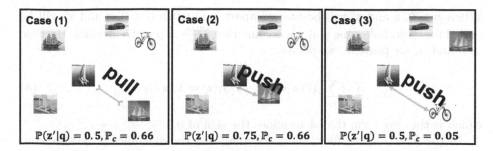

Fig. 3. Analysis of the relative contrastive loss with multiple criteria. Both $\mathbb{P}(\mathbf{z}'|\mathbf{q})$ and $\mathbb{P}_c$ represent the probability that $\mathbf{z}'$ and $\mathbf{q}$ have the same label. The difference is that $\mathbb{P}(\mathbf{z}'|\mathbf{q})$ is based on the cosine similarity of $\mathbf{z}'$ and $\mathbf{q}$, and $\mathbb{P}_c$ is based on the set of defined semantic criteria. Whether to pull $(\mathbf{q}, \mathbf{z})$ together or push $(\mathbf{q}, \mathbf{z})$ apart is determined by $\mathbb{P}(\mathbf{z}'|\mathbf{q}) - \mathbb{P}_c$. If $\mathbb{P}(\mathbf{z}'|\mathbf{q}) - \mathbb{P}_c < 0$, $(\mathbf{q}, \mathbf{z})$ should be pulled together. If $\mathbb{P}(\mathbf{z}'|\mathbf{q}) - \mathbb{P}_c > 0$, $(\mathbf{q}, \mathbf{z})$ should be pushed apart.

We derive the gradient of our relative contrastive loss. The gradient of $\mathcal{L}(\mathbf{z}, \mathbf{z}', \theta; \mathcal{M}_i)$ in Eq. 3 is

$$\frac{\partial \mathcal{L}(\mathbf{z}, \mathbf{z}', \theta; \mathcal{M}_i)}{\partial \mathbf{z}} = \frac{\partial \mathbf{q}_{\mathcal{M}_i}}{\partial \mathbf{z}} \frac{\partial \mathcal{L}(\mathbf{z}, \mathbf{z}', \theta; \mathcal{M}_i)}{\partial \mathbf{q}_{\mathcal{M}_i}}$$

$$= \left(\mathbb{P}\left(\mathbf{z}'|\mathbf{q}_{\mathcal{M}_i}\right) - \mathbb{I}\left[\mathcal{Y}_i(\mathbf{z}) = \mathcal{Y}_i(\mathbf{z}')\right] \right) \frac{\partial \mathbf{q}_{\mathcal{M}_i}}{\partial \mathbf{z}} \frac{\mathbf{z}'}{\tau} \tag{4}$$

$$+ \sum_{k=1}^{K} \frac{\partial \mathbf{q}_{\mathcal{M}_i}}{\partial \mathbf{z}} \mathbb{P}\left(\mathbf{s}_k|\mathbf{q}_{\mathcal{M}_i}\right) \frac{\mathbf{s}_k}{\tau},$$

where

$$\mathbb{P}\left(\mathbf{z}'|\mathbf{q}_{\mathcal{M}_i}\right) = \frac{\exp\left(\mathbf{q}_{\mathcal{M}_i}^{\top} \mathbf{z}'/\tau\right)}{\exp\left(\mathbf{q}_{\mathcal{M}_i}^{\top} \mathbf{z}'/\tau\right) + \sum_{k=1}^{K} \exp\left(\mathbf{q}_{\mathcal{M}_i}^{\top} \mathbf{s}_k/\tau\right)}, \tag{5}$$

$$\mathbb{P}\left(\mathbf{s}_k|\mathbf{q}_{\mathcal{M}_i}\right) = \frac{\exp\left(\mathbf{q}_{\mathcal{M}_i}^{\top} \mathbf{s}_k/\tau\right)}{\exp\left(\mathbf{q}_{\mathcal{M}_i}^{\top} \mathbf{z}')/\tau\right) + \sum_{k=1}^{K} \exp\left(\mathbf{q}_{\mathcal{M}_i}^{\top} \mathbf{s}_k/\tau\right)}. \tag{6}$$

The $\mathbb{P}\left(\mathbf{z}'|\mathbf{q}_{\mathcal{M}_i}\right)$ and $\mathbb{P}\left(\mathbf{s}_k|\mathbf{q}_{\mathcal{M}_i}\right)$ above are the conditional probabilities of assigning the query prediction $\mathbf{q}_{\mathcal{M}_i}$ to the label of projection $\mathbf{z}'$ and the label of negative samples $\mathbf{s}_k$. We skip the analysis to the query-negative pair $(\mathbf{z}, \mathbf{s}_k)$ and focus on analyzing the dynamics between query-key pair $(\mathbf{z}, \mathbf{z}')$. Therefore, we drop the terms $(\mathbf{q}_{\mathcal{M}_i}, \mathbf{s}_k)$ in Eq. 4. When the gradient above for $\mathcal{L}$ is considered for the loss $\mathcal{L}_{RCL}$ defined in Eq. 2, $\mathbf{z}$ is optimized by gradient descent with the learning rate γ as

$$\mathbf{z} \leftarrow \mathbf{z} - \frac{\gamma}{\tau} \underbrace{\sum_{i=1}^{H} \alpha_i \frac{\partial \mathbf{q}_{\mathcal{M}_i}}{\partial \mathbf{z}} \left(\mathbb{P}(\mathbf{z}'|\mathbf{q}_{\mathcal{M}_i}) - \mathbb{I}\left[\mathcal{Y}_i(\mathbf{z}) = \mathcal{Y}_i(\mathbf{z}')\right] \right) \mathbf{z}'}_{\eta}. \tag{7}$$

When $\eta > 0$, $\mathbf{z}$ and $\mathbf{z}'$ will be pushed apart, and when $\eta < 0$, $\mathbf{z}$ and $\mathbf{z}'$ will be pulled together. Following [44], we assume that $\frac{\partial \mathbf{q}_{\mathcal{M}_i}}{\partial \mathbf{z}}$ is positive definite. Because γ, τ and α_i are positive, we define

$$\eta' = \sum_{i=1}^{H} \left(\mathbb{P}(\mathbf{z}'|\mathbf{q}_{\mathcal{M}_i}) - \mathbb{I}\left[\mathcal{Y}_i(\mathbf{z}) = \mathcal{Y}_i(\mathbf{z}')\right] \right), \qquad (8)$$

which is the only term that determines the sign of η.

In the following, we focus on η' for analyzing the dynamics of relative contrastive loss on network optimization in Eq. 7. We will reveal that the relativeness of positive-negative samples is based on 1) the probability $\mathbb{P}(\mathbf{z}'|\mathbf{q}_{\mathcal{M}_i})$ of assigning the query prediction $\mathbf{q}_{\mathcal{M}_i}$ to the label of projection $\mathbf{z}'$, and 2) the constructed criteria that determines the labeling function $\mathcal{Y}_i(\cdot)$.

Single Criterion. When there is only one criterion for determining query-key pairs positive or negative, *i.e.*, $\eta' = (\mathbb{P}(\mathbf{z}'|\mathbf{q}_{\mathcal{M}_1}) - \mathbb{I}[\mathcal{Y}_1(\mathbf{z}) = \mathcal{Y}_1(\mathbf{z}')])$, our method collapses to the typical contrastive loss which pulls positive pairs close ($\mathbb{I}[\mathcal{Y}_1(\mathbf{z}) = \mathcal{Y}_1(\mathbf{z}')] = 1$, $\eta' < 0$) and pushes negative pairs apart ($\mathbb{I}[\mathcal{Y}_1(\mathbf{z}) = \mathcal{Y}_1(\mathbf{z}')] = 0$ and $\eta' > 0$).

Multiple Criteria. When there are multiple criteria, to facilitate analysis, we assume the criterion-specific predictors are identical $\mathcal{P}_i = \mathcal{P}, i \leq H$ and thus predictions $\mathbf{q}_{\mathcal{M}_i} = \mathbf{q}, i \leq H$ are the same. With these assumptions, Eq. 8 is modified as

$$\eta' = H(\mathbb{P}(\mathbf{z}'|\mathbf{q}) - \mathbb{P}_c), \qquad (9)$$

where $\mathbb{P}_c = \sum_{i=1}^{H} \mathbb{I}[\mathcal{Y}_i(\mathbf{z}) = \mathcal{Y}_i(\mathbf{z}')]/H$ is possibility of $(\mathbf{z}, \mathbf{z}')$ being labeled by the H criteria as positive pair. We show the difference between the probability $\mathbb{P}_c$ define by the criteria and the probability $\mathbb{P}(\mathbf{z}'|\mathbf{q})$ estimated from the model, *i.e.*, $\mathbb{P}(\mathbf{z}'|\mathbf{q}) - \mathbb{P}_c$, will adaptively determine the relative decision of pushing or pulling. We use three different cases for illustration (Fig. 3). (1) $\mathbb{P}(\mathbf{z}'|\mathbf{q}) = 0.50$ and $\mathbb{P}_c = 0.66$; (2) $\mathbb{P}(\mathbf{z}'|\mathbf{q}) = 0.75$ and $\mathbb{P}_c = 0.66$; (3) $\mathbb{P}(\mathbf{z}'|\mathbf{q}) = 0.50$ and $\mathbb{P}_c = 0.05$. **In case (1)**, $\mathbb{P}_c$ is large, *i.e.* most of the criteria label two samples as belonging to the same class. But $\mathbb{P}(\mathbf{z}'|\mathbf{q}) = 0.5$, *i.e.* the probability estimated from the learned features for $\mathbf{z}$ and $\mathbf{z}'$ belonging to the same class is not so high. In this case, because the term $\eta' = H(\mathbb{P}(\mathbf{z}'|\mathbf{q}) - \mathbb{P}_c)$ is negative, gradient descent will pull $\mathbf{z}$ towards $\mathbf{z}'$. **In case (2)**, since $\eta' = H(\mathbb{P}(\mathbf{z}'|\mathbf{q}) - \mathbb{P}_c) > 0$, the loss will pull $\mathbf{z}$ and $\mathbf{z}'$ together. Comparing cases (1) and (2), the loss changes its behavior from pushing samples away to pulling together because of the change of $\mathbb{P}(\mathbf{z}'|\mathbf{q})$. Cases (1) and (3) have the same estimated probability $\mathbb{P}(\mathbf{z}'|\mathbf{q})$. **In case (3)**, most of the criteria label the two samples as not belonging to the same class, *i.e.* $\mathbb{P}_c = 0.05$, and the loss will push $\mathbf{z}$ and $\mathbf{z}'$ away. Comparing cases (1) and (3), if the probability $\mathbb{P}_c$ defined by the criteria changes from high to low, the loss changes its behavior from pulling feature close to pushing features away.

4.3 Criteria Generation

In this section, we introduce an implementation of the semantic criteria $\mathcal{M}_{1:H} = \{\mathcal{M}_1, \mathcal{M}_2, ..., \mathcal{M}_H\}$ used in the relative contrastive loss, where $\mathcal{M}_h$ is used for defining query-key pair $(\mathbf{z}, \mathbf{z}')$ to be positive or negative. The criteria are implemented by online hierarchical clustering, which constrains the relativeness among different criteria with a hierarchy relationship, *i.e.*, $\mathcal{M}_1 \subset \mathcal{M}_2 \subset ... \subset \mathcal{M}_H$ (if $\mathcal{Y}_h(\mathbf{x}) = \mathcal{Y}_h(\mathbf{x}')$, then $\mathcal{Y}_j(\mathbf{x}) = \mathcal{Y}_j(\mathbf{x}'), \forall j > h$). At hierarchical clustering level h, a query-key pair $(\mathbf{x}, \mathbf{x}')$ in the same cluster are consider to be positive pair, $\mathcal{Y}_h(\mathbf{x}) = \mathcal{Y}_h(\mathbf{x}')$. Inspired by [55], the implementation of hierarchical clustering is required to conform with the following property.

Cluster Preserve Property: samples in the same cluster at the low level are also in the same cluster at higher levels.

There are two stages in the online hierarchical clustering: 1) warm-up stage to obtain the initial clustering results, 2) online cluster refinement stage along with feature learning.

Warm-Up Stage. Following other clustering-based methods [57], we train our model with the contrastive loss in Eq. 1 for 10 epochs. Then, the extracted features of all samples in the dataset are clustered by DBSCAN [18] to obtain initial clusters in level 2 to H. We use each sample as a cluster at level 1.

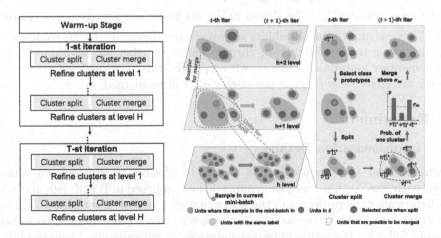

Fig. 4. Online hierarchical clustering. The label refinement at $(h+1)$-th level from the t-th to the $(t+1)$-th iteration is constrained by labels at h-th level and $(h+2)$-th level. The clusters at the h-th level are the basic units for cluster split at the $(h+1)$-th level, and the clusters at the $(h+2)$-th level provides a boarder to identify clusters at the $(h+1)$-th level that may be merged.

Online Cluster Refinement Stage. Initial clusters are not accurate due to the poor representations, and therefore need to be progressively adjusted along with the feature optimization. As illustrated in Fig. 4, for each training iteration t, the cluster refinement is conducted from the bottom to the top level, where a cluster contains the most samples. We take i-th cluster $\mathcal{C}_i^{h+1}$ at $(h+1)$-th level to elaborate the process of cluster split and merge.

Cluster Split. Cluster split aims to divide a cluster $\mathcal{C}_i^{h+1}$ into several smaller but more accurate clusters. To conform with the cluster preserve property, the basic units considered for splitting $\mathcal{C}_i^{h+1}$ are clusters in h-level whose samples all belong to $\mathcal{C}_i^{h+1}$, *i.e.*, $\mathcal{U}_i^{h+1} = \{\mathcal{C}_j^h | \mathcal{C}_j^h \subset \mathcal{C}_i^{h+1}, j = 1, \ldots, k^h\}$, where k^h is the number of clusters in $\mathcal{H}_h$. Each unit in $\mathcal{U}_i^{h+1}$ is a cluster. When splitting $\mathcal{C}_i^{h+1}$ into m smaller clusters $(m < k^h)$, m most dissimilar split units in $\mathcal{U}_i^{h+1}$ are selected using the density peak selection algorithm [37] as the prototype of m different clusters, each of which contains one selected unit. The remaining units in $\mathcal{U}_i$ are merged to the m clusters according to their nearest prototype or label propagation [31] (detailed in supplementary materials). With this procedure, cluster $\mathcal{C}_i^{h+1}$ is split into a set containing m divided clusters, denoted by $\mathcal{D}_i^{h+1} = \{\mathcal{D}_{i,j}'^{h+1}\}_{j=1}^m$.

Cluster Merge. Cluster merge aims to merge the divided clusters $\mathcal{D}_i^{h+1}$ and clusters at level $h+1$ if they are highly possible to one cluster. To conform with the cluster preserve property, we can only try to merge the clusters belonging to the same cluster $\mathcal{C}_{pa(i)}^{h+2}$ at the $(h+2)$-th level, where $\mathcal{C}_{pa(i)}^{h+2} \supset \mathcal{C}_i^{h+1}$ (clusters circled by the merge boarder in Fig. 4). Therefore, we construct a set of clusters that may be merged as $\mathcal{V}_i^{h+1} = \left\{ \bigcup_j \mathcal{C}_{pa(j)=pa(i)}^{h+1} \right\} \bigcup \mathcal{D}_i^{h+1}$, and all elements in $\mathcal{V}_i^{h+1}$ belong to the same cluster $\mathcal{C}_{pa(i)}^{h+2}$. As shown in Fig. 4(Cluster merge), to merge clusters in $\mathcal{V}_i^{h+1}$, we compute the possibility of two clusters belonging to the same class, *i.e.*, according to the distance of cluster centers or label propagation [23] (in supplementary materials). Clusters whose possibilities of belonging to the same cluster are larger than a hyper-parameter σ_m will be merged.

5 Experiment

5.1 Implementation Details

Architecture. Our architecture is similar to MoCo-v2 and MoCo-v3. Compared with MoCo-v2, we use the symmetric loss proposed in BYOL [19] and add predictors after the projector in the query branch. Compared with MoCo-v3, we construct a negative queue as MoCo-v2. Specifically, we use ResNet-50 as our encoder following the common implementations in self-supervised learning literature. We spatially average the output of ResNet-50 which makes the output of the encoder a 2048-dimensional embedding. The projection MLP is composed of 3 fully connected layers having output sizes $[2048, 2048, d]$, where d is the feature dimension applied in the loss, $d = 256$ if not specified. The projection MLP is fc-BN-ReLU for the first two MLP layers, and fc-BN for the last MLP layer. The architecture of the MLP predictor is 2 fully-connected layers of output size $[4096, d]$, which can be formulated as $fc_2(ReLU(BN(fc_1)))$.

Training. For fair comparison, we train our relative contrastive learning method on the ImageNet2012 dataset [14] which contains 1,281,167 images without using any annotation or class label. In the training stage, we train for 200, 400 and 800 epochs with a warm-up of 10 epochs and cosine annealing schedule using the LARS optimizer [49] by the relative contrastive loss Eq. 2. The base learning rate is set to 0.3. Weight decay of 10^{-6} is applied during training. As is common practice, we do not use weight decay on the bias. The training settings above are the same as BYOL. We also use the same data augmentation scheme as BYOL. For loss computation, we set temperature τ in Eq. 2 to 0.1.

Table 1. Comparison with other self-supervised learning methods under the linear evaluation protocol [21] on ImageNet. We omit the result for SwAV with multi-crop for fair comparison with other methods.

Method	Arch.	Epochs	Top1	Top5	Method	Arch	Epochs	Top1	Top5
ODC [52]	R50	100	57.6	–	PIRL [32]	R50	800	63.6	–
InstDisc [46]	R50	200	58.5	–	MoCo v2 [9]	R50	800	71.1	–
LocalAgg [57]	R50	200	58.8	–	SimSiam [10]	R50	800	71.3	90.7
MSF [39]	R50	200	71.4	–	SimCLR [7]	R50	800	69.3	89.0
MSF w/s [39]	R50	200	72.4	–	SwAV [5]	R50	800	71.8	–
CPC v2 [22]	R50	200	63.8	85.3	BYOL [19]	R50	1000	74.3	91.6
CMC [42]	R50	240	66.2	87.0	InfoMin Aug. [43]	R50	800	73.0	91.1
Adco [36]	R50	200	68.6	–	MoCo v3 [11]	R50	800	73.8	–
NNCLR [16]	R50	200	70.7	–	NNCLR [16]	R50	800	75.4	92.4
RCL (Ours)	R50	200	72.6	90.8	RCL (Ours)	R50	800	75.8	92.6

5.2 Comparison with State-of-the-Art Methods

Linear Evaluations. Following the standard linear evaluation protocol [9,21, 46,57], we train a linear classifier for 90 epochs on the frozen 2048-dimensional embeddings from the ResNet-50 encoder using LARS [49] with cosine annealed learning rate of 1 with Nesterov momentum of 0.9 and batch size of 4096. Comparison with state-of-the-art methods is presented in Table 1. Firstly, our proposed RCL achieves better performance compared to other state-of-the-art methods using a ResNet-50 encoder without multi-crop augmentations. Specifically, RCL improves MoCo v2 by 4.7% and MoCo v3 by 2.0%, which generates positive samples by implementing a different augmentation on the query image. Furthermore, our method is better than InfoMin Aug., which carefully designs the "good view" in the contrastive learning for providing positive samples, by 2.8%. The significant improvements empirically verifies one of our motivation that manually designed augmentations cannot cover the visual variations in a semantic class. Compared with other state-of-the-art methods, our method also achieves higher performance than BYOL by 1.5%. Clustering-based methods,

Table 2. Comparison with the state-of-the-art methods for semi-supervised learning. Pseudo Label, UDA, FixMatch and MPL are semi-supervised learning methods. † denotes using random augment [13]. We use the same subset as in SwAV.

Method	ImageNet 1%		ImageNet 10%	
	Top1	Top5	Top1	Top5
Supervised baseline [51]	25.4	48.4	56.4	80.4
Pseudo label [29]	–	–	51.6	82.4
UDA [47]	–	–	68.8†	88.5†
FixMatch [38]	–	–	71.5†	89.1†
MPL [35]	–	73.5†	–	–
InstDisc [46]	–	39.2	–	77.4
PCL [30]	–	75.6	–	86.2
SimCLR [7]	48.3	75.5	65.6	87.8
BYOL [19]	53.2	78.4	68.8	89.0
SwAV (multicrop) [5]	53.9	78.5	70.2	89.9
Barlow Twins [50]	55.0	79.2	69.7	89.3
NNCLR [16]	56.4	80.7	69.8	89.3
RCL (Ours)	57.2	81.0	70.3	89.9

e.g., SwAV [5], and nearest-neighbor-based methods go beyond *single positives*. Clustering-based methods utilize the cluster prototypes as the positive samples. However, our method also achieves 4.0% improvement without the multi-crop augmentation. SwAV leverages an online clustering algorithm and uses only its cluster centers as its positives, which ignores the relative proximity built by our relative contrastive loss. NNCLR [16] is the recent states-of-the-art method, which utilizes the nearest neighbor as the positive sample. Our method is better than NNCLR at 200 epochs are comparable at 800 epochs, because NNCLR defines positive samples without relativeness. Furthermore, our RCL can be the same as NNCLR when we set only one criterion and only cluster the nearest neighbor. We also compare our method with existing methods in various epochs, which is presented in Fig. 5 (a). Our method achieves better performance than SimCLR, Simsiam, MoCo-v3 and BYOL for 200, 400, 800 epochs.

Semi-supervised Learning Evaluations. To further evaluate the effectiveness of the learned features, we conduct experiments in a semi-supervised setting on ImageNet following the standard evaluation protocol [7,8], thus fine-tuning the whole base network on 1% or 10% ImageNet data with labels without regularization after unsupervised pre-training. The experimental results are presented in Table 2. Firstly, our method outperforms all the compared self-supervised learning methods with the semi-supervised learning setting on ImageNet 1% subset, even when compared with the SwAV method with strong multi-crop augmentation (our RCL does not use multi-crop augmentation). Second, in the ImageNet 10% setting, our method still leads to a better result than most popular self-supervised learning methods, such as SimCLR, BYOL, Barlow Twins and NNCLR. The results indicate the good generalization ability of the features learned by our relative contrastive loss.

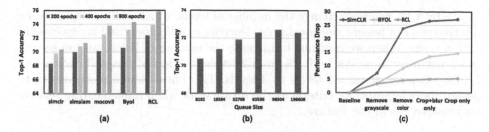

Fig. 5. Ablation studies. (a) Comparison with state-of-the-art methods when training 200, 400 and 800 epochs under linear evaluation on ImageNet. (b) ImageNet top-1 accuracy with different sizes of the support queue. (c) Top-1 Accuracy drop (Y-axis) by removing augmentations (X-axis).

5.3   Ablation Study

Default Settings. The size of the support set S is set to be 1.5×2^{16} and the batch size of our algorithm is 4096. We train for 200 epochs with a warm-up of 10 epochs. The learning rate is 0.3 and we leverage cosine annealing schedule using the LARS optimizer [49]. The results in this section are tested by linear evaluations on ImageNet.

Different Clustering Methods. To illustrate the effectiveness of our online hierarchical clustering method, we compare it with K-means and DBSCAN. Because both K-means and DBSCAN are offline clustering methods, we extract the features of all images in ImageNet-1K, and conduct clustering on these features before each epoch. For K-means, we set the number of clusters to (250000, 500000, 1000000), where we verify there are about 73.88% samples that conform the hierarchy in Sect. 4.3. For DBSCAN, we keep the minimum number of samples within r to 4, and select $r = 0.8, 0.7, 0.6$ to construct hierarchical label banks, leading to 97.3% samples conforming the hierarchy. As shown in Table 4, we can see that K-means improves the NNCLR by 1.1%, which verifies the effectiveness of relativeness. DBSCAN is better than K-means, which verifies the effectiveness of the hierarchical labels. Our online hierarchical clustering is better than above methods, because it can refine labels along with network optimization, which avoids the problem that label refinement is slower than network optimization when using offline clustering. Our online hierarchical clustering is faster than offline clustering algorithms, *e.g.*, kmeans and DBSCAN, because it only deals with samples in the current mini-batch while kmeans and DBSCAN needs to operate on the whole dataset. Compared with NNCLR, our method is about 18% slower, but shows better performance on 200 epochs setting.

Number of Levels in Online Hierarchical Clustering. To assess the effectiveness of relativeness, we ablate on different number of levels in the hierarchical label bank. As illustrated in Table 3, the top-1 accuracy improves from 70.2% to

71.3% by 1.1% when we change the number of levels, which indicates the adding relativeness can benefit the contrastive learning in self-supervised image classification tasks. When we continue to increase the number of levels, we can see the top-1 accuracy improves by 0.5% from 2 levels to 3 levels, but will decrease to 71.4% when we changes 3 levels to 4 levels. This phenomenon motivates us to design more appropriate criteria as the future work when implementing relative contrastive loss in the feature.

Table 3. Ablation studies on multiple predictions and the number of levels in the hierarchical clustering. #Predictors: number of criterion-specific predictors. #Hierarchies: number of levels in the hierarchical clustering.

No.	#Predictors	#Hierarchies	Top1
1	1	1	70.2
2	1	2	71.3
3	1	3	71.8
4	1	4	71.4
5	3	3	72.6

Table 4. Ablation studies on different clustering methods. Mixed precision time for training 1 epoch using 64 GeForce GTX 1080 Tis with 64 samples in each GPU is reported.

Method	Hierarchy	Online	Top1	Time/Ep
No (NNCLR [16])	×	×	70.7	659 s
K-means	low	×	71.8	1056 s
DBSCAN	high	×	72.3	986 s
Online Hierarchical Clustering	✓	✓	72.6	776 s

Multiple Predictors. Multiple predictors are used to predict the multiple projection expectations $\{\mathbb{E}_{\mathcal{T}_1}(\mathbf{z}_\theta), \mathbb{E}_{\mathcal{T}_2}(\mathbf{z}_\theta), ..., \mathbb{E}_{\mathcal{T}_H}(\mathbf{z}_\theta)\}$ based on the various image transformations that wilBl not change the label under different criteria. When implementing a single predictor after the projection, we actually impose to predict the expectation of the projection regardless of the semantic criterion. When using multiple predictors, we impose each predictor to predict the projection expectation based on the image transformation that will not change the label under a specific criterion. Comparing Exp. 3 and Exp. 5 in Table 3, we can conclude that multiple predictors can outperform single predictor by 0.7%.

Size of Support Queue. Similar with MoCo that utilizes a memory bank to store the representations of other samples, our method has a support queue to provide diverse image variations. We evaluate the performance of our method with different support queue size in Fig. 5(b). As can be observed, when the size of the support queue increases to 98304, the performance of our method also improves, reflecting the importance of using more diverse variation as positive samples. Specifically, increasing the size from 65536 to 98304 leads to 0.36% top-1 accuracy improvement. However, further increasing the size of the support queue does not provide further improvement.

Sensitivity to Augmentations. Previous methods leverage the manually designed augmentations to model the visual variation between a semantic class, and therefore augmentations are very critical to their self-supervised learning methods. In contrast, we utilize similar samples/images in the dataset to be positive samples. As illustrated in Fig. 5(c), Our proposed RCL is much less sensitive to image augmentations when compared with SimCLR and BYOL.

6   Limitations and Conclusions

In this paper, we propose a new relative contrastive loss for unsupervised learning. Different from typical contrastive loss that defines query-key pair to be absolutely positive or negative, relative contrastive loss can treat a query-key pair relatively positive, which is measured by a set of semantic criteria. The semantic criteria are instantiated by an online hierarchical clustering in our paper. Representations learnt by the relative contrastive loss can capture diverse semantic criteria, which is motivated by human recognition and fit the relationship among samples better. Extensive results on self-supervised learning, semi-supervised learning and transfer learning settings show the effectiveness of our relative contrastive loss. While our relative loss largely benefits from multiple criteria, the optimal criteria design is still under-explored.

Acknowledgement. This work was supported by the Australian Research Council Grant DP200103223, Australian Medical Research Future Fund MRFAI000085, CRC-P Smart Material Recovery Facility (SMRF) - Curby Soft Plastics, and CRC-P ARIA - Bionic Visual-Spatial Prosthesis for the Blind.

References

1. Agrawal, P., Carreira, J., Malik, J.: Learning to see by moving. In: Proceedings of the IEEE International Conference on Computer Vision, pp. 37–45 (2015)
2. Asano, Y.M., Rupprecht, C., Vedaldi, A.: Self-labelling via simultaneous clustering and representation learning. arXiv preprint arXiv:1911.05371 (2019)
3. Caron, M., Bojanowski, P., Joulin, A., Douze, M.: Deep clustering for unsupervised learning of visual features. In: Ferrari, V., Hebert, M., Sminchisescu, C., Weiss, Y. (eds.) Computer Vision – ECCV 2018. LNCS, vol. 11218, pp. 139–156. Springer, Cham (2018). https://doi.org/10.1007/978-3-030-01264-9_9
4. Caron, M., Bojanowski, P., Mairal, J., Joulin, A.: Unsupervised pre-training of image features on non-curated data. In: Proceedings of the IEEE/CVF International Conference on Computer Vision, pp. 2959–2968 (2019)

5. Caron, M., Misra, I., Mairal, J., Goyal, P., Bojanowski, P., Joulin, A.: Unsupervised learning of visual features by contrasting cluster assignments. arXiv preprint arXiv:2006.09882 (2020)
6. Chakrabarty, D., Khanna, S.: Better and simpler error analysis of the sinkhornknopp algorithm for matrix scaling. Math. Program. **188**(1), 395–407 (2020)
7. Chen, T., Kornblith, S., Norouzi, M., Hinton, G.: A simple framework for contrastive learning of visual representations. In: International Conference on Machine Learning, pp. 1597–1607. PMLR (2020)
8. Chen, T., Kornblith, S., Swersky, K., Norouzi, M., Hinton, G.: Big self-supervised models are strong semi-supervised learners. arXiv preprint arXiv:2006.10029 (2020)
9. Chen, X., Fan, H., Girshick, R., He, K.: Improved baselines with momentum contrastive learning. arXiv preprint arXiv:2003.04297 (2020)
10. Chen, X., He, K.: Exploring simple siamese representation learning. In: Proceedings of the IEEE/CVF Conference on Computer Vision and Pattern Recognition, pp. 15750–15758 (2021)
11. Chen, X., Xie, S., He, K.: An empirical study of training self-supervised visual transformers. arXiv e-prints pp. arXiv-2104 (2021)
12. Chen, X., et al.: Self-PU: self boosted and calibrated positive-unlabeled training. In: International Conference on Machine Learning, pp. 1510–1519. PMLR (2020)
13. Cubuk, E.D., Zoph, B., Shlens, J., Le, Q.V.: RandAugment: practical automated data augmentation with a reduced search space. In: Proceedings of the IEEE/CVF Conference on Computer Vision and Pattern Recognition Workshops, pp. 702–703 (2020)
14. Deng, J., Dong, W., Socher, R., Li, L.J., Li, K., Fei-Fei, L.: ImageNet: a large-scale hierarchical image database. In: 2009 IEEE Conference on Computer Vision and Pattern Recognition, pp. 248–255. IEEE (2009)
15. Doersch, C., Gupta, A., Efros, A.A.: Unsupervised visual representation learning by context prediction. In: Proceedings of the IEEE International Conference on Computer Vision, pp. 1422–1430 (2015)
16. Dwibedi, D., Aytar, Y., Tompson, J., Sermanet, P., Zisserman, A.: With a little help from my friends: nearest-neighbor contrastive learning of visual representations. arXiv preprint arXiv:2104.14548 (2021)
17. Ereshefsky, M.: The Poverty of the Linnaean Hierarchy: A Philosophical Study of Biological Taxonomy. Cambridge University Press (2000)
18. Ester, M., Kriegel, H.P., Sander, J., Xu, X., et al.: A density-based algorithm for discovering clusters in large spatial databases with noise. In: KDD, vol. 96, pp. 226–231 (1996)
19. Grill, J.B., et al.: Bootstrap your own latent: a new approach to self-supervised learning. arXiv preprint arXiv:2006.07733 (2020)
20. Han, T., Xie, W., Zisserman, A.: Self-supervised co-training for video representation learning. arXiv preprint arXiv:2010.09709 (2020)
21. He, K., Fan, H., Wu, Y., Xie, S., Girshick, R.: Momentum contrast for unsupervised visual representation learning. In: Proceedings of the IEEE/CVF Conference on Computer Vision and Pattern Recognition, pp. 9729–9738 (2020)
22. Henaff, O.: Data-efficient image recognition with contrastive predictive coding. In: International Conference on Machine Learning, pp. 4182–4192. PMLR (2020)
23. Hjelm, R.D., et al.: Learning deep representations by mutual information estimation and maximization. arXiv preprint arXiv:1808.06670 (2018)
24. Hu, Q., Wang, X., Hu, W., Qi, G.J.: AdCo: adversarial contrast for efficient learning of unsupervised representations from self-trained negative adversaries. In: Proceed-

ings of the IEEE/CVF Conference on Computer Vision and Pattern Recognition, pp. 1074–1083 (2021)

25. Jaiswal, A., Babu, A.R., Zadeh, M.Z., Banerjee, D., Makedon, F.: A survey on contrastive self-supervised learning. Technologies **9**(1), 2 (2021)

26. Kim, D., Cho, D., Yoo, D., Kweon, I.S.: Learning image representations by completing damaged jigsaw puzzles. In: 2018 IEEE Winter Conference on Applications of Computer Vision (WACV), pp. 793–802. IEEE (2018)

27. Knight, P.A.: The sinkhorn-knopp algorithm: convergence and applications. SIAM J. Matrix Anal. Appl. **30**(1), 261–275 (2008)

28. Larsson, G., Maire, M., Shakhnarovich, G.: Learning representations for automatic colorization. In: Leibe, B., Matas, J., Sebe, N., Welling, M. (eds.) ECCV 2016. LNCS, vol. 9908, pp. 577–593. Springer, Cham (2016). https://doi.org/10.1007/978-3-319-46493-0_35

29. Lee, D.H., et al.: Pseudo-label: the simple and efficient semi-supervised learning method for deep neural networks. In: Workshop on Challenges in Representation Learning (ICML), vol. 3, p. 896 (2013)

30. Li, J., Zhou, P., Xiong, C., Socher, R., Hoi, S.C.: Prototypical contrastive learning of unsupervised representations. arXiv preprint arXiv:2005.04966 (2020)

31. Liu, Y., et al.: Learning to propagate labels: transductive propagation network for few-shot learning. arXiv preprint arXiv:1805.10002 (2018)

32. Misra, I., Maaten, L.v.d.: Self-supervised learning of pretext-invariant representations. In: Proceedings of the IEEE/CVF Conference on Computer Vision and Pattern Recognition, pp. 6707–6717 (2020)

33. Noroozi, M., Favaro, P.: Unsupervised learning of visual representations by solving Jigsaw Puzzles. In: Leibe, B., Matas, J., Sebe, N., Welling, M. (eds.) ECCV 2016. LNCS, vol. 9910, pp. 69–84. Springer, Cham (2016). https://doi.org/10.1007/978-3-319-46466-4_5

34. Noroozi, M., Pirsiavash, H., Favaro, P.: Representation learning by learning to count. In: Proceedings of the IEEE International Conference on Computer Vision, pp. 5898–5906 (2017)

35. Pham, H., Dai, Z., Xie, Q., Le, Q.V.: Meta pseudo labels. In: Proceedings of the IEEE/CVF Conference on Computer Vision and Pattern Recognition, pp. 11557–11568 (2021)

36. Qi, G.J., Zhang, L., Lin, F., Wang, X.: Learning generalized transformation equivariant representations via autoencoding transformations. IEEE Trans. Pattern Anal. Mach. Intell. **44**(4), 2045–2057 (2020)

37. Rodriguez, A., Laio, A.: Clustering by fast search and find of density peaks. Science **344**(6191), 1492–1496 (2014)

38. Sohn, K., et al.: Fixmatch: simplifying semi-supervised learning with consistency and confidence. arXiv preprint arXiv:2001.07685 (2020)

39. Soroush Abbasi, K., Tejankar, A., Pirsiavash, H.: Mean shift for self-supervised learning. In: International Conference on Computer Vision (ICCV), pp. 10326–10335 (2021)

40. Tang, S., Chen, D., Bai, L., Liu, K., Ge, Y., Ouyang, W.: Mutual CRF-GNN for few-shot learning. In: Proceedings of the IEEE/CVF Conference on Computer Vision and Pattern Recognition, pp. 2329–2339 (2021)

41. Thomee, B.: YFCC100M: the new data in multimedia research. Commun. ACM **59**(2), 64–73 (2016)

42. Tian, Y., Krishnan, D., Isola, P.: Contrastive multiview coding. In: Vedaldi, A., Bischof, H., Brox, T., Frahm, J.-M. (eds.) ECCV 2020. LNCS, vol. 12356, pp. 776–794. Springer, Cham (2020). https://doi.org/10.1007/978-3-030-58621-8_45

43. Tian, Y., Sun, C., Poole, B., Krishnan, D., Schmid, C., Isola, P.: What makes for good views for contrastive learning. arXiv preprint arXiv:2005.10243 (2020)
44. Tian, Y., Chen, X., Ganguli, S.: Understanding self-supervised learning dynamics without contrastive pairs. arXiv preprint arXiv:2102.06810 (2021)
45. Van Horn, G., et al.: The inaturalist species classification and detection dataset. In: Proceedings of the IEEE Conference on Computer vision and Pattern Recognition, pp. 8769–8778 (2018)
46. Wu, Z., Xiong, Y., Yu, S.X., Lin, D.: Unsupervised feature learning via non-parametric instance discrimination. In: Proceedings of the IEEE Conference on Computer Vision and Pattern Recognition, pp. 3733–3742 (2018)
47. Xie, Q., Dai, Z., Hovy, E., Luong, M.T., Le, Q.V.: Unsupervised data augmentation for consistency training. arXiv preprint arXiv:1904.12848 (2019)
48. Xie, Z., Lin, Y., Zhang, Z., Cao, Y., Lin, S., Hu, H.: Propagate yourself: exploring pixel-level consistency for unsupervised visual representation learning. In: Proceedings of the IEEE/CVF Conference on Computer Vision and Pattern Recognition, pp. 16684–16693 (2021)
49. You, Y., Gitman, I., Ginsburg, B.: Large batch training of convolutional networks. arXiv preprint arXiv:1708.03888 (2017)
50. Zbontar, J., Jing, L., Misra, I., LeCun, Y., Deny, S.: Barlow twins: self-supervised learning via redundancy reduction. arXiv preprint arXiv:2103.03230 (2021)
51. Zhai, X., Oliver, A., Kolesnikov, A., Beyer, L.: S4L: self-supervised semi-supervised learning. In: Proceedings of the IEEE/CVF International Conference on Computer Vision, pp. 1476–1485 (2019)
52. Zhan, X., Xie, J., Liu, Z., Ong, Y.S., Loy, C.C.: Online deep clustering for unsupervised representation learning. In: Proceedings of the IEEE/CVF Conference on Computer Vision and Pattern Recognition, pp. 6688–6697 (2020)
53. Zhang, L., Qi, G.J., Wang, L., Luo, J.: AET vs. AED: unsupervised representation learning by auto-encoding transformations rather than data. In: Proceedings of the IEEE/CVF Conference on Computer Vision and Pattern Recognition, pp. 2547–2555 (2019)
54. Zhang, R., Isola, P., Efros, A.A.: Colorful image colorization. In: Leibe, B., Matas, J., Sebe, N., Welling, M. (eds.) ECCV 2016. LNCS, vol. 9907, pp. 649–666. Springer, Cham (2016). https://doi.org/10.1007/978-3-319-46487-9_40
55. Zheng, Y., et al.: Online pseudo label generation by hierarchical cluster dynamics for adaptive person re-identification. In: Proceedings of the IEEE/CVF International Conference on Computer Vision, pp. 8371–8381 (2021)
56. Zhou, B., Khosla, A., Lapedriza, A., Torralba, A., Oliva, A.: Places: an image database for deep scene understanding. arXiv preprint arXiv:1610.02055 (2016)
57. Zhuang, C., Zhai, A.L., Yamins, D.: Local aggregation for unsupervised learning of visual embeddings. In: Proceedings of the IEEE/CVF International Conference on Computer Vision, pp. 6002–6012 (2019)

Fine-Grained Fashion Representation Learning by Online Deep Clustering

Yang Jiao(✉), Ning Xie, Yan Gao, Chien-chih Wang, and Yi Sun

Amazon, Seattle, WA, USA
{jaoyan,xining,yanngao,ccwang,yisun}@amazon.com

Abstract. Fashion designs are rich in visual details associated with various visual attributes at both global and local levels. As a result, effective modeling and analyzing fashion requires fine-grained representations for individual attributes. In this work, we present a deep learning based online clustering method to jointly learn fine-grained fashion representations for all attributes at both instance and cluster level, where the attribute-specific cluster centers are online estimated. Based on the similarity between fine-grained representations and cluster centers, attribute-specific embedding spaces are further segmented into class-specific embedding spaces for fine-grained fashion retrieval. To better regulate the learning process, we design a three-stage learning scheme, to progressively incorporate different supervisions at both instance and cluster level, from both original and augmented data, and with ground-truth and pseudo labels. Experiments on FashionAI and DARN datasets in the retrieval task demonstrated the efficacy of our method compared with competing baselines.

Keywords: Fine-grained fashion representation learning · Online deep clustering · Image retrieval · Semi-supervised learning

1 Introduction

The pursuit of fashion is one of the most prominent incentives for consumers. Therefore, modeling and analyzing fashion is an essential step to understand customer preferences and behaviors. In online shopping, it facilitates fashion trend prediction, fashion search, fashion recommendation, fashion compatibility analysis, etc. Many previous works attempt to learn a generic representation [9, 12,17,21,28,29] to establish a metric embedding for fashions. However, they often fail to capture the subtle details of different fashion styles and hence are not sufficient to support fine-grained downstream applications, such as attribute based fashion manipulation [1,2,33] and search [20,26,27].

Supplementary Information The online version contains supplementary material available at https://doi.org/10.1007/978-3-031-19812-0_2.

Indeed, fashion designs are rich in visual details associated with a variety of fashion attributes at both global and local levels. Therefore, effective modeling and analyzing fashion necessitates fine-grained representations for individual attributes. A fashion attribute represents a specific aspect of fashion products. An example of a global fashion attribute is *"skirt length"*, depicting the overall characteristic of the fashion product. *"Neckline style"*, on the other hand, is a local attribute, which reflects the fashion design for a local product area. A naive way of learning such representations is to learn representations on each attribute independently. It is not ideal as it ignores the shared visual statistics among the attributes. A better way is to formulate it as a multi-task learning problem, such that the different fine-grained attribute-specific fashion representations may share a common backbone with a companion computing process to tailor to each specific attribute.

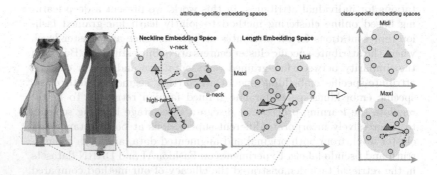

Fig. 1. Fine-grained representation learning by MODC. In each attribute-specific embedding space, a representation is learned by constraining it using the representations of the cluster centers (prototypes), other instances, and the augmented images. Based on the embedding similarity with cluster centers, class-specific embedding spaces for *Midi* and *Maxi* are segmented from *Length*. Solid arrow: the *cluster-level* constraint between instances and prototypes; dashed arrow: the *instance-level* constraint between instances; two-way arrow: the *augmentation constraint* between the two augmented images. More details are discussed in Sect. 3.

Attribute-Specific Embedding Network (ASEN) [20] and its extension ASEN++ [8] are the most recent prior state-of-the-art research to learn attribute-specific representations in the fashion domain. They address the problem by two attention modules, *i.e.*, an attribute-aware spatial attention module and an attribute-aware channel attention module, and learn fine-grained representations by a triplet loss, which is widely adopted in fashion related problems [1,2,13,20,33]. Notwithstanding their demonstrated efficacy, these works regularize multiple attribute embedding spaces with the triplet loss only at the instance level. We speculate the instance level loss is insufficient to learn representations that can well capture a global view of the cluster structure, and the performance can be further improved by constructing an attribute-specific clustering method.

Therefore, we propose a Multi-task Online Deep Clustering (MODC) method to learn fine-grained fashion representations. MODC leverages the generic representation power via multi-task learning, while simultaneously integrating cluster-level constraints with the global structure. In addition to the instance-level triplet loss, we further introduce a cluster-level triplet loss between cluster centers and instances, which strives for an explicit optimization of the global structures of the clusters. We treat cluster centers to be class prototypes, akin to that of prototypical networks [25], and use a memory bank to compute the prototypes. The cluster centers can be further leveraged in the inference stage to segment the fine-grained fashion retrieval space. As shown in Fig. 1, retrieval in class-specific embedding spaces prioritizes the positives (positives/negatives are assigned based on the embedding similarity to the given cluster center) compared with that in attribute-specific embedding spaces. Our proposed MODC is able to effectively leverage both labeled and unlabeled data for training, and we design a three-stage learning scheme to progressively guide the learning of the network parameters.

In summary, our contributions are:

- We propose the Multi-task Online Deep Clustering (MODC) method for efficient attribute-specific fine-grained representation learning for fashion products. MODC combines the instant-level loss function and a cluster-level triplet loss function to explicitly optimize the local and global structure of the fine-grained representation clusters in individual attribute-specific embedding spaces, which leads to improved clustering results.
- Using the cluster centers learned via MODC, we further segment the attribute-specific embedding spaces to class-specific embedding spaces to boost the fine-grained fashion retrieval.
- Our experiments on attribute-specific fashion retrieval, including supervised and semi-supervised learning, achieve state-of-the-art results, on the FashionAI [34] and DARN [15] datasets, demonstrating the efficacy of our proposed method.

2 Related Work

2.1 General Fashion Representation Learning

Fashion representation learning is a popular task-driven problem. In recent years, many researchers propose to learn representations by deep convolutional neural networks used for multiple tasks including in-shop fashion retrieval [17,24,29], street-to-shop fashion retrieval [5,9,12,15,18,19], compatibility search [14,16, 21,28], etc. One of the common approaches is to learn general representations [12,21,24]. The general fashion representations usually capture the patterns for the entire image, and are commonly used for general fashion image retrieval via conducting k nearest neighbor in the general representation space. Effective general fashion representations benefit tasks with similarity search for entire images.

2.2 Attribute-Specific Fashion Representation Learning

For fine-grained level tasks such as attribute-specific fashion retrieval, the fashion representations are asked to focus on specific attributes rather than the entire image. Therefore, for these tasks, instead of learning general representations, it is natural to involve attributes during the modeling stage. The attribute-specific fashion representation learning is usually formulated as a multi-task learning problem.

Attribute region proposal, classification, and ranking are popular components to involve attributes [1,2,13,15,33]. Huang *et al.* [15] proposes attribute region by Network-in-network, while [1,2,13] use global pooling layers to propose attribute activation maps. After extract attribute-specific representations, [33] further average the representations as the attribute prototypes to store in memory bank and achieve attribute manipulation. Although the aforementioned studies learn attribute-specific representations, region proposal with image cropping may result in losing global view. Furthermore, attribute-specific fully connected layer is the key component of these approaches, which is not scalable because it requires increased parameters with more attributes added.

To learn better representations and handle the scalability issue, another group of studies [8,20,27] apply attention masks to learn attribute-specific representations. Attention masks dynamically assign weights to different dimensions of the general representations for specific attributes. For instance, the state-of-the-art methods [8,20] enhance the participation of attribute in representation learning by attaching attribute-aware spatial and channel attention modules to the feature extraction network. In aforementioned works, attribute classification and attribute-specific triplet ranking is commonly applied.

In fact, most of the existing works focus on handling the fashion representation learning by optimizing the instance representation relationships such as optimizing the relative distance between a triplet instances, while ignoring the global structure and patterns of the attribute-specific embedding spaces. In our work, we propose the Multi-task Online Deep Clustering (MODC) method that models the global structure in the representation learning procedure.

2.3 Unsupervised Fashion Representation Learning

Learning attribute-specific fashion representations demands attribute annotations that is expensive because a fashion item could associate with many attributes. Therefore, unsupervised learning becomes a potential solution to relief this demand. Deep clustering [3], online deep clustering [4,32], and self-supervision [4,6,7,10,11,22,30,31] are commonly adopted techniques for unsupervised representation learning. Particularly in the fashion domain, Kim *et al.* [16] define pretexts such as color histogram prediction, patch discrimination, and pattern discrimination to conduct self-supervised learning. However, the representations learned via task-specific pretexts may not be generalizable to other tasks. Revanur *et al.* [23] build a semi-supervised representation learning with item ranking and self-supervision for labeled and unlabeled data. Similar to previous works [8,20,27], the method proposed by [23] optimizes the instance representation distribution but ignores the global representation distribution. In our work, the Multi-task Online Deep Clustering can effectively exploits unlabeled data via constructing online clustering with attribute-specific memory bank.

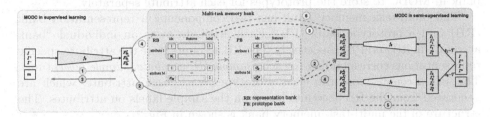

Fig. 2. The overall structure of the proposed *Multi-task Online Deep Clustering (MODC)*, where M tasks are involved, yielding M accounts in the representation bank (RB) and prototype bank (PB). MODC can adopt any multitask network that is denoted by f_θ. The proposed method works for both supervised learning and semi-supervised learning, which leverages two training schemes. The scheme details are shown in Algorithm 1 in Sect. 4, where the steps (for supervised learning: *step 1 to 4 on the left side*; for semi-supervised learning: *step 1 to 6 on the right side*) are consistent.

3 Multi-task Online Deep Clustering

To address the fine-grained fashion representation learning, each attribute is associated with its own embedding space to yield attribute-specific representations for a given input image. In order to provide an effective and scalable solution to capture visual details, we propose Multi-task Online Deep Clustering (MODC). MODC unifies classes and clusters for all attributes, and forms cluster centers as class prototypes. Furthermore, it learns not only the similarity between instances but also the similarity between instances and all class prototypes to constrain the fine-grained representations in a global manner. MODC is able to adopt unlabeled samples by assigning pseudo-labels and consequently can perform in both supervised and semi-supervised learning. Figure 2 illustrates the structure of MODC, and the training schemes for supervised and semi-supervised learning, which will be elaborated in Sect. 4.

3.1 Online Process with a Memory Bank

For a given attribute, a prototype is the "averaged" representation of samples belonging to the same class/cluster. Offline clustering methods like [3] commonly update prototypes after every training epoch, which have two drawbacks (1) the

representation generated during training is not reused when updating prototypes; (2) prototypes cannot accommodate the latest training outcome so that
the loss computation is always based on outdated prototypes. Online clustering,
however, addresses the drawbacks by storing and reusing the representations to
update cluster centers every n mini-batch. In this way, the training efficiency and
computational cost are optimized. In this work, we create a multi-task memory
bank in MODC to store the prototypes for each attribute separately.

The multi-task memory bank has two components: a representation bank
(RB) and a prototype bank (PB). Each attribute owns an individual "bank
account" in RB and PB respectively. The RB accounts store the attribute-specific
representations corresponding to each *(sample ID, attribute, sample label)* tuple.
The PB accounts store the class prototypes w.r.t. each attribute, which are
generated from the RB accounts based on the sample labels on attributes. The
structure of the multi-task memory bank is shown in Fig. 2.

Let's use $\{I, \{l_1, l_2, ..., l_M\}\}$ to denote a set of images and the corresponding
labels of each image for M different attributes. K_m is the total number of classes
in attribute m, where $m \in [1, M]$. The attribute-specific representation for an
arbitrary image I on a given attribute m is denoted as F_m^I, which is generated
via $F_m^I = f_\theta(I, m)$.

During training, when a new representation F_m^I is generated, we retrieve the
existing F_m^I from RB by *(sample id, attribute, sample label)* tuple. The F_m^I in
RB is then updated by

$$F_m^I \leftarrow \lambda F_m^I + (1 - \lambda) f_\theta(I, m), \tag{1}$$

where λ is a momentum coefficient for memory bank updating, and is set as 0.5
in our experiments. The storage limit of each attribute label is $1k$.

PB is updated along with RB. Suppose there are N_m^k representations belong
to class k ($k \in K_m$) in attribute m, we update the prototypes by

$$C_m^k = \frac{1}{N_m^k} \sum \{F_m | l_m = k\}, \tag{2}$$

where C_m^k is the prototype of class k for attribute m, and $\{F_m\}$ is the representation set for a group of images w.r.t. attribute m. We compute Eq. 2 every n
mini-batch, where n is set as 100 in our experiment. Only the representations of
labeled samples are stored into RB and used to update PB in the experiment.

For unlabeled samples, MODC generates pseudo-labels by searching for the
nearest prototype. For an unlabeled image sample I^u on attribute m, the representation is denoted as $F_m^{I^u}$, and the pseudo-labels $l_m^{\hat{u}}$ is calculated by

$$l_m^{\hat{u}} = \arg \min_{k \sim K_m} \{d(F_m^{I^u}, C_m^k)\}, \tag{3}$$

where d is the cosine similarity distance $d(a, b) = -\frac{a \cdot b}{\|a\| \|b\|}$.

3.2   MODC Learning Objectives

To learn the attribute-specific representations, we design three objective functions (defined by Eq. 4, 6, 7) covering both cluster-level and instance-level similarity learning, guiding the training of MODC in supervised and semi-supervised manners. If labels are involved in the objective function, MODC uses the ground truth label for labeled data, while using generated pseudo-labels for unlabeled data via Eq. 3.

Cluster-Level Similarity Objective: We define the cluster-level objective function in the form of a cluster-level triplet loss called *prototypical triplet loss*, which constructs triplet losses between a representation, the positive prototype, and the negative prototypes defined below. Let's use (I, l_m) to denote an image and label pair corresponding to attribute m, and the attribute-specific representation for this image I is F_m^I. In the embedding space of attribute m, there exist a positive prototype $C_m^+ = C_m^{l_m}$, and a negative prototype set with $K_m - 1$ prototypes $\{C_m^-\} = \{C_m^0, C_m^1, ..., C_m^{K_m}\} \backslash \{C_m^{l_m}\}$. We propose the prototypical triplet loss by averaging $K_m - 1$ triplet losses between the representation F_m^I, the positive prototype C_m^+, and the negative prototypes $\{C_m^-\}$,

$$\mathcal{L}_\mathcal{C}(I, m | l_m) = \frac{1}{K_m - 1} \sum_c^{\{C_m^-\}} max\{0, \alpha + d(F_m^I, C_m^+) - d(F_m^I, c)\}, \qquad (4)$$

where α is a predefined margin, which is 0.2 in our experiment.

Given that a prototype is the representation of a class "center", learning a cluster-level similarity implies learning the similarity between an instance and the "center" of all instances in a class. The prototypical triplet loss learns the similarity between an instance and all class prototypes in an attribute, and consequently constrains the representation learning in a global manner.

The prototypical triplet loss has two major benefits. First, it considers the global distribution of all class prototypes and efficiently pushes a representation closer to its positive class prototype. Second, unlike the objective function in [25], it allows a margin rather than intensely forcing a representation to its positive prototype. As a result, when learning with a tiny labeled dataset, it reduces over-fitting in semi-supervised learning.

Instance-Level Similarity Objective: For fashion representation learning, learning instance-level similarity is a popular training approach. While the cluster-level objective function aids in the learning of similarities between instances and class abstracts, the instance-level objective function aids in the learning of subtle similarities between single instances.

For an image and a label pair (I, l_m) on attribute m, to construct a set of instance triplets, we select a set of (image, label) pairs,

$$\mathcal{T} = \{(I, l_m), (I^+, l_m^+), (I^-, l_m^-) | m\}, \qquad (5)$$

where $l_m = l_m^+ \neq l_m^-$ on attribute m, indicating I and I^+ are more similar than I and I^- on attribute m. The instance-level similarity objective is defined as,

$$\mathcal{L}_\mathcal{I}(I, I^+, I^-, m) = max\{0, \alpha + d(F_m^I, F_m^{I^+}) - d(F_m^I, F_m^{I^-})\}, \qquad (6)$$

where α is a predefined margin.

Self-supervised Objective: When only limited labeled samples or unlabeled samples are applied during training, regularizing the representations through image augmentations often helps the learning. We further explore some recent research on data augmentation and self-supervised learning. Similar to [7], we build a simple Siamese network to leverage the self-supervised learning constraint. For an image I, we employ a set of image augmentation methods $\{\mathcal{T}_{\mathcal{AUG}}\}$, from which we randomly select $t_1, t_2 \sim \{\mathcal{T}_{\mathcal{AUG}}\}$ to generate image augmentations $I_1 = t_1(I)$, and $I_2 = t_2(I)$. The self-supervised objective function is,

$$\mathcal{L}_{\mathcal{A}}(I_1, I_2, m) = \frac{1}{2}d(F_m^{I_1}, \oslash F_m^{I_2}) + \frac{1}{2}d(\oslash F_m^{I_1}, F_m^{I_2}), \qquad (7)$$

where $\oslash$ is the stop-gradient operation, and $\oslash F_m^I$ is generated using the gradient-detached network in an iteration, as [7] defined.

3.3   Class-Specific Representation Space Segmentation

After the model is well trained via MODC, the cluster centers can be further leveraged during the inference stage to segment the attribute-specific embedding space into class-specific embedding spaces. Ideally, the class-specific embedding space only includes fine-grained representations that belong to this class, denoted as *space-positives*, while in practice, it may also include representations that do not belong to this class, denoted as *space-negatives*. Subsequently, the space construction finds the optimum trade-off between the accuracy of inclusion and coverage of space-positives.

We design a top_n segmentation strategy to allow elastic inclusion. Given an attribute m that has K_m classes, the prototypes (cluster centers) in the attribute-specific embedding space is denoted as $\{C_m^k\}$, which have been optimized by MODC. For a given image I_{new}, the attribute-specific image representation is $F_m^{I_{new}}$. Following the top_n segmentation strategy, $F_m^{I_{new}}$ is allowed to be assigned to n class-specific embedding spaces,

$$F_m^{I_{new}} \to S_m^{p_1}, ..., F_m^{I_{new}} \to S_m^{p_n}, \qquad (8)$$

where $\{p_1, ..., p_n\}$ is the classes whose prototypes are the top n closest to $F_m^{I_{new}}$, and S_m^p is the class-specific embedding space of class p ($p \in K_m$) in the attribute-specific embedding space of m. Therefore, a small n leads to high inclusion accuracy but low space-positive coverage because representations are only assigned to high-confident spaces. On the other hand, a large n leads to lower accuracy but higher coverage.

4   The Training Scheme

In this section, we explain the training scheme which integrates the cluster-level and instance-level objective constraints for attribute-specific fine-grained representation learning. The training steps for supervised and semi-supervised learning are also illustrated in Fig. 2.

The overall training scheme contains three stages: i) *a warm-up stage*, ii) *a supervised stage*, and iii) *a semi-supervised stage*. The warm-up stage is leveraged to form good initial representations for the prototypes, as the representations yielded based on a randomly initialized network may not be able to group images with the same labels closer in the representation space. In the warm-up stage, we only start with instance-level triplet loss on labeled samples to model convergence. The adopted network is updated using the loss function defined in Eq. 9.

After the warm-up, the supervised stage involves MODC with only labeled samples. To prepare for the MODC training, we initialize RB by pre-computing the representations for all training samples w.r.t. each attribute, and initialize PB by Eq. 2. To avoid immense memory bank but keep prototypes efficient, we limit the size of each RB account to 2,000 representations and refuse any extra representations. The cluster-level and instance-level objective functions are optimized together to learn the representations. An example of a supervised MODC iteration is shown in Algorithm 1 (*line 6–14*).

After the supervised stage, unlabeled samples are added to further guide the training in the semi-supervised stage. We incorporate the cluster-level and instance-level similarity learning for unlabeled data and also add the self-supervised learning constraints on augmented images. An example of a semi-supervised MODC iteration is shown in Algorithm 1 (*line 15–25*).

Algorithm 1. An MODC iteration

1: A multi-task embedding network Net.
2: A targeted attribute m, labeled image set S_l, and unlabeled image set S_u
3: A batch of image (with label) triplets $\{(I, l_m), (I^+, l_m^+), (I^-, l_m^-)|m\} \sim S_l$
4: A batch of unlabeled images $\{I^u|m\} \sim S_u$
5: Image augmentation methods t_1, t_2
6: **if** supervised stage **then**
7:     **for** I, I^+, I^- **do**
8:         ① Obtain representations $\leftarrow f_\theta$
9:     **end for**
10:     **for** I, I^+, I^- **do**
11:         ② Obtain positive and negative prototypes
12:     **end for**
13:     ③ Update Net by Eq. 10
14:     ④ Update RB by Eq. 1, update PB by Eq. 2 every n mini-batch
15: **else if** semi-supervised stage **then**
16:     **for** I, I^+, I^-, I^u **do**
17:         ① Obtain augmentations $\leftarrow t_1, t_2$, obtain representations $\leftarrow f_\theta$
18:     **end for**
19:     ② Assign pseudo-label $l_m^{\hat{u}}$ to I_1^u by Eq. 3
20:     ③ Based on $l_m^{\hat{u}}$, randomly index a pseudo-positive and a pseudo-negative image ($I^{\hat{u}+}|l_m^{\hat{u}+} = l_m^{\hat{u}}$), ($I^{\hat{u}-}|l_m^{\hat{u}-} \neq l_m^{\hat{u}}$) $\sim S_l$
21:     **for** I_1, I_1^+, I_1^-, I_1^u **do**
22:         ④ Obtain positive and negative prototypes
23:     **end for**
24:     ⑤ Update Net by Eq. 11
25:     ⑥ Update RB by Eq. 1, update PB by Eq. 2 every n mini-batch
26: **end if**

Supervised learning involves the first two stages, while semi-supervised learning involves all three stages. The next stage starts when the previous one converges. Equation 9, 10, 11 are the full objective functions for the warm-up, supervised, and semi-supervised stage, respectively,

$$\mathcal{L}_{warm} = \lambda_1 \mathcal{L}_{\mathcal{I}}(I, I^+, I^-, m),\tag{9}$$

$$\begin{aligned}
\mathcal{L}_{SL} = \lambda_1 \mathcal{L}_{\mathcal{I}}(I, I^+, I^-, m) + \lambda_1(\mathcal{L}_{\mathcal{C}}(I, m|l_m) \\
+ \mathcal{L}_{\mathcal{C}}(I^+, m|l_m^+) + \mathcal{L}_{\mathcal{C}}(I^-, m|l_m^-))/3,
\end{aligned}\tag{10}$$

$$\begin{aligned}
\mathcal{L}_{SSL} = \mathcal{L}_{SL} + \lambda_1 \mathcal{L}_{\mathcal{I}}(I_1^u, I^{\hat{u}+}, I^{\hat{u}-}, m) + \lambda_2 \mathcal{L}_{\mathcal{C}}(I_1^u, m|l_m^{\hat{u}}) \\
+ \lambda_1(\mathcal{L}_{\mathcal{A}}(I_1, I_2, m) + \mathcal{L}_{\mathcal{A}}(I_1^+, I_2^+, m) \\
+ \mathcal{L}_{\mathcal{A}}(I_1^-, I_2^-, m))/3 + \lambda_1 \mathcal{L}_{\mathcal{A}}(I_1^u, I_2^u, m),
\end{aligned}\tag{11}$$

where λ_1 is set to 10^0 and λ_2 is set to 10^{-1}.

5   Experiments

5.1   Datasets

FashionAI [34] is a public dataset for fashion challenges. It contains 180,335 fashion images and 8 fine-grained attribute annotations on coat length, dress length, collar design, and so on, with 5–10 classes. We adopt the labeled train/val/test split of [20], which contains 144k/18k/18k samples.

DARN [15] is a fashion attribute prediction and retrieval dataset with 253,983 images. DARN has 9 attributes with class numbers varying from 7 to 55. We follow the labeled train/val/test split of [20], which contains 163k/20k/20k images after excluding unavailable ones[1].

For semi-supervised learning, we further partition the full set of training split into "labeled"/"unlabeled" subsets by ratio 10%/90% and the ground truth labels for the "unlabeled" subsets is not used during model training, even though they are available in the original dataset.

5.2   Experimental Settings

We compare our proposed method with the state-of-the-art solutions [8,20] on the aforementioned two datasets.

Baselines. ASEN [20] attaches an attribute-aware spatial attention and an attribute-aware channel attention to a backbone network, and learns 1024 dimensional attribute-specific representations Compared with ASEN, $ASEN_{v2}$ [20] updates the attention module structures and achieves similar performance as ASEN with fewer training iterations. ASEN++ [8] is an extension of $ASEN_{v2}$ that further utilize the multi-scale information with a global branch and a local

---

[1] Note: Only 203,990 images are available due to broken URLs.

branch. The final representation is the composition of global and local representations with 2,048 dimensions.

Evaluation Tasks and Metrics. Mean Average Precision (MAP) and Recall are commonly used performance metrics for retrieval-related tasks [8,20]. We further utilize these at different scales, including MAP@100, MAP@all, and Recall@100, to comprehensively evaluate the performance. MAP@100 and Recall@100 are the evaluations for top 100 retrieval results. In the e-commerce fashion retrieval domain, customer satisfaction is usually influenced by the quality of top retrieval results. MAP@all further reports the evaluation considering all retrieval results.

5.3 Experimental Results

In this section, we discuss the experimental results of different models for two datasets[2]. Table 1 and Table 2 summarize the overall performance of baselines and MODC on supervised and semi-supervised learning. Table 3 and Table 4 show the detailed performance on each attribute of FashionAI and DARN. The best performers on each network are in **bold**. The global best performers are underlined.

In the experiment, MODC allows us to leverage the query image labels that are usually available in e-commerce fashion retrieval domain. With MODC, we prioritize the retrieval in class-specific embedding spaces to retrieve space-positives, and subsequently, process the retrieval in attribute-specific embedding spaces to retrieve all the rest candidates. If the query image labels are unknown, the prioritized retrieval strategy can still be applied by assigning the pseudo-label to the query image[3].

Table 1. Overall performance comparison on all attributes of FashionAI.

Model	100% labeled			10% labeled		
	MAP@100	MAP@all	Recall@100	MAP@100	MAP@all	Recall@100
$ASEN$	64.70	57.37	22.77	49.68	41.35	16.81
$MODC(ASEN)_{top1}$	**77.10**	**70.02**	**28.89**	<u>**65.29**</u>	<u>**56.64**</u>	<u>**24.32**</u>
$MODC(ASEN)_{top2}$	68.91	64.30	24.95	57.33	51.99	20.46
$ASEN_{v2}$	67.85	61.13	24.14	50.20	41.89	17.06
$MODC(ASEN_{v2})_{top1}$	**79.29**	**72.51**	**29.78**	**64.78**	**56.36**	**24.13**
$MODC(ASEN_{v2})_{top2}$	72.00	67.77	26.34	57.61	52.27	20.72
$ASEN++$	70.62	64.27	25.30	48.37	39.51	16.16
$MODC(ASEN++)_{top1}$	<u>**80.29**</u>	<u>**74.32**</u>	<u>**30.26**</u>	**61.61**	**52.00**	**22.73**
$MODC(ASEN++)_{top2}$	72.99	68.75	26.75	53.98	47.96	19.05

---

[2] *MODC(Net)* means *MODC* build upon a specific multi-task network *Net*. The subscript top_n means using top n similarity to segment class-specific embedding spaces.
[3] More experimental result of leveraging query image with pseudo labels is included in the Supplementary.

Table 2. Overall performance comparison on all attributes of DARN.

Model	100% labeled			10% labeled		
	MAP@100	MAP@all	Recall@100	MAP@100	MAP@all	Recall@100
ASEN	58.72	52.75	20.26	51.35	45.10	16.03
$MODC(ASEN)_{top1}$	**69.45**	**59.61**	**25.36**	**61.67**	53.21	21.53
$MODC(ASEN)_{top2}$	65.85	58.67	25.04	59.17	**53.55**	**21.72**
$ASEN_{v2}$	59.66	54.29	20.88	55.34	50.02	18.00
$MODC(ASEN_{v2})_{top1}$	**69.25**	**60.43**	**25.65**	**64.94**	**57.60**	**23.86**
$MODC(ASEN_{v2})_{top2}$	65.80	59.14	24.95	60.91	56.25	23.15
ASEN++	61.09	55.78	21.51	54.83	49.85	17.63
$MODC(ASEN++)_{top1}$	**72.16**	**62.56**	**26.76**	**65.35**	**57.07**	**23.05**
$MODC(ASEN++)_{top2}$	67.76	61.37	26.01	61.26	55.52	22.47

Table 3. Performance comparison on MAP@all of each attribute on FashionAI.

Model	MAP@all for each attribute								Overall
	Skirt length	Sleeve length	Coat length	Pant length	Collar design	Lapel design	Neckline design	Neck design	
ASEN	64.61	49.98	49.75	65.76	70.30	62.86	52.14	63.73	57.37
$MODC(ASEN)_{top1}$	**74.77**	62.79	64.70	76.62	80.50	74.33	66.99	69.52	70.02
$ASEN_{v2}$	65.58	54.42	52.03	67.41	71.36	66.76	60.91	59.58	61.13
$MODC(ASEN_{v2})_{top1}$	73.56	66.95	64.76	76.09	**81.63**	76.56	73.88	74.01	72.51
ASEN++	66.31	57.51	55.43	68.83	72.79	66.85	66.78	67.02	64.27
$MODC(ASEN++)_{top1}$	74.54	**67.48**	**68.25**	**77.69**	81.11	**76.90**	**77.46**	**77.10**	**74.32**

Table 4. Performance comparison on MAP@all of each attribute on DARN.

Model	MAP@all for each attribute									Overall
	Clothes category	Clothes button	Clothes color	Clothes length	Clothes pattern	Clothes shape	Collar shape	Sleeve length	Sleeve shape	
ASEN	36.62	46.01	52.76	56.85	54.89	56.85	34.40	79.95	58.08	52.75
$MODC(ASEN)_{top1}$	47.45	54.52	**59.37**	63.30	58.95	64.77	41.24	86.54	61.53	59.61
$ASEN_{v2}$	37.97	49.24	52.26	59.13	55.32	59.06	36.86	81.54	58.82	54.29
$MODC(ASEN_{v2})_{top1}$	46.67	59.13	58.94	64.60	61.49	65.95	42.25	84.61	61.58	60.43
ASEN++	40.21	50.04	53.14	59.83	57.41	59.70	37.45	83.70	60.41	55.78
$MODC(ASEN++)_{top1}$	**49.94**	**60.75**	58.79	**66.34**	**62.24**	**68.41**	**45.14**	**87.41**	**65.32**	**62.56**

Performance of MODC on Supervised Learning: Table 1 shows the experimental results on FashionAI dataset. When trained on 100% labeled FashionAI data, MODC with top_1 segmentation strategy shows significant improvement on all evaluation metrics (MAP@100, MAP@all, Recall@100) consistently for all adopted baseline networks (ASEN, $ASEN_{v2}$, ASEN++). Specifically, the best MAP@all is 74.32, which is achieved by $MODC(ASEN++)_{top1}$, exceeding the corresponding baseline model ASEN++ by 15.64%. We observe the top_1 segmentation results consistently outperform those of top_2 segmentation. The potential reason is, MODC with top_1 segmentation achieves 75% inclusion accuracy and 75% space-positive coverage, which is a better trade-off compared with the 46% inclusion accuracy and 91% space-positive coverage of top_2 segmentation. On DARN, we observe a similar improvement, as shown in Table 2. In supervised learning, the best MAP@all reaches to 62.56. Table 3 and Table 4 demonstrates the MAP@all is improved for each attribute on FashionAI and DARN, respectively.

Performance of MODC on Semi-supervised Learning: Similar performance improvement trend of adopting our method is also observed for semi-

Table 5. Ablation study on MODC components. Study on the overall performance on semi-supervised/supervised learning on FashionAI. Models are selected based on the best performers on these cases as we show in Table 1.

Component	10% labeled w. $MODC(ASEN)$			100% labeled w. $MODC(ASEN++)$		
	MAP@100	MAP@all	Recall@100	MAP@100	MAP@all	Recall@100
1 baseline network	49.68	41.35	16.81	70.62	64.27	25.30
2 +cluster-level loss	51.17	42.34	17.19	71.64	65.07	25.63
3 +augmentation	53.07	44.85	18.05	–	–	–
4 +pseudo label	54.19	46.25	18.66	–	–	–
5 +top_1 segmentation	65.29	56.64	24.32	80.29	74.32	30.26
6 +top_2 segmentation	57.33	51.99	20.46	72.99	68.75	26.75

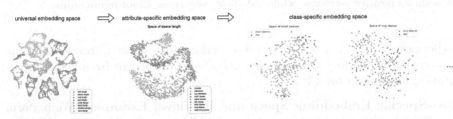

Fig. 3. Fine-grained representation distribution in the universal embedding space, attribute-specific embedding space, and class-specific embedding space. Model: $MODC(ASEN_{v2})_{top1}$. (Color figure online)

supervised settings[4], with an even larger margin. The potential reason of large margin performance improvement is, MODC is able to effectively leverage the global view and fully utilize the rich amount of unlabeled data via the designed objectives. On FashionAI, as shown in Table 1, MODC with $top1$ segmentation improves the most, compared with baseline approaches. $MODC(ASEN)_{top1}$ performs the best and reaches to 56.64 on MAP@all. On DARN, as shown in Table 2, the best MAP@all reaches to 57.60, which is 15.15% higher than the best baseline performance. Particularly, $MODC(ASEN)_{top2}$ on MAP@all and Recall@100 surpasses the top_1 MODC. With a deep-diving study, in this particular case, we find MODC with $top2$ segmentation has a better trade-off. MODC with $top2$ segmentation includes 57% space-positives with 28% accuracy, while the top_1 segmentation only includes 35% space-positives with 35% accuracy.

Ablation Study of MODC: To show the effectiveness of each component of MODC, we conduct an ablation study for the case of semi-supervised/supervised learning on FashionAI, and the results are shown in Table 5. This case leverages all the components of MODC. We observe that in the supervised learning stage (row 1 and 2), the cluster-level triplet loss helps improve the representation learning, as we hypothesized. Row 3 and 4 show the data augmentation and pseudo-label assignment in semi-supervised learning is able to effectively utilize the rich amount of unlabeled data, leading to further performance improvement.

---

[4] More results on various labeled and unlabeled data ratio are in Supplementary.

Fig. 4. Fine-grained fashion retrieval examples by MODC(ASEN$_{v2}$)$_{top1}$ on FashionAI. Green shows positive retrieves, while red shows negatives. Color figure online

Furthermore, row 5 and 6 illustrate the performance boost introduced by the class-specific embedding space segmentation, which is benefit from better representation learning in rows 1–4.

Class-Specific Embedding Space and Retrieval Examples: We perform the t-SNE algorithm for the three-scale embedding spaces and generate 2D visualizations as shown in Fig. 3. The left part is the universal multi-task embedding space that contains the representations of all attributes. The middle one shows the attribute-specific embedding space for a given attribute, where the instance-level and cluster level losses constrain the representation distribution. The right part is the class-specific embedding space for a given class belong to a specific attribute, which is generated based on the segmentation strategy introduced in Sect. 3.3. More detailed three-scale embedding spaces illustration is included in the supplementary. Figure 4 shows the fashion retrieval results in class-specific embedding spaces. We observe that most retrieved results share the same attribute class as the query image.

6 Conclusion

In this paper, we introduce Multi-task Online Deep Clustering (MODC), which learns at cluster-level and instance-level to optimize the representation distribution comprehensively. We design a three-stage training scheme to guide fine-grained representation learning in both supervised and semi-supervised fashion. MODC is able to fully utilize the rich amount of unlabeled data for performance boosting. By leveraging the cluster centers learned via MODC, the attribute-specific embedding spaces can be segmented into class-specific embedding spaces, enabling the prioritized retrieval strategy for fashion retrievals. We conduct experiments on FashionAI and DARN datasets, using evaluation metrics of MAP@100, MAP@all, and Recall@100. According to the experimental results, our proposed MODC is able to exceed the state-of-the-art solutions by a large margin, demonstrating the effectiveness of our method on fashion retrieval tasks.

References

1. Ak, K.E., Kassim, A.A., Lim, J.H., Tham, J.Y.: Learning attribute representations with localization for flexible fashion search. In: Proceedings of the IEEE Conference on Computer Vision and Pattern Recognition, pp. 7708–7717 (2018)
2. Ak, K.E., Lim, J.H., Tham, J.Y., Kassim, A.A.: Efficient multi-attribute similarity learning towards attribute-based fashion search. In: 2018 IEEE Winter Conference on Applications of Computer Vision (WACV), pp. 1671–1679. IEEE (2018)
3. Caron, M., Bojanowski, P., Joulin, A., Douze, M.: Deep clustering for unsupervised learning of visual features. In: Ferrari, V., Hebert, M., Sminchisescu, C., Weiss, Y. (eds.) Computer Vision – ECCV 2018. LNCS, vol. 11218, pp. 139–156. Springer, Cham (2018). https://doi.org/10.1007/978-3-030-01264-9_9
4. Caron, M., Misra, I., Mairal, J., Goyal, P., Bojanowski, P., Joulin, A.: Unsupervised learning of visual features by contrasting cluster assignments. In: Proceedings of Advances in Neural Information Processing Systems (NeurIPS) (2020)
5. Chen, Q., Huang, J., Feris, R., Brown, L.M., Dong, J., Yan, S.: Deep domain adaptation for describing people based on fine-grained clothing attributes. In: Proceedings of the IEEE Conference on Computer Vision and Pattern Recognition, pp. 5315–5324 (2015)
6. Chen, T., Kornblith, S., Norouzi, M., Hinton, G.: A simple framework for contrastive learning of visual representations. In: International Conference on Machine Learning, pp. 1597–1607. PMLR (2020)
7. Chen, X., He, K.: Exploring simple siamese representation learning. In: Proceedings of the IEEE/CVF Conference on Computer Vision and Pattern Recognition, pp. 15750–15758 (2021)
8. Dong, J., et al.: Fine-grained fashion similarity prediction by attribute-specific embedding learning. arXiv preprint arXiv:2104.02429 (2021)
9. Gajic, B., Baldrich, R.: Cross-domain fashion image retrieval. In: Proceedings of the IEEE Conference on Computer Vision and Pattern Recognition Workshops, pp. 1869–1871 (2018)
10. Gidaris, S., Singh, P., Komodakis, N.: Unsupervised representation learning by predicting image rotations. In: International Conference on Learning Representations (2018)
11. Grill, J.B., et al.: Bootstrap your own latent-a new approach to self-supervised learning. Adv. Neural. Inf. Process. Syst. 33, 21271–21284 (2020)
12. Hadi Kiapour, M., Han, X., Lazebnik, S., Berg, A.C., Berg, T.L.: Where to buy it: matching street clothing photos in online shops. In: Proceedings of the IEEE International Conference on Computer Vision, pp. 3343–3351 (2015)
13. Han, X., et al.: Automatic spatially-aware fashion concept discovery. In: Proceedings of the IEEE International Conference on Computer Vision, pp. 1463–1471 (2017)
14. He, R., Packer, C., McAuley, J.: Learning compatibility across categories for heterogeneous item recommendation. In: 2016 IEEE 16th International Conference on Data Mining (ICDM), pp. 937–942. IEEE (2016)
15. Huang, J., Feris, R.S., Chen, Q., Yan, S.: Cross-domain image retrieval with a dual attribute-aware ranking network. In: Proceedings of the IEEE International Conference on Computer Vision, pp. 1062–1070 (2015)
16. Kim, D., Saito, K., Mishra, S., Sclaroff, S., Saenko, K., Plummer, B.A.: Self-supervised visual attribute learning for fashion compatibility. In: Proceedings of the IEEE/CVF International Conference on Computer Vision, pp. 1057–1066 (2021)

17. Kinli, F., Ozcan, B., Kirac, F.: Fashion image retrieval with capsule networks. In: Proceedings of the IEEE/CVF International Conference on Computer Vision Workshops, pp. 0–0 (2019)
18. Kuang, Z., et al.: Fashion retrieval via graph reasoning networks on a similarity pyramid. In: Proceedings of the IEEE/CVF International Conference on Computer Vision, pp. 3066–3075 (2019)
19. Liu, Z., Luo, P., Qiu, S., Wang, X., Tang, X.: Deepfashion: powering robust clothes recognition and retrieval with rich annotations. In: Proceedings of the IEEE Conference on Computer Vision and Pattern Recognition, pp. 1096–1104 (2016)
20. Ma, Z., et al.: Fine-grained fashion similarity learning by attribute-specific embedding network. In: Proceedings of the AAAI Conference on Artificial Intelligence, pp. 11741–11748 (2020)
21. McAuley, J., Targett, C., Shi, Q., Van Den Hengel, A.: Image-based recommendations on styles and substitutes. In: Proceedings of the 38th International ACM SIGIR Conference on Research and Development in Information Retrieval, pp. 43–52 (2015)
22. Noroozi, M., Favaro, P.: Unsupervised learning of visual representations by solving jigsaw puzzles. In: Leibe, B., Matas, J., Sebe, N., Welling, M. (eds.) ECCV 2016. LNCS, vol. 9910, pp. 69–84. Springer, Cham (2016). https://doi.org/10.1007/978-3-319-46466-4_5
23. Revanur, A., Kumar, V., Sharma, D.: Semi-supervised visual representation learning for fashion compatibility. In: Fifteenth ACM Conference on Recommender Systems, pp. 463–472 (2021)
24. Shankar, D., Narumanchi, S., Ananya, H., Kompalli, P., Chaudhury, K.: Deep learning based large scale visual recommendation and search for e-commerce. arXiv preprint arXiv:1703.02344 (2017)
25. Snell, J., Swersky, K., Zemel, R.: Prototypical networks for few-shot learning. Adv. Neural. Inf. Process. Syst. **30**, 4077–4087 (2017)
26. Vasileva, M.I., Plummer, B.A., Dusad, K., Rajpal, S., Kumar, R., Forsyth, D.: Learning type-aware embeddings for fashion compatibility. In: Ferrari, V., Hebert, M., Sminchisescu, C., Weiss, Y. (eds.) ECCV 2018. LNCS, vol. 11220, pp. 405–421. Springer, Cham (2018). https://doi.org/10.1007/978-3-030-01270-0_24
27. Veit, A., Belongie, S., Karaletsos, T.: Conditional similarity networks. In: Proceedings of the IEEE conference on computer vision and pattern recognition. pp. 830–838 (2017)
28. Veit, A., Kovacs, B., Bell, S., McAuley, J., Bala, K., Belongie, S.: Learning visual clothing style with heterogeneous dyadic co-occurrences. In: Proceedings of the IEEE International Conference on Computer Vision, pp. 4642–4650 (2015)
29. Wang, Z., Gu, Y., Zhang, Y., Zhou, J., Gu, X.: Clothing retrieval with visual attention model. In: 2017 IEEE Visual Communications and Image Processing (VCIP), pp. 1–4. IEEE (2017)
30. Wu, Z., Xiong, Y., Yu, S.X., Lin, D.: Unsupervised feature learning via non-parametric instance discrimination. In: Proceedings of the IEEE Conference on Computer Vision and Pattern Recognition, pp. 3733–3742 (2018)
31. Zhai, X., Oliver, A., Kolesnikov, A., Beyer, L.: S4l: self-supervised semi-supervised learning. In: Proceedings of the IEEE/CVF International Conference on Computer Vision, pp. 1476–1485 (2019)
32. Zhan, X., Xie, J., Liu, Z., Ong, Y.S., Loy, C.C.: Online deep clustering for unsupervised representation learning. In: Proceedings of the IEEE/CVF Conference on Computer Vision and Pattern Recognition, pp. 6688–6697 (2020)

33. Zhao, B., Feng, J., Wu, X., Yan, S.: Memory-augmented attribute manipulation networks for interactive fashion search. In: Proceedings of the IEEE Conference on Computer Vision and Pattern Recognition, pp. 1520–1528 (2017)
34. Zou, X., Kong, X., Wong, W., Wang, C., Liu, Y., Cao, Y.: Fashionai: a hierarchical dataset for fashion understanding. In: Proceedings of the IEEE/CVF Conference on Computer Vision and Pattern Recognition Workshops, pp. 0–0 (2019)

NashAE: Disentangling Representations Through Adversarial Covariance Minimization

Eric Yeats[1]([✉]) [iD], Frank Liu[2] [iD], David Womble[2] [iD], and Hai Li[1] [iD]

[1] Duke University, Durham, NC 27708, USA
{eric.yeats,hai.li}@duke.edu
[2] Oak Ridge National Laboratory, Oak Ridge, TN 37830, USA
{liufy,wombalede}@ornl.gov

Abstract. We present a self-supervised method to disentangle factors of variation in high-dimensional data that does not rely on prior knowledge of the underlying variation profile (e.g., no assumptions on the number or distribution of the individual latent variables to be extracted). In this method which we call NashAE, high-dimensional feature disentanglement is accomplished in the low-dimensional latent space of a standard autoencoder (AE) by promoting the discrepancy between each encoding element and information of the element recovered from all other encoding elements. Disentanglement is promoted efficiently by framing this as a minmax game between the AE and an ensemble of regression networks which each provide an estimate of an element conditioned on an observation of all other elements. We quantitatively compare our approach with leading disentanglement methods using existing disentanglement metrics. Furthermore, we show that NashAE has increased reliability and increased capacity to capture salient data characteristics in the learned latent representation.

Keywords: Representation learning · Autoencoder · Adversarial · Minmax game

1 Introduction

Deep neural networks (DNNs) have proven to be extremely high-performing in the realms of computer vision [7], natural language processing [26], autonomous control [16], and deep generative models [5,13], among others. The huge successes of DNNs have made them almost ubiquitous as an engineering tool, and it is very common for them to appear in many new applications. However, as we rush to deploy DNNs in the real world, we have also exposed many of their shortcomings.

Supplementary Information The online version contains supplementary material available at https://doi.org/10.1007/978-3-031-19812-0_3.

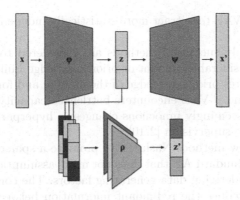

Fig. 1. Depiction of the proposed disentanglement method, NashAE, for a latent space dimensionality of $m = 3$. An autoencoder (AE), composed of the encoder ϕ and decoder ψ, compresses a high dimensional input $\mathbf{x} \in \mathbb{R}^n$ to a lower dimensional latent vector $\mathbf{z} \in \mathbb{R}^m$, and decompresses $\mathbf{z}$ to approximate $\mathbf{x}$ as $\mathbf{x}'$. An ensemble of m independently trained regression networks ρ takes m duplicates of $\mathbf{z}$ which each have an element removed, and each independent regression network tries to predict the value of its missing element using knowledge of the other elements. Disentanglement is achieved through equilibrium in an adversarial game in which ϕ minimizes the element-wise covariance between the true latent vector $\mathbf{z}$ and concatenated predictions vector $\mathbf{z}'$

One such shortcoming is that DNNs are extremely sensitive to minute pertur-bations in their inputs [6,25] or weights [8], causing otherwise high-performing models to suddenly be consistently incorrect. Additionally, DNNs trained on image classification tasks are observed to predict labels confidently even when the image shares no relationship with their in-distribution label space [9,17]. Fur-thermore, DNNs are known to perpetuate biases in their training data through their predictions, exacerbating salient issues such as racial and social inequity, and gender inequality [1]. While this small subset of examples may appear to be unrelated, they are all linked by a pervasive issue of DNNs: their lack of interpretability [23,24]. The fact that DNNs are treated as black boxes, where engineers lack a clear explanation or reasoning for why or how DNNs make decisions, makes the root cause of DNNs' shortcomings difficult to diagnose.

A promising remedy to this overarching issue is to clarify learning repre-sentations through feature disentanglement: the process of learning unique data representations that are each only sensitive to independent factors of the under-lying data distribution. It follows that a disentangled representation is an inher-ently interpretable representation, where each disentangled unit has a consistent, unique, and independent interpretation of the data across its domain.

Several works have pioneered the field of feature disentanglement, moving from supervised [14] to unsupervised approaches [2,4,10,11], which we focus on in this work. Chen et al. [4] present InfoGAN, an extension of the GAN frame-work [5] that enables better control of generated images using special noise vari-ables. Higgins et al. [10] introduce β-VAE, a generalization of the VAE framework

[13] that allows the VAE to extract more statistically independent, disentangled representations.

While these highly successful methods are considered to be unsupervised, they still have a considerable amount of prior knowledge built into their operation. InfoGAN requires prior knowledge of the number and form of disentangled factors to extract, and β-VAE encounters bottleneck capacity issues and inconsistent results with seemingly innocuous changes to hyperparameters, requiring finetuning with some supervision [2, 10].

We propose a new method, NashAE, to promote a sparse and disentangled latent space in the standard AE that does not make assumptions on the number or distribution of underlying data generating factors. The core intuition behind the approach is to reduce the redundant information between latent encoding elements, regardless of their distribution. To accomplish this, this work presents a new technique to reduce the information between encoded continuous and/or discrete random variables using just access to samples drawn from the unknown underlying distributions (Fig. 1). We empirically demonstrate that the method can reliably extract high-quality disentangled representations according to the metric presented in [10], and that the method has a higher latent feature capacity with respect to salient data characteristics.

The paper makes the following contributions:

- We develop a method to quantify the relationship between random variables with unknown distribution (arbitrary continuous or discrete/categorical), and show that it can be used to promote statistical independence among latent variables in an AE.
- We provide qualitative and quantitative evidence that NashAE reliably extracts a set of disentangled continuous and/or discrete factors of variation in a variety of scenarios, and we demonstrate the method's improved latent feature capacity with regard to salient data characteristics.
- We release the Beamsynthesis disentanglement dataset, a collection of time-series data based on particle physics studies and their associated data generating factor ground truth.

The code for all experiments and the Beamsynthesis dataset can be found at: https://github.com/ericyeats/nashae-beamsynthesis.

2   Related Work

Autoencoders. Much of this work derives from autoencoders (AE), which consist of an encoder function followed by a decoder function. The encoder transforms high-dimensional input $\mathbf{x} \sim X$ into a low-dimensional latent representation $\mathbf{z}$, and the decoder transforms $\mathbf{z}$ to a reconstruction of the high-dimensional input $\mathbf{x}'$. AE have numerous applications in the form of unsupervised feature learning, denoising, and feature disentanglement [11, 20, 22]. Variational autoencoders (VAEs) [13] take AEs further by using them to parameterize probability distributions for X. VAEs are trained by maximizing a lower bound of the likelihood of X, a process which involves conforming the encoded latent space $\mathbf{z} \sim Z$ with a prior distribution P. Adversarial AEs [21], like VAEs, match encoded distributions to a prior distribution, but do so through an adversarial procedure inspired by Generative Adversarial Networks (GANs) [5].

Unsupervised Disentanglement Methods. One of the most successful approaches to feature disentanglement is β-VAE [10], which builds on the VAE framework. β-VAE adjusts the VAE training framework by modulating the relative strength of the $D_{\mathrm{KL}}(Z\|P)$ term with hyperparameter β, effectively limiting the capacity of the VAE and encouraging disentanglement as β becomes larger. Higgins et al. [10] note a positive correlation between the size of the VAE latent dimension and the optimal β hyperparameter to do so, requiring some hyperparameter search and limited supervision. Another important contribution of Higgins et al. [10] is a metric for quantifying disentanglement which depends on the accuracy of a linear classifier in determining which data generating factor is held constant over a pair of data batches.

Multiple works have augmented β-VAE with loss functions that isolate the Total Correlation (TC) component of $D_{\mathrm{KL}}(Z\|P)$, further boosting quantitative disentanglement performance in certain scenarios [3,12]. Another VAE-based work proposed by Kumar et al. [15] directly minimizes the covariance of the encoded representation. However, simple covariance of the latent elements fails to capture more complex, nonlinear relationships between the elements. Our work employs regression neural networks to capture complex dependencies.

Chen et al. [4] present InfoGAN, which builds on the GAN framework [5]. InfoGAN augments the base GAN training procedure with a special set of independent noise inputs. A tractable lower bound on MI is maximized between the special noise inputs and output of the generator, leading to the special noise inputs resembling data generating factors. While the method claims to be unsupervised, choosing its special noise inputs requires prior knowledge of the number and nature (e.g. distribution) of factors to extract.

Limitations of Unsupervised Disentanglement. Locatello et al. [19] demonstrate that unsupervised disentanglement learning is fundamentally impossible without incorporating inductive biases on both models and data [19]. However, they assert that given the right inductive biases, the prospect of unsupervised disentanglement learning is not so bleak. We incorporate several inductive biases in our method to achieve unsupervised disentanglement. First, our approach assumes that disentangled learning representations are characterised by being statistically independent. Second, we posit that breaking up the latent factorization problem into multiple parts by individual masking and adversarial covariance minimization helps boost disentanglement reliability. In terms of models and data, we employ the network architectures and data preparation suggested by previous works in unsupervised disentanglement. Under such conditions, NashAE has demonstrated superior reliability in retrieving disentangled representations.

3   NashAE Methodology

Our approach starts with a purely deterministic encoder ϕ, which takes input observations $\mathbf{x} \sim X$ and creates a latent representation $\mathbf{z} = \phi(\mathbf{x})$. Where $\mathbf{x} \in \mathbb{R}^n$, $\mathbf{z} \in \mathbb{R}^m$, and typically $n \gg m$. Furthermore, ϕ employs a sigmoid activation function σ at its output to produce $\mathbf{z}$ such that $\mathbf{z} = \sigma(\zeta)$ and $\mathbf{z} \in [0,1]^m$, where ζ is the output of ϕ before it is passed through the sigmoid non-linearity. A deterministic decoder ψ maps the latent representation $\mathbf{z}$ back to the observation domain $\mathbf{x}' = \psi(\mathbf{z})$. To achieve disentanglement, the AE is trained with two complementary objectives: (1) reconstructing the observations, and (2) maximizing the discrepancy between each latent variable and predicted values of the variable using information of all other variables. The intuitions behind each are the following. First, reconstruction of the input observations $\mathbf{x}$ is standard of AEs and ensures that they learn features relevant to the distribution X. Second, promoting discrepancy between i-th latent element and its prediction (conditioned on all other $j \neq i$ elements) reduces the information between latent element i and all other elements $j \neq i$.

For the reconstruction objective, the goal is to minimize the mean squared error:

$$\mathcal{L}_R = \frac{1}{2n} \mathbb{E}_{\mathbf{x} \sim X} ||\mathbf{x}' - \mathbf{x}||_2^2. \tag{1}$$

Reconstructing the input observation $\mathbf{x}$ ensures that the features of the latent space are relevant to the underlying data distribution X. The following subsection describes the adversarial game loss objectives, which settle on an equilibrium and inspire the name of the proposed disentanglement method, NashAE.

Adversarial Covariance Minimization

In general, it is difficult to compute the information between latent variables when one only has access to samples of observations $\mathbf{z} \sim Z$. Since the underlying distribution Z is unknown, standard methods of computing the information directly are not possible. To overcome this challenge, we propose to reduce the information between latent variables indirectly using an ensemble of regression networks which attempt to capture the relationships between latent variables. The process is computationally efficient; it uses simple measures of linear statistical independence and an adversarial game.

Consider an ensemble of m independent regression networks ρ, where the output of the i-th network ρ_i corresponds to a missing i-th latent element. The objective of each ρ_i is to minimize the mean squared error:

$$\mathcal{L}_{\rho_i} = \frac{1}{2} \mathbb{E}_{\mathbf{x} \sim X} \left(\rho(\overline{\mathbf{z}}_i)_i - \mathbf{z}_i \right)^2, \tag{2}$$

where $\mathbf{z}_i$ is the i-th true latent element, and $\overline{\mathbf{z}}_i$ is the latent *vector* with the i-th latent element masked with 0 (i.e., all elements of the latent vector are present except $\mathbf{z}_i$).

We call ρ the predictors, since they are each optimized to predict one missing value of $\mathbf{z}$ given knowledge of all other $\mathbf{z}$. If all their individual predictions are concatenated together, they form $\mathbf{z}'$ such that each $\mathbf{z}'_i = \rho(\overline{\mathbf{z}_i})_i$.

For the disentanglement objective, we want to choose encodings $\mathbf{z} \sim \phi(X)$ that make it difficult to recover information of one element from all others. This leads to a natural minmax formulation for the AE and predictors:

$$\min_{\phi,\psi} \max_{\rho} \frac{1}{2}\mathbb{E}_{\mathbf{x}\sim X}\left[\frac{1}{n}||\mathbf{x}' - \mathbf{x}||_2^2 - ||\mathbf{z}' - \mathbf{z}||_2^2\right]. \tag{3}$$

In general, each predictor attempts to use information of $\overline{\mathbf{z}_i}$ to establish a one-to-one linear relationship between $\mathbf{z}'$ and $\mathbf{z}$. Hence we propose to use covariance between $\mathbf{z}'$ and $\mathbf{z}$ across a batch of examples to capture the degree to which they are related. In practice, we find that training the AE to minimize the summed covariance objective between each of the $\mathbf{z}'_i$ and $\mathbf{z}_i$ random variable pairs,

$$\mathcal{L}_A = \sum_{i=1}^{m} \mathrm{Cov}(\mathbf{z}'_i, \mathbf{z}_i), \tag{4}$$

is more stable than maximizing $\frac{1}{2}\mathbb{E}_{\mathbf{x}\sim X}||\mathbf{z}' - \mathbf{z}||$ and leads to more reliable disentanglement outcomes. Hence, in all the following experiments we train the AE to minimize this summed covariance measure, $\mathcal{L}_A$. Furthermore, one can show that the fixed points of the minmax objective (3) are the same as those of training ϕ to minimize $\mathcal{L}_R + \mathcal{L}_A$ for disentangled representations (see supplementary material).

In the adversarial loss $\mathcal{L}_A$, the optimization objective of the encoder ϕ is to adjust its latent representations to minimize the covariance between each $\mathbf{z}'_i$ and $\mathbf{z}_i$. Using minibatch stochastic gradient descent (SGD), the encoder ϕ can use gradient passed through the predictors ρ to learn exactly how to adjust its latent representations to minimize the adversarial loss. Assuming that ρ can learn faster than ϕ, each i-th covariance term will reach zero when $\mathbb{E}[\mathbf{z}_i|\mathbf{z}_j, \forall j \neq i] = \mathbb{E}[\mathbf{z}_i]$ everywhere.

In the following experiments, we weight the sum of $\mathcal{L}_R$ and $\mathcal{L}_A$ with the hyperparameter $\lambda \in [0,1)$ in order to establish a normalized balance between the reconstruction and adversarial objectives:

$$\mathcal{L}_{R,A}(\lambda) = (1 - \lambda)\mathcal{L}_R + \lambda\mathcal{L}_A. \tag{5}$$

Intuitively, higher values of λ result lower covariance between elements of $\mathbf{z}$ and $\mathbf{z}'$, and eventually the equilibrium covariance settles to zero. In the special case where all data generating factors are independent, the AE can theoretically achieve $\mathcal{L}_{R,A} = 0$.

Proposed Disentanglement Metric: TAD

In the following section, we find that NashAE and β-VAE could achieve equally high scores using the β-VAE metric. However, the β-VAE metric fails to capture a key aspect of a truly disentangled latent representation: change in one independent data generating factor should correspond to change in just one disentangled latent feature. This is not captured in the β-VAE disentanglement metric since the score can benefit from *spreading* the information of one data generating factor over multiple latent features. For example, duplicate latent representations of the same unique data generating factor can only increase the score of the β-VAE metric.

Furthermore, a disentanglement metric should quantify the degree to which its set of independent latent axes aligns with the independent data generating factor ground truth axes. In essence, a unique latent feature should be a confident predictor of a unique data generating factor, and all other latents should be orthogonal to the same data generating factor. Intuitively, the greater number of latent axes that align uniquely with the data generating factors and the more confident the latents are as predictors of the factors, the higher the metric score should be.

For these reasons, we design a disentanglement metric for datasets with binary attribute ground truth labels called Total AUROC Difference (TAD). For a large number l of examples which we collect a batch of latent representations z of the shape (l, m), we perform the following to calculate the TAD:

1. For each independent ground truth attribute, calculate the AUROC score of each latent variable in detecting the attribute.
2. For each independent ground truth attribute, find the maximum latent AUROC score $a_{1,i}$ and the next-largest latent AUROC score $a_{2,i}$, where i is the index of the independent ground truth attribute under consideration.
3. Take $\sum_i a_{1,i} - a_{2,i}$ as the TAD score, where i indexes over the independent ground truth attributes.

The TAD metric captures important aspects of a disentangled latent representation. First, each AUROC difference $a_{1,i} - a_{2,i}$ captures the degree to which a unique attribute is detected by a unique latent representation. Second, summing the AUROC difference scores for each independent ground truth attribute quantifies the degree to which the latent axes confidently replicate the ground truth axes. See the supplementary material for more details on how TAD is calculated and for a discussion relating it with other work.

4 Experiments

The following section contains a mix of qualitative and quantitative results for four unsupervised disentanglement algorithms: NashAE (this work), β-VAE [10], FactorVAE [12], and β-TCVAE [3]. The results are collected for disentanglement tasks on three datasets: Beamsynthesis, dSprites [10], and CelebA [18]. Please refer to the supplementary material for details on algorithm hyperparameters, network architectures, and data normalization for the different experiments.

Beamsynthesis is a simple dataset of 360 time-series data of current waveforms constructed from simulations of the LINAC (linear particle accelerator) portion of high-energy particle accelerators. The dataset contains two ground truth data generating factors: a categorical random variable representing the *frequency* of the particle waveform which can take on one of the three values $(10, 15, 20)$ and a continuous random variable constructed from a uniform sweep of 120 waveform *duty cycle* values $\in [0.2, 0.8)$. The Cartesian product of the two data generating factors forms the set of observations. The challenge in disentangling this dataset arises from the fact that both the *frequency* and *duty cycle* of a waveform affect the length of the "on" period of each wave. We visualize the complete latent space of different algorithms and evaluate the reliability of the algorithms in extracting the correct number of ground truth data generating factors using this dataset.

dSprites is a disentanglement dataset released by the authors of β-VAE - it is comprised of a set of $737,280$ images of white 2D shapes on a black background. The Cartesian product of the type of shape (categorical: square, ellipse, heart), scale (continuous: 6 values), orientation (continuous: 40 values), x-position (continuous: 32 values), and y-position (continuous: 32 values) forms the independent ground truth of the dataset. We measure the β-VAE disentanglement metric score for different algorithms using this dataset.

CelebA is a dataset comprised of $202,599$ images of the faces of $10,177$ different celebrities. Associated with each image are 40 different binary attribute labels such as *bangs, blond hair, black hair, chubby, male,* and *eyeglasses*. We measure the TAD score of different algorithms using this dataset.

Empirical Fixed Point Results

In Sect. 3, we indicate that higher values of $\lambda \in (0, 1)$ should result in a statistically independent NashAE latent space, and that redundant latent elements will not be learned. This is supported by observations of the fixed point of the optimization process for all experiments with nonzero λ: as λ is increased, the number of dead latent representations increases, and the average R^2 correlation statistic between latent representations and their predictions decreases.

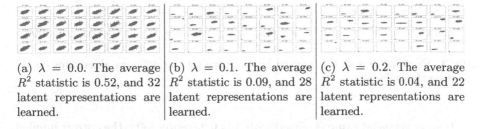

(a) $\lambda = 0.0$. The average R^2 statistic is 0.52, and 32 latent representations are learned.

(b) $\lambda = 0.1$. The average R^2 statistic is 0.09, and 28 latent representations are learned.

(c) $\lambda = 0.2$. The average R^2 statistic is 0.04, and 22 latent representations are learned.

Fig. 2. Visualization of true latent representations (*x-axis*) vs predicted latent representations (*y-axis*) on the CelebA dataset

Figure 2 depicts each of the 32 true latent representations vs their predictions for 1000 samples of the CelebA dataset after three different NashAE networks have converged. When $\lambda = 0$ (standard AE), all latent elements are employed towards the reconstruction objective, and the predictions exhibit a strong positive linear relationship with the true latent variables (average R^2 is 0.52). When $\lambda = 0.1$, only 28 latent representations are maintained, and the average R^2 statistic between true latents and their predictions becomes 0.09. The 4 unused latent representations are each isolated in a dead zone of the sigmoid non-linearity, respectively. When λ is increased to 0.2, only 22 latent representations are maintained and the average R^2 statistic decreases even further to 0.04. Note also that the predictions become constant and are each equal to the expected value of their respective true latent feature. This is consistent with the conditional expectation of each variable being equal to its marginal expectation everywhere, and it indicates that no useful information is given to the predictors towards their regression task.

Beamsynthesis Latent Space Visualization

Figure 3 depicts the complete latent space generated by encoding all 360 observations of the Beamsynthesis dataset for the different algorithms and their baselines with a starting latent size of $m = 4$.

A standard AE latent space (leftmost) employs all latent elements towards the reconstruction objective, and their relationship with the ground truth data generating factors, *frequency* (categorical) and *duty cycle* (continuous), is unclear. Similarly, when a standard VAE (center right) converges and the μ component of the latent space is plotted for all observations, all latent variables are employed towards the reconstruction objective, and no clear relationship can be established for the latent variables.

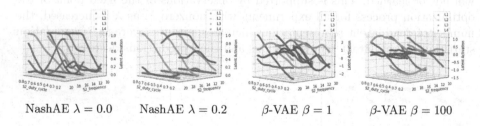

NashAE $\lambda = 0.0$ NashAE $\lambda = 0.2$ β-VAE $\beta = 1$ β-VAE $\beta = 100$

Fig. 3. Visualizations of the learned latent space for the different algorithms on the Beamsynthesis dataset

If an adversarial game is played with $\lambda = 0.2$ (center left), the correct number of latent dimensions is extracted, and each nontrivial latent representation aligns with just one data generating factor. In this case, $L1$ level-encodes the *frequency* categorical data generating factor, and $L2$ encodes the *duty cycle* continuous data generating factor with a consistent interpretation. The unused neurons remain in a dead zone of the sigmoid non-linearity.

β-VAE with $\beta = 100$ (rightmost) can disentangle the 360 observations in a similar fashion. In this example, $L2$ level-encodes the *frequency* categorical data generating factor, and $L3$ encodes the *duty cycle* continuous data generating factor with a consistent interpretation. The unused neurons each have approximately 0 variance in their μ component and an approximately constant value of 1 in their learned variance component.

Although all algorithms are capable of extracting a disentangled representation of the ground truth data generating factors, there is a stark difference in the reliability of the methods in extracting the correct number of latent variables when the starting latent space size m is changed. Reliability in this aspect is critical, as the dimensionality of the independent data generating factors is often an important unknown quantity to recover from new data. To determine this unknown dimensionality, one should start with a latent space size m which is larger than the number of latent factors that should be extracted.

Table 1. Average absolute difference between the number of learned latent dimensions and the number of ground truth factors for different starting latent space sizes m on the Beamsynthesis dataset. Lower is better, and the lowest for each latent space size configuration (m) are in bold. The results are averaged over 8 trials

Method	$m = 4$	$m = 8$	$m = 16$	$m = 32$
NashAE $\lambda = 0$	1.375	5.75	13.125	28.75
NashAE $\lambda = 0.2$	**0**	**0**	**0.25**	1
NashAE $\lambda = 0.3$	**0**	**0**	0.375	**0.5**
β-VAE $\beta = 1$	2	6	14	28.875
β-VAE $\beta = 50$	1.375	2	2.5	3.5
β-VAE $\beta = 100$	0	1	1.25	3.125
β-VAE $\beta = 125$	1.375	1.5	1.875	3.25
β-TCVAE $\beta = 1$	1.875	5.25	9.625	18.625
β-TCVAE $\beta = 50$	0.75	1.25	1	**0.5**
β-TCVAE $\beta = 75$	0.375	0.5	1	0.875
β-TCVAE $\beta = 100$	0.75	0.625	1.125	0.625
FactorVAE $\beta = 50$	0.5	1.25	0.875	0.625
FactorVAE $\beta = 75$	0.5	1	1.25	**0.5**
FactorVAE $\beta = 100$	0.25	0.75	1	0.75
FactorVAE $\beta = 125$	0.875	0.75	0.625	0.75

Table 1 depicts the results of an experiment in which all hyperparameters are held constant except the starting latent size m as each of the algorithms are trained to convergence on the Beamsynthesis dataset. Each entry in the table is the average absolute difference between the number of learned latent representations and the number of ground truth data generating factors (2 for

Beamsynthesis), collected over 8 trials. Both NashAE $\lambda = 0$ and β-(TC)VAE $\beta = 1$ learn far too many latent variables, and β-VAE $\beta = 125$ tends to learn too few latent variables when $m = 4$ and $m = 8$. NashAE $\lambda = 0.2$ and NashAE $\lambda = 0.3$ perform very well in comparison, keeping the average absolute difference less than or equal to one in all configurations of m. β-TCVAE and FactorVAE perform second-best overall, tending to learn too many latent variables. The results indicate that NashAE is the most consistent in recovering the correct number of data generating factors. See the supplementary material for a similar experiment with the dSprites dataset and details on how learned latent representations are counted.

β-VAE Metric on dSprites

Table 2 reports the disentanglement score of each algorithm averaged over 15 trials - please refer to Higgins et al. [10] for more details on the metric. In general, the standard AE (NashAE, $\lambda = 0$) and standard VAE (β-VAE, $\beta = 1$; β-TCVAE, $\beta = 1$) performed the worst on the β-VAE disentanglement metric. As λ and β are increased, the disentanglement score of NashAE and β-VAE increases to over 96%. We do not observe the difference between NashAE and β-VAE in top performance on this metric to be significant, so both are in bold. In general, β-TCVAE performed slightly worse on this metric than β-VAE and NashAE, achieving just over 95%. We observed that increasing λ or β beyond these values leads to poorer performance for all algorithms. All algorithms achieve higher disentanglement scores on some initializations than others, but no *outliers* are removed from the reported scores (as is done in [10]). Overall, the results indicate that NashAE scores at least as high as those of β-VAE and β-TCVAE algorithm on the β-VAE metric.

Table 2. β-VAE Metric Scores on dSprites averaged over 15 trials. Higher is better, and the highest scores of all models and hyperparameter configurations are in bold. Optimal λ values for disentanglement are different for this dataset because the dSprites image data is not normalized, following the precedent of previous works [10]

NashAE	$\lambda = 0.0$	$\lambda = 0.001$	$\lambda = 0.002$
	91.41%	92.58%	**96.57%**
β-VAE	$\beta = 1$	$\beta = 4$	$\beta = 8$
	84.63%	93.68%	**96.21%**
β-TCVAE	$\beta = 1$	$\beta = 2$	$\beta = 4$
	84.64%	95.01%	93.95%

Latent Traversals and TAD Metric on CelebA

We include traversals of latent representations that have the highest AUROC detector score for a small set of attributes on CelebA in Fig. 4. In each case, we

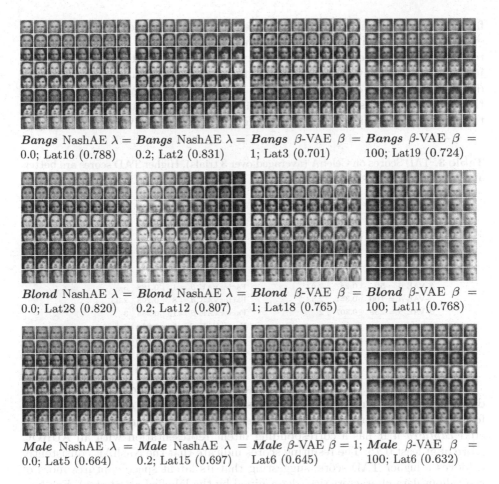

Bangs NashAE $\lambda =$ 0.0; Lat16 (0.788)   **Bangs** NashAE $\lambda =$ 0.2; Lat2 (0.831)   **Bangs** β-VAE $\beta =$ 1; Lat3 (0.701)   **Bangs** β-VAE $\beta =$ 100; Lat19 (0.724)

Blond NashAE $\lambda =$ 0.0; Lat28 (0.820)   **Blond** NashAE $\lambda =$ 0.2; Lat12 (0.807)   **Blond** β-VAE $\beta =$ 1; Lat18 (0.765)   **Blond** β-VAE $\beta =$ 100; Lat11 (0.768)

Male NashAE $\lambda =$ 0.0; Lat5 (0.664)   **Male** NashAE $\lambda =$ 0.2; Lat15 (0.697)   **Male** β-VAE $\beta = 1$; Lat6 (0.645)   **Male** β-VAE $\beta =$ 100; Lat6 (0.632)

Fig. 4. Traversals of latent features corresponding to the highest AUROC score for the **bangs**, **blond**, and **male** attributes for the different disentanglement algorithms. Each latent representation with maximum AUROC score and its corresponding score are reported

start with a random image from the dataset and hold all latent representations constant except the one identified to have the highest AUROC score for the attribute of interest. We vary that representation evenly from its minimum to its maximum (as observed across 1000 random samples) and decode the resulting latent representation to generate the images reported in Fig. 4.

Note that in all cases, employing disentanglement methods (NashAE $\lambda >$ 0 or β-VAE $\beta \gg$ 1) leads to a visual traversal that intuitively matches the attribute that the latent representation is a good detector for. Furthermore, the visual changes are significant and obvious. Contrarily, when there is no effort to disentangle the representations ($\lambda = 0$ or $\beta = 1$), the relationship between the representation's high AUROC score and its traversal visualization become far less clear. In some cases, the traversal does not make meaningful change or even causes odd artifacts during decoding. We hypothesize that this is due to redundant information being shared between the latent features, and changing just one may have either no significant effect or the combination will be "out of distribution" to the decoder, leading to unnatural decoding artifacts. The idea that standard latents hold redundant information is supported by Fig. 2, where the predictors establish a high average R^2 value on CelebA when $\lambda = 0$.

Table 3. TAD Scores on CelebA (averaged over 3 trials). Higher TAD scores are better, and the highest average score is in bold

Method	TAD	# Attributes	Method	TAD	# Attributes
NashAE $\lambda = 0$	0.235	5.33	β-TCVAE $\beta = 1$	0.165	3.33
NashAE $\lambda = 0.1$	0.362	4	β-TCVAE $\beta = 8$	0.359	4
NashAE $\lambda = 0.2$	**0.543**	5	β-TCVAE $\beta = 15$	0.446	4.33
NashAE $\lambda = 0.8$	0.474	5	β-TCVAE $\beta = 25$	0.403	3.67
β-VAE $\beta = 1$	0.158	3.67	β-TCVAE $\beta = 50$	0.362	3.67
β-VAE $\beta = 50$	0.287	2.67	FactorVAE $\beta = 1$	0.188	3
β-VAE $\beta = 100$	0.351	2.33	FactorVAE $\beta = 8$	0.208	2.33
β-VAE $\beta = 250$	0.307	2	FactorVAE $\beta = 15$	0.285	3
			FactorVAE $\beta = 50$	0.276	3
			FactorVAE $\beta = 75$	0.148	1.33

We employ the TAD metric to quantify disentanglement on the CelebA dataset. Table 3 summarizes the TAD results and number of captured attributes for each of the algorithms averaged over three trials. An attribute is considered *captured* if it has a corresponding latent representation with an AUROC score of at least 0.75. The resulting scores indicate that the NashAE consistently achieves a higher TAD score, suggesting that its latent space captures more of the salient data characteristics (determined by the labelled attributes). Furthermore, NashAE achieves high scores over a broad range for $\lambda \in (0, 1)$. β-TCVAE performs second best, achieving a TAD score of 0.446 when $\beta = 15$, yet it does not capture as many attributes as NashAE. In general, β-VAE and FactorVAE tend to capture fewer attributes and score lower TAD scores, suggesting that their latent spaces capture fewer of the salient data characteristics.

5   Discussion

We have shown with our quantitative experiments that NashAE can reliably extract disentangled representations. Furthermore, qualitative latent traversal inspection indicates that the latent variables of NashAE which are the best detectors for a given attribute indeed visually reflect independent traversals of the attribute. Hence, the adversarial covariance minimization objective presented in this work promotes learning of clarified, interpretable representations in neural networks. We believe that improvements in neural network interpretability can aid engineers in diagnosing and treating the current ailments of neural networks such as security vulnerability, lack of fairness, and out-of-distribution detection.

Future work will investigate more sophisticated latent distribution modeling and to make NashAE a generative model. This could further boost NashAE's disentanglement performance and provide deeper insight with information-theoretic approaches. It could be interesting to apply the adversarial covariance minimization objective to clarify the representations of DNNs for image classification.

6   Conclusion

We have presented NashAE, a new adversarial method to disentangle factors of variation which makes minimal assumptions on the number and form of factors to extract. We have shown that the method leads to a more statistically independent and disentangled AE latent space. Our quantitative experiments indicate that this flexible method is more reliable in retrieving the true number of data generating factors and has a higher capacity to align its latent representations with salient data characteristics than leading VAE-based algorithms.

Acknowledgements. This research is supported, in part, by the U.S. Department of Energy, through the Office of Advanced Scientific Computing Research's "Data-Driven Decision Control for Complex Systems (DnC2S)" project. Additionally this research is sponsored by the Artificial Intelligence Initiative as part of the Laboratory Directed Research and Development Program of Oak Ridge National Laboratory (ORNL). This research used resources of the Experimental Computing Laboratory (ExCL) at ORNL.

This manuscript has been authored by UT-Battelle, LLC, under contract DE-AC05-00OR22725 with the US Department of Energy (DOE). The US government retains and the publisher, by accepting the article for publication, acknowledges that the US government retains a nonexclusive, paid-up, irrevocable, worldwide license to publish or reproduce the published form of this manuscript, or allow others to do so, for US government purposes. DOE will provide public access to these results of federally sponsored research in accordance with the DOE Public Access Plan (http://energy.gov/downloads/doe-public-access-plan).

This research is further supported by US Army Research W911NF2220025 and the National Science Foundation OIA-2040588.

References

1. Alvi, M., Zisserman, A., Nellåker, C.: Turning a blind eye: explicit removal of biases and variation from deep neural network embeddings. In: Leal-Taixé, L., Roth, S. (eds.) ECCV 2018. LNCS, vol. 11129, pp. 556–572. Springer, Cham (2019). https://doi.org/10.1007/978-3-030-11009-3_34
2. Burgess, C.P., et al.: Understanding disentangling in β-vae. arXiv preprint arXiv:1804.03599 (2018)
3. Chen, R.T., Li, X., Grosse, R.B., Duvenaud, D.K.: Isolating sources of disentanglement in variational autoencoders. In: Advances in Neural Information Processing Systems, vol. 31 (2018)

4. Chen, X., Duan, Y., Houthooft, R., Schulman, J., Sutskever, I., Abbeel, P.: Info-gan: interpretable representation learning by information maximizing generative adversarial nets. In: Proceedings of the 30th International Conference on Neural Information Processing Systems, pp. 2180–2188 (2016)
5. Goodfellow, I., et al.: Generative adversarial nets. Advances in Neural Information Processing Systems, vol. 27 (2014)
6. Goodfellow, I.J., Shlens, J., Szegedy, C.: Explaining and harnessing adversarial examples. arXiv preprint arXiv:1412.6572 (2014)
7. He, K., Zhang, X., Ren, S., Sun, J.: Deep residual learning for image recognition. In: Proceedings of the IEEE Conference on Computer Vision and Pattern Recognition, pp. 770–778 (2016)
8. He, Z., Rakin, A.S., Li, J., Chakrabarti, C., Fan, D.: Defending and harnessing the bit-flip based adversarial weight attack. In: Proceedings of the IEEE/CVF Conference on Computer Vision and Pattern Recognition, pp. 14095–14103 (2020)
9. Hendrycks, D., Gimpel, K.: A baseline for detecting misclassified and out-of-distribution examples in neural networks. arXiv preprint arXiv:1610.02136 (2016)
10. Higgins, I., et al.: beta-vae: Learning basic visual concepts with a constrained variational framework (2016)
11. Hu, Q., Szabó, A., Portenier, T., Favaro, P., Zwicker, M.: Disentangling factors of variation by mixing them. In: Proceedings of the IEEE Conference on Computer Vision and Pattern Recognition, pp. 3399–3407 (2018)
12. Kim, H., Mnih, A.: Disentangling by factorising. In: International Conference on Machine Learning, pp. 2649–2658. PMLR (2018)
13. Kingma, D.P., Welling, M.: Auto-encoding variational bayes. arXiv preprint arXiv:1312.6114 (2013)
14. Kulkarni, T.D., Whitney, W., Kohli, P., Tenenbaum, J.B.: Deep convolutional inverse graphics network. arXiv preprint arXiv:1503.03167 (2015)
15. Kumar, A., Sattigeri, P., Balakrishnan, A.: Variational inference of disentangled latent concepts from unlabeled observations. arXiv preprint arXiv:1711.00848 (2017)
16. Li, D., Zhao, D., Zhang, Q., Chen, Y.: Reinforcement learning and deep learning based lateral control for autonomous driving [application notes]. IEEE Comput. Intell. Mag. 14(2), 83–98 (2019)
17. Liang, S., Li, Y., Srikant, R.: Enhancing the reliability of out-of-distribution image detection in neural networks. arXiv preprint arXiv:1706.02690 (2017)
18. Liu, Z., Luo, P., Wang, X., Tang, X.: Deep learning face attributes in the wild. In: Proceedings of International Conference on Computer Vision (ICCV), December 2015
19. Locatello, F., et al.: Challenging common assumptions in the unsupervised learning of disentangled representations. In: International Conference on Machine Learning, pp. 4114–4124. PMLR (2019)
20. Lu, X., Tsao, Y., Matsuda, S., Hori, C.: Speech enhancement based on deep denoising autoencoder. In: Interspeech, vol. 2013, pp. 436–440 (2013)
21. Makhzani, A., Shlens, J., Jaitly, N., Goodfellow, I., Frey, B.: Adversarial autoencoders. arXiv preprint arXiv:1511.05644 (2015)
22. Rifai, S., et al.: Higher order contractive auto-encoder. In: Gunopulos, D., Hofmann, T., Malerba, D., Vazirgiannis, M. (eds.) ECML PKDD 2011. LNCS (LNAI), vol. 6912, pp. 645–660. Springer, Heidelberg (2011). https://doi.org/10.1007/978-3-642-23783-6_41

23. Ross, A.S., Doshi-Velez, F.: Improving the adversarial robustness and interpretability of deep neural networks by regularizing their input gradients. In: Thirty-Second AAAI Conference on Artificial Intelligence (2018)
24. Rudin, C.: Stop explaining black box machine learning models for high stakes decisions and use interpretable models instead. Nature Mach. Intell. 1(5), 206–215 (2019)
25. Szegedy, C., et al.: Intriguing properties of neural networks. arXiv preprint arXiv:1312.6199 (2013)
26. Torfi, A., Shirvani, R.A., Keneshloo, Y., Tavaf, N., Fox, E.A.: Natural language processing advancements by deep learning: A survey. arXiv preprint arXiv:2003.01200 (2020)

A Gyrovector Space Approach
for Symmetric Positive Semi-definite
Matrix Learning

Xuan Son Nguyen(✉) [iD]

ETIS, UMR 8051, CY Cergy Paris Université, ENSEA, CNRS, Cergy, France
xuan-son.nguyen@ensea.fr

Abstract. Representation learning with Symmetric Positive Semi-definite (SPSD) matrices has proven effective in many machine learning problems. Recently, some SPSD neural networks have been proposed and shown promising performance. While these works share a common idea of generalizing some basic operations in deep neural networks (DNNs) to the SPSD manifold setting, their proposed generalizations are usually designed in an ad hoc manner. In this work, we make an attempt to propose a principled framework for building such generalizations. Our method is motivated by the success of hyperbolic neural networks (HNNs) that have demonstrated impressive performance in a variety of applications. At the heart of HNNs is the theory of gyrovector spaces that provides a powerful tool for studying hyperbolic geometry. Here we consider connecting the theory of gyrovector spaces and the Riemannian geometry of SPSD manifolds. We first propose a method to define basic operations, i.e., binary operation and scalar multiplication in gyrovector spaces of (full-rank) Symmetric Positive Definite (SPD) matrices. We then extend these operations to the low-rank SPSD manifold setting. Finally, we present an approach for building SPSD neural networks. Experimental evaluations on three benchmarks for human activity recognition demonstrate the efficacy of our proposed framework.

1 Introduction

SPSD matrices are computational objects that are commonly encountered in various applied areas such as medical imaging [2,35], shape analysis [42], drone classification [6], image recognition [10], and human behavior analysis [9,14, 15,17,32,41]. Due to the non-Euclidean nature of SPSD matrices, traditional machine learning algorithms usually fail to obtain good results when it comes to analyzing such data. This has led to extensive studies on the Riemannian geometry of SPSD matrices [2–4,24,30,36].

Supplementary Information The online version contains supplementary material available at https://doi.org/10.1007/978-3-031-19812-0_4.

In recent years, deep learning methods have brought breakthroughs in many fields of machine learning. Inspired by the success of deep learning and the modeling power of SPSD matrices, some recent works [6–9,17,32,34,47] have proposed different approaches for building SPSD neural networks. Although these networks have shown promising performance, their layers are usually designed in an ad hoc manner[1]. For example, in [8], the translation operation that is claimed to be analogous to adding a bias term in Euclidean neural networks is constructed from the action of the orthogonal group on SPD manifolds. However, this operation does not allow one to perform addition of two arbitrary SPD matrices and thus is not fully analogous to the vector addition in Euclidean spaces.

To tackle the above problem, we rely on the theory of gyrovector spaces [44, 45] that has been successfully applied in the context of HNNs [12,40]. However, in order to apply this theory to the SPSD manifold setting, we first need to define the basic operations in gyrovector spaces of SPSD matrices. Although there are some works [1,16,18–21,28] studying gyrovector spaces of SPD matrices with an Affine-invariant (AI) [36] geometry, none of them provides a rigorous mathematical formulation for the connection between the basic operations in these spaces and the Riemannian geometry of SPD manifolds. In this paper, we take one step further toward a deeper understanding of gyrovector spaces of SPD matrices by proposing a principled method to define the basic operations in these spaces. We focus on three different geometries of SPD manifolds, i.e., Affine-invariant, Log-Euclidean (LE) [2], Log-Cholesky (LC) [24], and derive compact expressions for the basic operations associated with these geometries. To extend our method to low-rank SPSD manifolds, we make use of their quotient geometry [3,4]. We show how to define the loose versions of the basic operations on these manifolds, and study some of their properties. For SPSD matrix learning, we consider the full-rank and low-rank learning settings, and develop a class of Recurrent Neural Networks (RNNs) with flexible learning strategies in these settings.

2 Gyrovector Spaces

Gyrovector spaces form the setting for hyperbolic geometry in the same way that vector spaces form the setting for Euclidean geometry [44–46]. We first recap the definitions of gyrogroups and gyrocommutative gyrogroups proposed in [44–46]. For greater mathematical detail and in-depth discussion, we refer the interested reader to these papers.

Definition 1 (Gyrogroups [46]). *A pair* $(G, \oplus)$ *is a groupoid in the sense that it is a nonempty set,* G*, with a binary operation,* $\oplus$*. A groupoid* $(G, \oplus)$ *is a gyrogroup if its binary operation satisfies the following axioms for* $a, b, c \in G$*:*

(G1) There is at least one element $e \in G$ *called a left identity such that* $e \oplus a = a$*.*
(G2) There is an element $\ominus a \in G$ *called a left inverse of* a *such that* $\ominus a \oplus a = e$*.*

---

[1] In terms of basic operations used to build the network layers.

(G3) There is an automorphism $\mathrm{gyr}[a,b] : G \to G$ *for each* $a, b \in G$ *such that*

$$a \oplus (b \oplus c) = (a \oplus b) \oplus \mathrm{gyr}[a,b]c \quad \text{(Left Gyroassociative Law)}.$$

The automorphism $\mathrm{gyr}[a,b]$ *is called the gyroautomorphism, or the gyration of* G *generated by* a, b.

(G4) $\mathrm{gyr}[a,b] = \mathrm{gyr}[a \oplus b, b]$ *(Left Reduction Property).*

Definition 2 (Gyrocommutative Gyrogroups [46]). *A gyrogroup* $(G, \oplus)$ *is gyrocommutative if it satisfies*

$$a \oplus b = \mathrm{gyr}[a,b](b \oplus a) \quad \text{(Gyrocommutative Law)}.$$

The following definition of gyrovector spaces is slightly different from Definition 3.2 in [46].

Definition 3 (Gyrovector Spaces). *A gyrocommutative gyrogroup* $(G, \oplus)$ *equipped with a scalar multiplication*

$$(t, x) \to t \odot x : \mathbb{R} \times G \to G$$

is called a gyrovector space if it satisfies the following axioms for $s, t \in \mathbb{R}$ *and* $a, b, c \in G$:

(V1) $1 \odot a = a, 0 \odot a = t \odot e = e,$ *and* $(-1) \odot a = \ominus a$.
(V2) $(s + t) \odot a = s \odot a \oplus t \odot a$.
(V3) $(st) \odot a = s \odot (t \odot a)$.
(V4) $\mathrm{gyr}[a,b](t \odot c) = t \odot \mathrm{gyr}[a,b]c$.
(V5) $\mathrm{gyr}[s \odot a, t \odot a] = \mathrm{Id},$ *where* Id *is the identity map.*

Note that the axioms of gyrovector spaces considered in our work are more strict than those in [18–21]. Thus, many results proved in these works can also be applied to our case, which gives rise to interesting applications.

3   Proposed Approach

For simplicity of exposition, we will concentrate on real matrices. Denote by Sym_n^+ the space of $n \times n$ SPD matrices, $\mathrm{S}_{n,p}^+$ the space of $n \times n$ SPSD matrices of rank $p < n$, $\mathrm{V}_{n,p}$ the space of $n \times p$ matrices with orthonormal columns, O_n the space of $n \times n$ orthonormal matrices. Let $\mathcal{M}$ be a Riemannian homogeneous space, $T_\mathbf{P}\mathcal{M}$ be the tangent space of $\mathcal{M}$ at $\mathbf{P} \in \mathcal{M}$. Denote by $\exp(\mathbf{P})$ and $\log(\mathbf{P})$ the usual matrix exponential and logarithm of $\mathbf{P}$, $\mathrm{Exp}_\mathbf{P}(\mathbf{W})$ the exponential map at $\mathbf{P}$ that associates to a tangent vector $\mathbf{W} \in T_\mathbf{P}\mathcal{M}$ a point of $\mathcal{M}$, $\mathrm{Log}_\mathbf{P}(\mathbf{Q})$ the logarithmic map of $\mathbf{Q} \in \mathcal{M}$ at $\mathbf{P}$. Let $\mathcal{T}_{\mathbf{P} \to \mathbf{Q}}(\mathbf{W})$ be the parallel transport of $\mathbf{W}$ from $\mathbf{P}$ to $\mathbf{Q}$ along geodesics connecting $\mathbf{P}$ and $\mathbf{Q}$.

Definition 4. *The binary operation* $\mathbf{P} \oplus \mathbf{Q}$ *where* $\mathbf{P}, \mathbf{Q} \in \mathcal{M}$ *is obtained by projecting* $\mathbf{Q}$ *in the tangent space at the identity element* $\mathbf{I} \in \mathcal{M}$ *with the logarithmic map, computing the parallel transport of this projection from* $\mathbf{I}$ *to* $\mathbf{P}$ *along geodesics connecting* $\mathbf{I}$ *and* $\mathbf{P}$, *and then projecting it back on the manifold with the exponential map, i.e.,*

$$\mathbf{P} \oplus \mathbf{Q} = \mathrm{Exp}_{\mathbf{P}}(\mathcal{T}_{\mathbf{I} \to \mathbf{P}}(\mathrm{Log}_{\mathbf{I}}(\mathbf{Q}))). \tag{1}$$

Definition 5. *The scalar multiplication* $t \otimes \mathbf{P}$ *where* $t \in \mathbb{R}$ *and* $\mathbf{P} \in \mathcal{M}$ *is obtained by projecting* $\mathbf{P}$ *in the tangent space at the identity element* $\mathbf{I} \in \mathcal{M}$ *with the logarithmic map, multiplying this projection by the scalar* t *in* $T_{\mathbf{I}}\mathcal{M}$, *and then projecting it back on the manifold with the exponential map, i.e.,*

$$t \otimes \mathbf{P} = \mathrm{Exp}_{\mathbf{I}}(t \, \mathrm{Log}_{\mathbf{I}}(\mathbf{P})). \tag{2}$$

In the next sections, we will define gyrovector spaces of SPD matrices with the Affine-invariant, Log-Euclidean, and Log-Cholesky geometries (see supplementary material for a review of these geometries).

3.1 Affine-Invariant Gyrovector Spaces

We first examine SPD manifolds with the Affine-invariant geometry. Lemma 1 gives a compact expression for the binary operation.

Lemma 1. *For* $\mathbf{P}, \mathbf{Q} \in \mathrm{Sym}_n^+$, *the binary operation* $\mathbf{P} \oplus_{ai} \mathbf{Q}$ *is given as*

$$\mathbf{P} \oplus_{ai} \mathbf{Q} = \mathbf{P}^{\frac{1}{2}} \mathbf{Q} \mathbf{P}^{\frac{1}{2}}. \tag{3}$$

Proof. See supplementary material.

The identity element of Sym_n^+ is the $n \times n$ identity matrix $\mathbf{I}_n$. Then, from Eq. (3), the inverse of $\mathbf{P}$ is given by

$$\ominus_{ai} \mathbf{P} = \mathbf{P}^{-1}.$$

Lemma 2. *For* $\mathbf{P} \in \mathrm{Sym}_n^+$, $t \in \mathbb{R}$, *the scalar multiplication* $t \otimes_{ai} \mathbf{P}$ *is given as*

$$t \otimes_{ai} \mathbf{P} = \mathbf{P}^t. \tag{4}$$

Proof. See supplementary material.

Definition 6 (Affine-invariant Gyrovector Spaces). *Define a binary operation* $\oplus_{ai}$ *and a scalar multiplication* $\otimes_{ai}$ *by Eqs. (3) and (4), respectively. Define a gyroautomorphism generated by* $\mathbf{P}$ *and* $\mathbf{Q}$ *as*

$$\mathrm{gyr}_{ai}[\mathbf{P}, \mathbf{Q}]\mathbf{R} = F_{ai}(\mathbf{P}, \mathbf{Q})\mathbf{R}(F_{ai}(\mathbf{P}, \mathbf{Q}))^{-1}, \tag{5}$$

where $F_{ai}(\mathbf{P}, \mathbf{Q}) = (\mathbf{P}^{\frac{1}{2}} \mathbf{Q} \mathbf{P}^{\frac{1}{2}})^{-\frac{1}{2}} \mathbf{P}^{\frac{1}{2}} \mathbf{Q}^{\frac{1}{2}}$.

Theorem 1. *Gyrogroups* $(\mathrm{Sym}_n^+, \oplus_{ai})$ *with the scalar multiplication* $\otimes_{ai}$ *form gyrovector spaces* $(\mathrm{Sym}_n^+, \oplus_{ai}, \otimes_{ai})$.

Proof. See supplementary material.

3.2 Log-Euclidean Gyrovector Spaces

We now study SPD manifolds with the Log-Euclidean geometry.

Lemma 3. *For* $\mathbf{P}, \mathbf{Q} \in \mathrm{Sym}_n^+$, *the binary operation* $\mathbf{P} \oplus_{le} \mathbf{Q}$ *is given as*

$$\mathbf{P} \oplus_{le} \mathbf{Q} = \exp(\log(\mathbf{P}) + \log(\mathbf{Q})). \tag{6}$$

Proof. See supplementary material.

From Lemma 3, the inverse of $\mathbf{P}$ is given by

$$\ominus_{le} \mathbf{P} = \mathbf{P}^{-1}.$$

Lemma 4. *For* $\mathbf{P} \in \mathrm{Sym}_n^+$, $t \in \mathbb{R}$, *the scalar multiplication* $t \otimes_{le} \mathbf{P}$ *is given by*

$$t \otimes_{le} \mathbf{P} = \mathbf{P}^t. \tag{7}$$

Proof. See supplementary material.

Definition 7 (Log-Euclidean Gyrovector Spaces). *Define a binary operation* $\oplus_{le}$ *and a scalar multiplication* $\otimes_{le}$ *by Eqs. (6) and (7), respectively. Define a gyroautomorphism generated by* $\mathbf{P}$ *and* $\mathbf{Q}$ *as*

$$\mathrm{gyr}_{le}[\mathbf{P}, \mathbf{Q}] = \mathrm{Id}.$$

Theorem 2. *Gyrogroups* $(\mathrm{Sym}_n^+, \oplus_{le})$ *with the scalar multiplication* $\otimes_{le}$ *form gyrovector spaces* $(\mathrm{Sym}_n^+, \oplus_{le}, \otimes_{le})$.

Proof. See supplementary material.

The conclusion of Theorem 2 is not surprising since it is known [2] that the space of SPD matrices with the Log-Euclidean geometry has a vector space structure. This vector space structure is given by the operations proposed in [2] that turn out to be the binary operation and scalar multiplication in Log-Euclidean gyrovector spaces.

3.3 Log-Cholesky Gyrovector Spaces

In this section, we focus on SPD manifolds with the Log-Cholesky geometry. Following the notations in [24], let $\lfloor \mathbf{A} \rfloor$ be a matrix of the same size as matrix $\mathbf{A}$ whose (i, j) element is $\mathbf{A}_{ij}$ if $i > j$ and is zero otherwise, $\mathbb{D}(\mathbf{A})$ is a diagonal matrix of the same size as matrix $\mathbf{A}$ whose (i, i) element is $\mathbf{A}_{ii}$. Denote by $\mathscr{L}(\mathbf{P})$ the lower triangular matrix obtained from the Cholesky decomposition of matrix $\mathbf{P} \in \mathrm{Sym}_n^+$, i.e., $\mathbf{P} = \mathscr{L}(\mathbf{P})\mathscr{L}(\mathbf{P})^T$.

Lemma 5. *For* $\mathbf{P}, \mathbf{Q} \in \mathrm{Sym}_n^+$, *the binary operation* $\mathbf{P} \oplus_{lc} \mathbf{Q}$ *is given as*

$$\begin{aligned}
\mathbf{P} \oplus_{lc} \mathbf{Q} = &\left(\lfloor \mathscr{L}(\mathbf{P}) \rfloor + \lfloor \mathscr{L}(\mathbf{Q}) \rfloor + \mathbb{D}(\mathscr{L}(\mathbf{P}))\mathbb{D}(\mathscr{L}(\mathbf{Q})) \right). \\
&\left(\lfloor \mathscr{L}(\mathbf{P}) \rfloor + \lfloor \mathscr{L}(\mathbf{Q}) \rfloor + \mathbb{D}(\mathscr{L}(\mathbf{P}))\mathbb{D}(\mathscr{L}(\mathbf{Q})) \right)^T.
\end{aligned} \tag{8}$$

Proof. See supplementary material.

From Eq. (8), the inverse of $\mathbf{P}$ is given by

$$\ominus_{lc}\mathbf{P} = \big(- \lfloor \mathscr{L}(\mathbf{P}) \rfloor + \mathbb{D}(\mathscr{L}(\mathbf{P}))^{-1} \big) \big(- \lfloor \mathscr{L}(\mathbf{P}) \rfloor + \mathbb{D}(\mathscr{L}(\mathbf{P}))^{-1} \big)^{T}.$$

Lemma 6. *For* $\mathbf{P} \in \mathrm{Sym}_n^+$, $t \in \mathbb{R}$, *the scalar multiplication* $t \otimes_{lc} \mathbf{P}$ *is given as*

$$t \otimes_{lc} \mathbf{P} = \big(t \lfloor \mathscr{L}(\mathbf{P}) \rfloor + \mathbb{D}(\mathscr{L}(\mathbf{P}))^t \big) \big(t \lfloor \mathscr{L}(\mathbf{P}) \rfloor + \mathbb{D}(\mathscr{L}(\mathbf{P}))^t \big)^{T}. \tag{9}$$

Proof. See supplementary material.

Definition 8 (Log-Cholesky Gyrovector Spaces). *Define a binary operation* $\oplus_{lc}$ *and a scalar multiplication* $\otimes_{lc}$ *by Eqs. (8) and (9), respectively. Define a gyroautomorphism generated by* $\mathbf{P}$ *and* $\mathbf{Q}$ *as*

$$\mathrm{gyr}_{lc}[\mathbf{P}, \mathbf{Q}] = \mathrm{Id}.$$

Theorem 3. *Gyrogroups* $(\mathrm{Sym}_n^+, \oplus_{lc})$ *with the scalar multiplication* $\otimes_{lc}$ *form gyrovector spaces* $(\mathrm{Sym}_n^+, \oplus_{lc}, \otimes_{lc})$.

Proof. See supplementary material.

3.4 Parallel Transport in Gyrovector Spaces of SPD Matrices

We now show a hidden analogy between Euclidean spaces and gyrovector spaces of SPD matrices studied in the previous sections. In the following, we drop the subscripts in the notations of the basic operations and the gyroautomorphism in these gyrovector spaces for simplicity of notation.

Lemma 7. *Let* $\mathbf{P}_0, \mathbf{P}_1, \mathbf{Q}_0, \mathbf{Q}_1 \in \mathrm{Sym}_n^+$. *If* $\mathrm{Log}_{\mathbf{P}_1}(\mathbf{Q}_1)$ *is the parallel transport of* $\mathrm{Log}_{\mathbf{P}_0}(\mathbf{Q}_0)$ *from* $\mathbf{P}_0$ *to* $\mathbf{P}_1$ *along geodesics connecting* $\mathbf{P}_0$ *and* $\mathbf{P}_1$, *then*

$$\ominus\mathbf{P}_1 \oplus \mathbf{Q}_1 = \mathrm{gyr}[\mathbf{P}_1, \ominus\mathbf{P}_0](\ominus\mathbf{P}_0 \oplus \mathbf{Q}_0).$$

Proof. See supplementary material.

Lemma 7 reveals a strong link between the Affine-invariant, Log-Euclidean, and Log-Cholesky geometries of SPD manifolds and hyperbolic geometry, as the algebraic definition [44] of parallel transport in a gyrovector space agrees with the classical parallel transport of differential geometry. In the gyrolanguage [44–46], Lemma 7 states that the gyrovector $\ominus\mathbf{P}_1 \oplus \mathbf{Q}_1$ is the gyrovector $\ominus\mathbf{P}_0 \oplus \mathbf{Q}_0$ gyrated by a gyroautomorphism. This gives a characterization of the parallel transport that is fully analogous to that of the parallel transport in Euclidean and hyperbolic spaces. Note that this characterization also agrees with the reinterpretation of addition and subtraction in a Riemannian manifold using logarithmic and exponential maps [36]. In the case of Log-Euclidean geometry, like the conclusion of Theorem 2, the result of Lemma 7 agrees with [2] which shows that the space of SPD matrices with the Log-Euclidean geometry has a vector space structure.

3.5   Low-Rank SPSD Manifolds

In this section, we extend the basic operations proposed in Sects. 3.1, 3.2, and 3.3 to the case of low-rank SPSD manifolds. We will see that defining a binary operation and a scalar multiplication on these manifolds that verify the axioms of gyrovector spaces is not trivial. However, based on the basic operations in gyrovector spaces of SPD matrices, one can still define the loose versions of these operations that are useful for applications.

We adopt the quotient manifold representation of $S_{n,p}^+$ proposed by [3,4], i.e.,

$$S_{n,p}^+ \cong (V_{n,p} \times \mathrm{Sym}_p^+) / O(p).$$

This representation is based on the decomposition

$$\mathbf{P} = \mathbf{U}_P \bar{\mathbf{P}} \mathbf{U}_P^T \tag{10}$$

of any matrix $\mathbf{P} \in S_{n,p}^+$, where $\mathbf{U}_P \in V_{n,p}$ and $\bar{\mathbf{P}} \in \mathrm{Sym}_p^+$. Here, each element of $S_{n,p}^+$ can be seen as a flat p-dimensional ellipsoid in $\mathbb{R}^n$ [3]. The flat ellipsoid belongs to a p-dimensional subspace spanned by the columns of $\mathbf{U}_P$, while the $p \times p$ SPD matrix $\bar{\mathbf{P}}$ defines the shape of the ellipsoid in Sym_p^+. This suggests a natural adaptation of the binary operations and scalar multiplications in gyrovector spaces of SPD matrices to the case of low-rank SPSD manifolds. That is, for any $\mathbf{P}, \mathbf{Q} \in S_{n,p}^+$, the binary operation will operate on the SPD matrices that define the shapes of $\mathbf{P}$ and $\mathbf{Q}$. Note, however, that the decomposition (10) is not unique and defined up to an orthogonal transformation

$$\mathbf{U}_P \mapsto \mathbf{U}_P \mathbf{O}, \bar{\mathbf{P}} \mapsto \mathbf{O}^T \bar{\mathbf{P}} \mathbf{O},$$

where $\mathbf{O} \in O_n$. In other words, $(\mathbf{U}_P \mathbf{O}, \mathbf{O}^T \bar{\mathbf{P}} \mathbf{O})$ also forms a decomposition of $\mathbf{P}$ for arbitrary $\mathbf{O} \in O_n$. This is problematic since in general, the binary operations defined in the previous sections is not invariant to orthogonal transformations. To resolve this ambiguity, we resort to canonical representation [3,4,11]. Our key idea is to identify a common subspace and then rotate the ranges of $\mathbf{P}$ and $\mathbf{Q}$ to this subspace. The SPD matrices that define the shapes of $\mathbf{P}$ and $\mathbf{Q}$ are rotated accordingly based on the corresponding rotations in order to reflect the changes of the ranges of $\mathbf{P}$ and $\mathbf{Q}$. These rotations are determined as follows. For any $\mathbf{U}, \mathbf{V} \in \mathrm{Gr}_{n,p}$, among all geodesics joining $\mathbf{U}$ and $\mathbf{V}$, we consider the one joining their canonical bases. Let $\mathbf{U}_V$ be the canonical base in the orbit of $\mathbf{U}$, $\mathbf{V}_U$ be the canonical base in the orbit of $\mathbf{V}$. These bases are given [3,4,11] by

$$\mathbf{U}_V = \mathbf{U}\mathbf{O}_{\mathbf{U} \to \mathbf{V}}, \mathbf{V}_U = \mathbf{V}\mathbf{O}_{\mathbf{V} \to \mathbf{U}},$$

where $\mathbf{O}_{\mathbf{U} \to \mathbf{V}}$ and $\mathbf{O}_{\mathbf{V} \to \mathbf{U}}$ are orthogonal matrices computed from a singular value decomposition (SVD) of $\mathbf{U}^T \mathbf{V}$, i.e.,

$$\mathbf{U}^T \mathbf{V} = \mathbf{O}_{\mathbf{U} \to \mathbf{V}} \mathbf{\Sigma} \mathbf{O}_{\mathbf{V} \to \mathbf{U}}^T,$$

where $\mathbf{\Sigma}$ is a diagonal matrix whose diagonal entries are the singular values of $\mathbf{U}^T \mathbf{V}$.

Let $\mathbf{U}_e$ be a common subspace used to define the loose versions of the basic operations on $\mathrm{S}_{n,p}^+$. In a special case where all matrices are supported by the same subspace, then $\mathbf{U}_e$ can be identified as this subspace. By abuse of language, we will use the same terminologies in gyrovector spaces to refer to the loose versions in the following definitions.

Definition 9. *Let* $\mathbf{P}, \mathbf{Q} \in \mathrm{S}_{n,p}^+$, $\mathbf{P} = \mathbf{U}_P \bar{\mathbf{P}} \mathbf{U}_P^T$, *and* $\mathbf{Q} = \mathbf{U}_Q \bar{\mathbf{Q}} \mathbf{U}_Q^T$. *The binary operation* $\mathbf{P} \oplus_{spsd} \mathbf{Q}$ *is defined as*

$$\mathbf{P} \oplus_{spsd} \mathbf{Q} = \mathbf{U}_e (\mathbf{O}_{\mathbf{U}_P \to \mathbf{U}_e}^T \bar{\mathbf{P}} \mathbf{O}_{\mathbf{U}_P \to \mathbf{U}_e} \oplus \mathbf{O}_{\mathbf{U}_Q \to \mathbf{U}_e}^T \bar{\mathbf{Q}} \mathbf{O}_{\mathbf{U}_Q \to \mathbf{U}_e}) \mathbf{U}_e^T.$$

Let $\mathbf{I}_{n,p} = \begin{bmatrix} \mathbf{I}_p & 0 \\ 0 & 0 \end{bmatrix}$ be the identity element of $\mathrm{S}_{n,p}^+$. The inverse of $\mathbf{P} \in \mathrm{S}_{n,p}^+$ where $\mathbf{P} = \mathbf{U}_P \bar{\mathbf{P}} \mathbf{U}_P^T$ is defined as

$$\ominus_{spsd} \mathbf{P} = \mathbf{U}_e \big(\ominus (\mathbf{O}_{\mathbf{U}_P \to \mathbf{U}_e}^T \bar{\mathbf{P}} \mathbf{O}_{\mathbf{U}_P \to \mathbf{U}_e}) \big) \mathbf{U}_e^T.$$

Definition 10. *Let* $\mathbf{P} \in \mathrm{S}_{n,p}^+$, $t \in \mathbb{R}$, *and* $\mathbf{P} = \mathbf{U}_P \bar{\mathbf{P}} \mathbf{U}_P^T$. *The scalar multiplication* $t \otimes_{spsd} \mathbf{P}$ *is defined as*

$$t \otimes_{spsd} \mathbf{P} = \mathbf{U}_e (t \otimes \mathbf{O}_{\mathbf{U}_P \to \mathbf{U}_e}^T \bar{\mathbf{P}} \mathbf{O}_{\mathbf{U}_P \to \mathbf{U}_e}) \mathbf{U}_e^T.$$

Definition 11. *Let* $\mathbf{P}, \mathbf{Q}, \mathbf{R} \in \mathrm{S}_{n,p}^+$, $\mathbf{P} = \mathbf{U}_P \bar{\mathbf{P}} \mathbf{U}_P^T$, $\mathbf{Q} = \mathbf{U}_Q \bar{\mathbf{Q}} \mathbf{U}_Q^T$, *and* $\mathbf{R} = \mathbf{U}_R \bar{\mathbf{R}} \mathbf{U}_R^T$. *The gyroautomorphism in* $\mathrm{S}_{n,p}^+$ *is defined by*

$$\mathrm{gyr}_{spsd}[\mathbf{P}, \mathbf{Q}]\mathbf{R}$$
$$= \mathbf{U}_e \big(\mathrm{gyr}[\mathbf{O}_{\mathbf{U}_P \to \mathbf{U}_e}^T \bar{\mathbf{P}} \mathbf{O}_{\mathbf{U}_P \to \mathbf{U}_e}, \mathbf{O}_{\mathbf{U}_Q \to \mathbf{U}_e}^T \bar{\mathbf{Q}} \mathbf{O}_{\mathbf{U}_Q \to \mathbf{U}_e}] \mathbf{O}_{\mathbf{U}_R \to \mathbf{U}_e}^T \bar{\mathbf{R}} \mathbf{O}_{\mathbf{U}_R \to \mathbf{U}_e}) \mathbf{U}_e^T.$$

It can be seen that spaces $\mathrm{S}_{n,p}^+$, when equipped with the basic operations defined in this section, do not form gyrovector spaces. However, Theorem 4 states that they still verify some important properties of gyrovector spaces.

Theorem 4. *The basic operations on* $\mathrm{S}_{n,p}^+$ *verify the Left Gyroassociative Law, Left Reduction Property, Gyrocommutative Law, and axioms (V2), (V3), and (V4).*

Proof. See supplementary material.

3.6   SPSD Neural Networks

Motivated by the work of [12] that develops RNNs on hyperbolic spaces, in this section, we propose a class of RNNs on SPSD manifolds. It is worth mentioning that the operations defined in Sects. 3.1, 3.2, and 3.3 as well as those constructed below can be used to build other types of neural networks on SPSD manifolds, e.g., convolutional neural networks. We leave this for future work.

In addition to the basic operations, we need to generalize some other operations of Euclidean RNNs to the SPSD manifold setting. Here we focus on two operations, i.e., vector-matrix multiplication and pointwise nonlinearity. Other operations [12] are left for future work.

Vector-Matrix Multiplication. If $\mathbf{P} \in S_{n,p}^+$ and $\mathbf{W} \in \mathbb{R}^p, \mathbf{W} \geq 0$, then the vector-matrix multiplication $\mathbf{W} \otimes_v \mathbf{P}$ is given by

$$\mathbf{W} \otimes_v \mathbf{P} = \mathbf{U} \operatorname{diag}(\mathbf{W} * \mathbf{V})\mathbf{U}^T,$$

where $\mathbf{P} = \mathbf{U} \operatorname{diag}(\mathbf{V})\mathbf{U}^T$ is the eigenvalue decomposition of $\mathbf{P}$, and $*$ denotes the element-wise multiplication.

Pointwise Nonlinearity. If φ is a pointwise nonlinear activation function, then the pointwise nonlinearity $\varphi^{\otimes_a}(\mathbf{P})$ is given by

$$\varphi^{\otimes_a}(\mathbf{P}) = \mathbf{U} \operatorname{diag}(\max(\epsilon\mathbf{I}, \varphi(\mathbf{V})))\mathbf{U}^T,$$

where $\epsilon > 0$ is a rectification threshold, and $\mathbf{P} = \mathbf{U} \operatorname{diag}(\mathbf{V})\mathbf{U}^T$ is the eigenvalue decomposition of $\mathbf{P}$. Note that the above operations preserve the range and the positive semi-definite property.

We first consider the case of full-rank learning. In this case, we adapt a class of models that are invariant to time rescaling [43] to the SPD manifold setting using the gyro-chain-rule in gyrovector spaces of SPD matrices (see supplementary material for the derivation). We obtain the following update equations:

$$\mathbf{P}_t = \varphi^{\otimes_a}(\mathbf{W}_h \otimes_v \mathbf{H}_{t-1} + \mathbf{W}_x \otimes_v \phi(\mathbf{X}_t)), \tag{11}$$

$$\mathbf{H}_t = \mathbf{H}_{t-1} \oplus \alpha \otimes ((\ominus\mathbf{H}_{t-1}) \oplus \mathbf{P}_t), \tag{12}$$

where $\mathbf{X}_t \in \operatorname{Sym}_n^+$ is the input at frame t, $\mathbf{H}_{t-1}, \mathbf{H}_t \in \operatorname{Sym}_n^+$ are the hidden states at frames $t - 1$ and t, respectively, $\mathbf{W}_h, \mathbf{W}_x \in \mathbb{R}^n$, $\mathbf{W}_h, \mathbf{W}_x > 0$, and $\alpha \in \mathbb{R}$ are learnable parameters, $\phi(\mathbf{X}_t)$ is any mapping[2] that transforms $\mathbf{X}_t$ into a SPD matrix.

The above model can be extended to the low-rank case by viewing $\mathbf{H}_{t-1}$ and $\mathbf{H}_t$ as the SPD matrices that define the shapes of the SPSD matrices representing the hidden states at frames $t - 1$ and t, respectively. If we assume that the hidden states are supported by the same subspace, then it is tempting to design the mapping $\phi(\mathbf{X}_t)$ such that it gives the SPD matrix that defines the shape of $\mathbf{X}_t$, once the range of $\mathbf{X}_t$ is rotated to that subspace. The algorithm in both the full-rank and low-rank cases can be summarized in Algorithm 1. The procedure SpdRotate() performs the computations of the mapping $\phi(.)$, and $\mathbf{X}^u[:,:p]$ denotes the matrix containing the first p columns of $\mathbf{X}^u$. The parameter $\mathbf{W}$ can be either learned or fixed up front which offers flexible learning strategies.

Complexity Analysis. In the full-rank learning setting, the most expensive operations are performed at steps 1, 3, 4, and 5, each of them has $O(n^3)$ complexity. In the low-rank learning setting, the most expensive operation is the eigenvalue decomposition at step 1 that has $O(n^3)$ complexity, while steps 3, 4, and 5 are $O(p^3)$ operations. Thus, when $p \ll n$, the algorithm in the low-rank learning setting is faster than the one in the full-rank learning setting.

---

[2] We drop parameters to simplify notations.

Algorithm 1: SPSD-RNN

Data: $\mathbf{X}_t \in \mathrm{S}_{n,p}^+, \mathbf{H}_{t-1}^{spd} \in \mathrm{Sym}_p^+, \mathbf{W} \in \mathrm{V}_{n,p}$

Result: $\mathbf{H}_t^{spd} \in \mathrm{Sym}_p^+$

1 $\mathbf{X}^s, \mathbf{X}^u \leftarrow \mathrm{EIG}(\mathbf{X}_t)$;   /* $\mathbf{X}^s$: eigenvalues, $\mathbf{X}^u$: eigenvectors */
2 $\mathbf{X}^u \leftarrow \mathbf{X}^u[:,:p]$;   /* Eigenvalues are arranged in descending order */
3 $\mathbf{X}^{spd} \leftarrow \mathrm{SpdRotate}(\mathbf{X}_t, \mathbf{X}^u, \mathbf{W})$;
4 $\mathbf{P}_t = \varphi^{\otimes a}(\mathbf{W}_h \otimes_v \mathbf{H}_{t-1}^{spd} + \mathbf{W}_x \otimes_v \mathbf{X}^{spd})$;
5 $\mathbf{H}_t^{spd} = \mathbf{H}_{t-1}^{spd} \oplus \alpha \otimes ((\ominus \mathbf{H}_{t-1}^{spd}) \oplus \mathbf{P}_t)$;

---

4 Experiments

Our networks, referred to as **SPSD-AI**, **SPSD-LE**, and **SPSD-LC** were implemented with Tensorflow framework. The networks were trained using Adadelta optimizer for 500 epochs. The ReLU function was used for the pointwise non-linearity. The learning rate and parameter ϵ for the pointwise nonlinearity were set respectively to 10^{-2} and 10^{-4}.

4.1 Datasets and Experimental Settings

We use HDM05 [31], FPHA [13], and NTU RBG+D 60 (NTU60) [39] datasets. These datasets include three different types of human activities: body actions (HDM05), hand actions (FPHA), and interaction actions (NTU60).

HDM05 Dataset. It has 2337 sequences of 3D skeleton data classified into 130 classes. Each frame contains the 3D coordinates of 31 body joints. We use all the action classes and follow the experimental protocol [15] in which 2 subjects are used for training and the remaining 3 subjects are used for testing.

FPHA Dataset. It has 1175 sequences of 3D skeleton data classified into 45 classes. Each frame contains the 3D coordinates of 21 hand joints. We follow the experimental protocol [13] in which 600 sequences are used for training and 575 sequences are used for testing.

NTU60 Dataset. It has 56880 sequences of 3D skeleton data classified into 60 classes. Each frame contains the 3D coordinates of 25 or 50 body joints. We use the mutual (interaction) actions and follow the cross-subject (X-Sub) and cross-view (X-View) experimental protocols [39]. For the X-Sub protocol, this results in 7319 and 3028 sequences for training and testing, respectively. For the X-View protocol, the numbers of training and testing sequences are 6889 and 3458, respectively.

4.2 Implementation Details

In order to retain the correlation of neighboring joints [5,49] and to increase feature interactions encoded by covariance matrices, we first identify a closest left (right) neighbor of every joint based on their distance to the hip (wrist) joint[3], and then combine the 3D coordinates of each joint and those of its left (right) neighbor to create a feature vector for the joint. Thus, a 6-dim feature vector is created for every joint. The input SPD data are computed as follows. For any frame t, a mean vector $\boldsymbol{\mu}_t$ and a covariance matrix $\boldsymbol{\Sigma}_t$ are computed from the set of feature vectors of the frame and then combined [29] to create a SPD matrix as

$$\mathbf{Y}_t = \begin{bmatrix} \boldsymbol{\Sigma}_t + \boldsymbol{\mu}_t(\boldsymbol{\mu}_t)^T & \boldsymbol{\mu}_t \\ (\boldsymbol{\mu}_t)^T & 1 \end{bmatrix}.$$

The lower part of matrix $\log(\mathbf{Y}_t)$ is flattened to obtain a vector $\tilde{\mathbf{v}}_t$. All vectors $\tilde{\mathbf{v}}_t$ within a time window $[t, t + c - 1]$ where c is a predefined value ($c = 10$ in our experiments) are used to compute a covariance matrix as $\mathbf{Z}_t = \frac{1}{c}\sum_{i=t}^{t+c-1}(\tilde{\mathbf{v}}_i - \bar{\mathbf{v}}_t)(\tilde{\mathbf{v}}_i - \bar{\mathbf{v}}_t)^T$, where $\bar{\mathbf{v}}_t = \frac{1}{c}\sum_{i=t}^{t+c-1}\tilde{\mathbf{v}}_i$. Matrix $\mathbf{Z}_t$ is then the input data at frame t of the networks.

Table 1. Accuracies and training times (minutes) per epoch of SPSD-AI for the full-rank (FR) and low-rank (LR) learning settings (the experiment is conducted on 1 NVIDIA 1080 GPU).

Dataset	HDM05		FPHA		NTU60 (X-Sub)		NTU60 (X-View)	
	FR	LR	FR	LR	FR	LR	FR	LR
Accuracy (%)	81.32	74.19	96.58	90.94	95.86	89.78	97.44	90.15
Training time (min)	1.09	0.66	0.64	0.39	9.19	5.61	8.56	5.26

Table 2. Accuracies of SPSD-AI when canonical representation is used (C) and not used (NC).

Dataset	HDM05		FPHA		NTU60 (X-Sub)		NTU60 (X-View)	
	C	NC	C	NC	C	NC	C	NC
Accuracy (%)	74.19	41.37	90.94	63.41	89.78	56.82	90.15	58.34

For classification, the network output is projected to the tangent space at the identity matrix using the logarithmic map. The lower part of the resulting matrix is flattened and fed to a fully-connected layer. Cross-entropy loss is used to optimize the network. Please refer to the supplementary material for more implementation details.

---

[3] For joints having more than one left (right) neighbor, one of them can be chosen.

Table 3. Accuracies of our networks and state-of-the-art methods on HDM05 dataset.

Method	Accuracy (%)	#Param. (MB)	Year
SPD-SRU [8]	42.26	0.05	2018
SPDNet [17]	58.44	0.12	2017
SPDNetBN [6]	62.54	0.13	2019
HypGRU [12]	55.47	0.23	2018
MS-G3D [27]	70.38	2.93	2020
ST-TR [38]	69.75	4.62	2021
SPSD-AI	**81.32**	0.31	
SPSD-LE	77.46	0.31	
SPSD-LC	73.52	0.31	

4.3 Ablation Study

In this section, we discuss the impact of different components of SPSD-AI on its performance.

Full-Rank vs. Low-Rank Learning. In this experiment, we compare the accuracies and computation times of SPSD-AI in the full-rank and low-rank learning settings. The value of p is set to 14. Results are reported in Table 1 (see supplementary material for more results w.r.t different settings of p). In terms of accuracy, the network trained in the full-rank learning setting overpasses the one trained in the low-rank learning setting. In terms of computation time, however, the former is slower than the latter. This experiment highlights the advantage of each of the learning settings. In practice, the value of p can be adjusted to offer a good compromise between accuracy and computation time.

Canonical Representation-Based Learning. This experiment is conducted to illustrate the efficacy of canonical representation in the low-rank case. For a fair comparison, we evaluate the accuracies of SPSD-AI in the two following settings. In the first setting, canonical representation is used and the parameter $\mathbf{W}$ is fixed up front ($\mathbf{W} = \mathbf{I}_{n,p}$). In the second setting, canonical representation is not used, i.e., $\mathbf{X}^{spd}$ at line 3 of Algorithm 1 is computed as

$$\mathbf{X}^{spd} = (\mathbf{X}^u)^T \operatorname{diag}(\mathbf{X}^s[: p]) \mathbf{X}^u, \tag{13}$$

where $\mathbf{X}^s[: p]$ denotes the vector containing the first p elements of $\mathbf{X}^s$, and $\operatorname{diag}(.)$ forms a diagonal matrix from a vector. The value of p is set to 14. Results are presented in Table 2. In all cases, canonical representation yields significant improvements in accuracy. The average performance gain over all the datasets is more than 30%.

In the following, we report results of our networks in the full-rank case.

Table 4. Accuracies of our networks and state-of-the-art methods on FPHA dataset.

Method	Accuracy (%)	#Param. (MB)	Year
SPD-SRU [8]	78.57	0.02	2018
SPDNet [17]	87.65	0.04	2017
SPDNetBN [6]	88.52	0.05	2019
HypGRU [12]	58.61	0.16	2018
ST-TS-HGR-NET [33]	93.22	–	2019
SRU-HOS-NET [34]	94.61	–	2020
HMM-HPEV-Net [25]	90.96	–	2020
SAGCN-RBi-IndRNN [22]	90.26	–	2021
MS-G3D [27]	88.61	2.90	2020
ST-TR [38]	86.32	4.59	2021
SPSD-AI	**96.58**	0.11	
SPSD-LE	91.84	0.11	
SPSD-LC	89.73	0.11	

Table 5. Accuracies (%) of our networks and state-of-the-art methods on NTU60 dataset (interaction actions).

Method	X-Sub	X-View	#Param. (X-Sub, MB)	Year
ST-LSTM [26]	83.0	87.3	–	2016
ST-GCN [48]	87.05	91.02	–	2018
AS-GCN [23]	91.22	93.46	–	2019
LSTM-IRN [37]	90.5	93.5	–	2019
SPD-SRU [8]	66.25	68.11	0.004	2018
SPDNet [17]	73.26	74.82	0.03	2017
SPDNetBN [6]	75.84	76.96	0.04	2019
HypGRU [12]	88.26	89.43	0.013	2018
MS-G3D [27]	93.25	95.73	2.89	2020
ST-TR [38]	92.18	94.69	4.58	2021
2S-DRAGCN$_{joint}$ [50]	93.20	95.58	3.57	2021
GeomNet [32]	93.62	96.32	–	2021
SPSD-AI	**95.86**	**97.44**	0.03	
SPSD-LE	90.74	91.18	0.03	
SPSD-LC	88.03	88.56	0.03	

4.4 Results on HDM05 Dataset

Results of our networks and state-of-the-art methods on HDM05 dataset are presented in Table 3. The implementations of SPD-SRU[4], SPDNet[5], SPDNetBN[6], HypGRU[7], MS-G3D[8], and ST-TR[9] are rendered publicly available by the authors of [8], [17], [6], [12], [27], and [38] respectively. HypGRU achieves the best results when the data are projected to hyperbolic spaces before they are fed to the networks, and all its layers are based on hyperbolic geometry. The hidden dimension for HypGRU is set to 200. For SPDNet and SPDNetBN, we compute a covariance matrix to represent an input sequence as in [17]. The sizes of the covariance matrix are 93×93. Our networks outperform all the competing networks. In particular, they beat the state-of-the-art MS-G3D for 3D skeleton-based action recognition. Furthermore, our networks have about 9 times fewer parameters than MS-G3D. Our networks also have superior performance than the SPD and HNN models.

4.5 Results on FPHA Dataset

For SPDNet and SPDNetBN, the sizes of the input covariance matrix are 60×60, and the sizes of the transformation matrices are set to 60×50, 50×40, and 40×30. Results of our networks and state-of-the-art methods on FPHA dataset are given in Table 4. SPSD-AI is the best performer on this dataset. SPSD-LE gives the second best result among our networks. It is slightly better than HMM-HPEV-Net and SAGCN-RBi-IndRNN, and outperforms MS-G3D and ST-TR by more than 3%. SPSD-LC achieves the lowest accuracy among our networks. However, it is superior to HypGRU and compares favorably to some state-of-the-art SPD models, i.e., SPD-SRU, SPDNet, and SPDNetBN. Note that MS-G3D is outperformed by our networks despite having 26 times more parameters.

4.6 Results on NTU60 Dataset

For SPDNet and SPDNetBN, the sizes of the input covariance matrix are 150×150, and the sizes of the transformation matrices are set to 150×100, 100×60, and 60×30. Results of our networks and state-of-the-art methods on NTU60 dataset are reported in Table 5. Again, SPSD-AI gives the best results among the competing methods. It outperforms the state-of-the-art methods 2S-DRAGCN and GeomNet for 3D skeleton-based human interaction recognition. We observe that on all the datasets, SPSD-AI trained in the low-rank learning setting (see Table 1) competes favorably with SPD-SRU, SPDNet, and SPDNetBN. This

---

[4] https://github.com/zhenxingjian/SPD-SRU/tree/master.

[5] https://github.com/zhiwu-huang/SPDNet.

[6] https://papers.nips.cc/paper/2019/hash/6e69ebbfad976d4637bb4b39de261bf7-Abstract.html.

[7] https://github.com/dalab/hyperbolic_nn.

[8] https://github.com/kenziyuliu/MS-G3D.

[9] https://github.com/Chiaraplizz/ST-TR.

suggests that integrating our method for low-rank matrix learning into these networks might also lead to effective solutions for SPSD matrix learning.

5   Conclusion

We presented a method for constructing the basic operations in gyrovector spaces of SPD matrices. We then studied gyrovector spaces of SPD matrices with the Affine-invariant, Log-Euclidean, and Log-Cholesky geometries. We proposed the loose versions of the basic operations in low-rank SPSD manifolds by extending those previously defined in gyrovector spaces of SPD matrices. Finally, we developed a class of RNNs for SPSD matrix learning, and provided the experimental evaluations on three benchmarks for human activity recognition to demonstrate the effectiveness of our networks.

References

1. Abe, T., Hatori, O.: Generalized gyrovector spaces and a Mazur-Ulam theorem. Publicationes Mathematicae Debrecen **87**, 393–413 (2015)
2. Arsigny, V., Fillard, P., Pennec, X., Ayache, N.: Fast and simple computations on tensors with log-euclidean metrics. Technical report RR-5584, INRIA (2005)
3. Bonnabel, S., Collard, A., Sepulchre, R.: Rank-preserving geometric means of positive semi-definite matrices. Linear Algebra Appl. **438**, 3202–3216 (2013)
4. Bonnabel, S., Sepulchre, R.: Riemannian metric and geometric mean for positive semidefinite matrices of fixed rank. SIAM J. Matrix Anal. Appl. **31**(3), 1055–1070 (2009)
5. Boureau, Y.L., Bach, F., LeCun, Y., Ponce, J.: Learning mid-level features for recognition. In: CVPR, pp. 2559–2566 (2010)
6. Brooks, D.A., Schwander, O., Barbaresco, F., Schneider, J.Y., Cord, M.: Riemannian batch normalization for SPD neural networks. In: NeurIPS, pp. 15463–15474 (2019)
7. Chakraborty, R., Bouza, J., Manton, J., Vemuri, B.C.: ManifoldNet: a deep neural network for manifold-valued data with applications. In: TPAMI, p. 1 (2020)
8. Chakraborty, R., et al.: A statistical recurrent model on the manifold of symmetric positive definite matrices. In: NeurIPS, pp. 8897–8908 (2018)
9. Dong, Z., Jia, S., Zhang, C., Pei, M., Wu, Y.: Deep manifold learning of symmetric positive definite matrices with application to face recognition. In: AAAI, pp. 4009–4015 (2017)
10. Engin, M., Wang, L., Zhou, L., Liu, X.: DeepKSPD: learning kernel-matrix-based SPD representation for fine-grained image recognition. In: Ferrari, V., Hebert, M., Sminchisescu, C., Weiss, Y. (eds.) ECCV 2018. LNCS, vol. 11206, pp. 629–645. Springer, Cham (2018). https://doi.org/10.1007/978-3-030-01216-8_38
11. Gallivan, K., Srivastava, A., Liu, X., Van Dooren, P.: Efficient algorithms for inferences on Grassmann manifolds. In: IEEE Workshop on Statistical Signal Processing, pp. 315–318 (2003)
12. Ganea, O., Becigneul, G., Hofmann, T.: Hyperbolic neural networks. In: NeurIPS, pp. 5350–5360 (2018)

13. Garcia-Hernando, G., Yuan, S., Baek, S., Kim, T.K.: First-person hand action benchmark with RGB-D videos and 3D hand pose annotations. In: CVPR, pp. 409–419 (2018)
14. Harandi, M., Salzmann, M., Hartley, R.: Dimensionality reduction on SPD manifolds: the emergence of geometry-aware methods. TPAMI **40**, 48–62 (2018)
15. Harandi, M.T., Salzmann, M., Hartley, R.: From manifold to manifold: geometry-aware dimensionality reduction for SPD matrices. In: Fleet, D., Pajdla, T., Schiele, B., Tuytelaars, T. (eds.) ECCV 2014. LNCS, vol. 8690, pp. 17–32. Springer, Cham (2014). https://doi.org/10.1007/978-3-319-10605-2_2
16. Hatori, O.: Examples and applications of generalized gyrovector spaces. RM **71**, 295–317 (2017)
17. Huang, Z., Gool, L.V.: A Riemannian network for SPD matrix learning. In: AAAI, pp. 2036–2042 (2017)
18. Kim, S.: Distributivity on the gyrovector spaces. Kyungpook Math. J. **55**, 13–20 (2015)
19. Kim, S.: Gyrovector spaces on the open convex cone of positive definite matrices. Math. Interdisc. Res. **1**(1), 173–185 (2016)
20. Kim, S.: Operator inequalities and gyrolines of the weighted geometric means. CoRR abs/2009.10274 (2020)
21. Kim, S.: Ordered gyrovector spaces. Symmetry **12**(6), 1041 (2020)
22. Li, C., Li, S., Gao, Y., Zhang, X., Li, W.: A two-stream neural network for pose-based hand gesture recognition. IEEE Trans. Cognit. Dev. Syst. 1 (2021)
23. Li, M., Chen, S., Chen, X., Zhang, Y., Wang, Y., Tian, Q.: Actional-structural graph convolutional networks for skeleton-based action recognition. In: CVPR, pp. 3595–3603 (2019)
24. Lin, Z.: Riemannian geometry of symmetric positive definite matrices via Cholesky decomposition. SIAM J. Matrix Anal. Appl. **40**(4), 1353–1370 (2019)
25. Liu, J., Liu, Y., Wang, Y., Prinet, V., Xiang, S., Pan, C.: Decoupled representation learning for skeleton-based gesture recognition. In: CVPR, pp. 5750–5759 (2020)
26. Liu, J., Shahroudy, A., Xu, D., Wang, G.: Spatio-temporal LSTM with trust gates for 3D human action recognition. In: Leibe, B., Matas, J., Sebe, N., Welling, M. (eds.) ECCV 2016. LNCS, vol. 9907, pp. 816–833. Springer, Cham (2016). https://doi.org/10.1007/978-3-319-46487-9_50
27. Liu, Z., Zhang, H., Chen, Z., Wang, Z., Ouyang, W.: disentangling and unifying graph convolutions for skeleton-based action recognition. In: CVPR, pp. 143–152 (2020)
28. López, F., Pozzetti, B., Trettel, S., Strube, M., Wienhard, A.: Vector-valued distance and gyrocalculus on the space of symmetric positive definite matrices. In: NeurIPS, pp. 18350–18366 (2021)
29. Lovrić, M., Min-Oo, M., Ruh, E.A.: Multivariate normal distributions parametrized as a Riemannian symmetric space. J. Multivar. Anal. **74**(1), 36–48 (2000)
30. Massart, E., Absil, P.A.: Quotient geometry with simple geodesics for the manifold of fixed-rank positive-semidefinite matrices. SIAM J. Matrix Anal. Appl. **41**(1), 171–198 (2020)
31. Müller, M., Röder, T., Clausen, M., Eberhardt, B., Krüger, B., Weber, A.: Documentation mocap database HDM05. Technical report. CG-2007-2, Universität Bonn, June 2007
32. Nguyen, X.S.: GeomNet: a neural network based on Riemannian geometries of SPD matrix space and Cholesky space for 3D skeleton-based interaction recognition. In: ICCV, pp. 13379–13389 (2021)

33. Nguyen, X.S., Brun, L., Lézoray, O., Bougleux, S.: A neural network based on SPD manifold learning for skeleton-based hand gesture recognition. In: CVPR, pp. 12036–12045 (2019)
34. Nguyen, X.S., Brun, L., Lézoray, O., Bougleux, S.: Learning recurrent high-order statistics for skeleton-based hand gesture recognition. In: ICPR, pp. 975–982 (2020)
35. Pennec, X.: Statistical Computing on Manifolds for Computational Anatomy. Habilitation à diriger des recherches, Université Nice Sophia-Antipolis (2006)
36. Pennec, X., Fillard, P., Ayache, N.: A Riemannian framework for tensor computing. Technical report. RR-5255, INRIA (2004)
37. Perez, M., Liu, J., Kot, A.C.: Interaction relational network for mutual action recognition. CoRR abs/1910.04963 (2019)
38. Plizzari, C., Cannici, M., Matteucci, M.: Skeleton-based action recognition via spatial and temporal transformer networks. Comput. Vis. Image Underst. **208**, 103219 (2021)
39. Shahroudy, A., Liu, J., Ng, T.T., Wang, G.: NTU RGB+D: a large scale dataset for 3D human activity analysis. In: CVPR, pp. 1010–1019 (2016)
40. Shimizu, R., Mukuta, Y., Harada, T.: Hyperbolic neural networks++. In: ICLR (2021)
41. Sukthanker, R.S., Huang, Z., Kumar, S., Endsjo, E.G., Wu, Y., Gool, L.V.: Neural architecture search of SPD manifold networks. In: IJCAI, pp. 3002–3009 (2021)
42. Tabia, H., Laga, H., Picard, D., Gosselin, P.H.: Covariance descriptors for 3D shape matching and retrieval. In: CVPR, pp. 4185–4192 (2014)
43. Tallec, C., Ollivier, Y.: Can recurrent neural networks warp time? In: ICLR (2018)
44. Ungar, A.A.: Beyond the Einstein Addition Law and Its Gyroscopic Thomas Precession: The Theory of Gyrogroups and Gyrovector Spaces. Fundamental Theories of Physics, vol. 117. Springer, Dordrecht (2002). https://doi.org/10.1007/0-306-47134-5
45. Ungar, A.A.: Analytic Hyperbolic Geometry: Mathematical Foundations and Applications. World Scientific Publishing Co., Pte. Ltd., Hackensack (2005)
46. Ungar, A.A.: Analytic Hyperbolic Geometry in N Dimensions: An Introduction. CRC Press, Boca Raton (2014)
47. Wang, R., Wu, X.J., Kittler, J.: SymNet: a simple symmetric positive definite manifold deep learning method for image set classification. IEEE Trans. Neural Netw. Learn. Syst. **33**, 1–15 (2021)
48. Yan, S., Xiong, Y., Lin, D.: Spatial temporal graph convolutional networks for skeleton-based action recognition. In: AAAI, pp. 7444–7452 (2018)
49. Yang, X., Tian, Y.: Super normal vector for activity recognition using depth sequences. In: CVPR, pp. 804–811 (2014)
50. Zhu, L., Wan, B., Li, C., Tian, G., Hou, Y., Yuan, K.: Dyadic relational graph convolutional networks for skeleton-based human interaction recognition. Pattern Recogn. **115**, 107920 (2021)

Learning Visual Representation from Modality-Shared Contrastive Language-Image Pre-training

Haoxuan You[1]([envelope]), Luowei Zhou[2], Bin Xiao[2], Noel Codella[2], Yu Cheng[3],
Ruochen Xu[2], Shih-Fu Chang[1], and Lu Yuan[2]

[1] Columbia University, New York, USA
{hy2612,sc250}@columbia.edu
[2] Microsoft Cloud and AI, Redmond, USA
{luozhou,bixi,ncodella,ruox,luyuan}@microsoft.com
[3] Microsoft Research, Redmond, USA
yu.cheng@microsoft.com

Abstract. Large-scale multi-modal contrastive pre-training has demonstrated great utility to learn transferable features for a range of downstream tasks by mapping multiple modalities into a shared embedding space. Typically, this has employed separate encoders for each modality. However, recent work suggests that transformers can support learning across multiple modalities and allow knowledge sharing. Inspired by this, we investigate a variety of Modality-Shared Contrastive Language-Image Pre-training (MS-CLIP) frameworks. More specifically, we question how many parameters of a transformer model can be shared across modalities during contrastive pre-training, and rigorously examine architectural design choices that position the proportion of parameters shared along a spectrum. In studied conditions, we observe that a mostly unified encoder for vision and language signals outperforms all other variations that separate more parameters. Additionally, we find that light-weight modality-specific parallel modules further improve performance. Experimental results show that the proposed MS-CLIP approach outperforms vanilla CLIP by up to 13% relative in zero-shot ImageNet classification (pre-trained on YFCC-100M), while simultaneously supporting a reduction of parameters. In addition, our approach outperforms vanilla CLIP by 1.6 points in linear probing on a collection of 24 downstream vision tasks. Furthermore, we discover that sharing parameters leads to semantic concepts from different modalities being encoded more closely in the embedding space, facilitating the transferring of common semantic structure (e.g., attention patterns) from language to vision. Code is available at https://github.com/Hxyou/MSCLIP.

H. You, L. Zhou, B. Xiao and N. Codella—Equal Contribution.

Supplementary Information The online version contains supplementary material available at https://doi.org/10.1007/978-3-031-19812-0_5.

S. Avidan et al. (Eds.): ECCV 2022, LNCS 13687, pp. 69–87, 2022.
https://doi.org/10.1007/978-3-031-19812-0_5

1 Introduction

Contrastive Language-Image Pre-training (CLIP) has drawn much attention recently in the field of Computer Vision and Natural Language Processing [21,47], where large-scale image-caption data are leveraged to learn generic vision representations from language supervision through contrastive loss. This allows the learning of open-set visual concepts and imbues the learned features with a robust capability to transfer to diverse vision tasks.

Prior work in this topic often employs separate language and image encoders, despite architectural similarities between the encoders for both modalities. For instance, the original CLIP work [47] uses a ViT [13] based image encoder, and a separate transformer [55] based language encoder. However, another work [38] recently discovered that transformer models pre-trained on language data could generalize well to visual tasks without altering the majority of parameters, suggesting patterns learned by one modality could transfer to another. These observations suggest that a unified encoder for CLIP may potentially be leveraged to promote learning commonly useful representations across modalities to realize performance and efficiency gains.

In this paper, we consequently investigate the feasibility of building a Modality-Shared CLIP (MS-CLIP) architecture, where parameters in vision encoder and text encoder can be shared. Through this framework, we seek answers to the following three questions: (*i*) Within each layer, which sub-module should be shared and which should not? (*ii*) In the CLIP training setting, which layers of the encoders for the two modalities should be shared, and which should be modality-specific? (*iii*) Lastly, what is the impact to performance and efficiency when including lightweight modality-specific auxiliary modules to accommodate specializations in each modality?

In order to answer these questions, we perform a comprehensive analysis on the impact of varying the degree of sharing of components across different layers. Our results show that in order to maximize performance, the input embedding, layer normalization (LN) [2], and output projection should be modality-specific. In contrast, all the remaining components can be shared across vision and text transformers, including the weights in self-attention and feed-forward modules. Addtionally, sharing all transformer layers even outperforms more complex strategies where we employ greedy selection of layers or use Neural Architecture Search (NAS) [12] to search for the optimal layer sharing policy.

Finally, we explore whether introducing lightweight modality-specific components to the shared backbone may yield a better balance between cross-modality modeling and specializations within each modality. Studied designs include: (*i*) *Early Specialization:* The first Transformer block is replaced by modules that are specialized for each modality, respectively. This includes a set of lightweight cascaded residual convolutional neural networks (CNNs) for vision, and a Transformer layer for language. This early adaption allows the representation in each modality to abstract to a higher level before unified encoding, and introduces shift invariance early in the visual branch. (*ii*) *Efficient Parallel Branch:* For the visual modality, we explore a lightweight multi-scale CNN network, parallel to the main modality-shared branch, and incorporate its multi-scale features to the main branch through depth-wise convolutional adaptors. This parallel branch enables augmenting the main branch with the benefits convolutions can instill from better modeling of spatial relationships.

We pre-train MS-CLIP architectures on YFCC100M [54] and a subset of Laion-400M [48] with a similar size, and evaluate on 25 downstream datasets that encompass a broad variety of vision tasks. The experimental results demonstrate that MS-CLIP architectures, while having fewer parameters, can outperform original CLIP on the majority of tasks, including zero-shot recognition, zero-shot retrieval, and linear probing. Moreover, in order to better understand why MS-CLIP architectures work so well, we conduct studies on the learned embedding space, namely with a measurement on multi-modal feature fusion degree [5], and quantitatively assess to what degree semantic structures (e.g., attention patterns) are shared across modalities. Our results reveal that sharing parameters can pull semantically-similar concepts from different modalities closer and facilitate the learning of common semantic structures (e.g., attention patterns).

The paper is subsequently organized as follows. Section 2 covers related work. In Sect. 3, we introduce the shareable modules and modality-specific designs. In Sect. 4, we present a rigorous study varying amount of parameters shared across modalities and measure the impact of both modality-shared parameters and modality-specific modules to downstream performance and efficiency. And we comprehensively compare proposed MS-CLIP architectures against CLIP on 25 downstream datasets. Section 5 concludes.

2 Related Work

Learning Visual Representation from Text: Our work is built on the recent success of learning visual representation from text supervision. VirTex [11] proposes to learn visual encoding through an image captioning objective. LocTex [34] introduces localized textual supervision to guide visual representation learning. Both studies are conducted on a relatively small scale. More recent work such as CLIP [47] and ALIGN [21] demonstrate that generic multi-modal pre-training could benefit from extremely large scale training (i.e., private datasets with hundreds of millions or billions of data pairs) and obtain strong zero-shot capability. They adopt a simple yet effective contrastive objective that attracts paired image and caption and repels unpaired ones. There have been several additional works following the line of CLIP/ALIGN [65]. Florence [64] and BASIC [45] scale up the dataset and training with various backbones. FILIP [63] focuses on generalizing the contrastive loss to local tokens for fine-grained supervision. DeCLIP [31], SLIP [40] and other recent works extend supervision signal from self-supervision, multi-view supervision, nearest-neighbor supervision, object detections [67], or external language knowledge [29]. Orthogonal to above mentioned works, this work focuses on the sharing of weights across vision and text modalities in large-scale contrastive pre-training.

Vision and Language Modeling: Another similar line of work is Vision-and-Language Pre-training (or VLP) [6,27,28,30,36,53,57–59,68], where both vision and language signals are fed into also a unified model to enable downstream multi-modal tasks. Moreover, [41] utilizes a set of shared tokens across different modalities to enable multi-modal fusion. But there are two main differences between VLPs and this work: First, in VLP approaches, the model input consists of both image and text modalities concurrently, where the model attends to both modalities at the same time (essentially conducting modality fusion). In CLIP and MS-CLIP, the Transformer's input is either image or text individually: each modality is processed in isolation, where the two modalities are never processed concurrently (except for computing the contrastive loss at the end). Secondly, VLP works focus on designing unified fusion modules to blend multi-modal input well and target at multi-modal tasks (*e.g.*, VQA, grounding), while the goal of our work is to allow parameter and knowledge sharing for uni-modal input and mainly serves visual-only downstream tasks.

Parameter-Sharing Across Modalities: As humans reason over various modalities simultaneously, sharing modules for multi-modal processing has attracted increasing interests recently from the research community. [26] proposes to share the parameters of Transformers across both layers and modalities to save parameters. They focus on video-audio multi-modal downstream tasks and have an additional multi-modal Transformer for modality fusion. [37] proposes to train a fully shared Multi-modal Transformer on 12 vision-language datasets. [20] further introduces a shared Transformer decoder for multi-task multi-modal learning. The most relevant work to ours is VATT [1]. VATT introduces a modality-agnostic transformer that can process video, text, and audio input and is pre-trained on a contrastive objective. The proposed model naively reuses the entire network for all modalities and yields results worse than the non-shared counterpart. In contrast, this work studies more than whether a model can be shared, but rather how various degrees of sharing and design nuances behave, and which of those design choices might be useful to improve performance.

3   Methods

3.1   Sharable Modules

Following [47], we use the Vision Transformer as the basic vision encoder (ViT-B/32 by default), and the transformer encoder as the basic text encoder, as shown in Fig. 1-1. The challenge is to merge these two architectures. To accomplish this, we adjust the hidden dimension of text transformer from 512 to 768 to match that in the vision transformer. The resulting additional baseline method is noted as CLIP (ViT-B/32, T768). After the adjustment, the resulting shared encoder uses 12 layers, with the vast majority of parameters able to be shared between two modalities, including the **attention modules, feedforward modules**, and **LayerNorm (LN) layers**. Modules that cannot be shared include

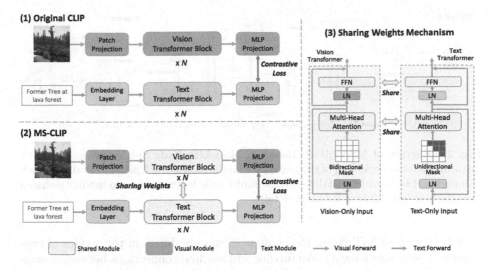

Fig. 1. Overview of the (1) vanilla CLIP and (2) our proposed baseline MS-CLIP, and (3) details of sharing mechanism MS-CLIP.

the input embedding layer (where the vision encoder deploys a projection layer to embed image patches, while the text encoder encodes word tokens), and the output projection layer.

We performed an experimental analysis to examine the impact of various degrees of weight sharing across modalities (see Sect. 4.3: *On Modality-Shared Components*). In summary, the observations of that study are as follows: (1) LNs need to be modality-specific while the rest can be modality-shared; (2) Sharing all layers is better than a subset. Subsequently, a model sharing the attention and feedforward modules, while keeping the LNs modality specific, across all 12 layers, is regarded as the baseline of our model family. We dub this Naïve modality sharing model MS-CLIP (see Fig. 1-2 and 1-3).

3.2   Modality-Specific Auxiliary Module Architecture

In this section we describe modifications introducing two lightweight modality-specific auxiliary modules, shown in Fig. 2. We name the full model with both modality-specific designs as MS-CLIP-S, where "S" indicates "Specialized branches".

Early Specialization: The first modality-specific design specializes only the first layer for visual and text modalities, leaving other layers shared. Concretely, on vision side, we employ a series of convolutional networks with residual connections as our specialization layer, in which the feature resolution is down-sampled and the channel dimension is increased. The detailed configuration is shown in Table 1, with ViT-B/32 as the visual encoder, inspired by [62]. For other visual

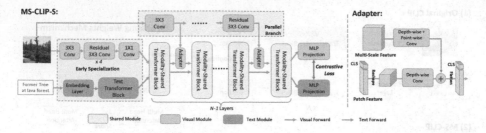

Fig. 2. Overview of MS-CLIP-S. Based on MS-CLIP, Early Specialization is further introduced at the beginning of the network. Simultaneously, an Efficient Parallel Branch is integrated to provide modality-specific multi-scale features to main modality-shared branch. See Sect. 3.2 text for more details.

encoders, such as ViT-B/16, the configuration only differs in the strides of convolutions (see Supplement). We further add residual connections between convolutional layers, which is empirically more stable for large-scale training. On the language side, we reuse the de-facto Transformer layer for language modeling.

Table 1. Setting of early specialization. $N \times N$ signifies the 2D kernel size of CNNs.

Module	Dim	Resolution
3×3 Conv	$3 \to 48$	$224 \to 112$
Residual 3×3 Conv	$48 \to 96$	$112 \to 56$
Residual 3×3 Conv	$96 \to 192$	$56 \to 28$
Residual 3×3 Conv	$192 \to 384$	$28 \to 14$
Residual 3×3 Conv	$384 \to 768$	$14 \to 7$
1×1 Conv	$768 \to 768$	$7 \to 7$
Total # Parameters	4.5M	

Table 2. Setting of efficient parallel branch. Fusion layer means fusing with which modality-shared layer.

Parallel module	Adapter module	Fusion layer	Resolution
3×3 Conv	16×16 DWConv	2	$224 \to 112$
Bottleneck 3×3 Conv	8×8 DWConv	4	$112 \to 56$
Bottleneck 3×3 Conv	4×4 DWConv	6	$56 \to 28$
Bottleneck 3×3 Conv	2×2 DWConv	8	$28 \to 14$
Bottleneck 3×3 Conv	1×1 DWConv	10	$14 \to 7$
Total # Parameters	3.9M		

Efficient Parallel Branch: For image representations, multi-scale information has been demonstrated to be valuable [4,52]. Vision Transformers [13], however, typically operate on a fixed scale. In recent works that introduce multi-scale information into ViT [33,60], the patch size is gradually reduced and the dimension of the channel is increased, stage by stage. Nevertheless, directly sharing weights between multi-scale ViT and the language Transformer is non-trivial, due to the discrepancy in their channel dimensions. Motivated by [16], we propose to have an auxiliary parallel vision branch alongside the shared Transformer, which consists of one convolution layer and four residual convolution layers, to decrease the resolution and increase the channel dimension (see Fig. 2). In contrast with the plain residual convolutions in Early Specialization, here we utilize the bottleneck design in ResNet [18] to be parameter efficient. The main function of the parallel branch is to supplement the shared branch with multi-scale features for image information. Therefore, we employ one adapter after each parallel layer to integrate features from varying scales into layers of the shared Transformer. For further efficiency, we adopt depth-wise convolutions (DWConv) and point-wise convolution (PWConv) in adapters to adjust the feature map size and depth. The adapter can be formulated as:

$$
\begin{aligned}
H_p' &= bn(\text{PWConv}(\text{DWConv}(H_p))) \\
H' &= ln(bn(\text{DWConv}(H)) + H_p'),
\end{aligned}
\tag{1}
$$

where H_p is the multi-scale feature in parallel branch, and (H, H') is the adapter's input and output, respectively. bn and ln denote batch normalization and layer normalization. Note that the CLS token is not fused with parallel branch and remains unchanged. The outputs of 5 parallel layers are fused with every other shared Transformer layers. The detailed configuration when ViT-B/32 being visual encoder is provided in Table 2. For other visual encoders, such as ViT-B/16, only the kernel size and stride differs, and we attach the configuration in Supplementary.

4   Experiments

Section 4.1 introduces the pre-training and evaluation setup. Sections 4.2 and 4.3 details the primary experimental results and related ablations. Section 4.4 presents experiments where the pretraining data is changed. Finally, Sect. 4.5 presents experiments to better elucidate why MS-CLIP works.

4.1   Setup

Training Details: Similar to the original CLIP paper [47], we maintain separate attention masks for image and text: vision transformer allows upper layers to attend to all tokens from lower layers with a bi-directional mask, while the mask in text transformer is auto-regressive. The optimizer is AdamW [35]. The learning rate is decayed from 1.6e−3 to 1.6e−4, with a cosine scheduler and a warm up at first 5 epochs. We train our models on 16 NVIDIA V100 GPUs with the batch size per GPU set to be 256. For MS-CLIP and MS-CLIP-S, the weight decay for non-shared parameters and shared parameters are separately set to 0.05 and 0.2. We found that a higher weight decay for shared parameters works better, simply because shared parameters are updated twice in each iteration, and a higher weight decay can mitigate over-fitting.

Pre-training Dataset: By default, we use YFCC100M [54] for pre-training. Following the filtering process in [47], we only keep image-text pairs where captions are in English. This leaves us around 22 million data pairs. All our results are reported on this data version, including the vanilla CLIP [47]. Subsequently, we also pre-train both our model and vanilla CLIP on a subset of the more recent dataset: LAION-400M [48]. More details can be found in Sect. 4.4.

Evaluation Datasets: In total, we adopt 25 public datasets for evaluation by either zero-shot learning or linear probing: ImageNet [10], Food-101 [3], CIFAR-10 [24], CIFAR-100 [24], SUN397 [61], Stanford Cars [23], FGVC Aircraft [39], Pascal Voc 2007 Classification [14], Describable Texture (DTD) [8], Oxford-IIIT Pets [44], Caltech-101 [15], Oxford Flowers 102 [42], MNIST [25], Facial Emotion Recognition (FER) [43], STL-10 [9], GTSRB [51], PatchCamelyon [56], UCF101 [50], Hateful Memes [22], Country211 [47], EuroSAT [19], Kitti-distance [17], Rendered-SST2 [49], Resisc45 [7], MSCOCO [32]. These datasets cover various categories, including generic objects, memes, scenes and etc. We perform linear probing with logistic regression on top of extracted image features, exactly following the protocol in the original CLIP paper [47]. For zero-shot recognition, we report zero-shot accuracy on the ImageNet [10] validation set. Following CLIP, we use an ensemble of multiple prompts to extract text features as category features. For zero-shot image-text retrieval, we report recall on MSCOCO [32]

4.2 Experimental Results

Compared Models: We conduct experiments on proposed MS-CLIP-S and vanilla CLIP [47]. Both ViT-B/32 and ViT-B/16 are adopted as visual encoders. As stated in Sect. 4.1, we strictly follow the implementation in [47].

Zero-Shot ImageNet Classification: The experimental results are reported in the row of ZS* in Table 3. By comparing the four columns, we find that, based on ViT-B/32 (ViT-B/16), MS-CLIP-S can outperform CLIP by 4.5 (2.1) percentage points, or 13.9% (5.6%) relative, in zero-shot recognition accuracy on ImageNet.

Linear Probing: To fully compare our model with vanilla CLIP, the results of linear probing on 24 various datasets are shown in Table 3. Overall, with ViT-B/32 (ViT-B/16) as backbone, MS-CLIP-S outperforms vanilla CLIP on 18 (17) out of 24 tasks, and the average improvement on 24 tasks is 1.62 (1.16) points.

Zero-Shot Image-Text Retrieval: We evaluate our MS-CLIP-S on two sub-tasks: image-to-text retrieval and text-to-image retrieval under zero-shot setting. The dataset we used is MSCOCO test set, which has 5,000 images. The comparison between MS-CLIP-S and vanilla CLIP, both pre-trained on YFCC, is shown in the last 4 rows of Table 3. With both ViT-B/32 and ViT-B/16, our MS-CLIP-S outperforms vanilla CLIP by a large margin across the board.

Table 3. Experimental results of zero-shot image classification (ZS*), linear probing and zero-shot image-text retrieval (ITR*) across 25 datasets.

Eval.	Datasets			CLIP (ViT-B/32)	MS-CLIP-S (ViT-B/32)	Δ	CLIP (ViT-B/16)	MS-CLIP-S (ViT-B/16)	Δ
Linear probing	Food-101			71.3	**76.0**	+4.7	80.1	81.5	+1.4
	SUN397			68.1	**71.7**	+3.6	72.3	**73.2**	+0.9
	Stanford Cars			21.8	**27.5**	+5.7	27.6	**32.0**	+4.4
	FGVC Aircraft			31.8	**32.9**	+1.1	33.6	**38.4**	+4.8
	Pascal Voc 2007			84.4	**86.1**	+1.7	85.6	**86.7**	+1.1
	DTD			64.1	**69.4**	+5.3	67.6	**71.9**	+4.3
	Oxford-IIIT Pets			61.1	**62.1**	+1.0	63.0	**63.7**	+0.7
	Caltech-101			**82.8**	81.6	−1.2	83.6	**83.8**	+0.2
	Oxford Flowers 102			90.7	**93.8**	+3.1	94.0	**95.2**	+1.2
	MNIST			96.5	**97.2**	+0.7	**96.9**	96.7	−0.2
	FER			**54.9**	53.6	−1.3	55.3	**56.2**	+0.9
	STL-10			**95.4**	95.1	−0.3	**96.9**	96.7	−0.2
	GTSRB			67.1	**69.9**	+2.8	72.5	**78.3**	+5.8
	PatchCamelyon			78.3	**81.3**	+3.0	**82**	80.4	−1.6
	UCF101			72.8	**74.6**	+1.8	74.6	**75.3**	+0.7
	CIFAR-10			**91.0**	87.2	−3.8	**91.1**	89.8	−1.3
	CIFAR-100			**71.9**	66.7	−5.2	**72.6**	71.5	−1.1
	Hateful Memes			50.6	**52.4**	+1.8	**51.6**	50.2	−1.4
	ImageNet			58.5	**63.7**	+5.1	64.7	66.7	+2.0
	Country211			19.9	**21.9**	+2.0	23.5	**23.6**	+0.1
	EuroSAT			**94.4**	93.5	−0.9	**94.6**	94.3	−0.3
	Kitti-distance			39.7	**45.1**	+5.4	35.7	**40.2**	+4.5
	Rendered-SST2			55.2	**56.0**	+0.8	56.8	**56.9**	+0.1
	Resisc45			83.3	**85.1**	+1.8	85.6	**86.5**	+0.9
	Avg.			66.9	**68.5**	+1.6	69.2	**70.4**	+1.2
ZS*	ImageNet			32.2	**36.7**	+4.5	36.9	**39.0**	+2.1
ITR*	MSCOCO	I2T	R@1	24.4	**28.5**	+4.1	27.5	**29.9**	+2.4
			R@5	48.5	**54.1**	+5.6	51.9	**56.8**	+4.9
		T2I	R@1	14.8	**19.4**	+4.6	17.7	**20.4**	+2.7
			R@5	34.9	**40.8**	+5.9	38.7	**42.9**	+4.2

4.3 Ablation Study

For the following ablation analysis, we use ViT-B/32, and report zero-shot accuracy on ImageNet validation set.

On Modality-Shared Components: We systematically study the impact of varying the degree of sharing of components across different layers, and make the following observations:

Table 4. Experimental results of sharing different components in transformer layer. First two rows are baselines without sharing. LN1 denotes the LN before Attn. LN2 denotes the LN before FFN.

Text width	# Params	Shared module	Non-shared module	Zero-shot Acc (%)
512	151M	–	Attn, FFN, LN1, LN2	32.15
768	209M	–	Attn, FFN, LN1, LN2	31.85
768	126M	Attn, FFN, LN1, LN2	–	28.40
768	126M	Attn, FFN, LN1	LN2	27.57
768	126M	Attn, FFN, LN2	LN1	32.16
768	126M	Attn, FFN	LN1, LN2	**32.99**

1. **LNs Need to be Modality-Specific.** We examine the shareable modules within each Transformer layer, excluding the input and output projection layers, which cannot be shared. As shown in Table 4, the first model variant shares all components (across all layers for simplicity), including two LN layers and transformation weights in the self-attention and feedforward modules, which results in worse performance (28.4%) compared to CLIP (ViT-B/32) (32.15%) and CLIP (ViT-B/32, T768)(31.85%). Then we examine making the two LN layers modality-specific, which yields better performance in both zero-shot accuracy (32.99%) and parameter efficiency. Note that the number of parameters in LNs is negligible compared with the transformation weights. Our observation echos the finding in FPT [38] that only tuning LNs in a mostly-frozen pre-trained language model yields satisfactory performance on vision tasks.

Table 5. Results of sharing different layers in transformer.

Share last X layers	12	11	10	8	6	4	2	0	NAS-Search
Zero-shot Acc (%)	32.99	31.25	32.21	32.39	32.85	30.91	nan	31.85	30.97
# Parameters	126M	132M	139M	153M	167M	181M	195M	209M	174M

2. **Less is More: Sharing all Layers is Better than Some.** We further study which layer should be modality-specific and which should be modality-shared. We conduct experiments on sharing the last N layers where N is ranging from 12 to 0. $N = 12$ indicates all layers are shared and $N = 0$ indicates the non-shared baseline CLIP (ViT-B/32, T768). Table 5 suggests that sharing all 12 layers performs the best while requiring the least number of parameters. This design of sharing all layers is what we refer to as MS-CLIP. Additionally, inspired by recent work on Neural Architecture Search (NAS) [12,66], we train a model that learns a policy to control which layer to (not) share via Gumbel Softmax [12]. Despite its sophistication, it still underperforms MS-CLIP.

On Modality-Specific Designs: We conduct experiments with the following settings: (1) CLIP (ViT-B/32): The same as [47], this uses ViT-B32 as the visual encoder, and Text Transformer with width set to 512. (2) CLIP (ViT-B/32, T768): This model sets the width of Text Transformer as 768 to unify the dimension of both encoders. (3) MS-CLIP (B/32): Compared with CLIP (ViT-B/32, T768), this model utilizes the modality-shared transformer blocks to substitute non-shared transformer blocks in visual and text encoders. We use the best setting found in Sect. 4.3: sharing all except for two layer normalizations. (4) MS-CLIP (B/32) + Early Specialization: Based on (3), we specialize the first layer of shared visual & text encoders following Sect. 3. (5) MS-CLIP (B/32) + Parallel Branch: Based on (3), we add a parallel branch to shared visual encoder. (6) MS-CLIP-S (B/32): Based on (3), we apply both early specialization and parallel branch to our shared visual & text encoders.

The result is summarized in Table 6. By comparing the 2nd row and the 3rd row, we find that directly increasing the capacity of the text transformer yields worse results. Then comparing 3-rd row and 4-th row, we find that sharing parameters in vision and text transformer improves the performance and even can outperform CLIP (ViT-B/32) (as also shown in previous ablation on modality-shared modules). Comparing 4th and 5th row against the 1st row, we notice that early specialization can contribute to 2.1% improvement with only a 4M parameters increase and auxiliary parallel branch on vision has a 1.1% boost. The full model in 6th row further advances to 36.66%, a 4.5% absolute gain over the baseline CLIP (ViT-B/32).

Table 6. Ablation on modality-specific designs.

Module name	# Parameters	Zero-shot Acc (%)
CLIP (ViT-B/32)	151M	32.15
CLIP (ViT-B/32, T768)	209M	31.85
MS-CLIP (B/32)	126M	32.99
$\cdots$ w/ Early specialization	129M	35.18
$\cdots$ w/ Parallel branch	129M	34.18
MS-CLIP-S (B/32)	132M	**36.66**

Table 7. Results of models pre-trained on Laion-20M: zero-shot image classification, linear probing and zero-shot image-text retrieval (ITR*).

	ImageNet zero-shot	MSCOCO Test ITR* I2T				Linear probing on 24 datasets	
	Acc (%)	R@1	R@5	R@1	R@5	Average	#Wins
CLIP	35.5	24.7	48.1	16.2	35.8	70.5	5
MS-CLIP-S	**40.2**	**31.2**	**57.4**	**20.6**	**43.6**	**73.3**	**19**
Δ	+4.7	+6.5	+9.3	+4.4	+7.8	+2.8	+14

4.4 Pre-training Data Quality

To verify that our proposed model can generalize to pre-training datasets of various quality, we pre-train both vanilla CLIP (ViT-B/32) and MS-CLIP-S (ViT-B/32) on a subset of the recently released public Laion-400M dataset [48]. This proof-of-concept subset contains 20M randomly-sampled image-caption pairs from Laion-400M, similar to the size of filtered YFCC. We name it Laion20M. The complete experimental results are shown in Table 7, where our model outperforms vanilla CLIP substantially. Since in the building of Laion-400M, a pre-trained CLIP is used to filter out the noisy image-text pairs, the dataset is believed to have higher data quality. This can also be proved by comparing vanilla CLIP's results in Laion and YFCC. Comparing Table 7 and Table 3 side by side, we find that the improvement brought by proposed MS-CLIP-S pre-trained on Laion-20M is generally higher than on YFCC (22M). It might imply that our method can benefit more when pre-training data quality is higher. Detailed performance of linear probing on 24 datasets is added in Supplementary.

4.5 Further Analysis

There are likely multiple reasons that explain observed improvements in performance. Firstly, sharing the majority of parameters across vision and language can implicitly encourage the model to focus on the common pattern across two modalities and alleviate overfitting of trivial vision (*e.g.*, illumination) or language cues (*e.g.* stop words). Additionally, the auxiliary modality-specific modules, *Early Specialization* and *Parallel Branch*, provide vision-specific multi-scale features and language-specific features to complement the shared modules. To have an in-depth understanding, we perform the following further analysis:

Table 8. Layer-wise NMI scores of models.

Layer	0	1	2	3	4	5	6	7	8	9	10	11	Avg.
CLIP (ViT-B/32, T768)	0.586	0.387	0.265	0.252	0.255	0.241	0.239	0.243	0.235	0.23	0.227	0.185	0.278
MS-CLIP (B/32)	0.589	0.332	0.235	0.211	0.2	0.21	0.2	0.202	0.214	0.197	0.192	0.173	0.246
··· w/ Early specialization	0.471	0.348	0.215	0.21	0.218	0.221	0.22	0.213	0.19	0.183	0.179	0.161	**0.235**
MS-CLIP-S (B/32)	0.519	0.536	0.243	0.216	0.199	0.221	0.19	0.247	0.216	0.215	0.224	0.217	0.270

NMI Score: Shared Model Exhibits Higher Multi-modal Fusion Degree. To probe the multi-modal fusion degree, following [5], we measure the Normalized Mutual Information (NMI) between visual features and text features at each layer. For each image-caption pair, we use K-means algorithm (K = 2) to group all feature vectors from the forward pass of visual input and text input into 2 clusters. Then, NMI is applied to measure the difference between the generated clusters and ground-truth clusters. The higher the NMI score is, the easier the visual features and text features can be separated, and the lower the multi-modal fusion degree is.

NMI scores are then used to probe the multi-modal fusion degree of the shared model (MS-CLIP (B/32)) vs. non-shared model (CLIP (ViT-B/32, T768)). Here we choose CLIP (ViT-B/32, T768) instead of CLIP (ViT-B/32) in that the feature dimensions of two modalities have to be the same for clustering. The measurement is performed on randomly sampled 50k image-caption pairs from YFCC100M dataset. NMI scores of all 12 layers and the average are listed in the first two rows of Table 8. Shared model has lower NMI scores than original CLIP on almost all the layers and the average, indicating a higher degree of multi-modal fusion.

Following the same procedure as above, we further report the NMI scores of MS-CLIP (B/32) + Early Specialization and MS-CLIP-S (B/32) (see Table 8). The result shows that sharing parameters and introducing early specialization can improve the multi-modal fusion degree, which coincides with our hypothesis mentioned above. However, adding parallel branch leads to a lower fusion score. This is somewhat conflicting with what we see in Table 6, where adding parallel branch enhances the learned representation. In the following subsection, we explore other metrics to further probe into what contributes to this behavior.

Table 9. Common semantic structure distance

Layer	0	1	2	3	4	5	6	7	8	9	10	11	Avg.
CLIP (ViT-B/32)	0.18	0.203	0.227	0.186	0.178	0.164	0.118	0.103	0.106	0.109	0.105	0.074	0.143
MS-CLIP (B/32)	0.175	0.128	0.153	0.132	0.136	0.136	0.106	0.119	0.092	0.106	0.083	0.058	0.113
... w/ Early specialization	–	0.107	0.142	0.16	0.12	0.12	0.103	0.103	0.096	0.111	0.11	0.058	0.111
MS-CLIP-S (B/32)	–	0.085	0.162	0.105	0.102	0.103	0.105	0.114	0.093	0.094	0.093	0.061	**0.101**

Multi-modal Common Semantic Structure: The Integration of Modality-Shared and Modality-Specific Modules Learns Better Common Patterns. One of the hypotheses on why MS-CLIP architectures perform better is that they better capture the common semantic structures inherent to concepts from different modalities.

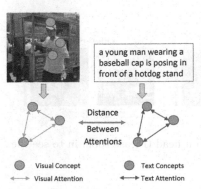

Fig. 3. Diagram of computing common semantic structure distance.

To justify this hypothesis, we propose to measure the similarity between attention weights on visual concepts and the corresponding language concepts (see Fig. 3). The measurement is performed on a surrogate dataset named Flick30K-Entities [46], where object regions in each image are grounded to their corresponding phrases in a caption, in the form of bounding boxes. Given an image, assuming there are grounded object regions (visual concepts) $\{vc_1, vc_2, ..., vc_n\}$ and corresponding object words (language concepts) $\{tc_1, tc_2, ..., tc_n\}$, where tc_i is associated with vc_i semantically. In the h-th head of l-th attention layer, we denote the raw visual attention matrix as M^{lh} and the raw text attention matrix as K^{lh}. We then regard the attention value between tc_i and tc_j as K^{lh}_{ij}, and attention value between vc_i and vc_j as M^{lh}_{ij}. We extract the attention values from concept i to all other concepts (i.e., j) and normalize for visual attention and language attention, respectively (denoted as "attention vectors"). The final attention vectors are averaged over all heads in that attention layer. We compute the attention vectors for all concept pairs i. Finally, we measure the $l1$ distance between the visual attention vector and the language attention vector and sum them up over all the concept pairs and treat it as the Common Semantic Structure (CSC) distance of that attention layer. A lower CSC distance means more common attention patterns learned across modalities. The whole process can be formulated as:

$$dis^l_{ij} = | \sum_{h=1}^{H} \frac{1}{H} softmax_i(M^{lh}_{ij}) - \sum_{h=1}^{H} \frac{1}{H} softmax_i(K^{lh}_{ij})| \qquad (2)$$

$$CSC^l = dis^l = \sum_{i=1}^{n} \sum_{j=1}^{n} (dis^l_{ij}). \qquad (3)$$

The layer-wise CSC distance of CLIP (ViT-B/32), MS-CLIP (B/32), MS-CLIP (B/32) + Early Specialization and MS-CLIP-S (B/32) are reported in Table 9. The first layers of MS-CLIP (B/32) + Early Specialization and MS-CLIP-S (B/32) are omitted as their vision branch do not contain any attention weights. The average score is computed based on the CSC distance on their last 11 layers. We find that our proposed modules lower the CSC distance and learn more modality-agnostic representation. Unsurprisingly, sharing parameters can enforce the attention to learn more common information. At the same time, it might reduce the overfitting brought by training separately. As for our proposed modality-specific modules, we suspect that these well designed modules can account for the discrepancy of individual modalities, especially by the vision-specific multi-scale feature, and thus facilitate the learning of the common patterns with the share component.

Fig. 4. Visualized attention maps of shared attention head (Please zoom in to see the caption).

Visualization of Shared Attention Head: In order to intuitively understand how shared attention module works, we visualize the visual attention patterns and text attention patterns of the same shared attention head during inference. More precisely, for vision, we visualize the attention weights at the final layer from the *CLS* token to all its input tokens. For text, we perform the same except on the *EOS* token. Note that both *CLS* token and *EOS* token are treated as the feature representation. Results on MS-CLIP-S (B/32) are shown in Fig. 4. Interestingly, some heads are able to attend on the same concepts from different modalities. We take Fig. 4(a) as an example. Given the image and caption respectively as input, the 1st head of 9th attention layer gives the highest attention value to the region of "cat" in image and token "cats" in text. It suggests the learning of co-reference across modalities.

5 Conclusion

We propose MS-CLIP, a modality-shared contrastive language-image pre-training approach, where most parameters in vision and text encoders are shared. To explore how many parameters/layers can be shared across modalities, we carefully investigate various architectural design choices through extensive experiments. In addition, we propose two modality-specific auxiliary designs: Early Specialization and Auxiliary Parallel Branch. Experiments on both zero-shot recognition and linear probing demonstrate the superiority of MS-CLIP architectures over the vanilla CLIP in both effectiveness and parameter efficiency. Finally, further analysis into the proposed architecture shows that sharing parameters can help map the two modalities into a closer embedding space and promote learning a common semantic structure.

Acknowledgement. This work is done during Haoxuan's internship at Microsoft. This work is also supported in part by DARPA MCS program under Cooperative Agreement N66001-19-2-4032.

References

1. Akbari, H., et al.: VATT: transformers for multimodal self-supervised learning from raw video, audio and text. arXiv preprint arXiv:2104.11178 (2021)
2. Ba, J.L., Kiros, J.R., Hinton, G.E.: Layer normalization. arXiv preprint arXiv:1607.06450 (2016)
3. Bossard, L., Guillaumin, M., Van Gool, L.: Food-101 – mining discriminative components with random forests. In: Fleet, D., Pajdla, T., Schiele, B., Tuytelaars, T. (eds.) ECCV 2014. LNCS, vol. 8694, pp. 446–461. Springer, Cham (2014). https://doi.org/10.1007/978-3-319-10599-4_29
4. Cai, Z., Fan, Q., Feris, R.S., Vasconcelos, N.: A unified multi-scale deep convolutional neural network for fast object detection. In: Leibe, B., Matas, J., Sebe, N., Welling, M. (eds.) ECCV 2016. LNCS, vol. 9908, pp. 354–370. Springer, Cham (2016). https://doi.org/10.1007/978-3-319-46493-0_22

5. Cao, J., Gan, Z., Cheng, Y., Yu, L., Chen, Y.-C., Liu, J.: Behind the scene: revealing the secrets of pre-trained vision-and-language models. In: Vedaldi, A., Bischof, H., Brox, T., Frahm, J.-M. (eds.) ECCV 2020. LNCS, vol. 12351, pp. 565–580. Springer, Cham (2020). https://doi.org/10.1007/978-3-030-58539-6_34

6. Chen, Y.C., et al.: UNITER: learning universal image-text representations (2019)

7. Cheng, G., Han, J., Lu, X.: Remote sensing image scene classification: benchmark and state of the art. Proc. IEEE **105**(10), 1865–1883 (2017)

8. Cimpoi, M., Maji, S., Kokkinos, I., Mohamed, S., Vedaldi, A.: Describing textures in the wild. In: Proceedings of the IEEE Conference on Computer Vision and Pattern Recognition (CVPR) (2014)

9. Coates, A., Ng, A., Lee, H.: An analysis of single-layer networks in unsupervised feature learning. In: Proceedings of the Fourteenth International Conference on Artificial Intelligence and Statistics. JMLR Workshop and Conference Proceedings, pp. 215–223 (2011)

10. Deng, J., Dong, W., Socher, R., Li, L.J., Li, K., Fei-Fei, L.: ImageNet: a large-scale hierarchical image database. In: 2009 IEEE Conference on Computer Vision and Pattern Recognition, pp. 248–255. IEEE (2009)

11. Desai, K., Johnson, J.: VirTex: learning visual representations from textual annotations. In: Proceedings of the IEEE/CVF Conference on Computer Vision and Pattern Recognition, pp. 11162–11173 (2021)

12. Dong, X., Yang, Y.: Searching for a robust neural architecture in four GPU hours. In: Proceedings of the IEEE/CVF Conference on Computer Vision and Pattern Recognition, pp. 1761–1770 (2019)

13. Dosovitskiy, A., et al.: An image is worth 16x16 words: transformers for image recognition at scale. arXiv preprint arXiv:2010.11929 (2020)

14. Everingham, M., Van Gool, L., Williams, C.K.I., Winn, J., Zisserman, A.: The PASCAL Visual Object Classes Challenge 2007 (VOC2007) Results (2007). http://www.pascal-network.org/challenges/VOC/voc2007/workshop/index.html

15. Fei-Fei, L., Fergus, R., Perona, P.: Learning generative visual models from few training examples: an incremental Bayesian approach tested on 101 object categories. In: 2004 Conference on Computer Vision and Pattern Recognition Workshop, p. 178. IEEE (2004)

16. Feichtenhofer, C., Fan, H., Malik, J., He, K.: SlowFast networks for video recognition. In: Proceedings of the IEEE/CVF International Conference on Computer Vision, pp. 6202–6211 (2019)

17. Geiger, A., Lenz, P., Urtasun, R.: Are we ready for autonomous driving? The kitti vision benchmark suite. In: 2012 IEEE Conference on Computer Vision And Pattern Recognition, pp. 3354–3361. IEEE (2012)

18. He, K., Zhang, X., Ren, S., Sun, J.: Deep residual learning for image recognition. In: Proceedings of the IEEE Conference on Computer Vision and Pattern Recognition, pp. 770–778 (2016)

19. Helber, P., Bischke, B., Dengel, A., Borth, D.: EuroSAT: a novel dataset and deep learning benchmark for land use and land cover classification. IEEE J. Sel. Topics Appl. Earth Obs. Remote Sens. **12**(7), 2217–2226 (2019)

20. Hu, R., Singh, A.: Unit: multimodal multitask learning with a unified transformer. arXiv preprint arXiv:2102.10772 (2021)

21. Jia, C., et al.: Scaling up visual and vision-language representation learning with noisy text supervision. arXiv preprint arXiv:2102.05918 (2021)

22. Kiela, D., et al.: The hateful memes challenge: detecting hate speech in multimodal memes. arXiv preprint arXiv:2005.04790 (2020)

23. Krause, J., Stark, M., Deng, J., Fei-Fei, L.: 3D object representations for fine-grained categorization. In: Proceedings of the IEEE International Conference on Computer Vision Workshops, pp. 554–561 (2013)
24. Krizhevsky, A., Hinton, G., et al.: Learning multiple layers of features from tiny images (2009)
25. LeCun, Y., Bottou, L., Bengio, Y., Haffner, P.: Gradient-based learning applied to document recognition. Proc. IEEE **86**(11), 2278–2324 (1998)
26. Lee, S., Yu, Y., Kim, G., Breuel, T., Kautz, J., Song, Y.: Parameter efficient multimodal transformers for video representation learning. arXiv preprint arXiv:2012.04124 (2020)
27. Li, J., Li, D., Xiong, C., Hoi, S.: BLIP: bootstrapping language-image pre-training for unified vision-language understanding and generation. arXiv preprint arXiv:2201.12086 (2022)
28. Li, L.H., Yatskar, M., Yin, D., Hsieh, C.J., Chang, K.W.: VisualBERT: a simple and performant baseline for vision and language. arXiv preprint arXiv:1908.03557 (2019)
29. Li, M., et al.: Clip-event: connecting text and images with event structures. In: Proceedings of the IEEE/CVF Conference on Computer Vision and Pattern Recognition, pp. 16420–16429 (2022)
30. Li, W., et al.: UNIMO: towards unified-modal understanding and generation via cross-modal contrastive learning. arXiv preprint arXiv:2012.15409 (2020)
31. Li, Y., et al.: Supervision exists everywhere: a data efficient contrastive language-image pre-training paradigm. arXiv preprint arXiv:2110.05208 (2021)
32. Lin, T.-Y., et al.: Microsoft COCO: common objects in context. In: Fleet, D., Pajdla, T., Schiele, B., Tuytelaars, T. (eds.) ECCV 2014. LNCS, vol. 8693, pp. 740–755. Springer, Cham (2014). https://doi.org/10.1007/978-3-319-10602-1_48
33. Liu, Z., et al.: Swin transformer: hierarchical vision transformer using shifted windows. arXiv preprint arXiv:2103.14030 (2021)
34. Liu, Z., Stent, S., Li, J., Gideon, J., Han, S.: LocTex: learning data-efficient visual representations from localized textual supervision. arXiv preprint arXiv:2108.11950 (2021)
35. Loshchilov, I., Hutter, F.: Decoupled weight decay regularization. arXiv preprint arXiv:1711.05101 (2017)
36. Lu, J., Batra, D., Parikh, D., Lee, S.: ViLBERT: pretraining task-agnostic visiolinguistic representations for vision-and-language tasks. arXiv preprint arXiv:1908.02265 (2019)
37. Lu, J., Goswami, V., Rohrbach, M., Parikh, D., Lee, S.: 12-in-1: multi-task vision and language representation learning. In: Proceedings of the IEEE/CVF Conference on Computer Vision and Pattern Recognition, pp. 10437–10446 (2020)
38. Lu, K., Grover, A., Abbeel, P., Mordatch, I.: Pretrained transformers as universal computation engines. arXiv preprint arXiv:2103.05247 (2021)
39. Maji, S., Rahtu, E., Kannala, J., Blaschko, M., Vedaldi, A.: Fine-grained visual classification of aircraft. arXiv preprint arXiv:1306.5151 (2013)
40. Mu, N., Kirillov, A., Wagner, D., Xie, S.: Slip: self-supervision meets language-image pre-training. arXiv preprint arXiv:2112.12750 (2021)
41. Nagrani, A., Yang, S., Arnab, A., Jansen, A., Schmid, C., Sun, C.: Attention bottlenecks for multimodal fusion. arXiv preprint arXiv:2107.00135 (2021)
42. Nilsback, M.E., Zisserman, A.: Automated flower classification over a large number of classes. In: 2008 Sixth Indian Conference on Computer Vision, Graphics & Image Processing, pp. 722–729. IEEE (2008)

43. Pantic, M., Valstar, M., Rademaker, R., Maat, L.: Web-based database for facial expression analysis. In: 2005 IEEE International Conference on Multimedia and Expo, pp. 5-pp. IEEE (2005)
44. Parkhi, O.M., Vedaldi, A., Zisserman, A., Jawahar, C.: Cats and dogs. In: 2012 IEEE Conference on Computer Vision and Pattern Recognition, pp. 3498–3505. IEEE (2012)
45. Pham, H., et al.: Combined scaling for zero-shot transfer learning. arXiv preprint arXiv:2111.10050 (2021)
46. Plummer, B.A., Wang, L., Cervantes, C.M., Caicedo, J.C., Hockenmaier, J., Lazebnik, S.: Flickr30k entities: collecting region-to-phrase correspondences for richer image-to-sentence models. In: Proceedings of the IEEE International Conference on Computer Vision, pp. 2641–2649 (2015)
47. Radford, A., et al.: Learning transferable visual models from natural language supervision. arXiv preprint arXiv:2103.00020 (2021)
48. Schuhmann, C., et al.: LAION-400M: open dataset of clip-filtered 400 million image-text pairs. arXiv preprint arXiv:2111.02114 (2021)
49. Socher, R., et al.: Recursive deep models for semantic compositionality over a sentiment treebank. In: Proceedings of the 2013 Conference on Empirical Methods in Natural Language Processing, pp. 1631–1642 (2013)
50. Soomro, K., Zamir, A.R., Shah, M.: UCF101: a dataset of 101 human actions classes from videos in the wild. arXiv preprint arXiv:1212.0402 (2012)
51. Stallkamp, J., Schlipsing, M., Salmen, J., Igel, C.: Man vs. computer: benchmarking machine learning algorithms for traffic sign recognition. Neural Netw. **32**, 323–332 (2012)
52. Szegedy, C., et al.: Going deeper with convolutions. In: Proceedings of the IEEE Conference on Computer Vision and Pattern Recognition, pp. 1–9 (2015)
53. Tan, H., Bansal, M.: LXMERT: learning cross-modality encoder representations from transformers. arXiv preprint arXiv:1908.07490 (2019)
54. Thomee, B., et al.: YFCC100M: the new data in multimedia research. Commun. ACM **59**(2), 64–73 (2016)
55. Vaswani, A., et al.: Attention is all you need. In: Advances in Neural Information Processing Systems, pp. 5998–6008 (2017)
56. Veeling, B.S., Linmans, J., Winkens, J., Cohen, T., Welling, M.: Rotation equivariant CNNs for digital pathology, June 2018
57. Wang, J., et al.: UFO: a unified transformer for vision-language representation learning. arXiv preprint arXiv:2111.10023 (2021)
58. Wang, W., Bao, H., Dong, L., Wei, F.: VLMO: unified vision-language pre-training with mixture-of-modality-experts. arXiv preprint arXiv:2111.02358 (2021)
59. Wang, Z., Yu, J., Yu, A.W., Dai, Z., Tsvetkov, Y., Cao, Y.: SimVLM: simple visual language model pretraining with weak supervision. arXiv preprint arXiv:2108.10904 (2021)
60. Wu, H., et al.: CVT: introducing convolutions to vision transformers. arXiv preprint arXiv:2103.15808 (2021)
61. Xiao, J., Hays, J., Ehinger, K.A., Oliva, A., Torralba, A.: Sun database: large-scale scene recognition from abbey to zoo. In: 2010 IEEE Computer Society Conference on Computer Vision and Pattern Recognition, pp. 3485–3492. IEEE (2010)
62. Xiao, T., Singh, M., Mintun, E., Darrell, T., Dollár, P., Girshick, R.: Early convolutions help transformers see better. arXiv preprint arXiv:2106.14881 (2021)
63. Yao, L., et al.: FILIP: fine-grained interactive language-image pre-training. arXiv preprint arXiv:2111.07783 (2021)

64. Yuan, L., et al.: Florence: a new foundation model for computer vision. arXiv preprint arXiv:2111.11432 (2021)
65. Zhai, X., et al.: LiT: zero-shot transfer with locked-image text tuning. arXiv preprint arXiv:2111.07991 (2021)
66. Zheng, X., et al.: MIGO-NAS: towards fast and generalizable neural architecture search. IEEE Trans. Pattern Anal. Mach. Intell. **43**(9), 2936–2952 (2021)
67. Zhong, Y., et al.: RegionCLIP: region-based language-image pretraining. In: Proceedings of the IEEE/CVF Conference on Computer Vision and Pattern Recognition, pp. 16793–16803 (2022)
68. Zhou, L., Palangi, H., Zhang, L., Hu, H., Corso, J., Gao, J.: Unified vision-language pre-training for image captioning and VQA. In: Proceedings of the AAAI Conference on Artificial Intelligence, vol. 34, pp. 13041–13049 (2020)

Contrasting Quadratic Assignments for Set-Based Representation Learning

Artem Moskalev[1]([✉]), Ivan Sosnovik[1], Volker Fischer[2], and Arnold Smeulders[1]

[1] UvA-Bosch Delta Lab, University of Amsterdam, Amsterdam, The Netherlands
{a.moskalev,i.sosnovik,a.w.m.smeulders}@uva.nl
[2] Bosch Center for AI (BCAI), Pittsburgh, USA
volker.fischer@de.bosch.com

Abstract. The standard approach to contrastive learning is to maximize the agreement between different views of the data. The views are ordered in pairs, such that they are either positive, encoding different views of the same object, or negative, corresponding to views of different objects. The supervisory signal comes from maximizing the total similarity over positive pairs, while the negative pairs are needed to avoid collapse. In this work, we note that the approach of considering individual pairs cannot account for both intra-set and inter-set similarities when the sets are formed from the views of the data. It thus limits the information content of the supervisory signal available to train representations. We propose to go beyond contrasting individual pairs of objects by focusing on contrasting objects as sets. For this, we use combinatorial quadratic assignment theory designed to evaluate set and graph similarities and derive set-contrastive objective as a regularizer for contrastive learning methods. We conduct experiments and demonstrate that our method improves learned representations for the tasks of metric learning and self-supervised classification.

Keywords: Contrastive learning · Representation learning · Self-supervised · Optimal assignment

1 Introduction

The common approach to contrastive learning is to maximize the agreement between individual views of the data [28,33]. The views are ordered in pairs, such that they either positive, encoding different views of the same object, or negative, corresponding to views of different objects. The pairs are compared against one another by a contrastive loss-objective [12,39,44]. Contrastive learning was successfully applied among others in metric learning [23], self-supervised

Source code: https://www.github.com/amoskalev/contrasting_quadratic.

Supplementary Information The online version contains supplementary material available at https://doi.org/10.1007/978-3-031-19812-0_6.

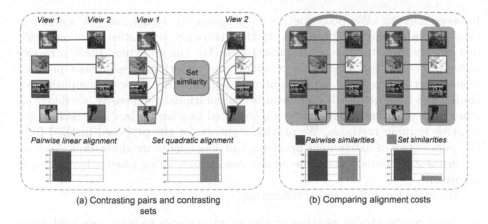

(a) Contrasting pairs and contrasting sets

(b) Comparing alignment costs

Fig. 1. (a) Contrasting views by similarity over pairs (pairwise linear alignment) versus similarity over sets with set-alignment (set-wise quadratic alignment). (b) Comparing total pairwise similarities versus set similarities for different configurations of representation graphs. In both configurations, the total similarity over pairs remains the same, being unable to discriminate between the internal structures of different views as quadratic alignment can.

classification [12, 21], and pre-training for dense prediction tasks [45]. However, when two views of an object are drastically different, the view of object A will resemble the same view of object B much more than it resembles the other view of object A. By comparing individual pairs, the common patterns in the differences between two views will not be exploited. In this paper, we propose to go beyond contrasting individual pairs of objects and focus on contrasting sets of objects.

In contrastive learning, the best alignment of objects follows from maximizing the total similarity over positive pairs, while the negative pairs are needed to encourage diversity. The diversity in representations is there to avoid collapse [42]. We note that one number, the total similarity from contrasting individual pairs, cannot both account for the inter-set similarities of the objects from the same view and the intra-set similarities with objects from another view. Therefore, considering the total similarity over pairs essentially limits the information content of the supervisory signal available to the model. We aim to exploit the information from contrasting sets of objects rather than contrasting objects pairwise only, further illustrated in Fig. 1a. From the perspective of set assignment theory [8], two sets may expose the same linear pairwise alignment costs, yet have different internal structures and hence have different set alignment costs, see Fig. 1b. Therefore, contrastive learning from sets provides a richer supervisory signal.

To contrast objects as sets, we turn to combinatorial quadratic assignment theory [8] designed to evaluate set and graph similarities. Quadratic assignment has advanced from linear assignment [9], which relies on pairwise similarities between objects. We pose contrastive learning by structural risk minimization [43] in assignment problems. In this, pairwise contrastive learning methods emerge from the linear assignment case. We aim to extend the contrastive objective to the set level by generalizing the underlying assignment problem from linear to quadratic, as illustrated in Fig. 1a. Since directly computing set similarities from quadratic alignment is computationally expensive, we derive an efficient approximation. It can be implemented as a regularizer for existing contrastive learning methods. We provide a theory for the proposed method from the perspective of assignment problems and dependence maximization. And, we experimentally demonstrate the advantages of contrasting objects by quadratic alignment.

We make the following contributions:

- Using combinatorial assignment theory, we propose to learn representations by contrasting objects as sets rather than as pairs of individual instances.
- We propose a computationally efficient implementation, where the set contrastive part is implemented as a regularizer for existing contrastive learning methods.
- We demonstrate that set-contrastive regularization improves recent contrastive learning methods for the tasks of metric learning and self-supervised classification.

As a byproduct of viewing representation learning through the lens of combinatorial assignment theory, we additionally propose SparseCLR contrastive loss, a modification of the popular InfoNCE [39] objective. Different from InfoNCE, SparseCLR enjoys sparse support over negative pairs, which permits better use of hard negative examples. Our experiments demonstrate that such an approach improves the quality of learned representations for self-supervised classification.

2　Related Work

2.1　Contrastive Learning

In contrastive learning, a model is trained to align representations of the data from different views (modalities), which dates back to the work of Becker *et al.* [4]. Contrastive learning is made up of a joint embedding architecture like Siamese networks [7] and a contrastive objective function. The network maps different views of the data into the embedding space, where the alignment between embeddings is measured by contrasting positive and negative pairs. The pairs either from a complete set of observations [12,13,40,41] or from partially-complete views [26,32,46,47]. And as a contrastive objective, contrastive loss functions are used [12,21,39,44]. Van den Oord *et al.* [39] derived the InfoNCE contrastive loss as a mutual information lower bound between different views of the signal. In computer vision, Chen *et al.* apply the InfoNCE to contrast the images with their distorted version. In PIRL [37], the authors propose to maintain a memory bank of image representations to improve the generalization of the model by sampling negative samples better. Along the same lines, MoCO [14,21] proposes a running queue of negative samples and a momentum-encoder to increase the contrasting effect of negative pairs. All of these contrastive methods are based on measuring the alignment between individual pairs of objects. This approach does not account for patterns in the views of objects beyond contrasting them pairwise. We aim to extend contrastive learning to include set similarities.

2.2 Information Maximization Methods

In contrastive learning information maximization methods aim to improve contrastive representations by maximizing the information content of the embeddings [2]. In W-MSE [16], batch representations are passed through a whitening, Karhunen-Loève transformation before computing the contrastive loss. Such transformations help to avoid collapsing representations when the contrastive objective can be minimized without learning the discriminative representations. In [48], the authors follow the redundancy-reduction principle to design a loss function to bring the cross-correlation matrix of representations from different views close to identity. In the recent work of Zbontar *et al.*, the authors extend the above formulation of Barlow Twins with an explicit variance term, which helps to stabilize the training. In this paper, we also seek to maximize the information content of the embeddings but we aim to do so by computing the rich representation of set similarities between data views. In contrast to existing methods, our approach does not require any additional transformations like whitening and can be easily incorporated into other contrastive learning methods.

2.3 Distillation Methods

Another branch of self-supervised methods is not based on contrastive learning but rather based on knowledge distillation [24]. Instead of contrasting positive and negative pairs of samples, these methods try to predict one positive view from another. We discuss them here for completeness. BYOL [19] uses a student network that learns to predict the output of a teacher network. SimSiam [15] simplifies the BYOL by demonstrating that the stop-gradient operation suffices to learn a generalized representation from distillation. In SWaV [11], the authors combine online clustering and distillation by predicting swapped cluster assignments. These self-supervised methods have demonstrated promising results in the task of learning representations. We prefer to follow a different path of contrastive learning, where we do not exclude the possibility that set-based methods may also be applicable to distillation.

2.4 Assignment Theory

Generally, optimal assignment problems can be categorized into linear and higher-order assignments. Linear assignment problems can be viewed as a transportation problem over a bipartite graph, where the transportation distances are defined on individual pairs of nodes. Linear assignment problems have many real-world applications such as scheduling or vehicle routing, we refer to [9]. Higher-order or in particular Quadratic assignment problems [8,17] extend the domain of the transportation distances from individual pairs to sets of objects. Where the linear assignment problem seeks to optimally match individual instances, its quadratic counterpart matches the inter-connected graphs of instances, bringing additional structure to the task. In this work, we aim to exploit linear and quadratic assignment theory to rethink contrastive learning.

2.5 Structured Predictions

In a structured prediction problem, the goal is to learn a structured object such as a sequence, a tree, or a permutation matrix [1]. Training a structure is non-trivial as one has to compute the loss on the manifold defined by the structured output space. In the seminal work of Tsochantaridis *et al.* [43], the authors derive a structured loss for support vector machines and apply it to a sequence labeling task. Later, structured prediction was applied to learn parameters of constraint optimization problems [6,20]. In this work, we utilize structured prediction principles to implement set similarities into contrastive losses.

3   Background

We start by formally introducing contrastive learning and linear assignment problems. Then, we argue about the connection between these two problems and demonstrate how one leads to another. This connection is essential for the derivation of our contrastive method.

3.1   Contrastive Representation Learning

Consider a dataset $\mathcal{D} = \{d_i\}_{i=1}^{N}$ and an encoder function $f_\theta : \mathcal{D} \longrightarrow \mathbb{R}^{N \times E}$, which outputs an embedding vector of dimension E for each of the objects in $\mathcal{D}$. The task is to learn a such f_θ that embeddings of objects belonging to the same category are pulled together, while the embeddings of objects from different categories are pushed apart.

As category labels are not available during training, the common strategy is to maximize the agreement between different views of the instances, i.e. to maximize the mutual information between different data modalities. The mutual information between two latent variables X, Y, can be expressed as:

$$MI(X, Y) = H(X) - H(X|Y) \tag{1}$$

where X and Y correspond to representations of two different views of a dataset. Minimizing the conditional entropy $H(X|Y)$ aims at reducing uncertainty in the representations from one view given the representations of another, while $H(X)$ enforces the diversity in representations and prevents trivial solutions. In practice, sample-based estimators of the mutual information such as InfoNCE [39] or NT-Xent [12] are used to maximize the objective in (1).

3.2   Linear Assignment Problem

Given two input sets, $\mathcal{A} = \{a_i\}_{i=1}^N$ and $\mathcal{B} = \{b_j\}_{j=1}^N$, we define the inter-set similarity matrix $\mathbf{S} \in \mathbb{R}^{N \times N}$ between each element in set $\mathcal{A}$ and each element in $\mathcal{B}$. This similarity matrix encodes *pairwise* distances between the elements of the sets, *i.e.* $[\mathbf{S}]_{i,j} = \phi(a_i, b_j)$, where ϕ is a distance metric. The goal of the linear assignment problem is to find a one-to-one assignment $\hat{y}(\mathbf{S})$, such that the sum of distances between assigned elements is optimal. Formally:

$$\hat{y}(\mathbf{S}) = \underset{\mathbf{Y} \in \Pi}{\text{argmin}}\ tr(\mathbf{S}\mathbf{Y}^T) \tag{2}$$

where Π corresponds to a set of all $N \times N$ permutation matrices.

The linear assignment problem in (2) is also known as the bipartite graph matching problem. It can be efficiently solved by linear programming algorithms [5].

3.3   Learning to Produce Correct Assignments

Consider two sets, $\mathcal{D}_{\mathcal{Z}_1}$ and $\mathcal{D}_{\mathcal{Z}_2}$, which encode two different views of the dataset $\mathcal{D}$ under two different views $\mathcal{Z}_1$ and $\mathcal{Z}_2$. By design, the two sets consist of the same instances, but the modalities and the order of the objects may differ. With the encoder, which maximizes the mutual information, objects in both sets can be uniquely associated with one another by comparing their representations as the uncertainty term in (1) should be minimized. In other words, $\hat{y}(\mathbf{S}) = \mathbf{Y}_{gt}$, where $\mathbf{Y}_{gt} \in \Pi$ is a ground truth assignment between elements of $\mathcal{D}_{\mathcal{Z}_1}$ and $\mathcal{D}_{\mathcal{Z}_2}$.

Thus, a natural objective to supervise an encoder function is to train it to produce the correct assignment between the different views of the data. As the assignment emerges as a result of the optimization problem, we employ a structured prediction framework [43] to define a structural loss from the linear assignment problem as follows:

$$L(\mathbf{S}, \mathbf{Y}_{gt}) = tr(\mathbf{S}\mathbf{Y}_{gt}^T) - \underset{\mathbf{Y} \in \Pi}{\min}\ tr(\mathbf{S}\mathbf{Y}^T) \tag{3}$$

where $\mathbf{S} = \phi\big(f_\theta(\mathcal{D}_{\mathcal{Z}_1}), f_\theta(\mathcal{D}_{\mathcal{Z}_2})\big)$. Note that $L \geq 0$ and $L = 0$ only when the similarities produced by an encoder lead to the correct optimal assignment. Intuitively, the structured linear[1] assignment loss in (3) encodes the discrepancy between the true cost of the assignment and the cost induced by an encoder.

By minimizing the objective in (3), we train the encoder f_θ to correctly assign objects from one view to another. In practice, it is desirable that such assignment is robust under small perturbations in the input data. The straightforward way to do so is to enforce a separation margin m in the input similarities as $\mathbf{S}_m = \mathbf{S} + m\mathbf{Y}_{gt}$. Then, the structured linear assignment loss with separation margin reduces to a known margin Triplet loss [23].

---

[1] We emphasize that the term *linear* here is only used with regard to an underlying assignment problem.

Proposition 1. *The structured linear assignment loss $L(S_m, Y_{gt})$ with separation margin $m \geq 0$ is equivalent to the margin triplet loss.*

Mining Strategies. By default, the loss in (3) enforces a one-to-one negative pair mining strategy due to the structural domain constraint $Y \in \Pi$. By relaxing this domain constraint to row-stochastic binary matrices, we arrive at the known batch-hard mining [23]. This is essential to have a computationally tractable implementation of structured assignment losses.

Smoothness. An immediate issue when directly optimizing the structured linear assignment loss is the non-smoothness of the minimum function in (3). It is known that optimizing smoothed functions can be more efficient than directly optimizing their non-smooth counterparts [3]. The common way to smooth a minimum is by *log-sum-exp* approximation. Thus, we can obtain a smoothed version of structured linear assignment loss:

$$L_\tau(\mathbf{S}, \mathbf{Y}_{gt}) = tr(\mathbf{S}\mathbf{Y}_{gt}^T) + \tau \log \sum_{\mathbf{Y} \in \Pi} \exp(-\frac{1}{\tau} tr(\mathbf{S}\mathbf{Y}^T)) \qquad (4)$$

where τ is a temperature parameter controlling the degree of smoothness. Practically, the formulation in (4) requires summing $N!$ terms, which makes it computationally intractable under the default structural constraints $\mathbf{Y} \in \Pi$. Fortunately, similar to the non-smooth case, we can utilize batch-hard mining, which leads to $O(N^2)$ computational complexity. The smoothed structured linear assignment loss with batch-hard mining reduces to known normalized-temperature cross entropy [12] also known as the InfoNCE [39] loss.

Proposition 2. *The smoothed structured linear assignment loss $L_\tau(S, Y_{gt})$ with batch-hard mining is equivalent to the normalized-temperature cross entropy loss.*

Connection to Mutual Information. It is known that the InfoNCE objective is a lower bound on the mutual information between the representations of data modalities [39]. Thus, Propositions 1 and 2 reveal a connection between mutual information maximization and minimization of structured losses for assignmnet problems. In fact, the assignment cost $tr(\mathbf{S}\mathbf{Y}_{gt}^T)$ in (2) is related to the conditional entropy $H(X|Y)$, while $\min_{\mathbf{Y} \in \Pi} tr(\mathbf{S}\mathbf{Y}^T)$ aims to maximize the diversity in representations. This connection allows for consideration of contrastive representation learning methods based on InfoNCE as a special case the structured linear assignment loss.

4   Extending Contrastive Losses

We next demonstrate how to exploit the connection between contrastive learning and assignment problems to extend contrastive losses the set level. As a byproduct of this connection, we also derive the SparseCLR contrastive objective.

4.1 Contrastive Learning with Quadratic Assignments on Sets

Quadratic Assignment Problem. As in the linear case, we are given two input sets $\mathcal{A}, \mathcal{B}$ and the inter-set similarity matrix $\mathbf{S}$. For the Quadratic Assignment Problem (QAP), we define intra-set similarity matrices $\mathbf{S}_\mathcal{A}$ and $\mathbf{S}_\mathcal{B}$ measuring similarities within the sets $\mathcal{A}$ and $\mathcal{B}$ respectively, $i.e.$ $[\mathbf{S}_\mathcal{A}]_{ij} = \phi(a_i, a_j)$. A goal of the quadratic assignment problem is to find a $one\text{-}to\text{-}one$ assignment $\hat{y}_\mathcal{Q}(\mathbf{S}, \mathbf{S}_\mathcal{A}, \mathbf{S}_\mathcal{B}) \in \Pi$ that maximizes the set similarity between $\mathcal{A}, \mathcal{B}$, where the set similarity is defined as follows:

$$\mathcal{Q}(\mathbf{S}, \mathbf{S}_\mathcal{A}, \mathbf{S}_\mathcal{B}) = \min_{\mathbf{Y} \in \Pi}\big\{ tr(\mathbf{S}\mathbf{Y}^T) + tr(\mathbf{S}_\mathcal{A}\mathbf{Y}\mathbf{S}_\mathcal{B}^T\mathbf{Y}^T) \big\} \tag{5}$$

Compared to the linear assignment problem, the quadratic term $\mathcal{Q}(\mathbf{S}, \mathbf{S}_\mathcal{A}, \mathbf{S}_\mathcal{B})$ in (5) additionally measures the discrepancy in internal structures between sets $\mathbf{S}_\mathcal{A}$ and $\mathbf{S}_\mathcal{B}$.

Learning with Quadratic Assignments. Following the similar steps as for the linear assignment problem in Sect. 3.3, we next define the structured quadratic assignment loss by extending the linear assignment problem in (3) with the quadratic term:

$$L_{QAP} = tr(\mathbf{S}\mathbf{Y}_{gt}) - \mathcal{Q}(\mathbf{S}, \mathbf{S}_\mathcal{A}, \mathbf{S}_\mathcal{B}) \tag{6}$$

Minimization of the structured quadratic assignment loss in (6) encourages the encoder to learn representations resulting in the same solutions of the linear and quadratic assignment problems, which is only possible when the inter-set and intra-set similarities are sufficiently close [8]. Note that we do not use a ground truth quadratic assignment in L_{QAP}, but a ground truth linear assignment objective is used for the supervision. This is due to a quadratic nature of $\mathcal{Q}$, where minimizing the discrepancy between ground truth and predicted assignments is a subtle optimization objective, e.g. for an equidistant set of points the costs of all quadratic assignments are identical.

To compute L_{QAP}, we first need to evaluate the quadratic term $\mathcal{Q}(\mathbf{S}, \mathbf{S}_\mathcal{A}, \mathbf{S}_\mathcal{B})$, which requires solving the quadratic assignment. This problem is known to be notoriously hard to solve exactly even when an input dimensionality is moderate [8]. To alleviate this, we use a computationally tractable upper-bound:

$$\begin{aligned} L_{QAP} &\leq tr(\mathbf{S}\mathbf{Y}_{gt}) - \min_{\mathbf{Y} \in \Pi} tr(\mathbf{S}\mathbf{Y}^T) - \min_{\mathbf{Y} \in \Pi} tr(\mathbf{S}_\mathcal{A}\mathbf{Y}\mathbf{S}_\mathcal{B}^T\mathbf{Y}^T) \\ &\leq L(\mathbf{S}, \mathbf{Y}_{gt}) - \langle\lambda_\mathcal{A}, \lambda_\mathcal{B}\rangle_- \end{aligned} \tag{7}$$

where $\langle\lambda_\mathcal{A}, \lambda_\mathcal{B}\rangle_-$ corresponds to a minimum dot product between eigenvalues of matrices $S_\mathcal{A}$ and $S_\mathcal{B}$.

The first inequality is derived from Jensen's inequality for (6) and the second inequality holds due to the fact that $\langle\lambda_F, \lambda_D\rangle_- \leq tr(\mathbf{F}\mathbf{X}\mathbf{D}^T\mathbf{X}^T) \leq \langle\lambda_F, \lambda_D\rangle_+$ for symmetric matrices $\mathbf{F}, \mathbf{D}$ and $\mathbf{X} \in \Pi$ as shown in *Theorem 5* by Burkard [8]. The above derivations are for the case when the similarity metric is a valid

Algorithm 1. Pseudocode for set-based InfoNCE with Euclidean distance similarity and Quadratic Assignment Regularization (QARe).

```
# f: encoder network
# alpha: weighting for the pairwise contrastive part (linear assignment)
# beta: weighting for the set contrastive part
# N: batch size
# E: dimensionality of the embeddings

for x in loader: # load a batch with N samples
    # two randomly augmented views of x
    y_a, y_b = augment(x)

    # compute embeddings
    z_a = f(y_a) # NxE
    z_b = f(y_b) # NxE

    # compute inter-set and intra-set similarities
    S_AB = similarity(z_a, z_b) # NxN
    S_A = similarity(z_a, z_a) # NxN
    S_B = similarity(z_b, z_b) # NxN

    # compute pairwise contrastive InfoNCE loss
    pairwise_term = infonce(S_AB)

    # compute eigenvalues
    eigs_a = eigenvalues(S_A) #N
    eigs_b = eigenvalues(S_B) #N

    # compute QARe from minimum dot product of eigenvalues
    eigs_a_sorted = sort(eigs_a, descending = True) #N
    eigs_b_sorted = sort(eigs_b, descending = False) #N
    qare = -1*(eigs_a_sorted.T@eigs_b_sorted)

    # combine pairwise contrastive loss with QARe
    loss = alpha*pairwise_term + beta*qare/(N^2)

    # optimization step
    loss.backward()
    optimizer.step()
```

distance function, i.e. minimizing a distances leads to maximizing a similarity. The derivation for the reverse case can be done analogously by replacing *min* with *max* in the optimal assignment problem formulation (we provide more details in supplementary material).

Optimizing the upper-bound in (7) is computationally tractable compared to optimizing the exact version of L_{QAP}. Another advantage is that the upper-bound in (7) breaks down towards minimizing the sum of the structured linear assignment loss $L(\mathbf{S}, \mathbf{Y}_{gt})$ and the regularizing term, which accounts for the set similarity. This allows to easily modify existing contrastive learning approaches like those in [12,23,36,39] that are based on pairwise similarities and thus stem from the linear assignment problem by simply plugging in the regularizing term. We provide a simple pseudocode example demonstrating InfoNCE with the quadratic assignment regularization (Algorithm 1).

Computational Complexity. Computing the upper-bound in (7) has a computational complexity of $O(N^3)$ as one needs to compute eigenvalues of the intra-set similarity matrices. This is opposed to (6) that requires directly computing quadratic assignments, for which it is known there exist no polynomial-time algorithms [8]. The computational complexity can be pushed further down to $O(k^2 N)$ by evaluating the only top-k eigenvalues instead of computing all eigenvalues. In supplementary materials, we also provide an empirical analysis of how the proposed approach influences a training time of a baseline contrastive method.

4.2 SparseCLR

In Sect. 3 we noted that the smoothness of a loss function is a desirable property for optimization and that the *log-sum-exp* smoothing of the structured linear assignment loss yields the normalized temperature cross-entropy objective as a special case. Such an approach, however, is known to have limitations. Specifically, the *log-sum-exp* smoothing yields dense support over samples, being unable to completely rule out irrelevant examples [38]. That can be statistically and computationally overwhelming and can distract the model from fully utilizing information from hard negative examples.

We propose to use *sparsemax* instead of *log-sum-exp* approximation to alleviate the non-smoothness of the structured linear assignment objective, yet keep the sparse support of the loss function. Here *sparsemax* is defined as the minimum distance Euclidean projection to a k-dimensional simplex as in [35, 38].

Let $\tilde{x} :\in \mathbb{R}^{N!}$ be a vector that consists of the realizations of all possible assignment costs for the similarity matrix **S**. With this we can define SparseCLR as follows:

$$L_{sparse}(\mathbf{S}, \mathbf{Y}_{gt}) = tr(\mathbf{S}\mathbf{Y}_{gt}^T) - \frac{1}{2} \sum_{j \in \Omega(\tilde{x})} \left(\tilde{x}_j^2 - \mathcal{T}^2(-\tilde{x}) \right) \tag{8}$$

where $\Omega(X) = \{j \in X : sparsemax(X)_j > 0\}$ is the support of *sparsemax* function, and $\mathcal{T}$ denotes the thresholding operator [35]. In practice, to avoid summing over a factorial number of terms, as well as for other methods, we use batch-hard mining strategy resulting in $O(N^2)$ computational complexity for SparseCLR.

5 Experiments

In this section, we evaluate the quality of representations trained with and without our Quadratic Assignment Regularization (QARe). We also evaluate the performance of SparseCLR and compare it with other contrastive losses. As we consider the representation learning from the perspective of the assignment theory, we firstly conduct the instance matching experiment, where the goal is to learn to predict the correct assignment between different views of the dataset. Then, we test the proposed method on the task of self-supervised classification and compare it with other contrastive learning approaches. Next, we present ablation studies to visualize the role of the weighting term, when combining QARe with the baseline contrastive learning method.

5.1   Matching Instances from Different Views

In this experiment, the goal is to train representations of objects from different views, such that the learned representations provide a correct matching between identities in the dataset. This problem is closely related to a metric learning and can be solved by contrasting views of the data [23].

Data. We adopt the CUHK-03 dataset [31] designed for the ReID [23] task. CUHK-03 consist of 1467 different identities recorded each from front and back views. To train and test the models, we randomly divide the dataset into 70/15/15 train/test/validation splits.

Evaluation. We evaluate the quality of representations learned with contrastive losses by computing the matching accuracy between front and back views. In practice, we first obtain the embeddings of the views of the instances from the encoder and then compute their inter-view similarity matrix using the Euclidean distance. Given this, the matching accuracy is defined as the mean Hamming distance between the optimal assignment from the inter-view similarity matrix and the ground truth assignment. We report the average matching accuracy and the standard deviation over 3 runs with the same fixed random seeds. As a baseline, we chose Triplet with batch-hard mining [23], InfoNCE [39] and NTLogistic [36] contrastive losses, which we extend with the proposed QARe.

Implementation Details. As the encoder, we use ResNet-18 [22] with the top classification layer replaced by the linear projection head that outputs feature vectors of dimension 64. To obtain representations, we normalize the feature vectors to be L2 unit-norm.

We train the models for 50 epochs using Adam optimizer [29] with the cosine annealing without restarts [34]. Initial learning rate is 0.01 and a batch size is set to 128. During the training, we apply random color jittering and horizontal flip augmentations. To compute the test matching accuracy, we select the best model over the epochs based on the validation split. We provide detailed hyperparameters of the losses, QARe weighting, and augmentations in the supplementary material.

Results. The results are reported in Table 1. As can be seen, adding QARe regularization to a baseline contrastive loss leads to a better matching accuracy, which indicates an improved quality of representations. Notably, QARe delivers 3.6% improvement when combined with Triplet loss and 4.1% increase in accuracy with the InfoNCE objective. This demonstrates that the quadratic assignment regularization on sets helps the model to learn generalized representation space.

Table 1. Matching accuracy for instances from different views of CUHK-03 dataset. The *pairwise* corresponds to the contrastive losses acting on the level of pairs. $+QARe$ denotes methods with quadratic assignment regularization. Best results are in bold.

Method	Triplet	SparseCLR	InfoNCE	NTLogistic
pairwise	54.85 ± 0.77	53.03 ± 0.43	57.87 ± 1.19	40.30 ± 0.42
$+QARe$	$\mathbf{58.48 \pm 1.67}$	$\mathbf{54.84 \pm 1.40}$	$\mathbf{61.96 \pm 1.38}$	$\mathbf{43.48 \pm 1.41}$

5.2 Self-supervised Classification

Next, we evaluate the quadratic assignments on sets in the task of self-supervised classification. The goal in this experiment is to learn a representation space from an unlabeled data that provides a linear separation between classes in a dataset. This is a common problem to test contrastive learning methods.

Evaluation. We follow the standard linear probing protocol [30]. The evaluation is performed by retrieving embeddings from a contrastively trained backbone and fitting a linear classifier on top of the embeddings. Since linear classifiers have a low discriminative power on their own, they heavily rely on input representations. Thus, a higher classification accuracy indicates a better quality of learned representations. As the baseline for pairwise contrastive learning methods, we select popular SimCLR and proposed SparseCLR. We extend the methods to the set level by adding the quadratic assignment regularization. We compare the set-level contrastive methods with other self-supervised [10,18] and contrastive approaches [11,12].

Table 2. Self-supervised training and linear probing for a self-supervised classification. Average classification accuracy (percentage) and standard deviation over 3 runs with common fixed random seeds are reported. * we report the results from our reimplementation of SimCLR.

Method	Conv-4			ResNet-32		
	CIFAR-10	CIFAR-100	tiny-ImageNet	CIFAR-10	CIFAR-100	tiny-ImageNet
Supervised (upper bound)	80.46 ± 0.39	49.29 ± 0.85	36.47 ± 0.36	90.87 ± 0.41	65.32 ± 0.22	50.09 ± 0.32
Random Weights (lower bound)	32.92 ± 1.88	10.79 ± 0.59	6.19 ± 0.13	27.47 ± 0.83	7.65 ± 0.44	3.24 ± 0.43
DeepCluster [10]	42.88 ± 0.21	21.03 ± 1.56	12.60 ± 1.23	43.31 ± 0.62	20.44 ± 0.80	11.64 ± 0.21
RotationNet [18]	56.73 ± 1.71	27.45 ± 0.80	18.40 ± 0.95	62.00 ± 0.79	29.02 ± 0.18	14.73 ± 0.48
Deep InfoMax [25]	44.60 ± 0.27	22.74 ± 0.21	14.19 ± 0.13	47.13 ± 0.45	24.07 ± 0.05	17.51 ± 0.15
SimCLR* [12]	59.64 ± 0.93	30.75 ± 0.23	21.15 ± 0.16	76.45 ± 0.10	40.18 ± 0.13	23.44 ± 0.27
SimCLR+QARe (Ours)	$\mathbf{61.54 \pm 1.17}$	$\mathbf{31.18 \pm 0.41}$	$\mathbf{21.33 \pm 0.18}$	$\mathbf{76.85 \pm 0.39}$	$\mathbf{41.20 \pm 0.34}$	$\mathbf{25.05 \pm 0.18}$

Implementation Details. We train shallow convolutional (Conv-4) and deep (ResNet-32) backbone encoders to obtain representations. We follow the standard approach and attach an MLP projection head that outputs feature vectors of dimension 64 to compute a contrastive loss. We use the cosine distance to get similarities between embeddings. We provide more details on the encoder architectures in the supplementary material.

We train the models for 200 epochs using Adam optimizer with a learning rate of 0.001 and a batch size is set to 128. For contrastive learning methods, we adopt a set of augmentations from [12] to form different views of the data. For linear probing, we freeze the encoder weights and train a logistic regression on top of the learned representation for 100 epochs with Adam optimizer, using a learning rate of 0.001 and a batch size of 128. We provide detailed hyperparameters of the contrastive losses and augmentations in the supplementary material.

We perform training and testing on standard CIFAR-10, CIFAR-100, and tiny-ImageNet datasets. For each dataset, we follow the same training procedure and fine-tune the optimal weighting of the quadratic assignment regularizer.

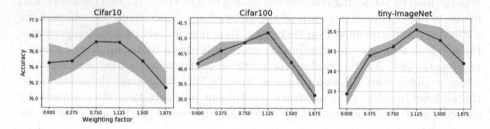

Fig. 2. Influence of the weighting of the QARe term in the self-supervised classification for ResNet-32 trained with SimCLR. The accuracy is recorded over 3 runs with common fixed random seeds.

Table 3. Self-supervised training on unlabeled data and linear evaluation on labeled data. Comparing SimCLR [12] with the proposed SparseCLR and SparseCLR with QARe. Average accuracy and standard deviation over three runs over 3 runs with common fixed random seeds.

Method	Conv-4			ResNet-32		
	CIFAR-10	CIFAR-100	tiny-ImageNet	CIFAR-10	CIFAR-100	tiny-ImageNet
SimCLR* [12]	59.64 ± 0.93	30.75 ± 0.23	21.15 ± 0.16	$\mathbf{76.45 \pm 0.10}$	40.18 ± 0.13	23.44 ± 0.27
SparseCLR (Ours)	59.86 ± 0.56	32.04 ± 0.26	$\mathbf{22.41 \pm 0.39}$	70.37 ± 0.12	41.05 ± 0.20	25.87 ± 0.59
SparseCLR+ QARe (Ours)	$\mathbf{61.06 \pm 0.39}$	$\mathbf{33.05 \pm 0.32}$	$\mathbf{22.45 \pm 0.30}$	71.39 ± 0.30	$\mathbf{42.07 \pm 0.35}$	$\mathbf{27.03 \pm 0.40}$

QARe Results. The results for the quadratic assignment regularization are reported in Table 2 for SimCLR and in Table 3 for proposed SparseCLR. For SimCLR, adding QARe delivers 1.9% accuracy improvement on CIFAR-10 for the shallow encoder network and up to 1.6% improvement for ResNet-32 on tiny-ImageNet. We observed a consistent improvement in other dataset-architecture setups, except tiny-ImageNet with shallow Conv-4 encoder, where the performance gain from adding QARe is modest. For this case, we investigated the training behavior of the models and observed that both SimCLR and SimCLR+QARe for Conv-4 architecture very quickly saturate to a saddle point, where the quality of representations stops improving. Since this does not happen with ResNet-32 architecture, we attribute this phenomenon to the limited discriminative power of the shallow Conv-4 backbone, which can not be extended by regularizing the loss.

For SparseCLR, we observed the same overall pattern. As can be seen from Table 3, extending SparseCLR to set level with QARe delivers 1.6% accuracy improvement for ResNet-32 on tiny-ImageNet and also steadily improve the performance on other datasets. This indicates that QARe helps to provide a richer supervisory signal for the model to train representations.

SparseCLR Results. Next, we compare SimCLR against the proposed SparseCLR. As can be seen in Table 3, SparseCLR consistently improves over the baseline on CIFAR-100 and tiny-ImageNet datasets, where it delivers 2.4% improvement. Surprisingly, we noticed a significant drop in performance for ResNet-32 on CIFAR-10. For this case, we investigated the training behavior of the model and observed that in the case of CIFAR-10, the batch often includes many false negative examples, which results in uninformative negative pairs. Since SparseCLR assigns the probability mass only to a few hardest negative pairs, a lot of false-negative examples in the batch impede obtaining a clear supervisory signal. We assume the problem can be alleviated by using false-negative cancellation techniques [27].

5.3 Ablation Study

Here we illustrate how the weighting of the QARe term influences the quality of representations learned with SimCLR under a linear probing evaluation. We search for the optimal weighting in the range from 0 to 1.875 with a step of 0.125. The results are depicted in Fig. 2. In practice, we observed that QARe is not too sensitive to a weighting and the values in the range 0.75–1.25 provide consistent improvement.

6 Discussion

In this work, we present set contrastive learning method based on quadratic assignments. Different from other contrastive learning approaches, our method works on the level of set similarities as opposed to only pairwise similarities, which allows improving the information content of the supervisory signal. For derivation, we view contrastive learning through the lens of combinatorial assignment theory. We show how pairwise contrastive methods emerge from learning to produce correct optimal assignments and then extend them to a set level by generalizing an underlying assignment problem, implemented as a regularization for existing methods. As a byproduct of viewing representation learning through the lens of assignment theory, we additionally propose SparceCLR contrastive loss.

Our experiments in instance matching and self-supervised classification suggest that adding quadratic assignment regularization improves the quality of representations learned by backbone methods. We suppose, that our approach would be most useful in the problems where the joint analysis of objects and their groups appears naturally and labeling is not readily available.

References

1. Baklr, G., Hofmann, T., Schölkopf, B., Smola, A.J., Taskar, B., Vishwanathan, S.: Predicting Structured Data. The MIT Press, Cambridge (2007)
2. Bardes, A., Ponce, J., LeCun, Y.: VICReg: variance-invariance-covariance regularization for self-supervised learning. In: ICLR (2022)
3. Beck, A., Teboulle, M.: Smoothing and first order methods: a unified framework. SIAM J. Optim. 22(2), 557–580 (2012)
4. Becker, S., Hinton, G.E.: Self-organizing neural network that discovers surfaces in random-dot stereograms. Nature 355, 161–163 (1992)
5. Bertsimas, D., Tsitsiklis, J.: Introduction to Linear Optimization. Athena Scientific, New Hampshire (1998)
6. Blondel, M., Martins, A., Niculae, V.: Learning classifiers with Fenchel-young losses: generalized entropies, margins, and algorithms. In: Proceedings of the Twenty-Second International Conference on Artificial Intelligence and Statistics. Proceedings of Machine Learning Research, vol. 89, pp. 606–615. PMLR (2019)
7. Bromley, J., Guyon, I., LeCun, Y., Säckinger, E., Shah, R.: Signature verification using a "Siamese" time delay neural network. In: Advances in Neural Information Processing Systems, vol. 6. Morgan-Kaufmann (1993)
8. Burkard, R.E.: Quadratic Assignment Problems, pp. 2741–2814. Springer, New York (2013). https://doi.org/10.1007/978-3-642-51576-7_7
9. Burkard, R.E., Çela, E.: Linear assignment problems and extensions. In: Handbook of Combinatorial Optimization (1999)
10. Caron, M., Bojanowski, P., Joulin, A., Douze, M.: Deep clustering for unsupervised learning of visual features. In: Ferrari, V., Hebert, M., Sminchisescu, C., Weiss, Y. (eds.) Computer Vision – ECCV 2018. LNCS, vol. 11218, pp. 139–156. Springer, Cham (2018). https://doi.org/10.1007/978-3-030-01264-9_9
11. Caron, M., Misra, I., Mairal, J., Goyal, P., Bojanowski, P., Joulin, A.: Unsupervised learning of visual features by contrasting cluster assignments. In: Advances in Neural Information Processing Systems, vol. 33, pp. 9912–9924 (2020)
12. Chen, T., Kornblith, S., Norouzi, M., Hinton, G.: A simple framework for contrastive learning of visual representations. In: International Conference on Machine Learning, pp. 1597–1607 (2020)

13. Chen, T., Kornblith, S., Swersky, K., Norouzi, M., Hinton, G.E.: Big self-supervised models are strong semi-supervised learners. Adv. Neural. Inf. Process. Syst. **33**, 22243–22255 (2020)
14. Chen, X., Fan, H., Girshick, R., He, K.: Improved baselines with momentum contrastive learning. arXiv preprint arXiv:2003.04297 (2020)
15. Chen, X., He, K.: Exploring simple Siamese representation learning. In: Proceedings of the IEEE/CVF Conference on Computer Vision and Pattern Recognition, pp. 15750–15758 (2021)
16. Ermolov, A., Siarohin, A., Sangineto, E., Sebe, N.: Whitening for self-supervised representation learning. In: International Conference on Machine Learning, pp. 3015–3024 (2021)
17. Finke, G., Burkard, R.E., Rendl, F.: Quadratic assignment problems. In: Surveys in Combinatorial Optimization, North-Holland Mathematics Studies, vol. 132, pp. 61–82. North-Holland (1987)
18. Gidaris, S., Singh, P., Komodakis, N.: Unsupervised representation learning by predicting image rotations. arXiv preprint arXiv:1803.07728 (2018)
19. Grill, J.B., et al.: Bootstrap your own latent-a new approach to self-supervised learning. Adv. Neural. Inf. Process. Syst. **33**, 21271–21284 (2020)
20. Hazan, T., Keshet, J., McAllester, D.: Direct loss minimization for structured prediction. In: Advances in Neural Information Processing Systems, vol. 23 (2010)
21. He, K., Fan, H., Wu, Y., Xie, S., Girshick, R.: Momentum contrast for unsupervised visual representation learning. In: Proceedings of the IEEE/CVF Conference on Computer Vision and Pattern Recognition, pp. 9729–9738 (2020)
22. He, K., Zhang, X., Ren, S., Sun, J.: Deep residual learning for image recognition. In: Proceedings of the IEEE Conference on Computer Vision and Pattern Recognition, pp. 770–778 (2016)
23. Hermans, A., Beyer, L., Leibe, B.: In defense of the triplet loss for person re-identification. arXiv preprint arXiv:1703.07737 (2017)
24. Hinton, G., Vinyals, O., Dean, J., et al.: Distilling the knowledge in a neural network. arXiv preprint arXiv:1503.02531 (2015)
25. Hjelm, D., et al.: Learning deep representations by mutual information estimation and maximization. ICLR (2019)
26. Huang, Z., Hu, P., Zhou, J.T., Lv, J., Peng, X.: Partially view-aligned clustering. Adv. Neural. Inf. Process. Syst. **33**, 2892–2902 (2020)
27. Huynh, T., Kornblith, S., Walter, M.R., Maire, M., Khademi, M.: Boosting contrastive self-supervised learning with false negative cancellation. In: Proceedings of the IEEE Winter Conference on Applications of Computer Vision (WACV) (2022)
28. Jaiswal, A., Babu, A.R., Zadeh, M.Z., Banerjee, D., Makedon, F.: A survey on contrastive self-supervised learning. Technologies **9**(1), 2 (2020)
29. Kingma, D.P., Ba, J.: Adam: a method for stochastic optimization. arXiv preprint arXiv:1412.6980 (2014)
30. Kolesnikov, A., Zhai, X., Beyer, L.: Revisiting self-supervised visual representation learning. In: Proceedings of the IEEE/CVF Conference on Computer Vision and Pattern Recognition (2019)
31. Li, W., Zhao, R., Xiao, T., Wang, X.: DeepReID: deep filter pairing neural network for person re-identification. In: Proceedings of the IEEE Conference on Computer Vision and Pattern Recognition (CVPR), pp. 152–159 (2014)
32. Lin, Y., Gou, Y., Liu, Z., Li, B., Lv, J., Peng, X.: Completer: incomplete multi-view clustering via contrastive prediction. In: Proceedings of the IEEE/CVF Conference on Computer Vision and Pattern Recognition (CVPR) (2021)

33. Linsker, R.: Self-organization in a perceptual network. IEEE Comput. **21**, 105–117 (1988). https://doi.org/10.1109/2.36
34. Loshchilov, I., Hutter, F.: SGDR: stochastic gradient descent with warm restarts. arXiv preprint arXiv:1608.03983 (2016)
35. Martins, A.F.T., Astudillo, R.F.: From softmax to sparsemax: a sparse model of attention and multi-label classification. In: Proceedings of the 33rd International Conference on International Conference on Machine Learning (ICML) (2016)
36. Mikolov, T., Chen, K., Corrado, G., Dean, J.: Efficient estimation of word representations in vector space. arXiv preprint arXiv:1301.3781 (2013)
37. Misra, I., Maaten, L.v.d.: Self-supervised learning of pretext-invariant representations. In: Proceedings of the IEEE/CVF Conference on Computer Vision and Pattern Recognition (CVPR), pp. 6707–6717 (2020)
38. Niculae, V., Martins, A., Blondel, M., Cardie, C.: SparseMAP: differentiable sparse structured inference. In: International Conference on Machine Learning (ICML), pp. 3799–3808 (2018)
39. Oord, A.v.d., Li, Y., Vinyals, O.: Representation learning with contrastive predictive coding. arXiv preprint arXiv:1807.03748 (2018)
40. Patacchiola, M., Storkey, A.: Self-supervised relational reasoning for representation learning. In: Advances in Neural Information Processing Systems (2020)
41. Peng, X., Huang, Z., Lv, J., Zhu, H., Zhou, J.T.: COMIC: multi-view clustering without parameter selection. In: International Conference on Machine Learning (ICML) (2019)
42. Tschannen, M., Djolonga, J., Rubenstein, P.K., Gelly, S., Lucic, M.: On mutual information maximization for representation learning. In: International Conference on Learning Representations (ICLR) (2020)
43. Tsochantaridis, I., Joachims, T., Hofmann, T., Altun, Y.: Large margin methods for structured and interdependent output variables. J. Mach. Learn. Res. **6**(50), 1453–1484 (2005)
44. Wang, T., Isola, P.: Understanding contrastive representation learning through alignment and uniformity on the hypersphere. In: International Conference on Machine Learning (ICML) (2020)
45. Wang, X., Zhang, R., Shen, C., Kong, T., Li, L.: Dense contrastive learning for self-supervised visual pre-training. In: Conference on Computer Vision and Pattern Recognition (CVPR) (2021)
46. Yang, M., Li, Y., Hu, P., Bai, J., Lv, J.C., Peng, X.: Robust multi-view clustering with incomplete information. IEEE Trans. Pattern Anal. Mach. Intell., 1 (2022)
47. Yang, M., Li, Y., Huang, Z., Liu, Z., Hu, P., Peng, X.: Partially view-aligned representation learning with noise-robust contrastive loss. In: Conference on Computer Vision and Pattern Recognition (CVPR) (2021)
48. Zbontar, J., Jing, L., Misra, I., LeCun, Y., Deny, S.: Barlow twins: self-supervised learning via redundancy reduction. In: International Conference on Machine Learning (ICML) (2021)

Class-Incremental Learning
with Cross-Space Clustering
and Controlled Transfer

Arjun Ashok[1,2]([✉])(ID), K. J. Joseph[1](ID), and Vineeth N. Balasubramanian[1](ID)

[1] Indian Institute of Technology Hyderabad, Sangareddy, India
{cs17m18p100001,vineethnb}@iith.ac.in
[2] PSG College of Technology, Coimbatore, India
arjun.ashok.psg@gmail.com
https://cscct.github.io

Abstract. In class-incremental learning, the model is expected to learn new classes continually while maintaining knowledge on previous classes. The challenge here lies in preserving the model's ability to effectively represent prior classes in the feature space, while adapting it to represent incoming new classes. We propose two distillation-based objectives for class incremental learning that leverage the structure of the feature space to maintain accuracy on previous classes, as well as enable learning the new classes. In our first objective, termed **cross-space clustering** (CSC), we propose to use the feature space structure of the previous model to characterize directions of optimization that maximally preserve the class - directions that all instances of a specific class should collectively optimize towards, and those directions that they should collectively optimize away from. Apart from minimizing forgetting, such a class-level constraint indirectly encourages the model to reliably cluster all instances of a class in the current feature space, and further gives rise to a sense of "herd-immunity", allowing all samples of a class to jointly combat the model from forgetting the class. Our second objective termed **controlled transfer** (CT) tackles incremental learning from an important and understudied perspective of inter-class transfer. CT explicitly approximates and conditions the current model on the semantic similarities between incrementally arriving classes and prior classes. This allows the model to learn the incoming classes in such a way that it maximizes positive forward transfer from similar prior classes, thus increasing plasticity, and minimizes negative backward transfer on dissimilar prior classes, whereby strengthening stability. We perform extensive experiments on two benchmark datasets, adding our method (CSCCT) on top of three prominent class-incremental learning methods. We observe consistent performance improvement on a variety of experimental settings.

Supplementary Information The online version contains supplementary material available at https://doi.org/10.1007/978-3-031-19812-0_7.

Keywords: Incremental learning · Continual learning · Knowledge distillation · Transfer learning

1   Introduction

Incremental learning is a paradigm of machine learning where learning objectives are introduced to a model incrementally in the form of *phases* or *tasks*, and the model must dynamically learn new tasks while maintaining knowledge on previously seen tasks. The differences of this setup from a *static training* scenario is that the model is not allowed to *retrain* from scratch on encountering new tasks, and no task information is available upfront. A fundamental challenge in incremental learning is in the stability-plasticity trade-off [36], where stability relates to maintaining accuracy on the previous tasks, while plasticity relates to learning the current task effectively. In their naive form, deep learning models are too plastic; the model changes significantly during training, and incurs *catastrophic forgetting* [16] of old tasks when exposed to new ones.

Class-incremental learning (CIL) [35,41] is a specific sub-paradigm of incremental learning where tasks are composed of *new classes* and we seek to learn a *unified* model that can *represent and classify* all classes seen so far equally well. The main challenge in class-incremental learning lies in how knowledge over the long stream of classes can be consolidated at every phase. Regularization-based methods [4,9,24,55] quantify and preserve important parameters corresponding to prior tasks. Another set of approaches [10,14,33,48] focus on modifying the learning algorithm to ensure that gradient updates do not conflict with the previous tasks. In dynamic architecture methods [1,30,40,50,53], the network architecture is modified by expansion or masking when encountering new tasks during learning. Replay-based methods [2,6–8,13,18,29,32,41,45,46,49,52] store a subset of each previous task in a separate memory, and replay the tasks when learning a new one, to directly preserve the knowledge on those tasks. A wide variety of such replay methods have been developed recently, and have attained promising results in the CIL setting. A number of these methods [2,7,8,13,18,29,41,46] use variants of knowledge distillation [17], where the model and its predictions corresponding to the previous task are utilized to prevent the current task's model from diverging too much from its previous state.

Our work herein falls under distillation-based methods. Prior work has advocated for utilizing distillation to directly constrain an example's position or angle using its position in the previous feature space [18], to preserve pooled convolutional outputs of an instance [13], or to maintain the distribution of logits that the model's classifier outputs on the data [2,41]. We argue that preserving the features or predictions of a model on independent individual instances are only useful to a certain extent, and do not characterize and preserve properties of a class captured globally by the model as a whole. *Class-level* semantics may be more important to be preserved in the *class-incremental* learning setting, to holistically prevent individual classes from being forgotten. To this end, we develop an objective termed **Cross-Space Clustering** (CSC) that characterizes *entire regions* in the feature space that classes should stay away from, and those that a class should belong to, and distills this information to the model. Our objective indirectly establishes multiple goals at once: (i) it encourages the model to cluster all instances of a given class; (ii) ensures that these clusters are well-separated; and (iii) regularizes to preserve *class cluster positions* as a single entity in the feature space. This provides for a class-consolidated distillation objective, prodding instances of a given class to "unite" and thus prevent the class from being forgotten.

Next, as part of our second objective, we tackle the class-incremental-learning problem from a different perspective. While all prior distillation objectives seek better ways to preserve properties of the learned representations in the feature space [2,7,8,13,18,29,41,46], we believe that controlling *inter-class transfer* is also critical for class-incremental learning. This comes from the observation that forgetting often results from *negative backward transfer* from new classes to previous classes, and plasticity is ensured when there is *positive forward transfer* from prior classes to new ones [33]. To this end, we develop an objective called **Controlled Transfer** (CT) that controls and regularizes transfer of features between classes at a fine-grained level. We formulate an objective that approximates the relative similarity between an incoming class and all previous classes, and conditions the current task's model on these estimated similarities. This encourages *new classes* to be situated optimally in the feature space, ensuring maximal positive transfer and minimal negative transfer.

A unique characteristic of our objectives is their ability to extend and enhance existing distillation-based CIL methodologies, without any change to their methodologies. We verify this by adding our objectives to three prominent and state-of-the art CIL methods that employ distillation in their formulation: iCARL [41], LUCIR [18] and PODNet [13]. We conduct thorough experimental evaluations on benchmark incremental versions of large-scale datasets like CIFAR-100 and ImageNet subset. We perform a comprehensive evaluation of our method, considering a wide variety of experimental settings. We show that our method consistently improves incremental learning performance across datasets and methods, at no additional cost. We further analyze and present ablation studies on our method, highlighting the contribution of each of our components.

2   Related Work

2.1   Incremental Learning

In an incremental setting, a model is required to consistently learn new tasks, without compromising performance on old tasks. Incremental learning methodologies can be split into five major categories, each of which we review below.

Regularization-based methods focus on quantifying the importance of each parameter in the network, to prevent the network from excessively changing the important parameters pertaining to a task. These methods include EWC [24], SI [55], MAS [4] and RWalk [9]. A recent method ELI [21], introduces an energy based implicit regularizer which helps to alleviate forgetting.

Algorithm-based methods seek to avoid forgetting from the perspective of the network training algorithm. They modify gradients such that updates to weights do not not deteriorate performance on previously seen tasks. Methods such as GEM [33], A-GEM [10], OGD [14] and NSCL [48] fall under this category. Meta-learning based methods [20,25] are also useful while learning continually.

Architecture-based methods modify the network architecture dynamically to fit more tasks, by expanding the model by adding more weights [50,53], or masking and allocating subnetworks to specific tasks [44], or by gating the parameters dynamically using a task identifier [1].

Exemplar-based methods (also called replay-based or rehearsal methods) assume that a small subset of every class can be stored in a memory at every phase. They replay the seen classes later along with the incoming new classes, directly preventing them from being forgotten. One set of works focus on reducing the recency bias due to the new classes being in majority at every phase [6,7, 18,49]. Another set of works focus on optimizing which samples to choose as exemplars to better represent the class distributions [5,32].

Distillation-based methods use the model learned until the previous task as a teacher and provide extra supervision to the model learning the current tasks (the student). Since the data of the previous tasks are inaccessible, these methods typically enforce distillation objectives on the current data [12,31], data from an exemplar memory [2,7,13,18,22,26,41], external data [29] or synthetic data [56]. Since our method falls under this category, we extend our discussion on related methods below.

Early works in this category distill logit scores [31,41] or attention maps [12] of the previous model. iCARL [41] proposes to enforce distillation on new tasks as well exemplars from old tasks, along with herding selection of exemplars and nearest-mean-of-exemplars (NME) based classification. GD [29] calibrates the confidence of the model's outputs using external unlabelled data, and propose to distill the calibrated outputs instead. LUCIR [18] introduces a less-forget constraint that encourages the orientation of a sample in the current feature space to be similar to its orientation in the old feature space. Apart from that, LUCIR proposes to use cosine-similarity based classifiers and a margin ranking loss that mines hard negatives from the new classes to better separate the old class, additionally avoiding ambiguities between old and new classes. PODNet [13] preserves an example's representation throughout the model with a spatial distillation loss. SS-IL [2] show that general KD preserves the recency bias in the distillation, and propose to use task-wise KD. Co2L [8] introduces a contrastive learning based self-supervised distillation loss that preserves the exact feature relations of a sample with its augmentations and other samples from the dataset. GeoDL [46] introduces a term that enhances knowledge distillation by performing KD across low-dimensions path between the subspaces of the two models, considering the gradual shift between models.

The main difference of our cross-space clustering objective from these works is that we do not optimize to preserve the properties of individual examples, and instead preserve the previously learned semantics or properties of each *class* in a *holistic manner*. Our formulation takes into account the global position of a class in the feature space, and optimizes all samples of the class towards the same region, making the model indifferent to instance-level semantics. Further, classes are supervised with specific "negative" regions all over the feature space, also intrinsically giving rise to better separation between class clusters.

Our controlled transfer objective, on the other hand, attempts to regularize transfer between tasks. MER [42], an algorithm-based method is related to our high-level objective. MER works in the online continual learning setup, combining meta-learning [15,37] with replay. Their method optimizes such that the model receives weight updates are restricted to those directions that agree with the gradients of prior tasks. Our objective proposes to utilize the *structure* of the feature space of the previous model to align the current feature space, in order to maximize transfer. Our novelty here lies in how we explicitly approximate *inter-class semantic similarities* in a *continual task stream*, and utilize them to appropriately position new tasks representations, regularizing transfer.

2.2 Knowledge Distillation

Hinton et al. [17] introduced knowledge distillation (KD) in their work as a way to transfer knowledge from an ensemble of teacher networks to a smaller student network. They show that there is dark knowledge in the logits of a trained network that can give more structure about the data, and use them as soft targets to train the student. Since then, a number of other works have explored variants of KD. Attention Transfer [54] focused on the attention maps of the network instead of the logits, while FitNets [43] also deal with intermediate activation maps of a network. Several other papers have enforced criteria based on multi-layer representations of a network [3,19,23,27,51].

Among these, our controlled transfer objective shares similarities with a few works that propose to exploit the mutual relation between data samples for distillation. Tung and Mori [47] propose a distillation objective that enforces an L2 loss in the student that constraints the similarities between activation maps of two examples to be consistent with those of the teacher. Relational KD [38] additionally propose to preserve the angle formed by the three examples in the feature space by means of a triplet distillation objective. Extending this direction, Correlation Congruence [39] models relations between examples through higher-order kernels, to enforce the same objectives with better relation estimates.

The difference of our controlled transfer objective from these works lies in the high-level objective in the context of the incremental learning setting, as well as the low-level formulation in terms of the loss objective. All the above works propose to use sample relations in the feature space to provide additional supervision to a student model by regularizing the feature relations of the student. The main challenge in incremental learning is how we can reduce the effect that a new class has on the representation space, to minimize forgetting.

Our objective also exploits sample relations in the feature space, however our novelty lies in how we estimate a measure of relative similarity between an *unseen class* and each previously seen class, and utilize them to control where the *new samples* are located in the embedding space, in relation to the old samples. Our specific formulation indirectly promotes forward transfer of features from prior classes similar to the new class, and simultaneously prevents negative backward transfer of features from the new class to dissimilar previous classes.

3   Method

We briefly introduce the problem setting in Sect. 3.1. Next, we explain in detail our learning objectives in Sect. 3.2 and Sect. 3.3 respectively, and discuss the overall objective function in Sect. 3.4.

3.1   Problem Setting

In the incremental learning paradigm, a set of tasks $\mathcal{T}_t = \{\tau_1, \tau_2, \cdots, \tau_t\}$ is introduced to the model over time, where $\mathcal{T}_t$ represents the tasks that the model has seen until time step t. τ_t denotes the task introduced at time step t, which is composed of images and labels sampled from its corresponding data distribution: $\tau_t = (\mathbf{x}_i^{\tau_t}, y_i^{\tau_t}) \sim p_{data}^{\tau_t}$. Each task τ_t contains instances from a disjoint set of classes. $\mathcal{F}^{\mathcal{T}_t}$ denotes the model at time step t. Without loss of generality, $\mathcal{F}^{\mathcal{T}_t}$ can be expressed as a composition of two functions: $\mathcal{F}^{\mathcal{T}_t}(\mathbf{x}) = (\mathcal{F}_\phi^{\mathcal{T}_t} \circ \mathcal{F}_\theta^{\mathcal{T}_t})(\mathbf{x})$, where $\mathcal{F}_\phi^{\mathcal{T}_t}$ represents a feature extractor, and $\mathcal{F}_\theta^{\mathcal{T}_t}$ denotes a classifier. The challenge in incremental learning is to learn a model that can represent and classify all seen classes equally well, at any point in the task stream.

While training the model $\mathcal{F}^{\mathcal{T}_t}$ on the task τ_t, the model does not have access to all the data from previous tasks. Exemplar-based methods [5,6,32,41,49] sample a very small subset of each task data $e_t \in \tau_t$ at the end of every task τ_t and store it in a memory buffer $\mathcal{M}_t = \{e_1, e_2, \cdots, e_t\}$, which contains a subset of data from all tasks seen until time t. When learning a new task at time step t, the task's data τ_t is combined with samples from the memory containing exemplars of each previous task $\mathcal{M}_{t-1}$. Therefore, the dataset that the model has at time step t is $\mathcal{D}_t = \tau_t \cup \mathcal{M}_{t-1}$. In distillation-based methods, we assume access to the previous model $\mathcal{F}^{\mathcal{T}_{t-1}}$ which has learned the stream of tasks $\mathcal{T}_{t-1}$. The model $\mathcal{F}^{\mathcal{T}_{t-1}}$ is frozen and not updated, and is instead used to guide the learning of the current model $\mathcal{F}^{\mathcal{T}_t}$. Effectively utilising the previous model is key to balancing stability and plasticity. Excess constraints tied to the model can prevent the current task from being learned, and poor constraints can lead to easy forgetting of previous tasks.

3.2   Cross-Space Clustering

Our *cross-space clustering (CSC)* objective alleviates forgetting by distilling class-level semantics and inducing tight clusters in the feature space. CSC leverages points across the entire feature space of the previous model $\mathcal{F}^{\mathcal{T}_{t-1}}$, to identify regions that a class is optimized to stay within, and other harmful regions

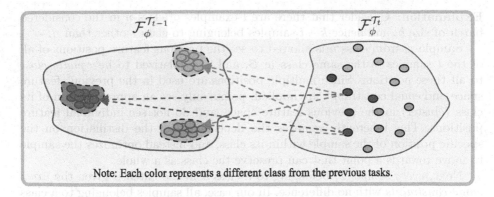

Note: Each color represents a different class from the previous tasks.

Fig. 1. We illustrate our cross-space clustering (CSC) objective. We show instances from 3 classes from the stream T_{t-1}, and their positions in $\mathcal{F}_\phi^{T_{t-1}}$ and $\mathcal{F}_\phi^{T_t}$ respectively. Classes are well represented in $\mathcal{F}_\phi^{T_{t-1}}$, however their representations are dispersed in the $\mathcal{F}_\phi^{T_t}$. Here we illustrate the constraint imposed on an instance of the violet class, based on the cluster position of its own class (indicated by the green arrows) and the positions of every other class (indicated by the red arrows). Note how the exact same constraint is applied on all instances of a class (illustrated here with 2 instances of the violet class). Best viewed in color. (Color figure online)

that it is prevented from drifting towards. We illustrate our cross-space clustering objective in Fig. 1.

Consider that the model $\mathcal{F}^{T_t}$ is trained on mini-batches $\mathcal{B} = \{x_i, y_i\}_{i=1}^k$ sampled from D_t. Our cross-space clustering objective enforces the following loss on the model:

$$L_{Cross-Cluster} = \frac{1}{k^2} \sum_{i=1}^k \sum_{j=1}^k \left(1 - \cos(\mathcal{F}_\phi^{T_t}(x_i), \mathcal{F}_\phi^{T_{t-1}}(x_j))\right) * ind(y_i == y_j) \quad (1)$$

where ind is an indicator function that returns 1 when its inputs are equal and -1 otherwise[1], and $\cos(a, b)$ denotes the cosine similarity between two vectors a and b.

Physical Interpretation: For pairs of samples x_i and x_j, $\mathcal{F}^{T_t}(x_i)$ is enforced to minimize cosine distance with $\mathcal{F}^{T_{t-1}}(x_j)$ when they are of the same class ($y_i == y_j$), and maximize cosine distance with $\mathcal{F}^{T_{t-1}}(x_j)$ when they are of different classes ($y_i! = y_j$). We expand upon the objective and its implications separately below.

---

[1] Note how this is different from a typical indicator function that returns 0 when the inputs are not equal.

Explanation: Consider that there are l examples of class n in the considered batch of size k, and hence $k - l$ samples belonging to classes other than n.

Sample x_i from class n is allowed to see the previous feature positions of all of the l samples of the same class in $\mathcal{B}$, and is regularized to be *equally close* to all these positions. Since multiple positions are used in the previous feature space and equal constraints are applied, points only see an approximation of its class (cluster) in the previous feature space, and do not see individual feature positions. This inherently removes the dependency of the distillation on the specific position of the sample within its class, and instead optimizes the sample to move towards a point that can preserve the class as a whole.

Next, *every sample x_i* belonging to a class n in the batch is given the *exact same constraints* with no difference. In our case, all samples belonging to a class are optimized towards the mean of the class's embeddings in the previous space. This leads to all of them being optimized *jointly* to a single stark region belonging to their class. Repeating this process for several iterations implicitly leads to model to implicitly *cluster* all samples of a class in the *current* feature space $\mathcal{F}^{\mathcal{T}_t}$ in the specific characterized regions. With respect to clustering, an important point is that our loss is *cross-space* in the sense, it does not encourage clustering of features of a class using features from the same model [8], that would neither exploits prior knowledge about the inter-class distances, nor imposes any constraints on the location of the classes. Our formulation instead encourages a model to keep all these clusters at specific points provided by the previous feature space, thereby directly distilling and preserving the *cluster positions* in the feature space as well. Hence, our objective uses approximate cluster positions from $\mathcal{F}^{\mathcal{T}_{t-1}}$ to in-turn cluster samples at specific positions in $\mathcal{F}^{\mathcal{T}_t}$. Since all samples are optimized towards the same region, all points of the class are optimized to *unite* and jointly protect and preserve the class. Such a formulation gives rise to a sense of *herd-immunity* of classes from forgetting, which better preserves the classes as the model drifts.

Finally, with very few exemplars stored per-class in the memory, our objective proposes to maximally utilize the memory[2] as well as the current task, leveraging them to identify *negative regions* that an instance is maintained to lie away from. Through multiple iterations of optimization, x_i belonging to class n is enforced to stay equally away from the positions of all other $k - l$ examples from the entire previous space. This indirectly tightens the cluster of class n in $\mathcal{F}^{\mathcal{T}_t}$ along multiple directions in the feature space.

Differences from Prior Work: Prior distillation-based methods [13,18,46] only apply *sample-to-sample* cross-space constraints, to preserve the representational properties of the previous space. The core difference of our method from all others lies in how it applies *class-to-region* constraints. Here, *class* denotes how all samples of a class are jointly optimized with the same constraints, and

---

[2] A batch of sufficient size typically contains at least one sample from each previous class, serving as a rough approximation of the memory.

region denotes how the samples are optimized towards and away from specific *regions* instead of towards individual points.

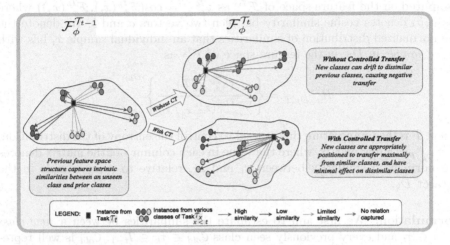

Fig. 2. We illustrate our **controlled transfer** objective. We show the positions of instances from five random classes taken from previous tasks $\tau_x; x < t$, and one unseen incoming class from the current task τ_t, in $\mathcal{F}_\phi^{\mathcal{T}_{t-1}}$ and $\mathcal{F}_\phi^{\mathcal{T}_t}$ respectively. With our objective, the new task instances are regularized to position themselves appropriately, to prevent negative transfer to dissimilar classes, and to encourage positive transfer from similar classes (best viewed in color) (Color figure online)

3.3 Controlled Transfer

Catastrophic forgetting has been previously characterized to arise due to a variety of reasons - the inability to access enough data of previous tasks [6,18,49], change in important parameters [4,24,55], representation drift [8,13,31], conflicting gradients [10,14,33,48] and insufficient capacity of models [1,50,53]. However, all these works ignore the semantic similarities between tasks and their relation to forgetting. We argue that knowing the degree of semantic similarity between two classes can, in fact, be very useful in incremental learning: When a previous class is *dissimilar* to the class currently being learned, the model must learn to treat the previous class distinctively and minimally impact it, so that the semantic specialities of that class are not erased. Conversely, when there is a previous class which is *similar* to the class currently being learned, the model must maximally transfer features from that class, to learn the current class in the best possible way. With these goals, we propose an incremental learning objective that *explicitly quantifies* inter-class similarities, and *controls* transfer between classes in every phase. Figure 2 illustrates our controlled transfer objective.

Notation: We first describe the general notation that we use to denote the similarity between samples in a space. Consider two samples x_i and x_j from a dataset D_k, and a model $\mathcal{F}^{T_k}$. We denote the similarity between x_i and x_j computed on the feature space of $\mathcal{F}^{T_k}$ as $z_{x_i,x_j}^{T_k} = \cos(\mathcal{F}_\phi^{T_k}(x_i), \mathcal{F}_\phi^{T_k}(x_j))$ where $\cos(a, b)$ denotes cosine similarity between two vectors a and b. We denote the the normalized distribution of similarities that an individual sample x_i has with *every sample* in D_k, in the feature space of $\mathcal{F}^{T_k}$ as

$$H_{x_i,D_k,T}^{T_k} = \left\{ \frac{(z_{x_i,x_j}^{T_k}/T)}{\sum_{g=1}^{|D_k|}(z_{x_i,x_g}^{T_k}/T)} \right\}_{j=1}^{|D_k|} \tag{2}$$

where T is the temperature that is used to control the entropy of the distribution. $H_{x_i,D_k,T}^{T_k}$ is a row matrix, where the value in each column j of the matrix denotes the normalized similarity between x_i and x_j, relative to every sample in the dataset D_k.

Formulation: We first aim to estimate the similarities between a *new class* $C_{new} \in \tau_t$ and every previously seen class $C_{old} \in \tau_k \in T_{t-1}$. C_{old} is well represented the model $\mathcal{F}^{T_{t-1}}$; the new class C_{new} has not yet been learned by any model. It is not possible to use the drifting feature space of $\mathcal{F}^{T_t}$ to represent C_{new}; even representing C_{new} once it has been learned by $\mathcal{F}^{T_t}$ would heavily bias the representations towards C_{new} due to the well-known recency bias [2, 49]. Our formulation instead proposes to utilize the *dark knowledge* that the *previous model* possesses about an *unseen class*: if the representations of an unseen class C_{new} lie relatively close to the class representations of a previous class in $\mathcal{F}^{T_{t-1}}$, it indicates that the two classes share semantic similarities. On the other hand, if the representations of an unseen class C_{new} lie relatively far from a previous class in $\mathcal{F}^{T_{t-1}}$, it indicates that the two classes do not have any semantic features in common. Note how the similarities for C_{new} given by $\mathcal{F}^{T_{t-1}}$ are *unbiased* as the model has never seen C_{new}, and hence can be used as approximations to the semantic similarities. We propose to use these approximate similarities captured by $\mathcal{F}^{T_{t-1}}$ in our objective explained below.

Consider a mini-batch of $B_n^{T_t}$ of size s that contains samples $\{(x_i^{T_t}, y_i^{T_t})\}$ randomly sampled from D_t. This mini-batch $B_n^{T_t}$ is composed of p samples from the current task denoted by $P = (x_i^{T_t}, y_i^{T_t})_{i=1}^p$, and q samples taken from the memory, denoted by $Q = (x_i^{T_k}, y_i^{T_k})_{i=1}^q$, where $k < t$. In an effort to control the transfer between a new and an old sample, our objective regularizes the normalized similarity (closeness) that a sample from the current task $(x_i^{T_t}, y_i^{T_t}) \in \tau_t$ has with every sample from any previous class $(x_i^{T_k}, y_i^{T_k})$, where $k < t$. This is enforced by minimizing the KL Divergence of the similarity distribution of $x_i^{T_t} \in P$ over Q, in the *current space* $\mathcal{F}_\phi^{T_t}$, with the similarity distribution computed in the *previous space* $\mathcal{F}_\phi^{T_{t-1}}$, as follows

$$L_{Transfer} = \frac{1}{p} \sum_{i=1}^p KL(H_{x_i,Q,T}^{T_t} || H_{x_i,Q,T}^{T_{t-1}}) \tag{3}$$

This loss modifies the position of the current classes in the current feature space $\mathcal{F}_\phi^{T_t}$ such that they have *high similarity* with (lie close to) prior classes that are *very similar*. This encourages *positive forward transfer* of features to the current classes from selected previous classes that are similar, as both their embeddings are optimized to have high similarity in the current space. This helps the model learn the current task better by leveraging transferred features, and lessens the impact that the new task has on the representation space. Conversely, as the embeddings are optimized to have *low similarity* with (lie far from) those previous classes that are *dissimilar* to it, it discourages (negative) backward transfer from the current classes to those dissimilar classes. Consequently, the features of these specific classes are further shielded from being erased, leading to the semantics of those classes being preserved more in the current space, which directly results in lesser forgetting of those classes.

3.4   Final Objective Function

The independent nature of our objectives make them suitable to be applied on top of any existing method to improve its performance. Our final objective combines $L_{Cross-Cluster}$ (1) and $L_{Transfer}$ (3) with appropriate coefficients:

$$L_{CSCCT} = L_{method} + \alpha * L_{Cross-Cluster} + \beta * L_{Transfer} \qquad (4)$$

where L_{method} denotes the objective function of the base method used, and α and β are loss coefficients for each of our objectives respectively. We term our method **CSCCT**, indicating **C**ross-**S**pace **C**lustering and **C**ontrolled **T**ransfer.

Table 1. The table shows results on **CIFAR100** when our method is added to three top-performing approaches [13,18,41]. The red subscript highlights the relative improvement. $\mathcal{B}$ denotes the number of classes in the first task. $\mathcal{C}$ denotes the number of classes in every subsequent task.

Dataset	CIFAR100					
Settings	$\mathcal{B} = 50$			$\mathcal{B} = \mathcal{C}$		
Methods	$\mathcal{C} = 1$	$\mathcal{C} = 2$	$\mathcal{C} = 5$	$\mathcal{C} = 1$	$\mathcal{C} = 2$	$\mathcal{C} = 5$
iCaRL [41]	43.39	48.31	54.42	30.92	36.80	44.19
iCaRL + CSCCT	$46.15_{+2.76}$	$51.62_{+3.31}$	$56.75_{+2.33}$	$34.02_{+3.1}$	$\mathbf{39.60}_{+2.8}$	$46.45_{+2.26}$
LUCIR [18]	50.26	55.38	59.40	25.40	31.93	42.28
LUCIR + CSCCT	$52.95_{+2.69}$	$56.49_{+1.13}$	$62.01_{+2.61}$	$28.12_{+2.72}$	$34.96_{+3.03}$	$44.03_{+1.55}$
PODNet [13]	56.88	59.98	62.66	33.58	36.68	45.27
PODNet + CSCCT	$\mathbf{58.80}_{+1.92}$	$\mathbf{61.10}_{+1.12}$	$\mathbf{63.72}_{+1.06}$	$\mathbf{36.23}_{+2.65}$	$39.3_{+2.62}$	$\mathbf{47.8}_{+2.53}$

4   Experiments and Results

We conduct extensive experiments adding our method to three prominent methods in class-incremental learning [13,18,41].

Protocols: Prior work has experimented with two CIL protocols: **a)** training with half the total number of classes in the first task, and equal number of classes in each subsequent task [13,18,49], and **b)** training with the same number of classes in each task, including the first [2,7,41]. The first setting has the advantage of gaining access to strong features in the first task, while the second tests an extreme continual learning setting; both these are plausible in a real-world incremental classification scenario. We experiment with both these protocols to demonstrate the applicability of our method. On CIFAR100, classes are grouped into 1, 2 and 5 classes per task. On ImageNet-Subset, the classes are split into 2, 5 and 10 classes per task. Hence, we experiment on both *long streams of small tasks*, as well as *short streams of large tasks*.

Datasets and Evaluation Metric: Following prior works [7,13,18,41], we test on the incremental versions of CIFAR-100 [28] and ImageNet-Subset [41]. CIFAR100 contains 100 classes, with 500 images per class, and each of dimension 32×32. ImageNet-Subset is a subset of the ImageNet-1k dataset [11], and contains 100 classes, with over 1300 images per class. Each image is of size 224×224. All our results denote average incremental accuracy. We follow the original papers in their inference methodology: On LUCIR [18] and PODNet [13], classification is performed as usual using the trained classifier, while on iCARL [41], classification is based on nearest-mean-of-exemplars.

Table 2. The table shows results on **ImageNet-Subset** when our method is added to three top-performing approaches [13,18,41]. The red subscript highlights the relative improvement. $\mathcal{B}$ denotes the number of classes in the first task. $\mathcal{C}$ denotes the number of classes in every subsequent task.

Dataset	ImageNet-Subset					
Settings	$\mathcal{B} = 50$			$\mathcal{B} = \mathcal{C}$		
Methods	$\mathcal{C} = 2$	$\mathcal{C} = 5$	$\mathcal{C} = 10$	$\mathcal{C} = 2$	$\mathcal{C} = 5$	$\mathcal{C} = 10$
iCaRL [41]	55.81	57.34	65.97	40.75	55.92	60.93
iCaRL + CSCCT	$57.01_{+1.2}$	$58.37_{+1.03}$	$66.82_{+0.8}$	$42.46_{+1.71}$	$57.45_{+1.53}$	$62.60_{+1.67}$
LUCIR [18]	60.44	66.55	70.18	36.84	46.40	56.78
LUCIR + CSCCT	$61.52_{+1.08}$	$67.91_{+1.36}$	$71.33_{+1.15}$	$37.86_{+1.02}$	$47.55_{+1.15}$	$58.07_{+1.29}$
PODNet [13]	67.27	73.01	75.32	44.94	58.23	66.24
PODNet + CSCCT	$68.91_{+1.64}$	$74.35_{+1.34}$	$76.41_{+1.09}$	$46.06_{+1.12}$	$59.43_{+1.2}$	$67.49_{+1.25}$

5   Implementation Details

Following prior work [13,18], we use a ResNet-32 and ResNet-18 on CIFAR100 and ImageNet-Subset respectively. On CIFAR100, we use a batch size of 128 and train for 160 epochs, with an initial learning rate of $4e^{-1}$ that is decayed by 0.1 at the 80th and 120th epochs respectively. On ImageNet-Subset, we use a batch size of 64 and train for 90 epochs, with an initial learning rate of $2e^{-2}$ that is decayed by 0.1 at the 30th and 60th epochs respectively. We use *herding selection* [41] for exemplar sampling, and an exemplar memory size of 20.

5.1 Quantitative Results

We add our method to three state-of-the-art class-incremental learning methodologies: iCARL [41], LUCIR [18] and PODNet [13]. Table 1 showcases results on CIFAR100, and Table 2 showcases results on ImageNet-Subset. We see a consistent improvement across all settings and methods when CSCCT is added to them. Specifically, on CIFAR100, adding CSCCT to iCARL [41], LUCIR [18] and PODNet [13] provides strong relative improvement of 2.76%, 2.28% and 1.99% respectively averaged across all settings, while on the much more high-dimensional ImageNet-Subset, adding our method to the respective baselines provides consistent relative improvements of 1.32%, 1.17% and 1.35%.

Evaluating iCARL [41], LUCIR [18] and PODNet [13] on the equal class protocol show that LUCIR [18] suffers from a severe performance degradation due to its inherent reliance on a large initial task, while iCARL [41] and PODNet [13] do not. On CIFAR100, simply adding our method to iCARL [41] gives it strong boosts of 2.2% − 3.1% in this setting, bringing it much closer to the state-of-the-art PODNet [13]. Overall, our method improves performance consistently across both settings, showing that our formulation *does not rely on a large initial task to learn strong representations.*

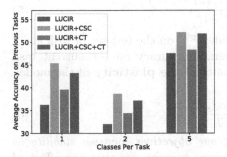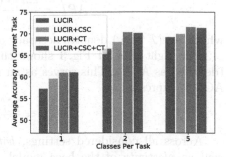

Fig. 3. Average accuracy on previous tasks (APT) and average accuracy on the current task (ACT), plotted across various settings on the CIFAR-100 dataset

6   Ablation Study and Analysis

6.1   Effect of Each Component on Average Incremental Accuracy

In Table 3, we ablate each component of our objective. Each of our objectives can improve accuracy independently. In particular, CSC is more effective when the number of classes per task is extremely low, while CT stands out in

Table 3. Ablating each objective on CIFAR100. Maroon denotes 2nd best result.

Settings	$\mathcal{B} = 50$			$\mathcal{B} = \mathcal{C}$		
Methods	$\mathcal{C} = 1$	$\mathcal{C} = 2$	$\mathcal{C} = 5$	$\mathcal{C} = 1$	$\mathcal{C} = 2$	$\mathcal{C} = 5$
LUCIR [18]	50.26	55.38	59.4	25.4	31.93	42.28
LUCIR + CSC	52.04	55.95	60.45	27.16	32.89	42.98
LUCIR + CT	51.5	55.87	61.97	26.53	33.98	43.69
LUCIR + CSCCT	52.95	56.49	62.01	28.12	34.96	44.03

the improvement it offers when there are more classes per task. Overall, combining our objectives achieves the best performance across all settings.

6.2   Effect of Each Component on Stability/Plasticity

To further investigate how each component is useful specifically in the incremental learning setup, we look into how each component improves the stability and plasticity of the model under various settings. The left plot of Fig. 3 shows the average accuracy on previous tasks (denotes as APT). This serves as an indicator of the **stability** of the model. Mathematically, APT can be expressed as

$$APT = \frac{\sum_{t=2}^{T} \left(\frac{\sum_{k=1}^{t-1} Acc(\mathcal{F}^{\mathcal{T}_t}, \tau_k)}{t-1} \right)}{T - 1} \tag{5}$$

where $Acc(\mathcal{F}^{\mathcal{T}_t}, \tau_k)$ denotes accuracy of model $\mathcal{F}^{\mathcal{T}_t}$ on the test set of task k.

The right plot of Fig. 3 shows the average accuracy on the current task (denoted as ACT). This serves as an indicator of the **plasticity** of the model. ACT is expressed as

$$ACT = \frac{\sum_{t=1}^{T} Acc(\mathcal{F}^{\mathcal{T}_t}, \tau_t)}{T} \tag{6}$$

Across all considered settings, *both of our objectives* increase *stability* as well as *plasticity* of the base model. However, one can see that the effect of the **CSC objective** is much more pronounced on the **stability** of the model. This aligns with intuition that the CSC helps in preserving previous classes better in the representation space. At the same time, the **CT objective** impacts the **plasticity** consistently more than the CSC objective, as it mainly aims at appropriately positioning the current task samples to maximize transfer.

6.3   Embedding Space Visualization

In Fig. 4, we present T-SNE [34] visualizations of the embedding space, without and with our Cross-Space Clustering (CSC) objective (1). The 50 classes learned

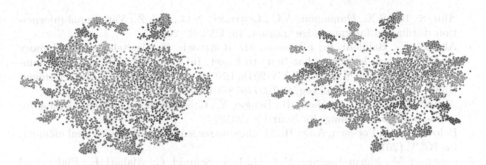

Fig. 4. T-SNE [34] visualizations of the base 50 classes of CIFAR100 in the embedding space, after all 100 classes have been learned (**Left**: LUCIR [18], **Right**: LUCIR+CSC)

in the initial task are plotted in the embedding spaces of both models, once all the 100 classes have been learned. It is seen that the CSC objective results in better clusters of prior classes in the feature space, compared to the baseline. The number of overlapping classes are reduced to a significant extent, as our objective ensures that the clusters are well-separated.

7 Conclusion

We introduced two complementary distillation-based objectives for class incremental learning. Our first objective called *cross-space clustering* positions classes appropriately in the embedding space and enables classes to counteract forgetting jointly. Our second objective called *controlled transfer* controls the positive and negative transfer between classes by estimating and utilizing inter-class relationships. We perform extensive experiments across a wide range of experimental settings to showcase the effectiveness of our objectives.

Acknowledgements. We are grateful to the Department of Science and Technology, India, as well as Intel India for the financial support of this project through the IMPRINT program (IMP/2019/000250) as well as the DST ICPS Data Science Cluster program. KJJ thanks TCS for their PhD Fellowship. We also thank the anonymous reviewers and Area Chairs for their valuable feedback in improving the presentation of this paper.

References

1. Abati, D., Tomczak, J.M., Blankevoort, T., Calderara, S., Cucchiara, R., Bejnordi, B.E.: Conditional channel gated networks for task-aware continual learning. In: CVPR (2020)
2. Ahn, H., Kwak, J., Lim, S.F., Bang, H., Kim, H., Moon, T.: SS-IL: separated softmax for incremental learning. In: ICCV (2021)

3. Ahn, S., Hu, S.X., Damianou, A.C., Lawrence, N.D., Dai, Z.: Variational information distillation for knowledge transfer. In: CVPR (2019)
4. Aljundi, R., Babiloni, F., Elhoseiny, M., Rohrbach, M., Tuytelaars, T.: Memory aware synapses: learning what (not) to forget. In: Ferrari, V., Hebert, M., Sminchisescu, C., Weiss, Y. (eds.) ECCV 2018. LNCS, vol. 11207, pp. 144–161. Springer, Cham (2018). https://doi.org/10.1007/978-3-030-01219-9_9
5. Aljundi, R., Lin, M., Goujaud, B., Bengio, Y.: Gradient based sample selection for online continual learning. In: NeurIPS (2019)
6. Belouadah, E., Popescu, A.D.: IL2M: class incremental learning with dual memory. In: ICCV (2019)
7. Castro, F.M., Marín-Jiménez, M.J., Guil, N., Schmid, C., Alahari, K.: End-to-end incremental learning. In: Ferrari, V., Hebert, M., Sminchisescu, C., Weiss, Y. (eds.) ECCV 2018. LNCS, vol. 11216, pp. 241–257. Springer, Cham (2018). https://doi.org/10.1007/978-3-030-01258-8_15
8. Cha, H., Lee, J., Shin, J.: Co2L: contrastive continual learning. In: ICCV (2021)
9. Chaudhry, A., Dokania, P.K., Ajanthan, T., Torr, P.H.S.: Riemannian walk for incremental learning: understanding forgetting and intransigence. In: Ferrari, V., Hebert, M., Sminchisescu, C., Weiss, Y. (eds.) ECCV 2018. LNCS, vol. 11215, pp. 556–572. Springer, Cham (2018). https://doi.org/10.1007/978-3-030-01252-6_33
10. Chaudhry, A., Ranzato, M., Rohrbach, M., Elhoseiny, M.: Efficient lifelong learning with a-GEM. In: ICLR (2019)
11. Deng, J., Dong, W., Socher, R., Li, L.J., Li, K., Fei-Fei, L.: ImageNet: a large-scale hierarchical image database. In: CVPR (2009)
12. Dhar, P., Singh, R.V., Peng, K.C., Wu, Z., Chellappa, R.: Learning without memorizing. In: CVPR (2019)
13. Douillard, A., Cord, M., Ollion, C., Robert, T., Valle, E.: PODNet: pooled outputs distillation for small-tasks incremental learning. In: Vedaldi, A., Bischof, H., Brox, T., Frahm, J.-M. (eds.) ECCV 2020. LNCS, vol. 12365, pp. 86–102. Springer, Cham (2020). https://doi.org/10.1007/978-3-030-58565-5_6
14. Farajtabar, M., Azizan, N., Mott, A., Li, A.: Orthogonal gradient descent for continual learning. In: AISTATS (2020)
15. Finn, C., Abbeel, P., Levine, S.: Model-agnostic meta-learning for fast adaptation of deep networks. In: ICML (2017)
16. French, R.M.: Catastrophic forgetting in connectionist networks. Trends Cogn. Sci. 3(4), 128–135 (1999)
17. Hinton, G.E., Vinyals, O., Dean, J.: Distilling the knowledge in a neural network. arXiv preprint arXiv:1503.02531 (2015)
18. Hou, S., Pan, X., Loy, C.C., Wang, Z., Lin, D.: Learning a unified classifier incrementally via rebalancing. In: CVPR (2019)
19. Huang, Z., Wang, N.: Like what you like: knowledge distill via neuron selectivity transfer. arXiv preprint arXiv:abs/1707.01219 (2017)
20. Javed, K., White, M.: Meta-learning representations for continual learning. In: NeurIPS (2019)
21. Joseph, K., Khan, S., Khan, F.S., Anwer, R.M., Balasubramanian, V.N.: Energy-based latent aligner for incremental learning. In: CVPR (2022)
22. Joseph, K., Khan, S., Khan, F.S., Balasubramanian, V.N.: Towards open world object detection. In: CVPR (2021)
23. Kim, J., Park, S., Kwak, N.: Paraphrasing complex network: network compression via factor transfer. In: NeurIPS (2018)
24. Kirkpatrick, J., et al.: Overcoming catastrophic forgetting in neural networks. In: PNAS (2017)

25. Joseph, K.J., Balasubramanian,V.N.: Meta-consolidation for continual learning. In: NeurIPS (2020)
26. Kj, J., Rajasegaran, J., Khan, S., Khan, F.S., Balasubramanian, V.N.: Incremental object detection via meta-learning. IEEE TPAMI (2021)
27. Koratana, A., Kang, D., Bailis, P., Zaharia, M.A.: LIT: learned intermediate representation training for model compression. In: ICML (2019)
28. Krizhevsky, A., Hinton, G.: Learning multiple layers of features from tiny images. In: CiteSeer (2009)
29. Lee, K., Lee, K., Shin, J., Lee, H.: Overcoming catastrophic forgetting with unlabeled data in the wild. arXiv preprint arXiv:1903.12648 (2019)
30. Li, X., Zhou, Y., Wu, T., Socher, R., Xiong, C.: Learn to grow: a continual structure learning framework for overcoming catastrophic forgetting. In: ICML (2019)
31. Li, Z., Hoiem, D.: Learning without forgetting. IEEE TPAMI (2018)
32. Liu, Y., Liu, A., Su, Y., Schiele, B., Sun, Q.: Mnemonics training: multi-class incremental learning without forgetting. In: CVPR (2020)
33. Lopez-Paz, D., Ranzato, M.: Gradient episodic memory for continual learning. In: NeurIPS (2017)
34. van der Maaten, L., Hinton, G.: Visualizing data using t-SNE. In: JMLR (2008)
35. Masana, M., Liu, X., Twardowski, B., Menta, M., Bagdanov, A.D., van de Weijer, J.: Class-incremental learning: survey and performance evaluation on image classification. arXiv preprint arXiv:2010.15277 (2021)
36. Mermillod, M., Bugaiska, A., Bonin, P.: The stability-plasticity dilemma: investigating the continuum from catastrophic forgetting to age-limited learning effects. Front. Psychol. **4**, 504 (2013)
37. Nichol, A., Achiam, J., Schulman, J.: On first-order meta-learning algorithms. arXiv preprint arXiv:1803.02999 (2018)
38. Park, W., Kim, D., Lu, Y., Cho, M.: Relational knowledge distillation. In: CVPR (2019)
39. Peng, B., et al.: Correlation congruence for knowledge distillation. In: ICCV (2019)
40. Rajasegaran, J., Hayat, M., Khan, S.H., Khan, F.S., Shao, L.: Random path selection for continual learning. In: NeurIPS (2019)
41. Rebuffi, S.A., Kolesnikov, A., Sperl, G., Lampert, C.H.: iCaRL: incremental classifier and representation learning. In: CVPR (2017)
42. Riemer, M., et al.: Learning to learn without forgetting by maximizing transfer and minimizing interference. In: ICLR (2019)
43. Romero, A., Ballas, N., Kahou, S.E., Chassang, A., Gatta, C., Bengio, Y.: FitNets: hints for thin deep nets. In: ICLR (2015)
44. Serrà, J., Surís, D., Miron, M., Karatzoglou, A.: Overcoming catastrophic forgetting with hard attention to the task. ICML (2018)
45. Shin, H., Lee, J.K., Kim, J., Kim, J.: Continual learning with deep generative replay. In: NeurIPS (2017)
46. Simon, C., Koniusz, P., Harandi, M.: On learning the geodesic path for incremental learning. In: CVPR (2021)
47. Tung, F., Mori, G.: Similarity-preserving knowledge distillation. In: ICCV (2019)
48. Wang, S., Li, X., Sun, J., Xu, Z.: Training networks in null space of feature covariance for continual learning. In: CVPR (2021)
49. Wu, Y., et al.: Large scale incremental learning. In: CVPR (2019)
50. Yan, S., Xie, J., He, X.: DER: dynamically expandable representation for class incremental learning. In: CVPR (2021)
51. Yim, J., Joo, D., Bae, J.H., Kim, J.: A gift from knowledge distillation: fast optimization, network minimization and transfer learning. In: CVPR (2017)

52. Yin, H., et al.: Dreaming to distill: data-free knowledge transfer via deepinversion. In: CVPR (2020)
53. Yoon, J., Yang, E., Lee, J., Hwang, S.J.: Lifelong learning with dynamically expandable networks. In: ICLR (2018)
54. Zagoruyko, S., Komodakis, N.: Paying more attention to attention: improving the performance of convolutional neural networks via attention transfer. In: ICLR (2017)
55. Zenke, F., Poole, B., Ganguli, S.: Continual learning through synaptic intelligence. In: ICML (2017)
56. Zhai, M., Chen, L., Tung, F., He, J., Nawhal, M., Mori, G.: Lifelong GAN: continual learning for conditional image generation. In: ICCV (2019)

Object Discovery and Representation Networks

Olivier J. Hénaff$^{(\boxtimes)}$, Skanda Koppula, Evan Shelhamer, Daniel Zoran,
Andrew Jaegle, Andrew Zisserman, João Carreira, and Relja Arandjelović

DeepMind, London, UK
henaff@google.com

Abstract. The promise of self-supervised learning (SSL) is to leverage large amounts of unlabeled data to solve complex tasks. While there has been excellent progress with simple, image-level learning, recent methods have shown the advantage of including knowledge of image structure. However, by introducing hand-crafted image segmentations to define regions of interest, or specialized augmentation strategies, these methods sacrifice the simplicity and generality that makes SSL so powerful. Instead, we propose a self-supervised learning paradigm that discovers this image structure by itself. Our method, **Odin**, couples object discovery and representation networks to discover meaningful image segmentations without any supervision. The resulting learning paradigm is simpler, less brittle, and more general, and achieves state-of-the-art transfer learning results for object detection and instance segmentation on COCO, and semantic segmentation on PASCAL and Cityscapes, while strongly surpassing supervised pre-training for video segmentation on DAVIS.

Keywords: Self-supervised learning · Object discovery · Transfer learning

1 Introduction

Self-supervised learning proposes to leverage large amounts of unlabeled data to solve complex visual tasks. Early attempts hand-designed pretext tasks, which required some semantic understanding of images and their layout to solve [21,60,64,89]. Contrastive learning departed from this tradition by radically simplifying the self-supervised protocol, in that the pretext task is specified by the data itself: representations must learn to distinguish a given example from the others in the dataset [25,36,62,81]. Modern instances of the contrastive framework have proven to be very powerful, leading to strong performance on a variety of downstream tasks [13,39,43]. More recent self-supervised methods have

---

Supplementary Information The online version contains supplementary material available at https://doi.org/10.1007/978-3-031-19812-0_8.

simplified the framework further, removing the need for negative samples [35], bespoke architectural components [15], and learning dynamics [87], suggesting that increasingly domain-agnostic and data-driven methods might enable learning from ever-larger and more general sources of data.

However, a parallel line of work has asked whether the current self-supervised paradigm—which maximizes the similarity of the same data-point under different views—is too simple. By treating data-points as monolithic instances, these methods overlook the complexity of real-world data: natural scenes are composed of many objects, natural speech of multiple speakers, and natural videos of many scenes. Ignoring this variability and encouraging models to represent different parts of an image in a similar manner risks dampening their selectivity for objects, their relationships, and layouts in real-world scenes. Indeed, several works have demonstrated the benefits of properly handling this variability when learning task-relevant representations [42,70,76,77,79]. While such object- and segmentation-aware approaches have yielded impressive empirical gains, they have relied on more domain-specific prior knowledge to expose the structure of the data—for example by using hand-crafted segmentation algorithms [42], or salience estimation networks trained on human annotations [77]—bounding how much they can learn from the data and what data they can be used on.

In this work we ask whether this knowledge can instead be derived from the data itself. To do so, we propose to couple two learning processes: object discovery and object representation. We use object discovery to uncover the structure of individual data-points, allowing the self-supervised task to focus on learning invariant representations of object-level instances. In turn, we use the resulting object representations as features for unsupervised object discovery, which feeds back into the representation learning process. These object discovery and representation networks thus engage in a virtuous cycle of representation and segmentation quality: better representations lead to better segmentations, and vice versa. Crucially, we derive the unsupervised segmentations with no prior knowledge about image structure or content, using a simple k-means clustering of local features to partition each image. We thus open the possibility of applying the algorithm to different domains, modalities, and their combination.

We make the following contributions: 1) Our object discovery networks uncover, in an entirely self-supervised manner and without any prior knowledge of image structure or segmentation, meaningful decompositions of real-world scenes. 2) Our object representation networks lead to state-of-the-art results in transfer learning to object detection and instance segmentation on COCO, and semantic segmentation on PASCAL and Cityscapes, surpassing prior works which exploit segmentation and saliency information, without requiring this prior knowledge. 3) Our object representation networks seamlessly generalize to video understanding, surpassing supervised pre-training for video object segmentation on DAVIS. Finally, we test the resilience of our method by varying its essential components, and find it to be very robust, supporting further computational benefits. Together these results suggest that knowledge of scene structure, and the benefits it confers in representing objects, can—with the right learning paradigm—be extracted from the data itself.

2 Related Work

Pre-Contrastive Self-supervised Learning: Hand-Designed Tasks.
Early self-supervised approaches focused on injecting human expertise and intuition into the design of proxy tasks for pretraining. For example, to stimulate the network to learn object parts, [21] designed the task of predicting the spatial arrangement between local image patches. A rich collection of such intuitions and objectives was further developed, ranging from pixel-wise reconstruction-based approaches, such as denoising [78], inpainting [64], colorization [49,89], and more [23,90], to higher-level pretext tasks, such as predicting spatial layouts [21,59,60], orientation [30], egomotion [1], and temporal ordering [58].

Contrastive Learning and its Variants. Instance discrimination [25] has proven to be a very powerful pretext task which, we argue, owes its superior performance to being minimally hand-designed and maximally data-driven. By minimizing a contrastive loss [36,62], the similarity of a representation across different 'views' of the same image is maximized, while minimizing their similarity with distracting negative samples. Multiple views of a single data-point can naturally be extracted from multimodal or multisensory data [2,48,56,63,68,72] while for a single image-only modality they are typically constructed via local and global cropping [5,43,44,62] or data-augmentation [13,22,25,39,81]. Positive pairs then correspond to views of the same data point, while negatives are sampled views of different data-points (typically from the same mini-batch), although the need for negative samples has recently been questioned [15,35,87].

Baking Prior Knowledge Back into Self-supervised Learning. A growing body of research has brought hand-designed supervisory signals back into the self-supervised paradigm. For example, [42,77,79,82,88] decompose input images into their constituent objects and regions of interest using supervised segmentation algorithms, or hand-crafted heuristics. Object-level features are then computed for each region, and optimized using a contrastive objective. Other approaches use object-agnostic learning objectives, but integrate knowledge from segmentation heuristics or models in their augmentation strategies [57,76,92].

This trend is reflected in the broader research in self-supervised learning for other modalities. For example, [50] uses domain-specific knowledge to improve the masking strategies of BERT and other masked-language models. [37,85] leverage motion and flow information to improve learning from video. And similar to previously described works in vision, [61] uses a segmentation step prior to applying SSL on point clouds. In all cases, we aim to remove the dependency on such prior knowledge while retaining its benefits for representation learning.

Clustering and Representation Learning. In parallel to the advent of contrastive methods, clustering-based representation learning methods have seen similar success, particularly in harnessing large amounts of uncurated images for transfer learning [4,9–11,33,45]. Although they differ in their formulation of the self-supervised objective, these works also treat entire images as monolithic entities.

In contrast, IIC [45] performs within-image clustering using similarity losses counterbalanced by information maximization, obtaining compelling results in unsupervised segmentation. PiCIE [17] improves on this approach by imposing carefully-chosen, modality-specific geometric data augmentations and corresponding invariance and equivariance constraints. Neither of these works explicitly leverage their unsupervised segmentations for transfer learning across datasets and tasks however, which we investigate here.

Object Discovery. Recent years have seen a growing interest in developing generative models that perform object discovery. By introducing different inductive biases such as mixture-model likelihoods [8,34], attention [54,93] and specific forms of factorization [46,47], such models are able to discover objects and their interactions [20,32,71]. While much progress has been made, models from this family have yet to be demonstrated to work on natural images [34] and their application has been limited to synthetic data and simple highly structured environments typically used in robotics. Here we investigate object discovery on natural images in the wild, leveraging contrastive representation learning to enable this with simple k-means clustering.

3   Method

3.1   Self-supervised Learning with Odin

Our method learns two sets of networks which work in collaboration. The *object discovery* network produces feature maps from high-resolution images. These feature maps are then spatially clustered to produce a segmentation of the image. The *object representation* networks learns better features via a contrastive loss which uses the masks proposed by the object discovery network. The resulting improved features are then used by the object discovery network to create better segmentations, and this process is continuously repeated. Figure 1 illustrates the full method, which we detail below.

Object Discovery Network: From Representations to Segmentations. Given an image x, we compute a spanning view v^0 which encompasses most of the area of the image (Fig. 1, *spanning view*, defined below) and which is simply cropped and resized. We use a feature extractor f_τ to encode this view into a spatial map of hidden vectors $h^0 = f_\tau(v^0)$ and projections $z^0 = g_\tau(h^0)$, where g_τ is a two-layer MLP which is applied to each vector independently, and τ are the parameters of the *object discovery network*. We apply K-means clustering

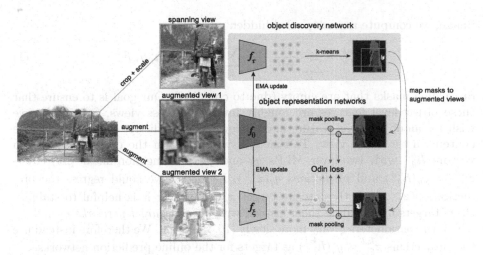

Fig. 1. Object discovery and representation networks. The object discovery network takes as input a cropped but otherwise un-augmented view of the image, and parses it using k-means clustering on its representation of it. The resulting segmentation is mapped into two augmented views of the same image, such that the masks are aligned across views and with the underlying image. The object representation networks take as input the augmented views of the image, and are trained using a self-supervised objective based on features pooled within each mask. The object discovery network is regularly updated with the parameters of the object representation network.

to the spatial map of features h^0 or z^0, segmenting it (independently across images) into K non-overlapping binary masks $m^{k,0}$ (Fig. 1, top row).

Object Representation Networks: From Segmentations to Representations. We produce two views v^1 and v^2 of the image by augmenting x twice, using the random preprocessing pipeline of BYOL [35], which includes random cropping, flipping, blurring, and point-wise color transformations (Fig. 1, *augmented views* and appendix).

The *spanning view* v^0 is chosen as the smallest crop which spans the spatial extent of the augmented views v^1 and v^2. We can therefore obtain two sets of masks $m^{k,1}, m^{k,2}$ which are consistent with each other and aligned with the underlying image content, by simply cropping, flipping, and resizing each mask $m^{k,0}$ as necessary (Fig. 1, right). Despite the significant differences in appearance across views, these masks contain the same underlying image content (up to differences in cropping), which we leverage in our objective.

Each augmented view $v^l \in \{v^1, v^2\}$ is encoded with a feature extractor f_θ into a spatial map of hidden vectors: $h_\theta^l = f_\theta(v^l)$ where θ are the parameters of the *object representation network* being optimized. For every mask $m^{k,l}$ in the image, we compute a mask-pooled hidden vector

$$h_\theta^{k,l} = \frac{1}{\sum_{i,j} m^{k,l}[i,j]} \sum_{i,j} m^{k,l}[i,j] \, h_\theta^l[i,j], \tag{1}$$

discarding masks that are empty (due to cropping). Our goal is to ensure that these object-level features are roughly invariant across views. Specifically, we wish for an object-level feature in one view to be predictive of the same image content in the other view. To that end we transform the object-level hidden vectors $h_\theta^{k,l}$ with two-layer MLPs g_θ and q_θ, yielding non-linear *projections* $z_\theta^{k,l} = g_\theta(h_\theta^{k,l})$ and *predictions* $q_\theta(z_\theta^{k,l})$. In theory, we could regress the prediction $q_\theta(z_\theta^{k,1})$ directly onto its target $z_\theta^{k,2}$, however it is helpful to stabilize these targets by encoding them instead with specific *target networks* g_ξ and f_ξ, where the parameters ξ vary more slowly [16,35,42,73]. We therefore instead use the projections $z_\xi^{k,l} = g_\xi(h_\xi^{k,l})$ as targets for the online prediction networks.

Jointly Learning to Discover and Represent Objects. Given a set of masks which approximately segment an image into objects, we wish to learn representations which distinguish these objects, while being invariant to identity-preserving transformations. Contrastive learning provides a straightforward objective for achieving this. Specifically, *contrastive detection* [42] trains a network to recognize object-level features across views, in the presence of many distracting "negative" features from other objects. The resulting objective maximizes the similarity between different views of the same object, while minimizing the similarity between different objects. We define the similarity between object-level features across views as

$$s_k^{1 \to 2} = \frac{1}{\alpha} \frac{\langle q_\theta(z_\theta^{k,1}), z_\xi^{k,2} \rangle}{\|q_\theta(z_\theta^{k,1})\| \|z_\xi^{k,2}\|} \tag{2}$$

where α is temperature hyper-parameter. We define the similarity between an object-level feature and a distracting negative sample $s_k^{1 \to n}$ analogously, by replacing the paired feature $z_\xi^{k,2}$ with one from a different mask in the same image, or a different image altogether. The contrastive loss function for an individual feature is then

$$\ell_k^{1 \to 2}(\theta; \xi, \tau) = -\log \frac{\exp(s_k^{1 \to 2})}{\exp(s_k^{1 \to 2}) + \sum_n \exp(s_k^{1 \to n})}, \tag{3}$$

which we sum across objects, views, and images in the mini-batch (summation across images not shown for clarity)

$$\mathcal{L}(\theta; \xi, \tau) = \frac{1}{K} \sum_{k=1}^K \ell_k^{1 \to 2}(\theta; \xi, \tau) + \ell_k^{2 \to 1}(\theta; \xi, \tau). \tag{4}$$

We optimize the object discovery and representation networks using a strategy inspired by BYOL [35]. One object representation network (the *online network* with parameters θ) is updated with gradients from the contrastive loss. The second object representation network (the *target network* with parameters ξ) and the object discovery network (with parameters τ) are updated using an exponential moving average of the online network:

$$\theta \leftarrow \text{optimizer}(\theta, \nabla_\theta \mathcal{L}(\theta; \xi, \tau), \lambda_\theta) \tag{5}$$

$$\xi \leftarrow (1 - \lambda_\xi)\xi + \lambda_\xi \theta \tag{6}$$

$$\tau \leftarrow (1 - \lambda_\tau)\tau + \lambda_\tau \theta, \tag{7}$$

where the optimizer is LARS [86], and λ_θ, λ_ξ, λ_τ are learning rates for the online, target, and discovery networks respectively. We adopt the learning rates for online and targets networks from BYOL without modification. For the object discovery network, we consider two schedules: a constant learning rate which continuously updates the object discovery network with the online one (e.g. $\lambda_\tau = 10^{-3}$), and a small number of discrete updates which copy the online representation network into the object discovery network (e.g. $\lambda_\tau = 1$ every 100 epochs and $\lambda_\tau = 0$ otherwise). The advantage of the second scheme is computational: if the object discovery network does not change between updates, the segments for training the object representation networks can be cached, removing the need to evaluate the object discovery network at every iteration.

Pretraining Details. We train object discovery and representation networks (Odin) on ImageNet [69] for 1000 epochs, using a ResNet-50 [41] or Swin Transformer [53] backbone equipped with Feature Pyramid Networks (FPN; [51]) as the feature extractor f. The FPN takes as input the hierarchy of latent vectors output by the ResNet or Swin backbone, and progressively upsamples them while adding information from intermediate feature arrays, yielding high-level and high-resolution representations of the input image. We use the highest-resolution output of the FPN (subsampling the image by a factor of 4) as the array of hidden vectors h.

After pretraining, we discard the target and object discovery networks, and use only the online object representation network for evaluation, facilitating the comparison to other methods which have their own means of learning the model.

3.2 Evaluating Object Discovery and Representation

Having trained object representation networks using the Odin framework, we evaluate the quality of their representation by fine-tuning them for object detection and instance segmentation on COCO, and segmentatic segmentation on PASCAL and Cityscapes. For consistency with prior work we retain only the pretrained backbone (ResNet or Swin transformer) for transfer learning, discarding feature pyramid networks and projection heads.

Object Detection and Instance Segmentation. For instance segmentation we use Mask-RCNN [40] while for object detection we report results for Mask-RCNN and FCOS*. Both methods are equipped with feature pyramid networks

[51] and cross-replica batch-norm [65]. For Mask-RCNN we adopt the Cloud TPU implementation [31] and use it without modification. FCOS* is our implementation of a single-stage detector based on FCOS [75], and improved with IoU prediction [80], ATSS [91] and T-Head [29]; full details are available in the appendix. We follow the common transfer setup and evaluate on COCO [52] – the pretrained network is used to initialize the backbone of a Mask-RCNN or FCOS* model, which is then fine-tuned on the train2017 set, and report bounding-box AP (AP^{bb}) and mask AP (AP^{mk}) on the val2017 set. We use two standard training schedules: 12 epochs and 24 epochs [39].

Semantic Segmentation with FCN. Following [39] we initialize the backbone of a fully-convolutional network (FCN, [55]) with our model. For PASCAL [27], we fine-tune on the train_aug2012 set for 45 epochs and report the mean intersection over union (mIoU) on the val2012 set. For Cityscapes [19], we fine-tune on the train_fine set for 160 epochs and evaluate on the val_fine set.

Object Discovery on COCO. We wish to assess whether our representations uncover the structure of real-world scenes during self-supervised pretraining. Simply visualizing saliency maps induced by the model only weakly tests this ability however [26], hence we use the COCO dataset comprised of complex scenes and human-annotated object segments. Specifically, we evaluate models on COCO images, cluster their features, and measure the overlap between the resulting segments and human-annotated ones. Given the diversity of object scales in COCO, we run multiple K-means segmentations (for K in $[1, 2, \ldots, 128]$) on the same set of latents, resulting in 255 object proposals which we resize to the input image resolution.

For each ground-truth segment g_t we compute the overlap with all proposals m_k using their intersection-over-union (IoU), and record the "best overlap" by taking the maximum across proposals. Averaging this metric across ground-truth segments, we obtain the "average best overlap" (ABO) metric [3], and computing the fraction of "best overlaps" greater than 50% yields the "object recovery" metric [18]. We then average each of these metrics across images.

Video Object Segmentation on DAVIS. As a further test of scene understanding, we assess whether learned representations can continue to recognize parts of an object as they evolve over time. Video object segmentation, specifically in its semi-supervised setting, captures this ability, which we evaluate on the DAVIS'17 benchmark [66]. Having evaluated a learned representation on a video independently across frames, we segment these features with nearest neighbor matching from frame to frame, given a segmentation of the first frame. In this way, the segmentation is propagated according to the similarity of the representation across space and time.

4 Experiments

4.1 Transfer Learning

Our first goal is to assess whether strong transfer learning performance can be obtained without resorting to prior knowledge of scene segmentations. To that end we train a ResNet-50 on ImageNet for 1000 epochs using the proposed Odin framework, and transfer it to object detection and instance segmentation on COCO, and semantic segmentation on PASCAL and Cityscapes.

Table 1. Transfer to COCO object detection and instance segmentation with Mask-RCNN: all methods pretrain a ResNet-50 on ImageNet before fine-tuning on COCO with Mask-RCNN for 12 epochs (1× schedule) or 24 epochs (2× schedule). We report average precision on object detection (AP^{bb}) and instance segmentation (AP^{mk})

Pretraining		Fine-tune 1×		Fine-tune 2×	
Method	Knows obj?	AP^{bb}	AP^{mk}	AP^{bb}	AP^{mk}
Supervised	no	39.6	35.6	41.6	37.6
VADeR [67]	no	39.2	35.6	–	–
MoCo [39]	no	39.4	35.6	41.7	37.5
SimCLR [13]	no	39.7	35.8	41.6	37.4
MoCo v2 [14]	no	40.1	36.3	41.7	37.6
InfoMin [74]	no	40.6	36.7	42.5	38.4
DeepCluster-v2 [11]	no	41.1	37.1	–	–
DINO [12]	no	41.2	37.1	42.3	38.1
PixPro [84]	no	41.4	–	–	–
BYOL [35]	no	41.6	37.2	42.4	38.0
SwAV [11]	no	41.6	37.8	–	–
ReLIC v2 [76]	yes	42.5	38.0	43.3	38.6
DetCon$_B$ [42]	yes	42.7	38.2	43.4	38.7
Odin	no	**42.9**	**38.4**	**43.8**	**39.1**

Object Detection and Instance Segmentation on COCO. Self-supervised learning has made steady gains on transfer learning from ImageNet to COCO, with a majority of methods surpassing supervised pretraining. The top-performing methods are ReLIC v2 and DetCon$_B$ which make heavy use of saliency or segmentation information in their learning paradigm. DetCon uses the same learning objective as Odin, but relies on a hand-crafted image segmentation algorithm [28] applied to the pixel lattice rather than a learned object discovery network. ReLIC v2 does not use segmentation information explicitly in its objective, but uses a hand-crafted saliency network to separate objects from their background in the data-augmentation pipeline. Both represent a step-change in performance relative to previous methods. Odin, which instead derives segmentations from its own learned representations, surpasses both of these methods (Table 1).

A recent self-supervised method, DINO [12], reports high-quality unsupervised segmentations, however it appears to do so at the cost of object representation. We fine-tune the publicly available ResNet checkpoint in our framework, and find it underperforms relative to simple methods such as BYOL. Other SSL methods such as SwAV and DeepCluster-v2 [11] which cluster representations *across* images rather than within also underperform in this setting.

Table 2. Transfer to PASCAL and Cityscapes semantic segmentation with fully convolutional networks: all methods pretrain a ResNet-50 on ImageNet before fine-tuning for semantic segmentation on PASCAL or Cityscapes, and report the mean intersection-over-union

Method	Knows obj?	PASCAL	Cityscapes
Supervised	no	74.4	74.9
BYOL [35]	no	75.7	74.6
DeepCluster-v2 [11]	no	75.8	76.8
SwAV [11]	no	76.0	76.2
DINO [12]	no	76.9	75.6
DetCon$_B$ [42]	yes	77.3	77.0
ReLIC v2 [76]	yes	77.9	75.2
Odin	no	**78.6**	**77.1**

Semantic Segmentation on PASCAL and Cityscapes. We assess the generality of these results by transferring them to two separate datasets and tasks, semantic segmetation on PASCAL and Cityscapes. Similarly to when transferring to COCO, DetCon and ReLIC v2 substantially outperform supervised and BYOL pretraining, confirming the utility of prior knowledge about segmentation and saliency. In this case as well, Odin successfully recovers this knowledge and surpasses both methods in a fully learned manner (Table 2).

In this setting DINO performs better, surpassing BYOL, possibly because semantic segmentation on PASCAL, which contains only 20 classes compared with 80 in COCO, weights object discovery more than object representation— isolating objects from the background rather than distinguishing object classes from each other. Nevertheless, Odin surpasses it as well, indicating that it achieves a better trade-off between object representation and discovery.

Transfer Learning with High-Performance Architectures. While Mask-RCNN has become a standard method for evaluating the quality of object-level representations, we asked whether the performance gains afforded by the Odin framework persisted with more sophisticated models. For this we turned to our FCOS* implementation, whose supervised baseline surpasses Mask-RCNN by 4.6% AP^{bb}. In this setting as well, Odin surpasses the supervised baseline and DINO (+1.3% AP^{bb}, Table 3, 1st column).

Table 3. Transfer to COCO object detection with FCOS*: all methods pretrain on ImageNet before fine-tuning on COCO with FCOS* for 30 epochs, and report average precision on object detection (AP^{bb}).

Pretraining	Knows obj?	ResNet-50	Swin-T	Swin-S
Supervised	no	44.2	46.7	48.3
DINO [12]	no	44.3	–	–
MOBY [83]	no	–	47.6	–
DetCon$_B$ [42]	yes	45.4	48.4	**50.4**
Odin	no	**45.6**	**48.5**	**50.4**

Swin transformers appear as a compelling candidate for general-purpose vision architectures, surpassing ResNet's in a variety of tasks [53]. Despite the almost universal success of self-supervised pretraining in improving the transfer learning performance of ResNet architectures, similar results have yet to become widespread for Swin transformers.

We therefore pretrain Swin-T and Swin-S transformers on ImageNet using Odin, and transfer them to COCO object detection using FCOS*. We also evaluate a pre-trained Moby checkpoint in the same setting. Moby pretraining marginally improves the performance of a Swin-T, whereas Odin furthers these gains (+1.8% AP^{bb}, Table 3, 2nd column). The benefits of Odin pretraining are emphasized when pretraining and transferring the larger Swin-S backbone (+2.1% AP^{bb}, Table 3, 3rd column).

We return to our original question of whether Odin has successfully recovered knowledge of scene structure by pretraining ResNet-50, Swin-T, and Swin-S with DetCon (which uses a hand-crafted segmentation algorithm instead of the object discovery network [28,42]), and transferring them with FCOS*. We find Odin to match or slightly surpass their performance, confirming our previous results.

4.2 Object Discovery in COCO

We have found thus far that Odin surpasses the transfer learning performance of state-of-the-art self-supervised methods which rely on prior knowledge of scene segmentations, suggesting it has derived this knowledge from the data itself. In this section, we directly evaluate the extent to which Odin has discovered objects in real-world scenes. We extract Odin features from COCO images, cluster them, and visualize the resulting segments (Fig. 2). Comparing unsupervised object proposals (last column) to human-annotated segments (2nd column) we see that Odin recovers a reasonable decomposition of real-world scenes: figures are separated from their background, small objects are isolated, and even different instances of the same class (such as cars, last row) are roughly separated from one-another. Failure modes, such as grouping multiple fruit—or two shirts—together, reflect the ambiguity of unsupervised object discovery.

Comparing these proposals to those obtained from a randomly-initialized network (3rd column) and an ImageNet supervised one (4th column), we appreciate the benefits of learning with the Odin framework. Both of these networks make erroneous proposals, failing to delineate object boundaries, or lacking the coherence and locality of real-world objects. We quantify this difference by evaluating the average best overlap (ABO) and fraction of recovered objects (OR) of the segments derived from each network. Consistently with the qualitative results, Odin strongly surpasses both baselines in all metrics (Table 4, left).

We also evaluate the accuracy of a recently-proposed self-supervised method, DINO, which specializes in object discovery. In this challenging task of discovering multiple objects in an unsupervised setting, we find that it underperforms relative to Odin. We test Odin in two regimes, one using the ResNet and FPN used for pretraining, the other with the ResNet only. Although its performance degrades slightly with the lower-resolution ResNet, it continues to outperform all other methods in all metrics. In particular, Odin surpasses DetCon by a large margin (+7% ABO, +16% OR), indicating that it has discovered more relevant image structure than the hand-crafted segmentations used in DetCon.

Finally, we note that the DINO method was primarily designed for use with vision transformers [24]. We therefore train a ViT-B/8 (as in DINO) on ImageNet for 100 epochs using the Odin framework (all other parameters unchanged). In this setting we find Odin to achieve compelling results, surpassing the high-resolution ResNet-FPN, and a supervised and DINO-pretrained vision-transformer (Table 4, right). Figure A.1. illustrates that Odin seems particularly effective at discovering small objects and differentiating instances of the same class. In sum, Odin provides a powerful means of discovering objects in real-world scenes irrespective of the architecture used.

Fig. 2. Object discovery with Odin. 1st column: original image, 2nd: human-annotated COCO segmentations, 3rd, 4th, 5th: segmentations obtained from k-means clustering on randomly intialized, ImageNet-supervised, and Odin-trained features, respectively.

Table 4. Object discovery on COCO: all methods pretrain on ImageNet before evaluating object discovery on COCO in an unsupervised manner, reporting average best overlap of instance masks (ABO^i) and categorical masks (ABO^c), and average object recovery (OR). By default we retain only the pretrained ResNet-50 from Odin's feature extractor, such that all methods are matched in their architecture. **Odin†** denotes the model equipped with the FPN used during training. ResNet's use 1024 × 1024 images for evaluation with a stride of 32, yielding a 32 × 32 feature grid. ViT's use 448 × 448 resolution with a patch size of 8, yielding 56 × 56 feature grids.

	ResNet-50			ViT-B		
Pretraining	ABO^i	ABO^c	OR	ABO^i	ABO^c	OR
Random init	28.1	33.6	17.0	27.8	33.6	17.5
DetCon$_B$ [42]	34.1	40.0	20.4	–	–	–
Supervised	35.8	41.1	23.8	43.9	53.6	41.9
DINO [12]	38.3	46.5	30.8	42.7	51.7	39.7
Odin	**41.5**	**48.6**	**36.5**	**45.9**	**53.9**	**44.1**
Odin†	**43.0**	**53.0**	**42.3**			

Table 5. Video Object Segmentation on DAVIS'17: we evaluate representation quality for video segmentation by nearest neighbor inference. We report the standard region $\mathcal{J}$ and contour $\mathcal{F}$ metrics and their mean. All representations are trained on ImageNet then evaluated without fine-tuning on the 30 validation videos of DAVIS'17. Odin† includes a feature pyramid network to reduce the output stride from 32× to 8×.

Pretraining	$(\mathcal{J}\&\mathcal{F})_m$	$\mathcal{J}$	$\mathcal{F}$
Random	15.2	15.9	14.6
Supervised	27.0	33.0	20.9
Odin	**35.6**	**41.3**	**29.9**
Odin†	**54.1**	**54.3**	**53.9**

4.3   Video Object Segmentation

We evaluate on the DAVIS'17 benchmark [66] following the experimental setup and nonparametric inference method of DINO [12]. Given a video and a segmentation of its first frame, we propagate the segmentation between consecutive frames by nearest neighbor matching of the extracted representation. In Table 5 we evaluate random, supervised, and our self-supervised representations with the ResNet-50 architecture. This evaluation does not fine-tune or train on the DAVIS benchmark, and so accuracy is a measure of object representation, as the fixed representation must support segmentation of the novel objects in these held-out videos. Consistently with our previous results, Odin strongly surpasses supervised pre-training in all metrics.

4.4   Ablations and Analysis

What components are necessary for driving Odin's ability to represent and discover objects? We systematically vary the two hyper-parameters governing the behavior of the object discovery network: the number of segments used for learning, and the schedule used for updating the network (Table 6). Starting with the number of segments K we find object discovery degrades substantially when using too coarse segmentations (e.g. $K = 8$). However, given a fine enough segmentations (K greater than 16) its performance is stable.

Regarding the rate at which the object discovery network is updated, we find both schemes to be viable: continuously updating the network leads to slightly better representations, whereas discrete updates lead to slightly better object discovery. The advantage of the later scheme is that the computational cost of the object discovery network becomes negligible, as it only needs to be evaluated every 100 epochs and resulting segmentations cached in-between.

Table 6. Ablating the components of Odin: We use the variant of Odin equipped with FPN for object discovery. Transfer learning is performed with the ResNet backbone only. K denotes the number of segments obtained through K-means during pretraining

Odin pretraining		Object discovery		Mask-RCNN transfer	
K	Update sched.	ABO^i	OR	AP^{bb}	AP^{mk}
8	every 100 ep.	38.3	34.6	42.6	38.1
16	Every 100 ep.	43.0	**42.3**	42.6	38.1
32	Every 100 ep.	**43.1**	42.0	42.5	38.0
16	$\lambda_\tau = 10^{-2}$	41.0	39.5	42.5	38.1
16	$\lambda_\tau = 10^{-3}$	41.3	39.9	**42.9**	**38.4**
16	$\lambda_\tau = 10^{-4}$	41.6	40.1	42.6	38.1

5   Conclusions

We have presented Odin, a new approach to self-supervised training which couples object discovery and representation learning. The resulting framework benefits from the same representation quality as methods which utilize explicit priors about image segmentation [42, 76], while deriving this knowledge from the data itself. The result is a simpler and more generally-applicable learning paradigm, and leads to state-of-the-art performance on a range of transfer learning tasks.

In this work, we have shown the utility of coupling representation learning and object discovery, for transfer learning and unsupervised scene understanding. Nevertheless, we have presented a single instance of this coupling, and there remain several open questions around how best to tie them together. This may require greater integration of the learning procedure and architecture—for example our self-supervised algorithm learns mask-pooled features which are different from those used in downstream tasks. The learning dynamics of Odin also warrant further investigation, as well as the objective used for representation learning. Recent work has revived interest in masked-autoencoding [7,24,38] and masked-distillation [6] as viable alternatives to contrastive learning. Odin, by proposing to leverage learned representations in the design of iteratively refined self-supervised tasks, is well positioned to benefit them as well.

References

1. Agrawal, P., Carreira, J., Malik, J.: Learning to see by moving. In: ICCV (2015)
2. Arandjelovic, R., Zisserman, A.: Look, listen and learn. In: Proceedings of the IEEE International Conference on Computer Vision, pp. 609–617 (2017)
3. Arbeláez, P., Pont-Tuset, J., Barron, J.T., Marques, F., Malik, J.: Multiscale combinatorial grouping. In: Proceedings of the IEEE conference on computer vision and pattern recognition, pp. 328–335 (2014)
4. Asano, Y.M., Rupprecht, C., Vedaldi, A.: Self-labelling via simultaneous clustering and representation learning. In: International Conference on Learning Representations (ICLR) (2020)
5. Bachman, P., Hjelm, R.D., Buchwalter, W.: Learning representations by maximizing mutual information across views. Adv. Neural. Inf. Process. Syst. **32**, 15535–15545 (2019)
6. Baevski, A., Hsu, W.N., Xu, Q., Babu, A., Gu, J., Auli, M.: Data2vec: a general framework for self-supervised learning in speech, vision and language. arXiv preprint arXiv:2202.03555 (2022)
7. Bao, H., Dong, L., Wei, F.: BEiT: BERT pre-training of image transformers. arXiv preprint arXiv:2106.08254 (2021)
8. Burgess, C.P., et al.: MONet: unsupervised scene decomposition and representation. CoRR **abs/1901.11390** (2019). http://arxiv.org/abs/1901.11390
9. Caron, M., Bojanowski, P., Joulin, A., Douze, M.: Deep clustering for unsupervised learning of visual features. In: Ferrari, V., Hebert, M., Sminchisescu, C., Weiss, Y. (eds.) Computer Vision – ECCV 2018. LNCS, vol. 11218, pp. 139–156. Springer, Cham (2018). https://doi.org/10.1007/978-3-030-01264-9_9
10. Caron, M., Bojanowski, P., Mairal, J., Joulin, A.: Unsupervised pre-training of image features on non-curated data. In: Proceedings of the IEEE/CVF International Conference on Computer Vision, pp. 2959–2968 (2019)
11. Caron, M., Misra, I., Mairal, J., Goyal, P., Bojanowski, P., Joulin, A.: Unsupervised learning of visual features by contrasting cluster assignments. Adv. Neural. Inf. Process. Syst. **33**, 9912–9924 (2020)
12. Caron, M., et al.: Emerging properties in self-supervised vision transformers. In: Proceedings of the IEEE/CVF International Conference on Computer Vision, pp. 9650–9660 (2021)
13. Chen, T., Kornblith, S., Norouzi, M., Hinton, G.: A simple framework for contrastive learning of visual representations. In: International Conference on Machine Learning, pp. 1597–1607. PMLR (2020)
14. Chen, X., Fan, H., Girshick, R., He, K.: Improved baselines with momentum contrastive learning. arXiv preprint arXiv:2003.04297 (2020)

15. Chen, X., He, K.: Exploring simple Siamese representation learning. In: Proceedings of the IEEE/CVF Conference on Computer Vision and Pattern Recognition, pp. 15750–15758 (2021)
16. Chen, X., Xie, S., He, K.: An empirical study of training self-supervised vision transformers. In: Proceedings of the IEEE/CVF International Conference on Computer Vision, pp. 9640–9649 (2021)
17. Cho, J.H., Mall, U., Bala, K., Hariharan, B.: PiCIE: unsupervised semantic segmentation using invariance and equivariance in clustering. In: CVPR, pp. 16794–16804 (2021)
18. Cho, M., Kwak, S., Schmid, C., Ponce, J.: Unsupervised object discovery and localization in the wild: part-based matching with bottom-up region proposals. In: Proceedings of the IEEE Conference on Computer Vision and Pattern Recognition, pp. 1201–1210 (2015)
19. Cordts, M., et al.: The cityscapes dataset for semantic urban scene understanding. In: Proceedings of the IEEE Conference on Computer Vision and Pattern Recognition, pp. 3213–3223 (2016)
20. Didolkar, A., et al.: Neural production systems (2021)
21. Doersch, C., Gupta, A., Efros, A.A.: Unsupervised visual representation learning by context prediction. In: Proceedings of the IEEE International Conference on Computer Vision, pp. 1422–1430 (2015)
22. Doersch, C., Zisserman, A.: Multi-task self-supervised visual learning. In: Proceedings of the IEEE International Conference on Computer Vision, pp. 2051–2060 (2017)
23. Donahue, J., Krähenbühl, P., Darrell, T.: Adversarial feature learning. In: International Conference on Learning Representations (ICLR) (2017)
24. Dosovitskiy, A., et al.: An image is worth 16x16 words: transformers for image recognition at scale. arXiv preprint arXiv:2010.11929 (2020)
25. Dosovitskiy, A., Springenberg, J.T., Riedmiller, M., Brox, T.: Discriminative unsupervised feature learning with convolutional neural networks. In: NIPS (2014)
26. Dwibedi, D., Aytar, Y., Tompson, J., Sermanet, P., Zisserman, A.: With a little help from my friends: Nearest-neighbor contrastive learning of visual representations. In: Proceedings of the IEEE/CVF International Conference on Computer Vision, pp. 9588–9597 (2021)
27. Everingham, M., Eslami, S.A., Van Gool, L., Williams, C.K., Winn, J., Zisserman, A.: The pascal visual object classes challenge: a retrospective. Int. J. Comput. Vision 111(1), 98–136 (2015)
28. Felzenszwalb, P.F., Huttenlocher, D.P.: Efficient graph-based image segmentation. Int. J. Comput. Vision 59(2), 167–181 (2004)
29. Feng, C., Zhong, Y., Gao, Y., Scott, M.R., Huang, W.: TOOD: task-aligned one-stage object detection. In: International Conference on Computer Vision (2021)
30. Gidaris, S., Singh, P., Komodakis, N.: Unsupervised representation learning by predicting image rotations. In: International Conference on Learning Representations (ICLR) (2018)
31. GitHub: TPU object detection and segmentation framework (2021). https://github.com/tensorflow/tpu/tree/master/models/official/detection
32. Goyal, A., et al.: Recurrent independent mechanisms. arXiv preprint arXiv:1909.10893 (2019)
33. Goyal, P., et al.: Self-supervised pretraining of visual features in the wild. arXiv preprint arXiv:2103.01988 (2021)

34. Greff, K., et al.: Multi-object representation learning with iterative variational inference. In: International Conference on Machine Learning, pp. 2424–2433. PMLR (2019)
35. Grill, J.B., et al.: Bootstrap your own latent-a new approach to self-supervised learning. In: Advances in Neural Information Processing Systems 33 (2020)
36. Hadsell, R., Chopra, S., LeCun, Y.: Dimensionality reduction by learning an invariant mapping. In: 2006 IEEE Computer Society Conference on Computer Vision and Pattern Recognition (CVPR2006), vol. 2, pp. 1735–1742. IEEE (2006)
37. Han, T., Xie, W., Zisserman, A.: Self-supervised co-training for video representation learning. Adv. Neural. Inf. Process. Syst. **33**, 5679–5690 (2020)
38. He, K., Chen, X., Xie, S., Li, Y., Dollár, P., Girshick, R.: Masked autoencoders are scalable vision learners. arXiv preprint arXiv:2111.06377 (2021)
39. He, K., Fan, H., Wu, Y., Xie, S., Girshick, R.: Momentum contrast for unsupervised visual representation learning. In: Proceedings of the IEEE/CVF Conference on Computer Vision and Pattern Recognition, pp. 9729–9738 (2020)
40. He, K., Gkioxari, G., Dollár, P., Girshick, R.: Mask R-CNN. In: Proceedings of the IEEE international conference on computer vision, pp. 2961–2969 (2017)
41. He, K., Zhang, X., Ren, S., Sun, J.: Deep residual learning for image recognition. In: Proceedings of the IEEE conference on computer vision and pattern recognition, pp. 770–778 (2016)
42. Hénaff, O.J., Koppula, S., Alayrac, J.B., van den Oord, A., Vinyals, O., Carreira, J.: Efficient visual pretraining with contrastive detection. In: ICCV (2021)
43. Hénaff, O.J., et al.: Data-efficient image recognition with contrastive predictive coding. arXiv preprint arXiv:1905.09272 (2019)
44. Hjelm, R.D., et al.: Learning deep representations by mutual information estimation and maximization. In: International Conference on Learning Representations (2018)
45. Ji, X., Henriques, J.F., Vedaldi, A.: Invariant information clustering for unsupervised image classification and segmentation. In: Proceedings of the IEEE/CVF International Conference on Computer Vision, pp. 9865–9874 (2019)
46. Kabra, R., et al.: Simone: view-invariant, temporally-abstracted object representations via unsupervised video decomposition. In: Advances in Neural Information Processing Systems 34 (2021)
47. Kipf, T., et al.: Conditional object-centric learning from video. arXiv preprint arXiv:2111.12594 (2021)
48. Korbar, B., Tran, D., Torresani, L.: Cooperative learning of audio and video models from self-supervised synchronization. In: Advances in Neural Information Processing Systems (2018)
49. Larsson, G., Maire, M., Shakhnarovich, G.: Colorization as a proxy task for visual understanding. In: CVPR, pp. 6874–6883 (2017)
50. Lin, C., Miller, T., Dligach, D., Bethard, S., Savova, G.: EntityBERT: entity-centric masking strategy for model pretraining for the clinical domain. In: Proceedings of the 20th Workshop on Biomedical Language Processing, pp. 191–201 (2021)
51. Lin, T.Y., Dollár, P., Girshick, R., He, K., Hariharan, B., Belongie, S.: Feature pyramid networks for object detection. In: Proceedings of the IEEE Conference on Computer Vision and Pattern Recognition, pp. 2117–2125 (2017)
52. Lin, T.-Y., et al.: Microsoft COCO: common objects in context. In: Fleet, D., Pajdla, T., Schiele, B., Tuytelaars, T. (eds.) ECCV 2014. LNCS, vol. 8693, pp. 740–755. Springer, Cham (2014). https://doi.org/10.1007/978-3-319-10602-1_48

53. Liu, Z., et al.: Swin transformer: hierarchical vision transformer using shifted windows. In: Proceedings of the IEEE/CVF International Conference on Computer Vision, pp. 10012–10022 (2021)
54. Locatello, F., et al.: Object-centric learning with slot attention. Adv. Neural. Inf. Process. Syst. **33**, 11525–11538 (2020)
55. Long, J., Shelhamer, E., Darrell, T.: Fully convolutional networks for semantic segmentation. In: Proceedings of the IEEE Conference on Computer Vision and Pattern Recognition, pp. 3431–3440 (2015)
56. Miech, A., Zhukov, D., Alayrac, J.B., Tapaswi, M., Laptev, I., Sivic, J.: Howto100M: learning a text-video embedding by watching hundred million narrated video clips. In: International Conference on Computer Vision (2019)
57. Mishra, S., et al.: Object-aware cropping for self-supervised learning. arXiv preprint arXiv:2112.00319 (2021)
58. Misra, I., Zitnick, C.L., Hebert, M.: Shuffle and learn: unsupervised learning using temporal order verification. In: Leibe, B., Matas, J., Sebe, N., Welling, M. (eds.) ECCV 2016. LNCS, vol. 9905, pp. 527–544. Springer, Cham (2016). https://doi.org/10.1007/978-3-319-46448-0_32
59. Nathan Mundhenk, T., Ho, D., Chen, B.Y.: Improvements to context based self-supervised learning. In: Proceedings of the IEEE Conference on Computer Vision and Pattern Recognition, pp. 9339–9348 (2018)
60. Noroozi, M., Favaro, P.: Unsupervised learning of visual representations by solving jigsaw puzzles. In: Leibe, B., Matas, J., Sebe, N., Welling, M. (eds.) ECCV 2016. LNCS, vol. 9910, pp. 69–84. Springer, Cham (2016). https://doi.org/10.1007/978-3-319-46466-4_5
61. Nunes, L., Marcuzzi, R., Chen, X., Behley, J., Stachniss, C.: Segcontrast: 3D point cloud feature representation learning through self-supervised segment discrimination. IEEE Robotics and Automation Letters (2022)
62. van den Oord, A., Li, Y., Vinyals, O.: Representation learning with contrastive predictive coding. arXiv preprint arXiv:1807.03748 (2018)
63. Owens, A., Efros, A.A.: Audio-visual scene analysis with self-supervised multisensory features. In: Ferrari, V., Hebert, M., Sminchisescu, C., Weiss, Y. (eds.) ECCV 2018. LNCS, vol. 11210, pp. 639–658. Springer, Cham (2018). https://doi.org/10.1007/978-3-030-01231-1_39
64. Pathak, D., Krahenbuhl, P., Donahue, J., Darrell, T., Efros, A.A.: Context encoders: feature learning by inpainting. In: Proceedings of the IEEE Conference on Computer Vision and Pattern Recognition, pp. 2536–2544 (2016)
65. Peng, C., et al.: MegDet: a large mini-batch object detector. In: Proceedings of the IEEE Conference on Computer Vision and Pattern Recognition, pp. 6181–6189 (2018)
66. Perazzi, F., Pont-Tuset, J., McWilliams, B., Van Gool, L., Gross, M., Sorkine-Hornung, A.: A benchmark dataset and evaluation methodology for video object segmentation. In: Proceedings of the IEEE conference on computer vision and pattern recognition, pp. 724–732 (2016)
67. Pinheiro, P.O., Almahairi, A., Benmalek, R.Y., Golemo, F., Courville, A.C.: Unsupervised learning of dense visual representations. In: NeurIPS (2020)
68. Recasens, A., et al.: Broaden your views for self-supervised video learning. In: International Conference on Computer Vision (2021)
69. Russakovsky, O., et al.: ImageNet large scale visual recognition challenge. Int. J. Comput. Vision **115**(3), 211–252 (2015)

70. Ryali, C., Schwab, D.J., Morcos, A.S.: Learning background invariance improves generalization and robustness in self-supervised learning on imageNet and beyond. In: Advances in Neural Information Processing Systems (2021)

71. Shanahan, M., Nikiforou, K., Creswell, A., Kaplanis, C., Barrett, D., Garnelo, M.: An explicitly relational neural network architecture. In: International Conference on Machine Learning, pp. 8593–8603. PMLR (2020)

72. Sun, C., Myers, A., Vondrick, C., Murphy, K., Schmid, C.: VideoBERT: a joint model for video and language representation learning. In: International Conference on Computer Vision (2019)

73. Tian, Y., Henaff, O.J., van den Oord, A.: Divide and contrast: self-supervised learning from uncurated data. In: Proceedings of the IEEE/CVF International Conference on Computer Vision, pp. 10063–10074 (2021)

74. Tian, Y., Sun, C., Poole, B., Krishnan, D., Schmid, C., Isola, P.: What makes for good views for contrastive learning. In: NeurIPS (2020)

75. Tian, Z., Shen, C., Chen, H., He, T.: FCOS: fully convolutional one-stage object detection. In: International Conference on Computer Vision (2019)

76. Tomasev, N., et al.: Pushing the limits of self-supervised resnets: can we outperform supervised learning without labels on imagenet? arXiv preprint arXiv:2201.05119 (2022)

77. Van Gansbeke, W., Vandenhende, S., Georgoulis, S., Van Gool, L.: Unsupervised semantic segmentation by contrasting object mask proposals. In: ICCV (2021)

78. Vincent, P., Larochelle, H., Bengio, Y., Manzagol, P.A.: Extracting and composing robust features with denoising autoencoders. In: Proceedings of the 25th international conference on Machine learning, pp. 1096–1103 (2008)

79. Wei, F., Gao, Y., Wu, Z., Hu, H., Lin, S.: Aligning pretraining for detection via object-level contrastive learning. In: Advances in Neural Information Processing Systems 34 (2021)

80. Wu, S., Li, X., Wang, X.: IoU-aware single-stage object detector for accurate localization. Image and Vision Computing (2020)

81. Wu, Z., Xiong, Y., Yu, S.X., Lin, D.: Unsupervised feature learning via nonparametric instance discrimination. In: Proceedings of the IEEE Conference on Computer Vision and Pattern Recognition, pp. 3733–3742 (2018)

82. Xie, J., Zhan, X., Liu, Z., Ong, Y., Loy, C.C.: Unsupervised object-level representation learning from scene images. In: Advances in Neural Information Processing Systems 34 (2021)

83. Xie, Z., et al.: Self-supervised learning with swin transformers. arXiv preprint arXiv:2105.04553 (2021)

84. Xie, Z., Lin, Y., Zhang, Z., Cao, Y., Lin, S., Hu, H.: Propagate yourself: exploring pixel-level consistency for unsupervised visual representation learning. In: Proceedings of the IEEE/CVF Conference on Computer Vision and Pattern Recognition, pp. 16684–16693 (2021)

85. Yang, C., Lamdouar, H., Lu, E., Zisserman, A., Xie, W.: Self-supervised video object segmentation by motion grouping. In: International Conference on Computer Vision (2021)

86. You, Y., Gitman, I., Ginsburg, B.: Large batch training of convolutional networks. arXiv preprint arXiv:1708.03888 (2017)

87. Zbontar, J., Jing, L., Misra, I., LeCun, Y., Deny, S.: Barlow twins: self-supervised learning via redundancy reduction. In: International Conference on Machine Learning, pp. 12310–12320. PMLR (2021)

88. Zhang, F., Torr, P., Ranftl, R., Richter, S.: Looking beyond single images for contrastive semantic segmentation learning. In: Advances in Neural Information Processing Systems 34 (2021)

89. Zhang, R., Isola, P., Efros, A.A.: Colorful image colorization. In: Leibe, B., Matas, J., Sebe, N., Welling, M. (eds.) ECCV 2016. LNCS, vol. 9907, pp. 649–666. Springer, Cham (2016). https://doi.org/10.1007/978-3-319-46487-9_40

90. Zhang, R., Isola, P., Efros, A.A.: Split-brain autoencoders: unsupervised learning by cross-channel prediction. In: Proceedings of the IEEE Conference on Computer Vision and Pattern Recognition, pp. 1058–1067 (2017)

91. Zhang, S., Chi, C., Yao, Y., Lei, Z., Li, S.Z.: Bridging the gap between anchor-based and anchor-free detection via adaptive training sample selection. In: IEEE Conference on Computer Vision and Pattern Recognition (2020)

92. Zhao, N., Wu, Z., Lau, R.W., Lin, S.: Distilling localization for self-supervised representation learning. arXiv preprint arXiv:2004.06638 (2020)

93. Zoran, D., Kabra, R., Lerchner, A., Rezende, D.J.: Parts: unsupervised segmentation with slots, attention and independence maximization. In: Proceedings of the IEEE/CVF International Conference on Computer Vision, pp. 10439–10447 (2021)

Trading Positional Complexity vs Deepness in Coordinate Networks

Jianqiao Zheng[✉], Sameera Ramasinghe, Xueqian Li, and Simon Lucey

Australian Institute for Machine Learning, University of Adelaide, Adelaide, Australia
jianqiao.zheng@adelaide.edu.au

Abstract. It is well noted that coordinate-based MLPs benefit—in terms of preserving high-frequency information—through the encoding of coordinate positions as an array of Fourier features. Hitherto, the rationale for the effectiveness of these *positional encodings* has been mainly studied through a Fourier lens. In this paper, we strive to broaden this understanding by showing that alternative non-Fourier embedding functions can indeed be used for positional encoding. Moreover, we show that their performance is entirely determined by a trade-off between the stable rank of the embedded matrix and the distance preservation between embedded coordinates. We further establish that the now ubiquitous Fourier feature mapping of position is a special case that fulfills these conditions. Consequently, we present a more general theory to analyze positional encoding in terms of shifted basis functions. In addition, we argue that employing a more complex positional encoding—that scales exponentially with the number of modes—requires only a linear (rather than deep) coordinate function to achieve comparable performance. Counter-intuitively, we demonstrate that trading positional embedding complexity for network deepness is orders of magnitude faster than current state-of-the-art; despite the additional embedding complexity. To this end, we develop the necessary theoretical formulae and empirically verify that our theoretical claims hold in practice.
Project page at https://osiriszjq.github.io/complex_encoding.

Keywords: Coordinate networks · Positional encoding · Signal reconstruction

1 Introduction

Positional encoding is an umbrella term used for representing the coordinates of a structured object as a finite-dimensional embedding. Such embeddings are fast becoming critical instruments in modern language models [2,6,9,15,35,37] and vision tasks that involve encoding a signal (*e.g.*, 2D image, 3D object, etc.) as weights of a neural network [3,8,16,18,19,22,23,38]. Of specific interest in this paper is the use of positional encodings when being used to enhance the performance of *coordinate-MLPs*.

J. Zheng and S. Ramasinghe—Contributed equally.

Supplementary Information The online version contains supplementary material available at https://doi.org/10.1007/978-3-031-19812-0_9.

S. Avidan et al. (Eds.): ECCV 2022, LNCS 13687, pp. 144–160, 2022.
https://doi.org/10.1007/978-3-031-19812-0_9

Coordinate-MLPs are fully connected networks, trained to learn the structure of an object as a continuous function, with coordinates as inputs. However, the major drawback of training coordinate-MLPs with raw input coordinates is their sub-optimal performance in learning high-frequency content [25].

As a remedy, recent studies empirically confirmed that projecting the coordinates to a higher dimensional space using sine and cosine functions of different frequencies (*i.e.*, Fourier frequency mapping) allows coordinate-MLPs to learn high-frequency information more effectively [19,38]. This observation was recently characterized theoretically by Tancik *et al.* [34], showing that the above projection permits tuning the spectrum of the neural tangent kernel (NTK) of the corresponding MLP, thereby enabling the network to learn high-frequency information. Despite impressive empirical results, encoding position through Fourier frequency mapping entails some unenviable attributes. First, prior research substantiates the belief that the performance of the Fourier feature mapping is sensitive to the choice of frequencies. Leading methods for frequency selection, however, employ a stochastic strategy (*i.e.*, random sampling) which can become volatile as one attempts to keep to a minimum the number of sampled frequencies. Second, viewing positional encoding solely through a Fourier lens obfuscates some of the fundamental principles behind its effectiveness. These concerns have heightened the need for an extended analysis of positional encoding.

This paper aims to overcome the aforesaid limitations by developing an alternative and more comprehensive understanding of positional encoding. The foremost benefit of our work is allowing non-Fourier embedding functions to be used in the positional encoding. Specifically, we show that positional encoding can be accomplished via systematic sampling of shifted continuous basis functions, where the shifts are determined by the coordinate positions. In comparison to the ambiguous frequency sampling in Fourier feature mapping, we derive a more interpretable relationship between the sampling density and the behavior of the embedding scheme. In particular, we discover that the effectiveness of the proposed embedding scheme primarily relies on two factors: (i) the approximate matrix rank of the embedded representation across positions, and (ii) the distance preservation between the embedded coordinates. Distance preservation measures the extent to which the inner product between the shifted functions correlates with the Euclidean distance between the corresponding coordinates. Intuitively, a higher approximate matrix rank causes better memorization of the training data, while the distance preservation correlates with generalization. Remarkably, we establish that any given continuous function can be used for positional encoding—as performance is simply determined by the trade-off between the aforementioned two factors. Further, we assert that the effectiveness and shortcomings of Fourier feature mapping can also be analyzed in the context of this newly developed framework. We also propose a complex positional encoding to relax the expressibility of the coordinate network into a single linear layer, which largely speedups the instance-based optimization. An essential idea here is the separation of the coordinates. For a simple 1D signal, the input is only embedded in one direction. As for 2D natural images and 3D video sequences, the coordinates are still separable, which enables us to use the Kronecker product to gather input embedding in every single direction. With signals that have non-separable coordinates, we add a blending matrix to linearly interpolate to get the final embedding. In summary, the contribution of this paper is four-fold:

- We expand the current understanding of positional encoding and show that it can be formulated as a systematic sampling scheme of shifted continuous basis functions. Compared to the popular Fourier frequency mapping, our formulation is more interpretative in nature and less restrictive.
- We develop theoretical formulae to show that the performance of the encoding is governed by the approximate rank of the embedding matrix (sampled at different positions) and the distance preservation between the embedded coordinates. We further solidify this new insight using empirical evaluations.
- As a practical example, we employ a Gaussian signal as the embedding function and show that it can deliver on-par performance with the Fourier frequency mapping. Most importantly, we demonstrate that the Gaussian embedding is more efficient in terms of the embedding dimension while being less volatile.
- We show that trading a complex positional encoding for a deep network allows us to encode high-frequency features with a substantial speedup by circumventing the heavy computation for a simple positional encoding combined with a deep neural network. Promising empirical reconstruction performance is obtained on 1D, 2D, and 3D signals using our proposed embedding function in conjunction with coordinate networks (Fig. 1).

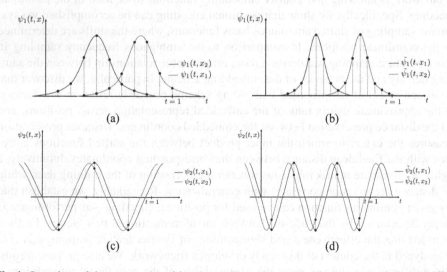

Fig. 1. Overview of the proposed positional encoding scheme. Positions are encoded as equidistant samples from shifted basis functions (embedders). The shifts are determined by the corresponding coordinate positions we are wanting to embed. In (a) and (b), x_1 and x_2 are encoded as samples from shifted Gaussians with a higher and a lower standard deviation, respectively. Note that we need a higher number of samples for (b) due to higher bandwidth (see Sect. 3). In (c) and (d), x_1 and x_2 are encoded with sinusoidal signals with a different frequencies. Note that although different sampling rates are employed for (c) and (d), the same two values are repeated across the samples. Hence, sampling more than twice is redundant.

2   Related Works

Positional encoding became a popular topic among the machine learning community after the seminal work on Transformers by Vaswani *et al.* [35] Since the attention mechanism used in the Transformers is position-insensitive, they employed a sinusoidal signal to encode the positions before feeding them to the higher blocks. A contemporary work by Gehring *et al.* [9] also proposed a convolutional seq2seq model, adapting a positional encoding mechanism. Since then, using positional encoding in language models became a common trend [5, 10, 13, 24, 30]. Notably, Wang *et al.* [36] extended the embedding space from real numbers to complex values. Another critical aspect of their work is replacing the pre-defined encoding mechanism with a learnable one. There have also been other exciting attempts to improve positional encoding, such as extending the sequential positional encoding to tree-based positional encoding [31], untying the correlations between words and positions while embedding coordinates [12], and modeling positional encoding using dynamical systems [17].

In parallel, positional encoding is also gaining attention in computer vision, specifically with coordinate-MLPs. Coordinate-MLPs provide an efficient method to encode objects such as images [20, 33] and 3D scenes [21, 29, 32] as their weights. Remarkably, Mildenhall *et al.* [19] and Zhong *et al.* [38] found that encoding coordinates with sinusoidal signals allow coordinate-MLPs to learn high frequency content better. One of the earliest roots of this approach can perhaps be traced to the work by Rahimi and Recht [26], where they used random Fourier features to approximate an arbitrary stationary kernel function by applying Bochner's theorem. More recently, Tancik *et al.* [34], leveraging the NTK theory [1, 4, 7, 11, 14], recently added theoretical rigor to this particular practice by showing that such embeddings enable tuning the spectrum of the NTK of the corresponding MLP. In contrast, the goal of this paper is to show that one does not have to be limited to the Fourier embedding for positional encoding. We demonstrate that alternative functions can be used for positional encoding while gaining similar or better performance compared to Fourier embedding.

3   Positional Encoding: A Theoretical Walk-Through

This section contains an exposition of the machinery and fundamentals necessary to understand the proposed framework. We begin our analysis by considering a simple linear learner since rigorous characterization of a linear learner is convenient compared to a non-linear model. Therefore, we study a linear learner and empirically show that the gathered insights are extendable to the non-linear models.

First, we show that the capacity to memorize a given set of training data entirely depends on the (approximate) rank of the embedding matrix. Next, we establish that for generalization, the rank should be upper-bounded against the number of coordinates, *i.e.*, the embedding function should be bandlimited[1]. We incur a crucial insight here that positional encoding essentially portrays a trade-off between memorization and generalization. Afterward, we discuss the importance of distance preservation between embedded coordinates and its relationship to bandlimited embedding functions. Finally,

---

[1] We assume that in regression, the smoothness of a model is implicitly related to generalization.

we consider several possible embedder functions and analyze their behavior using the developed tools.

3.1 Rank of the Embedded Representation

Let $\mathbf{x}=[x_1, x_2, \cdots, x_N]^T$ be a vector of 1D coordinates, in which $x_i \in [0, C]$. And let $\mathbf{y}=[y_1, y_2, \cdots, y_n]^T$ be the corresponding outputs of a function $f:\mathbb{R} \to \mathbb{R}$. Our goal is to find a d dimensional embedding $\Psi:\mathbb{R} \to \mathbb{R}^d$ for these positions, so that a linear model can be employed to learn the mapping f as,

$$\mathbf{w}^T \Psi(\mathbf{x}) + b \approx f(\cdot), \tag{1}$$

where $\mathbf{w} \in \mathbb{R}^d$ and $b \in \mathbb{R}$ are the learnable weights and the bias, respectively. Then, it is straightforward to show that for the perfect reconstruction of *any* given $\mathbf{y}$ using Eq. (1), the following condition should be satisfied:

$$\text{Rank} \{[\Psi(x_1)\, \Psi(x_2)\, \ldots\, \Psi(x_N)]\} = N. \tag{2}$$

Thus, we establish the following Proposition:

Proposition 1. *Consider a set of coordinates* $\mathbf{x}=[x_1, x_2, \cdots, x_N]^T$, *corresponding outputs* $\mathbf{y}=[y_1, y_2, \cdots, y_N]^T$, *and a d dimensional embedding* $\Psi:\mathbb{R} \to \mathbb{R}^d$. *Under perfect convergence, the sufficient condition for a linear model for perfectly memorizing the mapping between* $\mathbf{x}$ *and* $\mathbf{y}$ *is for* $\mathbf{X}=[\Psi(x_1), \Psi(x_2), \ldots, \Psi(x_N)]^T$ *to have full rank.*

3.2 Bandlimited Embedders

One possible way of enforcing the condition in Eq. (2) is to define an embedding scheme where the rank of the embedded matrix strictly monotonically increases with N (for a sufficiently large d). As depicted in Sect. 3.1, this would ensure that the model can memorize the training data and therefore perfectly reconstruct $\mathbf{y}$. However, memorization alone does not yield a good model. On the contrary, we also need our model to be generalizable to unseen coordinates.

To this end, let us define elements of $\Psi(\cdot)$ as sampled values from a function $\psi:\mathbb{R}^2 \to \mathbb{R}$ such that for a given x,

$$\Psi(x) = [\psi(0, x), \psi(s, x), \ldots, \psi((d-1)s, x)]^T, \tag{3}$$

where $s=Cd^{-1}$ is the sampling interval. We shall refer to $\psi(\cdot)$ as the *embedder*. As discussed above, for better generalization, we need,

$$\psi(t, x) \approx \sum_{b=0}^{B} \alpha_b \beta_b(t), \tag{4}$$

where α_b and $\beta_b(t)$ are weights and shifted basis functions, respectively, that can approximately estimate $\psi(t, x)$ at any arbitrary position x. We refer to such embedders as *bandlimited embedders* with a bandwidth B. This is equivalent to saying that the embedding matrix has a bounded rank, *i.e.*, the rank cannot increase arbitrarily with N. The intuition here is that if B is too small, the model will demonstrate poor memorization and overly smooth generalization. On the other hand, if B is extremely high, the model is capable of perfect memorization but poor generalization. Therefore we conclude that for ideal performance, the embedder should be chosen carefully, such that it is both bandlimited and has a sufficient rank. As we shall discuss the bandwidth B can also act as a guide for the minimal value of d.

3.3 Distance Preservation

Intuitively, the embedded coordinates should preserve the distance between the original coordinates, irrespective of the absolute position. The embedded distance (or similarity) $D(\cdot, \cdot)$ between two coordinates (x_1, x_2) can be measured via the inner product $D(x_1, x_2) = \int_0^1 \psi(t, x_1)\psi(t, x_2)dt$. For ideal distance preservation we need,

$$\|x_1 - x_2\| \propto D(x_1, x_2). \tag{5}$$

Interestingly, this property is also implicitly related to the limited bandwidth requirement. Note that in practice, we employ sampled embedders to construct Ψ as shown in Eq. (3). Hence, the dot product between the sampled $\psi(t, x_1)$ and $\psi(t, x_2)$ should be able to approximate D as,

$$D(x_1, x_2) = \int_0^C \psi(t, x_1)\psi(t, x_2)dt \approx \sum_{d=0}^{d-1} \psi(s \cdot d, x_1)\psi(s \cdot d, x_2), \tag{6}$$

which is possible, if and only if, ψ is bandlimited. In that case, $d=B$ is sufficient where B is the bandwidth of ψ (by Nyquist sampling theory). In practice, we choose $C=1$.

Remark 1. The embedder should be bandlimited for better generalization (equivalently, the rank of the embedded matrix should be upper-bounded). Further, the ideal embedder should essentially face a trade-off between memorization and generalization. Here, memorization correlates with the rank of the embedded matrix, while generalization relates to the distance preservation between the embedded coordinates.

4 Analysis of Possible Embedders

Although our derivations in Sect. 3 are generic, it is imperative to carefully choose a specific form of $\psi(\cdot, \cdot)$, such that properties of candidate embedders can be conveniently analyzed. Hence, we define embedders in terms of shifted basis functions, *i.e.*, $\psi(t, x) = \psi(t-x)$. Such a definition permits us to examine embedders in a unified manner, as we shall see below.

Moreover, the rank of a matrix can be extremely noisy in practice. Typically, we need to heuristically set an appropriate threshold to the singular values, leading to unstable calculations. Therefore, we use the stable rank [28] instead of the rank in all our experiments. In particular, the stable rank is a more stable surrogate for the rank, and is defined as $\frac{\|A\|_F^2}{\|A\|_2^2}$, where A is the matrix, $\|\cdot\|_F$ is the Frobenius norm, and $\|\cdot\|_2$ is the matrix norm. From here onwards, we will use the terms rank, approximate rank, and stable rank interchangeably.

Impulse Embedder. One simple way to satisfy the condition of Eq. (2) for an arbitrary large N is to define $\psi(t,x)=\delta(t-x)$, where $\delta(\cdot)$ is the impulse function. Note that using an impulse embedder essentially converts the embedding matrix to a set of one-hot encodings. With the impulse embedder, we can perfectly memorize a given set of data points, as the embedded matrix has full rank. The obvious drawback, however, is that the bandwidth of the impulse embedder is infinite, *i.e.*, assuming a continuous domain, d needs to reach infinity to learn outputs for all possible positions. Hence, the distance preservation is hampered, and consequently, the learned model lacks generalization.

Rectangle Embedder. As an approximation of impulse function (unit pulse), rectangular function $rect(x)=1$ when $|x|<\frac{1}{2}$ and $rect(x)=0$ when $|x|>\frac{1}{2}$. We can define $\psi(x)=rect\left(\frac{x-t}{d}\right)$, where d is the width of the impulse. Immediately we know the stable rank of rectangle embedder is $\min\left(N,\frac{1}{d}\right)$, where N is the number of sampled coordinates, the distance function $D(x_1,x_2)=tri(x_1-x_2)$, where $tri(\cdot)$ is triangular function. A physical way to understand rectangle embedder is nearest neighbour regression.

Triangle Embedder. A better choice to approximate impulse function may be triangular function, which is defined as $tri(x)=\max(1-|x|,0)$. Thus the embedder is defined as $\psi(x)=tri\left(\frac{x-t}{0.5d}\right)$. Here the factor 0.5 makes the width of the triangle to be d. The stable rank of triangular embedder is $\min\left(N,\frac{4/3}{d}\right)$. When d is the same, triangle embedder has a higher stable rank than rectangle embedder. The distance function of triangular embedder is $D(x_1,x_2)=\frac{1}{4}\max\left(d-|x_1-x_2|,0\right)^2$. This distance function looks really like Gaussian function, as illustrated in Fig. 3. A physical way to understand triangle embedder is linear interpolation.

Sine Embedder. Consider $\psi(t,x)=\sin(f(t-x))$ for an arbitrary fixed function f. Since $\sin(f(t-x))=\sin(ft)\cos(fx)-\cos(ft)\sin(fx)$, elements of any row of the embedding matrix can be written as a linear combination of the corresponding $\sin(ft)$ and $\cos(ft)$. Thus, the rank of the embedding matrix is upper-bounded at 2. Consequently, the expressiveness of the encoding is limited, leading to poor memorization and overly smooth generalization (interpolation) at unseen coordinates.

Square Embedder. Let us denote a square wave with unit amplitude and period 2π as $\text{sgn}(\sin(t))$, where sgn is the sign function. Then, define $\psi(t,x)=\text{sgn}(\sin(t-x))$. It is easy to deduce that the embedded distance $D(x_1,x_2)=1-2\|x_1-x_2\|, \forall|x|\leq1$ which implies perfect distance preservation. The drawback, however, is that the square wave is not bandlimited. Thus, it cannot approximate the inner product $\int \psi(t,x)\psi(t,x')$ using a finite set of samples as in Eq. (6). However, an interesting attribute of the square wave is that it can be decomposed into a series of sine waves with odd-integer harmonic frequencies as $\text{sgn}(\sin(t))=\frac{4}{\pi}\left[\sin(t)+\frac{1}{3}\sin(3t)+\frac{1}{5}\sin(5t)+\frac{1}{7}\sin(7t)+\dots\right]$. In other words, its highest energy (from a signal processing perspective) is contained in a sinusoidal with the same frequency. Thus, the square wave can be *almost* approximated by a sinusoidal signal. In fact, the square wave and the sinusoidal demonstrate similar properties in terms of the stable rank and the distance preservation (see Fig. 3).

Gaussian Embedder. We define the Gaussian embedder as $\psi(t,x)=\exp\left(-\frac{\|t-x\|^2}{2\sigma^2}\right)$ where σ is the standard deviation. The Gaussian embedder is also approximately bandlimited like the square embedder. However, the Gaussian embedder has a higher upper bound for the stable rank that can be controlled by σ. More precisely, when the embedding dimension is large enough, the stable rank of the Gaussian embedding matrix and the embedded distance between coordinates can be obtained analytically as shown below.

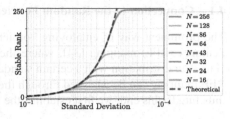

Fig. 2. Stable rank of the Gaussian embedder vs the standard deviation for different number of samples. The dash line is the theoretical stable rank $\frac{1}{2\sqrt{\pi}\sigma}$

Proposition 2. *Let the Gaussian embedder be denoted as* $\psi(t,x)=\exp\left(-\frac{\|t-x\|^2}{2\sigma^2}\right)$. *With a sufficient embedding dimension, the stable rank of the embedding matrix obtained using the Gaussian embedder is* $\min\left(N,\frac{1}{2\sqrt{\pi}\sigma}\right)$ *where N is the number of embedded coordinates. Under the same conditions, the embedded distance between two coordinates x_1 and x_2 is* $\mathrm{D}(x_1,x_2)=\exp\left(-\frac{\|x_1-x_2\|^2}{4\sigma^2}\right)$.

(see Fig. 2 for an experimental illustration). It is clear from Proposition 2 that as the number of sampled positions goes up, the stable rank of the Gaussian embedding matrix will linearly increase until it reaches its upper bound. Finally, Fig. 3 empirically validates the theoretically discussed properties of different embedders.

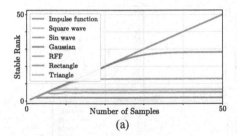
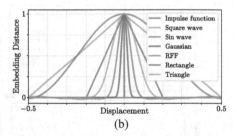

(a)   (b)

Fig. 3. Quantitative comparison of (a) the stable rank and (b) the distance preservation of different embedders and RFFs. As expected, the stable rank of the impulse embedder strictly increases with the number of sampled points, causing poor distance preservation. The stable rank of the sine embedder is upper-bounded at 2. The stable ranks of the square embedder and the sine embedder almost overlap. However, if the sample numbers are extremely high (not shown in the figure), their stable ranks begin to deviate. Similarly, the square embedder demonstrates perfect distance preservation, and the sine embedder is a close competitor. In contrast, the Gaussian embedder and the RFF showcase mid-range upper bounds for the stable rank and adequate distance preservation, advocating a much better trade-off between memorization and generalization.

4.1   Connection to the Random Fourier Features

The prominent way of employing Fourier frequency mapping is via Random Fourier Features (RFF) mapping [34], where the frequencies are randomly sampled from a Gaussian distribution with a certain standard deviation σ. In this Section, we show that RFF mapping can be analyzed through the lens of our theoretical framework discussed thus far. To this end, we first establish the following proposition:

Proposition 3. *Let the RFF embedding be denoted as $\gamma(x)=[\cos(2\pi \mathbf{b}x), \sin(2\pi \mathbf{b}x)]$, where $\mathbf{b}$ are sampled from a Gaussian distribution. When the embedding dimension is large enough, the stable rank of RFF will be $\min\left(N, \sqrt{2\pi}\sigma\right)$, where N is the numnber of embedded coordinates. Under the same conditions, the embedded distance between two coordinates x_1 and x_2 is $\mathrm{D}(x_1, x_2)=\sum_j \cos 2\pi b_j(x_1-x_2)$.*

As shown in Fig. 4, the stable rank of RFF increases linearly with the number of samples until it gets saturated at $\sqrt{2\pi}\sigma$. This indicates a relationship between RFF and Gaussian embedder. Let σ_g and σ_f be the standard deviations of Gaussian embedder and RFF. When their stable ranks are equal, $\frac{1}{2\sqrt{\pi}\sigma_g}=\sqrt{2\pi}\sigma_f$ (from Proposition 2, 3). This implies that when $\sigma_g\sigma_f=\frac{1}{2\sqrt{2\pi}}$, these two embedders are equivalent in terms of the stable rank and distance preservation (see Fig. 4 when $\sigma_g=0.01$ and $\sigma_f=0.1$).

A common observation with RFFs is that when σ_f is too low, the reconstruction is overly smooth and if σ_f is too high, it gives noisy interpolation [34]. This observation directly correlates to our theory. In Fig. 4, as the standard deviation increases, the stable rank increases and distance preservation decreases. Similarly, When the standard deviation is too low, the stable rank decreases while distance preservation increases.

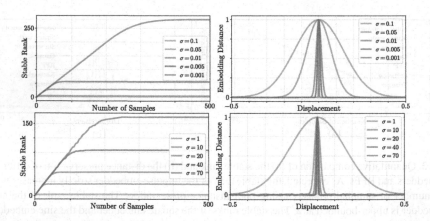

Fig. 4. The stable rank (left column) and distance preservation (right column) of Gaussian embedder (top row) and RFF (bottom row) across different standard deviations.

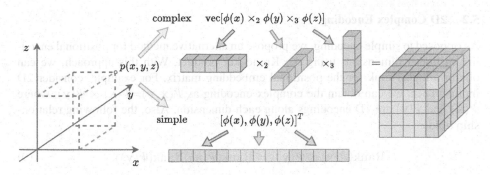

Fig. 5. Illustration of different methods to extend 1D encoding of length K to N-dimensional case. Simple encoding is the widely used method currently, which is only the concatenation of embeddings in each dimension to get a NK size encoding. We propose an alternative embedding method: conduct mode-n product to get the N dimensional cube, which we define as the complex embedding.

5 Simplicity vs Complexity in Positional Encoding

Thus far, we established that the positional encoding can achieved by sampling shifted basis functions, and the well-known RFF-embedding can also be analyzed through this lens. However, the analysis so far focused only on 1D coordinates. In this section, we shall investigate how to extend these positional embedding schemes to high-dimensional signals, *e.g.*, images and 3D signals.

5.1 2D Simple Encoding

Suppose $\psi(\cdot)$ is a an arbitrary positional encoding function. We define simple positional encoding as the concatenation of the 1D encoding in each dimension: $\Psi(x, y) = [\psi(x), \psi(y)]$. Then, with a linear model we have,

$$I(x, y) \approx \mathbf{w}^T \Psi(x, y) = \mathbf{w}_x^T \psi(x) + \mathbf{w}_y^T \psi(y). \tag{7}$$

The above formula can be written in the matrix form as,

$$
\begin{bmatrix} I(1,1) & \dots & I(N,1) \\ \vdots & \ddots & \vdots \\ I(1,N) & \dots & I(N,N) \end{bmatrix} \approx \underbrace{\begin{bmatrix} \mathbf{w}_x^T \psi(x_1) & \dots & \mathbf{w}_x^T \psi(x_N) \\ \vdots & \ddots & \vdots \\ \mathbf{w}_x^T \psi(x_1) & \dots & \mathbf{w}_x^T \psi(x_N) \end{bmatrix}}_{\mathbf{A}} + \underbrace{\begin{bmatrix} \mathbf{w}_y^T \psi(y_1) & \dots & \mathbf{w}_y^T \psi(y_1) \\ \vdots & \ddots & \vdots \\ \mathbf{w}_y^T \psi(y_N) & \dots & \mathbf{w}_y^T \psi(y_N) \end{bmatrix}}_{\mathbf{B}}.
$$
$$\tag{8}$$

Clearly, $\mathbf{A}$ and $\mathbf{B}$ are rank 1 matrices. Therefore, a linear network can only reconstruct a 2D image signal with at most rank 2. This drawback can be addressed in most practical cases using deeper non-linear MLPs, since the rank of the representations can be increased with multiple layers.

5.2   2D Complex Encoding

As opposed to simple encoding, we propose an alternative method for positional encoding in higher dimensions using the Kronecker product. With this approach, we can obtain a higher rank for the positional embedding matrix. For example, consider 2D inputs. Then, we can obtain the complex encoding as $\Psi(\mathbf{x}, \mathbf{y}) = \Psi(\mathbf{x}) \otimes \Psi(\mathbf{y})$, where $\Psi(\mathbf{x})$ and $\Psi(\mathbf{y})$ are 1D encodings along each dimension. Also, the following relationship holds:

$$\text{Rank}(\Psi(\mathbf{x}) \otimes \Psi(\mathbf{y})) = \text{Rank}(\Psi(\mathbf{x}))\text{Rank}(\Psi(\mathbf{y})). \tag{9}$$

However, the drawback is also obvious. The embedding dimension is squared, which takes significantly more memory and computational cost. However, we propose an elegant workaround for this problem given that the points are sampled on a regular grid, *i.e.*, when the coordinates are separable, using the following property of the Kronecker product,

$$\text{vec}(\text{S})^T \approx \text{vec}(\mathbf{W})^T(\Psi(\mathbf{x}) \otimes \Psi(\mathbf{y})) = \text{vec}(\Psi(\mathbf{y})^T\mathbf{W}\Psi(\mathbf{x}))^T, \tag{10}$$

where $\text{S}_{i,j} = I(x_i, y_j)$. For instance, suppose we have N^2 number of 2D separable points where the feature length is K for each dimension. The naive Kronecker product leads to $O(N^2K^2)$ computational complexity and $O(N^2K^2)$ memory complexity. Using Eq. (10), we reduce it dramatically to $O(NK(N + K))$ computational complexity and $O(2NK+K^2)$ memory complexity. The key advantage of the complex encoding mechanism is that although it leads to a larger encoding matrix, the ability to achieve full rank allows us to use a single linear layer instead of an MLP, which reduces the computational cost of the neural network substantially. In addition, this enables us to obtain a closed-form solution instead of using stochastic gradient descent, leading to dramatically faster optimization. More precisely, we need to solve,

$$\arg\min_{\mathbf{W}} \|\text{vec}(\text{S}) - (\Psi(\mathbf{x}) \otimes \Psi(\mathbf{y}))^T\text{vec}(\mathbf{W})\|_2^2, \tag{11}$$

where the solution can be obtained analytically as,

$$\mathbf{W} = (\Psi(\mathbf{y})\Psi(\mathbf{y})^T)^{-1}\Psi(\mathbf{y})\text{S}\Psi(\mathbf{x})^T(\Psi(\mathbf{x})\Psi(\mathbf{x})^T)^{-1}. \tag{12}$$

When the coordinates are not separable, we can still take advantage of Eq. (10) by adding a sparse blending matrix B as,

$$\text{vec}(I(\mathbf{x}, \mathbf{y}))^T \approx \text{vec}(\mathbf{W})^T(\Psi(\mathbf{x}) \otimes \Psi(\mathbf{y}))B = \text{vec}(\Psi(\mathbf{y})^T\mathbf{W}\Psi(\mathbf{x}))^TB. \tag{13}$$

This procedure is equivalent to evaluating virtual points (sampled on a regular grid) and interpolating to arbitrary coordinates using interpolation weights of B. The nature of the interpolation depends on the basis function used for positional encoding. Suppose x_0 and x_1 are two grid points and $x_0 \leq x \leq x_1$. We want $\psi(x) \approx \alpha_0\psi(x_0) + \alpha_1\psi(x_1)$. It can be solved by

$$\arg\min_{\alpha} \|\psi(x) - \left[\psi(x_0)\ \psi(x_1)\right]\alpha\|_2^2, \tag{14}$$

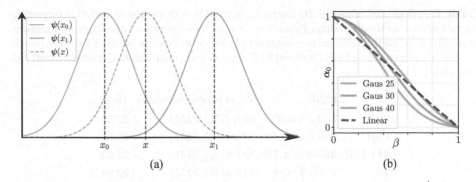

Fig. 6. Relationship between α_0 **and** β. (a) is an example positional encoding at x_0, x_1 and x. x-axis is along the feature dimension and y-axis is the encoding value. Here, we want to express $\psi(x)$ as a linear combination of $\psi(x_0)$ and $\psi(x_1)$. (b) is the relationship between the interpolation weight α_0 and the position ratio β. Instead of simple linear interpolation (dash line), the actual relation depends on the encoding function.

where $\alpha = \begin{bmatrix} \alpha_0 & \alpha_1 \end{bmatrix}^T$. With the definition $D(x)$ in Sect. 3.1, consider $d=x_1-x_0$, which is the grid interval. Then, $x=x_0+\beta d$, where $0\leq\beta\leq1$, and we have

$$\alpha = \frac{1}{D^2(0) - D^2(d)} \begin{bmatrix} D(0) & -D(d) \\ -D(d) & D(0) \end{bmatrix} \begin{bmatrix} D(\beta d) \\ D((1-\beta)d) \end{bmatrix}. \tag{15}$$

Please refer to the supplementary material for more details (Fig. 6).

5.3 High Dimensional Encoding

Both simple and complex encoding methods discussed in the previous sections can be extended easily to arbitrarily high dimensions. Suppose $\mathbf{x}=[x_1, x_2, \cdots, x_D]^T$ are the coordinates of a D dimensional point, $\psi:\mathbb{R}\rightarrow\mathbb{R}^K$ is the 1D encoder and $\Psi^{(D)}(\cdot)$ is the D dimensional encoding function. Then, the simple encoding is

$$\Psi^{(D)}(\mathbf{x}) = [\psi(x_1), \psi(x_2), \cdots, \psi(x_D)]^T. \tag{16}$$

Similarly, the complex encoding can be obtained via the Kronecker product between each encoding as,

$$\Psi^{(D)}(\mathbf{x}) = \text{vec}([\psi(x_1) \times_2 \psi(x_2) \times_3 \cdots \psi(x_3) \cdots \times_D \psi(x_D)]). \tag{17}$$

Then, we can again extend the workaround we used in Eq. 10 to multiple dimensions as,

$$\text{vec}(\mathbf{W})^T \Psi^{(D)}(\mathbf{x}) = \mathbf{W} \times_1 \psi(x_1) \times_2 \psi(x_2) \cdots \times_D \psi(x_D). \tag{18}$$

Figure 5 graphically illustrates the simple and complex positional encoding schemes.

Table 1. Performance of natural 2D image reconstruction without random sampling (separable coordinates). ● are simple positional encodings. ● are complex positional encodings with gradient descent. ● are complex positional encodings with closed-form solution. We did not show the result for the complex encoding LinF, LogF and RFF, since they are ill-conditioned (rank deficient) and unstable.

	PSNR	No. of params (memory)	Time (s)
● LinF	26.12 ± 3.99	$329, 475(1.32M)$	22.59
● LogF	26.11 ± 4.04	$329, 475(1.32M)$	22.67
● RFF [34]	$\mathbf{26.58 \pm 4.18}$	$329, 475(1.32M)$	22.62
● Tri	25.96 ± 3.88	$329, 475(1.32M)$	22.98
● Gau	26.17 ± 4.17	$329, 475(1.32M)$	23.12
● LinF	19.73 ± 2.49	$196, 608(0.79M)$	1.93
● LogF	23.55 ± 2.99	$196, 608(0.79M)$	1.85
● RFF [34]	24.34 ± 3.24	$196, 608(0.79M)$	1.55
● Tri	26.65 ± 3.57	$196, 608(0.79M)$	1.48
● Gau	$\mathbf{26.69 \pm 3.74}$	$196, 608(0.79M)$	2.01
● Tri	26.36 ± 3.39	$196, 608(0.79M)$	0.03
● Gau	$\mathbf{26.69 \pm 3.76}$	$196, 608(0.79M)$	0.18

6   Experiments

In this Section, we empirically confirm the advantages of using the proposed embedding procedure and verify that the theoretically predicted properties in the previous sections hold in practice. To this end, five encoding methods are compared: linearly sampled frequency (LinF), log-linearly sampled frequency (LogF), RFF, shifted Gaussian (Gau), and shifted triangle encoder (Tri).

6.1   1D: Rank of Input and Depth of Network

In this experiment, we randomly sample 16 columns and 16 rows from 512×512 natural images from the image dataset in [34]. And we used 256 equally spaced points for training and the rest 256 points for testing. The encoding length is set to be 256, the same as the number of training points. Parameters were chosen carefully for each encoder to show the relationship of the encoding rank and the depth of the network. The depth of the network changes from 0 (linear layer) to 2 with a fixed width of 256. From Fig. 4, we already know that the rank of the encoding matrix drops when σ of Gau increases or σ of RFF decreases. The result in Fig. 7 shows that when the rank is high, a linear network (0 depth) also works well. When the rank drops (*e.g.*, when the σ of Gau changes from 0.003 to 0.01 to 0.07), the performance of a single linear layer also drops. Adding one layer to the linear network makes up for the performance drop while adding more layers does not help a lot. In conclusion,as the rank drops, a deeper network is needed for better performance.

6.2 2D: Image Reconstruction

For this experiment, we used the image dataset in [34], which contains 32 natural images of size 512×512. For simple encoding, we used a 4 layer MLP with hidden units of 256 widths, and for complex encoding, we only used a single linear layer. The results discussed below are the average metrics for 16 images where the networks are trained for 2000 epochs.

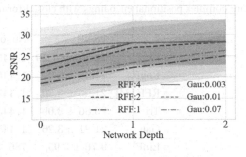

Fig. 7. The performance of the reconstruction depends on the deepness of the network and the rank of the input embedding.

Separable Coordinates. 256×256 grid points were evenly sampled for training and the rest were used for testing. As shown in Table 1, complex encoding is around 20 times faster compared to simple encoding. In fact, although both the encodings were trained for 2000 epochs, we observed that complex encodings achieved good performance in a significantly lower number of epochs. Complex encoding can also be solved in closed-form without training, which is orders of magnitude faster than simple encoding and maintains a good performance. Frequency encodings (LinF, LogF, RFF) did not perform well with complex encoding since they were rank deficient. Although complex frequency encodings did not perform as well as complex shifted encoding when combined with a single linear layer, they still outperformed simple encodings followed by a single linear layer.

Table 2. Performance of 2D image reconstruction with randomly sampled inputs (non-separable coordinates). ● are simple positional encodings. ● are complex positional encodings with stochastic gradient descent using smart indexing. The time of LinF and LogF is longer since we don't have the closed-form blending matrix.

	PSNR	No. of params (memory)	Time (s)
● LinF	24.58 ± 3.74	$329,475 (1.32M)$	21.97
● LogF	24.76 ± 3.82	$329,475 (1.32M)$	22.13
● RFF [34]	$\mathbf{24.90 \pm 3.78}$	$329,475 (1.32M)$	22.28
● Tri	24.24 ± 3.56	$329,475 (1.32M)$	22.50
● Gau	24.63 ± 3.70	$329,475 (1.32M)$	22.86
● LinF	19.64 ± 2.04	$196,608 (0.79M)$	11.51
● LogF	22.35 ± 2.82	$196,608 (0.79M)$	11.52
● RFF [34]	20.54 ± 2.61	$196,608 (0.79M)$	3.08
● Tri	23.21 ± 3.58	$196,608 (0.79M)$	1.90
● Gau	$\mathbf{23.97 \pm 3.44}$	$196,608 (0.79M)$	2.51

158   J. Zheng et al.

Table 3. Performance of video reconstruction without random sampling (separable coordinates). ● are simple positional encodings. ● are complex positional encodings with gradient descent; ● are complex positional encodings with closed-form solution.

	PSNR	No. of params (memory)	Time (s)
● LinF	**21.49 ± 3.29**	$1,445,891 (5.78M)$	77.06
● LogF	$21.46 ± 3.09$	$1,445,891 (5.78M)$	77.86
● RFF [34]	$21.06 ± 3.26$	$1,445,891 (5.78M)$	77.86
● Tri	$20.86 ± 3.09$	$1,445,891 (5.78M)$	78.91
● Gau	$21.21 ± 3.26$	$1,445,891 (5.78M)$	79.09
● LinF	$9.76 ± 3.95$	$786,432 (3.15M)$	0.69
● LogF	$9.98 ± 3.84$	$786,432 (3.15M)$	0.68
● RFF [34]	$20.33 ± 3.06$	$786,432 (3.15M)$	0.69
● Tri	**22.24 ± 2.89**	$786,432 (3.15M)$	0.68
● Gau	$22.11 ± 3.14$	$786,432 (3.15M)$	0.66
● RFF [34]	$18.05 ± 2.36$	$786,432 (3.15M)$	0.01
● Tri	**22.04 ± 2.95**	$786,432 (3.15M)$	0.009
● Gau	$21.83 ± 3.33$	$786,432 (3.15M)$	0.008

Non-separable Coordinates. For non-separable coordinates, the training points were randomly sampled 25% of the 512×512 natural images. Complex encoding contains a blending matrix representing virtual separable coordinates, which can be pre-computed. As illustrated in Table 2, the performance of complex encodings was comparably well and converged faster than the simple encodings.

6.3   3D: Video Reconstruction

As dimensionality of data increases, the faster convergence of the complex encoding becomes more notable. We use the Youtube video [27] for our experiments. In our experiments, we extracted 256 frames from 5 different videos and rescaled each frame to 256×256. Then, a central $128 \times 128 \times 128$ cube was cropped to create our dataset, since some videos contain borders. For simple encoding, a 5 layer MLP with 512-width was used, while for complex encoding, only a single linear layer was used. We trained the networks for 500 epochs. The training points were regularly sampled from a $64 \times 64 \times 64$ grid and the rest of the points were used for testing. The results are shown in Table 3.

7   Conclusion

In this paper, we show that the performance of a positional encoding scheme is mainly governed by the stable rank of the embedding matrix and the distance preservation between the embedded coordinates. In light of this discovery, we propose a novel framework that can incorporate arbitrary continuous signals as potential embedders, under certain constraints. We also propose a positional encoding scheme that enables dramatically faster convergence, allowing a single linear network to encode signals with high fidelity.

References

1. Arora, S., Du, S., Hu, W., Li, Z., Wang, R.: Fine-grained analysis of optimization and generalization for overparameterized two-layer neural networks. In: International Conference on Machine Learning, pp. 322–332. PMLR (2019)
2. Bao, H., et al.: UniLMv2: pseudo-masked language models for unified language model pre-training. In: International Conference on Machine Learning, pp. 642–652. PMLR (2020)
3. Barron, J.T., Mildenhall, B., Tancik, M., Hedman, P., Martin-Brualla, R., Srinivasan, P.P.: Mip-NeRF: a multiscale representation for anti-aliasing neural radiance fields. arXiv preprint arXiv:2103.13415 (2021)
4. Bietti, A., Mairal, J.: On the inductive bias of neural tangent kernels. arXiv preprint arXiv:1905.12173 (2019)
5. Dai, Z., et al.: Attentive language models beyond a fixed-length context. arXiv preprint arXiv:1901.02860 (2019)
6. Devlin, J., Chang, M.W., Lee, K., Toutanova, K.: BERT: pre-training of deep bidirectional transformers for language understanding. arXiv preprint arXiv:1810.04805 (2018)
7. Du, S.S., Zhai, X., Poczos, B., Singh, A.: Gradient descent provably optimizes overparameterized neural networks. arXiv preprint arXiv:1810.02054 (2018)
8. Gafni, G., Thies, J., Zollhöfer, M., Nießner, M.: Dynamic neural radiance fields for monocular 4d facial avatar reconstruction. arXiv preprint arXiv:2012.03065 (2020)
9. Gehring, J., Auli, M., Grangier, D., Yarats, D., Dauphin, Y.N.: Convolutional sequence to sequence learning. In: International Conference on Machine Learning, pp. 1243–1252. PMLR (2017)
10. He, P., Liu, X., Gao, J., Chen, W.: DeBERTa: decoding-enhanced BERT with disentangled attention. arXiv preprint arXiv:2006.03654 (2020)
11. Jacot, A., Gabriel, F., Hongler, C.: Neural tangent kernel: convergence and generalization in neural networks. arXiv preprint arXiv:1806.07572 (2018)
12. Ke, G., He, D., Liu, T.Y.: Rethinking positional encoding in language pre-training. arXiv preprint arXiv:2006.15595 (2020)
13. Kitaev, N., Klein, D.: Constituency parsing with a self-attentive encoder. arXiv preprint arXiv:1805.01052 (2018)
14. Lee, J., et al.: Wide neural networks of any depth evolve as linear models under gradient descent. arXiv preprint arXiv:1902.06720 (2019)
15. Lewis, M., et al.: BART: denoising sequence-to-sequence pre-training for natural language generation, translation, and comprehension. arXiv preprint arXiv:1910.13461 (2019)
16. Li, Z., Niklaus, S., Snavely, N., Wang, O.: Neural scene flow fields for space-time view synthesis of dynamic scenes. arXiv preprint arXiv:2011.13084 (2020)
17. Liu, X., Yu, H.F., Dhillon, I., Hsieh, C.J.: Learning to encode position for transformer with continuous dynamical model. In: International Conference on Machine Learning, pp. 6327–6335. PMLR (2020)
18. Martin-Brualla, R., Radwan, N., Sajjadi, M.S., Barron, J.T., Dosovitskiy, A., Duckworth, D.: NeRF in the wild: neural radiance fields for unconstrained photo collections. arXiv preprint arXiv:2008.02268 (2020)

19. Mildenhall, B., Srinivasan, P.P., Tancik, M., Barron, J.T., Ramamoorthi, R., Ng, R.: NeRF: representing scenes as neural radiance fields for view synthesis. In: Vedaldi, A., Bischof, H., Brox, T., Frahm, J.-M. (eds.) ECCV 2020. LNCS, vol. 12346, pp. 405–421. Springer, Cham (2020). https://doi.org/10.1007/978-3-030-58452-8_24

20. Nguyen, A., Yosinski, J., Clune, J.: Deep neural networks are easily fooled: high confidence predictions for unrecognizable images. In: Proceedings of the IEEE Conference on Computer Vision and Pattern Recognition, pp. 427–436 (2015)

21. Niemeyer, M., Mescheder, L., Oechsle, M., Geiger, A.: Differentiable volumetric rendering: learning implicit 3d representations without 3D supervision. In: Proceedings of the IEEE/CVF Conference on Computer Vision and Pattern Recognition, pp. 3504–3515 (2020)

22. Ost, J., Mannan, F., Thuerey, N., Knodt, J., Heide, F.: Neural scene graphs for dynamic scenes. arXiv preprint arXiv:2011.10379 (2020)

23. Park, K., et al.: Deformable neural radiance fields. arXiv preprint arXiv:2011.12948 (2020)

24. Raffel, C., et al.: Exploring the limits of transfer learning with a unified text-to-text transformer. arXiv preprint arXiv:1910.10683 (2019)

25. Rahaman, N., et al.: On the spectral bias of neural networks. In: International Conference on Machine Learning, pp. 5301–5310. PMLR (2019)

26. Rahimi, A., Recht, B.: Random features for large-scale kernel machines. In: Advances in Neural Information Processing Systems 20 (2007)

27. Real, E., Shlens, J., Mazzocchi, S., Pan, X., Vanhoucke, V.: Youtube-boundingboxes: a large high-precision human-annotated data set for object detection in video. In: proceedings of the IEEE Conference on Computer Vision and Pattern Recognition, pp. 5296–5305 (2017)

28. Rudelson, M., Vershynin, R.: Sampling from large matrices: an approach through geometric functional analysis. J. ACM (JACM) **54**(4), 21 (2007)

29. Saito, S., Huang, Z., Natsume, R., Morishima, S., Kanazawa, A., Li, H.: PiFu: pixel-aligned implicit function for high-resolution clothed human digitization. In: Proceedings of the IEEE/CVF International Conference on Computer Vision, pp. 2304–2314 (2019)

30. Shaw, P., Uszkoreit, J., Vaswani, A.: Self-attention with relative position representations. arXiv preprint arXiv:1803.02155 (2018)

31. Shiv, V., Quirk, C.: Novel positional encodings to enable tree-based transformers. Adv. Neural. Inf. Process. Syst. **32**, 12081–12091 (2019)

32. Sitzmann, V., Zollhöfer, M., Wetzstein, G.: Scene representation networks: continuous 3D-structure-aware neural scene representations. arXiv preprint arXiv:1906.01618 (2019)

33. Stanley, K.O.: Compositional pattern producing networks: a novel abstraction of development. Genet. Program Evolvable Mach. **8**(2), 131–162 (2007)

34. Tancik, M., et al.: Fourier features let networks learn high frequency functions in low dimensional domains. arXiv preprint arXiv:2006.10739 (2020)

35. Vaswani, A., et al.: Attention is all you need. arXiv preprint arXiv:1706.03762 (2017)

36. Wang, B., Zhao, D., Lioma, C., Li, Q., Zhang, P., Simonsen, J.G.: Encoding word order in complex embeddings. arXiv preprint arXiv:1912.12333 (2019)

37. Yang, Z., Dai, Z., Yang, Y., Carbonell, J., Salakhutdinov, R., Le, Q.V.: XLNet: generalized autoregressive pretraining for language understanding. arXiv preprint arXiv:1906.08237 (2019)

38. Zhong, E.D., Bepler, T., Davis, J.H., Berger, B.: Reconstructing continuous distributions of 3D protein structure from cryo-EM images. arXiv preprint arXiv:1909.05215 (2019)

MVDG: A Unified Multi-view Framework for Domain Generalization

Jian Zhang[1,2], Lei Qi[3(✉)], Yinghuan Shi[1,2(✉)], and Yang Gao[1,2]

[1] State Key Laboratory for Novel Software Technology, Nanjing University,
Nanjing, China
syh@nju.edu.cn
[2] National Institute of Healthcare Data Science, Nanjing University,
Nanjing, China
[3] School of Computer Science and Engineering, Southeast University,
Dhaka, China
qilei@seu.edu.cn

Abstract. To generalize the model trained in source domains to unseen target domains, domain generalization (DG) has recently attracted lots of attention. Since target domains can not be involved in training, overfitting source domains is inevitable. As a popular regularization technique, the meta-learning training scheme has shown its ability to resist overfitting. However, in the training stage, current meta-learning-based methods utilize only one task along a single optimization trajectory, which might produce a biased and noisy optimization direction. Beyond the training stage, overfitting could also cause unstable prediction in the test stage. In this paper, we propose a novel multi-view DG framework to effectively reduce the overfitting in both the training and test stage. Specifically, in the training stage, we develop a multi-view regularized meta-learning algorithm that employs multiple optimization trajectories to produce a suitable optimization direction for model updating. We also theoretically show that the generalization bound could be reduced by increasing the number of tasks in each trajectory. In the test stage, we utilize multiple augmented images to yield a multi-view prediction to alleviate unstable prediction, which significantly promotes model reliability. Extensive experiments on three benchmark datasets validate that our method can find a flat minimum to enhance generalization and outperform several state-of-the-art approaches. The code is available at https://github.com/koncle/MVRML.

1 Introduction

Traditional supervised learning assumes that training and test data are from the same distribution. However, this conventional assumption is not always

---

Supplementary Information The online version contains supplementary material available at https://doi.org/10.1007/978-3-031-19812-0_10.

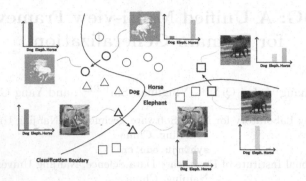

Fig. 1. The examples for the variation of the prediction probability when the test images are slightly perturbed in the unseen domain on the PACS dataset.

satisfied in the real world when domain shifts exist between training and test data. Recently, learning a robust and effective model against domain shift has raised considerable attention [3,20]. As one of the most representative learning paradigms under domain shift, unsupervised domain adaption (UDA) aims to tackle the adaptation from the labeled source domain to the unlabeled target domain under domain shift. Despite the great success of current UDA models [33,36,54], when deploying the previously trained UDA model to other unseen domains, we should re-train the model by incorporating the newly collected data from the unseen domain. This re-training process not only increases extra space/time costs but also violates privacy policy in some cases (e.g., clinical data), rendering these UDA methods not applicable to some real tasks.

The dilemma above motivates us to focus on a more applicable yet challenging setting, namely domain generalization (DG) [35]. In DG, by only learning the related knowledge from existing source domains, the trained model is required to be directly applied to previously unseen domains without any re-training procedure. To guarantee the model's efficacy on the unseen target domain, previous DG methods [25,35,41] intend to reduce the domain-specific influence from source domains via learning domain-invariant representations.

Well fitting source domains is easy, whereas well generalizing to an unseen target domain is hard. Previous methods inevitably suffer from overfitting when concentrating only on fitting source domains. Therefore, the meta-learning-based methods [10,24] have arisen as one of the most popular methods to resist overfitting during training, which simulates the domain shift episodically to perform regularization. However, these methods train their model with a single task at each iteration, which could cause a biased and noisy optimization direction.

Besides, after investigating the predictions of the trained model during the test stage, we notice that overfitting also results in unstable predictions. We conduct an experiment by perturbing (e.g., random crop and flip) the test images. As shown in Fig. 1, their predictions usually changed after being perturbed. It is because the feature representations of unseen images learned by the overfitted model are more likely to lie near the decision boundary. These representations are easily perturbed across the boundary, thus, producing different predictions. This phenomenon is more challenging in DG due to the domain discrepancy.

As aforementioned, the overfitting problem not only appears in the training stage but also largely influences the following test procedure. To fight against overfitting, we innovatively propose a multi-view framework to deal with the inferior generalization ability and unstable prediction. Specifically, in the training stage, we design a multi-view regularized meta-learning algorithm that can regularize the training process in a simple yet effective way. This algorithm contains two steps. The first step is to guide a model to pursue a suitable optimization direction via exploiting multi-view information. Unlike most previous methods (e.g., MLDG [24]) that train the model using only one task along a single optimization trajectory (i.e., the training path from the current model to another model) with limited single-view information, we propose to train the model using multiple trajectories with different sampled tasks to find a more accurate direction with integrated multi-view information. In the second step, we update the model with the learned direction. We present a theoretical analysis that the number of tasks is also critical for generalization ability. Besides, we empirically verify that integrating multiple trajectory information can help our method find a flat minimum for promising generalization.

In the test stage, we propose to deal with the unstable prediction caused by the overfitted model using multi-view prediction. We argue that current test images with a single view cannot prevent unstable prediction. Nevertheless, different augmentations applied to the test image can bring abundant information from different views. Thus, if using the image pre-processing perturbations in the test procedure (e.g., the cropping operation), we can obtain multi-view information for a single image. Therefore, we augment each test image into multiple views during the test stage and ensemble their predictions as the final output. By exploiting the multi-view predictions of a single image, we can eliminate the unreliability of predictions and obtain a more robust and accurate prediction.

In summary, we propose a unified multi-view framework to enhance the generalization of the model and stabilize the prediction in both training and test stages. Our contributions can be summarized as follows:

- During training, we design an effective multi-view regularized meta-learning scheme to prevent overfitting and find a flat minimum that generalizes better.
- We theoretically prove that increasing the number of tasks in the training stage results in a smaller generalization gap and better generalizability.
- During the test stage, we introduce a multi-view prediction strategy to boost the reliability of predictions by exploiting multi-view information.
- Our method is validated via conducting extensive experiments on multiple DG benchmark datasets and outperforms other state-of-the-art methods.

2   Related Work

Domain Generalization. Domain generalization (DG) has been proposed recently to deal with learning the generalizability to the unseen target domain.

Current DG methods can be roughly classified into three categories: *Domain-invariant feature learning*, *Data augmentation* and *Regularization*.

Domain-invariant feature learning-based methods aim to extract domain-invariant features that are applicable to any other domains. One widely employed technique is adversarial training [28,41,56], which learns the domain-invariant features by reducing the domain gap between multiple source domains. Instead of directly learning the domain-invariant features, several methods [4,8,39] try to disentangle it from domain-specific features.

Data augmentation based methods try to reduce the distance between source and unseen domains via augmenting unseen data. Most of them perform image-level augmentation [26,52,53,57] that generates images with generative adversarial networks [14] or adaptive instance normalization [16]. Since feature statistics contains style information and easy to manipulate, other methods augment features by modifying its statistics [19,38,59] or injecting generated noise [27,43].

As overfitting hurts the generalization ability of a model, regularization-based methods prevent this dilemma by regularizing the model during training. Several works [6,48] add auxiliary self-supervised loss to perform regularization. [10, 24,55] adopt a meta-learning framework to regularize the model by simulating domain shift during training. Ensemble learning [7,58] also has been employed to regularize training models. Our method also belongs to this category which can better prevent overfitting by exploiting multi-view information.

Meta-Learning. Meta-learning [45] is a long-standing topic that learns how to learn. Recently, MAML [11] has been proposed as a simple model-agnostic method to learn the meta-knowledge, attracting lots of attention. Due to the unpredictable large computational cost of second-order derivatives, first-order methods are thus developed [11,37] to reduce the cost. Later, meta-learning is introduced into DG to learn generalizable representation across domains. These methods perform regularization under the meta-learning framework. For example, MLDG [24] utilizes the episodic training paradigm and updates the network with simulated meta-train and meta-test data. MetaReg [2] explicitly learns regularization weights, and Feature-critic [29] designs a feature-critic loss to ensure that the updated network should perform better than the original network. Recent DG methods [30,40] all adopt the episodic training scheme similar to MLDG due to its effectiveness. Although these methods can alleviate overfitting by training on a single task, they may produce biased optimization direction. However, our method can mitigate this problem by learning from multiple tasks and optimization trajectories.

Test Time Augmentation. The test time augmentation (TTA) is originally proposed in [21], which integrates the predictions of several augmented images for improving the robustness of the final prediction. Besides, several methods [34,44] try to learn automatic augmentation strategy for TTA. Other methods apply TTA to estimate uncertainty in the model [1,22]. However, according to our best knowledge, TTA has not been explored in DG, which can alleviate prediction uncertainty via generating multi-view augmented test images.

3   Our Method

3.1   Episodic Training Framework

Given the data space and label space as $\mathcal{X}$ and $\mathcal{Y}$, respectively, we denote N source domains as $\mathcal{D}_1, \dots, \mathcal{D}_N$, where $\mathcal{D}_i = \{x_k, y_k\}_1^{N_i}$. N_i is the number of samples in the i-th source domain $\mathcal{D}_i$. We denote the model parameterized by θ as f. Given input x, the model outputs $f(x|\theta)$. As previously reviewed, meta-learning-based methods usually train the model with an episodic training paradigm. Similar to the meta-learning based methods [24] that split the source domains into meta-train and meta-test sets at each iteration, we leave one domain out as meta-test domain $\mathcal{D}_{te}$ and the remaining domains as meta-train domains $\mathcal{D}_{tr}$. Hereafter, we sample mini-batches from these domains and obtain meta-train $\mathcal{B}_{tr}$ and meta-test data $\mathcal{B}_{te}$. A *sub-DG task* is defined as a pair of them $t = (\mathcal{B}_{tr}, \mathcal{B}_{te})$. We define the loss on a batch $\mathcal{B} \in \{\mathcal{B}_{tr}, \mathcal{B}_{te}\}$ with parameter θ as:

$$\mathcal{L}(\mathcal{B}|\theta) = \sum_{(x_i, y_i) \in \mathcal{B}} \ell\big(f(x_i|\theta), y_i\big),$$

where ℓ is the traditional cross-entropy loss.

Different from previous meta-learning algorithms (e.g., MLDG [24]) that take second-order gradients to update model parameters, Reptile [37] is proposed as a first-order algorithm to reduce the computational cost. Therefore, we adopt Reptile version of MLDG. To be specific, given model parameter θ_j at the j-th iteration, we sample a task and train the model first with $\mathcal{L}(\mathcal{B}_{tr}|\theta_j)$ and then $\mathcal{L}(\mathcal{B}_{te}|\theta_j)$. Afterwards, we can obtain a temporarily updated parameter θ_{tmp} along this optimization tra-

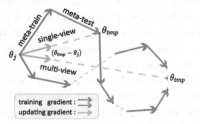

Fig. 2. An illustration of reptile and our multi-view regularized meta-learning algorithm (best viewed in color). (Color figure online)

jectory. Finally, we take $(\theta_{tmp} - \theta_j)$ as an optimization direction, i.e., the direction points from the temporary parameter to the original parameter, to update the original parameter θ_j:

$$\theta_{j+1} = \theta_j + \beta(\theta_{tmp} - \theta_j). \tag{1}$$

In this way, θ_{tmp} could exploit a part of current weight space and find a better optimization direction for current sampled tasks.

3.2 Multi-view Regularized Meta-Learning

Although Reptile reduces the computational cost, the training scheme
above suffers from several problems.
Firstly, the model is trained along
a single optimization trajectory, producing only one temporary parameter
θ_{tmp}. It is only a partial view of the
weight space for the current param-
eter θ_j, which is noisy and insufficient to produce a robust optimization direction. To better understand
this problem, we plot the loss surface
of three temporarily trained parame-

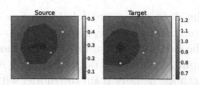

Fig. 3. The loss surface [13] of three temporarily trained parameters (denoted as
dot) starting from θ_j and optimized along
a different trajectory. The star denotes the
averaged parameter.

ters (denoted as a dot) in Fig. 3. Two of the three parameters have higher loss
values on both source and target domains. If we only consider one view (i.e.,
using a single temporary parameter), we may not find a good optimization
direction for updating. Recent researchs [7,12,18] find that the flat minimum
can produce better generalization performance than a sharp minimum, and simple weight averaging can achieve it if these weights share part of optimization
trajectory [12]. Inspired by this conclusion, we also plot the averaged parameter (denoted as a star) and find that it can produce a more robust parameter
with lower loss than most parameters on both training and test domains. Therefore, the ensembling of temporary models can produce a better and more stable
optimization direction.

Secondly, since the model is trained with a single task in each trajectory,
it cannot explore the weight space fully and is hard to escape from the local
minimum, resulting in the overfitting problem. We have theoretically proved
that more sampled tasks can help minimize the domain generalization error and
produce better performance in Sect. 3.3.

Aiming to better explore the weight space to obtain a more accurate optimization direction and erase the impact of overfitting, we develop a simple yet
effective multi-view regularized meta-learning (MVRML) algorithm by exploiting multi-view information at each iteration. Specifically, to find a robust optimization direction, we obtain T temporary parameters $\{\theta_{tmp}^1, ..., \theta_{tmp}^T\}$ along
different optimization trajectories. Different from MLDG, which only samples
a single task for the training stage, we train each temporary parameter with s
sampled tasks to help it escape from the local minimum. Besides, we sample
different tasks in different trajectories to encourage the diversity of temporary
models. Learning from these tasks allows to explore different information from
weight space with supplementary views. This sampling strategy plays an important role in our method, and we will verify it in Sect. 4.3. Then we average their
weights to obtain a robust parameter: $\theta_{tmp} = \frac{1}{T}\sum_{t=1}^{T}\theta_{tmp}^t$. Since these models
share a part of the optimization trajectory, ensembling their weights can help

find parameters located in the flat minimum that generalizes better. The full algorithm is shown in Algorithm 1 and illustrated in Fig. 2.

Algorithm 1. Multi-view Regularized Meta-Learning

Input: source data $\mathcal{D}_{src}$, network parametrized by θ, hyperparameters: inner loop learning rate α, outer loop learning rate β, the number of optimization trajectories T and the number of sampled tasks s.
Output: the trained parameter

1: $\theta_0 \leftarrow \theta; j \leftarrow 0$ // initialize parameter
2: **while** not converged **do**
3:     $\theta_j^0 \leftarrow$ Initialized by θ_j
4:     **for** $t \in \{1, ..., T\}$ **do** // train temporary models
5:         **for** $i \in \{1, ..., s\}$ **do**
6:             $\mathcal{D}_{tr}, \mathcal{D}_{te} \leftarrow$ Random split $\mathcal{D}_{src}$ // $\mathcal{D}_{tr} \cup \mathcal{D}_{te} = \mathcal{D}_{src}$, $\mathcal{D}_{tr} \cap \mathcal{D}_{te} = \emptyset$
7:             Sample mini-batch $\mathcal{B}_{tr}, \mathcal{B}_{te}$ from $\mathcal{D}_{tr}, \mathcal{D}_{te}$
8:             $\theta_j^{i-1} \leftarrow \theta_j^{i-1} - \alpha \nabla_\theta (\mathcal{L}(\mathcal{B}_{tr}|\theta_j^{i-1}))$ // train with meta-train data
9:             $\theta_j^i \leftarrow \theta_j^{i-1} - \alpha \nabla_\theta (\mathcal{L}(\mathcal{B}_{te}|\theta_j^{i-1}))$ // train with meta-test data
10:         **end for**
11:         $\theta_{tmp}^t \leftarrow \theta_j^i$ // assign current temporary parameter
12:     **end for**
13:     $\theta_{j+1} \leftarrow \theta_j + \beta(\frac{1}{T}\sum_{t=1}^T \theta_{tmp}^t - \theta_j)$ // update the original parameter
14:     $j \leftarrow j + 1$
15: **end while**

Relation to Reptile. Our algorithm is similar to the batch version of Reptile [37], but there are three key differences. Firstly, the goal is different. Reptile aims to find a good weight initialization that can be fast adapted to new tasks, while since our classification task is fixed, we are more interested in the generalization problem without adaptation. Secondly, the task sampling strategy is different. Reptile only samples a single task for each trajectory, while we sample multiple different tasks for better generalization. Finally, the training scheme is different. In Reptile, since its goal is to adapt to the current classification task, it trains the model on this task iteratively. However, it is easy to overfit this single task in DG since the performance of the training model is already good in the source domains. Differently, we train different tasks in each trajectory to find a more generalizable parameter and prevent the overfitting problem.

Relation to Ensemble Learning. There are two ensemble steps in our method. First, at each iteration, we ensemble several temporary model parameters to find a robust optimization direction. Second, if we change the formulation of Eq. (1) as $\theta_{i+1} = (1 - \beta)\theta_i + \beta\theta_{tmp}$, we can obtain an ensemble learning algorithm that combines the weights of current model and temporary model. Therefore, this training paradigm implicitly ensembles models in the weight space and can lead to a more robust model [18].

3.3   Theoretical Insight

Traditional meta-learning methods train the model with only one task, which could suffer from the overfitting problem. We theoretically prove that increasing the number of tasks can improve the generalizability in DG. We denote the source domain as $\mathcal{S} = \{\mathcal{D}_1, ...\mathcal{D}_N\}$ and target domain as $\mathcal{T} = \mathcal{D}_{N+1}$. A task is defined as $t = (\mathcal{B}_{tr}, \mathcal{B}_{te})$, which is obtained by sampling from $\mathcal{S}$. At each iteration, a sequence of sampled tasks along a single trajectory is defined as $\mathbf{T} = \{t_0, \ldots, t_m\}$ with a size of m. The training set of task sequences is defined as $\mathbb{T} = \{\mathbf{T}_0, \mathbf{T}_1, \ldots, \mathbf{T}_n\}$ with a size of n. A training algorithm $\mathbb{A}$ trained with $\mathbb{T}$ or $\mathbf{T}$ is denoted as $\theta = \mathbb{A}(\mathbb{T})$ or $\theta = \mathbb{A}(\mathbf{T})$. We define the expected risk as $\mathcal{E}_{\mathcal{P}}(\theta) = \mathbb{E}_{(x_i, y_i) \sim \mathcal{P}} \ell(f(x_i|\theta), y_i)$. With a little abuse of notation, we define the loss with respect to $\mathbf{T}$ as:

$$\mathcal{L}(\mathbf{T}; \theta) = \frac{1}{m} \sum_{(\mathcal{B}_{tr}, \mathcal{B}_{te}) \in \mathbf{T}} \frac{1}{2}(\mathcal{L}(\mathcal{B}_{tr}; \theta) + \mathcal{L}(\mathcal{B}_{te}; \theta)), \tag{2}$$

and the loss with respect to $\mathbb{T}$ as $\mathcal{L}(\mathbb{T}; \theta) = \frac{1}{n} \sum_{\mathbf{T} \in \mathbb{T}} \mathcal{L}(\mathbf{T}; \theta)$.

Theorem 1. Assume that algorithm $\mathbb{A}$ satisfies β_1-uniform stability [5] with respect to $\mathcal{L}(\mathbb{T}; \mathbf{A}(\mathbb{T}))$ and β_2-uniform stability with respect to $\mathcal{L}(\mathbf{T}; \mathbf{A}(\mathbf{T}))$. The following bound holds with probability at least $1 - \delta$:

$$\mathcal{E}_{\mathcal{T}}(\theta) \leq \hat{\mathcal{E}}_{\mathcal{S}}(\theta) + \frac{1}{2} \sup_{\mathcal{D}_i \in \mathcal{S}} \mathbf{Div}(\mathcal{D}_i, \mathcal{T}) + 2\beta_1 + (4n\beta_1 + M)\sqrt{\frac{\ln \frac{1}{\delta}}{2n}} + 2\beta_2, \tag{3}$$

where M is a bound of loss function ℓ and $\mathbf{Div}$ is KL divergence. β_1 and β_2 are functions of the number of task sequences n and the number of tasks m in each task samples. When $\beta_1 = o(1/n^a), a \geq 1/2$ and $\beta_2 = o(1/m^b), b \geq 0$, this bound becomes non-trivial. Proof is in **Supplementary Material**.

This bound contains three terms: (1) the empirical error estimated in the source domain; (2) the distance between the source and target domain; (3) the confidence bound related to the number of task sequences n and the number of tasks m in each sequence. Traditional meta-learning methods in DG train with a large number of task sequences (i.e., n). However, the number of tasks in the sequence is only one (i.e., m). *By increasing the number of sampled tasks in each sequence, we can obtain a lower error bound. In this case, we could expect a better generalization ability.*

3.4   Multi-view Prediction

As our model is trained in source domains, the feature representations of learned data are well clustered. However, when unseen images come, they are more likely to be near the decision boundary because of the overfitting and domain discrepancy, leading to unstable feature representations. When we apply small perturbations to the test images, their feature representations will be pushed across the boundary, as shown in Fig. 1.

However, current test images only present a single view (i.e., the original image) with limited information. As a result, it cannot completely prevent the unstable prediction caused by overfitting. Besides, we argue that different views of a single image could bring in more information than a single view. Therefore, instead of only using a single view to conduct the test, we propose to perform multi-view prediction (MVP). By performing multi-view predictions, we can integrate complementary information from these views and obtain a more robust and reliable prediction. Assuming we have an image x to be tested, we can generate different views of this image with some weak stochastic transformations $T(\cdot)$. Then the image prediction p is obtained by:

$$p = \text{softmax}\Big(\frac{1}{m}\sum_{i=1}^{m} f(T(x)|\theta)\Big),$$

where m is the number of views for a test image. We only apply the weak transformations (e.g., random flip) for MVP because we find that the strong augmentations (e.g., the color jittering) make the augmented images drift off the manifold of the original images, resulting in unsatisfactory prediction accuracy, which will be shown in **Supplementary Material**.

Note that the improvement brought by MVP does not mean the learned model has poor generalization capability on the simple transformations since our method without MVP has superior performance compared to other methods, and MVP can also improve other SOTA models. Besides, most predictions can not be changed if a model is robust. We will verify these claims in Sect. 4.3.

4 Experiments

We describe the details of datasets and implementation details as follows:

Datasets. To evaluate the performance of our method, we consider three popularly used domain generalization datasets: PACS, VLCS and OfficeHome. PACS [23] contains 9,991 images with 7 classes and 4 domains, and there is a large distribution discrepancy across domains. VLCS [46] consists of 10,729 images, including 5 classes and 4 domains with a small domain gap. Office-Home [47] contains 15,500 images, covering 4 domains and 65 categories which are significantly larger than PACS and VLCS.

Implementation Details. We choose ResNet-18 and Resnet-50 [15] pretrained on ImageNet [9] as our backbone, the same as previous methods [10]. All images are resized to 224×224, and the batch size is set to 64. The data augmentation consists of random resize and crop with an interval of [0.8, 1], random horizontal flip, and random color jittering with a ratio of 0.4. The model is trained for 30 epochs. We use SGD as our outer loop optimizer and Adam as the inner loop optimizer, both with a weight decay of 5×10^{-4}. Their initial learning rates are 0.05 and 0.001 for the first 24 epochs, respectively, and they are reduced to 5×10^{-3} and 1×10^{-4} for the last 6 epochs. The β_1 and β_2 are 0.9 and 0.999 for Adam optimizer, respectively. The number of optimization trajectories and sampled tasks are both 3. For multi-view prediction, we only apply weak augmentations, i.e., the random resized crop with an interval of $[0.8, 1]$ and random horizontal flip. The augmentation number t is set to 32. If not specially mentioned, we adopt this implementation as default.

We adopt the leave-one-out [23] experimental protocol that leaves one domain as an unseen domain and other domains as source domains. We conduct all experiments three times and average the results. Following the way in [23], we select the best model on the validation set of source domains. DeepAll indicates that the model is trained without any other domain generalization modules.

Table 1. Domain generalization accuracy (%) on PACS dataset with ResNet-18 (left) and ResNet-50 (right) backbone. The best performance is marked as **bold**.

Method	A	C	P	S	Avg.	Method	A	C	P	S	Avg.
DeepAll	78.40	75.76	**96.49**	66.21	79.21	DeepAll	86.72	76.25	**98.22**	76.31	84.37
MLDG [24]	79.50	77.30	94.30	71.50	80.70	MASF [10]	82.89	80.49	95.01	72.29	82.67
MASF [10]	80.29	77.17	94.99	71.69	81.04	MetaReg [2]	82.57	79.20	97.60	70.30	83.58
MetaReg [2]	83.70	77.20	95.50	70.30	81.70	MatchDG [31]	85.61	82.12	78.76	97.94	86.11
VDN [50]	82.60	78.50	94.00	82.70	84.50	DSON [42]	87.04	80.62	95.99	82.90	86.64
FACT [51]	85.37	78.38	95.15	79.15	84.51	RSC [17]	87.89	82.16	97.92	83.35	87.83
RSC [17]	83.43	80.31	95.99	80.85	85.15	FSDCL [19]	88.48	83.83	96.59	82.92	87.96
FSDCL [19]	85.30	**81.31**	95.63	81.19	85.86	SWAD [7]	89.30	83.40	97.30	82.50	88.10
MVDG (Ours)	**85.62**	79.98	95.54	**85.08**	**86.56**	MVDG (Ours)	**89.31**	**84.22**	97.43	**86.36**	**89.33**

4.1 Comparison with State-of-the-Art Methods

We evaluate our method (namely **MVDG**) to different kinds of recent state-of-the-art DG methods on several benchmarks to demonstrate its effectiveness.

Table 2. Domain generalization accuracy (%) on VLCS and OfficeHome datasets. The best performance is marked as **bold**.

Method	C	L	P	S	Avg.
DeepAll	96.98	62.00	73.83	68.66	75.37
JiGen [6]	96.17	62.06	70.93	71.40	75.14
MMLD [32]	97.01	62.20	73.01	**72.49**	76.18
RSC [17]	96.21	62.51	73.81	72.10	76.16
MVDG (Ours)	**98.40**	**63.79**	**75.26**	71.05	**77.13**

Method	A	C	P	R	Avg.
DeepAll	58.65	50.35	73.74	75.67	64.60
RSC [17]	58.42	47.90	71.63	74.54	63.12
DAEL [58]	59.40	55.10	74.00	75.70	66.10
FSDCL [19]	60.24	53.54	74.36	76.66	66.20
FACT [51]	**60.34**	**54.85**	74.48	76.55	66.56
MVDG (Ours)	60.25	54.32	**75.11**	**77.52**	**66.80**

PACS. We perform evaluation on PACS with ResNet-18 and ResNet-50 as our backbone. We compare with several meta-learning based methods (i.e., MLDG [24], MASF [10], MetaReg [2]), augmentation based methods (i.e., FACT [51], FSDCL [19]), ensemble learning based methods (i.e., SWAD [7]), domain-invariant feature learning (i.e., VDN [50]) and causal reasoning (i.e., MatchDG [31]). As shown in Table 1, our method can surpass traditional meta-learning methods in a large margin by 4.86% (86.56% vs. 81.70%) on ResNet-18 and 6.66% (89.33% vs. 82.67%) on ResNet-50. Besides, our method also achieves SOTA performance compared to recent other methods. Note that the improvement of our method on the hardest "sketch" domain is significant compared to the DeepAll (i.e., 85.08% vs. 66.21%), owing to its better regularization and robustness.

VLCS. To verify the trained model can also generalize to unseen domains with a small domain gap, we conduct an experiment on VLCS. As seen in Table 2, our method outperforms several SOTA methods and achieves the best performance on three domains (CALTECH, LABELME, and PASCAL), demonstrating that our method can also perform well in this case.

OfficeHome. We compare our method with SOTA methods on OfficeHome to prove the adaptation of our method to the dataset with a large number of classes. The result is reported in Table 2. Our method is able to achieve comparable performance to current SOTA methods.

4.2 Ablation Study

To further investigate our method, we conduct an ablation study on MVDG: i.e., 1) Reptile version of MLDG, 2) multi-view regularized meta-learning (MVRML), 3) multi-view prediction (MVP).

Table 3. The accuracy (%) of the ablation study on PACS dataset on each component: DeepAll, Reptile, and multi-view regularized meta-learning (MVRML), multi-view prediction (MVP).

Method	A	C	P	S	Avg.	Method	A	C	P	S	Avg.
Resnet-18	78.40	75.76	96.49	66.21	79.21±0.49	Resnet-50	86.72	76.25	98.22	76.31	84.37±0.42
+MVRML	85.20	79.97	95.29	83.11	85.89±0.27	+MVRML	89.02	84.47	97.09	85.24	88.95±0.06
+MVRML+MVP	85.62	79.98	95.54	85.08	86.56±0.18	+MVRML+MVP	89.31	84.22	97.43	86.36	89.33±0.18
+Reptile	80.49	76.23	94.91	77.65	82.34±0.71	+Reptile	85.48	78.58	97.07	77.31	84.61±0.15

Reptile. As seen in Table 3, the performance of Reptile can achieve satisfactory performance compared to DeepAll. Note that, although its performance in the "sketch" domain improves a lot (i.e., 77.65% vs. 66.21%), the performance in the "photo" domain decreases. We hypothesize that the feature spaces learned by meta-learning and DeepAll are different. Since ResNet-18 is pretrained on

ImageNet (photo-like dataset), it shows high performance in the "photo" domain at the beginning. When the training procedure continues, the model is hard to move far away from its initial weight space. Thus its performance is promising in the "photo" domain. However, when trained with meta-learning, it can obtain a good performance by the episodic training scheme but with a little sacrifice of its original performance in the "photo" domain.

Multi-view Regularized Meta-Learning. When we apply multi-view regularized meta-learning (MVRML), the performance is improved a lot on the baseline in Table 3, which shows its efficacy in dealing with the overfitting issue. We observe that the "photo" domain also decreases a little. It may be caused by the better weight space produced by the meta-learning algorithm, which is far away from the initial weight space (i.e., the initial model trained by ImageNet).

Multi-view Prediction. We employ multi-view prediction (MVP) to enhance model reliability. As shown in Table 3, the performance improves on both base-lines. We notice that there is a large improvement in the "sketch" domain because the "sketch" domain has only the outline of the object, and thus it is more sensitive to small perturbations. With MVP, the model's prediction can be more reliable and accurate.

4.3 Further Analysis

We further analyze the properties of our method with ResNet-18 as backbone. More experiments could be found in **Supplementary Material**.

Local Sharpness Comparison. As mentioned in Sect. 3.2, our method can achieve better performance because it can find a flat minimum. To verify it, we plot local flatness via the loss gap between the original parameter and perturbed parameter, i.e., $\mathbb{E}_{\theta'=\theta+\epsilon}[\mathcal{L}(\theta, \mathcal{D}) - \mathcal{L}(\theta', \mathcal{D})]$ [7], where ϵ is perturbation sampled from gaussian distribution with a radius of γ. We conduct an experiment on the target domain of PACS, and the results are shown in Fig. 4. With a larger radius, the sharpness of the three methods all increases. However, MVRML can find a better flat minimum where the loss increases the most slowly compared to the other methods, achieving better generalization performance.

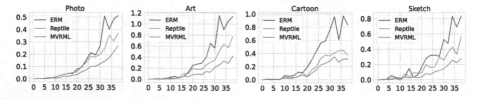

Fig. 4. Local sharpness comparison between ERM, Reptile, and MVRML on target domain of PACS. X-axis indicates the distance γ to the original parameter, and Y-axis indicates the sharpness of the loss surface (the lower, the flatter).

Table 4. The comparison of different task sampling strategies for MVRML on PACS dataset.

Strategies	A	C	P	S	Avg.
S1	82.81	76.85	94.65	82.78	84.27
S2	84.11	78.48	93.75	82.95	84.82
S3 (Ours)	85.20	79.97	95.29	83.11	85.89

Influence of Task Sampling Strategies. As mentioned in Sect. 3.2, task sampling strategy is crucial for performance improvement in MVRML. We compare different sampling strategies at each iteration: each trajectory samples 1) from the same domain, denoted as S1; 2) from all domains, denoted as S2; 3) from random split meta-train and meta-test domains, denoted as S3. As shown in Table 4, with a better sampling strategy, the generalizability of the trained model increases. We hypothesize that it is owing to the batch normalization layer that normalizes data with statistics calculated on a batch. When only sampling from a single domain, the diversity of BN statistics is limited to three domains. If we sample batches from different domains, although the diversity of BN statistics increases a little, the statistics in a batch tend to be the same on average. Finally, if we sample tasks from meta-train and meta-test splits, we can ensure that the diversity of statistics changes drastically, encouraging temporary models to explore diverse trajectories and produce a more robust optimization direction.

Impact of the Number of Tasks and Trajectories. For MVRML, we sample a sequence of tasks on multiple trajectories to train the model. Both the number of tasks and trajectories can affect the generalization performance. Therefore, we train our model with a different number of tasks and trajectories. When we experiment with one factor, we set the other to 3. The result can be shown in Fig. 5a and Fig. 5b. With the increasing number of tasks, the performance first improves, as our theory suggests that more tasks can benefit the generalizability. However, the performance plateaus afterward. We suspect that the first few tasks are critical for the optimization procedure of temporary models since it decides the direction to optimize. With more tasks to be learned, the optimization direction does not change too much. Thus, more tasks could not largely improve performance. There is a similar trend in the number of trajectories. Because three trajectories are good enough to provide a robust optimization direction, more trajectories also could not help too much. To reduce the computational cost, we choose three trajectories in our experiments.

Influence of the Number of Augmented Images in MVP. When applying multi-view prediction (MVP), we need to augment the test images into different views and ensemble their results. Therefore, the number of augmented images has an influence on the result. We apply MVP to both DeepAll and our model with a different number of augmented images. As shown in Fig. 5c, the performance improves when more augmented images are generated, which results from the increasing diversity of the test images. When the number is large enough (e.g.,

64), the diversity created by the weak augmentation cannot increase anymore, and the performance plateaus.

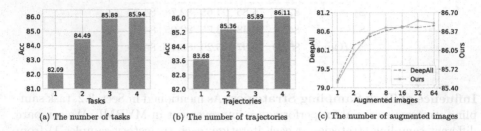

(a) The number of tasks   (b) The number of trajectories   (c) The number of augmented images

Fig. 5. The impact of the number of tasks (a) and trajectories (b) in MVRML. The number of augmented images (c) in MVP.

Table 5. The left table shows accuracy and prediction change rate (PCR) of different methods on PACS dataset with ResNet-18. The weak augmentation is denoted as WA. The right table shows the accuracy (%) of applying MVP to other SOTA methods on PACS dataset.

	Method	A	C	P	S	Avg.
Acc(%)	DeepAll (w/o WA)	77.90	70.60	96.41	66.03	77.73
	DeepAll	78.40	75.76	96.49	66.21	79.21
	MVRML	85.20	79.97	95.29	83.11	85.89
PCR(%)	DeepAll (w/o WA)	43.0	42.7	9.9	63.6	39.8
	DeepAll	36.5	37.6	8.1	49.3	32.9
	MVRML	27.7	28.4	8.7	25.4	22.6

Method	A	C	P	S	Avg.
MixStyle [59]	80.43	77.55	97.11	76.15	82.81
MixStyle+MVP	83.05	78.45	97.50	78.99	84.49
RSC [17]	84.67	76.75	95.81	82.59	84.96
RSC+MVP	84.91	76.83	96.41	83.81	85.49
FSR [49]	84.57	80.76	96.11	82.16	85.90
FSR+MVP	85.60	81.40	96.59	83.48	86.76

Unstable Prediction. In the previous sections, we argue that if the model overfits the source domains, it is easy to produce unstable predictions by perturbing the test images slightly (random resized crop and flip). By contrast, a robust model can reduce this effect and perform well. To verify it, we test several models in the unseen domain: DeepAll without weak augmentations (i.e., color jittering, random crop, and flip), DeepAll, and the model trained with MVRML. We introduce prediction change rate (PCR), calculated by the ratio of the number of predictions changed after applying the augmentations and the number of total predictions. We compare the test accuracy and PCR in Table 5. The larger this measure, the more unstable the model in the unseen domains. As seen, DeepAll without augmentation produces the highest PCR and lowest Acc because this model overfits source domains. Meanwhile, with data augmentation and a better training strategy, the performance of the model largely improves, and PCR decreases drastically.

MVP on SOTA Methods. MVP is a plug-and-play method that can be easily adapted to other methods. To validate its adaptation ability, we integrate it into three SOTA methods, i.e., Mixstyle [59], RSC [17] and FSR [49]. For RSC and FSR, we directly use their pre-trained model. For MixStyle, we implement it by ourselves. The result is shown in Table 5. MVP can improve all of these trained models, which suggests its effectiveness in DG.

5   Conclusion

In this paper, to resist overfitting, with the observation that the performance in DG models can be benefited by task-based augmentation in training and sample-based augmentation in testing, we propose a novel multi-view framework to boost generalization ability and reduce unstable prediction caused by overfitting. Specifically, during training, we designed a multi-view regularized meta-learning algorithm. During testing, we introduced multi-view prediction to generate different views of a single image for the ensemble to stabilize its prediction. We provide theoretical proof that increasing the number of tasks can boost generalizability, and we also empirically verified that our method can help find a flat minimum that generalizes better. By conducting extensive experiments on three DG benchmark datasets, we validated the effectiveness of our method.

Acknowledgement. This work was supported by NSFC Major Program (62192 783), CAAI-Huawei MindSpore Project (CAAIXSJLJJ-2021-042A), China Postdoctoral Science Foundation Project (2021M690609), Jiangsu Natural Science Foundation Project (BK20210224), and CCF-Lenovo Bule Ocean Research Fund.

References

1. Ayhan, M.S., Berens, P.: Test-time data augmentation for estimation of heteroscedastic aleatoric uncertainty in deep neural networks. In: MIDL (2018)
2. Balaji, Y., Sankaranarayanan, S., Chellappa, R.: MetaReg: towards domain generalization using meta-regularization. In: NeurIPS (2018)
3. Ben-David, S., Blitzer, J., Crammer, K., Pereira, F., et al.: Analysis of representations for domain adaptation. In: NeurIPS (2007)
4. Bousmalis, K., Trigeorgis, G., Silberman, N., Krishnan, D., Erhan, D.: Domain separation networks. In: NeurIPS (2016)
5. Bousquet, O., Elisseeff, A.: Stability and generalization. In: JMLR (2002)
6. Carlucci, F.M., D'Innocente, A., Bucci, S., Caputo, B., Tommasi, T.: Domain generalization by solving jigsaw puzzles. In: CVPR (2019)
7. Cha, J., et al.: SWAD: domain generalization by seeking flat minima. arXiv (2021)
8. Chattopadhyay, P., Balaji, Y., Hoffman, J.: Learning to balance specificity and invariance for in and out of domain generalization. In: ECCV (2020)
9. Deng, J., Dong, W., Socher, R., Li, L.J., Li, K., Fei-Fei, L.: ImageNet: a large-scale hierarchical image database. In: CVPR (2009)
10. Dou, Q., de Castro, D.C., Kamnitsas, K., Glocker, B.: Domain generalization via model-agnostic learning of semantic features. In: NeurIPS (2019)

11. Finn, C., Abbeel, P., Levine, S.: Model-agnostic meta-learning for fast adaptation of deep networks. In: ICML (2017)
12. Frankle, J., Dziugaite, G.K., Roy, D., Carbin, M.: Linear mode connectivity and the lottery ticket hypothesis. In: ICML (2020)
13. Garipov, T., Izmailov, P., Podoprikhin, D., Vetrov, D.P., Wilson, A.G.: Loss surfaces, mode connectivity, and fast ensembling of dnns. In: NeurIPS (2018)
14. Goodfellow, I., et al.: Generative adversarial nets. In: NeurIPS (2014)
15. He, K., Zhang, X., Ren, S., Sun, J.: Deep residual learning for image recognition. In: CVPR (2016)
16. Huang, X., Belongie, S.: Arbitrary style transfer in real-time with adaptive instance normalization. In: ICCV (2017)
17. Huang, Z., Wang, H., Xing, E.P., Huang, D.: Self-challenging improves cross-domain generalization. In: ECCV (2020)
18. Izmailov, P., Podoprikhin, D., Garipov, T., Vetrov, D., Wilson, A.G.: Averaging weights leads to wider optima and better generalization. arXiv (2018)
19. Jeon, S., Hong, K., Lee, P., Lee, J., Byun, H.: Feature stylization and domain-aware contrastive learning for domain generalization. In: ACMMM (2021)
20. Kouw, W.M., Loog, M.: A review of domain adaptation without target labels. In: TPAMI (2019)
21. Krizhevsky, A., Sutskever, I., Hinton, G.E.: ImageNet classification with deep convolutional neural networks. In: NeurIPS (2012)
22. Lee, H., Lee, H., Hong, H., Kim, J.: Test-time mixup augmentation for uncertainty estimation in skin lesion diagnosis. In: MIDL (2021)
23. Li, D., Yang, Y., Song, Y.Z., Hospedales, T.M.: Deeper, broader and artier domain generalization. In: ICCV (2017)
24. Li, D., Yang, Y., Song, Y.Z., Hospedales, T.M.: Learning to generalize: meta-learning for domain generalization. In: AAAI (2018)
25. Li, H., Jialin Pan, S., Wang, S., Kot, A.C.: Domain generalization with adversarial feature learning. In: CVPR (2018)
26. Li, L., et al.: Progressive domain expansion network for single domain generalization. In: CVPR (2021)
27. Li, P., Li, D., Li, W., Gong, S., Fu, Y., Hospedales, T.M.: A simple feature augmentation for domain generalization. In: ICCV (2021)
28. Li, Y., et al.: Deep domain generalization via conditional invariant adversarial networks. In: Ferrari, Vittorio, Hebert, Martial, Sminchisescu, Cristian, Weiss, Yair (eds.) ECCV 2018. LNCS, vol. 11219, pp. 647–663. Springer, Cham (2018). https://doi.org/10.1007/978-3-030-01267-0_38
29. Li, Y., Yang, Y., Zhou, W., Hospedales, T.M.: Feature-critic networks for heterogeneous domain generalizationx. arXiv (2019)
30. Liu, Q., Dou, Q., Heng, P.A.: Shape-aware meta-learning for generalizing prostate MRI segmentation to unseen domains. In: MICCAI (2020)
31. Mahajan, D., Tople, S., Sharma, A.: Domain generalization using causal matching. In: ICML (2021)
32. Matsuura, T., Harada, T.: Domain generalization using a mixture of multiple latent domains. In: AAAI (2020)
33. Melas-Kyriazi, L., Manrai, A.K.: PixMatch: unsupervised domain adaptation via pixelwise consistency training. In: CVPR (2021)
34. Molchanov, D., Lyzhov, A., Molchanova, Y., Ashukha, A., Vetrov, D.: Greedy policy search: a simple baseline for learnable test-time augmentation. arXiv (2020)
35. Muandet, K., Balduzzi, D., Schölkopf, B.: Domain generalization via invariant feature representation. In: ICML (2013)

36. Na, J., Jung, H., Chang, H.J., Hwang, W.: FixBi: bridging domain spaces for unsupervised domain adaptation. In: CVPR (2021)
37. Nichol, A., Schulman, J.: Reptile: a scalable metalearning algorithm. arXiv (2018)
38. Nuriel, O., Benaim, S., Wolf, L.: Permuted adain: Enhancing the representation of local cues in image classifiers. arXiv (2020)
39. Piratla, V., Netrapalli, P., Sarawagi, S.: Efficient domain generalization via common-specific low-rank decomposition. In: ICML (2020)
40. Qiao, F., Zhao, L., Peng, X.: Learning to learn single domain generalization. In: CVPR (2020)
41. Rahman, M.M., Fookes, C., Baktashmotlagh, M., Sridharan, S.: Correlation-aware adversarial domain adaptation and generalization. In: PR (2019)
42. Seo, S., Suh, Y., Kim, D., Han, J., Han, B.: Learning to optimize domain specific normalization for domain generalization. In: ECCV (2020)
43. Shu, M., Wu, Z., Goldblum, M., Goldstein, T.: Prepare for the worst: generalizing across domain shifts with adversarial batch normalization. arXiv (2020)
44. Sypetkowski, M., Jasiulewicz, J., Wojna, Z.: Augmentation inside the network. arXiv (2020)
45. Thrun, S., Pratt, L. (eds.): Larning to Learn(1998)
46. Torralba, A., Efros, A.A.: Unbiased look at dataset bias. In: CVPR (2011)
47. Venkateswara, H., Eusebio, J., Chakraborty, S., Panchanathan, S.: Deep hashing network for unsupervised domain adaptation. In: CVPR (2017)
48. Wang, S., Yu, L., Li, C., Fu, C.W., Heng, P.A.: Learning from extrinsic and intrinsic supervisions for domain generalization. In: ECCV (2020)
49. Wang, Y., Qi, L., Shi, Y., Gao, Y.: Feature-based style randomization for domain generalization. arXiv (2021)
50. Wang, Y., Li, H., Chau, L.P., Kot, A.C.: Variational disentanglement for domain generalization. arXiv (2021)
51. Xu, Q., Zhang, R., Zhang, Y., Wang, Y., Tian, Q.: A fourier-based framework for domain generalization. In: CVPR (2021)
52. Xu, Z., Liu, D., Yang, J., Raffel, C., Niethammer, M.: Robust and generalizable visual representation learning via random convolutions. arXiv (2020)
53. Yue, X., Zhang, Y., Zhao, S., Sangiovanni-Vincentelli, A., Keutzer, K., Gong, B.: Domain randomization and pyramid consistency: simulation-to-real generalization without accessing target domain data. In: ICCV (2019)
54. Yue, Z., Sun, Q., Hua, X.S., Zhang, H.: Transporting causal mechanisms for unsupervised domain adaptation. In: ICCV (2021)
55. Zhang, J., Qi, L., Shi, Y., Gao, Y.: Generalizable model-agnostic semantic segmentation via target-specific normalization. In: PR (2022)
56. Zhao, S., Gong, M., Liu, T., Fu, H., Tao, D.: Domain generalization via entropy regularization. In: NeurIPS (2020)
57. Zhou, K., Yang, Y., Hospedales, T.M., Xiang, T.: Deep domain-ad image generation for domain generalisation. In: AAAI (2020)
58. Zhou, K., Yang, Y., Qiao, Y., Xiang, T.: Domain adaptive ensemble learning. In: TIP (2021)
59. Zhou, K., Yang, Y., Qiao, Y., Xiang, T.: Mixstyle neural networks for domain generalization and adaptation. arXiv (2021)

Panoptic Scene Graph Generation

Jingkang Yang[1], Yi Zhe Ang[1], Zujin Guo[1], Kaiyang Zhou[1], Wayne Zhang[2],
and Ziwei Liu[1(✉)]

[1] S-Lab, Nanyang Technological University, Singapore, Singapore
{jingkang001,yizhe.ang,gu00008,kaiyang.zhou,ziwei.liu}@ntu.edu.sg
[2] SenseTime Research, Shenzhen, China
wayne.zhang@sensetime.com

Abstract. Existing research addresses scene graph generation (SGG)—
a critical technology for scene understanding in images—from a detection perspective, *i.e.*, objects are detected using bounding boxes followed by prediction of their pairwise relationships. We argue that such a
paradigm causes several problems that impede the progress of the field.
For instance, bounding box-based labels in current datasets usually contain redundant classes like hairs, and leave out background information
that is crucial to the understanding of context. In this work, we introduce *panoptic scene graph generation (PSG)*, a new problem task that
requires the model to generate a more comprehensive scene graph representation based on panoptic segmentations rather than rigid bounding boxes.
A high-quality *PSG dataset*, which contains 49k well-annotated overlapping images from COCO and Visual Genome, is created for the community to keep track of its progress. For benchmarking, we build four two-
stage baselines, which are modified from classic methods in SGG, and two
one-stage baselines called PSGTR and PSGFormer, which are based on
the efficient Transformer-based detector, *i.e.*, DETR. While PSGTR uses
a set of queries to directly learn triplets, PSGFormer separately models the
objects and relations in the form of queries from two Transformer decoders,
followed by a prompting-like relation-object matching mechanism. In the
end, we share insights on open challenges and future directions. We invite
users to explore the PSG dataset on our project page https://psgdataset.
org/, and try our codebase https://github.com/Jingkang50/OpenPSG.

1   Introduction

The goal of scene graph generation (SGG) task is to generate a graph-structured
representation from a given image to abstract out objects—grounded by bounding boxes—and their pairwise relationships [5,65]. Scene graphs aim to facilitate
the understanding of complex scenes in images and has potential for a wide
range of downstream applications, such as image retrieval [27,50,52], visual reasoning [1,53], visual question answering (VQA) [21], image captioning [8,16],
structured image generation and outpainting [13,26,66], and robotics [2,14].

Supplementary Information The online version contains supplementary material
available at https://doi.org/10.1007/978-3-031-19812-0_11.

S. Avidan et al. (Eds.): ECCV 2022, LNCS 13687, pp. 178–196, 2022.
https://doi.org/10.1007/978-3-031-19812-0_11

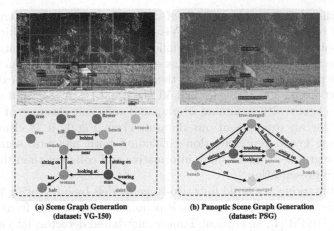

(a) Scene Graph Generation
(dataset: VG-150)

(b) Panoptic Scene Graph Generation
(dataset: PSG)

Fig. 1. Scene graph generation (a. SGG task) *vs.* panoptic scene graph generation (b. PSG task). The existing SGG task in (a) uses bounding box-based labels, which are often inaccurate—pixels covered by a bounding box do not necessarily belong to the annotated class—and cannot fully capture the background information. In contrast, the proposed PSG task in (b) presents a more comprehensive and clean scene graph representation, with more accurate localization of objects and including relationships with the background (known as stuff), *i.e.*, the trees and pavement.

Since the introduction of SGG [27], this problem has been addressed from a detection perspective, *i.e.*, using bounding boxes to detect objects followed by the prediction of their pairwise relationships [35,42,64]. We argue that such a bounding box-based paradigm is not ideal for solving the problem, and would instead cause a number of issues that impede the progress of the field. Firstly, bounding boxes—as labeled in current datasets [35]—only provide a coarse localization of objects and often contain noisy/ambiguous pixels belonging to different objects or categories (see the bounding boxes of the two persons in Fig. 1-a). Secondly, bounding boxes typically cannot cover the full scene of an image. For instance, the pavement region in Fig. 1-a is crucial for understanding the context but is completely ignored. Thirdly, current SGG datasets often include redundant classes and information like woman-has-hair in Fig. 1-a, which is mostly deemed trivial [42]. Furthermore, inconsistent and redundant labels are also observed in current datasets, *e.g.*, the trees and benches in Fig. 1-a are labeled multiple times, and some extra annotations do not contribute to the graph (see isolated nodes). Using such labels for learning might confuse the model.

Ideally, the grounding of objects should be clear and precise, and a scene graph should not only focus on salient regions and relationships in an image but also be comprehensive enough for scene understanding. We argue that as compared to bounding boxes, panoptic segmentation [33] labels would be a better choice for constructing scene graphs. To this end, we introduce a new problem, *panoptic scene graph generation*, or PSG, with a goal of generating scene graph representations based on panoptic segmentations rather than rigid bounding boxes.

To help the community keep track of the research progress, we create a new PSG dataset based on COCO [43] and Visual Genome (VG) [35], which contains 49k well-annotated images in total. We follow COCO's object annotation schema of 133 classes; comprising 80 thing classes and 53 stuff (background) classes. To construct predicates, we conduct a thorough investigation into existing VG-based datasets, e.g., VG-150 [64], VrR-VG [42] and GQA [24], and summarize 56 predicate classes with minimum overlap and sufficient coverage of semantics. See Fig. 1-b for an example of our dataset. From Fig. 1, it is clear that the panoptic scene graph representation—including both panoptic segmentations and the scene graph—is much more informative and coherent than the previous scene graph representation.

For benchmarking, we build four two-stage models by integrating four classic SGG methods [54,58,64,71] into a classic panoptic segmentation framework [32]. We also turn DETR [4], an efficient Transformer-based detector, into a one-stage PSG model dubbed as PSGTR, which has proved effective for the PSG task. We further provide another one-stage baseline called PSGFormer, which extends PSGTR with two improvements: 1) modeling objects and relations separately in the form of queries within two Transformer decoders, and 2) a prompting-like interaction mechanism. A comprehensive comparison of one-stage models and two-stage models is discussed in our experiments.

In summary, we make the following contributions to the SGG community:

- **A New Problem and Dataset**: We discuss several issues with current SGG research, especially those associated with existing datasets. To address them, we introduce a new problem that combines SGG with panoptic segmentation, and create a large PSG dataset with high-quality annotations.
- **A Comprehensive Benchmark**: We build strong two-stage and one-stage PSG baselines, and evaluate them comprehensively on our new dataset, so that the PSG task is solidified in its inception. We find that one-stage models, despite having a simplified training paradigm, have great potential for PSG as it achieves competitive results on the dataset.

2 Related Work

Scene Graph Generation. Existing scene graph generation (SGG) methods have been dominated by the two-stage pipeline that consists of object detection and pairwise predicate estimation. Given bounding boxes, early work predicts predicates using conditional random fields [11,27] or casts predicate prediction into a classification problem [34,49,75]. Inspired by knowledge graph embeddings, VTransE [74] and UVTransE [25] are proposed for explicit predicate modeling. Follow-up works have investigated various variants based on, e.g., RNN and graph-based modeling [9,38,44,58,64,67,71], energy-based models [54], external knowledge [18,46,58,69,70], and more recently language supervision [68,77]. Recent research has shifted the attention to problems associated with the SGG datasets, such as the long-tailed distribution of predicates [12,57],

Table 1. Comparsion between classic SGG datasets and PSG dataset. #PPI counts predicates per image. DupFree checks whether duplicated object groundings are cleaned up. Spvn indicates whether the objects are grounded by bounding boxes or segmentations.

Fig. 2. Word cloud for PSG predicates.

Dataset	#Image	#ObjCls	#RelCls	#PPI	DupFree	Spvn	Source
VG [35]	108K	34K	40K	21.4	✗	BBox	COCO & Flickr
VG-150 [64]	88K	150	50	5.7	✗	BBox	Clean VG
VrR-VG [42]	59K	1,600	117	3.4	✗	BBox	Clean VG
GQA [24]	85K	1,703	310	50.6	✓	BBox	Re-annotate VG
PSG	49K	133	56	5.7	✓	Seg	Annotate COCO

excessive visually-irrelevant predicates [42], and inaccurate localization of bounding boxes [29]. In particular, a very recent study [29] shows that training an SGG model to simultaneously generate scene graphs and predict semantic segmentation masks can bring about improvements, which inspires our research. In our work, we study panoptic segmentation-based scene graph generation in a more systematic way by formulating a new problem and building a new benchmark. We also notice that a closely-related topic human-object interaction (HOI) [19] shares a similar goal with SGG, *i.e.*, to detect prominent relations from the image. However, the HOI task restricts the model to only detect human-related relations while ignoring the valuable information between objects that is often critical to comprehensive scene understanding. Nevertheless, many HOI methods are applicable to SGG tasks [6,15,17,22,23,28,30,39,40,45,55,59–61,72,73,78], and some of them have inspired our PSG baselines [31,79].

Scene Graph Datasets. While early SGG works have constructed several smaller-size datasets such as RW-SGD [27], VRD [46], and UnRel-D [48], the large-scale Visual Genome (VG) [35] quickly became the standard SGG dataset as soon as it was released in 2017, prompting subsequent work to research in a more realistic setting. However, several critical drawbacks of VG were raised by the community, and therefore, some VG variants were gradually introduced to address some problems. Notice that VG contains an impractically large number of 33,877 object classes and 40,480 predicate classes, leading VG-150 [64] to only keep the most frequent 150 object classes and 50 predicate classes for a more realistic setting. Later, VrR-VG [42] argued that many predicates in VG-150 can be easily estimated by statistical priors, hence deciding to re-filter the original VG categories to only keep visually relevant predicate classes. However, by scrutinizing VrR-VG, we find many predicates are redundant (*e.g.*, alongside, beside, besides) and ambiguous (*e.g.*, beyond, down). Similar drawbacks appeared in another large-scale dataset with scene graph annotations called GQA [24]. In summary, although relations play a pivotal role in SGG tasks, a systematic definition of relations is unfortunately overlooked across all the existing SGG datasets. Therefore, in our proposed PSG dataset, we consider both comprehensive coverage and non-overlap between words, and carefully define a predicate dictionary with 56 classes to better formulate the scene graph problem. Figure 2 shows the word cloud of the predicate classes, where font size indicates frequency.

Apart from the problem of predicate definition, another critical issue of SGG datasets is that they all adopt bounding box-based object grounding, which inevitably causes a number of issues such as coarse localization (bounding boxes cannot reach pixel-level accuracy), inability to ground comprehensively (bounding boxes cannot ground backgrounds), tendency to provide trivial information (current datasets usually capture objects like head to form the trivial relation of person-has-head), and duplicate groundings (the same object could be grounded by multiple separate bounding boxes). These issues together have caused the low-quality of current SGG datasets, which impede the progress of the field. Therefore, the proposed PSG dataset tries to address all the above problems by grounding the images using accurate and comprehensive panoptic segmentations with COCO's appropriate granularity of object categories. Table 1 compares the statistics of the PSG dataset with classic SGG datasets.

Panoptic Segmentation. The panoptic segmentation task unifies semantic segmentation and instance segmentation [33] for comprehensive scene understanding, and the first approach is a simple combination of a semantic segmentation model and an instance segmentation model to produce stuff masks and thing masks respectively [33]. Follow-up work, such as Panoptic FPN [32] and UPSNet [63], aim to unify the two tasks in a single model through multitask learning to achieve gains in compute efficiency and segmentation performance. Recent approaches (e.g., MaskFormer [10], Panoptic Segformer [41] and K-Net [76]) have turned to more efficient architectures based on Transformers like DETR [4], which simplifies the detection pipeline by casting the detection task as a set prediction problem.

3   Problem and Dataset

Recap: Scene Graph Generation. We first briefly review the goal of the classic scene graph generation (SGG) task, which aims to model the distribution:

$$\Pr\left(\mathbf{G} \mid \mathbf{I}\right) = \Pr\left(\mathbf{B}, \mathbf{O}, \mathbf{R} \mid \mathbf{I}\right), \tag{1}$$

where $\mathbf{I} \in \mathbb{R}^{H \times W \times 3}$ is the input image, and $\mathbf{G}$ is the desired scene graph which comprises the bounding boxes $\mathbf{B} = \{\mathbf{b}_1, \ldots, \mathbf{b}_n\}$ and labels $\mathbf{O} = \{o_1, \ldots, o_n\}$ that correspond to each of the n objects in the image, and their relations in the set $\mathbf{R} = \{r_1, \ldots, r_l\}$. More specifically, $\mathbf{b}_i \in \mathbb{R}^4$ represents the box coordinates, $o_i \in \mathbb{C}^O$ and $r_i \in \mathbb{C}^R$ belong to the set of all object and relation classes.

Panoptic Scene Graph Generation. Instead of localizing each object by its bounding box coordinates, the new task of panoptic scene graph generation (PSG task) grounds each object with the more fine-grained panoptic segmentation. For conciseness, we refer to both objects and background as objects.

Formally, with panoptic segmentation, an image is segmented into a set of masks $\mathbf{M} = \{\mathbf{m}_1, \ldots, \mathbf{m}_n\}$, where $\mathbf{m}_i \in \{0, 1\}^{H \times W}$. Each mask is associated with an object with class label $o_i \in \mathcal{C}^O$. A set of relations $\mathbf{R}$ between objects are also predicted. The masks do not overlap, $i.e.$, $\sum_{i=1}^{n} \mathbf{m}_i \leq 1^{H \times W}$. Hence, PSG task models the following distribution:

$$\Pr(\mathbf{G} \mid \mathbf{I}) = \Pr(\mathbf{M}, \mathbf{O}, \mathbf{R} \mid \mathbf{I}). \tag{2}$$

PSG Dataset. To address the PSG task, we build our PSG dataset following these three major steps. Readers can find more details in the Appendix.

Step 1: A Coarse COCO & VG Fusion: To create a dataset with both panoptic segmentation and relation annotations, we use the 48,749 images in the intersection of the COCO and VG datasets with an automatic but coarse dataset fusion process. Specifically, we use an object category matching procedure to match COCO's segmentations with VG's bounding boxes, so that part of VG's predicates are applied to COCO's segmentation pairs. Due to the inherent mismatch between the label systems and localization annotations of VG and COCO, the auto-generated dataset is very noisy and requires further cleaning.

Step 2: A Concise Predicate Dictionary: Inspired by the appropriate granularity of COCO categories [43], we carefully identify 56 salient relations by taking reference from common predicates in the initial noisy PSG dataset and all VG-based datasets including VG-150 [64], VrR-VG [42] and GQA [24]. The selected 56 predicates are maximally independent (*e.g.*, we only keep "over/on" and do not have "under") and cover most common cases in the dataset.

Step 3: A Rigorous Annotation Process: Building upon the noisy PSG dataset, we require the annotators to *1) filter* out incorrect triplets, and *2) supplement* more relations between not only object-object, but also object-background and background-background pairs, using the predefined 56 predicates. To prevent ambiguity between predicates, we ask the annotators strictly not to annotate using general relations like on, in when a more precise predicate like parked on is applicable. With this rule, the PSG dataset allows the model to understand the scene more precisely and saliently.

Quality Control: The PSG dataset goes through a professional dataset construction process. The main authors first annotated 1000 images to construct a detailed documentation (available in project page), and then employed a professional annotation company (sponsored by SenseTime) to annotate the training set within a month (US$11K spent). Each image is annotated by two workers and examined by one head worker. All the test images are annotated by the authors.

Summary: Several merits worth highlighting by virtue of the novel and effective procedure of PSG dataset creation: *1) Good grounding annotation* from the pixel-wise panoptic segmentation from COCO dataset [43], *2) Clear category system* with 133 objects (*i.e.*, things plus stuff) and 56 predicates with appropriate granularity and minimal overlaps, and *3) Accurate and comprehensive relation annotations* from a rigorous annotation process that pays special attention to salient relations between object-object, object-background and background-background. These merits address the notorious shortcomings [37] of classic scene graph datasets discussed in Sect. 2.

Evaluation and Metrics. This section introduces the evaluation protocol for the PSG task. Following the settings of the classic SGG task [5,65], our PSG task comprises two sub-tasks: *predicate classification* (when applicable) and *scene graph generation* (main task) to evaluate the PSG models. *Predicate classification (PredCls)* aims to generate a scene graph given the ground-truth object labels and localization. The goal is to study the relation prediction performance without the interference of the segmentation performance. Notice that this metric is only applicable to two-stage PSG models in Sect. 4.1, since one-stage models cannot leverage the given segmentations to predict scene graph. *Scene graph generation (SGDet)* aims to generate scene graphs from scratch, which is the main result for the PSG task.

We also notice that classic SGG tasks contain another sub-task of scene graph classification (SGCls), which provide the ground-truth object groundings to simplify the scene graph generation process. We find SGCls is not applicable for PSG baselines. Unlike SGG tasks where object detectors such as Faster-RCNN [51] can utilize ground-truth object bounding boxes to replace predictions from the Region Proposal Network (RPN), panoptic segmentation models are unable to directly use the ground-truth segmentations for classification, so the SGCls task is inapplicable even for two-stage PSG methods.

The classic metrics of $R@K$ and $mR@K$ are used to evaluate the previous two sub-tasks, which calculates the triplet recall and mean recall for every predicate category, given the top K triplets from the PSG model. Notice that PSG grounds objects with segmentation, a successful recall requires both subject and object to have mask-based IOU larger than 0.5 compared to their ground-truth counterparts, with the correct classification on every position in the S-V-O triplet.

While the triplet recall rates that mentioned above are the main metric for PSG task, since objects are required to be grounded by segmentation masks, panoptic segmentation metrics [33] such as PQ [32] can be used for model diagnosis. However, it is not considered as the core evaluation metric of PSG task.

4   PSG Baselines

To build a comprehensive PSG benchmark, we refer to frameworks employed in the classic SGG task [5,65] and prepare two-stage and one-stage baselines.

4.1   Two-Stage PSG Baselines

Most prior SGG approaches tackle the problem in two stages: first performing object detection using off-the-shelf detectors like Faster-RCNN [51], then pairwise relationship prediction between these predicted objects. As shown in Fig. 3, we follow a similar approach in establishing two-stage baselines for the PSG task: **1)** using pretrained panoptic segmentation models of classic Panoptic FPN [32] to extract initial object features, masks and class predictions, and then **2)** processing them using a relation prediction module from classic scene graph generation methods like IMP [64], MOTIFS [71], VCTree [58], and GPSNet [44]

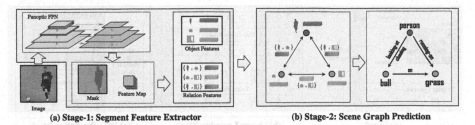

(a) Stage-1: Segment Feature Extractor   (b) Stage-2: Scene Graph Prediction

Fig. 3. Two-stage PSG baselines using Panoptic FPN. a) In stage one, for each thing/stuff object, Panoptic FPN [32] produces a segmentation mask with its tightest bounding box to crop out the object feature. The union of relevant objects can produce relation features. **b)** In the second stage, the extracted object and relation features are fed into by any existing SGG relation model to predict the relation triplets.

to obtain the final scene graph predictions. In this way, classic SGG methods can be adapted to solve the PSG task with minimal modification. Formally, the two-stage PSGG baselines decompose formulation from Eq. 1 to Eq. 3.

$$\Pr\left(\mathbf{G} \mid \mathbf{I}\right) = \Pr\left(\mathbf{M} \mid \mathbf{I}\right) \cdot \Pr\left(\mathbf{O} \mid \mathbf{M}, \mathbf{I}\right) \cdot \Pr\left(\mathbf{R} \mid \mathbf{O}, \mathbf{M}, \mathbf{I}\right). \tag{3}$$

4.2 A One-Stage PSG Baseline - PSGTR

Unlike classic dense prediction models (*e.g.*, Faster-RCNN [51]) with sophisticated design, the transformer-based architectures support flexible input and output specifications. Based on the end-to-end DETR [4] and its extension to the HOI task [79], we naturally design a one-stage PSG method named PSGTR to predict triples and localizations simultaneously, which can be directly modeled as Eq. 2 without decomposition.

Triplet Query Learning Block. As shown in Fig. 4, PSGTR first extracts image features from a CNN backbone and then feeds the features along with queries and position encoding into a transformer encoder-decoder. Here we expect the queries to learn the representation of scene graph triplets, so that for each triplet query, the subject/predicate/object predictions can be extracted by three individual Feed Forward Networks (FFNs), and the segmentation task can be completed by two panoptic heads for subject and object, respectively.

PSG Prediction Block. To train the model, we extend the DETR's Hungarian matcher [36] into a triplet Hungarian matcher. To match the triplet query $\mathcal{T}_i \in \mathbb{Q}^T$ with ground truth triplets $\mathcal{G}$, all contents in the triplet (*i.e.*, all outputs that are predicted from $\mathcal{T}_i$) are used, including the class of subject $\ddot{\mathcal{T}}_i^S$, relation $\ddot{\mathcal{T}}_i^R$, and object $\ddot{\mathcal{T}}_i^O$, and localization of subjects $\tilde{\mathcal{T}}_i^S$ and objects $\tilde{\mathcal{T}}_i^O$. Therefore, the triplet matching (tm) cost $\mathbf{C}_{\text{tm}}$ is designed with the combination of class matching $\mathbf{C}_{\text{cls}}$ and segments matching $\mathbf{C}_{\text{seg}}$:

$$\mathbf{C}_{\text{tm}}\left(\mathcal{T}_i, \mathcal{G}_{\sigma(i)}\right) = \sum_{k \in \{S, O\}} \mathbf{C}_{\text{seg}}\left(\tilde{\mathcal{T}}_i^k, \tilde{\mathcal{G}}_{\sigma(i)}^k\right) + \sum_{k \in \{S, R, O\}} \mathbf{C}_{\text{cls}}\left(\ddot{\mathcal{T}}_i^k, \ddot{\mathcal{G}}_{\sigma(i)}^k\right), \tag{4}$$

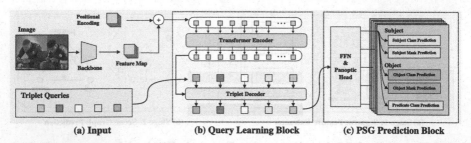

(a) Input   (b) Query Learning Block   (c) PSG Prediction Block

Fig. 4. PSGTR: One-stage PSG baseline. The one-stage model takes in a) features extracted by CNNs with positional encoding, and a set of queries aiming to represent triplets. b) Query learning block processes image features with Transformer encoder-decoder and use queries to represent triplet information. Then, c) the PSG prediction head concretes the triplet predictions by producing subject/object/predicate classes using simple FFNs, and uses panoptic heads for panoptic segmentation.

where σ is the mapping function to correspond each triplet query $\mathcal{T}_i \in \mathbb{Q}^T$ to the closest ground truth triplet. The triplet query set $\mathbb{Q}^T$ collects all the $|\mathbb{Q}^T|$ triplet queries. The optimization objective is thus:

$$\hat{\sigma} = \arg\max_{\sigma} \sum_{i=1}^{|\mathbb{Q}^T|} \mathbf{C}_{\text{tm}}\left(\mathcal{T}_i, \mathcal{G}_{\sigma(i)}\right). \tag{5}$$

Once the matching is done, the total loss $\mathcal{L}_{\text{total}}$ can be calculated by applying cross-entropy loss $\mathcal{L}_{\text{cls}}$ for labels and DICE/F-1 loss [47] for segmentation $\mathcal{L}_{\text{cls}}$:

$$\mathcal{L}_{\text{total}} = \sum_{i=1}^{|\mathbb{Q}^T|} \left(\sum_{k \in \{S,O\}} \mathcal{L}_{\text{seg}}\left(\tilde{\mathcal{T}}_i^k, \tilde{\mathcal{G}}_{\hat{\sigma}(i)}^k\right) + \sum_{k \in \{S,R,O\}} \mathcal{L}_{\text{cls}}\left(\ddot{\mathcal{T}}_i^k, \ddot{\mathcal{G}}_{\hat{\sigma}(i)}^k\right) \right). \tag{6}$$

4.3   Alternative One-Stage PSG Baseline - PSGFormer

Based on the PSGTR baseline that explained in Sect. 4.2, we extend another end-to-end HOI method [31] and further propose the alternative one-stage PSG baseline named PSGFormer, featured by an explicit relation modeling with a prompting-like matching mechanism. The model diagram is illustrated in Fig. 5 and will be elaborated as follows.

Object and Relation Query Learning Block. Compared to the classic object-oriented tasks such as object detection and segmentation, the most significant uniqueness of PSG task as well as SGG task is their extra requirements on the predictions of relations. Notice that the relation modeling in our two-stage baselines depends on features from object-pairs, while PSGTR implicitly models the objects and relations altogether within the triplets, the important relation modeling has not been given a serious treatment. Therefore, in the exploration

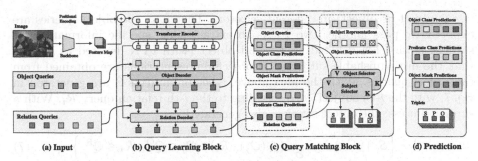

(a) Input   (b) Query Learning Block   (c) Query Matching Block   (d) Prediction

Fig. 5. PSGFormer: The proposed one-stage PSG method. a) Two types of queries, *i.e.*, object queries and relation queries, are fed into transformer block with CNN features and positional encoding. **b)** Query Learning Block processes image features with one encoder and output object or relation queries with the corresponding decoder. **c)** Object queries and relation queries interact with each other in the prompting-like query matching block, so that the triplets are formed and proceed to **d)** PSG prediction block to output results or compute loss as PSGTR behaves.

of PSGFormer, we explicitly model the relation query $\mathcal{R}_i \in \mathbb{Q}^R$, as well as object query $\mathcal{O}_i \in \mathbb{Q}^O$ separately, in hope that object queries to specially pay attentions to objects (*e.g.*, `person` and `phones`), and relation queries to focus on the area where the relationship takes place in the picture (*e.g.*, `person looking-at phone`). Similar to PSGTR in Fig. 4, both object and relation queries with CNN features and position encoding are fed into a transformer encoder, but being decoded with their corresponding decoder, *i.e.*, object or relation decoder, so that the queries can learn the corresponding representations.

Object and Relation Query Matching Block. In PSGFormer, each object query yields an object prediction with FFN and a mask prediction with a panoptic head, and each relation query yields a relation prediction. However, due to the parallel process of object queries and relation queries, the missing interdependence between different query types makes the triplet still not formed. To connect object and relation queries for compositing triplets, we are inspired by the design in HOTR [31] and implement a prompting-like query matching block.

Query matching block models the triplet composition task as a fill-in-the-blank question with prompts, *i.e.*, by prompting a relation, we expect a pair of suitable objects provided by their corresponding object queries can be selected, so that a complete `subject-predicate-object` triplet, can be generated. Therefore, two selectors, *i.e.*, subject selector and object selector, are required.

Given a relation query $\mathcal{R}_i \in \mathbb{Q}^R$ as prompt, both subject selector and object selector should return the most suitable candidate to form a complete triplet. We use the most standard cosine similarity between object queries and the provided relation query and pick the highest similarity to determine the subject and object candidates. It should also be noticed that subject and object selectors should rely on the level of association between objects and relation queries rather than the semantic similarity. Besides, object queries are regarded as different roles (*i.e.*, subject or object) in different selectors. Therefore, the object queries are expected to pass another two FFNs to extract some specific information for subject (with FFN denoted as f_S) and object (with FFN denoted as f_O), so that the distinguishable subject and object representations are obtained from the object queries. With the idea above, a set of subjects $\mathbb{S}$ are generated in Eq. 7, with the i-th subject corresponding to the i-th relation query $\mathcal{R}_i$. With a similar process, the object set $\mathbb{O}$ is also generated.

$$\mathbb{S} = \left\{ \mathcal{S}_i \mid \mathcal{S}_i = \arg\max_{\mathcal{O}} \left(f_S(\mathcal{O}_j) \cdot \mathcal{R}_i \right), \ \mathcal{O}_j \in \mathbb{Q}^O, \ \mathcal{R}_i \in \mathbb{Q}^R \right\}. \qquad (7)$$

Till now, the subject set $\mathbb{S}$ and the object set $\mathbb{O}$ are well-prepared by subject and object selectors, with the i-th subject query $\mathcal{S}_i$ and the i-th object $\mathcal{O}_i$ corresponding to the i-th relation query $\mathcal{R}_i$. Finally, it is straightforward to obtain all the matched triplet $\mathbb{T}$, which is shown in Eq. 8.

$$\mathbb{T} = \{(\mathcal{S}_i, \mathcal{R}_i, \mathcal{O}_i) \mid \mathcal{S}_i \in \mathbb{S}, \ \mathcal{R}_i \in \mathbb{R}, \ \mathcal{O}_i \in \mathbb{O}\}. \qquad (8)$$

Apart from interpreting the query matching as a prompt-like process, it can also be considered as a cross-attention mechanism. For a relation query (Q), the goal is to find the high-attention relations among all subject/object representations, which are considered as keys (K). The subject/object labels predicted by the corresponding representations are regarded as values (V), so that the QKV attention model outputs the labels of selected keys. Figure 5-c is generally depicted following this interpretation.

PSG Prediction Block. Similar to PSGTR, with the predicted triplets prepared, the prediction block can finally train the model using $\mathcal{L}_{\text{total}}$ from Eq. 6. In addition, with object labels and masks predicted by object queries, a standard training loss introduced in panoptic segmentation DETR [4] is used to enhance the object decoder and avoid duplicate object groundings.

5   Experiments

In this section, we first report the results of all PSG methods introduced in the paper. Implementation details are available in the appendix, and all codes are integrated in the OpenPSG codebase, which is developed based on MMDetection [7]. Most of the two-stage SGG implementations refer to MMScene-Graph [62] and Scene-Graph-Benchmark.pytorch [56].

5.1   Main Results

Table 2 reports the scene graph generation performance of all the methods mentioned in Sect. 4.1, Sect. 4.2, and Sect. 4.3 under the PSG dataset. Figure 6 reports the panoptic segmentation result using PQ and visualizes the segmentation results of two examples as well as the predicted scene graph in the form of triplet lists.

Table 2. Comparison between all baselines and PSGFormer. Recall (R) and mean recall (mR) are reported. IMP [64] (CVPR'17), MOTIFS [71] (CVPR'18), VCTree [58] (CVPR'19), and GPSNet [44] (CVPR'20) all originate from the SGG task and are adapted for the PSG task. Different backbones of ResNet-50 [20] and ResNet-101 [20] are used. Notice that predicate classification task is not applicable to one-stage PSG models, so the corresponding results are marked as '−'. Models are trained using 12 epochs by default. † denotes that the model is trained using 60 epochs.

Backbone	Method	Predicate Classification			Scene Graph Generation		
		R/mR@20	R/mR@50	R/mR@100	R/mR@20	R/mR@50	R/mR@100
ResNet-50	IMP	31.9/9.55	36.8/10.9	38.9/11.6	16.5/6.52	18.2/7.05	18.6/7.23
	MOTIFS	44.9/20.2	50.4/22.1	52.4/22.9	20.0/9.10	21.7/9.57	22.0/9.69
	VCTree	**45.3/20.5**	**50.8/22.6**	**52.7/23.3**	**20.6/9.70**	**22.1/10.2**	**22.5/10.2**
	GPSNet	31.5/13.2	39.9/16.4	44.7/18.3	17.8/7.03	19.6/7.49	20.1/7.67
	PSGTR	−	−	−	3.82/1.29	4.16/1.54	4.27/1.57
	PSGFormer	−	−	−	**16.8/14.5**	**19.2/17.4**	**20.2/18.7**
	PSGTR†	−	−	−	**28.4/16.6**	**34.4/20.8**	**36.3/22.1**
	PSGFormer†	−	−	−	18.0/14.8	19.6/17.0	20.1/17.6
ResNet-101	IMP	30.5/8.97	35.9/10.5	38.3/11.3	17.9/7.35	19.5/7.88	20.1/8.02
	MOTIFS	45.1/19.9	50.5/21.5	52.5/22.2	20.9/9.60	22.5/10.1	23.1/10.3
	VCTree	**45.9/21.4**	**51.2/23.1**	**53.1/23.8**	**21.7/9.68**	**23.3/10.2**	**23.7/10.3**
	GPSNet	38.8/17.1	46.6/20.2	50.0/21.3	18.4/6.52	20.0/6.97	20.6/7.17
	PSGTR	−	−	−	3.47/1.18	3.88/1.56	4.00/1.64
	PSGFormer	−	−	−	**18.0/14.2**	**20.1/18.3**	**21.0/19.8**
	PSGTR†	−	−	−	**28.2/15.4**	**32.1/20.3**	**35.3/21.5**
	PSGFormer†	−	−	−	18.6/16.7	20.4/19.3	20.7/19.7

Two-Stage Baselines Rely on First-Stage Performance. For predicate classification task (PredCls) that is only applicable to two-stage models, the provided ground-truth segmentation can significantly improve the triplet prediction performance. For example, even the most classic method IMP can reach over 30% R@20, which already exceeds all the available R@20 under the scene graph generation (SGDet) task (*cf.* 28.4% by PSGTR). This phenomenon indicates that a good panoptic segmentation performance could naturally benefit the PSG task. Further evidence where the performance of IMP on the SGDet task is almost halved (from 32% to 17% on R@20) strengthens the above conjecture.

Some SGG Techniques for VG are not Effective for PSG. Table 2 shows that the results of some two-stage baselines (*i.e.*, IMP, MOTIFS, and VCTree) are generally proportional to their performance on SGG tasks, indicating that the advantages of the two-stage models (*i.e.*, MOTIFS and VCTree) are transferable to PSG task. However, we notice that another two-stage baseline, GPSNet, does not seem to exceed its SGG baselines of MOTIFS and VCTree in the PSG task. The key advantage of GPSNet over MOTIFS and VCTree is that it explicitly models the direction of predicates. While the design can be effective in the VG dataset where many predicates are trivial with obvious direction of predicates (*e.g.*, of in `hair-of-man`, has in `man-has-head`), PSG dataset gets rid of these predicates, so the model may not be effective as expected.

Fig. 6. Visualization of segmentations and the top 20 predicted triplets of 5 PSG methods. The panoptic segmentation metric PQ is also reported. The colors of the subject and object in the triplet corresponds to the mask in the segmentation result. Reasonable triplets are marked by ticks. Triplets that match the ground-truth are marked by green ticks. One-stage models can provide more reasonable and diverse triplet predictions, but they are unable to achieve a good panoptic segmentation result. (Color figure online)

PSGFormer is an Unbiased PSG Model. When the training schedule is limited to 12 epochs, the end-to-end baseline PSGFormer outperforms the best two-stage model VCTree by significant 4.8% on mR@20 and 8.5% on mR@100. Although PSGFormer still cannot exceed two-stage methods on the metrics of R@20/50/100, its huge advantage in mean recall indicates that the model is unbiased in predicting relations. As Fig. 6 shows, PSGFormer can predict unusual but accurate relations such as person-going down-snow in the upper example, and the imperceptible relation person-driving-bus in the lower example. Also, in the upper example, PSGFormer predicts an interesting and exclusive triplet person-wearing-skis. This unique prediction should come from the design of the separate object/relation decoders, so that relation queries can independently capture the meaning of the predicates.

PSGTR Obtains SOTA Results with Long Training Time. In PSGTR, every triplet is expected to be captured by a query, which needs to predict everything in the triplet simultaneously, so the model is required to better focus on the connections between objects. Besides, the cross-attention mechanism in the transformer encoder and triplet decoder enable each triplet query access to the information of the entire image. Therefore, PSGTR is considered as the most straightforward and simplest one-stage PSG baseline with minimal constraints or prior knowledge. As a result, although PSGTR only achieves one-digit recall scores in 12 epochs, it surprisingly achieves SOTA results with a prolonged training time of 60 epochs.

6 Challenges and Outlook

Challenges. While some *prior knowledge* introduced by some two-stage SGG methods might not be effective in the PSG task, we expect that more creative knowledge-aided models can be developed for the PSG task in the era of multimodality, so that more interesting triplets can be extracted with extra priors. However, it should be noted that although priors can be useful to enhance performance, the PSG prediction should heavily rely on *visual clues*. For example, in Fig. 6, `person-walking on-pavement` should be identified if the model can perceive and understand the subtle visual differences between `walking` and `standing`. Also, PSG models are expected to *predict more meaningful and diverse relations*, such as rare relations like `feeding` and `kissing`, rather than only being content with statistically common or positional relations.

Relation between PSG and Panoptic Segmentation. Figure 6 visualizes the panoptic segmentation results of PSG methods, where PSGTR only obtains a miserable PQ result even with good PSG performance. The reason is that triplet queries in PSGTR produce object groundings independently, so that one object might be referred and segmented by several triplets, and the deduplication or the re-identification (Re-ID) process is non-trivial. Although the performance of Re-ID does not affect PSG metrics, it might still be critical to form an accurate and logical scene understanding for real-world applications.

Outlook. Apart from attracting more research on the learning of relations (either closed-set or open-set) and pushing the development of scene understanding, we also expect the PSG models to empower more exciting downstream tasks such as visual reasoning and segmentation-based scene graph-to-image generation.

Acknowledgements. This work is supported by NTU NAP, MOE AcRF Tier 2 (T2EP20221-0033), and under the RIE2020 Industry Alignment Fund – Industry Collaboration Projects (IAF-ICP) Funding Initiative, as well as cash and in-kind contribution from the industry partner(s).

References

1. Aditya, S., Yang, Y., Baral, C., Aloimonos, Y., Fermüller, C.: Image understanding using vision and reasoning through scene description graph. Comput. Vis. Image Understand. **173**, 33–45 (2018)
2. Amiri, S., Chandan, K., Zhang, S.: Reasoning with scene graphs for robot planning under partial observability. IEEE Robot. Autom. Lett. **7**, 5560–5567 (2022)
3. Bojanowski, P., Grave, E., Joulin, A., Mikolov, T.: Enriching word vectors with subword information. arXiv preprint arXiv:1607.04606 (2016)
4. Carion, N., Massa, F., Synnaeve, G., Usunier, N., Kirillov, A., Zagoruyko, S.: End-to-end object detection with transformers. arXiv preprint arXiv:2005.12872 (2020)
5. Chang, X., Ren, P., Xu, P., Li, Z., Chen, X., Hauptmann, A.: Scene graphs: a survey of generations and applications. arXiv preprint arXiv:2104.01111 (2021)
6. Chao, Y.W., Liu, Y., Liu, X., Zeng, H., Deng, J.: Learning to detect human-object interactions. In: Proceedings of the IEEE Winter Conference on Applications of Computer Vision (WACV) (2018)
7. Chen, K., et al.: Mmdetection: open mmlab detection toolbox and benchmark. arXiv preprint arXiv:1906.07155 (2019)
8. Chen, S., Jin, Q., Wang, P., Wu, Q.: Say as you wish: fine-grained control of image caption generation with abstract scene graphs. In: Proceedings of the IEEE/CVF Conference on Computer Vision and Pattern Recognition (CVPR) (2020)
9. Chen, T., Yu, W., Chen, R., Lin, L.: Knowledge-embedded routing network for scene graph generation. In: Proceedings of the IEEE/CVF Conference on Computer Vision and Pattern Recognition (CVPR) (2019)
10. Cheng, B., Schwing, A.G., Kirillov, A.: Per-pixel classification is not all you need for semantic segmentation. vol. abs/2107.06278 (2021)
11. Dai, B., Zhang, Y., Lin, D.: Detecting visual relationships with deep relational networks. In: Proceedings of the IEEE/CVF Conference on Computer Vision and Pattern Recognition (CVPR) (2017)
12. Desai, A., Wu, T.Y., Tripathi, S., Vasconcelos, N.: Learning of visual relations: the devil is in the tails. In: Proceedings of the IEEE/CVF International Conference on Computer Vision (ICCV) (2021)
13. Dhamo, H., et al.: Semantic image manipulation using scene graphs. In: Proceedings of the IEEE/CVF Conference on Computer Vision and Pattern Recognition (CVPR) (2020)
14. Gadre, S.Y., Ehsani, K., Song, S., Mottaghi, R.: Continuous scene representations for embodied AI. In: Proceedings of the IEEE/CVF Conference on Computer Vision and Pattern Recognition (CVPR) (2022)
15. Gao, C., Xu, J., Zou, Y., Huang, J.-B.: DRG: dual relation graph for human-object interaction detection. In: Vedaldi, A., Bischof, H., Brox, T., Frahm, J.-M. (eds.) ECCV 2020. LNCS, vol. 12357, pp. 696–712. Springer, Cham (2020). https://doi.org/10.1007/978-3-030-58610-2_41
16. Gao, L., Wang, B., Wang, W.: Image captioning with scene-graph based semantic concepts. In: Proceedings of the International Conference on Machine Learning and Computing (2018)
17. Gkioxari, G., Girshick, R., Dollár, P., He, K.: Detecting and recognizing human-object interactions. In: Proceedings of the IEEE/CVF Conference on Computer Vision and Pattern Recognition (CVPR) (2018)
18. Gu, J., Zhao, H., Lin, Z., Li, S., Cai, J., Ling, M.: Scene graph generation with external knowledge and image reconstruction. In: Proceedings of the IEEE/CVF Conference on Computer Vision and Pattern Recognition (CVPR) (2019)

19. Gupta, S., Malik, J.: Visual semantic role labeling. arXiv preprint arXiv:1505.04474 (2015)
20. He, K., Zhang, X., Ren, S., Sun, J.: Deep residual learning for image recognition. In: Proceedings of the IEEE/CVF Conference on Computer Vision and Pattern Recognition (CVPR) (2016)
21. Hildebrandt, M., Li, H., Koner, R., Tresp, V., Günnemann, S.: Scene graph reasoning for visual question answering. In: ICML Workshop Graph Representation Learning and Beyond (GRL+) (2020)
22. Hou, Z., Peng, X., Qiao, Yu., Tao, D.: Visual compositional learning for human-object interaction detection. In: Vedaldi, A., Bischof, H., Brox, T., Frahm, J.-M. (eds.) ECCV 2020. LNCS, vol. 12360, pp. 584–600. Springer, Cham (2020). https://doi.org/10.1007/978-3-030-58555-6_35
23. Hou, Z., Yu, B., Qiao, Y., Peng, X., Tao, D.: Affordance transfer learning for human-object interaction detection. In: Proceedings of the IEEE/CVF Conference on Computer Vision and Pattern Recognition (CVPR) (2021)
24. Hudson, D.A., Manning, C.D.: Gqa: A new dataset for real-world visual reasoning and compositional question answering. In: Proceedings of the IEEE/CVF Conference on Computer Vision and Pattern Recognition (CVPR) (2019)
25. Hung, Z.S., Mallya, A., Lazebnik, S.: Contextual translation embedding for visual relationship detection and scene graph generation. IEEE Trans. Pattern Anal. Mach. Intell. (TPAMI) 43, 3820–3832 (2020)
26. Johnson, J., Gupta, A., Fei-Fei, L.: Image generation from scene graphs. In: Proceedings of the IEEE/CVF Conference on Computer Vision and Pattern Recognition (CVPR) (2018)
27. Johnson, J., et al.: Image retrieval using scene graphs. In: Proceedings of the IEEE/CVF Conference on Computer Vision and Pattern Recognition (CVPR) (2015)
28. Kato, K., Li, Y., Gupta, A.: Compositional learning for human object interaction. In: Ferrari, V., Hebert, M., Sminchisescu, C., Weiss, Y. (eds.) Computer Vision – ECCV 2018. LNCS, vol. 11218, pp. 247–264. Springer, Cham (2018). https://doi.org/10.1007/978-3-030-01264-9_15
29. Khandelwal, S., Suhail, M., Sigal, L.: Segmentation-grounded scene graph generation. In: Proceedings of the IEEE/CVF International Conference on Computer Vision (ICCV) (2021)
30. Kim, B., Choi, T., Kang, J., Kim, H.J.: UnionDet: union-level detector towards real-time human-object interaction detection. In: Vedaldi, A., Bischof, H., Brox, T., Frahm, J.-M. (eds.) ECCV 2020. LNCS, vol. 12360, pp. 498–514. Springer, Cham (2020). https://doi.org/10.1007/978-3-030-58555-6_30
31. Kim, B., Lee, J., Kang, J., Kim, E.S., Kim, H.J.: Hotr: end-to-end human-object interaction detection with transformers. In: Proceedings of the IEEE/CVF Conference on Computer Vision and Pattern Recognition (CVPR) (2021)
32. Kirillov, A., Girshick, R., He, K., Dollár, P.: Panoptic feature pyramid networks. In: Proceedings of the IEEE/CVF Conference on Computer Vision and Pattern Recognition (CVPR) (2019)
33. Kirillov, A., He, K., Girshick, R., Rother, C., Dollár, P.: Panoptic segmentation. In: Proceedings of the IEEE/CVF Conference on Computer Vision and Pattern Recognition (CVPR) (2019)
34. Kolesnikov, A., Kuznetsova, A., Lampert, C., Ferrari, V.: Detecting visual relationships using box attention. In: Proceedings of the IEEE/CVF International Conference on Computer Vision Workshops (CVPR-W) (2019)

35. Krishna, R., et al.: Visual genome: connecting language and vision using crowd-sourced dense image annotations. Int. J. Comput. Vis. (IJCV) **123**, 32–73 (2017)
36. Kuhn, H.W.: The hungarian method for the assignment problem. Naval Res. Logist. Quart. **2**, 83–97 (1955)
37. Li, L., Chen, L., Huang, Y., Zhang, Z., Zhang, S., Xiao, J.: The devil is in the labels: noisy label correction for robust scene graph generation. In: Proceedings of the IEEE/CVF Conference on Computer Vision and Pattern Recognition (CVPR) (2022)
38. Li, Y., Ouyang, W., Zhou, B., Shi, J., Zhang, C., Wang, X.: Factorizable net: an efficient subgraph-based framework for scene graph generation. In: Ferrari, V., Hebert, M., Sminchisescu, C., Weiss, Y. (eds.) ECCV 2018. LNCS, vol. 11205, pp. 346–363. Springer, Cham (2018). https://doi.org/10.1007/978-3-030-01246-5_21
39. Li, Y.L., et al.: Detailed 2D–3D joint representation for human-object interaction. In: Proceedings of the IEEE/CVF Conference on Computer Vision and Pattern Recognition (CVPR) (2020)
40. Li, Y.L., et al.: Transferable interactiveness knowledge for human-object interaction detection. In: Proceedings of the IEEE/CVF Conference on Computer Vision and Pattern Recognition (CVPR) (2019)
41. Li, Z., et al.: Panoptic segformer. arXiv preprint arXiv:2109.03814 (2021)
42. Liang, Y., Bai, Y., Zhang, W., Qian, X., Zhu, L., Mei, T.: VRR-VG: refocusing visually-relevant relationships. In: Proceedings of the IEEE/CVF International Conference on Computer Vision (ICCV) (2019)
43. Lin, T.-Y., et al.: Microsoft COCO: common objects in context. In: Fleet, D., Pajdla, T., Schiele, B., Tuytelaars, T. (eds.) ECCV 2014. LNCS, vol. 8693, pp. 740–755. Springer, Cham (2014). https://doi.org/10.1007/978-3-319-10602-1_48
44. Lin, X., Ding, C., Zeng, J., Tao, D.: GPS-Net: graph property sensing network for scene graph generation. In: Proceedings of the IEEE/CVF Conference on Computer Vision and Pattern Recognition (CVPR) (2020)
45. Liu, Y., Chen, Q., Zisserman, A.: Amplifying key cues for human-object-interaction detection. In: Vedaldi, A., Bischof, H., Brox, T., Frahm, J.-M. (eds.) ECCV 2020. LNCS, vol. 12359, pp. 248–265. Springer, Cham (2020). https://doi.org/10.1007/978-3-030-58568-6_15
46. Lu, C., Krishna, R., Bernstein, M., Fei-Fei, L.: Visual relationship detection with language priors. In: Leibe, B., Matas, J., Sebe, N., Welling, M. (eds.) ECCV 2016. LNCS, vol. 9905, pp. 852–869. Springer, Cham (2016). https://doi.org/10.1007/978-3-319-46448-0_51
47. Milletari, F., Navab, N., Ahmadi, S.A.: V-net: Fully convolutional neural networks for volumetric medical image segmentation. In: International Conference on 3D Vision (3DV) (2016)
48. Peyre, J., Sivic, J., Laptev, I., Schmid, C.: Weakly-supervised learning of visual relations. In: Proceedings of the IEEE/CVF International Conference on Computer Vision (ICCV) (2017)
49. Qi, M., Li, W., Yang, Z., Wang, Y., Luo, J.: Attentive relational networks for mapping images to scene graphs. In: Proceedings of the IEEE/CVF Conference on Computer Vision and Pattern Recognition (CVPR) (2019)
50. Qi, M., Wang, Y., Li, A.: Online cross-modal scene retrieval by binary representation and semantic graph. In: Proceedings of the ACM International Conference on Multimedia (ACM MM) (2017)
51. Ren, S., He, K., Girshick, R., Sun, J.: Faster R-CNN: towards real-time object detection with region proposal networks. In: Advances in Neural Information Processing Systems (2015)

52. Schuster, S., Krishna, R., Chang, A., Fei-Fei, L., Manning, C.D.: Generating semantically precise scene graphs from textual descriptions for improved image retrieval. In: Proceedings of the Fourth Workshop on Vision and language (2015)
53. Shi, J., Zhang, H., Li, J.: Explainable and explicit visual reasoning over scene graphs. In: Proceedings of the IEEE/CVF Conference on Computer Vision and Pattern Recognition (CVPR) (2019)
54. Suhail, M., et al.: Energy-based learning for scene graph generation. In: Proceedings of the IEEE/CVF Conference on Computer Vision and Pattern Recognition (CVPR) (2021)
55. Tamura, M., Ohashi, H., Yoshinaga, T.: Qpic: query-based pairwise human-object interaction detection with image-wide contextual information. In: Proceedings of the IEEE/CVF Conference on Computer Vision and Pattern Recognition (CVPR) (2021)
56. Tang, K.: A scene graph generation codebase in pytorch (2020). https://github.com/KaihuaTang/Scene-Graph-Benchmark.pytorch
57. Tang, K., Niu, Y., Huang, J., Shi, J., Zhang, H.: Unbiased scene graph generation from biased training. In: Proceedings of the IEEE/CVF Conference on Computer Vision and Pattern Recognition (CVPR) (2020)
58. Tang, K., Zhang, H., Wu, B., Luo, W., Liu, W.: Learning to compose dynamic tree structures for visual contexts. In: Proceedings of the IEEE/CVF Conference on Computer Vision and Pattern Recognition (CVPR) (2019)
59. Wang, S., Duan, Y., Ding, H., Tan, Y.P., Yap, K.H., Yuan, J.: Learning transferable human-object interaction detector with natural language supervision. In: Proceedings of the IEEE/CVF Conference on Computer Vision and Pattern Recognition (CVPR) (2022)
60. Wang, T., et al.: Deep contextual attention for human-object interaction detection. In: Proceedings of the IEEE/CVF International Conference on Computer Vision (ICCV) (2019)
61. Wang, T., Yang, T., Danelljan, M., Khan, F.S., Zhang, X., Sun, J.: Learning human-object interaction detection using interaction points. In: Proceedings of the IEEE/CVF Conference on Computer Vision and Pattern Recognition (CVPR) (2020)
62. Wang, W.: Mmscenegraph (2021). https://github.com/Kenneth-Wong/MMScene Graph
63. Xiong, Y., et al.: Upsnet: A unified panoptic segmentation network. In: Proceedings of the IEEE/CVF Conference on Computer Vision and Pattern Recognition (CVPR) (2019)
64. Xu, D., Zhu, Y., Choy, C.B., Fei-Fei, L.: Scene graph generation by iterative message passing. In: Proceedings of the IEEE/CVF Conference on Computer Vision and Pattern Recognition (CVPR) (2017)
65. Xu, P., Chang, X., Guo, L., Huang, P.Y., Chen, X., Hauptmann, A.G.: A survey of scene graph: Generation and application. IEEE Trans. Neural Networks Learn. Syst. (TNNLS) (2020)
66. Yang, C.A., Tan, C.Y., Fan, W.C., Yang, C.F., Wu, M.L., Wang, Y.C.F.: Scene graph expansion for semantics-guided image outpainting. In: Proceedings of the IEEE/CVF Conference on Computer Vision and Pattern Recognition (CVPR) (2022)
67. Yang, J., Lu, J., Lee, S., Batra, D., Parikh, D.: Graph R-CNN for scene graph generation. In: Ferrari, V., Hebert, M., Sminchisescu, C., Weiss, Y. (eds.) ECCV 2018. LNCS, vol. 11205, pp. 690–706. Springer, Cham (2018). https://doi.org/10.1007/978-3-030-01246-5_41

68. Ye, K., Kovashka, A.: Linguistic structures as weak supervision for visual scene graph generation. In: Proceedings of the IEEE/CVF Conference on Computer Vision and Pattern Recognition (CVPR) (2021)
69. Zareian, A., Karaman, S., Chang, S.-F.: Bridging knowledge graphs to generate scene graphs. In: Vedaldi, A., Bischof, H., Brox, T., Frahm, J.-M. (eds.) ECCV 2020. LNCS, vol. 12368, pp. 606–623. Springer, Cham (2020). https://doi.org/10.1007/978-3-030-58592-1_36
70. Zareian, A., Wang, Z., You, H., Chang, S.-F.: Learning visual commonsense for robust scene graph generation. In: Vedaldi, A., Bischof, H., Brox, T., Frahm, J.-M. (eds.) ECCV 2020. LNCS, vol. 12368, pp. 642–657. Springer, Cham (2020). https://doi.org/10.1007/978-3-030-58592-1_38
71. Zellers, R., Yatskar, M., Thomson, S., Choi, Y.: Neural motifs: Scene graph parsing with global context. In: Proceedings of the IEEE/CVF Conference on Computer Vision and Pattern Recognition (CVPR) (2018)
72. Zhang, A., et al.: Mining the benefits of two-stage and one-stage hoi detection. In: Proceedings of Advances in Neural Information Processing Systems (NeurIPS) (2021)
73. Zhang, F.Z., Campbell, D., Gould, S.: Efficient two-stage detection of human-object interactions with a novel unary-pairwise transformer. In: Proceedings of the IEEE/CVF Conference on Computer Vision and Pattern Recognition (CVPR) (2022)
74. Zhang, H., Kyaw, Z., Chang, S.F., Chua, T.S.: Visual translation embedding network for visual relation detection. In: Proceedings of the IEEE/CVF Conference on Computer Vision and Pattern Recognition (CVPR) (2017)
75. Zhang, J., Elhoseiny, M., Cohen, S., Chang, W., Elgammal, A.: Relationship proposal networks. In: Proceedings of the IEEE/CVF Conference on Computer Vision and Pattern Recognition (CVPR) (2017)
76. Zhang, W., Pang, J., Chen, K., Loy, C.C.: K-Net: towards unified image segmentation. In: Proceedings of Advances in Neural Information Processing Systems (NeurIPS) (2021)
77. Zhong, Y., Shi, J., Yang, J., Xu, C., Li, Y.: Learning to generate scene graph from natural language supervision. In: Proceedings of the IEEE/CVF International Conference on Computer Vision (ICCV) (2021)
78. Zhou, T., Wang, W., Qi, S., Ling, H., Shen, J.: Cascaded human-object interaction recognition. In: Proceedings of the IEEE/CVF Conference on Computer Vision and Pattern Recognition (CVPR) (2020)
79. Zou, C., et al.: End-to-end human object interaction detection with hoi transformer. In: Proceedings of the IEEE/CVF Conference on Computer Vision and Pattern Recognition (CVPR) (2021)

Object-Compositional Neural Implicit Surfaces

Qianyi Wu[1](✉)(iD), Xian Liu[2](iD), Yuedong Chen[1](iD), Kejie Li[3](iD), Chuanxia Zheng[1](iD), Jianfei Cai[1](iD), and Jianmin Zheng[4](iD)

[1] Monash University, Melbourne, Australia
{qianyi.wu,yuedong.chen,jianfei.cai}@monash.edu, chuanxia001@e.ntu.edu.sg
[2] The Chinese University of Hong Kong, Hong Kong, China
alvinliu@ie.cuhk.edu.hk
[3] University of Oxford, Oxford, England
kejie.li@eng.ox.ac.uk
[4] Nanyang Technological University, Singapore, Singapore
asjmzheng@ntu.edu.sg

Abstract. The neural implicit representation has shown its effectiveness in novel view synthesis and high-quality 3D reconstruction from multi-view images. However, most approaches focus on holistic scene representation yet ignore individual objects inside it, thus limiting potential downstream applications. In order to learn object-compositional representation, a few works incorporate the 2D semantic map as a cue in training to grasp the difference between objects. But they neglect the strong connections between object geometry and instance semantic information, which leads to inaccurate modeling of individual instance. This paper proposes a novel framework, *ObjectSDF*, to build an object-compositional neural implicit representation with high fidelity in 3D reconstruction and object representation. Observing the ambiguity of conventional volume rendering pipelines, we model the scene by combining the Signed Distance Functions (SDF) of individual object to exert explicit surface constraint. The key in distinguishing different instances is to revisit the strong association between an individual object's SDF and semantic label. Particularly, we convert the semantic information to a function of object SDF and develop a unified and compact representation for scene and objects. Experimental results show the superiority of *ObjectSDF* framework in representing both the holistic object-compositional scene and the individual instances. Code can be found at https://qianyiwu. github.io/objectsdf/.

Keywords: Neural implicit representation · Object compositionality · Volume rendering · Signed distance function

Supplementary Information The online version contains supplementary material available at https://doi.org/10.1007/978-3-031-19812-0_12.

1   Introduction

This paper studies the problem of efficiently learning an object-compositional 3D scene representation from posed images and semantic masks, which defines the geometry and appearance of the whole scene and individual objects as well. Such a representation characterizes the compositional nature of scenes and provides additional inherent information, thus benefiting 3D scene understanding [8,11, 20] and context-sensitive application tasks such as robotic manipulation [16,30], object editing, and AR/VR [34,37]. Learning this representation yet imposes new challenges beyond those arising in the conventional 3D scene reconstruction.

The emerging neural implicit representation rendering approaches provide promising results in novel view synthesis [18] and 3D reconstruction [22,33,35]. A typical neural implicit representation encodes scene properties into a deep network, which is trained by minimizing the discrepancies between the rendered and real RGB images from different viewpoints. For example, NeRF [18] represents the volumetric radiance field of a scene with a neural network trained from images. The volume rendering method is used to compute pixel color, which samples points along each ray and performs $\alpha-$composition over the radiance of the sampled points. Despite not having direct supervision on the geometry, it is shown that neural implicit representations often implicitly learn the 3D geometry to render photorealistic images during training [18]. However, the scene-based neural rendering in these works is mostly *agnostic to individual object identities*.

To enable the model's object-level awareness, several works are developed to encode objects' semantics into the neural implicit representation. Zhi *et al.* propose an in-place scene labeling scheme [41], which trains the network to render not only RGB images but also 2D semantic maps. Decomposing a scene into objects can then be achieved by painting the scene-level geometric reconstruction using the predicted semantic labels. This workflow is not object-based modeling since the process of learning geometry is unaware of semantics. Therefore, the geometry and semantics are not strongly associated, which results in inaccurate object representation when the prediction of either geometry or semantics is bad. Yang *et al.* present an object-compositional NeRF [34], which is a unified rendering model for the scene but respecting individual object placement in the scene. The network consists of two branches: The scene branch encodes the scene geometry and appearance, and the object branch encodes each standalone object by conditioning the output only for a specific object with everything else removed. However, as proved in recent works [33,39], object supervision suffers from 3D space ambiguity in a clustered scene. It thus requires aids from extra components such as scene guidance and 3D guard masks, which are used to distill the scene information and protect the occluded object regions.

Inspired by these works, we suggest modeling the object-level geometry directly to learn the geometry and semantics simultaneously so that the representation captures "what" and "where" things are in the scene. The inherent challenge is how to get the supervision for the object-level geometry from RGB images and 2D instance semantic. Unlike the semantic label for a 3D position that is well constrained by multiple 2D semantic maps using multi-view consistency, finding a direct connection between object-level geometry and the 2D semantic labels is non-trivial. In this paper, we propose a novel method called *ObjectSDF* for object-compositional scene representations, aiming at more accurate geometry learning in highly composite scenes and more effective extraction of individual objects to facilitate 3D scene manipulation. First, ObjectSDF represents the scene at the level of objects using a multi-layer perceptron (MLP) that outputs the Signed Distance Function (SDF) of each object at any 3D position. Note that NeRF learns a volume density field, which has difficulty in extracting a high-quality surface [33,35,38–40]. In contrast, the SDF can more accurately define surfaces and the composition of all object SDFs via the minimum operation that gives the SDF of the scene. Moreover, a density distribution can be induced by the scene SDF, which allows us to apply the volume rendering to learn an object-compositional neural implicit representation with robust network training. Second, ObjectSDF builds an explicit connection between the desired semantic field and the level set prediction, which braces the insight that the geometry of each object is strongly associated with semantic guidance. Specifically, we define the semantic distribution in 3D space as a function of each object's SDF, which allows effective semantic guidance in learning the geometry of objects. As a result, ObjectSDF provides a unified, compact, and simple framework that can supervise the training by the input RGB and instance segmentation guidance naturally, and learn the neural implicit representation of the scene as a composition of object SDFs effectively. This is further demonstrated in our experiments.

In summary, the paper has the following contributions: **1)** We propose a novel neural implicit surface representation using the signed distance functions *in an object-compositional manner*. **2)** To grasp the strong associations between object geometry and instance segmentation, we propose a simple yet effective design to incorporate the segmentation guidance organically by updating each object's SDF. **3)** We conduct experiments that demonstrate the effectiveness of the proposed method in representing individual objects and compositional scene.

2   Related Work

Neural Implicit Representation. Occupancy Networks [17] and DeepSDF [24] are among those pioneers who introduced the idea of encoding objects or scenes implicitly using a neural network. Such a representation can be considered as a mapping function from a 3D position to the occupancy density or SDF of the input points, which is continuous and can achieve high spatial resolution. While these works require 3D ground-truth models, Scene Representation Networks (SRN) [31] and Neural Radiance Field (NeRF) [18] demonstrate that both geometry and appearance can be jointly learned only from multiple RGB images using multi-view consistency. Such an implicit representation idea is further used to predict the semantic segmentation label [13,41], deformation field [25,27], high-fidelity specular reflections [32].

This learning-by-rendering paradigm of NeRF has attracted broad interest. They also lay a foundation for many follow-up works including ours. Instead of rendering a neural radiance field, several works [5,14,22,33,35,36] demonstrate that rendering neural implicit surfaces, where gradients are concentrated around surface regions, is able to produce a high-quality 3D reconstruction. Particularly, a recent work, VolSDF [35], combines neural implicit surface with volume rendering and produces high fidelity reconstructed surfaces. Due to its superior modeling performance, our network is built upon VolSDF. The key difference is that VolSDF only has one SDF to model the entire scene while our work models the scene SDF as a composition of multiple object SDFs.

Object-Compositional Implicit Representation. Decomposing a holistic NeRF into several parts or object-centric representations could benefit efficient rendering of radiance fields and other applications like content generation [2,28, 29]. Several attempts are made to model the scene via a composition of object representations, which can be roughly categorized as category-specific [7,19,21, 23] and scene-specific [10,34,41] methods.

The category-specific methods learn the object representation of a limited number of object categories using a large amount of training data in those categories. They have difficulty in generalizing to objects in other unseen categories. For example, Guo *et al.* [7] propose a bottom-up method to learn one scattering field per object, which enables rendering scenes with moving objects and lights. Ost *et al.* [23] use a neural scene graph to represent dynamic scenes and particularly decompose objects in a street view dataset. Niemeyer and Geiger [21] propose GIRAFFE that conditions latent codes to get object-centric NeRFs and thus represents scenes as compositional generative neural feature fields.

The scene-specific methods directly learn a unified neural implicit representation for the whole scene, which also respects the object placement as in the scene [34,41]. Particularly, SemanticNeRF [41] augments NeRF to estimate the semantic label for any given 3D position. A semantic head is added into the network, which is trained by comparing the rendered and real semantic maps. Although SemanticNeRF is able to predict semantic labels, it does not explicitly model each semantic entity's geometry. The work closest to ours is ObjectNeRF [34], which uses a two-pathway architecture to capture the scene and object neural radiance fields. However, the design of ObjectNeRF requires a series of additional voxel feature embedding, object activation encoding, and separate modeling of the scene and object neural radiance fields to deal with occlusion issues and improve the rendering quality. In contrast, our approach is a simple and intuitive framework that uses SDF-based neural implicit surface representation and models scene and object geometry in one unified branch.

3   Method

Given a set of N posed images $\mathcal{A} = \{x_1, x_2, \cdots, x_N\}$ and the corresponding instance semantic segmentation masks $\mathcal{S} = \{s_1, s_2, \cdots, s_N\}$, our goal is to learn an *object-compositional implicit 3D representation* that captures the 3D shapes and appearances of not only the whole scene Ω but also individual *objects* $\mathcal{O}$ within the scene. Different from the conventional 3D scene modeling which typically models the scene as a whole without distinguishing individual objects within it, we consider the 3D scene as a composition of individual objects and the background. A unified simple yet effective framework is proposed for 3D scene and object modeling, which offers a better 3D modeling and understanding via inherent scene decomposition and recomposition.

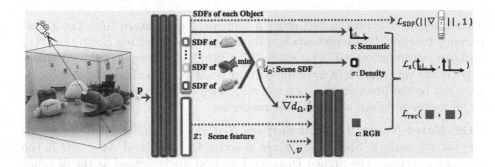

Fig. 1. Overview of our proposed *ObjectSDF* framework, consisting of two parts: an object-SDF part (left, yellow region) and a scene-SDF part (right, green region). The former predicts the SDF of each object, while the latter composites all object SDFs to predict the scene-level geometry and appearance. (Color figure online)

Figure 1 shows the proposed *ObjectSDF* framework of learning *object compositional neural implicit surfaces*. It consists of an object-SDF part that is responsible for modeling all instances including background (Fig. 1, yellow part) and a *scene*-SDF part that recomposes the decomposed objects in the scene (Fig. 1, green part). Note that here we use Signed Distance Function (SDF) based neural implicit surface representation to model the geometry of the scene and objects, instead of using the popular Neural Radiance Fields (NeRF). This is mainly because NeRF aims at high-quality view synthesis, not for accurate surface reconstruction, while the SDF-based neural surface representation is better for geometry modeling and SDF is also easier for the 3D composition of objects.

In the following, we first give the background of volume rendering and its combination with SDF-based neural implicit surface representation in Sect. 3.1. Then, we describe how to represent a scene as a composition of multiple objects within it under a unified neural implicit surface representation in Sect. 3.2, and emphasize our novel idea of leveraging semantic labels to supervise the modeling of individual object SDFs in Sect. 3.3, followed by a summary of the overall training loss in Sect. 3.4.

3.1 Background

Volume Rendering essentially takes the information from a radiance field. Considering a ray $\mathbf{r}(v) = \mathbf{o} + v\mathbf{d}$ emanated from a camera position $\mathbf{o}$ in the direction of $\mathbf{d}$, the color of the ray can be computed as an integral of the transparency $T(v)$, the density $\sigma(v)$ and the radiance $\mathbf{c}(v)$ over samples taken along near and far bounds v_n and v_f,

$$\hat{C}(\mathbf{r}) = \int_{v_n}^{v_f} T(v)\sigma(\mathbf{r}(v))\mathbf{c}(\mathbf{r}(v))dv. \tag{1}$$

This integral is approximated using a numerical quadrature [15]. The transparency function $T(v)$ represents how much light is transmitted along a ray $\mathbf{r}(v)$ and can be computed as $T(v) = \exp(-\int_{v_n}^{v} \sigma(\mathbf{r}(u))du)$, where the volume density $\sigma(\mathbf{p})$ is the rate that light is occluded at a point $\mathbf{p}$. Sometimes the radiance $\mathbf{c}$ may not be the function only of a ray $r(v)$, such as in [18,36]. We refer readers to [9] for more details about volume rendering.

SDF-Based Neural Implicit Surface. SDF directly characterizes the geometry at the surface. Specifically, given a scene $\Omega \subset \mathbb{R}^3$, and $\mathcal{M} = \partial\Omega$ is the boundary surface. The Signed Distance Function d_Ω is defined as the distance from point $\mathbf{p}$ to the boundary $\mathcal{M}$:

$$d_\Omega(\mathbf{p}) = (-1)^{\mathbb{1}_\Omega(\mathbf{p})} \min_{\mathbf{y}\in\mathcal{M}} ||\mathbf{p} - \mathbf{y}||_2, \tag{2}$$

where $\mathbb{1}_\Omega(\mathbf{p})$ is the indicator denoting whether $\mathbf{p}$ belongs to the scene Ω or not. If the point is outside the scene, $\mathbb{1}_\Omega(\mathbf{p})$ returns 0; otherwise returns 1. Typically, the standard l_2-norm is used to compute the distance.

The latest neural implicit surface works [33,35] combine SDF with neural implicit function and volume rendering for better geometry modeling, by replacing the NeRF volume density output $\sigma(\mathbf{p})$ with the SDF value $d_\Omega(\mathbf{p})$, which can be directly transferred into the density. Following [35], here we model the density $\sigma(\mathbf{p})$ using a specific tractable transformation:

$$\sigma(\mathbf{p}) = \alpha\Psi(d_\Omega(\mathbf{p})) = \begin{cases} \dfrac{1}{2\beta}\exp\left(\dfrac{d_\Omega(\mathbf{p})}{\beta}\right) & \text{if } d_\Omega(\mathbf{p}) \leq 0 \\ \dfrac{1}{\beta} - \dfrac{1}{2\beta}\exp\left(\dfrac{-d_\Omega(\mathbf{p})}{\beta}\right) & \text{if } d_\Omega(\mathbf{p}) > 0 \end{cases} \tag{3}$$

where β is a learnable parameter in our implementation.

3.2   The Scene as Object Composition

Unlike the existing SDF-based neural implicit surface modeling works [33,35], which either focus on a single object or treat the entire scene as one object, we consider the scene as a composition of multiple objects and aim to model their geometries and appearances jointly. Specifically, given a static scene Ω, it can be naturally represented by the spatial composition of k different objects $\{\mathcal{O}_i \subset \mathbb{R}^3 | i = 1, \ldots, k\}$, *i.e.*, $\Omega = \bigcup_{i=1}^{k} \mathcal{O}_i$ (including background, as an individual object). Using the SDF representation, we denote the scene geometry by *scene*-SDF $d_\Omega(\mathbf{p})$ and the object geometry as object-SDF $d_{\mathcal{O}_i}(\mathbf{p})$, and their relationship can be derived as: for any point $\mathbf{p} \in \mathbb{R}^3$, $d_\Omega(\mathbf{p}) = \min_{i=1...k} d_{\mathcal{O}_i}(\mathbf{p})$. This is fundamentally different from [33,35] that directly predict the SDF of the holistic scene Ω, while our neural implicit function outputs k distinct SDFs corresponding to different objects (see Fig. 1). The *scene*-SDF is just a minimum of the k object-SDFs, which can be implemented as a particular type of pooling.

Considering that we do not have any explicit supervision for the SDF values in any 3D position, we adopt the implicit geometric regulation loss [6] to regularize each object SDF $d_{\mathcal{O}_i}$ as:

$$\mathcal{L}_{SDF} = \sum_{i=1}^{k} \mathbb{E}_{d_{\mathcal{O}_i}}(\|\nabla d_{\mathcal{O}_i}(\mathbf{p})\| - 1)^2. \tag{4}$$

This will also constrain the scene SDF d_Ω. Once we obtain the scene SDF d_Ω, we use Eq. (3) to obtain the density in the holistic scene.

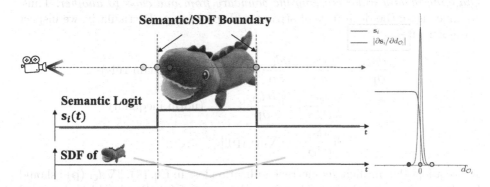

Fig. 2. Semantic as a function of object-SDF. Left: the desired 3D semantic field that should satisfy the requirement, *i.e.*, when the ray is crossing an object (the toy), the corresponding 3D semantic label should change rapidly. Thus, we propose to use the function (6) to approximate the 3D semantic field given object-SDF. Right: The plot of function (6) versus SDF.

3.3 Leveraging Semantics for Learning Object-SDFs

Although our idea of treating scene-SDF as a composition of multiple object-SDFs is simple and intuitive, it is extremely challenging to learn meaningful and accurate object-SDFs since there is no explicit SDF supervision. The only object information we have is the given 2D semantic masks $\mathcal{S} = \{s_1, s_2, \cdots, s_N\}$. So, the critical issue we need to address here is: *How to leverage 2D instance semantic masks to guide the learning of object-SDFs?*

The only existing solution we can find is the SemanticNeRF [41], which adds an additional head to predict a 3D "semantic field" **s** in the same way as predicting the radiance field **c**. Then, similar to Eq. (1), 2D semantic segmentation can be regarded as a volume rendering result from the 3D "semantic field" as:

$$\hat{S}(\mathbf{r}) = \int_{v_n}^{v_f} T(v)\sigma(\mathbf{r}(v))\mathbf{s}(\mathbf{r}(v))dv. \tag{5}$$

However, in our framework, σ is transformed from *scene*-SDF d_Ω, which is further obtained from object-SDFs. The supervision on the segmentation prediction $\hat{S}$ cannot ensure the object-SDFs to be meaningful.

Therefore, we turn to a new solution that represents the 3D semantic prediction **s** as a function of object-SDF. Our *key insight* is that the semantic information is strongly associated with the object geometry. Specifically, we analyze the property of a desired 3D "semantic field". Considering we have k objects $\{\mathcal{O}_i \subset \mathbb{R}^3 | i = 1, \ldots, k\}$ inside the scene including background, we expect that *a desired 3D semantic label should maintain consistency inside one object while changing rapidly when crossing the boundary from one class to another*. Thus, we investigate the derivative of $\mathbf{s}(\mathbf{p})$ at a 3D position $\mathbf{p}$. Particularly, we inspect the norm of $\frac{\partial \mathbf{s}_i}{\partial \mathbf{p}}$:

$$||\frac{\partial \mathbf{s}_i}{\partial \mathbf{p}}|| = ||\frac{\partial \mathbf{s}_i}{\partial d_{\mathcal{O}_i}} \cdot \frac{\partial d_{\mathcal{O}_i}}{\partial \mathbf{p}}|| \qquad \text{(chain rule)}$$

$$\leq ||\frac{\partial \mathbf{s}_i}{\partial d_{\mathcal{O}_i}}|| \cdot ||\frac{\partial d_{\mathcal{O}_i}}{\partial \mathbf{p}}|| \qquad \text{(norm inequality)}$$

$$= ||\frac{\partial \mathbf{s}_i}{\partial d_{\mathcal{O}_i}}|| \cdot ||\nabla d_{\mathcal{O}_i}(\mathbf{p})||.$$

As we adopt the implicit geometric regulization loss in Eq. (4), $||\nabla d_{\mathcal{O}_i}(\mathbf{p})||$ should be close to 1 after training. Therefore, the norm of $\partial \mathbf{s}_i/\partial \mathbf{p}$ should be bounded by the norm of $\partial \mathbf{s}_i/\partial d_{\mathcal{O}_i}$. In this way, we can convert the desired property of the 3D "semantic field" to $\partial \mathbf{s}_i/\partial d_{\mathcal{O}_i}$. Considering that crossing from one class to another class means $d_{\mathcal{O}_i}$ is passing zero-level set (see Fig. 2 left), we come up with a simple but effective function to satisfied the property. Concretely, we use the function:

$$\mathbf{s}_i = \gamma/(1 + \exp(\gamma d_{\mathcal{O}_i})), \tag{6}$$

which is a scaled sigmoid function and γ is a hyper-parameter to control the smoothness of the function. The absolute value of $\partial \mathbf{s}_i/\partial d_{\mathcal{O}_i}$ is $\gamma^2 \exp(\gamma d_{\mathcal{O}_i})/(1 + \exp(\gamma d_{\mathcal{O}_i}))^2$, which meets the requirement of desired 3D semantic field, *i.e.*, smooth inside the object but a rapid change at the boundary (see Fig. 2 right).

This is fundamentally different from [41]. Here we directly transform the object-SDF prediction $d_{\mathcal{O}_i}$ to a semantic label in 3D space. Thanks to this design, we can conduct volume rendering to convert the transformed SDF into the 2D semantic prediction using Eq. (5). With the corresponding semantic segmentation mask, we minimize the cross-entropy loss $\mathcal{L}_s$:

$$\mathcal{L}_s = \mathbb{E}_{\mathbf{r} \sim S}[-\log \hat{S}(\mathbf{r})]. \tag{7}$$

3.4   Model Training

Following [18,35], we first minimize the reconstruction error between the predicted color $\hat{C}(\mathbf{r})$ and the ground-truth color $C(\mathbf{r})$ with:

$$\mathcal{L}_{rec} = \mathbb{E}_\mathbf{r} ||\hat{C}(\mathbf{r}) - C(\mathbf{r})||_1. \tag{8}$$

Furthermore, we use the implicit geometric loss to regularize the SDF of each object as in Eq. (4). Moreover, the cross-entropy loss between the rendered semantic and ground-truth semantic is applied to guide the learning of object-SDFs as in Eq. (7). Overall, we train our model with the following three losses $\mathcal{L}_{total} = \mathcal{L}_{rec} + \lambda_1 \mathcal{L}_s + \lambda_2 \mathcal{L}_{SDF}$, where λ_1 and λ_2 are two trade-off hyperparameters. We set $\lambda_1 = 0.04$ and $\lambda_2 = 0.1$ empirically.

4   Experiments

The main purpose of our proposed method is to build an object-compositional neural implicit representation for scene rendering and object modeling. Therefore, we evaluate our approach in two real-world datasets from two aspects. Firstly, we quantitatively compare our scene representation ability with the state-of-the-art methods on standard scene rendering and modeling aspects. Then, we investigate the object representation ability of our method and compare it with NeRF-based object representation method [34]. Finally, we perform a model design ablation study to inspect the effectiveness of our framework.

4.1   Experimental Setting

Implementation Details. Our systems consists of two Multi-Layer Perceptrons (MLP). (i) The first MLP f_ϕ estimates each object SDF as well as a scene feature z of dimension 256 for further rendering branch, i.e., $f_\phi(\mathbf{p}) = [d_{\mathcal{O}_1}(\mathbf{p}), \dots, d_{\mathcal{O}_K}(\mathbf{p}), z(\mathbf{p})] \in \mathbb{R}^{K+256}$. f_ϕ consists of 6 layers with 256 channels. (ii) The second MLP f_θ is used to estimate the scene radiance field, which takes point position $\mathbf{p}$, point normal $\mathbf{n}$, view direction $\mathbf{d}$ and scene feature z as inputs and outputs the RGB color $\mathbf{c}$, i.e., $f_\theta(\mathbf{p}, \mathbf{n}, \mathbf{d}, z) = \mathbf{c}$. f_θ consists of 4 layers with 256 channels. We use the geometric network initialization technique [1,36] for both MLPs to initial the network weights to facilitate the learning of signed distance functions. We adopt the error-bounded sampling algorithm proposed by [35] to decide which points will be used in calculating volume rendering results. We also incorporate the positional encoding [18] with 6 levels for position $\mathbf{p}$ and 4 levels for view direction $\mathbf{d}$ to help the model capture high frequency information of the geometry and radiance field. Our model can be trained in a single GTX 2080Ti GPU with a batch size of 1024 rays. We set $\beta = 0.1$ in Eq. 3 in the initial stage of training.

Datasets. Following [34] and [41], we use two real datasets for comparisons.

- **ToyDesk** [34] contains scenes of a desk by placing several toys with two different layouts and capturing images in 360° by looking at the desk center. It also contains 2D instance segmentation for target objects as well as the camera pose for each image and a reconstructed mesh for each scene.
- **ScanNet** dataset [3] contains RGB-D indoor scene scans as well as 3D segmentation annotations and projected 2D segmentation masks. In our experiments, we use the 2D segmentation masks provided in the ScanNet dataset for training, and the provided 3D meshes for 3D reconstruction evaluation.

Comparison Baselines. We compare our method with the recent representative works in the realm of object-compositional neural implicit representation for the single static scene: **ObjectNeRF** [34] and **SemanticNeRF** [26]. ObjectNeRF uses a two-path architecture to represent object-compositional neural radiance, where one branch is used for individual object modeling while the other is for scene representation. To broaden the ability of the network to capture accurate scene information, ObjectNeRF utilizes voxel features for both scene and object branches training, as in [12], which significantly increases the model complexity. SemanticNeRF [26] is a NeRF-based framework that jointly predicts semantics and geometry in a single model for semantic labeling. The key design in this framework is an additional semantic prediction head extended from the NeRF backbone. Although this method does not directly represent objects, it can still extract an object by using semantic prediction.

Metric. We employ the following metrics for evaluation: **1) PSNR** to evaluate the quality of rendering; **2) mIOU** to evaluate the semantic segmentation; and **3) Chamfer Distance (CD)** to measure the quality of reconstructed 3D geometry. Besides these metrics, we also provide the number of neural network parameters (**#params**) of each method for comparing the model complexity.

Table 1. The quantitative results on scene representation. We compare our method against recent SOTA methods [34,41], ablation designs and Ground Truth

Methods ground truth (GT)	#Params	ToyDesk [34]			ScanNet [3]		
		PSNR ↑	mIOU ↑	CD ↓	PSNR ↑	mIOU ↑	CD ↓
	–	N/A	1.00	0.00	N/A	1.00	0.00
SemanticNeRF [41]	~1.26M	19.57	0.79	1.15	23.59	**0.57**	0.64
ObjectNeRF [34]	1.78M(+19.20M)	21.61	0.75	1.06	24.01	0.31	0.61
VolSDF [35]	**0.802M**	22.00	–	0.30	25.31	–	0.32
VolSDF w/ Semantic	~0.805M	22.00	**0.89**	0.34	**25.41**	0.56	0.28
Ours	~0.804M	22.00	0.88	**0.19**	25.23	0.53	**0.22**

Comparison Settings. We follow the comparison settings introduced by ObjectNeRF [34] and SemanticNeRF [41]. We use the same scene data used in [34] from ToyDesk and ScanNet for a fair comparison. To be consistent with SemanticNeRF [41], we predict the category semantic label rather than the instance semantic label for the quantitative evaluation on the ScanNet bench-mark. Note that we are unable to train SemanticNeRF in the original resolution in the official codebase due to memory overflow. Therefore, we downscale the images of ScanNet and train all methods with the same data. We also noticed that the ground truth mesh may lack points in some regions, for which we apply the same crop setting for all methods to evaluate the 3D region of interest.

It is worth noting that both our method and SemanticNeRF are able to pro-duce the semantic label in the output. However, ObjectNeRF does not explicitly predict the semantic label in their framework. Therefore, we calculate the depth of each object which is computed from the volume density predicted from each object branch in ObjectNeRF [4]. Then, we use the object with the nearest depth as the pixel semantic prediction of ObjectNeRF for calculating the mIOU metric. For scene rendering and the 3D reconstruction ability of ObjectNeRF, we adopt the result from the scene branch for evaluation. More details can be found in the supplementary.

4.2   Scene-Level Representation Ability

To evaluate the scene-level representation ability, we first compare the scene ren-dering, object segmentation, and 3D reconstruction results. As shown in Table 1, our framework outperforms other methods on the Toydesk benchmark and is comparable or even better than the SOTA methods on the ScanNet dataset. The qualitative results shown in Fig. 3 demonstrate that both our method and SemanticNeRF are able to produce fairly accurate segmentation masks. Object-NeRF, on the other hand, renders noisy semantic masks as shown in the third row of Fig. 3. We believe the volume density predicted by the object branch is susceptible to noisy semantic prediction for points that are further from the object surface. Therefore, when calculating the depth of each object, it results in artifacts and leads to noisy rendering.

In terms of 3D structure reconstruction, thanks to the accurate SDF in capturing surface information, our framework can recover much more accurate geometry compared with other methods. We also calculate the number of model parameters of each method. Due to the feature volume used in ObjectNeRF, their model needs additional 19.20 M parameters. In contrast, the number of parameters of our model is about 0.804 M, which is about 36% and 54% reduc-tions from ObjectNeRF and SemanticNeRF, respectively. This demonstrates the compactness and efficiency of our proposed method.

4.3   Object-Level Representation Ability

Besides the scene-level representation ability, our framework can naturally represent each object by selecting the specific output channel of object-SDFs for volume rendering. ObjectNeRF [34] can also isolate an object in a scene by computing the volume density and color of the object using the object branch network with a specific object activation code. We evaluate the object-level representation ability based on the quality of rendering and reconstruction of each object. Particularly, we compare our method against ObjectNeRF on Toydesk02 which contains five toys in the scene as shown in Fig. 4. We show the rendered opacity and RGB images of each toy from the same camera pose. It can be seen that our proposed method can render the objects more precisely with accurate opacity to describe each object. In contrast, ObjectNeRF often renders noisy images despite utilizing the opacity loss and 3D guided mask to stop gradient during training. Moreover, the accurate rendering of the occluded cubes (the last two columns in Fig. 4) demonstrates that our method handles occlusions much better than ObjectNeRF. We also compare the geometry reconstructions of all the five objects on the left of Fig. 4.

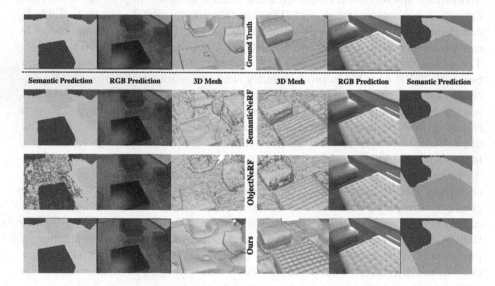

Fig. 3. Qualitative Comparison with SemanticNeRF [41] and Object-NeRF [34] on scene-level representation ability. We show the reconstructed meshes, predicted RGB images, and semantic masks of each method together with the ground truth results from two scenes in ScanNet.

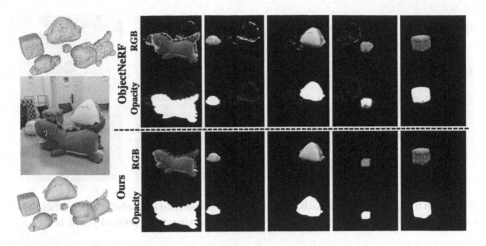

Fig. 4. Instance Results of ObjectNeRF [34] **and Ours.** We show the reconstructed mesh, rendered opacity, and RGB images of different objects.

4.4   Ablation Study

Our framework is built upon VolSDF [35] to develop an object-compositional neural implicit surface representation. Instead of modeling individual object SDFs, an alternative way to achieve the same goal is to add a semantic head to VolSDF to predict the semantic label given each 3D location, which is similar to the approach done in [41]. We name this variant as "VolSDF w/ Semantic".

We first evaluate the scene-level representation ability between our method and the variant "VolSDF w/ Semantic" in Table 1. For completeness, we also include the vanilla VolSDF, but due to the lack of semantic head, it cannot be evaluated on mIOU. While the comparing methods achieve similar performance on image rendering measured by PSNR, our method excels at geometric reconstruction. This is further demonstrated in Fig. 5, where we render the RGB image and normal map of each method. From the rendered normal maps, we can see that our method captures more accurate geometry compared with the two baselines. For example, our method can recover the geometry of the floor and the details of the sofa legs. The key difference between our method and the two variants is that we directly model each object SDF inside the scene. This indicates that our object-compositional modeling can improve the full understanding of 3D scene both semantically and geometrically.

To investigate the object representation ability of "VolSDF w/ semantic", we obtain an implicit object representation by using the prediction of semantic labels to determine the volume density of an object. In particular, given a semantic prediction in a 3D position, we can truncate the object semantic value by a threshold to decide whether to use the density to represent this object. We evaluate the object representation ability on two instances from ToyDesk and Scannet, respectively, in Fig. 6. We choose the object, which is not occluded to

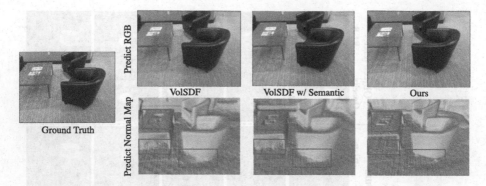

Fig. 5. Ablation study results on scene representation ability. We show the rendered RGB image and rendered normal map together with ground truth image.

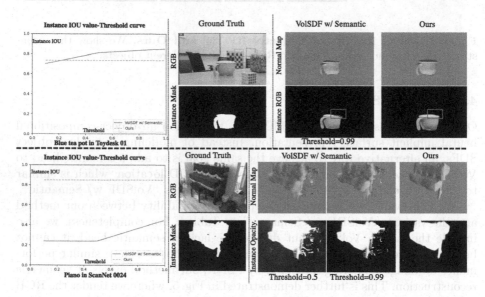

Fig. 6. Instance Results of Ours and "VolSDF w/ Semantic". We show the curve between instance IOU value and semantic value threshold (left), the ground truth instance image and mask (middle), the rendered normal map, and RGB/opacity of each instance under different threshold values (right).

extract the complete segmentation mask, and then use this mask to evaluate the semantic prediction result for each instance. Because the instance mask generated by "VolSDF w/ Semantic" is controlled by the semantic value threshold, we plot the curve of IOUs under different thresholds (blue line). This reveals an inherent challenge for "VolSDF w/ Semantic", *i.e.*, how to find a generally suitable threshold across different instances or scenes. For instance, we notice "VolSDF w/ Semantic" could gain a high IOU value with a high threshold of

0.99, but it will miss some information of the teapot (as highlighted by the red box). While using the same threshold of 0.99 on ScanNet 0024 (bottom), it fails in separating the piano. In contrast, our instance prediction is invariant to the threshold as shown in the yellow dash line. This suggests that the separate modeling of 3D structure and semantic information is undesirable to extract accurate instance representation when either prediction is inaccurate. We also observe that given a fairly rough segmentation mask during training, our framework can produce a smooth and high-fidelity object representation as shown in Fig. 6.

5   Conclusion and Future Work

We have presented an object-compositional neural implicit surface representation framework, namely *ObjectSDF*, which learns the signed distance functions of all objects in a scene from the guidance of 2D instance semantic segmentation masks and RGB images using a single network. Our model unifies the object and scene representations in one framework. The main idea behind it is building a strong association between semantic information and object geometry. Extensive experimental results on two datasets have demonstrated the strong ability of our framework in both 3D scene and object representation. Future work includes applying our model for various 3D scene editing applications and efficient training of neural implicit surfaces.

Acknowledgements. This research is partially supported by Monash FIT Start-up Grant and SenseTime Gift Fund.

References

1. Atzmon, M., Lipman, Y.: Sal: sign agnostic learning of shapes from raw data. In: IEEE/CVF Conference on Computer Vision and Pattern Recognition (CVPR), June 2020
2. Chen, Y., Wu, Q., Zheng, C., Cham, T.J., Cai, J.: Sem2nerf: converting single-view semantic masks to neural radiance fields. arXiv preprint arXiv:2203.10821 (2022)
3. Dai, A., Chang, A.X., Savva, M., Halber, M., Funkhouser, T., Nießner, M.: Scan-Net: Richly-annotated 3d reconstructions of indoor scenes. In: CVPR (2017)
4. Deng, K., Liu, A., Zhu, J.Y., Ramanan, D.: Depth-supervised nerf: Fewer views and faster training for free. arXiv preprint arXiv:2107.02791 (2021)
5. Deng, Y., Yang, J., Xiang, J., Tong, X.: Gram: Generative radiance manifolds for 3d-aware image generation. arXiv preprint arXiv:2112.08867 (2021)
6. Gropp, A., Yariv, L., Haim, N., Atzmon, M., Lipman, Y.: Implicit geometric regularization for learning shapes. arXiv preprint arXiv:2002.10099 (2020)
7. Guo, M., Fathi, A., Wu, J., Funkhouser, T.: Object-centric neural scene rendering. arXiv preprint arXiv:2012.08503 (2020)
8. Hassan, M., Choutas, V., Tzionas, D., Black, M.J.: Resolving 3d human pose ambiguities with 3d scene constraints. In: Proceedings of the IEEE/CVF International Conference on Computer Vision, pp. 2282–2292 (2019)

9. Kajiya, J.T., Von Herzen, B.P.: Ray tracing volume densities. ACM SIGGRAPH Comput. Graph. **18**(3), 165–174 (1984)
10. Kohli, A., Sitzmann, V., Wetzstein, G.: Semantic implicit neural scene representations with semi-supervised training. In: International Conference on 3D Vision (3DV) (2020)
11. Li, K., Rezatofighi, H., Reid, I.: Moltr: multiple object localization, tracking and reconstruction from monocular RGB videos. IEEE Robot. Autom. Lett. **6**(2), 3341–3348 (2021)
12. Liu, L., Gu, J., Lin, K.Z., Chua, T.S., Theobalt, C.: Neural sparse voxel fields. arXiv preprint arXiv:2007.11571 (2020)
13. Liu, X., Xu, Y., Wu, Q., Zhou, H., Wu, W., Zhou, B.: Semantic-aware implicit neural audio-driven video portrait generation. arXiv preprint arXiv:2201.07786 (2022)
14. Luan, F., Zhao, S., Bala, K., Dong, Z.: Unified shape and SVBRDF recovery using differentiable monte carlo rendering. In: Computer Graphics Forum, vol. 40, pp. 101–113. Wiley Online Library (2021)
15. Max, N.: Optical models for direct volume rendering. IEEE Trans. Vis. Comput. Graph. **1**(2), 99–108 (1995)
16. McCormac, J., Handa, A., Davison, A., Leutenegger, S.: SemanticFusion: dense 3d semantic mapping with convolutional neural networks. In: 2017 IEEE International Conference on Robotics and Automation (ICRA), pp. 4628–4635. IEEE (2017)
17. Mescheder, L., Oechsle, M., Niemeyer, M., Nowozin, S., Geiger, A.: Occupancy networks: learning 3d reconstruction in function space. In: Proceedings of the IEEE/CVF Conference on Computer Vision and Pattern Recognition, pp. 4460–4470 (2019)
18. Mildenhall, B., Srinivasan, P.P., Tancik, M., Barron, J.T., Ramamoorthi, R., Ng, R.: NeRF: representing scenes as neural radiance fields for view synthesis. In: Vedaldi, A., Bischof, H., Brox, T., Frahm, J.-M. (eds.) ECCV 2020. LNCS, vol. 12346, pp. 405–421. Springer, Cham (2020). https://doi.org/10.1007/978-3-030-58452-8_24
19. Nguyen-Phuoc, T.H., Richardt, C., Mai, L., Yang, Y., Mitra, N.: BlockGAN: learning 3d object-aware scene representations from unlabelled images. Adv. Neural Inf. Process. Syst. **33**, 6767–6778 (2020)
20. Nie, Y., Han, X., Guo, S., Zheng, Y., Chang, J., Zhang, J.J.: Total3DUnderstanding: joint layout, object pose and mesh reconstruction for indoor scenes from a single image. In: Proceedings of the IEEE/CVF Conference on Computer Vision and Pattern Recognition, pp. 55–64 (2020)
21. Niemeyer, M., Geiger, A.: Giraffe: representing scenes as compositional generative neural feature fields. In: Proceedings of the IEEE/CVF Conference on Computer Vision and Pattern Recognition, pp. 11453–11464 (2021)
22. Oechsle, M., Peng, S., Geiger, A.: UNISURF: unifying neural implicit surfaces and radiance fields for multi-view reconstruction. In: Proceedings of the IEEE/CVF International Conference on Computer Vision, pp. 5589–5599 (2021)
23. Ost, J., Mannan, F., Thuerey, N., Knodt, J., Heide, F.: Neural scene graphs for dynamic scenes. In: Proceedings of the IEEE/CVF Conference on Computer Vision and Pattern Recognition, pp. 2856–2865 (2021)
24. Park, J.J., Florence, P., Straub, J., Newcombe, R., Lovegrove, S.: DeepSDF: learning continuous signed distance functions for shape representation. In: Proceedings of the IEEE/CVF Conference on Computer Vision and Pattern Recognition, pp. 165–174 (2019)

25. Park, K., et al.: Nerfies: deformable neural radiance fields. In: Proceedings of the IEEE/CVF International Conference on Computer Vision, pp. 5865–5874 (2021)
26. Prajwal, K., Mukhopadhyay, R., Namboodiri, V.P., Jawahar, C.: A lip sync expert is all you need for speech to lip generation in the wild. In: Proceedings of the 28th ACM International Conference on Multimedia, pp. 484–492 (2020)
27. Pumarola, A., Corona, E., Pons-Moll, G., Moreno-Noguer, F.: D-nerf: neural radiance fields for dynamic scenes. In: Proceedings of the IEEE/CVF Conference on Computer Vision and Pattern Recognition, pp. 10318–10327 (2021)
28. Rebain, D., Jiang, W., Yazdani, S., Li, K., Yi, K.M., Tagliasacchi, A.: DeRF: decomposed radiance fields. In: Proceedings of the IEEE/CVF Conference on Computer Vision and Pattern Recognition, pp. 14153–14161 (2021)
29. Reiser, C., Peng, S., Liao, Y., Geiger, A.: KiloNeRF: speeding up neural radiance fields with thousands of tiny MLPs. In: Proceedings of the IEEE/CVF International Conference on Computer Vision, pp. 14335–14345 (2021)
30. Rosinol, A., Gupta, A., Abate, M., Shi, J., Carlone, L.: 3d dynamic scene graphs: actionable spatial perception with places, objects, and humans. arXiv preprint arXiv:2002.06289 (2020)
31. Sitzmann, V., Zollhöfer, M., Wetzstein, G.: Scene representation networks: continuous 3d-structure-aware neural scene representations. arXiv preprint arXiv:1906.01618 (2019)
32. Verbin, D., Hedman, P., Mildenhall, B., Zickler, T., Barron, J.T., Srinivasan, P.P.: Ref-NeRF: structured view-dependent appearance for neural radiance fields. In: CVPR (2022)
33. Wang, P., Liu, L., Liu, Y., Theobalt, C., Komura, T., Wang, W.: NeuS: learning neural implicit surfaces by volume rendering for multi-view reconstruction. In: NeurIPS (2021)
34. Yang, B., et al.: Learning object-compositional neural radiance field for editable scene rendering. In: International Conference on Computer Vision (ICCV), October 2021
35. Yariv, L., Gu, J., Kasten, Y., Lipman, Y.: Volume rendering of neural implicit surfaces. arXiv preprint arXiv:2106.12052 (2021)
36. Yariv, L., et al.: Multiview neural surface reconstruction by disentangling geometry and appearance. Adv. Neural Inf. Process. Syst. **33**, 2492–2502 (2020)
37. Yu, H.X., Guibas, L., Wu, J.: Unsupervised discovery of object radiance fields. In: International Conference on Learning Representations (2022). https://openreview.net/forum?id=rwE8SshAlxw
38. Zhang, K., Luan, F., Li, Z., Snavely, N.: IRON: Inverse rendering by optimizing neural SDFs and materials from photometric images. In: Proceedings of the IEEE/CVF Conference on Computer Vision and Pattern Recognition, pp. 5565–5574 (2022)
39. Zhang, K., Riegler, G., Snavely, N., Koltun, V.: Nerf++: analyzing and improving neural radiance fields. arXiv preprint arXiv:2010.07492 (2020)
40. Zhang, X., Srinivasan, P.P., Deng, B., Debevec, P., Freeman, W.T., Barron, J.T.: NeRFactor: neural factorization of shape and reflectance under an unknown illumination. ACM Trans. Graph (TOG) **40**(6), 1–18 (2021)
41. Zhi, S., Laidlow, T., Leutenegger, S., Davison, A.: In-place scene labelling and understanding with implicit scene representation. In: Proceedings of the International Conference on Computer Vision (ICCV) (2021)

RigNet: Repetitive Image Guided Network for Depth Completion

Zhiqiang Yan, Kun Wang, Xiang Li, Zhenyu Zhang, Jun Li[(✉)],
and Jian Yang[(✉)]

PCA Lab, Nanjing University of Science and Technology, Nanjing, China
{Yanzq,kunwang,xiang.li.implus,junli,csjyang}@njust.edu.cn

Abstract. Depth completion deals with the problem of recovering dense depth maps from sparse ones, where color images are often used to facilitate this task. Recent approaches mainly focus on image guided learning frameworks to predict dense depth. However, blurry guidance in the image and unclear structure in the depth still impede the performance of the image guided frameworks. To tackle these problems, we explore a repetitive design in our image guided network to gradually and sufficiently recover depth values. Specifically, the repetition is embodied in both the image guidance branch and depth generation branch. In the former branch, we design a repetitive hourglass network to extract discriminative image features of complex environments, which can provide powerful contextual instruction for depth prediction. In the latter branch, we introduce a repetitive guidance module based on dynamic convolution, in which an efficient convolution factorization is proposed to simultaneously reduce its complexity and progressively model high-frequency structures. Extensive experiments show that our method achieves superior or competitive results on KITTI benchmark and NYUv2 dataset.

Keywords: Depth completion · Image guidance · Repetitive design

1 Introduction

Depth completion, the technique of converting sparse depth measurements to dense ones, has a variety of applications in the computer vision field, such as autonomous driving [7,14,50], augmented reality [8,45], virtual reality [1], and 3D scene reconstruction [36,42,43,57]. The success of these applications heavily depends on reliable depth predictions. Recently, multi-modal information from various sensors is involved to help generate dependable depth results, such as color images [3,33], surface normals [38,57], confidence maps [10,49], and even binaural echoes [12,35]. Particularly, the latest image guided methods [17,29,47,59] principally concentrate on using color images to guide the recovery of dense depth maps, achieving outstanding performance. However, due to the challenging environments

Supplementary Information The online version contains supplementary material available at https://doi.org/10.1007/978-3-031-19812-0_13.

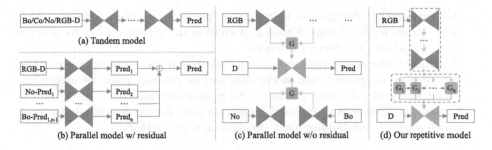

Fig. 1. To obtain dense depth **Pred**iction, most existing image guided methods employ tandem models [4,33,36] (a) or parallel models [17,29,47,59] (b,c) with various inputs (*e.g.*, **Bo**undary/**Co**nfidence/**No**rmal/RGB-D), whilst we propose the repetitive mechanism (d), aiming at providing gradually refined image/depth **G**uidance.

and limited depth measurements, it's difficult for existing image guided methods to produce clear image guidance and structure-detailed depth features (see Figs. 2 and 6). To deal with these issues, in this paper we develop a repetitive design in both the image guidance branch and depth generation branch.

In the image guidance branch: Existing image guided methods are not sufficient to produce very precise details to provide perspicuous image guidance, which limits the content-complete depth recovery. For example, the tandem models (Fig. 1(a)) tend to only utilize the final layer features of a hourglass unit. The parallel models conduct scarce interaction between multiple hourglass units (Fig. 1(b)), or refer to image guidance encoded only by single hourglass unit (Fig. 1(c)). Different from them, as shown in Fig. 1(d), we present a vertically repetitive hourglass network to make good use of RGB features in multi-scale layers, which contain image semantics with much clearer and richer contexts.

In the depth generation branch: It is known that gradients near boundaries usually have large mutations, which increase the difficulty of recovering structure-detailed depth for convolution [48]. As evidenced in plenty of methods [10,18,36], the depth values are usually hard to be predicted especially around the region with unclear boundaries. To moderate this issue, in this paper we propose a repetitive guidance module based on dynamic convolution [47]. It first extracts the high-frequency components by channel-wise and cross-channel convolution factorization, and then repeatedly stacks the guidance unit to progressively produce refined depth. We also design an adaptive fusion mechanism to effectively obtain better depth representations by aggregating depth features of each repetitive unit. However, an obvious drawback of the dynamic convolution is the large GPU memory consumption, especially under the case of our repetitive structure. Hence, we further introduce an efficient module to largely reduce the memory cost but maintain the accuracy.

Benefiting from the repetitive strategy with gradually refined image/depth representations, our method performs better than others, as shown in Figs. 4, 5 and 6, and reported in Tables 3, 4, 5 and 6. In short, our contributions are:

- We propose the effective but lightweight repetitive hourglass network, which can extract legible image features of challenging environments to provide clearer guidance for depth recovery.
- We present the repetitive guidance module based on dynamic convolution, including an adaptive fusion mechanism and an efficient guidance algorithm, which can gradually learn precise depth representations.
- Extensive experimental results demonstrate the effectiveness of our method, which achieves outstanding performances on three datasets.

2   Related Work

Depth only Approaches. For the first time in 2017, the work [48] proposes sparsity invariant CNNs to deal with sparse depth. Since then, lots of depth completion works [6,10,22,24,33,48,49] input depth without using color image. Distinctively, Lu *et al.* [32] take sparse depth as the only input with color image being auxiliary supervision when training. However, single-modal based methods are limited without other reference information. As technology quickly develops, plenty of multi-modal information is available, *e.g.*, surface normal and optic flow images, which can significantly facilitate the depth completion task.

Image Guided Methods. Existing image guided depth completion methods can be roughly divided into two patterns. One pattern is that various maps are together input into tandem hourglass networks [3–5,33,36,52]. For example, S2D [33] directly feeds the concatenation into a simple Unet [41]. CSPN [5] studies the affinity matrix to refine coarse depth maps with spatial propagation network (SPN). CSPN++ [4] further improves its effectiveness and efficiency by learning adaptive convolutional kernel sizes and the number of iterations for propagation. As an extension, NLSPN [36] presents non-local SPN which focuses on relevant non-local neighbors during propagation. Another pattern is using multiple independent branches to model different sensor information and then fuse them at multi-scale stages [17,26,29,47,49,53]. For example, PENet [17] employs feature addition to guide depth learning at different stages. ACMNet [59] chooses graph propagation to capture the observed spatial contexts. GuideNet [47] seeks to predict dynamic kernel weights from the guided image and then adaptively extract the depth features. However, these methods still cannot provide very sufficient semantic guidance for the specific depth completion task.

Repetitive Learning Models. To extract more accurate and abundant feature representations, many approaches [2,31,37,40] propose to repeatedly stack similar components. For example, PANet [30] adds an extra bottom-up path aggregation which is similar with its former top-down feature pyramid network (FPN). NAS-FPN [13] and BiFPN [46] conduct repetitive blocks to sufficiently encode discriminative image semantics for object detection. FCFRNet [29] argues that the feature extraction in one-stage frameworks is insufficient, and thus proposes a two-stage model, which can be regarded as a special case of the repetitive design. On this basis, PENet [17] further improves its performance by utilizing

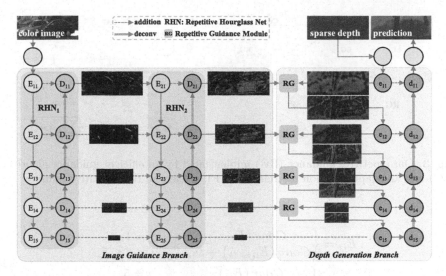

Fig. 2. Overview of our repetitive image guided network, which contains an image guidance branch and a depth generation branch. The former consists of a repetitive hourglass network (RHN) and the latter has the similar structure as RHN_1. In the depth branch, we perform our novel repetitive guidance module (RG, elaborated in Fig. 3) to refine depth. In addition, an efficient guidance algorithm (EG) and an adaptive fusion mechanism (AF) are proposed to further improve the performance of the module.

confidence maps and varietal CSPN++. Different from these methods, in our image branch we first conduct repetitive CNNs units to produce clearer guidance in multi-scale layers. Then in our depth branch we perform repetitive guidance module to generate structure-detailed depth.

3 Repetitive Design

In this section, we first introduce our repetitive hourglass network (RHN), then elaborate the proposed repetitive guidance module (RG), including an efficient guidance algorithm (EG) and an adaptive fusion mechanism (AF).

3.1 Repetitive Hourglass Network

For autonomous driving in challenging environments, it is important to understand the semantics of color images in view of the sparse depth measurement. The problem of blurry image guidance can be mitigated by a powerful feature extractor, which can obtain context-clear semantics. In this paper we present our repetitive hourglass network shown in Fig. 2. RHN_i is a symmetrical hourglass unit like Unet. The original color image is first encoded by a 5×5 convolution and then input into RHN_1. Next, we repeatedly utilize the similar but lightweight unit, each layer of which consists of two convolutions, to gradually extract high-level semantics. In the encoder of RHN_i, E_{ij} takes $E_{i(j-1)}$ and $D_{(i-1)j}$ as input. In the decoder of RHN_i, D_{ij} inputs E_{ij} and $D_{i(j+1)}$. When $i > 1$, the process is

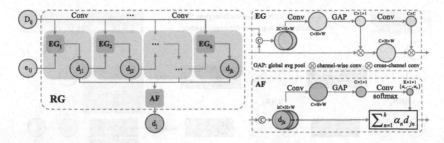

Fig. 3. Our repetitive guidance (RG) implemented by an efficient guidance algorithm (EG) and an adaptive fusion mechanism (AF). k refers to the repetitive number.

$$E_{ij} = \begin{cases} Conv\left(D_{(i-1)j}\right), & j = 1, \\ Conv\left(E_{i(j-1)}\right) + D_{(i-1)j}, & 1 < j \leq 5, \end{cases}$$
$$D_{ij} = \begin{cases} Conv\left(E_{i5}\right), & j = 5, \\ Deconv\left(D_{i(j+1)}\right) + E_{ij}, & 1 \leq j < 5, \end{cases} \tag{1}$$

where $Deconv\left(\cdot\right)$ denotes deconvolution function, and $E_{1j} = Conv(E_{1(j-1)})$.

3.2 Repetitive Guidance Module

Depth in challenging environments is not only extremely sparse but also diverse. Most of the existing methods suffer from unclear structures, especially near the object boundaries. Since gradual refinement is proven effective [4,36,52] to tackle this issue, we propose our repetitive guidance module to progressively generate dense and structure-detailed depth maps. As illustrated in Fig. 2, our depth generation branch has the same architecture as RHN_1. Given the sparse depth input and color image guidance features D_{ij} in the decoder of the last RHN, our depth branch generates final dense predictions. At the stage of the depth branch's encoder, our repetitive guidance module (left of Fig. 3) takes D_{ij} and e_{1j} as input and employs the efficient guidance algorithm (in Sect. 3.2) to produce refined depth d_{jk} step by step. Then we fuse the refined d_{jk} by our adaptive fusion mechanism (in Sect. 3.2), obtaining the depth d_j,

$$d_j = RG\left(D_{ij}, e_{1j}\right), \tag{2}$$

where $RG\left(\cdot\right)$ refers to the repetitve guidance function.

Efficient Guidance Algorithm. Suppose the size of inputs D_{ij} and e_{1j} are both $C \times H \times W$. It is easy to figure out the complexity of the dynamic convolution is $O(C \times C \times R^2 \times H \times W)$, which generates spatial-variant kernels according to color image features. R^2 is the size of the filter kernel window. In fact, C, H, and W are usually very large, it's thus necessary to reduce the complexity of the dynamic convolution. GuideNet [47] proposes channel-wise and cross-channel convolution factorization, whose complexity is $O(C \times R^2 \times H \times W + C \times C)$. However, our repetitive guidance module employs the convolution factorization many

Table 1. Theoretical analysis on GPU memory consumption.

$$\frac{M_{EG}}{M_{DC}} = \frac{C \times H \times W + C \times C}{C \times C \times R^2 \times H \times W} = \frac{H \times W + C}{C \times H \times W \times R^2}$$

$$\frac{M_{EG}}{M_{CF}} = \frac{C \times H \times W + C \times C}{C \times R^2 \times H \times W + C \times C} = \frac{H \times W + C}{C + H \times W \times R^2}$$

Table 2. Numerical analysis on GPU memory consumption.

Method	DC	CF	EG
Memory (GB)	42.75	0.334	0.037
Times (-/EG)	1155	9	1

times, where the channel-wise process still needs massive GPU memory consumption, which is $O(C \times R^2 \times H \times W)$. As a result, inspired by SENet [16] that captures high-frequency response with channel-wise differentiable operations, we design an efficient guidance unit to simultaneously reduce the complexity of the channel-wise convolution and encode high-frequency components, which is shown in the top right of Fig. 3. Specifically, we first concatenate the image and depth inputs and then conduct a 3×3 convolution. Next, we employ the global average pooling function to generate a $C \times 1 \times 1$ feature. At last, we perform pixel-wise dot between the feature and the depth input. The complexity of our channel-wise convolution is only $O(C \times H \times W)$, reduced to $1/R^2$. The process is defined as

$$d_{jk} = \begin{cases} EG\,(D_{ij}, e_{1j}), & k = 1, \\ EG\,(Conv\,(D_{ij}), d_{k-1}), & k > 1, \end{cases} \tag{3}$$

where $EG\,(\cdot)$ represents the efficient guidance function.

Suppose the memory consumptions of the common dynamic convolution, convolution factorization, and our EG are M_{DC}, M_{CF}, and M_{EG}, respectively.

Table 1 shows the theoretical analysis of GPU memory consumption ratio. Under the setting of the second (4 in total) fusion stage in our depth generation branch, using 4-byte floating precision and taking $C = 128$, $H = 128$, $W = 608$, and $R = 3$, as shown in Table 2, the GPU memory of EG is reduced from 42.75 GB to 0.037 GB compared with the common dynamic convolution, nearly 1155 times lower in one fusion stage. Compared to the convolution factorization in GuideNet [47], the memory of EG is reduced from 0.334 GB to 0.037 GB, nearly 9 times lower. Therefore, we can conduct our repetitive strategy easily without worrying much about GPU memory consumption.

Adaptive Fusion Mechanism. Since many coarse depth features $(d_{j1}, \cdots, d_{jk})$ are available in our repetitive guidance module, it comes naturally to jointly utilize them to generate refined depth maps, which has been proved effective in various related methods [4,17,28,36,45,58]. Inspired by the selective kernel convolution in SKNet [27], we propose the adaptive fusion mechanism to refine depth, which is illustrated in the bottom right of Fig. 3. Specifically, given inputs $(d_{j1}, \cdots, d_{jk})$, we first concatenate them and then perform a 3×3 convolution. Next, the global average pooling is employed to produce a $C \times 1 \times 1$ feature map. Then another 3×3 convolution and a softmax function are applied, obtaining $(\alpha_1, \cdots, \alpha_k)$,

$$\alpha_k = Soft\,(Conv\,(GAP\,(Conv\,(d_{j1}||\cdots||d_{jk})))), \tag{4}$$

where $Soft(\cdot)$ and $||$ refer to softmax function and concatenation. $GAP(\cdot)$ represents the global average pooling operation. Finally, we fuse the k coarse depth maps using α_k to produce the output d_j,

$$d_j = \sum_{n=1}^{k} \alpha_n d_{jn}. \tag{5}$$

The Eqs. 4 and 5 can be denoted as

$$d_j = AF(d_{j1}, d_{j2}, \cdots, d_{jk}), \tag{6}$$

where $AF(\cdot)$ represents the adaptive fusion function.

4   RigNet

In this section, we describe the network architecture and the loss function for training. The proposed RigNet mainly consists of two parts: (1) an image guidance branch for the generation of hierarchical and clear semantics based on the repetitive hourglass network, and (2) a depth generation branch for structure-detailed depth predictions based on the novel repetitive guidance module with an efficient guidance algorithm and an adaptive fusion mechanism.

4.1   Network Architecture

Figure 2 shows the overview of our network. In our image guidance branch, the RHN_1 encoder-decoder unit is built upon residual networks [15]. In addition, we adopt the common connection strategy [3,41] to simultaneously utilize low-level and high-level features. RHN_i ($i > 1$) has the similar but lightweight architecture with RHN_1, which is used to extract clearer image guidance semantics [54].

The depth generation branch has the same structure as RHN_1. In this branch, we perform repetitive guidance module based on dynamic convolution to gradually produce structure-detailed depth features at multiple stages, which is shown in Fig. 3 and described in Sect. 3.2.

4.2   Loss Function

During training, we adopt the mean squared error (MSE) to compute the loss, which is defined as

$$\mathcal{L} = \frac{1}{m} \sum_{q \in Q_v} \|GT_q - P_q\|^2, \tag{7}$$

where GT and P refer to ground truth depth and predicted depth respectively. Q_v represents the set of valid pixels in GT, m is the number of the valid pixels.

5   Experiments

In this section, we first introduce the related datasets, metrics, and implementation details. Then, we carry out extensive experiments to evaluate the performance of our method against other state-of-the-art approaches. Finally, a number of ablation studies are employed to verify the effectiveness of our method.

5.1 Datasets and Metrics

KITTI Depth Completion Dataset. [48] is a large autonomous driving real-world benchmark from a driving vehicle. It consists of 86,898 ground truth annotations with aligned sparse LiDAR maps and color images for training, 7,000 frames for validation, and another 1,000 frames for testing. The official 1,000 validation images are used during training while the remained images are ignored. Since there are rare LiDAR points at the top of depth maps, the input images are bottom center cropped [29, 47, 49, 59] to 1216×256.

Virtual KITTI Dataset. [11] is a synthetic dataset cloned from the real world KITTI video sequences. In addition, it also produces color images under various lighting (*e.g.*, sunset, morning) and weather (*e.g.*, rain, fog) conditions. Following GuideNet [47], we use the masks generated from sparse depths of KITTI dataset to obtain sparse samples. Such strategy makes it closed to real-world situation for the distribution of sparse depths. Sequences of 0001, 0002, 0006, and 0018 are used for training, 0020 with various lighting and weather conditions is used for testing. It contributes to 1,289 frames for fine-tuning and 837 frames for evaluating each condition.

NYUv2 Dataset. [44] is comprised of video sequences from a variety of indoor scenes as recorded by both the color and depth cameras from the Microsoft Kinect. Paired color images and depth maps in 464 indoor scenes are commonly used. Following previous depth completion methods [3, 33, 36, 38, 47], we train our model on 50K images from the official training split, and test on the 654 images from the official labeled test set. Each image is downsized to 320×240, and then 304×228 center-cropping is applied. As the input resolution of our network must be a multiple of 32, we further pad the images to 320×256, but evaluate only at the valid region of size 304×228 to keep fair comparison with other methods.

Metrics. For the outdoor KITTI depth completion dataset, following the KITTI benchmark and existing methods [17, 29, 36, 47], we use four standard metrics for evaluation, including RMSE, MAE, iRMSE, and iMAE. For the indoor NYUv2 dataset, following previous works [3, 29, 36, 38, 47], three metrics are selected for evaluation, including RMSE, REL, and δ_i ($i = 1.25, 1.25^2, 1.25^3$).

5.2 Implementation Details

The model is particularly trained with 4 TITAN RTX GPUs. We train it for 20 epochs with the loss defined in Eq. 7. We use ADAM [23] as the optimizer with the momentum of $\beta_1 = 0.9$, $\beta_2 = 0.999$, a starting learning rate of 1×10^{-3}, and weight decay of 1×10^{-6}. The learning rate drops by half every 5 epochs. The synchronized cross-GPU batch normalization [21, 55] is used when training.

Table 3. Quantitative comparisons on KITTI depth completion benchmark.

Method	RMSE mm	MAE mm	iRMSE 1/km	iMAE 1/km
CSPN [5]	1019.64	279.46	2.93	1.15
BDBF [39]	900.38	216.44	2.37	0.89
TWISE [19]	840.20	**195.58**	2.08	**0.82**
NConv [10]	829.98	233.26	2.60	1.03
S2D [33]	814.73	249.95	2.80	1.21
Fusion [49]	772.87	215.02	2.19	0.93
DLiDAR [38]	758.38	226.50	2.56	1.15
Zhu [60]	751.59	198.09	1.98	0.85
ACMNet [59]	744.91	206.09	2.08	0.90
CSPN++ [4]	743.69	209.28	2.07	0.90
NLSPN [36]	741.68	199.59	**1.99**	0.84
GuideNet [47]	736.24	218.83	2.25	0.99
FCFRNet [29]	735.81	217.15	2.20	0.98
PENet [17]	730.08	210.55	2.17	0.94
RigNet (ours)	**712.66**	203.25	2.08	0.90

Table 4. Quantitative comparisons on NYUv2 dataset.

Method	RMSE m	REL m	$\delta_{1.25}$	$\delta_{1.25^2}$	$\delta_{1.25^3}$
Bilateral [44]	0.479	0.084	92.4	97.6	98.9
Zhang [56]	0.228	0.042	97.1	99.3	99.7
S2D_18 [34]	0.230	0.044	97.1	99.4	99.8
DCoeff [20]	0.118	0.013	99.4	**99.9**	–
CSPN [5]	0.117	0.016	99.2	**99.9**	100.0
CSPN++ [4]	0.116	–	–	–	–
DLiDAR [38]	0.115	0.022	99.3	**99.9**	100.0
Xu et al. [51]	0.112	0.018	99.5	**99.9**	100.0
FCFRNet [29]	0.106	0.015	99.5	**99.9**	100.0
ACMNet [59]	0.105	0.015	99.4	**99.9**	100.0
PRNet [25]	0.104	0.014	99.4	**99.9**	100.0
GuideNet [47]	0.101	0.015	99.5	**99.9**	100.0
TWISE [19]	0.097	0.013	**99.6**	**99.9**	100.0
NLSPN [36]	0.092	**0.012**	**99.6**	**99.9**	100.0
RigNet (ours)	**0.090**	0.013	**99.6**	**99.9**	100.0

5.3   Evaluation on KITTI Dataset

Table 3 shows the quantitative results on KITTI benchmark, whose dominant evaluation metric is the RMSE. Our RigNet ranks 1st among publicly published papers when submitting, outperforming the 2nd with significant 17.42 mm improvement while the errors of other methods are very closed. Here, the performance of our RigNet is also better than those approaches that employ additional dataset, e.g., DLiDAR [38] utilizes CARLA [9] to predict surface normals for better depth predictions. Qualitative comparisons with several state-of-the-art works are shown in Fig. 4. While all methods provide visually good results in general, our estimated depth maps possess more details and more accurate object boundaries. The corresponding error maps can offer supports more clearly. For example, among the marked iron pillars in the first row of Fig. 4, the error of our prediction is significantly lower than the others.

5.4   Evaluation on NYUv2 Dataset

To verify the performance of proposed method on indoor scenes, following existing approaches [4,29,36,47], we train our repetitive image guided network on the NYUv2 dataset [44] with the setting 500 sparse samples. As illustrated in Table 4, our model achieves the best performance among all traditional and latest approaches without using additional datasets, which proves that our network possesses stronger generalization capability. Figure 5 demonstrates the qualitative visualization results. Obviously, compared with those state-of-the-art methods, our RigNet can recover more detailed structures with lower errors at most pixels, including sharper boundaries and more complete object shapes. For example, among the marked doors in the last row of Fig. 5, our prediction is very close

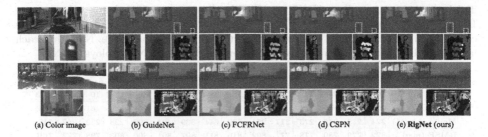

(a) Color image   (b) GuideNet   (c) FCFRNet   (d) CSPN   (e) RigNet (ours)

Fig. 4. Qualitative results on KITTI depth completion test set, including (b) GuideNet [47], (c) FCFRNet [29], and (d) CSPN [5]. Given sparse depth maps and the aligned color images (1st column), depth completion models output dense depth predictions (*e.g.*, 2nd column). We provide **error maps** borrowed from the KITTI leaderboard for detailed discrimination. Warmer color in error maps refer to higher error.

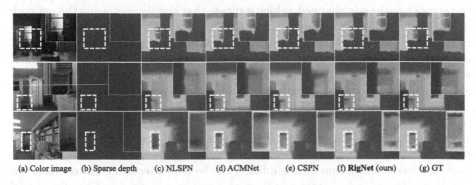

(a) Color image   (b) Sparse depth   (c) NLSPN   (d) ACMNet   (e) CSPN   (f) RigNet (ours)   (g) GT

Fig. 5. Qualitative results on NYUv2 test set. From left to right: (a) color image, (b) sparse depth, (c) NLSPN [36], (d) ACMNet [59], (e) CSPN [5], (f) our RigNet, and (g) ground truth. We present the results of these four methods under 500 samples. The circled rectangle areas show the recovery of object details.

to the ground truth, while others either have large errors in the whole regions or have blurry shapes on specific objects.

5.5   Ablation Studies

Here we employ extensive experiments to verify the effectiveness of each proposed component, including the repetitive hourglass network (RHN-Table 5) and the repetitive guidance module (RG-Table 6), which consists of the efficient guidance algorithm (EG) and the adaptive fusion mechanism (AF). **Note that** the batch size is set to 8 when computing the GPU memory consumption.

(1) Effect of Repetitive Hourglass Network
The state-of-the-art baseline GuideNet [47] employs 1 ResNet-18 as backbone and guided convolution G_1 to predict dense depth. To validate the effect of our RHN, we explore the backbone design of the image guidance branch for the specific depth completion task from four aspects, which are illustrated in Table 5.

Table 5. Ablation studies of RHN on KITTI validation set. 18-1 denotes that we use 1 ResNet-18 as backbone, which is also the baseline. 'Deeper'/'More' denotes that we conduct single&deeper/multiple&tandem hourglass units as backbone. Note that each layer of $RHN_{2,3}$ only contains two convolutions while the RHN_1 employs ResNet.

Method	Deeper					More			Deeper-More			Our parallel RHN			
	10-1	18-1	26-1	34-1	50-1	18-2	18-3	18-4	34-2	34-3	50-2	10-2	10-3	18-2	18-3
Parameter (M)	59	63	65	71	84	72	81	91	89	107	104	60	61	64	65
Model size (M)	224	239	246	273	317	274	309	344	339	407	398	228	232	242	246
RMSE (mm)	822	779	780	778	777	802	816	811	807	801	800	803	798	772	**769**

(i) Deeper single backbone vs. RHN. The second column of Table 5 shows that, when replacing the single ResNet-10 with ResNet-18, the error is reduced by 43 mm. However, when deepening the baseline from 18 to 26/34/50, the errors have barely changed, which indicate that simply increasing the network depth of image guidance branch cannot deal well with the specific depth completion task. Differently, with little sacrifice of parameters ($\sim$2 M), our RHN-10-3 and RHN-18-3 are 24 mm and 10 mm superior to Deeper-10-1 and Deeper-18-1, respectively. Figure 6 shows that the image feature of our parallel RHN-18-3 has much clearer and richer contexts than that of the baseline Deeper-18-1.

(ii) More tandem backbones vs. RHN. As shown in the third column of Table 5, we stack the hourglass unit in series. The models of More-18-2, More-18-3, and More-18-4 have worse performances than the baseline Deeper-18-1. It turns out that the combination of tandem hourglass units is not sufficient to provide clearer image semantic guidance for the depth recovery. In contrast, our parallel RHN achieves better results with fewer parameters and smaller model sizes. These facts give strong evidence that the parallel repetitive design in image guidance branch is effective for the depth completion task.

(iii) Deeper-More backbones vs. RHN. As illustrated in the fourth column of Table 5, deeper hourglass units are deployed in serial way. We can see that the Deeper-More combinations are also not very effective, since the errors of them are higher than the baseline while RHN's error is 10 mm lower. It verifies again the effectiveness of the lightweight RHN design.

(2) Effect of Repetitive Guidance Module

(i) Efficient guidance. Note that we directly output the features in EG_3 when not employing AF. Tables 1 and 2 have provided quantitative analysis in theory for EG design. Based on (a), we disable G_1 by replacing it with EG_1. Comparing (b) with (a) in Table 6, both of which carry out the guided convolution technology only once, although the error of (c) goes down a little bit, the GPU memory is heavily reduced by 11.95 GB. These results give strong evidence that our new guidance design is not only effective but also efficient.

(ii) Repetitive guidance. When the recursion number k of EG increases, the errors of (c) and (d) are 6.3 mm and 11.2 mm significantly lower than that of (b) respectively. Meanwhile, as illustrated in Fig. 6, since our repetition in depth (d) can continuously model high-frequency components, the intermediate depth feature possesses more detailed boundaries and the corresponding image

Table 6. Ablation studies of RG/AF on KITTI validation set. RG-EG$_k$ refer to the case where we repeatedly use EG k times. '±0' refers to 23.37 GB. G$_1$ represents the raw guided convolution in GuideNet [47], which is used only once in one fusion stage.

Method	RHN$_3$	RG				AF			Memory	RMSE
		G$_1$	EG$_1$	EG$_2$	EG$_3$	Add	Concat	Ours	(GB)	(mm)
Baseline		✓							±0	778.6
(a)	✓	✓							+1.35	769.0
(b)	✓		✓						−10.60	768.6
(c)	✓		✓	✓					+2.65	762.3
(d)	✓		✓	✓	✓				+13.22	757.4
(e)	✓		✓	✓	✓	✓			+13.22	755.8
(f)	✓		✓	✓	✓		✓		+13.22	754.6
(g)	✓		✓	✓	✓			✓	+13.28	**752.1**

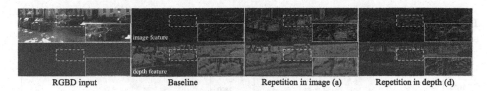

| RGBD input | Baseline | Repetition in image (a) | Repetition in depth (d) |

Fig. 6. Visual comparisons of intermediate features of the baseline and our repetition.

guidance branch consistently has a high response nearby the regions. These facts forcefully demonstrate the effectiveness of our repetitive guidance design.

(iii) Adaptive fusion. Based on (d) that directly outputs the feature of RG-EG$_3$, we choose to utilize all features of RG-EG$_k$ ($k = 1, 2, 3$) to produce better depth representations. (e), (f), and (g) refer to addition, concatenation, and our AF strategies, respectively. Specifically in (f), we conduct a 3×3 convolution to control the channel to be the same as RG-EG$_3$'s after concatenation. As we can see from the 'AF' column of Table 6, all of the three strategies improve the performance of the model with a little bit GPU memory sacrifice (about 0–0.06 GB), which demonstrates that aggregating multi-step features in repetitive procedure is effective. Furthermore, our AF mechanism obtains the best result among them, outperforming (d) 5.3 mm. These facts prove that our AF design benefits the system better than simple fusion strategies. Detailed difference of intermediate features produced by our repetitive design is shown in Figs. 2 and 6.

5.6 Generalization Capabilities

In this subsection, we further validate the generalization capabilities of our RigNet on different sparsity, including the number of valid points, various lighting and weather conditions, and the synthetic pattern of sparse data. The corresponding results are illustrated in Figs. 7 and 8.

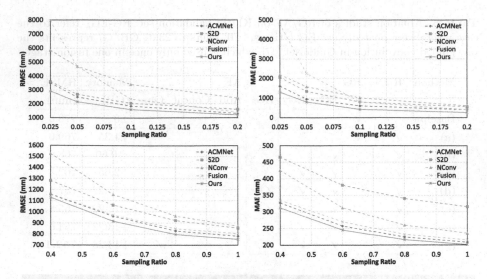

Fig. 7. Comparisons under different levels of sparsity on KITTI validation split. The solid lines refer to our method while the dotted ones represent other approaches.

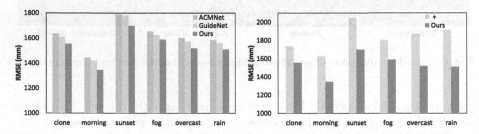

Fig. 8. Comparisons with existing methods (left) and itself (right) replacing 'RG' with '+', under different lighting and weather conditions on Virtual KITTI test split.

(1) Number of Valid Points

On KITTI selected validation split, we compare our method with four well-known approaches with available codes, *i.e.*, S2D [33], Fusion [49], NConv [10], and ACMNet [59]. Note that, all models are pretrained on KITTI training split with raw sparsity, which is equivalent to sampling ratios of 1.0, but not fine-tuned on the generated depth inputs. Specifically, we first uniformly sample the raw depth maps with ratios (0.025, 0.05, 0.1, 0.2) and (0.4, 0.6, 0.8, 1.0) to produce the sparse depth inputs. Then we test the pretrained models on the inputs. Figure 7 shows our RigNet significantly outperforms others under all levels of sparsity in terms of both RMSE and MAE metrics. These results indicates that our method can deal well with complex data inputs.

(2) Lighting and Weather Condition

The lighting condition of KITTI dataset is almost invariable and the weather condition is good. However, both lighting and weather conditions are vitally important for depth completion, especially for self-driving service. Therefore, we fine-tune our RigNet (trained on KITTI) on 'clone' of Virtual KITTI [11] and test under all other different lighting and weather conditions. As shown in the right of Fig. 8, we compare 'RG' with '+' (replace RG with addition), our method outperforms '+' with large margin on RMSE. The left of Fig. 8 further demonstrates that RigNet has better performance than GuideNet [47] and ACMNet [59] in complex environments. These results verify that our method is able to handle polytropic lighting and weather conditions.

In summary, all above-mentioned evidences demonstrate that the proposed approach has robust generalization capabilities.

6 Conclusion

In this paper, we explored the repetitive design in our image guided network for depth completion task. We pointed out that there were two issues impeding the performance of existing outstanding methods, *i.e.*, the blurry guidance in image and unclear structure in depth. To tackle the former issue, in our image guidance branch, we presented a repetitive hourglass network to produce discriminative image features. To alleviate the latter issue, in our depth generation branch, we designed a repetitive guidance module to gradually predict structure-detailed depth maps. Meanwhile, to model high-frequency components and reduce GPU memory consumption of the module, we proposed an efficient guidance algorithm. Furthermore, we designed an adaptive fusion mechanism to automatically fuse multi-stage depth features for better predictions. Extensive experiments show that our method achieves outstanding performances.

Acknowledgement. The authors would like to thank reviewers for their detailed comments and instructive suggestions. This work was supported by the National Science Fund of China under Grant Nos. U1713208, 62072242 and Postdoctoral Innovative Talent Support Program of China under Grant BX20200168, 2020M681608. Note that the PCA Lab is associated with, Key Lab of Intelligent Perception and Systems for High-Dimensional Information of Ministry of Education, and Jiangsu Key Lab of Image and Video Understanding for Social Security, Nanjing University of Science and Technology.

References

1. Armbrüster, C., Wolter, M., Kuhlen, T., Spijkers, W., Fimm, B.: Depth perception in virtual reality: distance estimations in peri-and extrapersonal space. Cyberpsychology & Behavior **11**(1), 9–15 (2008)
2. Cai, Z., Vasconcelos, N.: Cascade r-cnn: Delving into high quality object detection. In: CVPR. pp. 6154–6162 (2018)
3. Chen, Y., Yang, B., Liang, M., Urtasun, R.: Learning joint 2d–3d representations for depth completion. In: ICCV. pp. 10023–10032 (2019)
4. Cheng, X., Wang, P., Guan, C., Yang, R.: Cspn++: Learning context and resource aware convolutional spatial propagation networks for depth completion. In: AAAI. pp. 10615–10622 (2020)

5. Cheng, X., Wang, P., Yang, R.: Learning depth with convolutional spatial propagation network. In: ECCV, pp. 103–119 (2018)
6. Chodosh, N., Wang, C., Lucey, S.: Deep convolutional compressed sensing for lidar depth completion, In: ACCV. pp. 499–513 (2018)
7. Cui, Z., Heng, L., Yeo, Y.C., Geiger, A., Pollefeys, M., Sattler, T.: Real-time dense mapping for self-driving vehicles using fisheye cameras. In: ICR, pp. 6087–6093 (2019)
8. Dey, A., Jarvis, G., Sandor, C., Reitmayr, G.: Tablet versus phone: depth perception in handheld augmented reality. In: ISMAR, pp. 187–196 (2012)
9. Dosovitskiy, A., Ros, G., Codevilla, F., Lopez, A., Koltun, V.: Carla: an open urban driving simulator. In: CoRL, pp. 1–16. PMLR (2017)
10. Eldesokey, A., Felsberg, M., Khan, F.S.: Confidence propagation through CNNs for guided sparse depth regression. IEEE Trans. Pattern Anal. Mach. Intell. **42**(10), 2423–2436 (2020)
11. Gaidon, A., Wang, Q., Cabon, Y., Vig, E.: Virtual worlds as proxy for multi-object tracking analysis. In: CVPR, pp. 4340–4349 (2016)
12. Gao, R., Chen, C., Al-Halah, Z., Schissler, C., Grauman, K.: VISUALECHOES: spatial image representation learning through echolocation. In: Vedaldi, A., Bischof, H., Brox, T., Frahm, J.-M. (eds.) ECCV 2020. LNCS, vol. 12354, pp. 658–676. Springer, Cham (2020). https://doi.org/10.1007/978-3-030-58545-7_38
13. Ghiasi, G., Lin, T.Y., Le, Q.V.: NAS-FPN: learning scalable feature pyramid architecture for object detection. In: CVPR, pp. 7036–7045 (2019)
14. Häne, C., et al.: 3d visual perception for self-driving cars using a multi-camera system: calibration, mapping, localization, and obstacle detection. Image Vis. Comput. **68**, 14–27 (2017)
15. He, K., Zhang, X., Ren, S., Sun, J.: Deep residual learning for image recognition. In: CVPR, pp. 770–778 (2016)
16. Hu, J., Shen, L., Sun, G.: Squeeze-and-excitation networks. In: CVPR, pp. 7132–7141 (2018)
17. Hu, M., Wang, S., Li, B., Ning, S., Fan, L., Gong, X.: PENet: towards precise and efficient image guided depth completion. In: ICRA (2021)
18. Huang, Y.K., Wu, T.H., Liu, Y.C., Hsu, W.H.: Indoor depth completion with boundary consistency and self-attention. In: ICCV Workshops (2019)
19. Imran, S., Liu, X., Morris, D.: Depth completion with twin surface extrapolation at occlusion boundaries. In: CVPR, pp. 2583–2592 (2021)
20. Imran, S., Long, Y., Liu, X., Morris, D.: Depth coefficients for depth completion. In: CVPR, pp. 12438–12447. IEEE (2019)
21. Ioffe, S., Szegedy, C.: Batch normalization: Accelerating deep network training by reducing internal covariate shift. In: ICML, pp. 448–456. PMLR (2015)
22. Jaritz, M., De Charette, R., Wirbel, E., Perrotton, X., Nashashibi, F.: Sparse and dense data with CNNs: depth completion and semantic segmentation. In: 3DV, pp. 52–60 (2018)
23. Kingma, D.P., Ba, J.: Adam: a method for stochastic optimization. In: Computer Ence (2014)
24. Ku, J., Harakeh, A., Waslander, S.L.: In defense of classical image processing: Fast depth completion on the CPU. In: CRV, pp. 16–22 (2018)
25. Lee, B.U., Lee, K., Kweon, I.S.: Depth completion using plane-residual representation. In: CVPR, pp. 13916–13925 (2021)
26. Li, A., Yuan, Z., Ling, Y., Chi, W., Zhang, C., et al.: A multi-scale guided cascade hourglass network for depth completion. In: WACV, pp. 32–40 (2020)

27. Li, X., Wang, W., Hu, X., Yang, J.: Selective kernel networks. In: CVPR, pp. 510–519 (2019)
28. Lin, T.Y., Dollár, P., Girshick, R., He, K., Hariharan, B., Belongie, S.: Feature pyramid networks for object detection. In: CVPR, pp. 2117–2125 (2017)
29. Liu, L., et al.: FCFR-Net: feature fusion based coarse-to-fine residual learning for depth completion. In: AAAI, vol. 35, pp. 2136–2144 (2021)
30. Liu, S., Qi, L., Qin, H., Shi, J., Jia, J.: Path aggregation network for instance segmentation. In: CVPR, pp. 8759–8768 (2018)
31. Liu, Y., et al.: CBNet: a novel composite backbone network architecture for object detection. In: AAAI, vol. 34, pp. 11653–11660 (2020)
32. Lu, K., Barnes, N., Anwar, S., Zheng, L.: From depth what can you see? depth completion via auxiliary image reconstruction. In: CVPR, pp. 11306–11315 (2020)
33. Ma, F., Cavalheiro, G.V., Karaman, S.: Self-supervised sparse-to-dense: self-supervised depth completion from lidar and monocular camera. In: ICRA (2019)
34. Ma, F., Karaman, S.: Sparse-to-dense: depth prediction from sparse depth samples and a single image. In: ICRA, pp. 4796–4803. IEEE (2018)
35. Parida, K.K., Srivastava, S., Sharma, G.: Beyond image to depth: improving depth prediction using echoes. In: CVPR, pp. 8268–8277 (2021)
36. Park, J., Joo, K., Hu, Z., Liu, C.K., Kweon, I.S.: Non-local spatial propagation network for depth completion. In: ECCV (2020)
37. Qiao, S., Chen, L.C., Yuille, A.: Detectors: detecting objects with recursive feature pyramid and switchable atrous convolution. In: CVPR, pp. 10213–10224 (2021)
38. Qiu, J., et al.: DeepLiDAR: deep surface normal guided depth prediction for outdoor scene from sparse lidar data and single color image. In: CVPR, pp. 3313–3322 (2019)
39. Qu, C., Liu, W., Taylor, C.J.: Bayesian deep basis fitting for depth completion with uncertainty. In: ICCV, pp. 16147–16157 (2021)
40. Ren, S., He, K., Girshick, R., Sun, J.: Faster R-CNN: towards real-time object detection with region proposal networks. NeurIPS **28**, 91–99 (2015)
41. Ronneberger, O., Fischer, P., Brox, T.: U-net: convolutional networks for biomedical image segmentation. In: Navab, N., Hornegger, J., Wells, W.M., Frangi, A.F. (eds.) MICCAI 2015. LNCS, vol. 9351, pp. 234–241. Springer, Cham (2015). https://doi.org/10.1007/978-3-319-24574-4_28
42. Shen, Z., Lin, C., Liao, K., Nie, L., Zheng, Z., Zhao, Y.: PanoFormer: panorama transformer for indoor 360 depth estimation. arXiv e-prints pp. arXiv-2203 (2022)
43. Shen, Z., Lin, C., Nie, L., Liao, K., Zhao, Y.: Distortion-tolerant monocular depth estimation on omnidirectional images using dual-cubemap. In: ICME, pp. 1–6. IEEE (2021)
44. Silberman, N., Hoiem, D., Kohli, P., Fergus, R.: Indoor segmentation and support inference from RGBD images. In: Fitzgibbon, A., Lazebnik, S., Perona, P., Sato, Y., Schmid, C. (eds.) ECCV 2012. LNCS, vol. 7576, pp. 746–760. Springer, Heidelberg (2012). https://doi.org/10.1007/978-3-642-33715-4_54
45. Song, X., et al.: Channel attention based iterative residual learning for depth map super-resolution. In: CVPR, pp. 5631–5640 (2020)
46. Tan, M., Pang, R., Le, Q.V.: EfficientDet: scalable and efficient object detection. In: CVPR, pp. 10781–10790 (2020)
47. Tang, J., Tian, F.P., Feng, W., Li, J., Tan, P.: Learning guided convolutional network for depth completion. IEEE Trans. Image Process. **30**, 1116–1129 (2020)
48. Uhrig, J., Schneider, N., Schneider, L., Franke, U., Brox, T., Geiger, A.: Sparsity invariant CNNs. In: 3DV, pp. 11–20 (2017)

49. Van Gansbeke, W., Neven, D., De Brabandere, B., Van Gool, L.: Sparse and noisy lidar completion with RGB guidance and uncertainty. In: MVA, pp. 1–6 (2019)
50. Wang, K., et al.: Regularizing nighttime weirdness: efficient self-supervised monocular depth estimation in the dark. In: ICCV, pp. 16055–16064 (2021)
51. Xu, Y., Zhu, X., Shi, J., Zhang, G., Bao, H., Li, H.: Depth completion from sparse lidar data with depth-normal constraints. In: ICCV, pp. 2811–2820 (2019)
52. Xu, Z., Yin, H., Yao, J.: Deformable spatial propagation networks for depth completion. In: ICIP, pp. 913–917. IEEE (2020)
53. Yang, Y., Wong, A., Soatto, S.: Dense depth posterior (DDP) from single image and sparse range. In: CVPR, pp. 3353–3362 (2020)
54. Zeiler, M.D., Fergus, R.: Visualizing and understanding convolutional networks. In: Fleet, D., Pajdla, T., Schiele, B., Tuytelaars, T. (eds.) ECCV 2014. LNCS, vol. 8689, pp. 818–833. Springer, Cham (2014). https://doi.org/10.1007/978-3-319-10590-1_53
55. Zhang, H., et al.: Context encoding for semantic segmentation. In: CVPR, pp. 7151–7160 (2018)
56. Zhang, Y., Funkhouser, T.: Deep depth completion of a single RGB-d image. In: CVPR, pp. 175–185 (2018)
57. Zhang, Z., Cui, Z., Xu, C., Yan, Y., Sebe, N., Yang, J.: Pattern-affinitive propagation across depth, surface normal and semantic segmentation. In: CVPR, pp. 4106–4115 (2019)
58. Zhao, H., Shi, J., Qi, X., Wang, X., Jia, J.: Pyramid scene parsing network. In: CVPR, pp. 2881–2890 (2017)
59. Zhao, S., Gong, M., Fu, H., Tao, D.: Adaptive context-aware multi-modal network for depth completion. IEEE Trans. Image Process. **30**, 5264–5276 (2021)
60. Zhu, Y., Dong, W., Li, L., Wu, J., Li, X., Shi, G.: Robust depth completion with uncertainty-driven loss functions. arXiv preprint arXiv:2112.07895 (2021)

FADE: Fusing the Assets of Decoder and Encoder for Task-Agnostic Upsampling

Hao Lu, Wenze Liu, Hongtao Fu, and Zhiguo Cao

School of Artificial Intelligence and Automation, Huazhong University of Science and Technology, Wuhan 430074, China
{hlu,wzliu,htfu,zgcao}@hust.edu.cn

Abstract. We consider the problem of task-agnostic feature upsampling in dense prediction where an upsampling operator is required to facilitate both region-sensitive tasks like semantic segmentation and detail-sensitive tasks such as image matting. Existing upsampling operators often can work well in either type of the tasks, but not both. In this work, we present FADE, a novel, plug-and-play, and task-agnostic upsampling operator. FADE benefits from three design choices: i) considering encoder and decoder features jointly in upsampling kernel generation; ii) an efficient semi-shift convolutional operator that enables granular control over how each feature point contributes to upsampling kernels; iii) a decoder-dependent gating mechanism for enhanced detail delineation. We first study the upsampling properties of FADE on toy data and then evaluate it on large-scale semantic segmentation and image matting. In particular, FADE reveals its effectiveness and task-agnostic characteristic by consistently outperforming recent dynamic upsampling operators in different tasks. It also generalizes well across convolutional and transformer architectures with little computational overhead. Our work additionally provides thoughtful insights on what makes for task-agnostic upsampling. Code is available at: http://lnkiy.in/fade_in.

Keywords: Feature upsampling · Dense prediction · Dynamic networks · Semantic segmentation · Image matting

1 Introduction

Feature upsampling, which aims to recover the spatial resolution of features, is an indispensable stage in many dense prediction models [1,25,34,36,37,41]. Conventional upsampling operators, such as nearest neighbor (NN) or bilinear interpolation [15], deconvolution [40], and pixel shuffle [26], often have a preference of a specific task. For instance, bilinear interpolation is favored in semantic segmentation [4,37], and pixel shuffle is preferred in image super-resolution [14].

Supplementary Information The online version contains supplementary material available at https://doi.org/10.1007/978-3-031-19812-0_14.

S. Avidan et al. (Eds.): ECCV 2022, LNCS 13687, pp. 231–247, 2022.
https://doi.org/10.1007/978-3-031-19812-0_14

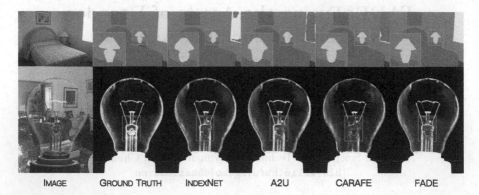

IMAGE   GROUND TRUTH   INDEXNET   A2U   CARAFE   FADE

Fig. 1. Inferred segmentation masks and alpha mattes with different upsampling operators. The compared operators include IndexNet [19], A2U [7], CARAFE [32], and our proposed FADE. Among all competitors, only FADE generates both the high-quality mask and the alpha matte.

A main reason is that each dense prediction task has its own focus: some tasks like semantic segmentation [18] and instance segmentation [11] are region-sensitive, while some tasks such as image super-resolution [8] and image matting [19,39] are detail-sensitive. If one expects an upsampling operator to generate semantically consistent features such that a region can share the same class label, it is often difficult for the same operator to recover boundary details simultaneously, and vice versa. Indeed empirical evidence shows that bilinear interpolation and max unpooling [1] have inverse behaviors in segmentation and matting [19,20], respectively.

In an effort to evade 'trials-and-errors' from choosing an upsampling operator for a certain task at hand, there has been a growing interest in developing a generic upsampling operator for dense prediction recently [7,19,20,22,30,32,33]. For example, CARAFE [32] demonstrates its benefits on four dense prediction tasks, including object detection, instance segmentation, semantic segmentation, and image inpainting. IndexNet [19] also boosts performance on several tasks such as image matting, image denoising, depth prediction, and image reconstruction. However, a comparison between CARAFE and IndexNet [20] indicates that neither CARAFE nor IndexNet can defeat its opponent on both region- and detail-sensitive tasks (CARAFE outperforms IndexNet on segmentation, while IndexNet is superior than CARAFE on matting), which can also be observed from the inferred segmentation masks and alpha mattes in Fig. 1. This raises an interesting question: *Does there exist a unified form of upsampling operator that is truly task-agnostic?*

To answer the question above, we present FADE, a novel, plug-and-play, and task-agnostic upsampling operator which Fuses the Assets of Decoder and Encoder (FADE). The name also implies its working mechanism: upsampling features in a 'fade-in' manner, from recovering spatial structure to delineating subtle details. In particular, we argue that an ideal upsampling operator should be able to preserve the semantic information and compensate the detailed information lost due to downsampling. The former is embedded in decoder features; the latter is abundant in encoder features. Therefore, we hypothesize that it is the insufficient use of encoder and decoder features bringing the task dependency of upsampling, and our idea is to design FADE to make the best use of encoder and decoder features, inspiring the following insights and contributions:

i) By exploring why CARAFE works well on region-sensitive tasks but poorly on detail-sensitive tasks, and why IndexNet and A2U [7] behave conversely, we observe that what features (encoder or decoder) to use to generate the upsampling kernels matters. Using decoder features can strengthen the regional continuity, while using encoder features helps recover details. It is thus natural to seek whether combining encoder and decoder features enjoys both merits, which underpins the core idea of FADE.

ii) To integrate encoder and decoder features, a subsequent problem is how to deal with the resolution mismatch between them. A standard way is to implement UNet-style fusion [25], including feature interpolation, feature concatenation, and convolution. However, we show that this naive implementation can have a negative effect on upsampling kernels. To solve this, we introduce a semi-shift convolutional operator that unifies channel compression, concatenation, and kernel generation. Particularly, it allows granular control over how each feature point participates in the computation of upsampling kernels. The operator is also fast and memory-efficient due to direct execution of cross-resolution convolution, without explicit feature interpolation for resolution matching.

iii) To enhance detail delineation, we further devise a gating mechanism, conditioned on decoder features. The gate allows selective pass of fine details in the encoder features as a refinement of upsampled features.

We conduct experiments on five data sets covering three dense prediction tasks. We first validate our motivation and the rationale of our design through several toy-level and small-scale experiments, such as binary image segmentation on Weizmann Horse [2], image reconstruction on Fashion-MNIST [35], and semantic segmentation on SUN RGBD [27]. We then present a thorough evaluation of FADE on large-scale semantic segmentation on ADE20K [42] and image matting on Adobe Composition-1K [39]. FADE reveals its task-agnostic characteristic by consistently outperforming state-of-the-art upsampling operators on both region- and detail-sensitive tasks, while also retaining the lightweight property by appending relatively few parameters and FLOPs. It has also good generalization across convolutional and transformer architectures [13,37].

To our knowledge, FADE is the first task-agnostic upsampling operator that performs favorably on both region- and detail-sensitive tasks.

2   Related Work

Feature Upsampling. Unlike joint image upsampling [12,31], feature upsampling operators are mostly developed in the deep learning era, to respond to the need for recovering spatial resolution of encoder features (decoding). Conventional upsampling operators typically use fixed/hand-crafted kernels. For instance, the kernels in the widely used NN and bilinear interpolation are defined by the relative distance between pixels. Deconvolution [40], *a.k.a.* transposed convolution, also applies a fixed kernel during inference, despite the kernel parameters are learned. Pixel shuffle [26] instead only includes memory operations but still follows a specific rule in upsampling by reshaping the depth channel into the spatial channels. Among hand-crafted operators, unpooling [1] perhaps is the only operator that has a dynamic upsampling behavior, *i.e.*, each upsampled position is data-dependent conditioned on the max operator. Recently the importance of the dynamic property has been proved by some dynamic upsampling operators [7,19,32]. CARAFE [32] implements context-aware reassembly of features, IndexNet [19] provides an indexing perspective of upsampling, and A2U [7] introduces affinity-aware upsampling. At the core of these operators is the data-dependent upsampling kernels whose kernel parameters are predicted by a sub-network. This points out a promising direction from considering generic feature upsampling. FADE follows the vein of dynamic feature upsampling.

Dense Prediction. Dense prediction covers a broad class of per-pixel labeling tasks, ranging from mainstream object detection [23], semantic segmentation [18], instance segmentation [11], and depth estimation [9] to low-level image restoration [21], image matting [39], edge detection [38], and optical flow estimation [29], to name a few. An interesting property about dense prediction is that a task can be region-sensitive or detail-sensitive. The sensitivity is closely related to what metric is used to assess the task. In this sense, semantic/instance segmentation is region-sensitive, because the standard Mask Intersection-over-Union (IoU) metric [10] is mostly affected by regional mask prediction quality, instead of boundary quality. On the contrary, image matting can be considered detail-sensitive, because the error metrics [24] are mainly computed from trimap regions that are full of subtle details or transparency. Note that, when we emphasize region sensitivity, we do not mean that details are not important, and vice versa. In fact, the emergence of Boundary IoU [5] implies that the limitation of a certain evaluation metric has been noticed by our community. The goal of developing a task-agnostic upsampling operator capable of both regional preservation and detail delineation can have a board impact on a number of dense prediction tasks. In this work, we mainly evaluate upsampling operators on semantic segmentation and image matting, which may be the most representative region- and detail-sensitive task, respectively.

3   Task-Agnostic Upsampling: A Trade-off Between Semantic Preservation and Detail Delineation

Before we present FADE, we share some of our view points towards task-agnostic upsampling, which may be helpful to understand our designs in FADE.

How Encoder and Decoder Features Affect Upsampling. In dense prediction models, downsampling stages are involved to acquire a large receptive field,

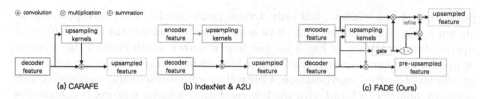

Fig. 2. Use of encoder and/or decoder features in different upsampling operators. (a) CARAFE generates upsampling kernels conditioned on decoder features, while (b) IndexNet and A2U generate kernels using encoder features only. By contrast, (c) FADE considers both encoder and decoder features not only in upsampling kernel generation but also in gated feature refinement.

bringing the need of peer-to-peer upsampling stages to recover the spatial resolution, which together constitutes the basic encoder-decoder architecture. During downsampling, details of high-resolution features are impaired or even lost, but the resulting low-resolution encoder features often have good semantic meanings that can pass to decoder features. Hence, we believe an ideal upsampling operator should appropriately resolve two issues: 1) preserve the semantic information already extracted; 2) compensate as many lost details as possible without deteriorating the semantic information. NN or bilinear interpolation only meets the former. This conforms to our intuition that interpolation often smooths features. A reason is that low-resolution decoder features have no prior knowledge about missing details. Other operators that directly upsample decoder features, such as deconvolution and pixel shuffle, can have the same problem with poor detail compensation. Compensating details requires high-resolution encoder features. This is why unpooling that stores indices before downsampling has good boundary delineation [19], but it hurts the semantic information due to zero-filling.

Dynamic upsampling operators, including CARAFE [32], IndexNet [19], and A2U [7], alleviate the problems above with data-dependent upsampling kernels. Their upsampling modes are illustrated in Fig. 2(a)-(b). From Fig. 2, it can be observed that, CARAFE generates upsampling kernels conditioned on decoder features, while IndexNet [19] and A2U [7] generate kernels via encoder features. This may explain the inverse behavior between CARAFE and IndexNet/A2U on region- or detail-sensitive tasks [20]. In this work, we find that generating upsampling kernels using either encoder or decoder features can lead to suboptimal results, and it is critical *to leverage both encoder and decoder features for task-agnostic upsampling*, as implemented in FADE (Fig. 2(c)).

How Each Feature Point Contributes to Upsampling Matters. After deciding what the features to use, the follow-up question is how to use the features effectively and efficiently. The main obstacle is the mismatched resolution between encoder and decoder feature maps. One may consider simple interpolation for resolution matching, but we find that this leads to sub-optimal upsampling. Considering the case of applying ×2 NN interpolation to decoder features, if we apply 3 × 3 convolution to generate the upsampling kernel, the effective receptive field of the kernel can be reduced to be < 50%: before interpolation there are 9 valid points in a 3 × 3 window, but only 4 valid points are left after interpolation, as shown in Fig. 5(a). Besides this, there is another more important issue. Still in ×2 upsampling, as shown in Fig. 5(a), the four windows which control the variance of upsampling kernels w.r.t. the 2 × 2 neighbors of high resolution are influenced by the hand-crafted interpolation. Controlling a high-resolution upsampling kernel map, however, is blind with the low-resolution decoder feature. It contributes little to an informative upsampling kernel, especially to the variance of the four neighbors in the upsampling kernel map. Interpolation as a bias of that variance can even worsen the kernel generation. A more reasonable choice may be to *let encoder and decoder features cooperate to control the overall upsampling kernel, but let the encoder feature alone control the variance of the four neighbors.* This insight exactly motivates the design of semi-shift convolution (Sect. 4).

Exploiting Encoder Features for Further Detail Refinement. Besides helping structural recovery via upsampling kernels, there remains much useful information in the encoder features. Since encoder features only go through a few layers of a network, they preserve 'fine details' of high resolution. In fact, nearly all dense prediction tasks require fine details, *e.g.*, despite regional prediction dominates in instance segmentation, accurate boundary prediction can also significantly boost performance [28], not to mention the stronger request of fine details in detail-sensitive tasks. *The demands of fine details in dense prediction need further exploitation of encoder features.* Instead of simply skipping the encoder features, we introduce a gating mechanism that leverages decoder features to guide where the encoder features can pass through.

4   Fusing the Assets of Decoder and Encoder

Dynamic Upsampling Revisited. Here we review some basic operations in recent dynamic upsampling operators such as CARAFE [32], IndexNet [19], and A2U [7]. Figure 2 briefly summarizes their upsampling modes. They share an identical pipeline, *i.e.*, first generating data-dependent upsampling kernels, and then reassembling the decoder features using the kernels. Typical dynamic upsampling kernels are content-aware, but channel-shared, which means each position has a unique upsampling kernel in the spatial dimension, but the same ones are shared in the channel dimension.

CARAFE learns upsampling kernels directly from decoder features and then reassembles them to high resolution. In particular, the decoder features pass through two consecutive convolutional layers to generate the upsampling kernels, of which the former is a channel compressor implemented by 1 × 1 convolution to reduce the computational complexity and the latter is a content encoder with 3 × 3 convolution, and finally the softmax function is used to normalize the kernel weights. IndexNet and A2U, however, adopt more sophisticated modules to leverage the merit of encoder features. Further details can be referred to [7,19,32].

FADE is designed to maintain the simplicity of dynamic upsampling. Hence, it generally follows the pipeline of CARAFE, but further optimizes the process

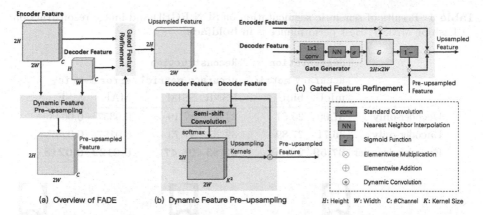

Fig. 3. Technical pipeline of FADE. From (a) the overview of FADE, feature upsampling is executed by jointly exploiting the encoder and decoder feature with two key modules. In (b) dynamic feature pre-upsampling, they are used to generate upsampling kernels using a semi-shift convolutional operator (Fig. 5). The kernels are then used to reassemble the decoder feature into pre-upsampled feature. In (c) gated feature refinement, the encoder and pre-upsampled features are modulated by a decoder-dependent gating mechanism to enhance detail delineation before generating the final upsampled feature.

of kernel generation with semi-shift convolution, and the channel compressor will also function as a way of pre-fusing encoder and decoder features. In addition, FADE also includes a gating mechanism for detail refinement. The overall pipeline of FADE is summarized in Fig. 3.

Generating Upsampling Kernels from Encoder and Decoder Features. We first showcase a few visualizations on some small-scale or toy-level data sets to highlight the importance of both encoder and decoder features for task-agnostic upsampling. We choose semantic segmentation on SUN RGBD [27] as the region-sensitive task and image reconstruction on Fashion MNIST [35] as the detail-sensitive one. We follow the network architectures and the experimental settings in [20]. Since we focus on upsampling, all downsampling stages use max pooling. Specifically, to show the impact of encoder and decoder features, in the segmentation experiments, we all use CARAFE but only modify the source of features used for generating upsampling kernels. We build three baselines: 1) *decoder-only*, the implementation of CARAFE; 2) *encoder-only*, where the upsampling kernels are generated from encoder features; 3) *encoder-decoder*, where the upsampling kernels are generated from the concatenation of encoder and NN-interpolated decoder features. We report Mask IoU (mIoU) [10] and Boundary IoU (bIoU) [5] for segmentation, and report Peak Signal-to-Noise Ratio (PSNR), Structural SIMilarity index (SSIM), Mean Absolute Error (MAE), and root Mean Square Error (MSE) for reconstruction. From Table 1, one can observe that the encoder-only baseline outperforms the decoder-only one in image reconstruction, but in semantic segmentation the trend is on the contrary. To understand why, we visualize the

238	H. Lu et al.

Table 1. Results of semantic segmentation on SUN RGBD and image reconstruction on Fashion MNIST. Best performance is in **boldface**.

| | Segmentation | | Reconstruction | | | |
| | accuracy metric↑ | | accuracy metric↑ | | error metric↓ | |
	mIoU	bIoU	PSNR	SSIM	MAE	MSE
Decoder-only	37.00	25.61	24.35	87.19	0.0357	0.0643
Encoder-only	36.71	27.89	32.25	97.73	0.0157	0.0257
Encoder-decoder	**37.59**	**28.80**	**33.83**	**98.47**	**0.0122**	**0.0218**

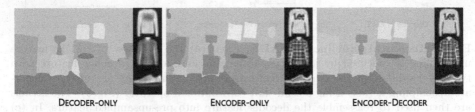

DECODER-ONLY   ENCODER-ONLY   ENCODER-DECODER

Fig. 4. Visualizations of inferred mask and reconstructed results on SUN RGBD and Fashion-MNIST. The decoder-only model generates good regional prediction but poor boundaries/textures, while the encoder-only one is on the contrary. When fusing encoder and decoder features, both region and detail predictions are improved, *e.g.*, the table lamp and stripes on clothes.

segmentation masks and reconstructed results in Fig. 4. We find that in segmentation the decoder-only model tends to produce region-continuous output, while the encoder-only one generates clear mask boundaries but blocky regions; in reconstruction, by contrast, the decoder-only model almost fails and can only generate low-fidelity reconstructions. It thus can be inferred that, encoder features help to predict details, while decoder features contribute to semantic preservation of regions. Indeed, by considering both encoder and decoder features, the resulting mask seems to integrate the merits of the former two, and the reconstructions are also full of details. Therefore, albeit a simple tweak, FADE significantly benefits from generating upsampling kernels with both encoder and decoder features, as illustrated in Fig. 2(c).

Semi-shift Convolution. Given encoder and decoder features, we next address how to use them to generate upsampling kernels. We investigate two implementations: a naive implementation and a customized implementation. The key difference between them is how each decoder feature point spatially corresponds to each encoder feature point. The naive implementation shown in Fig. 5(a) includes four operations: i) feature interpolation, ii) concatenation, iii) channel compression, iv) standard convolution for kernel generation, and v) softmax normalization. As aforementioned in Sect. 3, naive interpolation can have a few problems. To address them, we present semi-shift convolution that simplifies the first four operations above into a unified operator, which is schematically illustrated in Fig. 5(b). Note that the 4 convolution windows in encoder features all correspond to the same

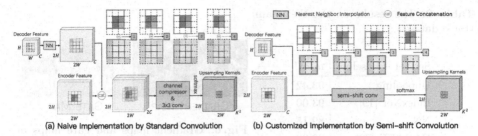

(a) Naive Implementation by Standard Convolution   (b) Customized Implementation by Semi–shift Convolution

Fig. 5. Two forms of implementations for generating upsampling kernels. Naive implementation requires matching resolution with explicit feature interpolation and concatenation, followed by channel compression and standard convolution for kernel prediction. Our customized implementation simplifies the whole process with only semi-shift convolution.

window in decoder features. This design has the following advantages: 1) the role of control in the kernel generation is made clear where the control of the variance of 2×2 neighbors is moved to encoder features completely; 2) the receptive field of decoder features is kept consistent with that of encoder features; 3) memory cost is reduced, because semi-shift convolution directly operates on low-resolution decoder features, without feature interpolation; 4) channel compression and 3×3 convolution can be merged in semi-shift convolution. Mathematically, the single window processing with naive implementation or semi-shift convolution has an identical form if ignoring the content of feature maps. For example, considering the top-left window ('1' in Fig. 5), the (unnormalized) upsampling kernel weight has the form

$$w_m = \sum_{l=1^d} \sum_{i=1^h} \sum_{j=1^h} \beta_{ijlm} \left(\sum_{k=1^{2C}} \alpha_{kl} x_{ijk} + a_l \right) + b_m \tag{1}$$

$$= \sum_{l=1^d} \sum_{i=1^h} \sum_{j=1^h} \beta_{ijlm} \left(\sum_{k=1^C} \alpha_{kl}^{en} x_{ijk}^{en} + \sum_{k=1^C} \alpha_{kl}^{de} x_{ijk}^{de} + a_l \right) + b_m \tag{2}$$

$$= \sum_{l=1^d} \sum_{i=1^h} \sum_{j=1^h} \beta_{ijlm} \sum_{k=1}^{C} \alpha_{kl}^{en} x_{ijk}^{en} + \sum_{l=1^d} \sum_{i=1^h} \sum_{j=1^h} \beta_{ijlm} \left(\sum_{k=1^C} \alpha_{kl}^{de} x_{ijk}^{de} + a_l \right) + b_m \tag{3}$$

where $w_m, m = 1, ..., K^2$, is the weight of the upsampling kernel, K the upsampling kernel size, h the convolution window size, C the number of input channel dimension of encoder and decoder features, and d the number of compressed channel dimension. α_{kl}^{en} and $\{\alpha_{kl}^+\text{de}, a_l\}$ are the parameters of 1×1 convolution specific to encoder and decoder features, respectively, and $\{\beta_{ijlm}, b_m\}$ the parameters of 3×3 convolution. Following CARAFE, we fix $h = 3$, $K = 5$ and $d = 64$.

According to Eq. (3), by the linearity of convolution, Eq. (1) and Eq. (2) are equivalent to applying two distinct 1×1 convolutions to C-channel encoder and C-channel decoder features, respectively, followed by a shared 3×3 convolution

Table 2. The results on the Weizmann Horse dataset.

SegNet – baseline	mIoU
Unpooling	93.42
IndexNet [19]	93.00
NN	89.15
CARAFE [32]	89.29
NN + Gate	95.26
CARAFE + Gate	95.25

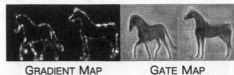

GRADIENT MAP   GATE MAP

Fig. 6. Gradient maps and gate maps of horses.

and summation. Equation (3) allows us to process encoder and decoder features without matching their resolution. To process the whole feature map, the window can move s steps on encoder features but only $\lfloor s/2 \rfloor$ steps on decoder features. This is why the operator is given the name 'semi-shift convolution'. To implement this efficiently, we split the process to 4 sub-processes; each sub-process focuses on the top-left, top-right, bottom-left, and bottom-right windows, respectively. Different sub-processes have also different prepossessing strategies. For example, for the top-left sub-process, we add full padding to the decoder feature, but only add padding on top and left to the encoder feature. Then all the top-left window correspondences can be satisfied by setting stride of 1 for the decoder feature and 2 for the encoder feature. Finally, after a few memory operations, the four sub-outputs can be reassembled to the expected upsampling kernel, and the kernel is used to reassemble decoder features to generate pre-upsampled features, as shown in Fig. 3(b).

Extracting Fine Details from Encoder Features. Here we further introduce a gating mechanism to complement fine details from encoder features to pre-upsampled features. We again use some experimental observations to showcase our motivation. We use a binary image segmentation dataset, Weizmann Horse [2]. The reasons for choosing this dataset are two-fold: (1) visualization is made simple; (2) the task is simple such that the impact of feature representation can be neglected. When all baselines have nearly perfect region predictions, the difference in detail prediction can be amplified. We use SegNet pretrained on ImageNet as the baseline and alter only the upsampling operators. Results are listed in Table 2. An interesting phenomenon is that CARAFE works almost the same as NN interpolation and even falls behind the default unpooling and IndexNet. An explanation is that the dataset is too simple such that the region smoothing property of CARAFE is wasted, but recovering details matters.

A common sense in segmentation is that, the interior of a certain class would be learned fast, while mask boundaries are difficult to predict. This can be observed from the gradient maps w.r.t. an intermediate decoder layer, as shown in Fig. 6. During the middle stage of training, most responses are near boundaries. Now that gradients reveal the demand of detail information, feature maps would also manifest this requisite with some distributions, e.g., in multi-class semantic segmentation a confident class prediction in a region would be a unimodal distribution along the channel dimension, and an uncertain prediction around boundaries would likely be a bimodal distribution. Hence, we assume that all decoder layers have gradient-imposed distribution priors and can be encoded to inform the requisite of detail or semantic information. In this way fine details can be chosen from encoder features without hurting the semantic property of decoder features. Hence, instead of directly skipping encoder features as in feature pyramid networks [16], we introduce a gating mechanism [6] to selectively refine pre-upsampled features using encoder features, conditioned on decoder features. The gate is generated through a 1×1 convolution layer, a NN interpolation layer, and a sigmoid function. As shown in Fig. 3(c), the decoder feature first goes through the gate generator, and the generator then outputs a gate map instantiated in Fig. 6. Finally, the gate map G modulates the encoder feature $\mathcal{F}_{encoder}$ and the pre-upsampled feature $\mathcal{F}_{pre-upsampled}$ to generate the final upsampled feature $\mathcal{F}_{upsampled}$ as

$$\mathcal{F}_{upsampled} = \mathcal{F}_{encoder} \cdot G + \mathcal{F}_{pre-upsampled} \cdot (1 - G). \qquad (4)$$

From Table 2, the gating mechanism works on both NN and CARAFE.

5 Results and Discussions

Here we formally validate FADE on large-scale dense prediction tasks, including image matting and semantic segmentation. We also conduct ablation studies to justify each design choice of FADE. In addition, we analyze computational complexity in terms of parameter counts and GFLOPs.

5.1 Image Matting

Image matting [39] is chosen as the representative of the detail-sensitive task. It requires a model to estimate the accurate alpha matte that smoothly splits foreground from background. Since ground-truth alpha mattes can exhibit significant differences among local regions, estimations are sensitive to a specific upsampling operator used [7,19].

Data Set, Metrics, Baseline, and Protocols. We conduct experiments on the Adobe Image Matting dataset [39], whose training set has 431 unique foreground objects and ground-truth alpha mattes. Following [7], instead of compositing each foreground with fixed 100 background images chosen from MS COCO [17], we randomly choose background images in each iteration and generate composited images on-the-fly. The Composition-1K testing set has 50 unique foreground objects, and each is composited with 20 background images from PASCAL VOC [10]. We report the widely used Sum of Absolute Differences (SAD), Mean Squared Error (MSE), Gradient (Grad), and Connectivity (Conn) and evaluate them using the code provided by [39].

Table 3. Image matting and semantic segmentation results on the Adobe Composition-1k and ADE20K data sets. ΔParam. indicates the additional number of parameters compared with the bilinear baseline. Best performance is in **boldface**.

A2U matting/	Matting – error↓					Segm – accuracy↑		
SegFormer	SAD	MSE	Grad	Conn	ΔParam	mIoU	bIoU	ΔParam
Bilinear	37.31	0.0103	21.38	35.39	8.05M	41.68	27.80	13.7M
CARAFE [32]	41.01	0.0118	21.39	39.01	+0.26M	42.82	29.84	+0.44M
IndexNet [19]	34.28	0.0081	15.94	31.91	+12.26M	41.50	28.27	+12.60M
A2U [7]	32.15	0.0082	16.39	29.25	+38K	41.45	27.31	+0.12M
FADE (Ours)	**31.10**	**0.0073**	**14.52**	**28.11**	+0.12M	**44.41**	**32.65**	+0.29M

A2U Matting [7] is adopted as the baseline. Following [7], the baseline network adopts a backbone of the first 11 layers of ResNet-34 with in-place activated batchnorm [3] and a decoder consisting of a few upsampling stages with short-cut connections. Readers can refer to [7] for the detailed architecture. To control variables, we use max pooling in downsampling stages consistently and only alter upsampling operators to train the model. We strictly follow the training configurations and data augmentation strategies used in [7].

Matting Results. We compare FADE with other state-of-the-art upsampling operators. Quantitative results are shown in Table 3. Results show that FADE consistently outperforms other competitors in all metrics, with also few additional parameters. It is worth noting that IndexNet and A2U are strong baselines that are delicately designed upsampling operators for image matting. Also the worst performance of CARAFE indicates that upsampling with only decoder features cannot meet a detail-sensitive task. Compared with standard bilinear upsampling, FADE invites 16%∼32% relative improvement, which suggests upsampling can indeed make a difference, and our community should shift more attention to upsampling. Qualitative results are shown in Fig. 1. FADE generates a high-fidelity alpha matte.

5.2 Semantic Segmentation

Semantic segmentation is chosen as the representative region-sensitive task. To prove that FADE is architecture-independent, SegFormer [37], a recent transformer based segmentation model, is used as the baseline.

Data Set, Metrics, Baseline, and Protocols. We use the ADE20K dataset [42], which is a standard benchmark used to evaluate segmentation models. ADE20K covers 150 fine-grained semantic concepts, including 20210 images in the training set and 2000 images in the validation set. In addition to reporting the standard Mask IoU (mIoU) metric [10], we also include the Boundary IoU (bIoU) metric [5] to assess boundary quality.

Table 4. Ablation study on the source of features, the way for upsampling kernel generation, and the effect of the gating mechanism. Best performance is in **boldface**. en: encoder; de: decoder.

No.	A2U MattingSegFormer			Matting - error ↓				Segm - accuracy ↑	
	source of feat	Kernel gen	Fusion	SAD	MSE	Grad	Conn	mIoU	bIoU
B1	en			34.22	0.0087	15.90	32.03	42.75	31.00
B2	de			41.01	0.0118	21.39	39.01	42.82	29.84
B3	en & de	naive		32.41	0.0083	16.56	29.82	43.27	31.55
B4	en & de	semi-shift		31.78	0.0075	15.12	28.95	43.33	32.06
B5	en & de	semi-shift	skipping	32.64	0.0076	15.90	29.92	43.22	31.85
B6	en & de	semi-shift	gating	**31.10**	**0.0073**	**14.52**	**28.11**	**44.41**	**32.65**

SegFormer-B1 [37] is chosen by considering both the effectiveness and computational sources at hand. We keep the default model architecture in SegFomer except for modifying the upsampling stage in the MLP head. All training settings and implementation details are kept the same as in [37].

Segmentation Results. Quantitative results of different upsampling operators are also listed in Table 3. Similar to matting, FADE is the best performing upsampling operator in both mIoU and bIoU metrics. Note that, among compared upsampling operators, FADE is the only operator that exhibits the task-agnostic property. A2U is the second best operator in matting, but turns out to be the worst one in segmentation. CARAFE is the second best operator in segmentation, but is the worst one in matting. This implies that current dynamic operators still have certain weaknesses to achieve task-agnostic upsampling. Qualitative results are shown in Fig. 1. FADE generates high-quality prediction both within mask regions and near mask boundaries.

5.3 Ablation Study

Here we justify how performance is affected by the source of features, the way for upsampling kernel generation, and the use of the gating mechanism. We build six baselines based on FADE:

1) B1: *encoder-only*. Only encoder features go through 1×1 convolution for channel compression (64 channels), followed by 3×3 convolution layer for kernel generation;
2) B2: *decoder-only*. This is the CARAFE baseline [32]. Only decoder features go through the same 1×1 and 3×3 convolution for kernel generation, followed by Pixel Shuffle as in CARAFE due to different spatial resolution;
3) B3: *encoder-decoder-naive*. NN-interpolated decoder features are first concatenated with encoder features, and then the same two convolutional layers are applied;
4) B4: *encoder-decoder-semi-shift*. Instead of using NN interpolation and standard convolutional layers, we use semi-shift convolution to generate kernels directly as in FADE;

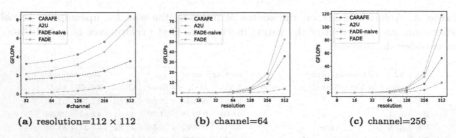

(a) resolution=112 × 112   (b) channel=64   (c) channel=256

Fig. 7. GFLOPs comparison between FADE and other upsampling operators.

5) B5: B4 with *skipping*. We directly skip the encoder features as in feature pyramid networks [16];
6) B6: B4 with *gating*. The full implementation of FADE.

Results are shown in Table 4. By comparing B1, B2, and B3, the experimental results give a further verification on the importance of both encoder and decoder features for upsampling kernel generation. By comparing B3 and B4, the results indicate a clear advantage of semi-shift convolution over naive implementation in the way of generating upsampling kernels. As aforementioned, the rationale that explains such a superiority can boil down to the granular control of the contribution of each feature point in kernels (Sect. 4). We also note that, even without gating, the performance of FADE already surpasses other upsampling operators (B4 vs. Table 3), which means the task-agnostic property is mainly due to the joint use of encoder and decoder features and the semi-shift convolution. In addition, skipping is clearly not the optimal way to move encoder details to decoder features, at least worse than the gating mechanism (B5 vs. B6).

5.4 Comparison of Computational Overhead

A favorable upsampling operator, being part of overall network architecture, should not significantly increase the computation cost. This issue is not well addressed in IndexNet as it significantly increases the number of parameters and computational overhead [19]. Here we measure GFLOPs of some upsampling operators by i) changing number of channels given fixed spatial resolution and by ii) varying spatial resolution given fixed number of channels. Figure 7 suggests FADE is also competitive in GFLOPs, especially when upsampling with relatively low spatial resolution and low channel numbers. In addition, semi-shift convolution can be considered a perfect replacement of the standard 'interpolation+convolution' paradigm for upsampling, not only superior in effectiveness but also in efficiency.

6 Conclusions

In this paper, we propose FADE, a novel, plug-and-play, and task-agnostic upsampling operator. For the first time, FADE demonstrates the feasibility of task-agnostic feature upsampling in both region- and detail-sensitive dense prediction tasks, outperforming the best upsampling operator A2U on image matting and the best operator CARAFE on semantic segmentation. With step-to-step analyses, we also share our view points from considering what makes for generic feature upsampling.

For future work, we plan to validate FADE on additional dense prediction tasks and also explore the peer-to-peer downsampling stage. So far, FADE is designed to maintain the simplicity by only implementing linear upsampling, which leaves much room for further improvement, e.g., with additional nonlinearity. In addition, we believe how to strengthen the coupling between encoder and decoder features to enable better cooperation can make a difference for feature upsampling.

Acknowledgement. This work is supported by the Natural Science Foundation of China under Grant No. 62106080.

References

1. Badrinarayanan, V., Kendall, A., Cipolla, R.: SegNet: a deep convolutional encoder-decoder architecture for image segmentation. IEEE Trans. Pattern Anal. Mach. Intell. **39**(12), 2481–2495 (2017)
2. Borenstein, E., Ullman, S.: Class-specific, top-down segmentation. In: Heyden, A., Sparr, G., Nielsen, M., Johansen, P. (eds.) ECCV 2002. LNCS, vol. 2351, pp. 109–122. Springer, Heidelberg (2002). https://doi.org/10.1007/3-540-47967-8_8
3. Bulo, S.R., Porzi, L., Kontschieder, P.: In-place activated batchnorm for memory-optimized training of DNNs. In: Proceedings of IEEE Conference on Computer Vision Pattern Recognition (CVPR), pp. 5639–5647 (2018)
4. Chen, L.-C., Zhu, Y., Papandreou, G., Schroff, F., Adam, H.: Encoder-decoder with atrous separable convolution for semantic image segmentation. In: Ferrari, V., Hebert, M., Sminchisescu, C., Weiss, Y. (eds.) Encoder-decoder with atrous separable convolution for semantic image segmentation. LNCS, vol. 11211, pp. 833–851. Springer, Cham (2018). https://doi.org/10.1007/978-3-030-01234-2_49
5. Cheng, B., Girshick, R., Dollár, P., Berg, A.C., Kirillov, A.: Boundary IOU: improving object-centric image segmentation evaluation. In: Proceedings of IEEE Conference on Computer Vision Pattern Recognition (CVPR), pp. 15334–15342 (2021)
6. Cho, K., Van Merriënboer, B., Bahdanau, D., Bengio, Y.: On the properties of neural machine translation: Encoder-decoder approaches. arXiv Computer Research Repository (2014)
7. Dai, Y., Lu, H., Shen, C.: Learning affinity-aware upsampling for deep image matting. In: Proceedings of IEEE Conference on Computer Vision Pattern Recognition (CVPR), pp. 6841–6850 (2021)
8. Dong, C., Loy, C.C., He, K., Tang, X.: Image super-resolution using deep convolutional networks. IEEE Trans. Pattern Anal. Mach. Intell. **38**(2), 295–307 (2015)
9. Eigen, D., Puhrsch, C., Fergus, R.: Depth map prediction from a single image using a multi-scale deep network. In: Proceedings of Annual Conference on Neural Information Processing Systems (NeurIPS), pp. 2366–2374 (2014)
10. Everingham, M., Van Gool, L., Williams, C.K., Winn, J., Zisserman, A.: The pascal visual object classes (VOC) challenge. Int. J. Comput. Vis. **88**(2), 303–338 (2010)

11. He, K., Gkioxari, G., Dollár, P., Girshick, R.: Mask R-CNN. In: Proceedings of IEEE International Conference on Computer Vision (ICCV), pp. 2961–2969 (2017)
12. He, K., Sun, J., Tang, X.: Guided image filtering. In: Daniilidis, K., Maragos, P., Paragios, N. (eds.) ECCV 2010. LNCS, vol. 6311, pp. 1–14. Springer, Heidelberg (2010). https://doi.org/10.1007/978-3-642-15549-9_1
13. He, K., Zhang, X., Ren, S., Sun, J.: Deep residual learning for image recognition. In: Proceedings of IEEE Conference on Computer Vision Pattern Recognition (CVPR), pp. 770–778 (2016)
14. Ignatov, A., Timofte, R., Denna, M., Younes, A.: Real-time quantized image super-resolution on mobile NPUS, mobile AI 2021 challenge: report. In: Proceedings of IEEE Conference on Computer Vision and Pattern Recognition (CVPR) Workshops, pp. 2525–2534, June 2021
15. Lin, G., Milan, A., Shen, C., Reid, I.: RefineNet: multi-path refinement networks for high-resolution semantic segmentation. In: Proceedings of IEEE Conference on Computer Vision Pattern Recognition (CVPR), pp. 1925–1934 (2017)
16. Lin, T.Y., Dollár, P., Girshick, R., He, K., Hariharan, B., Belongie, S.: Feature pyramid networks for object detection. In: Proceedings of IEEE Conference on Computer Vision Pattern Recognition (CVPR), pp. 2117–2125 (2017)
17. Lin, T.-Y., et al.: Microsoft COCO: common objects in context. In: Fleet, D., Pajdla, T., Schiele, B., Tuytelaars, T. (eds.) ECCV 2014. LNCS, vol. 8693, pp. 740–755. Springer, Cham (2014). https://doi.org/10.1007/978-3-319-10602-1_48
18. Long, J., Shelhamer, E., Darrell, T.: Fully convolutional networks for semantic segmentation. In: Proceedings of IEEE Conference on Computer Vision Pattern Recognition (CVPR), pp. 3431–3440 (2015)
19. Lu, H., Dai, Y., Shen, C., Xu, S.: Indices matter: learning to index for deep image matting. In: Proceedings of IEEE International Conference on Computer Vision (ICCV), pp. 3266–3275 (2019)
20. Lu, H., Dai, Y., Shen, C., Xu, S.: Index networks. IEEE Trans. Pattern Anal. Mach. Intell. **44**(1), 242–255 (2022)
21. Mao, X., Shen, C., Yang, Y.B.: Image restoration using very deep convolutional encoder-decoder networks with symmetric skip connections. In: Proceedings of Annual Conference on Neural Information Processing Systems (NeurIPS), pp. 2802–2810 (2016)
22. Mazzini, D.: Guided upsampling network for real-time semantic segmentation. In: Proceedings of British Machine Vision Conference (BMVC) (2018)
23. Ren, S., He, K., Girshick, R., Sun, J.: Faster R-CNN: towards real-time object detection with region proposal networks. In: Proceedings of Annual Conference on Neural Information Processing Systems (NeurIPS), 28 (2015)
24. Rhemann, C., Rother, C., Wang, J., Gelautz, M., Kohli, P., Rott, P.: A perceptually motivated online benchmark for image matting. In: Proceedings of IEEE Conference on Computer Vision Pattern Recognition (CVPR), pp. 1826–1833 (2009)
25. Ronneberger, O., Fischer, P., Brox, T.: U-net: convolutional networks for biomedical image segmentation. In: Navab, N., Hornegger, J., Wells, W.M., Frangi, A.F. (eds.) MICCAI 2015. LNCS, vol. 9351, pp. 234–241. Springer, Cham (2015). https://doi.org/10.1007/978-3-319-24574-4_28
26. Shi, W., et al.: Real-time single image and video super-resolution using an efficient sub-pixel convolutional neural network. In: Proceedings of IEEE Conference on Computer Vision Pattern Recognition (CVPR), pp. 1874–1883 (2016)
27. Song, S., Lichtenberg, S.P., Xiao, J.: SUN RGB-D: A RGB-D scene understanding benchmark suite. In: Proceedings of IEEE Conference on Computer Vision Pattern Recognition (CVPR), pp. 567–576 (2015)

28. Tang, C., Chen, H., Li, X., Li, J., Zhang, Z., Hu, X.: Look closer to segment better: Boundary patch refinement for instance segmentation. In: Proceedings of IEEE Conference on Computer Vision Pattern Recognition (CVPR), pp. 13926–13935 (2021)

29. Teed, Z., Deng, J.: RAFT: recurrent all-pairs field transforms for optical flow. In: Vedaldi, A., Bischof, H., Brox, T., Frahm, J.-M. (eds.) ECCV 2020. LNCS, vol. 12347, pp. 402–419. Springer, Cham (2020). https://doi.org/10.1007/978-3-030-58536-5_24

30. Tian, Z., He, T., Shen, C., Yan, Y.: Decoders matter for semantic segmentation: data-dependent decoding enables flexible feature aggregation. In: Proceedings of IEEE Conference on Computer Vision Pattern Recognition (CVPR), pp. 3126–3135 (2019)

31. Tomasi, C., Manduchi, R.: Bilateral filtering for gray and color images. In: Proceedings of IEEE International Conference on Computer Vision (ICCV), pp. 839–846. IEEE (1998)

32. Wang, J., Chen, K., Xu, R., Liu, Z., Loy, C.C., Lin, D.: CARAFE: context-aware reassembly of features. In: Proc. IEEE/CVF International Conference on Computer Vision (ICCV) (2019)

33. Wang, J., et al.: CARAFE++: unified content-aware ReAssembly of FEatures. IEEE Trans. Pattern Anal. Mach. Intell. (2021)

34. Wang, J., et al.: Deep high-resolution representation learning for visual recognition. IEEE Trans. Pattern Anal. Mach. Intell. 43(10), 3349–3364 (2020)

35. Xiao, H., Rasul, K., Vollgraf, R.: Fashion-MNIST: a novel image dataset for benchmarking machine learning algorithms. arXiv Computer Research Repository (2017)

36. Xiao, T., Liu, Y., Zhou, B., Jiang, Y., Sun, J.: Unified perceptual parsing for scene understanding. In: Ferrari, V., Hebert, M., Sminchisescu, C., Weiss, Y. (eds.) ECCV 2018. LNCS, vol. 11209, pp. 432–448. Springer, Cham (2018). https://doi.org/10.1007/978-3-030-01228-1_26

37. Xie, E., Wang, W., Yu, Z., Anandkumar, A., Alvarez, J.M., Luo, P.: SegFormer: simple and efficient design for semantic segmentation with transformers. In: Proceedings of Annual Conference on Neural Information Processing Systems (NeurIPS) (2021)

38. Xie, S., Tu, Z.: Holistically-nested edge detection. In: Proceedings of IEEE International Conference on Computer Vision (ICCV), pp. 1395–1403 (2015)

39. Xu, N., Price, B., Cohen, S., Huang, T.: Deep image matting. In: Proceedings of IEEE Conference on Computer Vision Pattern Recognition (CVPR), pp. 2970–2979 (2017)

40. Zeiler, M.D., Fergus, R.: Visualizing and understanding convolutional networks. In: Fleet, D., Pajdla, T., Schiele, B., Tuytelaars, T. (eds.) ECCV 2014. LNCS, vol. 8689, pp. 818–833. Springer, Cham (2014). https://doi.org/10.1007/978-3-319-10590-1_53

41. Zheng, S., et al.: Rethinking semantic segmentation from a sequence-to-sequence perspective with transformers. In: Proceedings of IEEE Conference on Computer Vision Pattern Recognition (CVPR), pp. 6881–6890 (2021)

42. Zhou, B., Zhao, H., Puig, X., Fidler, S., Barriuso, A., Torralba, A.: Scene parsing through ade20k dataset. In: Proceedings of IEEE Conference on Computer Vision Pattern Recognition (CVPR) (2017)

LiDAL: Inter-frame Uncertainty Based Active Learning for 3D LiDAR Semantic Segmentation

Zeyu Hu[1]([✉]) [iD], Xuyang Bai[1] [iD], Runze Zhang[2] [iD], Xin Wang[2] [iD],
Guangyuan Sun[2] [iD], Hongbo Fu[3] [iD], and Chiew-Lan Tai[1] [iD]

[1] Hong Kong University, Hong Kong, China
{zhuam,xbaiad,taicl}@cse.ust.hk
[2] Lightspeed & Quantum Studios, Tencent, Shenzhen, China
{ryanrzzhang,alexinwang,gerrysun}@tencent.com
[3] City University of Hong Kong, Hong Kong, China
hongbofu@cityu.edu.hk

Abstract. We propose LiDAL, a novel active learning method for 3D LiDAR semantic segmentation by exploiting inter-frame uncertainty among LiDAR frames. Our core idea is that a well-trained model should generate robust results irrespective of viewpoints for scene scanning and thus the inconsistencies in model predictions across frames provide a very reliable measure of uncertainty for active sample selection. To implement this uncertainty measure, we introduce new inter-frame divergence and entropy formulations, which serve as the metrics for active selection. Moreover, we demonstrate additional performance gains by predicting and incorporating pseudo-labels, which are also selected using the proposed inter-frame uncertainty measure. Experimental results validate the effectiveness of LiDAL: we achieve 95% of the performance of fully supervised learning with less than 5% of annotations on the SemanticKITTI and nuScenes datasets, outperforming state-of-the-art active learning methods. Code release: https://github.com/hzykent/LiDAL.

Keywords: Active learning · 3D LiDAR Semantic Segmentation

1 Introduction

Light detection and ranging (LiDAR) sensors capture more precise and farther-away distance measurements than conventional visual cameras, and have become a necessity for an accurate perception system of outdoor scenes. These sensors generate rich 3D geometry of real-world scenes as 3D point clouds to facilitate

---

Z. Hu—Intern at Tencent Lightspeed & Quantum Studios.

Supplementary Information The online version contains supplementary material available at https://doi.org/10.1007/978-3-031-19812-0_15.

a thorough scene understanding, in which 3D LiDAR semantic segmentation serves as a cornerstone. The semantic segmentation task is to parse a scene and assign an object class label to each point in 3D point clouds, thus providing point-wise perception information for numerous downstream applications like robotics [41] and autonomous vehicles [18].

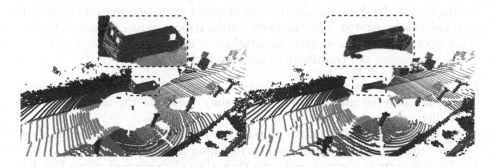

Fig. 1. Illustration of inter-frame uncertainty. While in one frame (Left) an object is correctly predicted as "vehicle" (highlighted in a red box), in the subsequent frame (Right) a large part of this object is mistakenly predicted as "fence" when scanned from a different viewpoint. (Color figure online)

Thanks to the large-scale LiDAR datasets [1,3] made publicly available in recent years, the state of the art in 3D LiDAR semantic segmentation has been significantly pushed forward [11,40,57]. However, the requirement of fully labeled point clouds for existing segmentation methods has become a major obstacle to scaling up the perception system or extending it to new scenarios. Typically, since a LiDAR sensor may perceive millions of points per second, exhaustively labeling all points is extremely laborious and time-consuming. It poses demands on developing label-efficient approaches for 3D LiDAR semantic segmentation.

Active learning provides a promising solution to reduce the costs associated with labeling. Its core idea is to design a learning algorithm that can interactively query a user to label new data samples according to a certain policy, leading to models trained with only a fraction of the data while yielding similar performances. Inspired by 2D counterparts [7,19,27,35,42], some previous works have explored active learning for 3D LiDAR semantic segmentation [21,26,34,49]. However, these methods almost exclusively operate on single LiDAR frames. Such a strategy is surprising since, unlike most 2D datasets, in which images are captured as independent samples, 3D LiDAR datasets are generally scanned as continuous point cloud frames. As a consequence, inter-frame constraints naturally embedded in the LiDAR scene sequences are largely ignored. We believe such constraints are particularly interesting for examining the quality of network predictions; i.e., the same object in a LiDAR scene should receive the same label when scanned from different viewpoints (see Fig. 1).

In this work, we propose to exploit inter-frame constraints in a novel view-consistency-based uncertainty measure. More specifically, we propose new inter-frame divergence and entropy formulations based on the variance of predicted score functions across continuous LiDAR frames. For a given (unlabeled) object (e.g., the one in a red box in Fig. 1), if its predicted labels differ across frames, we assume faulty network predictions and then strive to obtain user-specified labels for the most uncertain regions. In addition to the main active learning formulation, we also explore further improvements to the labeling efficiency with self-training by utilizing the proposed uncertainty measure in an inverse way. During each active learning iteration, we augment the user-specified labels with pseudo-labels generated from the most certain regions across frames to further boost performance without extra annotations or much computational cost.

To summarize, our contributions are threefold:

1. We propose a novel active learning strategy for 3D LiDAR semantic segmentation by estimating model uncertainty based on the inconsistency of predictions across frames.
2. We explore self-training in the proposed active learning framework and show that further gains can be realized by including pseudo-labels.
3. Through extensive experiments, we show that the proposed active learning strategy and self-training technique significantly improve labeling efficiency over baselines, and establish the state of the art in active learning for 3D LiDAR semantic segmentation.

2   Related Work

Compared to fully supervised methods [5,12,13,37,40,57], label-efficient 3D semantic segmentation is a relatively open research problem. Previous explorations can be roughly divided into five categories: transfer learning, unsupervised and self-supervised learning, weakly-supervised learning, active learning, and self-training. LiDAL falls into both the active learning and self-training categories.

Transfer Learning. Taking advantage of existing fully labeled datasets, transfer learning has been introduced to 3D semantic segmentation for reducing the annotation costs. Various domain adaptation approaches have been developed to make them perform well in novel scenarios given only labeled data from other domains [17,22,54] or even synthetic training sets [48]. They achieve fairly decent results but still require fully labeled data from a source domain and fail to generalize to new scenarios that are highly different from the source.

Unsupervised and Self-supervised Learning. Leveraging the colossal amount of unlabeled data, pre-trained models can be fine-tuned on a small set of labeled data to alleviate the over-dependence on labels and thus achieve satisfactory performances [8,14,36,39,51]. Pseudo tasks used for pre-training include reconstructing space [30], contrast learning [9,24,50], ball cover prediction [33], instance discrimination [56], and point completion [44], etc. Compared to other label-efficient counterparts, these methods require more labeled data and most of them only apply to object-level point clouds.

Weakly-Supervised Learning. Instead of point-by-point labeling in fully supervised learning, weak labels take various forms like scene-level or sub-cloud-level labels [28,46], 2D supervision [43], fewer point labels [4,10,47,53,55], seg-level labels [25,38], and box-level labels [23], etc. These methods can reduce the number of labeled samples, but either require intricate labeling processes or produce much more inferior results than the fully-supervised counterparts.

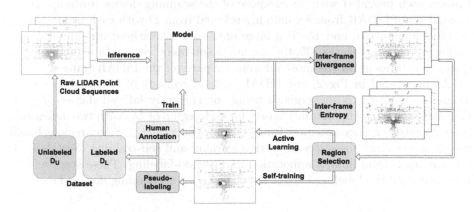

Fig. 2. Pipeline of LiDAL. In each round of active learning, we first train a 3D LiDAR semantic segmentation network in supervision with labeled dataset D_L. Second, we use the trained network to compute an inter-frame divergence score and an inter-frame entropy score for all regions from the unlabeled dataset D_U. We then select a batch of regions based on these scores for active learning and self-training, and finally request their respective labels from the human annotation and the pseudo-labeling. The process is repeated until the labeling budget is exhausted or all training data is labeled.

Active Learning. During network training, active learning methods iteratively select the most valuable data for label acquisition. The very few existing methods have explored uncertainty measurements like segment entropy [20], color discontinuity [49], and structural complexity [34,49]. The existing methods take LiDAR data as separated frames and only consider intra-frame information. Inspired by a 2D work operating on multi-view images [35], we take advantage of the inter-frame constraints for active learning in this work. Different from this 2D work, due to the distinct natures of 2D images and 3D point clouds, we design novel uncertainty formulations and selection strategies. Moreover, we propose a joint active learning and self-training framework to further exploit the inter-frame constraints.

Self-training. Building on the principle of knowledge distillation, previous methods generate pseudo labels to expand sparse labels [25,52] or to facilitate the network training using only scene-level supervision [28]. In this work, we develop a pseudo-labeling method applied in conjunction with our active learning framework to achieve even greater gains in efficiency.

3   Method

3.1   Overview

The goal of LiDAL is to train a well-performing 3D LiDAR semantic segmentation model with a constrained annotation budget. Specifically, we assume the availability of data $D = \{D_L, D_U\}$. The data consists of sequences of LiDAR frames, each provided with an ego-pose of the scanning device. Initially, D_L is a small set of LiDAR frames randomly selected from D with each frame having its label annotation, and D_U is a large unlabeled set without any annotations. Following previous works [35,49], we use a sub-scene region as a fundamental query unit to focus on the most informative parts of the LiDAR frames.

As illustrated in Fig. 2, our LiDAL method consists of four main steps: 1. Train the network to convergence using the currently labeled dataset D_L. 2. Calculate the model uncertainty scores for each region of D_U with two indicators: inter-frame divergence and inter-frame entropy (Sect. 3.2). 3. Select regions based on the uncertainty measures for active learning and self-training (Sect. 3.3). 4. Obtain labels from human annotation and pseudo-labeling. These steps will be repeated until the labeling budget is exhausted or all training data is labeled.

3.2   Uncertainty Scoring

At each iteration, after the first step of training the network on D_L, our active learning method LiDAL then aims at predicting which samples from D_U are the most informative to the network at the current state. To this end, we introduce two novel uncertainty scoring metrics named *inter-frame divergence* and *inter-frame entropy*. Figure 3 provides an overview of the scoring process.

Inter-frame Divergence. In a nutshell, the proposed inter-frame divergence score aims at estimating which objects are consistently predicted the same way, irrespective of the scanning viewpoints.

For each frame, we first calculate its point-wise class probability maps using the current trained segmentation network. To attain robust probability predictions, we perform data augmentations with random translation, rotation, scaling, and jittering. The probability P for a point p in frame F_i to belong to class c is given by:

$$P_i^p(c) = \frac{1}{D} \sum_{d=1}^{D} P_{i,d}^p(c), \tag{1}$$

where D is the number of augmented inference runs of the segmentation network, and $P_{i,d}^p(c)$ is the softmax probability of point p belonging to class c in the augmented inference run d.

Next, using the provided ego-pose, we register each frame in the world coordinate system. For each point in a given frame, we find its corresponding points in the neighboring frames and assign to it their associated probability distributions. Implementation details can be found in **Supplementary Section A**.

Each point p in frame F_i is now associated with a set of probability distributions Ω_i^p, each coming from a neighboring frame:

$$\Omega_i^p = \{P_j^p, j | F_j^p \text{ corresponds to } F_i^p\}, \tag{2}$$

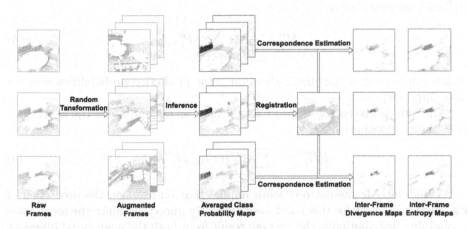

Fig. 3. Illustration of uncertainty scoring. For each unlabeled LiDAR frame in the dataset, we first obtain its averaged class probability predictions from augmented inference runs. Next, we register each frame with its provided ego-pose. For each point in the frame, we then find its corresponding points in neighboring frames and assign to it their associated class probability predictions. With the aggregated multiple class probability predictions per point, we compute the inter-frame divergence and entropy scores. We assign these two scores to each unlabeled region by averaging the scores of all the points contained in it.

where F_j^p denotes the point p in frame F_j, and F_j represents one of the neighboring frames of F_i.

In our setting, when estimating the point correspondences between neighboring frames, we assume that the objects in the scene are static and thus the points in the same registered position represent the same object. The moving objects are not specially treated for two reasons. First, they contribute only a small portion of the dataset. Second, when estimating correspondences after registration, the prediction disagreements introduced by the 3D motions can be seen as inter-frame inconsistency and help the system select these informative regions.

The inter-frame divergence corresponds to the average pairwise KL divergence between the class distribution at any given point and the class distributions assigned to that point from the neighboring frames. It effectively captures the degree of agreement between the prediction in the current frame with the predictions coming from the neighboring frames. Specifically, we define the inter-frame divergence score FD for a point p in frame F_i as follows:

$$FD_i^p = \frac{1}{|\Omega_i^p|} \sum_{P_j^p \in \Omega_i^p} D_{KL}(P_i^p || P_j^p), \tag{3}$$

where $D_{KL}(P_i^p || P_j^p)$ is the KL Divergence between distributions P_i^p and P_j^p.

Inter-frame Entropy. After measuring how inconsistent the predictions are across frames, we then define the inter-frame entropy score, which indicates the amount of uncertainty for the network to process a certain point. For a point p in frame F_i, with the aggregated probability distributions Ω_i^p, the mean distribution M_i^p can be calculated as:

$$M_i^p = \frac{1}{|\Omega_i^p|} \sum_{P_j^p \in \Omega_i^p} P_j^p, \tag{4}$$

which can be seen as the marginalization of the prediction probabilities over the scanning viewpoints.

The inter-frame entropy score FE is defined as the entropy of the mean class probability distribution M_i^p:

$$FE_i^p = -\sum_c M_i^p(c) \log(M_i^p(c)). \tag{5}$$

A high inter-frame entropy score implies that on average, the prediction of the current network for this point is significantly uncertain. Since the mean class probability distribution is the average result from both the augmented inference runs and the aggregation of corresponding points, the inter-frame entropy score estimates both the intra-frame uncertainty under random affine transformations and inter-frame uncertainty under viewpoint changes.

3.3   Region Selection

To select the most informative parts of the unlabeled dataset, we opt for using sub-scene regions as the fundamental label querying units, following previous works [35,49]. Our implementation uses the constrained K-means clustering [2] algorithm for region division. An ideal sub-scene region consists of one or several object classes and is lightweight to label for the annotator.

For each region r, the two scores FD_i^r and FE_i^r are computed as the average of the inter-frame divergence and inter-frame entropy scores of all the points contained in r:

$$FD_i^r = \frac{1}{|r|} \sum_{p \in r} FD_i^p, \tag{6}$$

$$FE_i^r = \frac{1}{|r|} \sum_{p \in r} FE_i^p, \tag{7}$$

where $|r|$ is the number of points contained in region r.

Active Learning. We now discuss our active learning strategy utilizing the proposed inter-frame uncertainty scores. Our strategy to select the next region for labeling consists of two steps. First, we look for the region r from frame F_i that has the highest inter-frame divergence score in D_U:

$$(i, r) = \underset{(j,s) \in D_U}{\arg\max} FD_j^s, \tag{8}$$

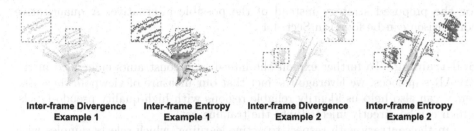

| Inter-frame Divergence | Inter-frame Entropy | Inter-frame Divergence | Inter-frame Entropy |
| Example 1 | Example 1 | Example 2 | Example 2 |

Fig. 4. Examples of Uncertainty Scores. Red and blue indicate inter-frame divergence and entropy, respectively. The darker the color, the higher the value. Due to the sparsity and varying-density property of LiDAR point clouds, neural networks tend to generate class distributions that are more uniform for farther away sparse points. As highlighted by the dotted red boxes, this property results in misleadingly high values for far away sparse points in terms of inter-frame entropy but affects less on the inter-frame divergence scores. (Color figure online)

where (j, s) refers to region s from frame F_j.

Since the inter-frame divergence indicates that for each region how inconsistent the predictions are across frames, the scores are similar for all the regions that are in correspondence. To determine which one of the regions in correspondence contains the largest amount of beneficial information to improve the network, we retrieve the set of regions representing the same part of the outdoor scene and denote this set as S. We then look for the region from S with the highest inter-frame entropy score:

$$(k, t) = \underset{(j,s)\in S}{\arg\max}\{FE_j^s|(j, s) \text{ and } (i, r) \text{ overlap}\}, \tag{9}$$

where (k, t) refers to the selected region t from frame F_k. Implementation details can be found in **Supplementary Section A**.

The selected region is added to D_L and all regions in set S are then removed from D_U to avoid label redundancy. The process is repeated until reaching the labeling budget. The active learning algorithm is summarized in Algorithm 1.

One possible alternative strategy is to first find the region with the highest inter-frame entropy score and then select the one with the highest inter-frame divergence score in the corresponding set. A similar strategy is implemented in a previous work operating on multi-view images [35]. However, unlike 2D images with dense and uniformly sampled pixels, 3D LiDAR frames have sparse and varying-density points. Specifically, the farther from the scanning viewpoint, the sparser the LiDAR points. As shown in Fig. 4, due to the sparsity, neural networks tend to predict uniform class distributions for peripheral points. This property will result in misleadingly high inter-frame entropy scores for points far away from the scanning viewpoint (Eq. 5), while the inter-frame divergence scores remain stable (Eq. 3). Considering the robustness of the system, we opt for the proposed strategy instead of the possible alternative. A quantitative comparison can be found in Sect. 4.4.

Self-training. To further exploit the inter-frame constraints embedded in the LiDAR sequences, we leverage the fact that our measure of viewpoint inconsistency can also help us identify reliable regions with high-quality pseudo-labels, which can be directly injected into the training set.

On the contrary with respect to active learning, which selects samples with the most uncertain predictions, self-training aims at acquiring confident and accurate pseudo-labels. To this end, we conduct a reversed process of the proposed active learning strategy. Specifically, we first look for the region r from frame F_i that has the lowest inter-frame divergence score in D_U:

$$(i, r) = \arg\min_{(j,s) \in D_U} FD_j^s, \tag{10}$$

We then look for the region from the corresponding set S that has the lowest inter-frame entropy score:

$$(k, t) = \arg\min_{(j,s) \in S} \{FE_j^s | (j, s) \text{ and } (i, r) \text{ overlap}\}, \tag{11}$$

The pseudo-label of the selected region is retrieved from the network predictions and all regions in set S will not be used for further pseudo-labeling. The process is repeated until reaching the target number of pseudo-labels. In order to prevent label drifting [6], we reset the pseudo label set at each iteration and only select regions that are not already selected in the previous iteration. The self-training algorithm is summarized in Algorithm 2.

Algorithm 1. Active Learning	**Algorithm 2.** Self-training
Input:	**Input:**
Data set D, labeled set D_L,	Data set D, labeled set D_L,
annotation budget B, metric M	previous pseudo set P,
Init:	target number T, metric M
Added samples $A \leftarrow \{\}$	**Init:**
Unlabeled set $D_U \leftarrow D \setminus D_L$	New pseudo set $P' \leftarrow \{\}$
repeat	$D'_U \leftarrow (D \setminus D_L) \setminus P$ ▷ No re-labeling
$\quad (i, r) \leftarrow \arg\max_{(j,s) \in D_U} M_{FD_j^s}$	**repeat**
$\quad$ Retrieve S ▷ Corresponding set	$\quad (i, r) \leftarrow \arg\min_{(j,s) \in D'_U} M_{FD_j^s}$
$\quad (k, t) \leftarrow \arg\max_{(j,s) \in S} M_{FE_j^s}$	$\quad$ Retrieve S ▷ Corresponding set
$\quad A \leftarrow A \cup (k, t)$	$\quad (k, t) \leftarrow \arg\min_{(j,s) \in S} M_{FE_j^s}$
$\quad D_L \leftarrow D_L \cup (k, t)$	$\quad P' \leftarrow P' \cup (k, t)$
$\quad D_U \leftarrow D_U \setminus S$	$\quad D'_U \leftarrow D'_U \setminus S$
until $|A| = B$ or $|D_U| = 0$	**until** $|P'| = T$ or $|D'_U| = 0$
return A	**return** P'

4   Experiments

To demonstrate the effectiveness of our proposed method, we now present various experiments conducted on two large-scale 3D LiDAR semantic segmentation datasets, i.e., SemanticKITTI [1] and nuScenes [3]. We first introduce the datasets and evaluation metrics in Sect. 4.1, and then present the experimental settings in Sect. 4.2. We report the results on the SemanticKITTI and nuScenes datasets in Sect. 4.3, and the ablation studies in Sect. 4.4.

4.1   Datasets and Metrics

SemanticKITTI [1]. SemanticKITTI is a large-scale driving-scene dataset derived from the KITTI Vision Odometry Benchmark and was collected in Germany with the Velodyne-HDLE64 LiDAR. The dataset consists of 22 sequences containing 43,552 point cloud scans. We perform all our experiments using the official training (seq 00-07 and 09-10) and validation (seq 08) split. 19 classes are used for segmentation.

nuScenes [3]. nuScenes was collected in Boston and Singapore with 32-beam LiDAR sensors. It contains 1,000 scenes of 20 s duration annotated 2 Hz frequency. Following the official train/val splits, we perform all label acquisition strategies on the 700 training sequences (28k scans) and evaluate them on 150 validation sequences (6k scans). 16 classes are used for segmentation.

Metrics. For evaluation, we report mean class intersection over union (mIoU) results for both the SemanticKITTI and nuScenes datasets following the official guidance.

4.2   Experimental Settings

Network Architectures. To verify the effectiveness of the proposed active learning strategy on various network architectures, we adopt MinkowskiNet [5] based on sparse convolution, and SPVCNN [37] based on point-voxel CNN, as our backbone networks for their great performance and high efficiency. We make the same choices for the network architectures as ReDAL [49], a recent state-of-the-art active learning method of 3D semantic segmentation, for better comparison.

Baseline Active Learning Methods. We select eight baseline methods for comparison, including random frame selection ($RAND_{fr}$), random region selection ($RAND_{re}$), segment-entropy (SEGENT) [20], softmax margin (MAR) [16, 29,45], softmax confidence (CONF) [32,45], softmax entropy (ENT) [15,45], core-set selection (CSET) [31], and ReDAL [49]. The implementation details for all the methods are explained in **Supplementary Section B**.

Learning Protocol. Following the same protocol as ReDAL [49], the model is initialized by training on x_{init}% of randomly selected LiDAR frames with full annotations. The active learning process consists of K rounds of the following

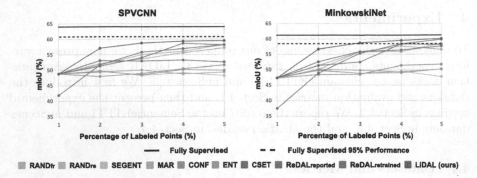

Fig. 5. Mean intersection over union scores on SemanticKITTI Val [1]. Detailed results can be found in **Supplementary Section C**.

actions: 1. Finetune the model on the current labeled set D_L. 2. Select $x_{active}\%$ of data from the current unlabeled set D_U for human annotation according to different active selection strategies. 3. Update D_L and D_U.

The labeling budget is measured by the percentage of labeled points. For both SemanticKITTI and nuScenes datasets, we use $x_{init} = 1\%$, $K = 4$, and $x_{active} = 1\%$. For self-training, the target number of pseudo-labels in terms of percentage of labeled points $T = 1\%$. To ensure the reliability of the results, all the experiments are performed three times and the average results are reported. More training details can be found in **Supplementary Section A**.

4.3   Results and Analysis

In this section, we present the performance of our approach compared to the baseline methods on the SemanticKITTI and nuScenes datasets. Figure 5 and Fig. 6 show the comparative results. In each subplot, the x-axis represents the percentage of labeled points and the y-axis indicates the mIoU score achieved by the respective networks, which are trained with data selected through different active learning strategies.

Since most of the baseline methods are not designed for LiDAR point clouds, we re-implement these methods for LiDAR data based on their official codes. For ReDAL [49], in its published paper, it is evaluated on the SemanticKITTI dataset but not on the nuScenes dataset. For the SemanticKITTI dataset, we find that the reported scores of its initial networks (trained with 1% of randomly selected frames) are way lower than our implementations (41.9 vs 48.8 for SPVCNN and 37.5 vs 47.3 for MinkowskiNet). We retrained its networks and got better results using its official code but with a finer training schedule (details can be found in **Supplementary Section A**). Both the retrained results and the reported results are presented in Fig. 5. For nuScenes, we adapt its official code and report the results.

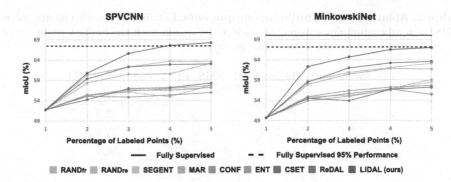

Fig. 6. Mean intersection over union scores on nuScenes Val [3]. Detailed results can be found in **Supplementary Section C**.

SemanticKITTI. As shown in Fig. 5, our proposed LiDAL significantly surpasses the existing active learning strategies using the same percentages of labeled data. Specifically, our method is able to reach nearly 95% of the fully supervised performance with only 5% of labeled data for the SPVCNN network and even achieve about 98% of the fully supervised result for the MinkowskiNet network.

In addition, we notice that many active learning strategies perform worse than the random baseline and some even bring negative effects on the network performance (e.g., the mIoU scores may drop after adding the data samples selected by SEGENT). For uncertainty-based methods, such as SEGENT and CONF, since the model uncertainty values are calculated only within each frame and are biased by the peripheral points due to the scanning property of LiDAR, their performances are degraded. Even for pure diversity-based approaches, such as CSET, since the LiDAR datasets are captured as continuous frames and have plenty of redundant information among neighboring frames, simply clustering features may fail to produce diverse label acquisition.

Moreover, we observe that the performance gap between $RAND_{re}$ and $RAND_{fr}$ is trivial. It showcases that if not combined with effective uncertainty measures, region-based training brings little benefit to the network performance.

NuScenes. We also evaluate our algorithm on the novel nuScenes dataset and report the results in Fig. 6. As shown in the figure, our method outperforms all the competitors in terms of mIoU under all the experimental settings. Specifically, for both SPVCNN and MinkowskiNet, our method achieves more than 95% of the fully supervised performances with only 5% of labeled data.

Compared to the results of SemanticKITTI, similar phenomena can be witnessed that many active learning strategies perform worse than the random baseline. However, the negative effects are alleviated and the mIoU scores consistently increase by adding data samples selected by most strategies. A possible explanation is that, since the nuScenes dataset contains 1,000 scenes of tens of

260   Z. Hu et al.

Table 1. Ablation study: building components. FD: inter-frame divergence score; NMS: non-maximum suppression, i.e., select the region with the highest score in the corresponding set; FE: inter-frame entropy score.

FD	Frame-level	Region-level	NMS	FE	Pseudo	mIoU(%)
✓	✓					51.8
✓		✓				52.5
✓		✓	✓			55.5
✓		✓		✓		56.4
✓		✓		✓	✓	57.1

frames while the SemanticKITTI dataset contains only 22 scenes of thousands of frames, the network is less likely to be biased by the data selected from nuScenes than that from SemanticKITTI.

4.4 Ablation Study

In this section, we conduct a number of controlled experiments that demonstrate the effectiveness of the building modules in LiDAL, and also examine some specific decisions in our LiDAL design. All the experiments are conducted on the SemanticKITTI validation set evaluating the performance of the SPVCNN network trained on the data selected in the first active learning round, keeping all the hyper-parameters the same. More ablation studies can be found in **Supplementary Section D.**

Building Components. In Table 1, we evaluate the effectiveness of each component of our method. **1. Effect of region-level labeling.** "FD + Frame-level" represents the baseline, which is to select frames with the highest average inter-frame divergence scores for training. By changing from "FD + Frame-level" to "FD + Region-level" (selecting regions), we can improve the performance by 0.7%. This improvement is brought by focusing on the most informative parts of the scenes. **2. Effect of active selection strategy.** "FD + Region-level + NMS" refers to selecting only the region with the highest inter-frame divergence score in the corresponding set. By avoiding the label redundancy, we can gain about 3% of improvement. "FD + Region-level + FE" refers to the proposed selection strategy described in Sect. 3.3. From the proposed inter-frame entropy measure, we further improve about 0.9%. **3. Effect of pseudo-labels.** "FD + Region-level + FE + Pseudo" denotes the complete strategy of LiDAL. The introduction of pseudo-labels brings around 0.7% of performance improvement.

Region Selection Strategies. In Sect. 3.3, we discuss two possible region selection strategies for both active learning and self-training. We advocate the proposed one that first finds corresponding sets using the inter-frame divergence

Table 2. Ablation study: (Left) Region selection strategy; (Right) Target number of pseudo-label.

Strategy	mIoU(%)
FE + FD	55.7
FD + FE	57.1

Target Number(%)	mIoU(%)
0.0	56.4
0.5	56.8
1.0	57.1
2.0	56.4

scores and then selects regions with the inter-frame entropy scores. To justify our choice, we implement both strategies and report the results in Table 2 (Left). "FD + FE" refers to the proposed strategy and "FE + FD" refers to the possible alternative strategy that first finds corresponding sets using the entropy scores and then selects regions with the divergence scores. As shown in the table, the proposed strategy significantly outperforms the possible alternative strategy. It may be caused by the misleadingly high entropy values of peripheral points, as illustrated in Fig. 4.

Target Number of Pseudo-labels. In Sect. 3.3, we explore self-training in the proposed active learning framework and show that further gains can be realized by including pseudo-labels in Table 1. To investigate the impact of pseudo-labels, we inject different numbers of pseudo-labels into the training set and report the results in Table 2 (Right). We observe that with the increasing number of pseudo-labels, the gain of network performance first increases and then decreases. We speculate that adding pseudo-labels with a reasonable number will improve the network performance but superfluous pseudo-labels may bring unhelpful training biases and label noises. A further study on pseudo-labels can be found in **Supplementary Section D**.

5 Conclusion

In this paper, we have presented a novel active learning strategy for 3D LiDAR semantic segmentation, named LiDAL. Aiming at exploiting the inter-frame constraints embedded in LiDAR sequences, we propose two uncertainty measures estimating the inconsistencies of network predictions among frames. We design a unified framework of both active learning and self-training by utilizing the proposed measures. Extensive experiments show that LiDAL achieves state-of-the-art results on the challenging SemanticKITTI and nuScenes datasets, significantly improving over strong baselines. For future works, one straightforward direction is to explore the potential of inter-frame constraints for RGB-D sequences of indoor scenes. Moreover, we believe that future works with special treatments for moving objects will further improve the performance.

Acknowledgements. This work is supported by Hong Kong RGC GRF 16206722 and a grant from City University of Hong Kong (Project No. 7005729).

References

1. Behley, J., et al.: SemanticKITTI: a dataset for semantic scene understanding of lidar sequences. In: Proceedings of the IEEE/CVF International Conference on Computer Vision, pp. 9297–9307 (2019)
2. Bradley, P.S., Bennett, K.P., Demiriz, A.: Constrained k-means clustering. Microsoft Res. Redmond **20**, 1–9 (2000)
3. Caesar, H., et al: nuscenes: a multimodal dataset for autonomous driving. In: Proceedings of the IEEE/CVF Conference on Computer Vision and Pattern Recognition, pp. 11621–11631 (2020)
4. Cheng, M., Hui, L., Xie, J., Yang, J.: SSPC-Net: semi-supervised semantic 3d point cloud segmentation network. In: Proceedings of the AAAI Conference on Artificial Intelligence, vol. 35, pp. 1140–1147 (2021)
5. Choy, C., Gwak, J., Savarese, S.: 4d spatio-temporal convnets: Minkowski convolutional neural networks. In: Proceedings of the IEEE/CVF Conference on Computer Vision and Pattern Recognition, pp. 3075–3084 (2019)
6. Feng, Q., He, K., Wen, H., Keskin, C., Ye, Y.: Active learning with pseudo-labels for multi-view 3d pose estimation. arXiv preprint arXiv:2112.13709 (2021)
7. Górriz, M., Giró Nieto, X., Carlier, A., Faure, E.: Cost-effective active learning for melanoma segmentation. In: ML4H: Machine Learning for Health NIPS, Workshop at NIPS 2017, pp. 1–5 (2017)
8. Hassani, K., Haley, M.: Unsupervised multi-task feature learning on point clouds. In: Proceedings of the IEEE/CVF International Conference on Computer Vision, pp. 8160–8171 (2019)
9. Hou, J., Graham, B., Nießner, M., Xie, S.: Exploring data-efficient 3d scene understanding with contrastive scene contexts. In: Proceedings of the IEEE/CVF Conference on Computer Vision and Pattern Recognition, pp. 15587–15597 (2021)
10. Hu, Q., et al.: SQN: weakly-supervised semantic segmentation of large-scale 3d point clouds with 1000× fewer labels. arXiv preprint arXiv:2104.04891 (2021)
11. Hu, Q., et al.: RANDLA-Net: efficient semantic segmentation of large-scale point clouds. In: Proceedings of the IEEE/CVF Conference on Computer Vision and Pattern Recognition, pp. 11108–11117 (2020)
12. Hu, Z., et al.: VMNet: voxel-mesh network for geodesic-aware 3d semantic segmentation. In: Proceedings of the IEEE/CVF International Conference on Computer Vision, pp. 15488–15498 (2021)
13. Hu, Z., Zhen, M., Bai, X., Fu, H., Tai, C.: JSENet: joint semantic segmentation and edge detection network for 3D point clouds. In: Vedaldi, A., Bischof, H., Brox, T., Frahm, J.-M. (eds.) ECCV 2020. LNCS, vol. 12365, pp. 222–239. Springer, Cham (2020). https://doi.org/10.1007/978-3-030-58565-5_14
14. Huang, S., Xie, Y., Zhu, S.C., Zhu, Y.: Spatio-temporal self-supervised representation learning for 3d point clouds. In: Proceedings of the IEEE/CVF International Conference on Computer Vision, pp. 6535–6545 (2021)
15. Hwa, R.: Sample selection for statistical parsing. Comput. Linguist. **30**(3), 253–276 (2004)
16. Joshi, A.J., Porikli, F., Papanikolopoulos, N.: Multi-class active learning for image classification. In: 2009 IEEE Conference on Computer Vision and Pattern Recognition, pp. 2372–2379. IEEE (2009)

17. Langer, F., Milioto, A., Haag, A., Behley, J., Stachniss, C.: Domain transfer for semantic segmentation of lidar data using deep neural networks. In: 2020 IEEE/RSJ International Conference on Intelligent Robots and Systems (IROS), pp. 8263–8270. IEEE (2020)

18. Li, B., Zhang, T., Xia, T.: Vehicle detection from 3d lidar using fully convolutional network. arXiv preprint arXiv:1608.07916 (2016)

19. Li, H., Yin, Z.: Attention, suggestion and annotation: a deep active learning framework for biomedical image segmentation. In: Martel, A.L. (ed.) MICCAI 2020. LNCS, vol. 12261, pp. 3–13. Springer, Cham (2020). https://doi.org/10.1007/978-3-030-59710-8_1

20. Lin, Y., Vosselman, G., Cao, Y., Yang, M.: Efficient training of semantic point cloud segmentation via active learning. ISPRS Ann. Photogramm. Remote Sens. Spat. Inf. Sci. **2**, 243–250 (2020)

21. Lin, Y., Vosselman, G., Cao, Y., Yang, M.Y.: Active and incremental learning for semantic ALS point cloud segmentation. ISPRS J. Photogramm. Remote. Sens. **169**, 73–92 (2020)

22. Liu, W., et al.: Adversarial unsupervised domain adaptation for 3d semantic segmentation with multi-modal learning. ISPRS J. Photogramm. Remote. Sens. **176**, 211–221 (2021)

23. Liu, Y., Hu, Q., Lei, Y., Xu, K., Li, J., Guo, Y.: Box2seg: learning semantics of 3d point clouds with box-level supervision. arXiv preprint arXiv:2201.02963 (2022)

24. Liu, Y., Yi, L., Zhang, S., Fan, Q., Funkhouser, T., Dong, H.: P4contrast: contrastive learning with pairs of point-pixel pairs for RGB-D scene understanding. arXiv e-prints, arXiv-2012 (2020)

25. Liu, Z., Qi, X., Fu, C.W.: One thing one click: a self-training approach for weakly supervised 3d semantic segmentation. In: Proceedings of the IEEE/CVF Conference on Computer Vision and Pattern Recognition, pp. 1726–1736 (2021)

26. Luo, H., et al.: Semantic labeling of mobile lidar point clouds via active learning and higher order MRF. IEEE Trans. Geosci. Remote Sens. **56**(7), 3631–3644 (2018)

27. Mackowiak, R., Lenz, P., Ghori, O., Diego, F., Lange, O., Rother, C.: Cereals-cost-effective region-based active learning for semantic segmentation. In: BMVC (2018)

28. Ren, Z., Misra, I., Schwing, A.G., Girdhar, R.: 3d spatial recognition without spatially labeled 3d. In: Proceedings of the IEEE/CVF Conference on Computer Vision and Pattern Recognition, pp. 13204–13213 (2021)

29. Roth, D., Small, K.: Margin-based active learning for structured output spaces. In: Fürnkranz, J., Scheffer, T., Spiliopoulou, M. (eds.) ECML 2006. LNCS (LNAI), vol. 4212, pp. 413–424. Springer, Heidelberg (2006). https://doi.org/10.1007/11871842_40

30. Sauder, J., Sievers, B.: Self-supervised deep learning on point clouds by reconstructing space. Adv. Neural. Inf. Process. Syst. **32**, 1–11 (2019)

31. Sener, O., Savarese, S.: Active learning for convolutional neural networks: a core-set approach. arXiv preprint arXiv:1708.00489 (2017)

32. Settles, B., Craven, M.: An analysis of active learning strategies for sequence labeling tasks. In: Proceedings of the 2008 Conference on Empirical Methods in Natural Language Processing, pp. 1070–1079 (2008)

33. Sharma, C., Kaul, M.: Self-supervised few-shot learning on point clouds. Adv. Neural. Inf. Process. Syst. **33**, 7212–7221 (2020)

34. Shi, X., Xu, X., Chen, K., Cai, L., Foo, C.S., Jia, K.: Label-efficient point cloud semantic segmentation: an active learning approach. arXiv preprint arXiv:2101.06931 (2021)

35. Siddiqui, Y., Valentin, J., Nießner, M.: Viewal: active learning with viewpoint entropy for semantic segmentation. In: Proceedings of the IEEE/CVF Conference on Computer Vision and Pattern Recognition, pp. 9433–9443 (2020)
36. Sun, W., Tagliasacchi, A., Deng, B., Sabour, S., Yazdani, S., Hinton, G., Yi, K.M.: Canonical capsules: unsupervised capsules in canonical pose. arXiv preprint arXiv:2012.04718 (2020)
37. Tang, H., Liu, Z., Zhao, S., Lin, Y., Lin, J., Wang, H., Han, S.: Searching efficient 3d architectures with sparse point-voxel convolution. In: Vedaldi, A., Bischof, H., Brox, T., Frahm, J.-M. (eds.) ECCV 2020. LNCS, vol. 12373, pp. 685–702. Springer, Cham (2020). https://doi.org/10.1007/978-3-030-58604-1_41
38. Tao, A., Duan, Y., Wei, Y., Lu, J., Zhou, J.: SegGroup: Seg-level supervision for 3d instance and semantic segmentation. arXiv preprint arXiv:2012.10217 (2020)
39. Thabet, A.K., Alwassel, H., Ghanem, B.: MortonNet: self-supervised learning of local features in 3d point clouds (2019)
40. Thomas, H., Qi, C.R., Deschaud, J.E., Marcotegui, B., Goulette, F., Guibas, L.J.: Kpconv: Flexible and deformable convolution for point clouds. In: Proceedings of the IEEE/CVF International Conference on Computer Vision, pp. 6411–6420 (2019)
41. Thrun, S., et al.: Stanley: the robot that won the DARPA grand challenge. J. Field Robot. **23**(9), 661–692 (2006)
42. Vezhnevets, A., Buhmann, J.M., Ferrari, V.: Active learning for semantic segmentation with expected change. In: 2012 IEEE Conference on Computer Vision and Pattern Recognition, pp. 3162–3169. IEEE (2012)
43. Wang, H., Rong, X., Yang, L., Feng, J., Xiao, J., Tian, Y.: Weakly supervised semantic segmentation in 3d graph-structured point clouds of wild scenes. arXiv preprint arXiv:2004.12498 (2020)
44. Wang, H., Liu, Q., Yue, X., Lasenby, J., Kusner, M.J.: Unsupervised point cloud pre-training via occlusion completion. In: Proceedings of the IEEE/CVF International Conference on Computer Vision, pp. 9782–9792 (2021)
45. Wang, K., Zhang, D., Li, Y., Zhang, R., Lin, L.: Cost-effective active learning for deep image classification. IEEE Trans. Circuits Syst. Video Technol. **27**(12), 2591–2600 (2016)
46. Wei, J., Lin, G., Yap, K.H., Hung, T.Y., Xie, L.: Multi-path region mining for weakly supervised 3d semantic segmentation on point clouds. In: Proceedings of the IEEE/CVF Conference on Computer Vision and Pattern Recognition, pp. 4384–4393 (2020)
47. Wei, J., Lin, G., Yap, K.H., Liu, F., Hung, T.Y.: Dense supervision propagation for weakly supervised semantic segmentation on 3d point clouds. arXiv preprint arXiv:2107.11267 (2021)
48. Wu, B., Zhou, X., Zhao, S., Yue, X., Keutzer, K.: SqueezeSegV2: Improved model structure and unsupervised domain adaptation for road-object segmentation from a lidar point cloud. In: 2019 International Conference on Robotics and Automation (ICRA), pp. 4376–4382. IEEE (2019)
49. Wu, T.H., et al.: ReDAL: region-based and diversity-aware active learning for point cloud semantic segmentation. In: Proceedings of the IEEE/CVF International Conference on Computer Vision, pp. 15510–15519 (2021)
50. Xie, S., Gu, J., Guo, D., Qi, C.R., Guibas, L., Litany, O.: PointContrast: unsupervised pre-training for 3d point cloud understanding. In: Vedaldi, A., Bischof, H., Brox, T., Frahm, J.-M. (eds.) ECCV 2020. LNCS, vol. 12348, pp. 574–591. Springer, Cham (2020). https://doi.org/10.1007/978-3-030-58580-8_34

51. Xu, C., et al.: Image2point: 3d point-cloud understanding with pretrained 2d convnets. arXiv preprint arXiv:2106.04180 (2021)
52. Xu, K., Yao, Y., Murasaki, K., Ando, S., Sagata, A.: Semantic segmentation of sparsely annotated 3d point clouds by pseudo-labelling. In: 2019 International Conference on 3D Vision (3DV), pp. 463–471. IEEE (2019)
53. Xu, X., Lee, G.H.: Weakly supervised semantic point cloud segmentation: towards 10× fewer labels. In: Proceedings of the IEEE/CVF Conference on Computer Vision and Pattern Recognition, pp. 13706–13715 (2020)
54. Yi, L., Gong, B., Funkhouser, T.: Complete & label: a domain adaptation approach to semantic segmentation of lidar point clouds. In: Proceedings of the IEEE/CVF Conference on Computer Vision and Pattern Recognition, pp. 15363–15373 (2021)
55. Zhang, Y., Li, Z., Xie, Y., Qu, Y., Li, C., Mei, T.: Weakly supervised semantic segmentation for large-scale point cloud. In: Proceedings of the AAAI Conference on Artificial Intelligence, vol. 35, pp. 3421–3429 (2021)
56. Zhang, Z., Girdhar, R., Joulin, A., Misra, I.: Self-supervised pretraining of 3d features on any point-cloud. In: Proceedings of the IEEE/CVF International Conference on Computer Vision, pp. 10252–10263 (2021)
57. Zhu, X., Zhou, H., Wang, T., Hong, F., Ma, Y., Li, W., Li, H., Lin, D.: Cylindrical and asymmetrical 3d convolution networks for lidar segmentation. In: Proceedings of the IEEE/CVF Conference on Computer Vision and Pattern Recognition, pp. 9939–9948 (2021)

Hierarchical Memory Learning
for Fine-Grained Scene Graph Generation

Youming Deng[1], Yansheng Li[1(✉)], Yongjun Zhang[1], Xiang Xiang[2],
Jian Wang[3], Jingdong Chen[3], and Jiayi Ma[4]

[1] School of Remote Sensing and Information Engineering, Wuhan University,
Wuhan, China
yansheng.li@whu.edu.cn
[2] School of Artificial Intelligence and Automation, Huazhong University of Science
and Technology, Wuhan, China
[3] Ant Group, Hangzhou, China
[4] Electronic Information School, Wuhan University, Wuhan, China

Abstract. Regarding Scene Graph Generation (SGG), coarse and fine predicates mix in the dataset due to the crowd-sourced labeling, and the long-tail problem is also pronounced. Given this tricky situation, many existing SGG methods treat the predicates equally and learn the model under the supervision of mixed-granularity predicates in one stage, leading to relatively coarse predictions. In order to alleviate the impact of the suboptimum mixed-granularity annotation and long-tail effect problems, this paper proposes a novel Hierarchical Memory Learning (HML) framework to learn the model from simple to complex, which is similar to the human beings' hierarchical memory learning process. After the autonomous partition of coarse and fine predicates, the model is first trained on the coarse predicates and then learns the fine predicates. In order to realize this hierarchical learning pattern, this paper, for the first time, formulates the HML framework using the new Concept Reconstruction (CR) and Model Reconstruction (MR) constraints. It is worth noticing that the HML framework can be taken as one general optimization strategy to improve various SGG models, and significant improvement can be achieved on the SGG benchmark.

Keywords: Scene graph generation · Mixed-granularity annotation ·
Hierarchical memory learning

Supplementary Information The online version contains supplementary material
available at https://doi.org/10.1007/978-3-031-19812-0_16.

1   Introduction

The task of Scene Graph Generation (SGG) [51] is a combination of visual object detection and relationship (i.e., predicate) recognition between visual objects. It builds up the bridge between computer vision and natural language. SGG receives increasing attention since an ideal informative scene graph has a huge potential for various downstream tasks such as image caption [17,54] and VQA [1,31]. To pursue the practical application value, SGG models keep working towards generating an informative scene graph where the fine-grained relationship between two objects should be predicted. Earlier works like [43,53,57] only design models for feature refinement and better representation. However, they ignore the dataset and task properties, limiting the performance. In order to deal with the long-tail effect and various biases [42] within the dataset, recent works including [7,16,39,42] move towards designing the learning framework to improve the overall performance of several classic SGG models. Even with this progress, making the fine-grained predicate prediction is still challenging.

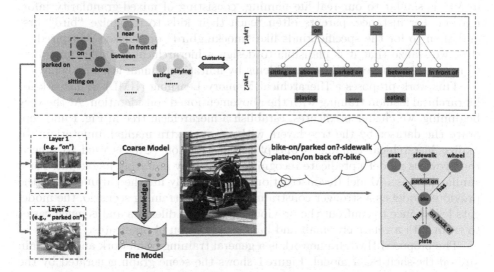

Fig. 1. Automatic Predicate Tree Construction and visualization of the HML Framework. After constructing a hierarchical predicate tree via clustering, the model is trained with the HML framework to make the fine-grained predicate prediction.

Generally speaking, two factors lead to a frustrating result. The first is the mixed-granularity predicates caused by artificial subjective annotation. The predicate recognition in the dataset is much trickier than the image classification tasks. For instance, although Microsoft coco [29] has super categories, it does not require a model to have the ability to make a different prediction like "bus" and "vehicle" for a visually identical object. However, in the SGG task, a more general predicate like "on" and a more informative one like "parked on" will be learned and predicted simultaneously. Under this training condition, it is a dilemma for models since machines cannot understand why almost identical visual features have different annotations and require them to make different prediction results. The second one is the long-tail effect which exists objectively in nature. Some of the dominant predicate classes are almost 1,000 times as many as less-frequent ones, leading to a bad performance on those less frequent predicates. Too many general predicates like "on" in training will lead to insufficient training for less-frequent ones like "eating" and drifting preference away from fine ones such as "parked on". Some methods, including re-weighting and re-sampling, seem to be suitable choices. However, due to the hierarchical annotation in the dataset, the improvement seems to be limited according to [42].

When training the deep network, problems like the long-tail effect and mixed-granularity annotation are universal but catastrophic to the deep network training. In contrast, humans seem capable of handling these complicated problems. As shown in cognitive psychology research [14], human beings appear to learn gradually and hierarchically. Coincidentally, the semantic structure of predicates in VG is similar to our real-life naming, consisting of mixed-granularity information. For instance, parents often teach their kids to recognize "bird" first and then go for the specific kinds like "mockingbird" or "cuckoo". Inspired by this, we realize that it is plausible to design a hierarchical training framework to resolve the abovementioned problems by imitating human learning behavior.

This work proposes a Hierarchical Memory Learning (HML) framework for hierarchical fashion training with the abovementioned consideration. At the very beginning, we cluster predicates, establish a hierarchical tree in Fig. 1 and separate the dataset by the tree layers without any extra manual annotation. To realize hierarchical training, Concept Reconstruction (CR) is used to inherit the previous model's predicate recognition ability by imitating its output. For a similar purpose, Model Reconstruction (MR) directly fits the parameters in the previous model as a stronger constraint. Under this training scenario, the model gets less chance to confront the previously discussed dilemma and is much easier to train with a relatively small and balanced fraction of predicates.

The proposed HML framework is a general training framework and can train any off-the-shelf SGG model. Figure 1 shows the scene graph generated by the hierarchical training scenario. The scene graph predicted by the model trained with the HML framework is more comprehensive and fine-grained. The predicted relationships such as "bike-parked on-sidewalk" and "plate-on back of-bike" are more informative and meaningful than "bike-on-sidewalk" and "plate-on-bike".

The main contributions of this work can be summarized as follows:

- Inspired by human learning behavior, we propose a novel HML framework, and its generality can be demonstrated by applying it to various classic models.
- We present two new CR and MR constraints to consolidate knowledge from coarse to fine.

- Our HML framework overperforms all existing optimization frameworks. Besides, one standard model trained under HML will also be competitive among various SGG methods with the trade-off between fine and coarse prediction.

2 Related Work

2.1 Scene Graph Generation

SGG [44,51,57] has received increasing attention in the computer vision community because of it's potential in various down-stream visual tasks [19,46,54]. Nevertheless, the prerequisite is the generation of fine-grained and informative scene graphs. Recent works consider SGG mainly from three perspectives.

Model Design. Initially, some works designed elaborate structures for better feature refinement. [51] leveraged GRUs to pass messages between edges and nodes. [59] explored that the feature of objects and predicates can be represented in low-dimensional space, which inspired works like [20,36,50] [57] chose BiLSTM for object and predicate context encoding. [43] encoded hierarchical and parallel relationships between objects and carried out a scoring matrix to find the existence of relationships between objects. Unfortunately, the improvement is limited to elaborate model design alone.

Framework Formulation. Later works tried to design the optimization framework to improve the model performance further. Based on causal inference, [42] used Total Direct Effect for unbiased SGG. [39] proposed an energy-based constraint to learn predicates in small numbers. [56] formulated the predicate tree structure and used tree-based class-balance loss for training. [56] and our work both focus on the granularity of predicates and share some similarities.

Dataset Property. The long-tail effect was particularly pronounced in VG, making studying this problem very important. [7] utilized dynamic frequency for the better training. [9] proposed a novel class-balance sampling strategy to capture entities and predicates distributions. [16] sought a semantic level balance of predicates. [27] used bipartite GNN and bi-level data re-sampling strategy to alleviate the imbalance. However, another problem (mixed-granularity annotation) in the dataset is not fully explored, which inspires this work. Our concurrent work [11] also borrowed the incremental idea to overcome this problem. We add semantic information for the separation and stronger distill constraint for better head knowledge preserving, while [11] learns better at the tail part.

2.2 Long-Tail Learning

Only a few works like [7,9,16,27] cast importance on the long-tail effect in VG. In fact, many long-tail learning strategies can be used in SGG. The previous works tackling the long-tail effect can be roughly divided into three strategies.

Re-sampling. Re-sampling is one of the most popular methods to resolve class imbalance. Simple methods like random over or under-sampling lead to over-fitting the tail and degrading the head. Thus, recent work like [13,21,47,61] monitored optimization process of depending only instance balance.

Cost-Sensitive Learning. Cost-sensitive learning realizes class balance by adjusting loss for different classes during training. [8,29,38] leveraged label frequency to adjust loss and prediction during the training. [40] regarded one positive sample as a negative sample for other classes in calculating softmax or sigmoid cross-entropy loss. Other works [4,22] tried to handle the long-tail problem by adjusting distances between representation features and the model classifier for different classes.

Transfer or Incremental Learning. Those methods help to transfer information or knowledge from head to tail and enhance models' performances. [30,55] proposed a guiding feature in the head to augment tail learning. [48] learned to map few-shot model parameters to many-shot ones for better training. Works like [15,28,32] helped to distill knowledge directly from the head to the tail.

3   Approach

We will first introduce how to automatically construct a hierarchical predicate tree via clustering (Sect. 3.1). And then turn back to explain our HML framework in (Sect. 3.2), along with loss formulation for CR (Sect. 3.3) and MR (Sect. 3.4).

3.1   Soft Construction of Predicate Tree

In order to form a predicate tree for our training scenario, we firstly embed all 50 predicates in the dataset into feature vectors with the pre-trained word representation model in [33]. After that, motivated by reporting bias [34], we cluster predicates into different groups and do some soft manual pruning (e.g., re-classifying some mistakes into different groups). We finally pick up the top-K frequent predicates within each group as the first K layers of the tree.

As for clustering, we choose the traditional distributed word embedding (DWE) algorithm [33], since we wish to eliminate the context from objects or subjects which can provide extra information [57] to the predicate embedding. We iterate through all 50 predicates from frequent to less-frequent for clustering. The first predicate is automatically divided into the first group and records its embedding vector to be the initial value of the first group representation $R_1 = DWE(x_1)$. As for the following ones, we calculate the cosine distance among all current group representations:

$$SS^{ij} = \frac{R_i \cdot DWE(x_j)}{||R_i|| \times ||DWE(x_j)||},$$ (1)

where SS^{ij} is the semantic similarity between current iterated predicate x_j and i^{th} group representations R_i. $DWE(x)$ represents distributed word embedding function on the predicate. Max cosine distance SS^{ij}_{max} will be recorded and compared with the empirical threshold T_{SS} whose setting is mentioned in Sect. 4.3. If SS^{ij} is larger than the threshold, the currently iterated predicate x_j will be added to the existing group. Otherwise, we create a new group for it. The group representations will be updated in the following rule:

$$\begin{cases} R_{N+1} = DWE(x_j), SS^{ij}_{max} < T_{SS} \\ R_i = \frac{n \cdot R_i + DWE(x_j)}{n+1}, SS^{ij}_{max} \geq T_{SS} \end{cases}, \qquad (2)$$

where N is the current number of groups and n is the number of predicates in the ith group.

After clustering, the most frequent predicates are assigned to the first layer, the second frequent predicates are assigned to the second layer, etc. It is worth noticing that during this clustering, some human actions such as "looking at", "playing", "says", "eating", and "walking in" will become a single group as one single predicate. We automatically divide them into the last layer since those human action predicates are almost 100 to 1000 times less than predicates in the other layer. The most suitable number of layers depends on the dataset itself. Section 4.6 analyzes the best layer number for the VG dataset.

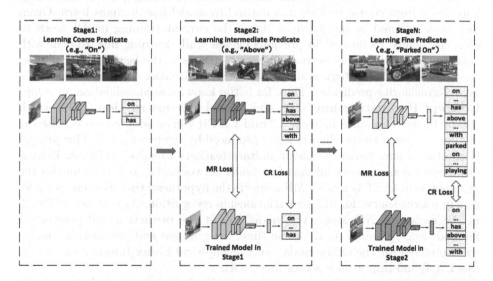

Fig. 2. Overview of HML Framework. We train the model in a coarse to fine fashion. In each step, the model calculates CR and MR for knowledge assimilation. Meanwhile, the importance scores and empirical Fisher Information Matrix are calculated after updating the model. The importance score and empirical Fisher Information Matrix are passed down at the end of each stage. For the VG dataset, we set the stage number to be 2 and explain in Sect. 4.6.

3.2   Hierarchical Memory Learning Framework

Most SGG models comprise two steps. In the beginning, an image is fed into an ordinary object detector to get bounding boxes, corresponding features of these regions, and the logits over each object class. These detection results are used to predict the scene graph in the next step. The feature of a node is initialized by box features, object labels, and position. Some structures like LSTM [37,57] are used to refine nodes' features by passing and incorporating the messages. After that, the object labels are obtained directly by refined feature, while the predicates are predicted from the union features refined by the structures of BiLSTM [57], BiTreeLSTM [37], GRU [10], or GNN [27].

Nevertheless, most models are still trained on the whole dataset at one time, making the task challenging. To address the long-tail effect and mixed-granularity annotation, we believe it is a better solution to disentangle semantic-confusing predicate classes by dealing with general relationships (e.g., "on", "has") and informative ones (e.g., "sitting on", "using") separately in different stages. In this training scenario, the model in its stage can only focus on a small fraction of predicates with relatively similar granularity and then congregate the knowledge from previous stages step by step.

Since the SGG task is similar to the human learning pattern, absorbing knowledge from coarse to fine, it is natural to model how humans learn. Given the model trained in the previous stage, the current training model needs to gain the ability to do well in previous classes while learning how to deal with new classes. A naive way is to sample some images in the last stage for review. Nevertheless, this strategy is unsuitable for our situation since it reintroduces mixed-granularity predicates. Thus, for better knowledge consolidation, we adopt **Concept Reconstruction (CR)** and **Model Reconstruction (MR)** which will be further explained in Sects. 3.3 and 3.4. CR will be adopted to decrease the distance between the prediction logits produced by the two models. This process is similar to how human students imitate teachers to solve problems. Human brain cortical areas have different functional networks [14]. It is the same for the parameters in an SGG model. MR respects the hypothesis that different parameters in a model serve for different relationship recognition. As is shown in Fig. 2, in the second to N^{th} stage, the model will fit the prediction and parameters for knowledge passing. At the same time, the gradient and parameters' change will be stored for the online update of the empirical Fisher Information Matrix (Sect. 3.4) and importance scores (Sect. 3.4).

Does a deep network have parameter redundancy? Some earlier work did answer this question. Hinton *et al.* [18] came up with knowledge distillation for the first time to compress and transfer knowledge from a complicated model to a more compact one that is easier to deploy. Moreover, it was verified in [3] that a cumbersome model can be compressed into a compact one. We assume that the whole model comprises many parameters based on these works. These parameters or "activated" neurons in an SGG network should target specific predicate classes, as shown in Fig. 1. To verify this assumption, we compare the mean of importance scores, which will be further illustrated in Sect. 3.4 and verified in supplementary material from the experimental perspective, of all the parameters in each layer and find out that the values vary between different stages. This mechanism is similar to how the human brain works. Each region in the brain has its' own function and works together to finish complex tasks [14]. After learning through all stages, the model will classify all classes with fine-grained preference.

The total loss for the HML framework is given by:

$$\ell = \ell_{new} + \ell_{CR} + \lambda \ell_{MR}, \tag{3}$$

where λ is a hyper-parameter. ℓ_{CR} is Concept Reconstruction loss, and ℓ_{MR} is Model Reconstruction loss.

ℓ_{new} in Eq. (3) is Class-Balance loss [8] and used to learn current stage predicates:

$$\ell_{new} = -W_B \sum_{i=1}^{C} y_i \log \frac{e^{z_i}}{\sum_{j=1}^{C} e^{z_j}}, \tag{4}$$

where z represents the model's output, y is the one-hot ground-truth label vector, and C is the number of predicate classes. $W_B = \frac{1-\gamma}{1-\gamma^{n_i}}$, γ denotes the hyper-parameter that represents the sample domain, and n_i denotes number of predicate i in current stage.

3.3 Concept Reconstruction Loss

In order to prevent activation drift [3], CR is applied. It is an implicit way to keep the prediction of previous predicates from drifting too much. Thus, we need to find the distance between two predictions from different stages of the same visual relationship and reduce it. The CR loss can be represented by:

$$\ell_{CR}(X_n, Z_n) = \frac{\sum_{i=1}^{N_n} \sum_{j=1}^{C_{old}} \left(\text{Softmax} \left(x_n^{ij} \right) - \text{Softmax} \left(z_n^{ij} \right) \right)^2}{N_n}, \tag{5}$$

where x_n^i and z_n^i are the output logits vector for the prediction. N_n is the number of outputs. We choose L2 distance [2] as the distance metric. Compared with the traditional loss function such as L1 loss and cross-entropy loss with the soft label, L2 loss is a stronger constraint but is sensitive to outliers. Fortunately, since the training process is coarse to fine, the representations will not drastically deviate, making L2 loss practical. With the consideration mentioned earlier, L2 distance is used in CR, receiving better performance in experiments. This is also verified in [60]. More ablation results of CR can be found in the supplementary material.

In a word, CR is used to help the current model learn how to make the same prediction as the previous model.

3.4 Model Reconstruction Loss

The parameters of the model determine the ability to recognize visual relationships. Thus, it is a more straightforward way to learn directly from parameters.

A feasible solution is to determine which parameters are crucial in the previous stage classification and fit them with greater attention in the following stage.

KL-divergence is a mathematical statistics measure of how a probability distribution is different from another one [25]. KL-divergence, denoted as in the form of $D_{KL}(p_\theta \| p_{\theta+\Delta\theta})$, can also be used to calculate the difference of the conditional likelihood between a model at θ and $\theta + \Delta\theta$. Since changes of parameters are subtle (i.e., $\Delta\theta \to 0$) during the optimization, we will get the second-order of Taylor approximation of KL-divergence, which is also the distance in Riemannian manifold induced by Fisher Information Matrix [26] and can be written as $D_{KL}(p_\theta \| p_{\theta+\Delta\theta}) \approx \frac{1}{2} \Delta\theta^\top F_\theta \Delta\theta$, where the F_θ is known as empirical Fisher Information Matrix [35] at θ and the approximate will be proved in supplementary material, is defined as:

$$F_\theta = \mathbb{E}_{(\mathbf{x},\mathbf{y}) \sim D} \left[\left(\frac{\partial \log p_\theta(\mathbf{y}|\mathbf{x})}{\partial \theta} \right) \left(\frac{\partial \log p_\theta(\mathbf{y}|\mathbf{x})}{\partial \theta} \right)^\top \right], \qquad (6)$$

where D is the dataset and $p_\theta(y|x)$ is the log-likelihood. However, in practice, if a model has P parameters, it means $F_\theta \in R^{P \times P}$, and it is computationally expensive. To solve this, we compromise and assume parameters are all independent, making F_θ diagonal. Then the approximation of KL-divergence looks like:

$$D_{KL}(p_\theta \| p_{\theta+\Delta\theta}) \approx \frac{1}{2} \sum_{i=1}^{P} F_{\theta_i} \Delta\theta_i^2, \qquad (7)$$

where θ_i is the ith parameters of the model and P is the total number of it.

F_θ will be updated in each iteration, following the rule:

$$F_\theta^t = \frac{F_\theta^t + (t-1) \cdot F_\theta^{t-1}}{t}, \qquad (8)$$

where t is the number of iterations.

Although the empirical Fisher Information Matrix captures static information of the model, it fails to capture the influence of each parameter during optimization in each stage. Thus, we adopt the method in [58] to search for essential parameters. Intuitively, if the value of a parameter changes a little in a single step, but it contributes a lot to the decrease of the loss, we think it is essential, at least for the current task. So, the importance of a parameter during an interval (from t to Δt) can be represented as:

$$\Omega_{raw}(\theta_i) = \sum_{t}^{t+\Delta t} \frac{\Delta \ell_t^{t+1}(\theta_i)}{\frac{1}{2} F_{\theta_i}^t (\theta_i(t+1) - \theta_i(t))^2 + \epsilon}, \qquad (9)$$

$$\Omega_t^{t+\Delta t}(\theta_i) = \sigma \left(\log_{10} \frac{P \times \Omega_{raw}(\theta_i)}{\sum_{i=1}^{P} \Omega_{raw}(\theta_i)} \right), \qquad (10)$$

where σ is the sigmoid function, numerator $\Delta \ell_t^{t+1}(\theta_i)$ is the change of loss caused by θ_i in one step, $\epsilon > 0$ aims to avoid the change of loss $\theta_i(t+1) - \theta_i(t) = 0$, and the denominator is the KL-divergence of θ_i between t and $t+1$.

To be more specific, $\Delta \ell_t^{t+1}(\theta_i)$ represents how much contribution does θ_i make to decrease the loss. Since the optimization trajectory is hard to track, to find the change in loss caused by θ_i, we need to figure out a way to split the overall loss form into the sum of each parameter's contributions. The solution is a first-order Taylor approximation:

$$\ell(\theta(t+1)) - \ell(\theta(t)) \approx -\sum_{i=1}^{P} \sum_{t=t}^{t+1} \frac{\partial \ell}{\partial \theta_i} (\theta_i(t+1) - \theta_i(t)) = -\sum_{i=1}^{P} \Delta \ell_t^{t+1}(\theta_i),$$

(11)

where $\frac{\partial \ell}{\partial \theta_i}$ is the gradient of θ_i and $\theta_i(t+1) - \theta_i(t)$ is the value change of θ_i during a single step. If $\ell(\theta(t+1)) - \ell(\theta(t)) > 0$, we set $\Delta \ell_t^{t+1}(\theta_i)$ to be 0, since we consider only when the loss become smaller, a step of optimization can be regarded as effective.

The empirical Fisher Information Matrix is used twice. The first is to calculate the difference in probability distributions of two models in different stages, and the second is to find the changes of a model in a nearby iteration within a single stage.

So, after figuring out how important each parameter is, the MR loss can be written as:

$$\ell_{MR} = \frac{\sum_{i=1}^{P} \left(F_{\theta_i}^{k-1} + (\Omega_{t_0}^{t_0 + \Delta t})^{k-1}(\theta_i) \right) \left(\theta_i^k - \theta_i^{k-1} \right)^2}{P},$$

(12)

where P is the number of parameters for relationship prediction in the model and k represents the current stage. $F_{\theta_i}^{k-1}$ and $(\Omega_{t_0}^{t_0 + \Delta t})^{k-1}$ are both calculated in previous stage.

Fisher Information Matrix F_{θ} and importance scores $\Omega_{t_0}^{t_{k-1}}$ are used to represent the importance of parameters from static and dynamic perspectives, respectively.

4 Experiment

4.1 Dataset and Model

Dataset. In the SGG task, we choose Visual Genome (VG) [24] as the dataset for both training and evaluation. It comprises 75k object categories and 40k predicate categories. However, due to the scarcity of over 90% predicates are less than ten instances, we applied the widely accepted split in [6,37,57], using the 150 highest frequency objects categories and 50 predicate categories. The training set is set to be 70%, and the testing set is 30%, with 5k images from the training set for finetuning. [42].

Model. We evaluate HML framework on three models and follow the setting in [41]: MOTIFS [57], Transformer [12,45], and VCTree [37].

4.2   Evaluation

Sub-Tasks: (1) **Predicate Classification**: given images, object bounding boxes, and object labels, predicting the relationship labels between objects. (2) **Scene Graph Classification**: given images and object bounding boxes, predicting object labels and relationship labels between objects. (3) **Scene Graph Detection**: localizing objects, recognizing objects, and predicting their relationships directly from images.

Table 1. Result of Relationship Retrieval mR@K [43] and R@K.

Model transformer [45]	Framework	Predicate classification			Scene graph classification			Scene graph detection		
		mR@20	mR@50	mR@100	mR@20	mR@50	mR@100	mR@20	mR@50	mR@100
MOTIFS [57]	Baseline	14.1	17.9	19.4	8.2	10.1	10.8	6.3	8.5	10.1
	CogTree [56]	22.9	28.4	31.0	13.0	15.7	16.7	7.9	11.1	12.7
	BPL+SA [16]	26.7	31.9	34.2	**15.7**	18.5	19.4	**11.4**	14.8	17.1
	HML(Ours)	**27.4**	**33.3**	**35.9**	**15.7**	**19.1**	**20.4**	**11.4**	**15.0**	**17.7**
VCTree [43]	Baseline	12.5	15.9	17.2	7.4	9.1	9.7	5.3	7.3	8.6
	EBM [39]	14.2	18.0	19.5	8.2	10.2	11.0	5.7	7.7	9.3
	SG [23]	14.5	18.5	20.2	8.9	11.2	12.1	6.4	8.3	9.2
	TDE [42]	18.5	25.5	29.1	9.8	13.1	14.9	5.8	8.2	9.8
	CogTree [56]	20.9	26.4	29.0	12.1	14.9	16.1	7.9	10.4	11.8
	DLFE [7]	22.1	26.9	28.8	12.8	15.2	15.9	8.6	11.7	13.8
	BPL+SA [16]	24.8	29.7	31.7	14.0	16.5	17.5	10.7	13.5	15.6
	GCL [11]	**30.5**	36.1	38.2	**18.0**	20.8	21.8	**12.9**	**16.8**	**19.3**
	HML(Ours)	30.1	**36.3**	**38.7**	17.1	**20.8**	**22.1**	10.8	14.6	17.3
	Baseline	13.4	16.8	18.1	8.5	10.5	11.2	5.9	8.2	9.6
	EBM [39]	14.2	18.2	19.7	10.4	12.5	13.5	5.7	7.7	9.1
	SG [23]	15.0	19.2	21.1	9.3	11.6	12.3	6.3	8.1	9.0
	TDE [42]	18.4	25.4	28.7	8.9	12.2	14.0	6.9	9.3	11.1
	CogTree [56]	22.0	27.6	29.7	15.4	18.8	19.9	7.8	10.4	12.1
	DLFE [7]	20.8	25.3	27.1	15.8	18.9	20.0	8.6	11.8	13.8
	BPL+SA [16]	26.2	30.6	32.6	17.2	20.1	21.2	10.6	13.5	15.7
	GCL [11]	**31.4**	**37.1**	39.1	19.5	22.5	23.5	**11.9**	**15.2**	**17.5**
	HML(Ours)	31.0	36.9	**39.2**	**20.5**	**25.0**	**26.8**	10.1	13.7	16.3

(a) Comparison between HML and various optimization frameworks.

Model+Framework	Predicate Classification		Scene Graph Classification		Scene Graph Detection		Mean@50/100
	mR@50/100	R@50/100	mR@50/100	R@50/100	mR@50/100	R@50/100	
MOTIFS-TDE [42]	25.5/29.1	46.2/51.4	13.1/14.9	27.7/29.9	8.2/9.8	16.9/20.3	22.9/25.9
MOTIFS-DLFE [7]	26.9/28.8	**52.5/54.2**	15.2/15.9	**32.3/33.1**	11.7/13.8	**25.4/29.4**	27.3/29.2
Transformer-CogTree [56]	28.4/31.0	38.4/39.7	15.7/16.7	22.9/23.4	11.1/12.7	19.5/21.7	22.7/24.2
PCPL [52]	35.2/37.8	50.8/52.6	18.6/19.6	27.6/28.4	9.5/11.7	14.6/18.6	26.1/28.1
DT2-ACBS [9]	35.9/39.7	23.3/25.6	24.8/**27.5**	16.2/17.6	**22.0/24.4**	15.0/16.3	22.9/25.2
SHA-GCL [11]	**41.6/44.1**	35.1/37.2	23.0/24.3	22.8/23.9	17.9/20.9	14.9/18.2	25.9/28.1
Transformer-HML(Ours)	33.3/35.9	45.6/47.8	19.1/20.4	22.5/23.8	15.0/17.7	15.4/18.6	25.2/27.4
MOTIFS-HML(Ours)	36.3/38.7	47.1/49.1	20.8/22.1	26.1/27.4	14.6/17.3	17.6/21.1	27.1/29.3
VCTree-HML(Ours)	36.9/39.2	47.0/48.8	**25.0/26.8**	27.0/28.4	13.7/16.3	17.6/21.0	**27.9/30.1**

(b) A more comprehensive comparison between HML and various SOTAs.

Relationship Recall. We choose **Mean Recall@K (mR@K)** [43] as a metric to evaluate the performance of SGG models. As is shown in [42], regular Recall@K (R@K) will lead to the reporting bias due to the imbalance that lies in the data (e.g., a model that only correctly classifies the top 5 frequent predicates can reach 75% of Recall@100). Thus, we introduce **Mean@K** which calculates the average score of all three sub-tasks R@K and mR@K under identical K. Mean@K is a metric to evaluate overall performance on both R@K and mR@K. We will further explain the reason and necessity of using this metric in the supplementary material.

4.3   Implementation Details

Object Detector. We pre-train a Faster-RCNN with ResNeXt-101-FPN [49] and freeze the previously trained weight during the SGG training period. The final detector reached 28 mAP on the VG test set.

Relationship Predictor. The backbone of baseline models is replaced with an identical one, and hierarchical trained in the same setting. We set the batch size to 12 and used SGD optimizer with an initial learning rate of 0.001, which will be decayed by 10 after the validation performance plateaus. The experiment was carried out on NVIDIA TITAN RTX GPUs.

Hierarchical Predicate Tree Construction. For Visual Genome (VG), the whole predicates are split into two disjoint subsets (tasks) following the construction in Sect. 3.1. The threshold is set to be $T_{SS} \in [0.65, 0.75]$ in Eq. (2). However, due to the small semantic variance within VG, this Predicate Tree Construction degenerates to simply separating frequent "on" or "has" with minority ones, similar to the separation in [11]. We believe a larger semantic variance dataset will need this kind of semantic information for more reasonable separation.

Hierarchical Training. In our experiment, two identical models will be trained separately in two stages. Moreover, the first model will be initialized randomly, and the previous stage models will not be used to initialize the following model. If not, the model will meet the intransigence [5] problem. Besides, we set the max iterations to 8000 and 16000 in the first and second stages. Nevertheless, models will usually converge around 8000 in both stages. The λ in an overall loss is set to 0.5 for the best performance, as is shown in Table 3a.

Fig. 3. Qualitative Results. The basic model generates yellow scene graphs, and the same basic model predicts pink ones under HML training. (Color figure online)

4.4   Quantitative Study

In Table 1a, our HML framework can consistently outperform the existing frameworks under various fundamental models. By applying the HML framework to different models, we notice that models will drastically improve the Mean Recall for all three sub-tasks. The improvement scale is similar to different models such as Motif, Transformer, and VCTree. In Table 1b, we compare HML with various SOTAs, which report R@K and mR@K simultaneously. After calculating Mean@K, it turns out that HML can make the fine-grained prediction (demonstrated by mR@K) and keep clear boundaries of general predicates (demonstrated by R@K).

In Table 2, we notice a vital decrease in R@K. After analyzing each predicate, we figure out that the decline mainly comes from the drop of general predicates such as "on" and "has". After HML training, the mR@100 of "on" and "has" dropped from 79.98 to 31.01 and 81.22 to 58.34. The model's preference for fine-grained prediction causes this decrease. Thus, we replace the fine-grained one with a general one and recalculate R@100, and the results of "on" and "has" re-bounce to be 71.72 and 86.91, respectively. Works like [7,9,42,52,56] compared in Table 1b can also make relatively fine-grained prediction (i.e., relatively high mR@K) but all suffer from decrease of R@K partially due to the reason mentioned above.

4.5   Qualitative Study

We visualize the qualitative result generated by original MOTIFS and MOTIFS trained with the HML framework in Fig. 3. Compared with the original model, the model trained under HML will make informative predictions such as "parked on", "growing on", "standing on", "riding", and "walking on" instead of the general one "on". Also, our model will tend to make fine-grained predictions such as "wearing" and "carrying" instead of "has". Besides, since we train a model hierarchically, the model will obtain the ability to capture tail part predicates such as "building-across-street" and position predicates such as "building-behind-bus" and "tree-behind-bus". Qualitative results with three stages are shown in the supplementary material.

4.6   Ablation Studies

CR and MR. We further explore the contributions of each term to our overall loss. In the SGG task, Recall@K and Mean Recall@K [43] restrict mutually with each other. Recall@K represents how well the model performs for the predicate classes' head part. Thus, it reflects how well a model can imitate the previous model. On the contrary, Mean Recall@K [43] evaluates the model's overall performance. Suppose we want to figure out the functionality of the knowledge consolidation term in the loss. In that case, it is reasonable to adopt Recall@K since two terms of knowledge reconstruction aim to prevent the model from

Table 2. Ablation on CR and MR. We explore the functionality of CR loss and MR loss.

Model	CR	MR	Predicate classification					
			mR@20	mR@50	mR@100	R@20	R@50	R@100
Transformer [45]			14.13	17.87	19.38	58.79	65.29	67.09
	✓		24.14	29.27	31.22	29.1	36.16	38.57
		✓	23.32	29.34	32.20	38.80	46.48	48.87
	✓	✓	**27.35**	**33.25**	**35.85**	38.81	45.61	47.78
MOTIFS [57]			12.54	15.89	17.19	59.12	65.45	67.20
	✓		24.69	30.00	32.79	33.92	41.34	43.95
		✓	21.56	27.43	30.05	44.30	51.87	54.14
	✓	✓	**30.10**	**36.28**	**38.67**	40.52	47.11	49.08
VCTree [43]			13.36	16.81	18.08	59.76	65.48	67.49
	✓		22.32	29.34	32.20	27.86	35.21	37.73
		✓	22.84	28.94	31.48	43.81	51.40	53.74
	✓	✓	**31.04**	**36.90**	**39.21**	40.28	46.47	48.36

forgetting previous knowledge. According to Table 2, if we add CR and MR separately, mR@K will get constant improvement. However, only when CR and MR are used simultaneously will we get the highest mR@K and prevent R@K from dropping too much. Also, after comparing the second and third row of each model on R@K, it is obvious that MR is a more powerful constraint than CR.

Table 3. Confusion matrix of one of the folds for the final classification of DGCNN-MS-T-W, with $W = 150$

Layer	Predicates cassification			time (hr)
	mR@20	mR@50	mR@100	
1	12.54	15.89	17.19	17.85
2	**30.10**	**36.28**	**38.67**	29.43
3	25.24	31.95	34.44	44.65
4	15.66	21.96	25.32	60.13

(a) **Ablation of layer number**

λ	Predicates classification		
	mR@20	mR@50	mR@100
0.00	25.24	31.95	34.44
0.25	**30.97**	35.91	37.88
0.50	30.10	**36.28**	**38.67**
0.75	29.73	34.36	36.79
1.00	29.20	33.47	35.69

(b) **Ablation of λ**

Layer Number. The number of layers (i.e., stage) depends on how many top-K frequent predicates we pick up after clustering. We conduct experiments in Table 3a on different layers. We figured out that 2 is suitable for the VG dataset, mainly due to the small number of predicate classes and limited granularity variance. HML training indeed needs more time to complete training during multi-stage training. Nevertheless, the increase ratio (125%) of model performance is way more significant than the one (65%) of training time. More time analysis will be shown in the supplementary material. All experiments were carried out on one identical GPU.

Hyperparameter λ. In order to figure out the effect of λ on the performance of the model, we set 5 values in ablation to $\lambda \in \{0, 0.25, 0.50, 0.75, 1.00\}$ in Table 3b. λ represents how much information will be passed down to the next stage. If λ is too high, the new model will stick to the original classes without learning new ones. In contrast, low λ can not guarantee effective information passing. Based on our experiment, $\lambda = 0.5$ is suitable for the HML framework on VG.

5   Conclusion

We propose a general framework to enable SGG models to make fine-grained predictions. In addition to the objective long-tail effect in the dataset, we uncover mixed-granularity predicates caused by subjective human annotation. The similarity between the human hierarchical learning pattern and the SGG problem is obvious under this condition. Based on that, we designed the HML framework with two new constraints (i.e., CR and MR) for efficient training. We observe that the HML framework can improve performance compared to the traditional training fashion models and achieves new state-of-the-art.

Acknowledgments. This work was partly supported by the National Natural Science Foundation of China under Grant 41971284; the Fundamental Research Funds for the Central Universities under Grant 2042022kf1201; Wuhan University-Huawei Geoinformatics Innovation Laboratory. We sincerely thank our reviewers and ACs for providing insightful suggestions.

References

1. Agrawal, A., Batra, D., Parikh, D., Kembhavi, A.: Don't just assume; look and answer: overcoming priors for visual question answering. In: CVPR, pp. 4971–4980 (2018)
2. Ba, J., Caruana, R.: Do deep nets really need to be deep? In: NIPS, pp. 2654–2662 (2014)
3. Buciluǎ, C., Caruana, R., Niculescu-Mizil, A.: Model compression. In: KDD, pp. 535–541 (2006)
4. Cao, D., Zhu, X., Huang, X., Guo, J., Lei, Z.: Domain balancing: face recognition on long-tailed domains. In: CVPR, pp. 5671–5679 (2020)
5. Chaudhry, A., Dokania, P.K., Ajanthan, T., Torr, P.H.S.: Riemannian walk for incremental learning: understanding forgetting and intransigence. In: Ferrari, V., Hebert, M., Sminchisescu, C., Weiss, Y. (eds.) ECCV 2018. LNCS, vol. 11215, pp. 556–572. Springer, Cham (2018). https://doi.org/10.1007/978-3-030-01252-6_33
6. Chen, L., Zhang, H., Xiao, J., He, X., Pu, S., Chang, S.F.: Counterfactual critic multi-agent training for scene graph generation. In: ICCV, pp. 4613–4623 (2019)
7. Chiou, M.J., Ding, H., Yan, H., Wang, C., Zimmermann, R., Feng, J.: Recovering the unbiased scene graphs from the biased ones. In: ACMMM, pp. 1581–1590 (2021)

8. Cui, Y., Jia, M., Lin, T.Y., Song, Y., Belongie, S.: Class-balanced loss based on effective number of samples. In: CVPR, pp. 9268–9277 (2019)
9. Desai, A., Wu, T.Y., Tripathi, S., Vasconcelos, N.: Learning of visual relations: the devil is in the tails. In: ICCV, pp. 15404–15413 (2021)
10. Dhingra, N., Ritter, F., Kunz, A.: BGT-Net: Bidirectional GRU transformer network for scene graph generation. In: CVPR, pp. 2150–2159 (2021)
11. Dong, X., Gan, T., Song, X., Wu, J., Cheng, Y., Nie, L.: Stacked hybrid-attention and group collaborative learning for unbiased scene graph generation. In: CVPR, pp. 19427–19436 (2022)
12. Dosovitskiy, A., et al.: An image is worth 16×16 words: transformers for image recognition at scale. In: ICLR (2021)
13. Feng, C., Zhong, Y., Huang, W.: Exploring classification equilibrium in long-tailed object detection. In: ICCV, pp. 3417–3426 (2021)
14. Genon, S., Reid, A., Langner, R., Amunts, K., Eickhoff, S.B.: How to characterize the function of a brain region. Trends Cogn. Sci. **22**(4), 350–364 (2018)
15. Goodfellow, I.J., Mirza, M., Xiao, D., Courville, A., Bengio, Y.: An empirical investigation of catastrophic forgetting in gradient-based neural networks. In: ICLR (2014)
16. Guo, Y., et al.: From general to specific: informative scene graph generation via balance adjustment. In: ICCV, pp. 16383–16392 (2021)
17. Hendricks, L.A., Burns, K., Saenko, K., Darrell, T., Rohrbach, A.: Women also snowboard: overcoming bias in captioning models. In: Ferrari, V., Hebert, M., Sminchisescu, C., Weiss, Y. (eds.) ECCV 2018. LNCS, vol. 11207, pp. 793–811. Springer, Cham (2018). https://doi.org/10.1007/978-3-030-01219-9_47
18. Hinton, G., Vinyals, O., Dean, J.: Distilling the knowledge in a neural network. CoRR (2015)
19. Hudson, D.A., Manning, C.D.: GQA: a new dataset for real-world visual reasoning and compositional question answering. In: CVPR, pp. 6700–6709 (2019)
20. Hung, Z., Mallya, A., Lazebnik, S.: Contextual translation embedding for visual relationship detection and scene graph generation. TPAMI **43**(11), 3820–3832 (2021)
21. Kang, B., et al.: Decoupling representation and classifier for long-tailed recognition. In: ICLR (2020)
22. Khan, S., Hayat, M., Zamir, S.W., Shen, J., Shao, L.: Striking the right balance with uncertainty. In: CVPR, pp. 103–112 (2019)
23. Khandelwal, S., Suhail, M., Sigal, L.: Segmentation-grounded scene graph generation. In: ICCV, pp. 15879–15889 (2021)
24. Krishna, R., et al.: Visual genome: Connecting language and vision using crowd-sourced dense image annotations. IJCV **123**(1), 32–73 (2017)
25. Kullback, S., Leibler, R.A.: On information and sufficiency. Ann. Math. Stat. **22**(1), 79–86 (1951)
26. Lee, J.M.: Riemannian Manifolds. GTM, vol. 176. Springer, New York (1997). https://doi.org/10.1007/b98852
27. Li, R., Zhang, S., Wan, B., He, X.: Bipartite graph network with adaptive message passing for unbiased scene graph generation. In: CVPR, pp. 11109–11119 (2021)
28. Li, T., Wang, L., Wu, G.: Self supervision to distillation for long-tailed visual recognition. In: ICCV, pp. 630–639 (2021)
29. Lin, T.-Y., et al.: Microsoft COCO: common objects in context. In: Fleet, D., Pajdla, T., Schiele, B., Tuytelaars, T. (eds.) ECCV 2014. LNCS, vol. 8693, pp. 740–755. Springer, Cham (2014). https://doi.org/10.1007/978-3-319-10602-1_48

30. Liu, J., Sun, Y., Han, C., Dou, Z., Li, W.: Deep representation learning on long-tailed data: a learnable embedding augmentation perspective. In: CVPR, pp. 2970–2979 (2020)
31. Manjunatha, V., Saini, N., Davis, L.S.: Explicit bias discovery in visual question answering models. In: CVPR, pp. 9562–9571 (2019)
32. McCloskey, M., Cohen, N.J.: Catastrophic interference in connectionist networks: the sequential learning problem. In: Psychology of Learning and Motivation, pp. 109–165 (1989)
33. Mikolov, T., Grave, E., Bojanowski, P., Puhrsch, C., Joulin, A.: Advances in pre-training distributed word representations. In: LREC (2018)
34. Misra, I., Lawrence Zitnick, C., Mitchell, M., Girshick, R.: Seeing through the human reporting bias: visual classifiers from noisy human-centric labels. In: CVPR, pp. 2930–2939 (2016)
35. Pascanu, R., Bengio, Y.: Revisiting natural gradient for deep networks. In: ICLR (2014)
36. Peyre, J., Laptev, I., Schmid, C., Sivic, J.: Detecting unseen visual relations using analogies. In: ICCV, pp. 1981–1990 (2019)
37. Rebuffi, S.A., Kolesnikov, A., Sperl, G., Lampert, C.H.: ICARL: Incremental classifier and representation learning. In: CVPR, July 2017
38. Ren, J., et al.: Balanced meta-softmax for long-tailed visual recognition. In: NIPS, pp. 4175–4186 (2020)
39. Suhail, M., et al.: Energy-based learning for scene graph generation. In: CVPR, pp. 13936–13945 (2021)
40. Tan, J., et al.: Equalization loss for long-tailed object recognition. In: CVPR, pp. 11662–11671 (2020)
41. Tang, K.: A scene graph generation codebase in pytorch (2020). https://github.com/KaihuaTang/Scene-Graph-Benchmark.pytorch
42. Tang, K., Niu, Y., Huang, J., Shi, J., 8 Zhang, H.: Unbiased scene graph generation from biased training. In: CVPR, pp. 3716–3725 (2020)
43. Tang, K., Zhang, H., Wu, B., Luo, W., Liu, W.: Learning to compose dynamic tree structures for visual contexts. In: CVPR, pp. 6619–6628 (2019)
44. Tao, L., Mi, L., Li, N., Cheng, X., Hu, Y., Chen, Z.: Predicate correlation learning for scene graph generation. TIP. 31, 4173–4185 (2022)
45. Vaswani, A., et al.: Attention is all you need. In: NIPS, pp. 5998–6008 (2017)
46. Wang, S., Wang, R., Yao, Z., Shan, S., Chen, X.: Cross-modal scene graph matching for relationship-aware image-text retrieval. In: WACV, pp. 1508–1517 (2020)
47. Wang, T., Li, Yu., Kang, B., Li, J., Liew, J., Tang, S., Hoi, S., Feng, J.: The devil is in classification: a simple framework for long-tail instance segmentation. In: Vedaldi, A., Bischof, H., Brox, T., Frahm, J.-M. (eds.) ECCV 2020. LNCS, vol. 12359, pp. 728–744. Springer, Cham (2020). https://doi.org/10.1007/978-3-030-58568-6_43
48. Wang, Y., Ramanan, D., Hebert, M.: Learning to model the tail. In: NIPS, pp. 7029–7039 (2017)
49. Xie, S., Girshick, R., Dollár, P., Tu, Z., He, K.: Aggregated residual transformations for deep neural networks. In: CVPR, pp. 1492–1500 (2017)
50. Xiong, S., Huang, W., Duan, P.: Knowledge graph embedding via relation paths and dynamic mapping matrix. In: Advances in Conceptual Modeling, pp. 106–118 (2018)
51. Xu, D., Zhu, Y., Choy, C.B., Fei-Fei, L.: Scene graph generation by iterative message passing. In: CVPR, pp. 5410–5419 (2017)

52. Yan, S., et al.: PCPL: predicate-correlation perception learning for unbiased scene graph generation. In: ACMMM, pp. 265–273 (2020)
53. Yang, J., Lu, J., Lee, S., Batra, D., Parikh, D.: Graph R-CNN for scene graph generation. In: Ferrari, V., Hebert, M., Sminchisescu, C., Weiss, Y. (eds.) ECCV 2018. LNCS, vol. 11205, pp. 690–706. Springer, Cham (2018). https://doi.org/10.1007/978-3-030-01246-5_41
54. Yang, X., Tang, K., Zhang, H., Cai, J.: Auto-encoding scene graphs for image captioning. In: CVPR, pp. 10685–10694 (2019)
55. Yin, X., Yu, X., Sohn, K., Liu, X., Chandraker, M.: Feature transfer learning for face recognition with under-represented data. In: CVPR, pp. 5704–5713 (2019)
56. Yu, J., Chai, Y., Wang, Y., Hu, Y., Wu, Q.: CogTree: cognition tree loss for unbiased scene graph generation. In: IJCAI, pp. 1274–1280 (2020)
57. Zellers, R., Yatskar, M., Thomson, S., Choi, Y.: Neural motifs: scene graph parsing with global context. In: CVPR, pp. 5831–5840 (2018)
58. Zenke, F., Poole, B., Ganguli, S.: Continual learning through synaptic intelligence. In: ICML, pp. 3987–3995 (2017)
59. Zhang, H., Kyaw, Z., Chang, S., Chua, T.: Visual translation embedding network for visual relation detection. In: CVPR, pp. 3107–3115 (2017)
60. Zhang, J., et al.: Class-incremental learning via deep model consolidation. In: WACV, pp. 1131–1140 (2020)
61. Zhang, X., et al.: VideoLT: large-scale long-tailed video recognition. In: ICCV, pp. 7960–7969 (2021)

DODA: Data-Oriented Sim-to-Real Domain Adaptation for 3D Semantic Segmentation

Runyu Ding[1], Jihan Yang[1], Li Jiang[2], and Xiaojuan Qi[1(✉)]

[1] The University of Hong Kong, Hong Kong, China
{ryding,jhyang,xjqi}@eee.hku.hk
[2] MPI for Informatics, Saarbürcken, Germany
lijiang@mpi-inf.mpg.de

Abstract. Deep learning approaches achieve prominent success in 3D semantic segmentation. However, collecting densely annotated real-world 3D datasets is extremely time-consuming and expensive. Training models on synthetic data and generalizing on real-world scenarios becomes an appealing alternative, but unfortunately suffers from notorious domain shifts. In this work, we propose a **D**ata-**O**riented **D**omain **A**daptation (DODA) framework to mitigate pattern and context gaps caused by different sensing mechanisms and layout placements across domains. Our DODA encompasses virtual scan simulation to imitate real-world point cloud patterns and tail-aware cuboid mixing to alleviate the interior context gap with a cuboid-based intermediate domain. The first unsupervised sim-to-real adaptation benchmark on 3D indoor semantic segmentation is also built on 3D-FRONT, ScanNet and S3DIS along with 8 popular Unsupervised Domain Adaptation (UDA) methods. Our DODA surpasses existing UDA approaches by over 13% on both 3D-FRONT → ScanNet and 3D-FRONT → S3DIS. Code is available at https://github.com/CVMI-Lab/DODA.

Keywords: Domain adaptation · 3D semantic segmentation

1 Introduction

3D semantic segmentation is a fundamental perception task receiving incredible attention from both industry and academia due to its wide applications in robotics, augmented reality, and human-computer interaction, to name a

---

R. Ding and J. Yang—Equal contribution.

Supplementary Information The online version contains supplementary material available at https://doi.org/10.1007/978-3-031-19812-0_17.

few. Data hungry deep learning approaches have attained remarkable success for 3D semantic segmentation [22,30,46,55,61,63]. Nevertheless, harvesting a large amount of annotated data is expensive and time-consuming [3,7].

An appealing avenue to overcome such data scarcity is to leverage simulation data where both data and labels can be obtained for free. Simulated datasets can be arbitrarily large, easily adapted to different label spaces and customized for various usages [8,18,26,34,53,72]. However, due to notorious domain gaps in point patterns and context (see Fig. 1), models trained on simulated scenes suffer drastic performance degradation when generalized to real-world scenarios. This motivates us to study sim-to-real unsupervised domain adaptation (UDA), leveraging labeled source data (simulation) and unlabeled target data (real) for effectively adapting knowledge across domains.

Recent efforts on 3D domain adaptation for outdoor scene parsing have obtained considerable progress [23,29,60,71]. However, they often adopt LiDAR-specific range image format, not applicable for indoor scenarios with scenes constructed by RGB-D sequences. Besides, such outdoor attempts could be suboptimal in addressing the indoor domain gaps raised from different scene construction processes. Further, indoor scenes have more sophisticated interior context than outdoor, which makes the context gap a more essential issue in indoor settings. Here, we explore sim-to-real UDA in the 3D indoor scenario which is challenging and largely under explored.

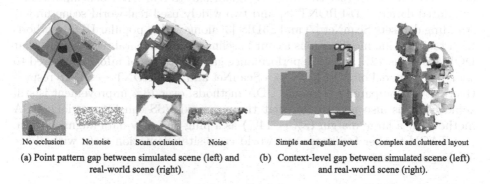

No occlusion   No noise   Scan occlusion   Noise   Simple and regular layout   Complex and cluttered layout

(a) Point pattern gap between simulated scene (left) and   (b) Context-level gap between simulated scene (left)
real-world scene (right).   and real-world scene (right).

Fig. 1. The domain gaps between simulated scenes from 3D-FRONT [8] and real-world scenes from ScanNet [7]. (a): The point pattern gap. The simulated scene is perfect without occlusions or noise, while the real-world scene inevitably contains scan occlusion and noise patterns such as rough surfaces. (b): The context gap. While the simulated scene applies simple layout with regularly placed objects, the real-world scene is complex with cluttered interiors.

Challenges. Our empirical studies on sim-to-real adaptation demonstrate two unique challenges in this setting: the *point pattern gap* owing to different sensing mechanisms, and the *context gap* due to dissimilar semantic layouts. As shown in Fig. 1(a), simulated scenes tend to contain complete objects as well as smooth surfaces, while real scenes include inevitable scan occlusions and noise patterns during reconstructing point clouds from RGB-D videos captured by depth cameras [3,7]. Also, even professionally designed layouts in simulated scenes are much simpler and more regular than real layouts as illustrated in Fig. 1(b).

To tackle the above domain gaps, we develop a holistic two stage pipeline DODA with a pretrain and a self-training stage, which is widely proved to be effective in UDA settings [49,64,73]. As the root of the challenges lies in "data", we thus design two data-oriented modules which are shown to dramatically reduce domain gaps without incurring any computational costs during inference. Specifically, we develop Virtual Scan Simulation (VSS) to mimic occlusion and noise patterns that occur during the construction of real scenes. Such pattern imitation yields a more transferable model to real-world data. Afterwards, to adapt the model to target domain, we design Tail-aware Cuboid Mixing (TACM) for boosting self-training. While source supervision is utilized to stabilize gradients with clean labels in self-training, it unfortunately introduces context bias. Thus, we propose TACM to create an intermediate domain by splitting, permuting, mixing and re-sampling source and target cuboids, which explicitly mitigates the context gap through breaking and rectifying source bias with target pseudo-labeled data, and simultaneously eases long-tail issue by oversampling tail cuboids.

To the best of our knowledge, we are the first to explore unsupervised domain adaptation on 3D indoor semantic segmentation. To verify the effectiveness of our DODA, we construct the first 3D indoor sim-to-real UDA benchmark on a simulated dataset 3D-FRONT [8] and two widely used real-world scene understanding datasets ScanNet [7] and S3DIS [3] along with 8 popular UDA methods with task-specific modifications as our baselines. Experimental results show that DODA obtains 22% and 19% performance gains in terms of mIoU compared to source only model on 3D-FRONT → ScanNet and 3D-FRONT → S3DIS respectively. Even compared to existing UDA methods, over 13% improvement is still achieved. It is also noteworthy that the proposed VSS can lift previous UDA methods by a large margin (8% ∼ 14%) as a plug-and-play data augmentation, and TACM further facilitates real-world cross-site adaptation tasks with 4% ∼ 5% improvements.

2   Related Work

3D Indoor Semantic Segmentation focuses on obtaining point-wise category predictions from point clouds, which is a fundamental while challenging task due to the irregularity and sparsity of 3D point clouds. Some previous works [41,53] feed 3D grids constructed from point clouds into 3D convolutional neural networks. Some approaches [6,16] further employ sparse convolution [17] to leverage the sparsity of 3D voxel representation to accelerate computation. Another line of works [25,45,46,61,70] directly extract feature embeddings from raw point clouds with hierarchical feature aggregation schemes. Recent methods [55,63] assign position-related kernel functions on local point areas to perform dynamic convolutions. Additionally, graph-based works [31,52,59] adopt graph convolutions to mimic point cloud structure for point representation learning. Although the above methods achieve prominent performance on various indoor scene datasets, they require large-scale human-annotated datasets which we aim to address using simulation data. Our experimental investigation is built upon the sparse-convolution-based U-Net [6,16] due to its high performance.

Unsupervised Domain Adaptation aims at adapting models obtained from annotated source data towards unlabeled target samples. The annotation efficiency of UDA and existing data-hungry deep neural networks make it receive great attention from the computer vision community. Some previous works [38,39] attempt to learn domain-invariant representations by minimizing maximum mean discrepancy [5]. Another line of research leverages adversarial training [14] to align distributions in feature [10,20,50], pixel [13,20,21] or output space [56] across domains. Adversarial attacks [15] have also been utilized in [35,66] to train domain-invariant classifiers. Recently, Self-training has been investigated in addressing this problem [49] which formulate UDA as a supervised learning problem guided by pseudo-labeled target data and achieves state-of-the-art performance in semantic segmentation [73] and object detection [28,48].

Lately, with the rising of 3D vision tasks, UDA has also attracted a lot of attention in such 3D tasks as 3D object classification [1,47], 3D outdoor semantic segmentation [23,29,44,60,67] and 3D outdoor object detection [40, 58,64,65,69]. Especially, Wu *et al.* [60] propose intensity rendering, geodesic alignment and domain calibration modules to align sim-to-real gaps of outdoor 3D semantic segmentation datasets. Jaritz *et al.* [23] explore multi-modality UDA by leveraging images and point clouds simultaneously. Nevertheless, no previous work studies UDA on 3D indoor scenes. The unique point pattern gap and the context gap also render 3D outdoor UDA approaches not readily applicable to indoor scenarios. Hence, in this work, we make the first attempt on UDA for 3D indoor semantic segmentation. Particularly, we focus on the most practical and challenging scenario – simulation to real adaptation.

Data Augmentation for UDA has also been investigated to remedy data-level gaps across domains. Data augmentation techniques have been widely employed to construct an intermediate domain   [13,29,48] to benefit optimization and facilitate gradual domain adaptation. However, they mainly focus on image-like input formats, which is not suitable for sparse and irregular raw 3D point clouds. Different from existing works, we build a holistic pipeline with two data-oriented modules on two stages to manipulate raw point clouds for mimicking target point cloud patterns and creating a cuboid-based intermediate domain.

3   Method

3.1   Overview

In this work, we aim at adapting a 3D semantic scene parsing model trained on a source domain $\mathcal{D}_s = \{(P_i^s, Y_i^s)\}_{i=1}^{N_s}$ of N_s samples to an unlabeled target

288   R. Ding et al.

domain $\mathcal{D}_t = \{P_i^t\}_{i=1}^{N_t}$ of N_t samples. P and Y represent the point cloud and the point-wise semantic labels respectively.

In this section, we present DODA, a data-oriented domain adaptation framework to simultaneously close pattern and context gaps by imitating target patterns as well as breaking source bias with the generated intermediate domain. Specifically, as shown in Fig. 2, DODA begins with pretraining the 3D scene parsing model F on labeled source data with our proposed virtual scan simulation module for better generalization. VSS puts virtual cameras on the feasible regions in source scenes to simulate occlusion patterns, and jitters source points to imitate sensing and reconstruction noise in the real scenes. The pseudo labels are then generated with the pretrained model. In the self-training stage, we develop tail-aware cuboid mixing to build an intermediate domain between source and target, which is constructed by splitting and mixing cuboids from both domains. Besides, cuboids including high percentage tail classes are over-sampled to overcome the class imbalance issue during learning with pseudo labeled data. Elaborations of our tailored VSS and TACM are presented in the following parts.

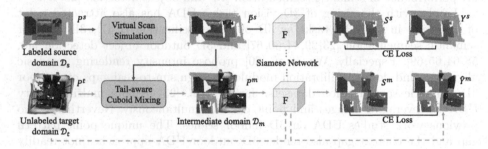

Fig. 2. Our DODA framework consists of two data-oriented modules: Virtual Scan Simulation (VSS) and Tail-aware Cuboid Mixing (TACM). VSS mimics real-world data patterns and TACM constructs an intermediate domain through mixing source and target cuboids. P denotes the point cloud; Y denotes the semantic labels and $\hat{Y}$ denotes the pseudo labels. The superscripts s, t and m stand for source, target and intermediate domain, respectively. The blue line denotes source training flow; the orange line denotes target training flow and the orange dotted line denotes target pseudo label generation procedure. Best viewed in color. (Color figure online)

3.2 Virtual Scan Simulation

DODA starts from training a 3D scene parsing network on labeled source data, to provide pseudo labels on the target domain in the next self-training stage. Hence, a model with a good generalization ability is highly desirable. As analyzed in Sect. 1, different scene construction procedures cause point pattern gaps across domains, significantly hindering the transferability of source-trained models. Specifically, we find that the missing of occlusion patterns and sensing or reconstruction noise in simulation scenes raises huge negative transfer during the adaptation, which cannot be readily addressed by previous UDA methods (see Sect. 5). This is potentially caused by the fact that models trained on clean source data are incapable of extracting useful features to handle real-world challenging scenarios with ubiquitous occlusions and noise. To this end, we propose a plug-and-play data augmentation technique, namely virtual scan simulation, to imitate camera scanning procedure for augmenting the simulation data.

VSS includes two parts: the occlusion simulation that puts virtual cameras in feasible regions of simulated scenes to imitate occlusions in the scanning process, and the noise simulation that randomly jitters point patterns to mimic sensing or reconstruction errors, through which the pattern gaps are largely bridged.

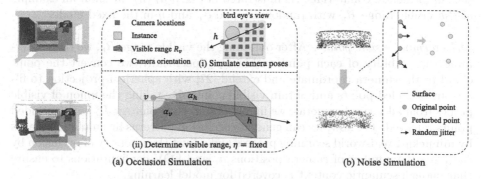

Fig. 3. Virtual scan simulation. (a): We simulate occlusion patterns by simulating camera poses and determining visible ranges. (b): We simulate noise by randomly jittering points to generate realistic irregular point patterns such as rough surfaces.

Occlusion Simulation.   Scenes in real-world datasets are reconstructed from RGB-D frame sequences suffering from inevitable occlusions, while simulated scenes contain complete objects without any hidden points. We attempt to mimic occlusion patterns on the simulation data by simulating the real-world data acquisition procedures. Specifically, we divide it into the following three steps:

a) Simulate camera poses. To put virtual cameras in a given simulation scene, we need to determine camera poses including camera positions and camera orientations. First, feasible camera positions where a handheld camera can be placed are determined by checking free space in the simulated environment. We voxelize and project P^s to bird eye's view and remove voxels containing instance or room boundary. The centers of remaining free-space voxels are considered as feasible x-y coordinates for virtual cameras, as shown in Fig. 3(a) (i). For the z axis, we randomly sample the camera height in the top half of the room.

Second, for each camera position v, we randomly generate a camera orientation using the direction from the camera position v to a corresponding randomly sampled point of interest h on the wall, as shown in Fig. 3(a) (i). This ensures that simulated camera orientations are uniformly distributed among all potential directions without being influenced by scene-specific layout bias.

b) Determine visible range. Given a virtual camera pose and a simulated 3D scene, we are now able to determine the spatial range that the camera can cover, i.e., R_v, which is determined by the camera field of view (FOV) (see Fig. 3(a) (ii)). To ease the modeling difficulties, we decompose FOV into the horizontal viewing angle α_h, the vertical viewing angle α_v and the viewing mode η that determine horizontal range, vertical range and the shape of viewing frustum, respectively. For the viewing mode η, we approximate three versions from simple to sophisticated, namely fixed, parallel and perspective, with details presented in the supplementary materials. As illustrated in Fig. 3(a) (ii), we show an example of the visible range R_v with random α_h and α_v and η in the fixed mode.

c) Determine visible points. After obtaining the visible range R_v, we then determine the visibility of each point within R_v. Specifically, we convert the point cloud to the camera coordinate and extend [27] with spherical projection to filter out occluded points and obtain visible points. By taking the union of visible points from all virtual cameras, we finally obtain the point set P_v^s with occluded points removed. Till now, we can generate occlusion patterns in simulation scenes by mimicking real-world scanning process and adjust the intensity of occlusion by changing the number of camera positions n_v and FOV configurations to ensure that enough semantic context is covered for model learning.

Noise Simulation. Besides occlusion patterns, sensing and reconstruction errors are unavoidable when generating 3D point clouds from sensor-captured RGB-D videos, which unfortunately results in non-uniform distributed points and rough surfaces in real-world datasets (See Fig. 1(a)). To address this issue, we equip our VSS with another noise simulation module, which injects perturbations to each point as follows:

$$\tilde{P}^s = \{p + \Delta p \mid p \in P_v^s\}, \tag{1}$$

where Δ_p denotes the point perturbation following a uniform distribution ranging from $-\delta_p$ to δ_p, and $\tilde{P}^s$ is the perturbed simulation point cloud. Though simple, we argue that this module efficiently imitates the noise in terms of non-uniform and irregular points patterns as illustrated in Fig. 3.

Model Pretraining on Source Data. By adopting VSS as a data augmentation for simulated data, we train a model with cross-entropy loss as Eq. (2) following settings in [24,37].

$$\min \mathcal{L}_{pre} = \sum_{i=1}^{N_s} \mathrm{CE}(S_i^s, Y_i^s), \tag{2}$$

where $\text{CE}(\cdot, \cdot)$ is the cross-entropy loss and S is the predicted semantic scores after performing *softmax* on logits.

3.3 Tail-aware Cuboid Mixing

After obtaining a more transferable scene parsing model with VSS augmentation, we further adopt self-training [32,54,62, 69,73], to adapt the model by directly utilizing target pseudo-labeled data for supervision. Since target pseudo label is rather noisy, containing incorrect pseudo labeled data and leading to erroneous supervisions [65], we also introduce source supervision to harvest its clean annotations and improve the percentage of correct labels. However, directly utilizing source data unfortunately brings source bias and large discrepancies in joint optimization. Even though point pattern gaps have already been alleviated with the proposed VSS, the model still suffers from the context gap due to different scene layouts.

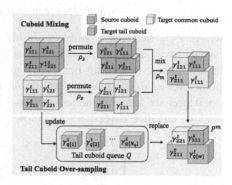

Fig. 4. An illustration of tail-aware cuboid mixing, which contains cuboid mixing and tail cuboid over-sampling. Notice that for clarity, we take $(n_x, n_y, n_z) = (2, 2, 1)$ as an example.

Fortunately, the availability of target domain data gives us the chance to rectify such context gaps. To this end, we design Tail-aware Cuboid Mixing (TACM) to construct an intermediate domain $\mathcal{D}_m$ that combines source and target cuboid-level patterns (see Fig. 4), which augments and rectifies source layouts with target domain context. Besides, it also decreases the difficulty of simultaneously optimizing source and target domains with huge distribution discrepancies by providing a bridge for adaptation. TACM further moderates the pseudo label class imbalance issue by cuboid-level tail class oversampling. Details on pseudo labeling, cuboid mixing and tail cuboid oversampling are as follows.

Pseudo Label Generation. To employ self-training after pretraining, we first need to generate pseudo labels $\hat{Y}^t$ for target scenes P^t. Similar to previous paradigms [24,62,65,73], we obtain pseudo labels via the following equation:

$$\hat{Y}_{i,j}^t = \begin{cases} 1 \text{ , if } \max(S_i^t) > T, j = \arg\max S_i^t, \\ 0 \text{ , otherwise,} \end{cases} \tag{3}$$

where $\hat{Y}_i^t = [\hat{Y}_{i,1}^t, \cdots, \hat{Y}_{i,c}^t]$, c is the number of classes and T is the confidence threshold to filter out uncertain predictions.

Cuboid Mixing. Here, given labeled source data and pseudo-labeled target data, we carry out the cuboid mixing to construct a new intermediate domain

$\mathcal{D}_m$ as shown in Fig. 2 and Fig. 4. For each target scene, we randomly sample a source scene to perform cuboid mixing. We first partition two scenes into several cuboids with varying sizes as the smallest units to mix cuboid as Eq. (4):

$$P = \{\gamma_{ijk}\}, i \in \{1, ..., n_x\}, j \in \{1, ..., n_y\}, k \in \{1, ..., n_z\},$$
$$\gamma_{ijk} = \{p \mid p \text{ in } [x_{i-1}, y_{j-1}, z_{k-1}, x_i, y_j, z_k]\}, \tag{4}$$

where γ_{ijk} denotes a single cuboid; n_x, n_y and n_z stand for the number of partitions in x, y and z axis, respectively; and each cuboid γ_{ijk} is constrained in a six-tuple bounding box $[x_{i-1}, y_{j-1}, z_{k-1}, x_i, y_j, z_k]$ defined by the partition positions x_i, y_j, z_k for corresponding dimensions, respectively. These partition positions are first initialized as equal-divisions and then injected with randomness to enhance diversities as below:

$$x_i = \begin{cases} \frac{i}{n_x}\max p_x + (1 - \frac{i}{n_x})\min p_x, & \text{if } i \in \{0, n_x\}, \\ \frac{i}{n_x}\max p_x + (1 - \frac{i}{n_x})\min p_x + \Delta\phi, & \text{otherwise,} \end{cases} \tag{5}$$

where $\Delta\phi$ is the random perturbation following uniform distribution ranging from $-\delta_\phi$ to δ_ϕ. The same formulation is also adopted for y_j and z_k. After partitioning, the source and target cuboids are first spatially permuted with a probability ρ_s and then randomly mixed with another probability ρ_m, as depicted in Fig. 4 and Fig. 2.

Though ConDA [29] shares some similarities with our cuboid mixing by mixing source and target, it aims to preserve cross-domain context consistency while ours attempts to mitigate context gaps. Besides, ConDA operates on 2D range images, inapplicable to reconstructed indoor scenes obtained by fusing depth images. Our cuboid mixing leverages the freedom of the raw 3D representation, i.e., point cloud, and thus is generalizable to arbitrary 3D scenarios.

Tail Cuboid Over-Sampling. Besides embedding target context to source data, our cuboid mixing technique also allows adjusting the category distributions by designing cuboid sampling strategies. Here, as an add-on advantage, we leverage this nice property to alleviate the biased pseudo label problem [2,19,36,73] in self-training: tail categories only occupy a small percentage of pseudo labeled data. Specifically, we sample cuboids with tail categories more frequently, namely tail cuboid over-sampling, detailed as follows.

We calculate per-class pseudo label ratio $r \in [0,1]^c$ and define n_r least common categories as tail categories. We then define tail cuboid whose pseudo label ratio is higher than the average value r on at least one of n_r tail categories. We construct a tail cuboid queue Q with size N_q to store tail cuboids. Formally, $\gamma^t_{q[w]}$ denotes the wth tail cuboid in Q, as shown in Fig. 4. Notice that through training, Q is dynamically updated with First In, First Out (FIFO) rule since cuboids are randomly split in each iteration as Eq. (4). In each training iteration, we ensure that at least u tail cuboids are in each mixed scene by sampling cuboids from Q and replacing existing cuboids if needed. With such a simple over-sampling strategy, we make the cuboid mixing process tail-aware, and relieve the class imbalance issue in the self-training. Experimental results in Sect. 6 further demonstrate the effectiveness of our tail cuboid over-sampling strategy.

Self-training with Target and Source data. In the self-training stage, for data augmentation, VSS is first adopted to augment the source domain data to reduce the pattern gap and then TACM mixes source and target scenes to construct a tail-aware intermediate domain $\mathcal{D}_m = \{P^m\}$ with labels $\hat{Y}^m$ mixed by source ground-truth and target pseudo labels. To alleviate the noisy supervisions from incorrect target pseudo labels, we minimize dense cross-entropy loss on source data $\tilde{P}^s$ and intermediate domain data P^m as below:

$$\min \mathcal{L}_{st} = \sum_{i=1}^{N_t} \text{CE}(S_i^m, \hat{Y}_i^m) + \lambda \sum_{i=1}^{N_s} \text{CE}(S_i^s, Y_i^s), \tag{6}$$

where λ denotes the trade-off factor between losses.

4   Benchmark Setup

4.1   Datasets

3D-FRONT [8] is a large-scale dataset of synthetic 3D indoor scenes, which contains 18,968 rooms with 13,151 CAD 3D furniture objects from 3D-FUTURE [9]. The layouts of rooms are created by professional designers and distinctively span 31 scene categories and 34 object semantic super-classes. We randomly select 4995 rooms as training samples and 500 rooms as validation samples after filtering out noisy rooms. Notice that we obtain source point clouds by uniformly sampling points from original mesh with CloudCompare [12] at 1250 surface density (number of points per square units). Comparison between 3D-FRONT and other simulation datasets are detailed in the nsupplemental materials.

ScanNet [7] is a popular real-world indoor 3D scene understanding dataset, consisting 1,613 real 3D scans with dense semantic annotations (*i.e.*,, 1,201 scans for training, 3,12 scans for validation and 100 scans for testing). It provides semantic annotations for 20 categories.

S3DIS [3] is also a well-known real-world indoor 3D point cloud dataset for semantic segmentation. It contains 271 scenes across six areas along with 13 categories with point-wise annotations. Similar to previous works [33,46], we use the fifth area as the validation split and other areas as the training split.

Label Mapping. Due to different category taxonomy of datasets, we condense 11 categories for 3D-FRONT → ScanNet and 3D-FRONT → S3DIS settings, individually. Besides, we condense 8 categories for cross-site settings between S3DIS and ScanNet. Please refer to the Suppl. for the detailed taxonomy.

4.2 UDA Baselines

As shown in Table 1 and 2, we reproduce 7 popular 2D UDA methods and 1 3D outdoor method as UDA baselines, encompassing MCD [51], AdaptSeg-Net [56], CBST [73], MinEnt [57], AdvEnt [57], Noisy Student [62], APO-DA [66] and SqueezeSegV2 [60]. These UDA baselines cover most existing streams such as adversarial alignment, discrepancy minimization, self-training and entropy guided adaptation. To perform these image-based methods on our setting, we carry out some task-specific modifications, which are detailed in supplemental materials.

5 Experiments

To validate our method, we benchmark DODA and other popular UDA methods with extensive experiments on 3D-FRONT [8], ScanNet [7] and S3DIS [3]. Moreover, we explore a more challenging setting, from simulated 3D-FRONT [8] to RGBD realistic dataset NYU-V2 [42], presented in the supplementary materials. To verify the generalizability of VSS and TACM, we further integrate VSS to previous UDA methods and adopt TACM in the real-world cross-site UDA setting. Note that since textures for some background classes are not provided in 3D-FRONT dataset, we only focus on adaptation using 3D point positions. The implementation details including network and training details are provided in the Suppl.

Comparison to Other UDA Methods. As shown in Table 1 and Table 2, compared to source only, DODA largely lifts the adaptation performance in terms of mIoU by around 21% and 19% on 3D-FRONT → ScanNet and 3D-FRONT → S3DIS, respectively. DODA also shows its superiority over other popular UDA methods, obtaining 14% ∼ 22% performance gain on 3D-FRONT → ScanNet and 13% ∼ 19% gain on 3D-FRONT → S3DIS. Even only equipping source only with VSS module, our DODA (only VSS) still outperforms UDA baselines by around 4% ∼ 10%, indicating that the pattern gap caused by different sensing mechanisms significantly harms adaptation results while previous methods have not readily addressed it. Comparing DODA with DODA (w/o TACM), we observe that TACM mainly contributes to the performance of instances such as bed and bookshelf on ScanNet, since cuboid mixing forces model to focus more on local semantic clues and object shapes itself inside cuboids. It is noteworthy that though DODA yields general improvement around almost all categories adaptation in both pretrain stage and self-training stage, challenging classes such as bed on ScanNet and sofa on S3DIS attain more conspicuous performance lift, demonstrating the predominance of DODA in tackling troublesome categories. However, the effectiveness of all UDA methods for column and beam on S3DIS are not obvious due to their large disparities in data patterns across domains and low appearing frequencies in source domain. To illustrate the reproducibility of our DODA, all results are repeated three times and reported as average performance along with standard variance.

Table 1. Adaptation results of 3D-FRONT → ScanNet in terms of mIoU. We indicate the best adaptation result in **bold**. † denotes pretrain generalization results with VSS

Method	mIoU	Wall	Floor	Cab	Bed	Chair	Sofa	Table	Door	Wind	Bksf	Desk
Source only	29.60	60.72	82.42	04.44	12.02	61.76	22.31	38.52	05.72	05.12	19.72	12.84
MCD [51]	32.27	62.86	88.70	03.81	38.50	57.51	21.48	41.67	05.78	01.29	18.81	15.69
AdaptSegNet [56]	34.51	61.81	83.90	03.64	36.06	55.05	34.26	44.21	06.59	05.54	31.87	16.64
CBST [73]	37.42	60.37	81.39	12.18	30.00	68.86	36.22	49.93	07.05	05.82	43.59	16.25
MinEnt [57]	34.61	63.35	85.54	04.66	26.05	61.98	33.05	48.38	05.20	03.15	35.84	13.49
AdvEnt [57]	32.81	64.31	79.21	04.39	35.01	61.05	24.36	41.64	05.97	01.60	29.07	14.32
Noisy student [62]	34.67	62.63	86.27	01.45	17.13	69.98	37.58	47.87	06.01	01.66	35.79	15.06
APO-DA [66]	31.73	62.84	85.43	02.77	15.08	64.24	34.41	46.41	03.94	03.59	18.88	11.41
SqueezeSegV2 [60]	29.77	61.85	72.74	02.50	16.89	58.79	16.81	38.19	05.08	03.24	35.68	15.72
DODA (only VSS)†	40.52±0.80	67.36	90.24	15.98	39.98	63.11	46.38	48.05	07.63	13.98	33.17	19.86
DODA (w/o TACM)	48.13±0.25	72.22	93.43	24.46	56.30	70.40	53.33	56.57	**09.44**	19.97	47.05	26.25
DODA	**51.42±0.90**	**72.71**	**93.86**	**27.61**	**64.31**	**71.64**	**55.30**	**58.43**	08.21	**24.95**	**56.49**	**32.06**
Oracle	75.19	83.39	95.11	69.62	81.15	88.95	85.11	71.63	47.67	62.74	82.63	59.05

Table 2. Adaptation results of 3D-FRONT → S3DIS in terms of mIoU. We indicate the best adaptation result in **bold**. † denotes pretrain generalization results with VSS

Method	mIoU	Wall	Floor	Chair	Sofa	Table	Door	Wind	Bkcase	Ceil	Beam	Col
Source only	36.72	67.95	88.68	57.69	04.15	38.96	06.99	00.14	44.90	94.42	00.00	00.00
MCD [51]	36.62	64.53	92.16	54.76	13.31	46.67	8.54	00.08	28.86	93.89	00.00	00.00
AdaptSegNet [56]	38.14	68.14	93.17	55.14	05.31	43.14	14.67	00.33	45.75	93.88	00.00	00.00
CBST [73]	42.47	71.60	92.07	68.09	03.28	60.45	17.13	00.18	58.45	95.87	00.00	00.00
MinEnt [57]	37.08	66.15	87.92	52.30	06.27	25.79	15.70	04.44	55.72	93.58	00.00	00.00
AdvEnt [57]	37.98	66.94	91.84	57.96	02.39	46.18	15.14	00.54	44.31	92.50	00.00	00.00
Noisy student [62]	39.44	68.84	91.78	65.53	06.65	48.67	02.27	00.00	53.67	**96.46**	00.00	00.00
APO-DA [66]	38.23	68.63	89.66	58.84	03.51	40.66	13.73	02.61	47.88	94.97	**00.04**	00.00
SqueezeSegV2 [60]	36.50	65.01	89.95	54.29	06.79	45.75	10.23	01.70	32.93	94.81	00.00	00.00
DODA (only VSS) †	46.85±0.78	70.96	96.12	68.70	25.47	58.47	17.87	27.65	54.39	95.66	00.00	00.00
DODA (w/o TACM)	53.86±0.49	75.75	95.14	76.12	60.11	64.07	25.24	31.75	**68.49**	95.82	00.00	00.00
DODA	**55.54±0.91**	**76.23**	**97.17**	**76.89**	**63.55**	**69.04**	25.76	**38.22**	68.18	95.85	00.00	00.00
Oracle	62.29	82.82	96.95	78.16	40.37	78.56	56.91	47.90	77.10	96.29	00.41	29.69

VSS Plug-and-Play Results to Other UDA Methods. Since VSS works as a data augmentation in our DODA, we argue that it can serve as a plug-and-play module to mimic occlusion and noise patterns on simulation data, and is orthogonal to existing UDA strategies. As demonstrated in Table 3, equipped with VSS, current popular UDA approaches consistently surpass their original performance by around 8% ∼ 13%. It also verifies that previous 2D-based methods fail to close the point pattern gap in 3D indoor scene adaptations, while our VSS can be incorporated into various pipelines to boost performance.

TACM Results in Cross-Site Adaptation. Serving as a general module to alleviate domain shifts across domains, we show that TACM can consistently mitigate domain discrepancies on even real-to-real adaptation settings. For cross-site adaptation, scenes collected from different sites or room types also suffer a considerable data distribution gap. As shown in Table 4, the domain gaps in real-to-real adaptation tasks are also large when comparing the source only and

Table 3. UDA results equipped with VSS on 3D-FRONT → ScanNet

Method	VSS w/o	w/	Improv.
MCD [51]	32.37	40.32	+7.95
AdaptSegNet [56]	34.51	45.75	+11.24
CBST [73]	36.30	47.70	+11.40
MinEnt [57]	34.61	43.26	+8.65
AdvEnt [57]	32.81	42.94	+10.13
Noisy Student [62]	34.67	48.30	+13.63
APO-DA [66]	31.73	43.98	+12.25
SqueezeSegV2 [60]	29.77	40.60	+10.83

Table 4. Cross-site adaptation results with TACM

Task	Method	mIoU
ScanNet→ S3DIS	Source only	54.09
	CBST [73]	60.13
	CBST+TACM	65.52
	Oracle	72.51
S3DIS → ScanNet	Source only	33.48
	Noisy student [62]	44.81
	Noisy student+TACM	48.47
	Oracle	80.06

oracle results. When adopting TACM in the self-training pipelines, they obtain 5.64% and 3.66% relative performance boost separately in ScanNet → S3DIS and S3DIS → ScanNet. These results verify that TACM is general in relieving data gaps, especially the context gap on various 3D scene UDA tasks. We provide the cross-site benchmark with more UDA methods in the Suppl.

6   Ablation Study

In this section, we conduct extensive ablation experiments to investigate the individual components of our DODA. All experiments are conducted on 3D-FRONT → ScanNet for simplicity. Default settings are marked in **bold**.

Component Analysis. Here, we investigate the effectiveness of each component and module in our DODA. As shown in Table 5, occlusion simulation brings the largest performance gain (around 9.7%), indicating that model trained on complete scenes is hard to adapt to scenes with occluded patterns. Noise simulation further supplements VSS to imitate sensing and reconstruction noise, obtaining about 1.3% boosts. Two sub-modules jointly mimic realistic scenes, largely alleviating the point distribution gap and leading to a more generalizable source only model. In the self-training stage, VSS also surpasses the baseline by around 13% due to its efficacy in reducing the point pattern gap and facilitating generating high-quality pseudo labels. Cuboid mixing combines cuboid patterns from source and target domains for moderating context-level bias, further boosting the performance by around 2.4%. Moreover, cuboid-level tail-class over-sampling yields 0.9% improvement with greater gains on tail classes. For instance, desk on ScanNet achieves 6% gain (see Suppl.).

VSS: Visible Range. Here, we study the effect of visible range of VSS, which is jointly determined by the horizontal angle α_h, vertical angle α_v, viewing mode η and the number of cameras n_v. As shown in Table 6, fewer cameras $n_v = 2$ and smaller viewing angle $\alpha_v = 45°$ draw around 2% performance degradation with

Table 5. Component Analysis for DODA on 3D-FRONT → ScanNet

Baseline	Virtual scan simulation		Tail-aware cuboid mixing		mIoU
	Occlusion sim	Noise sim	Cuboid mix	Tail samp	
Source only					29.60
Source only	✓				39.25 (+9.65)
Source only	✓	✓			40.52 (+1.27)
Noisy student					34.67
Noisy student	✓	✓			48.13 (+13.46)
Noisy student	✓	✓	✓		50.55 (+2.42)
Noisy student	✓	✓	✓	✓	**51.42** (+0.87)

Table 6. Ablation study of visible range design on 3D-FRONT → ScanNet

α_h	α_v	η	n_v	mIoU
180°	90°	Fixed	2	38.80
180°	90°	Fixed	4	**40.52**
90°	90°	Fixed	8	40.30
180°	90°	Parallel	4	39.08
180°	90°	Perspective	4	39.04
180°	45°	Perspective	4	36.64

Table 7. Ablation study of cuboid partitions on 3D-FRONT → ScanNet

(n_x, n_y, n_z)	# cuboid	mIoU
(1, 1, 1)	1	48.10
(2, 1, 1)	2	50.00
(2, 2, 1)	4	**50.55**
(3, 2, 1)	6	50.57
(3, 3, 1)	9	50.02
(1, 1, 2)	2	49.49
(2, 1, 2)	4	49.48

a smaller visible range. And decreasing α_h to 90° can also achieve similar performance with $\alpha_h = 180°$ with more cameras $n_v = 8$, demonstrating that enough semantic coverage is a vital factor. Besides, as for the three viewing modes η, the simplest fixed mode achieves the highest performance in comparison to parallel and perspective modes. Even though parallel and perspective are more similar to reality practice, they cannot cover sufficient range with limited cameras, since real-world scenes are reconstructed through hundreds or thousands of view frames. This again demonstrates that large spatial coverage is essential. To trade off between the effectiveness and efficiency of on-the-fly VSS, we use fixed mode with 4 camera positions by default here.

TACM: Cuboid Partition. We study various cuboid partition manners in Table 7. Notice that random rotation along z axis is performed before cuboid partition, so the partition on x or y axes can be treated as identical. While horizontal partitioning yields consistent performance beyond 50% mIoU, vertical partitioning does not show robust improvements, suggesting the mixing of vertical spatial context is not necessary. Simultaneous partitioning on x and y axes also improves performance (*i.e.*, (2,2,1) and (2,3,1)), while too small cuboid

Table 8. Ablation study of data-mixing methods on 3D-FRONT → ScanNet

Method	mIoU
Mix3D [43]	48.62
CutMix [68]	49.19
Copy-Paste [11]	48.51
TACM	**51.42**

Table 9. Investigation of pseudo label class imbalance issue on 3D-FRONT → ScanNet

Method	mIoU
Noisy student	48.13
TACM	**51.42**
CM + lovasz loss [4]	51.68
TACM + lovasz loss [4]	52.50

size (*i.e.*, (3,3,1)) results in insufficient context cues in each cuboid with a slight decrease in mIoU.

TACM: Data-Mixing Method. We compare TACM with other popular data-mixing methods in Table 8. Experimental results show the superiority of TACM since it outperforms Mix3D [43], CutMix [68] and Copy-Paste [11] by around 2.2% to 2.9%. TACM effectively alleviates the context gap while preserving local context clues. Mix3D, however, results in large overlapping areas, which is unnatural and causes semantic confusions. CutMix and Copy-Paste only disrupt local areas without enough perturbations of the broader context (see Suppl.).

TACM: Tail Cuboid Over-Sampling with Class-Balanced Loss. Tail cuboid over-sampling brings significant gains on tail classes as discussed in Sect. 6. As demonstrated in Table 9, the class-balanced lovasz loss [4] also boosts performance by considering each category more equally. We highlight that our TACM can also incorporate with other class-balancing methods during optimization since it eases long tail issue on the data-level.

7   Limitations and Open Problems

Although our model largely closes the domain gaps across simulation and real-world datasets, we still suffer from the inherent limitations of the simulation data. For some categories such as beam and column, the simulator fails to generate realistic shape patterns, resulting in huge negative transfer. Besides, room layouts need to be developed by experts, which may limit the diversity and complexity of the created scenes. Therefore, in order to make simulation data benefit real-world applications, there are still several open problems: how to handle the failure modes of the simulator, how to unify the adaptation and simulation stage in one pipeline, and how to automate the simulation process, to name a few.

8   Conclusions

We have presented DODA, a data-oriented domain adaptation method with virtual scan simulation and tail-aware cuboid mixing for 3D indoor sim-to-real unsupervised domain adaptation. Virtual scan simulation generates a more transferable model by mitigating the real-and-simulation point pattern gap. Tail-aware cuboid mixing rectifies context biases through creating a tail-aware intermediate domain and facilitating self-training to effectively leverage pseudo labeled target data, further reducing domain gaps. Our extensive experiments not only show the prominent performance of our DODA in two sim-to-real UDA tasks, but also illustrate the potential ability of TACM to solve general 3D UDA scene parsing tasks. More importantly, we have built the first benchmark for 3D indoor scene unsupervised domain adaptation, including sim to real adaptation and cross-site real-world adaptation. The benchmark suit will be publicly available. We hope our work could inspire further investigations on this problem.

Acknowledgement. This work has been supported by Hong Kong Research Grant Council - Early Career Scheme (Grant No. 27209621), HKU Startup Fund, and HKU Seed Fund for Basic Research.

References

1. Achituve, I., Maron, H., Chechik, G.: Self-supervised learning for domain adaptation on point clouds. In: Proceedings of the IEEE/CVF Winter Conference on Applications of Computer Vision, pp. 123–133 (2021)
2. Araslanov, N., Roth, S.: Self-supervised augmentation consistency for adapting semantic segmentation. In: Proceedings of the IEEE/CVF Conference on Computer Vision and Pattern Recognition, pp. 15384–15394 (2021)
3. Armeni, I., et al.: 3D semantic parsing of large-scale indoor spaces. In: Proceedings of the IEEE Conference on Computer Vision and Pattern Recognition, pp. 1534–1543 (2016)
4. Berman, M., Triki, A.R., Blaschko, M.B.: The lovász-softmax loss: a tractable surrogate for the optimization of the intersection-over-union measure in neural networks. In: Proceedings of the IEEE Conference on Computer Vision and Pattern Recognition, pp. 4413–4421 (2018)
5. Borgwardt, K.M., Gretton, A., Rasch, M.J., Kriegel, H.P., Schölkopf, B., Smola, A.J.: Integrating structured biological data by kernel maximum mean discrepancy. Bioinformatics **22**(14), e49–e57 (2006)
6. Choy, C., Gwak, J., Savarese, S.: 4d spatio-temporal convnets: minkowski convolutional neural networks. In: Proceedings of the IEEE/CVF Conference on Computer Vision and Pattern Recognition, pp. 3075–3084 (2019)
7. Dai, A., Chang, A.X., Savva, M., Halber, M., Funkhouser, T., Nießner, M.: Scannet: richly-annotated 3D reconstructions of indoor scenes. In: Proceedings of the IEEE Conference on Computer Vision and Pattern Recognition, pp. 5828–5839 (2017)
8. Fu, H., et al.: 3d-front: 3D furnished rooms with layouts and semantics. In: Proceedings of the IEEE/CVF International Conference on Computer Vision, pp. 10933–10942 (2021)
9. Fu, H., et al.: 3D-future: 3D furniture shape with texture. Int. J. Comput. Vision **129**, 1–25 (2021)
10. Ganin, Y., Lempitsky, V.: Unsupervised domain adaptation by backpropagation. In: International Conference on Machine Learning, pp. 1180–1189 (2015)
11. Ghiasi, G., et al.: Simple copy-paste is a strong data augmentation method for instance segmentation. In: Proceedings of the IEEE/CVF Conference on Computer Vision and Pattern Recognition, pp. 2918–2928 (2021)

12. Girardeau-Montaut, D.: Cloudcompare. EDF R&D Telecom ParisTech, France (2016)
13. Gong, R., Li, W., Chen, Y., Gool, L.V.: Dlow: domain flow for adaptation and generalization. In: Proceedings of the IEEE Conference on Computer Vision and Pattern Recognition, pp. 2477–2486 (2019)
14. Goodfellow, I., et al.: Generative adversarial nets. In: Advances in Neural Information Processing Systems, pp. 2672–2680 (2014)
15. Goodfellow, I.J., Shlens, J., Szegedy, C.: Explaining and harnessing adversarial examples. arXiv preprint arXiv:1412.6572 (2014)
16. Graham, B., Engelcke, M., Van Der Maaten, L.: 3D semantic segmentation with submanifold sparse convolutional networks. In: Proceedings of the IEEE Conference on Computer Vision and Pattern Recognition, pp. 9224–9232 (2018)
17. Graham, B., van der Maaten, L.: Submanifold sparse convolutional networks. arXiv preprint arXiv:1706.01307 (2017)
18. Handa, A., Patraucean, V., Badrinarayanan, V., Stent, S., Cipolla, R.: Understanding real world indoor scenes with synthetic data. In: Proceedings of the IEEE Conference on Computer Vision and Pattern Recognition, pp. 4077–4085 (2016)
19. He, R., Yang, J., Qi, X.: Re-distributing biased pseudo labels for semi-supervised semantic segmentation: a baseline investigation. In: Proceedings of the IEEE/CVF International Conference on Computer Vision, pp. 6930–6940 (2021)
20. Hoffman, J., et al.: Cycada: cycle-consistent adversarial domain adaptation. arXiv preprint arXiv:1711.03213 (2017)
21. Hoffman, J., Wang, D., Yu, F., Darrell, T.: Fcns in the wild: pixel-level adversarial and constraint-based adaptation. arXiv preprint arXiv:1612.02649 (2016)
22. Hu, Q., et al.: Randla-net: efficient semantic segmentation of large-scale point clouds. In: Proceedings of the IEEE/CVF Conference on Computer Vision and Pattern Recognition, pp. 11108–11117 (2020)
23. Jaritz, M., Vu, T.H., Charette, R.d., Wirbel, E., Pérez, P.: xmuda: cross-modal unsupervised domain adaptation for 3D semantic segmentation. In: Proceedings of the IEEE/CVF Conference on Computer Vision and Pattern Recognition, pp. 12605–12614 (2020)
24. Jiang, L., et al.: Guided point contrastive learning for semi-supervised point cloud semantic segmentation. In: Proceedings of the IEEE/CVF International Conference on Computer Vision, pp. 6423–6432 (2021)
25. Jiang, L., Zhao, H., Liu, S., Shen, X., Fu, C.W., Jia, J.: Hierarchical point-edge interaction network for point cloud semantic segmentation. In: Proceedings of the IEEE/CVF International Conference on Computer Vision, pp. 10433–10441 (2019)
26. Kar, A., et la.: Meta-sim: learning to generate synthetic datasets. In: Proceedings of the IEEE/CVF International Conference on Computer Vision, pp. 4551–4560 (2019)
27. Katz, S., Tal, A., Basri, R.: Direct visibility of point sets. In: ACM SIGGRAPH 2007 papers, pp. 24-es. x (2007)
28. Khodabandeh, M., Vahdat, A., Ranjbar, M., Macready, W.G.: A robust learning approach to domain adaptive object detection. In: Proceedings of the IEEE/CVF International Conference on Computer Vision, pp. 480–490 (2019)
29. Kong, L., Quader, N., Liong, V.E.: Conda: Unsupervised domain adaptation for lidar segmentation via regularized domain concatenation. arXiv preprint arXiv:2111.15242 (2021)
30. Lahoud, J., Ghanem, B., Pollefeys, M., Oswald, M.R.: 3D instance segmentation via multi-task metric learning. In: Proceedings of the IEEE/CVF International Conference on Computer Vision, pp. 9256–9266 (2019)

31. Landrieu, L., Simonovsky, M.: Large-scale point cloud semantic segmentation with superpoint graphs. In: Proceedings of the IEEE Conference on Computer Vision and Pattern Recognition, pp. 4558–4567 (2018)
32. Lee, D.H., et al.: Pseudo-label: the simple and efficient semi-supervised learning method for deep neural networks. In: Workshop on Challenges in Representation Learning, ICML, vol. 3, no. 2, p. 896 (2013)
33. Li, Y., Bu, R., Sun, M., Wu, W., Di, X., Chen, B.: Pointcnn: convolution on x-transformed points. Adv. Neural Inf. Process. Syst. 31, 820–830 (2018)
34. Li, Z., et al.: Openrooms: an end-to-end open framework for photorealistic indoor scene datasets. arXiv preprint arXiv:2007.12868 (2020)
35. Liu, H., Long, M., Wang, J., Jordan, M.: Transferable adversarial training: a general approach to adapting deep classifiers. In: International Conference on Machine Learning, pp. 4013–4022 (2019)
36. Liu, Y.C., et al.: Unbiased teacher for semi-supervised object detection. arXiv preprint arXiv:2102.09480 (2021)
37. Liu, Z., Qi, X., Fu, C.W.: One thing one click: a self-training approach for weakly supervised 3D semantic segmentation. In: Proceedings of the IEEE/CVF Conference on Computer Vision and Pattern Recognition, pp. 1726–1736 (2021)
38. Long, M., Cao, Y., Wang, J., Jordan, M.: Learning transferable features with deep adaptation networks. In: International Conference on Machine Learning, pp. 97–105 (2015)
39. Long, M., Zhu, H., Wang, J., Jordan, M.I.: Deep transfer learning with joint adaptation networks. In: International Conference on Machine Learning, pp. 2208–2217 (2017)
40. Luo, Z., et al.: Unsupervised domain adaptive 3D detection with multi-level consistency. arXiv preprint arXiv:2107.11355 (2021)
41. Maturana, D., Scherer, S.: Voxnet: a 3D convolutional neural network for real-time object recognition. In: 2015 IEEE/RSJ International Conference on Intelligent Robots and Systems (IROS), pp. 922–928. IEEE (2015)
42. Silberman, N., Hoiem, D., Kohli, P., Fergus, R.: Indoor segmentation and support inference from RGBD images. In: Fitzgibbon, A., Lazebnik, S., Perona, P., Sato, Y., Schmid, C. (eds.) ECCV 2012. LNCS, vol. 7576, pp. 746–760. Springer, Heidelberg (2012). https://doi.org/10.1007/978-3-642-33715-4_54
43. Nekrasov, A., Schult, J., Litany, O., Leibe, B., Engelmann, F.: Mix3d: out-of-context data augmentation for 3D scenes. In: 2021 International Conference on 3D Vision (3DV), pp. 116–125. IEEE (2021)
44. Peng, D., Lei, Y., Li, W., Zhang, P., Guo, Y.: Sparse-to-dense feature matching: Intra and inter domain cross-modal learning in domain adaptation for 3D semantic segmentation. In: Proceedings of the IEEE/CVF International Conference on Computer Vision (ICCV), pp. 7108–7117 (2021)
45. Qi, C.R., Su, H., Mo, K., Guibas, L.J.: Pointnet: deep learning on point sets for 3D classification and segmentation. In: Proceedings of the IEEE Conference on Computer Vision and Pattern Recognition, pp. 652–660 (2017)
46. Qi, C.R., Yi, L., Su, H., Guibas, L.J.: Pointnet++: deep hierarchical feature learning on point sets in a metric space. arXiv preprint arXiv:1706.02413 (2017)
47. Qin, C., You, H., Wang, L., Kuo, C.C.J., Fu, Y.: Pointdan: a multi-scale 3D domain adaption network for point cloud representation. arXiv preprint arXiv:1911.02744 (2019)
48. Ramamonjison, R., Banitalebi-Dehkordi, A., Kang, X., Bai, X., Zhang, Y.: Simrod: a simple adaptation method for robust object detection. In: Proceedings of the IEEE/CVF International Conference on Computer Vision, pp. 3570–3579 (2021)

49. Saito, K., Ushiku, Y., Harada, T.: Asymmetric tri-training for unsupervised domain adaptation. In: International Conference on Machine Learning, pp. 2988–2997. JMLR. org (2017)
50. Saito, K., Ushiku, Y., Harada, T., Saenko, K.: Strong-weak distribution alignment for adaptive object detection. In: Proceedings of the IEEE Conference on Computer Vision and Pattern Recognition, pp. 6956–6965 (2019)
51. Saito, K., Watanabe, K., Ushiku, Y., Harada, T.: Maximum classifier discrepancy for unsupervised domain adaptation. In: Proceedings of the IEEE/CVF Conference on Computer Vision and Pattern Recognition, pp. 3723–3732 (2018)
52. Simonovsky, M., Komodakis, N.: Dynamic edge-conditioned filters in convolutional neural networks on graphs. In: Proceedings of the IEEE Conference on Computer Vision and Pattern Recognition, pp. 3693–3702 (2017)
53. Song, S., Yu, F., Zeng, A., Chang, A.X., Savva, M., Funkhouser, T.: Semantic scene completion from a single depth image. In: Proceedings of the IEEE Conference on Computer Vision and Pattern Recognition, pp. 1746–1754 (2017)
54. Tarvainen, A., Valpola, H.: Mean teachers are better role models: weight-averaged consistency targets improve semi-supervised deep learning results. Adv. Neural Inf. Process. Syst. **30**, 1195–1204 (2017)
55. Thomas, H., Qi, C.R., Deschaud, J.E., Marcotegui, B., Goulette, F., Guibas, L.J.: Kpconv: flexible and deformable convolution for point clouds. In: Proceedings of the IEEE/CVF International Conference on Computer Vision, pp. 6411–6420 (2019)
56. Tsai, Y.H., Hung, W.C., Schulter, S., Sohn, K., Yang, M.H., Chandraker, M.: Learning to adapt structured output space for semantic segmentation. In: Proceedings of the IEEE/CVF Conference on Computer Vision and Pattern Recognition, pp. 7472–7481 (2018)
57. Vu, T.H., Jain, H., Bucher, M., Cord, M., Pérez, P.: Advent: adversarial entropy minimization for domain adaptation in semantic segmentation. In: Proceedings of the IEEE/CVF Conference on Computer Vision and Pattern Recognition, pp. 2517–2526 (2019)
58. Wang, Y., et al.: Train in Germany, test in the USA: making 3D object detectors generalize. In: Proceedings of the IEEE/CVF Conference on Computer Vision and Pattern Recognition, pp. 11713–11723 (2020)
59. Wang, Y., Sun, Y., Liu, Z., Sarma, S.E., Bronstein, M.M., Solomon, J.M.: Dynamic graph cnn for learning on point clouds. ACM Trans. Graph. (tog) **38**(5), 1–12 (2019)
60. Wu, B., Zhou, X., Zhao, S., Yue, X., Keutzer, K.: Squeezesegv 2: improved model structure and unsupervised domain adaptation for road-object segmentation from a lidar point cloud. In: 2019 International Conference on Robotics and Automation (ICRA), pp. 4376–4382. IEEE (2019)
61. Wu, W., Qi, Z., Fuxin, L.: Pointconv: deep convolutional networks on 3D point clouds. In: Proceedings of the IEEE/CVF Conference on Computer Vision and Pattern Recognition, pp. 9621–9630 (2019)
62. Xie, Q., Luong, M.T., Hovy, E., Le, Q.V.: Self-training with noisy student improves imagenet classification. In: Proceedings of the IEEE/CVF Conference on Computer Vision and Pattern Recognition, pp. 10687–10698 (2020)
63. Xu, M., Ding, R., Zhao, H., Qi, X.: Paconv: position adaptive convolution with dynamic kernel assembling on point clouds. In: Proceedings of the IEEE/CVF Conference on Computer Vision and Pattern Recognition, pp. 3173–3182 (2021)
64. Yang, J., Shi, S., Wang, Z., Li, H., Qi, X.: St3d++: denoised self-training for unsupervised domain adaptation on 3D object detection. arXiv preprint arXiv:2108.06682 (2021)

65. Yang, J., Shi, S., Wang, Z., Li, H., Qi, X.: St3d: self-training for unsupervised domain adaptation on 3D object detection. In: Proceedings of the IEEE/CVF Conference on Computer Vision and Pattern Recognition (2021)
66. Yang, J., et al.: An adversarial perturbation oriented domain adaptation approach for semantic segmentation. In: Proceedings of the AAAI Conference on Artificial Intelligence, pp. 12613–12620 (2020)
67. Yi, L., Gong, B., Funkhouser, T.: Complete & label: a domain adaptation approach to semantic segmentation of lidar point clouds. In: Proceedings of the IEEE/CVF Conference on Computer Vision and Pattern Recognition, pp. 15363–15373 (2021)
68. Yun, S., Han, D., Oh, S.J., Chun, S., Choe, J., Yoo, Y.: Cutmix: regularization strategy to train strong classifiers with localizable features. In: Proceedings of the IEEE/CVF International Conference on Computer Vision, pp. 6023–6032 (2019)
69. Zhang, W., Li, W., Xu, D.: Srdan: scale-aware and range-aware domain adaptation network for cross-dataset 3D object detection. In: Proceedings of the IEEE/CVF Conference on Computer Vision and Pattern Recognition, pp. 6769–6779 (2021)
70. Zhao, H., Jiang, L., Fu, C.W., Jia, J.: Pointweb: enhancing local neighborhood features for point cloud processing. In: Proceedings of the IEEE/CVF Conference on Computer Vision and Pattern Recognition, pp. 5565–5573 (2019)
71. Zhao, S., et al.: epointda: an end-to-end simulation-to-real domain adaptation framework for lidar point cloud segmentation, vol. 2, p. 3. arXiv preprint arXiv:2009.03456 (2020)
72. Zheng, J., Zhang, J., Li, J., Tang, R., Gao, S., Zhou, Z.: Structured3D: a large photo-realistic dataset for structured 3D modeling. In: Vedaldi, A., Bischof, H., Brox, T., Frahm, J.-M. (eds.) ECCV 2020. LNCS, vol. 12354, pp. 519–535. Springer, Cham (2020). https://doi.org/10.1007/978-3-030-58545-7_30
73. Zou, Y., Yu, Z., Vijaya Kumar, B., Wang, J.: Unsupervised domain adaptation for semantic segmentation via class-balanced self-training. In: European Conference on Computer Vision, pp. 289–305 (2018)

MTFormer: Multi-task Learning via Transformer and Cross-Task Reasoning

Xiaogang Xu[1], Hengshuang Zhao[2,3]($\boxtimes$), Vibhav Vineet[4], Ser-Nam Lim[5], and Antonio Torralba[2]

[1] CUHK, Hong Kong, China
[2] MIT, Cambridge, USA
hszhao@csail.mit.edu
[3] HKU, Hong Kong, China
[4] Microsoft Research, Redmond, USA
[5] Meta AI, New York, USA

Abstract. In this paper, we explore the advantages of utilizing transformer structures for addressing multi-task learning (MTL). Specifically, we demonstrate that models with transformer structures are more appropriate for MTL than convolutional neural networks (CNNs), and we propose a novel transformer-based architecture named MTFormer for MTL. In the framework, multiple tasks share the same transformer encoder and transformer decoder, and lightweight branches are introduced to harvest task-specific outputs, which increases the MTL performance and reduces the time-space complexity. Furthermore, information from different task domains can benefit each other, and we conduct cross-task reasoning. We propose a cross-task attention mechanism for further boosting the MTL results. The cross-task attention mechanism brings little parameters and computations while introducing extra performance improvements. Besides, we design a self-supervised cross-task contrastive learning algorithm for further boosting the MTL performance. Extensive experiments are conducted on two multi-task learning datasets, on which MTFormer achieves state-of-the-art results with limited network parameters and computations. It also demonstrates significant superiorities for few-shot learning and zero-shot learning.

Keywords: Multi-task learning · Transformer · Cross-task reasoning

1 Introduction

Multi-task learning (MTL) aims to improve the learning efficiency and accuracy by learning multiple objectives from shared representations [25,31,49]. It is of great importance for practical applications, e.g., autonomous driving [37], healthcare [51], agriculture [52], manufacturing [27], which cannot be addressed by merely seeking perfection on solving individual tasks.

X. Xu and H. Zhao—Indicates equal contribution.

S. Avidan et al. (Eds.): ECCV 2022, LNCS 13687, pp. 304–321, 2022.
https://doi.org/10.1007/978-3-031-19812-0_18

To tackle MTL for visual scene understanding in computer vision, various solutions have been proposed. They simultaneously handle multiple tasks by utilizing classic convolutional neural networks (CNNs) [4,25,31,36,42,49]. These approaches always meet performance drop compared to single-task learning (STL), or they need to add extra intricate loss functions and complex network structures with large network parameters and computations to overcome the performance decrease shortcoming. We own this phenomenon to the limited capacity of convolution operations and seek powerful structures with huge capacity like transformers for handling the MTL problem.

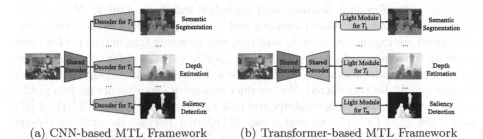

(a) CNN-based MTL Framework   (b) Transformer-based MTL Framework

Fig. 1. The differences between current CNN-based MTL framework (a) and our transformer-based MTL framework (b).

In contrast to the classical CNN-based MTL framework [4,25,31,36,42,49], in this work, we find there are significant advantages of utilizing transformers for MTL. We illustrate the differences in Fig. 1(a) and (b). For the traditional framework, as in (a), multiple task-specific decoders are needed to generate task-related predictions, resulting in considerable network parameters and computations. While for our transformer-based MTL framework named *MTFormer* as in (b), both the encoder and decoder parts are constructed based on transformers, and they are shared among different tasks. Only lightweight output branches are utilized for harvesting task-specific outputs. Such a design can vastly reduce the parameter number and inference time. Besides, transformer operations are of higher-order with complex capacity, and our experiments demonstrate they perform even better than STL methods with better performance.

Moreover, information from different tasks can benefit each other, and we further conduct cross-task reasoning to enhance the MTL performance. We propose a cross-task attention mechanism where information inside one task could be utilized to help the predictions of others and vice versa. For classical self-attention-based transformers, both query, key, and value are from the same task representation. Our design introduces similarity maps from other tasks (e.g., the query and key are from another task) for better information aggregation. Such cross-task attention is shown to be general for an arbitrary number of tasks and is proved to be more effective than self-attention.

Furthermore, to fully utilize the cross-task knowledge, we design a self-supervised cross-task contrastive learning algorithm for further enhancing the

MTL performance. As stated in [45], a powerful representation is the one that models view-invariant factors. In the MTL framework, the feature representations of different tasks are views of the same scene. They can be treated as positive pairs, and feature representations from different scenes are negative samples. Therefore, we innovatively propose the cross-task contrastive learning approach to maximize the mutual information between different views of the same scene, resulting in more compact and better feature representations. Simultaneously conducting multi-task learning and contrastive learning could further boost the performance of the MTL system.

Last but not least, we also explore the ability of MTFormer for knowledge transfer under few-shot learning and zero-shot learning settings. With shared feature extractors like shared encoder and decoder, the identical feature representations are expressive enough, and they can be easily transferred for few-shot learning where annotations are limited for specific tasks, and for zero-shot learning where no annotations are available for a dataset and knowledge from other datasets could be transferred. We conduct extensive experiments on two public datasets with various task numbers and task categories, including NYUD-v2 [40] and PASCAL VOC [15], on which our MTFormer harvest the state-of-the-art results on both MTL and knowledge transfer. We give all implementation details and will make our code and trained models publicly available. Our main contribution is three-fold:

- We investigate the advantages of transformers for MTL. We conduct an in-depth analysis and propose a novel MTL architecture named MTFormer, which performs better with smaller parameters and computations.
- We explore cross-task reasoning where both a cross-task attention mechanism and a cross-task contrastive learning algorithm are proposed, which further enhance the performance of MTL.
- We conduct extensive experiments on two competitive datasets. The state-of-the-art performance on MTL and transfer learning demonstrates the effectiveness and generality of the proposed MTFormer.

2   Related Work

Multi-task Learning. Multi-task learning is concerned with learning multiple tasks simultaneously, while exerting shared influence on model parameters [3,4, 12,16,17,25,28,29,42,43,56,62]. The potential benefits are manifold and include speed-up training or inference, higher accuracy, and lower parameters.

Many MTL methods perform multiple tasks by a single forward pass, using shared trunk [2,13,26,31,33,47], cross talk [36], or prediction distillation [54,59,60]. A recent work of MTI-Net [49] proposes to utilize the task interactions between multi-scale features. Another stream of MTL is based on task-conditional networks [24,34], which perform a separate forward pass and activate some task-specific modules for each task. Although the transformer-based MTL frameworks have been studied in the language-related domain [21,35,48], existing MTL frameworks for vision tasks mainly adopt CNNs while have not explored the effectiveness of vision transformers.

Vision Transformers. CNNs have dominated the computer vision field for many years and achieved tremendous successes [10,19,20,22,39,44]. Recently, the pioneering work ViT [14] demonstrates that transformer-based architectures can also achieve competitive results. Built upon the success of ViT, many efforts have been devoted to designing better transformer-based architectures for various vision tasks, including low-level image processing [6], image classification [11,18,23,46,50,53], object detection [5,63], semantic segmentation [41,61], depth estimation [38,55], saliency detection [30,57], etc. Rather than concentrating on one special task, some recent works [32,50,58] try to design a general vision transformer backbone for general-purpose vision tasks.

3   Method

In this section, we will first describe the details of our MTFormer in Sect. 3.1. Next, we will detail the cross-task attention in Sect. 3.2. Furthermore, the self-supervised cross-task contrastive learning algorithm and the final loss function of the framework will be depicted in Sects. 3.3 and 3.4.

3.1   MTFormer

Our MTL framework consists of only transformer blocks, and its visual illustration is shown in Fig. 2. It consists of two parts, i.e., the shared feature extractor and the lightweight task-specific branches. Their details are summarized below.

Shared Feature Extractor. The shared feature extractor consists of an encoder and a decoder. As illustrated in Fig. 2, the shared encoder is built based on a pre-trained transformer with a stack of down-sampling operations, e.g., the Swin-Transformer [32]. And the shared decoder consists of a stack of shared transformer blocks (with self-task attention only) with a flexible module design.

Lightweight Task-Specific Branches. The task-specific branch consists of two parts, i.e., the transformer-based feature transformation branch and the output head with non-linear projection. For different tasks, its related feature transformation follows the shared decoder, consisting of only a few transformer blocks thus is lightweight. The first part in each transformation branch includes only self-task attention modules to obtain unique representations. And the second part is a stack of transformer blocks with cross-task attention that will be detailed in Sect. 3.2. At the end of each branch, an output head with a non-linear projection is utilized to harvest the final prediction for the related task.

Self-task Attention for MTL. Suppose $T_1, ..., T_h$ are h input feature tokens, we flatten $T_1, ..., T_h$ into 1D features, and the transformer block with self-task attention is processed as

$$q = k = v = LN([T_1, ..., T_h]), \; [\widehat{T}_1, ..., \widehat{T}_h] = MSA(q, k, v) + [T_1, ..., T_h],$$
$$[\mathcal{T}_1, ..., \mathcal{T}_m] = FFN(LN([\widehat{T}_1, ..., \widehat{T}_h])) + [\widehat{T}_1, ..., \widehat{T}_h], \tag{1}$$

where LN denotes layer normalization, MSA denotes the multi-head self-attention module, q, k, and v denote the query, key, and value vector to complete the computation of MSA, FFN represents the forward module in the transformer block.

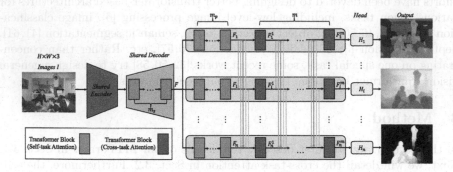

Fig. 2. The illustration of the proposed MTFormer framework.

Now we describe the self-task attention computation process, e.g., the $MSA()$. Suppose the head number is B for MSA, the b-th head self-attention calculation $Attention_b$ in one transformer block is formulated as

$$\mathbf{Q}_b = qW_b^q, \mathbf{K}_b = kW_b^k, \mathbf{V}_b = vW_b^v,\ Attention_b(\mathbf{Q}_b, \mathbf{K}_b, \mathbf{V}_b) = SoftMax(\frac{\mathbf{Q}_b \mathbf{K}_b^T}{\sqrt{d_b}})\mathbf{V}_b, \quad (2)$$

where q, k, v are features in Eq. 1; W_b^q, W_b^k, W_b^v represent the projection matrices for the b-th head; $\mathbf{Q}_b$, $\mathbf{K}_b$, $\mathbf{V}_b$ are the projected query, key, and value features, respectively. The cross-task attention for MTL will be introduced in Sect. 3.3.

Superiority Analysis. We summarize the structure of current MTL structures with CNNs and our transformer-only framework (MTFormer) as displayed in Fig. 1. The main difference is that the MTL framework with transformer allows the deep shared network module, including the shared encoder as well as the shared decoder. And as suggested by recent works [11,18,23,41,46,50,53,61], the transformer has strength in the computation of long-range attention and the general representation ability for various tasks. Such advantage is essential since the individual branches start from the same feature in MTL and need various long-range attention and a joint representation strategy.

Especially, as proved in Sect. 4.2, these advantages in the structures lead to significant superiority. 1) The superiority in the performance: combined with the simple MTL loss function (e.g., the uncertainty loss in [25]), the CNN-based MTL has worse performance than STL. On the other hand, the performance of the transformer-only MTL is better than STL on all tasks. 2) The superiority in the model parameters: we find that transformer-only MTL has a smaller parameter number ratio between MTL and STL, meaning that the superiority of the model parameter is more prominent for transformer-only MTL. This is because different tasks in MTFormer have a deeply shared backbone.

3.2 Cross-Task Attention for MTL

To achieve feature propagation across different tasks, previous methods mainly build the inter-task connections among different task-specific branches [36,49]. However, such a propagation mechanism has two significant drawbacks. First, different branches need to learn the task-common feature besides the task-specific part, which will impede the learning of each branch in MTL compared with STL since STL just needs to learn the task-specific feature. Second, the connections between different branches will increase the parameter number of the MTL system. To achieve the feature propagation among different tasks efficiently, we propose the cross-task attention, as shown in Fig. 3, novelly modifying the attention computation mechanism in the transformer block by merging attention maps from different tasks.

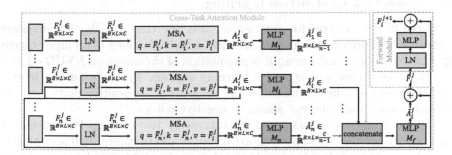

Fig. 3. Detailed structure of the proposed cross-task attention for MTL.

As shown in Fig. 3, suppose there are n tasks and thus corresponding n task features. The input features of the j-th transformer block with cross-task attention are denoted as $F_1^j, ..., F_n^j$. Without loss of generality, suppose we aim to compute the cross-task attention for F_i^j (the computations of cross-task attention for $F_1^j, ..., F_{i-1}^j, F_{i+1}^j, ..., F_n^j$ are similar). For $F_1^j, ..., F_n^j$, we can obtain n attention maps as $A_1^j, ..., A_n^j$, and how to fuse different attention maps, i.e., self-task attention map and the other attention maps, is the vital problem in the cross-task attention module. The combination of different attention maps can be achieved with n mapping functions $(M_1, ..., M_n)$ to adjust the dimension and one MLP (M_f) to fuse the adjusted outputs (as shown in Fig. 3), as

$$
\begin{aligned}
\bar{F}_1^j &= LN(F_1^j), ..., \bar{F}_n^j = LN(F_n^j), \\
A_1^j &= MSA(\bar{F}_1^j, \bar{F}_1^j, \bar{F}_i^j), ..., A_n^j = MSA(\bar{F}_n^j, \bar{F}_n^j, \bar{F}_i^j), \\
\widehat{A}_1^j &= M_1(A_1^j), ..., \widehat{A}_n^j = M_n(A_n^j), \\
\bar{A}_i^j &= M_f([\widehat{A}_1^j, ..., \widehat{A}_n^j]).
\end{aligned}
\tag{3}
$$

Especially, we find that the self-task attention output should take the primary role ($\widehat{A}_i^j \in \mathbb{R}^{B \times L \times C}$) while the cross-task attention outputs should take the auxiliary role (with smaller feature channel number, as $B \times L \times \frac{C}{n-1}$). This is verified by the ablation experiments in Sect. 4.

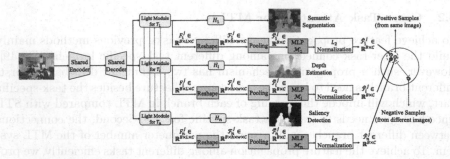

Fig. 4. Framework of self-supervised cross-task contrastive learning for MTL.

3.3 Cross-Task Contrastive Learning

As stated in [45], a powerful representation is one that models view-invariant factors. In MTFormer, the outputs are indeed multiple views of an input image, e.g., the depth value and semantic segmentation of the image on NYUD-v2 [40]. Therefore, we design a contrastive learning strategy by adopting the feature representations of different tasks for the same scene as positive pairs, and the representations from different scenes as negative pairs.

Suppose there are n tasks, and we take every two of them for contrastive learning. We set the features obtained from the intermediate representation in the task-specific branch as the inputs to compute the contrastive loss. The details of the contrastive loss can be viewed in Fig. 4. As we can see, for the intermediate features $F_1^j, ..., F_n^j$, we apply the global average pooling operation, and then a set of mapping functions for the processing, which is combined with an L_2 normalization operation. Note that the global average pooling operation, mapping functions, and the L_2 normalization operation are no longer needed during the inference of MTL. Suppose there are D negative samples, the loss for the task y and task z (the contrastive loss is computed for every two tasks) is

$$\mathcal{L}_{contrast}^y = -\mathbb{E}[\log\frac{g(\widehat{\mathcal{F}}_y, \widehat{\mathcal{F}}_z)}{\sum_{d=1}^{D} g(\widehat{\mathcal{F}}_y, \widehat{\mathcal{F}}_{z,d})}], \quad \mathcal{L}_{contrast}^z = -\mathbb{E}[\log\frac{g(\widehat{\mathcal{F}}_z, \widehat{\mathcal{F}}_y)}{\sum_{d=1}^{D} g(\widehat{\mathcal{F}}_z, \widehat{\mathcal{F}}_{y,d})}], \quad (4)$$

$$\mathcal{L}_{contrast}^{y,z} = \mathcal{L}_{contrast}^y + \mathcal{L}_{contrast}^z, \quad g(\widehat{\mathcal{F}}_y, \widehat{\mathcal{F}}_z) = exp(\frac{\widehat{\mathcal{F}}_y \cdot \widehat{\mathcal{F}}_z}{||\widehat{\mathcal{F}}_y|| \times ||\widehat{\mathcal{F}}_z||}), \quad (5)$$

where $g()$ is the function to measure similarity, $\mathbb{E}$ is the average operation, $\widehat{\mathcal{F}}_{z,d}$ and $\widehat{\mathcal{F}}_{y,d}$ are the d-th negative sample for $\widehat{\mathcal{F}}_z$ and $\widehat{\mathcal{F}}_y$, respectively. And the overall contrastive loss can be written as

$$\mathcal{L}_{contrast} = \sum_{1 \leq y \leq n, 1 \leq z \leq n} \mathcal{L}_{contrast}^{y,z}. \quad (6)$$

3.4 Loss Function

Different from existing MTL methods, our framework can achieve SOTA performance on different datasets without complex loss functions. We utilized the classical MTL loss function, which weighs multiple loss functions by considering the homoscedastic uncertainty of each task [25]. To implement such loss, we add the trainable values $\sigma_1, ..., \sigma_n$ to estimate the uncertainty of each task. And the final loss function can be written as

$$\mathcal{L}(\sigma_1, ..., \sigma_n) = \frac{1}{r_1 \sigma_1^2} \mathcal{L}_1 + ... + \frac{1}{r_2 \sigma_n^2} \mathcal{L}_n + \log \sigma_1 + ... + \log \sigma_n + \mathcal{L}_{contrast}, \qquad (7)$$

where $\mathcal{L}_1$ to $\mathcal{L}_n$ are n loss functions for n different tasks, r_1 to r_n belongs to $\{1, 2\}$ and their values are decided whether the corresponding outputs are modeled with Gaussian likelihood or softmax likelihood [25].

4   Experiments

4.1   Experimental Setting

Dataset. We follow the experimental setting of the recent MTL method [49], and perform the experimental evaluations on two competitive datasets, i.e. NYUD-v2 [40] and PASCAL VOC [15]. The NYUD-v2 dataset contains both semantic segmentation and depth estimation tasks, and it has 1449 images in total, with 795 images for training and the remaining 654 images for validation. For the PASCAL dataset, we use the split from PASCAL-Context [9], which has annotations for semantic segmentation, human part segmentation, and composited saliency labels from [34] that are distilled from pre-trained state-of-the-art models [1,8]. The dataset contains 10103 images, with 4998 and 5105 images for training and validation, respectively.

Evaluation Metric. The semantic segmentation, saliency estimation, and human part segmentation tasks are evaluated with the mean intersection over union (mIoU). The depth estimation task is evaluated using the root mean square error (rmse). Besides the metric for each task, we measure the multi-task learning performance Δ_m as in [34], where the MTL performance is defined as $\Delta_m = \frac{1}{n} \sum_{i=1}^{n} (-1)^{l_i} (M_{m,i} - M_{s,i}) / M_{s,i}$, where $M_{m,i}$ and $M_{s,i}$ are the MTL and STL performance on the i-th task, $l_i = 1$ if a lower value means better performance for task i, and 0 otherwise.

Implementation Detail. Theoretically speaking, the individual branch for each task can have an arbitrary number of cross-task attention modules. More cross-task attention modules mean more feature propagation, leading to better MTL performance. However, due to the limitation of computation resources, we only set $m = m_s = m_p = 2$ in the experiments. We adopt the Swin-Transformer [32] as the shared encoder for transformer-based MTL, ResNet50 [19] for CNN-based MTL. And for the transformer block in the decoder, we employ the strategy of W-MSA and SW-MSA in the Swin-Transformer [32] as the MSA module. For the individual branch in the CNN-based transformer, we use the ASPP in [7]. For the baseline STL with transformer, it consists of the shared encoder, decoder, one lightweight branch, and one head in Fig. 2.

Table 1. Results on NYUD-v2 of STL and MTL with CNN (C) and transformer (T). Cross-task attention and contrastive learning are not utilized.

Method	Seg↑	Dep↓	$\delta_m\%$ ↑
STL (C)	**43.11**	**0.507**	+0.00
MTL (C)	42.05	0.521	−2.61
STL (T)	47.96	0.497	+0.00
MTL (T)	**50.04**	**0.490**	+2.87

Table 2. Results on PASCAL of STL and MTL with CNN (C) and transformer (T). Cross-task attention and contrastive learning are not utilized.

Method	Seg↑	Part↑	Sal↑	$\delta_m\%$ ↑
STL (C)	**69.06**	**62.12**	**66.42**	+0.00
MTL (C)	61.87	60.97	64.68	−4.96
STL (T)	71.17	63.90	66.71	+0.00
MTL (T)	**73.52**	**64.26**	**67.24**	+1.55

Table 3. Resource analysis for Table 1. R-Params and R-FLOPS mean the ratio with the Params and FLOPs of STL.

Method	Params (M)	FLOPS (G)	R-Params	R-FLOPS
STL (C)	79.27	384.35	1.0	1.0
MTL (C)	**55.77**	**267.10**	0.704	0.695
STL (T)	114.26	157.52	1.0	1.0
MTL (T)	**62.45**	**94.62**	0.547	0.639

Table 4. Resource analysis for Table 2. R-Params and R-FLOPS mean the ratio with the Params and FLOPs of STL.

Method	Params (M)	FLOPS (G)	R-Params	R-FLOPS
STL (C)	118.91	491.93	1.0	1.0
MTL (C)	**71.89**	**291.83**	0.605	0.593
STL (T)	171.43	201.76	1.0	1.0
MTL (T)	**67.80**	**94.42**	0.395	0.519

4.2 MTFormer Superiority

The results of CNN-based and transformer-based STL/MTL frameworks on NYUD-v2 and PASCAL are shown in Tables 1 and 2, respectively. As we can see, combined with the simple MTL loss, the CNN-based MTL has worse performance than STL, while transformer-based MTL algorithm MTL (T) (a.k.a, vanilla MTFormer without cross-task reasoning) is better than STL on all tasks. Specifically, on NYUD-v2 and PASCAL, we observe a significant decrease of 2.61 and 4.96% points from STL to MTL for the CNN-based framework, while an improvement of 2.87 and 1.55% points from STL to MTL for the transformer-based framework MTFormer. We provide the qualitative analysis in Fig. 5 by providing the visual comparison for the transformer-based STL and the proposed MTFormer framework. As we can see, our MTFormer can bring noticeable improvement on all tasks compared with STL. We also conduct the resource analysis by computing the number of parameters, and computation FLOPS for different models, as displayed in Tables 3 and 4. Significantly, for the ratio between MTL's parameter-number/FLOPS and STL's parameter-number/FLOPS, the transformer-based MTL has a smaller value. Therefore, the transformer-based MTL has a more prominent advantage in reducing model parameters and computations w.r.t. STL. In conclusion, transformers have a larger capacity and are more suitable for MTL, and our proposed MTFormer achieves the best results with reduced parameters and computations.

4.3 Cross-Task Reasoning

The information inside different task domains can benefit the understanding of each other, and we conduct cross-task reasoning, which includes cross-task

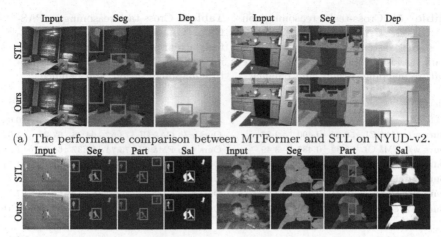

(a) The performance comparison between MTFormer and STL on NYUD-v2.

(b) The performance comparison between MTFormer and STL on PASCAL.

Fig. 5. Visual comparisons between the predictions of STL and our MTFormer. Regions highlighted by red rectangle show more clear differences. (Color figure online)

attention and cross-task contrastive learning. To demonstrate the effectiveness of our designed algorithms, we compare the results of the proposed MTFormer framework with self-task attention or cross-task attention, and with or without cross-task contrastive learning. The results on NYUD-v2 and PASCAL are shown in Tables 5 and 6 respectively.

Cross-Task Attention. Our cross-task attention mechanism is designed that attention maps and similarity relationships from other tasks are introduced to help the prediction of the current task. Comparing the two methods named "Ours wo CA&CL" and "Ours wo CL" in Tables 5 and 6, we can see that method with cross-task attention can get extra 0.5% points improvement for δ_m, which proves the effectiveness of the cross-task attention. We compute the parameter number/FLOPS for MTL frameworks with cross-task attention or with self-task attention only, and the results are shown in Tables 7 and 8. Compared with the framework with only self-task attention ("Ours w/o CA&CL"), the framework with cross-task attention ("Ours w/o CL") only increases a small number of model parameters (2.5% for NYUD-v2, 9.3% for PASCAL).

Ablation Study. To fuse the attention maps from different tasks, we first utilize feature mapping functions $(M_1, ...M_n)$ for attention outputs and then use an MLP (M_f) for feature fusion. Alternatively, we can use only an MLP instead of the mapping functions, and this setting is called "Ours w/o FM&CL"; if we remove the MLP for fusion, we can just add the outputs from mapping functions for fusion, and this setting is denoted as "Ours w/o FF&CL". The results are shown in Tables 5 and 6, and they are all weaker than our original strategy. As

Table 5. Cross-task reasoning on NYUD-v2. 'CA' and 'CL' stand for cross-task attention and contrastive learning, 'FM', 'FF', and 'FB' denote feature mapping, fusion, and balance.

Method	Seg↑	Dep↓	δ_m% ↑
STL (T)	47.96	0.497	+0.00
Ours w/o CA&CL	50.04	0.490	+2.87
Ours w/o FM&CL	50.34	0.487	+3.49
Ours w/o FF&CL	50.33	0.488	+3.38
Ours w/o FB&CL	–	–	–
Ours w/o CL	50.31	0.486	+3.56
Ours (MTFormer)	**50.56**	**0.483**	+4.12

Table 6. Cross-task reasoning on PAS-CAL. 'CA' and 'CL' stand for cross-task attention and contrastive learning, 'FM', 'FF', and 'FB' denote feature mapping, fusion, and balance.

Method	Seg↑	Part↑	Sal↑	δ_m% ↑
STL (T)	71.17	63.90	66.71	+0.00
Ours w/o CA&CL	73.52	64.26	67.24	+1.55
Ours w/o FM&CL	73.74	64.37	66.97	+1.58
Ours w/o FF&CL	73.84	64.42	67.14	+1.74
Ours w/o FB&CL	73.98	64.41	66.95	+1.70
Ours w/o CL	73.77	64.47	67.49	+1.91
Ours (MTFormer)	**74.15**	**64.89**	**67.71**	+2.41

Table 7. Resource analysis for Table 5.

Method	Params (M)	FLOPS (G)
Ours w/o CA&CL	62.45	94.62
Ours w/o CL	64.03	117.73

Table 8. Resource analysis for Table 6.

Method	Params (M)	FLOPS (G)
Ours w/o CA&CL	67.80	94.42
Ours w/o CL	74.12	128.77

stated in Sect. 3.2, the self-task attention output takes the primary role while the cross-task attention outputs take the auxiliary position. And we have feature dimension adaptation to balance their contributions. We conduct experiments to prove this claim by setting the feature channel of all attention outputs as $B \times L \times C$, and then use MLP for fusion. This setting is represented as "Ours w/o FB&CL", and the results are shown in Table 6, demonstrating the correctness of our claim since a decrease of 0.2% points for δ_m is caused by adopting "Ours w/o FB&CL" compared with "Ours w/o CL".

Cross-Task Contrastive Learning. We conduct cross-task contrastive learning to further enhance the MTL performance. We combine the contrastive loss with the supervised loss for MTL and optimize these two loss terms simultaneously. The results are in Tables 5 and 6 and our framework with contrastive learning is called "Ours (MTFormer)". We can see that extra cross-task contrastive learning introduces 0.56 and 0.50% points improvements for δ_m on NYUD-v2 and PASCAL, compared to those without cross-task contrastive learning ("Ours wo CL"). These results reveal the effectiveness of the proposed cross-task contrastive learning algorithm.

4.4   Comparison with Others

We conduct method comparisons with existing state-of-the-art MTL frameworks, which adopt various complex network structures and loss terms. The compared

Table 9. Results on NYUD-v2 for comparison with SOTA MTL methods.

Method	Seg↑	Dep↓	δ_m% ↑
STL (T)	47.96	0.497	+0.00
AST [34]	42.16	0.570	−13.39
Auto [3]	41.10	0.541	−11.58
Cross-stitch [36]	41.01	0.538	−11.37
NDDR-CNN [17]	40.88	0.536	−11.30
MTL-A [31]	42.03	0.519	−8.40
Repara [24]	43.22	0.521	−7.36
PAD-Net [54]	50.20	0.582	−6.22
ERC [4]	46.33	0.536	−5.62
Switching [42]	45.90	0.527	−5.17
MTI-Net [49]	49.00	0.529	−2.14
MTFormer	**50.56**	**0.483**	**+4.12**

Table 10. Results on PASCAL for comparison with SOTA MTL methods.

Method	Seg↑	Part↑	Sal↑	δ_m% ↑
STL (T)	71.17	63.90	66.71	+0.00
Repara [24]	56.63	55.85	59.32	−14.70
Switching [42]	64.20	55.03	63.31	−9.59
NDDR-CNN [17]	63.22	56.12	65.16	−8.56
MTL-A [31]	61.55	58.89	64.96	−7.99
Auto [3]	64.07	58.60	64.92	−6.99
PAD-Net [54]	60.12	60.70	67.20	−6.60
Cross-stitch [36]	63.28	60.21	65.13	−6.41
ERC [4]	62.69	59.42	67.94	−5.70
AST [34]	68.00	61.12	66.10	−3.24
MTI-Net [49]	64.98	62.90	**67.84**	−2.86
MTFormer	**74.15**	**64.89**	67.71	+2.41

Table 11. Results on PASCAL of few-shot learning with different tasks.

Method	Few-shot data	Seg↑	Part↑	Sal↑	δ_m% ↑
Single task	Seg	3.34	63.90	66.71	+0.00
Ours	Seg	**35.26**	**64.26**	**67.26**	+ 319.03
Single task	Part	71.17	11.27	66.71	+0.00
Ours	Part	**73.36**	**51.74**	**67.64**	+121.19
Single task	Sal	71.17	63.90	44.39	+0.00
Ours	Sal	**76.00**	**66.89**	**55.55**	+12.20

approaches on NYUD-v2 and PASCAL are MTL-A [31], Cross-stitch [36], MTI-Net [49], Switching [42], ERC [4], NDDR-CNN [17], PAD-Net [54], Repara [24], AST [34], and Auto [3]. The comparison results between our MTFormer framework and all the others on NYUD-v2 are shown in Table 9. It can be seen that our MTFormer's results are superior to the baselines in terms of both semantic segmentation and depth estimation results. The comparisons on PASCAL, as displayed in Table 10, also demonstrate the effectiveness of our MTFormer.

4.5 MTFormer for Few-Shot Learning

In Natural Language Processing (NLP) applications [35], it is observed that MTL's improvements (compared to STL) are usually focused on tasks that have fewer training samples. Here we explore the ability of MTFormer for transfer learning. And we demonstrate that our MTFormer can boost the few-shot learning performance on vision tasks without complex few-shot learning loss, which is due to the beneficial feature propagation among different tasks.

We take PASCAL dataset as an example. Annotating images with the accurate human segmentation ground truth label is more accessible than the human part segmentation, since human part segmentation needs more details. Therefore, we can set the human part segmentation's annotation as the few-shot samples. Specifically, for the PASCAL dataset, we take all the annotations for semantic segmentation and saliency detection, while randomly sampling only about 1% (40 out of 4998) human part segmentation annotations. We set the baseline as the STL with such few-shot samples. As shown in Tables 11, our MTFormer can significantly improve the performance on the few-shot learning task compared with STL (i.e., the accuracy is improved more than 40% points for human part segmentation), while keeping the performance on other tasks almost unchanged (compared to the results in Tables 10). And the few-shot learning settings for other tasks are also included in Tables 11. This shows MTFormer's strong ability to handle few-shot learning problems.

Table 12. Simultaneously training multiple datasets for zero-shot learning ('ZSL') does not affect the performance much.

Method	Seg↑ (NYUD-v2)	Dep↓ (NYUD-v2)	Seg↑ (PASCAL)	Part↑ (PASCAL)	Sal↑ (PASCAL)
Ours w/o ZSL	50.03	0.488	73.70	64.36	67.82
Ours w ZSL	48.26	0.480	70.18	61.47	67.59

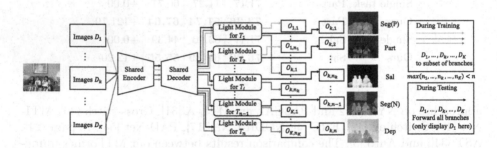

Fig. 6. Our MTFormer framework can be utilized for achieving zero-shot learning.

4.6   MTFormer for Zero-Shot Learning

Further, our MTFormer can also perform well on zero-shot learning. As exhibited in Fig. 6, MTFormer can be utilized to transfer the knowledge of one dataset to another dataset. Take the dataset of NYUD-v2 and PASCAL as an example. The NYUD-v2 dataset has the annotation of semantic segmentation and depth, and the PASCAL dataset has the annotation of semantic segmentation, human part segmentation, and saliency. We can simultaneously use the data of NYUD-v2 and PASCAL to train the proposed MTFormer, whose output includes semantic segmentation, depth estimation, human part segmentation, and saliency detection.

In the framework, we use the annotation of each dataset to train the corresponding output branch.

We are surprised to find that the trained framework can have comparable performances on the tasks which have annotations as shown in Table 12, i.e., the semantic segmentation and depth prediction on NYUD, the semantic segmentation, human part segmentation, and saliency detection on PASCAL. Meanwhile, the trained network can predict the outputs with no annotations, e.g., the saliency detection results on NYUD and the depth prediction on PASCAL VOC, as displayed in Fig. 7.

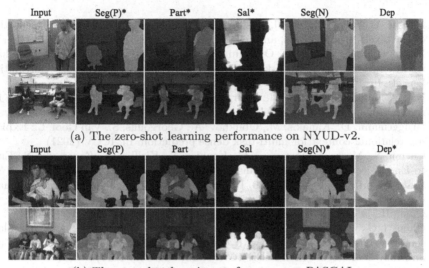

(a) The zero-shot learning performance on NYUD-v2.

(b) The zero-shot learning performance on PASCAL.

Fig. 7. Visual illustration of MTFormer for zero-shot learning on PASCAL and NYUD-v2. 'Seg(P)' and 'Seg(N)' denote the segmentation with PASCAL class and NYUD-v2 class, respectively. '*' means there is no training ground truth.

Such great property can be achieved because different tasks in our framework have a deeply shared backbone, and the branches for individual tasks are lightweight. Thus, different tasks can have a shared representation even with samples from various datasets. Besides, combined with our cross-task attention, the feature propagation can be implemented across different tasks, which also contributes to the zero-shot learning for the MTL framework.

5   Conclusion

In this paper, we first explore the superiority of using transformer structures for MTL and propose a transformer-based MTL framework named MTFormer. It is proved that MTL with deeply shared network parameters for different tasks can better reduce the time-space complexity and increase the performance compared with STL. Moreover, we also conduct cross-task reasoning and propose the cross-task attention mechanism to improve the MTL results, which can achieve effective feature propagation among different tasks. Besides, a contrastive learning algorithm is proposed to further enhance the MTL results. Extensive experiments on NYUD-v2 and PASCAL show that the proposed MTFormer can achieve state-of-the-art performance with fewer parameters and computations. And MTFormer also shows great superiorities for transfer learning tasks.

References

1. Bansal, A., Chen, X., Russell, B., Gupta, A., Ramanan, D.: Pixelnet: representation of the pixels, by the pixels, and for the pixels. arXiv:1702.06506 (2017)
2. Bragman, F.J., Tanno, R., Ourselin, S., Alexander, D.C., Cardoso, J.: Stochastic filter groups for multi-task cnns: learning specialist and generalist convolution kernels. In: ICCV (2019)
3. Bruggemann, D., Kanakis, M., Georgoulis, S., Van Gool, L.: Automated search for resource-efficient branched multi-task networks. In: BMVC (2020)
4. Bruggemann, D., Kanakis, M., Obukhov, A., Georgoulis, S., Van Gool, L.: Exploring relational context for multi-task dense prediction. In: ICCV (2021)
5. Carion, N., Massa, F., Synnaeve, G., Usunier, N., Kirillov, A., Zagoruyko, S.: End-to-End object detection with transformers. In: Vedaldi, A., Bischof, H., Brox, T., Frahm, J.-M. (eds.) ECCV 2020. LNCS, vol. 12346, pp. 213–229. Springer, Cham (2020). https://doi.org/10.1007/978-3-030-58452-8_13
6. Chen, H., et al.: Pre-trained image processing transformer. In: CVPR (2021)
7. Chen, L.C., Papandreou, G., Kokkinos, I., Murphy, K., Yuille, A.L.: Deeplab: semantic image segmentation with deep convolutional nets, atrous convolution, and fully connected CRFs. IEEE TPAMI **40**, 834–848 (2017)
8. Chen, L.-C., Zhu, Y., Papandreou, G., Schroff, F., Adam, H.: Encoder-decoder with atrous separable convolution for semantic image segmentation. In: Ferrari, V., Hebert, M., Sminchisescu, C., Weiss, Y. (eds.) ECCV 2018. LNCS, vol. 11211, pp. 833–851. Springer, Cham (2018). https://doi.org/10.1007/978-3-030-01234-2_49
9. Chen, X., Mottaghi, R., Liu, X., Fidler, S., Urtasun, R., Yuille, A.: Detect what you can: detecting and representing objects using holistic models and body parts. In: CVPR (2014)
10. Chen, Y., Li, J., Xiao, H., Jin, X., Yan, S., Feng, J.: Dual path networks. arXiv:1707.01629 (2017)
11. Chu, X., et al.: Twins: revisiting spatial attention design in vision transformers. arXiv:2104.13840 (2021)
12. Crawshaw, M.: Multi-task learning with deep neural networks: a survey. arXiv:2009.09796 (2020)
13. Doersch, C., Zisserman, A.: Multi-task self-supervised visual learning. In: ICCV (2017)
14. Dosovitskiy, A., et al.: An image is worth 16×16 words: transformers for image recognition at scale. arXiv:2010.11929 (2020)
15. Everingham, M., Van Gool, L., Williams, C.K., Winn, J., Zisserman, A.: The pascal visual object classes (voc) challenge. Int. J. Comput. Vision **88**, 303–338 (2010)
16. Gao, Y., Bai, H., Jie, Z., Ma, J., Jia, K., Liu, W.: Mtl-nas: task-agnostic neural architecture search towards general-purpose multi-task learning. In: CVPR (2020)

17. Gao, Y., Ma, J., Zhao, M., Liu, W., Yuille, A.L.: Nddr-cnn: layerwise feature fusing in multi-task cnns by neural discriminative dimensionality reduction. In: CVPR (2019)
18. Han, K., Xiao, A., Wu, E., Guo, J., Xu, C., Wang, Y.: Transformer in transformer. arXiv:2103.00112 (2021)
19. He, K., Zhang, X., Ren, S., Sun, J.: Deep residual learning for image recognition. In: CVPR (2016)
20. Hu, J., Shen, L., Sun, G.: Squeeze-and-excitation networks. In: CVPR (2018)
21. Hu, R., Singh, A.: Unit: multimodal multitask learning with a unified transformer. In: ICCV (2021)
22. Huang, G., Liu, Z., Van Der Maaten, L., Weinberger, K.Q.: Densely connected convolutional networks. In: CVPR (2017)
23. Jiang, Z., et al.: Token labeling: training a 85.5% top-1 accuracy vision transformer with 56m parameters on imagenet. arXiv:2104.10858 (2021)
24. Kanakis, M., Bruggemann, D., Saha, S., Georgoulis, S., Obukhov, A., Van Gool, L.: Reparameterizing convolutions for incremental multi-task learning without task interference. In: Vedaldi, A., Bischof, H., Brox, T., Frahm, J.-M. (eds.) ECCV 2020. LNCS, vol. 12365, pp. 689–707. Springer, Cham (2020). https://doi.org/10.1007/978-3-030-58565-5_41
25. Kendall, A., Gal, Y., Cipolla, R.: Multi-task learning using uncertainty to weigh losses for scene geometry and semantics. In: CVPR (2018)
26. Kokkinos, I.: Ubernet: training a universal convolutional neural network for low-, mid-, and high-level vision using diverse datasets and limited memory. In: CVPR (2017)
27. Li, Y., Yan, H., Jin, R.: Multi-task learning with latent variation decomposition for multivariate responses in a manufacturing network. IEEE Trans. Autom. Sci. Eng. (2022)
28. Liu, B., Liu, X., Jin, X., Stone, P., Liu, Q.: Conflict-averse gradient descent for multi-task learning. In: NIPS (2021)
29. Liu, L., et al.: Towards impartial multi-task learning. In: ICLR (2020)
30. Liu, N., Zhang, N., Wan, K., Shao, L., Han, J.: Visual saliency transformer. In: ICCV (2021)
31. Liu, S., Johns, E., Davison, A.J.: End-to-end multi-task learning with attention. In: CVPR (2019)
32. Liu, Z., et al.: Swin transformer: hierarchical vision transformer using shifted windows. In: ICCV (2021)
33. Lu, Y., Kumar, A., Zhai, S., Cheng, Y., Javidi, T., Feris, R.: Fully-adaptive feature sharing in multi-task networks with applications in person attribute classification. In: CVPR (2017)
34. Maninis, K.K., Radosavovic, I., Kokkinos, I.: Attentive single-tasking of multiple tasks. In: CVPR (2019)
35. McCann, B., Keskar, N.S., Xiong, C., Socher, R.: The natural language decathlon: multitask learning as question answering. arXiv:1806.08730 (2018)
36. Misra, I., Shrivastava, A., Gupta, A., Hebert, M.: Cross-stitch networks for multi-task learning. In: CVPR (2016)
37. Muhammad, K., Ullah, A., Lloret, J., Del Ser, J., de Albuquerque, V.H.C.: Deep learning for safe autonomous driving: current challenges and future directions. IEEE Trans. Intell. Transp. Syst. 22, 4316–4336 (2020)
38. Ranftl, R., Bochkovskiy, A., Koltun, V.: Vision transformers for dense prediction. In: CVPR (2021)

39. Sandler, M., Howard, A., Zhu, M., Zhmoginov, A., Chen, L.C.: Mobilenetv 2: inverted residuals and linear bottlenecks. In: CVPR (2018)
40. Silberman, N., Hoiem, D., Kohli, P., Fergus, R.: Indoor segmentation and support inference from RGBD images. In: Fitzgibbon, A., Lazebnik, S., Perona, P., Sato, Y., Schmid, C. (eds.) ECCV 2012. LNCS, vol. 7576, pp. 746–760. Springer, Heidelberg (2012). https://doi.org/10.1007/978-3-642-33715-4_54
41. Strudel, R., Garcia, R., Laptev, I., Schmid, C.: Segmenter: transformer for semantic segmentation. arXiv:2105.05633 (2021)
42. Sun, G., et al.: Task switching network for multi-task learning. In: ICCV (2021)
43. Sun, X., Panda, R., Feris, R., Saenko, K.: Adashare: learning what to share for efficient deep multi-task learning. In: NIPS (2020)
44. Tan, M., Le, Q.: Efficientnet: rethinking model scaling for convolutional neural networks. In: ICML, pp. 6105–6114 (2019)
45. Tian, Y., Krishnan, D., Isola, P.: Contrastive multiview coding. In: Vedaldi, A., Bischof, H., Brox, T., Frahm, J.-M. (eds.) ECCV 2020. LNCS, vol. 12356, pp. 776–794. Springer, Cham (2020). https://doi.org/10.1007/978-3-030-58621-8_45
46. Touvron, H., Cord, M., Sablayrolles, A., Synnaeve, G., Jégou, H.: Going deeper with image transformers. arXiv:2103.17239 (2021)
47. Vandenhende, S., Georgoulis, S., De Brabandere, B., Van Gool, L.: Branched multi-task networks: deciding what layers to share. In: BMVC (2019)
48. Vandenhende, S., Georgoulis, S., Van Gansbeke, W., Proesmans, M., Dai, D., Van Gool, L.: Multi-task learning for dense prediction tasks: a survey. IEEE TPAMI 44, 3614–3633 (2021)
49. Vandenhende, S., Georgoulis, S., Van Gool, L.: MTI-Net: multi-scale task interaction networks for multi-task learning. In: Vedaldi, A., Bischof, H., Brox, T., Frahm, J.-M. (eds.) ECCV 2020. LNCS, vol. 12349, pp. 527–543. Springer, Cham (2020). https://doi.org/10.1007/978-3-030-58548-8_31
50. Wang, W., et al.: Pyramid vision transformer: a versatile backbone for dense prediction without convolutions. arXiv:2102.12122 (2021)
51. Wang, W., et al.: Graph-driven generative models for heterogeneous multi-task learning. In: AAAI (2020)
52. Wen, C., et al.: Multi-scene citrus detection based on multi-task deep learning network. In: 2020 IEEE International Conference on Systems, Man, and Cybernetics (SMC) (2020)
53. Wu, H., et al.: Cvt: introducing convolutions to vision transformers. arXiv:2103.15808 (2021)
54. Xu, D., Ouyang, W., Wang, X., Sebe, N.: Pad-net: multi-tasks guided prediction-and-distillation network for simultaneous depth estimation and scene parsing. In: CVPR (2018)
55. Yang, G., Tang, H., Ding, M., Sebe, N., Ricci, E.: Transformer-based attention networks for continuous pixel-wise prediction. In: ICCV (2021)
56. Yu, T., Kumar, S., Gupta, A., Levine, S., Hausman, K., Finn, C.: Gradient surgery for multi-task learning. In: NIPS (2020)
57. Zhang, J., Xie, J., Barnes, N., Li, P.: Learning generative vision transformer with energy-based latent space for saliency prediction. In: NIPS (2021)
58. Zhang, P., et al.: Multi-scale vision longformer: a new vision transformer for high-resolution image encoding. arXiv:2103.15358 (2021)
59. Zhang, Z., Cui, Z., Xu, C., Jie, Z., Li, X., Yang, J.: Joint task-recursive learning for semantic segmentation and depth estimation. In: Ferrari, V., Hebert, M., Sminchisescu, C., Weiss, Y. (eds.) ECCV 2018. LNCS, vol. 11214, pp. 238–255. Springer, Cham (2018). https://doi.org/10.1007/978-3-030-01249-6_15

60. Zhang, Z., Cui, Z., Xu, C., Yan, Y., Sebe, N., Yang, J.: Pattern-affinitive propagation across depth, surface normal and semantic segmentation. In: CVPR (2019)
61. Zheng, S., et al.: Rethinking semantic segmentation from a sequence-to-sequence perspective with transformers. In: CVPR (2021)
62. Zhou, L., et al.: Pattern-structure diffusion for multi-task learning. In: CVPR (2020)
63. Zhu, X., Su, W., Lu, L., Li, B., Wang, X., Dai, J.: Deformable detr: deformable transformers for end-to-end object detection. arXiv:2010.04159 (2020)

MonoPLFlowNet: Permutohedral Lattice FlowNet for Real-Scale 3D Scene Flow Estimation with Monocular Images

Runfa Li[✉] and Truong Nguyen

UC San Diego, La Jolla, USA
{rul002,tqn001}@ucsd.edu

Abstract. Real-scale scene flow estimation has become increasingly important for 3D computer vision. Some works successfully estimate real-scale 3D scene flow with LiDAR. However, these ubiquitous and expensive sensors are still unlikely to be equipped widely for real application. Other works use monocular images to estimate scene flow, but their scene flow estimations are normalized with scale ambiguity, where additional depth or point cloud ground truth are required to recover the real scale. Even though they perform well in 2D, these works do not provide accurate and reliable 3D estimates. We present a deep learning architecture on permutohedral lattice - MonoPLFlowNet. Different from all previous works, our MonoPLFlowNet is the first work where only two consecutive monocular images are used as input, while both depth and 3D scene flow are estimated in real scale. Our real-scale scene flow estimation outperforms all state-of-the-art monocular-image based works recovered to real scale by ground truth, and is comparable to LiDAR approaches. As a by-product, our real-scale depth estimation is also comparable to other state-of-the-art works.

Keywords: Real-scale scene flow estimation · Monocular-image based · Permutohedral lattice · Real-scale depth estimation

1 Introduction

Scene flow are 3D vectors associating the corresponding 3D point-wise motion between consecutive frames, where scene flow can be recognized as lifting up pixel-wise 2D optical flow from the image plane to 3D space. Different to coarsely high-level motion cues such as bounding-box based tracking, 3D scene flow focuses on precisely low-level point-wise motion cues. With such advantage, scene flow can either serve for non-rigid motion as visual odometry and ego motion estimation, or rigid motion as multi-object tracking, which makes it increasingly

Supplementary Information The online version contains supplementary material available at https://doi.org/10.1007/978-3-031-19812-0_19.

important in motion perception/segmentation and applications in dynamic environments such as robotics, autonomous driving and human-computer interaction (Fig. 1).

Fig. 1. Results of our MonoPLFlowNet. With only two consecutive monocular images (*left*) as input, our MonoPLFlowNet estimates both the depth (*middle*) and 3D scene flow (*right*) in real scale. *Right* shows a zoom-in real-scale scene flow of the two vehicles from side view with the pseudo point cloud generating from the estimated depth map (middle), where blue points are from frame t, red and green points are blue points translated to frame $t + 1$ by ground truth and estimated 3D scene flow, respectively. The objective is to align green and red points. (Color figure online)

3D scene flow has been widely studied using LiDAR point cloud [3,15,27,33, 40,44,46] from two consecutive frames as input, where a few recent LiDAR works achieve very accurate performances. However, LiDARs are still too expensive to be equipped for real applications. Other sensors are also being explored for 3D scene flow estimation such as RGB-D cameras [16,20,29] and stereo cameras [2,22,30,39,42]. However, each sensor configuration also has its own limitation, such as RGB-D cameras are only reliable in the indoor environment, while stereo cameras require calibration for stereo rigs.

Since Monocular camera is ubiquitous and affordable for all real applications, it is a promising alternative to the complicated and expensive sensors. There are many works for monocular image-based scene flow estimation [8,18,19,28,37,48, 50,52,54], where CNN models are designed to jointly estimate monocular depth and optical/scene flow. However, their estimations are all with scale ambiguity. This problem exists in all monocular works where they estimate normalized depth and optical/scene flow. To recover to the real scale, they require depth and scene flow ground truth, which are possible to obtain for evaluation in labeled datasets but impossible for a real application.

Our motivation for this work is to take the advantages and overcome the limitations from both LiDAR-based (real-scale, accurate but expensive) and image-based (affordable, ubiquitous but scale-ambiguous) approaches. Our key contributions are:

– We build a deep learning architecture MonoPLFlowNet, which is the first work using only two consecutive monocular images to simultaneously estimate in real scale both the depth and 3D scene flow.
– Our 3D scene flow estimation outperforms all state-of-the-art monocular image-based works even after recovering their scale ambiguities with ground truth, and is comparable to LiDAR-based approaches.

- We introduce a novel method - "Pyramid-Level 2D-3D features alignment between Cartesian Coordinate and Permutohedral Lattice Network", which bridges the gap between features in monocular images and 3D points in our application, and inspires a new way to align 2D-3D information for computer vision tasks which could benefit other applications.
- As a byproduct, our linear-additive depth estimation from MonoPLFlowNet also outperforms state-of-the-art works on monocular depth estimation.

2   Related Works

Monocular Image-Based Scene Flow Estimation: Monocular 3D scene flow estimation originates from 2D optical flow estimation [9,48]. To get real-scale 3D scene flow from 2D optical flow, real-scale 3D coordinates are required which could be derived from real-scale depth map. Recently, following the success from SFM (Structure from Motion) [25,47], many works jointly estimate monocular depth and 2D optical flow [8,28,37,50,52,54]. However, as seen in most SFM models, the real scale decays in jointly training and leads to scale ambiguity. Although [18,19] jointly estimate depth and 3D scene flow directly, they suffer from scale ambiguity, which is the biggest issue for monocular image-based approaches.

3D Point Cloud Based Scene Flow Estimation: Following PointNet [6] and PointNet++ [35], it became possible to use CNN-based models to directly process point cloud for different tasks including 3D scene flow estimation. Since directly implementing on 3D points, there is no scale ambiguity. The success of CNN-based 2D optical flow networks also boost 3D scene flow. FlowNet3D [27] builds on PointNet++ and imitates the process used in 2D optical FlowNet [9] to build a 3D correlation layer. PointPWC-net [46] imitates another 2D optical flow network PWC-net [41] to build 3D cost volume layers. The most successful works are "Permutohedral Lattice family", where BCL [21], SplatNet [40], HPLFlowNet [15], PointFlowNet [3] all belong to the family. The lattice (more details will be provided in Sect. 3.1) is a very efficient representation for processing of high-dimensional data [1], including 3D point cloud. Point cloud based methods achieve better performance than image-based methods. However, with LiDAR scanning as the input, they are still too expensive for real applications.

Our MonoPLFlowNet takes advantages and overcomes limitations from both image (affordable, ubiquitous but scale-ambiguous) and LiDAR (real-scale, accurate but expensive) based approaches by only using monocular images to jointly estimate depth and 3D scene flow in real scale.

3   MonoPLFlowNet

Our MonoPLFlowNet is an encoder-decoder based model, which only takes two consecutive monocular images as input, while both the depth and 3D scene flow are estimated in real scale. Figure 2 shows our network architecture. While sharing the same encoder, we build depth and scene flow decoders, respectively. With

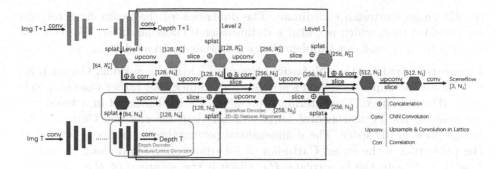

Fig. 2. MonoPLFlowNet Architecture: It shares the same encoder for two monocular images as the only input, and jointly estimates the depth and 3D scene flow in real scale by decoding separately with a *Depth decoder (purple box)* and a *Sceneflow Decoder (red box)*. Architectures of the two decoders are shown in Fig. 3 and 4, respectively. (Color figure online)

our designed mechanism, we align the 2D-3D features to boost the performance, where the real-scale 3D scene flow benefits from the depth estimation. In this section, we present the theory of permutohedral lattice, and then discuss how we design and align the two decoders.

3.1 Review of Permutohedral Lattice Filtering

High-Dimensional Gaussian Filtering: Value and position of the signal are two important components of filtering. Equation 1 shows a general form of high-dimensional Gaussian filtering:

$$\vec{v_i} = \sum_{j=1}^{n} exp^{-\frac{1}{2}(\vec{p_i}-\vec{p_j})^T \sum^{-1} (\vec{p_i}-\vec{p_j})^T} \vec{v_j} \tag{1}$$

$$\vec{v_i} = (r_i, g_i, b_i, 1), \ \vec{p_i} = (\frac{x_i}{\sigma_s}, \frac{y_i}{\sigma_s}) \tag{2}$$

$$\vec{v_i} = (r_i, g_i, b_i, 1), \ \vec{p_i} = (\frac{x_i}{\sigma_s}, \frac{y_i}{\sigma_s}, \frac{I_i}{\sigma_c}) \tag{3}$$

$$\vec{v_i} = (r_i, g_i, b_i, 1), \ \vec{p_i} = (\frac{x_i}{\sigma_s}, \frac{y_i}{\sigma_s}, \frac{r_i}{\sigma_c}, \frac{g_i}{\sigma_c}, \frac{b_i}{\sigma_c}) \tag{4}$$

where $exp^{-\frac{1}{2}(\vec{p_i}-\vec{p_j})^T \sum^{-1} (\vec{p_i}-\vec{p_j})^T}$ is a Gaussian distribution denoting the weight of the neighbor signal value $\vec{v_j}$ contributing to the target signal $\vec{v_i}$. Here $\vec{v}$ is the value vector of the signal, and $\vec{p}$ is the position vector of the signal. Equations 2, 3 and 4 denote Gaussian blur filter, gray-scale bilateral filter and color bilateral filter, respectively, where v_i and p_i are defined in Eq. 1. For these image filters, the signals are pixels, the signal values are 3D homogeneous color space, and signal positions are 2D, 3D and 5D, respectively, and the filtering processing is on 2D image Cartesian coordinate. The dimension of the position vector can be extended to d, which is called a d-dimensional Gaussian filter. We refer the readers to [1, 21] and our supplementary materials for more details.

Permutohedral Lattice Network: However, a high-dimensional Gaussian filter can also be implemented on features with n dimensions rather than on pixels with 3D color space. The filtering process can be implemented in a more efficient space, the Permutohedral Lattice rather than the classical Cartesian 2D image plane or 3D space. The d-dimensional permutohedral lattice is defined as the projection of the scaled Cartesian $(d + 1)$-dimensional grid along the vector $\vec{1} = [1, 1...1]$ onto the hyperplane H_d, which is the subspace of R_{d+1} in which coordinates sum to zero:

$$B_d = \begin{bmatrix} d & -1 & ... & -1 \\ -1 & d & ... & -1 \\ ... & ... & ... & ... \\ -1 & -1 & ... & d \end{bmatrix} \tag{5}$$

Therefore it is also spanned by the projection of the standard basis for the original $(d+1)$-dimensional Cartesian space to H_d. In other words, we can project a feature at Cartesian coordinate p_{cart} to Permutohedral Lattice coordinate p_{lat} as:

$$\vec{p_{lat}} = B_d \vec{p_{cart}} \tag{6}$$

With features embedding on lattice, [1] derived a maneuver pipeline "splatting-convolution-slicing" for feature processing in lattice; [21] improved the pipeline to be learnable BCL (Bilateral Convolutional Layers). Following CNN notion, [15] improved BCL to different levels of receptive fields.

To summarize, Permutohedral Lattice Network convolves the feature values $\vec{v_i}$ based on feature positions $\vec{p_i}$. While it is straightforward to derive $\vec{v_i}$ and $\vec{p_i}$ when feature positions and lattice have the same dimension, e.g. 3D Lidar points input to 3D lattice [15, 21, 40] or 2D to 2D [1, 45], it is challenging when dimensions are different, as in the case of our 2D image input to 3D lattice. The proposed MonoPLFlowNet is designed to overcome such a problem.

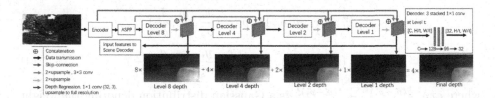

Fig. 3. Depth Decoder: Pyramid-Level Linearly-Additive Depth Estimation. Besides the accurate depth estimation, from a whole architecture view, our depth decoder also serves as the feature/lattice position generator, which is why we design it in linear-additive way.

3.2   Depth Decoder

We design our depth module as an encoder-decoder based network as shown in Fig. 3. Following the success of BTS DepthNet [24], we use their same encoder as a CNN-based feature extractor followed by the dilated convolution (ASPP) [7,49]. Our major contribution focuses on the decoder from three aspects.

Level-Based Decoder: First, while keeping a pyramid-level top-down reasoning, BTS designed "lpg" (local planar guidance) to regress depth at each level in an ambiguous scale. In our experiments, we found that "lpg" is a block where accuracy is sacrificed for efficiency. Instead, we replace the "lpg" with our "level-based decoder" as shown in Fig. 3, and improve the decoder to accommodate our sceneflow task.

Pyramid-Level Linearly-Additive Mechanism: BTS concatenates the estimated depth at each level and utilizes a final convolution to regress the final depth in a non-linear way, implying that the estimated depth at each level is not in a determined scale. Instead, we propose a "Pyramid-Level Linearly-Additive mechanism" as:

$$d_{final} = \frac{1}{4}(1 \times d_{lev1} + 2 \times d_{lev2} + 4 \times d_{lev4} + 8 \times d_{lev8}) \tag{7}$$

such that the final estimation is a linear combination over each level depth, where we force d_{lev1}, d_{lev2}, d_{lev4}, d_{lev8} to be in $1, \frac{1}{2}, \frac{1}{4}, \frac{1}{8}$ scale of the real-scale depth. To achieve this, we also derive a pyramid-level loss corresponding to the level of the decoder architecture to supervise the depth at each level as Eq. 11.

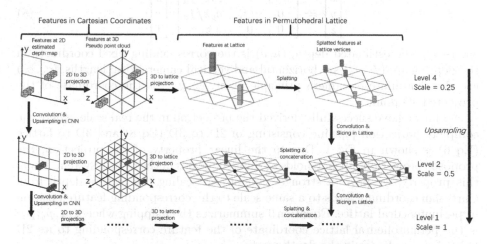

Fig. 4. 3D Scene Flow Decoder: Pyramid-Level 2D-3D features alignment between Cartesian Coordinate and Permutohedral Lattice Network. Horizontally it shows the feature embedding from Cartesian coordinate to permutohedral lattice. Vertically, it shows how the features are upsampled and concatenated for the next level.

Experiments show that with our improvement, our depth decoder outperforms the baseline BTS as well as other state-of-the-art works. More importantly, the objective is to design the depth decoder to generate feature/lattice for the scene flow decoder, which is our major contribution. More details are provided in the next section.

3.3 Scene Flow Decoder

Our scene flow decoder is designed as a two-stream pyramid-level model which decodes in parallel in two domains - 2D Cartesian coordinate and 3D permutalhedral lattice, as shown in Fig. 4. As mentioned in Sect. 3.1, feature values and positions are two key factors in filtering processing. For the feature values, we use the features decoded by level-based decoder from depth module as shown in Fig. 3, the features as the input to scene decoder (32 dimensions) are before regressing to the corresponding level depth (purple arrow), which means that the input features to the scene decoder are the high-level feature representation of the corresponding level depth. While values are trivial, positions are not straightforward. As the challenge mentioned in Sect. 3.1, the 2D feature position from our depth is not enough to project the feature values to 3D permutohedral lattice. We overcome it by projecting the estimated depth estimation into 3D space to generate real-scale pseudo point cloud. Since pseudo point cloud has real-scale 3D coordinates, we can first project the feature values from the 2D depth map to 3D point cloud in Cartesian coordinate, and then embed to the corresponding position in 3D permutohedral lattice. A 2D to 3D projection is defined as:

$$\begin{bmatrix} x \\ y \\ z \end{bmatrix} = \begin{bmatrix} z/f_u & 0 & -c_u z/f_u \\ 0 & z/f_v & -c_v z/f_v \\ 0 & 0 & z \end{bmatrix} \begin{bmatrix} u \\ v \\ 1 \end{bmatrix} \tag{8}$$

where z is the estimated depth, (u, v) is the corresponding pixel coordinate in the depth map, (f_u, f_v) are horizontal and vertical camera focal lengths, (c_u, c_v) are the coordinate of camera principle point. (x, y, z) is the coordinate of the projected 3D point.

So far we have successfully derived the projection in the real scale, where the complete projection pipeline consisting of 2D to 3D (Eq. 8) and 3D to lattice (Eq. 6) is shown in Fig. 4. Due to the linear property of the projection, the proposed projection pipeline holds at different scales in the overall system. Using this property, we prove a stronger conclusion: scaling the feature depth from Cartesian coordinate leads to a same scale to the corresponding feature position in permutohedral lattice. Equation 9 summarizes the mapping where (p_x, p_y, p_z) is the permutohedral lattice coordinate of the feature corresponding to its 2D Cartisian coordinate in the depth map.

$$\begin{bmatrix} p_x \\ p_y \\ p_z \end{bmatrix} = B_d \begin{bmatrix} x \\ y \\ z \end{bmatrix}$$

$$= B_d \begin{bmatrix} z/f_u & 0 & -c_u z/f_u \\ 0 & z/f_v & -c_u z/f_u \\ 0 & 0 & z \end{bmatrix} \begin{bmatrix} u \\ v \\ 1 \end{bmatrix}$$

$$= B_d \begin{bmatrix} \lambda z/\lambda f_u & 0 & -\lambda c_u \lambda z/\lambda f_u \\ 0 & \lambda z/\lambda f_v & -\lambda c_u \lambda z/\lambda f_u \\ 0 & 0 & \lambda z \end{bmatrix} \begin{bmatrix} u \\ v \\ 1 \end{bmatrix} \qquad (9)$$

$$= B_d \begin{bmatrix} z/f_u & 0 & -c_u \lambda z/f_u \\ 0 & z/f_v & -c_u \lambda z/f_u \\ 0 & 0 & \lambda z \end{bmatrix} \begin{bmatrix} \lambda u \\ \lambda v \\ 1 \end{bmatrix}$$

$$= B_d \begin{bmatrix} \lambda z/f_u & 0 & -c_u \lambda z/f_u \\ 0 & \lambda z/f_v & -c_u \lambda z/f_u \\ 0 & 0 & \lambda z \end{bmatrix} \begin{bmatrix} u \\ v \\ 1 \end{bmatrix}$$

B_d is defined in Eq. 5, λ is the scale, a "prime" sign denotes scaling the original value with λ. Comparing the final result of Eq. 9 to Eq. 8, the only difference is to replace z with λz, hence only scaling the depth in Cartesian coordinate will lead to a same scale to the position in permutohedral lattice. Using the proposed "Pyramid-Level 2D-3D features alignment" mechanism, we can embed the features from 2D Cartesian coordinate to 3D Permutohetral lattice, and then implement splating-convolution-slicing and concatenate different level features directly in the permutohedral lattice network. Please see the supplementary materials for more explanation. For the basic operations in permutohedral lattice, we directly refer to [15].

We further analysis into the motivation and intuition of model design. We design the explicit "linear regression" depth decoder (Eq. 7) to produce deep features and depth at each level for scene branch, implying that the depth estimation at level 2 is at scale 1/2 to the final depth, at level 4 is 1/4 and so on, which guarantees that we can embed the features at level n from the depth map to the corresponding level n lattice (Proved by Eq. 9). However, for the implicit "non-linear regression" in BTS 3, the depth estimation at level 2 is not 1/2 but an arbitrary and ambiguous scale to the final depth and so as other levels, which means that the features cannot be safely embedded to the lattice coordinate corresponding to the Euclidean coordinate. Note that this cannot be achieved by a simple concatenation of depth and scene branch, because not only the depth but also the deep features at corresponding position in 2D map are needed for scene branch. In other words, scene branch cannot work alone without depth module, and thus we take the two modules as a whole model rather than two independent models. This is the "Pyramid-Level 2D-3D features alignment between Cartesian Coordinate and Permutohedral Lattice Network" explained in Fig. 4. Our model design also considers the meta information aggregation, monocular input (like Mono-SF [18]) contains RGB, X, Y information, point cloud input (like HPLFlowNet [15]) contains X, Y, Z information, while our real-scale depth estimation from monocular input plus deep features extracted from the depth decoder contains information RGB, X, Y, Z. Moreover, the proposed network has advantage over Mono-SF/MonoSF-Multi [19] since our estimation is in real-scale whereas their estimation has scale ambiguity.

3.4   Loss

Depth Loss: Silog (scale-invariant log) loss is a widely-used loss [10] for depth estimation supervision defined as:

$$L_{silog}(\tilde{d}, d) = \alpha \sqrt{\frac{1}{T} \sum_i (g_i)^2 - \frac{\lambda}{T^2} \left(\sum_i g_i \right)^2} \tag{10}$$

where $g_i = \log \tilde{d}_i - \log d_i$, $\tilde{d}$ and d are estimated and ground truth depths, T is the number of valid pixels, λ and α are constants set to be 0.85 and 10. Since our depth decoder decodes a fixed-scale depth at each level, we do not directly supervise on final depth. Instead, we design a pyramid-level silog loss corresponding to our depth decoder to supervise the estimation from each level.

$$L_{depth} = \frac{1}{15}(8 \times L_1 + 4 \times L_2 + 2 \times L_4 + 1 \times L_8) \tag{11}$$

where $L_{level} = L_{silog}(\tilde{d}_{level}, d_{level}/n)$. Higher weight is assigned to low-level loss to stabilize the training process.

Scene Flow Loss: Following most LiDAR-based work, we first use a traditional End Point Error (EPE3D) loss as $L_{epe} = ||\tilde{sf} - sf||_2$, where $\tilde{sf}$ and sf are estimated and ground truth scene flows, respectively. To bring two sets of point clouds together, some self-supervised works leverage the Chamfer distance loss as:

$$L_{cham}(P, Q) = \sum_{p \in P} \min_{q \in Q} ||p - q||_2^2 + \sum_{q \in Q} \min_{p \in P} ||p - q||_2^2 \tag{12}$$

where P and Q are two sets of point clouds that optimized to be close to each other. While EPE loss supervises directly on scene flow 3D vectors, we improved canonical Chamfer loss to a forward-backward Chamfer distance loss supervising on our pseudo point cloud from depth estimates as:

$$
\begin{aligned}
L_{cham\_total} &= L_{cham\_f} + L_{cham\_b} \\
L_{cham\_f} &= L_{cham}(\tilde{P}_f, P_2) \\
L_{cham\_b} &= L_{cham}(\tilde{P}_b, P_1) \\
\tilde{P}_f &= P_1 + \tilde{sf}_f, \quad \tilde{P}_b = P_2 + \tilde{sf}_b
\end{aligned}
\tag{13}
$$

where P_1 and P_2 are pseudo point clouds generated from the estimated depth of two consecutive frames. $\tilde{sf}_f$ and $\tilde{sf}_b$ are estimated forward and backward scene flows.

4 Experiments

Datasets: We use Flyingthings3D [31] and KITTI [13] dataset in this work for training and evaluation. Flyingthings3D is a synthetic dataset with 19,460 pairs of images in its training split, and 3,824 pairs of images in its evaluation split. We use it for training and evaluation of both depth and scene flow estimation. For KITTI dataset, following most previous works, for depth training and evaluation, we use KITTI Eigen's [10] split which has 23,488 images of 32 scenes for training and 697 images of 29 scenes for evaluation. For scene flow evaluation, we use KITTI flow 2015 [32] split with 200 pairs of images labeled with flow ground truth. We do not train scene flow on KITTI.

4.1 Monocular Depth

We train the depth module in a fully-supervised manner using the pyramid-level silog loss derived in Eq. 11. For training simplicity, we first train the depth module free from scene flow decoder. Our model is completely trained from scratch.

Table 1. Monocular depth results comparison on KITTI Eigen's split. In the column *Output*, D denotes depth, *2DF* and *3DF* denote 2D optical flow and 3D scene flow. In the column *Scale*, ✓ denotes in real scale, ✗ denotes with scale ambiguity. DenseNet-121 as backbone more efficient than ResNext-101.

Method	Output	Scale	Higher is better			Lower is better			
			$\delta < 1.25$	$\delta < 1.25^2$	$\delta < 1.25^3$	Abs Rel	Sq Rel	RMSE	RMSE *log*
Make3D [38]	D	✓	0.601	0.820	0.926	0.280	3.012	8.734	0.361
Eigen et al. [10]	D	✓	0.702	0.898	0.967	0.203	1.548	6.307	0.282
Liu et al. [26]	D	✓	0.680	0.898	0.967	0.201	1.584	6.471	0.273
LRC (CS + K) [14]	D	✓	0.861	0.949	0.976	0.114	0.898	4.935	0.206
Kuznietsov et al. [23]	D	✓	0.862	0.960	0.986	0.113	0.741	4.621	0.189
Gan et al. [12]	D	✓	0.890	0.964	0.985	0.098	0.666	3.933	0.173
DORN [11]	D	✓	0.932	0.984	0.994	0.072	0.307	2.727	0.120
Yin et al. [51]	D	✓	0.938	0.990	0.998	0.072	-	3.258	0.117
BTS (DenseNet-121) [24]	D	✓	0.951	0.993	0.998	0.063	0.256	2.850	0.100
BTS (ResNext-101) [24]	D	✓	0.956	0.993	0.998	0.059	0.245	2.756	0.096
DPT-hybrid [36]	D	✓	0.959	**0.995**	**0.999**	0.062	0.256	**2.573**	**0.092**
GeoNet [52]	D + 2DF	✗	0.793	0.931	0.973	0.155	1.296	5.857	0.233
DFNet [54]	D + 2DF	✗	0.818	0.943	0.978	0.146	1.182	5.215	0.213
CC [37]	D + 2DF	✗	0.826	0.941	0.975	0.140	1.070	5.326	0.217
GLNet [8]	D + 2DF	✗	0.841	0.948	0.980	0.135	1.070	5.230	0.210
EPC [50]	D + 2DF	✗	0.847	0.926	0.969	0.127	1.239	6.247	0.214
EPC++ [28]	D + 2DF	✗	0.841	0.946	0.979	0.127	0.936	5.008	0.209
Mono-SF [18]	D + 3DF	✗	0.851	0.950	0.978	0.125	0.978	4.877	0.208
Ours (DenseNet-121)	**D + 3DF**	✓	**0.960**	0.993	0.998	**0.059**	**0.236**	2.691	0.095

KITTI: We first train on KITTI Eigen's training split, Table 1 shows the depth comparison on KITTI Eigen's evaluation split. We classify the previous works into two categories, joint-estimate monocular depth and flow, and single-estimate monocular depth alone. It is clearly from the table that the single estimation outperforms the joint estimation on average, and the joint estimation has scale ambiguity. With a similar design to our strongest single-estimate baseline BTS [24], our depth outperforms BTS with the same backbone DenseNet-121 [17] as well as the best BTS with ResNext-101 backbone. The joint-estimate works fail to estimate in real scale because they regress depth and scene flow together in self-supervised manner, which sacrifices the real depth. We design our model with separate decoders in a fully-supervised manner, and succeed to jointly estimate depth and scene flow in real scale, where our depth achieves a clear improvement to the strongest joint-estimate baseline Mono-SF [18]. The monocular depth evaluation metrics cannot show the difference of a normalized and real-scale depth, but real-scale depth is required for real-scale 3D scene flow estimation.

Flyingthings3D: Similarly, we train another version on Flyingthings3D from scratch and use it to train the scene flow decoder on Flyingthings3D. Since Flyingthings3D is not a typical dataset for depth training, very few previous works reported results. Because scene flow estimation is related to depth, we also evaluated two strongest baselines on Flyingthings3D as shown in Table 2. Then we use the trained depth module to train the scene flow decoder (Tables 3 and 5).

Table 2. Monocular depth results comparison on Flyingthings3D dataset. In the column *Train on*, K denotes KITTI, F denotes Flyingthings3D. In the column *Scale*, ✓ denotes in real scale, ✗ denotes with scale ambiguity.

Method	Train on	Scale	Higher is better			Lower is better			
			$\delta < 1.25$	$\delta < 1.25^2$	$\delta < 1.25^3$	Abs Rel	Sq Rel	RMSE	RMSE log
Mono-SF [18]	K	✗	0.259	0.483	0.648	0.943	19.250	14.676	0.667
Mono-SF-Multi [19]	K	✗	0.273	0.492	0.650	0.931	19.072	14.566	0.666
Ours	F	✓	**0.715**	**0.934**	**0.980**	**0.188**	**1.142**	**4.400**	**0.235**

Table 3. Monocular 3D scene flow results comparison on Flyingthings3D dataset.(image based evaluation standard) In the column *Train on*, K denotes KITTI, F denotes Flyingthings3D. In the column *Scale*, ✓ denotes in real scale, ✗ denotes with scale ambiguity.

Method	Train on	Scale	EPE3D(m)	ACC3DS	ACC3DR	Outlier3D	EPE2D(px)	ACC2D
Mono-SF [18]	K	✗	1.1288	0.0525	0.1017	0.9988	58.2761	0.2362
Mono-SF-Multi [19]	K	✗	1.5864	0.0020	0.0050	0.9988	48.3099	0.3162
Ours	F	✓	**0.3915**	**0.5424**	**0.6911**	**0.8279**	**22.4226**	**0.6659**

Table 4. Monocular 3D scene flow results comparison on KITTI flow 2015 dataset.(image based evaluation standard) In the column *Train on*, K denotes KITTI, F denotes Flyingthings3D. In the column *Scale*, ✓ denotes in real scale, ✗ denotes with scale ambiguity.

Method	Train on	Scale	EPE3D(m)	ACC3DS	ACC3DR	Outlier3D	EPE2D(px)	ACC2D
[18]depth + Mono-Exp [48]	K	✗	2.7079	0.0676	0.1467	0.9982	181.0699	0.2777
Our depth + Mono-Exp [48]	K	✗	1.6673	0.0838	0.1815	0.9953	78.7245	0.2837
Mono-SF [18]	K	✗	1.1288	0.0525	0.1017	0.9988	58.2761	0.2362
Mono-SF-Multi [19]	K	✗	0.7828	0.1725	0.2548	0.9477	35.9015	0.4886
Ours	F	✓	**0.6970**	**0.2453**	**0.3692**	**0.8630**	**33.4750**	**0.4968**

Table 5. 3D scene flow results comparison with different input data form on KITTI flow 2015 and Flyingthings3D. (LiDAR based evaluation standard) Since we also compare the LiDAR approaches here, we use the strict LiDAR-based evaluation standard. In the column *Dataset*, K denotes KITTI, F denotes Flyingthings3D. All works in the table are in real scale. Since our work is the first image-based work thoroughly evaluating 3D scene flow with 3D metrics, we lack of some 3D results from previous image-based works, but it is already enough to see our Monocular-image based work is comparable to LiDAR approaches

Dataset	Method	Input	EPE3D(m)	ACC3DS	ACC3DR	Outlier3D	EPE2D(px)	ACC2D
K	LDOF [5]	RGBD	0.498	-	-	-	-	-
	OSF [32]	RGBD	0.394	-	-	-	-	-
	PRSM [43]	RGBD	0.327	-	-	-	-	-
	PRSM [43]	Stereo	0.729	-	-	-	-	-
	Ours	Mono	0.6970	0.0035	0.0255	0.9907	33.4750	0.0330
	ICP(rigid) [4]	LiDAR	0.5185	0.0669	0.1667	0.8712	27.6752	0.1056
	FGR(rigid) [53]	LiDAR	0.4835	0.1331	0.2851	0.7761	18.7464	0.2876
	CPD(non-rigid) [34]	LiDAR	0.4144	0.2058	0.4001	0.7146	27.0583	0.1980
F	FlowNet-C [9]	Depth	0.7887	0.0020	0.0149	-	-	-
	FlowNet-C [9]	RGBD	0.7836	0.0025	0.0174	-	-	-
	Ours	Mono	0.3915	0.0125	0.0816	0.9874	22.4226	0.0724
	ICP(global) [4]	LiDAR	0.5019	0.0762	0.2198	-	-	-
	ICP(rigid) [4]	LiDAR	0.4062	0.1614	0.3038	0.8796	23.2280	0.2913
	FlowNet3D-EM [27]	LiDAR	0.5807	0.0264	0.1221	-	-	-
	FlowNet3D-LM [27]	LiDAR	0.7876	0.0027	0.0183	-	-	-
	FlowNet3D [27]	LiDAR	0.1136	0.4125	0.7706	0.6016	5.9740	0.5692

4.2 Real-Scale 3D Scene Flow

Most image-based scene flow works are trained on KITTI in a self-supervised manner, which leads to the scale ambiguity. We train our scene flow decoder in a fully-supervised manner with the EPE3D and forward-backward loss proposed in Sect. 3.4, which is able to estimate real-scale depth and scene flow. While real dataset like KITTI lacks 3D scene flow label, we only train our depth decoder on synthetic dataset Flyingthings3D.

Previous image-based scene flow works mostly use $d1, d2, f1, sf1$ for evaluation, but these metrics are designed for evaluating 2D optical flow or normalized scene flow, which themselves have the scale ambiguity. Instead, we use the metrics directly for evaluating real-scale 3D scene flow [15,27,46], which we refer as **LiDAR-based evaluation standard** (details in supplementary materials). However, since this LiDAR standard is too strict to image-based approaches, we slightly relax the LiDAR standard and use an **image-based evaluation standard**, EPE (end point error) 3D/2D are same to LiDAR standard:

- Acc3DS: the percentage of points with EPE3D < 0.3m or relative error < 0.1.
- Acc3DR: the percentage of points with EPE3D < 0.4m or relative error < 0.2.
- Outliers3D: the percentage of points with EPE3D > 0.5m or relative error > 0.3.
- Acc2D: the percentage of points whose EPE2D < 20px or relative error < 0.2.

Since we are the only monocular image-based approach estimating in real scale, to evaluate other works with our monocular approach, we need to recover other works to the real scale using the depth and scene flow ground truth (details in supplementary materials).

Flyingthings3D: Table 4 shows the monocular 3D scene flow comparison on Flyingthings3D. Even recovering [18,19] to real scale with ground truth, our result still outperforms the two strongest state-of-the-art baseline works by an overwhelming advantage. More importantly, we only need two consecutive images without any ground truth.

KITTI: We also directly evaluate scene flow on KITTI without any fine-tuning as shown in Table 4. The table also includes state-of-the-art 2D approach Mono-Expansion [48]. We first recover its direct output 2D optical flow to 3D scene flow, and then recover the scale. To recover 2D to 3D, Mono-Expansion proposed a strategy using LiDAR ground truth to expand 2D to 3D specifically for its own usage, but it is not able to extend to all works. For comparison, we recover 3D flow and scale in the same way with ground truth. In the table, the proposed approach still outperforms all state-of-the-art strong baseline works without any fine-tuning on KITTI. Since Mono-Expansion does not estimate depth, we use our depth and Mono-SF depth to help recovering 3D scene flow. Note that our scene flow decoder does not use the depth directly, but share the features and regress in parallel. In the table, by using our depth to recover Mono-Exp, it greatly outperforms by using depth from Mono-SF [18]. This comparison also shows the superiority of our depth estimation over others.

Ablation Study: We perform the ablation study for our scene flow decoder. The ablation study verifies the 2D-3D features alignment process, discussed in Sect. 3.3. As our MonoPLFlowNet architecture (Fig. 2) shows, we perform three-level 2D-3D features alignment in our full model and decode in parallel, which are level 1, 2, 4. In the ablation study, we train the model only with level1 and level1+level2, and compare to the full model trained to the same epoch. The results indicate that the performances get better with deeper levels involved, hence the concatenation of features from different levels in the lattice boost the training, which proves our 2D-3D features alignment mechanism (Table 6).

Table 6. Ablation study on our MonoPLFlowNet by changing level of the scene decoder. (image based evaluation standard) lev1 denotes only using the last level, lev1-lev2 denotes using the last two levels, full denotes using all levels. For fair comparison, we show all results after training epoch 22.

Method	EPE3D(m)	Scale	ACC3DS	ACC3DR	Outlier3D	EPE2D(px)	ACC2D
MonoPLFlowNet-lev1	0.4781	✓	0.4587	0.6146	0.8935	26.3133	0.6092
MonoPLFlowNet-lev1-lev2	0.4439	✓	0.4689	0.6333	0.8605	24.3198	0.6366
MonoPLFlowNet-full	**0.4248**	✓	**0.5099**	**0.6611**	**0.8595**	**23.7657**	**0.6456**

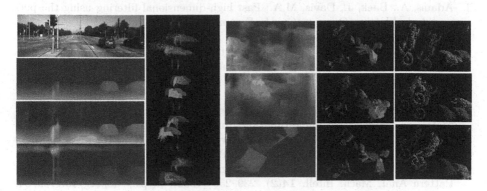

Fig. 5. Qualitative depth and real-scale 3D scene flow results of the proposed MonoPLFlowNet on KITTI and Flyingthins3D for a single pair of two consecutive frames. For KITTI (column 1&2), 1st row: 1st frame of the RGB input image, recovered scene flow of [48] by our depth. From 2nd to 4th row: depth and scene flow by Mono-sf [18], Mono-sf-multi [19] and ours. For Flyingthings3D (column3&4&5), from top to down: depth of the 1st frame, scene flow, zoom-in view scene flow by [18,19] and ours, original input RGB is shown in supplementary materials. Depth and scene flow of [18,19] are recovered to the real scale before generating point cloud.

4.3   Visual Results

We show our visual results of depth and real-scale scene flow in Fig. 5. 3D scene flow are visualized with the pseudo point cloud generating from the estimated depth map, where blue points are from 1st frame, red and green points are blue points translated to 2nd frame by ground truth and estimated 3D scene flow, respectively. The goal of the algorithm is to match the green points to the red points. Different to LiDAR-based works that have same shape of point cloud, the shapes of point cloud are different here because generating from different depth estimation. More visual results are provided in supplementary materials.

5   Conclusion

We present MonoPLFlowNet in this paper. It is the first deep learning architecture that can estimate both depth and 3D scene flow in real scale, using only two consecutive monocular images. Our depth and 3D scene flow estimation outperforms all the-state-of-art baseline monocular based works, and is comparable to LiDAR based works. In the future, we will explore the usage of more real datasets with specifically designed self-supervised loss to further improve the performance.

References

1. Adams, A., Baek, J., Davis, M.A.: Fast high-dimensional filtering using the permutohedral lattice. Comput. Graph. Forum **29** (2010)
2. Behl, A., Jafari, O.H., Mustikovela, S.K., Alhaija, H.A., Rother, C., Geiger, A.: Bounding boxes, segmentations and object coordinates: how important is recognition for 3d scene flow estimation in autonomous driving scenarios? In: 2017 IEEE International Conference on Computer Vision (ICCV), pp. 2593–2602 (2017). https://doi.org/10.1109/ICCV.2017.281
3. Behl, A., Paschalidou, D., Donné, S., Geiger, A.: PointFlowNet: learning representations for rigid motion estimation from point clouds. In: 2019 IEEE/CVF Conference on Computer Vision and Pattern Recognition (CVPR), pp. 7954–7963 (2019). https://doi.org/10.1109/CVPR.2019.00815
4. Besl, P., McKay, N.D.: A method for registration of 3-D shapes. IEEE Trans. Pattern Anal. Mach. Intell. **14**(2), 239–256 (1992). https://doi.org/10.1109/34.121791
5. Brox, T., Malik, J.: Large displacement optical flow: Descriptor matching in variational motion estimation. IEEE Trans. Pattern Anal. Mach. Intell. **33**(3), 500–513 (2011). https://doi.org/10.1109/TPAMI.2010.143
6. Charles, R.Q., Su, H., Kaichun, M., Guibas, L.J.: PointNet: deep learning on point sets for 3D classification and segmentation. In: 2017 IEEE Conference on Computer Vision and Pattern Recognition (CVPR), pp. 77–85 (2017). https://doi.org/10.1109/CVPR.2017.16
7. Chen, L.C., Papandreou, G., Kokkinos, I., Murphy, K., Yuille, A.L.: DeepLab: semantic image segmentation with deep convolutional nets, atrous convolution, and fully connected CRFs. IEEE Trans. Pattern Anal. Mach. Intell. **40**(4), 834–848 (2018). https://doi.org/10.1109/TPAMI.2017.2699184
8. Chen, Y., Schmid, C., Sminchisescu, C.: Self-supervised learning with geometric constraints in monocular video: connecting flow, depth, and camera. In: 2019 IEEE/CVF International Conference on Computer Vision (ICCV), pp. 7062–7071 (2019). https://doi.org/10.1109/ICCV.2019.00716
9. Dosovitskiy, A., et al.: FlowNet: learning optical flow with convolutional networks. In: 2015 IEEE International Conference on Computer Vision (ICCV), pp. 2758–2766 (2015). https://doi.org/10.1109/ICCV.2015.316
10. Eigen, D., Puhrsch, C., Fergus, R.: Depth map prediction from a single image using a multi-scale deep network. In: Ghahramani, Z., Welling, M., Cortes, C., Lawrence, N., Weinberger, K.Q. (eds.) Advances in Neural Information Processing Systems, vol. 27. Curran Associates, Inc. (2014). https://proceedings.neurips.cc/paper/2014/file/7bccfde7714a1ebadf06c5f4cea752c1-Paper.pdf
11. Fu, H., Gong, M., Wang, C., Batmanghelich, K., Tao, D.: Deep ordinal regression network for monocular depth estimation. In: 2018 IEEE/CVF Conference on Computer Vision and Pattern Recognition, pp. 2002–2011 (2018). https://doi.org/10.1109/CVPR.2018.00214

12. Gan, Y., Xu, X., Sun, W., Lin, L.: Monocular depth estimation with affinity, vertical pooling, and label enhancement. In: Ferrari, V., Hebert, M., Sminchisescu, C., Weiss, Y. (eds.) ECCV 2018. LNCS, vol. 11207, pp. 232–247. Springer, Cham (2018). https://doi.org/10.1007/978-3-030-01219-9_14

13. Geiger, A., Lenz, P., Urtasun, R.: Are we ready for autonomous driving? The kitti vision benchmark suite. In: Conference on Computer Vision and Pattern Recognition (CVPR) (2012)

14. Godard, C., Aodha, O.M., Brostow, G.J.: Unsupervised monocular depth estimation with left-right consistency. In: 2017 IEEE Conference on Computer Vision and Pattern Recognition (CVPR), pp. 6602–6611 (2017). https://doi.org/10.1109/CVPR.2017.699

15. Gu, X., Wang, Y., Wu, C., Lee, Y.J., Wang, P.: HPLFlowNet: hierarchical permutohedral lattice flownet for scene flow estimation on large-scale point clouds. In: 2019 IEEE/CVF Conference on Computer Vision and Pattern Recognition (CVPR), pp. 3249–3258 (2019). https://doi.org/10.1109/CVPR.2019.00337

16. Hornácek, M., Fitzgibbon, A., Rother, C.: SphereFlow: 6 DoF scene flow from RGB-D pairs. In: 2014 IEEE Conference on Computer Vision and Pattern Recognition, pp. 3526–3533 (2014). https://doi.org/10.1109/CVPR.2014.451

17. Huang, G., Liu, Z., Van Der Maaten, L., Weinberger, K.Q.: Densely connected convolutional networks. In: 2017 IEEE Conference on Computer Vision and Pattern Recognition (CVPR), pp. 2261–2269 (2017). https://doi.org/10.1109/CVPR.2017.243

18. Hur, J., Roth, S.: Self-supervised monocular scene flow estimation. In: 2020 IEEE/CVF Conference on Computer Vision and Pattern Recognition (CVPR), pp. 7394–7403 (2020). https://doi.org/10.1109/CVPR42600.2020.00742

19. Hur, J., Roth, S.: Self-supervised multi-frame monocular scene flow. In: Proceedings of the IEEE/CVF Conference on Computer Vision and Pattern Recognition (CVPR), pp. 2684–2694, June 2021

20. Jaimez, M., Souiai, M., Stückler, J., Gonzalez-Jimenez, J., Cremers, D.: Motion cooperation: smooth piece-wise rigid scene flow from RGB-D images. In: 2015 International Conference on 3D Vision, pp. 64–72 (2015). https://doi.org/10.1109/3DV.2015.15

21. Jampani, V., Kiefel, M., Gehler, P.V.: Learning sparse high dimensional filters: image filtering, dense CRFs and bilateral neural networks. In: 2016 IEEE Conference on Computer Vision and Pattern Recognition (CVPR), pp. 4452–4461 (2016). https://doi.org/10.1109/CVPR.2016.482

22. Jiang, H., Sun, D., Jampani, V., Lv, Z., Learned-Miller, E., Kautz, J.: Sense: a shared encoder network for scene-flow estimation. In: 2019 IEEE/CVF International Conference on Computer Vision (ICCV), pp. 3194–3203 (2019). https://doi.org/10.1109/ICCV.2019.00329

23. Kuznietsov, Y., Stückler, J., Leibe, B.: Semi-supervised deep learning for monocular depth map prediction. In: 2017 IEEE Conference on Computer Vision and Pattern Recognition (CVPR), pp. 2215–2223 (2017). https://doi.org/10.1109/CVPR.2017.238

24. Lee, J.H., Han, M.K., Ko, D.W., Suh, I.H.: From big to small: multi-scale local planar guidance for monocular depth estimation. arXiv preprint arXiv:1907.10326 (2019)

25. Li, R., Nguyen, T.: SM3D: simultaneous monocular mapping and 3D detection. In: 2021 IEEE International Conference on Image Processing (ICIP), pp. 3652–3656 (2021). https://doi.org/10.1109/ICIP42928.2021.9506302

26. Liu, F., Shen, C., Lin, G., Reid, I.: Learning depth from single monocular images using deep convolutional neural fields. IEEE Trans. Pattern Anal. Mach. Intell. **38**(10), 2024–2039 (2016). https://doi.org/10.1109/TPAMI.2015.2505283

27. Liu, X., Qi, C.R., Guibas, L.J.: FlowNet3D: learning scene flow in 3D point clouds. In: 2019 IEEE/CVF Conference on Computer Vision and Pattern Recognition (CVPR), pp. 529–537 (2019). https://doi.org/10.1109/CVPR.2019.00062

28. Luo, C., et al.: Every pixel counts ++: joint learning of geometry and motion with 3d holistic understanding. IEEE Trans. Pattern Anal. Mach. Intell. **42**(10), 2624–2641 (2020). https://doi.org/10.1109/TPAMI.2019.2930258

29. Lv, Z., Kim, K., Troccoli, A., Sun, D., Rehg, J.M., Kautz, J.: Learning rigidity in dynamic scenes with a moving camera for 3D motion field estimation. In: Ferrari, V., Hebert, M., Sminchisescu, C., Weiss, Y. (eds.) ECCV 2018. LNCS, vol. 11209, pp. 484–501. Springer, Cham (2018). https://doi.org/10.1007/978-3-030-01228-1_29

30. Ma, W.C., Wang, S., Hu, R., Xiong, Y., Urtasun, R.: Deep rigid instance scene flow. In: 2019 IEEE/CVF Conference on Computer Vision and Pattern Recognition (CVPR), pp. 3609–3617 (2019). https://doi.org/10.1109/CVPR.2019.00373

31. Mayer, N., et al.: A large dataset to train convolutional networks for disparity, optical flow, and scene flow estimation. In: 2016 IEEE Conference on Computer Vision and Pattern Recognition (CVPR), pp. 4040–4048 (2016). https://doi.org/10.1109/CVPR.2016.438

32. Menze, M., Geiger, A.: Object scene flow for autonomous vehicles. In: 2015 IEEE Conference on Computer Vision and Pattern Recognition (CVPR), pp. 3061–3070 (2015). https://doi.org/10.1109/CVPR.2015.7298925

33. Mittal, H., Okorn, B., Held, D.: Just go with the flow: self-supervised scene flow estimation. In: 2020 IEEE/CVF Conference on Computer Vision and Pattern Recognition (CVPR), pp. 11174–11182 (2020). https://doi.org/10.1109/CVPR42600.2020.01119

34. Myronenko, A., Song, X.: Point set registration: coherent point drift. IEEE Trans. Pattern Anal. Mach. Intell. **32**(12), 2262–2275 (2010). https://doi.org/10.1109/TPAMI.2010.46

35. Qi, C.R., Yi, L., Su, H., Guibas, L.J.: Pointnet++: deep hierarchical feature learning on point sets in a metric space. In: NIPS (2017)

36. Ranftl, R., Lasinger, K., Hafner, D., Schindler, K., Koltun, V.: Towards robust monocular depth estimation: mixing datasets for zero-shot cross-dataset transfer. IEEE Trans. Pattern Anal. Mach. Intell. (TPAMI) (2020)

37. Ranjan, A., et al.: Competitive collaboration: joint unsupervised learning of depth, camera motion, optical flow and motion segmentation. In: 2019 IEEE/CVF Conference on Computer Vision and Pattern Recognition (CVPR), pp. 12232–12241 (2019). https://doi.org/10.1109/CVPR.2019.01252

38. Saxena, A., Sun, M., Ng, A.Y.: MAKE3D: learning 3D scene structure from a single still image. IEEE Trans. Pattern Anal. Mach. Intell. **31**(5), 824–840 (2009). https://doi.org/10.1109/TPAMI.2008.132

39. Schuster, R., Wasenmuller, O., Kuschk, G., Bailer, C., Stricker, D.: SceneFlow-Fields: dense interpolation of sparse scene flow correspondences. In: 2018 IEEE Winter Conference on Applications of Computer Vision (WACV), pp. 1056–1065 (2018). https://doi.org/10.1109/WACV.2018.00121

40. Su, H., et al.: SplatNet: sparse lattice networks for point cloud processing. In: 2018 IEEE/CVF Conference on Computer Vision and Pattern Recognition, pp. 2530–2539 (2018). https://doi.org/10.1109/CVPR.2018.00268

41. Sun, D., Yang, X., Liu, M.Y., Kautz, J.: PWC-Net: CNNs for optical flow using pyramid, warping, and cost volume. In: 2018 IEEE/CVF Conference on Computer Vision and Pattern Recognition, pp. 8934–8943 (2018). https://doi.org/10.1109/CVPR.2018.00931

42. Taniai, T., Sinha, S.N., Sato, Y.: Fast multi-frame stereo scene flow with motion segmentation. In: 2017 IEEE Conference on Computer Vision and Pattern Recognition (CVPR), pp. 6891–6900 (2017). https://doi.org/10.1109/CVPR.2017.729

43. Vogel, C., Schindler, K., Roth, S.: 3D scene flow estimation with a piecewise rigid scene model. Int. J. Comput. Vision **115**(1), 1–28 (2015)

44. Wang, Z., Li, S., Howard-Jenkins, H., Prisacariu, V.A., Chen, M.: Flownet3d++: geometric losses for deep scene flow estimation. In: 2020 IEEE Winter Conference on Applications of Computer Vision (WACV), pp. 91–98 (2020). https://doi.org/10.1109/WACV45572.2020.9093302

45. Wannenwetsch, A.S., Kiefel, M., Gehler, P.V., Roth, S.: Learning task-specific generalized convolutions in the permutohedral lattice. In: Fink, G.A., Frintrop, S., Jiang, X. (eds.) DAGM GCPR 2019. LNCS, vol. 11824, pp. 345–359. Springer, Cham (2019). https://doi.org/10.1007/978-3-030-33676-9_24

46. Wu, W., Wang, Z.Y., Li, Z., Liu, W., Fuxin, L.: PointPWC-net: cost volume on point clouds for (self-)supervised scene flow estimation. In: Vedaldi, A., Bischof, H., Brox, T., Frahm, J.-M. (eds.) ECCV 2020. LNCS, vol. 12350, pp. 88–107. Springer, Cham (2020). https://doi.org/10.1007/978-3-030-58558-7_6

47. Xu, Y., Wang, Y., Guo, L.: Unsupervised ego-motion and dense depth estimation with monocular video. In: 2018 IEEE 18th International Conference on Communication Technology (ICCT), pp. 1306–1310 (2018). https://doi.org/10.1109/ICCT.2018.8600039

48. Yang, G., Ramanan, D.: Upgrading optical flow to 3D scene flow through optical expansion. In: 2020 IEEE/CVF Conference on Computer Vision and Pattern Recognition (CVPR), pp. 1331–1340 (2020). https://doi.org/10.1109/CVPR42600.2020.00141

49. Yang, M., Yu, K., Zhang, C., Li, Z., Yang, K.: DenseASPP for semantic segmentation in street scenes. In: 2018 IEEE/CVF Conference on Computer Vision and Pattern Recognition, pp. 3684–3692 (2018). https://doi.org/10.1109/CVPR.2018.00388

50. Yang, Z., Wang, P., Wang, Y., Xu, W., Nevatia, R.: Every pixel counts: unsupervised geometry learning with holistic 3D motion understanding (2018)

51. Yin, W., Liu, Y., Shen, C., Yan, Y.: Enforcing geometric constraints of virtual normal for depth prediction. In: 2019 IEEE/CVF International Conference on Computer Vision (ICCV), pp. 5683–5692 (2019). https://doi.org/10.1109/ICCV.2019.00578

52. Yin, Z., Shi, J.: GeoNet: unsupervised learning of dense depth, optical flow and camera pose. In: 2018 IEEE/CVF Conference on Computer Vision and Pattern Recognition, pp. 1983–1992 (2018). https://doi.org/10.1109/CVPR.2018.00212

53. Zhou, Q.-Y., Park, J., Koltun, V.: Fast global registration. In: Leibe, B., Matas, J., Sebe, N., Welling, M. (eds.) ECCV 2016. LNCS, vol. 9906, pp. 766–782. Springer, Cham (2016). https://doi.org/10.1007/978-3-319-46475-6_47

54. Zou, Y., Luo, Z., Huang, J.-B.: DF-net: unsupervised joint learning of depth and flow using cross-task consistency. In: Ferrari, V., Hebert, M., Sminchisescu, C., Weiss, Y. (eds.) ECCV 2018. LNCS, vol. 11209, pp. 38–55. Springer, Cham (2018). https://doi.org/10.1007/978-3-030-01228-1_3

TO-Scene: A Large-Scale Dataset for Understanding 3D Tabletop Scenes

Mutian Xu[1], Pei Chen[1], Haolin Liu[1,2], and Xiaoguang Han[1,2(✉)]

[1] School of Science and Engineering, The Chinese University of Hong Kong, Shenzhen, China
{mutianxu,peichen,haolinliu}@link.cuhk.edu.cn
[2] The Future Network of Intelligence Institute, CUHK-Shenzhen, Shenzhen, China
hanxiaoguang@cuhk.edu.cn

Abstract. Many basic indoor activities such as eating or writing are always conducted upon different *tabletops* (e.g., coffee tables, writing desks). It is indispensable to understanding tabletop scenes in 3D indoor scene parsing applications. Unfortunately, it is hard to meet this demand by directly deploying data-driven algorithms, since 3D tabletop scenes are rarely available in current datasets. To remedy this defect, we introduce TO-Scene, a large-scale dataset focusing on tabletop scenes, which contains 20,740 scenes with three variants. To acquire the data, we design an efficient and scalable framework, where a crowdsourcing UI is developed to transfer CAD objects from ModelNet [43] and ShapeNet [5] onto tables from ScanNet [10], then the output tabletop scenes are simulated into real scans and annotated automatically.

Further, a tabletop-aware learning strategy is proposed for better perceiving the small-sized tabletop instances. Notably, we also provide a *real* scanned test set TO-Real to verify the practical value of TO-Scene. Experiments show that the algorithms trained on TO-Scene indeed work on the realistic test data, and our proposed tabletop-aware learning strategy greatly improves the state-of-the-art results on both 3D semantic segmentation and object detection tasks. Dataset and code are available at https://github.com/GAP-LAB-CUHK-SZ/TO-Scene.

Keywords: 3D tabletop scenes · Efficient · Three variants · Tabletop-aware learning

1 Introduction

Understanding indoor scenes is a fundamental problem in many industrial applications, such as home automation, scene modeling, virtual reality, and percep-

M. Xu and P. Chen—Contribute equally.

Supplementary Information The online version contains supplementary material available at https://doi.org/10.1007/978-3-031-19812-0_20.

Fig. 1. Overview of data acquisition framework and TO-Scene dataset. We firstly transfer object CADs from ModelNet [43] and ShapeNet [5] onto real tables from ScanNet [10] via crowdsourcing Web UI. Then the tabletop scenes are simluated into real scans and annotated automatically. Three variants (TO_Vanilla, TO_Crowd and TO_ScanNet) are presented for various scenarios. A real-scanned test data TO-Real is provided to verify the practical value of TO-Scene.

tion assistance. While this topic spawns the recent development of 3D supervised deep learning methods [27,47,52], their performance directly depends on the availability of large labeled training datasets. Thanks to the progress of 3D scanning technologies and depth sensors (e.g., Kinect [51]), various 3D indoor scene datasets arised [2,4,10,21,34–36,38,46]. The most popular indoor scene benchmark among them, ScanNet [10], is consisted of richly annotated RGB-D scans in real world, which is produced by a scalable data acquisition framework.

Albeit the great advance on 3D indoor datasets allows us to train data-hungry algorithms for scene understanding tasks, one of the most frequent and widely-used setups under indoor environments is poorly investigated – the scene focusing on *tabletops*.

In indoor rooms, for satisfying the basic daily requirements (such as eating, writing, working), humans (or robots) need to frequently interact with or face to different tabletops (e.g., dining tables, coffee tables, kitchen cabinets, writing desks), and place, catch or use various tabletop objects (e.g., pencils, keyboards, mugs, phones, bowls). Thus, perceiving and understanding tabletop scenes is *indispensable* in indoor scene parsing applications. Unfortunately, it is hard to meet this demand by directly deploying the 3D networks, since existing indoor scene datasets lack either adequate samples, categories or annotations of tabletop objects (illustrated in Table 1), from where the models is not able to learn the corresponding representations. Therefore, it is substantially meaningful to build a dataset focusing on the tabletop objects with sufficient quantities and classes.

We attempt to construct such a dataset and present our work by answering the below questions:

(1) *Assumption – What is the Sample Pattern Supposed to Be?* Starting from our previous motivation, the dataset is expected to meet the practical demand in real applications. Thus, the sample is assumed to look similar with the real scanned tabletop scene, which is a bounded space filled by a table with multiple objects above it, and surrounded by some background furniture. This requires the model to perceive both the individual objects and their

inter-relationships, while assisted by the context information learned from finite indoor surroundings.

(**2**) *Acquisition – How to Build Such a Dataset with Decent Richness, Diversity, and Scalability, at a Low Cost?* Building large-scale datasets is always challenging, not only because of the laborious collection of large amounts of 3D data, but also the non-trivial annotation. As for our work, it is undoubtedly burdensome to manually place objects above real tables, then scan and label 3D data. Instead, we design an efficient and scalable framework (Fig. 1) to overcome this difficulty. We firstly develop a Web UI (Fig. 2) to help novices transfer CAD objects of ModelNet [43] and ShapeNet [5] to suitable tables extracted from ScanNet [10] scenes. The UI makes it possible to enlarge our dataset in the future. After that, we simulate the synthetic objects into real-world data, expecting that the model trained on our dataset can work on real scanned data. Last, an automatic annotation strategy is adopted to produce point-wise semantic labels on each reconstructed object's meshes, based on its bounding box that directly gained from the CAD model. So far, the complete acquisition pipeline enables us to construct a vanilla dataset as mentioned in (**1**), which contains 12,078 tabletop scenes with 60,174 tabletop instances belonging to 52 classes, called **TO_Vanilla**.

(**3**) *Enrichment – Can We Create More Variants of the Data to Bring New Challenges into the Indoor Scene Parsing Task?* i) In our daily life, the tabletops are sometimes full of crowded objects. To simulate this situation, we increase the instances above each table, producing a more challenging setup called **TO_Crowd**, which provides 3,999 tabletop scenes and 52,055 instances that are distinguished with TO_Vanilla. ii) Both TO_Vanilla and TO_Crowd assume to parse the tabletop scenes. Nevertheless, some real applications require to parse the *whole* room with all furniture including tabletop objects in one stage. To remedy this, another variants **TO_ScanNet** comes by directly using the tables in TO-Vanilla, but the complete scans of rooms that accommodate the corresponding tables are still kept. It covers 4663 scans holding around 137k tabletop instances, which can be treated as an *augmented ScanNet* [10]. Combining three variants, we introduce **TO-Scene**.

(**4**) *Strategies – How to Handle the open Challenges in our TO-Scene?* The tabletop objects in TO-Scene are mostly in smaller-size compared with other large-size background furniture, causing challenges to discriminate them. To better perceive the presence of tabletop instances, we propose a tabletop-aware learning strategy that can significantly improve upon the state-of-the-art results on our dataset, by jointly optimizing a tabletop-object discriminator and the main segmentation or detection targets in a single neural network.

(**5**) *Practicality – Can TO-Scene Indeed Serve for Real Applications?* To investigate this, we manually scan and annotate three sets of data, that corresponds to the three variants of TO-Scene. We denote the whole test data as **TO-Real**, which provides 197 *real* tabletop scans with 2373 objects and 22 indoor room scans holding 824 instances. Consequently, the models trained on TO-Scene get promising results on our realistic test data, which suggests the practical value of TO-Scene.

Here, the contributions of this paper are summarized as:

Table 1. Overview of 3D indoor scene datasets. "kit" indicates kitchen, "obj" denotes object, "bbox" means bounding boxes, "point segs" is point-wise segmentation. Our large-scale TO-Scene with three variants focuses on tabletop scenes, and is efficiently built by crowdsourcing UI and automatic annotation.

Dataset	Tabletop	#Scenes	Collection	Annotation
SUNCG [39]	✗	45k	synthetic, by designers	dense 3D
SceneNet [19]	✗	57	synthetic, by designers	dense 3D
OpenRooms [25]	✗	1068	synthetic, by designers	dense 3D
3D-FRONT [14]	✗	19k	synthetic, by designers	dense 3D
NYU v2 [36]	✗	464	scan, by experts	raw RGB-D [41]
SUN 3D [46]	✗	415	scan, by experts	2D polygons
S3DIS [2]	✗	265	scan, by experts	dense 3D [17]
ScanNet [10]	✗	1513	scan, by crowdsourcing UI [10]	dense 3D
WRGB-D [23]	✓, 5 sorts small obj	22	scan, by experts	point segs, 2D polygons
GMU Kit [16]	✓, 23 sorts kit obj	9	scan, by experts	dense 3D
TO-Scene (ours)	✓, various tables, 52 sorts obj	21k, 3 variants with augmented [10]	effortless transfer by our-own crowdsourcing UI	dense 3D: bboxes of [5,43] + auto point segs

- TO-Scene – To the best of our knowledge, the first large-scale dataset primarily for understanding tabletop scenes, with three different variants.
- An efficient and scalable data acquisition framework with an easy-to-use Web UI for untrained users.
- A tabletop-aware learning strategy, for better discriminating the small-sized tabletop instances in indoor rooms.
- A real scanned test set – TO-Real, with the same three variants as TO-Scene, for verifying the practical value of TO-Scene.
- Experiments demonstrate that the networks running on TO-Scene work well on TO-Real, and our proposed tabletop-aware learning strategy greatly improves the state-of-the-arts.
- TO-Scene and TO-Real, plus Web UI are all open source.

2 Related Work

3D Indoor Scene Datasets. 3D indoor scene datasets have been actively made over the past few years. NYU v2 [36] is an early real dataset for RGBD scene understanding, which contains 464 short RGB-D videos captured from 1449 frames, with 2D polygons annotations as LabelMe [41] system. SUN3D [46] captures a set of 415 sequences of 254 spaces, with 2D polygons annotation on key frames. The following SUN RGB-D [38] collects 10,335 RGB-D frames with diverse scenes. Yet it does not provide complete 3D surface reconstructions or dense 3D semantic segmentations. To remedy this, Hua et al. [21] introduce SceneNN, a larger scale RGB-D dataset consisting of 100 scenes. Another popular dataset S3DIS [2] includes manually labeled 3D meshes for 265 rooms captured with a Matterport camera. Later, Dai et al. [10] design an easy-to-use and scalable RGB-D capture system to produce ScanNet, the most widely-used and richly annotated indoor scene dataset, which contains 1513 RGB-D scans of over 707 indoor rooms with estimated camera parameters, surface reconstructions, textured meshes, semantic segmentations. Further, Matterport3D [4] provides 10,800 panoramic views from 194,400 RGB-D images of 90 building scenes. In [14,19,25,39], the synthetic 3D indoor scene data are generated. The recent 3D-FRONT [14] contains 18,797 rooms diversely furnished by 3D objects, surpassing all public scene datasets.

The aforementioned datasets ignore an important data form in indoor scene parsing applications – *tabletop* scenes, which is the basis of our dataset. There are two existing datasets emphasizing small objects that may appear on tables. WRGB-D Scenes [23] includes 22 annotated scene video sequences containing 5 sorts of small objects (subset of WRGB-D Object [23]). GMU kitchen [16] is comprised of multi-view kitchen counter-top scenes, each containing 10–15 hand-hold instances annotated with bounding boxes and in the 3D point cloud. However, their complex data collections and annotations cause the severe limitation on the data richness, diversity and scalability (see Table 1).

3D Shape and Object Datasets. The tabletop objects in TO-Scene are originated from ModelNet [43] containing 151,128 3D CAD models of 660 categories, and ShapeNetCore [5] covering 55 object classes with 51,300 3D models. As for 3D shape datasets, [3,5,22,43–45] provide CAD models, while [6,8,29,37,42] advocate the realistic data. [23,33] contain multi-view images of 3D objects, and the recent Objectron [1] is a collection of short object-centric videos. The aforesaid datasets deal with single 3D objects. In contrast, our TO-Scene highlights the holistic understanding and relationship exploration on various tabletop objects under indoor room environments.

Robot Grasping and Interacting Datasets. [12,13,24] contribute to the grasping of tabletop objects. Their annotations of object 6D poses and grasp poses exclude object categories, which are customized for the robot grasping, instead of understanding tabletop scenes. Garcia et al. [15] introduce a hyperrealistic indoor scene dataset, which is explored by robots interacting with objects in a simulated world, but still specifically for robotic vision tasks.

3D Indoor Scene Parsing Algorithms. The bloom of the indoor scene datasets opens the chances for training and benchmarking deep neural models in different 3D scene understanding tasks, such as 3D semantic segmentation [32,47,48,52] and 3D object detection [27,30,50]. Our TO-Scene raises a new challenge of discriminating the small-sized tabletop objects in indoor rooms. To tackle this, we propose a tabletop-aware learning strategy with a jointly optimized tabletop-object discriminator, for better perceiving tabletop instances.

Fig. 2. Our web-based crowdsourcing interface for transferring CADs onto real table-tops. The user chooses an suitable object and click somewhere on Bird's-Eye-View (BEV) (left) for placing it above 3D tables (right).

3   Data Acquisition

Building large-scale 3D datasets is always challenging, not only because of the laborious collection of large amounts of 3D data, but also the non-trivial annotation. This problem is especially severe even for expert users when collecting cluttered tabletop scenes under indoor environments, as in [16,23], which makes it non-trivial to replenish the dataset (i.e., inferior scalablity), and limits the richness and diversity of the dataset.

To solve this issue, we present an efficient and scalable framework for creating TO-Scene, with the ultimate goal of driving the deep networks to have a significant effect on the real world 3D data.

3.1   Transfer Object CADs into Indoor Scenes

In this work, rather than manually placing and scanning the tabletop objects in the real world, we propose to transfer the object CADs from ModelNet [43] and ShapeNet [5] into the tables located in ScanNet [10] rooms.

Source Datasets. ShapeNetCore [5] contains 55 object classes with 51,300 3D models and organizes them under the WordNet [28] taxonomy. Despite the tremendous size of ShapeNetCore, its quantity of tabletop objects are not able to meet our requirement. Thus, we also employ ModelNet [43] covering 151,128 3D CAD models of 660 classes. Both of them have the annotations of consistent rigid alignments and physical sizes. Leveraging their richness, we are able to agreeably borrow a large amount of CAD instances, belonging to 52 classes (detailed in Fig. 3) that are commonly seen on different tables in our daily life, as the tabletop objects of TO-Scene.

Another important source is ScanNet [10], which is a richly annotated real-world indoor scene dataset including 2.5M RGB-D images in 1513 scans acquired in 707 distinct spaces, especially covering diverse table instances. We extract the tables from ScanNet to place tabletop objects. Additionally, since the scanning of a tabletop scenes in real applications will also cover some background furniture, the ScanNet indoor environments around the tables also act as the context in our tabletop scenes.

User Interface. For allowing untrained users to create large-scale datasets, we develop a trivial-to-use Web UI to ease the object transfer process. As shown in Fig. 2, the Web UI shows up with a BEV (Bird's-Eye-View) of a table on the left and a 3D view of the surroundings on the right. The table are randomly selected from ScanNet with CADs picked from ModelNet and ShapeNet each time. The operation is friendly for untrained users. Specifically, when placing an object, the user does *not* need to perceive the *height* for placing it in 3D. The only action is just clicking at somewhere on the table in BEV, then the selected object will be automatically placed on the position as the user suggests, based on an encapsulated precise calibration algorithm. The flow of data through the system is handled by a tracking server. More details of UI can be found in the supplementary material.

The UI makes it possible to enlarge our dataset, endowing TO-Scene with decent scalability. Besides, similar transfer between different types of datasets can be achieved by revising the UI for creating new datasets or various purposes.

Transfer Rules. Notably, two implicit rules during transfer are achieved:

(1) *Rationality.* The function of a table is supposed to *match* with the objects above it. For instance, a mug will more likely to be appeared on coffee tables, while a pencil is possibly placed on writing desks. To achieve this, we set the UI to present objects only from the categories that fit the selected table, and the table label as well as its surroundings are shown to help users figure out the table function. Besides, users are guided to place objects according to their commonsense knowledge instead of reckless operations.

(2) *Diversity.* As mentioned in (1), the tables are randomly picked by UI with various instances shown to fit the table functions. Additionally, we employ around 500 users who may face with diverse tabletop scenes in their daily life, from different professions (e.g., teacher, doctor, student, cook, babysitter) and ages (20–50). After they finish, about 200 new users will double-check the samples, when they can rearrange, add or delete the objects.

Storage. Each time the user finishes a transfer, the UI will generate a file recording the file names of CADs and rooms, table ID, as well as the calibration parameters. This makes our dataset parameterized and editable, promoting us to store the results in a memory-saving way.

3.2 Simulate Tabletop Scenes into Real Scans

We realize a possible domain mismatch between the original synthetic tabletop objects and the real scanned data, which may result that the deep algorithms trained on TO-Scene are not able to directly work on real-world data. To avoid this, it is necessary to simulate the CAD objects into realistic data.

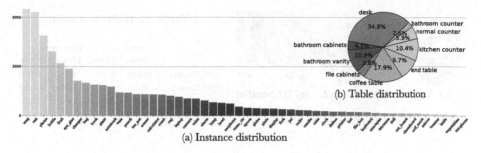

(b) Table distribution

(a) Instance distribution

Fig. 3. Semantic annotation statistics of TO_Vanilla.

According to the real-world data collection procedures, we firstly utilize Blender [9,11] to render CAD objects into several RGB-D sequences, via emulating the real depth camera. For instance, when a table is against walls, our simulated camera poses will only cover the views in front of tables. Generally, the objects are visible from different viewpoints and distances and may be partially or completely occluded in some frames. Then, the rendered RGB-D frames are sent to TSDF [49] reconstruction algorithms for generating the realistic 3D data.

So far, the whole process brings the occlusions and reconstruction errors, simulating the noise characteristics in real data scanned by depth sensors. As a matter of course, the data domain of tabletop objects are *unified* with the tables and background furniture that are extracted from real scanned ScanNet [10]. Table 5 demonstrates that the model trained on our dataset can be generalized to realistic data for practical applications.

3.3   Annotate Tabletop Instances

Agreeably, the bounding box annotations (i.e., the center coordinates of boxes, length, width, height, and semantic label) of tabletop objects are naturally gained from their CAD counterparts. Next, since the bounding box of an instance delineates an area covering its owning points, this promotes us to get the pointwise annotations straightforwardly and automatically.

Following above procedures, we build a dataset consisting of 12,078 tabletop scenes, with 60,174 tabletop object instances from 52 common classes. Figure 4 (a)) shows a sample of this vanilla dataset, denoted as **TO_Vanilla**, which is also the foundation of our dataset. Figure 3 shows the statistics for the semantic annotation of the major tabletop objects and the used table categories in TO_Vanilla.

3.4   Data Enrichment

We construct another two variants upon TO_Vanilla, for benchmarking existing algorithms under more real scenarios with new challenges.

Crowded Objects. The tabletops in our daily life are often full of crowded objects with more inter-occlusions, To simulate this challenge, we reload some

(a) TO_Vanilla   (b) TO_Crowd   (c) TO_ScanNet

Fig. 4. Three variants in TO-Scene.

Table 2. Train/Test split.

	Scenes		Instances	
	♯Train	♯Test	♯Train	♯Test
TO_Vanilla	10003	2075	49982	10192
TO_Crowd	3350	649	43390	8665
TO_ScanNet	3852	811	114631	23032

object-table sudo-mappings outputs when building TO_Vanilla (i.e., the table-tops after object transfers, yet not rendered or reconstructed), and employ novices to place much more tabletop CADs above each table. Then we render and reconstruct the new crowded set via the same way as before. Consequently, more occlusions with reconstruction flaws are introduced (see Fig. 4 (b)), yielding a more challenging setup of tabletop scenes, indicated by **TO_Crowd**. It covers 3,999 tabletop scenes and 52,055 instances

Parse Whole Room in One Stage. Previous TO_Vanilla and TO_Crowd assume to only parse tabletop scenes, but many real applications require to process the *whole* room with all furniture including tabletop objects in one stage. To make up this situation, we keep the complete scans of ScanNet [10] rooms in each data sample, from which the tables of TO_Vanilla are extracted. We maintain the semantic label on original room furniture from ScanNet. As a result, another variant **TO_ScanNet** is presented (see Fig. 4 (c)), which requires algorithms to comprehensively understand both tabletop objects and room furniture. TO_ScanNet can be regarded as an *augmented ScanNet*.

3.5 TO-Scene Dataset

Finally, **TO-Scene** is born by combining TO_Vanilla, TO_Crowd and TO_ScanNet. The train/validation split statistics of three variants are summarized in Table 2, with the per-category details shown in the supplementary material. Our TO-Scene contains totally 16,077 tabletop scenes with 52 common classes of tabletop objects. The annotation includes vertex semantic labels, 3D bounding boxes, and camera poses during rendering, which opens new opportunities for exploring the methods in various real-world scenarios.

Note: The stated three variants are currently organized separately for different uses. One may combine either of them to explore more research prospects. Furthermore, this paper just presents the current TO-Scene snapshot, we will keep replenishing our dataset and provide extra *private test set* for benchmarking in the future. More data samples can be found in the supplementary material.

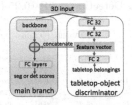

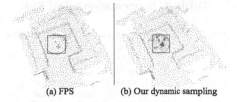

(a) FPS   (b) Our dynamic sampling

Fig. 5. Tabletop-aware learning.   **Fig. 6.** FPS V.S. dynamic sampling.

4   Tabletop-Aware Learning Strategy

For demonstrating the value of TO-Scene data, we focus on 3D semantic segmentation and 3D object detection tasks, towards understanding scenes from both point-wise and instance-level.

In TO-Scene, since tabletop objects are mostly in smaller-size compared with other large-size background furniture, it is naturally difficult to discriminate tabletop instances, especially for TO_ScanNet with lots of big furniture. Additionally, existing 3D networks mostly apply conventional downsampling such as farthest point sampling and grid sampling to enlarge the receptive field. Nevertheless, after being sampled by these schemes, the point densities of small tabletop objects are conspicuously sparser than big furniture (see Fig. 6 (a)), which hurts the perceiving of tabletop objects.

To handle these issues, our idea is to guide the network aware of the presence of tabletop objects, via adding a tabletop-object discriminator that is essentially a binary classifier. The loss is jointly optimized as the sum of the tabletop-object discriminator and segmentation (or detection) loss, which can be written as: $L_{total} = L_{seg\,or\,det} + \lambda L_{dis}$, where λ is the weight. For segmentation, the $0 - 1$ ground truth (gt) for L_{dis} can be directly gained from the point-wise semantic labels indicating if a point class belongs to tabletop objects, and L_{dis} is a cross-entropy loss. Yet the gt for detection only comes from bounding boxes. For fairly learning the discriminator, we employ a *soft* point-wise gt label that is a normalized per-point distance between each point and the center of a gt tabletop object bounding box, and compute the mean squared error as L_{dis}.

In this work, two operations are derived by tabletop-object discriminator:

(1) As shown in Fig. 5, the feature vector before the last fully connected layer of tabletop-object discriminator is concatenated with the features extracted by the main segmentation or detection branch, so that the predictions of the main branch are driven by the tabletop belongings information.

(2) A dynamic sampling strategy is proposed, where the points with higher tabletop-object discriminator score (i.e., points of tabletop objects) are more likely to be sampled (see Fig. 6 (b)). We replace the original sampling during the feature extraction in all backbone networks with our dynamic sampling.

In the practice, tabletop-object discriminator is implemented through a few fully-connected layers, assisted via max-pooling on K Nearest Neighbor (KNN)

Table 3. Segmentation mIoU (%).

Method	TO_Vanilla	TO_Crowd	TO_ScanNet
PointNet [31]	49.31	44.89	36.74
PointNet++ [32]	65.57	61.09	53.97
PointNet++ + FV	68.74	64.95	57.23
PointNet++ + DS	67.52	63.28	56.97
PointNet++ + FV + DS	69.87	65.15	58.80
PAConv [47]	75.68	71.28	65.15
Point Trans [52]	77.08	72.95	67.17
Point Trans + FV	79.01	75.06	69.09
Point Trans + DS	77.84	73.81	68.34
Point Trans + FV + DS	79.91	75.93	69.59

Table 4. Detection mAP@0.25 (%).

Method	TO_Vanilla	TO_Crowd	TO_ScanNet
VoteNet [30]	53.05	48.27	43.70
VoteNet + FV	59.33	50.32	48.36
VoteNet + DS	58.87	58.05	52.92
VoteNet + FV + DS	60.06	58.87	56.93
H3DNet [50]	59.64	57.25	52.39
Group-Free 3D [27]	61.75	59.61	49.04
Group-Free 3D + FV	62.26	59.63	53.66
Group-Free 3D + DS	62.19	59.69	55.71
Group-Free 3D + FV + DS	62.41	59.76	57.57

point features for fusing contextual information. Our joint learning concept can be promoted for tackling similar problems that requires to parse the objects with large size variance. The experimental results are listed in Sec. 5.

5   Benchmark on TO-Scene

For making the conclusions solid, extensive experiments are conducted on 3D semantic segmentation and 3D object detection tasks.

5.1   Common Notes

Below are common notes for both two tasks. The implementation details can be found in the supplementary material.

(1) We follow the original training strategies and data augmentations of all tested methods from their papers or open repositories.
(2) In Table 3 and Table 4, "FV" means applying feature vector of tabletop-object discriminator, "DS" indicates our dynamic sampling strategy.

5.2   3D Semantic Segmentation

Pre-voxelization. A common task on 3D data is semantic segmentation (i.e. labeling points with semantic classes). We advocate to pre-voxelize point clouds, which brings more regular structure and context information, as in [7,18,26, 40,52]. We set the voxel size to 4mm³ for matching the small sizes of tabletop objects. After voxelization, every voxel stores a surface point with object class annotation. Then we randomly sample 80,000 points from all voxels in a scene for training, and all points are adopted for testing.

Networks. We benchmark PointNet [31], PointNet++ [32], PAConv [47] and Point Transformer [52]. PointNet++ and Point Transformer are chosen as the backbones to plug our tabletop-aware learning modules.

Results and Analysis. Following the state-of-the-arts [20,47,52], we use mean of classwise intersection over union (mIoU) as the evaluation metrics. As we can

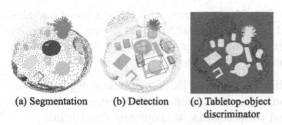 

(a) Segmentation   (b) Detection   (c) Tabletop-object discriminator

Fig. 7. Benchmark result.

Fig. 8. TO-Real test set.

see from Table 3, the state-of-the-arts learned from the training data are able to perform well in the test set based on the geometric input. Moreover, our tabletop-aware learning modules stably improve the model performance, especially when they are applied together.

5.3 3D Object Detection

Data-Preprocessing. Understanding indoor scenes at the instance level is also important. We follow the original pre-processing schemes of the selected state-of-the-arts.

Networks. We run VoteNet [30], H3DNet [50] and Group-Free 3D [27] on TO-Scene. VoteNet and Group-Free 3D are picked as the backbones to integrate our tabletop-aware learning strategies.

Results and Analysis. For the evaluation metrics, we use mAP@0.25, mean of average precision across all semantic classes with 3D IoU threshold 0.25, following the state-of-the-arts. As shown in Table 4, the deep networks achieve good results based on the geometric input. Our tabletop-aware learning methods again significantly improve the model performance.

A sample of segmentation, detection result and the predicted tabletop-belongings is visualized in Fig. 7. We can see that the networks successfully segment or detect the objects with tabletop-awareness. Both the segmentation and detection results show that TO_Crowd is more challenging than TO_Vanilla, and TO_ScanNet is most difficult. More result visualizations, the result of each class, and the ablations of tabletop-aware learning strategies are presented in the supplementary material.

6 Real-World Test

The ultimate target of our dataset is for serving the real applications. For a clearer picture of this goal, the below steps are performed.

Data. Since there is no real dataset that perfectly match with the three variants of TO-Scene, the first thing is to acquire real-world data. We employ expert users to manually scan and annotate **TO-Real** including three sets of data (see Fig. 8), which are respectively denoted as Real_Vanilla, Real_Crowd, Real_Scan.

Specifically, Real_Vanilla contains 97 tabletop scenes, while Real_Crowd includes 100 tabletop scenes with crowded objects. In Real_Scan, 22 scenes are scanned with both big furniture and small tabletop objects. The categories in TO-Real cover a subset of our TO-Scene objects (see Table 5).

Implementations. We train Point Transformer [52] for semantic segmentation and VoteNet [30] for detection on different variants of TO-Scene, and *directly* test on the corresponding TO-Real counterparts, without any fine-tuning.

Results and Analysis. Table 5 enumerates the segmentation mIoU and detection mAP of each class, where we find *two important phenomenons*:

(1) Under both Vanilla and Crowd settings that *specifically* for parsing tabletop objects, the variance between the results tested on TO-Scene and TO-Real is stably acceptable. For detection task, the test mAP (highlighted in red bold) of some categories on TO-Real is even better than it on TO-Scene. This definitely proves the practical value of the *tabletop*-scenes data in TO-Scene.

Table 5. Per-category test results on TO-Scene/TO-Real.

Class in	Segmentation mIoU (%)			Detection mAP@0.25(%)		
Real Data	Vanilla	Crowd	Scan	Vanilla	Crowd	Scan
Big furniture:						
wall	-	-	76.8/10.0	-	-	-
floor	-	-	94.9/46.5	-	-	-
cabinet	-	-	59.5/19.3	-	-	78.5/3.8
chair	-	-	80.4/33.6	-	-	92.3/55.7
sofa	-	-	75.3/39.2	-	-	98.7/62.2
table	-	-	71.9/23.5	-	-	83.4/16.3
door	-	-	55.6/19.2	-	-	69.5/10.1
window	-	-	59.5/5.9	-	-	57.1/1.5
bookshelf	-	-	64.0/10.2	-	-	69.6/10.5
picture	-	-	20.8/21.8	-	-	16.7/18.5
counter	-	-	58.5/6.2	-	-	86.0/8.7
desk	-	-	62.8/4.1	-	-	95.2/3.3
curtain	-	-	58.3/4.6	-	-	76.6/41.7
refrigerator	-	-	61.8/1.2	-	-	93.9/21.3
sink	-	-	58.1/34.0	-	-	67.9/70.0
Tabletop object:						
bottle	88.3/62.5	87.9/70.3	85.3/23.6	64.3/67.3	72.4/49.3	91.4/33.9
bowl	89.5/61.1	87.5/51.2	85.7/1.8	75.5/45.7	77.0/69.2	90.4/49.2
camera	89.0/74.4	85.3/77.9	81.2/1.2	81.0/91.7	74.7/50.5	95.2/3.1
cap	92.1/64.2	87.8/63.1	85.4/28.0	87.1/62.8	88.2/71.7	97.8/40.0
keyboard	86.0/75.7	89.3/77.1	-	51.2/67.4	37.7/36.1	-
display	93.6/81.4	91.4/80.6	-	93.9/92.14	84.8/80.2	-
lamp	86.0/72.6	90.0/78.4	72.2/10.9	84.7/84.2	85.6/67.5	98.4/61.6
laptop	94.3/81.6	96.9/66.2	95.5/52.7	90.3/62.8	96.8/69.2	97.7/80.1
mug	94.2/48.8	96.4/72.0	92.0/31.2	81.8/77.3	90.1/67.0	94.6/32.1
alarm	66.7/52.2	66.0/54.0	51.5/2.7	59.2/32.5	48.9/38.9	94.7/9.5
book	77.5/58.6	67.3/41.5	68.6/28.2	60.0/57.2	62.7/69.8	92.8/11.8
fruit	94.1/47.4	88.7/42.1	81.6/16.6	76.1/55.9	77.9/44.9	88.8/31.1
globe	96.0/85.1	98.0/75.4	96.4/17.6	87.9/88.6	95.9/91.1	99.9/31.1
plant	93.9/65.0	96.9/65.6	92.0/21.0	87.7/89.2	89.7/80.7	97.2/13.3

(2) The more interesting case lies on whole-room Scan (emphasized in gray shadow). As for the big furniture categories (highlighted in blue), the result variance of these categories are obviously undesirable. Note that these categories in TO-Scene all come from ScanNet [10]. Additionally, the results of tabletop object classes *particularly degrade* under whole room Scan setup, which is probably influenced by ScanNet big furniture that are simultaneously learned with tabletop objects during training on TO-ScanNet.

Here we discuss some possible reasons. Scanning big furniture around large room spaces is physically hard to control, causing various unstable noise (point density, *incompleteness*), and instance *arrangements/layouts* greatly change geographically. These unavoidable factors possibly cause the poor model generalization on big furniture across various data collections. As for tabletop objects, we guess the domain gap is small because scanning tabletops is physically controllable, bringing less unstable noise.

More details of TO-Real and the result visualizations are illustrated in the supplementary material.

7 Discussion and Conclusion

This paper presents TO-Scene, a large-scale 3D indoor dataset focusing on tabletop scenes, built through an efficient data acquisition framework. Moreover, a tabletop-aware learning strategy is proposed to better discriminate the small-sized tabletop instances, which improve the state-of-the-art results on both 3D semantic segmentation and object detection tasks. A real scanned test set, TO-Real, is provided to verify the practical value of TO-Scene. One of the variants of our dataset, TO-ScanNet, includes totally 4663 scans with 137k instances, which can possibly serve as a platform for *pre-training* data-hungry algorithms in 3D tasks towards individual shape-level or holistic scene-level.

Acknowledgements. The work was supported in part by the National Key R&D Program of China with grant No. 2018YFB1800800, the Basic Research Project No. HZQB-KCZYZ-2021067 of Hetao Shenzhen-HK S&T Cooperation Zone, by Shenzhen Outstanding Talents Training Fund 202002, by Guangdong Research Projects No. 2017ZT07X152 and No. 2019CX01X104, and by the Guangdong Provincial Key Laboratory of Future Networks of Intelligence (Grant No. 2022B1212010001). It was also supported by NSFC-62172348, NSFC-61902334 and Shenzhen General Project (No. JCYJ20190814112007258). We also thank the High-Performance Computing Portal under the administration of the Information Technology Services Office at CUHK-Shenzhen.

References

1. Ahmadyan, A., Zhang, L., Ablavatski, A., Wei, J., Grundmann, M.: Objectron: A large scale dataset of object-centric videos in the wild with pose annotations. In: CVPR (2021)

2. Armeni, I., et al.: 3D semantic parsing of large-scale indoor spaces. In: CVPR (2016)
3. Avetisyan, A., Dahnert, M., Dai, A., Savva, M., Chang, A.X., Niessner, M.: Scan2CAD: learning cad model alignment in RGB-D scans. In: CVPR (2019)
4. Chang, A., et al.: Matterport3D: learning from RGB-D data in indoor environments. In: 3DV (2017)
5. Chang, A.X., et al.: ShapeNet: an information-rich 3D model repository. arXiv preprint arXiv:1512.03012 (2015)
6. Choi, S., Zhou, Q.Y., Miller, S., Koltun, V.: A large dataset of object scans. arXiv preprint arXiv:1602.02481 (2016)
7. Choy, C., Gwak, J., Savarese, S.: 4D spatio-temporal convnets: Minkowski convolutional neural networks. In: CVPR (2019)
8. Collins, J., et al.: ABO: dataset and benchmarks for real-world 3D object understanding. arXiv preprint arXiv:2110.06199 (2021)
9. Blender Online Community: Blender - a 3D modelling and rendering package. Blender Foundation, Stichting Blender Foundation, Amsterdam (2018). http://www.blender.org
10. Dai, A., Chang, A.X., Savva, M., Halber, M., Funkhouser, T., Nießner, M.: ScanNet: richly-annotated 3D reconstructions of indoor scenes. In: CVPR (2017)
11. Denninger, M., et al.: BlenderProc. arXiv preprint arXiv:1911.01911 (2019)
12. Depierre, A., Dellandréa, E., Chen, L.: Jacquard: a large scale dataset for robotic grasp detection. In: IROS (2018)
13. Fang, H.S., Wang, C., Gou, M., Lu, C.: GraspNet-1billion: a large-scale benchmark for general object grasping. In: CVPR (2020)
14. Fu, H., et al.: 3D-front: 3D furnished rooms with layouts and semantics. In: CVPR (2021)
15. Garcia-Garcia, A., et al.: The RobotriX: an extremely photorealistic and very-large-scale indoor dataset of sequences with robot trajectories and interactions. In: IROS (2018)
16. Georgakis, G., Reza, M.A., Mousavian, A., Le, P., Kosecka, J.: Multiview RGB-D dataset for object instance detection. In: 3DV (2016)
17. Girardeau-Montaut, D.: CloudCompare3D point cloud and mesh processing software. OpenSource Project (2011)
18. Graham, B., Engelcke, M., van der Maaten, L.: 3D semantic segmentation with submanifold sparse convolutional networks. In: CVPR (2018)
19. Handa, A., Patraucean, V., Badrinarayanan, V., Stent, S., Cipolla, R.: SceneNet: understanding real world indoor scenes with synthetic data. In: CVPR (2016)
20. Hu, W., Zhao, H., Jiang, L., Jia, J., Wong, T.T.: Bidirectional projection network for cross dimensional scene understanding. In: CVPR (2021)
21. Hua, B.S., Pham, Q.H., Nguyen, D.T., Tran, M.K., Yu, L.F., Yeung, S.K.: SceneNN: a scene meshes dataset with annotations. In: 3DV (2016)
22. Koch, S., et al.: ABC: a big cad model dataset for geometric deep learning. In: CVPR (2019)
23. Lai, K., Bo, L., Ren, X., Fox, D.: A large-scale hierarchical multi-view RGB-D object dataset. In: ICRA (2011)
24. Lenz, I., Lee, H., Saxena, A.: Deep learning for detecting robotic grasps. IJRR **34**, 705–724 (2015)
25. Li, Z., et al.: OpenRooms: an open framework for photorealistic indoor scene datasets. In: CVPR (2021)

26. Liu, Z., Hu, H., Cao, Y., Zhang, Z., Tong, X.: A closer look at local aggregation operators in point cloud analysis. In: Vedaldi, A., Bischof, H., Brox, T., Frahm, J.-M. (eds.) ECCV 2020. LNCS, vol. 12368, pp. 326–342. Springer, Cham (2020). https://doi.org/10.1007/978-3-030-58592-1_20

27. Liu, Z., Zhang, Z., Cao, Y., Hu, H., Tong, X.: Group-free 3D object detection via transformers. In: ICCV (2021)

28. Miller, G.A.: WordNet: a lexical database for English. ACM Commun. **38**, 39–41 (1995)

29. Park, K., Rematas, K., Farhadi, A., Seitz, S.M.: PhotoShape: photorealistic materials for large-scale shape collections. ACM Trans. Graph **37**, 1–12 (2018)

30. Qi, C.R., Litany, O., He, K., Guibas, L.J.: Deep hough voting for 3D object detection in point clouds. In: ICCV (2019)

31. Qi, C.R., Su, H., Mo, K., Guibas, L.J.: PointNet: deep learning on point sets for 3D classification and segmentation. In: CVPR (2017)

32. Qi, C.R., Yi, L., Su, H., Guibas, L.J.: PointNet++: deep hierarchical feature learning on point sets in a metric space. In: NeurIPS (2017)

33. Reizenstein, J., Shapovalov, R., Henzler, P., Sbordone, L., Labatut, P., Novotny, D.: Common objects in 3D: large-scale learning and evaluation of real-life 3D category reconstruction. In: ICCV (2021)

34. Savva, M., Chang, A.X., Hanrahan, P., Fisher, M., Nießner, M.: PiGraphs: learning Interaction Snapshots from Observations. ACM Trans. Graph **35**, 1–12 (2016)

35. Silberman, N., Fergus, R.: Indoor scene segmentation using a structured light sensor. In: ICCV Workshops (2011)

36. Silberman, N., Hoiem, D., Kohli, P., Fergus, R.: Indoor segmentation and support inference from RGBD images. In: Fitzgibbon, A., Lazebnik, S., Perona, P., Sato, Y., Schmid, C. (eds.) ECCV 2012. LNCS, vol. 7576, pp. 746–760. Springer, Heidelberg (2012). https://doi.org/10.1007/978-3-642-33715-4_54

37. Singh, A., Sha, J., Narayan, K.S., Achim, T., Abbeel, P.: BigBIRD: a large-scale 3D database of object instances. In: ICRA (2014)

38. Song, S., Lichtenberg, S.P., Xiao, J.: Sun RGB-D: a RGB-D scene understanding benchmark suite. In: CVPR (2015)

39. Song, S., Yu, F., Zeng, A., Chang, A.X., Savva, M., Funkhouser, T.: Semantic scene completion from a single depth image. In: CVPR (2017)

40. Thomas, H., Qi, C.R., Deschaud, J.E., Marcotegui, B., Goulette, F., Guibas, L.J.: KPConv: flexible and deformable convolution for point clouds. In: ICCV (2019)

41. Torralba, A., Russell, B.C., Yuen, J.: LabeLMe: online image annotation and applications. IJCV (2010)

42. Uy, M.A., Pham, Q.H., Hua, B.S., Nguyen, D.T., Yeung, S.K.: Revisiting point cloud classification: a new benchmark dataset and classification model on real-world data. In: ICCV (2019)

43. Wu, Z., et al.: 3D ShapeNets: a deep representation for volumetric shapes. In: CVPR (2015)

44. Xiang, Yu., et al.: ObjectNet3D: a large scale database for 3D object recognition. In: Leibe, B., Matas, J., Sebe, N., Welling, M. (eds.) ECCV 2016. LNCS, vol. 9912, pp. 160–176. Springer, Cham (2016). https://doi.org/10.1007/978-3-319-46484-8_10

45. Xiang, Y., Mottaghi, R., Savarese, S.: Beyond PASCAL: a benchmark for 3D object detection in the wild. In: WACV (2014)

46. Xiao, J., Owens, A., Torralba, A.: Sun3D: a database of big spaces reconstructed using SFM and object labels. In: ICCV (2013)

47. Xu, M., Ding, R., Zhao, H., Qi, X.: PAConv: position adaptive convolution with dynamic kernel assembling on point clouds. In: CVPR (2021)
48. Xu, M., Zhang, J., Zhou, Z., Xu, M., Qi, X., Qiao, Y.: Learning geometry-disentangled representation for complementary understanding of 3D object point cloud. In: AAAI (2021)
49. Zeng, A., Song, S., Nießner, M., Fisher, M., Xiao, J., Funkhouser, T.: 3DMatch: learning local geometric descriptors from RGB-D reconstructions. In: CVPR (2017)
50. Zhang, Z., Sun, B., Yang, H., Huang, Q.: H3DNet: 3D object detection using hybrid geometric primitives. In: Vedaldi, A., Bischof, H., Brox, T., Frahm, J.-M. (eds.) ECCV 2020. LNCS, vol. 12357, pp. 311–329. Springer, Cham (2020). https://doi.org/10.1007/978-3-030-58610-2_19
51. Zhang, Z.: Microsoft Kinect sensor and its effect. IEEE MultiMedia (2012)
52. Zhao, H., Jiang, L., Jia, J., Torr, P., Koltun, V.: Point transformer. In: ICCV (2021)

Is It Necessary to Transfer Temporal Knowledge for Domain Adaptive Video Semantic Segmentation?

Xinyi Wu[1], Zhenyao Wu[1], Jin Wan[2], Lili Ju[1(✉)], and Song Wang[1(✉)]

[1] University of South Carolina, Columbia, USA
{xinyiw,zhenyao}@email.sc.edu, ju@math.sc.edu, songwang@cec.sc.edu
[2] Beijing Jiaotong University, Beijing, China
jinwan@bjtu.edu.cn

Abstract. Video semantic segmentation is a fundamental and important task in computer vision, and it usually requires large-scale labeled data for training deep neural network models. To avoid laborious manual labeling, domain adaptive video segmentation approaches were recently introduced by transferring the knowledge from the source domain of self-labeled simulated videos to the target domain of unlabeled real-world videos. However, it leads to an interesting question – while video-to-video adaptation is a natural idea, **are the source data required to be videos?** In this paper, we argue that it is not necessary to transfer temporal knowledge since the temporal continuity of video segmentation in the target domain can be estimated and enforced without reference to videos in the source domain. This motivates a new framework of Image-to-Video Domain Adaptive Semantic Segmentation (**I2VDA**), where the source domain is a set of images without temporal information. Under this setting, we bridge the domain gap via adversarial training based only on the spatial knowledge, and develop a novel temporal augmentation strategy, through which the temporal consistency in the target domain is well-exploited and learned. In addition, we introduce a new training scheme by leveraging a proxy network to produce pseudo-labels on-the-fly, which is very effective to improve the stability of adversarial training. Experimental results on two synthetic-to-real scenarios show that the proposed I2VDA method can achieve even better performance on video semantic segmentation than existing state-of-the-art video-to-video domain adaption approaches.

1 Introduction

Generating a dense prediction map for each frame to indicate specific class of each pixel, video semantic segmentation is a fundamental task in computer vision with

L. Ju and S. Wang—Code is available at github.com/W-zx-Y/I2VDA.

Supplementary Information The online version contains supplementary material available at https://doi.org/10.1007/978-3-031-19812-0_21.

important applications in autonomous driving and robotics [6, 7]. Just like image semantic segmentation [3, 24, 43], state-of-the-art supervised learning methods for video semantic segmentation require large-scale labeled training data, which is costly and laborious to annotate manually [9, 10, 22, 30, 46]. Semi-supervised training [2, 29, 30, 47] can help relieve the manual-annotation burden but still requires to annotate sparsely sampled video frames from the same domain.

One way to avoid completely manual annotation is to train segmentation models on simulated data that are easily rendered by video game engines and therefore self-annotated, and then transfer the learned knowledge into real-world video data for improving semantic segmentation. Underlying this is actually an important concept of

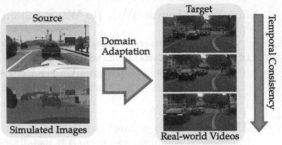

Fig. 1. An illustration of the framework setting for the proposed image-to-video domain adaptive semantic segmentation (I2VDA).

domain adaptation – from the source domain of simulated data to the target domain of real-world data – which was initially studied for image semantic segmentation [4, 15, 37, 38, 41, 42], *e.g.*, from GTA5 [33] to Cityscapes [6] and from SYNTHIA [34] to Cityscapes with much success. This concept of domain adaptation also has been extended to tackle video semantic segmentation – a straightforward approach is to treat each video frame as an image and directly perform image-to-image domain adaptation to segment each frame independently [11]. By ignoring the temporal information along the videos, these approaches usually exhibit limited performance on video semantic segmentation.

Recent progress on video semantic segmentation witnesses two inspirational works [11, 36] that coincidentally suggest video-to-video domain adaptation. Both of them employ adversarial learning of the video predictions between the source and target domains and therefore consider spatial-temporal information in both domains. While we can generate large-scale simulated videos to well reflect the source domain, it may lead to high complexity of the network and its training in the source domain. Motivated by such observation and with the goal to reduce the cost, we aim to develop a new concept of *image-to-video domain adaptive semantic segmentation* (I2VDA), where the source domain contains only simulated images and the target domain consists of real-world videos, as illustrated in Fig. 1.

Videos contain spatial-temporal information and video-to-video domain adaption can exploit and pass both spatial and temporal knowledge from the source domain to the target domain. The fundamental hypothesis of the proposed image-to-video domain adaptation for semantic segmentation is that we only need to pass the spatial knowledge from the source domain to the target domain, not the temporal one. In principle, we have two major arguments for this hypothesis: 1) the between-frame continuity is the most important temporal knowledge for video semantic segmentation and such continuity can be well exploited from videos in the target domain, *e.g.*, the optical flow along each video; and 2) the temporal information between the source and target domains practically may not show a systematic domain gap that has to be filled by adaptation. On the other hand, using images, instead of videos, in the source domain can significantly reduce the required training-data size and the network complexity.

In this paper, we verify the above fundamental hypothesis by developing a new image-to-video domain adaptive semantic segmentation method. In our method, we propose a novel temporal augmentation strategy to make use of the temporal consistency in the target domain and improve the target predictions. Moreover, the domain gap is bridged by the widely-used adversarial learning strategy which only considers the spatial features in the two domains. To relieve the instability of the adversarial learning, we further introduce a new training scheme that leverages a proxy network to generate pseudo labels for target predictions on-the-fly. We conduct extensive experiments to demonstrate the effectiveness of the proposed method and each of its strategy. The main contributions of this paper are summarized as follows:

- We propose and verify a new finding – for segmenting real videos, it is sufficient to perform domain adaptation from synthetic *images*, instead of synthetic *videos*, i.e., there is no need to adapt and transfer temporal information in practice.
- We introduce for the first time the setting of image-to-video domain adaptive semantic segmentation, *i.e.*, which uses labeled images as the source domain in domain adaptation for video semantic segmentation.
- We successfully develop an I2VDA method with two novel designs: 1) a temporal augmentation strategy to better exploit and learn diverse temporal consistency patterns in the target domain; and 2) a training scheme to achieve more stable adversarial training with the help of a proxy network.
- Experimental results on two synthetic-to-real scenarios demonstrate the effectiveness of the proposed method and verify our fundamental hypothesis. Without simulating/adapting temporal information in the source domain, our method still outperforms existing state-of-the-art video-to-video domain adaptation methods.

2   Related Works

Video Semantic Segmentation.   Existing video semantic segmentation approaches can be categorized into accuracy-oriented and efficiency-oriented ones. Optical-flow-based representation warping and multi-frame prediction fusion have been employed to achieve more robust and accurate results [10,22,46]. An alternative solution is to use the gated recurrent layers to extract the temporal information [9] or propagate labels to unlabeled frames by means of optical flow [30]. Many strategies have been studied to improve efficiency.

For example, features in each frame can be reused by adjacent frames to reduce the overall cost [35,40,46]. Li *et al.* [19] further proposed to reduce both of computational cost and maximum latency by adaptive feature propagation and key-frame allocation. More recently, Liu *et al.* [23] proposed to train a compact model via temporal knowledge distillation for real-time inference.

All of the above video semantic segmentation methods need the labeling on densely or sparsely sampled frames from the target domain for training. In this paper, we instead use self-labeled simulated images for training and then adapt to the target domain for video semantic segmentation.

Domain Adaptive Image Segmentation.   In recent years, many domain adaptation approaches have been proposed for image semantic segmentation to relieve the burden of dense pixel-level labeling. Hoffman *et al.* [15] introduced the first unsupervised domain adaptation method for transferring segmentation FCNs [24] by applying adversarial learning on feature representations, which has become a standard strategy for domain adaptive semantic segmentation [4,25]. More recently, the adversarial learning has been further extended to image level [5,14], output level [1,37] and entropy level [31,38] for this task.

In [48], Zou *et al.* first suggested the self-training in the form of a self-paced curriculum learning scheme for segmentation by generating and selecting pseudo labels based on confidence scores. Following this, many alter works on semantic segmentation directly integrate self-training [18,20,41] or refine it by confidence regularization [49], self-motivated curriculum learning [21], uncertainty estimation [44], instance adaptive selection [27], prototypical pseudo label denoising [42] and domain-aware meta-learning [12].

As mentioned earlier, while these image-to-image domain adaptation methods can be applied to video segmentation by processing each frame independently [11], their performance is usually limited by ignoring the temporal information in the videos.

Domain Adaptive Video Segmentation.   Recently, Guan *et al.* [11] made the first attempt at video-to-video domain adaptive semantic segmentation, in which both cross-domain and intra-domain temporal consistencies are considered to regularize the learning. The former is achieved by the adversarial learning of the spatial-temporal information between the source and target domains and the latter by passing the confident part of the flow-propagated prediction between adjacent frames. Concurrently, Shin *et al.* [36] also introduced the concept of domain adaptive video segmentation and propose a two-stage solution – the adversarial learning at the clip level first, followed by the target-domain learning with the refined pseudo labels. As mentioned earlier, while our work also performs domain adaptive video segmentation, it differs from the above two works in terms of the source domain setting – they use videos but we instead use images.

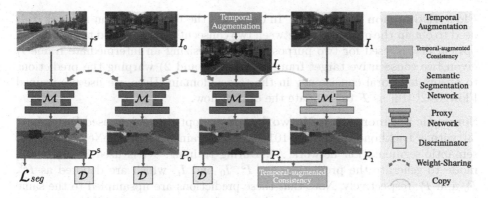

Fig. 2. The framework of the proposed image-to-video domain adaptive semantic segmentation. During training, the framework requires three inputs including a source image I^S and two consecutive frames I_0 and I_1 from a target video I^T. First, an intermediate target frame I_t $(0 < t < 1)$ is synthesized using I_0 and I_1 via a frame interpolation with temporal augmentation. Then, I^S, I_0 and I_t are fed into a weight-sharing semantic segmentation network $\mathcal{M}$ to obtain the corresponding predictions. A semantic segmentation loss $\mathcal{L}_{seg}$ is computed using the prediction of I^S and its label GT^S. A discriminator $\mathcal{D}$ is employed to distinguish outputs from the source domain S and target domain T. Besides, a proxy network $\mathcal{M}'$ takes I_1 as the input to generate its pseudo label which is used for ensuring the temporal consistency of the target predictions. Note that the parameters of $\mathcal{M}'$ are updated via copying from $\mathcal{M}$ instead of back propagation.

3   Proposed Method

3.1   Problem Setting

The goal of image-to-video domain adaptive semantic segmentation is to transfer only spatial knowledge from a labeled source domain S to an unlabeled target domain T. Same as the setting of domain adaptive video segmentation [11,36], the target domain is in the format of video sequences $I^T := \{I_0^T, I_1^T, ..., I_n^T, ...\}$ with $I^T \in$ T. In contrast, the source domain consists of a set of image-label pairs that are not in chronological order, $(I^S, GT^S) \in$ S.

3.2   Framework Overview

Our work bridges the spatial domain gap between the source and the target via adversarial learning and further considers the augmented temporal consistency in the target domain to achieve accurate predictions for the videos. In addition, a novel training scheme is introduced to improve the stability of the adversarial training. The proposed image-to-video domain adaptive semantic segmentation framework is illustrated in Fig. 2. The main components include flow estimation network $\mathcal{F}$ (for temporal augmentation and consistency learning), semantic segmentation network $\mathcal{M}$ and its proxy $\mathcal{M}'$, and discriminator $\mathcal{D}$.

Flow Estimation Network.   In our work, the flow estimation network $\mathcal{F}$ is used to obtain the optical flow between two consecutive frames and the computed optical flow is used for two purposes: 1) synthesizing an intermediate frame I_t given two consecutive target frames I_0 and I_1; and 2) warping the predictions to ensure temporal consistency in the target domain. Here, we use pre-trained FlowNet2[1] [16] as $\mathcal{F}$ to estimate the optical flow.

Semantic Segmentation Network.   We adopt the widely-used Deeplab-v2 [3] with a backbone of ResNet-101 [13] (pre-trained on ImageNet [8]) as the semantic segmentation network $\mathcal{M}$. During training, $\mathcal{M}$ is used in a training mode to generate the predictions for I^S, I_0 and I_t, which are denoted as P^S, P_0 and P_t, respectively. Note that these predictions are upsampled to the same resolution as the input images. In addition, the proxy network $\mathcal{M}'$ has the same architecture as $\mathcal{M}$, which instead is used in an evaluation mode to generate pseudo labels given I_1 as the input. The parameters of $\mathcal{M}'$ are updated via a copy from $\mathcal{M}$ at a certain frequency.

Discriminator.   To perform the adversarial learning, we employ the discriminator $\mathcal{D}$ to distinguish whether the prediction is from the source domain or the target one by following [37].

3.3   The Temporal Augmentation Strategy

From our perspective, the source does not require to be an ordered video sequence, but the temporal patterns such as frame rate and the speed of the ego-vehicle in the target domain do matter for performance improvements. As stated in [26], the temporal constraint is sensitive to object occlusions and lost frames. Here we propose a novel temporal augmentation strategy to achieve robust temporal consistency in the target domain, which is implemented based on a well-studied task – video frame interpolation [17]. Different from images, videos have the unique temporal dimension where more choices on data augmentation strategies can be applied other than those only focusing on the spatial dimension, *e.g.*, random flipping and rotation. In [47], Zhu *et al.* proposed to synthesize more image-label pairs by transforming a past frame and its corresponding label via video prediction technique for video semantic segmentation. This method can tackle the general video semantic segmentation task where only sparsely sampled video frames are labeled – the labels can be propagated to the unlabeled or synthesized frames. However, it is not applicable to our setting because of no labels in the target videos.

We carefully design a temporal augmentation strategy that is suitable for robust unlabeled video representation to improve the diversity of temporal consistency in the target domain. Specifically, given two consecutive target frames I_0 and I_1, we first extract the bi-directional optical flows using the pre-trained $\mathcal{F}$ as follows:

$$F_{0 \to 1} = \mathcal{F}(I_0, I_1), \quad F_{1 \to 0} = \mathcal{F}(I_1, I_0). \tag{1}$$

---

[1] https://github.com/NVIDIA/flownet2-pytorch.

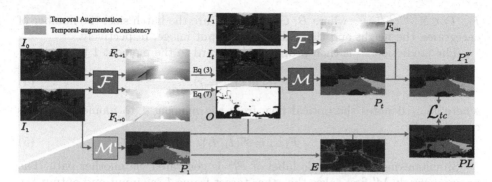

Fig. 3. An illustration of the proposed temporal augmentation strategy (Sect. 3.3) and temporal-augmented consistency learning (Sect. 3.4) in the target domain. (Color figure online)

By assuming that the optical flow field is locally smooth as [17], $F_{t \to 0}$ and $F_{t \to 1}$, for some $t \in (0,1)$ randomly generated in each training iteration, can be approximated by:

$$F_{t \to 0} \approx t F_{1 \to 0}, \quad F_{t \to 1} \approx (1 - t) F_{0 \to 1}. \tag{2}$$

Then, an intermediate frame I_t can be formulated as:

$$I_t = \alpha \mathcal{W}(I_0, F_{t \to 0}) + (1 - \alpha)\mathcal{W}(I_1, F_{t \to 1}), \tag{3}$$

where the parameter α controls the contribution of I_0 and I_1 and is set to 0.5 in all experiments, and $\mathcal{W}(\cdot, \cdot)$ is a backward warping function implemented using the bilinear interpolation [17,45].

The blue region of Fig. 3 illustrated the process of the proposed temporal augmentation strategy. Next, we will show how to use the produced synthesized frame to achieve better temporal-augmented consistency learning in the target domain.

3.4 The Temporal-Augmented Consistency Learning

Temporal consistency learning is a commonly-used constraint for video-level tasks [11,23,28,30,39]. In this work, we extend this idea and propose the temporal-augmented consistency learning leveraging the synthesized frame I_t obtained via Eq. (3). The goal of this operation is to not only improve the prediction consistency between consecutive frames, but more importantly, fulfil the on-the-fly self-training to stabilize the adversarial training. As illustrated in the green part of Fig. 3, the temporal-augmented consistency loss computed between a propagated prediction P_1^W of I_t and a corresponding pseudo label PL. Below we detail how to achieve this temporal-augmented consistency learning.

Firstly, the target frame I_0 and the synthesized frame I_t are fed into the segmentation network $\mathcal{M}$ to obtain the corresponding segmentation predictions

P_0, $P_t \in \mathbb{R}^{B \times C \times H \times W}$, where B, C, H and W are the batch size, the number of categories, the height and the width of the input image, respectively.

The prediction P_t is then propagated forward to the moment 1 to generate

$$P_1^W = \mathcal{W}(P_t, F_{1 \to t}), \tag{4}$$

where $F_{1 \to t}$ denotes the optical flow from the moment 1 to moment t and is computed by:

$$F_{1 \to t} = \mathcal{F}(I_1, I_t). \tag{5}$$

Simultaneously, the pseudo label of P_1^W is generated via another path. The proxy network $\mathcal{M}'$ first takes the other target frame I_1 as input and output the prediction P_1 (More details related to the usage of $\mathcal{M}'$ are introduced later in Sect. 3.5). Then the prediction P_1 is rectified according to its own confidence and only the predictions with the high confidence will be kept as the pseudo labels. Following [38], we first compute the entropy map $E \in [0, 1]^{B \times H \times W}$ via:

$$E = -\frac{1}{\log(C)} \sum_{k=1}^{C} \left(P_1^{(k)} \cdot \log(P_1^{(k)}) \right). \tag{6}$$

Since the synthesized frame I_t is not perfect, especially in the occlusion region, we further exclude the occlusion region in P_1 during the temporal-augmented consistency learning. Specifically, the occlusion region $O \in \mathbb{R}^{B \times H \times W}$ is defined as:

$$O = \begin{cases} 1, & \text{if } \mathcal{W}(F_{1 \to 0}, F_{0 \to 1}) + F_{0 \to 1} < \eta. \\ 0, & \text{otherwise}, \end{cases} \tag{7}$$

where η is a hyper-parameter (set to 1 in all experiments). The final rectified pseudo label PL is then given by:

$$PL = \begin{cases} \text{ArgMax}(P_1), & \text{if } E < \delta \text{ and } O = 1. \\ i, & \text{otherwise}, \end{cases} \tag{8}$$

where the threshold $\delta = 0.8$, and i is the ignored class label which is not considered during training. The rectified pseudo label PL is used to guide the prediction P_1^W which is achieved by minimizing the following **temporal-augmented consistency loss** $\mathcal{L}_{tc}$:

$$\mathcal{L}_{tc} = CE(P_1^W, PL). \tag{9}$$

Different from [11,23] which compute the L1 distance for temporal consistency, we employ the cross-entropy (CE) instead. Note that this is a non-trivial design, since Eq. (9) is also used to achieve the on-the-fly self-training. The CE loss is a common choice for self-training-based approaches [18,20,41] in domain adaptive semantic segmentation.

3.5   Proxy Network for On-the-Fly Self-training

The usage of the proxy network is motivated by two observations: 1) the instability of the adversarial training strategy in existing domain adaptation approaches [37,38]; and 2) the self-training technique requires multiple training stages but is not able to improve the performance on the target domain. Therefore, in this paper we propose to employ a proxy network $\mathcal{M}'$ to implicitly generate the pseudo labels for P_t on-the-fly. Specifically, $\mathcal{M}'$ gets starting to work after a few training iterations and it is used only in an evaluation mode. The parameters of $\mathcal{M}'$ will be updated via copying from M at every a fixed number of iterations.

3.6   Pipeline and Other Training Objectives

In summary, we describe the whole training pipeline in Algorithm 1 with the involved loss functions listed and discussed below.

Algorithm 1. – I2VDA

Input: Source images $\{I^s\}$, source labels $\{GT^s\}$, two consecutive frames $\{I_0, I_1\}$ from target videos, the base segmentor $\mathcal{M}$ with parameter $\theta_{\mathcal{M}}$, the proxy network $\mathcal{M}'$ with parameter $\theta_{\mathcal{M}'}$ and discriminator $\mathcal{D}$ with parameter $\theta_{\mathcal{D}}$, the max number of training iterations MAX_ITER, the copying frequency ITER_COPY, the training iterations ITER_LAUNCH before launching $\mathcal{M}'$.
Output: Optimal $\theta_{\mathcal{M}}$
 1: iter $= 0$
 2: **for** iter<MAX_ITER **do**
 3:     Synthesize I_t via Eq. (3);
 4:     Feed I^s, I_0 and I_t into $\mathcal{M}$ to obtain the predictions;
 5:     **if** iter % ITER_COPY **then**
 6:         Update the parameters: $\theta_{\mathcal{M}'} \leftarrow \theta_{\mathcal{M}}$;
 7:     **end if**
 8:     **if** iter $<$ ITER_LAUNCH **then**
 9:         Update $\theta_{\mathcal{M}}$ using $(\mathcal{L}_{seg} + 0.01\mathcal{L}_{adv})$;
10:     **else**
11:         Feed I_1 into $\mathcal{M}'$ and obtain PL;
12:         Compute $\mathcal{L}_{tc}$ using Eq. (9);
13:         Update $\theta_{\mathcal{M}}$ using $(\mathcal{L}_{seg} + 0.01\mathcal{L}_{adv} + \mathcal{L}_{tc})$;
14:     **end if**
15:     Update $\theta_{\mathcal{D}}$ using $\mathcal{L}_d$ defined in Eq. (12); iter $+= 1$;
16: **end for**
17: Return $\theta_{\mathcal{M}}$;

We compute the **Semantic segmentation loss** based on CE to train $\mathcal{M}$ to learn knowledge from the source domain:

$$\mathcal{L}_{seg} = CE(P^s, GT^s). \tag{10}$$

Minimizing the **adversarial loss** can close the gap between the source and target predictions so that the target prediction can fool the discriminator. The adversarial loss $\mathcal{L}_{adv}$ is defined as:

$$\mathcal{L}_{adv} = (\mathcal{D}(P_0) - r)^2 + (\mathcal{D}(P_t) - r)^2, \tag{11}$$

where r is the label indicating the source domain which has the same resolution as the output of the discriminator. The final loss of semantic segmentation network can be expressed as $\mathcal{L} = \mathcal{L}_{seg} + \mathcal{L}_{tc} + 0.01\mathcal{L}_{adv}$. Besides, the goal of the discriminator is to distinguish between the source and target predictions which is trained with the following objective function:

$$\mathcal{L}_d = (\mathcal{D}(P^S) - r)^2 + \frac{1}{2}(\mathcal{D}(P_0) - f)^2 + \frac{1}{2}(\mathcal{D}(P_t) - f)^2, \tag{12}$$

where f is the label indicating the target domain with the same resolution as the output of discriminator.

4   Experimental Results

4.1   Datasets

VIPER [32] dataset comprises 254,064 fully annotated video frames for training, validation and testing rendered from a computer game. We use 13,367 images marked as *0[2] with their labels as one of our source datasets. The frame resolution is $1,920 \times 1,080$. Following [11], 15 classes are considered for adaptation.

SYNTHIA [34] dataset is a synthetic dataset that consists of photo-realistic video frames rendered from a virtual city. It contains 8,000 labeled frames with a resolution of $1,280 \times 720$. We use the 850 labeled images from SYNTHIA-SEQS-04-DAWN[3] as another source dataset. Note that we remove the temporal constraint by randomly shuffling the frames in time. Following [11], 11 classes are considered for adaptation.

Cityscapes [6] dataset focuses on semantic understanding of real urban street scenes. It contains 5,000 images with fine annotations that are split into 2,975/ 500/1,525 for training/validation/testing. Each annotated image is the 20th image from a 30 frame video snippets. The resolution of each image is $2,048 \times 1,024$. We use it as the target domain in this work.

4.2   Experimental Settings

We implement the proposed I2VDA method using Pytorch. Following [37], our semantic segmentation network $\mathcal{M}$ is trained using Stochastic Gradient Descent (SGD) optimizer with a momentum of 0.9 and its initial learning rate is $2.5 \times$

---

[2] https://playing-for-benchmarks.org/download/.
[3] https://synthia-dataset.net/downloads/.

Table 1. Quantitative comparison results on the VIPER $\rightarrow$ Cityscapes domain adaptive video segmentation task. The best results are presented in **bold**, with the second best results underlined.

Methods	Road	Sidewalk	Building	Fence	Traffic light	Traffic sign	Vegetation	Terrain	Sky	Person	Car	Truck	Bus	Motorcycle	Bicycle	mIoU (%)
Source only	56.7	18.7	78.7	6.0	22.0	15.6	81.6	18.3	80.4	59.9	66.3	4.5	16.8	20.4	10.3	37.1
AdvEnt [38]	78.5	31.0	81.5	22.1	29.2	26.6	81.8	13.7	80.5	58.3	64.0	6.9	38.4	4.6	1.3	41.2
CBST [48]	48.1	20.2	**84.8**	12.0	20.6	19.2	83.8	18.4	**84.9**	59.2	71.5	3.2	38.0	23.8	**37.7**	41.7
IDA [31]	78.7	33.9	82.3	22.7	28.5	26.7	82.5	15.6	79.7	58.1	64.2	6.4	41.2	6.2	3.1	42.0
CRST [49]	56.0	23.1	82.1	11.6	18.7	17.2	85.5	17.5	82.3	60.8	73.6	3.6	38.9	30.5	35.0	42.4
FDA [41]	70.3	27.7	81.3	17.6	25.8	20.0	83.7	31.3	82.9	57.1	72.2	22.4	49.0	17.2	7.5	44.4
DA-VSN [11]	**86.8**	**36.7**	83.5	22.9	30.2	27.7	83.6	26.7	80.3	60.0	79.1	20.3	47.2	21.2	11.4	47.8
I2VDA	84.8	36.1	84.0	**28.0**	**36.5**	**36.0**	**85.9**	**32.5**	74.0	**63.2**	**81.9**	**33.0**	**51.8**	**39.9**	0.1	**51.2**

10^{-4}. The discriminator $\mathcal{D}$ is optimized using Adam with a β of $(0.9, 0.99)$ and its initial learning rate is 1.0×10^{-4}. We employ the polynomial decay with a power of 0.9 on the learning rates of both $\mathcal{M}$ and $\mathcal{D}$. The images in VIPER [32], SYNTHIA [34], Cityscapes [6] are resized to 896×512, 1280×768 and 1024×512, respectively. We don't perform any spatial-level data augmentation strategy during training and testing. Each experiment in this paper is run for 50,000 iterations with a batch size of 2 on two Tesla V100 GPUs. Especially for testing, we only feed each frame independently into $\mathcal{M}$ to achieve the prediction without using optical flow. The mean intersection-over-union (mIoU) is used as the main evaluation metric, for which the higher the better. We also report video-specific metric of "Temporal Consistency" (TC) [23], which is again the higher the better.

4.3 Comparison with State-of-the-Art Methods

VIPER $\rightarrow$ Cityscapes. We first compare our I2VDA method with the existing state-of-the-art methods, including [11,31,38,41,48,48,49] as in [11], for the VIPER $\rightarrow$ Cityscapes scenario. The quantitative results are reported in Table 1. We find our method significantly outperforms (51.2% mIoU) all the others that are trained with VIPER videos, *i.e.*, use additional unlabeled frames that are adjacent to the labeled one for temporal modeling. Besides, these video-to-video domain adaptation approaches require two images and a pre-computed optical flow as inputs during testing, while our method performs only a per-frame inference without optical-flow computation. On the video-level evaluation, our method achieves 66.01% on TC metric, while DAVSN [11] obtain 63.82%. This shows that our proposed method can generate more consistent prediction across frames. The video samples that we provide in the supplemental materials also verify this conclusion. We also present sample qualitative results for VIPER $\rightarrow$ Cityscapes scenario in Fig. 4. It can be observed that our method visually achieves better performance than the second best approach DA-VSN (but the

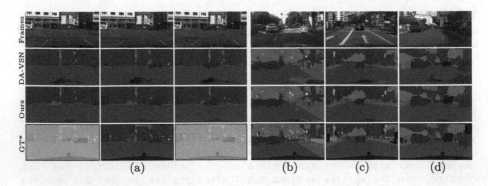

Fig. 4. Qualitative comparison results on the VIPER → Cityscapes domain adaptive video segmentation task. (a) The first three columns show the predictions of three consecutive frames. *Only one frame has ground truth in each video (30 frames). (b)–(d) show three other independent results from the Cityscapes validation set.

Table 2. Quantitative comparison results on the SYNTHIA → Cityscapes domain adaptive video segmentation task.

Methods	Road	Sidewalk	Building	Pole	Traffic light	Traffic sign	Vegetation	Sky	Person	Rider	Car	mIoU (%)
Source only	56.3	26.6	75.6	25.5	5.7	15.6	71.0	58.5	41.7	17.1	27.9	38.3
AdvEnt [38]	85.7	21.3	70.9	21.8	4.8	15.3	59.5	62.4	46.8	16.3	64.6	42.7
CBST [48]	64.1	30.5	78.2	28.9	14.3	21.3	75.8	62.6	46.9	20.2	33.9	43.3
IDA [31]	87.0	23.2	71.3	22.1	4.1	14.9	58.8	67.5	45.2	17.0	73.4	44.0
CRST [49]	70.4	31.4	79.1	27.6	11.5	20.7	78.0	67.2	49.5	17.1	39.6	44.7
FDA [41]	84.1	32.8	67.6	28.1	5.5	20.3	61.1	64.8	43.1	19.0	70.6	45.2
DA-VSN [11]	89.4	31.0	77.4	26.1	9.1	20.4	75.4	74.6	42.9	16.1	82.4	49.5
I2VDA (Ours)	**89.9**	**40.5**	77.6	27.3	**18.7**	**23.6**	76.1	76.3	48.5	22.4	82.1	**53.0**

best among all existing ones). Although our method does not contain temporal modeling during testing, our predictions in Fig. 4 (a) still show better temporal consistency than those by DA-VSN. In the spatial level, our segmentation results look also more accurate, *e.g.*, bus in (a), person in (a) and (c), car in (a)–(d).

SYNTHIA → Cityscapes. The quantitative comparison results for SYN-THIA → Cityscapes scenario are reported in Table 2, where our method still achieves the best performance and surpasses the second best (DA-VSN) by 2.6% mIoU. Sample qualitative comparison results for this adaptation scenario are shown in Fig. 5, and our method still achieves more consistent and accurate segmentation results.

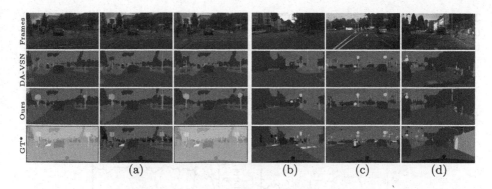

(a)   (b)   (c)   (d)

Fig. 5. Qualitative comparison results on the SYNTHIA → Cityscapes domain adaptive video segmentation task. (a) The first three columns show the predictions of three consecutive frames. *Only one frame has ground truth in each video (30 frames). (b)–(d) show three other independent results from the Cityscapes validation set.

Table 3. Ablation study on the I2VDA framework designs under the VIPER → Cityscapes scenario.

Variants	mIoU (%)
Baseline	44.0
w/o Temporal Augmentation	47.0
w/o Temporal-augmented Consistency	45.6
w/o Occlusion O in Eq. (8)	49.7
w/o Entropy Map E in Eq. (8)	49.6
Full I2VDA settings	**51.2**

4.4   Ablation Studies

On the Framework Design. To verify the effectiveness of each component of the I2VDA framework, we conduct a comprehensive ablation study with several model variants. The results under the VIPER → Cityscapes scenario are reported in Table 3. The variant in the first row serves as the baseline which trains the semantic segmentation network with the labeled source domain and employs the adversarial learning to close the domain gap [37], and the last row is the I2VDA method with full settings. We find that the proposed temporal augmentation strategy and temporal consistency learning are both very effective and can achieve 4.2% and 5.6% gains, respectively, over the baseline. Another observation is that the temporal augmentation strategy only obtain 1.6% mIoU gain on its own, but it will play a much greater role (51.2% vs. 44.0%) when combined with the temporal consistency learning. In addition, rows 4–5 show the effectiveness of some designs inside the temporal consistency learning including the consideration of occlusion and entropy.

On the Proxy Network. The proxy network also plays an important role in the temporal-augmented consistency learning. We conduct experiments on the

Table 4. Ablation study on ITER_COPY and ITER_LAUNCH for the proxy network under the VIPER → Cityscapes scenario. The ITER_LAUNCH is fixed to 8,000 for the first sub-table and the ITER_LAUNCH is fixed to 8,000 for the second sub-table.

ITER_COPY	1k	8k	15k	ITER_LAUNCH	1k	8k	15k
mIoU(%)	48.9	**51.2**	49.6	mIoU(%)	48.3	**51.2**	50.2

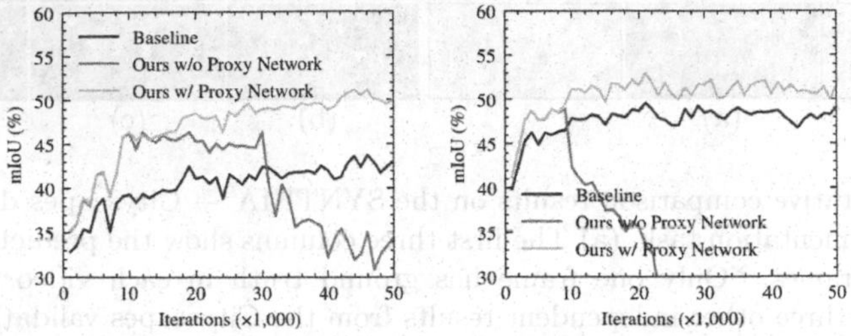

(a) VIPER → Cityscapes   (b) SYNTHIA → Cityscapes

Fig. 6. The mIoU performance vs. varying adaptation iterations.

Table 5. Ablation study on η, δ, t and α under the VIPER → Cityscapes scenario.

η	0.1	1.0	2.0	δ	0.1	0.3	0.5
mIoU(%)	50.4	**51.2**	50.2	mIoU(%)	48.5	**51.2**	49.7

t	0	0.25	0.5	0.75	1	Random	α	0.1	0.3	0.5	0.7	0.9
mIoU	47.0	47.0	48.4	48.1	47.4	**51.2**	mIoU	49.2	49.7	**51.2**	49.6	48.8

choice of copying frequency (ITER_COPY) and the training iterations before launching (ITER_LAUNCH). From Table 4, we find that copying every 8,000 iterations and launching the proxy network after 8,000 iterations achieves the best performance. In addition, as shown in Fig. 6, the use of the proxy network does improve the training stability effectively. The baseline here is the same as the one in Table 3.

On Some Hyper-parameters. We also conduct experiments to explore the choice of hyper-parameters involved in the temporal-augmented consistency learning. The results are reported in Table 5 where we find that our method achieves better performance when $\eta = 1.0$, $\delta = 0.3$ and $\alpha = 0.5$ and using randomly generated t.

5   Conclusion

In this paper, we found that it is not necessary to transfer temporal knowledge for domain-adaptive video semantic segmentation and have introduced for the first time the setting of image-to-video domain adaptive semantic segmentation which transfers knowledge from simulated images to real-world videos. Our I2VDA method reduces the domain gap between the source and target via adversarial training on only spatial knowledge. On the other hand, our method enhances the temporal consistency learning in the target domain by performing the temporal augmentation via frame interpolation to explore more temporal patterns and leveraging the proxy network to provide the pseudo labels on-the-fly to improve the stability of adversarial training. Experimental results on two synthetic-to-real scenarios showed that our method can outperform existing state-of-the-art video-to-video domain adaptation methods.

Acknowledgment. Dr. Lili Ju's work is partially supported by U.S. Department of Energy, Office of Advanced Scientific Computing Research through Applied Mathematics program under grant DE-SC0022254. This work used GPUs provided by the NSF MRI-2018966.

References

1. Chang, W.L., Wang, H.P., Peng, W.H., Chiu, W.C.: All about structure: adapting structural information across domains for boosting semantic segmentation. In: CVPR, pp. 1900–1909 (2019)
2. Chen, L.-C., et al.: Naive-student: leveraging semi-supervised learning in video sequences for urban scene segmentation. In: Vedaldi, A., Bischof, H., Brox, T., Frahm, J.-M. (eds.) ECCV 2020. LNCS, vol. 12354, pp. 695–714. Springer, Cham (2020). https://doi.org/10.1007/978-3-030-58545-7_40
3. Chen, L.C., Papandreou, G., Kokkinos, I., Murphy, K., Yuille, A.L.: DeepLab: semantic image segmentation with deep convolutional nets, atrous convolution, and fully connected CRFs. IEEE TPAMI **40**(4), 834–848 (2017)
4. Chen, Y.H., Chen, W.Y., Chen, Y.T., Tsai, B.C., Frank Wang, Y.C., Sun, M.: No more discrimination: Cross city adaptation of road scene segmenters. In: ICCV, pp. 1992–2001 (2017)
5. Chen, Y.C., Lin, Y.Y., Yang, M.H., Huang, J.B.: CrDoCo: pixel-level domain transfer with cross-domain consistency. In: CVPR, pp. 1791–1800 (2019)
6. Cordts, M., et al.: The cityscapes dataset for semantic urban scene understanding. In: CVPR, pp. 3213–3223 (2016)
7. Couprie, C., Farabet, C., Najman, L., LeCun, Y.: Indoor semantic segmentation using depth information. arXiv preprint arXiv:1301.3572 (2013)
8. Deng, J., Dong, W., Socher, R., Li, L.J., Li, K., Fei-Fei, L.: ImageNet: a large-scale hierarchical image database. In: CVPR, pp. 248–255. IEEE (2009)
9. Fayyaz, M., Saffar, M.H., Sabokrou, M., Fathy, M., Klette, R., Huang, F.: STFCN: spatio-temporal FCN for semantic video segmentation. arXiv preprint arXiv:1608.05971 (2016)
10. Gadde, R., Jampani, V., Gehler, P.V.: Semantic video CNNs through representation warping. In: ICCV, pp. 4453–4462 (2017)
11. Guan, D., Huang, J., Xiao, A., Lu, S.: Domain adaptive video segmentation via temporal consistency regularization. In: ICCV, pp. 8053–8064 (2021)
12. Guo, X., Yang, C., Li, B., Yuan, Y.: MetaCorrection: domain-aware meta loss correction for unsupervised domain adaptation in semantic segmentation. In: CVPR, pp. 3927–3936 (2021)

13. He, K., Zhang, X., Ren, S., Sun, J.: Deep residual learning for image recognition. In: CVPR, pp. 770–778 (2016)
14. Hoffman, J., et al.: CyCADA: cycle-consistent adversarial domain adaptation. In: International Conference Machine Learning, pp. 1989–1998. PMLR (2018)
15. Hoffman, J., Wang, D., Yu, F., Darrell, T.: FCNs in the wild: pixel-level adversarial and constraint-based adaptation. arXiv preprint arXiv:1612.02649 (2016)
16. Ilg, E., Mayer, N., Saikia, T., Keuper, M., Dosovitskiy, A., Brox, T.: FlowNet 2.0: evolution of optical flow estimation with deep networks. In: CVPR, pp. 2462–2470 (2017)
17. Jiang, H., Sun, D., Jampani, V., Yang, M.H., Learned-Miller, E., Kautz, J.: Super SloMo: high quality estimation of multiple intermediate frames for video interpolation. In: CVPR, pp. 9000–9008 (2018)
18. Kim, M., Byun, H.: Learning texture invariant representation for domain adaptation of semantic segmentation. In: CVPR, pp. 12975–12984 (2020)
19. Li, Y., Shi, J., Lin, D.: Low-latency video semantic segmentation. In: CVPR, pp. 5997–6005 (2018)
20. Li, Y., Yuan, L., Vasconcelos, N.: Bidirectional learning for domain adaptation of semantic segmentation. In: CVPR, pp. 6936–6945 (2019)
21. Lian, Q., Lv, F., Duan, L., Gong, B.: Constructing self-motivated pyramid curriculums for cross-domain semantic segmentation: a non-adversarial approach. In: ICCV, pp. 6758–6767 (2019)
22. Liu, S., Wang, C., Qian, R., Yu, H., Bao, R., Sun, Y.: Surveillance video parsing with single frame supervision. In: CVPR, pp. 413–421 (2017)
23. Liu, Y., Shen, C., Yu, C., Wang, J.: Efficient semantic video segmentation with per-frame inference. In: Vedaldi, A., Bischof, H., Brox, T., Frahm, J.-M. (eds.) ECCV 2020. LNCS, vol. 12355, pp. 352–368. Springer, Cham (2020). https://doi.org/10.1007/978-3-030-58607-2_21
24. Long, J., Shelhamer, E., Darrell, T.: Fully convolutional networks for semantic segmentation. In: CVPR, pp. 3431–3440 (2015)
25. Luo, Y., Liu, P., Guan, T., Yu, J., Yang, Y.: Significance-aware information bottleneck for domain adaptive semantic segmentation. In: ICCV, pp. 6778–6787 (2019)
26. Maninis, K.K., et al.: Video object segmentation without temporal information. IEEE TPAMI 41(6), 1515–1530 (2018)
27. Mei, K., Zhu, C., Zou, J., Zhang, S.: Instance adaptive self-training for unsupervised domain adaptation. In: Vedaldi, A., Bischof, H., Brox, T., Frahm, J.-M. (eds.) ECCV 2020. LNCS, vol. 12371, pp. 415–430. Springer, Cham (2020). https://doi.org/10.1007/978-3-030-58574-7_25
28. Miksik, O., Munoz, D., Bagnell, J.A., Hebert, M.: Efficient temporal consistency for streaming video scene analysis. In: International Conference on Robotics and Automation, pp. 133–139. IEEE (2013)
29. Mustikovela, S.K., Yang, M.Y., Rother, C.: Can ground truth label propagation from video help semantic segmentation? In: Hua, G., Jégou, H. (eds.) ECCV 2016. LNCS, vol. 9915, pp. 804–820. Springer, Cham (2016). https://doi.org/10.1007/978-3-319-49409-8_66
30. Nilsson, D., Sminchisescu, C.: Semantic video segmentation by gated recurrent flow propagation. In: CVPR, pp. 6819–6828 (2018)
31. Pan, F., Shin, I., Rameau, F., Lee, S., Kweon, I.S.: Unsupervised intra-domain adaptation for semantic segmentation through self-supervision. In: CVPR, pp. 3764–3773 (2020)
32. Richter, S.R., Hayder, Z., Koltun, V.: Playing for benchmarks. In: ICCV, pp. 2213–2222 (2017)

33. Richter, S.R., Vineet, V., Roth, S., Koltun, V.: Playing for data: ground truth from computer games. In: Leibe, B., Matas, J., Sebe, N., Welling, M. (eds.) ECCV 2016. LNCS, vol. 9906, pp. 102–118. Springer, Cham (2016). https://doi.org/10.1007/978-3-319-46475-6_7

34. Ros, G., Sellart, L., Materzynska, J., Vazquez, D., Lopez, A.M.: The SYNTHIA dataset: a large collection of synthetic images for semantic segmentation of urban scenes. In: CVPR, pp. 3234–3243 (2016)

35. Shelhamer, E., Rakelly, K., Hoffman, J., Darrell, T.: Clockwork convnets for video semantic segmentation. In: Hua, G., Jégou, H. (eds.) ECCV 2016. LNCS, vol. 9915, pp. 852–868. Springer, Cham (2016). https://doi.org/10.1007/978-3-319-49409-8_69

36. Shin, I., Park, K., Woo, S., Kweon, I.S.: Unsupervised domain adaptation for video semantic segmentation. arXiv preprint arXiv:2107.11052 (2021)

37. Tsai, Y.H., Hung, W.C., Schulter, S., Sohn, K., Yang, M.H., Chandraker, M.: Learning to adapt structured output space for semantic segmentation. In: CVPR, pp. 7472–7481 (2018)

38. Vu, T.H., Jain, H., Bucher, M., Cord, M., Pérez, P.: ADVENT: adversarial entropy minimization for domain adaptation in semantic segmentation. In: CVPR, pp. 2517–2526 (2019)

39. Xu, T., Feng, Z.H., Wu, X.J., Kittler, J.: Learning adaptive discriminative correlation filters via temporal consistency preserving spatial feature selection for robust visual object tracking. IEEE TIP **28**(11), 5596–5609 (2019)

40. Xu, Y.S., Fu, T.J., Yang, H.K., Lee, C.Y.: Dynamic video segmentation network. In: CVPR, pp. 6556–6565 (2018)

41. Yang, Y., Soatto, S.: FDA: Fourier domain adaptation for semantic segmentation. In: CVPR, pp. 4085–4095 (2020)

42. Zhang, P., Zhang, B., Zhang, T., Chen, D., Wang, Y., Wen, F.: Prototypical pseudo label denoising and target structure learning for domain adaptive semantic segmentation. In: CVPR, pp. 12414–12424 (2021)

43. Zhao, H., Shi, J., Qi, X., Wang, X., Jia, J.: Pyramid scene parsing network. In: CVPR, pp. 2881–2890 (2017)

44. Zheng, Z., Yang, Y.: Rectifying pseudo label learning via uncertainty estimation for domain adaptive semantic segmentation. IJCV **129**(4), 1106–1120 (2021)

45. Zhou, T., Tulsiani, S., Sun, W., Malik, J., Efros, A.A.: View synthesis by appearance flow. In: Leibe, B., Matas, J., Sebe, N., Welling, M. (eds.) ECCV 2016. LNCS, vol. 9908, pp. 286–301. Springer, Cham (2016). https://doi.org/10.1007/978-3-319-46493-0_18

46. Zhu, X., Xiong, Y., Dai, J., Yuan, L., Wei, Y.: Deep feature flow for video recognition. In: CVPR, pp. 2349–2358 (2017)

47. Zhu, Y., et al.: Improving semantic segmentation via video propagation and label relaxation. In: CVPR, pp. 8856–8865 (2019)

48. Zou, Y., Yu, Z., Vijaya Kumar, B.V.K., Wang, J.: Unsupervised domain adaptation for semantic segmentation via class-balanced self-training. In: Ferrari, V., Hebert, M., Sminchisescu, C., Weiss, Y. (eds.) ECCV 2018. LNCS, vol. 11207, pp. 297–313. Springer, Cham (2018). https://doi.org/10.1007/978-3-030-01219-9_18

49. Zou, Y., Yu, Z., Liu, X., Kumar, B., Wang, J.: Confidence regularized self-training. In: ICCV, pp. 5982–5991 (2019)

Meta Spatio-Temporal Debiasing
for Video Scene Graph Generation

Li Xu[1], Haoxuan Qu[1], Jason Kuen[2], Jiuxiang Gu[2], and Jun Liu[1(✉)]

[1] Singapore University of Technology and Design, Singapore, Singapore
{li_xu,haoxuan_qu}@mymail.sutd.edu.sg, jun_liu@sutd.edu.sg
[2] Adobe Research, San Jose, USA
{kuen,jigu}@adobe.com

Abstract. Video scene graph generation (VidSGG) aims to parse the video content into scene graphs, which involves modeling the spatio-temporal contextual information in the video. However, due to the long-tailed training data in datasets, the generalization performance of existing VidSGG models can be affected by the **spatio-temporal conditional bias** problem. In this work, from the perspective of meta-learning, we propose a novel Meta Video Scene Graph Generation (**MVSGG**) framework to address such a bias problem. Specifically, to handle various types of spatio-temporal conditional biases, our framework first constructs a support set and a group of query sets from the training data, where the data distribution of each query set is different from that of the support set w.r.t. a type of conditional bias. Then, by performing a novel **meta training and testing** process to optimize the model to obtain good testing performance on these query sets after training on the support set, our framework can effectively guide the model to learn to well generalize against biases. Extensive experiments demonstrate the efficacy of our proposed framework.

Keywords: VidSGG · Long-tailed bias · Meta learning

1 Introduction

A scene graph is a graph-based representation, which encodes different visual entities as nodes and the pairwise relationships between them as edges, i.e., in the form of `subject predicate object` relation triplets [13,29]. Correspondingly, the task of video scene graph generation (VidSGG) aims to parse the video content into a sequence of spatio-temporal relationships between different objects of interest [29,40]. Since it can provide refined and structured scene understanding, the video scene graph representation has been widely used in

---

L. Xu and H. Qu—Contributed equally to the work.

Supplementary Information The online version contains supplementary material available at https://doi.org/10.1007/978-3-031-19812-0_22.

various higher-level video tasks, such as video question answering [15,35], video captioning [8,38], and video retrieval [7,16].

However, despite of the great progress of VidSGG [2,5,22,36], most existing approaches tackling this task may suffer from the problem of *spatio-temporal conditional biases*. Specifically, as shown by previous works [4,19,33], there exist long-tailed training data issues in existing SGG datasets. While in the context of VidSGG, given the complex spatio-temporal nature of this task, such long-tailed issues can lead to spatio-temporal conditional biases that affect the model generalization performance. Here conditional biases mean the problem that once the model detects certain context information (i.e., conditions) in the visual content, it is likely to directly predict certain labels (i.e., biased prediction), which however may contradict with the ground-truth. Some works [27,43] also refer to this problem as spurious correlation. In particular, in the VidSGG task, this conditional bias issue can be further divided into two sub-problems: temporal conditional bias and spatial conditional bias.

For **temporal** conditional bias, as shown in the example of Fig. 1 (a), if `person hold bottle` appears first (i.e., **temporal** context) in the video, and in most cases, `person drink from bottle` happens next, then a conditional bias can be established towards `person drink from bottle` conditioned on `person hold bottle` along the temporal axis in the video. Due to such temporal conditional bias, once the previous video part involves `person hold bottle`, the trained model is very likely to simply predict `person drink from bottle` for the next part, which however can contradict with the ground truth as in the example.

(a) Example of temporal conditional bias.

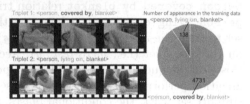

(b) Example of spatial conditional bias.

Such a conditional bias problem also exists in the **spatial** domain when tackling the VidSGG task. For example, as shown in Fig. 1 (b), there are many more videos containing `person covered by blanket` than `person lying on blanket` in the VidSGG dataset: Action Genome [12]. This can lead to a conditional bias towards the predicate (`covered by`) given the **spatial**

Fig. 1. Illustration of spatio-temporal conditional biases examples from Action Genome dataset [12]. (a) illustrates an example of temporal conditional bias towards `person drink from bottle` conditioned on `person hold bottle` in consecutive video parts, and (b) presents an example of spatial conditional bias towards the predicate of `covered by` conditioned on the subject-object pair of `person` and `blanket`. Such spatio-temporal conditional biases can affect the performance of VidSGG models.

contexts of `person` and `blanket`. Due to such spatial conditional bias, once person and blanket appear in the video, the model tends to directly predict person covered by blanket that however can be incorrect.

We observe that such spatio-temporal conditional bias problems widely exist in VidSGG datasets [12,29]. Meanwhile, to correctly infer the relation triplets, VidSGG models need to effectively model the spatio-temporal context information in the video [5,29,36]. Thus the models can be easily prone to exploiting the conditional biases w.r.t. the relation triplet components (e.g., the predicate) based on the spatio-temporal contexts during training, and then fail to generalize to data samples in which such conditional biases no longer hold as shown in Fig. 1. Therefore, to address this issue for obtaining better generalization performance, we propose a novel meta-learning based framework, Meta Video Scene Graph Generation (**MVSGG**).

Meta learning, also known as learning to learn, aims to enhance the model generalization capacity by incorporating *virtual testing* during model training [6,11,23]. Inspired by this, to improve the generalization performance of VidSGG models against the conditional biases, our framework incorporates a *meta training and testing* scheme. More concretely, we can split the training set to construct a support set for *meta training* and a query set for *meta testing*, which have different data distributions w.r.t. the conditional biases, i.e., creating a virtual testing scenario where simply exploiting the conditional biases during training would lead to poor testing performance. For example, given the same subject-object pair of person and blanket, if the support set contains more person covered by blanket relation triplets, the query set can contain more person lying on blanket triplets on the contrary. We first use the support set to train the model (i.e., *meta training*), and then evaluate the trained model on the query set (i.e., *meta testing*). According to the evaluation performance (loss) on the query set, we can further update the model to obtain better generalization performance. Since the query set is distributionally different from the support set w.r.t. the conditional biases, by improving the testing performance on the query set after training on support set via *meta training and testing*, our model is driven to learn to capture the "truly" generalizable features in the data instead of relying on the biases. Thus our model can "learn to generalize" well, even when handling the "difficult" testing samples that contradict the biases in training data.

Moreover, there can exist various types of conditional biases besides the ones shown in Fig. 1. For example, there can also exist a conditional bias w.r.t. the object based on subject-predicate pair in relation triplets, if an object appears more frequently given the same subject-predicate pair in the training data. Thus to better handle such a range of conditional biases, we can construct a group of query sets, where each query set is distributionally different from the support set w.r.t. one type of conditional bias. In this manner, by utilizing all these query sets to improve the model generalization performance via *meta training and testing*, our framework can effectively address various types of conditional biases in the video, and enhance the robustness of the VidSGG model.

Our MVSGG framework is general since it only changes the model training scheme (i.e., via *meta training and testing*), and thus can be flexibly applied to various off-the-shelf VidSGG models. We experiment with multiple models, and achieve consistent improvement of model performance.

The contributions of our work are summarized as follows. 1) We propose a novel *meta training and testing* framework, MVSGG, for effectively addressing the spatio-temporal conditional bias problem in VidSGG. 2) By constructing a support set and multiple query sets w.r.t. various types of conditional biases, our framework can enable the trained model to learn to generalize well against various types of conditional biases simultaneously. 3) Our framework achieves significant performance improvement when applied on state-of-the-art models on the evaluation benchmarks [12, 29].

2 Related Work

Scene Graph Generation (SGG). Being able to provide structured graph-based representation of an image or a video, scene graph generation (SGG) has attracted extensive research attention [3, 10, 13, 18, 21, 29, 31, 34, 36, 40]. For image SGG (ImgSGG), a variety of methods [34, 44–46] have been proposed. Suhail et al. [31] proposed an energy-based framework to improve the model performance by learning the scene graph structure. Yang et al. [41] investigated the diverse predictions for predicates in SGG from a probabilistic view.

Besides ImgSGG, there are also increasing research efforts exploring the task of video scene graph generation (VidSGG) [2, 20, 29, 36]. This task provides two task settings based on the granularity of the generated video scene graphs: video-level [2, 20, 24, 28, 29, 37] and frame-level [5, 36]. For video-level VidSGG, models generate scene graphs based on the video clip, where each node encodes the spatio-temporal trajectory of an object, and the connecting edge denotes the relation between two objects. Shang et al. [29] first investigated this problem setting, and proposed to extract improved Dense Trajectories features [39] for handling this problem. Later on, some other methods have been proposed to solve this video-level VidSGG problem from different perspectives, including the fully-connected spatio-temporal graph [37], and iterative relation inference [28]. For frame-level VidSGG, a scene graph is generated for each video frame [5, 36]. To handle this problem setting, Teng et al. [36] proposed to use a hierarchical relation tree to capture the spatio-temporal context information. Cong et al. [5] proposed to solve this problem via a spatio-temporal transformer.

For SGG, there often exists the long-tailed data bias issue that hinders models from obtaining better performance. To solve this problem, various debiasing methods have been proposed. Tang et al. [33] introduced a debiasing framework by utilizing the Total Direct Effect (TDE) analysis. Guo et al. [10] proposed a balance adjustment method to handle this issue. Li et al. [19] explored a causality-inspired interventional approach to reduce the data bias in VidSGG. Differently, to cope with the spatio-temporal conditional bias problem in SGG, from the perspective of meta learning, we propose a novel learning framework that can train the SGG model to learn to better generalize against biases.

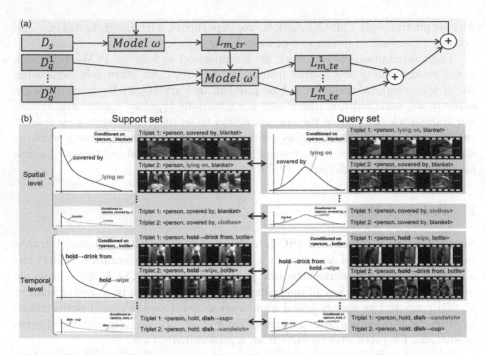

Fig. 2. Overview of our framework. (a) illustrates our *meta training and testing* scheme. 1) We first train the model (with parameters ω) on the support set (D_s) by optimizing the loss function (L_{m_tr}), and thus obtain the model with updated parameters (ω'), i.e., *meta training* process. 2) We evaluate the updated model on a group of query sets ($\{D_q^n\}_{n=1}^N$), by computing the losses ($\{L_{m\_te}^n(\omega')\}_{n=1}^N$) on these query sets (i.e., *meta testing* process). 3) Finally, based on the evaluation losses, we perform meta-optimization to update the model to improve its generalization performance. (b) shows that to address various types of **spatial level** and **temporal level** conditional biases, we construct a support set and a group of query sets for *meta training and testing*. The data distribution of each query set (see right side of (b)) is different from that of the support set (see left side of (b)) w.r.t. a type of conditional bias.

Meta Learning. As a group of representative works in meta learning, MAML [6] and its following works [23,26,32] mainly tackle the few-shot learning problem. These approaches often need to perform test-time model update for fast adaptation to new few-shot tasks. While recently, meta learning techniques have also been explored in other tasks [1,9,11,17,25] to improve the model performance without the need of test-time update, such as in domain generalization [1] and point cloud classification [11]. Different from existing works, here to address the challenging spatio-temporal conditional bias problem in SGG, we propose a framework that optimizes the model via *meta training and testing* over the constructed support set and query sets with different data distributions w.r.t. the conditional biases.

3   Method

As discussed above, affected by the conditional biases in the dataset, the VidSGG model can fail to generalize to the data samples where the biases do not hold. To address this problem, we aim to train the model to learn generalizable features in the data instead of exploiting biases. Here generalizable features refer to the learned features that can enable the model to make unbiased predictions, i.e., obtaining robust performance. How to achieve this goal? We notice that some meta-learning works [6,23,32] propose to boost the model learning ability via *meta training and testing*. Concretely, these works use *meta training and testing* to mimic the model training and testing for improving model generalization performance. Inspired by this, we propose a novel MVSGG framework, that optimizes the VidSGG model via *meta training and testing* for robust generalization performance against the biases.

More specifically, our framework first splits the training set (D_{train}) into a support set (D_s) for *meta training*, and a group of (N) query sets $(\{D_q^n\}_{n=1}^N)$ for *meta testing*, where each query set is distributionally different from the support set w.r.t. one type of conditional bias. Then we first train the model using the support set (i.e., *meta training*), and then evaluate the model testing performance on each of the query sets (i.e., *meta testing*). Since the biases in meta-training data (support set) do not hold in meta-testing data (query sets) due to their different data distributions, if the model trained on the support set can still obtain good testing performance under this condition, it indicates the model has learned more generalizable features rather than biases during the training process. As a result, we can optimize the model performance in *meta testing*, which can serve as a *generalization feedback*, to drive and adjust the model training on the support set towards learning more generalizable features. Below, we first introduce the *meta training and testing* scheme in our framework, and then describe how to construct the support set and query sets.

3.1   Meta Training and Testing

Meta Training. Using the support set D_s, we first train a VidSGG model (with parameters ω), via conventional gradient update. Specifically, we compute the model loss on the support set as:

$$L_{m\_tr}(\omega) = L(D_s; \omega) \tag{1}$$

where $L(\cdot)$ denotes the loss function (e.g., cross-entropy loss) for training the VidSGG model. Then we update the model parameters via gradient descent as:

$$\omega' = \omega - \alpha \nabla_\omega L_{m\_tr}(\omega) \tag{2}$$

where α is the learning rate for *meta training*. Note that the parameters update in this step is virtual (i.e., the updated parameters ω' is merely intermediate parameters), and the actual update for parameters ω will be performed in the meta-optimization step.

Meta Testing. After *meta training* on the support set (D_s), we then evaluate the generalization performance of the model with the updated parameters (ω'), on the query sets $(\{D_q^n\}_{n=1}^N)$. In particular, for each query set D_q^n, we compute the model loss $L_{m\_te}^n$ on this query set as:

$$L_{m\_te}^n(\omega') = L(D_q^n; \omega') \tag{3}$$

This computed loss can measure the model generalization performance on the query set after training on the support set, and will be used to provide feedback on *how the model should be updated so that it can generalize to different data distributions against the biases* in the following meta-optimization step.

Meta-optimization. As discussed above, we aim to optimize the model parameters (ω), so that *after the training (update) on the support set (i.e., $\omega \rightarrow \omega'$), it can also obtain good testing performance (i.e., lower $L_{m\_te}^n(\omega')$) on all the query sets against the biases in training data*. Towards this goal, inspired by MAML [6], the meta-optimization objective can be formulated as:

$$\min_\omega L_{m\_tr}(\omega) + \sum_{n=1}^N L_{m\_te}^n(\omega')$$
$$= \min_\omega L_{m\_tr}(\omega) + \sum_{n=1}^N L_{m\_te}^n(\omega - \alpha \nabla_\omega L_{m\_tr}(\omega)) \tag{4}$$

where the first term denotes the model training performance, while the second term denotes the model *generalization* performance (with the updated parameters ω'). Note that the above meta-optimization is performed over the initial model parameters ω, while ω' is merely intermediate parameters for evaluating the model generalization performance ($L_{m\_te}^n(\omega')$) during *meta testing*. Based on the meta-optimization objective in Eq. 4, we can update the model parameters ω as:

$$\omega \leftarrow \omega - \beta \nabla_\omega \left(L_{m\_tr}(\omega) + \sum_{n=1}^N L_{m\_te}^n(\omega - \alpha \nabla_\omega L_{m\_tr}(\omega)) \right) \tag{5}$$

where β denotes the learning rate for meta-optimization. Via such optimization, the model is driven to learn to capture more generalizable features to generalize well against biases.

Here we provide an intuitive analysis of such meta-optimization. During the above "learning to learn" process, the model is first trained (updated) over the support set (i.e., $\omega \rightarrow \omega'$). In this step, the biases in meta-training data (support set) can be learned by the model, since such biases can contribute to model performance on meta-training data. However, to generalize well to the meta-testing data (query sets) where biases in meta-training data (support set) no longer hold, the model needs to learn to avoid learning biases and instead capture more generalizable features during *meta training*. This means that the second term in Eq. 5 that involves the second-order gradients of ω (i.e., meta-gradients): $\nabla_\omega L_{m\_te}^n(\omega - \alpha \nabla_\omega L_{m\_tr}(\omega))$, serves as a *generalization feedback* to the model learning process $(\omega \rightarrow \omega')$ on the support set about how to learn more generalizable features.

From the above analysis, we can also conclude that the efficacy of our framework for debiasing lies in the simulated difficult testing scenarios where training data biases no longer hold. This also implies that we are not using the query sets to simulate the data distribution of the real testing set, which is unknown during model training. Instead, we only need to make the difference between the data distribution of meta-testing data (query sets) and that of meta-training data (support set) to be as large as possible w.r.t. the biases, so as to drive the model learning to learn more generalizable features. We also provide theoretical analysis of the efficacy of this framework for alleviating the bias learning in the supplementary. We perform the above three steps (i.e., meta training, meta testing and meta-optimization) iteratively until the model converges.

3.2   Dataset Split

As mentioned above, to handle various types of conditional biases, we split the original training set to construct a support set and a group of N query sets for *meta training and testing*. In this way, the purpose of the following dataset split strategy is to make each query set distributionally different from the support set w.r.t. one type of conditional bias. Under the guidance of this strategy, we can easily construct the support set and query sets. Below we first discuss the details of the support set and query sets, and then introduce the strategy for constructing each query set by selecting the data samples, of which the data distributions have the largest KL divergences to the support set w.r.t. the corresponding type of conditional bias. Some visualization examples of data distributions of the support set and query sets can refer to supplementary.

Support Set and Query Sets. We first randomly select a part of the training set data as the support set (D_s), and the remaining part of the training set will be used to construct various query sets $(\{D_q^n\}_{n=1}^N)$, where each query set is designed to address one type of conditional bias. Since the conditional biases in VidSGG can be roughly grouped into the spatial level and the temporal level, we correspondingly construct our query sets based on these two levels, as follows.

Spatial Level. There can exist conditional biases between a part of the relation triplet (e.g., the predicate) and the remaining parts (i.e., the spatial contexts). For example, as shown in Fig. 1 (b), given the same subject-object pair of human and blanket, the corresponding predicate is covered by in most triplets. To reduce such spatial conditional bias w.r.t. the **predicate** conditioned on subject-object pair, we can construct a query set, in which the distribution of the predicates conditioned on the same subject-object pair is different from the support set, as shown in Fig. 2.

Similarly, conditional bias can also exist w.r.t. the **predicate conditioned on subject**. For instance, if there are many more triplets containing bear play than the triplets containing bear bite in the dataset, a conditional bias can be established towards the predicate play given the subject bear. Thus we can build a query set where the distribution of the predicates (e.g., play, bite) conditioned on the same subject (e.g., bear) is different from that of the support set. In a similar way, we can also construct a query set to handle the conditional bias w.r.t. the **predicate conditioned on object**.

Therefore, 3 query sets can be constructed to handle the corresponding 3 types of conditional biases w.r.t. the *predicate* (*predicate-centered*) conditioned on other parts of the relation triplet (i.e., the subject-object pair, or the subject, or the object), as discussed above. Similarly, when considering the conditional biases w.r.t. the *subject* (*subject-centered*) conditioned on other parts of the triplet, we can also construct 3 query sets, and the same goes for the *object-centered* scenario. Thus we will construct a total of **9** query sets for handling these different types of spatial conditional biases.

Temporal Level. In VidSGG, when predicting a relation triplet, besides spatial contexts, there can also exist conditional biases between the current triplet and its temporal contexts. Specifically, temporal conditional bias can exist between the current triplet and the triplets that appear before it, and for simplicity, we refer to this case as *forward case*. Similarly, conditional bias can also exist between the current triplet and the triplets that appear after it (*backward case*). For these two cases, the query set construction procedures are similar, and below we take the forward case as the example to describe such procedures.

For example, as shown in Fig. 1 (a), if `human hold bottle` happens first in the video, and then `human drink from bottle` follows in most cases, then there can exist temporal conditional bias between the **previous predicate** (e.g., hold) **and current predicate** (e.g., `drink from`), based on the subject-object pair (e.g., `human` and `bottle`). To handle such temporal conditional bias, we can construct a query set, in which the distribution w.r.t. the temporal change of predicates, conditioned on the same subject-object pair, is different from that in the support set. For example, if the support set has more videos containing `human hold bottle`→`human drink from bottle`, the query set will involve more videos containing other cases w.r.t. the temporal change of predicates, such as `human hold bottle`→`human wipe bottle`.

Similarly, temporal conditional bias can also exist between the **previous subject and current subject**, and we can construct a query set for handling this type of conditional bias. In a similar manner, we can also construct a query set for handling the temporal conditional bias between the **previous object and current object**. Therefore, we construct 3 query sets to handle the above 3 types of temporal conditional biases in the *forward case*. Similarly, we can also construct 3 query sets for the *backward case*, and thus a total of **6** query sets for handling various types of temporal conditional biases can be obtained.

As a result, considering both spatial-level and temporal-level conditional biases, we construct **9 + 6 = 15** query sets ($N = 15$) in total from the training data.

Query Sets Construction Strategy. For constructing each query set, we need to select suitable video samples from the candidate video samples, so that the difference between the data distribution of the triplets in the selected videos (i.e., query sets) and that of the support set is as large as possible w.r.t. the corresponding type of conditional bias. Here to achieve this goal, we adopt an efficient and generalizable strategy by maximizing the KL divergence between the data distributions of the query set and support set w.r.t. the biases, which can be applied to construct each of the 15 query sets. Below we take the process of constructing the query set for handling the spatial conditional biases w.r.t. the **predicate conditioned on subject** as an example, to describe such a strategy.

As mentioned before, for handling this conditional bias, we aim to construct a query set, of which the distribution of the **predicates** (e.g., play, bite) given the same **subject** (e.g., bear), is different from the support set. For simplicity, we use ϕ_q to denote such a distribution of the query set, and ϕ_s to denote this distribution of the support set. Then since the KL divergence can be used to measure the difference of two distributions, we here aim to construct a query set, so that the KL divergence between ϕ_q and ϕ_s (i.e., $D_{KL}(\phi_q \parallel \phi_s)$) is large.

To this end, we perform the following four steps. (1) We first compute the distribution ϕ_s, i.e., computing the probability of the occurrence of each **predicate** conditioned on the same **subject** (e.g., $p(\text{play}|\text{bear})$, $p(\text{bite}|\text{bear})$) in the support set. (2) Then, assuming we have a total of N_c candidate video samples for constructing the query sets, since each candidate video sample (i) contains multiple relation triplets, we can also compute its corresponding data distribution (ϕ_c^i, $i \in \{1, ..., N_c\}$). (3) Since we aim to select a set of video samples to construct the query set, so that ϕ_q is different from ϕ_s (i.e., large $D_{KL}(\phi_q \parallel \phi_s)$), we compute the KL divergence between ϕ_c^i of each candidate video sample and ϕ_s (i.e., $D_{KL}(\phi_c^i \parallel \phi_s)$) that can be computed efficiently. (4) Finally, we can select the set of video samples that have the largest KL divergences w.r.t. ϕ_s, to construct the query set.

In a similar manner, we can apply the above strategy to automatically construct other query sets. Note that different query sets can share common data samples. Moreover, to help cover the wide range of possible conditional biases in the dataset, instead of fixing the support set and query sets during the whole training process, at the beginning of each training epoch, we *randomly* select a part of the training set to re-construct the support set, and use the remaining part to automatically re-construct various query sets via the above strategy. In this way, by performing *meta training and testing*, during the whole training process, our model can learn to effectively handle various types of possible conditional biases.

3.3   Training and Testing

We can flexibly apply our framework to train the off-the-shelf VidSGG models. During training, at each epoch, we first split the training set to construct a support set and a group of query sets as discussed above. Then we perform *meta training and testing* over the support set and query sets, to iteratively optimize the VidSGG model. During testing, we can evaluate the trained model on the testing set in the conventional manner.

4   Experiments

We evaluate our framework on two datasets for two evaluation settings in VidSGG respectively: ImageNet-VidVRD [29] for video-level VidSGG, and Action Genome [12] for frame-level VidSGG. More experiment results are in supplementary.

ImageNet-VidVRD (VidVRD). VidVRD dataset [29] contains 1000 video samples with 35 object categories and 132 predicate categories. For each video in VidVRD dataset, the model needs to predict a set of relation instances, and each relation instance contains a relation triplet with the subject and object trajectories. Following [28,29], we use two evaluation protocols on this dataset: relation detection and relation tagging. For relation detection, we count a predicted relation instance as a correct one, if its relation triplet is the same with a ground truth, and their trajectory vIoU (volume IoU) of the subject and object are both larger than the threshold of 0.5. In the same way as [28,29], we adopt Mean Average Precision (mAP), Recall@50 (R@50) and Recall@100 (R@100) to evaluate the model performance on relation detection. While in relation tagging, for a predicted relation instance, following [28,29] we only consider the correctness of its relation triplet, and ignore the precision of its subject and object trajectories. The evaluation metrics of Precision@1 (P@1), Precision@5 (P@5) and Precision@10 (P@10) are used in relation tagging [28,29].

Action Genome (AG). AG dataset [12] provides scene graph annotation for each video frame, i.e., the model needs to predict the scene graph of each frame. AG dataset contains 234253 video frames with 35 object categories and 25 predicate categories. Following [5,12,36], we evaluate models on three standard sub-tasks on this dataset: predicate classification (PredCls), scene graph classification (SGCls) and scene graph detection (SGDet). For these three sub-tasks, in line with [36], we use Recall (R@20, R@50), Mean Recall (MR@20, MR@50), mAP_{rel} and $wmAP_{rel}$ to measure model performance.

4.1 Implementation Details

We conduct our experiments on an RTX 3090 GPU. For experiments of video-level VidSGG on VidVRD dataset, we use the VidVRD-II network [28] as the backbone of our framework, which exploits the spatio-temporal contexts via iterative relation inference. For experiments of frame-level VidSGG on AG dataset, we use TRACE network [36] as the backbone of our framework, which adaptively aggregates contextual information to infer the scene graph.

On these two datasets, at each training epoch, we randomly select 60% of the training samples as the support set, and the remaining training samples are used to construct the query sets. We set the size of each query set to 100 on VidVRD, and 200 on AG. Note that in AG dataset, since the subject of all relation triplets is fixed to "person", we skip the query sets for handling the conditional biases w.r.t. the prediction of subject (e.g., *subject-centered* group) in this dataset. We set the learning rate (α) for *meta training* to 0.0005, and the learning rate (β) for meta-optimization to 0.01.

4.2 Experimental Results

On VidVRD dataset, compared to existing approaches, our method achieves the best performance across all metrics on both relation detection and relation tagging as shown in Table 1. This demonstrates that by reducing various

Table 1. Comparison with state-of-the-arts on VidVRD dataset.

Method	Relation detection			Relation tagging		
	mAP	R@50	R@100	P@1	P@5	P@10
VidVRD [29]	8.58	5.54	6.37	43.00	28.90	20.80
GSTEG [37]	9.52	7.05	8.67	51.50	39.50	28.23
VRD-GCN [24]	14.23	7.43	8.75	59.50	40.50	27.85
VRD-GCN+siamese [24]	16.26	8.07	9.33	57.50	41.00	28.50
VRD-STGC [20]	18.38	11.21	13.69	60.00	43.10	32.24
VidVRD+MHA [30]	15.71	7.40	8.58	40.00	26.70	18.25
VRD-GCN+MHA [30]	19.03	9.53	10.38	57.50	41.40	29.45
TRACE [36]	17.57	9.08	11.15	61.00	45.30	33.50
Social Fabric [2]	20.08	13.73	16.88	62.50	49.20	38.45
IVRD [19]	22.97	12.40	14.46	68.83	49.87	35.57
VidVRD-II [28]	29.37	19.63	22.92	70.40	53.88	40.16
VidVRD-II [28] + Reweight [33]	29.52	19.80	22.96	71.50	54.30	40.20
VidVRD-II [28] + TDE [33]	29.78	19.90	23.04	72.50	54.50	40.65
VidVRD-II [28] + DLFE [4]	29.92	19.98	23.16	73.50	54.90	41.10
Ours	**31.57**	**21.16**	**24.57**	**79.00**	**57.60**	**43.20**

Table 2. We apply our framework on various models, and obtain consistent performance improvement on VidVRD dataset.

Method	Relation detection			Relation tagging		
	mAP	R@50	R@100	P@1	P@5	P@10
VRD-STGC [20]	18.38	11.21	13.69	60.00	43.10	32.24
VRD-STGC + Ours	20.76	12.62	15.78	65.50	44.90	33.15
Independent baseline [28]	27.49	18.18	21.28	67.10	50.18	38.02
Independent baseline + Ours	30.02	19.86	23.10	75.50	53.60	40.80
VidVRD-II [28]	29.37	19.63	22.92	70.40	53.88	40.16
VidVRD-II + Ours	31.57	21.16	24.57	79.00	57.60	43.20

Table 3. We apply our framework on different SOTA models for image SGG, and obtain consistent performance improvement.

Method	SGGen			SGCls			PredCls		
	mR@20	mR@50	mR@100	mR@20	mR@50	mR@100	mR@20	mR@50	mR@100
VCTree [34]	5.2	7.1	8.3	9.1	11.3	12.0	14.1	17.7	19.1
VCTree+Ours	10.1	13.1	15.4	16.9	19.6	20.6	25.7	29.8	31.4
BGNN [18]	–	10.7	12.6	–	14.3	16.5	–	30.4	32.9
BGNN + Ours	11.1	14.2	16.4	15.9	17.4	18.6	27.3	31.6	34.1

types of conditional biases, our method can effectively enhance the model performance. Moreover, we also compare our method to other debiasing methods in SGG, including two representative methods (Reweight [33] and TDE [33]) and a recently proposed one (DLFE [4]). For Reweight, we follow the idea in [33]. These methods use the same backbone (VidVRD-II [28]) with ours. The results in Table 1 show that compared to these methods, our method achieves superior performance, demonstrating that by considering the spatio-temporal structure of VidSGG, our method can better handle the biases in this task.

On AG dataset, as shown in Table 4 and Table 5, our method outperforms other methods on all metrics. Our method also outperforms other debiasing methods [4,33] that use the same backbone (TRACE [36]) with ours. Moreover, note that the metric of Mean Recall is designed to measure the model performance considering the imbalanced data distribution [33,36], and our method achieves more performance improvements on this metric, demonstrating that our framework can effectively mitigate the spatio-temporal conditional bias problem caused by biased data distribution in the dataset.

4.3 Ablation Studies

We conduct extensive ablation experiments to evaluate our framework on VidVRD dataset.

Table 4. Recall (%) of various models on AG dataset following the setting in [36].

Top k predictions for each pair	Method	SGDet				SGCls				PredCls			
		Image		Video		Image		Video		Image		Video	
		R@20	R@50	R@20	R@50	R@20	R@50	R@20	R@50	R@20	R@50	R@20	R@50
k = 7	Freq Prior [45]	34.41	44.34	32.50	41.11	45.10	48.87	44.47	46.39	87.95	93.02	86.01	88.59
	G-RCNN [42]	34.28	44.47	32.60	41.29	45.57	49.75	45.11	47.22	88.73	93.73	86.28	88.93
	RelDN [46]	34.92	45.27	33.18	42.10	46.47	50.31	45.87	47.78	90.89	96.09	88.77	91.43
	TRACE [36]	35.09	45.34	33.38	42.18	46.66	50.46	46.03	47.92	91.60	96.35	89.31	91.72
	TRACE [36] + Reweight [33]	35.15	45.37	33.42	42.24	46.68	50.50	46.07	47.94	91.61	96.35	89.32	91.74
	TRACE [36] + TDE [33]	35.20	45.41	33.49	42.30	46.71	50.55	46.12	48.00	91.63	96.36	89.32	91.76
	TRACE [36] + DLFE [4]	35.29	45.47	33.58	42.41	46.75	50.63	46.18	48.04	91.64	96.36	89.35	91.77
	Ours	**36.59**	**47.00**	**34.88**	**43.81**	**47.40**	**51.06**	**46.71**	**48.56**	**91.74**	**96.43**	**89.44**	**91.85**
k = 6	Freq Prior [45]	34.47	43.69	32.38	40.24	44.90	47.15	43.57	44.63	85.89	89.43	83.33	84.99
	G-RCNN [42]	34.60	43.98	32.75	40.65	45.82	48.31	44.60	45.77	87.03	90.60	84.02	85.74
	RelDN [46]	35.22	44.94	33.39	41.64	46.76	49.11	45.48	46.57	89.63	93.56	87.01	88.86
	TRACE [36]	35.41	45.06	33.59	41.76	47.00	49.32	45.71	46.79	90.34	93.94	87.56	89.24
	TRACE [36] + Reweight [33]	35.44	45.10	33.64	41.83	47.01	49.35	45.73	46.82	90.36	93.95	87.58	89.27
	TRACE [36] + TDE [33]	35.49	45.16	33.68	41.90	47.04	49.36	45.76	46.89	90.37	93.96	87.61	89.27
	TRACE [36] + DLFE [4]	35.56	45.28	33.76	41.99	47.08	49.41	45.83	46.92	90.39	93.99	87.65	89.29
	Ours	**36.80**	**46.73**	**34.99**	**43.39**	**47.66**	**49.96**	**46.41**	**47.47**	**90.49**	**94.11**	**87.78**	**89.50**

Table 5. Mean Recall (%) and Average Precision (%) of various models on AG dataset following the setting in [36].

Method	SGDet				SGCls				PredCls			
	Mean recall		Average precision		Mean recall		Average precision		Mean recall		Average precision	
	@20	@50	mAP_r	wmAP_r	@20	@50	mAP_r	wmAP_r	@20	@50	mAP_r	wmAP_r
Freq Prior [45]	24.89	34.07	9.45	15.58	34.30	36.96	14.29	22.68	55.17	63.67	33.10	65.92
G-RCNN [42]	27.79	34.99	11.76	15.90	36.19	38.29	17.64	22.53	56.32	61.31	41.21	70.89
RelDN [46]	30.39	39.53	12.93	15.94	39.92	41.93	20.07	23.88	59.81	63.47	50.08	72.26
TRACE [36]	30.84	40.12	13.43	16.56	41.19	43.21	20.71	24.61	61.80	65.37	53.27	75.45
TRACE [36] + Reweight [33]	30.87	40.21	13.44	16.59	41.31	43.44	20.75	24.63	61.97	65.77	53.30	75.46
TRACE [36] + TDE [33]	31.01	40.40	13.47	16.60	41.56	43.70	20.79	24.66	62.12	65.89	53.34	75.50
TRACE [36] + DLFE [4]	31.24	40.75	13.48	16.62	41.77	43.98	20.83	24.70	62.44	66.31	53.35	75.52
Ours	**32.43**	**43.13**	**14.00**	**17.47**	**43.43**	**47.26**	**21.25**	**25.32**	**67.67**	**75.72**	**53.88**	**75.96**

Impact of Different Backbone Networks.

To validate the general effectiveness of our framework, we apply it on different models [20,28], and obtain consistent performance improvement as shown in Table 2, showing our framework can be flexibly applied on various models to improve their performance.

Impact of Spatio-Temporal Conditional Biases.

To investigate the impact of spatial and temporal conditional biases on model performance, we evaluate the following variants. For spatial conditional biases, we test 4 variants.

Specifically, one model variant (*w/o Spatial Level (all)*) ignores *all* groups of spatial conditional biases and handles only temporal conditional biases, i.e., optimizing the model without the query sets for handling *all* types of spatial conditional biases. Moreover, as discussed in Sect. 3.2, we have 3 groups of spatial con-

Table 6. We evaluate various variants to investigate the impact of each group of spatio-temporal conditional biases.

Method	Relation detection			Relation tagging		
	mAP	R@50	R@100	P@1	P@5	P@10
Baseline (VidVRD-II)	29.37	19.63	22.92	70.40	53.88	40.16
w/o Spatial Level (all)	30.49	20.35	23.61	75.50	55.30	41.50
w/o Predicate-centered	30.98	20.67	23.94	76.50	56.40	42.35
w/o Subject-centered	31.10	20.87	24.04	78.00	56.80	42.75
w/o Object-centered	31.05	20.80	23.98	77.50	56.60	42.60
w/o Temporal Level (all)	30.47	20.48	23.63	75.00	55.60	41.70
w/o Forward Case	30.94	20.78	23.95	76.50	56.50	42.60
w/o Backward Case	31.00	20.75	24.01	77.50	56.80	42.45
Ours	**31.57**	**21.16**	**24.57**	**79.00**	**57.60**	**43.20**

ditional biases, i.e., the conditional bias between *predicate/subject/object* and their corresponding spatial contexts. Thus to explore the impact of each group of conditional biases, we correspondingly implement 3 variants (*w/o Predicate-centered, w/o Subject-centered* and *w/o Object-centered*), and each variant ignores the corresponding group of query sets during the model training.

Similarly, for temporal conditional biases, we have 3 variants. One model variant (*w/o Temporal Level (all)*) ignores *all* groups of temporal conditional biases, and handles only spatial conditional biases. Furthermore, since we have 2 groups of temporal conditional biases, i.e., the conditional bias between the current triplet and the triplets appear before or appear after, we evaluate 2 more variants (*w/o Forward Case* and *w/o Backward Case*).

As shown in Table 6, ignoring any group of conditional biases would lead to performance drop compared to our framework, showing that each group of conditional biases can affect the model performance. More ablation study and qualitative results are in our supplementary.

4.4   Experiments on Image SGG

Besides the VidSGG task, there can also exist spatial conditional biases in the task of image SGG. Thus if we remove the query sets for handling the temporal conditional biases, our framework can then be adapted to handle the image SGG task.

Table 7. Experiment results of ours and other debiasing methods in image SGG.

Method	SGGen		SGCls		PredCls	
	mR@20	mR@50	mR@20	mR@50	mR@20	mR@50
VCTree [34]	5.2	7.1	9.1	11.3	14.1	17.7
VCTree+Reweight [33]	6.6	8.7	10.6	12.5	16.3	19.4
VCTree+TDE [33]	6.8	9.5	11.2	15.2	19.2	26.2
VCTree+DLFE [4]	8.6	11.8	15.8	18.9	20.8	25.3
VCTree+Ours	13.1	15.4	19.6	20.6	29.8	31.4

Therefore, we also evaluate our method on the widely used SGG benchmark: Visual Genome [14], by constructing and incorporating only the query sets for handling the spatial conditional biases. As shown in Table 3, we apply our framework on different SGG models [18,34], and consistently enhance their performances. Besides, as shown in Table 7, based on the same backbone (VCTree [34]), our method achieves better performance than other debiasing strategies.

5   Conclusion

To address the spatio-temporal conditional bias problem in VidSGG, we propose a novel Meta Video Scene Graph Generation (**MVSGG**) framework. By constructing a support set and various query sets w.r.t. various types of conditional biases, and optimizing the model on these constructed sets via *meta training and testing*, our framework can effectively train the model to handle various types of conditional biases. Moreover, our framework is general, and can be flexibly applied to various models. Our framework achieves superior performance.

Acknowledgement. This work is supported by National Research Foundation, Singapore under its AI Singapore Programme (AISG Award No: AISG-100E-2020-065), Ministry of Education Tier 1 Grant and SUTD Startup Research Grant.

References

1. Bai, Y., et al.: Person30K: a dual-meta generalization network for person re-identification. In: Proceedings of the IEEE/CVF Conference on Computer Vision and Pattern Recognition, pp. 2123–2132 (2021)
2. Chen, S., Shi, Z., Mettes, P., Snoek, C.G.: Social fabric: tubelet compositions for video relation detection. In: Proceedings of the IEEE/CVF International Conference on Computer Vision, pp. 13485–13494 (2021)
3. Chen, T., Yu, W., Chen, R., Lin, L.: Knowledge-embedded routing network for scene graph generation. In: Proceedings of the IEEE/CVF Conference on Computer Vision and Pattern Recognition, pp. 6163–6171 (2019)
4. Chiou, M.J., Ding, H., Yan, H., Wang, C., Zimmermann, R., Feng, J.: Recovering the unbiased scene graphs from the biased ones. In: Proceedings of the 29th ACM International Conference on Multimedia, pp. 1581–1590 (2021)
5. Cong, Y., Liao, W., Ackermann, H., Rosenhahn, B., Yang, M.Y.: Spatial-temporal transformer for dynamic scene graph generation. In: Proceedings of the IEEE/CVF International Conference on Computer Vision, pp. 16372–16382 (2021)
6. Finn, C., Abbeel, P., Levine, S.: Model-agnostic meta-learning for fast adaptation of deep networks. In: International Conference on Machine Learning, pp. 1126–1135. PMLR (2017)
7. Gao, J., Sun, C., Yang, Z., Nevatia, R.: TALL: temporal activity localization via language query. In: Proceedings of the IEEE International Conference on Computer Vision, pp. 5267–5275 (2017)
8. Guadarrama, S., et al.: YouTube2Text: recognizing and describing arbitrary activities using semantic hierarchies and zero-shot recognition. In: Proceedings of the IEEE International Conference on Computer Vision, pp. 2712–2719 (2013)
9. Guo, J., Zhu, X., Zhao, C., Cao, D., Lei, Z., Li, S.Z.: Learning meta face recognition in unseen domains. In: Proceedings of the IEEE/CVF Conference on Computer Vision and Pattern Recognition, pp. 6163–6172 (2020)
10. Guo, Y., et al.: From general to specific: informative scene graph generation via balance adjustment. In: Proceedings of the IEEE/CVF International Conference on Computer Vision, pp. 16383–16392 (2021)
11. Huang, C., Cao, Z., Wang, Y., Wang, J., Long, M.: MetaSets: meta-learning on point sets for generalizable representations. In: Proceedings of the IEEE/CVF Conference on Computer Vision and Pattern Recognition, pp. 8863–8872 (2021)
12. Ji, J., Krishna, R., Fei-Fei, L., Niebles, J.C.: Action genome: actions as compositions of spatio-temporal scene graphs. In: Proceedings of the IEEE/CVF Conference on Computer Vision and Pattern Recognition, pp. 10236–10247 (2020)
13. Johnson, J., et al.: Image retrieval using scene graphs. In: Proceedings of the IEEE Conference on Computer Vision and Pattern Recognition, pp. 3668–3678 (2015)
14. Krishna, R., et al.: Visual genome: connecting language and vision using crowd-sourced dense image annotations. Int. J. Comput. Vision **123**(1), 32–73 (2017)
15. Lei, J., Yu, L., Bansal, M., Berg, T.L.: TVQA: localized, compositional video question answering. arXiv preprint arXiv:1809.01696 (2018)

16. Lei, J., Yu, L., Berg, T.L., Bansal, M.: TVR: a large-scale dataset for video-subtitle moment retrieval. In: Vedaldi, A., Bischof, H., Brox, T., Frahm, J.-M. (eds.) ECCV 2020. LNCS, vol. 12366, pp. 447–463. Springer, Cham (2020). https://doi.org/10.1007/978-3-030-58589-1_27

17. Li, D., Yang, Y., Song, Y.Z., Hospedales, T.: Learning to generalize: meta-learning for domain generalization. In: Proceedings of the AAAI Conference on Artificial Intelligence, vol. 32, April 2018

18. Li, R., Zhang, S., Wan, B., He, X.: Bipartite graph network with adaptive message passing for unbiased scene graph generation. In: Proceedings of the IEEE/CVF Conference on Computer Vision and Pattern Recognition, pp. 11109–11119 (2021)

19. Li, Y., Yang, X., Shang, X., Chua, T.S.: Interventional video relation detection. In: Proceedings of the 29th ACM International Conference on Multimedia, pp. 4091–4099 (2021)

20. Liu, C., Jin, Y., Xu, K., Gong, G., Mu, Y.: Beyond short-term snippet: video relation detection with spatio-temporal global context. In: Proceedings of the IEEE/CVF Conference on Computer Vision and Pattern Recognition, pp. 10840–10849 (2020)

21. Liu, H., Yan, N., Mortazavi, M., Bhanu, B.: Fully convolutional scene graph generation. In: Proceedings of the IEEE/CVF Conference on Computer Vision and Pattern Recognition, pp. 11546–11556 (2021)

22. Lu, Y., et al.: Context-aware scene graph generation with seq2seq transformers. In: Proceedings of the IEEE/CVF International Conference on Computer Vision, pp. 15931–15941 (2021)

23. Nichol, A., Achiam, J., Schulman, J.: On first-order meta-learning algorithms. arXiv preprint arXiv:1803.02999 (2018)

24. Qian, X., Zhuang, Y., Li, Y., Xiao, S., Pu, S., Xiao, J.: Video relation detection with spatio-temporal graph. In: Proceedings of the 27th ACM International Conference on Multimedia, pp. 84–93 (2019)

25. Qu, H., Li, Y., Foo, L.G., Kuen, J., Gu, J., Liu, J.: Improving the reliability for confidence estimation. In: Farinella, T. (ed.) ECCV 2022, LNCS 13687, pp. 391–408 (2022)

26. Rajeswaran, A., Finn, C., Kakade, S.M., Levine, S.: Meta-learning with implicit gradients. In: Advances in Neural Information Processing Systems, vol. 32 (2019)

27. Seo, S., Lee, J.Y., Han, B.: Information-theoretic bias reduction via causal view of spurious correlation. arXiv preprint arXiv:2201.03121 (2022)

28. Shang, X., Li, Y., Xiao, J., Li, W., Chua, T.S.: Video visual relation detection via iterative inference. In: Proceedings of the 29th ACM International Conference on Multimedia (2021)

29. Shang, X., Ren, T., Guo, J., Zhang, H., Chua, T.S.: Video visual relation detection. In: Proceedings of the 25th ACM International Conference on Multimedia, pp. 1300–1308 (2017)

30. Su, Z., Shang, X., Chen, J., Jiang, Y.G., Qiu, Z., Chua, T.S.: Video relation detection via multiple hypothesis association. In: Proceedings of the 28th ACM International Conference on Multimedia, pp. 3127–3135 (2020)

31. Suhail, M., et al.: Energy-based learning for scene graph generation. In: Proceedings of the IEEE/CVF Conference on Computer Vision and Pattern Recognition, pp. 13936–13945 (2021)

32. Sun, Q., Liu, Y., Chua, T.S., Schiele, B.: Meta-transfer learning for few-shot learning. In: Proceedings of the IEEE/CVF Conference on Computer Vision and Pattern Recognition, pp. 403–412 (2019)

33. Tang, K., Niu, Y., Huang, J., Shi, J., Zhang, H.: Unbiased scene graph generation from biased training. In: Proceedings of the IEEE/CVF Conference on Computer Vision and Pattern Recognition, pp. 3716–3725 (2020)

34. Tang, K., Zhang, H., Wu, B., Luo, W., Liu, W.: Learning to compose dynamic tree structures for visual contexts. In: Proceedings of the IEEE/CVF Conference on Computer Vision and Pattern Recognition, pp. 6619–6628 (2019)

35. Tapaswi, M., Zhu, Y., Stiefelhagen, R., Torralba, A., Urtasun, R., Fidler, S.: MovieQA: understanding stories in movies through question-answering. In: Proceedings of the IEEE Conference on Computer Vision and Pattern Recognition, pp. 4631–4640 (2016)

36. Teng, Y., Wang, L., Li, Z., Wu, G.: Target adaptive context aggregation for video scene graph generation. In: Proceedings of the IEEE/CVF International Conference on Computer Vision, pp. 13688–13697 (2021)

37. Tsai, Y.H.H., Divvala, S., Morency, L.P., Salakhutdinov, R., Farhadi, A.: Video relationship reasoning using gated spatio-temporal energy graph. In: Proceedings of the IEEE/CVF Conference on Computer Vision and Pattern Recognition, pp. 10424–10433 (2019)

38. Venugopalan, S., Rohrbach, M., Donahue, J., Mooney, R., Darrell, T., Saenko, K.: Sequence to sequence-video to text. In: Proceedings of the IEEE International Conference on Computer Vision, pp. 4534–4542 (2015)

39. Wang, H., Schmid, C.: Action recognition with improved trajectories. In: Proceedings of the IEEE International Conference on Computer Vision, pp. 3551–3558 (2013)

40. Xu, D., Zhu, Y., Choy, C.B., Fei-Fei, L.: Scene graph generation by iterative message passing. In: Proceedings of the IEEE Conference on Computer Vision and Pattern Recognition, pp. 5410–5419 (2017)

41. Yang, G., Zhang, J., Zhang, Y., Wu, B., Yang, Y.: Probabilistic modeling of semantic ambiguity for scene graph generation. In: Proceedings of the IEEE/CVF Conference on Computer Vision and Pattern Recognition, pp. 12527–12536 (2021)

42. Yang, J., Lu, J., Lee, S., Batra, D., Parikh, D.: Graph R-CNN for scene graph generation. In: Ferrari, V., Hebert, M., Sminchisescu, C., Weiss, Y. (eds.) ECCV 2018. LNCS, vol. 11205, pp. 690–706. Springer, Cham (2018). https://doi.org/10.1007/978-3-030-01246-5_41

43. Ye, N., et al.: Adversarial invariant learning. In: 2021 IEEE/CVF Conference on Computer Vision and Pattern Recognition (CVPR), pp. 12441–12449. IEEE (2021)

44. Yu, J., Chai, Y., Hu, Y., Wu, Q.: CogTree: cognition tree loss for unbiased scene graph generation. arXiv preprint arXiv:2009.07526 (2020)

45. Zellers, R., Yatskar, M., Thomson, S., Choi, Y.: Neural motifs: scene graph parsing with global context. In: Proceedings of the IEEE Conference on Computer Vision and Pattern Recognition, pp. 5831–5840 (2018)

46. Zhang, J., Shih, K.J., Elgammal, A., Tao, A., Catanzaro, B.: Graphical contrastive losses for scene graph parsing. In: Proceedings of the IEEE/CVF Conference on Computer Vision and Pattern Recognition, pp. 11535–11543 (2019)

Improving the Reliability for Confidence Estimation

Haoxuan Qu[1], Yanchao Li[1], Lin Geng Foo[1], Jason Kuen[2], Jiuxiang Gu[2], and Jun Liu[1(✉)]

[1] Singapore University of Technology and Design, Singapore, Singapore
{haoxuan_qu,lingeng_foo}@mymail.sutd.edu.sg,
{yanchao_li,jun_liu}@sutd.edu.sg
[2] Adobe Research, San Jose, USA
{kuen,jigu}@adobe.com

Abstract. Confidence estimation, a task that aims to evaluate the trustworthiness of the model's prediction output during deployment, has received lots of research attention recently, due to its importance for the safe deployment of deep models. Previous works have outlined two important qualities that a reliable confidence estimation model should possess, i.e., the ability to perform well under label imbalance and the ability to handle various out-of-distribution data inputs. In this work, we propose a meta-learning framework that can simultaneously improve upon both qualities in a confidence estimation model. Specifically, we first construct virtual training and testing sets with some intentionally designed distribution differences between them. Our framework then uses the constructed sets to train the confidence estimation model through a *virtual training and testing* scheme leading it to learn knowledge that generalizes to diverse distributions. We show the effectiveness of our framework on both monocular depth estimation and image classification.

Keywords: Confidence estimation · Meta-learning

1 Introduction

With the continuous development of deep learning techniques, deep models are becoming increasingly accurate on various computer vision tasks, such as image classification [22] and monocular depth estimation [25]. However, even highly accurate models might still commit errors [1,10,18], and these errors can potentially lead to serious consequences, especially in safety-critical fields, such as nuclear power plant monitoring [30], disease diagnosis [39], and self-driving vehicles [40]. Due to the severe implications of errors in these applications, it is crucial for us to be able to assess whether we can place confidence in the model

---

H. Qu and Y. Li—Contributed equally to the work.

Supplementary Information The online version contains supplementary material available at https://doi.org/10.1007/978-3-031-19812-0_23.

predictions, before acting according to them. Hence, the task of confidence estimation (also known as trustworthiness prediction), which aims to evaluate the confidence of the model's prediction during deployment, has received a lot of research attention recently [5,19,32].

Specifically, in confidence estimation, we would like to compute the confidence estimate $S \in \{0,1\}$ for a prediction P made by a model regarding input I, where S estimates if prediction P is correct (1) or not (0). In this paper, for clarity, the *task model* refers to the deep model that produces predictions P on the main task; confidence estimation for P is performed by a separate confidence estimation model, which we refer to as the *confidence estimator*, as shown in Fig. 1. Many previous works [5,26,32,47] have proposed to train such a confidence estimator to conduct confidence estimation more reliably.

Some recent works [26,32] have noted that a reliable confidence estimator should *perform well under label imbalance*. This is because confidence estimators use the *correctness of task model predictions* (C) *as labels*, which are often imbalanced. As shown

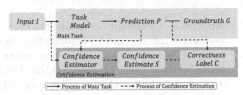

Fig. 1. Illustration of confidence estimation.

in Fig. 1, correctness labels C are produced by checking for consistency between predictions P and ground truths G, where $C = 1$ if P is correct and $C = 0$ otherwise. Thus, since many task models have achieved good performance on computer vision tasks (e.g., Small ConvNet [19] achieves $> 99\%$ for MNIST [24] and VGG-16 [31,41] achieves $> 93\%$ for CIFAR-10 [21] in image classification), there are often many more correct predictions (where $C = 1$) than incorrect ones (where $C = 0$), which leads to label imbalance for the confidence estimation task. If this label imbalance is not accounted for during training, the confidence estimator is likely to be overly confident [26,32] for incorrect predictions (where $C = 0$), which is undesirable.

On the other hand, some other works [35,43] have suggested that the ability to handle *out-of-distribution data inputs* (I) is important for confidence estimation. Out-of-distribution data occurs due to distribution shifts in the data – such data distribution shifts can occur within the same dataset [33], but are generally more severe between different datasets, e.g. between the training data from existing datasets and testing data received during deployment under real-world conditions. If the confidence estimator does not learn to handle out-of-distribution inputs, it will tend to perform badly whenever an out-of-distribution input sample I is fed into the task model, which affects its utility in practical applications.

In this paper, we aim to improve the reliability of our confidence estimator in terms of both the above-mentioned qualities; we improve its ability to tackle label imbalance of C, as well as to handle various out-of-distribution inputs I. Specifically, we observe that these qualities actually share a common point – they are acquired when the confidence estimator learns to *generalize to diverse distributions*. If a confidence estimator learns knowledge that can generalize to diverse distributions, it will be able to tackle diverse correctness label (C) distributions, which includes distributions where $C = 0$ is more common, and can thus better tackle the imbalanced label problem; it will also be able to tackle diverse input (I) distributions, which improves performance on out-of-distribution data. Based on this novel perspective, we propose to improve upon both of these qualities *simultaneously through a unified framework*, that allows the confidence estimator to learn to generalize, and perform well on distributions that might be different from the distributions (of both C and I) seen during training. In order to achieve this, we incorporate *meta-learning* into our framework.

Meta-learning, also known as *"learning to learn"*, allows us to train a model that can *generalize well to different distributions*. Specifically, in some meta-learning works [2,9,13,16,28,46], a *virtual testing set* is used to mimic the testing conditions during training, so that even though training is mainly done on a *virtual training set* consisting of training data, performance on the testing scenario is improved. In our work, we construct our virtual testing sets such that they simulate various distributions that are different from the virtual training set, which will push our model to learn *distribution-generalizable knowledge to perform well on diverse distributions*, instead of learning *distribution-specific knowledge that only performs well on the training distribution*. In particular, for our confidence estimator to learn distribution-generalizable knowledge and tackle diverse distributions of C and I, we intentionally construct virtual training and testing sets that simulate the different distribution shifts of C and I, and use them for meta-learning.

The contributions of our work are summarized as follows. 1) We propose a novel framework, which incorporates meta-learning to learn a *confidence estimator* to produce confidence estimates more reliably. 2) By carefully constructing virtual training and testing sets that simulate the training and various testing scenarios, our framework can learn to generalize well to different correctness label distributions and input distributions. 3) We apply our framework upon state-of-the-art confidence estimation methods [5,47] across various computer vision tasks, including image classification and monocular depth estimation, and achieve consistent performance enhancement throughout.

2 Related Work

Confidence Estimation. Being an important task that helps determine whether a deep predictor's predictions can be trusted, confidence estimation has been studied extensively across various computer vision tasks [4,5,11,14,19, 26,32,34–36,43,44,47]. At the beginning, Hendrycks and Gimpel [14] proposed Maximum Class Probability utilizing the classifier softmax distribution, Gal and Ghahramani [11] proposed MCDropout from the perspective of uncertainty estimation, and Jiang et al. [19] proposed Trust Score to calculate the agreement between the classifier and a modified nearest-neighbor classifier in the testing set. More recently, the idea of *separate confidence estimator* was introduced by several works [5,47]. Specifically, these works proposed to fix the task model, and instead conduct confidence estimation via a separate confidence estimator. Notably, Corbiere et al. [5] proposed a separate confidence estimator called Confidnet and a new loss function called True Class Probability. Subsequently, Yu et al. [47] proposed SLURP, a generic confidence estimator for regression tasks, that is specially targeted at task models that perform monocular depth estimation.

In this paper, we also build a separate confidence estimator, since it has the benefit of not affecting the main task performance. Different from previous works, we propose a novel meta-learning framework that simultaneously improves the performance of the confidence estimator under label imbalance and on out-of-distribution input data, in a unified manner.

Label Imbalance in Confidence Estimation. Recently, using the correctness of task model predictions (C) as labels, many existing confidence estimation methods [5,11,14] have been shown to suffer from the label imbalance problem. To solve this problem and enable the *confidence estimator* to perform well under label imbalance, various methods have been proposed. Luo et al. [32] proposed a loss function called Steep Slope Loss to separate features w.r.t. correct and incorrect task model predictions from each other. Afterwards, Li et al. [26] proposed an extension to True Class Probability [5] that uses a Distributional Focal Loss to focus more on predictions with higher uncertainty. Unlike previous methods that design strategies to handle a specific imbalanced distribution of correct and incorrect labels, we adopt a novel perspective, and tackle the label imbalance problem through meta-learning, which allows our confidence estimator to learn *distribution-generalizable knowledge to tackle a variety of diverse label distributions*. This is done through construction of virtual testing sets that *simulate various different label distributions*.

Confidence Estimation on Out-of-distribution Data. As various distribution shifts exist between the training and testing data in real-world applications, the handling of out-of-distribution data inputs (I) is important for reliable confidence estimation. To this end, Mukhoti et al. [35] proposed to replace the cross entropy loss with the focal loss [29], and utilize its implicit regularization effects to handle out-of-distribution data. Tomani et al. [43] proposed to handle out-of-distribution data via applying perturbations on data from the validation set. However, as these previous methods either emphasizes on the rare samples or fine-tunes on an additional set of samples, they can still be prone to overfit these rare samples or the additional set of samples. Differently, in this work, we propose to use meta-learning and optimize the model through feedbacks from diverse virtual sets with diverse distributions. Thus, we can enable our model to learn knowledge that is more generalizable to various out-of-distribution data.

Meta-learning. MAML [9], a popular meta-learning method, was originally designed to learn a good weight initialization that can quickly adapt to new tasks in testing, which showed promise in few-shot learning. Subsequently, its extension [28], which requires no model updating on the unseen testing scenarios, has been applied beyond few-shot learning, to enhance model performance [2,13,16,46]. Differently, we propose a novel framework via meta-learning to perform *more reliable confidence estimation*. Through performing meta-learning on carefully constructed virtual training and virtual testing sets, we simultaneously improve the ability of our confidence estimator to generalize well to different distributions of C and I.

3   Method

To conduct confidence estimation reliably, previous works have suggested two important qualities that a model should possess: the ability to *perform well under label imbalance*, and the ability to *handle various out-of-distribution data inputs*. We find that both qualities are actually acquired when the confidence estimator is trained to perform well across different distributions (w.r.t. either the correctness label C or the data input I). Hence, to train a more reliable confidence estimator, we leverage upon meta-learning that allows our confidence estimator to learn more distribution-generalizable knowledge to better tackle diverse distributions – which is achieved by obtaining feedback from a *virtual testing set* while concurrently updating using a *virtual training set*. A crucial part of our meta-learning algorithm is the virtual testing set construction, which needs to simulate diverse distributions to provide good feedback to the confidence estimator. Specifically, at the start of each iteration, from the training set D, we first construct a virtual training set D_{v_tr} and a virtual testing set D_{v_te}, such that there are *intentionally designed distribution differences between them*. To optimize the confidence estimator to possess both qualities discussed above, the virtual training set D_{v_tr} and the virtual testing set D_{v_te} are constructed to have different distributions of correctness labels C every odd-numbered iteration and different distributions of data inputs I every even-numbered iteration. After constructing D_{v_tr} and D_{v_te}, our framework then uses them to train the confidence estimator through a *virtual training and testing* procedure based on meta-learning.

Below, we first describe the *virtual training and testing* scheme we use to train the confidence estimator in Sect. 3.1. Next, in Sect. 3.2, we discuss how we construct our virtual training and virtual testing sets at the start of each iteration. Finally, we describe our framework as a whole in Sect. 3.3.

3.1   Virtual Training and Testing

As mentioned above, at the start of each iteration, we first construct a virtual training set D_{v_tr} and a virtual testing set D_{v_te}, such that there are intentionally designed distribution differences between them. In this section, we assume that D_{v_tr} and D_{v_te} have been constructed, and describe how we utilize them via the *virtual training and testing* scheme to train the confidence estimator to generalize to different distributions.

Specifically, each iteration of the *virtual training and testing* scheme contains three steps: (1) **Virtual training**. We first virtually train the confidence estimator using the virtual training set D_{v_tr} to simulate the conventional training procedure of the confidence estimator. (2) **Virtual testing**. After that, the confidence estimator is assessed (i.e., virtually tested) on the virtual testing set

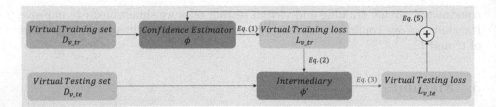

Fig. 2. Illustration of our virtual training and testing scheme. (1) In the virtual training step, we conduct updates on the confidence estimator parameters ϕ with the virtual training set D_{v_tr}, and obtain an intermediary ϕ' (which is indicated with red arrows). (2) The intermediary ϕ' is then evaluated on the virtual testing set D_{v_te} with a different distribution from D_{v_tr} to obtain the virtual testing loss L_{v_te} (which is indicated with the yellow arrow). (3) Lastly, the virtual training loss L_{v_tr} and the virtual testing loss L_{v_te} are used to update confidence estimator ϕ (indicated with blue arrows), such that it can generalize over diverse distributions and become more reliable. (Color figure online)

D_{v_te}, which evaluates the performance on a different distribution from the virtual training set D_{v_tr}. (3) **Meta Optimization (Actual update)**. Finally, we incorporate the evaluation result (loss) calculated during virtual testing as a feedback to actually update the confidence estimator. This provides a feedback to the confidence estimator, that allows it to learn generalizable knowledge to tackle diverse distributions while training using the virtual training set D_{v_tr}. Below, we describe these three steps of the *virtual training and testing* scheme in more detail. We also demonstrate these three steps in Fig. 2.

Virtual Training. During virtual training, we simulate the conventional training procedure of the confidence estimator, and first train the confidence estimator via gradient descent with data from the virtual training set D_{v_tr}. Here we denote the confidence estimator parameters as ϕ, the learning rate for virtual training as α, and the loss function of the confidence estimator as L (e.g., binary cross entropy loss). We can calculate the virtual training loss L_{v_tr} as:

$$L_{v\_tr}(\phi) = L(\phi, D_{v\_tr}) \tag{1}$$

Using this loss, we can update our confidence estimator parameters ϕ via gradient descent:

$$\phi' = \phi - \alpha \nabla_\phi L_{v\_tr}(\phi) \tag{2}$$

Note that we do not actually update the confidence estimator to be ϕ' (hence the term "virtual"). Instead, the *virtually trained* ϕ' is just an intermediary to calculate L_{v_te} in next step, and simulates what training on D_{v_tr} would be like.

Virtual Testing. In this step, we evaluate how the virtually updated confidence estimator ϕ' (that is trained on D_{v_tr}) performs on the virtual testing set D_{v_te}, which has a different distribution to D_{v_tr}.

$$L_{v\_te}(\phi') = L(\phi', D_{v\_te}) \tag{3}$$

The computed virtual testing loss L_{v_te} measures the confidence estimator performance on D_{v_te}, after one simulated training step on D_{v_tr}, and can be used to provide feedback on how we can update the confidence estimator parameters such that it can better generalize to different distributions (as is done in next step).

Meta-optimization (Actual Update). In the virtual training and virtual testing steps, we have computed the losses L_{v_tr} and L_{v_te} respectively. In this step, we use them to optimize our confidence estimator to perform well on diverse distributions, by obtaining feedback from L_{v_te} while concurrently updating using L_{v_tr}. We first formulate our overall objective as:

$$\min_{\phi} \left\{ L_{v\_tr}(\phi) + L_{v\_te}(\phi') \right\}$$
$$= \min_{\phi} \left\{ L_{v\_tr}(\phi) + L_{v\_te}\left(\phi - \alpha \nabla_{\phi} L_{v\_tr}(\phi)\right) \right\} \tag{4}$$

We highlight that, in Eq. 4, our goal is to optimize ϕ, and ϕ' is just used as a helpful intermediary in calculating $L_{v\_te}(\phi')$. After constructing our overall objective, we can then update ϕ via gradient descent for meta-optimization as:

$$\phi \leftarrow \phi - \beta \nabla_{\phi} \left(L_{v\_tr}(\phi) + L_{v\_te}\left(\phi - \alpha \nabla_{\phi} L_{v\_tr}(\phi)\right) \right) \tag{5}$$

where β denotes the learning rate for meta-optimization. By updating the confidence estimator with the meta-optimization update rule in Eq. 5, the confidence estimator is updated with knowledge that is more *distribution-generalizable*, leading to a more reliable confidence estimator that is applicable to diverse distributions. We explain this in more detail below.

During virtual training, we first update the confidence estimator ϕ to an intermediary ϕ' in Eq. 2. In this step, the intermediary ϕ' can learn *distribution-specific knowledge* (that is only specifically applicable to the distribution of D_{v_tr}), as such knowledge can help improve performance on D_{v_tr}. On the other hand, we note that for the intermediary (trained on D_{v_tr}) to generalize well to the virtual testing set D_{v_te} in Eq. 3 (which has a *different distribution* compared to D_{v_tr} and where *distribution-specific knowledge from D_{v_tr} does not apply*), the intermediary needs to *avoid learning distribution-specific knowledge* when learning on D_{v_tr}, and instead *learn more distribution-generalizable knowledge*. This means that, the term $L_{v\_te}(\phi')$ in Eq. 3 provides a feedback which guides the learning towards acquiring more distribution-generalizable knowledge.

Importantly, based on our analysis above, as long as D_{v_tr} and D_{v_te} have *different distributions and cannot be tackled with the same distribution-specific knowledge*, the confidence estimator will be encouraged to avoid learning distribution-specific knowledge, and focus on learning more distribution-generalizable knowledge in the meta-optimization step. This also implies that, we do not aim to use the distribution of virtual testing set D_{v_te} to simulate the distribution of the real testing scenario (which is unknown during training) to learn distribution-generalizable knowledge that can tackle real testing scenarios. We also present a more theoretical analysis of the efficacy of the meta-optimization rule in the supplementary material.

3.2 Set Construction

In this section, we discuss how we construct a virtual training set D_{v_tr} and a virtual testing set D_{v_te} to have different distributions in each iteration of our virtual training and testing scheme (that is described in Sect. 3.1). Specifically, *at the start of each epoch*, we first split the training set D into two halves: D^C and D^I, which will be used to tackle the two different problems (w.r.t correctness labels C and data inputs I). Within the epoch, at the start of every odd-numbered iteration, we construct virtual training and testing sets from D^C to tackle the label imbalance problem; on the other hand, at the start of every even-numbered iteration, we construct virtual training and testing sets from D^I to tackle the out-of-distribution data input problem.

As there exist some differences between the distribution of C and the distribution of I (e.g., it is more difficult to characterize the distribution of data input I and find input distributions that are different), we propose different set construction methods for each of them that provide diverse testing distributions in practice. We highlight that, due to the *unified nature of our framework*, tackling of these two different problems have now been reduced to a more straightforward designing of their respective set construction methods. Below, we separately discuss each construction method.

Constructing Sets for Correctness Label C. With respect to the correctness label C, we construct virtual training and testing sets with different distributions in two steps. **Step (C1)** *At the start of each epoch*, we first randomly split D^C into two subsets D_1^C and D_2^C, where the first subset D_1^C will be used to construct batches of D_{v_tr}, and the second subset D_2^C will be used to construct batches of D_{v_te}. Then, we pre-compute the correctness label C w.r.t. every sample in the second subset D_2^C to facilitate D_{v_te} construction in that epoch. **Step (C2)** *At the start of every odd-numbered iteration*, we randomly select a batch of data from the first subset D_1^C to construct a virtual training set D_{v_tr}. Next, we construct the virtual testing set D_{v_te} – we want its distribution of C to vary between iterations constantly, to simulate various distributions that are different from D_{v_tr}. Hence, we randomly select a percentage from 0 to 100% to set as the percentage of correct task model predictions (where $C = 1$) in D_{v_te} each time. Based on the sampled percentage of correct task model predictions, we randomly select a batch of samples from the second subset D_2^C to construct the virtual testing set D_{v_te} to approximately match that percentage. This way, our virtual testing set D_{v_te} will have a different distribution of C compared to D_{v_tr}, with a high probability.

Constructing Sets for Data Input I. Besides, we also construct virtual training and testing sets to have different distributions w.r.t. the data input I. Note that, when using only a single dataset, constructing virtual training and testing sets to have different data input distributions is a difficult problem. Here we follow a simple and effective technique proposed in previous works [17, 27, 33] that can help to simulate a distribution shift within a dataset. Specifically, they found that the statistics (i.e., mean and standard deviation) computed spatially over the pixels within the convolutional feature map of an input image, are a *compact representation that effectively captures the style and domain character-istics of this image.* Hence, we concatenate the convolutional feature statistics from all convolutional layers of our confidence estimator (into a single vector) as a representation of each input sample. Then, following [33], we use a K-means clustering technique to separate the convolutional feature statistics vectors of all the data in D^I into different clusters, such that a data distribution shift is simulated between clusters, that will be used for constructing virtual training and testing sets with different distributions.

Specifically, our set construction for data input I is done in two steps. **Step (I1)** *At the start of each epoch*, we first cluster D^I into N clusters by applying the K-means algorithm on the convolutional feature statistics vectors of samples in D^I. Among the N clusters, we randomly select one cluster as D_1^I that will be used to construct D_{v_tr} in this epoch. **Step (I2)** *Then at the start of every even-numbered iteration*, we first randomly select a batch of data from the selected cluster D_1^I to construct the virtual training set D_{v_tr}. After that, we randomly select a cluster from the remaining $N - 1$ clusters, and select a batch of data from this cluster to construct the virtual testing set D_{v_te}. For more details, please refer to the Supplementary.

After constructing virtual training and testing sets as discussed above, during experiments, we empirically observe consistent performance enhancement, as shown in Sect. 4, which shows the effectiveness of our set construction method.

3.3 Overall Training and Testing Scheme

In the above two sections, we have described the *virtual training and testing* scheme and how we construct our virtual training and virtual testing sets. In this section, we summarize them and discuss the overall training and testing scheme of our framework. Specifically, in the training procedure of the confidence estimator, at the start of each iteration, we first construct the virtual training and testing sets to have different distributions (w.r.t correctness label C in odd-numbered iterations and data input I in even-numbered iterations) following Sect. 3.2. After that, the constructed virtual training and testing sets are used to train the confidence estimator through the *virtual training and testing* scheme as discussed in Sect. 3.1. Hence, we alternatingly deal with the label imbalance problem and the handling of out-of-distribution inputs over iterations, resulting a simulatenous tackling of both problems. We demonstrate the overall training scheme of our framework in Alg. 1. During testing, we follow the evaluation procedure of previous works [5,47].

4 Experiments

In this section, in order to verify the effectiveness of our proposed framework, we conduct experiments on various different tasks including monocular depth estimation and image classification. For monocular depth estimation, we only modify the training procedure by adding our framework and follow all the other

---

Algorithm 1: Overall Training Scheme

---

1 Initialize ϕ.
2 **for** E epochs **do**
3   Randomly split D into two halves: D^C and D^I.
4   Process D^C and D^I following Step (C1) and Step (I1) in Sect. 3.2 respectively.
5   **for** T iterations **do**
6   **if** T is odd **then**
7   Construct D_{v_tr} and D_{v_te} from D^C, following Step (C2) in Sect. 3.2.
8   **else**
9   Construct D_{v_tr} and D_{v_te} from D^I, following Step (I2) in Sect. 3.2.
10   Calculate the virtual training loss L_{v_tr} on D_{v_tr} using Eq. 1:
        $L_{v\_tr}(\phi) = L(\phi, D_{v\_tr})$.
11   Calculate an updated version of confidence estimator (ϕ) using Eq. 2:
        $\phi = \phi - \alpha\nabla_\phi L_{v\_tr}(\phi)$.
12   Calculate the virtual testing loss L_{v_te} on D_{v_te} using Eq. 3:
        $L_{v\_te}(\phi') = L(\phi', D_{v\_te})$.
13   Update using Eq. 5: $\phi \leftarrow \phi - \beta\nabla_\phi\Big(L_{v\_tr}(\phi) + L_{v\_te}\big(\phi - \alpha\nabla_\phi L_{v\_tr}(\phi)\big)\Big)$.

---

experiment settings of [47] for evaluation on various testing scenarios. For image classification, similarly, we merely change the training procedure to include our framework, and follow all the other experiment settings of [5] to test our proposed method. We conduct all our experiments on an RTX 3090 GPU, and fix the task model during confidence estimator training.

4.1 Confidence Estimation on Monocular Depth Estimation

Settings and Implementation Details. For monocular depth estimation, we follow [47] and conduct two groups of experiments to evaluate our proposed framework. In the first experiment, we train our confidence estimator on KITTI Eigen-split training set [8,12,45], and evaluate the trained confidence estimator on two testing scenarios: KITTI Eigen-split testing set from the *same dataset*, and Cityscapes [6] testing set from a *different dataset*.

In the second experiment, we further evaluate our framework under *different weather conditions*. We fine tune our trained confidence estimator on Cityscapes training set, and evaluate it on several testing scenarios: Cityscapes testing set, Foggy Cityscapes-DBF [38] testing set with three severity levels, and Rainy Cityscapes [15] testing set with three severity levels.

Table 1. Experiment results of confidence estimation on monocular depth estimation, with our model **trained on KITTI Eigen-split training set** following the setting in [47]. Our method performs the best across all metrics.

Method	KITTI [8,12,45]			CityScapes [6]		
	AUSE-RMSE↓	AUSE-Absrel↓	AUROC↑	AUSE-RMSE↓	AUSE-Absrel↓	AUROC↑
MCDropout [11]	8.14	9.48	0.686	9.42	9.52	0.420
Empirical Ensembles	3.17	5.02	0.882	11.56	13.14	0.504
Single PU [20]	1.89	4.59	0.882	9.91	9.96	0.386
Deep Ensembles [23]	1.68	4.32	0.897	11.47	9.36	0.501
True Class Probability [5]	1.76	4.24	0.892	10.48	5.75	0.519
SLURP [47]	1.68	4.38	0.895	9.48	10.90	0.400
SLURP + Reweight	1.67	4.29	0.896	9.39	10.41	0.402
SLURP + Resample [3]	1.67	4.28	0.896	9.37	10.35	0.404
SLURP + Dropout [42]	1.67	4.20	0.896	9.29	10.01	0.412
SLURP + Focal loss [29]	1.67	4.18	0.895	9.30	10.14	0.410
SLURP + Mixup [48]	1.67	4.15	0.896	9.17	10.01	0.420
SLURP + Resampling + Mixup	1.67	4.07	0.896	8.99	9.84	0.431
SLURP + Ours(tackling label imbalance only)	1.66	3.84	0.897	8.75	7.79	0.509
SLURP + Ours(tackling out-of-distribution inputs only)	1.66	3.90	0.897	8.54	6.90	0.524
SLURP + Ours(full)	**1.65**	**3.62**	**0.898**	**8.26**	**5.32**	**0.601**

Table 2. Experiment results of confidence estimation on monocular depth estimation, with our model **fine-tuned on CityScapes** [6] following the setting in [47]. In this table, s indicates severity. The higher s is, more severe the rain or the fog is. Our method performs the best across all metrics and testing scenarios.

Method	CityScapes [6]			CityScapes Foggy s = 1 [38]			CityScapes Foggy s = 2 [38]			CityScapes Foggy s = 3 [38]			CityScapes Rainy s = 1 [15]			CityScapes Rainy s = 2 [15]			CityScapes Rainy s = 3 [15]		
	AUSE-RMSE↓	AUSE-Absrel↓	AUROC↑	AUSE-RMSE↓	AUSE-Absrel↓	AUROC↑	AUSE-RMSE↓	AUSE-Absrel↓	AUROC↑	AUSE-RMSE↓	AUSE-Absrel↓	AUROC↑	AUSE-RMSE↓	AUSE-Absrel↓	AUROC↑	AUSE-RMSE↓	AUSE-Absrel↓	AUROC↑	AUSE-RMSE↓	AUSE-Absrel↓	AUROC↑
MCDropout [11]	7.72	8.13	0.705	7.06	8.73	0.659	7.14	8.36	0.667	7.30	8.27	0.665	7.80	8.36	0.700	7.82	8.20	0.704	7.84	7.87	0.715
Empirical Ensemble	8.20	7.50	0.796	7.29	6.92	0.757	6.90	6.48	0.767	6.66	6.03	0.778	7.82	7.33	0.783	7.53	7.09	0.791	7.28	6.80	0.801
Single PU [20]	4.35	6.44	0.741	4.17	6.55	0.731	4.27	6.79	0.731	4.35	6.44	0.742	3.42	6.78	0.842	3.42	6.55	0.847	3.48	6.19	0.851
Deep Ensembles [23]	3.03	6.81	0.856	3.42	6.68	0.746	3.35	6.24	0.756	3.28	5.85	0.767	3.05	6.58	0.852	2.98	6.35	0.857	2.93	6.01	0.863
True Class Probability [5]	4.05	6.34	0.821	4.89	7.26	0.697	4.68	6.86	0.714	4.59	6.64	0.729	3.98	6.21	0.824	3.86	6.02	0.833	3.70	5.78	0.846
SLURP [47]	3.05	6.55	0.849	3.39	5.62	0.788	3.36	5.28	0.794	3.41	5.05	0.801	3.04	6.25	0.847	3.01	6.06	0.852	3.08	5.80	0.857
SLURP + Reweight	2.56	5.47	0.861	2.71	5.14	0.804	2.89	5.06	0.811	2.93	4.46	0.819	2.85	6.07	0.854	2.89	5.87	0.868	2.45	5.14	0.864
SLURP + Resample [3]	2.51	5.32	0.865	2.69	5.11	0.805	2.76	4.99	0.813	2.89	4.27	0.823	2.73	5.99	0.857	2.77	5.84	0.871	2.31	4.85	0.866
SLURP + Dropout [42]	2.88	5.39	0.857	2.52	4.91	0.813	2.55	4.78	0.819	2.74	4.01	0.835	2.56	5.68	0.863	2.65	5.47	0.880	2.27	4.77	0.870
SLURP + Focal loss [29]	2.75	5.20	0.859	2.49	4.87	0.816	2.47	4.69	0.825	2.67	4.09	0.830	2.49	5.55	0.867	2.41	5.23	0.884	2.18	4.81	0.867
SLURP + Mixup [48]	2.49	5.13	0.866	2.28	4.59	0.827	2.33	4.41	0.830	2.44	3.92	0.847	2.41	5.44	0.869	2.34	5.11	0.889	2.03	4.51	0.872
SLURP + Resample + Mixup	2.31	4.97	0.869	2.05	4.29	0.836	2.08	4.24	0.842	2.29	3.79	0.853	2.33	5.14	0.880	2.09	4.98	0.877	1.94	3.77	0.877
SLURP + Ours(tackling label imbalance only)	1.33	1.76	0.908	1.84	2.64	0.874	1.90	2.51	0.871	1.98	2.34	0.864	1.81	3.17	0.889	1.77	3.10	0.891	1.71	2.55	0.889
SLURP + Ours(tackling out-of-distribution inputs only)	1.42	1.88	0.900	1.61	2.19	0.890	1.66	2.20	0.891	1.76	2.09	0.881	1.59	2.78	0.901	1.60	2.75	0.904	1.63	1.97	0.890
SLURP + Ours(full)	0.60	0.62	0.933	0.73	0.63	0.934	0.80	0.58	0.937	0.93	0.58	0.938	0.85	0.69	0.923	0.96	0.68	0.925	1.08	0.80	0.909

We emphasize that in these experiments, the distribution of I will face a large shift from training conditions due to the cross-dataset/cross-weather setting. Moreover, there is also obvious imbalance in the distribution of C. Specifically, **the distribution of correct and incorrect labels of C in the KITTI Eigen-split training set is quite imbalanced (99.8%:0.2%)**. This means, there are both obvious label (C) imbalance problem and input (I) out-of-distribution problem.

In both above-mentioned experiments, we use the same backbone as SLURP [47], which is described in more detail in the supplementary material. Following the setting in [47], we use the area under sparsification error corresponding to square error (**AUSE-RMSE**), the area under sparsification error corresponding to absolute relative error (**AUSE-Absrel**) [8], and the area under the receiver operating characteristic (**AUROC**) as our evaluation metrics for the confidence estimator. We also follow [47] to regard the depth prediction of *each single pixel* to be correct ($C = 1$) if the relative difference between the depth prediction and the ground truth is less than 25%. Correspondingly, we also regard the depth prediction of *an input image* to be correct ($C = 1$) if the average relative difference among all its pixels (w.r.t the ground truth image) is less than 25%.

At the start of every training epoch, we randomly select 60% of data from D^C to construct the first subset D_1^C, and use the remaining as the second subset D_2^C. On the other hand, D^I is clustered into 6 clusters (i.e., $N = 6$), and one cluster is randomly selected to be D_1^I. We ablate these decisions in Sect. 4.3. During training, we set the learning rate (α) for *virtual training* to $5e - 4$, and the learning rate (β) for meta-optimization to $1e - 4$.

Experiment Results. In both experiments as shown in Tables 1 and 2, we compare our framework with both existing confidence estimation methods and other representative methods on tackling label imbalance problem (Reweight and

Resample [3]) and improving out-of-distribution data generalization (Dropout [42], Focal loss [29], and Mixup [48]). Besides, we also compare with the combination of Resample [3] and Mixup [48], which have been shown to effectively tackle label imbalance problem and improving out-of-distribution data generalization respectively. We reimplement all these methods on the same backbone (densenet161) as SLURP and ours. Furthermore, to better assess the effectiveness of our framework in tackling either of the two problems individually, we also assess the following two variants of our framework, i.e., the variant (**tackling label imbalance only**) that only constructs virtual training and testing sets w.r.t. distribution of the correctness label C, and the variant (**tackling out-of-distribution inputs only**) that only constructs virtual training and testing sets w.r.t. distribution of the data input I.

As shown in Table 1, as compared to all other methods, our confidence estimator that is trained on KITTI Eigen-split training set achieves the *best performance across all metrics and testing scenarios*, including both the KITTI Eigen-split testing set from the same dataset and Cityscapes testing set from a different dataset. This demonstrates that, by training the confidence estimator towards improvements on both qualities with our framework, the confidence estimator can become more reliable. Besides, as shown in Table 1, both variants of our framework improve the performance of the SLURP baseline, demonstrating that both individual set construction methods can lead to a more reliable confidence estimator, through our *virtual training and testing* scheme.

In Table 2, we evaluate the reliability of our confidence estimator under different weather conditions, and report results on the testing sets of Cityscapes, Foggy Cityscapes-DBF and Rainy Cityscapes, where three different weather severity levels are reported for the latter two datasets. We highlight that, under different weather conditions with different severity levels, there are fluctuating degrees of distribution shifts (of C and I) as compared to the Cityscapes training set that are challenging for a confidence estimator to handle. Our framework *outperforms all other methods on all reported metrics*, demonstrating that our framework effectively leads the confidence estimator to learn knowledge that can generalize to diverse distributions.

4.2   Confidence Estimation on Image Classification

Settings and Implementation Details. To evaluate our proposed framework on image classification, we follow previous works [5,19] and conduct experiments on both MNIST [24] and CIFAR-10 [21]. On MNIST, the confidence estimator is trained on MNIST training set and tested on MNIST testing set; and on CIFAR-10, the confidence estimator is trained on CIFAR-10 training set and tested on CIFAR-10 testing set. Note that, in these experiments, even though training/testing are done on same dataset, there are still data distribution shift issues, as shown in [33,37].

On both datasets, we use the same backbone (Confidnet) as TCP [5], which is described in more detail in the supplementary material. Following [5,14], we report scores on 4 evaluation metrics: the False positive rate at 95% True positive rate (**FPR-95%-TPR**), the area under the precision-recall curve with respect to $C = 0$ labels (**AUPR-Error**), the area under the precision-recall curve with respect to $C = 1$ labels (**AUPR-Success**), and the area under the receiver operating characteristic (**AUROC**).

Our set construction hyperparameters are set similarly to the monocular depth estimation experiments. At the start of every training epoch, we randomly select 60% of data from D^C to construct D_1^C and designate the rest as D_2^C, while D^I is split into 6 clusters (i.e., $N = 6$). On MNIST, we set the learning rate (α) for *virtual training* to $1e - 4$, and the learning rate (β) for meta-optimization to $1e - 4$. On CIFAR-10, we set the learning rate (α) for *virtual training* to $1e - 5$, and the learning rate (β) for meta-optimization to $1e - 5$.

Results and Analysis. In Table 3 we report results using our framework, as well as existing image classification confidence estimation methods and various other representative methods introduced previously (i.e., Reweight and Resample [3], Dropout [42], Focal loss [29], Mixup [48], and Resample [3] + Mixup [48]). As shown in Table 3, on both the MNIST testing set and the CIFAR-10 testing set, our framework achieves the *best performance across all metrics*, which demonstrates that our framework can improve confidence estimator performance effectively. The variants of our framework also achieves improvements, which shows the superiority of our framework both in tackling label imbalance problem and improving generalization to distribution shifts in input data. In particular, the

Table 3. Results on MNIST and CIFAR-10 using same backbone as [5]. When using our variant that tackles label imbalance only, we obtain obvious improvements in the AUPR-Error metric, showing efficacy on tackling cases where $C = 0$.

Dataset	Method	FPR-95%-TPR↓	AUSE-Error↑	AUSE-Success↑	AUROC↑
MNIST [24]	Maximum Class Probability [14]	5.56	35.05	99.99	98.63
	MCDropout [11]	5.26	38.50	99.99	98.65
	Trust Score [19]	10.00	35.88	99.98	98.20
	Steep Slope Loss [32]	2.22	40.86	99.99	98.83
	True Class Probability (TCP) [5]	3.33	45.89	99.99	98.82
	Balanced TCP [26]	4.44	43.03	99.99	98.67
	TCP + Reweight	7.78	31.67	99.98	98.06
	TCP + Resample [3]	6.67	33.57	99.98	98.32
	TCP + Dropout [42]	3.33	43.05	99.99	98.79
	TCP + Focal loss [29]	4.44	42.65	99.99	98.73
	TCP + Mixup [48]	4.44	45.73	99.99	98.80
	TCP + Resample + Mixup	4.44	45.45	99.99	98.78
	TCP + Ours(tackling label imbalance only)	2.22	46.71	99.99	98.87
	TCP + Ours(tackling out-of-distribution inputs only)	3.33	45.91	99.99	98.85
	TCP + Ours(full)	**2.22**	**47.05**	**99.99**	**98.91**
CIFAR-10 [21]	Maximum Class Probability [14]	47.50	45.36	99.19	91.53
	MCDropout [11]	49.02	46.40	99.27	92.08
	Trust Score [19]	55.70	38.10	98.76	88.47
	Steep Slope Loss [32]	44.69	50.28	99.26	92.22
	True Class Probability (TCP) [5]	44.94	49.94	99.24	92.12
	Balanced TCP [26]	45.33	49.79	99.25	92.19
	TCP + Reweight	45.20	49.77	99.25	92.18
	TCP + Resample [3]	45.71	49.81	99.25	92.20
	TCP + Dropout [42]	45.45	49.63	99.25	92.19
	TCP + Focal loss [29]	45.07	49.46	99.24	92.09
	TCP + Mixup [48]	45.33	49.68	99.25	92.18
	TCP + Resample + Mixup	45.20	49.66	99.25	92.18
	TCP + Ours(tackling label imbalance only)	44.81	50.27	99.26	92.23
	TCP + Ours(tackling out-of-distribution inputs only)	44.81	50.26	99.26	92.23
	TCP + Ours(full)	**44.69**	**50.30**	**99.27**	**92.26**

variant tackling the label imbalance problem achieves an obvious improvement gain on the AUPR-Error metric which focuses on the performance where $C = 0$.

Experiments on Imagenet. For confidence estimation on image classification, besides evaluating our framework on small scale datasets including MNIST [24] and CIFAR-10 [21] following many previous works [5,19], we also evaluate our framework on the large-scale dataset Imagenet [7] following [32]. Here, we use the same backbone as [32]. As shown in Table 4, after incorporating our framework, we observe a significant performance improvement, which further shows the effectiveness of our method in a large-scale scenario with more classes and larger images, which is more realistic.

4.3 Additional Ablation Studies

In this section and in the supplementary material, we conduct more extensive ablation studies on the monocular depth estimation task, with a confidence estimator that is fine-tuned on CityScapes training set. Specifically, our framework is evaluated on the CityScapes testing set, as well as both the Foggy Cityscapes-DBF testing set and Rainy Cityscapes testing set with the highest severity level (i.e., s = 3).

Table 4. Experiment results on Imagenet [7], where our framework is applied on Steep Slope Loss [32], which is the current state-of-the-art. We obtain a significant performance improvement.

Method	FPR-95%-TPR↓	AUSE-Error↑	AUSE-Success↑	AUROC↑
Steep Slope Loss [32]	80.48	10.26	93.01	73.68
Steep Slope Loss + Ours(full)	76.70	10.33	94.11	78.60

Table 5. Ablation studies conducted on the effectiveness of the virtual training and testing scheme.

Method	CityScapes [6]			CityScapes Foggy s = 3 [38]			CityScapes Rainy s = 3 [15]		
	AUSE-RMSE↓	AUSE-Absrel↓	AUROC↑	AUSE-RMSE↓	AUSE-Absrel↓	AUROC↑	AUSE-RMSE↓	AUSE-Absrel↓	AUROC↑
Baseline(SLURP)	3.05	6.55	0.849	3.41	5.05	0.801	3.08	5.80	0.857
Joint-training scheme	2.47	5.11	0.867	2.63	4.01	0.829	2.12	3.98	0.869
Meta-learning scheme	0.60	0.62	0.933	0.93	0.58	0.938	1.08	0.80	0.909

Impact of Second-Order Gradient. In our framework, we update the confidence estimator utilizing the *virtual training and testing* scheme through a second-order gradient $\nabla_\phi \big(L_{v\_tr}(\phi) + L_{v\_te}(\phi - \alpha \nabla_\phi L_{v\_tr}(\phi)) \big)$. To investigate the impact of such a second-order gradient, we compare our framework (**meta-learning scheme**) with a variant (**joint-training scheme**) that still constructs virtual training and testing sets in the same way, but optimizes the confidence estimator through $\nabla_\phi \big(L_{v\_tr}(\phi) + L_{v\_te}(\phi) \big)$ without utilizing the *virtual training and testing* scheme. As shown in Table 5, our framework consistently outperforms this variant, which shows effectiveness of the *virtual training and testing* scheme.

5 Conclusion

In this paper, we propose a unified framework that improves the reliability of confidence estimators, through simultaneously improving their performance under label imbalance and their handling of various out-of-distribution data inputs. Through carefully constructing virtual training and testing sets with different distributions w.r.t. both the correctness label C and the data input I, our framework trains the confidence estimator with a *virtual training and testing* scheme and leads it to learn knowledge that is more generalizable to different distributions (w.r.t. both the C and I). To validate the general effectiveness of our framework, we apply our framework to confidence estimation methods on both monocular depth estimation and image classification tasks, and show consistent improvements on both.

Acknowledgement. This work is supported by National Research Foundation, Singapore under its AI Singapore Programme (AISG Award No: AISG-100E-2020-065), Ministry of Education Tier 1 Grant and SUTD Startup Research Grant.

References

1. Amodei, D., Olah, C., Steinhardt, J., Christiano, P., Schulman, J., Mané, D.: Concrete problems in AI safety. arXiv preprint arXiv:1606.06565 (2016)
2. Bai, Y., et al.: Person30K: a dual-meta generalization network for person re-identification. In: Proceedings of the IEEE/CVF Conference on Computer Vision and Pattern Recognition, pp. 2123–2132 (2021)
3. Burnaev, E., Erofeev, P., Papanov, A.: Influence of resampling on accuracy of imbalanced classification. In: Eighth international Conference on Machine Vision (ICMV 2015), vol. 9875, pp. 423–427. SPIE (2015)
4. Chen, J., Liu, F., Avci, B., Wu, X., Liang, Y., Jha, S.: Detecting errors and estimating accuracy on unlabeled data with self-training ensembles. In: Advances in Neural Information Processing Systems 34 (2021)
5. Corbière, C., Thome, N., Bar-Hen, A., Cord, M., Pérez, P.: Addressing failure prediction by learning model confidence. In: Advances in Neural Information Processing Systems 32 (2019)
6. Cordts, M., et al.: The cityscapes dataset for semantic urban scene understanding. In: Proceedings of the IEEE Conference on Computer Vision and Pattern Recognition, pp. 3213–3223 (2016)
7. Deng, J., Dong, W., Socher, R., Li, L.J., Li, K., Fei-Fei, L.: ImageNet: a large-scale hierarchical image database. In: 2009 IEEE Conference on Computer Vision and Pattern Recognition, pp. 248–255. IEEE (2009)
8. Eigen, D., Puhrsch, C., Fergus, R.: Depth map prediction from a single image using a multi-scale deep network. In: Advances in Neural Information Processing Systems 27 (2014)
9. Finn, C., Abbeel, P., Levine, S.: Model-agnostic meta-learning for fast adaptation of deep networks. In: International Conference on Machine Learning, pp. 1126–1135. PMLR (2017)
10. Floridi, L.: Establishing the rules for building trustworthy AI. Nat. Mach. Intell. **1**(6), 261–262 (2019)
11. Gal, Y., Ghahramani, Z.: Dropout as a Bayesian approximation: representing model uncertainty in deep learning. In: International Conference on Machine Learning, pp. 1050–1059. PMLR (2016)
12. Geiger, A., Lenz, P., Stiller, C., Urtasun, R.: Vision meets robotics: the KITTI dataset. In: International Journal of Robotics Research (IJRR) (2013)

13. Guo, J., Zhu, X., Zhao, C., Cao, D., Lei, Z., Li, S.Z.: Learning meta face recognition in unseen domains. In: Proceedings of the IEEE/CVF Conference on Computer Vision and Pattern Recognition, pp. 6163–6172 (2020)
14. Hendrycks, D., Gimpel, K.: A baseline for detecting misclassified and out-of-distribution examples in neural networks. In: Proceedings of International Conference on Learning Representations (2017)
15. Hu, X., Fu, C.W., Zhu, L., Heng, P.A.: Depth-attentional features for single-image rain removal. In: Proceedings of the IEEE/CVF Conference on Computer Vision and Pattern Recognition, pp. 8022–8031 (2019)
16. Huang, C., Cao, Z., Wang, Y., Wang, J., Long, M.: Metasets: meta-learning on point sets for generalizable representations. In: Proceedings of the IEEE/CVF Conference on Computer Vision and Pattern Recognition, pp. 8863–8872 (2021)
17. Huang, X., Belongie, S.: Arbitrary style transfer in real-time with adaptive instance normalization. In: Proceedings of the IEEE International Conference on Computer Vision, pp. 1501–1510 (2017)
18. Janai, J., Güney, F., Behl, A., Geiger, A., et al.: Computer vision for autonomous vehicles: problems, datasets and state of the art. Found. Trends® Comput. Graph. Vis. **12**(3), 1–308 (2020)
19. Jiang, H., Kim, B., Guan, M., Gupta, M.: To trust or not to trust a classifier. In: Advances in neural information processing systems 31 (2018)
20. Kendall, A., Gal, Y.: What uncertainties do we need in Bayesian deep learning for computer vision? In: Advances in Neural Information Processing Systems 30 (2017)
21. Krizhevsky, A., Hinton, G., et al.: Learning multiple layers of features from tiny images (2009)
22. Krizhevsky, A., Sutskever, I., Hinton, G.E.: ImageNet classification with deep convolutional neural networks. Adv. Neural. Inf. Process. Syst. **25**, 1097–1105 (2012)
23. Lakshminarayanan, B., Pritzel, A., Blundell, C.: Simple and scalable predictive uncertainty estimation using deep ensembles. In: Advances in neural information processing systems 30 (2017)
24. LeCun, Y., Bottou, L., Bengio, Y., Haffner, P.: Gradient-based learning applied to document recognition. Proc. IEEE **86**(11), 2278–2324 (1998)
25. Lee, J.H., Han, M.K., Ko, D.W., Suh, I.H.: From big to small: multi-scale local planar guidance for monocular depth estimation. arXiv preprint arXiv:1907.10326 (2019)
26. Li, B., Zheng, Z., Zhang, C.: Identifying incorrect classifications with balanced uncertainty. arXiv preprint arXiv:2110.08030 (2021)
27. Li, B., Wu, F., Lim, S.N., Belongie, S., Weinberger, K.Q.: On feature normalization and data augmentation. In: Proceedings of the IEEE/CVF Conference on Computer Vision and Pattern Recognition, pp. 12383–12392 (2021)
28. Li, D., Yang, Y., Song, Y.Z., Hospedales, T.M.: Learning to generalize: meta-learning for domain generalization. In: Thirty-Second AAAI Conference on Artificial Intelligence (2018)
29. Lin, T.Y., Goyal, P., Girshick, R., He, K., Dollár, P.: Focal loss for dense object detection. In: Proceedings of the IEEE International Conference on Computer Vision, pp. 2980–2988 (2017)
30. Linda, O., Vollmer, T., Manic, M.: Neural network based intrusion detection system for critical infrastructures. In: 2009 International Joint Conference on Neural Networks,. pp. 1827–1834. IEEE (2009)

31. Liu, S., Deng, W.: Very deep convolutional neural network based image classification using small training sample size. In: 2015 3rd IAPR Asian Conference on Pattern Recognition (ACPR), pp. 730–734. IEEE (2015)
32. Luo, Y., Wong, Y., Kankanhalli, M.S., Zhao, Q.: Learning to predict trustworthiness with steep slope loss. In: Advances in Neural Information Processing Systems 34 (2021)
33. Matsuura, T., Harada, T.: Domain generalization using a mixture of multiple latent domains. In: Proceedings of the AAAI Conference on Artificial Intelligence, vol. 34, pp. 11749–11756 (2020)
34. Moon, J., Kim, J., Shin, Y., Hwang, S.: Confidence-aware learning for deep neural networks. In: International Conference on Machine Learning, pp. 7034–7044. PMLR (2020)
35. Mukhoti, J., Kulharia, V., Sanyal, A., Golodetz, S., Torr, P., Dokania, P.: Calibrating deep neural networks using focal loss. Adv. Neural. Inf. Process. Syst. **33**, 15288–15299 (2020)
36. Qiu, X., Miikkulainen, R.: Detecting misclassification errors in neural networks with a gaussian process model. arXiv preprint arXiv:2010.02065 (2020)
37. Rabanser, S., Günnemann, S., Lipton, Z.: Failing loudly: an empirical study of methods for detecting dataset shift. In: Advances in Neural Information Processing Systems 32 (2019)
38. Sakaridis, C., Dai, D., Hecker, S., Van Gool, L.: Model adaptation with synthetic and real data for semantic dense foggy scene understanding. In: Proceedings of the European Conference on Computer Vision (ECCV), pp. 687–704 (2018)
39. Sanz, J.A., Galar, M., Jurio, A., Brugos, A., Pagola, M., Bustince, H.: Medical diagnosis of cardiovascular diseases using an interval-valued fuzzy rule-based classification system. Appl. Soft Comput. **20**, 103–111 (2014)
40. Shafaei, S., Kugele, S., Osman, M.H., Knoll, A.: Uncertainty in machine learning: a safety perspective on autonomous driving. In: Gallina, B., Skavhaug, A., Schoitsch, E., Bitsch, F. (eds.) SAFECOMP 2018. LNCS, vol. 11094, pp. 458–464. Springer, Cham (2018). https://doi.org/10.1007/978-3-319-99229-7_39
41. Simonyan, K., Zisserman, A.: Very deep convolutional networks for large-scale image recognition. In: Bengio, Y., LeCun, Y. (eds.) 3rd International Conference on Learning Representations, ICLR 2015, San Diego, CA, USA, May 7–9, 2015, Conference Track Proceedings (2015). http://arxiv.org/abs/1409.1556
42. Srivastava, N., Hinton, G., Krizhevsky, A., Sutskever, I., Salakhutdinov, R.: Dropout: a simple way to prevent neural networks from overfitting. J. Mach. Learn. Res. **15**(1), 1929–1958 (2014)
43. Tomani, C., Gruber, S., Erdem, M.E., Cremers, D., Buettner, F.: Post-hoc uncertainty calibration for domain drift scenarios. In: Proceedings of the IEEE/CVF Conference on Computer Vision and Pattern Recognition, pp. 10124–10132 (2021)
44. Tsiligkaridis, T.: Failure prediction by confidence estimation of uncertainty-aware dirichlet networks. In: ICASSP 2021–2021 IEEE International Conference on Acoustics, Speech and Signal Processing (ICASSP), pp. 3525–3529. IEEE (2021)
45. Uhrig, J., Schneider, N., Schneider, L., Franke, U., Brox, T., Geiger, A.: Sparsity invariant CNNs. In: 2017 International Conference on 3D Vision (3DV), pp. 11–20. IEEE (2017)
46. Xu, L., Qu, H., Kuen, J., Gu, J., Liu, J.: Meta spatio-temporal debiasing for video scene graph generation. In: Proceedings of the European Conference on Computer Vision (ECCV) (2022)

47. Yu, X., Franchi, G., Aldea, E.: SLURP: side learning uncertainty for regression problems. In: 32nd British Machine Vision Conference, BMVC 2021, Virtual Event/November 22–25, 2021 (2021)

48. Zhang, H., Cisse, M., Dauphin, Y.N., Lopez-Paz, D.: mixup: Beyond empirical risk minimization. In: International Conference on Learning Representations (2018)

Fine-Grained Scene Graph Generation with Data Transfer

Ao Zhang[1,2], Yuan Yao[3,4], Qianyu Chen[3,4], Wei Ji[1,2(✉)], Zhiyuan Liu[3,4(✉)], Maosong Sun[3,4], and Tat-Seng Chua[1,2]

[1] Sea-NExT Joint Lab, Singapore, Singapore
[2] School of Computing, National University of Singapore, Singapore, Singapore
`aozhang@u.nus.edu, jiwei@nus.edu.sg`
[3] Department of Computer Science and Technology, Institute for Artificial Intelligence, Tsinghua University, Beijing, China
`liuzy@tsinghua.edu.cn`
[4] Beijing National Research Center for Information Science and Technology, Beijing, China

Abstract. Scene graph generation (SGG) is designed to extract (*subject*, `predicate`, *object*) triplets in images. Recent works have made a steady progress on SGG, and provide useful tools for high-level vision and language understanding. However, due to the data distribution problems including long-tail distribution and semantic ambiguity, the predictions of current SGG models tend to collapse to several frequent but uninformative predicates (*e.g.*, `on`, `at`), which limits practical application of these models in downstream tasks. To deal with the problems above, we propose a novel Internal and External Data Transfer (IETrans) method, which can be applied in a plug-and-play fashion and expanded to large SGG with 1,807 predicate classes. Our IETrans tries to relieve the data distribution problem by automatically creating an enhanced dataset that provides more sufficient and coherent annotations for all predicates. By applying our proposed method, a Neural Motif model doubles the macro performance for informative SGG. The code and data are publicly available at https://github.com/waxnkw/IETrans-SGG.pytorch.

Keywords: Scene graph generation · Plug-and-play · Large-scale

1 Introduction

Scene graph generation (SGG) aims to detect relational triplets (*e.g.*(*man*, `riding`, *bike*)) in images. As an essential task for connecting vision and language, it can serve as a fundamental tool for high-level vision and language

---

A. Zhang and Y. Yao—Indicates equal contribution.

Supplementary Information The online version contains supplementary material available at https://doi.org/10.1007/978-3-031-19812-0_24.

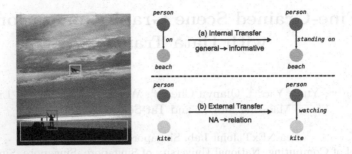

Fig. 1. Generate an enhanced dataset automatically for better model training with: (a) **Internal Transfer**: Specify general predicate annotations as informative ones. (b) **External Transfer**: Relabel missed relations from NA.

tasks, such as visual question answering [2,13,24,28], image captioning [6,32], and image retrieval [9,26,27]. However, existing SGG methods can only make correct predictions on a limited number of predicate classes (*e.g.*, 29 out of 50 pre-defined classes [38]), among which a majority of predicates are trivial and uninformative (*e.g.*, on, and, near). This undermines the application of SGG for downstream tasks. To address the limitation, we first identify two main problems that need to deal with:

- **Long-tail problem:** the problem refers to the phenomenon that annotations mainly concentrate on a few head predicate classes, and are much sparse in most tail predicate classes. For example, in Visual Genome [11], there are over 100K samples for the top 5 predicate classes, while over 90% of predicate classes have less than 10 samples. As a result, the performance of tail predicate classes is poor due to the lack of effective supervision.
- **Semantic ambiguity:** many samples can be described as either general predicate class (*e.g.*, on) or an informative one (*e.g.*, riding). However, data annotators prefer some general (and thus uninformative) predicate classes to informative ones for simplicity. This causes conflicts in the widely adopted single-label optimization since different labels are annotated for the same type of instances. Thus, even when the informative predicates have enough training samples, the prediction will easily collapse to the general ones.

To address the problems mentioned above, recent works propose to use resampling [5,12], reweighting [31], and post-processing methods [7,22]. However, we argue that these problems can be better alleviated by enhancing the existing dataset into a reasonable dataset, that contains more abundant training samples for tail classes and also provides coherent annotations for different classes.

To this end, we propose a novel framework named Internal and External data **Transfer** (**IETrans**), which can be equipped to different baseline models in a plug-and-play applied in a fashion. As shown in Fig. 1, we automatically transfer data from general predicates to informative ones (**Internal Transfer**) and relabel relational triplets missed by annotators (**External Transfer**). (1) **For internal transfer**, we first identify the general-informative relational pairs based on the confusion matrix, and then conduct a triplet-level data transfer from general ones to informative ones. The internal transfer will not only alleviate the optimization conflict caused by semantic ambiguity but also provide more data for tail classes; (2) **For external transfer**, there exist many positive samples missed by annotators [11,18], which are usually treated as negative samples by current methods. However, this kind of data can be considered as a potential data source, covering a wide range of predicate categories. Inspired by Visual Distant Supervision [34] which employs NA samples for pre-training, we also consider the NA samples, which are the union of negative and missed annotated samples. The missed annotated samples can be relabeled to provide more training samples.

It is worth noting that both internal transfer and external transfer are indispensable for improving SGG performance. Without the internal transfer, the external transfer will suffer from the semantic ambiguity problem. Meanwhile, the external transfer can further provide training samples for tail classes, especially for those that have weak semantic connection with head classes.

Exhaustive experiments show that our method is both adaptive to different baseline models and expansible to large-scale SGG. We equip our data augmentation method with 4 different baseline models and find that it can significantly boost all models' macro performance and achieve SOTA performance for F@K metric, a metric for overall evaluation. For example, a Neural Motif Model with our proposed method can double the mR@100 performance and achieve the highest F@100 among all model-agnostic methods on predicate classification task of the widely adopted VG-50 [30] benchmark.

To validate the scalability of our proposed method, we additionally propose a new benchmark with 1,807 predicate classes (VG-1800), which is more practical and challenging. To provide a reliable and stable evaluation, we manually remove unreasonable predicate classes and make sure there are over 5 samples for each predicate class on the test set. On VG-1800, our method achieves SOTA performance with significant superiority compared with all baselines. The proposed IETrans can make correct predictions on 467 categories, compared with all other baselines that can only correctly predict less than 70 categories. While the baseline model can only predict relations like (*cloud*, in, *sky*) and (*window*, on, *building*), our method enables to generate informative ones like (*cloud*, floating through, *sky*) and (*window*, on exterior of, *building*).

Our main contributions are summarized as follows: (1) To cope with the long-tail problem and semantic ambiguity in SGG, we propose a novel IETrans framework to generate an enhanced training set, which can be applied in a plug-and-play fashion. (2) We propose a new VG-1800 benchmark, which can provide reliable and stable evaluation for large-scale SGG. (3) Comprehensive experiments demonstrate the effectiveness of our IETrans in training SGG models.

2   Related Works

2.1   Scene Graph Generation

As an important tool of connecting vision and language, SGG [14,18,30] has drawn widespread attention from the community. SGG is first proposed as visual relation detection (VRD) [18], in which each relation is detected independently. Considering that relations are highly dependent on their context, [30] further proposes to formulate VRD as a dual-graph generation task, which can incorporate context information. Based on [30], different methods [17,23,38] are proposed to refine the object and relation representations in the scene graph. For example, [17] proposes a novel message passing mechanism that can encode edge directions into node representations. Recently, CPT [35] and PEVL [33] propose to employ pre-trained vision-language models for SGG. CPT shows promising few-shot ability and PEVL shows much better performance than models training from scratch.

2.2 Informative Scene Graph Generation

Although making steady progress on improving recall on SGG task, [3,23] point out that the predictions of current SGG models are easy to collapse to several general and trivial predicate classes. Instead of only focusing on recall metric, [3,23] propose a new metric named mean recall, which is the average recall of all predicate classes. [22] employs a causal inference framework, which can eliminate data bias during the inference process. CogTree [36] proposes to leverage the semantic relationship between different predicate classes, and design a novel CogTree loss to train models that can make informative predictions. In BGNN [12], the authors design a bi-level resampling strategy, which can help to provide a more balanced data distribution during the training process. However, previous works of designing new loss or conducting resampling, only focus on predicate-level adjustment, while the visual relation is triplet-level. For example, given the subject *man* and object *skateboard*, the predicate `riding` is an informative version of `standing on`, while given the subject *man* and object *horse*, `riding` will not be an informative alternative of `standing on`. Thus, instead of using less precise predicate-level manipulation, we employ a triplet-level transfer.

2.3 Large-Scale Scene Graph Generation

In the last few years, there are some works [1,34,39,40] focusing on large-scale SGG. Then, how to provide a reliable evaluation is an important problem. [39] first proposes to study large-scale scene graph generation and makes a new split of Visual Genome dataset named VG80K, which contains 29,086 predicate categories. However, the annotations are too noisy to provide reliable evaluation. To cope with this problem, [1] further cleans the dataset, and finally reserves 2,000 predicate classes. However, only 1,429 predicate classes are contained in the test set, among which 903 relation categories have no more than 5 samples. To provide enough samples for each predicate class' evaluation, we re-split the Visual Genome to ensure each predicate class on the test set has more than 5 samples, and the total predicate class number is 1,807. For the proposed methods, [39] employs a triplet loss to regularize the visual representation with the constraint on word embedding space. RelMix [1] proposes to conduct data augmentation with the format of feature mixup. Visual distant supervision [34] pre-trains the model on relabeled NA data with the help of a knowledge base and achieve significant improvement on a well-defined VG setting without semantic ambiguity.

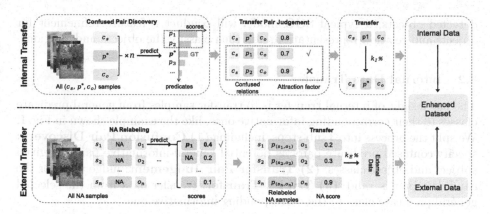

Fig. 2. Illustration of our proposed IETrans to generate an enhanced dataset. **Internal transfer** is designed to transfer data from general predicate to informative ones. **External transfer** is designed to relabel NA data. To avoid misunderstanding, (c_s, p^*, c_o) is a relational triplet class. $(s_i, p_{(s_i,o_i)}, o_i)$ represents a single relational triplet instance.

However, the data extension will be significantly limited by the semantic ambiguity problem. To deal with this problem, we propose an internal transfer method to generate informative triplets.

3   Method

In this section, we first introduce the internal data transfer and external data transfer, respectively, and then elaborate how to utilize them collaboratively. Figure 2 shows the pipeline of our proposed IETrans.

The goal of our method is to generate an enhanced dataset automatically, which should provide more training samples for tail classes, and also specify general predicate classes as informative ones. Concretely, as shown in Fig. 1, the general relation on between (*person, beach*) need to be specified as more informative one **standing on**, and the missed annotations between (*person, kite*) can be labeled so as to provide more training samples.

3.1   Problem Definition

Scene Graph Generation. Given an image I, a scene graph corresponding to I has a set of objects $O = \{(b_i, c_i)\}_{i=1}^{N_o}$ and a set of relational triplets $E = \{(s_i, p_{(s_i,o_i)}, o_i)\}_{i=1}^{N_e}$. For each object (b_i, c_i), it consists of an object bounding box $b_i \in \mathbb{R}^4$ and an object class c_i which belongs to the pre-defined object class set $\mathcal{C}$. With $s_i \in O$ and $o_i \in O$, p_i is defined as relation between them and belongs to the pre-defined predicate class set $\mathcal{P}$.

Inference. SGG is defined as a joint detection of objects and relations. Generally, an SGG model will first detect the objects in the image I. Based on the detected objects, a typical SGG model will conduct a feature refinement for objects and relation representation, and then classify the objects and relations.

3.2 Internal Data Transfer

The key insight of internal transfer is to transfer samples from general predicate classes to their corresponding informative ones, like the example shown in Fig. 1. We split the process into 3 sub-steps, including **(1) Confusion Pair Discovery**: specify confused predicate pairs as potential general-informative pairs for given subject and object classes. **(2) Transfer Pair Judgement**: judge whether the candidate pair is valid. **(3) Triplet Transfer**: transfer data from the selected general predicate class to the corresponding informative one.

Confusion Pair Discovery. To find general predicate classes and corresponding informative ones, a straightforward way is to annotate the possible relation transitions manually. However, relations are highly dependent on the subject and object classes, i.e. relation is triplet-level rather than predicate-level. For example, given the entity pair *man* and *bike*, `riding` is a sub-type of `sitting on`, while for *man* and *skateboard*, `riding` shares different meaning with `sitting on`. In this condition, even under 50 predicate classes settings, the possible relation elements will scale up to an infeasible number for human annotation. Another promising alternative is to employ pre-defined knowledge bases, such as WordNet [19] and VerbNet [10]. However, existing knowledge bases are not specifically designed to cope with visual relation problems, which result in a gap between visual and textual hierarchies [25].

Thus, in this work, we try to specify the general-informative pairs by taking advantage of information within the dataset, and leave the exploration of external knowledge sources for future work. A basic observation is that **informative predicate classes are easily confused by general ones**. Thus, we can first find confusion pairs as candidate general-informative pairs. By observing the predictions of the pre-trained Motif [38] model, we find that the collapse from informative predicate classes to general ones, appears not only on the test set but also on the training set. As shown in Fig. 3, the predicate classes `riding` and `sitting on` are significantly confused by a more general predicate class `on`.

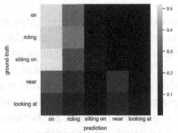

Fig. 3. Confusion matrix of Motif [38]'s prediction score on all entity pairs in VG training set with the subject *man* and the object *motorcycle*.

On the training set, given a relational triplet class (c_s, p, c_o), we use a pre-trained baseline model to predict predicate labels of all samples belonging to (c_s, p, c_o), and average their score vectors. We denote the aggregated scores for all predicates as $S = \{s_{p_i} | p_i \in \mathcal{P}\}$. From S, we select all predicate classes with higher prediction scores than the ground-truth annotation p, which can be formulated as $\mathcal{P}_c = \{p_i | s_{p_i} > s_p\}$. $\mathcal{P}_c$ can be considered as the most confusing predicate set for (c_s, p, c_o), which can serve as candidate transfer sources.

Transfer Pair Judgement. However, a confused predicate class does not equal to a general one. Sometimes, a general predicate can also be confused by an informative predicate. For example, in Fig. 3, under the constraint of $c_s = man$ and $c_o = motorcycle$, the less informative predicate sitting on is confused by the more informative predicate riding. In this condition, it is not a good choice to transfer from riding to sitting on. Thus, we need to further select the truly general predicates from the candidate set $\mathcal{P}_c$.

To select the most possible general predicate classes from $\mathcal{P}_c$, we first introduce an important feature that is useful to recognize general predicate classes. As observed by [36], **the general predicate classes usually cover more diverse relational triplets**, while informative ones are limited. Based on this observation, we can define the attraction factor of a triplet category (c_s, p, c_o) as:

$$A(c_s, p, c_o) = \frac{1}{\sum_{c_i, c_j \in \mathcal{C}} \mathcal{I}(c_i, p, c_j)}, \tag{1}$$

where $\mathcal{C}$ is the object categories set and $\mathcal{I}(t)$ indicates whether the triplet category t exists in the training set, which can be formulated as:

$$\mathcal{I}(t) = \begin{cases} 1, & \text{if } t \in \text{ training set} \\ 0, & \text{otherwise} \end{cases} \tag{2}$$

The denominator of $A(c_s, p_i, c_o)$ is the number of relational triplet types containing p_i. Thus, $A(c_s, p_i, c_o)$ with smaller value means p_i is more likely to be a general predicate. Concretely, when $A(c_s, p_i, c_o) < A(c_s, p, c_o)$, we transfer data from (c_s, p_i, c_o) to (c_s, p, c_o).

However, only considering the number of relational triplet types also has drawbacks: some relational triplets with very limited number of samples (*e.g.*, only 1 or 2 samples) might be annotation noise, while these relational triplets are easily selected as transfer targets. Transferring too much data to such uncertain relational triplets will significantly degenerate models' performance. Thus, we further consider the number of each relational triplet and modify the attraction factor as:

$$A(c_s, p, c_o) = \frac{N(c_s, p, c_o)}{\sum_{c_i, c_j \in \mathcal{C}} \mathcal{I}(c_i, p, c_j) \cdot N(c_i, p, c_j)}, \tag{3}$$

where $N(t)$ denotes the number of instances with relational type t in the training set. With the attraction factor, we can further filter the candidate confusion set $\mathcal{P}_c$ to the valid transfer source for (c_s, p, c_o):

$$\mathcal{P}_s = \{p_i | (p_i \in \mathcal{P}_c) \wedge (A(c_s, p_i, c_o) < A(c_s, p, c_o))\}, \tag{4}$$

where $\wedge$ denotes the logical conjunction operator.

Triplet Transfer. Given the transfer source $\mathcal{P}_s$, we collect all samples in the training set satisfying:

$$T = \{(o_i, p_k, o_j)|(c_{o_i} = c_s) \wedge (p_k \in \mathcal{P}_s) \wedge (c_{o_j} = c_o)\}. \tag{5}$$

Then, we sort T by model's prediction score of p, and transfer the top $k_I\%$ samples to the target triplet category (c_s, p, c_o). Note that, a triplet instance may need to be transferred to more than one relational triplets. To deal with the conflict, we choose the target predicate with the highest attraction factor.

3.3   External Data Transfer

The goal of our external transfer is to relabel unannotated samples to excavate missed relational triplets, as the example shown in Fig. 1.

NA Relabeling. NA samples refer to all unannotated samples in the training set, including both truly negative samples and missed positive samples. In external transfer, NA samples are directly considered as the transfer source and are relabeled as existing relational triplet types.

To get the NA samples, we first traverse all unannotated object pairs in images. However, considering that data transfer from all NA samples to all possible predicate classes will bring heavy computational burden, and inevitably increase the difficulty of conducting precise transfer, so as to sacrifice the quality of transferred data. Thus, we only focus on object pairs whose bounding boxes have overlaps and limit the possible transfer targets to existing relational triplet types. The exploration of borrowing zero-shot relational triplets from NA is left for future work.

Given a sample (s, NA, o), we can get its candidate target predicate set as:

$$\text{Tar}(s, \text{NA}, o) = \{p|(p \in \mathcal{P}) \wedge (N(c_s, p, c_o) > 0) \wedge (\text{IoU}(b_s, b_o) > 0)\}, \tag{6}$$

where $\mathcal{P}$ denotes pre-defined predicate classes, b_s and b_o denote bounding boxes of s and o, and IoU denotes the intersection over union.

Given a triplet (s, NA, o), the predicate class with the highest prediction score except for NA is chosen. The label assignment can be formulated as:

$$p_{(s,o)} = \underset{p \in \text{Tar}(s,\text{NA},o)}{\arg\max} (\phi^p(s, o)), \tag{7}$$

where $\phi^p(\cdot)$ denotes the prediction score of predicate p.

NA Triplet Transfer. To decide transfer or not, we rank all chosen (s, NA, o) samples according to NA scores in an ascending order. The lower NA score means the sample is more likely to be a missed positive sample. Similar with internal transfer, we simply transfer the top $k_E\%$ data.

3.4   Integration

Internal transfer is conducted on annotated data and external transfer is conducted on unannotated data, which are orthogonal to each other. Thus, we can simply merge the data without conflicts. After obtaining the enhanced dataset, we re-train a new model from scratch and use the new model to make inferences on the test set.

4 Experiments

In this section, we first show the generalizability of our method with different baseline models and the expansibility to large-scale SGG. We also make ablation studies to explore the influence of different modules and hyperparameters. Finally, analysis is conducted to show the effectiveness of our method in enhancing the current dataset.

4.1 Generalizability with Different Baseline Models

We first validate the generalizability of our method with different baseline models and its effectiveness when compared with current SOTA methods.

Datasets. Popular VG-50 [30] benchmark is employed, which consists of 50 predicate classes and 150 object classes.

Tasks. Following previous works [22,30,38], we evaluate our model on three widely used SGG tasks: (1) **Predicate Classification (PREDCLS)** provides both localization and object classes, and requires models to recognize predicate classes. (2) **Scene Graph Classification (SGCLS)** provides only correct localization and asks models to recognize both object and predicate classes. (3) In **Scene Graph Detection (SGDET)**, models are required to first detect the bounding boxes and then recognize both object and predicate classes.

Metrics. Following previous works [23,36], we use Recall@K (**R@K**) and mean Recall@K (**mR@K**) as our metrics. However, different trade-offs between R@K and mR@K are made in different methods, which makes it hard to make a direct comparison. Therefore, we further propose an overall metric **F@K** to jointly evaluate R@K and mR@K, which is the harmonic average of R@K and mR@K.

Baselines. We categorize several baseline methods into two categories: (1) **Model-agnostic baselines.** They refers to methods that can be applied in a plug-and-play fashion. For this part, we include Resampling [12], TDE [22], CogTree [36], EBM [21], DeC [8], and DLFE [4]. (2) **Specific models.** We also include some dedicated designed models with strong performance, including KERN [3], KERN [3], GBNet [37], BGNN [12], DT2-ACBS [5], and PCPL [31].

Implementation Details. Following [22], we employ a pre-trained Faster-RCNN [20] with ResNeXt-101-FPN [15,29] backbone. In the training process, the parameters of the detector are fixed to reduce the computation cost. The batch size is set to 12, and the learning rate is 0.12, except for Transformer. We optimize all models with an SGD optimizer. Specifically, to better balance the data distribution, the external transfer will not be conducted for the top 15 frequent predicate classes. To avoid deviating too much from the original data distribution, the frequency bias item calculated from the original dataset is applied to our IETrans in the inference stage. For internal and external transfer, the k_I is set to 70% and k_E is set to 100%. Please refer to the Appendix for more details.

418   A. Zhang et al.

Table 1. Performance (%) of our method and other baselines on VG-50 dataset. **IETrans** denotes different models equipped with our IETrans. **Rwt** denotes using the reweighting strategy.

Models		Predicate classification			Scene graph classification			Scene graph detection		
		R@50/100	mR@50/100	F@50/100	R@50/100	mR@50/100	F@50/100	R@50/100	mR@50/100	F@50/100
Specific	KERN [3]	65.8/67.6	17.7/19.2	27.9/29.9	36.7/37.4	9.4/10.0	15.0/15.8	27.1/29.8	6.4/7.3	10.4/11.7
	GBNet [37]	66.6/68.2	22.1/24.0	33.2/35.5	37.3/38.0	12.7/13.4	18.9/19.8	26.3/29.9	7.1/8.5	11.2/13.2
	BGNN [12]	59.2/61.3	30.4/32.9	40.2/42.8	37.4/38.5	14.3/16.5	20.7/23.1	31.0/35.8	10.7/12.6	15.9/18.6
	DT2-ACBS [5]	23.3/25.6	35.9/39.7	28.3/31.1	16.2/17.6	24.8/27.5	19.6/21.5	15.0/16.3	22.0/24.0	17.8/19.4
	PCPL [31]	50.8/52.6	35.2/37.8	41.6/44.0	27.6/28.4	18.6/19.6	22.2/23.2	14.6/18.6	9.5/11.7	11.5/14.4
Model-Agnostic	Motif [38]	64.0/66.0	15.2/16.2	24.6/26.0	38.0/38.9	8.7/9.3	14.2/15.0	31.0/35.1	6.7/7.7	11.0/12.6
	-TDE [22]	46.2/51.4	25.5/29.1	32.9/37.2	27.7/29.9	13.1/14.9	17.8/19.9	16.9/20.3	8.2/9.8	11.0/13.2
	-CogTree [36]	35.6/36.8	26.4/29.0	30.3/32.4	21.6/22.2	14.9/16.1	17.6/18.7	20.0/22.1	10.4/11.8	13.7/15.4
	-EBM [21]	—/—	18.0/19.5	—/—	—/—	10.2/11.0	-/-	—/—	7.7/9.3	—/—
	-DeC [8]	—/—	35.7/38.9	—/—	—/—	18.4/19.1	—/—	—/—	13.2/15.6	-/-
	-DLFE [4]	52.5/54.2	26.9/28.8	35.6/37.6	32.3/33.1	15.2 /15.9	20.7/21.5	25.4/29.4	11.7 /13.8	16.0/18.8
	-IETrans (ours)	54.7/56.7	30.9/33.6	39.5/42.2	32.5/33.4	16.8/17.9	22.2/23.3	26.4/30.6	12.4/14.9	16.9/20.0
	-IETrans+Rwt (ours)	48.6/50.5	**35.8/39.1**	**41.2/44.1**	29.4/30.2	**21.5/22.8**	**24.8/26.0**	23.5/27.2	**15.5/18.0**	**18.7/21.7**
	VCTree [23]	64.5/66.5	16.3/17.7	26.0/28.0	39.3/40.2	8.9/9.5	14.5/15.4	30.2/34.6	6.7/8.0	11.0/13.0
	-TDE [22]	47.2/51.6	25.4/28.7	33.0/36.9	25.4/27.9	12.2/14.0	16.5/18.6	19.4/23.2	9.3/11.1	12.6/15.0
	-CogTree [36]	44.0/45.4	27.6/29.7	33.9/35.9	30.9/31.7	18.8/19.9	23.4/24.5	18.2/20.4	10.4/12.1	13.2/15.2
	-EBM [21]	-/-	18.2/19.7	-/-	-/-	12.5/13.5	-/-	-/-	7.7/9.1	-/-
	-DLFE [4]	51.8/53.5	25.3/27.1	34.0/36.0	33.5/34.6	18.9 /20.0	**24.2/25.3**	22.7/26.3	11.8 /13.8	15.5/18.1
	-IETrans (ours)	53.0/55.0	30.3/33.9	38.6/41.9	32.9/33.8	16.5/18.1	22.0/23.6	25.4/29.3	11.5/14.0	15.8/18.9
	-IETrans+Rwt (ours)	48.0/49.9	**37.0/39.7**	**41.8/44.2**	30.0/30.9	**19.9/21.8**	23.9/25.6	23.6/27.8	**12.0/14.9**	**15.9/19.4**
	GPS-Net [17]	65.1/66.9	15.0/16.0	24.4/25.8	36.9/38.0	8.2/8.7	13.4/14.2	30.3/35.0	5.9/7.1	9.9/11.8
	-Resampling [12]	64.4/66.7	19.2/21.4	29.6/32.4	37.5/38.6	11.7/12.5	17.8/18.9	27.8/32.1	7.4/9.5	11.7/14.7
	-DeC [8]	—/—	35.9/38.4	-/-	-/-	17.4/18.5	-/-	-/-	11.2/15.2	-/-
	-IETrans (ours)	52.3/54.3	31.0/34.5	38.9/42.2	31.8/32.7	17.0/18.3	22.2/23.5	25.9/28.1	14.6/16.5	18.7/20.8
	-IETrans+Rwt (ours)	47.5/49.4	34.9/**38.6**	**40.2/43.3**	29.3/30.3	**19.8/21.6**	**23.6/25.2**	23.1/25.0	**16.2/18.8**	**19.0/21.5**
	Transformer [22]	63.6/65.7	17.9/19.6	27.9/30.2	38.1/39.2	9.9/10.5	15.7/16.6	30.0/34.3	7.4/8.8	11.9/14.0
	-CogTree [36]	38.4/39.7	28.4/31.0	32.7/34.8	22.9/23.4	15.7/16.7	18.6/19.5	19.5/21.7	11.1/12.7	14.1/16.0
	-IETrans (ours)	51.8/53.8	30.8/34.7	38.6/42.2	32.6/33.5	17.4/19.1	22.7/24.3	25.5/29.6	12.5/15.0	16.8/19.9
	-IETrans+Rwt (ours)	49.0/50.8	**35.0/38.0**	**40.8/43.5**	29.6/30.5	**20.8/22.3**	**24.4/25.8**	23.1/27.1	**15.0/18.1**	**18.2/21.7**

Comparison with SOTAs. We report the results of our IETrans and baselines for VG-50 in Table 1. Based on the observation of experimental results, we have summarized the following conclusions:

Our IETrans is Adaptive to Different Baseline Models. We equip our method with 4 different models, including Motif [38], VCTree [23], GPS-Net [17], and Transformer [22]. The module architectures range from conventional CNN to TreeLSTM (VCTree) and self-attention layers (Transformer). The training algorithm contains both supervised training and reinforcement learning (VCTree). Despite the model diversity, our IETrans can boost all models' mR@K metric and also achieve competitive F@K performance. For example, our IETrans can double mR@50/100 and improve the overall metric F@50/100 for over 9 points across all 3 tasks for GPS-Net.

Compared with Other Model-Agnostic Methods, Our Method Outperforms all of them in Nearly All Metrics. For example, when applying IETrans to Motif on PREDCLS, our model can achieve the highest R@50/100 and mR@50/100 among all model-agnostic baselines except for DeC. After adding the reweighting strategy, our IETrans can outperform DeC on mR@K.

Compared with Strong Specific Baselines, Our Method Can Also Achieve Competitive Performance on mR@50/100, and Best Overall Performance on F@50/100. Considering mR@50/100, our method with reweighting strategy is slightly lower than DT2-ACBS on SGCLS and SGDET tasks, while our method performs much better than them on R@50/100 (*e.g.*, 24.3 points of VCTree on PREDCLS task). For overall comparison considering F@50/100 metrics, our VCTree+IETrans+Rwt can achieve the best F@50/100 on PREDCLS and Motif+IETrans+Rwt achieves the best F@50/100 in SGCLS and SGDET task.

4.2 Expansibility to Large-Scale SGG

We also validate our IETrans on VG-1800 dataset to show its expansibility to large-scale scenarios.

Datasets. We re-split the Visual Genome dataset to create a VG-1800 benchmark, which contains 70,098 object categories and 1,807 predicate categories. Different from previous large-scale VG split [1,39], we clean the misspellings and unreasonable relations manually and make sure all 1,807 predicate categories appear on both training and test set. For each predicate category, there are over 5 samples on the test set to provide a reliable evaluation. Detailed statistics of VG-1800 dataset are provided in Appendix.

Tasks. In this work, we mainly focus on the predicate-level recognition ability and thus compare models on PREDCLS in the main paper. For SGCLS results, please refer to the Appendix.

Metrics. Following [1,39], we use accuracy (**Acc**) and mean accuracy upon all predicate classes (**mAcc**). Similar to VG-50, the harmonic average of two metrics is reported as **F-Acc**. In addition, we also report the number of predicate classes that the model can make at least one correct prediction, denoted as **Non-Zero**.

Baselines. We also include model-agnostic baselines including Focal Loss [16], TDE [22], and RelMix [1], and a specific model BGNN [12].

Implementation Details. Please refer to the Appendix for details.

Table 2. Performance of our method and baselines on VG-1800 dataset. **IETrans** denotes the Motif [38] model trained using our IETrans. To better compare with baselines, we show different Acc and mAcc trade-offs by setting different k_I.

Models	Top-1				Top-5				Top-10			
	Acc	mAcc	F-Acc	Non-Zero	Acc	mAcc	F-Acc	Non-Zero	Acc	mAcc	F-Acc	Non-Zero
BGNN [12]	**61.55**	0.59	1.16	37	**85.64**	2.33	4.5	111	**90.07**	3.91	7.50	139
Motif [38]	59.63	0.61	1.21	47	84.82	2.68	5.20	112	89.44	4.37	8.33	139
-Focal Loss	54.65	0.26	0.52	14	79.69	0.79	1.56	27	85.21	1.36	2.68	41
-TDE [22]	60.00	0.62	1.23	45	85.29	2.77	5.37	119	89.92	4.65	8.84	152
-RelMix [1]	60.16	0.81	1.60	65	85.31	3.27	6.30	134	89.91	5.17	9.78	177
-IETrans ($k_I = 10\%$) (ours)	56.66	1.89	3.66	202	83.99	8.23	14.99	419	89.71	13.06	22.80	530
-IETrans ($k_I = 90\%$) (ours)	27.40	**4.70**	**8.02**	**467**	72.48	**13.34**	**22.53**	**741**	83.50	**19.12**	**31.12**	**865**

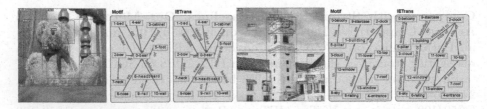

Fig. 4. Visualization of raw Motif model and Motif equipped with our IETrans.

Comparison with SOTAs. Performance of our method and baselines are shown in Table 2. Based on the observation of experimental results, we have summarized the following conclusions:

Our Model Can Successfully Work on Large-Scale Settings. On VG-1800 dataset, the long-tail problem is even exacerbated, where hundreds of predicate classes have only less than 10 samples. Simply increasing loss weight (Focal Loss) on tail classes can not work well. Different from these methods, our IETrans can successfully boost the performance on mAcc while keeping competitive results on Acc. For quantitative comparison, our **IETrans ($k_I = 10\%$)** can significantly improve the performance on top-10 mAcc (e.g., 19.12% vs. 4.37%) while maintaining comparable performance on Acc.

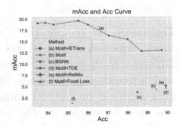

Fig. 5. The mAcc and Acc curve. (a) is our IETrans method. k_I is tuned to generate the blue curve. (b-f) are baselines. (Color figure online)

Compared with Different Baselines, Our Method can Outperform them for Overall Evaluation. As shown in Table 2, our **IETrans ($k_I = 90\%$)** can achieve best performance on F-Acc, which is over 3 times of the second highest baseline, RelMix, a method specifically designed for large-scale SGG. To make the visualized comparison, we plot a curve of IETrans with different Acc and mAcc trade-offs by tuning k_I, and show the performance of other baselines as points. As shown in Fig. 5, all baselines drawn as points are under our curve, which means our method can achieve better performance than them. Moreover, our IETrans ($k_I = 90\%$) can make correct predictions on 467 predicate classes for top-1 results, while the **Non-Zero** value of all other baselines are less than 70.

Case Studies. To show the potential of our method for real-world application, we provide some cases in Fig. 4. We can observe that our IETrans can help to generate more informative predicate classes while keeping faithful to the image content. For example, when the Motif model only predict relational triplets like (foot, of, bear), (nose, on, bear) and (cloud, in, sky), our IETrans can generate more informative ones as (foot, belonging to, bear), (nose, sewn onto, bear), and (cloud, floating through, sky).

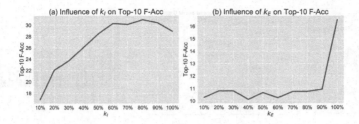

Fig. 7. (a) The influence of k_I in the Top-10 F-Acc with only internal transfer. (b) The influence of k_E in the Top-10 F-Acc with only external transfer.

4.3 Ablation Studies

In this part, we analyse the influence of internal transfer, external transfer, and corresponding parameters, k_I and k_E.

Influence of Internal Transfer. As shown in Fig. 6, only using external transfer (yellow cube) is hard to boost the mAcc performance as much as IETrans. The reason is that although introducing samples for tail classes, they will still be suppressed by corresponding general ones. However, by introducing internal transfer (green point) to cope with semantic ambiguity problem, the performance (red cross) can be improved significantly on mAcc, together with minor performance drop on Acc.

Influence of External Transfer. Although internal transfer can achieve huge improvement on mAcc compared with Motif, its performance is poor compared with IETrans, which shows the importance of further introducing training data by external transfer. Integration of two methods can maximize the advantages of data transfer.

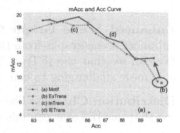

Influence of k_I. As shown in Fig. 7 (a), with the increase of k_I, the top-10 F-Acc will increase until $k_I = 80\%$, and begin to decrease when $k_I > 80\%$. The phenomenon indicates that a large number of general predicates can be interpreted as informative ones. Moving these predicates to informative ones will boost the overall performance. However, there also exists some predicates that can not be interpreted as informative ones or be modified suitably by current methods, which is harmful to the performance of models.

Fig. 6. The mAcc and Acc curve. (a) Normally trained Motif. (b) ExTrans: external transfer. (c) InTrans: internal transfer. (d) Our proposed IETrans. k_I is tuned to generate a curve. The blue circle and arrow mean that combining ExTrans and InTrans can lead to the pointed result. (Color figure online)

Influence of k_E. As shown in Fig. 7 (b), the overall performance increases slowly with the initial 90% transferred data, but improves significantly with the rest 10%. Note that, the data is ranked according to the NA score, which means

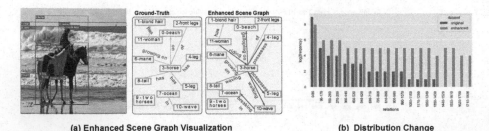

(a) Enhanced Scene Graph Visualization   **(b) Distribution Change**

Fig. 8. (a) **Enhanced Scene Graph Visualization.** Gray line denotes unchanged relation. Blue line denotes changed and reasonable relation. Red line denotes changed but unreasonable relation. (b) **Distribution Change.** The comparison between distributions of original dataset and enhanced dataset for VG-1800. The x-axis is the relation id intervals from head to tail classes. The y-axis is the corresponding log-frequency. (Color figure online)

that the last 10% data is actually what the model considered as most likely to be truly negative. The phenomenon indicates that the model may easily classify tail classes as negative samples, while this part of data is of vital significance for improving the model's ability of making informative predictions.

4.4   Analysis of Enhanced Dataset

Enhanced Scene Graph Correctness. We investigate the correctness of enhanced scene graphs from the instance level. An example is shown in Fig. 8(a). We can see that the IETrans is less accurate on VG-1800, which indicates that it is more challenging to conduct precise data transfer on VG-1800.

Distribution Change. The distribution change is shown in Fig. 8(b). We can see that our IETrans can effectively supply samples for non-head classes.

5   Conclusion

In this paper, we design a data transfer method named IETrans to generate an enhanced dataset for the SGG. The proposed IETrans consists of an internal transfer module to relabel general predicate classes as informative ones and an external transfer module to complete missed annotations. Comprehensive experiments are conducted to show the effectiveness of our method. In the future, we hope to extend our method to other large-scale visual recognition problems (*e.g.*, image classification, semantic segmentation) with similar challenges.

Acknowledgements. This research is funded by Sea-NExT Joint Lab, Singapore. The research is also supported by the National Key Research and Development Program of China (No. 2020AAA0106500).

References

1. Abdelkarim, S., Agarwal, A., Achlioptas, P., Chen, J., Huang, J., Li, B., Church, K., Elhoseiny, M.: Exploring long tail visual relationship recognition with large vocabulary. In: Proceedings of ICCV, pp. 15921–15930 (2021)
2. Antol, S., Agrawal, A., Lu, J., Mitchell, M., Batra, D., Zitnick, C.L., Parikh, D.: VQA: Visual question answering. In: Proceedings of ICCV, pp. 2425–2433 (2015)
3. Chen, T., Yu, W., Chen, R., Lin, L.: Knowledge-embedded routing network for scene graph generation. In: Proceedings of CVPR, pp. 6163–6171 (2019)
4. Chiou, M.J., Ding, H., Yan, H., Wang, C., Zimmermann, R., Feng, J.: Recovering the unbiased scene graphs from the biased ones. In: Proceedings of ACM Multimedia, pp. 1581–1590 (2021)
5. Desai, A., Wu, T.Y., Tripathi, S., Vasconcelos, N.: Learning of visual relations: The devil is in the tails. In: Proceedings of ICCV, pp. 15404–15413 (2021)
6. Gu, J., Joty, S., Cai, J., Zhao, H., Yang, X., Wang, G.: Unpaired image captioning via scene graph alignments. In: Proceedings of ICCV, pp. 10323–10332 (2019)
7. Guo, Y., et al.: From general to specific: Informative scene graph generation via balance adjustment. In: Proceedings of ICCV, pp. 16383–16392 (2021)
8. He, T., Gao, L., Song, J., Cai, J., Li, Y.F.: Semantic compositional learning for low-shot scene graph generation. In: Proceedings of ICCV, pp. 2961–2969 (2021)
9. Johnson, J., et al.: Image retrieval using scene graphs. In: Proceedings of CVPR, pp. 3668–3678 (2015)
10. Kipper, K., Korhonen, A., Ryant, N., Palmer, M.: Extending VerbNet with novel verb classes. In: LREC, pp. 1027–1032 (2006)
11. Krishna, R., Zhu, Y., et al.: Visual Genome: Connecting language and vision using crowdsourced dense image annotations. In: IJCV, pp. 32–73 (2017)
12. Li, R., Zhang, S., Wan, B., He, X.: Bipartite graph network with adaptive message passing for unbiased scene graph generation. In: Proceedings of CVPR, pp. 11109–11119 (2021)
13. Li, Y., Wang, X., Xiao, J., Ji, W., Chua, T.S.: Invariant grounding for video question answering. In: Proceedings of CVPR, pp. 2928–2937 (2022)
14. Li, Y., Yang, X., Shang, X., Chua, T.S.: Interventional video relation detection. In: Proceedings of ACM Multimedia, pp. 4091–4099 (2021)
15. Lin, T.Y., Dollár, P., Girshick, R., He, K., Hariharan, B., Belongie, S.: Feature pyramid networks for object detection. In: Proceedings of CVPR, pp. 2117–2125 (2017)
16. Lin, T.Y., Goyal, P., Girshick, R., He, K., Dollár, P.: Focal loss for dense object detection. In: Proceedings of ICCV, pp. 2980–2988 (2017)
17. Lin, X., Ding, C., Zeng, J., Tao, D.: Gps-Net: Graph property sensing network for scene graph generation. In: Proceedings of CVPR, pp. 3746–3753 (2020)
18. Lu, C., Krishna, R., Bernstein, M., Fei-Fei, L.: Visual relationship detection with language priors. In: Leibe, B., Matas, J., Sebe, N., Welling, M. (eds.) ECCV 2016. LNCS, vol. 9905, pp. 852–869. Springer, Cham (2016). https://doi.org/10.1007/978-3-319-46448-0_51
19. Miller, G.A.: WordNet: a lexical database for english. Commun. ACM 39–41 (1995)
20. Ren, S., He, K., Girshick, R., Sun, J.: Faster R-CNN: Towards real-time object detection with region proposal networks. In: Proceedings of NIPS, pp. 91–99 (2015)
21. Suhail, M., et al.: Energy-based learning for scene graph generation. In: Proceedings of CVPR, pp. 13936–13945 (2021)

22. Tang, K., Niu, Y., Huang, J., Shi, J., Zhang, H.: Unbiased scene graph generation from biased training. In: Proceedings of CVPR, pp. 3716–3725 (2020)
23. Tang, K., Zhang, H., Wu, B., Luo, W., Liu, W.: Learning to compose dynamic tree structures for visual contexts. In: Proceedings of CVPR, pp. 6619–6628 (2019)
24. Teney, D., Liu, L., van Den Hengel, A.: Graph-structured representations for visual question answering. In: Proceedings of CVPR, pp. 1–9 (2017)
25. Wan, A., et al.: NBDT: Neural-backed decision trees, pp. 1027–1032 (2021)
26. Wang, S., Wang, R., Yao, Z., Shan, S., Chen, X.: Cross-modal scene graph matching for relationship-aware image-text retrieval. In: Proceedings of WACV, pp. 1508–1517 (2020)
27. Wei, M., Chen, L., Ji, W., Yue, X., Chua, T.S.: Rethinking the two-stage framework for grounded situation recognition. In: Proceedings of AAAI, pp. 2651–2658 (2022)
28. Xiao, J., Yao, A., Liu, Z., Li, Y., Ji, W., Chua, T.S.: Video as conditional graph hierarchy for multi-granular question answering. In: Proceedings of AAAI, pp. 2804–2812 (2022)
29. Xie, S., Girshick, R., Dollár, P., Tu, Z., He, K.: Aggregated residual transformations for deep neural networks. In: Proceedings of CVPR, pp. 1492–1500 (2017)
30. Xu, D., Zhu, Y., Choy, C.B., Fei-Fei, L.: Scene graph generation by iterative message passing. In: Proceedings of CVPR, pp. 5410–5419 (2017)
31. Yan, S., et al.: PCPL: Predicate-correlation perception learning for unbiased scene graph generation. In: Proceedings of ACM Multimedia, pp. 265–273 (2020)
32. Yang, X., Tang, K., Zhang, H., Cai, J.: Auto-encoding scene graphs for image captioning. In: Proceedings of CVPR, pp. 10685–10694 (2019)
33. Yao, Y., et al.: PEVL: Position-enhanced pre-training and prompt tuning for vision-language models. arXiv preprint arXiv:2205.11169 (2022)
34. Yao, Y., et al.: Visual distant supervision for scene graph generation. In: Proceedings of ICCV, pp. 15816–15826 (2021)
35. Yao, Y., Zhang, A., Zhang, Z., Liu, Z., Chua, T.S., Sun, M.: CPT: Colorful prompt tuning for pre-trained vision-language models. arXiv preprint arXiv:2109.11797 (2021)
36. Yu, J., Chai, Y., Wang, Y., Hu, Y., Wu, Q.: CogTree: Cognition tree loss for unbiased scene graph generation, pp. 1274–1280 (2021)
37. Zareian, A., Karaman, S., Chang, S.-F.: Bridging knowledge graphs to generate scene graphs. In: Vedaldi, A., Bischof, H., Brox, T., Frahm, J.-M. (eds.) ECCV 2020. LNCS, vol. 12368, pp. 606–623. Springer, Cham (2020). https://doi.org/10.1007/978-3-030-58592-1_36
38. Zellers, R., Yatskar, M., Thomson, S., Choi, Y.: Neural Motifs: Scene graph parsing with global context. In: Proceedings of CVPR, pp. 5831–5840 (2018)
39. Zhang, J., Kalantidis, Y., Rohrbach, M., Paluri, M., Elgammal, A., Elhoseiny, M.: Large-scale visual relationship understanding. In: Proceedings of the AAAI, pp. 9185–9194 (2019)
40. Zhuang, B., Wu, Q., Shen, C., Reid, I., van den Hengel, A.: HCVRD: a benchmark for large-scale human-centered visual relationship detection. In: Proceedings of AAAI, pp. 7631–7638 (2018)

Pose2Room: Understanding 3D Scenes from Human Activities

Yinyu Nie[1]([✉]), Angela Dai[1], Xiaoguang Han[2], and Matthias Nießner[1]

[1] Technical University of Munich, Munich, Germany
yinyu.nie@tum.de
[2] The Chinese University of Hong Kong, Shenzhen, China

Abstract. With wearable IMU sensors, one can estimate human poses from wearable devices without requiring visual input. In this work, we pose the question: Can we reason about object structure in real-world environments solely from human trajectory information? Crucially, we observe that human motion and interactions tend to give strong information about the objects in a scene – for instance a person sitting indicates the likely presence of a chair or sofa. To this end, we propose P2R-Net to learn a probabilistic 3D model of the objects in a scene characterized by their class categories and oriented 3D bounding boxes, based on an input observed human trajectory in the environment. P2R-Net models the probability distribution of object class as well as a deep Gaussian mixture model for object boxes, enabling sampling of multiple, diverse, likely modes of object configurations from an observed human trajectory. In our experiments we show that P2R-Net can effectively learn multi-modal distributions of likely objects for human motions, and produce a variety of plausible object structures of the environment, even without any visual information. The results demonstrate that P2R-Net consistently outperforms the baselines on the PROX dataset and the VirtualHome platform.

Keywords: 3D Scene Understanding · Shape-from-X · Probabilistic model

1 Introduction

Understanding the structure of real-world 3D environments is fundamental to many computer vision tasks, with a well-studied history of research into 3D reconstruction from various visual input mediums, such as RGB video [13, 43, 53, 55], RGB-D video [6, 9, 45, 47, 66], or single images [8, 14, 27, 35, 36, 46, 50, 72]. Such approaches with active cameras have shown impressive capture of geometric structures leveraging strong visual signals. We consider an unconventional view of passive 3D scene perception: in the case of a lack of any visual signal, we look to human pose data, which for instance can be estimated from wearable IMU

Supplementary Information The online version contains supplementary material available at https://doi.org/10.1007/978-3-031-19812-0_25.

S. Avidan et al. (Eds.): ECCV 2022, LNCS 13687, pp. 425–443, 2022.
https://doi.org/10.1007/978-3-031-19812-0_25

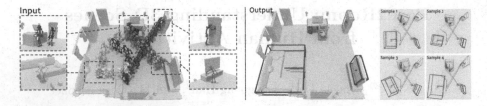

Fig. 1. From an observed pose trajectory of a person performing daily activities in an indoor scene (left), we learn to estimate likely object configurations of the scene underlying these interactions, as set of object class labels and oriented 3D bounding boxes (middle). By sampling from our probabilistic decoder, we synthesize multiple plausible object arrangements (right). (Scene geometry is shown only for visualization.)

sensors [19,28,62], and ask "What can we learn about a 3D environment from only human pose trajectory information?". This opens up new possibilities to explore information embedded in wearable devices (e.g., phones, fitness watches, etc.) towards understanding mapping, interactions, and content creation.

In particular, we observe that human movement in a 3D environment often interacts both passively and actively with objects in the environment, giving strong cues about likely objects and their locations. For instance, walking around a room indicates where empty floor space is available, a sitting motion indicates high likelihood of a chair or sofa to support the sitting pose, and a single out-stretched arm suggests picking up/putting down an object to furniture that supports the object. We thus propose to address a new scene estimation task: from only a sequence observation of 3D human poses, to estimate the object arrangement in the scene of the objects the person has interacted with, as a set of object class categories and 3D oriented bounding boxes (see Fig. 1).

As there are inherent ambiguities that lie in 3D object localization from only a human pose trajectory in the scene, we propose P2R-Net to learn a probabilistic model of the most likely modes of object configurations in the scene. From the sequence of poses, P2R-Net leverages the pose joint locations to vote for potential object centers that participate in the observed pose interactions. We then introduce a probabilistic decoder that learns a Gaussian mixture model for object box parameters, from which we can sample multiple diverse hypotheses of object arrangements. To enable massive training, we introduce a large-scale dataset with VirtualHome [51] platform to learn object configurations from human motions. Experiments on VirtualHome and the real dataset PROX [24,70] demonstrate our superiority against the baseline methods.

In summary, we present the following contributions:

- We propose a new perspective on 3D scene understanding by studying estimation of 3D object configurations from solely observing 3D human pose sequences of interactions in an environment, without any visual input, and predicting the object class categories and 3D oriented bounding boxes of the interacted objects in the scene.

- To address this task, we introduce a new, end-to-end, learned probabilistic model that estimates probability distributions for the object class categories and bounding box parameters.
- We demonstrate that our model captures complex, multi-modal distributions of likely object configurations, which can be sampled to produce diverse hypotheses that have accurate coverage over the ground truth object arrangement. Experiments also demonstrates the superiority of our method against the baselines in terms of accuracy and diversity.

2   Related Work

Predicting Human Interactions in Scenes. Capturing and modeling interactions between human and scenes has seen impressive progress in recent years, following significant advances in 3D reconstruction and 3D deep learning. From a visual observation of a scene, interactions and human-object relations are estimated. Several methods have been proposed for understanding the relations between scene and human poses via object functionality prediction [20,26,49,75] and affordance analysis [12,21,54,57,58,64].

By parsing the physics and semantics in human interactions, further works have been proposed towards synthesizing static human poses or human body models into 3D scenes [20,21,24,25,34,56,57,73,74]. These works focus on how to place human avatars into a 3D scene with semantic and physical plausibility (e.g., support or occlusion constraints). Various approaches have additionally explored synthesizing dynamic motions for a given scene geometry. Early methods retrieve and integrate existing avatar motions from database to make them compatible with scene geometry [2,32,37,38,60]. Given a goal pose or a task, more works learn to search for a possible motion path and estimate plausible contact motions [5,7,23,41,61,63]. These methods explore human-scene interaction understanding by estimating object functionalities or human interactions as poses in a given 3D scene environment. In contrast, we take a converse perspective, and aim to estimate the 3D scene arrangement from human pose trajectory observations.

Scene Understanding with Human Priors. As many environments, particularly indoor scenes, have been designed for people's daily usage, human behavioral priors can be leveraged to additionally reason about 2D or 3D scene observations. Various methods have been proposed to leverage human context as extra signal towards holistic perception to improve performance in scene understanding tasks such as semantic segmentation [10], layout detection from images [16,59], 3D object labeling [29], 3D object detection and segmentation [65], and 3D reconstruction [17,18,70].

Additionally, several methods learn joint distributions of human interactions with 3D scenes or RGB video that can be leveraged to re-synthesize the observed scene as an arranged set of synthetic, labeled CAD models [15,30,31,42,57]. Recently, HPS [22] proposed to simultaneously estimate pose trajectory and scene reconstruction from wearable visual and inertial sensors on a person. We also aim to understand 3D scenes as arrangements of objects, but do not require any labeled interactions nor consider any visual (RGB, RGB-D, etc.) information as input. The recent approach of Mura et al. [44] poses the task of floor plan estimation from 2D human walk trajectories, and proposes to predict occupancy-based floor plans that indicate structure and object footprints, but without object instance distinction and employs a fully-deterministic prediction. To the best of our knowledge, we introduce the first method to learn 3D object arrangement distributions from only human pose trajectories, without any visual input.

Pose Tracking with IMUs. Our method takes the input of human pose trajectories, which is built on the success of motion tracking techniques. Seminal work on pose estimation from wearable sensors have demonstrated effective pose estimation from wearable sensors, such as optical markers [4,23] or IMUs [19,28,33,39,62]. Our work is motivated by the capability of reliably estimating human pose from these sensor setups without visual data, from which we aim to learn human-object interaction priors to estimate scene object configurations.

3 Method

From only a human pose trajectory as input, we aim to estimate a distribution of likely object configurations, from which we can sample plausible hypotheses of objects in the scene as sets of class category labels and oriented 3D bounding boxes. We observe that most human interactions in an environment are targeted towards specific objects, and that general motion behavior is often influenced by the object arrangement in the scene. We thus aim to discover potential objects that each pose may be interacting with.

We first extract meaningful features from the human pose sequence with a *position encoder* to disentangle each frame into a relative position encoding and a position-agnostic pose, as well as a *pose encoder* to learn the local spatio-temporal feature for each pose in consecutive frames. We then leverage these features to vote for a potential interacting object for each pose. From these votes, we learn a *probabilistic mixture decoder* to propose box proposals for each object, characterizing likely modes for objectness, class label, and box parameters. An illustration of our approach is shown in Fig. 2.

3.1 Relative Position Encoding

We consider an input pose trajectory with N frames and J joints as the sequence of 3D locations $T \in \mathbb{R}^{N \times J \times 3}$. We also denote the root joint of each pose by $r \in \mathbb{R}^{N \times 3}$, where the root joint of a pose is the centroid of the joints corresponding to the body hip (for the skeleton configuration, we refer to the supplemental). To learn informative pose features, we first disentangle for each frame the absolute pose joint coordinates into a relative position encoding $Q \in \mathbb{R}^{N \times d_1}$ and a position-agnostic pose feature $P \in \mathbb{R}^{N \times J \times d_1}$, which are formulated as:

$$Q = \text{Pool}\left[f_1\left(\mathcal{N}\left(r\right) - r\right)\right],$$
$$P = f_2\left(T - r\right), \quad \mathcal{N}\left(r\right) \in \mathbb{R}^{N \times k \times 3}, \tag{1}$$

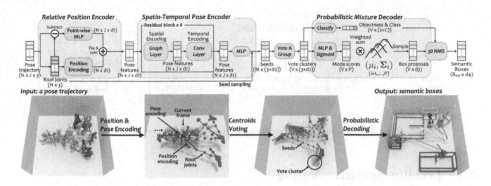

Fig. 2. Overview of P2R-Net. Given a pose trajectory with N frames and J joints, a position encoder decouples each skeleton frame into a relative position encoding (from its root joint as the hip centroid) and a position-agnostic pose. After combining them, a pose encoder learns local pose features from both body joints per skeleton (spatial encoding) and their changes in consecutive frames (temporal encoding). Root joints as seeds are then used to vote for the center of a nearby object that each pose is potentially interacting with. A probabilistic mixture network learns likely object box distributions, from which object class labels and oriented 3D boxes can be sampled.

where $f_1(*)$, $f_2(*)$ are point-wise MLP layers. $\mathcal{N}(r)$ is the set of k temporal neighbors to each root joint in r, and Pool($*$) denotes neighbor-wise average pooling. By broadcast summation, we output $P^r = P + Q$ for further spatio-temporal pose encoding. Understanding relative positions rather than absolute positions helps to provide more generalizable features to understand common pose motion in various object interactions, as these human-object interactions typically occur locally in a scene.

3.2 Spatio-Temporal Pose Encoding

The encoding P^r provides signal for the relative pose trajectory of a person. We then further encode these features to capture the joint movement to understand local human-object interactions. That is, from P^r, we learn joint movement in spatio-temporal domain: (1) in the spatial domain, we learn from intra-skeleton joints to capture per-frame pose features; (2) in the temporal domain, we learn from inter-frame relations to perceive each joint's movement.

Inspired by [69] in 2D pose recognition, we first use a graph convolution layer to learn intra-skeleton joint features. Edges in the graph convolution are constructed following the skeleton bones, which encodes skeleton-wise spatial information. For each joint, we then use a 1-D convolution layer to capture temporal features from its inter-frame neighbors. A graph layer and an 1-D convolution layer are linked into a block with a residual connection to process the input P^r (see Fig. 3). By stacking six blocks, we obtain a deeper spatio-temporal pose encoder with a wider receptive field in temporal domain, enabling reasoning over more temporal neighbors for object box estimation. Finally, we adopt an MLP to process all joints per skeleton to obtain pose features $P^{st} \in \mathbb{R}^{N \times d_2}$.

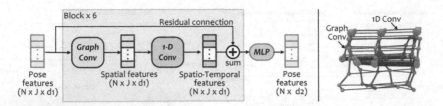

Fig. 3. Pose encoding with spatio-temporal convolutions.

3.3 Locality-Sensitive Voting

With pose features P^{st}, we then learn to vote for all the objects a person could have interacted with in a trajectory (see Fig. 2). For each pose frame, we predict the center of an object it potentially interacts with. Since we do not know when interactions begin or end, each pose votes for a potential object interaction. As human motion in a scene will tend to active interaction with an object or movement to an object, we aim to learn these patterns by encouraging votes for objects close to the respective pose, encouraging locality-based consideration.

For each pose feature $p^{st} \in P^{st}$, we use its root joint $r \in r$ as a seed location, and vote for an object center by learning the displacement from the seed:

$$
\begin{aligned}
v &= r_s + f_3\left(P_s^{st}\right), \quad r_s, v \in \mathbb{R}^{M \times 3}, \\
P^v &= P_s^{st} + f_4\left(P_s^{st}\right), \quad P_s^{st}, P^v \in \mathbb{R}^{M \times d_2},
\end{aligned}
\tag{2}
$$

where r_s are the evenly sampled M seeds from r; P_s^{st} are the corresponding pose features of r_s; f_3, f_4 are MLP layers; v, P^v denote the vote coordinates and features learned from P_s^{st}. We evenly sample seeds r_s from r to make them cover the whole trajectory and adaptive to sequences with different length.

Since there are several objects in a scene, for each seed in r_s, we vote for the center to the nearest one (see Fig. 4). The nearest object is both likely to participate in a nearby interaction, and affect motion around the object if not directly participating in an interaction. This strategy helps to reduce the ambiguities in scene object configuration estimation from a pose trajectory by capturing both direct and indirect effects of object location on pose movement.

For the seeds which vote for the same object, we group their votes to a cluster following [52]. This outputs cluster centers $v^c \in \mathbb{R}^{V \times 3}$ with aggregated cluster feature $P^c \in \mathbb{R}^{V \times d_2}$ where V denotes the number of vote clusters. We then use the P^c to decode to distributions that characterize semantic 3D boxes, which is described in Sect. 3.4. For poses whose root joint is not close to any object during training (beyond a distance threshold t_d), we consider them to have little connection with the objects, and do not train them to vote for any object.

3.4 Probabilistic Mixture Decoder

We decode vote clusters (v^c, P^c) to propose oriented 3D bounding boxes for each object, along with their class label and objectness score. Each box is represented

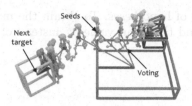

Fig. 4. Voting to objects that potentially influence the motion trajectory in approaching the target.

by a 3D center c, 3D size s and 1D orientation θ, where we represent the size by $\log(s)$ and orientation by $(\sin(\theta), \cos(\theta))$ for regression, similar to [71]. Since the nature of our task is inherently ambiguous (e.g., it may be unclear from observing a person sit if they are sitting on a chair or a sofa, or the size of the sofa), we propose to learn a probabilistic mixture decoder to predict the box centroid, size and orientation with multiple modes, from a vote cluster $v^c \in \boldsymbol{v}^c, P^c \in \boldsymbol{P}^c$:

$$
\begin{aligned}
y_\tau &= \sum_{k=1}^{P} f_\tau^k(P^c) \cdot y_\tau^k, \quad \tau \in \{c, s, \theta\}, \\
y_c^* &= v^c + y_c, \quad y_\tau^k \sim \mathcal{N}(\mu_\tau^k, \Sigma_\tau^k), \quad y_\tau, y_\tau^k \in \mathbb{R}^{d_\tau},
\end{aligned}
\tag{3}
$$

where $\tau \in \{c, s, \theta\}$ denote the regression targets for center, size, and orientation; $\mathcal{N}(\mu_\tau^k, \Sigma_\tau^k)$ is the learned multivariate Gaussian distribution of the k-th mode for τ, where y_τ^k is sampled from; P is the number of Gaussian distributions (i.e., modes); $f_\tau^k(*) \in [0, 1]$ is the learned score for the k-th mode; y_τ is the weighted sum of the samples from all modes, which is the prediction of the center/size/orientation; and d_τ is their output dimension ($d_c = 3$, $d_s = 3$, $d_\theta = 2$). Note that the box center y_c^* is obtained by regressing the offset y_c from cluster center v^c. We predict the proposal objectness and the probability distribution for class category directly from P^c, using an MLP.

Multi-modal Prediction. In Eq. 3, the learnable parameters are $f_\tau(*)$ and (μ_τ, Σ_τ). $f_\tau(*)$ is realized with an MLP followed by a sigmoid function, and (μ_τ, Σ_τ) are the learned embeddings shared among all samples. During training, we sample y_τ^k from each mode $\mathcal{N}(\mu_\tau^k, \Sigma_\tau^k)$ and predict y_τ using Eq. 3. To generate diverse and plausible hypotheses during inference, we not only sample y_τ^k, but also sample various different modes by randomly disregarding mixture elements based on their probabilities $f_\tau(*)$. Then we obtain y_τ as follows:

$$
y_\tau = \sum_{k=1}^{P} I_\tau^k \cdot y_\tau^k, \quad I_\tau^k \sim \mathrm{Bern}(f_\tau^k), \quad y_\tau^k \sim \mathcal{N}(\mu_\tau^k, \Sigma_\tau^k),
\tag{4}
$$

where I_τ^k is sampled from Bernoulli distribution with probability of $f_\tau^k(*)$. We also sample the object classes by the predicted classification probabilities, and discard proposed object boxes with low objectness ($\leq t_o$) after 3D NMS.

We can then generate N_h hypotheses in a scene; each hypothesis is an average of N_s samples of y_τ, which empirically strikes a good balance between diversity and accuracy of the set of hypotheses. To obtain the maximum likelihood prediction, we use $f_\tau^k(*)$ and the mean value μ_τ^k instead of I_τ^k and y_τ^k to estimate the boxes with Eq. 3.

3.5   Loss Function

The loss consists of classification losses for objectness $\mathcal{L}_{obj}$ and class label $\mathcal{L}_{cls}$, and regression losses for votes $\mathcal{L}_v$, box center $\mathcal{L}_c$, size $\mathcal{L}_s$ and orientation $\mathcal{L}_\theta$.

Classification Losses. Similar to [52], $\mathcal{L}_{obj}$ and $\mathcal{L}_{cls}$ are supervised by cross entropy losses, wherein the objectness score is used to classify if a vote cluster center is close to (≤ 0.3 m, positive) or far from (≥ 0.6 m, negative) the ground truth. Proposals from the clusters with positive objectness are further supervised with box regression losses.

Regression Losses. We supervise all the predicted votes, box centers, sizes and orientations with a Huber loss. For poses that are located within d_p to objects ($d_p = 1$ m), we use the closest object center to supervise their vote. Votes from those poses that are far from all objects are not considered. For center predictions, we use their nearest ground-truth center to calculate $\mathcal{L}_c$. Since box sizes and orientations are predicted from vote clusters, we use the counterpart from the ground-truth box that is nearest to the vote cluster for supervision. Then the final loss function is $\mathcal{L} = \sum_\tau \lambda_\tau \mathcal{L}_\tau$, where $\mathcal{L}_\tau \in \{\mathcal{L}_{obj}, \mathcal{L}_{cls}, \mathcal{L}_v, \mathcal{L}_c, \mathcal{L}_s, \mathcal{L}_\theta\}$ and $\{\lambda_\tau\}$ are constant weights that balance the losses.

4   Experiment Setup

Datasets. To the best of our knowledge, existing 3D human pose trajectory datasets are either with very few sequences (≤ 102) [3,24,57,70,74], or without instance annotations [3,24,74], or focused on single objects [23]. To this end, we introduce a new large-scale dataset using the simulation platform **Virtual-Home** [51] for the task of estimating multiple scene objects from a human pose trajectory observation. To demonstrate our applicability to real data, we also evaluate on real human motions from the **PROX** dataset [24,70].

   We construct our dataset on VirtualHome [51], which is built on the Unity3D game engine. It consists of 29 rooms, with each room containing 88 objects on average; each object is annotated with available interaction types. VirtualHome allows customization of action scripts and control over humanoid agents to execute a series of complex interactive tasks. We refer readers to [51] for the details of the scene and action types. In our work, we focus on the interactable objects under 17 common class categories. In each room, we select up to 10 random static objects to define the scene, and script the agent to interact with each of the objects in a sequential fashion. For each object, we also select a random interaction type associated with the object class category. Then we randomly sample 13,913 different sequences with corresponding object boxes to construct the dataset. During training, we also randomly flip, rotate and translate the scenes and poses for data augmentation. For additional detail about data generation, we refer to the supplemental. For the PROX dataset [24], we use its human motions with the 3D instance boxes labeled by [70], which has 46 motion sequences interacting with four object categories (i.e., bed, chair, sofa, table) in 10 rooms. For more details, we refer readers to [24,70].

Implementation. We train P2R-Net end-to-end from scratch with the batch size at 32 on 4 NVIDIA 2080 Ti GPUs for 180 epochs, where Adam is used as the optimizer. The initial learning rate is at 1e-3 in the first 80 epochs, which is decayed by 0.1× every 40 epochs after that. The losses are weighted by $\lambda_{obj} = 5$, $\lambda_{cls} = 1$, $\{\lambda_v, \lambda_c, \lambda_s, \lambda_\theta\} = 10$ to balance the loss values. During training, we use pose distance threshold $t_d = 1$ m. At inference time, we output box predictions after 3D NMS with an IoU threshold of 0.1. We use an objectness threshold of $t_o = 0.5$. For the layer and data specifications, we refer to the supplemental.

Evaluation. We evaluate our task both on our dataset and on PROX. For our dataset, we consider two types of evaluation splits: a sequence-level split $\mathcal{S}_1$ across different interaction sequences, and room-level split $\mathcal{S}_2$ across different rooms as well as interaction sequences. Note that sequences are trained with and evaluated against only the objects that are interacted with during the input observation, resulting in different variants of each room under different interaction sequences. For $\mathcal{S}_1$, the train/test split ratio is 4:1 over the generated sequences. $\mathcal{S}_2$ is a more challenging setup, with 27 train rooms and 2 test rooms, resulting in 13K/1K sequences. Since the task is inherently ambiguous, and only a single ground truth configuration of each room is available, we evaluate multi-modal predictions by several metrics: $mAP@0.5$ evaluates the mean average precision with the IoU threshold at 0.5 of the maximum likelihood prediction; MMD evaluates the Minimal Matching Distance [1] of the best matching prediction with the ground truth out of 10 sampled hypotheses to measure their quality; TMD evaluates the Total Mutual Diversity [68] to measure the diversity of the 10 hypotheses. We provide additional detail about MMD and TMD in the supplemental. For PROX dataset, we split the train/test set by 8:1 considering the very limited number of sequences (46) and use $mAP@0.5$ for detection evaluation.

5 Results and Analysis

We evaluate our approach on the task of scene object configuration estimation from a pose trajectory observation, in comparison with baselines constructed from state-of-the-art 3D detection and pose understanding methods, as well as an ablation analysis of our multi-modal prediction.

5.1 Baselines

Since there are no prior works that tackle the task of predicting the object configuration of a scene from solely a 3D pose trajectory, we construct several baselines leveraging state-of-the-art techniques as well as various approaches

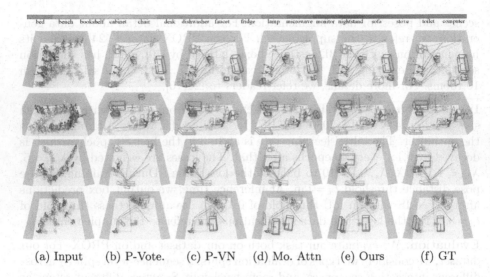

(a) Input   (b) P-Vote.   (c) P-VN   (d) Mo. Attn   (e) Ours   (f) GT

Fig. 5. Qualitative results of object detection from a pose trajectory on the sequence-level split S_1 (unseen interaction sequences).

to estimate multi-modal distributions. We consider the following baselines: **1)** **Pose-VoteNet** [52]. Since VoteNet is designed for detection from point clouds, we replace their PointNet++ encoder with our position encoder + MLPs to learn joint features for seeds. **2) Pose-VN**, Pose-VoteNet based on Vector Neurons [11] which replaces MLP layers in Pose-VoteNet with SO(3)-equivariant operators that can capture arbitrary rotations of poses to estimate objects. **3) Motion Attention** [40]. Since our task can be also regarded as a sequence-to-sequence problem, we adopt a frame-wise attention encoder to extract repetitive pose patterns in the temporal domain which then inform a VoteNet decoder to regress boxes. Additionally, we also ablate our probabilistic mixture decoder with other alternatives: **4) Deterministic P2R-Net** (P2R-Net-D), where we use VoteNet decoder [52] in our method for box regression to produce deterministic results; **5) Generative P2R-Net** (P2R-Net-G), where our P2R-Net decoder is designed with a probabilistic generative model [67] to decode boxes from a learned latent variable; **6) Heatmap P2R-Net** (P2R-Net-H), where the box center, size and orientation are discretized into binary heatmaps, and the box regression is converted into a classification task. Detailed architecture specifications for these networks are given in the supplemental material.

5.2 Qualitative Comparisons

Comparisons on S_1. Figure 5 visualizes predictions on the test set of unseen interaction sequences. Pose-VoteNet struggles to identify the existence of an object, leading to many missed detections, but can estimate reasonable object locations when an object is predicted. Pose-VN alleviates this problem of under-

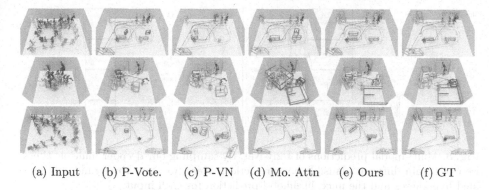

(a) Input   (b) P-Vote.   (c) P-VN   (d) Mo. Attn   (e) Ours   (f) GT

Fig. 6. Qualitative results of object detection from a pose trajectory on the room-level split $\mathcal{S}_2$ (unseen interaction sequences and rooms).

detection, but struggles to estimate object box sizes (rows 1,3). These baselines indicate the difficulty in detecting objects without sharing pose features among temporal neighbors. Motion Attention [40] addresses this by involving global context with inter-frame attention. However, it does not take advantage of the skeleton's spatial layout in continuous frames and struggles to detect the existence of objects (row 1,2). In contrast, our method leverages both target-dependent poses and object occupancy context, that learns the implicit interrelations between poses and objects to infer object boxes, and achieves better estimate of the scene configuration.

Comparisons on $\mathcal{S}_2$. In Fig. 6, we illustrate the qualitative comparisons on the test set of unseen interaction sequences in unknown rooms. In this scenario, most baselines fail to localize objects, while our method can nonetheless produce plausible object layouts.

Multi-modal Predictions. We visualize various sampled hypotheses from our model $\mathcal{S}_1$ in Fig. 8, showing that our method is able to deduce the spatial occupancy of objects from motion trajectories, and enables diverse, plausible estimation of object locations, orientation, and sizes for interactions.

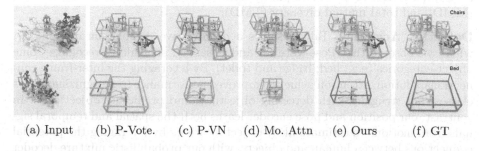

(a) Input   (b) P-Vote.   (c) P-VN   (d) Mo. Attn   (e) Ours   (f) GT

Fig. 7. Qualitative results of object detection on the PROX dataset [24,70].

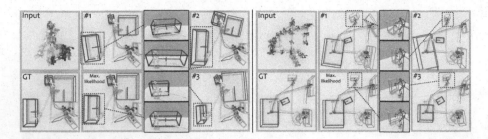

Fig. 8. Multi-modal predictions of P2R-Net. By sampling our decoder multiple times, we can obtain different plausible box predictions. Here, we show three randomly sampled hypotheses and the max. likelihood prediction for each input.

Table 1. Quantitative evaluation on split $\mathcal{S}_1$. For P2R-Net-G, P2R-Net-H and ours, we use the maximum likelihood predictions to calculate mAP scores. The mAP@0.5 is averaged over all 17 classes (see the full table with all classes in the supplementary file).

	Bed	Bench	Cabinet	Chair	Desk	Dishwasher	Fridge	Lamp	Sofa	Stove	Toilet	Computer	mAP@0.5
Pose-VoteNet	2.90	15.00	33.14	18.77	58.52	32.14	0.00	**6.07**	62.32	49.82	0.00	3.06	25.70
Pose-VN	20.81	**18.13**	49.76	18.68	70.92	33.56	0.00	5.60	67.24	46.76	0.00	6.11	29.90
Motion Attention	36.42	7.54	23.35	**19.50**	77.71	15.59	17.13	2.35	78.61	51.03	14.81	5.50	28.39
P2R-Net-D	93.77	12.63	11.98	5.77	**95.93**	61.80	73.95	0.58	88.44	**70.42**	0.00	14.17	34.91
P2R-Net-G	91.69	7.56	36.61	10.05	93.47	**67.53**	**77.45**	1.21	**92.97**	64.86	5.56	18.67	37.48
P2R-Net-H	85.84	8.04	22.04	10.91	76.08	55.20	55.15	0.00	83.92	57.60	5.00	4.33	31.41
P2R-Net	**94.21**	10.12	**54.72**	8.02	93.32	56.33	59.89	3.25	90.92	57.86	**61.11**	**19.94**	**42.20**

Comparisons on PROX. We additionally show qualitative results on real motion data from PROX [24,70] in Fig. 7. Since there are only 46 sequences labeled with object boxes, we pretrain each method on our dataset first before finetuning them on PROX. As PROX uses SMPL-X human body model [48], we manually map its skeleton joint indexes to ours for transfer learning. The results show that our approach can effectively handle real, noisy pose trajectory inputs.

5.3   Quantitative Comparisons

We use mAP@0.5 to measure object detection accuracy, and evaluate the accuracy and diversity of a set of output hypotheses using minimal matching distance (MMD) and total mutual diversity (TMD).

Detection Accuracy. Table 1 shows a quantitative comparison on split $\mathcal{S}_1$, where we observe that Pose-VoteNet and Pose-VN, struggle to recognize some object categories (e.g., bed, fridge and toilet). By leveraging the inter-frame connections, Motion Attention achieves improved performance in recognizing object classes, but struggles with detecting objectness and predicting object sizes. In contrast, our position and pose encoder learns both the spatial and temporal signals from motions to estimate likely object locations by leveraging the potential connections between human and objects, with our probabilistic mixture decoder better capturing likely modalities in various challenging ambiguous interactions

Table 2. Comparisons on detection accuracy, and multi-modal quality and diversity on S_1 and S_2. TMD=1 indicates no diversity.

	S_1			S_2		
	mAP	MMD	TMD	mAP	MMD	TMD
Pose-VoteNet	25.70	–	–	10.23	–	–
Pose-VN	29.90	–	–	6.12	–	–
Motion Attn	28.39	–	–	6.53	–	–
P2R-Net-D	34.91	–	–	31.56	–	–
P2R-Net-G	37.48	37.43	1.73	31.59	31.83	1.98
P2R-Net-H	31.41	21.10	2.39	27.96	20.71	3.28
P2R-Net	**42.20**	**38.28**	**3.34**	**35.34**	**32.47**	**4.35**

Table 3. Comparisons on detection accuracy (mAP@0.5) using PROX.

	w/o pretrain	w/ pretrain
Pose-VoteNet	2.29	27.97
Pose-VN	1.92	9.23
Motion Attn	2.68	6.25
P2R-Net	5.36	**31.38**

(e.g., toilet and cabinet). In Table 2, we compare mAP@0.5 scores on split S_2, with increased relative improvement in the challenging scenario of scene object configuration estimation in new rooms.

Quality and Diversity of Multi-modal Predictions. We study the multi-modal predictions with our ablation variants P2R-Net-G and P2R-Net-H, and use MMD and TMD to evaluate the quality and diversity of 10 randomly sampled predictions for each method. From the 10 predictions, MMD records the best detection score (mAP@0.5), and TMD measures the average variance of the 10 semantic boxes per object. Table 2 presents the MMD and TMD scores on S_1 and S_2 respectively. P2R-Net-G tends to predict with low diversity, as seen in low TMD score (TMD=1 indicates identical samples) and similar mAP@0.5 and MMD scores. P2R-Net-H shows better diversity but with lower accuracy in both of the two splits. Our final model not only achieves best detection accuracy, it also provides reasonable and diverse object configurations, with a notable performance improvement in the challenging S_2 split.

Comparisons on PROX. We quantitatively compare with baselines on real human motion data from PROX [24,70] in Table 3. We evaluate our method and baselines with and without pretraining on our synthetic dataset, considering the very limited number (46) of motion sequences in PROX. The results demonstrate that pretraining on our dataset can significantly improve all methods' performance on real data, with our approach outperforming all baselines.

Ablations. In Table 4, we explore the effects of each individual module (relative position encoder, spatio-temporal pose encoder and probabilistic mixture decoder). We ablate P2R-Net by gradually adding components from the baseline c_0: without relative position encoding (Pstn-Enc), where we use joints' global coordinates relative to the room center; without spatio-temporal pose encoding (Pose-Enc), where we use MLPs to learn pose features from joint coordinates; without probabilistic mixture decoder (P-Dec), where we use two-layer MLPs to regress box parameters.

Table 4. Ablation study of our design choices. Note that c_1 and c_2 are different with Pose-VoteNet and P2R-Net-D since our method parameterizes boxes differently from VoteNet (see Sect. 3.4)

$\mathcal{S}_1/\mathcal{S}_2$	Pstn-Enc	Pose-Enc	P-Dec	mAP@0.5
c_0	–	–	–	8.71 / 3.12
c_1	✓	–	–	34.43/19.07
c_2	✓	✓	–	39.98/29.25
Full	✓	✓	✓	**42.20/35.34**

From the comparisons, we observe that relative position encoding plays the most significant role. It allows our model to pick up on local pose signal, as many human-object interactions present with strong locality. The spatio-temporal pose encoder then enhances the pose feature learning, and enables our model to learn the joint changes both in spatial and temporal domains. This design largely improves our generalization ability, particularly in unseen rooms (from 19.07 to 29.25). The probabilistic decoder further alleviates the ambiguity of this problem, and combining all the modules together produces the best results.

Limitations. Although P2R-Net achieves plausible scene estimations from only pose trajectories, it operates on several assumptions that can lead to potential limitations: (1) Objects should be interactable, e.g., our method may not detect objects that do not induce strong pose interactions like mirror or picture; (2) Interactions occur at close range, e.g., we may struggle to detect a TV from a person switching on it with a remote control. Additionally, we currently focus on estimating static object boxes. We believe an interesting avenue for future work is to characterize objects in motion (e.g., due to grabbing) or articulated objects (e.g., laptops).

6 Conclusion

We have presented a first exploration to the ill-posed problem of estimating the 3D object configuration in a scene from only a 3D pose trajectory observation of a person interacting with the scene. Our proposed model P2R-Net leverages spatio-temporal features from the pose trajectory to vote for likely object positions and inform a new probabilistic mixture decoder that captures multi-modal distributions of object box parameters. We demonstrate that such a probabilistic approach can effectively model likely object configurations in scene, producing plausible object layout hypotheses from an input pose trajectory. We hope that this establishes a step towards object-based 3D understanding of environments using non-visual signal and opens up new possibilities in leveraging ego-centric motion for 3D perception and understanding.

Acknowledgments. This project is funded by the Bavarian State Ministry of Science and the Arts and coordinated by the Bavarian Research Institute for Digital Transformation (bidt), the TUM Institute of Advanced Studies (TUM-IAS), the ERC Starting Grant Scan2CAD (804724), and the German Research Foundation (DFG) Grant Making Machine Learning on Static and Dynamic 3D Data Practical.

References

1. Achlioptas, P., Diamanti, O., Mitliagkas, I., Guibas, L.: Learning representations and generative models for 3d point clouds. In: International Conference on Machine Learning. pp. 40–49. PMLR (2018)
2. Agrawal, S., van de Panne, M.: Task-based locomotion. ACM Trans. Graph. (TOG) **35**(4), 1–11 (2016)
3. Cao, Z., Gao, H., Mangalam, K., Cai, Q.-Z., Vo, M., Malik, J.: Long-term human motion prediction with scene context. In: Vedaldi, A., Bischof, H., Brox, T., Frahm, J.-M. (eds.) ECCV 2020. LNCS, vol. 12346, pp. 387–404. Springer, Cham (2020). https://doi.org/10.1007/978-3-030-58452-8_23
4. Chai, J., Hodgins, J.K.: Performance animation from low-dimensional control signals. In: ACM SIGGRAPH 2005 Papers, pp. 686–696 (2005)
5. Chao, Y.W., Yang, J., Chen, W., Deng, J.: Learning to sit: Synthesizing human-chair interactions via hierarchical control. arXiv preprint arXiv:1908.07423 (2019)
6. Choi, S., Zhou, Q.Y., Koltun, V.: Robust reconstruction of indoor scenes. In: Proceedings of the IEEE Conference on Computer Vision and Pattern Recognition, pp. 5556–5565 (2015)
7. Corona, E., Pumarola, A., Alenya, G., Moreno-Noguer, F.: Context-aware human motion prediction. In: Proceedings of the IEEE/CVF Conference on Computer Vision and Pattern Recognition, pp. 6992–7001 (2020)
8. Dahnert, M., Hou, J., Nießner, M., Dai, A.: Panoptic 3d scene reconstruction from a single rgb image. In: Proceedings of the Neural Information Processing Systems (NeurIPS) (2021)
9. Dai, A., Nießner, M., Zollhöfer, M., Izadi, S., Theobalt, C.: Bundlefusion: Real-time globally consistent 3d reconstruction using on-the-fly surface reintegration. ACM Trans. Graph. (ToG) **36**(4), 1 (2017)
10. Delaitre, V., Fouhey, D.F., Laptev, I., Sivic, J., Gupta, A., Efros, A.A.: Scene semantics from long-term observation of people. In: Fitzgibbon, A., Lazebnik, S., Perona, P., Sato, Y., Schmid, C. (eds.) ECCV 2012. LNCS, vol. 7577, pp. 284–298. Springer, Heidelberg (2012). https://doi.org/10.1007/978-3-642-33783-3_21
11. Deng, C., Litany, O., Duan, Y., Poulenard, A., Tagliasacchi, A., Guibas, L.: Vector neurons: a general framework for so(3)-equivariant networks. arXiv preprint arXiv:2104.12229 (2021)
12. Deng, S., Xu, X., Wu, C., Chen, K., Jia, K.: 3d affordancenet: A benchmark for visual object affordance understanding. In: Proceedings of the IEEE/CVF Conference on Computer Vision and Pattern Recognition, pp. 1778–1787 (2021)
13. Engel, J., Schöps, T., Cremers, D.: LSD-SLAM: Large-scale direct monocular SLAM. In: Fleet, D., Pajdla, T., Schiele, B., Tuytelaars, T. (eds.) ECCV 2014. LNCS, vol. 8690, pp. 834–849. Springer, Cham (2014). https://doi.org/10.1007/978-3-319-10605-2_54
14. Engelmann, F., Rematas, K., Leibe, B., Ferrari, V.: From points to multi-object 3d reconstruction. In: Proceedings of the IEEE/CVF Conference on Computer Vision and Pattern Recognition, pp. 4588–4597 (2021)

15. Fisher, M., Savva, M., Li, Y., Hanrahan, P., Nießner, M.: Activity-centric scene synthesis for functional 3d scene modeling. ACM Trans. Graph. (TOG) **34**(6), 1–13 (2015)

16. Fouhey, D.F., Delaitre, V., Gupta, A., Efros, A.A., Laptev, I., Sivic, J.: People watching: human actions as a cue for single view geometry. In: Fitzgibbon, A., Lazebnik, S., Perona, P., Sato, Y., Schmid, C. (eds.) ECCV 2012. LNCS, vol. 7576, pp. 732–745. Springer, Heidelberg (2012). https://doi.org/10.1007/978-3-642-33715-4_53

17. Fowler, S., Kim, H., Hilton, A.: Towards complete scene reconstruction from single-view depth and human motion. In: BMVC (2017)

18. Fowler, S., Kim, H., Hilton, A.: Human-centric scene understanding from single view 360 video. In: 2018 International Conference on 3D Vision (3DV), pp. 334–342. IEEE (2018)

19. Glauser, O., Wu, S., Panozzo, D., Hilliges, O., Sorkine-Hornung, O.: Interactive hand pose estimation using a stretch-sensing soft glove. ACM Trans. Graph. (TOG) **38**(4), 1–15 (2019)

20. Grabner, H., Gall, J., Van Gool, L.: What makes a chair a chair? In: CVPR 2011, pp. 1529–1536. IEEE (2011)

21. Gupta, A., Satkin, S., Efros, A.A., Hebert, M.: From 3d scene geometry to human workspace. In: CVPR 2011, pp. 1961–1968. IEEE (2011)

22. Guzov, V., Mir, A., Sattler, T., Pons-Moll, G.: Human poseitioning system (hps): 3d human pose estimation and self-localization in large scenes from body-mounted sensors. In: Proceedings of the IEEE/CVF Conference on Computer Vision and Pattern Recognition, pp. 4318–4329 (2021)

23. Hassan, M., et al.: Stochastic scene-aware motion prediction. In: Proceedings of the IEEE/CVF International Conference on Computer Vision, pp. 11374–11384 (2021)

24. Hassan, M., Choutas, V., Tzionas, D., Black, M.J.: Resolving 3d human pose ambiguities with 3d scene constraints. In: Proceedings of the IEEE/CVF International Conference on Computer Vision, pp. 2282–2292 (2019)

25. Hassan, M., Ghosh, P., Tesch, J., Tzionas, D., Black, M.J.: Populating 3d scenes by learning human-scene interaction. In: Proceedings of the IEEE/CVF Conference on Computer Vision and Pattern Recognition, pp. 14708–14718 (2021)

26. Hu, R., van Kaick, O., Wu, B., Huang, H., Shamir, A., Zhang, H.: Learning how objects function via co-analysis of interactions. ACM Trans. Graph. (TOG) **35**(4), 1–13 (2016)

27. Huang, S., Qi, S., Zhu, Y., Xiao, Y., Xu, Y., Zhu, S.-C.: Holistic 3d scene parsing and reconstruction from a single RGB image. In: Ferrari, V., Hebert, M., Sminchis-escu, C., Weiss, Y. (eds.) ECCV 2018. LNCS, vol. 11211, pp. 194–211. Springer, Cham (2018). https://doi.org/10.1007/978-3-030-01234-2_12

28. Huang, Y., Kaufmann, M., Aksan, E., Black, M.J., Hilliges, O., Pons-Moll, G.: Deep inertial poser: Learning to reconstruct human pose from sparse inertial measurements in real time. ACM Trans. Graph. (TOG) **37**(6), 1–15 (2018)

29. Jiang, Y., Koppula, H., Saxena, A.: Hallucinated humans as the hidden context for labeling 3d scenes. In: Proceedings of the IEEE Conference on Computer Vision and Pattern Recognition, pp. 2993–3000 (2013)

30. Jiang, Y., Koppula, H.S., Saxena, A.: Modeling 3d environments through hidden human context. IEEE Trans. Pattern Anal. Mach. Intell. **38**(10), 2040–2053 (2015)

31. Jiang, Y., Lim, M., Saxena, A.: Learning object arrangements in 3d scenes using human context. arXiv preprint arXiv:1206.6462 (2012)

32. Kapadia, M., et al.: Precision: Precomputing environment semantics for contact-rich character animation. In: Proceedings of the 20th ACM SIGGRAPH Symposium on Interactive 3D Graphics and Games, pp. 29–37 (2016)
33. Kaufmann, M., et al.: Em-pose: 3d human pose estimation from sparse electromagnetic trackers. In: Proceedings of the IEEE/CVF International Conference on Computer Vision, pp. 11510–11520 (2021)
34. Kim, V.G., Chaudhuri, S., Guibas, L., Funkhouser, T.: Shape2pose: Human-centric shape analysis. ACM Trans. Graph. (TOG) **33**(4), 1–12 (2014)
35. Kuo, W., Angelova, A., Lin, T.-Y., Dai, A.: Mask2CAD: 3D shape prediction by learning to segment and retrieve. In: Vedaldi, A., Bischof, H., Brox, T., Frahm, J.-M. (eds.) ECCV 2020. LNCS, vol. 12348, pp. 260–277. Springer, Cham (2020). https://doi.org/10.1007/978-3-030-58580-8_16
36. Kuo, W., Angelova, A., Lin, T.Y., Dai, A.: Patch2cad: Patchwise embedding learning for in-the-wild shape retrieval from a single image. In: Proceedings of the IEEE/CVF International Conference on Computer Vision, pp. 12589–12599 (2021)
37. Lee, J., Chai, J., Reitsma, P.S., Hodgins, J.K., Pollard, N.S.: Interactive control of avatars animated with human motion data. In: Proceedings of the 29th Annual Conference on Computer Graphics and Interactive Techniques, pp. 491–500 (2002)
38. Lee, K.H., Choi, M.G., Lee, J.: Motion patches: building blocks for virtual environments annotated with motion data. In: ACM SIGGRAPH 2006 Papers, pp. 898–906 (2006)
39. Liu, H., Wei, X., Chai, J., Ha, I., Rhee, T.: Realtime human motion control with a small number of inertial sensors. In: Symposium on Interactive 3D Graphics and Games, pp. 133–140 (2011)
40. Mao, W., Liu, M., Salzmann, M.: History repeats itself: Human motion prediction via motion attention. In: Vedaldi, A., Bischof, H., Brox, T., Frahm, J.-M. (eds.) ECCV 2020. LNCS, vol. 12359, pp. 474–489. Springer, Cham (2020). https://doi.org/10.1007/978-3-030-58568-6_28
41. Merel, J., et al.: Catch & carry: reusable neural controllers for vision-guided whole-body tasks. ACM Trans. Graph. (TOG) **39**(4), 1–39 (2020)
42. Monszpart, A., Guerrero, P., Ceylan, D., Yumer, E., Mitra, N.J.: imapper: interaction-guided scene mapping from monocular videos. ACM Trans. Graph. (TOG) **38**(4), 1–15 (2019)
43. Mur-Artal, R., Montiel, J.M.M., Tardos, J.D.: Orb-slam: a versatile and accurate monocular slam system. IEEE Trans. Rob. **31**(5), 1147–1163 (2015)
44. Mura, C., Pajarola, R., Schindler, K., Mitra, N.: Walk2map: Extracting floor plans from indoor walk trajectories. In: Computer Graphics Forum, vol. 40, pp. 375–388. Wiley Online Library (2021)
45. Newcombe, R.A., et alA.: Kinectfusion: Real-time dense surface mapping and tracking. In: 2011 10th IEEE International Symposium on Mixed and Augmented Reality, pp. 127–136. IEEE (2011)
46. Nie, Y., Han, X., Guo, S., Zheng, Y., Chang, J., Zhang, J.J.: Total3dunderstanding: Joint layout, object pose and mesh reconstruction for indoor scenes from a single image. In: IEEE/CVF Conference on Computer Vision and Pattern Recognition (CVPR) (June 2020)
47. Nießner, M., Zollhöfer, M., Izadi, S., Stamminger, M.: Real-time 3d reconstruction at scale using voxel hashing. ACM Trans. Graph. (ToG) **32**(6), 1–11 (2013)
48. Pavlakos, G., et al.: Expressive body capture: 3d hands, face, and body from a single image. In: Proceedings of the IEEE/CVF Conference on Computer Vision and Pattern Recognition, pp. 10975–10985 (2019)

49. Pieropan, A., Ek, C.H., Kjellström, H.: Functional object descriptors for human activity modeling. In: 2013 IEEE International Conference on Robotics and Automation, pp. 1282–1289. IEEE (2013)

50. Popov, S., Bauszat, P., Ferrari, V.: CoReNet: coherent 3D scene reconstruction from a single RGB image. In: Vedaldi, A., Bischof, H., Brox, T., Frahm, J.-M. (eds.) ECCV 2020. LNCS, vol. 12347, pp. 366–383. Springer, Cham (2020). https://doi.org/10.1007/978-3-030-58536-5_22

51. Puig, X., et al.: Virtualhome: Simulating household activities via programs. In: Proceedings of the IEEE Conference on Computer Vision and Pattern Recognition, pp. 8494–8502 (2018)

52. Qi, C.R., Litany, O., He, K., Guibas, L.J.: Deep hough voting for 3d object detection in point clouds. In: Proceedings of the IEEE/CVF International Conference on Computer Vision (ICCV) (October 2019)

53. Qian, S., Jin, L., Fouhey, D.F.: Associative3D: Volumetric reconstruction from sparse views. In: Vedaldi, A., Bischof, H., Brox, T., Frahm, J.-M. (eds.) ECCV 2020. LNCS, vol. 12360, pp. 140–157. Springer, Cham (2020). https://doi.org/10.1007/978-3-030-58555-6_9

54. Ruiz, E., Mayol-Cuevas, W.: Where can i do this? geometric affordances from a single example with the interaction tensor. In: 2018 IEEE International Conference on Robotics and Automation (ICRA), pp. 2192–2199. IEEE (2018)

55. Runz, M., et al.: Frodo: From detections to 3d objects. In: Proceedings of the IEEE/CVF Conference on Computer Vision and Pattern Recognition, pp. 14720–14729 (2020)

56. Savva, M., Chang, A.X., Hanrahan, P., Fisher, M., Nießner, M.: Scenegrok: Inferring action maps in 3d environments. ACM Trans. Graph. (TOG) 33(6), 1–10 (2014)

57. Savva, M., Chang, A.X., Hanrahan, P., Fisher, M., Nießner, M.: Pigraphs: learning interaction snapshots from observations. ACM Trans. Graph. (TOG) 35(4), 1–12 (2016)

58. Sawatzky, J., Srikantha, A., Gall, J.: Weakly supervised affordance detection. In: Proceedings of the IEEE Conference on Computer Vision and Pattern Recognition, pp. 2795–2804 (2017)

59. Shoaib, M., Yang, M.Y., Rosenhahn, B., Ostermann, J.: Estimating layout of cluttered indoor scenes using trajectory-based priors. Image Vis. Comput. 32(11), 870–883 (2014)

60. Shum, H.P., Komura, T., Shiraishi, M., Yamazaki, S.: Interaction patches for multi-character animation. ACM Trans. Graph. (TOG) 27(5), 1–8 (2008)

61. Starke, S., Zhang, H., Komura, T., Saito, J.: Neural state machine for character-scene interactions. ACM Trans. Graph. 38(6), 1–209 (2019)

62. Von Marcard, T., Rosenhahn, B., Black, M.J., Pons-Moll, G.: Sparse inertial poser: Automatic 3d human pose estimation from sparse imus. In: Computer Graphics Forum, vol. 36, pp. 349–360. Wiley Online Library (2017)

63. Wang, J., Xu, H., Xu, J., Liu, S., Wang, X.: Synthesizing long-term 3d human motion and interaction in 3d scenes. In: Proceedings of the IEEE/CVF Conference on Computer Vision and Pattern Recognition, pp. 9401–9411 (2021)

64. Wang, Z., Chen, L., Rathore, S., Shin, D., Fowlkes, C.: Geometric pose affordance: 3d human pose with scene constraints. arXiv preprint arXiv:1905.07718 (2019)

65. Wei, P., Zhao, Y., Zheng, N., Zhu, S.C.: Modeling 4d human-object interactions for joint event segmentation, recognition, and object localization. IEEE Trans. Pattern Anal. Mach. Intell. 39(6), 1165–1179 (2016)

66. Whelan, T., Leutenegger, S., Salas-Moreno, R., Glocker, B., Davison, A.: Elastic-fusion: Dense slam without a pose graph. Robotics: Science and Systems (2015)
67. Wu, J., Zhang, C., Xue, T., Freeman, W.T., Tenenbaum, J.B.: Learning a probabilistic latent space of object shapes via 3d generative-adversarial modeling. In: Proceedings of the 30th International Conference on Neural Information Processing Systems, pp. 82–90 (2016)
68. Wu, R., Chen, X., Zhuang, Y., Chen, B.: Multimodal shape completion via conditional generative adversarial networks. In: Vedaldi, A., Bischof, H., Brox, T., Frahm, J.-M. (eds.) ECCV 2020. LNCS, vol. 12349, pp. 281–296. Springer, Cham (2020). https://doi.org/10.1007/978-3-030-58548-8_17
69. Yan, S., Xiong, Y., Lin, D.: Spatial temporal graph convolutional networks for skeleton-based action recognition. In: Thirty-second AAAI Conference on Artificial Intelligence (2018)
70. Yi, H., et al.: Human-aware object placement for visual environment reconstruction. In: Computer Vision and Pattern Recognition (CVPR) (2022)
71. Yin, T., Zhou, X., Krahenbuhl, P.: Center-based 3d object detection and tracking. In: Proceedings of the IEEE/CVF Conference on Computer Vision and Pattern Recognition, pp. 11784–11793 (2021)
72. Zhang, C., Cui, Z., Zhang, Y., Zeng, B., Pollefeys, M., Liu, S.: Holistic 3d scene understanding from a single image with implicit representation. In: Proceedings of the IEEE/CVF Conference on Computer Vision and Pattern Recognition (CVPR), pp. 8833–8842 (June 2021)
73. Zhang, S., Zhang, Y., Ma, Q., Black, M.J., Tang, S.: Place: Proximity learning of articulation and contact in 3d environments. In: 2020 International Conference on 3D Vision (3DV), pp. 642–651. IEEE (2020)
74. Zhang, Y., Hassan, M., Neumann, H., Black, M.J., Tang, S.: Generating 3d people in scenes without people. In: Proceedings of the IEEE/CVF Conference on Computer Vision and Pattern Recognition, pp. 6194–6204 (2020)
75. Zhu, Y., Zhao, Y., Chun Zhu, S.: Understanding tools: Task-oriented object modeling, learning and recognition. In: Proceedings of the IEEE Conference on Computer Vision and Pattern Recognition, pp. 2855–2864 (2015)

Towards Hard-Positive Query Mining for DETR-Based Human-Object Interaction Detection

Xubin Zhong[1], Changxing Ding[1,2](✉), Zijian Li[1], and Shaoli Huang[3]

[1] South China University of Technology, Guangzhou, China
{eexubin,eezijianli}@mail.scut.edu.cn, chxding@scut.edu.cn
[2] Pazhou Lab, Guangzhou, China
[3] Tencent AI-Lab, Shenzhen, China
shaolihuang@tencent.com

Abstract. Human-Object Interaction (HOI) detection is a core task for high-level image understanding. Recently, Detection Transformer (DETR)-based HOI detectors have become popular due to their superior performance and efficient structure. However, these approaches typically adopt fixed HOI queries for all testing images, which is vulnerable to the location change of objects in one specific image. Accordingly, in this paper, we propose to enhance DETR's robustness by mining hard-positive queries, which are forced to make correct predictions using partial visual cues. First, we explicitly compose hard-positive queries according to the ground-truth (GT) position of labeled human-object pairs for each training image. Specifically, we shift the GT bounding boxes of each labeled human-object pair so that the shifted boxes cover only a certain portion of the GT ones. We encode the coordinates of the shifted boxes for each labeled human-object pair into an HOI query. Second, we implicitly construct another set of hard-positive queries by masking the top scores in cross-attention maps of the decoder layers. The masked attention maps then only cover partial important cues for HOI predictions. Finally, an alternate strategy is proposed that efficiently combines both types of hard queries. In each iteration, both DETR's learnable queries and one selected type of hard-positive queries are adopted for loss computation. Experimental results show that our proposed approach can be widely applied to existing DETR-based HOI detectors. Moreover, we consistently achieve state-of-the-art performance on three benchmarks: HICO-DET, V-COCO, and HOI-A. Code is available at https://github.com/MuchHair/HQM.

Keywords: Human-object interaction · Detection transformer · Hard example mining

Supplementary Information The online version contains supplementary material available at https://doi.org/10.1007/978-3-031-19812-0_26.

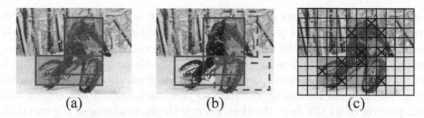

(a) (b) (c)

Fig. 1. Illustration of the hard-positive queries. (a) The green area represents important visual cues for HOI prediction of one human-object pair. (b) The dashed boxes are produced via Ground-truth Bounding-box Shifting (GBS), which only cover part of important image area and are then encoded into hard-positive queries. (c) Part of important visual cues are removed via Attention Map Masking (AMM), which increases the prediction difficulty of one positive query to infer HOI triplets. Best viewed in color. (Color figure online)

1 Introduction

Human-Object Interaction (HOI) detection is a fundamental task for human-centric scene understanding [2,3,51,53,54]. It aims to infer a set of HOI triplets $< human, interaction, object >$ from a given image [1,2]. In other words, it involves identifying not only the categories and locations of objects in an individual image, but also the interactions between each human-object pair. Recently, Detection Transformer (DETR)-based methods [4–7,52] have become popular in the field of HOI detection due to their superior performance and efficient structure. These methods typically adopt a set of learnable queries, each of which employs the cross-attention mechanism [33] to aggregate image-wide context information in order to predict potential HOI triplets at specific locations.

However, the learnable queries are usually weight-fixed after training [4,52]. Since each query targets a specific location [5,8], DETR-based methods are typically sensitive to changes in the object locations in testing images. Recent works improve DETR's robustness through the use of adaptive queries. For example, CDN [7] performs human-object pair detection before interaction classification occurs, generating adaptive interaction queries based on the output of the object detection part. However, its queries for object detection remain fixed. Moreover, two other object detection works [39,43] opt to update each object query according to the output embedding of each decoder layer. An object query is typically formulated as a single reference point of one potential object. Notably, this strategy may not be easy to apply in the context of HOI detection, since the interaction area for one human-object pair is usually more complex to formulate [13,28,29]. Therefore, current DETR-based methods still suffer from poor-quality queries.

In this paper, we enhance the robustness of DETR-based HOI detection methods from a novel perspective, namely that of Hard-positive Query Mining (HQM). In our approach, the robustness refers to the ability of DETR model to correctly predict HOI instances even using poor-quality queries with limited visual cues (or say inaccurate position). Accordingly, a hard-positive query refers to a query that corresponds to one labeled human-object pair, but is restricted to employ limited visual cues to make correct HOI predictions. First, as illustrated in Fig. 1(b), we explicitly generate such queries via Ground-truth Bounding-box Shifting (GBS). In more detail, we shift the two ground-truth (GT) bounding boxes in one labeled human-object pair so that each shifted box covers only a certain portion of its GT box. We then encode the coordinates of the two shifted boxes into an HOI query. Accordingly, the resultant query contains only rough location information about the pair. This strategy models the extreme conditions caused by variations in object location for fixed HOI queries.

Second, as shown in Fig. 1(c), we increase the prediction difficulty of positive queries by means of Attention Map Masking (AMM). The positive queries in AMM are those DETR's learnable queries matched with ground-truth according to bipartite matching [35]. In more detail, for each positive query, a proportion of the top scores in the cross-attention maps are masked. In this way, the positive query employs only part of the visual cues for prediction purposes. Specially, as our goal is to enhance the robustness of learnable queries, we select the masked elements according to the value of their counterparts in the learnable queries. Queries generated via GBS and AMM are less vulnerable to overfitting and capable of producing valuable gradients for DETR-based models. Finally, the robustness of DETR-based models is enhanced for the test images.

During each iteration of the training stage, the DETR's learnable queries and our hard-positive queries are utilized sequentially for prediction with shared model parameters and loss functions. To promote efficiency, GBS and AMM are alternately selected in each iteration. This Alternate Joint Learning (AJL) strategy is more efficient and achieves better performance than other joint learning strategies. Moreover, during inference, both GBT and AMM are removed; therefore, our method does not increase the complexity of DETR-based models in the testing stage.

To the best of our knowledge, HQM is the first approach that promotes the robustness of DETR-based models from the perspective of hard example mining. Moreover, HQM is plug-and-play and can be readily applied to many DETR-based HOI detection methods. Exhaustive experiments are conducted on three HOI benchmarks, namely HICO-DET [2], V-COCO [1], and HOI-A [13]. Experimental results show that HQM not only achieves superior performance, but also significantly accelerates the training convergence speed.

2   Related Works

Human-Object Interaction Detection. Based on the model architecture adopted, existing HOI detection approaches can be divided into two categories: Convolutional Neural Networks (CNN)-based methods [11,13,25] and transformer-based methods [4–7,30].

CNN-based methods can be further categorized into two-stage approaches [10,11,14,17,25,26] and one-stage approaches [13,28,29]. In general terms, two-stage approaches first adopt a pre-trained object detector [9] to generate human and object proposals, after which they feed the features of human-object pairs into verb classifiers for interaction prediction. Various types of features can be utilized to improve interaction classification, including human pose [10,11], human-object spatial information [15,21,24], and language features [14,25,26]. Although two-stage methods are flexible to include diverse features, they are usually time-consuming due to the cascaded steps. By contrast, one-stage methods are usually more efficient because they perform object detection and interaction prediction in parallel [13,28,29]. These methods typically depend on predefined interaction areas for interaction prediction. For example, UnionDet [29] used the union box of a human-object pair as interaction area, while PPDM [13] employed a single interaction point to represent interaction area. Recently, GGNet [28] utilized a set of dynamic points to cover larger interaction areas. However, the above predefined interaction areas may not fully explore the image-wide context information.

Recently, the transformer architecture has become popular for HOI detection. Most such methods are DETR-based [4–7,30,44,45]. These methods can be further divided into two categories: methods that employ one set of learnable queries for both object detection and interaction classification [4,6,44,45], and methods that utilize separate sets of queries for object detection and interaction prediction [5,7,30]. The above methods have achieved superior performance through their utilization of image-wide context information for HOI prediction. However, due to their use of weight-fixed queries, their performance is usually sensitive to location change of humans or objects.

DETR-Based Object Detection. The DETR model realizes end-to-end object detection by formulating the task as a set prediction problem [8]. However, due to its use of weight-fixed and semantically obscure HOI queries queries, it suffers from slow training convergence [39–43]. To solve this problem, recent works have largely adopted one of two main strategies. The first of these is to impose spatial priors on attention maps in the decoder layers to reduce semantic ambiguity. For example, Dynamic DETR [41] estimates a Region of Interest (ROI) based on the embedding of each decoder layer, then constrains the cross-attention operation in the next decoder layer within the ROI region. The second strategy involves updating queries according to the output decoder embeddings from each decoder layer [39,43]. Each query in these works is typically formulated through a single reference point of the object instance. However, it may not be straightforward to make similar formulations in the context of HOI detection. This is because HOI detection is a more challenging task that involves not only the detection of a single object, but also detection of the human instance and interaction category.

In this paper, we enhance the robustness of DETR-based models from a novel perspective, namely that of hard-positive query mining. Compared with existing approaches, our method is easier to implement and does not increase model complexity during inference. In the experimentation section, we further demonstrate that our approach achieves better performance than existing methods.

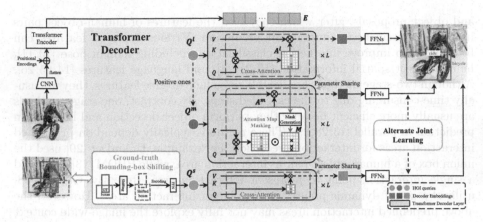

Fig. 2. Overview of HQM in the training stage based on QPIC [4]. In the interest of simplicity, only one learnable query Q^l and two hard-positive queries are illustrated. The hard-positive query Q^s is produced by GBS that encodes the coordinates of shifted bounding boxes of one human-object pair into a query. Another positive query Q^m is selected from the learnable queries according to bipartite matching with the ground-truth. The cross-attention maps of Q^m are partially masked to increase prediction difficulty. The two types of hard-positive queries are alternately selected in each iteration, and the chosen type of queries are utilized together with the learnble queries for loss computation. $\otimes$ and $\odot$ denote matrix multiplication and Hadamard product, respectively. In the inference stage, HQM is removed and therefore brings no extra computational cost. Best viewed in color. (Color figure online)

Hard Example Mining. HQM can be regarded as a hard example mining (HEM) approach to transformer-based HOI detection. HEM has demonstrated its effectiveness in improving the inference accuracy of CNN-based object detection models [49,50]. However, this strategy has rarely been explored in HOI detection. Recently, Zhong et al. [28] devised a hard negative attentive loss to overcome the problem of class imbalance between positive and negative samples for keypoint-based HOI detection models [12,13]. In comparison, HQM modifies DETR's model architecture in the training stage and resolves the problem caused by its use of poor-quality queries.

3 Method

HQM is plug-and-play and can be applied to many existing DETR-based HOI detection models. [4–7,30,44,45]. In this section, we take the representative work QPIC [4] as an example. The overall framework of QPIC [4] equipped with HQM is shown in Fig. 2. In the following, we first give a brief review of QPIC, which is followed by descriptions of two novel hard-positive query mining methods, e.g., GBS (Sect. 3.2) and AMM (Sect. 3.3). Finally, we introduce an alternate joint learning strategy to apply GBS and AMM (Sect. 3.4) efficiently.

3.1   Overview of Our Method

Revisit to QPIC. As shown in Fig. 2, QPIC is constructed by a CNN-based backbone, a transformer encoder, a transformer decoder, and feed-forward networks (FFNs). Each input image $\mathbf{I} \in \mathbb{R}^{H_0 \times W_0 \times 3}$ is first fed into the CNN backbone and the transformer encoder to extract flattened visual features $\mathbf{E} \in \mathbb{R}^{(H \times W) \times D}$. QPIC then performs cross-attention between learnable queries $\mathbf{Q}^l \in \mathbb{R}^{N_q \times D}$ and $\mathbf{E}$ in the transformer decoder. N_q is the number of learnable queries fixed after training. $H \times W$ and D denote the number of the image patches and feature dimension for each patch, respectively. Besides, the transformer decoder is typically composed of multiple stacked layers. For clarity, we only present the cross-attention operation in one decoder layer. The output embedding $\mathbf{C}_i \in \mathbb{R}^{N_q \times D}$ of the i-th decoder layer can be formulated as follows:

$$\mathbf{C}_i = \text{Concat}([\mathbf{A}_h^l \mathbf{E} \mathbf{W}_h^V]_{h=1}^T), \tag{1}$$

$$\mathbf{A}_h^l = \text{Softmax}(Att_h(\mathbf{Q}^l, \mathbf{C}_{i-1}, \mathbf{E})), \tag{2}$$

where T is the number of cross-attention heads. $\mathbf{A}_h^l \in \mathbb{R}^{N_q \times (H \times W)}$ is the normalized cross-attention map for the h-th head. $\mathbf{W}_h^V$ is a linear projection matrix. $Att_h(\cdot)$ is a function for similarity computation. Finally, as illustrated in Fig. 2, each output decoder embedding is sent to detection heads based on FFNs to obtain object class scores, interaction category scores, and position of the human and object instances.

Hard-Positive Query Mining. Most DETR-based HOI detection methods, e.g., QPIC, adopt poor-quality queries after training. As analyzed in Sect. 1, performance of weight-fixed queries is sensitive to the location change of human and object instances in testing images. In the following, we propose to promote the robustness of DETR-based models via hard-positive query mining. One hard-positive query refers to a query that corresponds to one labeled human-object pair, but is restricted to employ limited visual cues to infer correct HOI triplets (shown in Fig. 1).

As illustrated in Fig. 2, two strategies are introduced to produce hard-positive queries, i.e., GBS and AMM. Their generated queries are denoted as $\mathbf{Q}^s \in \mathbb{R}^{N_g \times D}$ and $\mathbf{Q}^m \in \mathbb{R}^{N_g \times D}$, respectively. N_g is the number of labeled human-object pairs in one training image. Similar to $\mathbf{Q}^l$, $\mathbf{Q}^s$ and $\mathbf{Q}^m$ are sent to the transformer decoder and their output decoder embeddings are forced to infer correct HOI triplets. $\mathbf{Q}^l$, $\mathbf{Q}^s$ and $\mathbf{Q}^m$ share all model layers and loss functions.

3.2   Ground-Truth Bounding-Box Shifting

Previous works have shown that each query attends to specific locations in one image [5,8]. To enhance DETR's robustness against the spatial variance of human-object pairs, we here explicitly compose hard-positive queries $\mathbf{Q}^s$ according to the GT position of labeled human-object pairs for each training image. As shown in Fig. 1(b), we shift the bounding boxes of labeled human-object pairs such that the shifted boxes only contain partial visual cues for HOI prediction.

Algorithm 1. Attention Map Masking for Each Attention Head

1: **Input:** attention maps $\mathbf{A}^m$, $\mathbf{A}^l \in \mathbb{R}^{H \times W}$ for a hard-positive query, K, γ
2: Get the indices I_K of the top-K elements in $\mathbf{A}^l$
3: Initialize a random binary mask $\mathbf{M} \in \mathbb{R}^{H \times W}$: $\mathbf{M}_{i,j} \sim Bernoulli(\gamma)$
4: **for** $\mathbf{M}_{i,j} \in \mathbf{M}$ **do**
5:     **if** $(i,j) \notin I_K$ **then**
6:         $\mathbf{M}_{i,j} = 1$
7:     **end if**
8: **end for**
9: **Output:** Masked attention map $\mathbf{A}^m = \mathbf{A}^m \odot \mathbf{M}$

Specifically, we encode a hard-positive query $\mathbf{q}^s \in \mathbf{Q}^s$ for one labeled human-object pair as follows:

$$\mathbf{q}^s = L_n(F_p(Shift(\mathbf{p}^s))), \tag{3}$$

where

$$\mathbf{p}^s = [x_h, y_h, w_h, h_h, x_o, y_o, w_o, h_o, x_h - x_o, y_h - y_o, w_h h_h, w_o h_o]^T. \tag{4}$$

The first eight elements in $\mathbf{p}^s$ are the center coordinates, width, and height of one GT human-object pair, respectively. $[x_h - x_o, y_h - y_o]$ denotes the relative position between the two boxes, respectively; while the last two elements are the areas of the two boxes. $Shift(\cdot)$ represents the shifting operation to GT bounding boxes (as illustrated in Fig. 2). $F_p(\cdot)$ is an FFN with two layers whose dimensions are both D. It projects $\mathbf{p}^s$ to another D-dimensional space. $L_n(\cdot)$ is a $tanh$ normalization function, which ensures the amplitudes of elements in $\mathbf{q}^s$ and the positional embeddings for $\mathbf{E}$ are consistent [52].

Compared with one concurrent work DN-DETR [55], GBS focuses on hard-positive query mining. To ensure the query is both positive and hard, we control the Intersection-over-Unions (IoUs) between each shifted box and its ground truth. We adopt low IoUs ranging from 0.4 to 0.6 in our experiment and find that GBS significantly improves the inference performance of DETR-based models.

3.3 Attention Map Masking

One popular way to enhance model robustness is Dropout [34]. However, applying Dropout directly to features or attention maps of $\mathbf{Q}^l$ may cause interference to bipartite matching [35], since the feature quality of the query is artificially degraded. To solve this problem, we implicitly construct another set of hard-positive queries $\mathbf{Q}^m$ via AMM after the bipartite matching of $\mathbf{Q}^l$. Queries in $\mathbf{Q}^m$ are copied from the positive queries in $\mathbf{Q}^l$ according to results by bipartite matching. As shown in Fig. 2, to increase the prediction difficulty of $\mathbf{Q}^m$, some elements in the cross-attention maps for each query in $\mathbf{Q}^m$ are masked. In this way, each query in $\mathbf{Q}^m$ is forced to capture more visual cues from the non-masked regions.

Detailed operations of AMM are presented in Algorithm 1. For clarity, only one hard-positive query $\mathbf{q}^m \in \mathbf{Q}^m$ is taken as an example, whose attention maps are denoted as $\mathbf{A}_h^m$ $(1 \leq h \leq T)$. For simplicity, we drop the subscripts of both $\mathbf{A}_h^m$ and $\mathbf{A}_h^l$ in the following.

AMM has two parameters, i.e., K and γ. Since our ultimate goal is to enhance the robustness of $\mathbf{Q}^l$ rather than $\mathbf{Q}^m$, we select dropped elements in $\mathbf{A}^m$ according to the value of their counterparts in $\mathbf{A}^l$. Specifically, we first select the top K elements according to the value in $\mathbf{A}^l$. Then, we randomly mask the selected K elements in $\mathbf{A}^m$ with a ratio of γ.

Discussion. AMM is related but different from Dropout and its variants [34, 36]. Their main difference lies in the way to select dropped elements. First, AMM drops elements with high values, while Dropout drops elements randomly. Second, AMM requires a reference, i.e., $\mathbf{A}^l$, for dropped element selection in $\mathbf{A}^m$. Dropout requires no reference. In the experimentation section, we show that AMM achieves notably better performance than the naive Dropout.

3.4 Alternate Joint Learning

The two hard-positive query mining methods, i.e., GBS and AMM, can be applied jointly to generate diverse hard queries. However, as DETR-based HOI detection methods typically require large number of training epochs to converge, it is inefficient to adopt both methods together in each iteration. We here present the Alternate Joint Learning (AJL) strategy, in which GBS and AMM are applied alternately for each training iteration. Concretely, the learnable queries of DETR and our hard queries are fed into the transformer decoder sequentially. The main reason for this lies in the design of AMM. The masked attention scores for hard queries are selected according to those of learnable queries (in Sect. 3.3). Therefore, learnable queries should pass the model first to provide attention scores. Compared to applying GBS and AMM together for each iteration, AJL is more efficient and achieves better performance in our experiments.

Overall Loss Function. We adopt the same loss functions for object detection and interaction prediction as those in QPIC [4]. The overall loss function in the training phase can be represented as follows:

$$\mathcal{L} = \alpha \mathcal{L}_l + \beta \mathcal{L}_h, \tag{5}$$

where

$$\mathcal{L}_l = \lambda_b \mathcal{L}_{l_b} + \lambda_u \mathcal{L}_{l_u} + \lambda_c \mathcal{L}_{l_c} + \lambda_a \mathcal{L}_{l_a}, \tag{6}$$

$$\mathcal{L}_h = \lambda_b \mathcal{L}_{h_b} + \lambda_u \mathcal{L}_{h_u} + \lambda_c \mathcal{L}_{h_c} + \lambda_a \mathcal{L}_{h_a}. \tag{7}$$

$\mathcal{L}_l$ and $\mathcal{L}_h$ denote the loss for learnable queries and hard-positive queries, respectively. $\mathcal{L}_{k_b}$, $\mathcal{L}_{k_u}$, $\mathcal{L}_{k_c}$, and $\mathcal{L}_{k_a}$ $(k \in \{l, h\})$ denote the L1 loss, GIOU loss [47] for bounding box regression, cross-entropy loss for object classification, and focal loss [48] for interaction prediction, respectively. These loss functions are realized in the same way as in [4]. Moreover, both α and β are set as 1 for simplicity; while λ_b, λ_u, λ_c and λ_a are set as 2.5, 1, 1, 1, which are the same as those in [4].

4 Experimental Setup

4.1 Datasets and Evaluation Metrics

HICO-DET. HICO-DET [2] is the most popular large-scale HOI detection dataset, which provides more than 150,000 annotated instances. It consists of 38,118 and 9,658 images for training and testing, respectively. There are 80 object categories, 117 verb categories, and 600 HOI categories in total.

V-COCO. V-COCO [1] was constructed based on the MS-COCO database [31]. The training and validation sets contain 5,400 images in total, while its testing set includes 4,946 images. It covers 80 object categories, 26 interaction categories, and 234 HOI categories. The mean average precision of Scenario 1 role (mAP_{role}) [1] is commonly used for evaluation.

HOI-A. HOI-A was recently proposed in [13]. The images are collected from wild; it is composed of 38,629 images, with 29,842 used for training and 8,787 for testing. HOI-A contains 11 object categories and 10 interaction categories.

4.2 Implementation Details

We adopt ResNet-50 [32] as our backbone model. Following QPIC [4], we initialize parameters of our models using those of DETR that was pre-trained on the MS-COCO database as an object detection task. We adopt the AdamW [46] optimizer and conduct experiments with a batch size of 16 on 8 GPUs. The initial learning rate is set as 1e-4 and then decayed to 1e-5 after 50 epochs; the total number of training epochs is 80. N_q and D are set as 100 and 256, respectively. For GBS, the IoUs between the shifted and ground-truth bounding boxes range from 0.4 to 0.6; while for AMM, K and γ are set as 100 and 0.4, respectively.

4.3 Ablation Studies

We perform ablation studies on HICO-DET, V-COCO, and HOI-A datasets to demonstrate the effectiveness of each proposed component. We adopt QPIC [4] as the baseline and all experiments are performed using ResNet-50 as the backbone. Experimental results are tabulated in Table 1.

Effectiveness of GBS. GBS is devised to explicitly generate hard-positive queries leveraging the bounding box coordinates of labeled human-object pairs. When GBS is incorporated, performance of QPIC is promoted by 1.50%, 1.39% and 1.13% mAP on HICO-DET, V-COCO, and HOI-A datasets, respectively. Moreover, as shown in Fig. 3(a), GBS also significantly accelerates the training

Table 1. Ablation studies on each key component of HQM. For HICO-DET, the DT mode is adopted for evaluation.

Method	Components					mAP			# Epochs
	GBS	AMM	CJL	PJL	AJL	HICO-DET	V-COCO	HOI-A	HICO-DET
Baseline	–	–	–	–	–	29.07	61.80	74.10	150
Incremental	✓	-	-	–	–	30.57	63.19	75.23	80
	-	✓	-	-	-	30.58	63.28	75.30	80
	✓	✓	✓	–	–	30.11	63.03	75.01	80
	✓	✓	–	✓	–	30.81	63.39	75.59	80
Our method	✓	✓	–	–	✓	**31.34**	**63.60**	**76.13**	80

convergence of QPIC. It justifies the superiority of GBS in improving DETR-based HOI detectors. We further evaluate the optimal values of IoUs and provide experimental results in the supplementary material.

Effectiveness of AMM. AMM is proposed to implicitly construct hard-positive queries using masking to cross-attention maps. As illustrated in Table 1, the performance of QPIC is notably improved by 1.51%, 1.48%, and 1.20% mAP on HICO-DET, V-COCO, and HOI-A datasets, respectively. Furthermore, as shown in Fig. 3(b), AMM also significantly reduces the number of training epochs required on the HICO-DET dataset. We also provide a detailed analysis for K and γ values in the supplementary material.

Combination of GBS and AMM. We here investigate three possible strategies that combine GBS and AMM for more effective DETR training, namely, Cascaded Joint Learning (CJL), Parallel Joint Learning (PJL) and Alternate Joint Learning (AJL).

Cascaded Joint Learning. In this strategy, we formulate GBS and AMM as two successive steps to produce one single set of hard-positive queries. In more details, we first apply GBS to produce one set of hard-positive queries. Then, we apply AMM to cross-attention maps of queries generated by GBS. As shown in Table 1, CJL achieves worse performance than the model using GBS or AMM alone. This may be because queries generated by CJL contain rare cues for HOI prediction, thereby introducing difficulties in optimizing DETR-based models.

Parallel Joint Learning. In this strategy, GBS and AMM are employed to generate one set of hard-positive queries, respectively. Then, both sets of hard-positive queries are employed for HOI prediction. To strike a balance between the loss of learnable queries and hard-positive queries, the loss weight for each type of hard-positive queries is reduced by one-half. Moreover, they are independent, which means there is no interaction between these two types of queries. As shown in Table 1, PJL achieves better performance than the model using GBS or AMM alone. Moreover, it outperforms QPIC by 1.74%, 1.59%, and 1.49% mAP on HICO-DET, V-COCO, and HOI-A datasets, respectively. However, PJL lowers the computational efficiency due to the increased number of hard-positive queries.

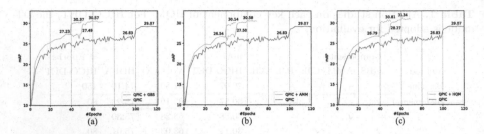

Fig. 3. The mAP and training convergence curves for QPIC and our method on HICO-DET. Our method significantly improves QPIC in both mAP accuracy and convergence rate.

Table 2. Effectiveness of GBS and AMM on HOTR and CDN in the DT Mode of HICO-DET.

Baseline	Incremental components			mAP		
	GBS	AMM	AJL	Full	Rare	Non-rare
HOTR	–	–	–	23.46	16.21	25.62
	✓	–	–	24.67	23.29	25.34
	–	✓	–	24.73	23.52	25.09
	✓	✓	✓	**25.69**	**24.70**	**25.98**
CDN	–	–	–	31.44	27.39	32.64
	✓	–	–	32.07	27.52	33.43
	–	✓	–	32.05	27.15	33.51
	✓	✓	✓	**32.47**	**28.15**	**33.76**

Table 3. Comparisons with variants of GBS on HICO-DET.

	Full	Rare	Non-rare
QPIC [4]	29.07	21.85	31.23
w/o $Shift(\cdot)$	29.61	22.67	31.68
w Gaussian noise	30.05	24.08	31.82
QPIC + GBS	**30.57**	**24.64**	**32.34**

Alternate Joint Learning. In this strategy, GBS and AMM are applied alternately for each training iteration. The learnable queries of DETR and our hard-positive queries are fed into the transformer decoder sequentially, meaning there is no interference between each other. As tabulated in Table 1, AJL outperforms other joint learning strategies. AJL also has clear advantages in efficiency compared with PJL. Moreover, it significantly promotes the performance of QPIC by 2.27%, 1.80%, and 2.03% mAP on the three datasets, respectively. The above experimental results justify the effectiveness of AJL.

Application to Other DETR-Based Models. Both GBS and AMM are plug-and-play methods that can be readily applied to other DETR-based HOI detection models, e.g., HOTR [5] and CDN [7]. The main difference between HOTR [5] and QPIC is that HOTR performs object detection and interaction prediction in parallel branches with independent queries. Here, we mainly apply HQM to its interaction detection branch. As presented in Table 2, HOTR+GBS (AMM) outperform HOTR by 1.21% (1.27%) mAP in DT mode for the full HOI categories. When AJL is adopted, the performance of HOTR is considerably improved by 2.23%, 8.49% and 0.36% mAP in DT mode for the full, rare and non-rare HOI categories, respectively. Besides, significant improvements can also be observed by applying our methods to CDN. Impressively, when incorporated with our method, performance of CDN is promoted by 1.03% mAP for the full HOI categories.

Table 4. Comparisons with variants of AMM on HICO-DET.

	Full	Rare	Non-rare
QPIC [4]	29.07	21.85	31.23
w/o top-K	30.06	24.10	31.84
w/o $\mathbf{A}^l$	30.11	24.28	31.85
w/o $\mathbf{Q}^m$	28.75	21.97	30.78
QPIC [4] + AMM	**30.58**	**25.48**	**32.10**

Table 5. Performance comparisons on HOI-A. D-based is short for DETR-based.

	Methods	Backbone	mAP
CNN-based	iCAN [25]	ResNet-50	44.23
	TIN [10]	ResNet-50	48.64
	GMVM [38]	ResNet-50	60.26
	C-HOI [37]	ResNet-50	66.04
	PPDM [13]	Hourglass-104	71.23
D-based	AS-Net [30]	ResNet-50	72.19
	QPIC [4]	ResNet-50	74.10
	QPIC [4] + **HQM**	ResNet-50	**76.13**

4.4 Comparisons with Variants of GBS and AMM

Comparisons with Variants of GBS. We compare the performance of GBS with its two possible variants. Experimental results are tabulated in Table 3.

First, 'w/o $Shift(\cdot)$' means removing the box-shifting operation in Eq. (4). This indicates that the ground-truth position of one human-object pair is leveraged for query encoding. Therefore, the obtained queries in this setting are easy-positives rather than hard-positives. It is shown that the performance of this variant is lower than our GBS by 0.96%, 1.97% and 0.66% mAP in DT mode for the full, rare and non-rare HOI categories respectively. This experimental result provides direct evidence for the effectiveness of hard-positive queries.

Second, 'w Gaussian noise' represents that we remove $Shift(\cdot)$ and add Gaussian noise to $\mathbf{q}^s$ in Eq. 3. This variant provides another strategy to generate hard-positive queries. Table 3 shows that GBS outperforms this variant by 0.52% mAP for the full HOI categories. The main reason is that operations in GBS are more explainable and physically meaningful than adding random Gaussian noise. This experiment justifies the superiority of GBS for producing hard-positive queries.

Comparisons with Variants of AMM. We here compare the performance of AMM with some possible variants, namely, 'w/o top-K', 'w/o $\mathbf{A}^l$', and 'w/o $\mathbf{Q}^l$'. Experimental results are tabulated in Table 4.

First, 'w/o top-K' is a variant that randomly masks elements rather than the large-value elements in an attention map with the same γ ratio. We can observe that the performance of this variant is lower than AMM by 0.52% in terms of DT mAP for the full HOI categories. Compared with this variant, AMM is more challenging since visual cues are partially removed. Therefore, AMM forces each query to explore more visual cues in unmasked regions, which avoids overfitting. This experiment further demonstrates the necessity of mining hard queries.

Second, 'w/o $\mathbf{A}^l$' means that we select the masked elements according to $\mathbf{A}^m$ rather than $\mathbf{A}^l$ in Algorithm 1. Compared with AMM, the mAP of this variant drops by 0.47%, 1.20%, 0.25% for the full, rare and non-rare HOI categories. This may be because the learnable queries rather than the hard-positive queries are employed during inference. Therefore, masking according to $\mathbf{A}^l$ can push the hard-positive queries to explore complementary features to those attended by the learnable ones. In this way, more visual cues can be mined and the inference power of learnable queries can be enhanced during inference.

Table 6. Performance comparisons on HICO-DET.

	Methods	Backbone	DT Mode		
			Full	Rare	Non-rare
CNN-based	InteractNet [27]	ResNet-50-FPN	9.94	7.16	10.77
	UnionDet [29]	ResNet-50-FPN	17.58	11.72	19.33
	PD-Net [16]	ResNet-152	20.81	15.90	22.28
	DJ-RN [15]	ResNet-50	21.34	18.53	22.18
	PPDM [13]	Hourglass-104	21.73	13.78	24.10
	GGNet [28]	Hourglass-104	23.47	16.48	25.60
	VCL [19]	ResNet-101	23.63	17.21	25.55
DETR-based	HOTR [5]	ResNet-50	23.46	16.21	25.62
	HOI-Trans [6]	ResNet-50	23.46	16.91	25.41
	AS-Net [29]	ResNet-50	28.87	24.25	30.25
	QPIC [4]	ResNet-50	29.07	21.85	31.23
	ConditionDETR [39]	ResNet-50	29.65	22.64	31.75
	CDN-S [7]	ResNet-50	31.44	27.39	32.64
	HOTR [5] + HQM	ResNet-50	25.69	24.70	25.98
	QPIC [4] + HQM	ResNet-50	31.34	26.54	32.78
	CDN-S [7] + HQM	ResNet-50	32.47	28.15	33.76

Table 7. Performance comparisons on V-COCO.

	Methods	Backbone	AP_{role}
CNN-based	DRG [18]	ResNet-50-FPN	51.0
	PMFNet [24]	ResNet-50-FPN	52.0
	PD-Net [16]	ResNet-152	52.6
	ACP [20]	ResNet-152	52.9
	FCMNet [22]	ResNet-50	53.1
	ConsNet [23]	ResNet-50-FPN	53.2
	InteractNet [27]	ResNet-50-FPN	40.0
	UnionDet [29]	ResNet-50-FPN	47.5
	IP-Net [12]	Hourglass-104	51.0
	GGNet [28]	Hourglass-104	54.7
DETR-based	HOI-Trans [6]	ResNet-101	52.9
	AS-Net [30]	ResNet-50	53.9
	HOTR [5]	ResNet-50	55.2
	QPIC [4]	ResNet-50	58.8
	CDN-S [7]	ResNet-50	61.7
	QPIC [4] + HQM	ResNet-50	**63.6**

Finally, 'w/o $\mathbf{Q}^m$' indicates that we apply the same masking operations as AMM to the attention maps of $\mathbf{Q}^l$ rather than those of $\mathbf{Q}^m$. In this variant, $\mathbf{Q}^m$ are removed and only $\mathbf{Q}^l$ are adopted as queries. It is shown that the performance of this setting is significantly lower than those of AMM. As analyzed in Sect. 3.3, applying dropout directly to attention maps of $\mathbf{Q}^l$ may degrade the quality of their decoder embeddings, bringing in interference to bipartite matching and therefore causing difficulties in optimizing the entire model.

4.5 Comparisons with State-of-the-Art Methods

Comparisons on HICO-DET. As shown in Table 6, our method outperforms all state-of-the-art methods by considerable margins. Impressively, QPIC + HQM outperforms QPIC by 2.27%, 4.69%, and 1.55% in mAP on the full, rare and non-rare HOI categories of the DT mode, respectively. When our method is applied to HOTR and CDN-S with ResNet-50 as the backbone, HOTR (CDN-S) + HQM achieves a 2.23% (1.03%) mAP performance gain in DT mode for the full HOI categories over the HOTR (CDN-S) baseline. These experiments justify the effectiveness of HQM in enhancing DETR's robustness. Comparisons under the KO mode are presented in the supplementary material.

Moreover, we compare the performance of HQM with Conditional DETR [39]. Conditional DETR relieves the weight-fixed query problem via updating queries according to decoder embeddings in each decoder layer. We extend this approach to HOI detection by using an interaction point to represent one potential human-object pair. To facilitate fair comparison, all the other settings are kept the same for HQM and Conditional DETR. Table 6 shows that HQM achieves better performance. The above experiments justify the superiority of HQM for improving the robustness of DETR-based models in HOI detection.

Comparisons on HOI-A. Comparison results on the HOI-A database are summarized in Table 5. The same as results on HICO-DET, our approach outperforms all state-of-the-art methods. In particular, QPIC + HQM significantly outperforms QPIC by 2.03% in mAP when the same backbone adopted.

Comparisons on V-COCO. Comparisons on V-COCO are tabulated in Table 7. It is observed that our method still outperforms all other approaches, achieving 63.6% in terms of AP_{role}. These experiments demonstrate that HQM can consistently improve the robustness of DETR-based models on HICO-DET, VCOCO, and HOI-A datasets.

4.6 Qualitative Visualization Results

As presented in Fig. 4, we visualize some HOI detection results and cross-attention maps from QPIC (the first row) and QPIC + HQM (the second row). It can be observed that QPIC + HQM captures richer visual cues. One main reason for this may be that QPIC + HQM is trained using hard-positive queries. Therefore, QPIC + HQM is forced to mine more visual cues to improve the model prediction accuracy during inference. More qualitative comparisons results are provided in the supplementary material.

Fig. 4. Visualization of HOI detection results and the cross-attention maps in one decoder layer on HICO-DET. Images in the first and second rows represent results for QPIC and QPIC+HQM, respectively. Best viewed in color. (Color figure online)

5   Conclusions

This paper promotes the robustness of existing DETR-based HOI detection models. We creatively propose Hard-positive Queries Mining (HQM) that enhances the robustness of DETR-based models from the perspective of hard example mining. HQM is composed of three key components: Ground-truth Bounding-box Shifting (GBS), Attention Map Masking (AMM), and Alternate Joint Learning (AJL). GBS explicitly encodes hard-positive queries leveraging coordinates of shifted bounding boxes of labeled human-object pairs. At the same time, AMM implicitly constructs hard-positive queries by masking high-value elements in the cross-attention scores. Finally, AJL is adopted to alternately select one type of the hard positive queries during each iteration for efficiency training. Exhaustive ablation studies on three HOI datasets are performed to demonstrate the effectiveness of each proposed component. Experimental results show that our proposed approach can be widely applied to existing DETR-based HOI detectors. Moreover, we consistently achieve state-of-the-art performance on three benchmarks: HICO-DET, V-COCO, and HOI-A.

Acknowledgments. This work was supported by the National Natural Science Foundation of China under Grant 62076101 and 61702193, the Program for Guangdong Introducing Innovative and Entrepreneurial Teams under Grant 2017ZT07X183, Guangdong Basic and Applied Basic Research Foundation under Grant 2022A1515011549, and Guangdong Provincial Key Laboratory of Human Digital Twin under Grant 2022B1212010004.

References

1. Gupta, S., Malik, J.: Visual semantic role labeling. arXiv preprint arXiv:1505.04474 (2015)
2. Chao, Y., Liu, Y., Liu, X., Zeng, H., Deng, J.: Learning to detect human-object interactions. In: WACV (2018)
3. Ji, J., Krishna, R., Fei-Fei, L., Niebles, J.: Action genome: Actions as compositions of spatio-temporal scene graphs. In: CVPR (2020)
4. Tamura, M., Ohashi, H., Yoshinaga, T.: QPIC: query-based pairwise human-object interaction detection with image-wide contextual information. In: CVPR (2021)
5. Kim, B., Lee, J., Kang, J., Kim, E., Kim, H.: HOTR: end-to-end human-object interaction detection with transformers. In: CVPR (2021)
6. Zou, C., et al.: End-to-end human object interaction detection with hoi transformer. In: CVPR (2021)
7. Zhang, A., et al.: Mining the Benefits of Two-stage and One-stage HOI Detection. In: NeurIPS (2021)
8. Carion, N., Massa, F., Synnaeve, G., Usunier, N., Kirillov, A., Zagoruyko, S.: End-to-end object detection with transformers. In: Vedaldi, A., Bischof, H., Brox, T., Frahm, J.-M. (eds.) ECCV 2020. LNCS, vol. 12346, pp. 213–229. Springer, Cham (2020). https://doi.org/10.1007/978-3-030-58452-8_13
9. Ren, S., He, K., Girshick, R., Sun, J.: Faster r-cnn: Towards real-time object detection with region proposal networks. In: NeurIPS (2015)
10. Li, Y., et al.: Transferable Interactiveness Knowledge for Human-Object Interaction Detection. In: CVPR (2019)
11. Gupta, T., Schwing, A., Hoiem, D.: No-frills human-object interaction detection: factorization, layout encodings, and training techniques. In: ICCV (2019)
12. Wang, T., Yang, T., Danelljan, M., Khan, F., Zhang, X., Sun, J.: Learning human-object interaction detection using interaction points. In: CVPR (2020)
13. Liao, Y., Liu, S., Wang, F., Chen, Y., Qian, C., Feng, J.: Ppdm: Parallel point detection and matching for real-time human-object interaction detection. In: CVPR (2020)

14. Ulutan, O., Iftekhar, A., Manjunath, B.: VSGNet: Spatial attention network for detecting human object interactions using graph convolutions. In: CVPR (2020)
15. Li, Y.: Detailed 2D–3D joint representation for human-object interaction. In: CVPR (2020)
16. Zhong, X., Ding, C., Qu, X., Tao, D.: Polysemy deciphering network for human-object interaction detection. In: Vedaldi, A., Bischof, H., Brox, T., Frahm, J.-M. (eds.) ECCV 2020. LNCS, vol. 12365, pp. 69–85. Springer, Cham (2020). https://doi.org/10.1007/978-3-030-58565-5_5
17. Zhong, X., Ding, C., Qu, X., Tao, D.: Polysemy deciphering network for robust human-object interaction detection. In: IJCV (2021)
18. Gao, C., Xu, J., Zou, Y., Huang, J.-B.: DRG: Dual relation graph for human-object interaction detection. In: Vedaldi, A., Bischof, H., Brox, T., Frahm, J.-M. (eds.) ECCV 2020. LNCS, vol. 12357, pp. 696–712. Springer, Cham (2020). https://doi.org/10.1007/978-3-030-58610-2_41
19. Hou, Z., Peng, X., Qiao, Yu., Tao, D.: Visual compositional learning for human-object interaction detection. In: Vedaldi, A., Bischof, H., Brox, T., Frahm, J.-M. (eds.) ECCV 2020. LNCS, vol. 12360, pp. 584–600. Springer, Cham (2020). https://doi.org/10.1007/978-3-030-58555-6_35
20. Kim, D.-J., Sun, X., Choi, J., Lin, S., Kweon, I.S.: Detecting human-object interactions with action co-occurrence priors. In: Vedaldi, A., Bischof, H., Brox, T., Frahm, J.-M. (eds.) ECCV 2020. LNCS, vol. 12366, pp. 718–736. Springer, Cham (2020). https://doi.org/10.1007/978-3-030-58589-1_43
21. Zhou, P., Chi, M.: Relation parsing neural network for human-object interaction detection. In: ICCV (2019)
22. Liu, Y., Chen, Q., Zisserman, A.: Amplifying key cues for human-object-interaction detection. In: Vedaldi, A., Bischof, H., Brox, T., Frahm, J.-M. (eds.) ECCV 2020. LNCS, vol. 12359, pp. 248–265. Springer, Cham (2020). https://doi.org/10.1007/978-3-030-58568-6_15
23. Liu, Y., Yuan, J., Chen, C.: ConsNet: learning consistency graph for zero-shot human-object interaction detection. In: ACM MM (2020)
24. Wan, B., Zhou, D., Liu, Y., Li, R., He, X.: Pose-aware Multi-level Feature Network for Human Object Interaction Detection. In: ICCV (2019)
25. Gao, C., Zou, Y., Huang, J.: ican: Instance-centric attention network for human-object interaction detection. In: BMVC (2018)
26. Wang, T., et al.: Deep contextual attention for human-object interaction detection. In: ICCV (2019)
27. Gkioxari, G., Girshick, R.: Detecting and recognizing human-object interactions. In: CVPR (2018)
28. Zhong, X., Qu, X., Ding, C., Tao, D.: Glance and gaze: inferring action-aware points for one-stage human-object interaction detection. In: CVPR (2021)
29. Kim, B., Choi, T., Kang, J., Kim, H.J.: Uniondet: Union-level detector towards real-time human-object interaction detection. In: Vedaldi, A., Bischof, H., Brox, T., Frahm, J.-M. (eds.) ECCV 2020. LNCS, vol. 12360, pp. 498–514. Springer, Cham (2020). https://doi.org/10.1007/978-3-030-58555-6_30
30. Chen, M., Liao, Y., Liu, S., Chen, Z., Wang, F., Qian, C.: Reformulating hoi detection as adaptive set prediction. In: CVPR (2021)
31. Lin, T.-Y., et al.: Microsoft COCO: common objects in context. In: Fleet, D., Pajdla, T., Schiele, B., Tuytelaars, T. (eds.) ECCV 2014. LNCS, vol. 8693, pp. 740–755. Springer, Cham (2014). https://doi.org/10.1007/978-3-319-10602-1_48
32. He, K., Zhang, X., Ren, S., Sun, J.: Deep residual learning for image recognition. In: CVPR (2016)

33. Vaswani, A., Shazeer, N., Parmar, N., Uszkoreit, J., Jones, L., Gomez, A.: Attention is all you need. In: NeurIPS (2017)
34. Srivastava, N., Hinton, G., Krizhevsky, A., Sutskever, I., Salakhutdinov, R.: Dropout: a simple way to prevent neural networks from overfitting. J. Mach. Learn. Res. **15**, 1929–1958 (2014)
35. Kuhn, H.: The Hungarian method for the assignment problem. In: Naval Research Logistics Quarterly (2020)
36. Ghiasi, G., Lin, T., Le, Q.: Dropblock: A regularization method for convolutional networks. In: Wiley Online Library (1955)
37. Zhou, T., Wang, W., Qi, S., Ling, H., Shen, J.: Cascaded human-object interaction recognition. In: CVPR (2020)
38. Pic leaderboard (2019). http://www.picdataset.com/challenge/leaderboard/hoi2019,
39. Meng, D.: Conditional DETR for fast training convergence. In: ICCV (2021)
40. Gao, P., Zheng, M., Wang, X., Dai, J., Li, H.: Fast convergence of DETR with spatially modulated CoAttention. In: ICCV (2021)
41. Dai, X., Chen, Y., Yang, J., Zhang, P., Yuan, L., Zhang, L.: Dynamic DETR: end-to-end object detection with dynamic attention. In: ICCV (2021)
42. Zhu, X., Su, W., Lu, L., Li, B., Wang, X., Dai, J.: Deformable DETR: deformable transformers for end- to-end object detection. In: ICLR (2020)
43. Liu, S., et al.: DAB-DETR: dynamic anchor boxes are better queries for DETR. In: ICLR (2022)
44. Yuan, H., Wang, M., Ni, D., Xu, L.: Detecting human-object interactions with object-guided cross-modal calibrated semantics. In: AAAI (2022)
45. Li, Z., Zou, C., Zhao, Y., Li, B., Zhong, S.: Improving human-object interaction detection via phrase learning and label composition. In: AAAI (2022)
46. Loshchilov, I., Hutter, F.: Decoupled weight decay regularization. In: ICLR (2018)
47. Rezatofighi, H., Tsoi, N., Gwak, J., Sadeghian, A., Reid, I., Savarese, S.: Generalized intersection over union: A metric and a loss for bounding box regression. In: CVPR (2019)
48. Lin, T., Goyal, P., Girshick, R., He, K., Dollar, P.: Focal loss for dense object detection. In: ICCV (2017)
49. Wang, X., Shrivastava, A., Gupta, A.: A-fast-rcnn: Hard positive generation via adversary for object detection. arXiv preprint arXiv:2201.12329 (2022)
50. Shrivastava, A., Gupta, A., Girshick, R.: Training region-based object detectors with online hard example mining. In: CVPR (2017)
51. Wang, K., Wang, P., Ding, C., Tao, D.: Batch coherence-driven network for part-aware person re-identification. In: TIP (2021)
52. Qu, X., Ding, C., Li, X., Zhong, X., Tao, D.: Distillation using oracle queries for transformer-based human-object interaction detection. In: CVPR (2022)
53. Lin, X., Ding, C., Zhang, J., Zhan, Y., Tao, D.: RU-Net: regularized unrolling network for scene graph generation. In: CVPR (2022)
54. Lin, X., Ding, C., Zhan, Y., Li, Z., Tao, D.: HL-Net: Heterophily learning network for scene graph generation. In: CVPR (2022)
55. Li, F., Zhang, H., Liu, S., Guo, J., Ni, L., Zhang, L.: Dn-detr: Accelerate detr training by introducing query denoising. In: CVPR (2022)

Discovering Human-Object Interaction Concepts via Self-Compositional Learning

Zhi Hou[1], Baosheng Yu[1(✉)], and Dacheng Tao[1,2]

[1] The University of Sydney, Sydney, Australia
zhou9878@uni.sydney.edu.au, baosheng.yu@sydney.edu.au
[2] JD Explore Academy, Beijing, China

Abstract. A comprehensive understanding of human-object interaction (HOI) requires detecting not only a small portion of predefined HOI concepts (or categories) but also other reasonable HOI concepts, while current approaches usually fail to explore a huge portion of unknown HOI concepts (i.e., unknown but reasonable combinations of verbs and objects). In this paper, 1) we introduce a novel and challenging task for a comprehensive HOI understanding, which is termed as **HOI Concept Discovery**; and 2) we devise a self-compositional learning framework (or **SCL**) for HOI concept discovery. Specifically, we maintain an online updated concept confidence matrix during training: 1) we assign pseudo labels for all composite HOI instances according to the concept confidence matrix for self-training; and 2) we update the concept confidence matrix using the predictions of all composite HOI instances. Therefore, the proposed method enables the learning on both known and unknown HOI concepts. We perform extensive experiments on several popular HOI datasets to demonstrate the effectiveness of the proposed method for HOI concept discovery, object affordance recognition and HOI detection. For example, the proposed self-compositional learning framework significantly improves the performance of 1) HOI concept discovery by over **10%** on HICO-DET and over **3%** on V-COCO, respectively; 2) object affordance recognition by over **9%** mAP on MS-COCO and HICO-DET; and 3) rare-first and non-rare-first unknown HOI detection relatively over **30%** and **20%**, respectively. Code is publicly available at https://github.com/zhihou7/HOI-CL.

Keywords: Human-object interaction · Hoi concept discovery · Object affordance recognition

1 Introduction

Human-object interaction (HOI) plays a key role in analyzing the relationships between humans and their surrounding objects [21], which is of great importance

Supplementary Information The online version contains supplementary material available at https://doi.org/10.1007/978-3-031-19812-0_27.

for deep understanding on human activities/behaviors. Human-object interaction understanding has attracted extensive interests from the community, including image-based [5,7,17,38,52], video-based visual relationship analysis [11,40], video generation [42], and scene reconstruction [63]. However, the distribution of HOI samples is naturally long-tailed: most interactions are rare and some interactions do not even occur in most scenarios, since we can not obtain an interaction between human and object until someone conducts such action in real-world scenarios. Therefore, recent HOI approaches mainly focus on the analysis of very limited predefined HOI concepts/categories, leaving the learning on a huge number of unknown HOI concepts [3,9] poorly investigated, including HOI detection and object affordance recognition [25,26,50]. For example, there are only 600 HOI categories known in HICO-DET [6], while we can find 9,360 possible verb-object combinations from 117 verbs and 80 objects.

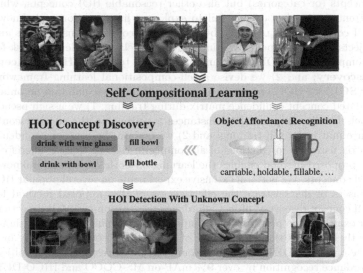

Fig. 1. An illustration of unknown HOI detection via concept discovery. Given some known HOI concepts (*e.g.*, "drink_with cup", "drink_with bottle", and "hold bowl"), the task of concept discovery aims to identify novel HOI concepts (i.e., reasonable combinations between verbs and objects). For example, here we have some novel HOI concepts, "drink_with wine_glass", "fill bowl", and "fill bottle". Specifically, the proposed self-compositional learning framework jointly optimizes HOI concept discovery and HOI detection on unknown concepts in an end-to-end manner.

Object affordance is closely related to HOI understanding from an object-centric perspective. Specifically, two objects with similar attributes usually share the same affordance, *i.e.* , humans usually interact with similar objects in a similar way [18]. For example, cup, bowl, and bottle share the same attributes (*e.g.*, hollow), and all of these objects can be used to "drink with". Therefore, object affordance [18,26] indicates whether each action can be applied into an object, *i.e.* , if a verb-object combination is reasonable, we then find a novel HOI concept/category. An illustration of unknown HOI detection via concept discovery is shown in Fig. 1. Recently, it has turned out that an HOI model is not only capable of detecting interactions, but also able to recognize object affordances [26], especially novel object affordances using the composite HOI features. Particularly, novel object affordance recognition also indicates discovering novel reasonable verb-object combinations or HOI concepts. Inspired by this, we can introduce a simple baseline for HOI concept discovery by averaging the affordance predictions of training dataset into each object category [26].

Nevertheless, there are two main limitations when directly utilizing object affordance prediction [26] for concept discovery. First, the affordance prediction approach in [26] is time-consuming and unsuitable to be utilized during training phrase, since it requires to predict all possible combinations of verbs and objects using the whole training set. By contrast, we introduce an online HOI concept discovery method, which is able to collect concept confidence in a running mean manner with verb scores of all composite features in mini-batches during training. Second, also more importantly, the compositional learning approach [26] merely optimizes the composite samples with known concepts (*e.g.*, 600 categories on HICO-DET), ignoring a large number of composite samples with unknown concepts (unlabeled composite samples). As a result, the model is inevitably biased to known object affordances (or HOI concepts), and leads to the similar inferior performance to the one in Positive-Unlabeled learning [12, 14, 46]. That is, without negative samples for training, the network will tend to predict high confidence on those impossible verb-object combinations or overfit verb patterns (please refer to Appendix A for more analysis). Considering that the online concept discovery branch is able to predict concept confidence during optimization, we can then construct pseudo labels [35] for all composite HOIs belonging to either known or unknown categories. Inspired by this, we introduce a self-compositional learning strategy (or SCL) to jointly optimize all composite representations and improve concept predictions in an iterative manner. Specifically, SCL combines the object representations with different verb representations to compose new samples for optimization, and thus implicitly pays attention to the object representations and improves the discrimination of composite representations. By doing this, we can improve the object affordance learning, and then facilitate the HOI concept discovery.

Our main contributions can be summarized as follows: 1) we introduce a new task for a better and comprehensive understanding on human-object interactions; 2) we devise a self-compositional learning framework for HOI concept discovery and object affordance recognition simultaneously; and 3) we evaluate the proposed approach on two extended benchmarks, and it significantly improves the performance of HOI concept discovery, facilitates object affordance recognition with HOI model, and also enables HOI detection with novel concepts.

2   Related Work

2.1   Human-Object Interaction

HOI understanding [21] is of great importance for visual relationship reasoning [58] and action understanding [4,64]. Different approaches have been investigated for HOI understanding from various aspects, including HOI detection [6,8,32,37,38,52,62,65,67], HOI recognition [7,28,31], video HOI [11,30], compositional action recognition [40], 3D scene reconstruction [10,63], video generation [42], and object affordance reasoning [15,26]. Recently, compositional approaches (e.g., VCL [25]) have been intensively proposed for HOI understanding using the structural characteristic [25,26,31,36,42]. Meanwhile, DETR-based methods (e.g., Qpic [52]) achieve superior performance on HOI detection. However, these approaches mainly consider the perception of known HOI concepts, and pay no attention to HOI concept discovery. To fulfill the gap between learning on known and unknown concepts, a novel task, i.e. , HOI concept discovery, is explored in this paper. Currently, zero-shot HOI detection also attracts massive interests from the community [2,25,27,45,50]. However, those approaches merely consider known concepts and are unable to discover HOI concepts. Some HOI approaches [2,45,55,56] expand the known concepts via leveraging language priors. However, that is limited to existing knowledge and can not discover concepts that never appear in the language prior knowledge. HOI concept discovery is able to address the problem, and enable unknown HOI concept detection.

2.2   Object Affordance Learning

The notation of affordance is formally introduced in   [18], where object affordances are usually those action possibilities that are perceivable by an actor [18,19,43]. Noticeably, the action possibilities of an object also indicate the HOI concepts related to the object. Therefore, object affordance can also represent the existence of HOI concepts. Recent object affordance approaches mainly focus on the pixel-level affordance learning from human interaction demonstration [13,15,16,23,34,41,61]. Yao et al. [60] present a weakly supervised approach to discover object functionalities from HOI data in the musical instrument environment. Zhu et al. [66] introduce to reason affordances in knowledge-based representation. Recent approaches propose to generalize HOI detection to unseen HOIs via functionality generalization [2] or analogies [45]. However those approaches focus on HOI detection, ignoring object affordance recognition. Specifically, Hou et al. [26] introduce an affordance transfer learning (ATL) framework to enable HOI model to not only detect interactions but also recognize object affordances. Inspired by this, we further develop a self-compositional learning framework to facilitate the object affordance recognition with HOI model to discover novel HOI concepts for downstream HOI tasks.

2.3   Semi-supervised Learning

Semi-supervised learning is a learning paradigm for constructing models that use both labeled and unlabeled data [59]. There are a wide variety of Deep Semi-supervised Learning methods, such as Generative Networks [33,51], Graph-Based methods [20,54], Pseudo-Labeling methods [24,35,57]. HOI concept discovery shares a similar characteristic to semi-supervised learning approaches. HOI concept discovery has instances of labeled HOI concepts, but no instances of unknown concepts. We thus compose HOI representations for unknown concepts according to [47]. With composite HOIs, concept discovery and object affordance recognition can be treated as PU learning [12]. Moreover, HOI concept discovery requires to discriminate whether the combinations (possible HOI concepts) are reasonable and existing. Considering each value of the concept confidences also represents the possibility of the composite HOI, we construct pseudo labels [35,47] for composite features from the concept confidence matrix, and optimize the composite HOIs in an end-to-end way.

3   Approach

In this section, we first formulate the problem of HOI concept discovery and introduce the compositional learning framework. We then describe a baseline for HOI concept discovery via affordance prediction. Lastly, we introduce the proposed self-compositional learning framework for online HOI concept discovery and object affordance recognition.

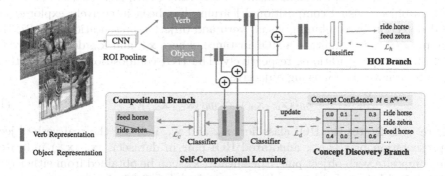

Fig. 2. Illustration of Self-Compositional Learning for HOI Concept Discovery. Specifically, following [25], verb and object features are extracted via RoI-Pooling from union box and object box respectively, which are then used to construct HOI features in HOI branch according to HOI annotation. Following [25], for SCL, verb and object features are further mutually combined to generate composite HOI features. Then, the feasible composite HOI features belonging to the known concepts are directly used to train the network in Compositional Branch. Here the classifier predicts verb classes directly. Meanwhile, we update the concept confidence $\mathbf{M} \in R^{N_v \times N_o}$, where N_v and N_o are the number of verb classes and object classes respectively, with the predictions of all composite HOI features. The concept discovery branch is optimized via a self-training approach to learn from composite HOI features with the concept confidence $\mathbf{M}$.

3.1   Problem Definition

HOI concept discovery aims to discover novel HOI concepts/categories using HOI instances from existing known HOI categories. Given a set of verb categories $\mathcal{V}$ and a set of object categories $\mathcal{O}$, let $\mathcal{S} = \mathcal{V} \times \mathcal{O}$ indicate the set of all possible verb-object combinations. Let $\mathcal{S}^k$, $\mathcal{S}^u$, and $\mathcal{S}^o$ denote three disjoint sets, known HOI concepts, unknown HOI concepts, and invalid concepts (or impossible verb-object combinations), respectively. That is, we have $\mathcal{S}^k \cap \mathcal{S}^u = \varnothing$ and $\mathcal{S}^k \cup \mathcal{S}^u = \mathcal{S}$ if $\mathcal{S}^o = \varnothing$. Let $\mathcal{T} = \{(h_i, c_i)\}_{i=1}^{L}$ indicate the training dataset, where h_i is a HOI instance (*i.e.* , verb-object visual representation pair), $c_i \in \mathcal{S}^k$ indicates the label of the i-th HOI instance and L is the total number of HOI instance.

We would also like to clarify the difference between the notations of "unknown HOI categories" and "unseen HOI categories" in current HOI approaches as follows. Let $\mathcal{S}^z$ indicate the set of "unseen HOI categories" and we then have $\mathcal{S}^z \subseteq \mathcal{S}^k$. Specifically, "unseen HOI category" indicates that the HOI concept is known but no corresponding HOI instances can be observed in the training data. Current HOI methods usually assume that unseen HOI categories $\mathcal{S}^z$ are known HOI categories via the prior knowledge [2,25,31,45,50]. Therefore, existing HOI methods can not directly detect/recognize HOIs with unknown HOI concepts. HOI concept discovery aims to find $\mathcal{S}^u$ from the existing HOI instances in $\mathcal{T}$ with only known HOI concepts in $\mathcal{S}^k$.

3.2   HOI Compositional Learning

Inspired by the compositional nature of HOI, *i.e.* , each HOI consists of a verb and an object, visual compositional learning has been intensively explored for HOI detection by combining visual verb and object representations [25–27,31]. Let $h_i = \langle \mathbf{x}_{v_i}, \mathbf{x}_{o_i} \rangle$ indicate a HOI instance, where $\mathbf{x}_{v_i}$ and $\mathbf{x}_{o_i}$ denote the verb and object representations, respectively. The HOI compositional learning then aims to achieve the following objective,

$$g_h(\langle \widetilde{\mathbf{x}}_{v_i}, \widetilde{\mathbf{x}}_{o_i} \rangle) \approx g_h(\langle \mathbf{x}_{v_i}, \mathbf{x}_{o_i} \rangle), \tag{1}$$

where g_h indicates the HOI classifier, $\mathbf{x}_{v_i}$ and $\mathbf{x}_{o_i}$ indicate the real verb-object representation pair (*i.e.* , annotated HOI pair in dataset), $\langle \widetilde{\mathbf{x}}_{v_i}, \widetilde{\mathbf{x}}_{o_i} \rangle$ indicates the composite verb-object pair. Specifically, $\widetilde{\mathbf{x}}_{o_i}$ can be obtained from either real HOIs [25], fabricated objects or language embedding [2,27,45], or external object datasets [26], while $\widetilde{\mathbf{x}}_{v_i}$ can be from real HOIs (annotated verb-object pair) and language embeddings [31,45]. As a result, when composite HOIs are similar to real HOIs, we are then able to augment HOI training samples in a compositional manner. However, current compositional approaches for HOI detection [25,26] simply remove the composite HOI instances out of the label space, which may also remove a large number of feasible HOIs (*e.g.*, "ride zebra" as shown Fig. 2). Furthermore, the compositional approach can not only augment the training data for HOI recognition, but also provide a method to determinate whether $\widetilde{\mathbf{x}}_{v_i}$ and $\widetilde{\mathbf{x}}_{o_i}$ are combinable to form a new HOI or not [26], *i.e.* , discovering the HOI concepts.

3.3   Self-compositional Learning

In this subsection, we introduce the proposed self-compositional learning framework for HOI concept discovery as follows. As shown in Fig. 2, the main HOI concept discovery framework falls into the popular two-stage HOI detection framework [25]. Specifically, we compose novel HOI samples from pair-wise images to optimize the typical HOI branch (annotated HOIs), compositional branch (the composite HOIs out of the label space are removed [25,26]) and the new concept discovery branch (all composite HOIs are used). The main challenge of HOI concept discovery is the lack of instances for unknown HOI concepts, but we can infer to discover new concepts according to the shared verbs and objects. Specifically, we find that the affordance transfer learning [26] can be used for not only the object affordance recognition but also the HOI concept discovery, and we thus first introduce the affordance-based method as a baseline as follows.

Affordance Prediction. The affordance transfer learning [26] or ATL is introduced for affordance recognition using the HOI detection model. However, it has been ignored that the affordance prediction can also enable HOI concept discovery, *i.e.* , predicting a new affordance for an object although the affordance is not labeled during training. We describe a vanilla approach for HOI concept discovery using affordance prediction [26]. Specifically, we predict the affordances for all objects in the training set according to [26]. Then, we average the affordance predictions according to each object category to obtain the HOI concept confidence matrix $\mathbf{M} \in R^{N_v \times N_o}$, where each value represents the concept confidence of the corresponding combination between a verb and an object. N_v and N_o are the numbers of verb and object categories, respectively. For simplicity, we may use both vector and matrix forms of the confidence matrix $\mathbf{M} \in R^{N_v N_o}$ and $\mathbf{M} \in R^{N_v \times N_o}$ in this paper. Though affordance prediction can be used for HOI concept discovery, it is time-consuming since it requires to predict affordances of all objects in training set. Specifically, we need an extra offline affordance prediction process to infer concepts with the computational complexity $O(N^2)$ in [26], where N is the number of total training HOIs, *e.g.*, it takes 8 h with one GPU to infer the concept matrix $\mathbf{M}$ on HICO-DET. However, we can treat the verb representation as affordance representation [26], and obtain the affordance predictions for all objects in each mini-batch during training stage. Inspired by the running mean manner in [29], we devise an online HOI concept discovery framework via averaging the predictions in each mini-batch.

Online Concept Discovery. As shown in Fig. 2, we keep a HOI concept confidence vector during training, $\mathbf{M} \in R^{N_v N_o}$, where each value represents the concept confidence of the corresponding combination between a verb and an object. To achieve this, we first extract all verb and object representations among pair-wise images in each batch as $\mathbf{x}_v$ and $\mathbf{x}_o$. We then combine each verb representation and all object representations to generate the composite HOI representations $\mathbf{x}_h$. After that, we use the composite HOI representations as the input to the verb classifier and obtain the corresponding verb predictions $\hat{\mathbf{Y}}_v \in R^{NN \times N_v}$, where N indicates the number of real HOI instances (*i.e.*, verb-object pair) in each mini-batch and NN is then the number of all composite verb-object pairs (including unknown HOI concepts). Let $\mathbf{Y}_v \in R^{N \times N_v}$ and $\mathbf{Y}_o \in R^{N \times N_o}$ denote the label of verb representations $\mathbf{x}_v$ and object representations $\mathbf{x}_o$, respectively. We then have all composite HOI labels $\mathbf{Y}_h = \mathbf{Y}_v \otimes \mathbf{Y}_o$, where $\mathbf{Y}_h \in R^{NN \times N_v N_o}$, and the superscripts h, v, and o indicate HOI, verb, and object, respectively. Similar to affordance prediction, we repeat $\hat{\mathbf{Y}}_v$ by N_o times to obtain concept predictions $\hat{\mathbf{Y}}_h \in R^{NN \times N_v N_o}$. Finally, we update $\mathbf{M}$ in a running mean manner [29] as follows,

$$\mathbf{M} \leftarrow \frac{\mathbf{M} \odot \mathbf{C} + \sum_i^{NN} \hat{\mathbf{Y}}_h(i,:) \odot \mathbf{Y}_h(i,:)}{\mathbf{C} + \sum_i^{NN} \mathbf{Y}_h(i,:)}, \tag{2}$$

$$\mathbf{C} \leftarrow \mathbf{C} + \sum_i^{NN} \mathbf{Y}_h(i,:), \tag{3}$$

where $\odot$ indicates the element-wise multiplication, $\hat{\mathbf{Y}}_h(i,:) \odot \mathbf{Y}_h(i,:)$ aims to filter out predictions whose labels are not $\mathbf{Y}_h(i,:)$, each value of $\mathbf{C} \in R^{N_v N_o}$ indicates the total number of composite HOI instances in each verb-object pair (including unknown HOI categories). Actually, $\hat{\mathbf{Y}}_h(i,:) \odot \mathbf{Y}_h(i,:)$ follows the affordance prediction process [26]. The normalization with $\mathbf{C}$ is to avoid the model bias to frequent categories. Specifically, both $\mathbf{M}$ and $\mathbf{C}$ are zero-initialized. With the optimization of HOI detection, we can obtain the vector $\mathbf{M}$ to indicate the HOI concept confidence of each combination between verbs and objects.

Self-Training. Existing HOI compositional learning approaches [25–27] usually only consider the known HOI concepts and simply discard the composite HOIs out of label space during optimization. Therefore, there are only positive data for object affordance learning, leaving a large number of unlabeled composite HOIs ignored. Considering that the concept confidence on HOI concept discovery also demonstrates the confidence of affordances (verbs) that can be applied to an object category, we thus try to explore the potential of all composite HOIs, i.e., both labeled and unlabeled composite HOIs, in a semi-supervised way. Inspired by the way used in PU learning [12] and pseudo-label learning [35], we devise a self-training strategy by assigning the pseudo labels to each verb-object combination instance using the concept confidence matrix $\mathbf{M}$, and optimize the network with the pseudo labels in an end-to-end way. With the self-training, the online concept discovery can gradually improve the concept confidence $\mathbf{M}$, and in turn optimize the HOI model for object affordance learning with the concept confidence. Specifically, we construct the pseudo labels $\tilde{\mathbf{Y}}_v \in R^{NN \times N_v}$ from the concept confidence matrix $\mathbf{M} \in R^{N_v \times N_o}$ for composite HOIs $\mathbf{x}_h$ as follows,

$$\tilde{\mathbf{Y}}_v(i,:) = \sum_j^{N_o} \frac{\mathbf{M}(:,j)}{\max(\mathbf{M})} \odot \mathbf{Y}_h(i,:,j), \tag{4}$$

where $0 \leq j < N_o$ indicates the index of object category, $0 \leq i < NN$ is the index of HOI representations. Here, N is the number of HOIs in each mini-batch, and is usually very small on HICO-DET and V-COCO. Thus the time complexity of Eq. 4 is small. The labels of composite HOIs are reshaped as $\mathbf{Y}_h \in R^{NN \times N_v \times N_o}$. Noticeably, in each label $\mathbf{Y}_h(i,:,:)$, there is only one vector $\mathbf{Y}_h(i,:,j)$ larger than 0 because each HOI has only one object. As a result, we obtain pseudo verb label $\tilde{\mathbf{Y}}_v(i,:)$ for HOI $\mathbf{x}_{h_i}$. Finally, we use composite HOIs with pseudo labels to train the models, and the loss function is defined as follows,

$$\mathcal{L}_d = \frac{1}{NN} \sum_i^{NN} (\frac{1}{N_v} \sum_k^{N_v} \mathcal{L}_{\text{BCE}}(\frac{\mathbf{Z}(i,k)}{T}, \tilde{\mathbf{Y}}_v(i,k))), \qquad (5)$$

where $\mathbf{Z}(i,:)$ is the prediction of the i-th composite HOI, $0 \leq k < N_v$ means the index of predictions, T is the temperature hyper-parameter to smooth the predictions (the default value is 1 in experiment), $\mathcal{L}_{\text{BCE}}$ indicates the binary cross entropy loss. Finally, we optimize the network using $\mathcal{L}_d$, $\mathcal{L}_h$ and $\mathcal{L}_c$ in an end-to-end way, where $\mathcal{L}_h$ indicate the typical classification loss for known HOIs and $\mathcal{L}_c$ is the compositional learning loss [25].

4   Experiments

In this section, we first introduce the datasets and evaluation metrics. We then compare the baseline and the proposed method for HOI concept discovery and object affordance recognition. We also demonstrate the effectiveness of the proposed method for HOI detection with unknown concepts and zero-shot HOI detection. Lastly, we provide some visualizations results of self-compositional learning. Moreover, ablation studies and the full results of HOI detection with self-compositional learning are provided in Appendix D, F, respectively.

4.1   Datasets and Evaluation Metrics

Datasets. We extend two popular HOI detection datasets, HICO-DET [6] and V-COCO [22], to evaluate the performance of different methods for HOI concept discovery. Specifically, we first manually annotate all the possible verb-object combinations on HICO-DET (117 verbs and 80 objects) and V-COCO (24 verbs and 80 objects). As a result, we obtain 1,681 concepts on HICO-DET and 401 concepts on V-COCO, *i.e.* , 1,681 of 9,360 verb-object combinations on HICO-DET and 401 of 1,920 verb-object combinations on V-COCO are reasonable. Besides, 600 of 1,681 HOI concepts on HICO-DET and 222 of 401 HOI concepts on V-COCO are known according to existing annotations. Thus, the HOI concept discovery task requires to discover the other 1,081 concepts on HICO-DET and 179 concepts on V-COCO. See more details about the annotation process, the statistics of annotations, and the novel HOI concepts in Appendix B.

Evaluation Metrics. HOI concept discovery aims to discover all reasonable combinations between verbs and objects according to existing HOI training samples. We report the performance by using the average precision (AP) for concept discovery and mean AP (or mAP) for object affordance recognition. For HOI detection, we also report the performance using mAP. We follow [26] to evaluate object affordance recognition with HOI model on COCO validation 2017 [39], Object 365 validation [49], HICO-DET test set [6] and Novel Objects from Object 365 [49].

4.2   Implementation Details

We implement the proposed method with TensorFlow [1]. During training, we have two HOI images (randomly selected) in each mini-batch and we follow [17] to augment ground truth boxes via random crop and random shift. We use a modified HOI compositional learning framework, *i.e.*, we directly predict the verb classes and optimize the composite HOIs using SCL. Following [25,27], the overall loss function is defined as $\mathcal{L} = \lambda_1 \mathcal{L}_h + \lambda_2 \mathcal{L}_c + \lambda_3 \mathcal{L}_d$, where $\lambda_1 = 2$, $\lambda_2 = 0.5$, $\lambda_3 = 0.5$ on HICO-DET, and $\lambda_1 = 0.5$, $\lambda_2 = 0.5$, $\lambda_3 = 0.5$ on V-COCO, respectively. Following [27], we also include a sigmoid loss for verb representation and the loss weight is 0.3 on HICO-DET. For self-training, we remove the composite HOIs when its corresponding concept confidence is 0, *i.e.*, the concept confidence has not been updated. If not stated, the backbone is ResNet-101. The Classifier is a two-layer MLP. We train the model for 3.0M iterations on HICO-DET and 300K iterations on HOI-COCO with an initial learning rate of 0.01. For zero-shot HOI detection, we keep human and objects with the score larger than 0.3 and 0.1 on HICO-DET, respectively. See more ablation studies (*e.g.*, hyper-parameters, modules) in Appendix. Experiments are conducted using a single Tesla V100 GPU (16 GB), except for experiments on Qpic [52], which uses four V100 GPUs with PyTorch [44].

4.3   HOI Concept Discovery

Baseline and Methods. We perform experiments to evaluate the effectiveness of our proposed method for HOI concept discovery. For a fair comparison, we build several baselines and methods as follows,

- **Random**: we randomly generate the concept confidence to evaluate the performance.
- **Affordance**: discover concepts via affordance prediction [26] as described in Sect. 3.3.
- **GAT** [53]: build a graph attention network to mine the relationship among verbs during HOI detection, and discover concepts via affordance prediction.
- **Qpic*** [52]: convert verb and object predictions of [52] to concept confidence similar as online discovery.
- **Qpic*** [52] **+SCL**: utilize concept confidence to update verb labels, and optimize the network (Self-Training). Here, we have no composite HOIs.

Table 1. The performance of the proposed method for HOI concept discovery. We report all performance using the average precision (AP) (%). SCL means self-compositional learning. SCL− means online concept discovery without self-training.

Method	HICO-DET		V-COCO	
	Unknown (%)	Known (%)	Unknown (%)	Known (%)
Random	12.52	6.56	12.53	13.54
Affordance [26]	24.38	57.92	20.91	95.71
GAT [53]	26.35	76.05	18.35	98.09
Qpic* [52]	27.53	87.68	15.03	13.21
SCL−	22.25	83.04	24.89	96.70
Qpic* [52] + SCL	28.44	88.91	15.48	13.34
SCL	**33.58**	**92.65**	**28.77**	**98.95**

Please refer to the Appendix for more details, comparisons (*e.g.*, re-training, language embedding), and qualitative discovered concepts with analysis.

Results Comparison. Table 1 shows affordance prediction is capable of HOI concept discovery since affordance transfer learning [26] also transfers affordances to novel objects. Affordance prediction achieves 24.38% mAP on HICO-DET and 21.36% mAP on V-COCO, respectively, significantly better than the random baseline. With graph attention network, the performance is further improved a bit. Noticeably, [26] completely ignores the possibility of HOI concept discovery via affordance prediction. Due to the strong ability of verb and object prediction, Qpic achieves 27.42% on HICO-DET, better than affordance prediction. However, Qpic has poor performance on V-COCO. The inference process of affordance prediction for concept discovery is time-consuming (over 8 h with one GPU). Thus we devise an efficient online concept discovery method which directly predicts all concept confidences. Specifically, the online concept discovery method (SCL−) achieves 22.25% mAP on HICO-DET, which is slightly worse than the result of affordance prediction. On V-COCO, the online concept discovery method improves the performance of concept discovery by **3.98%** compared to the affordance prediction. The main reason for the above observation might be due to that V-COCO is a small dataset and the HOI model can easily overfit known concepts on V-COCO. Particularly, SCL significantly improves the performance of HOI concept discovery from 22.36% to **33.58%** on HICO-DET and from 24.89% to **28.77%** on V-COCO, respectively. We find we can also utilize self-training to improve concept discovery on Qpic [52] (ResNet-50) though the improvement is limited, which might be because verbs and objects are entangled with Qpic. Lastly, we meanwhile find SCL largely improves concept discovery of known concepts on both HICO-DET and V-COCO.

4.4   Object Affordance Recognition

Following [26] that has discussed average precision (AP) is more robust for evaluating object affordance, we evaluate object affordance recognition with AP on HICO-DET. Table 2 illustrates SCL largely improves SCL− (without self-training) by **over 9%** on Val2017, Object365, HICO-DET under the same training iterations. SCL requires more iterations to converge, and SCL greatly improves previous methods on all datasets with 3M iterations (Please refer to Appendix for convergence analysis). Noticeably, SCL directly predicts verb rather than HOI categories, and removes the spatial branch. Thus, SCL without self-training (SCL−) is a bit worse than ATL. Previous approaches ignore the unknown affordance recognition. We use the released models of [26] to evaluate the results on novel affordance recognition. Here, affordances of novel classes (annotated by hand [26]) are the same in the two settings. We find SCL improves the performance considerably by **over 10%** on Val2017 and HICO-DET.

Table 2. Comparison of object affordance recognition with HOI network (trained on HICO-DET) among different datasets. Val2017 is the validation 2017 of COCO [39]. Obj365 is the validation of Object365 [49] with only COCO labels. Novel classes are selected from Object365 with non-COCO labels. ATL* means ATL optimized with COCO data. Numbers are copied from the appendix in [26]. Unknown affordances indicate we evaluate with our annotated affordances. Previous approaches [25,26] are usually trained by less 0.8M iterations (Please refer to the released checkpoint in [25, 26]). We thus also illustrate SCL under 0.8M iterations by default. SCL− means SCL without self-training. Results are reported by Mean Average Precision (%).

Method	Known affordances				Unknown affordances			
	Val2017	Obj365	HICO	Novel	Val2017	Obj365	HICO	Novel
FCL [27]	25.11	25.21	37.32	6.80	–	–	–	–
VCL [25]	36.74	35.73	43.15	12.05	28.71	27.58	32.76	12.05
ATL [26]	52.01	50.94	59.44	15.64	36.80	34.38	42.00	15.64
ATL* [26]	56.05	40.83	57.41	8.52	37.01	30.21	43.29	8.52
SCL−	50.51	43.52	57.29	14.46	44.21	41.37	48.68	14.46
SCL	**59.64**	**52.70**	**67.05**	14.90	**47.68**	**42.05**	**52.95**	14.90
SCL (3M iters)	72.08	57.53	82.47	18.55	56.19	46.32	64.50	18.55

4.5   HOI Detection with Unknown Concepts

HOI concept discovery enables zero-shot HOI detection with unknown concepts by first discovering unknown concepts and then performing HOI detection. The experimental results of HOI detection with unknown concepts are shown in Table 3. We follow [25] to evaluate HOI detection with 120 unknown concepts in two settings: rare first selection and non-rare first selection, *i.e.* , we select

Table 3. Illustration of HOI detection with unknown concepts and zero-shot HOI detection with SCL. K is the number of selected unknown concepts. HOI detection results are reported by mean average precision (mAP)(%). We also report the recall rate of the unseen categories in the top-K novel concepts. "K = all" indicates the results of selecting all concepts, $i.e.$, common zero-shot. * means we train Qpic [52] (ResNet-50) with the released code in zero-shot setting and use the discovered concepts of SCL to evaluate HOI detection with unknown concepts. Un indicates Unknown/Unseen, Kn indicates Known/Seen, while Rec indicates Recall.

Method	K	Rare first				Non-rare first			
		Un	Kn	Full	Rec (%)	Un	Kn	Full	Rec (%)
SCL	0	1.68	22.72	18.52	0.00	5.86	16.70	14.53	0.00
SCL	120	2.26	22.72	18.71	10.83	7.05	16.70	14.77	21.67
SCL	240	3.66	22.72	18.91	15.00	7.17	16.70	14.80	25.00
SCL	360	4.09	22.72	19.00	15.83	7.91	16.70	14.94	30.83
SCL	all	9.64	22.72	19.78	100.00	13.30	16.70	16.02	100.00
Qpic* [52]	0	0.0	**30.47**	24.37	0.00	0.0	23.73	18.98	0.0
Qpic* [52]	120	2.32	30.47	24.84	10.83	14.90	22.19	20.58	21.67
Qpic* [52]	240	3.35	30.47	25.04	15.00	14.90	22.79	21.22	25.00
Qpic* [52]	360	3.72	30.47	25.12	15.83	14.91	23.13	21.48	30.83
Qpic* [52]	all	15.24	30.44	27.40	100.00	21.03	23.73	23.19	100.00
ATL [26]	all	9.18	24.67	21.57	100.00	18.25	18.78	18.67	100.00
FCL [27]	all	13.16	24.23	22.01	100.00	18.66	19.55	19.37	100.00
Qpic + SCL	all	**19.07**	30.39	**28.08**	100.00	**21.73**	**25.00**	**24.34**	100.00

120 unknown concepts from head and tail classes respectively. Different from [25,27] where the existence of unseen categories is known and the HOI samples for unseen categories are composed during optimization, HOI detection with unknown concepts does not know the existence of unseen categories. Therefore, we select top-K concepts according to the confidence score during inference to evaluate the performance of HOI detection with unknown concepts (that is also zero-shot) in the default mode [6].

As shown in Table 3, with more selected unknown concepts according to concept confidence, the proposed approach further improves the performance on unseen categories on both rare first and non-rare first settings. Specifically, it demonstrates a large difference between rare first unknown concepts HOI detection and non-rare first unknown concepts HOI detection in Table 3. Considering that the factors (verbs and objects) of rare-first unknown concepts are rare in the training set [27], the recall is very low and thus degrades the performance on unknown categories. However, with concept discovery, the results with top 120 concepts on unknown category are improved by relatively **34.52%** (absolutely 0.58%) on rare first unknown concepts setting and by relatively **20.31%**

(absolutely 1.19%) on non-rare first setting, respectively. with more concepts, the performance on unknown categories is also increasingly improved.

We also utilize the discovered concept confidences with SCL to evaluate HOI detection with unknown concepts on Qpic [52]. For a fair comparison, we use the same concept confidences to SCL. Without concept discovery, the performance of Qpic [52] degrades to 0 on Unseen categories though Qpic significantly improves zero-shot HOI detection. Lastly, we show zero-shot HOI detection (the unseen categories are known) in Table 3 (Those rows where K is all). We find that SCL significantly improves Qpic, and *forms a new state-of-the-art* on zero-shot setting though we merely use ResNet-50 as backbone in Qpic. We consider SCL improves the detection of rare classes (include unseen categories in rare first and seen categories in non-rare first) via stating the distribution of verb and object. See Appendix D for more analysis, *e.g.*, SCL improves Qpic particularly for rare category on Full HICO-DET.

4.6   Visualization

Figure 3 illustrates the Grad-CAM under different methods. We find the proposed SCL focus the details of objects and small objects, while the baseline and VCL mainly highlight the region of human and the interaction region, *e.g.*, SCL highlights the details of the motorbike, particularly the front-wheel (last row). Besides, SCL also helps the model via emphasizing the learning of small objects (*e.g.*, frisbee and bottle in the last two columns), while previous works ignore the small objects. This demonstrates SCL facilitates affordance recognition and HOI concept discovery via exploring more details of objects. A similar trend can be observed in Appedix G (Qpic+SCL).

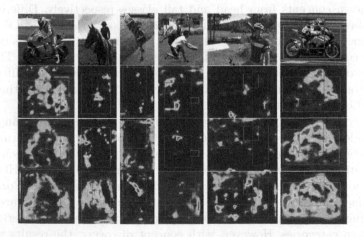

Fig. 3. A visual comparison of recent methods using the Grad-CAM [48] tool. The first row is input image, the second row is baseline without compositional approach, the third row is VCL [25] and the last row is the proposed SCL. We do not compare with ATL [26], since that ATL uses extra training datasets. Here, we compare all models using the same dataset.

5   Conclusion

We propose a novel task, Human-Object Interaction Concept Discovery, which aims to discover all reasonable combinations (*i.e.*, HOI concepts) between verbs and objects according to a few training samples of known HOI concepts/categories. Furthermore, we introduce a self-compositional learning or SCL framework for HOI concept discovery. SCL maintains an online updated concept confidence matrix, and assigns pseudo labels according to the matrix for all composite HOI features, and thus optimize both known and unknown composite HOI features via self-training. SCL facilitates affordance recognition of HOI model and HOI concept discovery via enabling the learning on both known and unknown HOI concepts. Extensive experiments demonstrate SCL improves HOI concept discovery on HICO-DET and V-COCO and object affordance recognition with HOI model, enables HOI detection with unknown concepts, and improves zero-shot HOI detection.

Acknowledgments. Mr. Zhi Hou and Dr. Baosheng Yu are supported by ARC FL-170100117, DP-180103424, IC-190100031, and LE-200100049.

References

1. Abadi, M., et al.: Tensorflow: a system for large-scale machine learning. In: 12th Symposium on Operating Systems Design and Implementation (OSDI), pp. 265–283 (2016)
2. Bansal, A., Rambhatla, S.S., Shrivastava, A., Chellappa, R.: Detecting human-object interactions via functional generalization. In: AAAI (2020)
3. Best, J.B.: Cognitive psychology. West Publishing Co (1986)
4. Carreira, J., Zisserman, A.: Quo vadis, action recognition? a new model and the kinetics dataset. In: CVPR, pp. 6299–6308 (2017)
5. Chao, Y.W., Liu, Y., Liu, X., Zeng, H., Deng, J.: Learning to detect human-object interactions. In: 2018 IEEE Winter Conference on Applications of Computer Vision (WACV), pp. 381–389. IEEE (2018)
6. Chao, Y.W., Liu, Y., Liu, X., Zeng, H., Deng, J.: Learning to detect human-object interactions. In: WACV, pp. 381–389. IEEE (2018)
7. Chao, Y.W., Wang, Z., He, Y., Wang, J., Deng, J.: HICO: a benchmark for recognizing human-object interactions in images. In: ICCV, pp. 1017–1025 (2015)
8. Chen, M., Liao, Y., Liu, S., Chen, Z., Wang, F., Qian, C.: Reformulating hoi detection as adaptive set prediction. In: CVPR, pp. 9004–9013 (2021)
9. Coren, S.: Sensation and perception. Handbook of psychology, pp. 85–108 (2003)
10. Dabral, R., Shimada, S., Jain, A., Theobalt, C., Golyanik, V.: Gravity-aware monocular 3d human-object reconstruction. In: ICCV, pp. 12365–12374 (2021)
11. Damen, D., et al.: Scaling egocentric vision: the dataset. In: Ferrari, V., Hebert, M., Sminchisescu, C., Weiss, Y. (eds.) ECCV 2018. LNCS, vol. 11208, pp. 753–771. Springer, Cham (2018). https://doi.org/10.1007/978-3-030-01225-0_44
12. De Comité, F., Denis, F., Gilleron, R., Letouzey, F.: Positive and unlabeled examples help learning. In: Watanabe, O., Yokomori, T. (eds.) ALT 1999. LNCS (LNAI), vol. 1720, pp. 219–230. Springer, Heidelberg (1999). https://doi.org/10.1007/3-540-46769-6_18

13. Deng, S., Xu, X., Wu, C., Chen, K., Jia, K.: 3D affordanceNet: a benchmark for visual object affordance understanding. In: Proceedings of the IEEE/CVF Conference on Computer Vision and Pattern Recognition, pp. 1778–1787 (2021)
14. Elkan, C., Noto, K.: Learning classifiers from only positive and unlabeled data. In: Proceedings of the 14th ACM SIGKDD international conference on Knowledge Discovery and Data Mining, pp. 213–220 (2008)
15. Fang, K., Wu, T.L., Yang, D., Savarese, S., Lim, J.J.: Demo2vec: reasoning object affordances from online videos. In: CVPR (2018)
16. Fouhey, D.F., Delaitre, V., Gupta, A., Efros, A.A., Laptev, I., Sivic, J.: People watching: human actions as a cue for single view geometry. IJCV **110**, 259–274 (2014)
17. Gao, C., Zou, Y., Huang, J.B.: iCAN: instance-centric attention network for human-object interaction detection. In: BMVC (2018)
18. Gibson, J.J.: The ecological approach to visual perception (1979)
19. Gibson, J.J.: The ecological approach to visual perception: classic edition. Psychology Press (2014)
20. Gilmer, J., Schoenholz, S.S., Riley, P.F., Vinyals, O., Dahl, G.E.: Neural message passing for quantum chemistry. In: ICML, pp. 1263–1272. PMLR (2017)
21. Gupta, A., Kembhavi, A., Davis, L.S.: Observing human-object interactions: using spatial and functional compatibility for recognition. IEEE PAMI **31**(10), 1775–1789 (2009)
22. Gupta, S., Malik, J.: Visual semantic role labeling. arXiv preprint arXiv:1505.04474 (2015)
23. Hassan, M., Dharmaratne, A.: Attribute based affordance detection from human-object interaction images. In: Huang, F., Sugimoto, A. (eds.) PSIVT 2015. LNCS, vol. 9555, pp. 220–232. Springer, Cham (2016). https://doi.org/10.1007/978-3-319-30285-0_18
24. Hinton, G., Vinyals, O., Dean, J.: Distilling the knowledge in a neural network. arXiv preprint arXiv:1503.02531 (2015)
25. Hou, Z., Peng, X., Qiao, Yu., Tao, D.: Visual compositional learning for human-object interaction detection. In: Vedaldi, A., Bischof, H., Brox, T., Frahm, J.-M. (eds.) ECCV 2020. LNCS, vol. 12360, pp. 584–600. Springer, Cham (2020). https://doi.org/10.1007/978-3-030-58555-6_35
26. Hou, Z., Yu, B., Qiao, Y., Peng, X., Tao, D.: Affordance transfer learning for human-object interaction detection. In: CVPR (2021)
27. Hou, Z., Yu, B., Qiao, Y., Peng, X., Tao, D.: Detecting human-object interaction via fabricated compositional learning. In: CVPR (2021)
28. Huynh, D., Elhamifar, E.: Interaction compass: Multi-label zero-shot learning of human-object interactions via spatial relations. In: ICCV, pp. 8472–8483 (2021)
29. Ioffe, S., Szegedy, C.: Batch normalization: accelerating deep network training by reducing internal covariate shift. In: ICML, pp. 448–456. PMLR (2015)
30. Ji, J., Desai, R., Niebles, J.C.: Detecting human-object relationships in videos. In: ICCV, pp. 8106–8116 (2021)
31. Kato, K., Li, Y., Gupta, A.: Compositional learning for human object interaction. In: Ferrari, V., Hebert, M., Sminchisescu, C., Weiss, Y. (eds.) Computer Vision – ECCV 2018. LNCS, vol. 11218, pp. 247–264. Springer, Cham (2018). https://doi.org/10.1007/978-3-030-01264-9_15
32. Kim, B., Lee, J., Kang, J., Kim, E.S., Kim, H.J.: HOTR: end-to-end human-object interaction detection with transformers. In: CVPR, pp. 74–83 (2021)
33. Kingma, D.P., Mohamed, S., Rezende, D.J., Welling, M.: Semi-supervised learning with deep generative models. In: NIPS (2014)

34. Kjellström, H., Romero, J., Kragić, D.: Visual object-action recognition: inferring object affordances from human demonstration. Comput. Vis. Image Underst. **115**(1), 81–90 (2011)
35. Lee, D.H., et al.: Pseudo-label: the simple and efficient semi-supervised learning method for deep neural networks. In: Workshop on challenges in representation learning, ICML (2013)
36. Li, Y.L., Liu, X., Wu, X., Li, Y., Lu, C.: Hoi analysis: integrating and decomposing human-object interaction. In: NeuIPS 33 (2020)
37. Li, Y.L., et al.: Transferable interactiveness prior for human-object interaction detection. In: CVPR (2019)
38. Liao, Y., Liu, S., Wang, F., Chen, Y., Feng, J.: PPDM: parallel point detection and matching for real-time human-object interaction detection. In: CVPR (2020)
39. Lin, T.-Y.: Microsoft COCO: common objects in context. In: Fleet, D., Pajdla, T., Schiele, B., Tuytelaars, T. (eds.) ECCV 2014. LNCS, vol. 8693, pp. 740–755. Springer, Cham (2014). https://doi.org/10.1007/978-3-319-10602-1_48
40. Materzynska, J., Xiao, T., Herzig, R., Xu, H., Wang, X., Darrell, T.: Something-else: Compositional action recognition with spatial-temporal interaction networks. In: CVPR, pp. 1049–1059 (2020)
41. Nagarajan, T., Grauman, K.: Learning affordance landscapes for interaction exploration in 3D environments. Adv. Neural. Inf. Process. Syst. **33**, 2005–2015 (2020)
42. Nawhal, M., Zhai, M., Lehrmann, A., Sigal, L., Mori, G.: Generating videos of zero-shot compositions of actions and objects. In: Vedaldi, A., Bischof, H., Brox, T., Frahm, J.-M. (eds.) ECCV 2020. LNCS, vol. 12357, pp. 382–401. Springer, Cham (2020). https://doi.org/10.1007/978-3-030-58610-2_23
43. Norman, D.A.: The design of everyday things. Basic Books Inc, USA (2002)
44. Paszke, A., et al.: PyTorch: an imperative style, high-performance deep learning library. In: Wallach, H., Larochelle, H., Beygelzimer, A., d'Alché-Buc, F., Fox, E., Garnett, R. (eds.) NeurIPS, pp. 8024–8035. Curran Associates, Inc. (2019). https://papers.neurips.cc/paper/9015-pytorch-an-imperative-style-high-performance-deep-learning-library.pdf
45. Peyre, J., Laptev, I., Schmid, C., Sivic, J.: Detecting unseen visual relations using analogies. In: ICCV (2019)
46. Scott, C., Blanchard, G.: Novelty detection: Unlabeled data definitely help. In: Artificial intelligence and statistics, pp. 464–471. PMLR (2009)
47. Scudder, H.: Probability of error of some adaptive pattern-recognition machines. IEEE Trans. Inf. Theory **11**(3), 363–371 (1965)
48. Selvaraju, R.R., Cogswell, M., Das, A., Vedantam, R., Parikh, D., Batra, D.: Grad-cam: Visual explanations from deep networks via gradient-based localization. In: ICCV (2017)
49. Shao, S., Li, Z., Zhang, T., Peng, C., Sun, J.: Objects365: a large-scale, high-quality dataset for object detection. In: ICCV (2019)
50. Shen, L., Yeung, S., Hoffman, J., Mori, G., Fei-Fei, L.: Scaling human-object interaction recognition through zero-shot learning. In: WACV, pp. 1568–1576. IEEE (2018)
51. Springenberg, J.T.: Unsupervised and semi-supervised learning with categorical generative adversarial networks. arXiv preprint arXiv:1511.06390 (2015)
52. Tamura, M., Ohashi, H., Yoshinaga, T.: QPIC: Query-based pairwise human-object interaction detection with image-wide contextual information. In: CVPR (2021)
53. Veličković, P., Cucurull, G., Casanova, A., Romero, A., Lio, P., Bengio, Y.: Graph attention networks. In: ICLR (2017)

54. Wang, D., Cui, P., Zhu, W.: Structural deep network embedding. In: Proceedings of the 22nd ACM SIGKDD international conference on Knowledge Discovery and Data Mining, pp. 1225–1234 (2016)
55. Wang, S., Yap, K.H., Ding, H., Wu, J., Yuan, J., Tan, Y.P.: Discovering human interactions with large-vocabulary objects via query and multi-scale detection. In: Proceedings of the IEEE/CVF International Conference on Computer Vision, pp. 13475–13484 (2021)
56. Wang, S., Yap, K.H., Yuan, J., Tan, Y.P.: Discovering human interactions with novel objects via zero-shot learning. In: CVPR, pp. 11652–11661 (2020)
57. Xie, Q., Luong, M.T., Hovy, E., Le, Q.V.: Self-training with noisy student improves imageNet classification. In: CVPR, pp. 10687–10698 (2020)
58. Xu, D., Zhu, Y., Choy, C.B., Fei-Fei, L.: Scene graph generation by iterative message passing. In: Proceedings of the IEEE Conference on Computer Vision and Pattern Recognition, pp. 5410–5419 (2017)
59. Yang, X., Song, Z., King, I., Xu, Z.: A survey on deep semi-supervised learning. arXiv preprint arXiv:2103.00550 (2021)
60. Yao, B., Ma, J., Li, F.F.: Discovering object functionality. In: ICCV (2013)
61. Zhai, W., Luo, H., Zhang, J., Cao, Y., Tao, D.: One-shot object affordance detection in the wild. arXiv preprint arXiv:2108.03658 (2021)
62. Zhang, A., et al.: Mining the benefits of two-stage and one-stage hoi detection. In: Advances in Neural Information Processing Systems, vol. 34 (2021)
63. Zhang, J.Y., Pepose, S., Joo, H., Ramanan, D., Malik, J., Kanazawa, A.: Perceiving 3D human-object spatial arrangements from a single image in the wild. In: Vedaldi, A., Bischof, H., Brox, T., Frahm, J.-M. (eds.) ECCV 2020. LNCS, vol. 12357, pp. 34–51. Springer, Cham (2020). https://doi.org/10.1007/978-3-030-58610-2_3
64. Zheng, S., Chen, S., Jin, Q.: Skeleton-based interactive graph network for human object interaction detection. In: 2020 IEEE International Conference on Multimedia and Expo (ICME), pp. 1–6. IEEE (2020)
65. Zhong, X., Ding, C., Qu, X., Tao, D.: Polysemy deciphering network for human-object interaction detection. In: Vedaldi, A., Bischof, H., Brox, T., Frahm, J.-M. (eds.) ECCV 2020. LNCS, vol. 12365, pp. 69–85. Springer, Cham (2020). https://doi.org/10.1007/978-3-030-58565-5_5
66. Zhu, Y., Fathi, A., Fei-Fei, L.: Reasoning about object affordances in a knowledge base representation. In: Fleet, D., Pajdla, T., Schiele, B., Tuytelaars, T. (eds.) ECCV 2014. LNCS, vol. 8690, pp. 408–424. Springer, Cham (2014). https://doi.org/10.1007/978-3-319-10605-2_27
67. Zou, C., et al.: End-to-end human object interaction detection with hoi transformer. In: CVPR, pp. 11825–11834 (2021)

Primitive-Based Shape Abstraction
via Nonparametric Bayesian Inference

Yuwei Wu[1], Weixiao Liu[1,2], Sipu Ruan[1], and Gregory S. Chirikjian[1(✉)]

[1] National University of Singapore, Singapore, Singapore
{yw.wu,mpewxl,ruansp,mpegre}@nus.edu.sg
[2] Johns Hopkins University, Baltimore, USA

Abstract. 3D shape abstraction has drawn great interest over the years. Apart from low-level representations such as meshes and voxels, researchers also seek to semantically abstract complex objects with basic geometric primitives. Recent deep learning methods rely heavily on datasets, with limited generality to unseen categories. Furthermore, abstracting an object accurately yet with a small number of primitives still remains a challenge. In this paper, we propose a novel nonparametric Bayesian statistical method to infer an abstraction, consisting of an unknown number of geometric primitives, from a point cloud. We model the generation of points as observations sampled from an infinite mixture of Gaussian Superquadric Taper Models (GSTM). Our approach formulates the abstraction as a clustering problem, in which: 1) each point is assigned to a cluster via the Chinese Restaurant Process (CRP); 2) a primitive representation is optimized for each cluster, and 3) a merging post-process is incorporated to provide a concise representation. We conduct extensive experiments on two datasets. The results indicate that our method outperforms the state-of-the-art in terms of accuracy and is generalizable to various types of objects.

Keywords: Superquadrics · Nonparametric Bayesian · Shape abstraction

1 Introduction

Over the years, 3D shape abstraction has received considerable attention. Low-level representations such as meshes [12,19], voxels [2,10], point clouds [1,13] and implicit surfaces [16,27] have succeeded in representing 3D shapes with accuracy and rich features. However, they cannot reveal the part-level geometric features of an object. Humans, on the other hand, are inclined to perceive the environment by parts [34]. Studies have shown that the human visual system

Supplementary Information The online version contains supplementary material available at https://doi.org/10.1007/978-3-031-19812-0_28.

makes tremendous use of part-level description to guide the perception of the environment [43]. As a result, the part-based abstraction of an object appears to be a promising way to allow a machine to perceive the environment more intelligently and hence perform higher-level tasks like decision-making and planning. Inspired by those advantages, researchers seek to abstract objects with volumetric primitives, such as polyhedral shapes [37], spheres [21] and cuboids [28,42,47,48]. Those primitives, however, are very limited in shape expressivity and suffer from accuracy issues. Superquadrics, on the other hand, are a family of geometric surfaces that include common shapes such as spheres, cuboids, cylinders, octahedra, and shapes in between, but are only encoded by five parameters. By further applying global deformations, they can express shapes such as square frustums, cones, and teardrop shapes. Due to their rich shape vocabulary, superquadrics have been widely applied in robotics, *e.g.* grasping [35,44,45], collision detection [39], and motion planning [38] (Fig. 1).

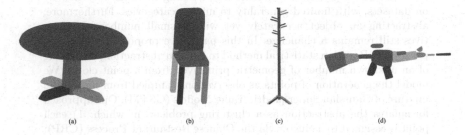

Fig. 1. (a)–(d) Examples of multi-tapered-superquadric-based structures of a table, chair, cloth rack, and rifle, inferred by our proposed method.

The authors of [8,25] pioneered abstracting superquadric-based representations from complex objects. Recently, the authors in [26] developed a hierarchical process to abstract superquadric-based structures. But, their method necessitates that an object has a hierarchical geometric structure. In [31,33], the authors utilize deep learning techniques to infer superquadric representations from voxels or images. However, the data-driven approaches show limitations in abstraction accuracy and generality beyond the training dataset.

Our work focuses on accurately abstracting a multi-tapered-superquadric-based representation of a point cloud using a small number of primitives. By assuming that an object is composed of superquadric-like components, we can regard the problem as a clustering task, which provides a means for us to reason about which portion of the point set can be properly fitted by a single tapered superquadric and thus belongs to the same cluster. The collection of tapered superquadrics fitted to each cluster constitutes the multi-tapered-superquadric-based model. Inspired by the work [26] in which the authors construct a Gaussian model around a superquadric, we build a probabilistic model by mixing Gaussian components to account for numerous components of an object. Since the number of components of an object is unknown in advance and varies case by case, we adapt our model to a nonparametric perspective to assure generality. Gibbs sampling is applied to infer the posterior distribution, in which we incorporate both an optimization method [26] for recovering superquadrics accurately from the point set and a merging process for minimizing the number of primitives, leading to a more exact, compact, and interpretable representation. Evaluations on Shapenet [7] and D-FAUST [6] corroborate the superior performance of our method in the abstraction of 3D objects.

2 Related Work

In this section, we cover the mathematical definition of superquadrics and discuss relevant work on 3D representations.

2.1 Superquadrics

Superquadrics [4] are a family of geometric surfaces that include common shapes, such as spheres, cuboids, cylinders, and octahedra, but only encoded by five parameters. A superquadric surface can be parameterized by $\omega \in (-\pi, \pi]$ and $\eta \in [-\frac{\pi}{2}, \frac{\pi}{2}]$:

$$\mathbf{p}(\eta, \omega) = \begin{bmatrix} C_\eta^{\varepsilon_1} \\ a_z S_\eta^{\varepsilon_1} \end{bmatrix} \otimes \begin{bmatrix} a_x C_\omega^{\varepsilon_2} \\ a_y S_\omega^{\varepsilon_2} \end{bmatrix} = \begin{bmatrix} a_x C_\eta^{\varepsilon_1} C_\omega^{\varepsilon_2} \\ a_y C_\eta^{\varepsilon_1} S_\omega^{\varepsilon_2} \\ a_z S_\eta^{\varepsilon_1} \end{bmatrix} \tag{1}$$

$$C_\alpha^\varepsilon \triangleq \mathrm{sgn}(\cos(\alpha))|\cos(\alpha)|^\varepsilon, \ S_\alpha^\varepsilon \triangleq \mathrm{sgn}(\sin(\alpha))|\sin(\alpha)|^\varepsilon,$$

where $\otimes$ denotes the spherical product [4], ε_1 and ε_2 define the sharpness of the shape, and a_x, a_y, and a_z control the size and aspect ratio. Equation 1 is defined within the superquadric canonical frame. The expressiveness of a superquadric can be further extended with global deformations such as bending, tapering, and twisting [5]. In our work, we apply a linear tapering transformation along z-axis defined as follows:

$$x' = \left(\frac{k_x}{a_3} z + 1\right) x, \ y' = \left(\frac{k_y}{a_3} z + 1\right) y, \ z' = z, \tag{2}$$

where $-1 \leq k_x, k_y \leq 1$ are tapering factors, (x, y, z) and (x', y', z') are untapered and tapered coordinates, respectively. To have a superquadric with a general pose, we apply a Euclidean transformation $g = [\mathbf{R} \in SO(3), \mathbf{t} \in \mathbb{R}^3] \in SE(3)$ to it. Thus, a tapered superquadric $\mathcal{S}_\theta$ is fully parameterized by $\theta = [\varepsilon_1, \varepsilon_2, a_x, a_y, a_z, g, k_x, k_y]$ (Fig. 2).

2.2 3D Representations

Based on how a 3D shape is represented, we can categorize it as a low-level or semantic representation.

Fig. 2. (a) Examples of tapering: a cylinder can be tapered to a cone and a cuboid can be tapered to a square frustum. (b) Part-based models inferred by SQs [33]. The left one is the original mesh; the middle one is the superquadrics representation inferred from the network trained on the chair category; the right one is inferred from the network trained on the table category, indicating a limited generality of the DL approach.

Low-Level Representations. Standard 3D representations such as voxels, point clouds, and meshes have been extensively studied. In the work of [2,10,20,36,40,41], the authors try to recover voxel models from images, which represents the 3D shapes as a regular grid. A high-resolution voxel model requires a large amount of memory, which limits its applications. Point clouds are a more memory-efficient way to represent 3D shapes that are utilized in [1,13], but they fail to reveal surface connectivity. Hence, researchers also turn to exploiting meshes [12,19,23,24,29,46] to show connections between points. Additionally, using implicit surface functions to represent 3D shapes has gained a lot of popularity [3,9,15,16,27,30]. Although those representations can capture detailed 3D shapes, they lack interpretability as they cannot identify the semantic structures of objects.

Part-Based Semantic Representations. To abstract the semantic structures of objects, researchers have attempted to exploit various kinds of volumetric primitives such as polyhedral shapes [37], spheres [21] and cuboids [28,42,48]. However, their results are limited due to the shape-expressiveness of the primitives. Superquadrics, on the other hand, are more expressive. The authors of [8,25] are pioneers in abstracting part-based structures from complex objects using superquadrics. They first segmented a complex object into parts and then fitted a single superquadric for each part. However, their work suffers from limited accuracy. Recently, the authors in [26] proposed a fast, robust, and accurate method to recover a single superquadric from point clouds. They exploited the symmetry of the superquadrics to avoid local optima and constructed a probabilistic model to reject outliers. Based on the single superquadric recovery, they developed a hierarchical way to represent a complex object with multiple superquadrics. The method is effective but requires that an object possess an inherent hierarchical structure. Another line of primitive-based abstraction is by deep learning [31–33]. Their networks demonstrate the ability to capture fine details of complex objects. However, the data-driven DL approaches are less generalizable to unseen categories. Besides, they are of a semantic-level approximation, which is lack accuracy. Instead, our method builds a probabilistic model to reason about primitive-based structures case by case, ensuring generality. Moreover, optimizations are incorporated to yield a more accurate representation for each semantic part.

3 Method

3.1 Nonparametric Clustering Formulation

In this section, we will show how to cast the problem of superquadric-based abstraction into the nonparametric clustering framework. To begin with, we model how a random point (observation) x is sampled from a superquadric primitive. First, for a superquadric parameterized by $\boldsymbol{\theta} = [\varepsilon_1, \varepsilon_2, a_x, a_y, a_z, g, k_x, k_y]$, a point $\boldsymbol{\mu} \in \mathcal{S}_{\bar{\theta}}$, where $\bar{\boldsymbol{\theta}} = [\varepsilon_1, \varepsilon_2, a_x, a_y, a_z, (I_3, \mathbf{0}), 0, 0]$, is randomly selected across the whole surface; a noise factor τ is sampled from an univariate Gaussian distribution $\tau \sim \mathcal{N}(0, \sigma^2)$. Then, an point $\bar{x}$ is generated as

$$\bar{x} = (1 + \frac{\tau}{|\boldsymbol{\mu}|})\boldsymbol{\mu}, \tag{3}$$

where τ denotes the noise level that shows how far a point deflects the surface. After that, we obtain the point x by applying tapering and rigid transformation to $\bar{x}$, $i.e.$ $x = g \circ Taper(\bar{x})$. We call the above generative process the *Gaussian Superquadric Taper Model* (GSTM), denoted by:

$$x \sim GSTM(\boldsymbol{\theta}, \sigma^2). \tag{4}$$

Subsequently, given a point cloud of an object $X = \{x_i \in \mathbb{R}^3 | i = 1, 2, ..., N\}$, we assume that each element x_i is generated from some GSTM parameterized by $(\boldsymbol{\theta}_j, \sigma_j^2)$. As a result, we consider the point cloud X as sample points generated by a mixture model as follows:

$$X = \{x_i | x_i \sim \sum_{j=1}^{K} \omega_j GSTM(\boldsymbol{\theta}_j, \sigma_j^2)\}, \tag{5}$$

where $\sum_{j=1}^{K} \omega_j = 1$, and each ω_j denotes the probability that an observation is drawn from $(\boldsymbol{\theta}_j, \sigma_j^2)$. Given the observation, we can estimate a set of $\boldsymbol{\theta}$ from the mixture model. Subsequently, we assume each $\boldsymbol{\theta}_j$ is a shape representation for one semantic part of the object. And thus, we attain a set of tapered superquadrics representing the semantic structures for the object.

The EM algorithm [11] is a classical inference to solve a mixture model problem. However, EM implementation requires knowledge of K – the number of components, which in our case is hard to determine beforehand from a raw

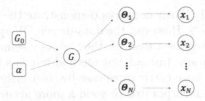

Fig. 3. Generative process of a point cloud. Notice that x_i and x_j where $i \neq j$ could be sampled from the same Θ. Since we only draw finite samples, the number of cluster is in fact finite.

point cloud. Therefore, we handle this difficulty by adapting our model to a nonparametric clustering framework, where we consider K to be infinite.

To deal with the mixture model with infinitely many components, we introduce the *Dirichlet Process* (DP) into our formulation. A DP, parameterized by a base distribution G_0 and a concentration factor α, is a distribution over distributions:

$$G \sim DP(G_0, \alpha), \tag{6}$$

which is equivalent to

$$G = \sum_{j=1}^{\infty} \omega_j \delta_{\Theta_j}, \ \Theta_j \sim G_0, \ \pi \sim GEM(\alpha), \tag{7}$$

where $\Theta_j = (\theta_j, \sigma_j^2)$, sampled from G_0, is the parameter of the jth GSTM, δ is the indicator function which evaluates to zero everywhere, except for $\delta_{\Theta_j}(\Theta_j) = 1$, $\pi = (\omega_1, \omega_2, ...)$, $\sum_{i=1}^{\infty} \omega_i = 1$, and GEM is the Griffiths, Engen and McCloskey distribution [17]. Therefore, an observation $\mathbf{x}_i$ is regarded as sampled from:

$$z_i \sim \pi, \mathbf{x}_i \sim GSTM(\Theta_{z_i}), \tag{8}$$

where z_i is a latent variable sampled from a categorical distribution parameterized by π, indicating the membership of $\mathbf{x}_i$. Figure 3 illustrates the process.

Even though we have an infinite mixture model, in practice we only draw finite samples, which means the number of clusters is actually finite. One advantage of our formulation is that we do not need to impose any constraints on K, which is inferred from the observation $\mathbf{X}$. On the other hand, unlike learning-based approaches that require a large amount of training data, our method reasons about primitive-based structures case by case, relying entirely on the geometric shapes of the object. These two facts contribute to increasing the generality of being able to cope with objects of varying shapes and component counts.

3.2   Optimization-Based Gibbs Sampling

We apply Bayesian inference to solve the mixture model problem, where the goal is to infer the posterior distribution of the parameters $\tilde{\boldsymbol{\theta}} = \{\boldsymbol{\theta}_1, \boldsymbol{\theta}_2, ..., \boldsymbol{\theta}_K\}, \tilde{\sigma}^2 =$

$\{\sigma_1^2, \sigma_2^2, ..., \sigma_K^2\}$ and the latent variables $\boldsymbol{Z} = \{z_1, z_2, ..., z_N\}$ given the observation $\boldsymbol{X}$:

$$p(\tilde{\boldsymbol{\theta}}, \tilde{\sigma}^2, \boldsymbol{Z} \mid \boldsymbol{X}). \tag{9}$$

Algorithm 1. Optimization-based Gibbs sampling

Input: $\boldsymbol{X} = \{\boldsymbol{x}_1, \boldsymbol{x}_2, ..., \boldsymbol{x}_N\}$
Output: $\{\tilde{\boldsymbol{\theta}}^t, \tilde{\sigma}^{2^t}, \boldsymbol{Z}^t\}_{t=1}^T$
initialize $\{\tilde{\boldsymbol{\theta}}^t, \tilde{\sigma}^{2^t}, \boldsymbol{Z}^t\}$ for $t = 0$ by K-means clustering
for $t = 1, 2, ..., T$ **do**
    1. draw a sample $\boldsymbol{Z}'$ for $\boldsymbol{Z}$, where $\boldsymbol{Z}' \sim p(\boldsymbol{Z} \mid \boldsymbol{X}, \tilde{\boldsymbol{\theta}}^t, \tilde{\sigma}^{2^t})$
    2. optimize each element $\boldsymbol{\theta}_j$ of $\tilde{\boldsymbol{\theta}}$ conditioned on $\{\boldsymbol{Z}', \boldsymbol{X}, \tilde{\sigma}^{2^t}\}$, and let $\tilde{\boldsymbol{\theta}}'$ be the optimized $\tilde{\boldsymbol{\theta}}$
    3. draw a sample $\tilde{\sigma}^{2'}$ for $\tilde{\sigma}^2$, where $\tilde{\sigma}^{2'} \sim p(\tilde{\sigma}^2 \mid \boldsymbol{X}, \boldsymbol{Z}', \tilde{\boldsymbol{\theta}}')$
    4. let $\{\tilde{\boldsymbol{\theta}}^{t+1}, \tilde{\sigma}^{2^{t+1}}, \boldsymbol{Z}^{t+1}\} = \{\tilde{\boldsymbol{\theta}}', \tilde{\sigma}^{2'}, \boldsymbol{Z}'\}$
end for

However, in practice, the Eq. 9 is intractable to obtain in a closed-form. Thus, we apply Gibbs sampling [14], an approach to estimating the desired probability distribution via sampling. Apart from sampling, we also incorporate an optimization process, which is used to obtain an accurate superquadric representation for each cluster. The following algorithm 1 shows how optimization-based Gibbs sampling works in our case. In the following sections, we will derive and demonstrate explicitly how to obtain each parameter.

Sample $\boldsymbol{Z}$. To begin with, as defined in Eq. 3, we have the sampling distribution of $\boldsymbol{x}$

$$p(\boldsymbol{x} \mid \boldsymbol{\theta}, \sigma^2) = \frac{1}{2\sqrt{2\pi}\sigma} \exp\left(-\frac{\|\boldsymbol{x} - \boldsymbol{\mu}_1(\boldsymbol{\theta}, \boldsymbol{x})\|_2^2}{2\sigma^2}\right)$$
$$+ \frac{1}{2\sqrt{2\pi}\sigma} \exp\left(-\frac{\|\boldsymbol{x} - \boldsymbol{\mu}_2(\boldsymbol{\theta}, \boldsymbol{x})\|_2^2}{2\sigma^2}\right), \tag{10}$$

where $\boldsymbol{\mu}_1$ and $\boldsymbol{\mu}_2$ are two intersection points between the superquadric surface and the line joining the superqadric's origin and $\boldsymbol{x}$, as Fig. 4 shows.

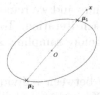

Fig. 4. Demonstration for computing sampling density of $\boldsymbol{x}$. According to GSTM, $\boldsymbol{\mu}_1$ and $\boldsymbol{\mu}_2$ are the only two points accounting for the generation of $\boldsymbol{x}$.

We denote $\boldsymbol{\mu}_1$ as the closer intersection point to $\boldsymbol{x}$. In the general case, Eq. 10 is dominated by the former part, and hence we let

$$p(\boldsymbol{x} \mid \boldsymbol{\theta}, \sigma^2) \approx \frac{1}{2\sqrt{2\pi}\sigma} \exp\left(-\frac{\|\boldsymbol{x} - \boldsymbol{\mu}_1(\boldsymbol{\theta}, \boldsymbol{x})\|_2^2}{2\sigma^2}\right). \qquad (11)$$

By further examination, we discover that the term $\|\boldsymbol{x} - \boldsymbol{\mu}_1(\boldsymbol{\theta}, \boldsymbol{x})\|_2$ is the radial distance between a point and a superquadric as defined in [18]. We denote it by $d(\boldsymbol{\theta}, \boldsymbol{x})$. Integrating out the $\boldsymbol{\theta}$ and σ^2 gives:

$$p(\boldsymbol{x}) = \int_{\boldsymbol{\theta},\sigma^2} p(\boldsymbol{x} \mid \boldsymbol{\theta}, \sigma^2) p(\boldsymbol{\theta}, \sigma^2) \, d\boldsymbol{\theta}d\sigma^2 \approx \int_{\boldsymbol{\theta},\sigma^2} \frac{p(\boldsymbol{\theta}, \sigma^2)}{2\sqrt{2\pi}\sigma} \exp\left(-\frac{d^2(\boldsymbol{\theta}, \boldsymbol{x})}{2\sigma^2}\right) \, d\boldsymbol{\theta}d\sigma^2.$$

$$(12)$$

Eq. 12 denotes the prior predictive density of $\boldsymbol{x}$ and is intractable to compute in closed form. It can be approximated by Monte Carlo sampling or approximated by a constant [22]. In our work, we treat $p(\boldsymbol{x})$ as a tunable hyper-parameter and denote it as p_0. To sample membership for each point $\boldsymbol{x}_i$, we have

$$p\left(z_i = j \mid \boldsymbol{Z}_{-i}, \boldsymbol{\theta}_j, \sigma_j^2, \boldsymbol{X}, \alpha\right) \propto p\left(z_i = j \mid \boldsymbol{Z}_{-i}, \alpha\right) p\left(\boldsymbol{x}_i \mid \boldsymbol{\theta}_j, \sigma_j^2, \boldsymbol{Z}_{-i}\right)$$

$$\propto \frac{n_{-i,j}}{N-1+\alpha} p(\boldsymbol{x}_i \mid \boldsymbol{\theta}_j, \sigma_j^2) = \frac{n_{-i,j}}{N-1+\alpha} \frac{1}{2\sqrt{2\pi}\sigma_j} \exp\left(-\frac{d^2(\boldsymbol{\theta}_j, \boldsymbol{x}_i)}{2\sigma_j^2}\right), \qquad (13)$$

and

$$p\left(z_i = K+1 \mid \boldsymbol{Z}_{-i}, \boldsymbol{\theta}_j, \sigma_j^2, \boldsymbol{X}, \alpha\right) \propto p\left(z_i = K+1 \mid \alpha\right) p\left(\boldsymbol{x}_i \mid \boldsymbol{\theta}_j, \sigma_j^2, \boldsymbol{Z}_{-i}\right)$$

$$\propto \frac{\alpha}{N-1+\alpha} p(\boldsymbol{x}_i) = \frac{\alpha}{N-1+\alpha} p_0, \qquad (14)$$

where α is the concentration factor of DP, $\boldsymbol{Z}_{-i}$ denotes $\boldsymbol{Z}$ excluding z_i, and $n_{-i,j}$ is the number of points belonging to cluster j, excluding $\boldsymbol{x}_i$. Equation 13 computes the probability that $\boldsymbol{x}_i$ belongs to some existing cluster, whereas Eq. 14 determines the probability of generating a new cluster. The term $p\left(z_i = j \mid \boldsymbol{Z}_{-i}, \alpha\right)$ of Eq. 13 and $p\left(z_i = K+1 \mid \alpha\right)$ of Eq. 14 come from the *Chinese Restaurant Process* (CRP), where a point tends to be attracted by a larger population and has a fixed probability to generate a new group. The term $p\left(\boldsymbol{x}_i \mid \boldsymbol{\theta}_j, \sigma_j^2, \boldsymbol{Z}_{-i}\right)$ reasons about what the likelihood is that $\boldsymbol{x}_i$ belongs to some existing cluster or a new one, based on the current $\tilde{\boldsymbol{\theta}} = \{\boldsymbol{\theta}_1, \boldsymbol{\theta}_2, ..., \boldsymbol{\theta}_K\}$ and $\tilde{\sigma}^2 = \{\sigma_1^2, \sigma_2^2, ..., \sigma_K^2\}$. After the assignment of all points, some existing clusters may be assigned with none of the points and we remove those empty clusters. Thus, the K keeps changing during each iteration. To increase the performance, we incorporate a splitting process before sampling $\boldsymbol{Z}$. Details are presented in the supplementary.

Optimize $\tilde{\boldsymbol{\theta}}$. By independence between individual $\boldsymbol{\theta}$, the density function of each $\boldsymbol{\theta}_j$ is conditioned only on $\boldsymbol{X}^j$ and σ_j^2 as follows:

$$p(\boldsymbol{\theta}_j \mid \boldsymbol{X}^j, \sigma_j^2), \qquad (15)$$

where $\boldsymbol{X}^j = \{\boldsymbol{x}_l \mid \boldsymbol{x}_l \in \boldsymbol{X}, z_l = j\}$, $i.e.$ the set of points belonging to cluster j. By assuming that the prior for $\boldsymbol{\theta}$ is an uniform distribution, we have

$$p(\boldsymbol{\theta}_j \mid \boldsymbol{X}^j, \sigma_j^2) \propto p(\boldsymbol{\theta}_j)p(\boldsymbol{X}^j \mid \boldsymbol{\theta}_j, \sigma_j^2) \propto p(\boldsymbol{X}^j \mid \boldsymbol{\theta}_j, \sigma_j^2), \tag{16}$$

where

$$p(\boldsymbol{X}^j \mid \boldsymbol{\theta}_j, \sigma_j^2) = \prod_l \frac{1}{2\sqrt{2\pi}\sigma_j} \exp\left(-\frac{d^2(\boldsymbol{\theta}_j, \boldsymbol{x}_l)}{2\sigma_j^2}\right). \tag{17}$$

Combining Eq. 16 and Eq. 17 gives

$$p(\boldsymbol{\theta}_j \mid \boldsymbol{X}^j, \sigma_j^2) \propto \prod_l \exp\left(-\frac{d^2(\boldsymbol{\theta}_j, \boldsymbol{x}_l)}{2\sigma_j^2}\right) = \exp\left(-\sum_l \frac{d^2(\boldsymbol{\theta}_j, \boldsymbol{x}_l)}{2\sigma_j^2}\right). \tag{18}$$

Gibbs sampling requires sampling $\boldsymbol{\theta}_j$ from Eq. 18. However, directly sampling from Eq. 18 is difficult due to its complexity. Instead, optimization is used as a substitute for the sampling process, which, we believe, is a reasonable replacement. By inspecting Eq. 18 more closely, we discover that the $\boldsymbol{\theta}_j$ minimizing $\sum_l d^2(\boldsymbol{\theta}_j, \boldsymbol{x}_l)$ maximizes the density function. Therefore, an optimized $\boldsymbol{\theta}_j$ has relatively higher likelihood to be close to the actual sample of $\boldsymbol{\theta}_j$ drawn from $p(\boldsymbol{\theta}_j \mid \boldsymbol{X}^j, \sigma_j^2)$. And closeness implies similar shapes. Additionally, we recognize that optimizing Eq. 18 can be regarded as a single superquadric recovery problem, which requires the abstraction of an optimal superquadric primitive from the cluster points $\boldsymbol{X}^j$. In other words, we fit an optimal superquadric to each cluster, and those superquadrics will affect the membership of each point in the subsequent iteration, which is a process similar to EM. As a result, we use the robust and accurate recovery algorithm [26], which yields an optimal superquadric with high fidelity, to acquire each $\boldsymbol{\theta}_j$ in replacement of the sampling.

Sample $\tilde{\sigma}^2$. Similarly, by independence, we have

$$\begin{aligned} \sigma_j^{2'} &\sim p(\sigma_j^2 \mid \boldsymbol{X}^j, \boldsymbol{\theta}_j) \\ \tilde{\sigma}^{2'} &= \{\sigma_1^{2'}, \sigma_2^{2'}, ..., \sigma_K^{2'}\}. \end{aligned} \tag{19}$$

We also assume the non-informative prior for σ^2 is the uniform distribution, which gives

$$p(\sigma_j^2 \mid \boldsymbol{X}^j, \boldsymbol{\theta}_j) \propto p(\sigma_j^2)p(\boldsymbol{X}^j \mid \boldsymbol{\theta}_j, \sigma_j^2) \propto p(\boldsymbol{X}^j \mid \boldsymbol{\theta}_j, \sigma_j^2). \tag{20}$$

Combining Eq. 17 and Eq. 20 gives

$$\begin{aligned} p(\sigma_j^2 \mid \boldsymbol{X}^j, \boldsymbol{\theta}_j) &\propto \prod_l \frac{1}{2\sqrt{2\pi}\sigma_j} \exp\left(-\frac{d^2(\boldsymbol{\theta}_j, \boldsymbol{x}_l)}{2\sigma_j^2}\right) \\ &\propto \left(\frac{1}{\sigma_j}\right)^{n_j} \exp\left(-\sum_l \frac{d^2(\boldsymbol{\theta}_j, \boldsymbol{x}_l)}{2\sigma_j^2}\right), \end{aligned} \tag{21}$$

where n_j is the number of $\boldsymbol{X}^j$. Let $D = \sum_l d^2(\boldsymbol{\theta}_j, \boldsymbol{x}_l)$ and $\gamma_j = \frac{1}{\sigma_j^2}$. By change of variable, we have

$$\gamma_j' \sim p(\gamma_j \mid \boldsymbol{X}^j, \boldsymbol{\theta}_j) \propto \gamma_j^{\frac{n_j-3}{2}} \exp(-\frac{D}{2}\gamma_j). \tag{22}$$

Hence, γ_j follows a gamma distribution with shape parameter $\frac{n_j-1}{2}$ and scale parameter $\frac{2}{D}$. In other words,

$$\sigma_j^{2'} = \frac{1}{\gamma_j'}$$

$$\gamma_j' \sim \Gamma\left(\frac{n_j-1}{2}, \frac{2}{D}\right). \tag{23}$$

D reflects how good the optimized superquadric fits the cluster points. With lower value of D, γ_j' will have a better chance to be higher and hence $\sigma_j^{2'}$ will be smaller. In other words, the better the fitting is, the smaller the noise level will be.

3.3   Merging Process

We observe that our method yields structures consisting of excessive components, resulting in less interpretability. Therefore, we design a merging post-process minimizing component numbers while maintaining accuracy. Specifically, for any two clusters represented by two superquadrics, we make a union of the two sets of points into one set, from which we recover a superquadric. If the newly recovered superquadric turns out to be a good fit for the new point set, we will merge these two clusters into one, and replace the two original superquadrics with the newly fitted one. Detailed formulations and procedures are presented in the supplementary.

4   Experiment

In this section, we demonstrate our approach to abstracting part-level structures exhibits high accuracy, compared with state-of-the-art part-based abstraction method [33]. We do not compare with the work of [31,32] since their work focuses mainly on abstracting 3D shapes from 2D images. We also include a simple clustering method as a baseline, where the point cloud is parsed into K clusters via K-means and each cluster is then represented by an optimized superquadric [26]. We conduct experiments on the ShapeNet dataset [7] and the D-FAUST dataset [6]. The ShapeNet is a collection of CAD models of various common objects such as tables, chairs, bottles, etc. On the other hand, the D-FAUST dataset contains point clouds of 129 sequences of 10 humans performing various movements, e.g., punching, shaking arms, and running. Following [33], we evaluate the results with two metrics, Chamfer L_1-distance and Intersection over Union (IoU). Detailed computations of the two metrics are discussed in the supplementary.

Initialization: we parse the point cloud into K components based on the K-means clustering algorithm. Although we specify the value of K initially, the final value of K will be inferred by our nonparametric model and vary from case to case. The latent variable z_i of each point x_i is assigned accordingly. Subsequently, each cluster is represented by an ellipsoid θ_j^0 whose moment-of-inertial (MoI) is four times smaller than the MoI of the cluster points; each $\sigma_j^{2^0}$ is randomly sampled within $(0, 1]$. We set the number of the sampling iteration to be $T = 30$, concentration factor $\alpha = 0.5$, and $p_0 = 0.1$.

Fig. 5. Qualitative results of 3D abstraction on various objects. The left ones are the original meshes, the middle ones are our inferred results, and the right ones are inferred from SQs [33]. (a) Bottle, (b) chair, (c) lamp, (d) table, and (e) mailbox.

4.1 Evaluation on ShapeNet

We choose seven different types of objects among all of the categories. For deep learning training, we randomly divide the data of each object into two sets – a training set (80%) and a testing set (20%), and we compare the results on the testing set. Since ShapeNet only provides meshes, we first densely sample points on the mesh surfaces and then downsample the point clouds to be around 3500 points. For all categories, we set the $K = 30$. The result is summarized in Table 1, where w/om denotes our method excluding the merging process. Our method outperforms the state-of-the-art [33] and the K-means baseline significantly on all object types. Excluding the merging process improves accuracy but increases the number of primitives, making the abstracted models less interpretable. Therefore, we believe merging is beneficial and important because it reduces the primitive numbers while maintaining excellent accuracy, which improves interpretability. Unlike the learning-based method, which is a semantic-level approximation, our method infers the part-based representation in an optimization-based manner. As a result, our method yields a more geometrically accurate primitive-based structure, yet with a compact number of primitives. A qualitative comparison between our method and SQs [33] is depicted in Fig. 5.

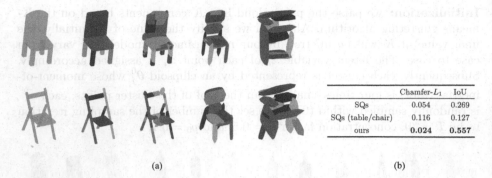

	Chamfer-L_1	IoU
SQs	0.054	0.269
SQs (table/chair)	0.116	0.127
ours	**0.024**	**0.557**

(a)   (b)

Fig. 6. (a) Comparison between different results inferred by different models. From left to right: the original meshes, results inferred by our method, results inferred by our method excluding merging, results inferred by the baseline trained on the chair category, and results inferred by the baseline trained on the table category, (b) quantitative results showing that the baseline method has limited generality. The (table/chair) means that a network trained on the table category is used to predict the chair category.

Table 1. Quantitative results on ShapeNet

Category	Chamfer-L_1				IoU			
	K-means	SQs [33]	w/om	Ours	K-means	SQs	w/om	Ours
bottle	0.064	0.037	0.026	**0.019**	0.552	0.596	0.618	**0.656**
can	0.086	0.032	0.028	**0.014**	0.690	0.736	**0.803**	0.802
chair	0.065	0.054	**0.018**	0.024	0.433	0.269	**0.577**	0.557
lamp	0.066	0.065	**0.020**	0.024	0.354	0.190	**0.425**	0.414
mailbox	0.054	0.059	0.019	**0.019**	0.529	0.400	**0.687**	0.686
rifle	0.018	0.022	**0.009**	0.013	0.517	0.291	**0.594**	0.536
table	0.060	0.057	**0.018**	0.021	0.374	0.194	**0.536**	0.512
mean	0.057	0.053	**0.017**	0.021	0.410	0.242	**0.547**	0.526

Category	#primitives			
	K-means	SQs	w/om	Ours
bottle	30	8	7.4	6.8
can	30	7	13.6	1.1
chair	30	10	26.9	13.6
lamp	30	10	24.8	9.5
mailbox	30	10	18.8	3.1
rifle	30	7	20.0	7.6
table	30	11	25.1	9.5

Furthermore, generality is noteworthy. To attain the reported accuracy, the baseline method needs to be trained on a dataset of a specified item category, respectively. A network trained on one item is difficult to generalize to another as Fig. 6 shows. In contrast, our probabilistic formulation reasons about the part-based representation case by case, and the nonparametric formulation makes it possible to adapt to various shapes with varying component numbers.

4.2 Evaluation on D-FAUST

We follow the same split strategy in [31] and divide the dataset into training (91), testing (29), and validation (9). Likewise, we compare results on the testing set. For our method, we downsample the point clouds to be around 5500 points and set K to be 30, as well. The results are shown in Table 2. Figure 7 illustrates examples of inferred representations. We can observe that our model can accurately capture the major parts of humans, *i.e.* heads, chests, arms, forearms, hips, thighs, legs, and feet, even when they are performing different movements.

Table 2. Quantitative results on D-FAUST

	Chamfer-L_1	IoU
SQs [33]	0.0473	0.7138
Ours	**0.0335**	**0.7709**

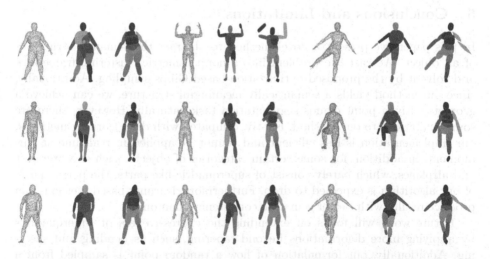

Fig. 7. Abstraction results on D-FAUST dataset. The left ones are the original point clouds, the middle ones are inferred by our method, and the right ones are from SQs [33].

4.3   Extension: Point Cloud Segmentation

Due to the fact that our method yields a geometrically accurate structure, we can achieve a geometry-driven point clouds segmentation task naturally. All points in the point clouds have been well clustered after we obtain the abstraction of an object and we segment the point clouds accordingly. Figure 8 illustrates some examples of point clouds segmentation on different objects, inferred by our method.

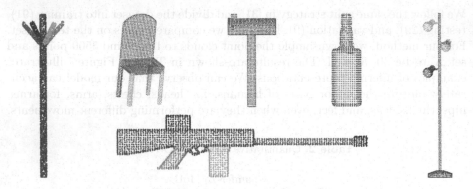

Fig. 8. Examples of point clouds segmentation inferred by our method.

5   Conclusions and Limitations

In this paper, we present a novel method to abstract the semantic structures of an object. We cast the problem into a nonparametric clustering framework and solve it by the proposed optimization-based Gibbs sampling. Additionally, since our method yields a semantically meaningful structure, we can achieve a geometry-driven point clouds segmentation task naturally. However, there are some limitations to our method. Firstly, compared with deep learning methods, our implementation is less efficient and cannot be applied in real-time at this moment. In addition, for some certain categories of objects, such as watercraft and airplanes, which barely consist of superquadric-like parts, the performance of our algorithm is expected to drop. Furthermore, learning-based methods can produce results with better semantic consistency than ours.

Future work will focus on extending the expressiveness of superquadrics by applying more deformations beyond tapering, such as bending and sheering. Additionally, our formulation of how a random point is sampled from a tapered superquadric primitive can be extended to a more general surface beyond superquadrics. Moreover, trying different priors for both θ and σ^2 other than uniform distributions is also an auspicious way to improve performance.

Acknowledgments. This research is supported by the National Research Foundation, Singapore, under its Medium Sized Centre Programme - Centre for Advanced Robotics Technology Innovation (CARTIN) R-261-521-002-592.

References

1. Achlioptas, P., Diamanti, O., Mitliagkas, I., Guibas, L.: Learning representations and generative models for 3D point clouds. In: International Conference on Machine Learning, pp. 40–49. PMLR (2018)
2. Anwar, Z., Ferrie, F.: Towards robust voxel-coloring: handling camera calibration errors and partial emptiness of surface voxels. In: 18th International Conference on Pattern Recognition (ICPR), vol. 1, pp. 98–102. IEEE (2006)
3. Atzmon, M., Lipman, Y.: SAL: sign agnostic learning of shapes from raw data. In: Proceedings of the IEEE/CVF Conference on Computer Vision and Pattern Recognition (CVPR), pp. 2565–2574 (2020)
4. Barr, A.H.: Superquadrics and angle-preserving transformations. IEEE Comput. Graph. Appl. **1**(1), 11–23 (1981)
5. Barr, A.H.: Global and local deformations of solid primitives. In: Readings in Computer Vision, pp. 661–670. Elsevier, Amsterdam (1987)
6. Bogo, F., Romero, J., Pons-Moll, G., Black, M.J.: Dynamic FAUST: registering human bodies in motion. In: IEEE Conference on Computer Vision and Pattern Recognition (CVPR) (2017)
7. Chang, A.X., et al.: ShapeNet: an information-rich 3D model repository. arXiv preprint arXiv:1512.03012 (2015)
8. Chevalier, L., Jaillet, F., Baskurt, A.: Segmentation and superquadric modeling of 3D objects. In: WSCG (2003)
9. Chibane, J., Alldieck, T., Pons-Moll, G.: Implicit functions in feature space for 3D shape reconstruction and completion. In: Proceedings of the IEEE/CVF Conference on Computer Vision and Pattern Recognition (CVPR), pp. 6970–6981 (2020)
10. Choy, C.B., Xu, D., Gwak, J.Y., Chen, K., Savarese, S.: 3D-R2N2: a unified approach for single and multi-view 3D object reconstruction. In: Leibe, B., Matas, J., Sebe, N., Welling, M. (eds.) ECCV 2016. LNCS, vol. 9912, pp. 628–644. Springer, Cham (2016). https://doi.org/10.1007/978-3-319-46484-8_38
11. Dempster, A.P., Laird, N.M., Rubin, D.B.: Maximum likelihood from incomplete data via the EM algorithm. J. Roy. Stat. Soc.: Ser. B (Methodol.) **39**(1), 1–22 (1977)
12. Deng, B., Genova, K., Yazdani, S., Bouaziz, S., Hinton, G., Tagliasacchi, A.: CVXNet: learnable convex decomposition. In: Proceedings of the IEEE/CVF Conference on Computer Vision and Pattern Recognition (CVPR), pp. 31–44 (2020)
13. Fan, H., Su, H., Guibas, L.J.: A point set generation network for 3D object reconstruction from a single image. In: Proceedings of the IEEE/CVF Conference on Computer Vision and Pattern Recognition (CVPR), pp. 605–613 (2017)
14. Gelfand, A.E.: Gibbs sampling. J. Am. Stat. Assoc. **95**(452), 1300–1304 (2000)
15. Genova, K., Cole, F., Sud, A., Sarna, A., Funkhouser, T.: Local deep implicit functions for 3D shape. In: Proceedings of the IEEE/CVF Conference on Computer Vision and Pattern Recognition (CVPR), pp. 4857–4866 (2020)
16. Genova, K., Cole, F., Vlasic, D., Sarna, A., Freeman, W.T., Funkhouser, T.: Learning shape templates with structured implicit functions. In: Proceedings of the IEEE/CVF International Conference on Computer Vision (ICCV), pp. 7154–7164 (2019)

17. Gnedin, A., Kerov, S.: A characterization of gem distributions. Comb. Probab. Comput. **10**(3), 213–217 (2001)
18. Gross, A.D., Boult, T.E.: Error of fit measures for recovering parametric solids. In: Proceedings of the IEEE International Conference on Computer Vision (ICCV) (1988)
19. Groueix, T., Fisher, M., Kim, V.G., Russell, B.C., Aubry, M.: A papier-mâché approach to learning 3D surface generation. In: Proceedings of the IEEE Conference on Computer Vision and Pattern Recognition (CVPR), pp. 216–224 (2018)
20. Häne, C., Tulsiani, S., Malik, J.: Hierarchical surface prediction for 3D object reconstruction. In: 2017 International Conference on 3D Vision (3DV), pp. 412–420. IEEE (2017)
21. Hao, Z., Averbuch-Elor, H., Snavely, N., Belongie, S.: DualSDF: semantic shape manipulation using a two-level representation. In: Proceedings of the IEEE/CVF Conference on Computer Vision and Pattern Recognition (CVPR), pp. 7631–7641 (2020)
22. Hayden, D.S., Pacheco, J., Fisher, J.W.: Nonparametric object and parts modeling with lie group dynamics. In: Proceedings of the IEEE/CVF Conference on Computer Vision and Pattern Recognition (CVPR), pp. 7426–7435 (2020)
23. Jimenez Rezende, D., Eslami, S., Mohamed, S., Battaglia, P., Jaderberg, M., Heess, N.: Unsupervised learning of 3D structure from images. In: Advances in Neural Information Processing Systems, vol. 29 (2016)
24. Kanazawa, A., Tulsiani, S., Efros, A.A., Malik, J.: Learning category-specific mesh reconstruction from image collections. In: Ferrari, V., Hebert, M., Sminchisescu, C., Weiss, Y. (eds.) ECCV 2018. LNCS, vol. 11219, pp. 386–402. Springer, Cham (2018). https://doi.org/10.1007/978-3-030-01267-0_23
25. Leonardis, A., Jaklic, A., Solina, F.: Superquadrics for segmenting and modeling range data. IEEE Trans. Pattern Anal. Mach. Intell. **19**(11), 1289–1295 (1997)
26. Liu, W., Wu, Y., Ruan, S., Chirikjian, G.S.: Robust and accurate superquadric recovery: a probabilistic approach. In: Proceedings of the IEEE/CVF Conference on Computer Vision and Pattern Recognition (CVPR), pp. 2676–2685 (2022)
27. Mescheder, L., Oechsle, M., Niemeyer, M., Nowozin, S., Geiger, A.: Occupancy networks: learning 3D reconstruction in function space. In: Proceedings of the IEEE/CVF Conference on Computer Vision and Pattern Recognition (CVPR), pp. 4460–4470 (2019)
28. Niu, C., Li, J., Xu, K.: IM2Struct: recovering 3D shape structure from a single RGB image. In: Proceedings of the IEEE Conference on Computer Vision and Pattern Recognition (CVPR), pp. 4521–4529 (2018)
29. Pan, J., Han, X., Chen, W., Tang, J., Jia, K.: Deep mesh reconstruction from single RGB images via topology modification networks. In: Proceedings of the IEEE/CVF International Conference on Computer Vision (ICCV), pp. 9964–9973 (2019)
30. Park, J.J., Florence, P., Straub, J., Newcombe, R., Lovegrove, S.: DeepSDF: learning continuous signed distance functions for shape representation. In: Proceedings of the IEEE/CVF Conference on Computer Vision and Pattern Recognition (CVPR), pp. 165–174 (2019)
31. Paschalidou, D., Gool, L.V., Geiger, A.: Learning unsupervised hierarchical part decomposition of 3D objects from a single RGB image. In: Proceedings of the IEEE/CVF Conference on Computer Vision and Pattern Recognition (CVPR), pp. 1060–1070 (2020)

32. Paschalidou, D., Katharopoulos, A., Geiger, A., Fidler, S.: Neural parts: learning expressive 3D shape abstractions with invertible neural networks. In: Proceedings of the IEEE/CVF Conference on Computer Vision and Pattern Recognition (CVPR), pp. 3204–3215 (2021)

33. Paschalidou, D., Ulusoy, A.O., Geiger, A.: Superquadrics revisited: learning 3D shape parsing beyond cuboids. In: Proceedings of the IEEE/CVF Conference on Computer Vision and Pattern Recognition (CVPR), pp. 10344–10353 (2019)

34. Pentland, A.P.: Perceptual organization and the representation of natural form. In: Readings in Computer Vision, pp. 680–699. Elsevier, Amsterdam (1987)

35. Quispe, A.H., et al.: Exploiting symmetries and extrusions for grasping household objects. In: 2015 IEEE International Conference on Robotics and Automation (ICRA), pp. 3702–3708. IEEE (2015)

36. Riegler, G., Osman Ulusoy, A., Geiger, A.: OCTNet: learning deep 3D representations at high resolutions. In: Proceedings of the IEEE Conference on Computer Vision and Pattern Recognition (CVPR), pp. 3577–3586 (2017)

37. Roberts, L.G.: Machine perception of three-dimensional solids. Ph.D. thesis, Massachusetts Institute of Technology (1963)

38. Ruan, S., Chirikjian, G.S.: Closed-form Minkowski sums of convex bodies with smooth positively curved boundaries. Comput. Aided Des. **143**, 103133 (2022)

39. Ruan, S., Poblete, K.L., Li, Y., Lin, Q., Ma, Q., Chirikjian, G.S.: Efficient exact collision detection between ellipsoids and superquadrics via closed-form minkowski sums. In: 2019 International Conference on Robotics and Automation (ICRA), pp. 1765–1771. IEEE (2019)

40. Slabaugh, G.G., Culbertson, W.B., Malzbender, T., Stevens, M.R., Schafer, R.W.: Methods for volumetric reconstruction of visual scenes. Int. J. Comput. Vision **57**(3), 179–199 (2004)

41. Tatarchenko, M., Dosovitskiy, A., Brox, T.: Octree generating networks: efficient convolutional architectures for high-resolution 3d outputs. In: Proceedings of the IEEE International Conference on Computer Vision (ICCV), pp. 2088–2096 (2017)

42. Tulsiani, S., Su, H., Guibas, L.J., Efros, A.A., Malik, J.: Learning shape abstractions by assembling volumetric primitives. In: Proceedings of the IEEE Conference on Computer Vision and Pattern Recognition (CVPR), pp. 2635–2643 (2017)

43. Tversky, B., Hemenway, K.: Objects, parts, and categories. J. Exp. Psychol. Gen. **113**(2), 169 (1984)

44. Vezzani, G., Pattacini, U., Natale, L.: A grasping approach based on superquadric models. In: 2017 IEEE International Conference on Robotics and Automation (ICRA), pp. 1579–1586. IEEE (2017)

45. Vezzani, G., Pattacini, U., Pasquale, G., Natale, L.: Improving superquadric modeling and grasping with prior on object shapes. In: 2018 IEEE International Conference on Robotics and Automation (ICRA), pp. 6875–6882. IEEE (2018)

46. Wang, N., Zhang, Y., Li, Z., Fu, Y., Liu, W., Jiang, Y.-G.: Pixel2Mesh: generating 3D mesh models from single RGB images. In: Ferrari, V., Hebert, M., Sminchisescu, C., Weiss, Y. (eds.) ECCV 2018. LNCS, vol. 11215, pp. 55–71. Springer, Cham (2018). https://doi.org/10.1007/978-3-030-01252-6_4

47. Yang, K., Chen, X.: Unsupervised learning for cuboid shape abstraction via joint segmentation from point clouds. ACM Trans. Graph. (TOG) **40**(4), 1–11 (2021)

48. Zou, C., Yumer, E., Yang, J., Ceylan, D., Hoiem, D.: 3D-PRNN: generating shape primitives with recurrent neural networks. In: Proceedings of the IEEE International Conference on Computer Vision (ICCV), pp. 900–909 (2017)

Stereo Depth Estimation with Echoes

Chenghao Zhang[1,2], Kun Tian[1,2], Bolin Ni[1,2], Gaofeng Meng[1,2,3(✉)], Bin Fan[4],
Zhaoxiang Zhang[1,2,3], and Chunhong Pan[1]

[1] NLPR, Institute of Automation, Chinese Academy of Sciences, Beijing, China
{chenghao.zhang,gfmeng}@nlpr.ia.ac.cn
[2] School of Artificial Intelligence, University of Chinese Academy of Sciences,
Beijing, China
[3] CAIR, HK Institute of Science and Innovation, Chinese Academy of Sciences,
Hong Kong, China
[4] University of Science and Technology Beijing, Beijing, China

Abstract. Stereo depth estimation is particularly amenable to local textured regions while echoes have good depth estimations for global textureless regions, thus the two modalities complement each other. Motivated by the reciprocal relationship between both modalities, in this paper, we propose an end-to-end framework named *StereoEchoes* for stereo depth estimation with echoes. A Cross-modal Volume Refinement module is designed to transfer the complementary knowledge of the audio modality to the visual modality at feature level. A Relative Depth Uncertainty Estimation module is further proposed to yield pixel-wise confidence for multimodal depth fusion at output space. As there is no dataset for this new problem, we introduce two Stereo-Echo datasets named Stereo-Replica and Stereo-Matterport3D for the first time. Remarkably, we show empirically that our StereoEchoes, on Stereo-Replica and Stereo-Matterport3D, outperforms stereo depth estimation methods by 25%/13.8% RMSE, and surpasses the state-of-the-art audio-visual depth prediction method by 25.3%/42.3% RMSE.

Keywords: Depth estimation · Multimodal learning · Cross-modal volume refinement · Relative depth uncertainty estimation

1 Introduction

Recent years have witnessed exciting attempts to leverage audio visual multimodal learning for depth estimation [8,12,28]. For the visual modality, learning depth from stereo images is appropriate for textured regions though not accurate in textureless areas due to matching ambiguity. In contrast, in the audio modality, the echo has a good depth estimation for textureless regions in spite of large errors in local details. This suggests that the two modalities can complement

Supplementary Information The online version contains supplementary material available at https://doi.org/10.1007/978-3-031-19812-0_29.

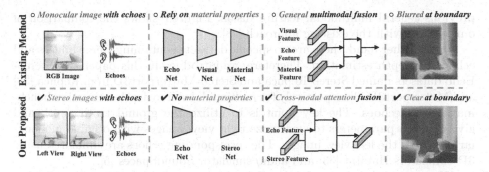

Fig. 1. Comparison of our method with the existing approach [28]. Our StereoEchoes learns depth from stereo images and echoes with no need for material properties estimation. Our method produces depth maps with clear object boundary.

each other, which is also reflected in psychology and perception that auditory grouping helps solve visual ambiguity [44] while visual information helps calibrate the auditory information [20].

Previous work in audio-visual depth estimation dates back to BatVision [8], which predicts depth directly from binaural echoes. The performance was improved by concatenating features of monocular images and echoes in [12]. Parida *et al.* [28] explored the idea further by integrating a material properties estimation network with an attention mechanism, and achieved state-of-the-art performance. Unfortunately, material properties which rely on additional collected data with material annotations, are difficult to obtain for many environments. Besides, monocular depth estimation is an ill-posed problem thus the estimated depth maps are still blurry at local details and object boundaries.

To address these challenges, we argue that the above mentioned stereo depth estimation with echoes is a better configuration without demands on material properties. In general, the material of the object is usually reflected in the visual texture. Rich textures on objects are particularly amenable to stereo matching. From this point of view, stereo learning can be a good substitute for both monocular learning and material properties estimation. Although depth is not well estimated in textureless regions for stereo, the echo can play a complementary role for these areas. The multimodal learning of stereo images and echoes will make a dramatic leap on the performance of depth prediction.

Deriving from the above motivation, in this work, we propose an end-to-end framework named *StereoEchoes* for stereo depth estimation with echoes. To fully exploit the reciprocal relationship between the audio and visual modalities, we integrate both modalities at internal feature level and output space, respectively. At feature level, we propose a Cross-modal Volume Refinement module to transfer the complementary knowledge of echoes into the stereo features. On output space, we introduce a Relative Depth Uncertainty Estimation module to yield pixel-wise confidence for subsequent multimodal depth maps fusion. Our carefully designed cross-modal attention based fusion is empirically superior to previous general multimodal feature fusion. Figure 1 shows the comparison of our method with the existing approach [28].

On the other hand, there are no specific datasets containing stereo images and echoes for depth estimation. Therefore, we introduce in this paper two Stereo-Echo datasets named Stereo-Replica and Stereo-Matterport3D from Replica [38] and Matterport3D [3] respectively for multimodal stereo depth estimation benchmarks with echoes. The key point is to utilize the ground truth depth and given camera parameters to synthesize right-view images with original monocular images as the left-view images. The corresponding echoes are simulated using 3D simulators Habitat [33] and audio simulator SoundSpaces [5].

We evaluate the proposed StereoEchoes framework on the introduced Stereo-Echo datasets. We show in experiments that our method outperforms the state-of-the-art audio-visual depth prediction method [28] by 25.3% and 42.3% RMSE on Stereo-Replica and Stereo-Matterport3D. Compared with the challenging baselines that directly learn depth from the stereo, the improvements of our StereoEchoes are 25% and 13.8% respectively, demonstrating the superiority of incorporating echoes. Quantitative visualization shows that our method can produce more accurate depth maps on foreground objects and boundaries. Furthermore, extensive ablations validate the effectiveness of our methods.

Our contributions are summarized as follows:

- We propose to formulate the problem of stereo depth estimation with echoes, and introduce the StereoEchoes framework for this problem by utilizing the reciprocal relationship between the audio and visual modalities.
- Two modules of Cross-modal Volume Refinement and Relative Depth Uncertainty Estimation are designed for multimodal fusion at feature level and output space, which are superior to previous general fusion strategies.
- We further introduce two Stereo-Echo datasets named Stereo-Replica and Stereo-Matterport3D for evaluating the problem of multimodal stereo depth estimation with echoes.
- Experiments show that, on Stereo-Replica and Stereo-Matterport3D datasets, the proposed StereoEchoes outperforms the state-of-the-art audio-visual depth prediction method by 25.3% and 42.3% RMSE, and surpasses the challenging baseline of stereo depth estimation by 25% and 13.8%.

2   Related Work

Audio-Visual Learning. Most videos contain both audio and visual information, which bridges the link between the two domains. The close connection between the two modalities has made a dramatic leap in audio-visual learning in recent years. In one line of work, the corresponding of the two modalities is used to learn the cross-modal representation in a self-supervised manner, which can be transferred well to a series of downstream tasks [1,2,6,26,50]. The representations can be learned by an auxiliary task of predicting the audio-visual correspondence [2], by predicting whether the audio and video frames are temporally synchronized [26] or spatially aligned [50], or by using cross-modal prediction for co-clustering [1]. One of the recent approaches further employs compositional contrastive learning to transfer audio-visual knowledge for better video representation learning [6]. In another line of work, the integration of both audio and visual modalities is exploited, which has promoted a variety of tasks such as audio source separation [11,13,15,54], audio spatialization [14,24], audio-visual instance discrimination [23,25], saliency prediction [40], and action recognition [16]. Our work can be understood as exploring the complementary knowledge between audio and visual modality for the task of depth estimation.

Deep Stereo Matching. Depth is preferentially recovered by well-posed stereo matching due to its simple settings, high accuracy, and acceptable cost. Most deep stereo methods directly leverage rectified RGB stereo images to estimate disparity, which can be converted to depth with known camera baseline and focal length. One category of approaches utilizes correlation layers to encode matching information of left and right views [22,27,48], in which semantic [49] and edge information [36] are also incorporated as additional cues to improve performance. Another category of approaches focuses on building a 4D cost volume and leveraging 3D convolutions for cost aggregation to regress disparity or depth [4,7,17,19,52]. A few other methods work on combining other modalities to obtain accurate dense depth maps, like sparse LiDAR point clouds [30] or proxy disparity labels from a dedicated platform on-board the camera [31]. However, none of these techniques has been intended to cope with audio information, whereas this work demonstrates the ability of the audio modality to help predict better depth when combined with stereo images.

Multimodal Monocular Depth Estimation. Monocular depth estimation methods span from only monocular image based methods to multimodal methods. The former involves estimating dense depth maps from a single RGB image [53]. The latter usually increases other modalities including sparse depth maps [47], LiDAR point clouds [46,51], bird's eye views [37], and surface normal [32]. Recently, the audio modality is shown to be able to estimate the depth of the scene, like echoes from two ears [8] or binaural sounds of the object itself [41]. To fuse multimodal information from the audio and visual modalities to improve the performance, the authors in [12] leverage echolocation as a proxy task to learn better visual representations. They show that simply concatenating visual and audio features can yield better depth maps. This idea was further extended in [28] where a material properties estimation network is added and a multimodal fusion module is proposed with attention mechanisms for better depth estimation. Going beyond the ill-posed monocular depth estimation and inaccessible material properties, in this study, we propose to learn depth from stereo images using echoes with no requirements for material properties. Stereo learning on visual textures and the complementary knowledge from echoes can boost the performance of depth estimation to a further level.

3 Methods

3.1 Problem Formulation

In this paper, we focus on learning depth from stereo images with echoes. Given a pair of RGB stereo images, $(I_l, I_r) \in \mathbb{R}^{3 \times W \times H}$, a Stereo Net is adopted to predict the disparity map, $D_v \in \mathbb{R}^{W \times H}$, where W, H are the width and height of images. With known camera baseline B and focal length f, the depth map Z_v from the visual modality can be obtained by $Z_v = \frac{Bf}{D_v}$. The corresponding time-domain echo response is also given, which can be converted into a frequency spectrogram representation, $E \in \mathbb{R}^{2 \times P \times Q}$, where P is the number of discrete time steps and Q is the number of frequency bins. An Echo Net is employed to regress the depth map Z_a from the audio modality. The final depth map Z is obtained by fusing the depth maps predicted by both modalities.

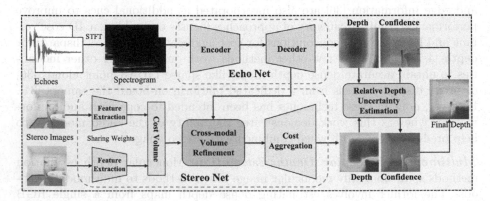

Fig. 2. Framework overview of our StereoEchoes. The multimodal data of stereo images and echoes pass through the Stereo Net and the Echo Net to yield their respective depth maps. The two networks interact at feature level through the Cross-modal Volume Refinement module. The final depth map is fused by the pixel-wise confidence produced by the Relative Depth Uncertainty Estimation module.

3.2 Framework Overview

Figure 2 depicts the framework of our method. As mentioned in Sect. 3.1, we take multimodal data of stereo images and echoes as input. The Echo Net and Stereo Net are adopted to yield the depth maps of the respective modalities. The Echo Net is an encoder-decoder network used in [12]. The Stereo Net inspired from [17] consists of feature extraction, cost volume construction, cost aggregation, and disparity regression. To fully exploit the reciprocal relationship between the audio and visual modalities, we integrate both modalities at internal feature level and output space, respectively. For feature-level integration, we propose a Cross-modal Volume Refinement module to transfer the complementary knowledge of echoes into the stereo cost volume for refinement. On the output space, we introduce a Relative Depth Uncertainty Estimation module to yield pixel-wise confidence of each modality. The final depth maps are obtained by fusing depth maps of both modalities with respective pixel-wise confidence.

3.3 Cross-modal Volume Refinement

Stereo matching approaches aim at learning structural information by comparing the similarity of local left and right patches to obtain the optimal disparity. As a result, stereo methods often succeed on richly-textured foreground objects but struggle to deal with textureless areas such as white walls. In contrast, depth prediction from echoes reported in earlier work [5,8,28] shows that the audio modality has a good estimation for textureless global regions like white walls despite large errors in the details. To fully exploit the reciprocal relationship between the two modalities, we propose to transfer the complementary knowledge of the audio modality to the visual modality at internal feature level.

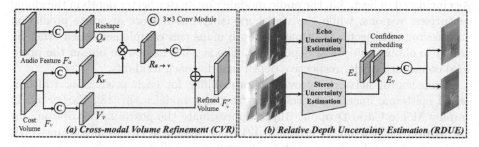

Fig. 3. Schematic diagram of Cross-modal Volume Refinement module (a) and Relative Depth Uncertainty Estimation module (b).

Cost volume is the most significant internal feature in deep stereo networks, encoding all necessary information for succeeding disparity regression. The decoder features of the Echo Net also contain global characteristics related to depth regression. To this end, we design a Cross-modal Volume Refinement (CVR) module that utilizes echo features as a guide to help refine the cost volume of the Stereo Net. Figure 3(a) shows the schematic diagram of CVR. Inspired by the cross-attention mechanism [42], we adopt audio features as query features and visual features as key-value features to learn audio-visual multimodal features for volume refinement.

Specifically, the CVR has two inputs: the audio feature $F_a \in \mathbb{R}^{B \times C_1 \times H \times W}$ and the cost volume $F_v \in \mathbb{R}^{B \times C_2 \times D \times H \times W}$. The convolutional modules with the kernel size 3×3 followed by BN and ReLU (W_Q^a, W_K^v, and W_V^v) are used to transform F_a and F_v to obtain the embeddings Q_a, K_v, and V_v:

$$Q_a = W_Q^a(F_a), K_v = W_K^v(F_v), V_v = W_V^v(F_v). \tag{1}$$

The audio-visual correlation $R_{a \to v}$ is computed by the Hadamard product $\circ$ between K_v and the reshaped $Q_a \in \mathbb{R}^{B \times (C_2 D) \times H \times W}$ under the constraint of $C_1 = C_2 \times D$:

$$R_{a \to v} = \text{Reshape}(Q_a) \circ K_v. \tag{2}$$

The residual volume is learned from the multimodal correlation $R_{a \to v}$, which is further added to the input to yield the refined volume F_v^r as:

$$F_v^r = W_M(R_{a \to v}) + V_v, \tag{3}$$

where W_M denotes a convolutional module with the kernel size 3×3 followed by BN and ReLU.

In practice, we employ CVR at multi-scale audio and visual features, and the resolutions of feature maps of both modalities are aligned by upsampling or downsampling operations.

3.4   Relative Depth Uncertainty Estimation

As elucidated in Sect. 3.3, the audio modality estimates better depth in the global textureless regions, while the visual modality has a more accurate prediction on foreground objects. Multimodal depth maps can complement each other by fusion to obtain an optical depth map. The key lies in how to obtain the pixel-wise confidence of the respective depth map for each modality.

Deep neural networks provide a probability for each prediction, which is called epistemic uncertainty resulting from the model itself [18]. Earlier works employ Monte Carlo Dropout [10] to approximate the posterior distribution for uncertainty estimation, or ensemble [21]. For binocular vision, uncertainty estimation evolves into stereo confidence estimation. Various methods have been proposed for this that use the single-modal or bi-modal input [29,35,39]. These works mostly focus on the absolute confidence estimation of depth maps from the visual modality, but rarely explore the relative confidence estimation between two modalities. To this end, we propose a Relative Depth Uncertainty Estimation module (RDUE) to obtain the relative confidence of the visual modality compared to the audio modality for depth map fusion. Figure 3(b) shows the architecture of RDUE.

Specifically, we first use the input left image I_l and the generated disparity map D to obtain the corresponding warped right image $\tilde{I}_r$ based on stereo reconstruction. Then, a small modal-specific fully-convolutional network (W_C^a and W_C^v) takes the concatenation of I_l, the respective depth map (Z_a and Z_v), and the corresponding pixel-wise error map (O_a and O_v) as inputs, which produces stereo confidence embeddings E_a and E_v. For both modalities, this can be expressed as:

$$\begin{aligned} E_a &= W_C^a(\text{Cat}(I_l, Z_a, O_a)), \\ E_v &= W_C^v(\text{Cat}(I_l, Z_v, O_v)), \end{aligned} \tag{4}$$

where the error map is calculated by the l_1 norm between the input right image and the warped one as $O = |I_r - \tilde{I}_r|$. Next, the relative depth confidence map $\mathcal{M}$

are learned from the stereo confidence embeddings of both modalities followed by a Sigmoid layer to normalize the values to $[0, 1]$:

$$\mathcal{M} = \text{Sigmoid}(W_o(\text{Cat}(E_a, E_v))), \qquad (5)$$

where W_o denotes a small fully-convolutional network for relative confidence estimation.

We use the relative confidence map $\mathcal{M}$ for weighting the depth map Z_v from stereo and $1 - \mathcal{M}$ for weighting the depth map Z_a from echoes. Thus the final depth map Z can be obtained by

$$Z = \mathcal{M} \odot Z_v + (1 - \mathcal{M}) \odot Z_a, \qquad (6)$$

where $\odot$ denotes the element-wise product.

3.5   Objective Function

We train the Echo Net and Stereo Net jointly in an end-to-end manner following [28], and adopt the logarithm of depth errors as the loss function:

$$\mathcal{L}(Z, Z^*) = \ln(1 + ||Z - Z^*||_1), \qquad (7)$$

where Z^* is the ground truth depth map.

4   Stereo-Echo Datasets

Lacking specific datasets for evaluating depth estimation from stereo images with echoes, we introduce two Stereo-Echo datasets named **Stereo-Replica** and **Stereo-Matterport3D** from two indoor visual scenes Replica [38] and Matterport3D [3], respectively. We describe the details of the visual scenes, echoes simulation, and stereo images synthesis as below.

Visual Scenes. Both Replica and Matterport3D datasets are rendered using open source 3D simulators, Habitat [33]. Replica has 18 scenes in total from 1740 images and 4 orientations ($90°, 180°, 270°, 360°$), which covers hotels, apartments, rooms, and offices. Following [12], we use 15 scenes for training and 3 scenes for testing. On Matterport3D, we use 77 scenes of real-world homes from 16844 images and 4 orientations for evaluation following [28]. The training, validation, and testing sets consist of 59, 10, and 8 scenes, respectively.

Echoes Simulation. We use the audio simulator SoundSpaces [5] for realistic echoes simulation. The visual scene of the respective dataset is firstly divided into grids along navigation points. We place the source and receiver at the same point for sending the audio signal and receiving the echoes, respectively. Following [12], a 3 ms sweep signal is adopted as the source audio spanning the human hearing range (20 Hz to 20 kHz). The Room Impulse Response (RIR) is then calculated in four orientations using audio ray tracing [43]. Finally, we obtain the echoes by convolving the input audio signal with the RIR. Here, the sampling rates of the source and received echoes are 44.1 kHz and 16 kHz for Replica and Matterport3D, respectively. We encourage the interested readers to refer to [12] for more details.

Stereo Images Synthesis. We utilize RGB images and their ground truth depth to generate stereo image pairs similar to [45]. To simulate camera baselines and focal lengths, we directly convert the depth Z to disparity D with $D = \frac{Z_{max}}{Z}$. The RGB image is regarded as the left image I_l and the right image I_r is synthesized via forward warping [34]. Specifically, we translate each pixel of left image D pixels to the left side and perform linear interpolation to obtain the right image. However, pixels in I_r with no matching pixels in I_l may manifest themselves as holes in the synthesized image I_r. To address this, following image painting techniques [9], we fill the missing regions with a texture from a randomly selected image from the same scene. In this way, the interference from black holes with depth prediction is mitigated. Figure 4 presents several synthesized examples with corresponding disparity maps. The datasets are available at https://github.com/chzhang18/Stereo-Echo-Datasets.

Fig. 4. Synthesized examples of stereo image pairs and disparity maps on Stereo-Replica dataset [38] (left three cases) and Stereo-Matterport3D dataset [3] (right four cases). Brighter colors indicate larger disparity values. (Color figure online)

5   Experiments

In this section, we first introduce the implementation details and evaluation metrics. We then conduct experiments on our Stereo-Echo datasets, Stereo-Replica and Stereo-Matterport3D, to demonstrate the superiority of our method. Next, extensive ablation studies are provided to analyze the contribution of each proposed module in our framework, as well as the extensions for other stereo networks. Finally, we show the qualitative results to further validate the effectiveness of our method.

5.1   Experimental Setup

Our method is implemented with PyTorch. The input to the Stereo Net is 128×128 RGB stereo images. Color normalization is used for data preprocessing without any data augmentation. The maximum disparity is set to 32. For input to the Echo Net, following [28], 60ms echo signal is used to compute spectrogram with FFT size of 512. For Replica, a $2 \times 257 \times 166$ spectrogram is obtained using Hanning window of length 64 and hop length of 16. For Matterport3D, a $2 \times 257 \times 121$ spectrogram is produced using Hanning window of length 32 and hop length of 8. For network architecture, the Echo Net is used in [28] and the Stereo Net is adopted from [48]. Detailed architectures of the two networks and the proposed Cross-modal Volume Refinement and Relative Depth Uncertainty Estimation are provided in Supplementary Materials.

In training, we employ Adam ($\beta_1 = 0.9$, $\beta_2 = 0.999$) as the optimizer with learning rate of 0.001. The batch size is set to 50 on a single TITAN-RTX GPU. The entire model is trained from scratch. The training epoch is set to 100 for Replica and 50 for Matterport3D. The code is available at https://github.com/chzhang18/StereoEchoes.

Table 1. Evaluation results on the Stereo-Replica dataset. E refers to echoes, M refers to monocular images, and S refers to stereo images.

Methods	Modality	RMSE ($\downarrow$)	REL ($\downarrow$)	log10 ($\downarrow$)	$\delta_{1.25}$ ($\uparrow$)	$\delta_{1.25^2}$ ($\uparrow$)	$\delta_{1.25^3}$ ($\uparrow$)
ECHO2DEPTH	E	0.713	0.347	0.134	0.580	0.772	0.868
RGB2DEPTH	M	0.374	0.202	0.076	0.749	0.883	0.945
VisualEchoes [12]	$E + M$	0.346	0.172	0.068	0.798	0.905	0.950
BI2D [28]	$E + M$	0.249	0.118	0.046	0.869	0.943	0.970
STEREO2DEPTH	S	0.248	0.069	0.030	0.945	0.980	0.989
StereoEchoes	$E + S$	**0.186**	**0.051**	**0.022**	**0.964**	**0.985**	**0.993**

Table 2. Evaluation results on the Stereo-Matterport3D dataset. E refers to echoes, M refers to monocular images, and S refers to stereo images.

Methods	Modality	RMSE ($\downarrow$)	REL ($\downarrow$)	log10 ($\downarrow$)	$\delta_{1.25}$ ($\uparrow$)	$\delta_{1.25^2}$ ($\uparrow$)	$\delta_{1.25^3}$ ($\uparrow$)
ECHO2DEPTH	E	1.778	0.507	0.192	0.464	0.642	0.759
RGB2DEPTH	M	1.090	0.260	0.111	0.592	0.802	0.910
VisualEchoes [12]	$E + M$	0.998	0.193	0.083	0.711	0.878	0.945
BI2D [28]	$E + M$	0.950	0.175	0.079	0.733	0.886	0.948
STEREO2DEPTH	S	0.636	0.058	0.026	0.943	0.979	0.990
StereoEchoes	$E + S$	**0.548**	**0.049**	**0.021**	**0.958**	**0.984**	**0.992**

5.2   Comparison with State-of-the-Art Methods

We compare on Stereo-Replica and Stereo-Matterport3D datasets with state-of-the-art methods: VisualEchoes [12] and Beyond-Image-to-Depth [28] (mark it as BI2D for convenience). We also compare with three competitive baselines: ECHO2DEPTH that predicts depth only from Echo Net, STEREO2DEPTH that predicts depth only from Stereo Net, and RGB2DEPTH that predicts depth only from monocular images.

Table 1 shows the comparison results with the above methods on the Stereo-Replica dataset. Our proposed method outperforms all the compared methods on all the metrics. We observe that STEREO2DEPTH achieves comparable performance to BI2D on RMSE, and surpasses it on other metrics benefiting from the advantage of binocular vision. When adding the audio modality, our StereoEchoes outperforms BI2D by 25.3% (0.186 cf. 0.249 RMSE). It is also worth noting that our StereoEchoes achieves an order of magnitude lower than VisualEchoes by 50.3% (0.186 cf. 0.374 RMSE).

Table 2 shows the comparison results on the Stereo-Matterport3D dataset. Our StereoEchoes achieves the best performance, notably outperforming BI2D by 42.3% on RMSE. Although the performance of STEREO2DEPTH is quite remarkable, our StereoEchoes further improves it by 13.8% on RMSE. This is surprisingly higher than the improvement of BI2D w.r.t. RGB2DEPTH (0.950 cf. 1.090 i.e. 12.8%). This validates our claim that the configuration of stereo inputs with echoes is better than that of monocular inputs with echoes. Stereo depth prediction with echoes can fully utilize the complementary knowledge to achieve higher performance without the help of the material network.

Table 3. Ablation study of key components on the Stereo-Replica and Stereo-Matterport3D datasets.

Datasets	Methods	CVR	RDUE	RMSE ($\downarrow$)	REL ($\downarrow$)	log10 ($\downarrow$)	$\delta_{1.25}$ ($\uparrow$)	$\delta_{1.25^2}$ ($\uparrow$)	$\delta_{1.25^3}$ ($\uparrow$)
Replica	STEREO2DEPTH			0.248	0.069	0.030	0.945	0.980	0.989
	Ours w/o RDUE	✓		0.202	0.054	0.024	0.958	0.983	0.991
	Ours w/o CVR		✓	0.193	0.057	0.023	0.958	0.984	0.991
	Ours (full)	✓	✓	**0.186**	**0.051**	**0.022**	**0.964**	**0.985**	**0.993**
Mp3D	STEREO2DEPTH			0.636	0.058	0.026	0.943	0.979	0.990
	Ours w/o RDUE	✓		0.593	0.054	0.023	0.951	0.980	0.990
	Ours w/o CVR		✓	0.599	0.050	0.022	0.951	0.980	0.990
	Ours (full)	✓	✓	**0.548**	**0.049**	**0.021**	**0.958**	**0.984**	**0.992**

Table 4. Performance of different feature fusion strategies on Stereo-Replica.

Methods	RMSE ($\downarrow$)	REL ($\downarrow$)	log10 ($\downarrow$)	$\delta_{1.25}$ ($\uparrow$)	$\delta_{1.25^2}$ ($\uparrow$)	$\delta_{1.25^3}$ ($\uparrow$)
BI2D [28]	0.249	0.118	0.046	0.869	0.943	0.970
Concat	0.228	0.065	0.028	0.953	**0.983**	**0.991**
Bilinear	0.234	0.065	0.029	0.952	**0.983**	**0.991**
CVR	**0.202**	**0.054**	**0.024**	**0.958**	0.983	0.991

5.3   Ablation Study

In this section, we conduct detailed ablation studies to demonstrate the following points. (i) Using stereo images and echoes together with either CVR or RDUE improves the performance over only using stereo images. (ii) Among different fusion strategies at feature level or output space, our proposed method achieves the best performance. (iii) Our method can be embedded into other stereo networks.

Effectiveness of Key Components. We adopt STEREO2DEPTH as the ablation baseline to show the impact of CVR and RDUE as shown in Table 3. As can be seen, applying the Cross-modal Volume Refinement can significantly reduce the RMSE, *e.g.*, 18.5% on Stereo-Replica and 6.8% on Stereo-Mp3D. We conjecture that since the visual scenes in Replica have more textureless regions, the echo guidance is more effective thus the improvement on Replica is more. The δ metrics are also improved indicating that the complementary knowledge from the audio modality also helps reduce the pixel-wise relative errors.

In addition, compared with the baselines, RMSE is reduced by 22.2% and 5.8% on Stereo-Replica and Stereo-Matterport3D respectively by integrating the proposed Relative Depth Uncertainty Estimation. The results validate that the depth fusion is able to fully exploit the reciprocal relationship between the audio and visual modalities on textureless and textured areas through the pixel-wise confidence map.

Furthermore, using both CVR and RDUE can further reduce the RMSE by 3.6%–8.5% on the two datasets, though the performance is already encouraging by adding either of them. As a result, our full method significantly outperforms the corresponding baselines on both datasets, especially an improvement of 25% RMSE on the Stereo-Replica dataset.

Different Fusion Strategies. To further demonstrate the effectiveness of each module, we perform exhaustive comparisons with other alternative methods respectively. In Table 4, for the feature level fusion, two strategies are chosen for comparison, which are *concat* of audio and stereo features and *bilinear* transformation used in [28] with an attention network. We observe that our CVR, with RMSE of 0.202, achieves the best performance among the alternative strategies. Note that *concat* and *bilinear* perform better than BI2D benefiting from stereo settings, but are still inferior to our CVR. This highlights that our elaborately designed CVR for stereo and echo feature fusion is better than generic multi-modal features fusion with attention.

In Table 5, for the fusion at output space, we take the average value and linear weighting[1] of the estimated depth from two modalities as baselines. We also compare with single-modal uncertainty-aware depth fusion strategies that leverage only audio or visual modality. One can observe that our method significantly outperforms these four compared strategies, indicating that multimodal relative uncertainty estimation is able to learn better pixel-wise confidence than single-modal absolute uncertainty estimation for depth fusion.

---

[1] The depth maps from stereo images and echoes are fused using weights of 0.9:0.1.

Table 5. Performance of different depth fusion strategies at output space on the Stereo-Replica dataset.

Methods	RMSE (↓)	REL (↓)	log10 (↓)	$\delta_{1.25}$ (↑)	$\delta_{1.25^2}$ (↑)	$\delta_{1.25^3}$ (↑)
Average	0.281	0.069	0.030	0.941	0.978	0.989
Linear weighting	0.246	0.066	0.029	0.946	0.980	0.990
Echo uncertainty	0.242	0.066	0.029	0.948	0.981	0.990
Stereo uncertainty	0.234	0.065	0.029	0.950	0.982	0.990
Relative uncertainty	**0.193**	**0.057**	**0.023**	**0.958**	**0.984**	**0.991**

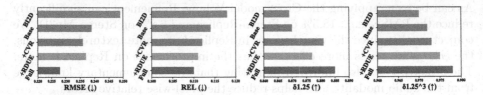

Fig. 5. Performance improvements by gradually adding proposed modules to AANet [48] on the Stereo-Replica dataset. The tag "full" refers to Base+CVR+RDUE.

Stereo Backbone Network. We further extend our method to correlation-based stereo networks, *e.g.*, the lightweight stereo network AANet [48]. Since the aggregation network in AANet employs 2D convolutions, our CVR can adapt to the 3D matching volume while the RDUE remains constant. We reimplement all models with the training protocols detailed in Sec. 5.1. Figure 5 depicts the results. It can be seen that our method delivers better performance using different stereo networks. This suggests that our designed method generalizes well to various stereo networks to improve their performance with echoes.

5.4   Qualitative Results and Analysis

In addition to quantitative comparisons, we further provide qualitative visual analysis to illustrate the superiority of our method. Figure 6 visualizes the depth map comparison with competing methods on the Stereo-Replica dataset. Compared to VisualEchoes and BI2D, STEREO2DEPTH is able to generate more accurate depth maps for foreground objects, such as chairs, benches, and clothes. This is mainly due to the rich texture and large disparity of foreground objects that are suitable for stereo learning. When echoes are integrated, the complementarity of both modalities makes the depth boundary sharper, since the audio modality is conducive to depth estimation for textureless backgrounds. Figure 7 further shows the comparison results on the Stereo-Matterport3D dataset. Our method produces more accurate depth maps on both foreground objects and backgrounds. The reasons are two-fold. Firstly, the scenes in Matterport3D are rich in textures thus enhancing the stereo performance. Secondly, complemen-

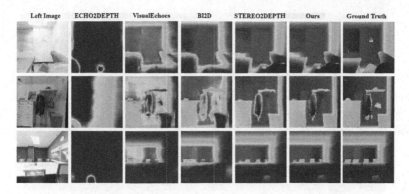

Fig. 6. Qualitative comparisons of different methods on Stereo-Replica. Our method produces better depth maps with fine structures and clear object boundaries.

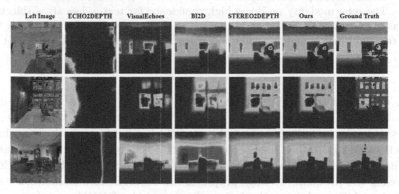

Fig. 7. Qualitative comparisons on Stereo-Matterport3D. Our method produces more accurate depth maps on both foregrounds and backgrounds.

tary knowledge of echoes further improves the depth maps of background objects that are far away, such as windows and murals on walls.

We further visualize the confidence maps for Echo Net and Stereo Net in Fig. 8. On Stereo-Replica, the audio modality is generally more confident in textureless regions (*e.g.*, white walls in the backgrounds) while the visual modality is more confident in textured foreground objects (*e.g.*, sofa and table). On Stereo-Matterport3D, the visual modality produces higher confidence in most regions, since most scenes have rich textures suitable for matching. Unfortunately, visual modalities tend to exhibit poor confidence in dark textureless regions, where audio modalities are mainly relied upon. An example is marked using a black box in the rightmost case in Fig. 8. The above analysis suggests that the audio and visual modalities can complement each other. Our method tries to leverage the best of the strengths of both modalities to yield the final depth.

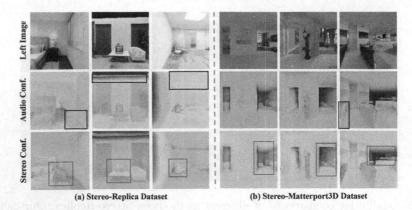

(a) Stereo-Replica Dataset   (b) Stereo-Matterport3D Dataset

Fig. 8. Confidence map visualization on Stereo-Replica (left) and Stereo-Matterport3D (right). The echo modality produces high confidence for textureless areas (black box) whereas the visual modality attends more on richly-textured regions (red box). Warm colors represent high confidence while cool colors represent low confidence. (Color figure online)

6   Conclusion and Future Work

In this paper, we propose a new problem of predicting depth with stereo images and echoes and introduce the Stereo-Replica and Stereo-Matterport3D datasets as benchmarks. To exploit the reciprocal relationship of both modalities for addressing the problem, we have proposed the *StereoEchoes* framework consisting of the CVR module at the feature level and the RDUE module for multimodal depth fusion. Extensive experiments on the two datasets validate that our method improves stereo depth estimation by adding echoes. In future work, we plan to extend our method to unsupervised conditions without ground truth depth and deploy our model on edge devices for robot navigation.

Acknowledgements. This research was supported by the National Key Research and Development Program of China under Grant No. 2018AAA0100400, and the National Natural Science Foundation of China under Grants 61976208, 62076242, 62071466, and the InnoHK project.

References

1. Alwassel, H., Mahajan, D., Korbar, B., Torresani, L., Ghanem, B., Tran, D.: Self-supervised learning by cross-modal audio-video clustering. In: NeurIPS, pp. 9758–9770 (2020)
2. Arandjelovic, R., Zisserman, A.: Look, listen and learn. In: ICCV, pp. 609–617 (2017)
3. Chang, A., et al.: Matterport3D: learning from RGB-D data in indoor environments. In: 3DV, pp. 667–676 (2017)

4. Chang, J.R., Chen, Y.S.: Pyramid stereo matching network. In: CVPR, pp. 5410–5418 (2018)
5. Chen, C., et al.: SoundSpaces: audio-visual navigation in 3D environments. In: Vedaldi, A., Bischof, H., Brox, T., Frahm, J.-M. (eds.) ECCV 2020. LNCS, vol. 12351, pp. 17–36. Springer, Cham (2020). https://doi.org/10.1007/978-3-030-58539-6_2
6. Chen, Y., Xian, Y., Koepke, A., Shan, Y., Akata, Z.: Distilling audio-visual knowledge by compositional contrastive learning. In: CVPR, pp. 7016–7025 (2021)
7. Cheng, X., et al.: Hierarchical neural architecture search for deep stereo matching. In: NeurIPS, pp. 22158–22169 (2020)
8. Christensen, J.H., Hornauer, S., Stella, X.Y.: BatVision: learning to see 3D spatial layout with two ears. In: ICRA, pp. 1581–1587 (2020)
9. Dwibedi, D., Misra, I., Hebert, M.: Cut, paste and learn: surprisingly easy synthesis for instance detection. In: ICCV, pp. 1301–1310 (2017)
10. Gal, Y., Ghahramani, Z.: Dropout as a Bayesian approximation: representing model uncertainty in deep learning. In: ICML, pp. 1050–1059 (2016)
11. Gan, C., Huang, D., Zhao, H., Tenenbaum, J.B., Torralba, A.: Music gesture for visual sound separation. In: CVPR, pp. 10478–10487 (2020)
12. Gao, R., Chen, C., Al-Halah, Z., Schissler, C., Grauman, K.: VISUALECHOES: spatial image representation learning through echolocation. In: Vedaldi, A., Bischof, H., Brox, T., Frahm, J.-M. (eds.) ECCV 2020. LNCS, vol. 12354, pp. 658–676. Springer, Cham (2020). https://doi.org/10.1007/978-3-030-58545-7_38
13. Gao, R., Feris, R., Grauman, K.: Learning to separate object sounds by watching unlabeled video. In: Ferrari, V., Hebert, M., Sminchisescu, C., Weiss, Y. (eds.) ECCV 2018. LNCS, vol. 11207, pp. 36–54. Springer, Cham (2018). https://doi.org/10.1007/978-3-030-01219-9_3
14. Gao, R., Grauman, K.: 2.5 d visual sound. In: CVPR, pp. 324–333 (2019)
15. Gao, R., Grauman, K.: Co-separating sounds of visual objects. In: ICCV, pp. 3879–3888 (2019)
16. Gao, R., Oh, T.H., Grauman, K., Torresani, L.: Listen to look: action recognition by previewing audio. In: CVPR, pp. 10457–10467 (2020)
17. Guo, X., Yang, K., Yang, W., Wang, X., Li, H.: Group-wise correlation stereo network. In: CVPR, pp. 3273–3282 (2019)
18. Kendall, A., Gal, Y.: What uncertainties do we need in Bayesian deep learning for computer vision? In: NeurIPS (2017)
19. Kendall, A., Martirosyan, H., Dasgupta, S., Henry, P.: End-to-end learning of geometry and context for deep stereo regression. In: ICCV, pp. 66–75 (2017)
20. Kolarik, A.J., Moore, B.C., Zahorik, P., Cirstea, S., Pardhan, S.: Auditory distance perception in humans: a review of cues, development, neuronal bases, and effects of sensory loss. Attention Percept. Psychophys. **78**(2), 373–395 (2016)
21. Lakshminarayanan, B., Pritzel, A., Blundell, C.: Simple and scalable predictive uncertainty estimation using deep ensembles. In: NeurIPS (2017)
22. Liang, Z., et al.: Learning for disparity estimation through feature constancy. In: CVPR, pp. 2811–2820 (2018)
23. Morgado, P., Misra, I., Vasconcelos, N.: Robust audio-visual instance discrimination. In: CVPR, pp. 12934–12945 (2021)
24. Morgado, P., Nvasconcelos, N., Langlois, T., Wang, O.: Self-supervised generation of spatial audio for 360 video. In: NeurIPS (2018)
25. Morgado, P., Vasconcelos, N., Misra, I.: Audio-visual instance discrimination with cross-modal agreement. In: CVPR, pp. 12475–12486 (2021)

26. Owens, A., Efros, A.A.: Audio-visual scene analysis with self-supervised multisensory features. In: Ferrari, V., Hebert, M., Sminchisescu, C., Weiss, Y. (eds.) ECCV 2018. LNCS, vol. 11210, pp. 639–658. Springer, Cham (2018). https://doi.org/10.1007/978-3-030-01231-1_39
27. Pang, J., Sun, W., Ren, J., Yang, C., Yan, Q.: Cascade residual learning: a two-stage convolutional neural network for stereo matching. In: ICCV, pp. 878–886 (2017)
28. Parida, K.K., Srivastava, S., Sharma, G.: Beyond image to depth: improving depth prediction using echoes. In: CVPR, pp. 8268–8277 (2021)
29. Poggi, M., Mattoccia, S.: Learning from scratch a confidence measure. In: BMVC, vol. 2, p. 4 (2016)
30. Poggi, M., Pallotti, D., Tosi, F., Mattoccia, S.: Guided stereo matching. In: CVPR, pp. 979–988 (2019)
31. Poggi, M., Tonioni, A., Tosi, F., Mattoccia, S., Di Stefano, L.: Continual adaptation for deep stereo. IEEE Trans. Pattern Anal. Mach. Intell. (2021)
32. Qiu, J., et al.: DeepLidar: deep surface normal guided depth prediction for outdoor scene from sparse lidar data and single color image. In: CVPR, pp. 3313–3322 (2019)
33. Savva, M., et al.: Habitat: a platform for embodied AI research. In: ICCV, pp. 9339–9347 (2019)
34. Schwarz, L.A.: Non-rigid registration using free-form deformations. Technische Universität München 6 (2007)
35. Shaked, A., Wolf, L.: Improved stereo matching with constant highway networks and reflective confidence learning. In: CVPR, pp. 4641–4650 (2017)
36. Song, X., Zhao, X., Fang, L., Hu, H., Yu, Y.: EdgeStereo: an effective multi-task learning network for stereo matching and edge detection. Int. J. Comput. Vision 128(4), 910–930 (2020)
37. Srivastava, S., Jurie, F., Sharma, G.: Learning 2D to 3D lifting for object detection in 3D for autonomous vehicles. In: IROS, pp. 4504–4511 (2019)
38. Straub, J., et al.: The replica dataset: a digital replica of indoor spaces. arXiv preprint arXiv:1906.05797 (2019)
39. Tosi, F., Poggi, M., Benincasa, A., Mattoccia, S.: Beyond local reasoning for stereo confidence estimation with deep learning. In: Ferrari, V., Hebert, M., Sminchisescu, C., Weiss, Y. (eds.) ECCV 2018. LNCS, vol. 11210, pp. 323–338. Springer, Cham (2018). https://doi.org/10.1007/978-3-030-01231-1_20
40. Tsiami, A., Koutras, P., Maragos, P.: Stavis: spatio-temporal audiovisual saliency network. In: CVPR, pp. 4766–4776 (2020)
41. Vasudevan, A.B., Dai, D., Van Gool, L.: Semantic object prediction and spatial sound super-resolution with binaural sounds. In: Vedaldi, A., Bischof, H., Brox, T., Frahm, J.-M. (eds.) ECCV 2020. LNCS, vol. 12349, pp. 638–655. Springer, Cham (2020). https://doi.org/10.1007/978-3-030-58548-8_37
42. Vaswani, A., et al.: Attention is all you need. In: NeurIPS (2017)
43. Veach, E., Guibas, L.: Bidirectional estimators for light transport. In: Photorealistic Rendering Techniques, pp. 145–167 (1995)
44. Watanabe, K., Shimojo, S.: When sound affects vision: effects of auditory grouping on visual motion perception. Psychol. Sci. 12(2), 109–116 (2001)
45. Watson, J., Aodha, O.M., Turmukhambetov, D., Brostow, G.J., Firman, M.: Learning stereo from single images. In: Vedaldi, A., Bischof, H., Brox, T., Frahm, J.-M. (eds.) ECCV 2020. LNCS, vol. 12346, pp. 722–740. Springer, Cham (2020). https://doi.org/10.1007/978-3-030-58452-8_42

46. Weng, X., Kitani, K.: Monocular 3D object detection with pseudo-lidar point cloud. In: ICCVW (2019)
47. Xiong, X., Xiong, H., Xian, K., Zhao, C., Cao, Z., Li, X.: Sparse-to-dense depth completion revisited: sampling strategy and graph construction. In: Vedaldi, A., Bischof, H., Brox, T., Frahm, J.-M. (eds.) ECCV 2020. LNCS, vol. 12366, pp. 682–699. Springer, Cham (2020). https://doi.org/10.1007/978-3-030-58589-1_41
48. Xu, H., Zhang, J.: AANet: adaptive aggregation network for efficient stereo matching. In: CVPR, pp. 1959–1968 (2020)
49. Yang, G., Zhao, H., Shi, J., Deng, Z., Jia, J.: SegStereo: exploiting semantic information for disparity estimation. In: Ferrari, V., Hebert, M., Sminchisescu, C., Weiss, Y. (eds.) ECCV 2018. LNCS, vol. 11211, pp. 660–676. Springer, Cham (2018). https://doi.org/10.1007/978-3-030-01234-2_39
50. Yang, K., Russell, B., Salamon, J.: Telling left from right: learning spatial correspondence of sight and sound. In: CVPR, pp. 9932–9941 (2020)
51. You, Y., et al.: Pseudo-lidar++: accurate depth for 3D object detection in autonomous driving. In: ICLR (2019)
52. Zhang, F., Prisacariu, V., Yang, R., Torr, P.H.: GA-Net: guided aggregation net for end-to-end stereo matching. In: CVPR, pp. 185–194 (2019)
53. Zhao, C.Q., Sun, Q.Y., Zhang, C.Z., Tang, Y., Qian, F.: Monocular depth estimation based on deep learning: an overview. SCIENCE CHINA Technol. Sci. **63**(9), 1612–1627 (2020). https://doi.org/10.1007/s11431-020-1582-8
54. Zhao, H., Gan, C., Rouditchenko, A., Vondrick, C., McDermott, J., Torralba, A.: The sound of pixels. In: Ferrari, V., Hebert, M., Sminchisescu, C., Weiss, Y. (eds.) ECCV 2018. LNCS, vol. 11205, pp. 587–604. Springer, Cham (2018). https://doi.org/10.1007/978-3-030-01246-5_35

Inverted Pyramid Multi-task Transformer for Dense Scene Understanding

Hanrong Ye and Dan Xu[(✉)]

Department of Computer Science and Engineering, HKUST, Clear Water Bay,
Kowloon, Hong Kong
{hyeae,danxu}@cse.ust.hk

Abstract. Multi-task dense scene understanding is a thriving research domain that requires simultaneous perception and reasoning on a series of correlated tasks with pixel-wise prediction. Most existing works encounter a severe limitation of modeling in the locality due to heavy utilization of convolution operations, while learning interactions and inference in a global spatial-position and multi-task context is critical for this problem. In this paper, we propose a novel end-to-end Inverted Pyramid multi-task Transformer (**InvPT**) to perform simultaneous modeling of spatial positions and multiple tasks in a unified framework. To the best of our knowledge, this is the first work that explores designing a transformer structure for multi-task dense prediction for scene understanding. Besides, it is widely demonstrated that a higher spatial resolution is remarkably beneficial for dense predictions, while it is very challenging for existing transformers to go deeper with higher resolutions due to huge complexity to large spatial size. InvPT presents an efficient UP-Transformer block to learn multi-task feature interaction at gradually increased resolutions, which also incorporates effective self-attention message passing and multi-scale feature aggregation to produce task-specific prediction at a high resolution. Our method achieves superior multi-task performance on NYUD-v2 and PASCAL-Context datasets respectively, and significantly outperforms previous state-of-the-arts. The code is available at https://github.com/prismformore/InvPT.

1 Introduction

Multi-task visual scene understanding typically requires joint learning and reasoning on a bunch of correlated tasks [41], which is highly important in computer vision and has a wide range of application scenarios such as autonomous driving, robotics, and augmented or virtual reality (AR/VR). Many of visual scene understanding tasks produce pixel-wise predictions for dense understanding of the scene such as semantic segmentation, monocular depth estimation, and human parsing. These dense prediction tasks essentially have abundant explicit

---

Supplementary Information The online version contains supplementary material available at https://doi.org/10.1007/978-3-031-19812-0_30.

S. Avidan et al. (Eds.): ECCV 2022, LNCS 13687, pp. 514–530, 2022.
https://doi.org/10.1007/978-3-031-19812-0_30

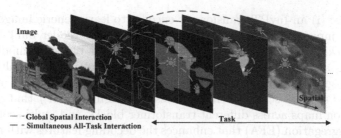

Fig. 1. Joint learning and inference of global spatial interaction and simultaneous all-task interaction are critically important for multi-task dense prediction.

and implicit correlation at the pixel level [48], which is very beneficial and can be fully utilized to improve the overall performance of multi-task models. However, how to effectively learn and exploit the cross-task correlation (*e.g.* complementarity and consistency) in a single model remains a challenging open issue.

To advance the multi-task dense scene understanding, existing works mostly rely on the powerful Convolutional Neural Networks (CNN), and significant effort has been made by developing multi-task optimization losses [19] and designing [48] or searching [16] multi-task information sharing strategies and network structures. Although promising performance has been achieved, these works are still limited by the nature of convolution kernels that are heavily used in their deep learning frameworks, which model critical spatial and task related contexts in relatively local perceptive fields (*i.e.* locality discussed by previous works [3,45]). Although the recently proposed attention based methods address this issue [5,52,55], the scope of their cross-task interaction is still highly limited. However, for multi-task dense scene understanding, the capability of capturing long-range dependency and *simultaneously* modeling global relationships of *all* tasks is crucially important for this pixel-wise multi-task problem (see Fig. 1).

On the other hand, recently the transformer models have been introduced to model the long-range spatial relationship for dense prediction problems [34,50] but they only target the setting of *single-task* learning, while the joint modeling of multiple dense prediction tasks with transformer is rarely explored in the literature, and it is not a trivial problem to globally model both the spatial and the cross-task correlations in a unified transformer framework. Besides, the performance of dense prediction tasks is greatly affected by the resolution of the final feature maps produced from the model, while it is very difficult for existing transformers to go deeper with higher resolution because of huge complexity brought by large spatial size, and typically many transformers downsample the spatial resolution dramatically to reduce the computation overhead [14,44].

To tackle the above-mentioned issues, in this work we propose a novel end-to-end Inverted Pyramid Multi-task Transformer (InvPT) framework, which can jointly model the long-range dependency within spatial and all-task contexts, and also efficiently learn fine-grained dense prediction maps at a higher resolution, for multi-task dense scene understanding. Specifically, it consists of three core designs: (i) an InvPT transformer encoder to learn generic image representations for input images, (ii) an InvPT Transformer decoder built by consecutively stacking a proposed efficient UP-Transformer block, to model implicit correlations among all the dense prediction tasks and produce multi-task features with gradually increased resolutions, and (iii) two effective multi-scale strategies, *i.e.* cross-scale Attention Message Passing (AMP) that aggregates self-attention maps across different transformer blocks, and multi-scale Encoder Feature Aggregation (EFA) that enhances the decoding features with multi-scale information from the InvPT transformer encoder.

The proposed method yields strong multi-task performance measured by the relative improvement metric [25], which is 2.59% and 1.76% on NYUD-v2 and PASCAL-Context datasets respectively. The proposed method also *largely* outperforms other state-of-the-art methods on all 9 evaluation metrics of these two benchmarks. Notably on NYUD-v2, it surpasses the best competitor by **7.23** points (mIoU) on semantic segmentation, while on PASCAL-Context it outperforms the previous best result by **11.36** and **4.68** points (mIoU) on semantic segmentation and human parsing, respectively.

In summary, our main contribution is three-fold:

- We propose a novel end-to-end Inverted Pyramid Multi-task Transformer (InvPT) framework for jointly learning multiple dense prediction tasks, which can effectively model long-range interaction in both spatial and all-task contexts in a unified architecture. As far as we know, it is the *first* work to present a transformer structure for this problem.
- We design an efficient UP-Transformer block, which allows for multi-task feature interaction and refinement at gradually *increased* resolutions, and can construct a multi-layer InvPT decoder by consecutively stacking multiple blocks to produce final feature maps with a high resolution to largely boost dense predictions. The UP-Transformer block can also flexibly embed multi-scale information through two designed strategies, *i.e.* cross-scale self-attention message passing and InvPT encoder feature aggregation.
- The proposed framework obtains superior performance on multi-task dense prediction and *remarkably* outperforms the previous state-of-the-arts on two challenging benchmarks (*i.e.* Pascal-Context and NYUD-v2).

2   Related Work

We review the most related works in the literature from two angles, *i.e.* multi-task deep learning for scene understanding and visual transformers.

Multi-task Deep Learning for Scene Understanding. As an active research field [20,25,48], multi-task deep learning can greatly help to improve the efficiency of training, as it only needs to optimize once for multiple tasks, and the overall performance of scene understanding when compared with performing several scene understanding tasks separately [42]. Multi-task deep learning methods mainly focus on two directions [41], *i.e.* multi-task optimization and

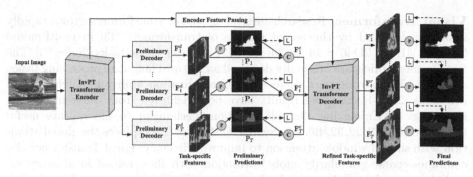

Fig. 2. Framework overview of the proposed Inverted Pyramid Multi-task Transformer (InvPT) for dense scene understanding. The task-shared transformer encoder learns generic visual representations from the input image. Then for each task $t \in \{1 \dots T\}$, the preliminary decoder produces task-specific feature $\mathbf{F}_t^d$ and preliminary prediction $\mathbf{P}_t$, which are combined as $\mathbf{F}_t^c$, serving as the input of the InvPT decoder to generate *refined and resolution-enlarged* task-specific features via globally modeling spatial and all-task interactions for the final prediction. ©, ⓟ and L denote the channel-wise concatenation, linear projection layer and loss function, respectively.

network architecture design. Previous works in the former direction typically investigate loss balancing techniques in the optimization process to address the problem of task competition [10, 11, 19]. In the latter direction researchers design explicit or implicit mechanisms for modeling cross-task interaction and embed them into the whole deep model [17, 27, 35] or only the decoder stage [51, 52, 55].

Regarding the multi-task dense scene understanding where all the tasks require pixel-wise predictions, many pioneering research works [17, 19, 25, 27, 48] have explored this field. Specifically, Xu *et al.* [48] propose PAD-Net with an effective information distillation module with attention guided cross-task message passing on multi-task predictions. MTI-Net [42] designs a sophisticated multi-scale and multi-task CNN architecture to distill information at multiple feature scales. However, most of these methods adopt CNN to learn multi-task representation and model it in a limited local context. To address this issue, there are also some exciting works developing attention-based mechanisms. For instance, [52, 55] and [51] design spatial global or local attention learning strategies within each task-specific branch, and propagate the attention to refine features among all the tasks. Concurrent to our work, [5] proposes to build up decoder via searching for proper cross-task attention structures with neural architecture search (NAS). Despite their innovative designs, these works still fail to jointly model spatial and cross-task contexts in a global manner.

Different from these works, we propose a novel multi-task transformer framework to learn long-range interactions of spatial and cross-task relationships in global contexts, which is critical for this complex multi-task problem.

Visual Transformer. Research interest in visual transformers grows rapidly nowadays inspired by the recent success of transformers [43] in multi-modal learning [31,33], 2D [6–8,14,18,29] and 3D computer vision tasks [26,28,53]. The transformer models are originally designed for natural language processing tasks, and then show strong performance and generalization ability in solving vision problems [2,4,14]. Exciting results have been achieved from different aspects including: (i) Enhancing the self-attention mechanism to incorporate useful inductive bias [12,22,32,49]. *e.g.* Swin Transformer [22] replaces the global attention with shifted window attention to improve efficiency; Focal Transformer [49] combines coarse-granularity global attention with fine-grained local attention to balance model efficiency and effectiveness; (ii) Combining transformer with CNNs [38,44,46]. *e.g.* BOTNet [38] uses a specially designed multi-head self-attention head to replace final three bottleneck blocks of ResNet; PVT [44] and CVT [46] embed convolutional layers in a hierarchical transformer framework and demonstrate that they can help improve the performance; (iii) Designing special training techniques [21,39,40]. *e.g.* DEIT [39] proposes a special transformer token for knowledge distillation from CNNs; DRLOC [21] designs a self-supervised auxiliary task to make transformer learn spatial relations. Regarding dense scene understanding tasks [44,47], Ranftl *et al.* [34] recently propose a visual transformer framework with transpose convolution for dealing with dense prediction, while HRFormer [50] adopts local attention to keep multi-scale features efficiently in the network.

To the best of our knowledge, this is the first exploration of simultaneously modeling multiple dense prediction tasks in a unified transformer framework for scene understanding. The proposed framework jointly learns spatial and all-task interactions in a global context at gradually *increased* resolutions with a novel and efficient UP-Transformer block, which can produce spatially higher-resolution feature maps to significantly boost dense predictions, and effectively incorporate multi-scale information via the proposed strategies of self-attention message passing and encoder feature aggregation.

3   InvPT for Multi-task Dense Prediction

3.1   Framework Overview

The overall framework of the proposed Inverted Pyramid Multi-task Transformer (InvPT) is depicted in Fig. 2. It mainly consists of three core parts, *i.e.* a task-shared InvPT transformer encoder, the task-specific preliminary decoders, and the InvPT transformer decoder. Specifically, the transformer encoder learns *generic* visual representations from the input images for all tasks. Then, the preliminary decoders produce *task-specific* features and preliminary predictions, which are supervised by the ground-truth labels. The task-specific feature and preliminary prediction of each task are combined and concatenated as a sequence serving as input of the InvPT Transformer decoder, to learn to produce refined task-specific representations within global spatial and task contexts, which are further used to produce the final predictions with task-specific linear projection layers. The details of these parts are introduced as follows.

3.2 InvPT Transformer Encoder

The transformer encoder is shared for different tasks to learn generic visual representations from the input image. The self-attention mechanism of the transformer can help to learn a global feature representation of the input via long-range modeling of the spatial dependency of image pixels or patches. In our implementation, we consider different alternatives for the encoder including ViT [14] and Swin Transformer [22]. We obtain from the encoder a feature sequence and reshape it as a spatial feature map with resolution $H_0 \times W_0$ where H_0 and W_0 denote its height and width respectively. The feature map is then input into T preliminary decoders to learn the T task-specific feature maps.

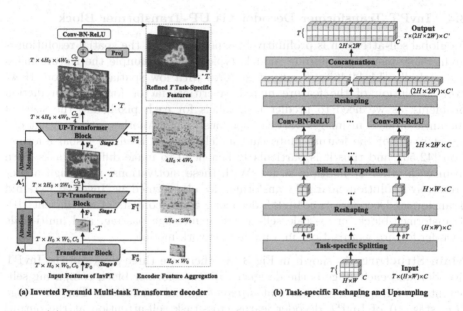

Fig. 3. (a) Illustration of InvPT Transformer decoder. Stage 0 uses a transformer block which keeps the feature resolution unchanged, while stage 1 and 2 employ the proposed UP-Transformer block which enlarges the spatial resolution by 2×. The Attention Message Passing (AMP) enables cross-scale self-attention interaction, and the Encoder Feature aggregation incorporates multi-scale information from the InvPT encoder. "⊕" and "Proj" denote the accumulation operation and the linear projection layer, respectively. **(b)** Pipeline of task-specific reshaping and upsampling block.

3.3 Task-Specific Preliminary Decoders

To learn task-specific representations for different tasks, we construct a decoding block consisting of a 3×3 convolutional layer, a batch normalization layer, and a ReLU activation function (*i.e.* "Conv-BN-ReLU"). The preliminary decoder uses two such blocks to produce task-specific feature for each task. Then suppose that we have T tasks in total, for the t-th task, the output task-specific feature $\mathbf{F}_t^d$ from the preliminary decoder is projected by a linear projection layer (*i.e.* 1×1 convolution) to produce a preliminary task prediction $\mathbf{P}_t$, which is supervised by the ground-truth labels. Then, we concatenate $\mathbf{F}_t^d$ and $\mathbf{P}_t$ along the channel dimension, and adjust the channel number to C_0 with a linear projection layer, to make the different task-specific features with the same channel dimension to facilitate the processing in the transformer decoder. The combined output is denoted as $\mathbf{F}_t^c$. We flatten $\mathbf{F}_t^c$ spatially to a sequence, and concatenate all T sequences as $\mathbf{F}^c$ with $\mathbf{F}^c \in \mathbb{R}^{TH_0W_0 \times C_0}$. $\mathbf{F}^c$ serves as the input of the proposed InvPT transformer decoder, which enables global task interaction and progressively generates refined task-specific feature maps with a high-resolution.

3.4   InvPT Transformer Decoder via UP-Transformer Block

As global self-attention is prohibitively expensive when the spatial resolution is high, many visual transformer models typically downsample the feature maps dramatically [14,44,46] and output features with low spatial resolution. However, resolution of the feature map is a critical factor for dense prediction problems, as we need to predict task labels for each pixel, and the sizes of semantic objects in images vary tremendously [54]. Another point is that different scales of the feature maps can model different levels of visual information [42,50], and thus it is particularly beneficial to make different tasks learn from each other at multiple scales. With these motivations, we design a progressively resolution-enlarged transformer decoder termed as "Inverted Pyramid Transformer Decoder" (*i.e.* InvPT decoder), which consists of an efficient UP-Transformer block, cross-scale self-attention message passing, and multi-scale encoder feature aggregation, in a unified network module.

Main Structure. As shown in Fig. 3 (a), there are three stages in the InvPT decoder, and each stage is the designed UP-Transformer block computing self-attention and updating features at *different* spatial resolutions. The first stage (*i.e.* stage 0) of InvPT decoder learns cross-task self-attention at the output resolution of the InvPT encoder (*i.e.* $H_0 \times W_0$), while the following two stages enlarge the spatial resolution of the feature maps, and calculate cross-task self-attention at higher resolutions. The latter two stages (*i.e.* stage 1 and 2) use the proposed UP-Transformer blocks which refine features at higher resolution and enable cross-scale self-attention propagation as well as multi-scale transformer feature aggregation from the transformer encoder.

To simplify the description, for the s-th stage (*e.g.* $s = 0, 1, 2$), we denote its input feature as $\mathbf{F}_s$ with $\mathbf{F}_s \in \mathbb{R}^{TH_sW_s \times C_s}$, where H_s and W_s are the spatial height and width of the feature, and C_s is the channel number. Thus, the input of stage 0 (*i.e.* $\mathbf{F}_0$) is $\mathbf{F}^c$, which is a combination of a set of T task-specific features as introduced in Sect. 3.3. For the output of InvPT decoder, we add up the feature maps from different stages after the alignment of feature resolution

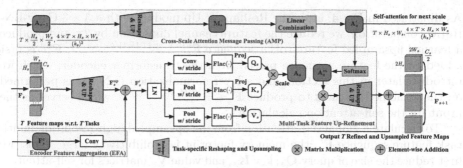

Fig. 4. Illustration of the proposed UP-Transformer Block. **Input:** $\mathbf{A}_{s-1}$ is the attention score matrix of the $(s-1)$-th stage, $\mathbf{F}_s$ is the input multi-task feature sequence of the s-th stage, and $\mathbf{F}_s^e$ is the feature passed from the transformer encoder. **Output:** $\mathbf{A}_s'$ is the enhanced attention score matrix passing to the next stage and $\mathbf{F}_{s+1}$ is the refined and upsampled feature sequence.

and channel dimension with bilinear interpolation and a linear projection layer, and then pass it to a Conv-BN-ReLU block to produce T upsampled and refined task-specific features for the final prediction.

Task-Specific Reshaping and Upsampling. The transformer computing block typically operates on 2D feature-token sequences with the spatial structure of the feature map broken down, while the spatial structure is critical for dense prediction tasks, and it is not straightforward to directly perform upsampling on the feature sequence with the consideration of spatial structure. Another issue is that the input features into the InvPT decoder consist of multiple different task-specific features, we need to perform feature upsampling and refinement for each single task separately to avoid feature corruption by other tasks. To address these issues, we design a task-specific reshaping and upsampling computation block for the InvPT decoder, *i.e.* the Reshape & UP module as illustrated in Fig. 3 (b) and Fig. 4. Reshape & Up first splits the feature tokens of $\mathbf{F}_s \in \mathbb{R}^{TH_sW_s \times C_s}$ in the first dimension into T (*i.e.* the number of tasks) groups of features with tensor slicing, and reshapes each of them back to a spatial feature map with a shape of $\mathbb{R}^{H_s \times W_s \times C_s}$. Then a bilinear interpolation with a scaling factor of 2 is performed to enlarge the height and width by $2\times$. Each scaled task-specific feature map is further fed into a Conv-BN-Relu block to perform feature fusion and reduction of channel dimension if necessary. Finally, The T feature maps are reshaped back to token sequences and finally concatenated as an upsampled multi-task token sequence.

Multi-task UP-Transformer Block. The multi-task UP-Transformer block (see Fig. 4) is employed in both stage 1 and 2 (*i.e.* $s = 1, 2$) and learns to gradually increase the spatial resolution of the multi-task feature and also perform feature interaction and refinement among *all* the tasks in a global manner.

As illustrated in Fig. 4, after the Reshape & Up module with a 3×3 Conv-BN-ReLU computation, we reduce the feature channel dimension by $2\times$ and produce a learned upsampled feature-token sequence $\mathbf{F}_s^{up} \in \mathbb{R}^{4TH_sW_s \times (C_s/2)}$. $\mathbf{F}_s^{up}$ is first added by the feature sequence passed from the transformer encoder, which we introduce later in this section, and a layer normalization (LN) [1] is performed on the combined features to produce $\mathbf{F}_s' \in \mathbb{R}^{4TH_sW_s \times (C_s/2)}$, which serves as the input for the self-attention calculation.

To calculate a global self-attention from the upsampled high-resolution multi-task feature sequence $\mathbf{F}_s'$, the memory footprint is prohibitively large. Thus, we first reduce the size of query $\mathbf{Q}_s$, key $\mathbf{K}_s$, and value $\mathbf{V}_s$ matrices for self-attention computation following works [44,46]. Specifically, we first split and reshape the feature-token sequence $\mathbf{F}_s'$ into T groups of spatial feature maps corresponding to the T tasks, each with a shape of $\mathbb{R}^{2H_s \times 2W_s \times (C_s/2)}$. To generate the query embedding from each feature map, we use a convolution with a fixed kernel size $k_c = 3$ and a stride 2 for each group, denoted as $\mathrm{Conv}(\cdot, k_c)$. To generate the key and value embeddings, we use an average pooling operation $\mathrm{Pool}(\cdot, k_s)$ with a kernel size k_s ($k_s = 2^{s+1}$ for the s-th stage). By controlling the kernel parameters of the convolution and pooling operations, we can largely improve the memory and computation efficiency of the global self-attention calculation, which makes the utilization of multiple consecutive UP-Transformer blocks possible. Then, we define $\mathbf{Flac}(\cdot)$ as a function that first flattens the T groups of spatial feature maps and then performs concatenation to produce a multi-task feature-token sequence. Then we can perform global interaction among all the tasks with a multi-task self-attention. Let $\mathbf{W}_s^q$, $\mathbf{W}_s^k$, and $\mathbf{W}_s^v$ be the parameter matrices of three linear projection layers, the calculation of $\mathbf{Q}_s$, $\mathbf{K}_s$, and $\mathbf{V}_s$ can be formulated as follows:

$$
\begin{aligned}
\mathbf{Q}_s &= \mathbf{W}_s^q \times \mathbf{Flac}\big(\mathrm{Conv}(\mathbf{F}_s', k_c)\big), \ \mathbf{Q}_s \in \mathbb{R}^{TH_sW_s \times \frac{C_s}{2}}, \\
\mathbf{K}_s &= \mathbf{W}_s^k \times \mathbf{Flac}\big(\mathrm{Pool}(\mathbf{F}_s', k_s)\big), \ \mathbf{K}_s \in \mathbb{R}^{\frac{4TH_sW_s}{(k_s)^2} \times \frac{C_s}{2}}, \\
\mathbf{V}_s &= \mathbf{W}_s^v \times \mathbf{Flac}\big(\mathrm{Pool}(\mathbf{F}_s', k_s)\big), \ \mathbf{V}_s \in \mathbb{R}^{\frac{4TH_sW_s}{(k_s)^2} \times \frac{C_s}{2}}.
\end{aligned}
\tag{1}
$$

With $\mathbf{Q}_s$ and $\mathbf{K}_s$, the self-attention score matrix $\mathbf{A}_s$ for the s-th stage can be calculated as:

$$
\mathbf{A}_s = \frac{\mathbf{Q}_s \mathbf{K}_s^T}{\sqrt{C_s'}}, \ \mathbf{A}_s \in \mathbb{R}^{TH_sW_s \times \frac{4TH_sW_s}{(k_s)^2}},
\tag{2}
$$

where $\sqrt{C_s'}$ with $C_s' = \frac{C_s}{2}$ is a scaling factor to address the magnitude problem [43]. In vanilla transformers, the self-attention map is directly calculated with a softmax function on $\mathbf{A}_s$. We propose a mechanism of Attention Message Passing (AMP) to enhance the attention $\mathbf{A}_s$ before the Softmax normalization, using multi-scale information from different transformer stages.

Cross-scale Self-Attention Message Passing. To enable the InvPT decoder to model the cross-task interaction at different scales more effectively, we pass attention message to the attention score matrix $\mathbf{A}_s$ at the current s-th stage from $\mathbf{A}_{s-1} \in \mathbb{R}^{\frac{TH_sW_s}{4} \times \frac{4TH_sW_s}{(k_s)^2}}$, which is computed at the $(s-1)$-th stage. It can be noted that the second dimension of $\mathbf{A}_s$ at different stages maintain the same size due to the design of the kernel size k_s. An illustration of AMP is shown in Fig. 4. Specifically, we perform 'Reshape & Up' operation to first adjust the shape of $\mathbf{A}_{s-1}$ to $\mathbb{R}^{\frac{H_s}{2} \times \frac{W_s}{2} \times \frac{TH_sW_s}{(k_s)^2}}$, and then perform $2\times$ bilinear interpolation in the first two spatial dimensions, and finally flatten it to have the attention message matrix $\mathbf{M}_{s-1} \in \mathbb{R}^{TH_sW_s \times \frac{4TH_sW_s}{(k_s)^2}}$ which has the same dimension as $\mathbf{A}_s$. Finally, we perform a linear combination of the self-attention maps $\mathbf{A}_s$ and $\mathbf{M}_{s-1}$ to pass attention message from the $(s-1)$-th stage to the s-th stage as:

$$\mathbf{A}_s' = \alpha_s^1 \mathbf{A}_s + \alpha_s^2 \mathbf{M}_{s-1},$$
$$\mathbf{A}_s^m = \mathrm{Softmax}(\mathbf{A}_s'), \tag{3}$$

where α_s^1 and α_s^2 are learnable weights for $\mathbf{A}_s$ and $\mathbf{M}_{s-1}$, respectively; $\mathrm{Softmax}(\cdot)$ is a *row-wise* softmax function. After multiplying with the new attention map $\mathbf{A}_s^m$ with the value matrix $\mathbf{V}_s$, we obtain the final multi-task feature $\mathbf{F}_{s+1}$ as output, which is refined and upsampled, and can be further fed into the next UP-Transformer block. The whole process can be formulated as follows:

$$\mathbf{F}_{s+1} = \mathrm{Reshape\_Up}(\mathbf{A}_s^m \times \mathbf{V}_s) + \mathbf{F}_s', \tag{4}$$

where the function $\mathrm{Reshape\_Up}(\cdot)$ denotes the task-specific reshaping and upsampling. It enlarges the feature map by $2\times$ to be the same spatial resolution as $\mathbf{F}_s'$ which is a residual feature map from the input.

Efficient Multi-scale Encoder Feature Aggregation. For dense scene understanding, some basic tasks such as object boundary detection require lower-level visual representation. However, it is tricky to efficiently use the multi-scale features in transformer as standard transformer structures have a quadratic computational complexity regarding the image resolution, and typically only operate on small-resolution feature maps. To gradually increase the feature map size and also incorporate multi-scale features is very challenging to GPU memory. Therefore, we design an efficient yet effective multi-scale encoder feature aggregation (EFA) strategy. As shown in Fig. 4, in each upsampling stage s of the InvPT decoder, we obtain a corresponding-scale feature sequence $\mathbf{F}_s^e$ with channel number C_s^e from the transformer encoder. We reshape it to a spatial feature map and apply a 3×3 convolution to produce a new feature map with channel dimension C_s, and then reshape and expand it T times to align with the dimension of $\mathbf{F}_s^{up}$ and add to it. Benefiting from the proposed efficient UP-Transformer block, we can still maintain high efficiency even if at each consecutive stage of the decoder, the resolution is gradually enlarged by two times.

4   Experiments

We present extensive experiments to demonstrate the effectiveness of the proposed InvPT framework for multi-task dense prediction.

Datasets. The experiments are conducted on two popular scene understanding datasets with multi-task labels, *i.e.* NYUD-v2 [37] and PASCAL-Context [9]. **NYUD-v2** contains various indoor scenes such as offices and living rooms with 795 training and 654 testing images. It provides different dense labels, including semantic segmentation, monocular depth estimation, surface normal estimation and object boundary detection. **PASCAL-Context** is formed from PASCAL dataset [15]. It has 4,998 images in the training split and 5,105 in the testing split, covering both indoor and outdoor scenes. This dataset provides pixel-wise labels for semantic segmentation, human parsing and object boundary detection. Additionally, [25] generates surface normal and saliency labels for this dataset. We perform experiments on *all* tasks in both datasets for evaluation.

Table 1. Ablation study on the InvPT decoder. The proposed InvPT and its components yield consistent improvement on different datasets and achieve clear overall improvement on each single task and the multi-task (MT) performance Δ_m. The gain shows absolute performance point improvement. The different variants of the InvPT all use Swin-tiny as its encoder structure. '↓' means lower better and '↑' means higher better.

Model	NYUD-v2				PASCAL-Context				
	Semseg mIoU ↑	Depth RMSE ↓	Normal mErr ↓	Boundary odsF ↑	Semseg mIoU ↑	Parsing mIoU ↑	Saliency maxF ↑	Normal mErr ↓	Boundary odsF ↑
InvPT Baseline (ST)	43.29	0.5975	20.80	76.10	72.43	61.13	83.43	14.38	71.50
InvPT Baseline (MT)	41.06	0.6350	21.47	76.00	70.92	59.63	82.63	14.63	71.30
InvPT w/ UTB	43.18	0.5643	21.05	76.10	72.34	61.08	83.99	14.49	71.60
InvPT w/ UTB+AMP	43.64	0.5617	20.87	76.10	73.29	61.78	84.03	14.37	71.80
InvPT w/ UTB+AMP+EFA (Full)	44.27	0.5589	20.46	76.10	73.93	62.73	84.24	14.15	72.60
Gain on Each Task (vs. MT)	△3.21	△0.0761	△1.01	△0.10	△3.01	△3.10	△1.61	△0.48	△1.30
MT Performance Δ_m (vs. ST) [25]	+2.59				+1.76				

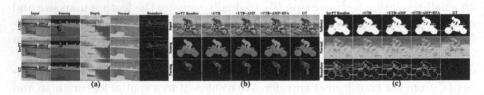

Fig. 5. (a): Qualitative comparison with the previous best method ATRC [5] on NYUD-v2. (b)&(c): Qualitative analysis of InvPT decoder on PASCAL-Context. Results of different model variants are shown by columns.

Evaluation. Semantic segmentation (Semseg) and human parsing (Parsing) are evaluated with mean Intersection over Union (mIoU); monocular depth estimation (Depth) is evaluated with Root Mean Square Error (RMSE); surface normal estimation (Normal) is evaluated by the mean error (mErr) of predicted angles; saliency detection (Saliency) is evaluated with maximal F-measure (maxF);

object boundary detection (Boundary) is evaluated with the optimal-dataset-scale F-measure (odsF). To evaluate the average performance gain of multi-task models against single-task models, we adopt the "multi-task learning performance" (MT Performance) metric Δ_m introduced in [25], which is an important metric to reflect the performance of a multi-task model (the higher the better).

Implementation Details. For the ablation study, we adopt Swin-Tiny transformer [22] pre-trained on ImageNet-22K [13] as the transformer encoder. The models for different evaluation experiments are trained for 40,000 iterations on both datasets, with a batch size of 6. For the transformer models, Adam optimizer is adopted with a learning rate of 2×10^{-5}, and a weight decay rate of 1×10^{-6}. Polynomial learning rate scheduler is used. The output channel number of preliminary decoder is 768. More details are in supplemental materials.

4.1 Model Analysis

Baselines and Model Variants. To have a deep analysis of the proposed InvPT framework, we first define several model baselines and variants (see Table 1): (i) "InvPT Baseline (MT)" denotes a strong multi-task baseline model of the proposed InvPT framework. It uses Swin-tiny encoder and two 3×3 Conv-BN-ReLU blocks as decoder for each task, which is equivalent to the preliminary decoder in InvPT. The encoder feature map is upsampled by $8\times$ before the final prediction. It also combines multi-scale features from the encoder to help boost performance. This is a typical multi-task baseline structure as in previous works [5,42]. (ii) "InvPT Baseline (ST)" has a similar structure as "InvPT Baseline" but it is trained under single-task setting. (iii) "InvPT w/ UTB" indicates adding the proposed UP-Transformer block upon "InvPT Baseline (MT)"; Similarly, "InvPT w/ UTB + AMP" indicates further adding the cross-scale Attention Message Passing, and "InvPT w/ UTB + AMP + EFA" denotes the full model by further adding multi-scale Encoder Feature Aggregation.

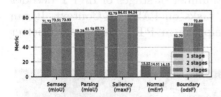

Fig. 6. Investigation of the number of stages in the InvPT decoder.

Table 2. Performance comparison of using different transformer encoder structures in InvPT on PASCAL-Context.

Encoder	Semseg mIoU ↑	Parsing mIoU ↑	Saliency maxF ↑	Normal mErr ↓	Boundary odsF ↑
Swin-T	73.93	62.73	**84.24**	**14.15**	72.60
Swin-B	77.50	66.83	83.65	14.63	73.00
Swin-L	**78.53**	**68.58**	83.71	14.56	**73.60**
Vit-B	77.33	66.62	**85.14**	**13.78**	73.20
Vit-L	**79.03**	**67.61**	84.81	14.15	73.00

Effectiveness of InvPT Decoder. In this part, we investigate the effectiveness of the proposed three modules to demonstrate the proposed InvPT decoder, *i.e.* UP-Transformer Block (UTB), cross-scale Attention Message Passing (AMP), and Encoder Feature Aggregation (EFA), on both datasets. The experimental results for this investigation are shown in Table 1. It can be observed that the UTB, AMP and EFA modules all achieve clear improvement. Specifically, as a core module of the proposed InvPT framework, UTB significantly improves the task Semseg by 2.12 (mIoU), Depth by 0.0707 (RMSE) and Normal by 0.42 (mErr) on NYUD-v2. Finally, the full model of InvPT achieves remarkable performance gain compared against both the Single-task (ST) baseline (see MT performance Δ_m) and the multi-task (MT) baseline (see the Gain on each task), clearly verifying the effectiveness of the proposed InvPT decoder.

For qualitative comparison, in Fig. 5, we show prediction examples generated by different model variants which add these modules one by one on PASCAL-Context. It is intuitively to observe that the proposed UTB, AMP and EFA all help produce visually more accurate predictions to against the baseline.

Multi-task Improvement Against Single-Task Setting. To validate the effectiveness of the proposed multi-task model, we compare it with its single-task variant "InvPT Baseline (ST)" on both datasets in Table 1. Our full model achieves strong performance improvement against the single-task model, yielding **2.59%** multi-task performance on NYUD-v2 and **1.76%** on PASCAL-Context.

Effect of Different Transformer Encoders. We also compare the model performance using two families of transformer encoders, *i.e.* Swin Transformer (Swin-T, Swin-B, and Swin-L) [22] and ViT (ViT-B and ViT-L) [14], used as our InvPT encoder. The results on PASCAL-Context are shown in Table 2. We observe that the models with higher capacity in the same family can generally obtain consistent performance gain on semantic tasks including Semseg and Parsing, while on other tasks (*e.g.* Saliency) the improvement is however not clear. One possible reason for the difference of performance gain is the task competition problem in training as discussed in previous works [19,36].

Effect of the Number of Stages. Our UP-Transformer block typically consists of three stages. In Fig. 6, we show how the number of stages of InvPT decoder influences the performance of the different tasks on PASCAL-Context. It can be observed that using more stages can help the InvPT decoder learn better

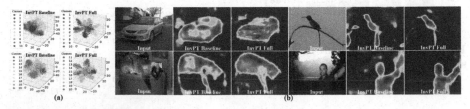

Fig. 7. (a): Statistics of learned features with t-SNE [23] of all 20 classes on Pascal-Context. (b): Visualization of examples of learned feature of semantic segmentation. From both (a) and (b), we observe that features learned by InvPT is effectively improved and is more discriminative compared to the baseline.

predictions for all tasks. Our efficient design makes the multi-task decoding feature maps with gradually increased resolutions possible.

Qualitative Study of learned Features with InvPT. In Fig. 7, we show visualization comparison of the learned final features between the transformer baseline (*i.e.* InvPT Baseline (MT)) and our InvPT full model, to further demonstrate how the features are improved using our proposed InvPT model. The statistics of the learned feature points is visualized with t-SNE [24] on all 20 semantic classes of Pascal-Context dataset. It is obvious that our model helps learn more discriminative features, thus resulting in higher quantitative results. The generated spatial feature maps for segmentation are also intuitively better.

Generalization Performance. To qualitatively study the generalization performance of the proposed multi-task transformer for dense scene understanding, we compare it with the best performing methods, including ATRC [5] and PAD-Net [48], on the challenging DAVIS video segmentation Dataset [30]. The results are shown in the video demo in the github page. All the models are trained on PASCAL-Context with all the five tasks. Then the models are directly tested on DAVIS to generate multi-task predictions on video sequences. One example frame is shown in Fig. 8, which clearly shows our advantage on this perspective.

4.2 State-of-the-Art Comparison

Table 3 shows a comparison of the proposed InvPT method against existing state-of-the-arts, including PAD-Net [48], MTI-Net [42] and ATRC [5], on both NYUD-v2 and PASCAL-Context. On all the 9 metrics from these two benchmarks, the proposed InvPT achieves clearly superior performance, especially for higher-level scene understanding tasks such as Semseg and Parsing. Notably, on NYUD-v2, our InvPT surpasses the previous best performing method (*i.e.* ATRC) by **+7.23** (mIoU) on Semseg, while on PASCAL-Context, InvPT outperforms ATRC by **+11.36** (mIoU) and **+4.68** (mIoU) on Semseg and Parsing, respectively. A qualitative comparison with ATRC is shown in Fig. 5.

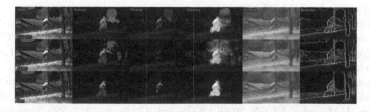

Fig. 8. Study on generalization performance. Models are all trained on PASCAL-Context [9] and tested on DAVIS video dataset [30]. The proposed method yields better generalization performance compared to PAD-Net [48] and ATRC [5].

Table 3. State-of-the-art comparison on NYUD-v2 (*left*) and PASCAL-Context (*right*). Our InvPT significantly outperforms the previous state-of-the-arts by a large margin. '↓' means lower better and '↑' means higher better.

Model	Semseg mIoU ↑	Depth RMSE ↓	Normal mErr ↓	Boundary odsF ↑	Model	Semseg mIoU ↑	Parsing mIoU ↑	Saliency maxF ↑	Normal mErr ↓	Boundary odsF ↑
Cross-Stitch [27]	36.34	0.6290	20.88	76.38	ASTMT [25]	68.00	61.10	65.70	14.70	72.40
PAP [52]	36.72	0.6178	20.82	76.42	PAD-Net [48]	53.60	59.60	65.80	15.30	72.50
PSD [55]	36.69	0.6246	20.87	76.42	MTI-Net [42]	61.70	60.18	84.78	14.23	70.80
PAD-Net [48]	36.61	0.6270	20.85	76.38	ATRC [5]	62.69	59.42	84.70	14.20	70.96
MTI-Net [42]	45.97	0.5365	20.27	77.86	ATRC-ASPP [5]	63.60	60.23	83.91	14.30	70.86
ATRC [5]	46.33	0.5363	20.18	77.94	ATRC-BMTAS [5]	67.67	62.93	82.29	14.24	72.42
InvPT (ours)	**53.56**	**0.5183**	**19.04**	**78.10**	InvPT (ours)	**79.03**	**67.61**	**84.81**	**14.15**	**73.00**

5   Conclusion

This paper presented a novel transformer framework, Inverted Pyramid Multi-task Transformer (InvPT), for the multi-task dense prediction for visual scene understanding. InvPT is able to effectively learn the long-range interaction in both spatial and all-task contexts on the multi-task feature maps with gradually increased spatial resolution for dense prediction. Extensive experiments demonstrated the effectiveness of the proposed method, and also showed its significantly better performance on two popular benchmarks compared to the previous state-of-the-art methods.

Acknowledgements. This research is supported in part by the Early Career Scheme of the Research Grants Council (RGC) of the Hong Kong SAR under grant No. 26202321 and HKUST Startup Fund No. R9253.

References

1. Ba, J.L., Kiros, J.R., Hinton, G.E.: Layer normalization. arXiv preprint arXiv:1607.06450 (2016)
2. Bai, Y., Mei, J., Yuille, A., Xie, C.: Are transformers more robust than CNNs? In: NeurIPS (2021)
3. Bello, I., Zoph, B., Le, Q., Vaswani, A., Shlens, J.: Attention augmented convolutional networks. In: ICCV (2019)
4. Bhojanapalli, S., Chakrabarti, A., Glasner, D., Li, D., Unterthiner, T., Veit, A.: Understanding robustness of transformers for image classification. In: ICCV (2021)
5. Bruggemann, D., Kanakis, M., Obukhov, A., Georgoulis, S., Van Gool, L.: Exploring relational context for multi-task dense prediction. In: ICCV (2021)
6. Carion, N., Massa, F., Synnaeve, G., Usunier, N., Kirillov, A., Zagoruyko, S.: End-to-end object detection with transformers. In: Vedaldi, A., Bischof, H., Brox, T., Frahm, J.-M. (eds.) ECCV 2020. LNCS, vol. 12346, pp. 213–229. Springer, Cham (2020). https://doi.org/10.1007/978-3-030-58452-8_13
7. Chen, H., et al.: Pre-trained image processing transformer. In: CVPR (2021)
8. Chen, T., Saxena, S., Li, L., Fleet, D.J., Hinton, G.: Pix2Seq: a language modeling framework for object detection. arXiv preprint arXiv:2109.10852 (2021)

9. Chen, X., Mottaghi, R., Liu, X., Fidler, S., Urtasun, R., Yuille, A.: Detect what you can: detecting and representing objects using holistic models and body parts. In: CVPR (2014)

10. Chen, Z., Badrinarayanan, V., Lee, C.Y., Rabinovich, A.: GradNorm: gradient normalization for adaptive loss balancing in deep multitask networks. In: ICML (2018)

11. Chen, Z., et al.: Just pick a sign: optimizing deep multitask models with gradient sign dropout. In: NeurIPS (2020)

12. d'Ascoli, S., Touvron, H., Leavitt, M., Morcos, A., Biroli, G., Sagun, L.: ConViT: improving vision transformers with soft convolutional inductive biases. In: ICML (2021)

13. Deng, J., Dong, W., Socher, R., Li, L.J., Li, K., Fei-Fei, L.: ImageNet: a large-scale hierarchical image database. In: CVPR (2009)

14. Dosovitskiy, A., et al.: An image is worth 16x16 words: transformers for image recognition at scale. In: ICLR (2021)

15. Everingham, M., Van Gool, L., Williams, C.K., Winn, J., Zisserman, A.: The pascal visual object classes (VOC) challenge. IJCV **88**(2), 303–338 (2010)

16. Gao, Y., Bai, H., Jie, Z., Ma, J., Jia, K., Liu, W.: MTL-NAS: task-agnostic neural architecture search towards general-purpose multi-task learning. In: CVPR (2020)

17. Gao, Y., Ma, J., Zhao, M., Liu, W., Yuille, A.L.: NDDR-CNN: layerwise feature fusing in multi-task CNNs by neural discriminative dimensionality reduction. In: CVPR (2019)

18. Han, K., Xiao, A., Wu, E., Guo, J., Xu, C., Wang, Y.: Transformer in transformer. In: NeurIPS (2021)

19. Kendall, A., Gal, Y., Cipolla, R.: Multi-task learning using uncertainty to weigh losses for scene geometry and semantics. In: CVPR (2018)

20. Liang, M., Yang, B., Chen, Y., Hu, R., Urtasun, R.: Multi-task multi-sensor fusion for 3D object detection. In: CVPR (2019)

21. Liu, Y., Sangineto, E., Bi, W., Sebe, N., Lepri, B., De Nadai, M.: Efficient training of visual transformers with small-size datasets. arXiv preprint arXiv:2106.03746 (2021)

22. Liu, Z., et al.: Swin transformer: hierarchical vision transformer using shifted windows. In: ICCV (2021)

23. Van der Maaten, L., Hinton, G.: Visualizing data using t-SNE. J. Mach. Learn. Res. **9**(11) (2008)

24. Van der Maaten, L., Hinton, G.: Visualizing data using t-SNE. JMLR **9**(11) (2008)

25. Maninis, K.K., Radosavovic, I., Kokkinos, I.: Attentive single-tasking of multiple tasks. In: CVPR (2019)

26. Mao, J., et al.: Voxel transformer for 3D object detection. In: ICCV (2021)

27. Misra, I., Shrivastava, A., Gupta, A., Hebert, M.: Cross-stitch networks for multi-task learning. In: CVPR (2016)

28. Pan, X., Xia, Z., Song, S., Li, L.E., Huang, G.: 3D object detection with point-former. In: CVPR (2021)

29. Parmar, N., et al.: Image transformer. In: ICML (2018)

30. Perazzi, F., Pont-Tuset, J., McWilliams, B., Gool, L.V., Gross, M., Sorkine-Hornung, A.: A benchmark dataset and evaluation methodology for video object segmentation. In: CVPR (2016)

31. Radford, A., et al.: Learning transferable visual models from natural language supervision. arXiv preprint arXiv:2103.00020 (2021)

32. Ramachandran, P., Parmar, N., Vaswani, A., Bello, I., Levskaya, A., Shlens, J.: Stand-alone self-attention in vision models. In: NeurIPS (2019)

33. Ramesh, A., et al.: Zero-shot text-to-image generation. In: ICML (2021)
34. Ranftl, R., Bochkovskiy, A., Koltun, V.: Vision transformers for dense prediction. In: ICCV (2021)
35. Ruder, S., Bingel, J., Augenstein, I., Søgaard, A.: Latent multi-task architecture learning. In: AAAI (2019)
36. Sener, O., Koltun, V.: Multi-task learning as multi-objective optimization. In: NeurIPS (2018)
37. Silberman, N., Hoiem, D., Kohli, P., Fergus, R.: Indoor segmentation and support inference from RGBD images. In: Fitzgibbon, A., Lazebnik, S., Perona, P., Sato, Y., Schmid, C. (eds.) ECCV 2012. LNCS, vol. 7576, pp. 746–760. Springer, Heidelberg (2012). https://doi.org/10.1007/978-3-642-33715-4_54
38. Srinivas, A., Lin, T.Y., Parmar, N., Shlens, J., Abbeel, P., Vaswani, A.: Bottleneck transformers for visual recognition. In: CVPR (2021)
39. Touvron, H., Cord, M., Douze, M., Massa, F., Sablayrolles, A., Jegou, H.: Training data-efficient image transformers & distillation through attention. In: ICML (2021)
40. Touvron, H., Cord, M., Sablayrolles, A., Synnaeve, G., Jégou, H.: Going deeper with image transformers. In: ICCV (2021)
41. Vandenhende, S., Georgoulis, S., Van Gansbeke, W., Proesmans, M., Dai, D., Van Gool, L.: Multi-task learning for dense prediction tasks: a survey. TPAMI (2021)
42. Vandenhende, S., Georgoulis, S., Van Gool, L.: MTI-net: multi-scale task interaction networks for multi-task learning. In: Vedaldi, A., Bischof, H., Brox, T., Frahm, J.-M. (eds.) ECCV 2020. LNCS, vol. 12349, pp. 527–543. Springer, Cham (2020). https://doi.org/10.1007/978-3-030-58548-8_31
43. Vaswani, A., et al.: Attention is all you need. In: NeurIPS (2017)
44. Wang, W., et al.: Pyramid vision transformer: a versatile backbone for dense prediction without convolutions. In: ICCV (2021)
45. Wang, X., Girshick, R., Gupta, A., He, K.: Non-local neural networks. In: CVPR (2018)
46. Wu, H., et al.: CVT: introducing convolutions to vision transformers. arXiv preprint arXiv:2103.15808 (2021)
47. Xie, E., Wang, W., Yu, Z., Anandkumar, A., Alvarez, J.M., Luo, P.: SegFormer: simple and efficient design for semantic segmentation with transformers. In: NeurIPS (2021)
48. Xu, D., Ouyang, W., Wang, X., Sebe, N.: Pad-net: multi-tasks guided prediction-and-distillation network for simultaneous depth estimation and scene parsing. In: CVPR (2018)
49. Yang, J., et al.: Focal self-attention for local-global interactions in vision transformers. In: NeurIPS (2021)
50. Yuan, Y., et al.: HRFormer: high-resolution transformer for dense prediction. In: NeurIPS (2021)
51. Zhang, X., Zhou, L., Li, Y., Cui, Z., Xie, J., Yang, J.: Transfer vision patterns for multi-task pixel learning. In: ACMMM (2021)
52. Zhang, Z., Cui, Z., Xu, C., Yan, Y., Sebe, N., Yang, J.: Pattern-affinitive propagation across depth, surface normal and semantic segmentation. In: CVPR (2019)
53. Zhao, H., Jiang, L., Jia, J., Torr, P.H., Koltun, V.: Point transformer. In: ICCV (2021)
54. Zhao, H., Shi, J., Qi, X., Wang, X., Jia, J.: Pyramid scene parsing network. In: CVPR (2017)
55. Zhou, L., et al.: Pattern-structure diffusion for multi-task learning. In: CVPR (2020)

PETR: Position Embedding Transformation for Multi-view 3D Object Detection

Yingfei Liu$^{(\boxtimes)}$, Tiancai Wang, Xiangyu Zhang, and Jian Sun

MEGVII Technology, Beijing, China
{liuyingfei,wangtiancai,zhangxiangyu,sunjian}@megvii.com

Abstract. In this paper, we develop position embedding transformation (PETR) for multi-view 3D object detection. PETR encodes the position information of 3D coordinates into image features, producing the 3D position-aware features. Object query can perceive the 3D position-aware features and perform end-to-end object detection. PETR achieves state-of-the-art performance (**50.4%** NDS and **44.1%** mAP) on standard nuScenes dataset and ranks 1*st* place on the benchmark. It can serve as a simple yet strong baseline for future research. Code is available at https://github.com/megvii-research/PETR.

Keywords: Position embedding · Transformer · 3D object detection

1 Introduction

3D object detection from multi-view images is appealing due to its low cost in autonomous driving system. Previous works [6,33,34,48,49] mainly solved this problem from the perspective of monocular object detection. Recently, DETR [4] has gained remarkable attention due to its contribution on end-to-end object detection. In DETR [4], each object query represents an object and interacts with the 2D features in transformer decoder to produce the predictions (see Fig. 1(a)). Simply extended from DETR [4] framework, DETR3D [51] provides an intuitive solution for end-to-end 3D object detection. The 3D reference point, predicted by object query, is projected back into the image spaces by the camera parameters and used to sample the 2D features from all camera views (see Fig. 1(b)). The decoder will take the sampled features and the queries as input and update the representations of object queries.

However, such 2D-to-3D transformation in DETR3D [51] may introduce several problems. First, the predicted coordinates of reference point may not that accurate, making the sampled features out of the object region. Second, only the image feature at the projected point will be collected, which fails to perform the representation learning from global view. Also, the complex feature sampling

---

Y. Liu and T. Wang—Equal contribution.

© The Author(s), under exclusive license to Springer Nature Switzerland AG 2022
S. Avidan et al. (Eds.): ECCV 2022, LNCS 13687, pp. 531–548, 2022.
https://doi.org/10.1007/978-3-031-19812-0_31

procedure will hinder the detector from practical application. Thus, building an end-to-end 3D object detection framework without the online 2D-to-3D transformation and feature sampling is still a remaining problem.

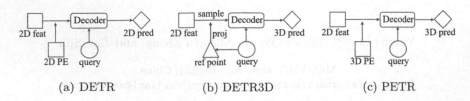

(a) DETR   (b) DETR3D   (c) PETR

Fig. 1. Comparison of DETR, DETR3D, and our proposed PETR. (a) In DETR, the object queries interact with 2D features to perform 2D detection. (b) DETR3D repeatedly projects the generated 3D reference points into image plane and samples the 2D features to interact with object queries in decoder. (c) PETR generates the 3D position-aware features by encoding the 3D position embedding (3D PE) into 2D image features. The object queries directly interact with 3D position-aware features and output 3D detection results.

In this paper, we aim to develop a simple and elegant framework based on DETR [4] for 3D object detection. We wonder if it is possible that we transform the 2D features from multi-view into 3D-aware features. In this way, the object query can be directly updated under the 3D environment. Our work is inspired by these advances in implicit neural representation [8,17,32]. In MetaSR [17] and LIIF [8], the high-resolution (HR) RGB values are generated from low-resolution (LR) input by encoding HR coordinates information into the LR features. In this paper, we try to transform the 2D features from multi-view images into the 3D representation by encoding 3D position embedding (see Fig. 1(c)).

To achieve this goal, the camera frustum space, shared by different views, is first discretized into meshgrid coordinates. The coordinates are then transformed by different camera parameters to obtain the coordinates of 3D world space. Then 2D image features extracted from backbone and 3D coordinates are input to a simple 3D position encoder to produce the 3D position-aware features. The 3D position-aware features will interact with the object queries in transformer decoder and the updated object queries are further used to predict the object class and the 3D bounding boxes.

The proposed PETR architecture brings many advantages compared to the DETR3D [51]. It keeps the end-to-end spirit of original DETR [4] while avoiding the complex 2D-to-3D projection and feature sampling. During inference time, the 3D position coordinates can be generated in an offline manner and served as an extra input position embedding. It is relatively easier for practical application.

To summarize, our contributions are:

- We propose a simple and elegant framework, termed PETR, for multi-view 3D object detection. The multi-view features are transformed into 3D domain by encoding the 3D coordinates. Object queries can be updated by interacting with the 3D position-aware features and generate 3D predictions.

- A new 3D position-aware representation is introduced for multi-view 3D object detection. A simple implicit function is introduced to encode the 3D position information into 2D multi-view features.
- Experiments show that PETR achieves state-of-the-art performance (**50.4%** NDS and **44.1%** mAP) on standard nuScenes dataset and ranks $1st$ place on 3D object detection leaderboard.

2 Related Work

2.1 Transformer-Based Object Detection

Transformer [47] is an attention block that widely applied to model the long-range dependency. In transformer, the features are usually added with position embedding, which provides the position information of the image [13,27,53], sequence [10,11,15,47,54], and video [1,24,52]. Transformer-XL [10] uses the relative position embedding to encode the relative distance of the pairwise tokens. ViT [13] adds the learned position embedding to the patch representations that encode distance of different patches. MViT [24] decomposes the distance computation of the relative position embedding and model the space-time structure.

Recently, DETR [4] involves the transformer into 2D object detection task for end-to-end detection. In DETR [4], each object is represented as an object query which interacts with 2D images features through transformer decoder. However, DETR [4] suffers from the slow convergence. [44] attributes the slow convergence to the cross attention mechanism and designs a encoder-only DETR. Furthermore, many works accelerate the convergence by adding position priors. SMAC [14] predicts 2D Gaussian-like weight map as spatial prior for each query. Deformable DETR [58] associates the object queries with 2D reference points and proposes deformable cross-attention to perform sparse interaction. [26,30,50] generate the object queries from anchor points or anchors that use position prior for fast convergence. Extended from DETR [58], SOLQ [12] uses object queries to perform classification, box regression and instance segmentation simultaneously.

2.2 Vision-Based 3D Object Detection

Vision-based 3D object detection is to detect 3D bounding boxes from camera images. Many previous works [2,6,19–21,33,41,48,49] perform 3D object detection in the image view. M3D-RPN [2] introduces the depth-aware convolution, which learns position-aware features for 3D object detection. FCOS3D [49] transforms the 3D ground-truths to image view and extends FCOS [46] to predict 3D cuboid parameters. PGD [48] follows the FCOS3D [49] and uses a probabilistic representation to capture the uncertainty of depth. It greatly alleviates the depth estimation problem while introducing more computation budget and larger inference latency. DD3D [34] shows that depth pre-training on large-scale depth dataset can significantly improve the performance of 3D object detection.

Recently, several works attempt to conduct the 3D object detection in 3D world space. OFT [39] and CaDDN [38] map the monocular image features into the bird's eye view (BEV) and detect 3D objects in BEV space. ImVoxel-Net [40] builds a 3D volume in 3D world space and samples multi-view features to obtain the voxel representation. Then 3D convolutions and domain-specific heads are used to detect objects in both indoor and outdoor scenes. Similar to CaDDN [38], BEVDet [18] employs the Lift-Splat-Shoot [37] to transform 2D multi-view features into BEV representation. With the BEV representation, a CenterPoint [55] head is used to detect 3D objects in an intuitive way. Following DETR [4], DETR3D [51] represents 3D objects as object queries. The 3D reference points, generated from object queries, are repeatedly projected back to all camera views and sample the 2D features.

BEV-based methods tend to introduce the Z-axis error, resulting in poor performance for other 3D-aware tasks (e.g., 3D lane detection). DETR-based methods can enjoy more benefits from end-to-end modeling with more training augmentations. Our method is DETR-based that detects 3D objects in a simple and effective manner. We encode the 3D position information into 2D features, producing the 3D position-aware features. The object queries can directly interact with such 3D position-aware representation without projection error.

2.3 Implicit Neural Representation

Implicit neural representation (INR) usually maps the coordinates to visual signal by a multi-layer perceptron (MLP). It is a high efficiency way for modeling 3D objects [9,31,35], 3D scenes [5,32,36,43] and 2D images [8,17,42,45]. NeRF [32] employs a fully-connected network to denote a specific scene. To synthesize a novel view, the 5D coordinates along camera rays are input to the network as queries and output the volume density and view-dependent emitted radiance. In MetaSR [17] and LIIF [8], the HR coordinates are encoded into the LR features and HR images of arbitrary size can be generated. Our method can be regarded as an extension of INR in 3D object detection. The 2D images are encoded with 3D coordinates to obtain 3D position-aware features. The anchor points in 3D space are transformed to object queries by a MLP and further interact with 3D position-aware features to predict the corresponding 3D objects.

3   Method

3.1   Overall Architecture

Figure 2 shows the overall architecture of the proposed PETR. Given the images $I = \{I_i \in R^{3 \times H_I \times W_I}, i = 1, 2, \ldots, N\}$ from N views, the images are input to the backbone network (e.g. ResNet-50 [16]) to extract the 2D multi-view features $F^{2d} = \{F_i^{2d} \in R^{C \times H_F \times W_F}, i = 1, 2, \ldots, N\}$. In 3D coordinates generator, the camera frustum space is first discretized into a 3D meshgrid. Then the coordinates of meshgrid are transformed by camera parameters and generate the coordinates in 3D world space. The 3D coordinates together with the 2D multi-view features are input to the 3D position encoder, producing the 3D position-aware features $F^{3d} = \{F_i^{3d} \in R^{C \times H_F \times W_F}, i = 1, 2, \ldots, N\}$. The 3D features are further input to the transformer decoder and interact with the object queries, generated from query generator. The updated object queries are used to predict the object class as well as the 3D bounding boxes.

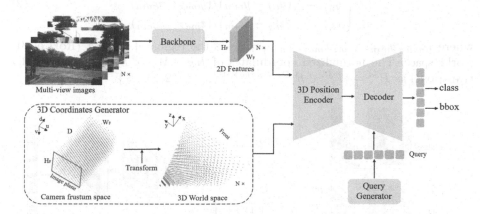

Fig. 2. The architecture of the proposed PETR paradigm. The multi-view images are input to the backbone network (e.g. ResNet) to extract the multi-view 2D image features. In 3D coordinates generator, the camera frustum space shared by all views is discretized into a 3D meshgrid. The meshgrid coordinates are transformed by different camera parameters, resulting in the coordinates in 3D world space. Then 2D image features and 3D coordinates are injected to proposed 3D position encoder to generate the 3D position-aware features. Object queries, generated from query generator, are updated through the interaction with 3D position-aware features in transformer decoder. The updated queries are further used to predict the 3D bounding boxes and the object classes.

3.2   3D Coordinates Generator

To build the relation between the 2D images and 3D space, we project the points in camera frustum space to 3D space since the points between these two spaces are one-to-one assignment. Similar to DGSN [7], we first discretize the camera frustum space to generate a meshgrid of size (W_F, H_F, D). Each point in the meshgrid can be represented as $p_j^m = (u_j \times d_j, v_j \times d_j, d_j, 1)^T$, where (u_j, v_j) is a pixel coordinate in the image, d_j is the depth value along the axis orthogonal to the image plane. Since the meshgrid is shared by different views, the corresponding 3D coordinate $p_{i,j}^{3d} = (x_{i,j}, y_{i,j}, z_{i,j}, 1)^T$ in 3D world space can be calculated by reversing 3D projection:

$$p_{i,j}^{3d} = K_i^{-1} p_j^m \qquad (1)$$

where $K_i \in R^{4 \times 4}$ is the transformation matrix of i-th view that establish the transformation from 3D world space to camera frustum space. As illustrated in Fig. 2, the 3D coordinates of all views cover the panorama of the scene after the transformation. We further normalize the 3D coordinates as in Eq. 2.

$$\begin{cases} x_{i,j} = (x_{i,j} - x_{min})/(x_{max} - x_{min}) \\ y_{i,j} = (y_{i,j} - y_{min})/(y_{max} - y_{min}) \\ z_{i,j} = (z_{i,j} - z_{min})/(z_{max} - z_{min}) \end{cases} \quad (2)$$

where $[x_{min}, y_{min}, z_{min}, x_{max}, y_{max}, z_{max}]$ is the region of interest (RoI) of 3D world space. The normalized coordinates of $H_F \times W_F \times D$ points are finally transposed as $P^{3d} = \{P_i^{3d} \in R^{(D \times 4) \times H_F \times W_F}, i = 1, 2, \dots, N\}$.

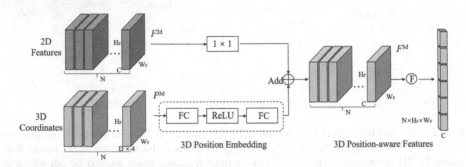

Fig. 3. Illustration of the proposed 3D Position Encoder. The multi-view 2D image features are input to a 1×1 convolution layer for dimension reduction. The 3D coordinates produced by the 3D coordinates generator are transformed into 3D position embedding by a multi-layer perception. The 3D position embeddings are added with the 2D image features of the same view, producing the 3D position-aware features. Finally, the 3D position-aware features are flattened and serve as the input of the transformer decoder. (F) is the flatten operation.

3.3   3D Position Encoder

The purpose of the 3D position encoder is to obtain 3D features $F^{3d} = \{F_i^{3d} \in R^{C \times H_F \times W_F}, i = 1, 2, \dots, N\}$ by associating 2D image features $F^{2d} = \{F_i^{2d} \in R^{C \times H_F \times W_F}, i = 1, 2, \dots, N\}$ with 3D position information. Analogously to Meta SR [17], the 3D position encoder can be formulated as:

$$F_i^{3d} = \psi(F_i^{2d}, P_i^{3d}), \quad i = 1, 2, \dots, N \quad (3)$$

where $\psi(.)$ is the position encoding function that is illustrated in Fig. 3. Next, we describe the detailed implementation of $\psi(.)$. Given the 2D features F^{2d} and 3D coordinates P^{3d}, the P^{3d} is first feed into a multi-layer perception (MLP) network and transformed to the 3D position embedding (PE). Then, the 2D features F^{2d} is transformed by a 1×1 convolution layer and added with the 3D PE to formulate the 3D position-aware features. Finally, we flatten the 3D position-aware features as the key component of transformer decoder.

Analysis on 3D PE: To demonstrate the effect of 3D PE, we randomly select the PE at three points in the front view and compute the PE similarity between these three points and all multi-view PEs. As shown in Fig. 4, the regions close to these points tend to have the higher similarity. For example, when we select the left point in the front view, the right region of front-left view will have relatively higher response. It indicates that 3D PE implicitly establishes the position correlation of different views in 3D space.

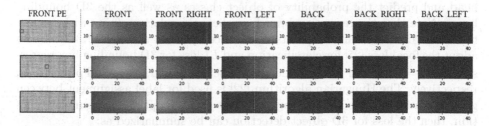

Fig. 4. 3D position embedding similarity. The red points are selected positions in the front view. We calculated the similarity between the position embedding of these selected positions and all image views. It shows that the regions close to these selective points tend to have higher similarity. (Color figure online)

3.4 Query Generator and Decoder

Query Generator: Original DETR [4] directly uses a set of learnable parameters as the initial object queries. Following Deformable-DETR [58], DETR3D [51] predicts the reference points based on the initialized object queries. To ease the convergence difficulty in 3D scene, similar to Anchor-DETR [50], we first initialize a set of learnable anchor points in 3D world space with uniform distribution from 0 to 1. Then the coordinates of 3D anchor points are input to a small MLP network with two linear layers and generate the initial object queries Q_0. In our practice, employing anchor points in 3D space can guarantee the convergence of PETR while adopting the setting in DETR or generating the anchor points in BEV space fail to achieve satisfying detection performance. For more details, please kindly refer to our experimental section.

Decoder: For the decoder network, we follow the standard transformer decoder in DETR [4], which includes L decoder layers. Here, we formulate the interaction process in decoder layer as:

$$Q_l = \Omega_l(F^{3d}, Q_{l-1}), \quad l = 1, \dots, L \tag{4}$$

where Ω_l is the l-th layer of the decoder. $Q_l \in R^{M \times C}$ is the updated object queries of l-th layer. M and C are the number of queries and channels, respectively. In each decoder layer, object queries interact with 3D position-aware features through the multi-head attention and feed-forward network. After iterative interaction, the updated object queries have the high-level representations and can be used to predict corresponding objects.

3.5   Head and Loss

The detection head mainly includes two branches for classification and regression. The updated object queries from the decoder are input to the detection head and predict the probability of object classes as well as the 3D bounding boxes. Note that the regression branch predicts the relative offsets with respect to the coordinates of anchor points. For fair comparison with DETR3D, we also adopt the focal loss [25] for classification and $L1$ loss for 3D bounding box regression. Let $y = (c, b)$ and $\hat{y} = (\hat{c}, \hat{b})$ denote the set of ground truths and predictions, respectively. The Hungarian algorithm [22] is used for label assignment between ground-truths and predictions. Suppose that σ is the optimal assignment function, then the loss for 3D object detection can be summarized as:

$$L(y, \hat{y}) = \lambda_{cls} * L_{cls}(c, \sigma(\hat{c})) + L_{reg}(b, \sigma(\hat{b})) \tag{5}$$

Here L_{cls} denotes the focal loss for classification, L_{reg} is $L1$ loss for regression. λ_{cls} is a hyper-parameter to balance different losses.

4   Experiments

4.1   Datasets and Metrics

We validate our method on nuScenes benchmark [3]. NuScenes is a large-scale multimodal dataset that is composed of data collected from 6 cameras, 1 lidar and 5 radars. The dataset has 1000 scenes and is officially divided into 700/150/150 scenes for training/validation/testing, respectively. Each scene has 20s video frames and is fully annotated with 3D bounding boxes every 0.5s. Consistent with official evaluation metrics, we report nuScenes Detection Score (NDS) and mean Average Precision (mAP), along with mean Average Translation Error (mATE), mean Average Scale Error (mASE), mean Average Orientation Error(mAOE), mean Average Velocity Error(mAVE), mean Average Attribute Error(mAAE).

4.2   Implementation Details

To extract the 2D features, ResNet [16], Swin-Transformer [27] or VoVNetV2 [23] are employed as the backbone network. The C5 feature (output of 5th stage) is upsampled and fused with C4 feature (output of 4th stage) to produce the P4 feature. The P4 feature with 1/16 input resolution is used as the 2D feature. For 3D coordinates generation, we sample 64 points along the depth axis following the linear-increasing discretization (LID) in CaDDN [38]. We set the region to $[-61.2\,m, 61.2\,m]$ for the X and Y axis, and $[-10\,m, 10\,m]$ for Z axis. The 3D coordinates in 3D world space are normalized to $[0, 1]$. Following DETR3D [51], we set $\lambda_{cls} = 2.0$ to balance classification and regression.

PETR is trained using AdamW [29] optimizer with weight decay of 0.01. The learning rate is initialized with 2.0×10^{-4} and decayed with cosine annealing policy [28]. Multi-scale training strategy is adopted, where the shorter side is randomly chosen within $[640, 900]$ and the longer side is less or equal to 1600. Following CenterPoint [55], the ground-truths of instances are randomly rotated with a range of $[-22.5°, 22.5°]$ in 3D space. All experiments are trained for 24 epochs (2x schedule) on 8 T V100 GPUs with a batch size of 8. No test time augmentation methods are used during inference.

Table 1. Comparison of recent works on the nuScenes val set. The results of FCOS3D and PGD are fine-tuned and tested with test time augmentation. The DETR3D, BEVDet and PETR are trained with CBGS [57]. † is initialized from an FCOS3D backbone.

Methods	Backbone	Size	NDS↑	mAP↑	mATE↓	mASE↓	mAOE↓	mAVE↓	mAAE↓
CenterNet	DLA	–	0.328	0.306	0.716	0.264	0.609	1.426	0.658
FCOS3D	Res-101	1600 × 900	0.415	0.343	0.725	0.263	0.422	1.292	0.153
PGD	Res-101	1600 × 900	0.428	0.369	0.683	0.260	0.439	1.268	0.185
BEVDet	Res-50	1056 × 384	0.381	0.304	0.719	0.272	0.555	0.903	0.257
BEVDet	Res-101	1056 × 384	0.389	0.317	0.704	0.273	0.531	0.940	0.250
BEVDet	Swin-T	1408 × 512	0.417	0.349	**0.637**	**0.269**	0.490	0.914	0.268
PETR	Res-50	1056 × 384	0.381	0.313	0.768	0.278	0.564	0.923	0.225
PETR	Res-50	1408 × 512	0.403	0.339	0.748	0.273	0.539	0.907	0.203
PETR	Res-101	1056 × 384	0.399	0.333	0.735	0.275	0.559	0.899	0.205
PETR	Res-101	1408 × 512	0.421	0.357	0.710	0.270	**0.490**	0.885	0.224
PETR	Swin-T	1408 × 512	**0.431**	**0.361**	0.732	0.273	0.497	**0.808**	**0.185**
DETR3D†	Res-101	1600 × 900	0.434	0.349	0.716	0.268	**0.379**	0.842	0.200
PETR†	Res-101	1056 × 384	0.423	0.347	0.736	0.269	0.448	0.844	0.202
PETR†	Res-101	1408 × 512	0.441	0.366	0.717	0.267	0.412	**0.834**	**0.190**
PETR†	Res-101	1600 × 900	**0.442**	**0.370**	**0.711**	**0.267**	0.383	0.865	0.201

4.3 State-of-the-Art Comparison

As shown in Table 1, we first compare the performance with state-of-the-art methods on nuScenes val set. It shows that PETR achieves the best performance on both NDS and mAP metrics. CenterNet [56], FCOS3D [49] and PGD [48] are typical monocular 3D object detection methods. When compare with FCOS3D [49] and PGD [48], PETR with ResNet-101 [16] surpasses them on NDS by 2.7% and 1.4%, respectively. However, PGD [48] achieves relatively lower mATE because of the explicit depth supervision. Besides, we also compare PETR with multi-view 3D object detection methods DETR3D [51] and BEVDet [18], which detect 3D objects in a unified view. Since the DETR3D [51] and BEVDet [18] follow different settings on the image size and backbone initialization, we individually compare the PETR with them for fair comparison. Our method outperforms them 0.8% and 1.4% in NDS, respectively.

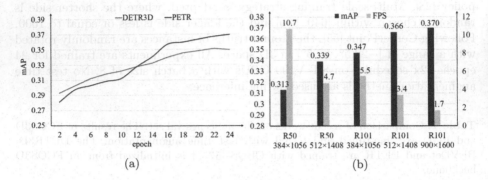

(a)   (b)

Fig. 5. Convergence and speed analysis on PETR. (a) The convergence comparison between PETR and DETR3D [51]. PETR converges slower at initial stage and requires a relatively longer training schedule for fully convergence. (b) The performance and speed analysis with different backbones and input sizes.

Table 2. Comparison of recent works on the nuScenes test set. * are trained with external data. ‡ is test time augmentation.

Methods	Backbone	NDS↑	mAP↑	mATE↓	mASE↓	mAOE↓	mAVE↓	mAAE↓
FCOS3D‡	Res-101	0.428	0.358	0.690	0.249	0.452	1.434	**0.124**
PGD‡	Res-101	0.448	0.386	0.626	0.245	0.451	1.509	0.127
DD3D*‡	V2-99	0.477	0.418	0.572	0.249	**0.368**	1.014	**0.124**
DETR3D*	V2-99	0.479	0.412	0.641	0.255	0.394	0.845	0.133
BEVDet	Swin-S	0.463	0.398	0.556	**0.239**	0.414	1.010	0.153
BEVDet*	V2-99	0.488	0.424	**0.524**	0.242	0.373	0.950	0.148
PETR	Res-101	0.455	0.391	0.647	0.251	0.433	0.933	0.143
PETR	Swin-T	0.450	0.411	0.664	0.256	0.522	0.971	0.137
PETR	Swin-S	0.481	0.434	0.641	0.248	0.437	0.894	0.143
PETR	Swin-B	0.483	**0.445**	0.627	0.249	0.449	0.927	0.141
PETR*	V2-99	**0.504**	0.441	0.593	0.249	0.383	**0.808**	0.132

Table 2 shows the performance comparison on nuScenes test set. Our method also achieves the best performance on both NDS and mAP. For fair comparison with BEVDet [18], PETR with Swin-S backbone is also trained with an image size of 2112×768. It shows that PETR surpasses BEVDet [18] by 3.6% in mAP and 1.8% in NDS, respectively. It is worth noting that PETR with Swin-B achieves a comparable performance compared to existing methods using external data. When using the external data, PETR with VOVNetV2 [23] backbone achieves 50.4% NDS and 44.1% mAP. As far as we know, PETR is the first vision-based method that surpasses 50.0% NDS.

We also perform the analysis on the convergence and detection speed of PETR. We first compare the convergence of DETR3D [51] and PETR (see Fig. 5(a)). PETR converges relatively slower than DETR3D [51] within the first 12 epochs and finally achieves much better detection performance. It indicates that PETR requires a relatively longer training schedule for fully convergence. We guess the reason is that PETR learns the 3D correlation through global attention while DETR3D [51] perceives the 3D scene within local regions. Figure 5(b) further reports the detection performance and speed of PETR with different input sizes. The FPS is measured on a single Tesla V100 GPU. For the same image size (e.g., 1056×384), our PETR infers with 10.7 FPS compared to the BEVDet [18] with 4.2 FPS. Note that the speed of BEVDet [18] is measured on NVIDIA 3090 GPU, which is stronger than Tesla V100 GPU.

Table 3. The impact of 3D Position Embedding. 2D PE is the common position embedding used in DETR. MV is multi-view position embedding to distinguish different views. 3D PE is the 3D position embedding proposed in our methods.

PE	2D	MV	3D	NDS↑	mAP↑	mATE↓	mASE↓	mAOE↓	mAVE↓	mAAE↓
1	✓			0.208	0.069	1.165	0.290	0.773	0.936	0.259
2	✓	✓		0.224	0.089	1.165	0.287	0.738	**0.929**	0.251
3			✓	0.356	0.305	**0.835**	**0.238**	0.639	0.971	**0.237**
4	✓		✓	0.351	0.305	0.838	0.283	**0.633**	1.048	0.256
5	✓	✓	✓	**0.359**	**0.309**	0.844	0.278	0.653	0.945	0.241

Table 4. Analysis of different methods to discrete the camera frustum space and different region of interest (ROI) ranges to normalized the 3D coordinates. UD is the Uniform discretization while LID is the linear-increasing discretization.

Depth Range	$(x_{min}, y_{min}, z_{min}, x_{max}, y_{max}, z_{max})$	UD	LID	NDS↑	mAP↑	mATE↓
(1,51.2)	(−51.2, −51.2, −10.0, 51.2, 51.2, 10.0)	✓		0.352	0.303	0.862
(1,51.2)	(−51.2, −51.2, −5, 51.2, 51.2, 3)	✓		0.352	0.305	0.854
(1,61.2)	(−61.2, −61.2, −10.0, 61.2, 61.2, 10.0)	✓		**0.358**	**0.308**	**0.850**
(1,61.2)	(−61.2, −61.2, −5, 61.2, 61.2, 3)	✓		0.342	0.297	0.860
(1,51.2)	(−51.2, −51.2, −10.0, 51.2, 51.2, 10.0)		✓	0.350	**0.310**	0.843
(1,51.2)	(−51.2, −51.2, −5, 51.2, 51.2, 3)		✓	0.355	0.306	**0.838**
(1,61.2)	(−61.2, −61.2, −10.0, 61.2, 61.2, 10.0)		✓	**0.359**	0.309	0.839
(1,61.2)	(−61.2, −61.2, −5, 61.2, 61.2, 3)		✓	0.346	0.304	0.842

4.4 Ablation Study

In this section, we perform the ablation study on some important components of PETR. All the experiments are conducted using single-level C5 feature of ResNet-50 backbone without the CBGS [57].

Impact of 3D Position Embedding. We evaluate the impact of different position embedding (PE) (see Table 3). When only the standard 2D PE in DETR is used, the model can only converge to 6.9% mAP. Then we add the multi-view prior (convert the view numbers into PE) to distinguish different views and it brings a slight improvement. When only using the 3D PE generated by 3D coordinates, PETR can directly achieve 30.5% mAP. It indicates that 3D PE provides a strong position prior to perceive the 3D scene. In addition, the performance can be improved when we combine the 3D PE with both 2D PE and multi-view prior. It should be noted that the main improvements are from the 3D PE and the 2D PE/multi-view prior can be selectively used in practice.

3D Coordinate Generator. In 3D coordinates generator, the perspective view in camera frustum space is discretized into 3D meshgrid. The transformed coordinates in 3D world space are further normalized with a region of interest (RoI). Here, we explore the effectiveness of different discretization methods and RoI range (see Table 4). The Uniform discretization (UD)

Table 5. The ablation studies of different components in the proposed PETR.

PE Networks	NDS↑	mAP↑	mATE↓
None	0.311	0.256	1.00
1×1 ReLU 1 × 1	**0.359**	**0.309**	**0.839**
3×3 ReLU 3 × 3	0.017	0.000	1.054

(a) The network to generate the 3D PE. "None" means that the normalized 3D coordinates are directly used as 3D PE.

Fusion Ways	NDS↑	mAP↑	mATE↓
Add	**0.359**	**0.309**	0.839
Concat	0.358	0.309	**0.832**
Multiply	0.357	0.303	0.848

(b) Different ways to fuse the 2D multi-view features with 3D PE in the 3D position encoder.

Anc-Points	NDS↑	mAP↑	mATE↓
None	–	–	–
Fix-BEV	0.337	0.295	0.852
Fix-3D	0.343	0.303	0.864
Learned-3D	**0.359**	**0.309**	**0.839**

(c) "None" means no anchor points following DETR. "Fix-BEV" and "Fix-3D" mean the grid anchor points in BEV space and 3D space respectively.

Points-Num	NDS↑	mAP↑	mATE↓
600	0.339	0.300	0.847
900	0.351	0.303	0.860
1200	0.354	0.303	0.854
1500	**0.359**	**0.309**	**0.839**

(d) Results with different numbers of anchor points. We explored anchor point numbers ranging from 600 to 1500. More points perform better.

shows similar performance compared to the linear-increasing discretization (LID). We also tried several common ROI regions and the RoI range of $(-61.2\,m, -61.2\,m, -10.0\,m, 61.2\,m, 61.2\,m, 10.0\,m)$ achieves better performance than others.

3D Position Encoder. The 3D position encoder is used to encode the 3D position into the 2D features. Here we first explore the effect of the multi-layer perception (MLP) that converts the 3D coordinates into 3D position embedding. It can be seen in Table 5(a) that the network with a simple MLP can improve the performance by 4.8% and 5.3% on NDS and mAP compared to the baseline without MLP (aligning the channel number of 2D features to $D \times 4$). When using two 3×3 convolution layers, the model will not converge as the 3×3 convolution destroys the correspondence between 2D feature and 3D position. Furthermore, we compare different ways to fuse the 2D image features with 3D PE in Table 5(b). The concatenation operation achieves similar performance compared to addition while surpassing the multiply fusion.

Query Generator. Table 5(c) shows the effect of different anchor points to generate queries. Here, we compare four types of anchor points: "None", "Fix-BEV", "Fix-3D" and "Learned-3D". Original DETR ("None") directly employs a set of learnable parameters as object queries without anchor points. The global feature of object query fail to make the model converge. "Fix-BEV" is the fixed anchor points are generated with the number of 39×39 in BEV space. "Fix-3D" means the fixed anchor points are with the number of $16 \times 16 \times 6$ in 3D world

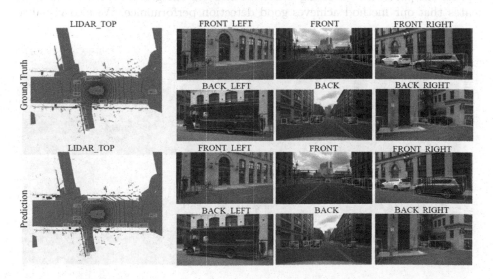

Fig. 6. Qualitative analysis of detection results in BEV and image views. The score threshold is 0.25, while the backbone is ResNet-101. The 3D bounding boxes are drawn with different colors to distinguish different classes.

544   Y. Liu et al.

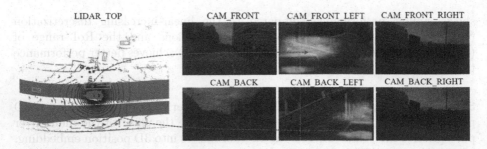

Fig. 7. Visualization of attention maps, generated from an object query (corresponding to the truck) on multi-view images. Both front-left and back-left views have a high response on the attention map.

space. "Learned-3D" are the learnable anchor points defined in 3D space. We find the performance of both "Fix-BEV" and "Fix-3D" are lower than learned anchor points. We also explore the number of anchor points (see Table 5(d)), which ranges from 600 to 1500. The model achieve the best performance with 1500 anchor points. Considering of the computation cost is increasing with the number of anchor points, we simply use 1500 anchor points to make a trade-off.

4.5 Visualization

Figure 6 shows some qualitative detection results. The 3D bounding boxes are projected and drawn in BEV space as well as image view. As shown in the BEV space, the predicted bounding boxes are close to the ground-truths. This indicates that our method achieves good detection performance. We also visualize

Fig. 8. Failure cases of PETR. We mark the failure cases by red and green circles. The red circles are some small objects that are not detected. The green circles are objects that are wrongly classified. (Color figure online)

the attention maps generated from an object query on multi-view images. As shown in Fig. 7, the object query tends to pay attention to the same object, even in different views. It indicates that 3D position embedding can establish the position correlation between different views. Finally, we provide some failure cases (see Fig. 8). The failure cases are marked by red and green circles. The red circles show some small objects that are not detected. The objects in green circle are wrongly classified. The wrong detection mainly occurs when different vehicles share high similarity on appearance.

5   Conclusions

The paper provides a simple and elegant solution for multi-view 3D object detection. By the 3D coordinates generation and position encoding, 2D features can be transformed into 3D position-aware feature representation. Such 3D representation can be directly incorporated into query-based DETR architecture and achieves end-to-end detection. It achieves state-of-the-art performance and can serve as a strong baseline for future research.

Acknowledgements. This research was supported by National Key R&D Program of China (No. 2017YFA0700800) and Beijing Academy of Artificial Intelligence (BAAI).

References

1. Bertasius, G., Wang, H., Torresani, L.: Is space-time attention all you need for video understanding. arXiv preprint arXiv:2102.05095 2(3), 4 (2021)
2. Brazil, G., Liu, X.: M3d-rpn: Monocular 3d region proposal network for object detection. In: Proceedings of the IEEE/CVF International Conference on Computer Vision, pp. 9287–9296 (2019)
3. Caesar, H., et al.: nuscenes: A multimodal dataset for autonomous driving. In: Proceedings of the IEEE/CVF Conference on Computer Vision and Pattern Recognition, pp. 11621–11631 (2020)
4. Carion, N., Massa, F., Synnaeve, G., Usunier, N., Kirillov, A., Zagoruyko, S.: End-to-end object detection with transformers. In: Vedaldi, A., Bischof, H., Brox, T., Frahm, J.-M. (eds.) ECCV 2020. LNCS, vol. 12346, pp. 213–229. Springer, Cham (2020). https://doi.org/10.1007/978-3-030-58452-8_13
5. Chabra, R., et al.: Deep local shapes: learning local SDF priors for detailed 3D reconstruction. In: Vedaldi, A., Bischof, H., Brox, T., Frahm, J.-M. (eds.) ECCV 2020. LNCS, vol. 12374, pp. 608–625. Springer, Cham (2020). https://doi.org/10.1007/978-3-030-58526-6_36
6. Chen, X., Kundu, K., Zhang, Z., Ma, H., Fidler, S., Urtasun, R.: Monocular 3d object detection for autonomous driving. In: Proceedings of the IEEE conference on computer vision and pattern recognition, pp. 2147–2156 (2016)
7. Chen, Y., Liu, S., Shen, X., Jia, J.: Dsgn: Deep stereo geometry network for 3d object detection. In: Proceedings of the IEEE/CVF conference on computer vision and pattern recognition, pp. 12536–12545 (2020)
8. Chen, Y., Liu, S., Wang, X.: Learning continuous image representation with local implicit image function. In: Proceedings of the IEEE/CVF Conference on Computer Vision and Pattern Recognition, pp. 8628–8638 (2021)

9. Chen, Z., Zhang, H.: Learning implicit fields for generative shape modeling. In: Proceedings of the IEEE/CVF Conference on Computer Vision and Pattern Recognition, pp. 5939–5948 (2019)

10. Dai, Z., Yang, Z., Yang, Y., Carbonell, J., Le, Q.V., Salakhutdinov, R.: Transformer-xl: Attentive language models beyond a fixed-length context. arXiv preprint arXiv:1901.02860 (2019)

11. Devlin, J., Chang, M.W., Lee, K., Toutanova, K.: Bert: Pre-training of deep bidirectional transformers for language understanding. arXiv preprint arXiv:1810.04805 (2018)

12. Dong, B., Zeng, F., Wang, T., Zhang, X., Wei, Y.: Solq: Segmenting objects by learning queries. In: Advances in Neural Information Processing Systems vol. 34 (2021)

13. Dosovitskiy, A., et al.: An image is worth 16x16 words: Transformers for image recognition at scale. arXiv preprint arXiv:2010.11929 (2020)

14. Gao, P., Zheng, M., Wang, X., Dai, J., Li, H.: Fast convergence of detr with spatially modulated co-attention. In: Proceedings of the IEEE/CVF International Conference on Computer Vision, pp. 3621–3630 (2021)

15. Gehring, J., Auli, M., Grangier, D., Yarats, D., Dauphin, Y.N.: Convolutional sequence to sequence learning. In: International Conference on Machine Learning, pp. 1243–1252. PMLR (2017)

16. He, K., Zhang, X., Ren, S., Sun, J.: Deep residual learning for image recognition. In: Proceedings of the IEEE conference on computer vision and pattern recognition, pp. 770–778 (2016)

17. Hu, X., Mu, H., Zhang, X., Wang, Z., Tan, T., Sun, J.: Meta-sr: A magnification-arbitrary network for super-resolution. In: Proceedings of the IEEE/CVF Conference on Computer Vision and Pattern Recognition, pp. 1575–1584 (2019)

18. Huang, J., Huang, G., Zhu, Z., Du, D.: Bevdet: High-performance multi-camera 3d object detection in bird-eye-view. arXiv preprint arXiv:2112.11790 (2021)

19. Jörgensen, E., Zach, C., Kahl, F.: Monocular 3d object detection and box fitting trained end-to-end using intersection-over-union loss. arXiv preprint arXiv:1906.08070 (2019)

20. Kehl, W., Manhardt, F., Tombari, F., Ilic, S., Navab, N.: Ssd-6d: Making rgb-based 3d detection and 6d pose estimation great again. In: Proceedings of the IEEE international conference on computer vision, pp. 1521–1529 (2017)

21. Ku, J., Pon, A.D., Waslander, S.L.: Monocular 3d object detection leveraging accurate proposals and shape reconstruction. In: Proceedings of the IEEE/CVF Conference on Computer Vision and Pattern Recognition, pp. 11867–11876 (2019)

22. Kuhn, H.W.: The hungarian method for the assignment problem. Naval Res. Logistics Q. **2**(1–2), 83–97 (1955)

23. Lee, Y., Park, J.: Centermask: Real-time anchor-free instance segmentation. In: Proceedings of the IEEE/CVF Conference on Computer Vision and Pattern Recognition, pp. 13906–13915 (2020)

24. Li, Y., et al.: Improved multiscale vision transformers for classification and detection. arXiv preprint arXiv:2112.01526 (2021)

25. Lin, T.Y., Goyal, P., Girshick, R., He, K., Dollár, P.: Focal loss for dense object detection. In: Proceedings of the IEEE international conference on computer vision, pp. 2980–2988 (2017)

26. Liu, S., et al.: Dab-detr: Dynamic anchor boxes are better queries for detr. arXiv preprint arXiv:2201.12329 (2022)

27. Liu, Z., et al.: Swin transformer: Hierarchical vision transformer using shifted windows. In: Proceedings of the IEEE/CVF International Conference on Computer Vision, pp. 10012–10022 (2021)
28. Loshchilov, I., Hutter, F.: Sgdr: Stochastic gradient descent with warm restarts. arXiv preprint arXiv:1608.03983 (2016)
29. Loshchilov, I., Hutter, F.: Decoupled weight decay regularization. arXiv preprint arXiv:1711.05101 (2017)
30. Meng, D., et al.: Conditional detr for fast training convergence. In: Proceedings of the IEEE/CVF International Conference on Computer Vision, pp. 3651–3660 (2021)
31. Mescheder, L., Oechsle, M., Niemeyer, M., Nowozin, S., Geiger, A.: Occupancy networks: Learning 3d reconstruction in function space. In: Proceedings of the IEEE/CVF Conference on Computer Vision and Pattern Recognition, pp. 4460–4470 (2019)
32. Mildenhall, B., Srinivasan, P.P., Tancik, M., Barron, J.T., Ramamoorthi, R., Ng, R.: NeRF: representing scenes as neural radiance fields for view synthesis. In: Vedaldi, A., Bischof, H., Brox, T., Frahm, J.-M. (eds.) ECCV 2020. LNCS, vol. 12346, pp. 405–421. Springer, Cham (2020). https://doi.org/10.1007/978-3-030-58452-8_24
33. Mousavian, A., Anguelov, D., Flynn, J., Kosecka, J.: 3d bounding box estimation using deep learning and geometry. In: Proceedings of the IEEE conference on Computer Vision and Pattern Recognition, pp. 7074–7082 (2017)
34. Park, D., Ambrus, R., Guizilini, V., Li, J., Gaidon, A.: Is pseudo-lidar needed for monocular 3d object detection? In: Proceedings of the IEEE/CVF International Conference on Computer Vision, pp. 3142–3152 (2021)
35. Park, J.J., Florence, P., Straub, J., Newcombe, R., Lovegrove, S.: Deepsdf: Learning continuous signed distance functions for shape representation. In: Proceedings of the IEEE/CVF Conference on Computer Vision and Pattern Recognition, pp. 165–174 (2019)
36. Peng, S., Niemeyer, M., Mescheder, L., Pollefeys, M., Geiger, A.: Convolutional occupancy networks. In: Vedaldi, A., Bischof, H., Brox, T., Frahm, J.-M. (eds.) ECCV 2020. LNCS, vol. 12348, pp. 523–540. Springer, Cham (2020). https://doi.org/10.1007/978-3-030-58580-8_31
37. Philion, J., Fidler, S.: Lift, splat, shoot: encoding images from arbitrary camera rigs by implicitly unprojecting to 3D. In: Vedaldi, A., Bischof, H., Brox, T., Frahm, J.-M. (eds.) ECCV 2020. LNCS, vol. 12359, pp. 194–210. Springer, Cham (2020). https://doi.org/10.1007/978-3-030-58568-6_12
38. Reading, C., Harakeh, A., Chae, J., Waslander, S.L.: Categorical depth distribution network for monocular 3d object detection. In: Proceedings of the IEEE/CVF Conference on Computer Vision and Pattern Recognition, pp. 8555–8564 (2021)
39. Roddick, T., Kendall, A., Cipolla, R.: Orthographic feature transform for monocular 3d object detection. arXiv preprint arXiv:1811.08188 (2018)
40. Rukhovich, D., Vorontsova, A., Konushin, A.: Imvoxelnet: Image to voxels projection for monocular and multi-view general-purpose 3d object detection. In: Proceedings of the IEEE/CVF Winter Conference on Applications of Computer Vision, pp. 2397–2406 (2022)
41. Simonelli, A., Bulo, S.R., Porzi, L., López-Antequera, M., Kontschieder, P.: Disentangling monocular 3d object detection. In: Proceedings of the IEEE/CVF International Conference on Computer Vision, pp. 1991–1999 (2019)

42. Sitzmann, V., Martel, J., Bergman, A., Lindell, D., Wetzstein, G.: Implicit neural representations with periodic activation functions. Adv. Neural. Inf. Process. Syst. **33**, 7462–7473 (2020)
43. Sitzmann, V., Zollhöfer, M., Wetzstein, G.: Scene representation networks: Continuous 3d-structure-aware neural scene representations. In: Advances in Neural Information Processing Systems vol. 32 (2019)
44. Sun, Z., Cao, S., Yang, Y., Kitani, K.M.: Rethinking transformer-based set prediction for object detection. In: Proceedings of the IEEE/CVF International Conference on Computer Vision, pp. 3611–3620 (2021)
45. Tancik, M., et al.: Fourier features let networks learn high frequency functions in low dimensional domains. Adv. Neural. Inf. Process. Syst. **33**, 7537–7547 (2020)
46. Tian, Z., Shen, C., Chen, H., He, T.: Fcos: Fully convolutional one-stage object detection. In: Proceedings of the IEEE/CVF International Conference on Computer Vision, pp. 9627–9636 (2019)
47. Vaswani, A.: Attention is all you need. In: Advances in Neural Information Processing Systems, vol. 30 (2017)
48. Wang, T., Xinge, Z., Pang, J., Lin, D.: Probabilistic and geometric depth: Detecting objects in perspective. In: Conference on Robot Learning, pp. 1475–1485. PMLR (2022)
49. Wang, T., Zhu, X., Pang, J., Lin, D.: Fcos3d: Fully convolutional one-stage monocular 3d object detection. In: Proceedings of the IEEE/CVF International Conference on Computer Vision, pp. 913–922 (2021)
50. Wang, Y., Zhang, X., Yang, T., Sun, J.: Anchor detr: Query design for transformer-based detector. arXiv preprint arXiv:2109.07107 (2021)
51. Wang, Y., Vitor Campagnolo, G., Zhang, T., Zhao, H., Solomon, J.: Detr3d: 3d object detection from multi-view images via 3d-to-2d queries. In: In Conference on Robot Learning, pp. 180–191 (2022)
52. Wu, C.Y., et al.: Memvit: Memory-augmented multiscale vision transformer for efficient long-term video recognition. arXiv preprint arXiv:2201.08383 (2022)
53. Wu, K., Peng, H., Chen, M., Fu, J., Chao, H.: Rethinking and improving relative position encoding for vision transformer. In: Proceedings of the IEEE/CVF International Conference on Computer Vision, pp. 10033–10041 (2021)
54. Yang, Z., Dai, Z., Yang, Y., Carbonell, J., Salakhutdinov, R.R., Le, Q.V.: Xlnet: Generalized autoregressive pretraining for language understanding. In: Advances in Neural Information Processing Systems, vol. 32 (2019)
55. Yin, T., Zhou, X., Krahenbuhl, P.: Center-based 3d object detection and tracking. In: Proceedings of the IEEE/CVF Conference on Computer Vision and Pattern Recognition, pp. 11784–11793 (2021)
56. Zhou, X., Wang, D., Krähenbühl, P.: Objects as points. arXiv preprint arXiv:1904.07850 (2019)
57. Zhu, B., Jiang, Z., Zhou, X., Li, Z., Yu, G.: Class-balanced grouping and sampling for point cloud 3d object detection. arXiv preprint arXiv:1908.09492 (2019)
58. Zhu, X., Su, W., Lu, L., Li, B., Wang, X., Dai, J.: Deformable detr: Deformable transformers for end-to-end object detection. arXiv preprint arXiv:2010.04159 (2020)

S2Net: Stochastic Sequential Pointcloud Forecasting

Xinshuo Weng[1]([⊠]), Junyu Nan[1], Kuan-Hui Lee[2], Rowan McAllister[2], Adrien Gaidon[2], Nicholas Rhinehart[3], and Kris M. Kitani[1]

[1] Robotics Institute, Carnegie Mellon University, Pittsburgh, USA
{xinshuow,jnan1,kkitani}@andrew.cmu.edu
[2] Toyota Research Institute, Palo Alto, USA
{kuan.lee,rowan.mcallister,adrien.gaidon}@tri.global
[3] Berkeley Artificial Intelligence Research Lab, University of California, Berkeley, USA
nrhinehart@berkeley.edu

Abstract. Predicting futures of surrounding agents is critical for autonomous systems such as self-driving cars. Instead of requiring accurate detection and tracking prior to trajectory prediction, an object agnostic Sequential Pointcloud Forecasting (SPF) task was proposed [28], which enables a forecast-then-detect pipeline effective for downstream detection and trajectory prediction. One limitation of prior work is that it forecasts only a deterministic sequence of future point clouds, despite the inherent uncertainty of dynamic scenes. In this work, we tackle the stochastic SPF problem by proposing a generative model with two main components: (1) a conditional variational recurrent neural network that models a temporally-dependent latent space; (2) a pyramid-LSTM that increases the fidelity of predictions with temporally-aligned skip connections. Through experiments on real-world autonomous driving datasets, our stochastic SPF model produces higher-fidelity predictions, reducing Chamfer distances by up to 56.6% compared to its deterministic counterpart. In addition, our model can estimate the uncertainty of predicted points, which can be helpful to downstream tasks.

Keywords: Sequential point cloud forecasting · Variational recurrent neural network · Future uncertainty · Self-driving cars

1 Introduction

Uncertainty is an inherent challenge associated with different future prediction tasks such as video prediction [4,23,30,31], trajectory prediction [15,18,29,33] and sequential pointcloud forecasting (SPF) [21,28]. For SPF [28], given a sequence of past point clouds captured by the LiDAR sensor, future point clouds are uncertain because the future behaviors of entities in the scene are uncertain.

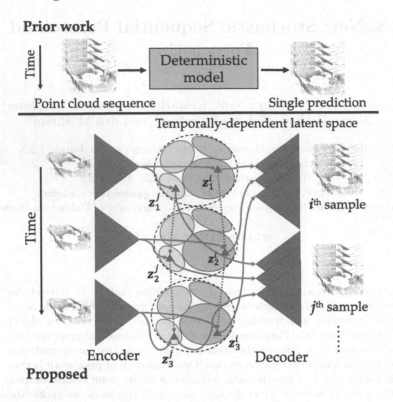

Fig. 1. Different from prior work (top) that uses a deterministic model to predict a single future of point clouds, our S2Net (bottom) can sample (*e.g.*, green and brown) sequences of latent variables to tackle future uncertainty. Also, each sequence of latent variables is temporally-dependent to ensure consistency of forecasting. (Color figure online)

Although prior work in video prediction [7,20] and trajectory prediction [25,33] has made significant advancements in developing generative models to handle future uncertainty, prior work in SPF is limited by predicting a deterministic sequence of future point clouds.

In this work, we propose S2Net[1], a *Stochastic* SPFNet that, for the first time, enables prediction of stochastic future point clouds. Specifically, we follow the LSTM (Long Short-Term Memory) encoder-decoder style as in [28] but extend it with a conditional variational LSTM. At each frame, the LSTM hidden state propagates past information up to the current frame, which we use as the context and map to a prior distribution. Then, we can sample from this prior distribution to predict the point cloud in the next frame through a decoder. As future point clouds are supposed to be temporally-consistent, the uncertainty at each frame

---

[1] Our project website is at https://www.xinshuoweng.com/projects/S2Net.

should depend on the last frame. Therefore, we enforce the temporal dependency between sampled latent variables across time as shown in Fig. 1.

Another limitation of prior work is blurry predictions or excessive smoothness in the predicted point clouds. We alleviate this issue and improve the fidelity of predicted point clouds by adding skip connections between encoders and decoders. Specifically, a pyramid of features at different levels of encoders are fed into the decoders, which reduces the complexity of training the decoder because now it only needs to learn residuals of features. However, naively adding skip connections performs poorly in the SPF task as the timestamp of features in the encoder is not aligned with the timestamp of features in the decoder. To tackle this issue, we add additional LSTMs at every level of the pyramids before skip connection so that we fuse temporally-aligned features in the decoder.

Through experiments on KITTI and nuScenes, we show that the pyramid LSTMs is a key to produce sharper and more accurate point clouds than the simple LSTM encoder-decoder framework in [28]. Combining with the conditional variational LSTM, we reduce predictions errors by 56.6% relative to its deterministic counterpart when sampling five predictions. By computing the standard deviation of every point across five samples, we can measure how certain the network is about every predicted point, which can be useful to downstream tasks. Also, compared to [28], the addition of conditional variational LSTM and temporally-aligned skip connections does not add significant computational overhead, so our method is still efficient and able to predict a sequence of large-scale LiDAR point clouds (*e.g.*, 122,880 points per frame) for a time horizon of 3 s. Our contributions are summarized below:

1. a *stochastic* SPF model (S2Net) with temporally-dependent latent space that can sample predictions of point clouds to tackle future uncertainty;
2. a pyramid-LSTM module that can increase the fidelity and sharpness of the predicted future point clouds over prior work;
3. an efficient network design that allows prediction of a sequence of large-scale LiDAR point clouds over a long horizon.

2   Related Work

Sequential Pointcloud Forecasting was proposed in [28] for large-scale LiDAR point clouds. It has been shown that, by scaling up the learning of SPF in a fully unsupervised manner, the downstream trajectory prediction task can be improved. Instead of using 1D-LSTM, [27] proposed to use ConvLSTM for SPF. Instead of directly predicting point locations, [9] proposes to predict flow which can be added to the input point cloud to generate future point locations. However, [9] only predicts the next frame of point cloud, which does not strictly follow the design of sequence prediction. Recently, [21] proposes to use 3D convolutions to jointly encode spatial and temporal information for SPF, which shows improved performance over [28]. However, all these prior works propose deterministic models, whereas our method can predict stochastic futures of point cloud sequences to tackle future uncertainty.

Sequence Point Cloud Processing is closely related to SPF as it also processes a sequence of point clouds. The difference to SPF is that, the term "point cloud" here is loose and does not necessarily mean large-scale LiDAR point cloud. For example, it can be processing of image pixels such as moving MNIST [12] with $64 \times 64 = 4096$ pixels as in [14], or processing severely downsampled LiDAR point clouds of about $1,024$ points as in [12], or processing mobile traffic with about $5,000$ points as in [34], or processing human hand joints with less than 50 points as in [22]. Because it does not necessarily process large-scale LiDAR point clouds, network efficiency is not a critical concern in prior work of sequence point cloud processing. As a result, these works may not be directly transferred to SPF and process full LiDAR point cloud data, although we can draw inspiration from these works in designing our method for SPF. In contrast, our method is designed specifically for SPF, and can operate on a sequence of $\geq 100,000$ points, *i.e.*, a total of $\geq 1M$ points for 10 frames.

Variational Models in Sequence Modeling. Stochastic recurrent networks [3,6,8] are commonly used to model variations and uncertainty in sequential data, which is significantly different from standard VAE/CVAE [16] that is designed to model variations for a single frame of data. STORNs [3] incorporates a latent variable into every timestamp of the recurrent network, where the latent variables are independent across time. VRNN [8] models the dependency between the RNN's hidden state at the current timestamp and the latent variable in the last timestamp. As the latent variable in the current timestamp also depends on the RNN's hidden state, there is an indirect temporal dependency between latent variables. [6] further improves VRNN by allowing direct temporal dependency between latent variables[2]. However, the use of these stochastic recurrent networks in large-scale future prediction tasks is still under-explored, and in this work we explore how we can adapt them to stochastic SPF.

Point Cloud Generation. Most prior work focuses on generating a point cloud of a single object at a single frame. [11] proposes to optimize object point cloud generation using Chamfer distance [11] and Earth Mover's distance [24]. [19] projects the point cloud into 2d images from multiple views and optimizes for the re-projection error. Other works focus on stochastic object point cloud generation, where normalizing flow [32], generative adversarial networks (GANs) [26], or variational autoencoders (VAEs) [17] can be used. Different from these works which are designed to generate the point cloud for an object or a scene at a single frame, our work aims to *predict* a *long horizon* of *large-scale* point clouds.

3   Approach: S2Net

The goal of stochastic SPF (Sequential Pointcloud Forecasting) is to learn a function that can sample different sequences of future point clouds given a sequence

---

[2] An illustrative comparison between these works can be found in [6].

of observed past point clouds. Let $\mathcal{S}_p = \{\boldsymbol{S}_{1-M}, \ldots, \boldsymbol{S}_0\}$ denote M frames of past point clouds of a scene and $\mathcal{S}_f = \{\boldsymbol{S}_1, \ldots, \boldsymbol{S}_N\}$ denote N frames of future point clouds. Each frame of point cloud $\boldsymbol{S}_t = \{(x,y,z)_j\}_{j=1}^{K_t} = \{\boldsymbol{u}_j\}_{j=1}^{K_t}$ contains a set of unordered points, where $t \in [1-M, \cdots, N]$ denotes the frame index, $j \in [1, \cdots, K_t]$ denotes the index of point and K_t denotes the number of points at frame t. Then, we aim to learn a function $\mathcal{F}$ that can map $\mathcal{S}_p$ and sampled latent variables $\mathcal{Z} = \{\boldsymbol{z}_1, \ldots, \boldsymbol{z}_N\}$ to a sequence of future point clouds $\mathcal{S}_f$:

$$\mathcal{S}_f = \mathcal{F}(\mathcal{S}_p, \mathcal{Z}). \tag{1}$$

In this work, we use LiDAR point clouds as $\mathcal{S}$ to validate our approach, but our approach can also be applied to other types of point clouds such as those captured by indoor RGB-D cameras or generated by stereo images. The main challenge of working with LiDAR point clouds is that the data is typically large-scale, that is more than $100,000$ points per frame or 1 million of points for a sequence of 10 frames, so efficiency is the key in approach design.

The network architecture of our approach is illustrated in Fig. 2, which contains the following parts: 1) a shared encoder to obtain features $\boldsymbol{r}_t^l$ at different levels of the pyramid and at all frames, where $t \in [1-M, \cdots, N]$ denotes the frame index and $l \in [1, \cdots, L]$ denotes the pyramid level; 2) a pyramid of LSTMs to propagate features from the past frame $\boldsymbol{h}_{t-1}^l$ to the future $\boldsymbol{h}_t^l$; 3) a temporally-dependent latent model that computes the prior distribution and sample latent variable $\boldsymbol{z}_t$ conditioned on previous latent $\boldsymbol{z}_{t-1}$ and current hidden state $\boldsymbol{h}_t^1$; 4) a shared decoder to predict the next frame's point cloud $\mathcal{S}_t^l$ given $\boldsymbol{z}_t$, $\boldsymbol{h}_t^l$, where $l \in [1, \cdots, L]$. Here we omit the details about how to compute the prior and posterior distribution to sample latent variables during training and testing, which can be found in Sect. 3.4. During testing, our model performs auto-regressive prediction, which uses the predicted point cloud as input for the next frame.

3.1 Input/Output Representation: Range Map

To represent a point cloud $\boldsymbol{S} = \{(x,y,z)_j\}_{j=1}^K$, we follow prior work [21,28] and use the range map representation $\mathcal{R} \in \mathbb{R}^{H \times W \times 1}$. Each range map can be viewed as a 1-channel image, with every pixel corresponding to a point in 3D and the pixel value storing the Euclidean distance $d = \sqrt{x^2 + y^2 + z^2}$ of the point to the LiDAR sensor. To convert a point cloud to a range map, we use spherical projection. Specifically, for a point $p = (x,y,z)$ in the Cartesian coordinate (z is the height), its coordinate in the range map $q = (\theta, \phi)$ can be computed as:

$$\theta = \arctan(y/x), \phi = \arcsin(z/\sqrt{x^2 + y^2 + z^2}) = \arcsin(z/d), \tag{2}$$

where θ, ϕ are the azimuth, elevation angle. Since d is stored in the range map, one can also apply inverse spherical projection to recover the $p = (x,y,z)$ as:

$$z = \sin(\phi) \times d, \qquad d_{\text{ground}} = \cos(\phi) \times d, \tag{3}$$

where d_{ground} is the projected distance on the x-y ground plane. Then,

$$x = \cos(\theta) \times d_{\text{ground}}, \qquad y = \sin(\theta) \times d_{\text{ground}}. \tag{4}$$

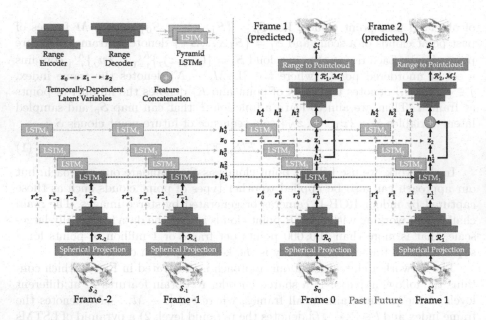

Fig. 2. (Left) **Extracting features from past frames**. Given a point cloud $\mathcal{S}_t$ in the past, we first convert it into a 2D range map $\mathcal{R}_t$ (spherical projection) and then extract features $r_t^l = \{r_t^1, r_t^2, \cdots, r_t^L\}$ at different layers with a 2D CNN (range encoder). To learn temporal dynamics, features at different layers r_t^l are propagated through time via pyramid LSTMs and output hidden states $h_0^l = \{h_0^1, h_0^2, \cdots, h_0^L\}$. (Right) **Autoregressive future prediction**. To begin at input frame 0, given propagated hidden states h_0^l and extracted feature pyramids r_0^l, we further propagate the LSTM hidden states into frame 1. Combining h_1^1 with the initialized latent variable z_0, a prior distribution is computed during testing where we can sample multiple z_1. We then predict the range map $\mathcal{R}_1'$ and range mask $\mathcal{M}_1'$ via the range decoder, conditioned on the propagated hidden states $(h_1^1, h_1^2, \cdots, h_1^L)$ and sampled latent variable z_1. For illustration, we only show using three past frames of inputs $(\mathcal{S}_{-2}, \mathcal{S}_{-1}, \mathcal{S}_0)$ to predict two frames of future $(\mathcal{S}_1', \mathcal{S}_2')$. Also, only one branch of the encoder-decoder is shown while we have two sets of encoders and decoders for range map and range mask separately. (Color figure online)

Although range map is an image representation, it is very different from other image representations which often involves loss of information during projection such as the camera image with perspective projection (losing depth information) or the Bird's eye view projection (losing height information). In contrast, there is no loss of information in theory[3] when converting a point cloud to range map since the range map preserves full LiDAR data. Also, it is very efficient to process range maps with CNNs (Convolutional Neural Networks) due to the nature of image representation, which is the key to our efficient network design.

---

[3] There might be still a small amount of information loss due to discretization unless one uses very high-resolution range map as we do in the experiments.

3.2 Range Encoder

To process the range map $\mathcal{R}_t$ converted from the point cloud $\mathcal{S}_t$, we follow [28] and use a 2D CNNs as shown in reddish-brown in Fig. 2. This 2D CNNs contains a series of blocks, with each block having a 2D convolution, batch normalization (BN) and LeakyReLU activation, except for the last block which does not have BN and LeakyReLU. The output of the encoder is a pyramid of features $[r_t^1, \cdots, r_t^L]$ after each layer of convolution. The range encoder is shared for all past frames $(\mathcal{R}_{1-M}, \cdots, \mathcal{R}_0)$ and also used to extract features from the predicted range maps $(\mathcal{R}_1', \cdots, \mathcal{R}_{N-1}')$.

In addition to the range map encoder, we have another range mask encoder that has the exactly same architecture as the range map encoder, which we omit in Fig. 2 for simplicity. The goal of the range mask encoder is to learn features to predict the range mask $\mathcal{M}_t'$, which masks out "empty" pixels[4] in the predicted range map $\mathcal{R}_t'$. The inputs to the range mask encoder are the same as the range map encoder, *i.e.*, $\mathcal{R}_t$, while the weights of two encoders are not shared.

3.3 Pyramid LSTMs

After extracting features at different levels r_t^l for all past frames, we propagate them through time using LSTMs to learn temporal dynamics of the point cloud sequence. As the encoder CNNs output a vector in the last layer r_t^1, we use standard LSTM as shown in blue in Fig. 2 to propagate r_t^1 through time. However, for features at other levels except for the last layer, we use Convolutional LSTMs (ConvLSTM) as shown in orangish-yellow in Fig. 2 because r_t^l is a 2D feature map when $l > 1$. The outputs of pyramid LSTMs at frame $t - 1$ are propagated to obtain hidden states h_t^l (with a shift of one timestep), where $l \in [1, \cdots, L]$.

The motivation to keep other levels of features (besides r_t^1) being propagated through time is to prepare for temporally-aligned skip connection in the decoder at multiple pyramid levels, which we realize is a key to increase the prediction accuracy compared to using only one level of features as shown in the ablation in Table 3 (right). Also, if only extracting feature pyramids for naive skip connection without propagating them through time, *e.g.*, directly feeding r_0^2, r_0^3, r_0^4 (rather than h_1^2, h_1^3, h_1^4) to the decoder at frame 0, the timestamps of features in the decoder are not consistent which turns out can mess up the training.

3.4 CVAE Prior and Posterior

To enable prediction of stochastic futures, we adapt standard CVAE (Conditional Variational Auto-encoder) framework to our sequence-to-sequence problem. As shown in related stochastic video prediction work [10], learnable prior $\mathcal{N}(\boldsymbol{\mu}, \boldsymbol{\sigma}^2)$, where $\boldsymbol{\mu}$ and $\boldsymbol{\sigma}$ of the Gaussian are conditioned on context features, works better

---

[4] Unlike RGB images, not every pixel in the range map is valid. This is because there are pixels without corresponding points in 3D due to no return of the LiDAR beam in that direction, *e.g.*, when the LiDAR beam shots to the sky.

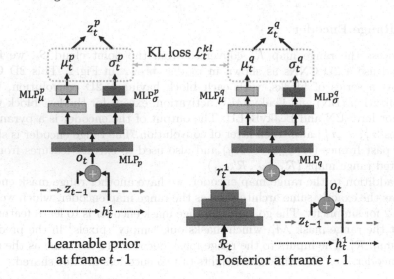

Fig. 3. (Left) **Computing the prior**. To better accommodate prediction at a long horizon, we learn the prior $\mathcal{N}(\boldsymbol{\mu}_t^p, \boldsymbol{\sigma}_t^{p2}) = \mathcal{N}(\mu_{\phi_1}(\mathcal{S}_{1-M:t-1}), \sigma_{\phi_2}(\mathcal{S}_{1-M:t-1}))$, instead of using a fixed Gaussian $\mathcal{N}(0, \mathbf{I})$. The inputs are the concatenated feature of $\boldsymbol{z}_{t-1}$ and $\boldsymbol{h}_t^1$, where $\boldsymbol{h}_t^1$ is the context feature while $\boldsymbol{z}_{t-1}$ enforces temporal dependency in the latent space. We then compute the mean $\boldsymbol{\mu}_t^p$ and variance $\boldsymbol{\sigma}_t^p$ via MLPs so we can sample latent variable $\boldsymbol{z}_t^p$. (Right) **Computing the posterior**. Except for one additional input, that is the future range map $\mathcal{R}_t$ and its extracted feature $\boldsymbol{r}_t^1$, we use the same architecture as the learnable prior to compute the posterior, although weights are not shared between posterior and prior computation. A KL divergence loss $\mathcal{L}_t^{kl}$ is applied between the computed prior and posterior distributions during training.

than fixed Gaussian prior $\mathcal{N}(0, \mathbf{I})$ in the sequence-to-sequence problem, so we also use learnable prior for our S2Net.

As shown in Fig. 3 (left), the inputs to compute the prior at frame $t - 1$ are sampled latent variable $\boldsymbol{z}_{t-1}$ and the context feature $\boldsymbol{h}_t^1$ (propagated LSTM hidden state). Two inputs are first concatenated to obtain an intermediate feature $\boldsymbol{o}_t$, which is then fed into a joint MLP_p (Multi-Layer Perceptron) followed by two separate MLP_μ^p and MLP_σ^p to compute the mean $\boldsymbol{\mu}_t^p$ and variance $\boldsymbol{\sigma}_t^p$ of the prior distribution at frame $t - 1$. During testing time, we can then randomly sample latent variables $\boldsymbol{z}_t^p$ from the prior distribution $\mathcal{N}(\boldsymbol{\mu}_t^p, \boldsymbol{\sigma}_t^{p2}) = \mathcal{N}(\mu_{\phi_1}(\mathcal{S}_{1-M:t-1}), \sigma_{\phi_2}(\mathcal{S}_{1-M:t-1}))$ to enable stochastic prediction, where the MLPs are parametrized by ϕ_1 and ϕ_2. The process can be summarized below:

$$\boldsymbol{o}_t = \boldsymbol{z}_{t-1} \oplus \boldsymbol{h}_t^1, \tag{5}$$

$$\boldsymbol{\mu}_t^p = \text{MLP}_\mu^p(\text{MLP}_p(\boldsymbol{o}_t)), \ \boldsymbol{\sigma}_t^p = \text{MLP}_\sigma^p(\text{MLP}_p(\boldsymbol{o}_t)), \tag{6}$$

$$\boldsymbol{z}_t \sim \mathcal{N}(\boldsymbol{\mu}_t^p, \boldsymbol{\sigma}_t^{p2}). \tag{7}$$

Similar to computing the prior distribution during testing, we compute the posterior distribution $\mathcal{N}(\boldsymbol{\mu}_t^q, \boldsymbol{\sigma}_t^{q2})$ (Fig. 3 right) during training for the KL loss.

The main difference when computing the posterior at frame $t - 1$ is the use of future range map $\mathcal{R}_t$ as input, in addition to z_{t-1} and the context h_t^1. Here, a future range encoder that has the same architecture as the range encoder (Sect. 3.2) is used to extract features from the future range data $\mathcal{R}_t$. Similarly, we can sample latent variable $z_t^q \sim \mathcal{N}(\mu_t^q, \sigma_t^{q^2}) = \mathcal{N}(\mu_{\phi_3}(\mathcal{S}_{1-M:t}), \sigma_{\phi_4}(\mathcal{S}_{1-M:t}))$, where ϕ_3 and ϕ_4 summarize parameters of the $\mathrm{MLP}_q, \mathrm{MLP}_\mu^q, \mathrm{MLP}_\sigma^q$ and the future range encoder. Then, the latent variable z_t^q is passed to the decoder during training. Note that during testing, we only compute the prior as in the standard CVAE formulation because we do not need the KL loss and also the future range data (ground truth) $\mathcal{R}_t$ is not available at testing.

3.5 Temporally-Dependent Latent Space

Given the prior and posterior, we can sample the latent variable at every frame. However, if we sample latent variables independently at every frame, it is not likely to generate temporally-consistent variations in the predicted point clouds as the uncertainty is drawn from independent samples. This motivates us to enforce temporal dependency in the latent space, that is the latent variable z_t is directly conditioned on the latent variable z_{t-1} sampled in the previous frame as shown in Fig. 3. We realize that this temporally-dependent latent space is especially useful to improve the performance of point cloud prediction for a long time horizon. The first latent variable z_0 is initialized with all zeros.

3.6 Range Decoder

To obtain predicted point clouds at every future frame, we first predict the range map $\mathcal{R}_t'$ and range mask $\mathcal{M}_t'$. Then, the range map $\mathcal{R}_t'$ is used to generate point clouds via inverse spherical projection as explained in Eq. 3 and 4, and the range mask is used in a mask operation to prevent "empty" pixels in the range map to generate "bad" points. The mask decoder has the architecture as the range map decoder except that the weights of decoders are different.

Now we describe how we predict the range map or mask. As we formulate the stochastic SPF in a CVAE framework, the range decoder at frame $t - 1$ is conditioned on the context feature (LSTM hidden state h_t^1), in addition to the sampled latent variable z_t. Two inputs are concatenated before feeding into the range decoder, as shown in Fig. 2. To reduce the complexity of predicting full-resolution range map $\mathcal{R}_t'$ from only two low-dimensional features (h_t^1 and z_t), we add the temporally-aligned skip connections from pyramid LSTMs. As higher-resolution feature maps are added as inputs to the decoder, we only need to learn the residual of features for small local changes after one frame, which increases the fidelity of point cloud prediction. In terms of the architecture, the range decoder has the inverse structure as the range encoder introduced in Sect. 3.2 except that the input channel of the first layer is increased to accommodate the added dimension of the latent variable z_t.

3.7 Training Objective

Since we formulate our stochastic SPF in a sequential CVAE framework, we use the negative evidence lower bound (ELBO) $\mathcal{L}_{\text{elbo}}$ as our loss function:

$$\mathcal{L}_{\text{elbo}} = \mathbb{E}_{q(z_{\leq N}|S_{\leq N})}\left[\sum_{t=1}^{N}\left(-\log p(S_t|z_{\leq t}, S_{<t}) + \text{KL}(q(z_t|S_{\leq t}, z_{<t}) \| p(z_t|S_{<t}, z_{<t}))\right)\right], \quad (8)$$

where the KL loss aims to minimize the difference between the prior distribution $p(z_t|S_{<t}, z_{<t})$ and posterior distribution $q(z_t|S_{\leq t}, z_{<t})$. Also, to maximize the log-likelihood $\log p(S_t|z_{\leq t}, S_{<t})$, we use the following reconstruction losses:

1. Chamfer distance [11] $\mathcal{L}_t^{\text{cd}}$ between the predicted point cloud S_t' (after points masking) and ground truth (GT) point cloud S_t:

$$\mathcal{L}_t^{\text{cd}} = \sum_{u' \in S_t'} \min_{u \in S_t} \|u - u'\|_2^2 + \sum_{u \in S_t} \min_{u' \in S_t'} \|u - u'\|_2^2, \quad (9)$$

2. L_1 distance $\mathcal{L}_t^{L1}$ between the predicted range map $\mathcal{R}_t'$ and GT range map $\mathcal{R}_t \in \mathbb{R}^{H \times W \times 2}$ at every valid pixel:

$$\mathcal{L}_t^{L1} = \sum_i^H \sum_j^W \|\mathcal{M}_{ti,j}(\mathcal{R}_{ti,j}' - \mathcal{R}_{ti,j})\|_1, \quad (10)$$

3. A binary cross-entropy loss $\mathcal{L}_t^{bce}$ between the predicted mask $\mathcal{M}_t'$ and GT mask $\mathcal{M}_t$ at every pixel:

$$\mathcal{L}_t^{bce} = \sum_i^H \sum_j^W -\mathcal{M}_{ti,j}\log(\mathcal{M}_{ti,j}') - (1 - \mathcal{M}_{ti,j})\log(1 - \mathcal{M}_{ti,j}'), \quad (11)$$

Combining the reconstruction losses with the KL loss, our full loss function is:

$$\mathcal{L} = \sum_{t=1}^{N}(\mathcal{L}_t^{kl} + \mathcal{L}_t^{\text{reconstruction}}) = \sum_{t=1}^{N}(\beta\mathcal{L}_t^{kl} + \alpha\mathcal{L}_t^{\text{cd}} + \kappa\mathcal{L}_t^{L1} + \omega\mathcal{L}_t^{bce}). \quad (12)$$

We note that our $\mathcal{L}_{\text{elbo}}$ is different from many CVAE-based methods [25,33] because our reconstruction loss has three components (rather than only a L2 loss for regression). But we will show in the supplementary that all three components are necessary to achieve strong practical performance.

3.8 Training and Testing Details

To stabilize the LSTM training, especially for large-scale data over a long time horizon, we apply teacher forcing [9]. This means that, at the beginning of the training when prediction is of low quality, we use GT point clouds $(S_1, S_2, \cdots)$ as inputs at future frames to ease the training. Then, we gradually increase the probability of using predicted point clouds $(S_1', S_2', \cdots)$ as inputs, which matches the style of autoregressive prediction during testing.

When generating GT range mask for training, we let all pixels have a value of 1 if they have corresponding 3D points after spherical projection, while let all pixels have a value of 0 if they do not have corresponding projected points. During testing, as the predicted range mask $\mathcal{M}_t'$ contains scalars between 0 and 1 after the softmax function, we use a threshold T_m to determine whether to mask out the point generated from every pixel of the predicted range map.

4 Experiments

Hyper-parameters. For KITTI [13], we use $H = 60$ and $W = 2048$ for the input range map, which results in a total of $K = 122880$ points per frame. For nuScenes [5], we use $H = 28$ and $W = 1024$ for the input range map, which results in a total of $K = 28672$ points per frame. We use $\alpha = \kappa = \omega = 1$ and $\beta = 3e - 5$ for the loss weights, and $T_m = 0.05$ as the threshold of the mask.

Network Details. To extract features from the range map, we use a 2D CNN with 8 blocks of convolution, BN and LeakyReLU by increasing the channel dimensions from the input of 2 to the output of 512 ($2 \rightarrow 4 \rightarrow 8 \rightarrow 16 \rightarrow 32 \rightarrow 64 \rightarrow 128 \rightarrow 256 \rightarrow 512$). Then, we use output features at all layers as inputs to our pyramid LSTMs so $L = 8$. The feature dimension of latent variables z_t is 32 and the feature dimension of hidden states h_t^1 is 512.

4.1 Evaluation Methodology

Datasets. We use real-world autonomous driving datasets (KITTI [13] and nuScenes [5]) for training and evaluation. For nuScenes, we use the official data split [2] of the nuScenes prediction challenge (500, 200, 150 sequences for train, val, test). We evaluate the prediction horizon of 1 and 3 seconds. For KITTI, we use the raw dataset [1], which is a superset of the KITTI odometry, tracking, detection datasets, *etc.*. As there is no official data split for the KITTI raw dataset, we created our own balanced data split.

Metrics. To evaluate the accuracy of predicted point clouds, we use standard Chamfer Distance (CD) [11] (Sect. 3.7) and Earth Mover's Distance (EMD) [24] to measure the distance between a sequence of GT future point clouds $\mathcal{S}_f$ and a sequence of predicted future point clouds $\mathcal{S}'_f$:

$$\text{EMD}(\mathcal{S}_f, \mathcal{S}'_f) = \frac{1}{N} \sum_{t=1}^{N} \min_{\phi: \mathcal{S}'_t \rightarrow \mathcal{S}_t} \sum_{u' \in \mathcal{S}'_t} \|u' - \phi(u')\|_2. \qquad (13)$$

To adapt standard EMD and CD to evaluate our stochastic model, we follow similar idea in the domain of trajectory prediction by computing the best of k CD and EMD ($\text{minCD}_k, \text{minEMD}_k$) over K_{sa} predicted samples, where each sample $\mathcal{S}'_{f_k}$ is a sequence of predicted point clouds:

$$\text{minCD}_k = \min_{k \in (1, \cdots, K_{\text{sa}})} \text{CD}(\mathcal{S}_f, \mathcal{S}'_{f_k}), \text{minEMD}_k = \min_{k \in (1, \cdots, K_{\text{sa}})} \text{EMD}(\mathcal{S}_f, \mathcal{S}'_{f_k}), \quad (14)$$

where we use $K_{\text{sa}} = 5$ for evaluation on both nuScenes and KITTI. To measure the accuracy of predicted range maps, we use standard L_1, L_2 distance and also the perceptual metrics including Structural Similarity Index Measure (SSIM) and Peak Signal-to-Noise Ratio (PSNR).

Baselines. As SPF is still under-explored, there are mainly two baselines to our knowledge which strictly follows the SPF design, *i.e.*, [28] and [21]. We evaluate SPFNet [28][5] on both KITTI/nuScenes, while we evaluate [21] only on the KITTI dataset because [21][6] did not provide method description or configuration files on the nuScenes or other datasets.

Table 1. Comparison on the test split of the KITTI raw dataset.

Prediction horizon	Methods	Range map				Point cloud	
		L1↓	L2↓	SSIM↑	PSNR↑	CD↓	EMD↓
1 s	SPFNet [28]	0.865	3.108	0.845	24.610	0.341	123.826
	[21]	0.707	3.603	**0.873**	**30.453**	0.202	96.426
	S2Net (w/ Pyramid LSTMs only)	0.723	2.745	0.754	25.801	0.203	106.830
	S2Net (w/ Pyramid LSTMs + Temporally-dependent latent)	**0.675**	**2.433**	0.868	30.294	**0.148**	**84.418**
3 s	SPFNet [28]	1.086	4.586	0.827	27.092	0.562	135.690
	[21]	1.187	6.069	0.795	25.935	0.379	143.194
	S2Net (w/ Pyramid LSTMs only)	1.008	4.413	0.869	29.668	0.360	130.325
	S2Net (w/ Pyramid LSTMs + Temporally-dependent latent)	**0.983**	**4.374**	**0.894**	**31.647**	**0.293**	**120.874**

Table 2. Comparison on the test split of the nuScenes prediction dataset.

Prediction horizon	Methods	Range map				Point cloud	
		L1↓	L2↓	SSIM↑	PSNR↑	CD↓	EMD↓
1 s	SPFNet [28]	0.669	1.406	0.708	**23.545**	0.456	239.798
	S2Net (w/ Pyramid LSTMs only)	0.622	**1.196**	0.759	21.118	0.366	189.336
	S2Net (w/ Pyramid LSTMs + Temporally-dependent latent)	**0.545**	1.285	**0.785**	23.274	**0.321**	**172.069**
3 s	SPFNet [28]	0.706	1.869	**0.717**	**23.587**	0.522	238.239
	S2Net (w/ Pyramid LSTMs only)	0.712	1.644	0.702	21.452	0.421	**205.269**
	S2Net (w/ Pyramid LSTMs + Temporally-dependent latent)	**0.560**	**1.261**	0.685	20.870	**0.381**	209.267

4.2   Results and Analysis

Results on KITTI. Results on the test set are summarized in Table 1. Unsurprisingly, our method outperforms SPFNet [28] and the most recent work [21] in all settings (1 or 3 s of horizon). Also, it is important to note that both of the key innovations of our method (Pyramid LSTMs and temporally-dependent latent space) are effective for the SPF task! For example, our method reduces the CD in the 1-second setting by 40.5% (from 0.341 to 0.203) after adding Pyramid LSTMs, and then reduces the CD in the 1-second setting by 27.1% (from 0.203 to 0.148) after adding temporally-dependent latent space, with an overall of 56.6% error reduction (from 0.341 to 0.148) compared to SPFNet.

---

[5] Note that the original numbers reported in [28] are different due to various changes including improved network architectures, balanced data split, improved implementation of the metrics, *etc.*

[6] Even for KITTI, [21] has only evaluated on the odometry dataset with only 22 sequences, *i.e.*, a subset of the raw dataset, so we have re-trained their model on the full KITTI raw dataset using the official code and KITTI configuration files.

Results on nuScenes. We summarize the results in Table 2. Similar to the trend in the KITTI experiments, S2Net also outperforms the SPFNet baseline for both 1-second and 3-seconds settings. One interesting finding is that the overall magnitude of CD and EMD on nuScenes is higher than those on KITTI. We believe that this is due to sparser point clouds[7] in nuScenes. In other words, for each point, its nearest neighbor point in the GT point cloud generally has a larger distance in nuScenes.

Table 3. Ablation study. **(Left)**: Effect of temporal dependency of the latent space. **(Right)**: Effect of pyramid LSTMs on the KITTI dataset.

Datasets	Horizon	Methods	CD	EMD
KITTI	1 s	No dependency	0.171	87.564
		Indirect dependency	0.155	92.586
		Direct dependency	**0.148**	**84.418**
	3 s	No dependency	0.357	**120.391**
		Indirect dependency	0.316	126.498
		Direct dependency	**0.293**	120.874
nuScenes	1 second	No dependency	0.352	194.640
		Indirect dependency	0.334	173.642
		Direct dependency	**0.321**	**172.069**
	3 s	No dependency	0.485	212.755
		Indirect dependency	0.482	222.665
		Direct dependency	**0.381**	**209.267**

Horizon	Pyramid LSTMs	No. of pyramids	CD	EMD
1 s		7	0.366	130.586
	✓	1	0.196	110.593
	✓	3	0.176	100.439
	✓	5	0.163	94.427
	✓	7	**0.148**	**84.418**
3 s		7	0.472	169.110
	✓	1	0.381	130.898
	✓	3	0.345	123.225
	✓	5	0.349	124.010
	✓	7	**0.293**	**120.874**

Effect of Temporally-Dependent Latent Space. To validate this key innovation of our stochastic SPF approach, we experiment with two other variants of our method: 1) No dependency. We remove the dependency between z_{t-1} and z_t when computing the prior and posterior; 2) Indirect dependency. Instead of using z_{t-1} as a conditioning variable to z_t, we now let h_t^1 depends on z_{t-1}. As z_t depends on the context h_t^1, so there is an indirect dependency between z_{t-1} and z_t. The results for three variants are summarized in Table 3 (left), where our method with direct dependency between latent variables achieves the best performance consistently, compared to indirect dependency and no dependency.

Effect of Pyramid LSTMs. To validate the effectiveness of another key innovation of our S2Net, *i.e.*, pyramid LSTMs, we experiment with the following variants of our method: 1) Decrease the number of pyramids we use in pyramid LSTMs, *e.g.*, $L = 1, 3, 5$, compared to $L = 7$ we use in our full model; 2) Keep $L = 7$ but remove the temporal alignment of the pyramid features, *i.e.*, removing the orangish-yellow ConvLSTM as shown in Fig. 2.

Results are summarized in Table 3 (right), where we use the temporally-dependent latent space for all variants. First, when we compare the 5th row with the 2nd, 3rd, 4th rows for both 1-s and 3-s settings, we can see that using

---

[7] We did not aggregate point clouds along the temporal dimension.

all levels of feature pyramids $L = 7$ achieves the best performance compared to using fewer number of pyramids. This shows that adding the pyramid features is indeed useful. Also, when we compare the 1st row and all other rows, we can see that the prediction performance drops significantly if we remove the LSTMs between feature pyramids across timestamps. This confirms that naively adding skip connection to our prediction model is not sufficient and our design of pyramid LSTMs is reasonable.

Uncertainty Measurement. As our S2Net is a generative model, we can compute the standard deviation (SD) of the pixel value from multiple samples of predictions. We use this SD as the uncertainty measurement for each point. To understand which predicted points our S2Net is uncertain about, we visualize the predicted point cloud (1-s horizon) in Fig. 4 (right) where each point is colorized with the SD computed from 5 samples. We can see that points with high uncertainty (red) are mostly around the object boundary, which is reasonable since object's future motion is inherently uncertain.

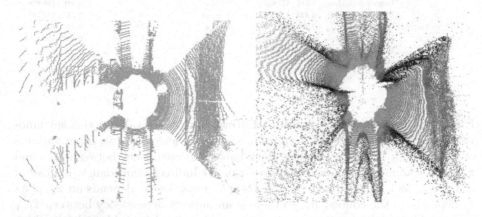

Fig. 4. (Left) GT point cloud. (Right) Predicted point cloud at the same frame colorized with computer point-wise uncertainty. The more red, the higher uncertainty. (Color figure online)

Qualitative Results. Due to limited space, we refer readers to the supplementary for high-resolution visualization. The takeaway is that, with the addition of pyramid LSTMs and temporally-dependent latent space, our S2Net can predict higher-fidelity point clouds (better global structure, more clear freespace and sharper object boundary) compared to SPFNet on different scenes with pedestrians and cars. Also, we provide more visualization of uncertainty measurements in the supplementary, to show the inherent future uncertainty and the potential benefits to the downstream tasks.

5   Conclusion

Our work opened a new direction of predicting stochastic futures of large-scale LiDAR point clouds, which can deal with the inherent future uncertainty and strengthen the forecast-then-detect pipeline proposed in [28] for autonomous systems. We showed that both the addition of temporally-dependent latent space and pyramid LSTMs are critical to obtaining significantly better performance. In future work, we plan to investigate how this new stochastic SPF model can be applied to downstream tasks such as tracking and planning.

References

1. KITTI Raw Dataset. http://www.cvlibs.net/datasets/kitti/raw_data.php
2. nuScenes Prediction Data Split. https://github.com/nutonomy/nuscenes-devkit/blob/master/python-sdk/nuscenes/eval/prediction/splits.py
3. Bayer, J., Osendorfer, C.: Learning Stochastic Recurrent Networks. arXiv:1411.7610 (2014)
4. Bei, X., Yang, Y., Soatto, S.: Learning Semantic-Aware Dynamics for Video Prediction. CVPR (2021)
5. Caesar, H., Bankiti, V., Lang, A.H., Vora, S., Liong, V.E., Xu, Q.: nuScenes: A Multimodal Dataset for Autonomous Driving. CVPR (2020)
6. Castrejón, L., Ballas, N., Courville, A.C.: Improved conditional vrnns for video prediction. In: 2019 IEEE/CVF International Conference on Computer Vision (ICCV), pp. 7607–7616 (2019)
7. Chatterjee, M., Ahuja, N., Cherian, A.: A Hierarchical Variational Neural Uncertainty Model for Stochastic Video Prediction. ICCV (2021)
8. Chung, J., Kastner, K., Dinh, L., Goel, K., Courville, A.C., Bengio, Y.: A Recurrent Latent Variable Model for Sequential Data. NIPS (2015)
9. Deng, D., Zakhor, A.: Temporal LiDAR Frame Prediction for Autonomous Driving. 3DV (2020)
10. Denton, E., Fergus, R.: Stochastic Video Generation with a Learned Prior. ICML (2018)
11. Fan, H., Su, H., Guibas, L.: A Point Set Generation Network for 3D Object Reconstruction from a Single Image. CVPR (2017)
12. Fan, H., Yang, Y.: PointRNN: Point Recurrent Neural Network for Moving Point Cloud Processing. arXiv:1910.08287 (2019)
13. Geiger, A., Lenz, P., Urtasun, R.: Are We Ready for Autonomous Driving? the KITTI Vision Benchmark Suite. CVPR (2012)
14. Gomes, P., Rossi, S., Toni, L.: Spatio-Temporal Graph-RNN for Point Cloud Prediction. ICIP (2021)
15. Gupta, A., Johnson, J., Fei-Fei, L., Savarese, S., Alahi, A.: Social GAN: Socially Acceptable Trajectories with Generative Adversarial Networks. CVPR (2018)
16. Kingma, D.P., Welling, M.: Auto-Encoding Variational Bayes. arXiv:1312.6114 (2013)
17. Klokov, R., Verbeek, J.J., Boyer, E.: Probabilistic reconstruction networks for 3d shape inference from a single image. In: BMVC (2019)
18. Liang, J., Jiang, L., Murphy, K., Yu, T., Hauptmann, A.: The Garden of Forking Paths: Towards Multi-Future Trajectory Prediction. CVPR (2020)

19. Lin, C.H., Kong, C., Lucey, S.: Learning efficient point cloud generation for dense 3d object reconstruction. In: AAAI (2018)
20. Liu, B., Chen, Y., Liu, S., Kim, H.S.: Deep Learning in Latent Space for Video Prediction and Compression. CVPR (2021)
21. Mersch, B., Chen, X., Behley, J., Stachniss, C.: Self-Supervised Point Cloud Prediction Using 3D Spatio-temporal Convolutional Networks. CoRL (2021)
22. Min, Y., Zhang, Y., Chai, X., Chen, X.: An Efficient PointLSTM for Point Clouds Based Gesture Recognition. CVPR (2020)
23. Nair, S., Savarese, S., Finn, C.: Goal-Aware Prediction: Learning to Model What Matters. ICML (2020)
24. Rubner, Y., Tomasi, C., Guibas, L.J.: The Earth Mover's Distance as a Metric for Image Retrieval. IJCV (2000)
25. Salzmann, T., Ivanovic, B., Chakravarty, P., Pavone, M.: Trajectron++: dynamically-feasible trajectory forecasting with heterogeneous data. In: Vedaldi, A., Bischof, H., Brox, T., Frahm, J.-M. (eds.) ECCV 2020. LNCS, vol. 12363, pp. 683–700. Springer, Cham (2020). https://doi.org/10.1007/978-3-030-58523-5_40
26. Shu, D.W., Park, S.W., Kwon, J.: 3d point cloud generative adversarial network based on tree structured graph convolutions. In: 2019 IEEE/CVF International Conference on Computer Vision (ICCV), pp. 3858–3867 (2019)
27. Sun, X., Wang, S., Wang, M., Wang, Z., Liu, M.: A Novel Coding Architecture for LiDAR Point Cloud Sequence. RA-L (2020)
28. Weng, X., Wang, J., Levine, S., Kitani, K., Rhinehart, N.: Inverting the Pose Forecasting Pipeline with SPF2: Sequential Pointcloud Forecasting for Sequential Pose Forecasting. CoRL (2020)
29. Weng, X., Yuan, Y., Kitani, K.: PTP: Parallelized Tracking and Prediction with Graph Neural Networks and Diversity Sampling. Robot. Autom. Lett. **6**(3), 4640–4647 (2021)
30. Wu, B., Nair, S., Martin-Martin, R., Fei-Fei, L., Finn, C.: Greedy Hierarchical Variational Autoencoders for Large-Scale Video Prediction. CVPR (2021)
31. Wu, Y., Gao, R., Park, J., Chen, Q.: Future Video Synthesis with Object Motion Prediction. CVPR (2020)
32. Yang, G., Huang, X., Hao, Z., Liu, M.Y., Belongie, S.J., Hariharan, B.: Pointflow: 3d point cloud generation with continuous normalizing flows. In: 2019 IEEE/CVF International Conference on Computer Vision (ICCV), pp. 4540–4549 (2019)
33. Yuan, Y., Weng, X., Ou, Y., Kitani, K.: AgentFormer: Agent-Aware Transformers for Socio-Temporal Multi-Agent Forecasting. ICCV (2021)
34. Zhang, C., Fiore, M., Murray, I., Patras, P.: CloudLSTM: A Recurrent Neural Model for Spatiotemporal Point-cloud Stream Forecasting. AAAI (2021)

RA-Depth: Resolution Adaptive Self-supervised Monocular Depth Estimation

Mu He, Le Hui, Yikai Bian, Jian Ren, Jin Xie$^{(\boxtimes)}$, and Jian Yang$^{(\boxtimes)}$

Key Lab of Intelligent Perception and Systems for High-Dimensional Information of Ministry of Education, Jiangsu Key Lab of Image and Video Understanding for Social Security PCA Lab, School of Computer Science and Engineering, Nanjing University of Science and Technology, Nanjing, China
{muhe,le.hui,yikai.bian,renjian,csjxie,csjyang}@njust.edu.cn

Abstract. Existing self-supervised monocular depth estimation methods can get rid of expensive annotations and achieve promising results. However, these methods suffer from severe performance degradation when directly adopting a model trained on a fixed resolution to evaluate at other different resolutions. In this paper, we propose a resolution adaptive self-supervised monocular depth estimation method (RA-Depth) by learning the scale invariance of the scene depth. Specifically, we propose a simple yet efficient data augmentation method to generate images with arbitrary scales for the same scene. Then, we develop a dual high-resolution network that uses the multi-path encoder and decoder with dense interactions to aggregate multi-scale features for accurate depth inference. Finally, to explicitly learn the scale invariance of the scene depth, we formulate a cross-scale depth consistency loss on depth predictions with different scales. Extensive experiments on the KITTI, Make3D and NYU-V2 datasets demonstrate that RA-Depth not only achieves state-of-the-art performance, but also exhibits a good ability of resolution adaptation. Source code is available at https://github.com/hmhemu/RA-Depth.

Keywords: Self-supervised learning · Monocular depth estimation · Resolution adaptation

1 Introduction

Monocular depth estimation [5,6,20,21,25,38] recovers a pixel-wise depth map from a single image, which is a challenging but essential task in computer vision. It has promoted the development of various applications such as autonomous driving, robot navigation, 3D scene reconstruction, and augmented reality.

Supplementary Information The online version contains supplementary material available at https://doi.org/10.1007/978-3-031-19812-0_33.

S. Avidan et al. (Eds.): ECCV 2022, LNCS 13687, pp. 565–581, 2022.
https://doi.org/10.1007/978-3-031-19812-0_33

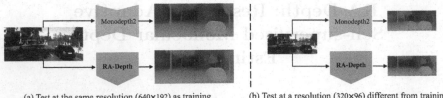

(a) Test at the same resolution (640×192) as training   (b) Test at a resolution (320×96) different from training

Fig. 1. Depth predictions for different resolutions. We compare the depth predictions of Monodepth2 [10] and our RA-Depth at different resolutions. Both Monodepth2 and RA-Depth are trained at the fixed resolution of 640×192, and then tested at 640×192 (a) and 320×96 (b). RA-Depth exhibits the good resolution adaptation ability when tested at a resolution different from training.

Due to the difference of acquisition devices in different application scenarios, the resolutions of the acquired images are different. Thus, to reduce resource consumption, how to make a single trained model of monocular depth estimation adaptive to the changes of image resolution in a self-supervised manner is a valuable and open problem.

Existing self-supervised monocular depth estimation methods [9,10,27,28,49] usually use geometrical constraints on stereo pairs or monocular sequences as the sole source of supervision and have made great progress. However, these supervision methods cannot adapt to the changes of image resolution at inference, whose performance drops severely when the test resolution is inconsistent with the training resolution. As shown in Fig. 1, we compare the depth prediction results of existing advanced work Monodepth2 [10] and our RA-Depth. Both Monodepth2 and RA-Depth are trained at the fixed resolution of 640×192 and then tested at two resolutions 640×192 and 320×96. It can be seen that Monodepth2 predicts inconsistent and poor depth maps when tested at different resolutions. To test at different resolutions, existing methods train an individual model for each resolution. As a result, this not only requires unavoidable training overhead and high storage cost, but also limits the flexibility and practicality of monocular depth estimation models.

In this paper, we propose a resolution adaptive self-supervised monocular depth estimation method named as RA-Depth. First, we propose an arbitrary-scale data augmentation method to generate images with arbitrary scales for the same scene. Specifically, we change the scale of the input image while maintaining the image resolution/size (*i.e.*, width × height) through randomly resizing, cropping, and stitching (details in Sect. 3.2). These generated images with arbitrary scales can mimic the scale variations at different image resolutions, thus prompting the model to implicitly learn the scale invariance of scene depth. Then, we propose an efficient monocular depth estimation framework with multi-scale feature fusion. In our framework, we use the superior high-resolution representation network HRNet [40] as encoder, and design a decoder with efficient multi-scale feature fusion. As a result, the encoder and decoder form a dual HRNet architecture, which can fully exploit and aggregate multi-scale features to infer the accurate depth. Thanks to this efficient design, we can achieve better depth estimation performance with the lower network overhead. Finally, we propose a novel cross-scale depth consistency loss to explicitly learn the scale invariance of scene depth. Thus, the monocular depth estimation model can predict the consistent depth maps for the same scene, even if the scales of input images are different. Extensive experiments on the KITTI [8], Make3D [38], and NYU-V2 [39] datasets demonstrate that RA-Depth achieves state-of-the-art performance on monocular depth estimation and shows a good ability of resolution adaptation.

To summarize, the main contributions of our work are as follows:

– To the best of our knowledge, our RA-Depth is the first work to tackle the image resolution adaptation for self-supervised monocular depth estimation.
– We propose an arbitrary-scale data augmentation method to promote the model to learn depths from images with different scales.
– We develop an efficient dual high-resolution network with multi-scale feature fusion for monocular depth estimation, which is trained with a novel cross-scale depth consistency loss.
– Extensive experiments demonstrate that our RA-Depth achieves state-of-the-art performance on monocular depth estimation, and has a good generalization ability to different resolutions.

2   Related Work

2.1   Supervised Monocular Depth Estimation

Monocular depth estimation aims to predict the scene depth from single color image. Early works [5,16,21,22,24,43,44] estimated continuous depth maps pixel by pixel using convolutional neural networks by minimizing the error between the prediction and ground-truth depths. Furthermore, the geometry [31,44] or multi-task constraints [35,47] are imposed on the depth estimation network to predict more accurate depth maps. However, these continuous regression methods usually suffer from slow convergence and unsatisfactory local solutions. Deep ordinal regression network [6] thus introduced a spacing-increasing discretization strategy to discretize depth, where the depth estimation problem is converted into the ordinal depth regression problem. AdaBins [1] proposed a Transformer based depth estimation scheme by dividing the depth range into different bins. Recently, some works [23,29] employed the multimodel learning for depth estimation and further improved its performance.

2.2   Self-supervised Monocular Depth Estimation

Self-supervised methods convert the monocular depth estimation task into an image reconstruction problem, and they use the photometric loss on stereo pairs or monocular sequences as the supervisory signal to train networks.

One type of self-supervised monocular depth estimation methods employ the geometric constraints on stereo pairs to learn depth. Garg *et al.* [7] first propose a self-supervised monocular depth estimation framework, where depth is estimated from synchronized stereo image pairs. Following this framework, Monodepth [9] designs a left-right disparity consistency loss to produce more accurate prediction results, while 3Net [34] introduces a trinocular stereo assumption to solve the occlusion problem between stereo pairs. Based on these methods, Depth Hints [42] uses the off-the-shelf Semi-Global Matching (SGM) algorithm [14,15] to obtain complementary depth hints, which can enhance existing photometric loss and guide the network to learn more accurate weights. Recently, EPCDepth [32] adopted a data grafting technique to make the model focus on non-vertical image positions for accurate depth inference.

Another type of depth estimation methods with self-supervision come from unlabelled monocular videos. SfM-Learner [49] is a pioneering work that jointly learns monocular depth and ego-motion from monocular videos in a self-supervised way. Based on SfM-Learner, SC-SfMLearner [2] proposes a geometry consistency loss to ensure the scale-consistency of depth. Monodepth2 [10] introduces a minimum reprojection loss and an auto-masking loss to solve the problem of occlusions and moving objects. Poggi *et al.* [33] explore the uncertainty of self-supervised monocular depth estimation and propose a novel peculiar technique specifically designed for self-supervised depth estimation. Besides, many recent works [3,4,12,19,50] utilize extra semantic supervision to aid self-supervised monocular depth estimation. More recently, some works [27, 48] have developed high-performance monocular depth estimation models through efficient network architecture designs.

3   Method

3.1   Problem Formulation

Self-supervised methods exploit geometric constraints on stereo pairs or monocular videos as the supervision signal for training. In this paper, our proposed framework uses unlabelled monocular videos for training, each training instance contains a target frame I_t and two source frames I_s ($s \in \{t-1, t+1\}$) adjacent to I_t temporally. With the depth D_t of the target view and the camera pose $T_{t \to s}$ between the target view and source view, the image synthesis process from the source view to the target view can be expressed as $I_{s \to t} = I_s \langle proj(D_t, T_{t \to s}, K) \rangle$, where K represents the known camera intrinsics, $\langle \rangle$ is the sampling operator [17] and $proj()$ is the coordinate projection operation [49]. The photometric error is composed of L_1 and SSIM [41]:

$$pe(I_a, I_b) = \frac{\alpha}{2}(1 - SSIM(I_a, I_b)) + (1 - \alpha)\|I_a - I_b\|_1. \tag{1}$$

Following [10], in order to handle the issue of occlusion, we adopt the per-pixel minimum reprojection loss as our photometric loss:

$$\mathcal{L}_{ph}(I_t, I_{s \to t}) = \min_s pe(I_t, I_{s \to t}). \tag{2}$$

The edge-aware smoothness loss is used to deal with disparity discontinuities:

$$\mathcal{L}_{sm}(D_t, I_t) = |\partial_x D_t^*| e^{-|\partial_x I_t|} + |\partial_y D_t^*| e^{-|\partial_y I_t|} \qquad (3)$$

where ∂_x and ∂_y are the gradients in the horizontal and vertical direction respectively. Besides, $D_t^* = D_t / \overline{D_t}$ is the mean-normalized inverse depth from [10] to discourage shrinking of the estimated depth.

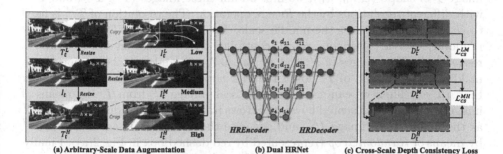

(a) Arbitrary-Scale Data Augmentation   (b) Dual HRNet   (c) Cross-Scale Depth Consistency Loss

Fig. 2. Overview of RA-Depth. (a) First, given an original instance $\{I_t, I_s\}$ ($s \in \{t-1, t+1\}$, t for target image and s for source image), we use our arbitrary-scale data augmentation to generate three training instances with different scales: $\{I_t^L, I_s^L\}$, $\{I_t^M, I_s^M\}$, and $\{I_t^H, I_s^H\}$. For simplicity, only target images I_t^L, I_t^M, and I_t^H are shown in this figure. (b) Then, we use our proposed efficient Dual HRNet to separately predict depth maps (D_t^L, D_t^M, D_t^H) for these target images. Note that Dual HRNet only inputs a single target image and then outputs the corresponding depth map at a time, and all target images share the same Dual HRNet. (c) Finally, we compute the proposed cross-scale depth consistency losses $\mathcal{L}_{cs}^{LM}$ (between D_t^L and D_t^M) and $\mathcal{L}_{cs}^{MH}$ (between D_t^M and D_t^H) to constrain the network to learn the scale invariance of the scene depth.

3.2 Resolution Adaptive Self-supervised Framework

Overview. An overview of our proposed method can be seen in Fig. 2. Given an original instance $\{I_t, I_s\}$ ($s \in \{t-1, t+1\}$, t for target image and s for source image), we employ our proposed arbitrary-scale data augmentation to expand three training instances: $\{I_t^L, I_s^L\}$, $\{I_t^M, I_s^M\}$, and $\{I_t^H, I_s^H\}$, where L, M and H denote the low, middle and high scales, respectively. For simplicity, we only show I_t^L, I_t^M, and I_t^H in Fig. 2(a). Then, we use our proposed efficient Dual HRNet to separately predict depth maps (D_t^L, D_t^M, D_t^H) of these target views, and use the pose network to predict the relative 6D camera pose $T_{t \to s}$ from the target view to the source view. With D_t^L and $T_{t \to s}$, we can synthesize image $\tilde{I}_{s \to t}^L$ by interpolating the source image I_s^L. In the same way, we can synthesize images $\tilde{I}_{s \to t}^M$ and $\tilde{I}_{s \to t}^H$. Then we compute the photometric losses between real images (I_t^L, I_t^M, I_t^H) and synthesized images ($\tilde{I}_{s \to t}^L, \tilde{I}_{s \to t}^M, \tilde{I}_{s \to t}^H$). Note that all image synthesis processes use the same camera pose $T_{t \to s}$ predicted from I_t^M to I_s^M. Finally, the proposed cross-scale depth consistency losses $\mathcal{L}_{cs}^{LM}$ (between D_t^L and D_t^M) and $\mathcal{L}_{cs}^{MH}$ (between D_t^M and D_t^H) are computed. For clarity, the pose network, photometric loss, and smoothness loss are not shown in Fig. 2.

Arbitrary-Scale Data Augmentation. The details of arbitrary-scale data augmentation for a single input are shown in Algorithm 1. For a single original image I of shape (c, h_0, w_0), we first obtain three images $(T^L, T^M, \text{and } T^H)$ with different resolutions by the *Resize* operation. The resolution of T^M is fixed to (h, w), which denotes the middle scale. The resolutions of T^L and T^H vary randomly over a continuous range, controlled by the scale factors s^L and s^H, respectively. The ranges of s^L and s^H are [0.7, 0.9] and [1.1, 2.0], respectively, making the resolution of T^L lower than (h, w) and the resolution of T^H higher than (h, w). Then we can generate a low scale image I^L from T^L by means of image stitching (represented by white arrows in Fig. 2(a)), and directly treat T^M as the middle scale image I^M, and generate the high scale image I^H from T^H by means of *RandomCrop* (represented by red dashed box in Fig. 2(a)). Finally, we obtain three images I^L, I^M, and I^H with the same shape of (c, h, w) at different scales, which served as the input of the network. Note, in this paper, (c, h_0, w_0) is (3, 375, 1242), and (c, h, w) is (3, 192, 640).

Dual HRNet for Monocular Depth Estimation. As shown in Fig. 2(b), we develop an efficient dual high-resolution network (Dual HRNet) with multi-scale feature fusion for monocular depth estimation. We use the superior high-resolution representation network HRNet18 [40] as the encoder, named HREncoder. The core idea of HRNet [40] is to perform efficient multi-scale feature fusion while maintaining high-resolution feature representations, so as to obtain semantically richer and spatially more precise multi-scale features. Inspired by HRNet [40], we design a decoder with efficient multi-scale feature fusion named HRDecoder. Specifically, HRDecoder first inherits the multi-scale features of the encoder, and then gradually fuses low-scale features while maintaining the high-resolution feature representations. Let e_i denote the feature of the encoder at the i-th level, d_{ji} denote the feature of the decoder at the i-th level and the j-th stage, and d_{ji}^m denote the feature after multi-scale feature fusion at the i-th level and the j-th stage. Let us take the calculation of d_{1i} and d_{1i}^m (refer to Fig. 2(b)) at the first stage as an example:

$$\begin{cases} d_{1i} = \text{CONV}_{3\times3}(e_i), & i = 1, 2, 3, 4 \\ d_{1i}^m = d_{1i} + [\text{CONV}_{1\times1}(\mu(d_{1k}))] & i = 1, 2, 3, k = i+1, \ldots, 4 \end{cases} \quad (4)$$

where $\text{CONV}_{3\times3}$ represents a 3×3 convolution layer, and $\text{CONV}_{1\times1}$ represents an 1×1 convolution layer. In addition, $\mu(\cdot)$ is an upsampling operator, and $[\cdot]$ is a summation operator. By exploiting the HRDecoder, the multi-scale features can be fully fused from the low-resolution feature map to the high-resolution feature map. It is desired that the Dual HRNet can effectively learn depth information of different scales for accurate depth estimation at different test resolutions.

Algorithm 1. Arbitrary-Scale Data Augmentation.

Input: An original image I of shape (c, h_0, w_0).
Output: Three training images I^L, I^M, I^H of shape (c, h, w).
1: Random initializing the scale factors s^L and s^H with respective ranges of $[0.7, 0.9]$ and $[1.1, 2.0]$; Zero initializing I^L, I^M, I^H of shape (c, h, w);
2: $(h^L, w^L), (h^M, w^M), (h^H, w^H) = int((h, w) \times s^L), (h, w), int((h, w) \times s^H)$;
3: Generating the low-resolution image (I^L);
   (a) Resizing the original image I
      $T^L \leftarrow Resize(I)$ to (c, h^L, w^L)
   (b) Slicing and copying T^L
      $I^L[:, : h^L, : w^L] \leftarrow T^L[:, :, :]$
      $I^L[:, h^L : h, : w^L] \leftarrow T^L[:, (2 \times h^L - h) : h^L, : w^L]$
      $I^L[:, : h^L, w^L : w] \leftarrow T^L[:, : h^L, (2 \times w^L - w) : w^L]$
      $I^L[:, h^L : h, w^L : w] \leftarrow T^L[:, (2 \times h^L - h) : h^L, (2 \times w^L - w) : w^L]$
4: Generating the middle-resolution image (I^M);
   (a) Resizing the original image I
      $T^M \leftarrow Resize(I)$ to (c, h^M, w^M)
   (b) Copying T^M
      $I^M[:, :, :] \leftarrow T^M[:, :, :]$
5: Generating the high-resolution image (I^H);
   (a) Resizing the original image I
      $T^H \leftarrow Resize(I)$ to (c, h^H, w^H)
   (b) Randomly cropping T^H
      $I^H[:, :, :] \leftarrow RandomCrop(T^H)$ to (c, h, w)
6: Return I^L, I^M, I^H;

Cross-Scale Depth Consistency Loss. As shown in Fig. 2(c), we compute the cross-scale depth consistency losses $\mathcal{L}_{cs}^{ML}$ (between D_t^M and D_t^L) and $\mathcal{L}_{cs}^{MH}$ (between D_t^M and D_t^H) to constrain the model to explicitly learn the scale invariance of scene depth. For example, the same pillar or car among D_t^L, D_t^M and D_t^H should have the same depth as shown in Fig. 2(c). Specifically, according to the known scale factors s^L and s^H as well as the cropped position of $RandomCrop$ in Algorithm 1, we can obtain the pixel correspondence among D_t^L, D_t^M and D_t^H. For D_t^M and D_t^H, we first find the corresponding position of D_t^H in D_t^M, which is represented by the black dashed box (named as $\tilde{D}_t^M$) in D_t^M. Then we resize D_t^H to keep the same size as $\tilde{D}_t^M$ to obtain $\tilde{D}_t^H$. Finally, we calculate the scene depth consistency loss between $\tilde{D}_t^M$ and $\tilde{D}_t^H$:

$$\mathcal{L}_{cs}^{MH} = \frac{\alpha}{2}(1 - SSIM(\tilde{D}_t^M, \tilde{D}_t^H)) + (1 - \alpha)\left\|\tilde{D}_t^M - \tilde{D}_t^H\right\|_1. \quad (5)$$

Similarly, for D_t^L and D_t^M, we first find the corresponding position of D_t^M in D_t^L, which is represented by the black dashed box (named as $\hat{D}_t^L$) in D_t^L. Then we resize D_t^M to keep the same size as $\hat{D}_t^L$ to obtain $\hat{D}_t^M$. Finally, we calculate the cross-scale depth consistency loss between $\hat{D}_t^L$ and $\hat{D}_t^M$:

$$\mathcal{L}_{cs}^{LM} = \frac{\alpha}{2}(1 - SSIM(\hat{D}_t^L, \hat{D}_t^M)) + (1 - \alpha)\left\|\hat{D}_t^L - \hat{D}_t^M\right\|_1. \quad (6)$$

Final Training Loss. Our overall loss function can be formulated as follows:

$$
\begin{aligned}
\mathcal{L}_f = &\gamma(\mathcal{L}_{ph}(\boldsymbol{I}_t^L, \tilde{\boldsymbol{I}}_{s\to t}^L) + \mathcal{L}_{ph}(\boldsymbol{I}_t^M, \tilde{\boldsymbol{I}}_{s\to t}^M) + \mathcal{L}_{ph}(\boldsymbol{I}_t^H, \tilde{\boldsymbol{I}}_{s\to t}^H)) \\
&+ \lambda(\mathcal{L}_{sm}(\tilde{\boldsymbol{D}}_t^L, \boldsymbol{I}_t^L) + \mathcal{L}_{sm}(\tilde{\boldsymbol{D}}_t^M, \boldsymbol{I}_t^M) + \mathcal{L}_{sm}(\tilde{\boldsymbol{D}}_t^H, \boldsymbol{I}_t^H)) \\
&+ \beta(\mathcal{L}_{cs}^{LM} + \mathcal{L}_{cs}^{MH})
\end{aligned}
\tag{7}
$$

Here, γ, λ, and β are the hyper-parameters of the photometric loss, smoothness loss, and our proposed scene depth consistency loss.

4   Experiments

4.1   Implementation Details

Our proposed method is implemented in PyTorch [30] and trained on a single Titan RTX GPU. Our models are trained for 20 epochs using Adam optimizer [18], with a batch size of 12. The learning rate for the first 15 epochs is 10^{-4} and then dropped to 10^{-5} for the last 5 epochs. The hyper-parameters γ, λ, and β of the final training loss in Eq. (7) are set to 1.0, 0.001, and 1.0, respectively. We set $\alpha = 0.85$ in Eq. (1), Eq. (5), and Eq. (6). For the monocular depth estimation network, We implement our proposed Dual HRNet described in Sect. 3.2, which uses HRNet18 [40] as the encoder and performs efficient multi-scale feature fusion on the decoder. For the pose estimation network, we use the same architecture as Monodepth2 [10], which contains ResNet18 [13] followed by several convolutional layers. Similar to [10,48], we use the weights pretrained on ImageNet [37] to initialize HRNet18 and ResNet18. During training, the input resolution of networks is 640×192. To improve the training speed, we only output a single-scale depth for the depth estimation network and compute the loss on the single-scale depth, instead of computing losses on multi-scale outputs of the depth estimation network (4 scales in [10,49] and 6 scales in [36]).

4.2   Results

Basic Results. We evaluate the monocular depth estimation performance of our single model on the KITTI dataset [8] using the data split of Eigen et al. [5]. Following Zhou et al. [49], we remove static frames, using 39810, 4424, and 697 images for training, validation, and test, respectively. During the evaluation, we cap depth to 80m and adopt the same conventional metrics as [5]. Since we use monocular videos for training, we perform median scaling introduced by [49] on our predicted depths when evaluating. Table 1 shows the basic quantitative results and all models are tested at the same resolution as training. Our proposed method outperforms all existing self-supervised monocular depth estimation approaches significantly. In particular, RA-Depth achieves the SqRel error of 0.632, the error reduction rate of 17% over the best-published result 0.764.

Table 1. Quantitative monocular depth estimation results on the KITTI dataset [8] using the Eigen split [5]. We divide compared methods into three categories based on training data. In each category, the best results are in **bold** and the second are underlined. The test resolution is the same as the training resolution for all these methods. S: trained on stereo pairs; M: trained on monocular videos; Se: trained with semantic labels.

Method	Train	Resolution	Error Metric ↓				Accuracy Metric ↑		
			AbsRel	SqRel	RMSE	RMSElog	$\delta < 1.25$	$\delta < 1.25^2$	$\delta < 1.25^3$
Monodepth [9]	S	512 × 256	0.148	1.344	5.927	0.247	0.803	0.922	0.964
3Net [34]	S	512 × 256	0.142	1.207	5.702	0.240	0.809	0.928	0.967
Chen [3]	S+Se	512 × 256	0.118	0.905	5.096	0.211	0.839	0.945	0.977
Monodepth2 [10]	S	640 × 192	0.109	0.873	4.960	0.209	0.864	0.948	0.975
Depth Hints [42]	S	640 × 192	0.106	0.780	4.695	0.193	0.875	0.958	0.980
EPCDepth [32]	S	640 × 192	**0.099**	**0.754**	**4.490**	**0.183**	**0.888**	**0.963**	**0.982**
Zhan [46]	M+S	608 × 160	0.135	1.132	5.585	0.229	0.820	0.933	0.971
EPC++ [26]	M+S	832 × 256	0.128	0.935	5.011	0.209	0.831	0.945	0.979
Monodepth2 [10]	M+S	640 × 192	0.106	0.818	4.750	0.196	0.874	0.957	0.979
HR-Depth [27]	M+S	640 × 192	0.107	0.785	4.612	0.185	0.887	0.962	0.982
Depth Hints [42]	M+S	640 × 192	0.105	0.769	4.627	0.189	0.875	0.959	0.982
DIFFNet [48]	M+S	640 × 192	**0.101**	**0.749**	**4.445**	**0.179**	**0.898**	**0.965**	**0.983**
SfMLearner [49]	M	640 × 192	0.183	1.595	6.709	0.270	0.734	0.902	0.959
EPC++ [26]	M	832 × 256	0.141	1.029	5.350	0.216	0.816	0.941	0.976
SC-SfMLearner [2]	M	832 × 256	0.114	0.813	4.706	0.191	0.873	0.960	0.982
Monodepth2 [10]	M	640 × 192	0.115	0.903	4.863	0.193	0.877	0.959	0.981
SGDDepth [19]	M+Se	640 × 192	0.113	0.835	4.693	0.191	0.879	0.961	0.981
SAFENet [4]	M+Se	640 × 192	0.112	0.788	4.582	0.187	0.878	0.963	0.983
PackNet-SfM [11]	M	640 × 192	0.111	0.785	4.601	0.189	0.878	0.960	0.982
Mono-Uncertainty [33]	M	640 × 192	0.111	0.863	4.756	0.188	0.881	0.961	0.982
HR-Depth [27]	M	640 × 192	0.109	0.792	4.632	0.185	0.884	0.962	0.983
DIFFNet [48]	M	640 × 192	0.102	0.764	4.483	0.180	0.896	0.965	0.983
RA-Depth	M	640 × 192	**0.096**	**0.632**	**4.216**	**0.171**	**0.903**	**0.968**	**0.985**

Resolution Adaptation Results. As shown in Table 2, we compare our single model RA-Depth with existing three advanced approaches including Monodepth2 [10], HR-Depth [27], and DIFFNet [48] in terms of resolution adaptation on the KITTI dataset [8] using the Eigen split [5]. All these models are trained at the resolution of 640 × 192 and then tested at four different resolutions including 416 × 128, 512 × 160, 832 × 256, and 1024 × 320. Note, we directly resize the original image to generate four resolution images without using the scale augmentation strategy in the training process. The results show that existing methods perform poorly in terms of resolution adaptation. That is to say, existing methods cannot adapt to the changes of image resolution during testing. In contrast, our single model RA-Depth maintains high performance across different test resolutions, significantly outperforming existing self-supervised methods. Figure 3 also shows the resolution adaptation results of different models on two error metrics SqRel and RMSE and one accuracy metric $\delta < 1.25$. It can be seen that our single model RA-Depth achieves the lowest error on two error

Table 2. Resolution adaptive comparison results on the KITTI dataset [8] using the Eigen split [5]. All these models are trained at the resolution of 640×192 and then tested at four different resolutions including 416×128, 512×160, 832×256, and 1024×320.

Method	Test resolution	Error Metric ↓				Accuracy metric ↑		
		AbsRel	SqRel	RMSE	RMSElog	$\delta < 1.25$	$\delta < 1.25^2$	$\delta < 1.25^3$
Monodepth2 [10]	416×128	0.184	1.365	6.146	0.268	0.719	0.911	0.966
HR-Depth [27]	416×128	0.157	1.120	5.669	0.231	0.787	0.938	0.976
DIFFNet [48]	416×128	<u>0.142</u>	<u>1.068</u>	<u>5.552</u>	<u>0.218</u>	<u>0.826</u>	<u>0.948</u>	<u>0.979</u>
RA-Depth	416×128	**0.111**	**0.723**	**4.768**	**0.187**	**0.874**	**0.961**	**0.984**
Monodepth2 [10]	512×160	0.132	1.062	5.318	0.209	0.846	0.951	0.978
HR-Depth [27]	512×160	0.128	<u>0.978</u>	<u>4.999</u>	0.199	0.855	0.957	<u>0.981</u>
DIFFNet [48]	512×160	<u>0.121</u>	1.007	5.107	<u>0.196</u>	<u>0.870</u>	<u>0.958</u>	<u>0.981</u>
RA-Depth	512×160	**0.101**	**0.658**	**4.373**	**0.175**	**0.895**	**0.967**	**0.985**
Monodepth2 [10]	832×256	0.131	0.992	5.451	0.222	0.815	0.947	0.978
HR-Depth [27]	832×256	0.136	0.920	<u>5.321</u>	0.218	0.817	0.949	<u>0.980</u>
DIFFNet [48]	832×256	<u>0.128</u>	<u>0.896</u>	5.328	<u>0.214</u>	<u>0.834</u>	<u>0.950</u>	<u>0.980</u>
RA-Depth	832×256	**0.095**	**0.613**	**4.106**	**0.170**	**0.906**	**0.969**	**0.985**
Monodepth2 [10]	1024×320	0.193	1.335	6.058	0.271	0.673	0.921	0.972
HR-Depth [27]	1024×320	0.183	1.241	6.054	0.267	0.687	0.920	0.972
DIFFNet [48]	1024×320	<u>0.163</u>	<u>1.153</u>	<u>6.011</u>	<u>0.251</u>	<u>0.743</u>	<u>0.928</u>	<u>0.974</u>
RA-Depth	1024×320	**0.097**	**0.608**	**4.131**	**0.174**	**0.901**	**0.968**	**0.985**

metrics at all resolutions, even lower than the errors of these individual models trained separately at each test resolution. Moreover, our single model achieves the highest accuracy at all resolutions compared with other single models and is comparable to these individual models. Figure 4 illustrates the visualization results of our RA-Depth and Monodepth2 [10] for resolution adaptation in the depth estimation. It can be observed that the depth maps predicted by the single model Monodepth2 are inconsistent at different resolutions (see green rectangles). In contrast, our single model RA-Depth shows credible and consistent depth predictions at different resolutions, which demonstrates that RA-Depth can learn the scale-invariance of scene depth.

Generalization Results Across Datasets. In Table 3, we report the generalization performance on the Make3D [38] and NYU-V2 [39] datasets using models trained at the resolution of 640×192 on the KITTI dataset [8]. For a fair comparison, we adopt the same evaluation criteria, cropping approach [10] and data preprocessing strategy [45] for all models. When the test resolution is the same as the training resolution (640×192), we achieve state-of-the-art results whether generalizing to the outdoor dataset Make3D or the indoor dataset NYU-V2. Moreover, we also test our model at four different resolutions (416×128, 512×160, 832×256, 1024×320) and take the average results as the resolution adaptation results across datasets. These results demonstrate that our model still has the good resolution adaptation ability when tested across datasets.

4.3 Ablation Study

To better comprehend how the components of our method contribute to the overall performance as well as the resolution adaptation ability, we perform sufficient ablation experiments in this section. As shown in Table 4, we perform ablation studies by changing various components of our method, where all models are trained at the resolution of 640×192 on the KITTI dataset [8].

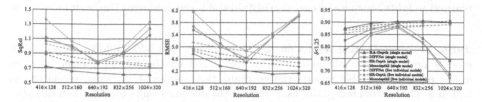

Fig. 3. Resolution adaptation results on the error metrics (SqRel, RMSE) and the accuracy metric ($\delta < 1.25$). Solid lines denote the resolution adaptation results tested at five different resolutions using a single model trained on 640×192. Dotted lines denote results tested at five different resolutions using five individual models trained on each test resolution. Our single model RA-Depth outperforms other single models significantly on all metrics and is comparable to these individual models trained separately at each test resolution. This figure is best viewed in a zoomed-in document.

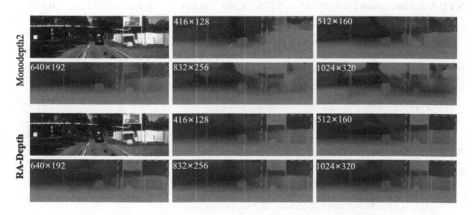

Fig. 4. Visualization results of resolution adaptation. We use models trained at the resolution of 640×192 to predict depths at various test resolutions.

We conduct ablation experiments to verify the effectiveness of each component on overall performance at the same resolution as training (640×192). Moreover, we also verify the effectiveness of each component on the resolution adaptation ability at four different resolutions (416×128, 512×160, 832×256,

1024×320), where the average results are reported at four resolutions. For the baseline model, we use HRNet18 [40] as the encoder and use the same decoder as Monodepth2 [10]. The ablation results show that our proposed arbitrary-scale data augmentation (AS-Aug), Dual HRNet (D-HRNet), and cross-scale depth consistency loss (CS-Loss) can bring obvious improvements individually. Since the CS-Loss is imposed on the AS-Aug, experiments involving the CS-Loss must include the AS-Aug operation. All combined components can yield the best performance (RA-Depth). Besides, even without using ImageNet pre-trained weights, our model can also obtain the large gain over the baseline model.

Table 3. Generalization results on the Make3D [38] and NYU-V2 [39] datasets. All models are trained at the resolution of 640×192 on the KITTI dataset [8]. The upper part of this table reports the generalization results at the same resolution as training. The bottom half of this table reports the average results tested at four different resolutions (416×128, 512×160, 832×256, 1024×320), which represent the results of resolution adaptation across datasets.

Dataset	Method	Error Metric ↓				Accuracy Metric ↑		
		AbsRel	SqRel	RMSE	RMSElog	$\delta < 1.25$	$\delta < 1.25^2$	$\delta < 1.25^3$
(a) Results at the same resolution as training								
Make3D	Monodepth2 [10]	0.322	3.589	7.418	0.163	0.559	0.799	0.909
	HR-Depth [27]	0.315	3.208	7.024	0.159	0.562	0.798	0.913
	DIFFNet [48]	0.309	3.313	7.008	0.155	0.575	0.815	0.919
	RA-Depth	**0.277**	**2.703**	**6.548**	**0.143**	**0.612**	**0.846**	**0.933**
NYU-V2	Monodepth2 [10]	0.377	0.778	1.388	0.414	0.442	0.728	0.879
	HR-Depth [27]	0.321	0.521	1.150	0.367	0.490	0.774	0.913
	DIFFNet [48]	0.307	0.481	1.095	0.352	0.518	0.796	0.921
	RA-Depth	**0.250**	**0.286**	**0.843**	**0.293**	**0.605**	**0.861**	**0.955**
(b) Average results of resolution adaptation at four different resolutions								
Make3D	Monodepth2 [10]	0.342	3.862	7.921	0.172	0.509	0.776	0.901
	HR-Depth [27]	0.340	3.527	7.577	0.171	0.502	0.773	0.903
	DIFFNet [48]	0.333	3.753	7.700	0.167	0.528	0.790	0.909
	RA-Depth	**0.278**	**2.722**	**6.655**	**0.146**	**0.601**	**0.844**	**0.932**
NYU-V2	Monodepth2 [10]	0.380	0.778	1.384	0.413	0.445	0.730	0.882
	HR-Depth [27]	0.325	0.520	1.147	0.377	0.491	0.778	0.915
	DIFFNet [48]	0.322	0.508	1.167	0.364	0.500	0.781	0.913
	RA-Depth	**0.265**	**0.326**	**0.890**	**0.304**	**0.586**	**0.848**	**0.948**

Effects of Arbitrary-Scale Data Augmentation. As shown in Table 4(a), our proposed arbitrary-scale data augmentation (AS-Aug) significantly improves performance when tested at the same resolution as training. Moreover, results in Table 4(b) demonstrate that AS-Aug brings large gains over the baseline in terms of resolution adaptation performance. In particular, when combining AS-Aug to

Table 4. Ablation results for each component of our method. All models are trained at the resolution of 640 × 192 on the KITTI dataset [8] using the Eigen split [5]. AS-Aug: arbitrary-scale data augmentation. D-HRNet: Dual HRNet. CS-Loss: cross-scale depth consistency loss. pt: pretrained weights on the ImageNet dataset. (a) We test the effects of each component on overall performance at the same resolution as training. (b) We report the average results tested at four different resolutions (416 × 128, 512 × 160, 832 × 256, 1024 × 320) to verify the effectiveness of each component on the resolution adaptation ability.

	Pretrained	AS-Aug	D-HRNet	CS-Loss	Error Metric ↓				Accuracy Metric ↑		
					AbsRel	SqRel	RMSE	RMSElog	$\delta < 1.25$	$\delta < 1.25^2$	$\delta < 1.25^3$
(a) Results at the same resolution as training											
Baseline	✓				0.107	0.866	4.680	0.183	0.890	0.963	0.982
Baseline + AS-Aug	✓	✓			0.102	0.716	4.395	0.178	0.899	0.965	0.984
Baseline + D-HRNet	✓		✓		0.102	0.746	4.466	0.178	0.897	0.965	0.983
RA-Depth w/o D-HRNet	✓	✓		✓	0.097	0.651	4.246	0.172	0.902	0.967	0.984
RA-Depth w/o CS-Loss	✓	✓	✓		0.101	0.732	4.382	0.176	0.900	0.967	0.984
RA-Depth	✓	✓	✓	✓	**0.096**	**0.632**	**4.216**	**0.171**	**0.903**	**0.968**	**0.985**
Baseline w/o pt					0.122	0.957	4.955	0.199	0.860	0.954	0.979
RA-Depth w/o pt		✓	✓	✓	**0.115**	**0.806**	**4.633**	**0.189**	**0.873**	**0.959**	**0.982**
(b) Average results of resolution adaptation at four different resolutions											
Baseline	✓				0.152	1.239	5.745	0.225	0.799	0.945	0.978
Baseline + AS-Aug	✓	✓			0.107	0.730	4.470	0.182	0.890	0.964	0.983
Baseline + D-HRNet	✓		✓		0.145	0.994	5.332	0.220	0.801	0.950	0.980
RA-Depth w/o D-HRNet	✓	✓		✓	0.102	0.664	4.375	**0.177**	0.893	**0.966**	**0.985**
RA-Depth w/o CS-Loss	✓	✓	✓		0.107	0.724	4.467	0.182	0.891	0.965	0.984
RA-Depth	✓	✓	✓	✓	**0.101**	**0.651**	**4.345**	**0.177**	**0.894**	**0.966**	**0.985**
Baseline w/o pt					0.209	2.179	7.285	0.290	0.678	0.890	0.955
RA-Depth w/o pt		✓	✓	✓✓	**0.124**	**0.856**	**4.844**	**0.198**	**0.856**	**0.955**	**0.981**

the baseline model, we achieve the error reduction rates of 29.6%, 41.4%, and 22.2% in terms of AbsRel, SqRel, and RMSE, respectively, and the accuracy gain of 11.4% in terms of $\delta < 1.25$. As described in Algorithm 1, given an original image, AS-Aug generates three training images with three different scales to let the model implicitly learn the scale invariance of the scene depth. When generating only one training image from an original image, we compare our AS-Aug component with the data augmentation (dubbed Bian-Aug) proposed by Bian et al. [2] as shown in Table 5(a). Although Bian-Aug also uses randomly resizing and cropping to change the scale of images, the differences between us are two-fold. On the one hand, Bian-Aug first downsizes the original image and then upsamples the downsized image to high resolution for cropping. However, our AS-Aug directly crops on the original image so that the detailed information of the images can be remained. On the other hand, [2] only inputs one-scale image to the network, while our method inputs three-scale images to the network so that three kinds of camera intrinsics can be simulated. By imposing the cross-scale depth consistency loss among them, we can learn the scale invariance of different image resolutions. Therefore, the proposed AS-Aug significantly outperforms the Bian-Aug in terms of resolution adaptation of depth estimation. Table 5(b) reports how the number of images generated by AS-Aug affects the resolution adaptation performance. Since the performance is better when generating multiple images and the proposed cross-scale depth consistency loss needs to be implemented based on multiple images, we generate three training images for each input.

Effects of Cross-Scale Depth Consistency Loss. As shown in Table 4, whether testing at the same resolution as training or four different resolutions, the addition of cross-scale depth consistency loss (CS-Loss) brings significant improvements. Moreover, as shown in Table 5(c), for different settings of AS-Aug, combining CS-Loss can obviously improve the resolution adaptation performance of the model. These experiments demonstrate that the explicit constraint of CS-Loss can further help the model learn the scale invariance of scene depth, so as to enhance the resolution adaptation ability of the model. This verifies that our depth estimation model can explicitly learn the scale invariance of scene depth with our proposed cross-scale depth consistency loss.

Effects of Dual HRNet. Table 6 reports the parameter complexity (#Params) and computation complexity (GFLOPs) of our model RA-Depth. Compared with existing state-of-the-art models as well as the baseline model, our model is the most efficient in terms of parameter complexity and computation complexity. That is, thanks to the efficient design of depth network Dual HRNet with multi-scale feature fusion, our model can achieve the best performance with the lowest network overhead.

Table 5. Additional ablation studies for AS-Aug and CS-Loss. Bian-Aug represents the data augmentation method of Bian *et al.* [2]. All models are trained at the resolution of 640×192 on the KITTI dataset [8]. We report the average results of resolution adaptation tested at four different resolutions (416×128, 512×160, 832×256, 1024×320).

		Error Metric ↓				Accuracy Metric ↑		
		AbsRel	SqRel	RMSE	RMSElog	$\delta < 1.25$	$\delta < 1.25^2$	$\delta < 1.25^3$
(a)	Baseline	0.152	1.239	5.745	0.225	0.799	0.945	0.978
	Baseline + Bian-Aug (1 image)	0.128	0.847	4.770	0.200	0.850	0.960	0.981
	Baseline + AS-Aug (1 image)	**0.108**	**0.742**	**4.491**	**0.184**	**0.885**	**0.961**	**0.982**
(b)	Baseline + AS-Aug (1 image)	0.108	0.742	4.491	0.184	0.885	0.961	0.982
	Baseline + AS-Aug (2 images)	**0.107**	0.734	4.478	**0.182**	0.888	0.963	**0.983**
	Baseline + AS-Aug (3 images)	**0.107**	**0.730**	**4.470**	**0.182**	**0.890**	**0.964**	**0.983**
(c)	Baseline + AS-Aug (2 images) + CS-Loss	0.103	0.670	4.383	0.178	0.891	0.965	0.984
	Baseline + AS-Aug (3 images) + CS-Loss	**0.102**	**0.664**	**4.375**	**0.177**	**0.893**	**0.966**	**0.985**

Table 6. Parameters and GFLOPs of the depth estimation network.

Method	Encoder	#Params	GFLOPs	Error Metric ↓				Accuracy Metric ↑		
				AbsRel	SqRel	RMSE	RMSElog	$\delta < 1.25$	$\delta < 1.25^2$	$\delta < 1.25^3$
Monodepth2 [10]	ResNet50	34.57M	16.63	0.110	0.831	4.642	0.187	0.883	0.962	0.982
HR-Depth [27]	ResNet18	14.61M	11.27	0.109	0.792	4.632	0.185	0.884	0.962	0.983
DIFF-Net [48]	HRNet18	10.87M	15.77	0.102	0.764	4.483	0.180	0.896	0.965	0.983
Baseline	HRNet18	11.31M	10.99	0.107	0.866	4.680	0.183	0.890	0.963	0.982
RA-Depth	HRNet18	**9.98M**	**10.78**	**0.096**	**0.632**	**4.216**	**0.171**	**0.903**	**0.968**	**0.985**

5 Conclusions

We proposed RA-Depth, a self-supervised monocular depth estimation method to efficiently predict depth maps of images when the resolutions of images are inconsistent during training and testing. Based on our proposed arbitrary-scale data augmentation method, we developed a dual high-resolution network to efficiently fuse multi-scale features for the accurate depth prediction. RA-Depth achieves state-of-the-art results on various public datasets, and exhibits the good ability of resolution adaptation. Moreover, benefiting from the constructed dual HRNet, our RA-Depth model is efficient in terms of the parameter and computation complexity.

Acknowledgments. The authors would like to thank reviewers for their detailed comments and instructive suggestions. Thank Beibei Zhou and Kun Wang for their valuable suggestions and discussions. This work was supported by the National Science Fund of China (Grant Nos. U1713208, 61876084).

References

1. Bhat, S.F., Alhashim, I., Wonka, P.: AdaBins: depth estimation using adaptive bins. In: CVPR (2021)
2. Bian, J.W., et al.: Unsupervised scale-consistent depth and ego-motion learning from monocular video. In: NeurIPS (2019)
3. Chen, P.Y., Liu, A.H., Liu, Y.C., Wang, Y.C.F.: Towards scene understanding: unsupervised monocular depth estimation with semantic-aware representation. In: CVPR (2019)
4. Choi, J., Jung, D., Lee, D., Kim, C.: Safenet: self-supervised monocular depth estimation with semantic-aware feature extraction. arXiv preprint arXiv:2010.02893 (2020)
5. Eigen, D., Puhrsch, C., Fergus, R.: Depth map prediction from a single image using a multi-scale deep network. arXiv preprint arXiv:1406.2283 (2014)
6. Fu, H., Gong, M., Wang, C., Batmanghelich, K., Tao, D.: Deep ordinal regression network for monocular depth estimation. In: CVPR (2018)
7. Garg, R., B.G., V.K., Carneiro, G., Reid, I.: Unsupervised CNN for single view depth estimation: geometry to the rescue. In: Leibe, B., Matas, J., Sebe, N., Welling, M. (eds.) ECCV 2016. LNCS, vol. 9912, pp. 740–756. Springer, Cham (2016). https://doi.org/10.1007/978-3-319-46484-8_45
8. Geiger, A., Lenz, P., Stiller, C., Urtasun, R.: Vision meets robotics: the kitti dataset. Int. J. Robot. Res. **32**(11), 1231–1237 (2013)
9. Godard, C., Mac Aodha, O., Brostow, G.J.: Unsupervised monocular depth estimation with left-right consistency. In: CVPR (2017)
10. Godard, C., Mac Aodha, O., Firman, M., Brostow, G.J.: Digging into self-supervised monocular depth estimation. In: ICCV (2019)
11. Guizilini, V., Ambrus, R., Pillai, S., Raventos, A., Gaidon, A.: 3D packing for self-supervised monocular depth estimation. In: CVPR (2020)
12. Guizilini, V., Hou, R., Li, J., Ambrus, R., Gaidon, A.: Semantically-guided representation learning for self-supervised monocular depth. arXiv preprint arXiv:2002.12319 (2020)

13. He, K., Zhang, X., Ren, S., Sun, J.: Deep residual learning for image recognition. In: CVPR (2016)
14. Hirschmuller, H.: Accurate and efficient stereo processing by semi-global matching and mutual information. In: CVPR (2005)
15. Hirschmuller, H.: Stereo processing by semiglobal matching and mutual information. IEEE Trans. Pattern Anal. Mach. Intell. **30**(2), 328–341 (2007)
16. Hu, J., Ozay, M., Zhang, Y., Okatani, T.: Revisiting single image depth estimation: toward higher resolution maps with accurate object boundaries. In: WACV (2019)
17. Jaderberg, M., Simonyan, K., Zisserman, A., Kavukcuoglu, K.: Spatial transformer networks. arXiv preprint arXiv:1506.02025 (2015)
18. Kingma, D.P., Ba, J.: Adam: a method for stochastic optimization. arXiv preprint arXiv:1412.6980 (2014)
19. Klingner, M., Termöhlen, J.-A., Mikolajczyk, J., Fingscheidt, T.: Self-supervised monocular depth estimation: solving the dynamic object problem by semantic guidance. In: Vedaldi, A., Bischof, H., Brox, T., Frahm, J.-M. (eds.) ECCV 2020. LNCS, vol. 12365, pp. 582–600. Springer, Cham (2020). https://doi.org/10.1007/978-3-030-58565-5_35
20. Ladicky, L., Shi, J., Pollefeys, M.: Pulling things out of perspective. In: CVPR (2014)
21. Laina, I., Rupprecht, C., Belagiannis, V., Tombari, F., Navab, N.: Deeper depth prediction with fully convolutional residual networks. In: 3DV (2016)
22. Lee, J.H., Han, M.K., Ko, D.W., Suh, I.H.: From big to small: multi-scale local planar guidance for monocular depth estimation. arXiv preprint arXiv:1907.10326 (2019)
23. Leistner, T., Mackowiak, R., Ardizzone, L., Köthe, U., Rother, C.: Towards multimodal depth estimation from light fields. In: CVPR (2022)
24. Liu, F., Shen, C., Lin, G.: Deep convolutional neural fields for depth estimation from a single image. In: CVPR (2015)
25. Liu, F., Shen, C., Lin, G., Reid, I.: Learning depth from single monocular images using deep convolutional neural fields. IEEE Trans. Pattern Anal. Mach. Intell. **38**(10), 2024–2039 (2015)
26. Luo, C., et al.: Every pixel Counts++: joint learning of geometry and motion with 3D holistic understanding. IEEE Trans. Pattern Anal. Mach. Intell. **42**(10), 2624–2641 (2019)
27. Lyu, X., et al.: HR-depth: high resolution self-supervised monocular depth estimation. In: AAAI (2020)
28. Mahjourian, R., Wicke, M., Angelova, A.: Unsupervised learning of depth and ego-motion from monocular video using 3D geometric constraints. In: CVPR (2018)
29. Parida, K.K., Srivastava, S., Sharma, G.: Beyond image to depth: improving depth prediction using echoes. In: CVPR (2021)
30. Paszke, A., et al.: Automatic differentiation in pytorch (2017)
31. Patil, V., Sakaridis, C., Liniger, A., Van Gool, L.: P3Depth: monocular depth estimation with a piecewise planarity prior. In: Proceedings of the IEEE/CVF Conference on Computer Vision and Pattern Recognition, pp. 1610–1621 (2022)
32. Peng, R., Wang, R., Lai, Y., Tang, L., Cai, Y.: Excavating the potential capacity of self-supervised monocular depth estimation. In: ICCV (2021)
33. Poggi, M., Aleotti, F., Tosi, F., Mattoccia, S.: On the uncertainty of self-supervised monocular depth estimation. In: CVPR (2020)
34. Poggi, M., Tosi, F., Mattoccia, S.: Learning monocular depth estimation with unsupervised trinocular assumptions. In: 3DV (2018)

35. Qi, X., Liao, R., Liu, Z., Urtasun, R., Jia, J.: GeoNet: geometric neural network for joint depth and surface normal estimation. In: CVPR (2018)
36. Ranjan, A., et al.: Competitive collaboration: joint unsupervised learning of depth, camera motion, optical flow and motion segmentation. In: CVPR (2019)
37. Russakovsky, O., et al.: Imagenet large scale visual recognition challenge. Int. J. Comput. Vision **115**(3), 211–252 (2015)
38. Saxena, A., Sun, M., Ng, A.Y.: Make3D: learning 3D scene structure from a single still image. IEEE Trans. Pattern Anal. Mach. Intell. **31**(5), 824–840 (2008)
39. Silberman, N., Hoiem, D., Kohli, P., Fergus, R.: Indoor segmentation and support inference from RGBD images. In: Fitzgibbon, A., Lazebnik, S., Perona, P., Sato, Y., Schmid, C. (eds.) ECCV 2012. LNCS, vol. 7576, pp. 746–760. Springer, Heidelberg (2012). https://doi.org/10.1007/978-3-642-33715-4_54
40. Wang, J., Sun, K., Cheng, T.: Deep high-resolution representation learning for visual recognition. IEEE Trans. Pattern Anal. Mach. Intell. **43**(10), 3349–3364 (2019)
41. Wang, Z., Bovik, A.C., Sheikh, H.R., Simoncelli, E.P.: Image quality assessment: from error visibility to structural similarity. IEEE Trans. Image Process. **13**(4), 600–612 (2004)
42. Watson, J., Firman, M., Brostow, G.J., Turmukhambetov, D.: Self-supervised monocular depth hints. In: ICCV (2019)
43. Xu, D., Wang, W., Tang, H., Liu, H., Sebe, N., Ricci, E.: Structured attention guided convolutional neural fields for monocular depth estimation. In: CVPR (2018)
44. Yin, W., Liu, Y., Shen, C., Yan, Y.: Enforcing geometric constraints of virtual normal for depth prediction. In: ICCV (2019)
45. Yu, Z., Jin, L., Gao, S.: P^2Net: patch-match and plane-regularization for unsupervised indoor depth estimation. In: Vedaldi, A., Bischof, H., Brox, T., Frahm, J.-M. (eds.) ECCV 2020. LNCS, vol. 12369, pp. 206–222. Springer, Cham (2020). https://doi.org/10.1007/978-3-030-58586-0_13
46. Zhan, H., Garg, R., Weerasekera, C.S., Li, K., Agarwal, H., Reid, I.: Unsupervised learning of monocular depth estimation and visual odometry with deep feature reconstruction. In: CVPR (2018)
47. Zhang, Z., Cui, Z., Xu, C., Yan, Y., Sebe, N., Yang, J.: Pattern-affinitive propagation across depth, surface normal and semantic segmentation. In: CVPR (2019)
48. Zhou, H., Greenwood, D., Taylor, S.: Self-supervised monocular depth estimation with internal feature fusion. In: BMVC (2021)
49. Zhou, T., Brown, M., Snavely, N., Lowe, D.G.: Unsupervised learning of depth and ego-motion from video. In: CVPR (2017)
50. Zhu, S., Brazil, G., Liu, X.: The edge of depth: explicit constraints between segmentation and depth. In: CVPR (2020)

PolyphonicFormer: Unified Query Learning for Depth-Aware Video Panoptic Segmentation

Haobo Yuan[1], Xiangtai Li[3], Yibo Yang[4(✉)], Guangliang Cheng[5], Jing Zhang[6], Yunhai Tong[3], Lefei Zhang[1,2(✉)], and Dacheng Tao[4]

[1] Institute of Artificial Intelligence and School of Computer Science, Wuhan University, Wuhan 430072, People's Republic of China
{yuanhaobo,zhanglefei}@whu.edu.cn
[2] Hubei Luojia Laboratory, Wuhan 430072, People's Republic of China
[3] Key Laboratory of Machine Perception, MOE, School of Artificial Intelligence, Peking University, Beijing 100871, People's Republic of China
lxtpku@pku.edu.cn
[4] JD Explore Academy, Beijing, People's Republic of China
ibo@pku.edu.cn
[5] SenseTime Research, Beijing, People's Republic of China
[6] The University of Sydney, Sydney, Australia

Abstract. The Depth-aware Video Panoptic Segmentation (DVPS) is a new challenging vision problem that aims to predict panoptic segmentation and depth in a video simultaneously. The previous work solves this task by extending the existing panoptic segmentation method with an extra dense depth prediction and instance tracking head. However, the relationship between the depth and panoptic segmentation is not well explored – simply combining existing methods leads to competition and needs carefully weight balancing. In this paper, we present Polyphonic-Former, a vision transformer to unify these sub-tasks under the DVPS task and lead to more robust results. Our principal insight is that the depth can be harmonized with the panoptic segmentation with our proposed new paradigm of predicting instance level depth maps with object queries. Then the relationship between the two tasks via query-based learning is explored. From the experiments, we demonstrate the benefits of our design from both depth estimation and panoptic segmentation aspects. Since each thing query also encodes the instance-wise information, it is natural to perform tracking directly with appearance learning. Our method achieves state-of-the-art results on two DVPS datasets (Semantic KITTI, Cityscapes), and ranks **1st** on the ICCV-2021 BMTT Challenge video + depth track. Code is available here.

H. Yuan and X. Li—Contributed equally to the work.

Supplementary Information The online version contains supplementary material available at https://doi.org/10.1007/978-3-031-19812-0_34.

Keywords: Depth-aware video panoptic segmentation · Scene understanding · Multi-task learning

1 Introduction

To enable machines to perceive the 3D world from 2D video clips, Depth-aware Video Panoptic Segmentation (DVPS) [43] is proposed by extending the video panoptic segmentation [21,61] with monocular depth estimation [46] which is a challenging and not trivial task for scene understanding. It predicts temporally consistent instance-level semantic results along with per-pixel depth prediction. Achieving accurate and robust DVPS methods in real-world scenarios can greatly promote the development of autonomous driving [10,15].

To tackle this problem, previous work [43] builds two DVPS datasets, including Cityscapes-DVPS and SemKITTI-DVPS by extending two existing datasets Cityscape-VPS [21] and Semantic-KITTI [1]. It also offers a strong baseline ViP-Deeplab [43] by adding two separate task heads based on Panoptic-Deeplab [8] including one dense depth estimation prediction head and one center prediction head for offline tracking as shown in Fig. 1(a). However, the separate-head design will damage the performance on both the depth estimation and panoptic segmentation since both fight for suitable backbone features and conflict with each other as observed in previous work [43]. Besides, the model is sensitive to the loss weights of depth estimation and panoptic segmentation, and thus requires a careful balance between the two tasks to enable satisfying performances for both. Therefore, a unified framework that stably facilitates the mutual benefit of the two tasks remains to be developed.

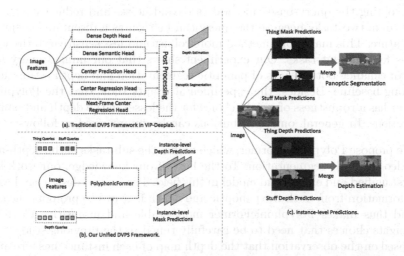

Fig. 1. The principal idea of PolyphonicFormer. (a) Previous work's pipeline [43]. (b), Illustration of our unified framework. (c). Key insights of our PolyphonicFormer: The queries are extracted from instance-level information and used to predict instance-level mask and depth results in a unified manner. Best view it on screen.

Recently, transformers [11,34] make great progress on vision tasks. Except for the global perception property of vision transformers, the query-based set prediction design in Detection Transformer (DETR) [3] has been proved to be effective in modeling the interactions between instance-level and global contexts. Following the DETR formulation, the query-based design has been applied with good performances on various tasks [9,13,53,73]. In our task, the instance-level semantic contexts have a strong connection with depth information, since the boundary of an instance in the image corresponds to the region where sharp changes occur in the depth map. So it is natural to utilize query-based reasoning to fulfill the mutual benefit between semantic context and geometry information.

Motivated by such analysis, in this paper, we develop a novel unified query-based representation for things, stuff, and depth, and propose **Polyphonic-Former** (Polyphonic Transformer) where different queries come from different sources (depth or panoptic) but can benefit each other. This is just like the **polyphony** used in the music field. As shown in Fig. 1(b), the PolyphonicFormer builds a unified query learning framework to enable the interaction between panoptic context and depth information and make them benefit from each other iteratively. We further link both panoptic and depth queries to facilitate mutual benefit. Our insight is that both depth prediction and panoptic prediction can be linked via the corresponding *instance-wised masks and queries*, which are shown in Fig. 1(c), since one unique mask corresponds to one unique query. As a result, the joint modeling can inject semantic information from thing and stuff queries into depth prediction. Moreover, the query-based depth prediction can be seen as regularization items to force semantic consistency during training, which also improves the segmentation results. In terms of temporal modeling, our model directly links to the thing query, which avoids the complex offline post-processing that is used in ViP-Deeplab [43].

Adopting the query-based method can avoid noises and reduce the resource battle from two tasks because the query can be seen as a disentanglement from the feature. This makes our method more robust and less sensitive to the weight of loss for different tasks. Our experiment shows that our unified query learning can enhance both results of panoptic segmentation and depth estimation on a strong baseline. Besides, the experimental results show that the Polyphonic-Former has a robustness of weight choice for the losses in the depth and panoptic predictions. In general, our contributions can be summarized as follows:

- We propose PolyphonicFormer, which unifies the sub-tasks of the depth-aware video panoptic segmentation. To the best of our knowledge, our work is the first unified and end-to-end model in this field. The unified design can leverage information from both the panoptic and depth features to promote the other, and thus makes PolyphonicFormer more stable and insensitive to the loss weights choices that need to be carefully tuned in the previous study.
- Based on the observation that the depth map of each instance has a relatively simple structure than the whole scene, we propose a novel query-based depth estimation scheme to predict the depth map of each instance and merge them

into a complete depth map. The query-based depth estimation scheme takes full advantages of the instance boundaries and has better accuracy.
- We conduct extensive experiments on Cityscapes-DVPS, Cityscapes-VPS, and SemKITTI-DVPS to verify the effectiveness of PolyphonicFormer. Our method achieves 64.6 DSTQ on the SemKITTI-DVPS Challenge and won the ICCV-2021 BMTT Challenge video + depth track. Ablation studies show that our framework can boost the *mutual benefit* between depth and panoptic predictions as well as has *robustness on weight choice for losses*.

2   Related Work

Panoptic Segmentation. The earlier work [23] directly combines predictions of things and stuff from different models. To alleviate computation cost, many works [7,22,26,30,41,64,70] are proposed to model both stuff segmentation and thing segmentation in one model with different task heads. Detection based methods [20,22,31,42,65] usually represent thing within the box prediction, while several bottom-up models [8,14,54,69] perform grouping instance via the pixel-level affinities or instance centers from semantic segmentation results. Recently, several works [3,9,53,73] use transformer-like architecture and use object queries to encode thing and stuff masks in an end-to-end manner. Our method is inspired by these works and takes a further step by jointly modeling depth estimation into panoptic segmentation to build a unified framework.

Joint Depth and Semantic Modeling. Several works [6,36,44,45] model the depth estimation and semantic (panoptic) segmentation as a naive multi-task learning procedure and bond them with a series of consistent losses. Some other works [17,27,55] utilize semantic segmentation to guide depth estimation learning. From the perspective of 3D geometry, previous works [4,24,25] use semantic or instance segmentation to tackle the object motion problem left in the self-supervised monocular depth estimation [16]. Recently, ViP-Deeplab [43] extends Panoptic-Deeplab [8] by adding extra dense depth prediction heads, and builds a holistic perception framework. Different from the previous works, where depth and segmentation are tackled separately, we link both parts via object queries in a unified manner, so enjoy the mutual benefit of both tasks.

Segmentation and Tracking in Video. Several tasks including Video Object Segmentation (VOS) [37,40,51], Video Instance Segmentation (VIS) [68], Multi-Object Tracking and Segmentation (MOTS) [52], and Video Panoptic Segmentation (VPS) [21] are very close to DVPS. Previous works [2,21,29,63,76] mainly model the temporal consistency for these tasks. VisTR [58] solves VIS problem using transformer [50] in an end-to-end manner. However, this method is limited by the complex scene and long video clip inputs. Recently, STEP [61] proposes a new metric named Segmentation Tracking Quality (STQ) for better evaluating video panoptic segmentation. There are also several tracking methods [38,47,59,60,75] for MOT in terms of transformer architecture and appearance learning. Our PolyphonicFormer simply applies an appearance-based method, Quasi-Dense [38] to extract tracking embeddings as the tracking head.

Vision Transformer. Many researchers have adopted Transformer [50] to solve computer vision problems [11,34,49,54,56,57,67,72]. With the help of vision transformers, DETR [3] reformulates the object detection task to output set predictions with an end-to-end framework. The key component is the object query design, which serves as a learnable anchor to detect each instance. This novelty has been also used in panoptic segmentation [9,28,32,53,66,71,73,74] where the pure mask classification can work well on panoptic segmentation. In this paper, inspired by DETR-like segmentation methods [3,9], we borrow the merits of query-based reasoning and into joint depth and panoptic prediction.

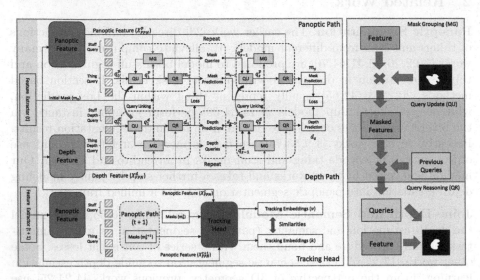

Fig. 2. Illustration of our proposed PolyphonicFormer (left). Our method contains three parts: (1) Feature Extractor to obtain two parallel features for depth estimation and panoptic segmentation. The extracted panoptic (red) and depth (green) features are directly used to predict the final output. (2) Polyphonic Head containing the panoptic path and depth path to refine all the queries at the same time (middle). We use the instance masks to group (orange) the panoptic and depth features for query-based learning. (3) Tracking Head to learn the feature embedding among the frames (bottom). The Mask Grouping (MG), Query Update (QU), and Query Reasoning (QR) (right). (Color figure online)

3   Method

We explain the architecture design of PolyphonicFormer in detail. As shown in Fig. 2, our PolyphonicFormer is composed of three parts: (1) A feature extractor to extract features for each frame. (2) a unified query learning sub-network, which takes three different types of queries and backbone features as inputs and outputs both panoptic segmentation and depth estimation predictions. It contains two paths: depth path and panoptic path, which are interacted with each other iteratively. (3) A lightweight tracking head with several convolution layers to learn the instance-wise tracking embeddings for each thing query.

3.1 Feature Extractor

We use a shared backbone network (Residual Network [19] or Swin Transformer [34]) along with Feature Pyramid Network as the feature extractor. We adopt the semantic FPN [22] design to simply fuse the multiscale information since both the depth and panoptic predictions need the high-resolution feature to find the fine structures as well as high-level semantic information. In particular, leveraging a shared backbone, the neck generates different feature maps for panoptic and depth predictions in parallel. These feature maps output from FPN are denoted as X_{FPN}^{p} and X_{FPN}^{d}, respectively. They are directly used to generate the final and intermediate predictions of depth estimation and panoptic segmentation with the queries in each stage, as described in Sect. 3.2.

3.2 Unified Query Learning

The unified query learning sub-network is composed of two parallel paths for panoptic and depth predictions, respectively. Each path takes the panoptic or depth feature as input and uses *mask grouping* and *query update* to iteratively update the queries. The updated queries are adopted to refine the corresponding mask and depth predictions by the *query reasoning* module.

Mask Grouping. At each stage s, we first use the mask results generated at the former stage $s - 1$ to group the X_{FPN}^{p} and X_{FPN}^{d}. The key motivation has two folds: The first is that using grouping can avoid noise and select the most salient part for query learning. The second is that adopting grouping or pooling can speed up the learning process of DETR-like models [29,48,73]. Thus, we formulate the process as follows:

$$X_{s}^{(n,c)} = \sum_{u}^{W} \sum_{v}^{H} m_{s-1}^{n}(u,v) \cdot X_{\mathrm{FPN}}^{c}(u,v), \tag{1}$$

where m_{s-1} is the mask predictions from former stage. The X_{FPN}^{p} is with a $C \times H \times W$ shape, m is with a $N \times H \times W$ shape, if we use C and N to represent number of channels and instances respectively. In PolyphonicFormer, we set $C = 256$ and $N = 100$, respectively. For each mask, we generate a corresponding feature to represent the instance-level information. The instance-level features $(N \times C)$ are used to update the queries better focusing on each instance. This process is done in both panoptic path and depth path, with the same former stage mask m_{s-1}, as shown in Fig. 2 with orange line. With the help of previous stage masks, both the depth and panoptic predictions can be refined with instance-level features.

For the first stage, since the former stage is not available, we use an initial stage (denoted as stage 0), to generate the initial depth and panotpic results. Specifically, we use different convolution module to generate dense predictions on instance segmentation, semantic segmentation, and depth estimation, which are all guided with the ground truth. The initial panoptic segmentation results are delivered to the first stage for mask grouping. The convolution kernels are also transferred to the first stage as the initial queries. Mask Grouping operation is conducted on both panoptic path and depth path separately.

Query Update. The masked instance-level features are then delivered to update panoptic and depth queries. We describe the panoptic path first. Inspired by K-Net [73], we adopt an adaptive query update process. The query update process avoids the heavy pixel-wised affinity calculation that is used in DETR-like models [3,9]. The query update process forces the model to learn the instance-aware feature to speed up the training procedure. Specifically, we use a gated fusion design to capture the information from queries and features. We first calculate the gate features F_G as follows:

$$F_G^p = \phi(\boldsymbol{X}_s^p) \cdot \phi(q_{s-1}^p), \tag{2}$$

where ϕ is linear transformations, and all of the ϕs in this section are independent. The F_G has the information from both the queries and the instance-level features. With F_G, we can calculate gates for features and queries with the following formulation:

$$G_q^p = \sigma(\psi(F_G^p)), G_{\boldsymbol{X}}^p = \sigma(\psi(F_G^p)), \tag{3}$$

where ψs are independent fully connected layers and σ are sigmoid functions. With the gates, for the panoptic queries, the updated queries can be calculated as follows:

$$q_s^p = G_{\boldsymbol{X}}^p \cdot \psi(\boldsymbol{X}_s^p) + G_q^p \cdot \psi(q_{s-1}^p), \tag{4}$$

where ψs are also independent fully connected layers. The updated queries in this stage take advantages of both the queries from the former stage and the grouped features with the former stage masks.

For the depth path, we adopt a similar process as Eq. 2 and Eq. 3 to calculate depth features F_G^d and gates G_q^d, $G_{\boldsymbol{X}}^d$. The features and queries from both the panoptic path and depth path will contribute to the current stage depth query:

$$q_s^d = G_{\boldsymbol{X}}^d \cdot \psi(\boldsymbol{X}_s^d) + G_q^d \cdot \psi(q_{s-1}^d) + q_s^p. \tag{5}$$

We call this process Query Linking. The query linking process will make the depth query get the instance-level information from both the panoptic path and the depth path, and further bolster the mutual benefit between depth and panoptic predictions.

Query Reasoning. With the updated queries, we perform QR to predict the depth and mask results. We simply adopt Multi-Head Self Attention [50] (MSA), Feed-Forward Neural Network [50] (FFN), followed by FC-LN-ReLU layers on queries, which has been proved to be effective in [73]. The depth and mask predictions are then calculated by:

$$m_s = FFN\left(MSA\left(q_s^m\right)\right) \cdot X_{\text{FPN}}^m,$$
$$d_s = FFN\left(MSA\left(q_s^d\right)\right) \cdot X_{\text{FPN}}^d. \tag{6}$$

The m_s and d_s are instance-level predictions of stage s. Note that both query updating and reasoning perform individually (Panoptic Path and Depth Path in Fig. 2). The effect of each component can be found in the experiment part.

In our framework, the queries are refined in each stage to be applied to the features from FPN for panoptic and depth paths to get the predictions. The predictions are conducted with the bipartite match for calculating loss during training and merged into dense predictions when inference. All predictions contribute to the final loss, but only the final stage predictions are used when inference. Please refer to Sect. 3.5 for details about merging the instance-level depth prediction d_s into the final dense depth map.

3.3 Tracking with Thing Query

For the tracking part, we adopt previous work design [38,68] and add a tracking head, where we directly learn appearance embeddings among the different frames. During training, we first match predicted thing masks from the panoptic path to ground truth thing mask according to mask IoU. Then, we use the bound box generated by the ground truth thing mask to conduct ROIAlign [18] for extracting the tracking embeddings. We denote tracking embeddings for each instance from the source frame as v, and positive and negative tracking embeddings as k^+ and k^-. The tracking embedding loss can be calculated as:

$$\mathcal{L}_{\text{track}} = \log[1 + \sum_{k^+} \sum_{k^-} \exp(v \cdot k^- - v \cdot k^+)]. \tag{7}$$

During the inference, we use the thing masks, which are generated from the thing queries to obtain final tracking embeddings for tracking, as shown in the bottom part of Fig. 2. The bi-directional softmax is calculated to associate the instances between two frames (annotated as $\mathbf{n}$ and $\mathbf{m}$):

$$\mathbf{f}(i,j) = [\frac{\exp(\mathbf{n}_i \cdot \mathbf{m}_j)}{\sum_{k=0}^{M-1} \exp(\mathbf{n}_i \cdot \mathbf{m}_k)} + \frac{\exp(\mathbf{n}_i \cdot \mathbf{m}_j)}{\sum_{k=0}^{N-1} \exp(\mathbf{n}_k \cdot \mathbf{m}_j)}]/2. \tag{8}$$

3.4 Training

To train the proposed PolyphonicFormer, we need to assign ground truth according to cost since all the outputs are encoded via queries. We also assign ground truth for the initial-stage instance segmentation. In particular, we mainly follow the design of MaskFormer and Max-Deeplab [9,53] to use bipartite matching via a cost considering both segmentation mask and classification results of them.

For depth prediction, we use the same bipartite matching results to assign depth ground truth for each query.

After the bipartite matching, we apply a loss jointly considering depth estimation, mask prediction, and classification for each thing or stuff. For depth loss, following ViP-Deeplab [43], we use a joint loss including scale-invariant depth loss [12], absolute relative loss, and square relative loss. We did not find an advantage in our framework with the monodepth2 [16] activation strategy, so we use a sigmoid activation function and multiply the max distance for simplicity. For panoptic segmentation, we apply focal loss [33] on classification and adopt dice loss, focal loss, and cross-entropy loss on mask predictions. The loss for each stage can be formulated as follows:

$$\mathcal{L}_i = \lambda_{depth} \cdot \mathcal{L}_{depth} + \lambda_{mask} \cdot \mathcal{L}_{mask} + \lambda_{cls} \cdot \mathcal{L}_{cls}. \tag{9}$$

Note that the losses are applied to each stage, i.e.,

$$\mathcal{L}_{final} = \sum_i^N (\lambda_i \cdot \mathcal{L}_i) + \lambda_{track} \cdot \mathcal{L}_{track}, \tag{10}$$

where N is the total stages applied to the framework. We adopt $N = 3$ in PolyphonicFormer, and we set $\lambda_i = 1$ for all stages. The λ_{track} is set to 0.25.

3.5 Inference

We directly get the instance-level panoptic and depth predictions from the corresponding queries. For final panoptic segmentation results, we adopt the method used in Panoptic-FPN [22] to merge panoptic masks. Since the depth queries and panoptic queries have a one-to-one correspondence, the panoptic segmentation results are used to merge the instance-level depth predictions, i.e.:

$$D(u,v) = d(I(u,v), u, v), D \in R^{H \times W}, \tag{11}$$

where d is the instance-level depth predictions with a $N \times H \times W$ shape from the last stage, I is the instance ID for each pixel, which is from the panoptic segmentation results. The dense depth prediction D $(H \times W)$ is then calculated.

For tracking, after getting the embeddings of each instance, we calculate the similarities between the embeddings stored before with the bidirectional softmax similarity. If we detect a new instance embedding that does not appear before, we will store the embedding for future matching. We note that this process only needs *single image input* for each sample during the inference process.

4   Experiment

Experimental Setup. We implement our models with Pytorch [39], and follow the same training settings from Panoptic Deeplab [8] and ViP-Deeplab [43] where we first pretrain our model on both Mapillary [35] and Cityscapes [10] datasets for Panoptic Segmentation, and then we fine-tune the model with our depth query on Cityscapes-DVPS and SemKITTI-DVPS. During pretraining, we randomly resize the origin images with the scale from 1.0 to 2.0, and then we perform random crops with the 2048×1024 for Cityscapes-DVPS and 1280×384 for SemKITTI-DVPS. The batch size is set to 16, and we adopt the synchronized batch normalization during the training. For video training settings, we randomly sample one nearly frame to learn the tracking embeddings. All the models use the *single scale inference*. We adopt Swin-B and Resnet-50 backbones, and we add RFP [42] following ViP-Deeplab [43] but for Swin-B backbone only. We carry out ablation studies on Cityscapes-DVPS datasets for evaluating panoptic segmentation results and depth results.

Evaluation Metrics. We use DVPQ metric following ViP-Deeplab [43]. Let P and Q be the prediction and ground truth respectively, k be the window size, and λ be the depth threshold. We use P^c, P^{id}, and P^d to represent semantic segmentation, the instance segmentation, and depth estimation results respectively; Q^c, Q^{id}, and Q^d are alike but for ground truth. The $DVPQ^k_\lambda$ metric can be formulated as: $\mathrm{PQ}\Big(\Big[\|_{i=t}^{t+k-1}\big(\hat{P}_i^c, P_i^{id}\big), \|_{i=t}^{t+k-1}\big(Q_i^c, Q_i^{id}\big)\Big]_{t=1}^{T-k+1}\Big)$. where $\hat{P}_i^c := P_i^c$ for pixels that have an absolute relative depth error inside the error threshold (λ) and $\hat{P}_i^c := void$ otherwise. $\|_{i=t}^{t+k-1}(P_i^c, P_i^{id})$ denotes the horizontal concatenation of the pair (P_i^c, P_i^{id}) from t to $t + k - 1$.

Table 1. Experiment results on Cityscapes-DVPS and SemKITTI-DVPS. Each cell shows $DVPQ^k_\lambda$ | $DVPQ^k_\lambda$-Thing | $DVPQ^k_\lambda$-Stuff where λ is the threshold of relative depth error, and k is the number of frames. Smaller λ and larger k correspond to a higher accuracy requirement. PolyphonicFormer adopts Swin-B backbone in this table.

$DVPQ^k_\lambda$ on Cityscapes-DVPS	k = 1			k = 2			k = 3			k = 4			Average			FLOPs
PolyphonicFormer $\lambda = 0.50$	70.6	63.0	76.0	62.9	49.2	72.9	59.3	42.3	71.7	56.5	36.9	70.8	62.3	47.9	72.9	–
PolyphonicFormer $\lambda = 0.25$	67.8	61.0	72.8	60.4	47.6	69.8	56.9	40.8	68.6	54.3	35.8	67.8	59.9	46.3	69.8	–
PolyphonicFormer $\lambda = 0.10$	50.2	43.4	55.2	44.4	33.4	52.4	41.5	28.6	51.0	39.5	24.7	50.4	43.9	32.5	52.3	–
Average: PolyphonicFormer	62.9	55.8	68.0	55.9	43.4	65.0	52.6	37.2	63.8	50.1	32.5	63.0	**55.4**	42.2	65.0	1,675G
Average: ViP-Deeplab [43]	61.9	55.9	66.3	55.6	44.3	63.8	52.4	38.4	62.6	50.4	34.6	61.9	55.1	43.3	63.6	9,451G
$DVPQ^k_\lambda$ on SemKITTI-DVPS	k = 1			k = 5			k = 10			k = 20			Average			FLOPs
PolyphonicFormer $\lambda = 0.50$	58.5	55.1	61.0	52.0	42.3	59.1	50.6	39.9	58.5	49.9	38.6	58.0	52.8	44.0	59.2	–
PolyphonicFormer $\lambda = 0.25$	56.3	54.0	57.9	49.7	41.1	56.0	48.4	38.7	55.5	47.7	37.6	55.0	50.5	42.9	56.1	–
PolyphonicFormer $\lambda = 0.10$	41.8	41.1	42.4	35.1	28.2	40.1	33.7	26.0	39.3	33.0	25.1	38.7	35.9	30.1	40.1	–
Average: PolyphonicFormer	52.2	50.1	53.8	45.6	37.2	51.7	44.2	34.9	51.1	43.4	33.8	50.6	**46.4**	39.0	51.8	402G
Average: ViP-Deeplab [43]	48.9	42.0	53.9	45.8	36.9	52.3	44.4	34.6	51.6	43.4	33.0	51.1	45.6	36.6	52.2	2,267G

However, the $DVPQ^k_\lambda$ metric does not measure the depth quality and tracking quality explicitly; instead, they are observed by the $DVPQ^k_\lambda$ dropping when k and λ are getting larger. Therefore, we also report $DSTQ$, which is an extension of STQ [61]. The definition of $DSTQ$ is: $DSTQ = (AQ \times SQ \times DQ)^{\frac{1}{3}}$, where the AQ and SQ are association quality (tracking quality) and segmentation quality (mIoU) respectively [61]. DQ is depth prediction quality. In the ablation study, we report widely used PQ [23] and absolute relative error (abs rel) for panoptic segmentation and depth map quality assessment.

4.1 Experimental Results

Cityscapes-(D)VPS. The Cityscapes-DVPS dataset [43] is an extension of the Cityscapes-VPS [21] dataset, which contains extra depth annotations. Different from VPSNet [21], we only use the keyframes for training and inference, which means our setting needs fewer inputs and execution rounds to get the results compared to VPSNet [21], and thus might be more challenging. The results on the Cityscapes-VPS dataset are shown in Table 2. In the Cityscapes-VPS dataset, with the very same ResNet-50 backbone, the proposed PolyphonicFormer outperforms the existing methods, VPSNet [21] and SiamTrack [63] drastically, although we successfully get rid of the optical flow input. Note that we did not fine-tune our methods on Cityscapes-VPS after training on Cityscapes-DVPS since depth estimation in our framework will not damage the performance of panoptic segmentation performance in our framework. As shown in Table 1, in the Cityscapes-DVPS dataset, our methods achieve 55.4 average DVPQ with a Swin-B [34] backbone. The DVPQ results demonstrate that the proposed PolyphonicFormer has a good performance on the DVPS task and its sub-tasks.

SemKITTI-DVPS. The SemKITTI-DVPS dataset has 19,130 / 4,071 / 4,342 images for training, evaluation, and testing respectively. SemKITTI-DVPS is a challenging dataset since the annotation of both the depth and panoptic segmentation are sparse. As the sparse nature of annotations of SemKITTI-DVPS, following ViP-Deeplab [43], we consider the unannotated pixels as unknown when performing the evaluation. The Table 1 reports our DVPQ results on SemKITTI-DVPS validation set. The PolyphonicFomer achieves a 46.4 average DVPQ. On the test set (ICCV-2021 SemKITTI-DVPS challenge), our method won the championship with 63.6 DSTQ, as shown in Table 2. Beyond that, we re-train the proposed PolyphonicFormer with the additional validation set and achieve 64.6 DSTQ, which is the state-of-the-art result on the test set.

Table 2. (Left) Experiment results on Cityscapes-VPS validation set. $k = \{0, 5, 10, 15\}$ in [21] correspond to $k = \{1, 2, 3, 4\}$ in this paper as we use different notations. All the methods in this table is *without* test-time augmentation. (Right) Results on ICCV-2021 SemKITTI-DVPS challenge. * indicates post-challenge submission.

Method	k = 1	k = 2	k = 3	k = 4	VPQ
VPSNet [21]	65.0	57.6	54.4	52.8	57.5
SiamTrack [63]	64.6	57.6	54.2	52.7	57.3
ViP-Deeplab [43]	69.2	62.3	59.2	57.0	61.9
Ours (ResNet50)	65.4	58.6	55.4	53.3	58.2
Ours (Swin-b)	70.8	63.1	59.5	56.8	62.3

Method	DSTQ
rl-lab	54.8
yang26	55.6
Vip-Deeplab	63.3
PolyphonicFormer	63.6
PolyphonicFormer*	64.6

Comparison on DVPQ. As in Table 1, we compare our proposed Polyphonic-Former (with Swin-B backbone) with previous work ViP-Deeplab [43], and Poly-phonicFormer outperforms ViP-Deeplab on both datasets. On Cityscapes-DVPS dataset, the proposed PolyphonicFormer / ViP-Deeplab has ~1675 GFLOPs / ~9451 GFLOPs, respectively. And on SemKITTI-DVPS dataset, Polyphonic-Former / ViP-Deeplab has ~402 GFLOPs / ~2267 GFLOPs, respectively. Note that we do not do the experiments on the much larger WR-41 backbone [5], which is the backbone used in ViP-Deeplab [43], due to the limitation of computational resources. We also do not apply *test-time augmentation* and *semi-supervised learning* (both proved to be effective in [43]) for simplicity.

4.2 Ablation Studies and Analysis

(a) Effect of Unified Framework. We evaluate the effect of the unified framework, and the results can be found in Table 3a. In Table 3a, **Depth** refers to the dense prediction baseline of depth estimation. **Panoptic** refers to the panoptic segmentation baseline via query learning, i.e., panoptic path only design in Fig. 2. **Hybrid** means that PolyphonicFormer removes the instance-level depth prediction scheme (**Ins** in the table) but only contains the initial dense prediction head. As shown in the table, although the single-task baselines are strong for multi-task methods, our method still improves beyond two single-task baselines on both depth and panoptic segmentation via query learning. The performance enhancement on depth estimation from **Hybrid** to **PolyphonicFormer** indicates the effectiveness of instance-level depth estimation scheme. We also notice that the performance on panoptic segmentation increased from **Panoptic** to **Hybrid**, and we think it may be because depth supervision at least does not affect and may have some benefits on segmentation in our framework.

Table 3. Ablation studies on PolyphonicFormer. **N/A** indicates **"not applicable"**, and **w/o** indicates **"without"**. "↑" indicates higher is better, and "↓" indicates lower is better. Please refer to each paragraph for the description of the abbreviations and results analysis. All experiments use ResNet-50 backbone if no further description.

Method	Depth	Panoptic	Ins	PQ ↑	abs rel ↓
ViP-Deeplab [43]	✓	✓	-	60.6	0.112
Depth	✓	-	-	N/A	0.084
Panoptic	-	✓	-	63.7	N/A
Hybrid (ours)	✓	✓	-	65.1	0.089
PolyphonicFormer (ours)	✓	✓	✓	65.2	0.080

(a)

L_{depth}	PQ ↑	abs rel ↓
0.1	65.4	0.101
1.0	65.3	0.089
5.0	65.2	0.080
10	65.4	0.079

(b)

Method	PQ ↑	abs rel ↓
PolyphonicFormer	65.2	0.080
w/o Query Linking	64.8	0.088
w/o Dense Init	63.2	0.094
w/o Both	63.0	0.104

(c)

Method	PQ ↑	abs rel ↓
P	65.2	0.080
B	63.8	0.087
A	65.3	0.081

(d)

Method	DSTQ ↑	AQ ↑
PolyphonicFormer + DeepSort [62]	51.8	25.9
PolyphonicFormer + Unitrack [59]	49.3	22.5
PolyphonicFormer + QuasiDense [38]	63.6	46.2

(e)

Stages	PQ ↑	abs rel ↓
1	64.1	0.081
2	64.6	0.081
3	65.2	0.080

(f)

(b) Robustness of PolyphonicFormer. We modify the depth loss weight to evaluate the robustness of setting different depth loss weights. We set the depth loss weights from 0.1, 1, to 5 and 10. The results are shown in Table 3b. We found that with different depth loss weights, the PQ results do not change drastically. The phenomenon is different from ViP-Deeplab [43] where the depth estimation and panoptic segmentation are with two separate heads and sensitive to the loss choices. We speculate that it is the unified framework that makes two different tasks "polyphonic" instead of battling with each other.

(c) Ablation Study on Panoptic Depth Interaction. We perform ablation study on panoptic depth interaction. As shown in Table 3c, we do experiments on the original settings along with dismissing the "Query Linking" and "Dense Init" (Dense Depth Initialization). "Dense Depth Initialization" is a strategy to initialize the depth queries. We empirically found that instead of initializing the depth queries randomly, initializing it with the queries at the initial stage of depth path is with a better performance. We also found that the "Query Linking" module is a simple but effective module to boost the mutual benefit.

(d) Effect of Query Linking Module Design. We have tried different forms of query linking module design. In Table 3d, "**P**" refers to the current PolyphonicFormer design, which simply uses an addition from the panoptic queries to the depth queries. We try to replace the current design to "**B**", a bidirectional query linking module that links queries not only from panoptic to depth but also from depth to panoptic. We found that the information from depth queries may not be that helpful to panoptic queries. We also try to apply a more advanced query linking module, for instance, a self-attention module to fuse panoptic queries and depth queries ("**A**" in the table). The results may indicate that the query linking itself is more important than the linking module design choice. So, we would like to keep it simple and use the current query linking design, an **ADD** module, to propagate the semantic context to the geometry context.

Fig. 3. Visualizations of PolyphonicFormer on Cityscapes-DVPS and SemKITTI-DVPS. From top to down: input image, temporally consistent panoptic segmentation prediction, and monocular depth prediction. The red box is a failure case example. (Color figure online)

(e) Ablation Study on Tracking Head Design. The DVPQ [43] does not have an explicit tracking quality metric, so we apply Association Quality (AQ) in DSTQ metric [61] for tracking head evaluation. To alleviate the deviation of tracking quality caused by the mask prediction's inaccuracy, we choose to use Swin-B backbone [34] here. As demonstrated in Table 3e, we explore three different tracking methods including DeepSort [62], Unitrack [59] and Quansi-Dense [38]. We found the QuansiDense tracker works best and is chosen as the final tracking head. The QuansiDense tracker is an online tracker and only uses appearance embeddings. For the fair comparison with ViP-Deeplab [43], we do not explore the geometry information for tracking in the current framework.

(f) Ablation Study on Iterative Rounds. The PolyphonicFormer performs in an iterative manner. We carry out the ablation study on the choice of iterative stages. We perform studies from 1 to 3 stages to study the effectiveness of iterative design. The results can be found in Table 3f. With more iterative rounds, as we expected, the instance-level information from the features could be more used to refine the query to predict more accurate mask and depth results. We have also tried to use more iterative rounds and do not found salient performance enhancement, so we choose to set the number of stages to 3 following [73].

4.3 Visualization and Limitation Analysis

Visualization and Analysis. We do visualization analysis on the two DVPS datasets. As shown in Fig. 3, the PolyphonicFormer can predict frame-consistent panoptic segmentation along with depth in a unified manner. In the panoptic segmentation map, things with the same color are a single identity over the different frames. Figure 4 shows that the depth estimation task could benefit from the polyphonic design. We take the patch cropped from the depth map (bottom) as an example. The dense prediction neural network has an uncertainty on the boundary and tend to predict vague results. Instead, our PolyphonicFormer can clearly distinguish the boundary of the car and thus predicts a depth map with a clearer boundary. Then we measure the depth-aware capability of the PolyphonicFormer and compare it with the traditional dense depth estimation. Specifically, we verify the depth prediction accuracy of each instance. We consider each instance as **depth awareness** when less than a specific proportion (10%) of pixels with absolute relative errors in depth estimation exceeds a certain threshold (25%). The thresholds here follow the design of DQ. Simply combination of depth estimation and panoptic segmentation (similar structure as

Fig. 4. The depth estimation results of the traditional dense depth estimation (middle) and PolyphonicFormer (right). For the small objects, the proposed unified framework could successfully distinguish the boundary for enhancing depth results.

in [43]) leads to 5,851 depth-aware instances out of 7,998 (73.2%) instances in total, while the PolyphonicFormer achieves 6,119 out of 7,998 (76.5%) results on the Cityscapes-DVPS validation set. The depth-aware capability of PolyphonicFormer is consistent with the visualization results and demonstrates the effectiveness of the unified framework for the DVPS task.

Limitation and Future Work. As shown in Fig. 3, the tracking head may fail when handling extreme occlusion cases (e.g. the car in the red box). This is because PolyphonicFormer mainly performs tracking with appearance embeddings like the previous work. When applying PolyphonicFormer directly to safety-critical tasks like autonomous driving, the failure cases may cause accidents. The reliability needs further consideration and is potentially future work.

5   Conclusion

In this paper, we explore the relationship between semantics and geometry and build PolyphonicFormer for joint modeling panoptic segmentation and depth estimation. Our key insight is to unify all scene queries (thing, stuff) and depth queries into one framework. Based on our experiments, the PolyphonicFormer enhances the robustness towards panoptic segmentation as well as improves the performance of depth estimation. The proposed PolyphonicFormer achieves state-of-the-art results on both Cityscapes-DVPS and SemKITTI-DVPS datasets, and outperforms other methods on the SemKITTI-DVPS challenge. We hope PolyphonicFormer could serve as a good baseline in the DVPS task.

Acknowledgments. This work was supported by the National Natural Science Foundation of China under Grants 62122060 and 62076188, and the Special Fund of Hubei Luojia Laboratory under Grant 220100014. The numerical calculations in this work had been supported by the supercomputing system in the Supercomputing Center of Wuhan University. This research is also supported by the National Key Research and Development Program of China under Grant No.2020YFB2103402.

References

1. Behley, J., Garbade, M., Milioto, A., Quenzel, J., Behnke, S., Stachniss, C., Gall, J.: SemanticKITTI: A Dataset for Semantic Scene Understanding of LiDAR Sequences. In: ICCV (2019)
2. Bertasius, G., Torresani, L.: Classifying, segmenting, and tracking object instances in video with mask propagation. In: CVPR (2020)
3. Carion, N., Massa, F., Synnaeve, G., Usunier, N., Kirillov, A., Zagoruyko, S.: End-to-end object detection with transformers. In: ECCV (2020)
4. Casser, V., Pirk, S., Mahjourian, R., Angelova, A.: Depth prediction without the sensors: leveraging structure for unsupervised learning from monocular videos. In: AAAI (2019)
5. Chen, L.C., et al.: Naive-Student: leveraging semi-supervised learning in video sequences for urban scene segmentation. In: ECCV (2020)

6. Chen, P.Y., Liu, A.H., Liu, Y.C., Wang, Y.C.F.: Towards scene understanding: unsupervised monocular depth estimation with semantic-aware representation. In: CVPR (2019)
7. Chen, Y., et al.: BANet: bidirectional aggregation network with occlusion handling for panoptic segmentation. In: CVPR (2020)
8. Cheng, B., et al.: Panoptic-DeepLab: a simple, strong, and fast baseline for bottom-up panoptic segmentation. In: CVPR (2020)
9. Cheng, B., Schwing, A.G., Kirillov, A.: Per-pixel classification is not all you need for semantic segmentation. In: NeurIPS (2021)
10. Cordts, M., et al.: The cityscapes dataset for semantic urban scene understanding. In: CVPR (2016)
11. Dosovitskiy, A., et al.: An image is worth 16×16 words: transformers for image recognition at scale. In: ICLR (2020)
12. Eigen, D., Puhrsch, C., Fergus, R.: Depth map prediction from a single image using a multi-scale deep network. NIPS (2014)
13. Fang, Y., et al.: Instances as queries. In: ICCV (2021)
14. Gao, N., et al.: SSAP: single-shot instance segmentation with affinity pyramid. In: ICCV (2019)
15. Geiger, A., Lenz, P., Urtasun, R.: Are we ready for autonomous driving? the KITTI vision benchmark suite. In: CVPR (2012)
16. Godard, C., Mac Aodha, O., Firman, M., Brostow, G.J.: Digging into self-supervised monocular depth estimation. In: ICCV (2019)
17. Guizilini, V., Hou, R., Li, J., Ambrus, R., Gaidon, A.: Semantically-guided representation learning for self-supervised monocular depth. In: ICLR (2019)
18. He, K., Gkioxari, G., Dollár, P., Girshick, R.: Mask R-CNN. In: ICCV (2017)
19. He, K., Zhang, X., Ren, S., Sun, J.: Deep residual learning for image recognition. In: CVPR (2016)
20. Hou, R., et al.: Real-time panoptic segmentation from dense detections. In: CVPR (2020)
21. Kim, D., Woo, S., Lee, J.Y., Kweon, I.S.: Video panoptic segmentation. In: CVPR (2020)
22. Kirillov, A., Girshick, R., He, K., Dollár, P.: Panoptic feature pyramid networks. In: CVPR (2019)
23. Kirillov, A., He, K., Girshick, R., Rother, C., Dollár, P.: Panoptic segmentation. In: CVPR (2019)
24. Klingner, M., Termöhlen, J.A., Mikolajczyk, J., Fingscheidt, T.: Self-supervised monocular depth estimation: Solving the dynamic object problem by semantic guidance. In: ECCV (2020)
25. Lee, S., Im, S., Lin, S., Kweon, I.S.: Learning monocular depth in dynamic scenes via instance-aware projection consistency. In: AAAI (2021)
26. Li, J., Raventos, A., Bhargava, A., Tagawa, T., Gaidon, A.: Learning to fuse things and stuff. arXiv:1812.01192 (2018)
27. Li, R., et al.: Semantic-guided representation enhancement for self-supervised monocular trained depth estimation. arXiv preprint arXiv:2012.08048 (2020)
28. Li, X., Xu, S., Yang, Y., Cheng, G., Tong, Y., Tao, D.: Panoptic-PartFormer: learning a unified model for panoptic part segmentation. In: ECCV (2022)
29. Li, X., et al.: Video K-Net: a simple, strong, and unified baseline for video segmentation. In: CVPR (2022)
30. Li, Y., et al.: Attention-guided unified network for panoptic segmentation. In: CVPR (2019)

31. Li, Y., et al.: Fully convolutional networks for panoptic segmentation. CVPR (2021)
32. Li, Z., et al.: Panoptic SegFormer. arXiv preprint arXiv:2109.03814 (2021)
33. Lin, T.Y., Goyal, P., Girshick, R., He, K., Dollár, P.: Focal loss for dense object detection. In: ICCV (2017)
34. Liu, Z., et al.: Swin transformer: hierarchical vision transformer using shifted windows. In: ICCV (2021)
35. Neuhold, G., Ollmann, T., Rota Bulo, S., Kontschieder, P.: The Mapillary vistas dataset for semantic understanding of street scenes. In: ICCV (2017)
36. Ochs, M., Kretz, A., Mester, R.: SDNet: semantically guided depth estimation network. arXiv preprint arXiv:1907.10659 (2019)
37. Oh, S.W., Lee, J.Y., Xu, N., Kim, S.J.: Video object segmentation using space-time memory networks. In: ICCV (2019)
38. Pang, J., et al.: Quasi-dense similarity learning for multiple object tracking. In: CVPR (2021)
39. Paszke, A., et al.: PyTorch: An imperative style, high-performance deep learning library. In: NeurIPS (2019)
40. Perazzi, F., Pont-Tuset, J., McWilliams, B., Van Gool, L., Gross, M., Sorkine-Hornung, A.: A benchmark dataset and evaluation methodology for video object segmentation. In: CVPR (2016)
41. Porzi, L., Bulo, S.R., Colovic, A., Kontschieder, P.: Seamless scene segmentation. In: CVPR (2019)
42. Qiao, S., Chen, L.C., Yuille, A.: DetectoRS: detecting objects with recursive feature pyramid and switchable atrous convolution. In: CVPR (2021)
43. Qiao, S., Zhu, Y., Adam, H., Yuille, A., Chen, L.C.: ViP-DeepLab: learning visual perception with depth-aware video panoptic segmentation. In: CVPR (2021)
44. Ramirez, P.Z., Poggi, M., Tosi, F., Mattoccia, S., Di Stefano, L.: Geometry meets semantics for semi-supervised monocular depth estimation. In: ACCV (2018)
45. Saeedan, F., Roth, S.: Boosting monocular depth with panoptic segmentation maps. In: WACV (2021)
46. Saxena, A., Chung, S.H., Ng, A.Y., et al.: Learning depth from single monocular images. In: NIPS (2005)
47. Sun, P., et al.: TransTrack: multiple-object tracking with transformer. arXiv preprint arXiv: 2012.15460 (2020)
48. Sun, P., et al.: Sparse R-CNN: end-to-end object detection with learnable proposals. In: CVPR (2021)
49. Touvron, H., Cord, M., Douze, M., Massa, F., Sablayrolles, A., Jégou, H.: Training data-efficient image transformers & distillation through attention. In: ICML (2021)
50. Vaswani, A., et al.: Attention is all you need. In: NIPS (2017)
51. Voigtlaender, P., Chai, Y., Schroff, F., Adam, H., Leibe, B., Chen, L.C.: FEELVOS: fast end-to-end embedding learning for video object segmentation. In: CVPR (2019)
52. Voigtlaender, P., et al.: MOTS: multi-object tracking and segmentation. In: CVPR (2019)
53. Wang, H., Zhu, Y., Adam, H., Yuille, A., Chen, L.C.: MaX-DeepLab: end-to-end panoptic segmentation with mask transformers. In: CVPR (2021)
54. Wang, H., Zhu, Y., Green, B., Adam, H., Yuille, A., Chen, L.C.: Axial-DeepLab: stand-alone axial-attention for panoptic segmentation. In: ECCV (2020)
55. Wang, L., Zhang, J., Wang, O., Lin, Z., Lu, H.: SDC-depth: semantic divide-and-conquer network for monocular depth estimation. In: CVPR (2020)
56. Wang, W., Cao, Y., Zhang, J., Tao, D.: FP-DETR: detection transformer advanced by fully pre-training. In: ICLR (2021)

57. Wang, W., Zhang, J., Cao, Y., Shen, Y., Tao, D.: Towards data-efficient detection transformers. In: ECCV (2022)
58. Wang, Y., et al.: End-to-end video instance segmentation with transformers. In: CVPR (2021)
59. Wang, Z., Zhao, H., Li, Y.L., Wang, S., Torr, P.H., Bertinetto, L.: Do different tracking tasks require different appearance models? In: NeurIPS (2021)
60. Wang, Z., Zheng, L., Liu, Y., Li, Y., Wang, S.: Towards real-time multi-object tracking. In: ECCV (2020)
61. Weber, M., et al.: STEP: segmenting and tracking every pixel. In: NeurIPS (2021)
62. Wojke, N., Bewley, A., Paulus, D.: Simple online and realtime tracking with a deep association metric. In: ICIP (2017)
63. Woo, S., Kim, D., Lee, J.Y., Kweon, I.S.: Learning to associate every segment for video panoptic segmentation. In: CVPR (2021)
64. Wu, Y., Zhang, G., Xu, H., Liang, X., Lin, L.: Auto-Panoptic: cooperative multi-component architecture search for panoptic segmentation. In: NeurIPS (2020)
65. Xiong, Y., et al.: UPSNet: a unified panoptic segmentation network. In: CVPR (2019)
66. Xu, S., Li, X., Wang, J., Cheng, G., Tong, Y., Tao, D.: Fashionformer: a simple, effective and unified baseline for human fashion segmentation and recognition. In: ECCV (2022)
67. Xu, Y., Zhang, Q., Zhang, J., Tao, D.: ViTAE: vision transformer advanced by exploring intrinsic inductive bias. In: NeurIPS (2021)
68. Yang, L., Fan, Y., Xu, N.: Video instance segmentation. In: ICCV (2019)
69. Yang, T.J., et al.: DeeperLab: single-shot image parser. arXiv:1902.05093 (2019)
70. Yang, Y., Li, H., Li, X., Zhao, Q., Wu, J., Lin, Z.: SogNet: scene overlap graph network for panoptic segmentation. In: AAAI (2020)
71. Zhang, J., et al.: EatFormer: improving vision transformer inspired by evolutionary algorithm. arXiv preprint arXiv:2206.09325 (2022)
72. Zhang, Q., Xu, Y., Zhang, J., Tao, D.: ViTAEv2: vision transformer advanced by exploring inductive bias for image recognition and beyond. arXiv preprint arXiv:2202.10108 (2022)
73. Zhang, W., Pang, J., Chen, K., Loy, C.C.: K-NET: towards unified image segmentation. In: NeurIPS (2021)
74. Zhou, Q., et al.: TransVOD: end-to-end video object detection with spatial-temporal transformers. arXiv preprint arXiv:2201.05047 (2022)
75. Zhou, X., Koltun, V., Krähenbühl, P.: Tracking objects as points. In: ECCV (2020)
76. Zhu, X., Xiong, Y., Dai, J., Yuan, L., Wei, Y.: Deep feature flow for video recognition. In: CVPR (2017)

SQN: Weakly-Supervised Semantic Segmentation of Large-Scale 3D Point Clouds

Qingyong Hu[1] , Bo Yang[2(✉)] , Guangchi Fang[3], Yulan Guo[3] ,
Aleš Leonardis[4] , Niki Trigoni[1] , and Andrew Markham[1]

[1] University of Oxford, Oxford, UK
qingyong.hu@cs.ox.ac.uk
[2] vLAR Group, The Hong Kong Polytechnic University, Hung Hom, Hong Kong
bo.yang@polyu.edu.hk
[3] Sun Yat-sen University, Guangzhou, China
[4] Huawei Noah's Ark Lab, Birmingham, UK
https://github.com/QingyongHu/SQN

Abstract. Labelling point clouds fully is highly time-consuming and costly. As larger point cloud datasets with billions of points become more common, we ask whether the full annotation is even necessary, demonstrating that existing baselines designed under a fully annotated assumption only degrade slightly even when faced with 1% random point annotations. However, beyond this point, *e.g.*, at 0.1% annotations, segmentation accuracy is unacceptably low. We observe that, as point clouds are samples of the 3D world, the distribution of points in a local neighbourhood is relatively homogeneous, exhibiting strong semantic similarity. Motivated by this, we propose a new weak supervision method to implicitly augment highly sparse supervision signals. Extensive experiments demonstrate the proposed Semantic Query Network (SQN) achieves promising performance on seven large-scale open datasets under weak supervision schemes, while requiring only 0.1% randomly annotated points for training, greatly reducing annotation cost and effort.

Keywords: Semantic query · Weak supervision · Large-scale point clouds

1 Introduction

Learning precise semantic meanings of large-scale point clouds is crucial for intelligent machines to truly understand complex 3D scenes in the real world. This is a key enabler for autonomous vehicles, augmented reality devices, *etc.*, to quickly interpret the surrounding environment for better navigation and planning.

Supplementary Information The online version contains supplementary material available at https://doi.org/10.1007/978-3-031-19812-0_35.

Raw Point Clouds   Ground Truth   RandLA-Net   Our SQN
                                    trained with 100% labels   trained with 0.1% labels

■ floor ■ wall ■ door ■ chair ■ board ■ bookcase ■ table ■ clutter

Fig. 1. Qualitative results of RandLA-Net [24] and our SQN on the S3DIS dataset. Trained with only 0.1% annotations, SQN achieves comparable or even better results than the fully-supervised RandLA-Net. Red bounding boxes highlight the superior segmentation accuracy of our SQN. (Color figure online)

With the availability of large amounts of labeled 3D data for fully-supervised learning, the task of 3D semantic segmentation has made significant progress in the past four years. Following the seminal works PointNet [46] and SparseConv [16], a series of sophisticated neural architectures [10,11,24,34,38,47,66,103] have been proposed in the literature, greatly improving the accuracy and efficiency of semantic estimation on raw point clouds. The performance of these fully-supervised methods can be further boosted with the aid of self-supervised pre-training representation learning as seen in recent studies [7,36,64,73,85,96]. The success of these approaches primarily relies on densely annotated per-point semantic labels to train the deep neural networks. However, it is extremely costly to fully annotate 3D point clouds due to the unordered, unstructured, and non-uniform data format (*e.g.*, over 1700 person-hours to annotate a typical dataset [3] and around 22.3 min for a single indoor scene (5 m × 5 m × 2 m) [14]). In fact, for very large-scale scenarios *e.g.*, an entire city, it becomes infeasible to manually label every point in practice.

Inspired by the success of weakly-supervised learning techniques in 2D images, a few recent works have started to tackle 3D semantic segmentation using fewer point labels to train neural networks. These methods can be generally divided into five categories: 1) Using 2D image labels for training as in [72,102]; 2) Using fewer 3D labels with gradient approximation/supervision propagation/perturbation consistency [75,79,87,94]; 3) Generating pseudo 3D labels from limited indirect annotations [60,78]; 4) Using superpoint annotations from over-segmentation [9,37,60], and 5) Contrastive pretraining followed by fine-tuning with fewer 3D labels [22,85,97]. Although they achieve encouraging results on multiple datasets, there are a number of limitations still to be resolved.

Firstly, existing approaches usually use custom methods to annotate different amounts of data (*e.g.*, 10%/5%/1% of raw points or superpoints) for training. It is thus unclear what proportion of raw points should be annotated and how, making fair comparison impossible. **Secondly**, to fully utilize the sparse annotations, existing weak-labelling pipelines usually involve multiple stages including careful data augmentation, self-pretraining, fine-tuning, and/or post-processing such as the use of dense CRF [28]. As a consequence, it tends to be more difficult to tune the parameters and deploy them in practical applications, compared with the standard end-to-end training scheme. **Thirdly**, these techniques do not adequately consider the strong local semantic homogeneity of point neighbors in large-scale point clouds, or do so ineffectively, resulting in the limited, yet valuable, annotations being under-exploited.

Motivated by these issues, we propose a new paradigm for weakly-supervised semantic segmentation on large-scale point clouds, addressing the above shortcomings. In particular, we first explore weak-supervision schemes purely based on existing fully-supervised methods, and then introduce an effective approach to learn accurate semantics given extremely limited point annotations.

To explore weak supervision schemes, we take into account two key questions: 1) *whether, and how, do existing fully-supervised methods deteriorate given different amounts of annotated data for training?* 2) *given fewer and fewer labels, where the weakly supervised regime actually begins?* Fundamentally, by doing so, we aim to explore the limit of current fully-supervised methods. This allows us to draw insights about the use of mature architectures when addressing this challenging task, instead of naïvely borrowing off-the-shelf techniques developed in 2D images [61]. Surprisingly, we find that the accuracy of existing fully-supervised baselines drops only slightly when faced with 1% of random labelled points. However, beyond this point, *e.g.*, 0.1% of the full annotations, the performance degrades rapidly.

With this insight, we propose a novel yet simple **S**emantic **Q**uery **N**etwork, named **SQN**, for semantic segmentation given as few as 0.1% labeled points for training. Our SQN firstly encodes the entire raw point cloud into a set of hierarchical latent representations via an existing feature extractor, and then takes an arbitrary 3D point position as input to query a subset of latent representations within a local neighborhood. These queried representations are summarized into a compact vector and then fed into a series of multilayer perceptrons (MLPs) to predict the final semantic label. Fundamentally, our SQN explicitly and effectively considers the semantic similarity between neighboring 3D points, allowing the extremely sparse training signals to be back-propagated to a much wider spatial region, thereby achieving superior performance under weak supervision.

Overall, this paper takes a step to bridge the gap between the highly successful fully-supervised methods to the emerging weakly-supervised schemes, in an attempt to reduce the time and labour cost of point-cloud annotation. However, unlike the existing weak-supervision methods, our SQN does not require any self-supervised pretraining, hand-crafted constraints, or complicated post-processing steps, whilst obtaining close to fully-supervised accuracy using as few as 0.1% training labels on multiple large-scale open datasets. Remarkably, for similar accuracy, we find that labelling costs (time) can be reduced up to 98% according to our empirical evaluation in Appendix. Figure 1 shows the qualitative results of our method. Our key contributions are:

- We propose a new weakly supervised method that leverages a point neighbourhood query to fully utilize the sparse training signals.
- We observe that existing fully-supervised methods degrade slowly until 1% point annotations, showing that dense labelling is redundant and unnecessary.
- We demonstrate a significant improvement over baselines in our benchmark, and surpass the state-of-the-art weak-supervision methods by large margins.

2   Related Work

2.1   Learning with Full Supervision

End-to-End Full Supervision. With the availability of densely-annotated point cloud datasets [2,3,18,23,52,58,68], deep learning-based approaches have achieved unprecedented development in semantic segmentation in recent years. The majority of existing approaches follow the standard end-to-end training strategy. They can be roughly divided into three categories according to the representation of 3D point clouds [17]: **1) Voxel-based methods.** They [10,16,42,88] usually voxelize the irregular 3D point clouds into regular cubes [11,63], cylinders [103], or spheres [33]. **2) 2D Projection-based methods.** This pipeline projects the unstructured 3D points into 2D images through multiview [4,29], bird-eye-view [1], or spherical projections [13,43,80,81,86], and then uses the mature 2D architectures [21,39] for semantic learning. **3) Point-based methods.** These methods [24,34,46,47,66,83,100] directly operate on raw point clouds using shared MLPs. Hybrid representations, such as point-voxel representation [38,49,59], 2D-3D representation [26,92], are also studied.

Self-supervised Pretraining + Full Finetuning. Inspired by the success of self-supervised pre-training representation learning in 2D images [7,20], several recent studies [8,27,36,53,64,73,85,96] apply contrastive techniques for 3D semantic segmentation. These methods usually pretrain the networks on additional 3D source datasets to learn initial per-point representations via self-supervised contrastive losses, after which the networks are carefully finetuned on the target datasets with full labels. This noticeably improves the overall accuracy.

Although these methods have achieved remarkable results on existing datasets, they rely on a large amount of labeled data for training, which is costly and prohibitive in real applications. By contrast, this paper aims to learn semantics from a small fraction of annotations, which is cheaper and more realistic in practice.

2.2   Unsupervised Learning

Saudar and Sievers [53] learn the point semantics by recovering the correct voxel position of every 3D point after the point cloud is randomly shuffled. Sun et al. propose Canonical Capsules [57] to decompose point clouds into object parts and elements via self-canonicalization and auto-encoding. Although they have obtained promising results, they are limited to simple objects and cannot process the complex large-scale point clouds.

2.3   Learning with Weak Supervision

Limited Indirect Annotations. Instead of having point-level semantic annotations, only sub-cloud level or seg-level labels are available. Wei et al. [78] firstly train a classifier with sub-cloud labels, and then generate point-level pseudo labels using class activation mapping technique [101]. Tao et al. [60] present a grouping network to learn semantic and instance segmentation of 3D point clouds, with the seg-level labels generated by over-segmentation pre-processing. Ren et al. [48] present a multi-task learning framework for both semantic segmentation and 3D object detection with scene-level tags.

Limited Point Annotations. Given a small fraction of points with accurate semantic labels for training, Xu and Lee [87] propose a weakly supervised point cloud segmentation method by approximating gradients and using handcrafted spatial and color smoothness constraints. Zhang et al. [94] explicitly added a perturbed branch, and achieve weakly-supervised learning on 3D point clouds by enforcing predictive consistency. Shi et al. [55] further investigate label-efficient learning by introducing a super-point-based active learning strategy. In addition, self-supervised pre-training methods [22,36,54,85,96,97] are also flexible to fine-tune networks on limited annotations. Our SQN is designed for limited point annotations which we believe has greater potential in practical applications. It does not require any pre-training, post-processing, or active labelling strategies, while achieving similar or even higher performance than the fully-supervised counterpart with only 0.1% randomly annotated points for training.

Fair Comparison with 1T1C [37]. In the interests of fair and reproducible comparison, we point out that a few published works claim state-of-the-art results yet make misleading assumptions. Specifically, 1T1C [37] reports impressive results in the paper. However, a deeper investigation of its official GitHub codebase reveals two serious issues:

– **Ground truth label leakage.** 1T1C [37] uses the ground truth instance segments as the super-voxel partition for training on ScanNet[1]. However, given the semantic label of 1 click on ground truth instance segments, the super-voxel semantic labels used by 1T1C are actually dense and full ground truth semantic labels, rather than weak labels.
– **Misleading (over-exaggerated) labeling ratios.** 1T1C calculates its labeling ratio by using the number of labeled instances divided by the total number of raw points, resulting in a fantastically low labeling ratio (*e.g.*, 0.02%)[2]. A fairer method, as used in prior art [87,93,97], is to use the total number of labelled points (*i.e.*, to keep consistency) divided by the total number of points.

For these reasons, 1T1C [37] and its follow-up work PointMatch [84] can be regarded as almost full supervision (all instances are fully annotated) methods on ScanNet. Therefore, our method cannot directly compare with them on ScanNet.

---

[1] https://github.com/liuzhengzhe/One-Thing-One-Click/issues/13.
[2] https://github.com/liuzhengzhe/One-Thing-One-Click/issues/8.

3   Exploring Weak Supervision

As weakly-supervised 3D semantic segmentation is still in its infancy, there is no consensus about what are the sensible formulations of weak training signals, and what approach should be used to sparsely annotate a dataset such that a direct comparison is possible. We first explore this, then we investigate how existing fully supervised techniques perform under a weak labelling regime.

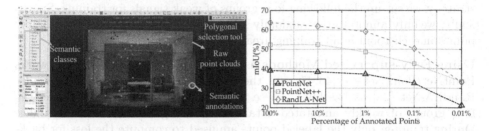

Fig. 2. Left: Illustration of the sparse annotation tool. Right: Degradation of three baselines in the *Area-5* of S3DIS [2] when decreasing proportions of points that are randomly annotated. (Logarithmic scale used in horizontal axis).

Weak Annotation Strategy: The fundamental objective of weakly-supervised segmentation is to obtain accurate estimations with as low as possible annotation cost, in terms of labeller time. However, it is non-trivial to compare the cost of different annotation methods in practice. Existing annotation options include 1) randomly annotating sparse point labels [87,93,94], 2) actively annotating sparse point labels [22,55] or region-wise labels [82], 3) annotating seg-level labels or superpoint labels [9,37,60] and 4) annotating sub-cloud labels [78]. All methods have merits. For the purpose of fair reproducibility, we opt for the random point annotation strategy, considering the practical simplicity of building such an annotation tool.

Annotation Tool: To verify the feasibility of random sparse annotations in practice, we develop a user-friendly labelling pipeline based on the off-the-shelf CloudCompare[3] software. Specifically, we first import raw 3D point clouds to the software and randomly downsample them to 10%/1%/0.1% of the total points for sparse annotation. Considering the sparsity of the remaining points, we explicitly enlarge the size of selected points and take the original full point clouds as a reference. As illustrated in left part of Fig. 2, we then use the standard labelling mode such as polygonal edition for point-wise annotating. (Details and video recordings of our annotation pipeline are supplied in the appendix).

Annotation Cost: With the developed annotation tool, it takes less than 2 min to annotate 0.1% of points of a standard room in the S3DIS dataset. For

---

[3] https://www.cloudcompare.org/.

comparison, it requires more than 20 min to fully annotate all points for the same room. Note that, the sparse annotation scheme is particularly suitable for large-scale 3D point clouds with billions of points. As detailed in the appendix, it only takes about 18 h to annotate 0.1% of the urban-scale SensatUrban dataset [23], while annotating all points requires more than 600 person-hours.

Experimental Settings: We choose the well-known S3DIS dataset [2] as the testbed. The Areas {1/2/3/4/6} are selected as the training point clouds, the Area 5 is fully annotated for testing only. With the random sparse annotation strategy, we set up the following four groups of weak signals for training. Specifically, we only annotate the randomly selected 10%/1%/0.1%/0.01% of the 3D points in each room in all training areas.

Using Fully-supervised Methods as Baselines. We select the seminal works PointNet/PointNet++ [46,47] and the recent large-scale-point-cloud friendly RandLA-Net [24] as baselines. These methods are end-to-end trained on the four groups of weakly annotated data without using any additional modules. During training, only the labeled points are used to compute the loss for back-propagation. In total, 12 models (3 models/group × 4 groups) are trained for evaluation on the full Area 5. Detailed results can be found in Appendix.

Results and Findings. Figure 2 shows the mIoU scores of all models for segmenting the total 13 classes. The results under full supervision (100% annotations for all training data) are included for comparison. It can be seen that:

- The performance of all baselines only decreases marginally (less than 4%) even though the proportion of point annotations drops significantly from 100% to 1%. This clearly shows that the dense annotations are actually unnecessary to obtain a comparable and favorable segmentation accuracy under the simple random annotation strategy.
- The performance of all baselines drops significantly once the annotated points are lower than 0.1%. This critical point indicates that keeping a certain amount of training signals is also essential for weak supervision.

Above all, we may conclude that for segmenting large-scale point clouds which are usually dominated by major classes and have numerous repeatable local patterns, it is desirable to develop weakly-supervised methods which have an excellent trade-off between annotation costs and estimation accuracy. With this motivation, we propose SQN which achieves close to fully-supervised accuracy using only 0.1% labels for training.

4   SQN

4.1   Overview

Given point clouds with sparse annotations, the fundamental challenge for weakly-supervised learning is how to fully utilize the sparse yet valuable training

signals to update the network parameters, such that more geometrically meaningful local patterns can be learned. To resolve this, we design a simple SQN
which consists of two major components: 1) a point local feature extractor to
learn diverse visual patterns; 2) a flexible point feature query network to collect
as many as possible relevant semantic features for weakly-supervised training.
As shown in Fig. 3, our two sub-networks are illustrated by the stacked blocks.

4.2 Point Local Feature Extractor

This component aims to extract local features for all points. As discussed in
Sect. 2.1, there are many excellent backbone networks that are able to extract
per-point features. In general, these networks stack multiple encoding layers
together with downsampling operations to extract hierarchical local features.
In this paper, we use the encoder of RandLA-Net [24] as our feature extractor thanks to its efficiency on large-scale point clouds. Note that SQN is not
restricted to any particular backbone network $e.g.$ as we demonstrate in the
Appendix with MinkowskiNet [11].

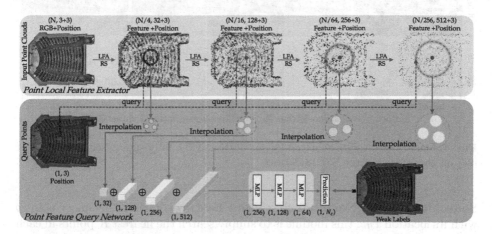

Fig. 3. The pipeline of our SQN at the training stage with weak supervision. We only
show one query point for simplicity.

As shown in the top block of Fig. 3, the encoder includes four layers of Local
Feature Aggregation (LFA) followed by a Random Sampling (RS) operation.
Details refer to RandLA-Net [24]. Given an input point cloud $\mathcal{P}$ with N points,
four levels of hierarchical point features are extracted after each encoding layer,
$i.e.$, 1) $\frac{N}{4} \times 32$, 2) $\frac{N}{16} \times 128$, 3) $\frac{N}{64} \times 256$, and 4) $\frac{N}{256} \times 512$. To facilitate the subsequent query network, the corresponding point location xyz are always preserved
for each hierarchical feature vector.

4.3   Point Feature Query Network

Given the extracted point features, this query network is designed to collect as many relevant features, to be trained using the available sparse signals. In particular, as shown in the bottom block of Fig. 3, it takes a specific 3D query point as input and then acquires a set of learned point features relevant to that point. Fundamentally, this is assumed that the query point shares similar semantic information with the collected point features, such that the training signals from the query points can be shared and back-propagated for the relevant points. The network consists of: 1) Searching Spatial Neighbouring Point Features, 2) Interpolating Query Point Features, 3) Inferring Query Point Semantics.

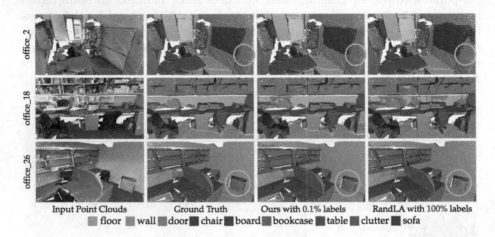

Input Point Clouds   Ground Truth   Ours with 0.1% labels   RandLA with 100% labels
■ floor ■ wall ■ door ■ chair ■ board ■ bookcase ■ table ■ clutter ■ sofa

Fig. 4. Qualitative results achieved by our SQN and the fully-supervised RandLA-Net [24] on the *Area-5* of the S3DIS dataset.

Searching Spatial Neighbouring Point Features. Given a 3D query point p with its location xyz, this module is to simply search the nearest K points in each of the previous 4-level encoded features, according to the point-wise Euclidean distance. For example, as to the first level of extracted point features, the most relevant K points are selected, acquiring the raw features $\{\boldsymbol{F}_p^1, \dots \boldsymbol{F}_p^K\}$.

Interpolating Query Point Features. For each level of features, the queried K vectors are compressed into a compact representation for the query point p. For simplicity, we apply the trilinear interpolation method to compute a feature vector for p, according to the Euclidean distance between p and each of K points. Eventually, four hierarchical feature vectors are concatenated together, representing all relevant point features from the entire 3D point cloud.

Inferring Query Point Semantics. After obtaining the unique and representative feature vector for the query point p, we feed it into a series of MLPs, directly inferring the point semantic category.

Overall, given a sparse number of annotated points, we query their neighbouring point features in parallel for training. This allows the valuable training signals to be back-propagated to a much wider spatial context. During testing, all 3D points are fed into the two sub-networks for semantic estimation. In fact, our simple query mechanism allows the network to infer the point semantic category from a significantly larger receptive field.

4.4 Implementation Details

The hyperparameter K is empirically set to 3 for semantic query in our framework and kept consistent for all experiments. Our SQN follows the dataset pre-processing used in RandLA-Net [24], and is trained end-to-end with 0.1% randomly annotated points. All experiments are conducted on a PC with an Intel Core™ i9-10900X CPU and an NVIDIA RTX Titan GPU. Note that, the proposed SQN framework allows flexible use of different backbone networks such as voxel-based MinkowskiNet [11], please refer to the appendix for more details.

Table 1. Quantitative results of different methods on the *Area-5* of S3DIS dataset. Mean IoU (mIoU, %), and per-class IoU (%) scores are reported. Bold represents the best result in weakly labelled settings and underlined represents the best under fully labelled settings. †As mentioned in Sect. 2.3, misleading labeling ratio is reported, and hence a direct comparison is not possible.

	Methods	mIoU(%)	Ceiling	Floor	Wall	Beam	Column	Window	Door	Table	Chair	Sofa	Bookcase	Board	Clutter
Full supervision	PointNet [46]	41.1	88.8	97.3	69.8	0.1	3.9	46.3	10.8	58.9	52.6	5.9	40.3	26.4	33.2
	PointCNN [34]	57.3	92.3	98.2	79.4	0.0	17.6	22.8	62.1	74.4	80.6	31.7	66.7	62.1	56.7
	SPGraph [31]	58.0	89.4	96.9	78.1	0.0	42.8	48.9	61.6	84.7	75.4	69.8	52.6	2.1	52.2
	SPH3D [33]	59.5	93.3	97.1	81.1	0.0	33.2	45.8	43.8	79.7	86.9	33.2	71.5	54.1	53.7
	PointWeb [99]	60.3	92.0	98.5	79.4	0.0	21.1	59.7	34.8	76.3	88.3	46.9	69.3	64.9	52.5
	RandLA-Net [24]	63.0	92.4	96.7	80.6	0.0	18.3	61.3	43.3	77.2	85.2	71.5	71.0	69.2	52.3
	KPConv rigid [66]	65.4	92.6	97.3	81.4	0.0	16.5	54.5	69.5	80.2	90.1	66.4	74.6	63.7	58.1
Limited superpoint labels†	1T1C (0.02%) [37]	50.1	-	-	-	-	-	-	-	-	-	-	-	-	-
	SSPC-Net (0.01%) [9]	51.5	-	-	-	-	-	-	-	-	-	-	-	-	-
Limited point-wise labels	Π Model (10%) [30]	46.3	91.8	97.1	73.8	0.0	5.1	42.0	19.6	67.2	66.7	47.9	19.1	30.6	41.3
	MT (10%) [61]	47.9	92.2	96.8	74.1	0.0	10.4	46.2	17.7	70.7	67.0	50.2	24.4	30.7	42.2
	Xu (10%) [87]	48.0	90.9	97.3	74.8	0.0	8.4	49.3	27.3	71.7	69.0	53.2	16.5	23.3	42.8
	Zhang et al. (1%) [93]	61.8	91.5	96.9	80.6	0.0	18.2	58.1	47.2	75.8	85.7	65.2	68.9	65.0	50.2
	PSD (1%) [94]	63.5	92.3	97.7	80.7	0.0	27.8	56.2	62.5	78.7	84.1	63.1	70.4	58.9	53.2
	Π Model (0.2%) [30]	44.3	89.1	97.0	71.5	0.0	3.6	43.2	27.4	63.1	62.1	43.7	14.7	24.0	36.7
	MT (0.2%) [61]	44.4	88.9	96.8	70.1	0.1	3.0	44.3	28.8	63.7	63.6	47.7	15.5	23.0	35.8
	Xu (0.2%) [87]	44.5	90.1	97.1	71.9	0.0	1.9	47.2	29.3	64.0	62.9	42.2	15.9	18.9	37.5
	RandLA-Net (0.1%)	52.9	89.9	95.9	75.3	0.0	7.5	52.4	26.5	62.2	74.5	49.1	60.2	49.3	45.1
	Ours (0.1%)	**61.4**	**91.7**	95.6	**78.7**	0.0	**24.2**	**55.9**	**63.1**	**70.5**	**83.1**	**60.7**	**67.8**	**56.1**	**50.6**

5 Experiments

5.1 Comparison with SOTA Approaches

We first evaluate the performance of our SQN on three commonly-used benchmarks including S3DIS [2], ScanNet [14] and Semantic3D [18]. Following [24], we use the Overall Accuracy (OA) and mean Intersection-over-Union (mIoU) as the main evaluation metrics.

Evaluation on S3DIS. Following [87], we report the results on Area-5 in Table 1. Note that, our SQN is compared with three groups of approaches: 1) Fully-supervised methods including SPGraph [31], KPConv [66] and RandLA-Net with 100% training labels; 2) Weakly supervised approaches that learn from limited superpoint annotations including 1T1C [37] and SSPC-Net [9]; 3) Weakly-supervised methods [30,61,87] that learning from limited annotations. We also list the proportion of annotations used for training.

Considering different backbones and different labelling ratios are used by existing methods, we focus on the comparison of our SQN and the baseline RandLA-Net, which under the same weakly-supervised settings. It can be seen that our SQN outperforms RandLA-Net by nearly 9% under the same 0.1% random sparse annotations. In particular, our SQN is also comparable to the fully-supervised RandLA-Net [24]. Figure 4 shows qualitative comparisons of RandLA-Net and our SQN.

Table 2. Quantitative results on Scan-Net (online test set). *MPRM [78] takes sub-cloud labels as supervision signal.

Settings	Methods	mIoU(%)
Full supervision	PointNet++ [47]	33.9
	SPLATNet [56]	39.3
	TangentConv [62]	43.8
	PointCNN [34]	45.8
	PointConv [83]	55.6
	SPH3D-GCN [33]	61.0
	KPConv [66]	68.4
	RandLA-Net [24]	64.5
Weak supervision	MPRM* [78]	41.1
	Zhang et al. (1%) [93]	51.1
	PSD (1%) [94]	54.7
	Ours (0.1%)	**56.9**

Table 3. Quantitative results on Semantic3D [18]. The scores are obtained from the recent publications.

	Methods	Semantic8		Reduced8	
		OA(%)	mIoU(%)	OA(%)	mIoU(%)
Full sup.	SnapNet [4]	91.0	67.4	88.6	59.1
	PointNet++ [47]	85.7	63.1	–	–
	ShellNet [98]	–	–	93.2	69.3
	GACNet [74]	–	–	91.9	70.8
	RGNet [67]	90.6	72.0	94.5	74.7
	SPG [31]	92.9	76.2	94.0	73.2
	KPConv [66]	–	–	92.9	74.6
	ConvPoint [6]	93.4	76.5	–	–
	WreathProdNet [76]	94.6	77.1	–	–
	RandLA-Net [24]	95.0	75.8	94.8	77.4
Weak sup.	Zhang et al. (1%) [93]	–	–	–	72.6
	PSD (1%) [94]	–	–	–	75.8
	Ours (0.1%)	**94.8**	**72.3**	**93.7**	**74.7**
	Ours (0.01%)	91.9	58.8	90.3	65.6

Evaluation on ScanNet. We report the quantitative results achieved by different approaches on the hidden test set in Table 2 . It can be seen that our SQN achieves higher mIoU scores with only 0.1% training labels, compared with MPRM [78] which is trained with sub-cloud labels, and Zhang et al. [93] and PSD [94] trained with 1% annotations. Considering that the actual training settings in the ScanNet Data-Efficient benchmark cannot be verified, hence we do not provide the comparison in this benchmark.

Evaluation on Semantic3D. Table 3 compares our SQN with a number of fully-supervised methods. It can be seen that our SQN trained with 0.1% labels achieves competitive performance with fully-supervised baselines on both *Semantic8* and *Reduced8* subsets. This clearly demonstrates the effectiveness of our semantic query framework, which takes full advantage of the limited annotations. Additionally, we also train our SQN with only 0.01% randomly annotated points, considering the extremely large amount of 3D points scanned. We can see that our SQN trained with 0.01% labels also achieves satisfactory accuracy, though there is space to be improved in the future.

5.2 Evaluation on Large-Scale 3D Benchmarks

To validate the versatility of our SQN, we further evaluate our SQN on four point cloud datasets with different density and quality, including SensatUrban [23], Toronto3D [58], DALES [68], and SemanticKITTI [3]. Note that, all existing weakly supervised approaches are only evaluated on the dataset with dense point clouds, and there are no results reported on these datasets. Therefore, we only compare our approach with existing fully-supervised methods in this section.

Table 4. Quantitative results of different approaches on the DALES [68], SensatUrban [23], Toronto3D [58] and SemanticKITTI [3].

Settings	Methods	DALES [68]		SensatUrban [23]			Toronto3D [58]		SemanticKITTI [3]
		OA(%)	mIoU(%)	OA(%)	mAcc (%)	mIoU(%)	OA(%)	mIoU(%)	mIoU(%)
Full supervision	PointNet [46]	–	–	80.8	30.3	23.7	–	–	14.6
	PointNet++ [47]	95.7	68.3	84.3	40.0	32.9	84.9	41.8	20.1
	PointCNN [34]	97.2	58.4	–	–	–	–	–	–
	TangentConv [62]	–	–	77.0	43.7	33.3	–	–	40.9
	ShellNet [98]	96.4	57.4	–	–	–	–	–	–
	DGCNN [77]	–	–	–	–	–	94.2	61.8	–
	SPG [31]	95.5	60.6	85.3	44.4	37.3	–	–	17.4
	SparseConv [16]	–	–	88.7	63.3	42.7	–	–	–
	KPConv [66]	97.8	81.1	93.2	63.8	57.6	95.4	69.1	58.1
	ConvPoint [5]	97.2	67.4	–	–	–	–	–	–
	RandLA-Net [24]	97.1	80.0	89.8	69.6	52.7	92.9	77.7	53.9
Weak supervision	**Ours (0.1%)**	97.0	72.0	**91.0**	**70.9**	**54.0**	96.7	**77.7**	50.8
	Ours (0.01%)	95.9	60.4	85.6	49.4	37.2	94.2	68.2	39.1

As shown in Table 4, the performance of our SQN is on par with the fully-supervised counterpart RandLA-Net on several datasets, whilst the model is only supplied with 0.1% labels for training. In particular, our SQN trained with 0.1% labels even outperforms the fully supervised RandLA-Net on the SensatUrban dataset. This shows the great potential of our method, especially for extremely large-scale point clouds with billions of points, where the manual annotation is unrealistic and impractical. The detailed results can be found in Appendix.

5.3 Ablation Study

To evaluate the effectiveness of each module in our framework, we conduct the following ablation studies. All ablated networks are trained on Areas{1/2/3/4/6} with 0.1% labels, and tested on the *Area-5* of the S3DIS dataset.

(1) Varying Number of Queried Neighbours. Intuitively, querying a larger neighborhood is more likely to achieve better results. However, an overly large neighborhood may include points with very different semantics, diminishing overall performance. To investigate the impact of the number of neighboring points

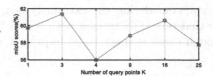

Fig. 5. The results of our SQN with different number of query points on the *Area-5* of the S3DIS dataset.

used in our semantic query, we conduct experiments by varying the number of neighboring points from 1 to 25. As shown in Fig. 5, the overall performance with differing numbers of neighboring points does not change significantly, showing that our simple query mechanism is robust to the size of the neighboring patch. Instead, the mixture of different feature levels plays a more important role (Table 5).

(2) Variants of Semantic Queries. The hierarchical point feature query mechanism is the major component of our SQN. To evaluate this component, we perform semantic query at different encoding layers. In particular, we train four additional models, each of which has a different combination of queried neighbouring point features. From Table 5 we can see that the segmentation performance drops significantly if we only collect the relevant point features at a single layer (*e.g.*, the first or the last layer), whilst querying at the last layer can achieve much better results than in the first layer. This is because the points in the last encoding layer are quite sparse but representative, aggregating a large number of neighboring points. Additionally, querying at different encoding layers and combining them is likely to achieve better segmentation results, mainly because it integrates different spatial levels of semantic content and considers more neighboring points.

Table 5. Ablations of different levels of semantic query.

Model	1st	2nd	3rd	4st	OA (%)	mIoU (%)
A	✓				48.66	22.89
B				✓	75.54	46.02
C	✓	✓			70.76	38.18
D	✓	✓	✓		82.37	54.21
E	✓	✓	✓	✓	**86.15**	**61.41**

Table 6. Sensitivity analysis of the proposed SQN on S3DIS dataset (*Area 5*) over 5 runs.

	OA (%)	mIoU (%)
Trial1	86.15	61.41
Trial2	85.63	59.24
Trial3	86.39	60.93
Trial4	86.32	59.40
Trial5	**86.40**	**61.56**
Mean	86.25	60.42
STD	0.32	0.93

(3) Varying Annotated Points. To verify the sensitivity of our SQN to different randomly annotated points, we train our models five times with exactly same architectures, *i.e.*, the only change is that different subsets of randomly selected 0.1% of points are labeled. The results are reported in Table 6. It can be seen that there are slight, but not significant, differences between different runs. This indicates that the proposed SQN is robust to the choice of randomly annotated points. We also notice that the major performance change lies in minor categories such as *door*, *sofa*, and *board*, showing that the underrepresented classes are more sensitive to weak annotation. Please refer to appendix for details.

(4) Varying Proportion of Annotated Points. We further examine the performance of SQN with differing amounts of annotated points. As shown in Table 7, the proposed SQN can achieve satisfactory segmentation performance when there are only 0.1% labels available, but the performance drops significantly when there are only 0.01% labeled points available, primarily because the supervision signal is too sparse and limited in this case. It is also interesting to see that our framework achieves slightly better mIoU performance when using 10% labels compared with full supervision. In particular, the performance on minority categories such as *column/window/door* has improved by 2%–5%. This implies that: 1) In a sense, the supervision signal is sufficient in this case; 2) Another way to address the critical issue of imbalanced class distribution may be to use a portion of training data (*i.e.*, weak supervision). This is an interesting direction for further research, and we leave it for future exploration.

Table 7. Quantitative results achieved by our SQN on *Area-5* of S3DIS under different amounts of labeled points.

Settings	Methods	mIoU(%)	Ceil.	Floor	Wall	Beam	Col.	Win.	Door	Chair	Table	Book.	Sofa	Board	Clutter
100%	SQN	63.73	92.76	96.92	**81.84**	0.00	25.93	50.53	65.88	79.52	85.31	55.66	**72.51**	65.78	55.85
10%	SQN	**64.67**	**93.04**	**97.45**	81.55	0.00	**28.01**	55.77	68.68	**80.11**	**87.67**	55.25	72.31	63.91	**57.02**
1%	SQN	63.65	92.03	96.41	81.32	0.00	21.42	53.71	**73.17**	77.80	85.95	56.72	69.91	66.57	52.49
0.1%	SQN	61.41	91.72	95.63	78.71	0.00	24.23	**55.89**	63.14	70.50	83.13	**60.67**	67.82	56.14	50.63
0.01%	SQN	45.30	89.16	93.49	71.28	0.00	4.14	34.67	41.02	54.88	66.85	25.68	55.37	12.80	39.57

(5) Extension to Region-wise Annotated Data. Beyond evaluating on randomly point-wise annotated datasets, we also extend our SQN on the region-wise sparsely labeled S3DIS dataset. Following [82], point clouds are firstly grouped into regions by unsupervised over-segmentation methods [45], and then a sparse number of regions are manually annotated through various active learning strategies [15,71,82]. As shown in Table 8, our SQN can consistently achieve better results than vanilla SPVCNN [59] and MinkowskiNet [11] under the same supervision signal (10 iterations of active selection), regardless of the active learning strategy used. This is likely because the SparseConv based methods [11,59] usually have larger models and more trainable parameters compared with our point-based lightweight SQN, thus naturally exhibiting a stronger demand and dependence for more supervision signals. On the other hand, this result further validates the effectiveness and superiority of our SQN under weak supervision.

614   Q. Hu et al.

Table 8. Quantitative results achieved by different methods on the region-wise labeled S3DIS dataset.

	SPVCNN [59]	MinkowskiUnet [11]	**SQN (Ours)**
Random	49.61	46.15	**60.19**
Softmax confidence [71]	51.05	45.45	**57.24**
Softmax margin [71]	50.80	44.33	**57.94**
Softmax entropy [71]	50.35	49.99	**57.98**
MC dropout [15]	50.39	49.94	**58.30**
ReDAL [82]	50.89	47.88	**54.24**

6 Conclusion

In this paper, we propose SQN, a conceptually simple and elegant framework to learn the semantics of large-scale point clouds, with as few as 0.1% supplied labels for training. We first point out the redundancy of dense 3D annotations through extensive experiments, and then propose an effective semantic query framework based on the assumption of semantic similarity of neighboring points in 3D space. The proposed SQN simply follows the concept of wider label propagation, but shows great potential for weakly-supervised semantic segmentation of large-scale point clouds. It would be interesting to extend this method for weakly-supervised instance segmentation, panoptic segmentation, and further integrate it into semantic surface reconstruction [70].

Acknowledgements. This work was partially supported by the National Natural Science Foundation of China (No. 61972435, U20A20185), China Scholarship Council (CSC) scholarship, and Huawei UK AI Fellowship. Qingyong Hu and Bo Yang were partially supported by Shenzhen Science and Technology Innovation Commission (JCYJ20210324120603011).

References

1. Aksoy, E.E., Baci, S., Cavdar, S.: Salsanet: fast road and vehicle segmentation in LiDAR point clouds for autonomous driving. In: IV, pp. 926–932 (2019)
2. Armeni, I., Sax, S., Zamir, A.R., Savarese, S.: Joint 2D–3D-semantic data for indoor scene understanding. In: ICCV (2017)
3. Behley, J., et al.: SemanticKITTI: a dataset for semantic scene understanding of LiDAR sequences. In: ICCV, pp. 9297–9307 (2019)
4. Boulch, A., Saux, B.L., Audebert, N.: Unstructured point cloud semantic labeling using deep segmentation networks. In: 3DOR, pp. 17–24 (2017)
5. Boulch, A.: Generalizing discrete convolutions for unstructured point clouds. In: 3DOR. pp. 71–78 (2019)
6. Boulch, A., Puy, G., Marlet, R.: Fkaconv: feature-kernel alignment for point cloud convolution. In: ACCV (2020)
7. Chen, T., Kornblith, S., Norouzi, M., Hinton, G.: A simple framework for contrastive learning of visual representations. In: ICML, pp. 1597–1607 (2020)

8. Chen, Y., et al.: Shape self-correction for unsupervised point cloud understanding. In: ICCV (2021)

9. Cheng, M., Hui, L., Xie, J., Yang, J.: Sspc-net: Semi-supervised semantic 3d point cloud segmentation network. arXiv preprint arXiv:2104.07861 (2021)

10. Cheng, R., Razani, R., Taghavi, E., Li, E., Liu, B.: 2–S3Net: attentive feature fusion with adaptive feature selection for sparse semantic segmentation network. arXiv preprint arXiv:2102.04530 (2021)

11. Choy, C., Gwak, J., Savarese, S.: 4D spatio-temporal convnets: Minkowski convolutional neural networks. In: CVPR, pp. 3075–3084 (2019)

12. Contreras, J., Denzler, J.: Edge-convolution point net for semantic segmentation of large-scale point clouds. In: IGARSS, pp. 5236–5239 (2019)

13. Cortinhal, T., Tzelepis, G., Aksoy, E.E.: SalsaNext: fast semantic segmentation of LiDAR point clouds for autonomous driving. In: ISVC (2020)

14. Dai, A., Chang, A.X., Savva, M., Halber, M., Funkhouser, T., Nießner, M.: ScanNet: richly-annotated 3D reconstructions of indoor scenes. In: CVPR, pp. 5828–5839 (2017)

15. Gal, Y., Ghahramani, Z.: Dropout as a bayesian approximation: representing model uncertainty in deep learning. In: ICML (2016)

16. Graham, B., Engelcke, M., van der Maaten, L.: 3D semantic segmentation with submanifold sparse convolutional networks. In: CVPR (2018)

17. Guo, Y., Wang, H., Hu, Q., Liu, H., Liu, L., Bennamoun, M.: Deep learning for 3D point clouds: a survey. IEEE TPAMI (2020)

18. Hackel, T., Savinov, N., Ladicky, L., Wegner, J.D., Schindler, K., Pollefeys, M.: Semantic3D.Net: a new large-scale point cloud classification benchmark. ISPRS (2017)

19. Hackel, T., Wegner, J.D., Schindler, K.: Fast semantic segmentation of 3D point clouds with strongly varying density. ISPRS **3**, 177–184 (2016)

20. He, K., Fan, H., Wu, Y., Xie, S., Girshick, R.: Momentum contrast for unsupervised visual representation learning. In: CVPR, pp. 9729–9738 (2020)

21. He, K., Zhang, X., Ren, S., Sun, J.: Deep residual learning for image recognition. In: CVPR (2016)

22. Hou, J., Graham, B., Nießner, M., Xie, S.: Exploring data-efficient 3D scene understanding with contrastive scene contexts. In: CVPR (2021)

23. Hu, Q., Yang, B., Khalid, S., Xiao, W., Trigoni, N., Markham, A.: Towards semantic segmentation of urban-scale 3D point clouds: A dataset, benchmarks and challenges. In: CVPR (2021)

24. Hu, Q., et al.: RandLA-Net: efficient semantic segmentation of large-scale point clouds. In: CVPR (2020)

25. Huang, Q., Wang, W., Neumann, U.: Recurrent slice networks for 3D segmentation of point clouds. In: ICCV (2018)

26. Jaritz, M., Gu, J., Su, H.: Multi-view pointnet for 3D scene understanding. In: ICCVW (2019)

27. Jiang, L., et al.: Guided point contrastive learning for semi-supervised point cloud semantic segmentation. In: ICCV (2021)

28. Krähenbühl, P., Koltun, V.: Efficient inference in fully connected CRFs with gaussian edge potentials. In: NeurIPS, pp. 109–117 (2011)

29. Kundu, A., Yin, X., Fathi, A., Ross, D., Brewington, B., Funkhouser, T., Pantofaru, C.: Virtual multi-view fusion for 3D semantic segmentation. In: Vedaldi, A., Bischof, H., Brox, T., Frahm, J.-M. (eds.) ECCV 2020. LNCS, vol. 12369, pp. 518–535. Springer, Cham (2020). https://doi.org/10.1007/978-3-030-58586-0_31

30. Laine, S., Aila, T.: Temporal ensembling for semi-supervised learning. In: ICLR (2017)
31. Landrieu, L., Simonovsky, M.: Large-scale point cloud semantic segmentation with superpoint graphs. In: CVPR, pp. 4558–4567 (2018)
32. Lei, H., Akhtar, N., Mian, A.: SegGCN: efficient 3D point cloud segmentation with fuzzy spherical kernel. In: CVPR (2020)
33. Lei, H., Akhtar, N., Mian, A.: Spherical kernel for efficient graph convolution on 3D point clouds. IEEE TPAMI (2020)
34. Li, Y., Bu, R., Sun, M., Wu, W., Di, X., Chen, B.: PointCNN: convolution on X-transformed points. In: NeurIPS (2018)
35. Li, Y., Ma, L., Zhong, Z., Cao, D., Li, J.: TGNet: geometric graph CNN on 3D point cloud segmentation. IEEE TGRS (2019)
36. Liu, Y., Yi, L., Zhang, S., Fan, Q., Funkhouser, T., Dong, H.: P4contrast: contrastive learning with pairs of point-pixel pairs for rgb-d scene understanding. arXiv preprint arXiv:2012.13089 (2020)
37. Liu, Z., Qi, X., Fu, C.W.: One thing one click: a self-training approach for weakly supervised 3d semantic segmentation. In: CVPR, pp. 1726–1736 (2021)
38. Liu, Z., Tang, H., Lin, Y., Han, S.: Point-voxel CNN for efficient 3D deep learning. In: NeurIPS (2019)
39. Long, J., Shelhamer, E., Darrell, T.: Fully convolutional networks for semantic segmentation. In: CVPR, pp. 3431–3440 (2015)
40. Ma, L., Li, Y., Li, J., Tan, W., Yu, Y., Chapman, M.A.: Multi-scale point-wise convolutional neural networks for 3D object segmentation from LiDAR point clouds in large-scale environments. IEEE TITS (2019)
41. Ma, Y., Guo, Y., Liu, H., Lei, Y., Wen, G.: Global context reasoning for semantic segmentation of 3D point clouds. WACV (2020)
42. Meng, H.Y., Gao, L., Lai, Y.K., Manocha, D.: VV-Net: voxel vae net with group convolutions for point cloud segmentation. In: ICCV (2019)
43. Milioto, A., Vizzo, I., Behley, J., Stachniss, C.: Rangenet++: Fast and accurate LiDAR semantic segmentation. In: IROS, pp. 4213–4220 (2019)
44. Montoya-Zegarra, J.A., Wegner, J.D., Ladický, L., Schindler, K.: Mind the gap: modeling local and global context in (road) networks. In: GCPR (2014)
45. Papon, J., Abramov, A., Schoeler, M., Worgotter, F.: Voxel cloud connectivity segmentation-supervoxels for point clouds. In: CVPR (2013)
46. Qi, C.R., Su, H., Mo, K., Guibas, L.J.: PointNet: deep learning on point sets for 3D classification and segmentation. In: CVPR, pp. 652–660 (2017)
47. Qi, C.R., Yi, L., Su, H., Guibas, L.J.: PointNet++: deep hierarchical feature learning on point sets in a metric space. In: NeurIPS (2017)
48. Ren, Z., Misra, I., Schwing, A.G., Girdhar, R.: 3d spatial recognition without spatially labeled 3d. In: Proceedings of the IEEE/CVF Conference on Computer Vision and Pattern Recognition, pp. 13204–13213 (2021)
49. Rethage, D., Wald, J., Sturm, J., Navab, N., Tombari, F.: Fully-convolutional point networks for large-scale point clouds. In: Ferrari, V., Hebert, M., Sminchisescu, C., Weiss, Y. (eds.) ECCV 2018. LNCS, vol. 11208, pp. 625–640. Springer, Cham (2018). https://doi.org/10.1007/978-3-030-01225-0_37
50. Rosu, R.A., Schütt, P., Quenzel, J., Behnke, S.: LatticeNet: fast point cloud segmentation using permutohedral lattices. In: RSS (2020)
51. Roynard, X., Deschaud, J.E., Goulette, F.: Classification of point cloud for road scene understanding with multiscale voxel deep network. In: PPNIV (2018)

52. Roynard, X., Deschaud, J.E., Goulette, F.: Paris-Lille-3D: a large and high-quality ground-truth urban point cloud dataset for automatic segmentation and classification. IJRR **37**(6), 545–557 (2018)
53. Sauder, J., Sievers, B.: Self-supervised deep learning on point clouds by reconstructing space. In: NeurIPS, pp. 12962–12972 (2019)
54. Sharma, C., Kaul, M.: Self-supervised few-shot learning on point clouds. In: NeurIPS (2020)
55. Shi, X., Xu, X., Chen, K., Cai, L., Foo, C.S., Jia, K.: Label-efficient point cloud semantic segmentation: An active learning approach. arXiv preprint arXiv:2101.06931 (2021)
56. Su, H., et al.: SPLATNet: sparse lattice networks for point cloud processing. In: CVPR, pp. 2530–2539 (2018)
57. Sun, W., et al.: Canonical capsules: unsupervised capsules in canonical pose. arXiv preprint arXiv:2012.04718 (2020)
58. Tan, W., Qin, N., Ma, L., Li, Y., Du, J., Cai, G., Yang, K., Li, J.: Toronto-3D: A large-scale mobile LiDAR dataset for semantic segmentation of urban roadways. In: CVPRW. pp. 202–203 (2020)
59. Tang, H., Liu, Z., Zhao, S., Lin, Y., Lin, J., Wang, H., Han, S.: Searching efficient 3D architectures with sparse point-voxel convolution. In: Vedaldi, A., Bischof, H., Brox, T., Frahm, J.-M. (eds.) ECCV 2020. LNCS, vol. 12373, pp. 685–702. Springer, Cham (2020). https://doi.org/10.1007/978-3-030-58604-1_41
60. Tao, A., Duan, Y., Wei, Y., Lu, J., Zhou, J.: Seggroup: seg-level supervision for 3D instance and semantic segmentation. arXiv preprint arXiv:2012.10217 (2020)
61. Tarvainen, A., Valpola, H.: Mean teachers are better role models: Weight-averaged consistency targets improve semi-supervised deep learning results. In: NeurIPS, pp. 1195–1204 (2017)
62. Tatarchenko, M., Park, J., Koltun, V., Zhou, Q.Y.: Tangent convolutions for dense prediction in 3D. In: CVPR, pp. 3887–3896 (2018)
63. Tchapmi, L., Choy, C., Armeni, I., Gwak, J., Savarese, S.: Segcloud: semantic segmentation of 3D point clouds. In: 3DV, pp. 537–547 (2017)
64. Thabet, A., Alwassel, H., Ghanem, B.: Self-supervised learning of local features in 3D point clouds. In: CVPRW, pp. 938–939 (2020)
65. Thomas, H., Goulette, F., Deschaud, J.E., Marcotegui, B., LeGall, Y.: Semantic classification of 3D point clouds with multiscale spherical neighborhoods. In: 3DV, pp. 390–398 (2018)
66. Thomas, H., Qi, C.R., Deschaud, J.E., Marcotegui, B., Goulette, F., Guibas, L.J.: KPConv: flexible and deformable convolution for point clouds. In: ICCV, pp. 6411–6420 (2019)
67. Truong, G., Gilani, S.Z., Islam, S.M.S., Suter, D.: Fast point cloud registration using semantic segmentation. In: DICTA, pp. 1–8 (2019)
68. Varney, N., Asari, V.K., Graehling, Q.: DALES: a large-scale aerial LiDAR data set for semantic segmentation. In: CVPRW, pp. 186–187 (2020)
69. Varney, N., Asari, V.K., Graehling, Q.: Pyramid point: a multi-level focusing network for revisiting feature layers. arXiv preprint arXiv:2011.08692 (2020)
70. Wang, B., et al.: RangUDF: semantic surface reconstruction from 3d point clouds. arXiv preprint arXiv:2204.09138 (2022)
71. Wang, D., Shang, Y.: A new active labeling method for deep learning. In: IJCNN, pp. 112–119. IEEE (2014)
72. Wang, H., Rong, X., Yang, L., Wang, S., Tian, Y.: Towards weakly supervised semantic segmentation in 3D graph-structured point clouds of wild scenes. In: BMVC, p. 284 (2019)

73. Wang, H., Liu, Q., Yue, X., Lasenby, J., Kusner, M.J.: Pre-training by completing point clouds. arXiv preprint arXiv:2010.01089 (2020)

74. Wang, L., Huang, Y., Hou, Y., Zhang, S., Shan, J.: Graph attention convolution for point cloud semantic segmentation. In: CVPR (2019)

75. Wang, P., Yao, W.: A new weakly supervised approach for als point cloud semantic segmentation. arXiv preprint arXiv:2110.01462 (2021)

76. Wang, R., Albooyeh, M., Ravanbakhsh, S.: Equivariant maps for hierarchical structures. arXiv preprint arXiv:2006.03627 (2020)

77. Wang, Y., Sun, Y., Liu, Z., Sarma, S.E., Bronstein, M.M., Solomon, J.M.: Dynamic graph CNN for learning on point clouds. ACM TOG **38**(5), 1–12 (2019)

78. Wei, J., Lin, G., Yap, K.H., Hung, T.Y., Xie, L.: Multi-path region mining for weakly supervised 3D semantic segmentation on point clouds. In: CVPR, pp. 4384–4393 (2020)

79. Wei, J., Lin, G., Yap, K.H., Liu, F., Hung, T.Y.: Dense supervision propagation for weakly supervised semantic segmentation on 3d point clouds. arXiv preprint arXiv:2107.11267 (2021)

80. Wu, B., Wan, A., Yue, X., Keutzer, K.: SqueezeSeg: convolutional neural nets with recurrent CRF for real-time road-object segmentation from 3D LiDAR point cloud. In: ICRA, pp. 1887–1893 (2018)

81. Wu, B., Zhou, X., Zhao, S., Yue, X., Keutzer, K.: SqueezeSegV2: improved model structure and unsupervised domain adaptation for road-object segmentation from a LiDAR point cloud. In: ICRA, pp. 4376–4382 (2019)

82. Wu, T.H., et al.: Redal: region-based and diversity-aware active learning for point cloud semantic segmentation. In: ICCV, pp. 15510–15519 (2021)

83. Wu, W., Qi, Z., Fuxin, L.: PointConv: Deep convolutional networks on 3D point clouds. In: CVPR, pp. 9621–9630 (2018)

84. Wu, Y., et al.: Pointmatch: a consistency training framework for weakly supervisedsemantic segmentation of 3d point clouds. arXiv preprint arXiv:2202.10705 (2022)

85. Xie, S., Gu, J., Guo, D., Qi, C.R., Guibas, L., Litany, O.: PointContrast: unsupervised pre-training for 3D point cloud understanding. In: Vedaldi, A., Bischof, H., Brox, T., Frahm, J.-M. (eds.) ECCV 2020. LNCS, vol. 12348, pp. 574–591. Springer, Cham (2020). https://doi.org/10.1007/978-3-030-58580-8_34

86. Xu, C., Wu, B., Wang, Z., Zhan, W., Vajda, P., Keutzer, K., Tomizuka, M.: SqueezeSegV3: spatially-adaptive convolution for efficient point-cloud segmentation. In: Vedaldi, A., Bischof, H., Brox, T., Frahm, J.-M. (eds.) ECCV 2020. LNCS, vol. 12373, pp. 1–19. Springer, Cham (2020). https://doi.org/10.1007/978-3-030-58604-1_1

87. Xu, X., Lee, G.H.: Weakly supervised semantic point cloud segmentation: Towards 10x fewer labels. In: CVPR, pp. 13706–13715 (2020)

88. Yan, X., Gao, J., Li, J., Zhang, R., Li, Z., Huang, R., Cui, S.: Sparse single sweep lidar point cloud segmentation via learning contextual shape priors from scene completion. In: AAAI (2020)

89. Yan, X., Zheng, C., Li, Z., Wang, S., Cui, S.: PointASNL: robust point clouds processing using nonlocal neural networks with adaptive sampling. In: ICCV, pp. 5589–5598 (2020)

90. Ye, X., Li, J., Huang, H., Du, L., Zhang, X.: 3D recurrent neural networks with context fusion for point cloud semantic segmentation. In: Ferrari, V., Hebert, M., Sminchisescu, C., Weiss, Y. (eds.) ECCV 2018. LNCS, vol. 11211, pp. 415–430. Springer, Cham (2018). https://doi.org/10.1007/978-3-030-01234-2_25

91. Zhang, B., Wang, Y., Hou, W., Wu, H., Wang, J., Okumura, M., Shinozaki, T.: Flexmatch: Boosting semi-supervised learning with curriculum pseudo labeling. Advances in Neural Information Processing Systems 34 (2021)

92. Zhang, F., Fang, J., Wah, B., Torr, P.: Deep FusionNet for point cloud semantic segmentation. In: Vedaldi, A., Bischof, H., Brox, T., Frahm, J.-M. (eds.) ECCV 2020. LNCS, vol. 12369, pp. 644–663. Springer, Cham (2020). https://doi.org/10.1007/978-3-030-58586-0_38

93. Zhang, Y., Li, Z., Xie, Y., Qu, Y., Li, C., Mei, T.: Weakly supervised semantic segmentation for large-scale point cloud. In: AAAI (2021)

94. Zhang, Y., Qu, Y., Xie, Y., Li, Z., Zheng, S., Li, C.: Perturbed self-distillation: Weakly supervised large-scale point cloud semantic segmentation. In: ICCV, pp. 15520–15528 (2021)

95. Zhang, Y., et al.: PolarNet: an improved grid representation for online LiDAR point clouds semantic segmentation. In: CVPR, pp. 9601–9610 (2020)

96. Zhang, Z., Girdhar, R., Joulin, A., Misra, I.: Self-supervised pretraining of 3D features on any point-cloud. arXiv preprint arXiv:2101.02691 (2021)

97. Zhang, Z., Girdhar, R., Joulin, A., Misra, I.: Self-supervised pretraining of 3d features on any point-cloud. In: ICCV (2021)

98. Zhang, Z., Hua, B.S., Yeung, S.K.: ShellNet: efficient point cloud convolutional neural networks using concentric shells statistics. In: ICCV, pp. 1607–1616 (2019)

99. Zhao, H., Jiang, L., Fu, C.W., Jia, J.: PointWeb: enhancing local neighborhood features for point cloud processing. In: CVPR (2019)

100. Zhao, H., Jiang, L., Jia, J., Torr, P., Koltun, V.: Point Transformer. arXiv preprint arXiv:2012.09164 (2020)

101. Zhou, B., Khosla, A., Lapedriza, A., Oliva, A., Torralba, A.: Learning deep features for discriminative localization. In: CVPR, pp. 2921–2929 (2016)

102. Zhu, X., et al.: Weakly supervised 3d semantic segmentation using cross-image consensus and inter-voxel affinity relations. In: ICCV (2021)

103. Zhu, X., et al.: Cylindrical and asymmetrical 3D convolution networks for LiDAR segmentation. In: CVPR (2021)

PointMixer: MLP-Mixer for Point Cloud Understanding

Jaesung Choe[1]([✉]) [ID], Chunghyun Park[2] [ID], Francois Rameau[1] [ID],
Jaesik Park[2] [ID], and In So Kweon[1] [ID]

[1] Korea Advanced Institute of Science and Technology (KAIST),
Daejeon, South Korea
{jaesung.choe,frameau,iskweon77}@kaist.ac.kr
[2] Pohang University of Science and Technology (POSTECH), Pohang, South Korea
{p0125ch,jaesik.park}@postech.ac.kr
https://github.com/LifeBeyondExpectations/ECCV22-PointMixer

Abstract. MLP-Mixer has newly appeared as a new challenger against
the realm of CNNs and Transformer. Despite its simplicity compared
to Transformer, the concept of channel-mixing MLPs and token-mixing
MLPs achieves noticeable performance in image recognition tasks. Unlike
images, point clouds are inherently sparse, unordered and irregular,
which limits the direct use of MLP-Mixer for point cloud understanding. To overcome these limitations, we propose **PointMixer**, a universal
point set operator that facilitates information sharing among unstructured 3D point cloud. By simply replacing token-mixing MLPs with
Softmax function, PointMixer can "mix" features within/between point
sets. By doing so, PointMixer can be broadly used for intra-set, inter-set,
and hierarchical-set mixing. We demonstrate that various channel-wise
feature aggregation in numerous point sets is better than self-attention
layers or dense token-wise interaction in a view of parameter efficiency
and accuracy. Extensive experiments show the competitive or superior
performance of PointMixer in semantic segmentation, classification, and
reconstruction against Transformer-based methods.

1 Introduction

3D scanning devices, such as LiDAR or RGB-D sensors, are widely used to
capture a scene as 3D point clouds. Unlike images, point clouds are inherently sparse, unordered, and irregular. These properties make standard neural network architectures [21,62] hardly applicable. To tackle these challenges,

---

J. Choe and C. Park—Both authors have equally contributed to this work.

Supplementary Information The online version contains supplementary material
available at https://doi.org/10.1007/978-3-031-19812-0_36.

there have been numerous ad hoc solutions, such as sparse convolution networks [8,15], graph neural networks [6,57,61,74,75,78,84], and point convolution networks [48,67,76,83]. Despite their structural differences, these techniques have all been designed to extract meaningful feature representation from point clouds [18]. Among existing solutions, Transformer [7,17,54,73,96] appears to be particularly beneficial to extract features from point clouds. Indeed, the self-attention layer that encompasses the dense token-wise relations is specifically relevant in the context of processing irregular and unordered 3D points.

Beyond the well established realm of CNNs and Transformer, MLP-Mixer [68] proposes a new architecture that exclusively uses MLPs. Based on the pioneering study [68], concurrent works [5,16,23,35,41,69,88,89] address the locality issue of MLPs [5,12,23,39,88,89] and discuss the necessity of self-attention [41,65,92]. More recently, Yu *et al.* [90] claim that the general architecture formulation is more important than the specific token-wise interaction strategies, such as self-attention and token-mixing MLPs. Despite an increasing interest, the MLP-like architectures for point clouds have not yet been fully explored.

In this paper, we introduce the *PointMixer* that newly extends the philosophy of MLP-like architectures to point cloud analysis. Specifically, we demonstrate the dense token-wise interaction are not essential factors in this context. Instead of using token-mixing MLPs, we extend the usage of channel-mixing MLPs into numerous point sets. As illustrated in Fig. 1 and Table 1, PointMixer layer shares and mixes point features (1) within grouped points (intra-set), (2) between point sets (inter-set), or (3) points in different hierarchical sets. In particular, we newly introduce the concepts of the inter-set mixing and the hierarchical-set mixing, which is clearly different from previous studies [47,56,96] that only

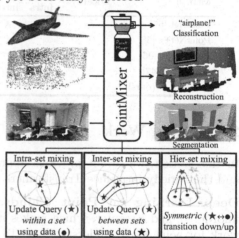

Fig. 1. We present a MLP-like architecture for various point cloud processing, which considers numerous point sets with larger receptive fields to "mix" information.

focus on the intra-set mixing. To this end, PointMixer layer is a universal point set operator that can propagate point responses into various point sets. We claim that various channel MLPs on numerous point sets can outperform self-attention layers or token-mixing MLPs for point clouds. Moreover, the PointMixer network is a general architecture that has symmetric encoder-decoder blocks fully equipped with PointMixer layers.

We conduct extensive experiments on various 3D tasks. These large-scale experiments demonstrate that our method achieves compelling performance among Transformer-based studies [51,96]. Our contributions are summarized as below:

- PointMixer as a universal point set operator that facilitates mixing of point features through various point sets: intra-set, inter-set, and hierarchical-set.
- Highly accurate and parameter-efficient block design that purely consists of channel-mixing MLPs without token-mixing MLPs.
- Symmetric encoder-decoder network to propagate hierarchical point responses through PointMixer layer, instead of trilinear interpolation.
- Extensive experiments in various 3D point cloud tasks that highlight the efficacy of PointMixer network against recent Transformer-based studies.

Table 1. Technical comparisons. Locality represents the local feature aggregation among sampled points. We split the function of the set operator as "intra"-set mix, "inter"-set mix, and "hierarchical"-set mix. Also, we present the symmetric property of encoder-decoder architecture of related work [55,56,96].

Method	Locality	Set operator			Symmetric pyramid arch	Token-mix
		Intra	Inter	Hier		
PointNet [55]	✗	✗	✗	✗	✗	Pooling
PointNet++ [56]	✓	✓	✗	✗	✗	Pooling
PointTrans [96]	✓	✓	✗	✗	✗	Self-attn
PointMLP [47]	✓	✓	✗	✗	✗	Affine
PointMixer (ours)	✓	✓	✓	✓	✓	Softmax

2 Related Work

In this section, we revisit previous approaches for point cloud understanding, and then briefly introduce Transformers and MLP-like architectures.

Deep Learning on Point Clouds. Point clouds are naturally sparse, unordered, and irregular, which makes it difficult to design a deep neural network for point cloud understanding. To handle such complex data structures, two distinct philosophies have been investigated: voxel-based and point-based methods.

Voxel-based methods [8,14,34,50,63,98] first quantize an irregular point cloud into the regular voxel grids, which makes it efficient to search neighbor voxels. However, the voxelization process inevitably loses the geometric details of the original point cloud. This issue often leads to infer inaccurate predictions though several recent methods [45,64,93] try to alleviate the quantization artifacts. Therefore, point-based methods have been actively studied.

PointNet [55] is a pioneering paper that processes an unordered and irregular points in deep neural architectures. Based on this seminal work, PointNet++ [56] presents the ways of involving feature hierarchy as well as points' locality. In details, this paper adopts k-Nearest Neighbor (kNN) for local neighborhood sampling and the Farthest Point Sampling algorithm (FPS) for feature hierarchy (e.g., transition downsampling). This pyramid encoder-decoder network largely influences on the MLP-based methods [25,26,28,31,36,42,58,82,85,95], point convolution studies [33,38,40,43,48,79,83], and graph-based networks [57, 61,75,78,84]. However, as stated in Table 1, PointNet++ is limited to capture local point responses within the scope of intra-set. Moreover, we found that this vanilla architecture is asymmetric between transition down layers and transition up layers. While downsampling layers adopt pooling with kNN and FPS, upsampling layers re-compute kNN and trilinear interpolation, which brings asymmetric feature propagation in the encoder-decoder architecture. More recently, Transformer-based study for point cloud processing [96] still suffers from the same issue in the pyramid architecture design.

Our work unifies a local feature aggregation layer, a downsampling layer, and an upsampling layer into *an universal set operator*, named PointMixer layer. This novel layer brings the symmetric and learnable down/upsampling architecture for various 3D perception tasks such as object shape classification [80], semantic segmentation [2] and point cloud reconstruction tasks [7].

Transformers and MLP-Like Architectures. Transformer-based architecture has recently become a game changer in both natural language processing [11,59,65,73] and computer vision [3,13,19,44,49,60,70,91,96].

Vision Transformer (ViT) [13] has opened the applicability of Transformers on visual recognition tasks. Because of the quadratic runtime of the self-attention layers in Transformers, ViT adopts tokenized inputs that divide the image into small region of patches [71]. The idea of patch embeddings is widely used in the following studies that focus on various issues in ViT [30,66]: locality [10,24,60,72] and hierarchy [4,44,77,81]. With those self-attention layers [60,94], Transformer-based point cloud studies [17,51,96] demonstrate accurate predictions in both 3D shape classification [80] and semantic segmentation [2]. However, a general-purpose layer for both local feature learning and down/upsampling has drawn little attention in handling 3D points.

Recently, there exist trials to go beyond the hegemony of CNNs and Transformer by introducing MLP-like architectures. The pioneering paper, MLP-Mixer [68], presents a MLP-like network constituted of token-mixing MLPs and channel-mixing MLPs for image classification task. Especially in computer vision, this MLP-like architectures appear to be a new paradigm with their simple formulation and superior performance given large-scale training data. Subsequent papers raise issues and develop potentials in MLP-like architectures: (1) can MLPs handle position-sensitive information or locality [5,12,23,39,88]? and (2) does self-attention is truly needed [41,65,92]? Though these issues are still controversial, more recent paper, Metaformer [90], addresses the importance of general architecture formulation instead of the specific dense token-wise interaction strategies such as self-attention layers [13,73] or token-mixing MLPs [68]. Simply, by replacing complicated token-mixing operators with the average pooling layer, MetaFormer achieves remarkable performance against the recent MLP-based and Transformer-based studies.

Despite their success, modern MLP-like approaches have not yet been fully exploited to point clouds. In contrast to recent Transformer-based point cloud studies [17,51,54,96], our PointMixer network is a general-purpose architecture that symmetrically upsamples/downsamples points' responses and truly exploits the strength of MLPs to operate mixing within/beyond sets of points. By doing so, we successfully conduct various tasks, 3D semantic segmentation, point cloud reconstruction, and object classification tasks [2,7,80].

3   Method

In this section, we describe the details of our PointMixer design. For the sake of clarity, we compare the general formulation of MLP-Mixer with representative point-based approaches, such as PointNet++ and Point Transformer (Sect. 3.1). Then, we examine whether MLP-Mixer is of relevance to a point set operator (Sect. 3.2). Finally, we introduce our PointMixer layer (Sect. 3.3) that is adopted in our entire network (Sect. 3.4).

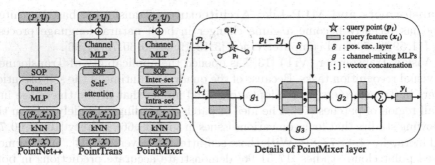

Fig. 2. Block design comparison and PointMixer layer details. Note that SOP means symmetric operation, such as pooling and summation.

3.1   Preliminary

Let's assume a point cloud $\mathcal{P} = \{\mathbf{p}_i\}_{i=1}^{N}$ and its corresponding point features $\mathcal{X} = \{\mathbf{x}_i\}_{i=1}^{N}$ where $\mathbf{p}_i \in \mathbb{R}^3$ is the position of the i-th point and $\mathbf{x}_i \in \mathbb{R}^C$ is its corresponding feature. The objective is to learn a function $f : \mathcal{X} \to \mathcal{Y}$ to produce the output point features $\mathcal{Y} = \{\mathbf{y}_i\}_{i=1}^{N}$. Instead of processing the entire point cloud directly, most approaches treat data locally based on points' proximity. For this purpose, k-Nearest Neighbor (kNN) [29,52,97] is widely used to get an index map of neighbor points, which is denoted as:

$$\mathcal{M}_i = k\text{NN}(\mathcal{P}, \mathbf{p}_i), \tag{1}$$

where $\mathcal{M}_i$ is an index map of the K closest points for a query point $\mathbf{p}_i \in \mathbb{R}^3$. In other words, given a query index i, the index map $\mathcal{M}_i$ is defined as a set of K nearest neighbor indices ($K = |\mathcal{M}_i|$). Accordingly, kNN can be understood as a directional graph that links each query point $\mathbf{p}_i$ to its K closest neighbor points $\mathcal{P}_i = \{\mathbf{p}_j \in \mathcal{P} | j \in \mathcal{M}_i\}$ and the corresponding features $\mathcal{X}_i = \{\mathbf{x}_j \in \mathcal{X} | j \in \mathcal{M}_i\}$.

PointNet++ [56] addresses the problem of PointNet [55] that has difficulty in capturing local responses. To cope with this problem, it utilizes kNN and Farthest Point Sampling algorithm and builds asymmetric encoder-decoder network. Instead of dealing with the entire point cloud directly, PointNet++ aggregates set-level responses locally as follows:

$$\mathbf{y}_i = \text{maxpool}_{j \in \mathcal{M}_i} \Big(\text{MLP}\left([\mathbf{x}_j; \mathbf{p}_i - \mathbf{p}_j]\right) \Big), \tag{2}$$

where $\mathbf{y}_i$ is the output feature vector for the i-th point and $[;]$ denotes vector concatenation. By adopting this grouping and sampling strategy, MLPs can capture local responses from unordered 3D points.

Point Transformer [96] adopts vector subtraction attention as a similarity measurement for token-wise communication. Following PointNet++, Point Transformer also uses kNN to compute local responses. Given a query point feature $\mathbf{x}_i$ and its neighbor feature set $\mathcal{X}_i$, Point Transformer operates self-attention layers to densely relate token interaction as:

$$\mathbf{y}_i = \sum_{j \in \mathcal{M}_i} \text{softmax}\Big(\psi\big(\mathbf{W}_1\mathbf{x}_i - \mathbf{W}_2\mathbf{x}_j + \delta(\mathbf{p}_i - \mathbf{p}_j)\big)\Big)\Big(\mathbf{W}_3\mathbf{x}_j + \delta(\mathbf{p}_i - \mathbf{p}_j)\Big), \tag{3}$$

where $\mathbf{W}$ indicates a linear transformation matrix, $\psi(\cdot)$ denotes an MLPs to calculate vector similarities, $\delta(\mathbf{p}_i - \mathbf{p}_j)$ is a positional encoding vector to embed local structures of 3D points, and $\mathbf{p}_i - \mathbf{p}_j$ is the relative distance between a query point $\mathbf{p}_i$ and its neighbor point $\mathbf{p}_j$.

3.2 MLP-Mixer as Point Set Operator

MLP-Mixer [68] has achieved remarkable success by only using MLPs for image classification. However, when dealing with sparse and unordered points, the direct application of the MLP-Mixer network is restricted. Let us revisit MLP-Mixer to ease the understanding of our PointMixer.

The MLP-Mixer layer[1] consists of token-mixing MLPs and channel-mixing MLPs. MLP-Mixer takes K tokens having C-dimensional features, denoted as $\mathbf{X} \in \mathbb{R}^{K \times C}$, where tokens are features from image patches. It begins with token-mixing MLPs that transposes the spatial axis and channel axis to mix spatial information. Then, it continues with channel-mixing MLPs so that input tokens are mixed in spatial and channel dimensions.

$$\mathbf{X}' = \mathbf{X} + (\mathbf{W}_2\, \rho(\mathbf{W}_1(\text{LayerNorm}(\mathbf{X}))^\top))^\top, \tag{4}$$

$$\mathbf{Y} = \mathbf{X}' + \mathbf{W}_4\, \rho(\mathbf{W}_3\, \text{LayerNorm}(\mathbf{X}')), \tag{5}$$

where $\mathbf{W}$ is the weight matrix of a linear function and ρ is GELU [22]. By Eq. (4), token-mixing MLPs are sensitive to the order of the input tokens, which

---

[1] We set the relation of terminologies as layer $\subset$ block $\subset$ network.

is permutation-variant property. Due to its property, positional encoding is not required in the vanilla MLP-Mixer as stated in the paper [68]. However, this property is not desirable for processing irregular and unordered point clouds, which is different characteristics of uniform and ordered pixels in the image. To cope with this issue, previous point-based layers [56, 96] are independent to orders of input point, $i.e.$, permutation-invariance[2]. Moreover, as a point set operator, vanilla MLP-Mixer layer only computes $intra\text{-}set$ relations as PointNet++ and Point Transformer do. From this analysis, we observe room for improvement in point cloud understanding. We propose PointMixer layer that is permutation-invariant and can also be used for a learnable upsampling in Sect. 3.3.

3.3 PointMixer: Universal Point Set Operator

We introduce an approach to embed geometric relations between points' features into the MLP-Mixer's framework. As illustrated in Fig. 2, the PointMixer layer takes a point set $\mathcal{P}_i = \{\mathbf{p}_j\}$ and its associated point features set $\mathcal{X}_i = \{\mathbf{x}_j\}$ as inputs in order to compute the output feature vector $\mathbf{y}_i$. For a point $\mathbf{p}_i$, we first compute a score vector $\mathbf{s} = [s_1, ..., s_K]$ to aggregate $\mathcal{X}_i$ as follows:

$$s_j = g_2\Big(\big[g_1(\mathbf{x}_j); \delta(\mathbf{p}_i - \mathbf{p}_j)\big] \Big) \quad \text{where} \quad \forall j \in \mathcal{M}_i, \tag{6}$$

where $g(\cdot)$ is the channel-mixing MLPs, $\delta(\cdot)$ is the positional encoding MLPs, and $\mathbf{x}_j$ is a j-th element of the feature vector set $\mathcal{X}_i$. Note that we follow the relative positional encoding scheme [56, 96] to deal with unstructured 3D points. As a result, we obtain the score vector $\mathbf{s} \in \mathbb{R}^K$. Finally, the features of the K adjacent points are gathered to produce a new feature vector $\mathbf{y}_i$ as:

$$\mathbf{y}_i = \sum_{j \in \mathcal{M}_i} \text{softmax}(s_j) \odot g_3(\mathbf{x}_j), \tag{7}$$

where $\text{softmax}(\cdot)$ is the Softmax function that normalizes the spatial dimension, and $\odot$ indicates an element-wise multiplication. Note that this symmetric operation (SOP) in the proposed PointMixer is different from both the average pooling in MLP-Mixer and the max pooling in PointNet++, as described in Table 1.

As a set operator, PointMixer layer has different characteristics compared to both MLP-Mixer layer [68]. First, PointMixer layer sees relative positional information $\delta(\mathbf{p}_i - \mathbf{p}_j)$ to encode the local structure of a point set. Second, the vanilla MLP-Mixer layer does not have the Softmax function. Last, PointMixer layer does not have token-mixing MLPs for scalability to arbitrary number of neighbor points and for permutation-invariance to deal with unordered points. Let us explain the reasons behind these differences.

No Token-Mixing MLPs. There are two reasons that we do not put token-mixing MLPs into PointMixer layer. First, token-mixing MLPs are permutation-variant, which makes it incompatible with unordered point clouds. As stated in

---

[2] To deal with unordered points, layers are permutation-invariant ($f_{\text{layer}} : \mathcal{X}_i \rightarrow \mathbf{y}_i$) and blocks are permutation-equivariant ($f_{\text{block}} : \mathcal{X} \rightarrow \mathcal{Y}$).

Point Transformer [96], permutation-invariant property is a necessary condition, also for PointMixer layer. Second, while a given pixel in an image systematically admits 8 adjacent pixels, each 3D point does not have pre-defined number of neighbors, which is determined by the clustering algorithms, such as kNN [56, 78,96], radius neighborhood [67], or hash table [7,8]. Since token-mixing MLPs can only take fixed number of input points[3], token-mixing MLPs are not suitable for handling various cardinality of point sets.

Inspired by Synthesizer [65], we alleviate this problem by replacing the token-mixing MLPs with the Softmax function. We conjecture that the Softmax function weakly binds token-wise information in a non-parametric manner (*i.e.*, normalization). By doing so, PointMixer layer can calculate arbitrary cardinality of point sets and have a permutation-invariant property. As described in Fig. 3 and in Table 1, PointMixer layer can be used as a universal point operator for mixing various types of point sets: intra-set, intra-set, and hierarchical-set.

Intra-set Mixing. Given a point set $\mathcal{P}_i$ and its corresponding feature set $\mathcal{X}_i$, intra-set mixing aims to compute point-wise interaction within each set. Usually, kNN is widely used to cluster neighbor points into groups. For example in Fig. 3-(a), we apply kNN on each query point where $K=3$. As a result, a red point ($\bigstar$) has three neighbor points ($\bullet$). Based on the index map $\mathcal{M}_i$ from kNN, the PointMixer layer updates a query feature $\mathbf{x}_i$ using its neighbor feature set $\mathcal{X}_i$, as in Eq. (6) and Eq. (7). While intra-set mixing is proven to be useful in various methods [18], the receptive field is bounded within a set, as depicted in Fig. 3-(a). To overcome this restriction, we propose the inter-set mixing operation.

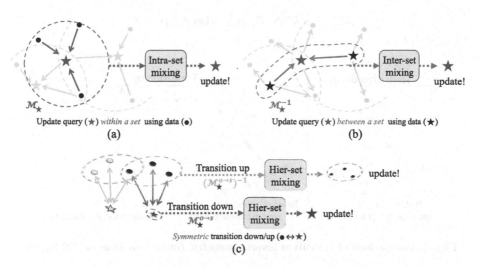

Update query ($\bigstar$) *within a set* using data ($\bullet$)
(a)

Update query ($\bigstar$) *between a set* using data ($\bigstar$)
(b)

Symmetric transition down/up ($\bullet \leftrightarrow \bigstar$)
(c)

Fig. 3. PointMixer is a universal point set operator: (a) intra-set mixing, (b) inter-set mixing, and (c) hierarchical-set mixing.

---

[3] Please refer to the supplementary material for further details.

Inter-set Mixing. This is a new concept of spreading point features between different sets. Using the index mapping $\mathcal{M}_i$, we can trace back to find another set $\mathcal{P}_j$ that includes a query point $\mathbf{p}_i$ as their neighbors. This process can be viewed as the inverse version of kNN, and we define the inverse mapping of $\mathcal{M}_i$ as $\mathcal{M}_i^{-1} = \{j|i \in \mathcal{M}_j\}$. For example in Fig. 3-(b), given index mapping $\mathcal{M}_\star$, we compute inverse index mapping $\mathcal{M}_\star^{-1}$. Then, we can find the two adjacent sets whose query points are black points ($\star$). It implies the red point is included in two adjacent sets, as drawn in Fig. 3-(b)[4]. In shorts, inverse mapping $\mathcal{M}_i^{-1}$ finds the set index j that includes a point $\mathbf{p}_i$. By doing so, inter-set mixing can aggregate point responses between neighbor sets $\mathcal{P}_j$ into the query point $\mathbf{p}_i$.

Hierarchical-Set Mixing. The PointMixer layer is universally applicable for the transition down/up layers as shown in Fig. 3-(c). For instance, let's prepare a point set $\mathcal{P}_s = \{\mathbf{p}_j\}_{j=1}^{N'}$ that is sampled from original point set $\mathcal{P}_o = \{\mathbf{p}_i\}_{i=1}^N$ ($\mathcal{P}_s \subset \mathcal{P}_o$). Using a point $\mathbf{p}_j \in \mathcal{P}_s$, we calculate its neighbors from $\mathcal{P}_o$ and obtain index mapping $\mathcal{M}_j^{o \rightarrow s}$. By putting $\mathcal{M}_j^{o \rightarrow s}$ in Eq. (6) and Eq. (7), we readily pass the feature from $\mathcal{P}_o$ to $\mathcal{P}_s$ (*i.e.*, point *downsampling*), which is computed as:

$$\mathcal{M}_j^{o \rightarrow s} = k\text{NN}(\mathcal{P}_o, \mathbf{p}_j) \quad \text{where} \quad \forall \mathbf{p}_j \in \mathcal{P}_s. \tag{8}$$

For point *upsampling*, we notice that conventional U-Net in both PointNet++ and Point Transformer is *not symmetric* in terms of downsampling and upsampling. This is because the spatial grouping is performed asymmetrically as visualized in Fig. 4. In details, conventional approaches [56,95,96] build another kNN map $\mathcal{M}_i^{s \rightarrow o}$ for the upsampling as below:

$$\mathcal{M}_i^{s \rightarrow o} = k\text{NN}(\mathcal{P}_s, \mathbf{p}_i) \quad \text{where} \quad \forall \mathbf{p}_i \in \mathcal{P}_o. \tag{9}$$

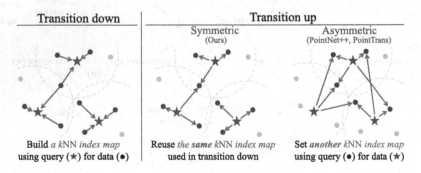

Transition down	Transition up	
	Symmetric (Ours)	Asymmetric (PointNet++, PointTrans)
Build *a kNN index map* using query (★) for data (●)	Reuse *the same kNN index map* used in transition down	Set *another kNN index map* using query (●) for data (★)

Fig. 4. Comparison of transition layer: symmetric (ours), asymmetric [56,95,96].

However, this is not symmetric because *nearest neighbor is not a symmetric function*: even if $\mathbf{p}_i$'s nearest neighbor is $\mathbf{p}_j$, $\mathbf{p}_j$'s nearest neighbor may not $\mathbf{p}_i$.

---

[4] There is a chance to collect variable number of points after an inverse mapping $\mathcal{M}_i^{-1}$.

Instead of creating a new index map $\mathcal{M}_i^{s \to o}$, our PointMixer layer can use $\left(\mathcal{M}_j^{o \to s}\right)^{-1}$ for upsampling (Fig. 3-(b)) by re-using the original index mapping from the downsampling $\mathcal{M}_j^{o \to s}$. See Fig. 4 for the symmetric upsampling. The benefit of this approach is that it does not introduce additional k-Nearest Neighbor search. Furthermore, we can propagate point responses in different hierarchy based on their scores computed by our PointMixer, instead of using trilinear interpolation [56,96]. These technical differences results in higher performance than that of asymmetric design on dense prediction tasks (see Sect. 4.4).

As illustrated in Fig. 5-(b) of the transition down block, we use Farthest Point Sampling algorithm to produce $\mathcal{P}_s$ from $\mathcal{P}_o$. Then, we utilize kNN to sample $\mathcal{P}_s$ from $\mathcal{P}_o$. The resulting point locations are used to calculate the relative distance $\mathbf{p}_i - \mathbf{p}_j$. In the transition up block, we keep using the index map $\mathcal{M}_j^{o \to s}$ calculated in the transition down block. To this end, we apply the PointMixer layer in transition up/down while maintaining the symmetric relation between the sampled point cloud $\mathcal{P}_s$ and the original points $\mathcal{P}_o$. We empirically prove that this symmetric upsampling layer helps the network to predict dense point-level representations accurately in Sect. 4.

3.4 Network Architecture

In this section, we describe the details of our MLP-like encoder-decoder architecture as shown in Fig. 5. Our network is composed of several MLP blocks, such as the transition down blocks, transition up blocks, and Mixer blocks. For a fair comparison, our network mainly follows the proposed hyper-parameters in Point Transformer [96] for network composition. Overall, our network takes a deep pyramid-style network that progressively downsamples points to obtain global features. For dense prediction tasks, such as semantic segmentation or point reconstruction, we include upsampling blocks for per-point estimation.

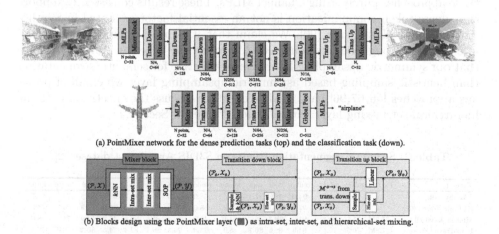

(a) PointMixer network for the dense prediction tasks (top) and the classification task (down).

(b) Blocks design using the PointMixer layer (■) as intra-set, inter-set, and hierarchical-set mixing.

Fig. 5. Overall architecture of PointMixer network.

Finally, our header block is designed for task-specific solutions. For classification, we take fully-connected layers, dropout layers, and global pooling layer. For semantic segmentation and point reconstruction, the header block consists of MLPs without pooling layers.

4   Experiments

In this section, we evaluate the efficacy and versatility of the proposed Point-Mixer for various point cloud understanding tasks: semantic segmentation [2], point reconstruction [7], and object classification [80].

4.1   Semantic Segmentation

To validate the effectiveness of PointMixer for semantic segmentation, we propose an evaluation on the large-scale point cloud dataset S3DIS [2] consisting of 271 room reconstructions. Each 3D point of this dataset is assigned to one label among 13 semantic categories. For the sake of fairness, we meticulously follow the widely used evaluation protocol proposed by Point Transformer [96]. For training, we set the batch size as 4 and use the SGD optimizer with momentum and weight decay set to 0.9 and 0.0001 respectively. For evaluation, we use the class-wise mean Intersection of Union (mIoU), class-wise mean accuracy (mAcc), and overall point-wise accuracy (OA).

As shown in Table 2 and Fig. 6, PointMixer achieves the state-of-the-art performance in S3DIS [2] Area 5, though PointMixer network consumes less parameters (**6.5M**) than that of Point Transformer (7.8M). Even in class-wise IoU, PointMixer network outperforms Point Transformer [96], except for a few classes. While various studies [17,51,96] underline the necessity of dense point-wise interaction (*i.e.*, self-attention layer), PointMixer successfully outperforms these approaches purely using Channel MLPs. These results consistently support that dense token communication is not an essential factor as stated in Synthesizer [65] and Metaformer [90]. We claim that it is much more crucial to mix information through various point sets. Moreover, the experimental result shows that our symmetric upsampling layer is more effective for semantic segmentation than heuristic sampling-based asymmetric upsampling layer which all of previous approaches [56,67,96] have used. We further discuss the effectiveness of our hierarchical-set mixing layer with ablation studies in Sect. 4.4.

Table 2. Semantic segmentation results on S3DIS Area 5 test dataset [2].

Method	Param.	mAcc	mIoU	ceiling	floor	wall	column	window	door	table	chair	sofa	book.	board	clutter
PAConv [83]	-	73.0	66.6	**94.6**	98.6	82.4	26.4	58.0	60.0	80.4	89.7	69.8	74.3	73.5	57.7
KPConv *deform* [67]	-	72.8	67.1	92.8	97.3	82.4	23.9	58.0	69.0	81.5	**91.0**	**75.4**	75.3	66.7	58.9
MinkowskiNet [8]	37.9M	71.7	65.4	91.8	**98.7**	86.2	34.1	48.9	62.4	81.6	89.8	47.2	74.9	74.4	58.6
PointTrans [96]	7.8M	76.5	70.4	94.0	98.5	**86.3**	38.0	**63.4**	74.3	89.1	82.4	74.3	**80.2**	76.0	59.3
FastPointTrans [54]	37.9M	**77.9**	70.3	94.2	98.0	86.0	**53.8**	61.2	77.3	81.3	89.4	60.1	72.8	**80.4**	58.9
PointMixer (ours)	**6.5M**	77.4	**71.4**	94.2	98.2	86.0	43.8	62.1	**78.5**	**90.6**	82.2	73.9	79.8	78.5	**59.4**

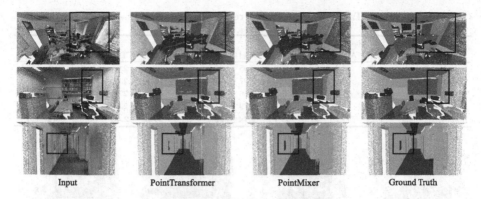

Input   PointTransformer   PointMixer   Ground Truth

Fig. 6. Qualitative results in semantic segmentation on S3DIS Area 5 test dataset [2].

4.2 Point Cloud Reconstruction

To highlight the versatility of our approach, we propose a large-scale assessment for the newly introduced task of point cloud reconstruction [7] where an inaccurate point cloud is jointly denoised, densified, and completed. This experiment is also particularly interesting to evaluate the generalization capabilities of networks since it allows us to test methods in unmet environments. Specifically, we train on the synthetic objects of ShapeNetPart [87] and evaluate the reconstruction accuracy on unmet indoor scenes from ScanNet [9] (real reconstruction) and ICL-NUIM [20] (synthetic data). Note that in [7], the point reconstruction is performed in two stages: 1) point upsampling via a sparse hourglass network, 2) denoising and refinement via Transformer network. For this evaluation, we propose to replace the second stage of this pipeline with various architectures (*i.e.*, PointMixer network and previous studies [55,56,96]) to compare their performances. Under the same data augmentation and data pre-processing as in [7,37], we train PointMixer and previous studies [55,56,96]. For evaluation, we utilize the Chamfer distance (CD) to measure the distance between the predictions and the ground truth point clouds. Additionally, we use the accuracy (Acc.), completeness (Cp.), and F1 score to measure the performance in occupancy aspects [1,27,32,86].

Though our network is solely trained in a synthetic/object dataset, our network can generalize towards unmet scenes including real-world 3D scans [9] and synthetic/room-scale point clouds [20] as in Table 3 and Fig. 7. Moreover, our method compares favorably to previous Transformer-based [7,96] and MLP-based [55,56] studies. In particular, the performance gap between ours and previous studies become larger in the ScanNet [9] and ICL-NUIM dataset [20], which indicates better generalization performance.

Table 3. Point cloud reconstruction results.

Method	ShapeNet-Part [87]				ScanNet [9]				ICL-NUIM [20]			
	CD($\downarrow$)	Acc.($\uparrow$)	Cp.($\uparrow$)	F1($\uparrow$)	CD($\downarrow$)	Acc.($\uparrow$)	Cp.($\uparrow$)	F1($\uparrow$)	CD($\downarrow$)	Acc.($\uparrow$)	Cp.($\uparrow$)	F1($\uparrow$)
PointNet [55]	1.33	63.2	38.8	48.2	3.05	37.5	27.8	32.6	2.98	46.9	33.2	38.1
PointNet++ [56]	1.25	65.1	39.0	50.1	2.97	38.3	29.5	33.4	2.88	48.8	35.8	39.9
PointRecon [7]	1.19	81.0	40.4	53.4	2.86	40.4	30.2	34.1	2.78	54.1	38.1	43.6
PointTrans [96]	1.12	75.9	40.9	52.7	2.79	41.1	32.1	35.6	2.57	51.1	36.4	41.6
PointMixer (ours)	**1.11**	77.1	**41.5**	**53.7**	**2.74**	**42.1**	**33.5**	**37.8**	**2.43**	**56.5**	**38.2**	**44.7**

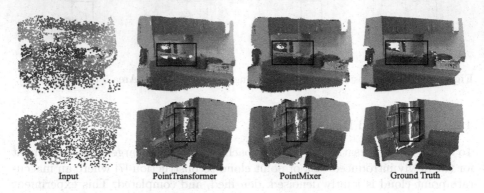

Input   PointTransformer   PointMixer   Ground Truth

Fig. 7. Qualitative results in point reconstruction on ScanNet dataset [9].

4.3 Shape Classification

The ModelNet40 [80] dataset has 12K CAD models with 40 object categories. We follow the official train/test splits to train and evaluate ours and the previous studies. For fair comparison, we follow the data augmentation and pre-processing as proposed in PointNet++ [56], which is also adopted in the recent studies [48,67,83,96]. For evaluation, we adopt the mean accuracy within each category (mAcc), and the overall accu-

Table 4. Shape classification results on ModelNet40 dataset [80].

Method	Param.	mAcc	OA
PointNet [55]	-	86.2	89.2
PointNet++ [56]	**1.4M**	-	90.7
PointConv [79]	18.6M	-	92.5
DGCNN [78]	-	90.2	92.9
KPConv *rigid* [67]	15.2M	-	92.9
PointTrans [96]	5.3M	90.6	**93.7**
PointMixer (ours)	3.9M	**91.4**	93.6

racy over all classes (OA) with the same evaluation protocol with previous approaches [56,83,96]. The results presented in Table 4 show that our approach outperforms the recently proposed techniques. Especially, PointMixer achieves the highest mAcc with outperforming other methods by a large margin as 0.8 mAcc, using 1024 points without normals. Moreover, our network shows this competitive performance with less parameters (**3.9M**) against previous studies (Point Transformer[5] 5.3M, KPConv 15.2M). Based on these comparisons with Point Transformer and related work, we conclude that PointMixer network effec-

---

[5] Since there is no official release of codes, we use the best implementation of Point Transformer available in the public domain, which contains the official code provided by the authors of Point Transformer and reproduces the reported accuracy.

tively and efficiently aggregates various point responses through intra-set mixing, inter-set mixing, and downsampling layers, even for shape classification task.

4.4 Ablation Study

We conduct an extensive ablation study about the proposed PointMixer in semantic segmentation on the S3DIS dataset [2] and in point cloud reconstruction on the ShapeNet-Part dataset [87]. First, we proceed the case study of our PointMixer (Table 5, top-right one). Second, we analyze the influence of positional encoding on PointMixer (Table 5, left one). Last, we compare PointMixer that is free from token-mixing MLPs (Table 5, bottom-right one).

Universal Point Set Operator. PointMixer can be applicable to act as intra-set mixing, inter-set mixing, and hierarchical-set mixing. Technically speacking, intra-set mixing and hierarchical-set mixing for point downsampling utilizes $\mathcal{M}_i$, but inter-set mixing and hierarchical-set mixing for point upsampling use $\mathcal{M}_i^{-1}$. This ablation study aims to validate the inverse mapping as well as a functionality of PointMixer layer. As in Table 5, especially, when we combine the usage of hierarchical-set mixing and inter-set mixing, the synergy brings large performance improvement in both two tasks, 2.2 mIoU in semantic segmentation and 0.02 Chamfer distance in point reconstruction. It implies that the various ways of sharing points' responses are beneficial for point cloud understanding.

Unnecessary Token-Mixing MLPs. We validate our claims about the role of the Softmax function, *i.e.*, weakly binding tokens. For this purpose, we replace the Softmax functions with token-mixing MLPs, as proposed in the vanilla MLP-Mixers. Table 5 demonstrates that even without explicit use of token-mixing MLPs, our PointMixer successfully achieves similar accuracy in semantic segmentation and point reconstruction. Moreover, it takes 3 days for training the PointMixer with token-mixing MLPs while our original PointMixer requires a day (twice faster) with less parameter consumption (18% less). These results are consistently support to Metaformer [90] and Synthesizer [65] in that dense token-wise interaction is not an essential choice.

Positional Encoding. MLP-Mixer does not use positional encoding since token-mixing MLPs are sensitive to the order of tokens. However, relative position information is an important factor to handle unstructured 3D points. Also, our PointMixer layer is free from token-mixing MLPs to obtain permutation-invariant property to function as a universal point set operator. Without any modification on the layer except positional encoding layers $\delta(\mathbf{p}_i - \mathbf{p}_j)$, we experiment the effectiveness of positional encoding in all of these usages. As in Table 5, there is large performance drop when we intentionally omit positional encodings in our PointMixer layer. Different from MLP-Mixer, we claim the relative positional encoding is a necessary condition to deal with 3D points.

Symmetric Architecture. When we think of the convolutional neural networks for image recognition, it is natural to design symmetric encoder network and decoder network. For instance in the previous paper [53], this paper verify the importance of symmetric transposed convolution layer design for semantic segmentation task. In contrast, point-based studies [95, 96] dominantly rely on the asymmetric PointNet++ architecture, which is similar to FCN [46].

The top-right sub-table in Table 5 supports our claim. When we do not use hierarchical-set mixing, the architecture become asymmetric, and transition down and up layers are identical to that in PointNet++ [56] and Point Transformer [96]. It turns out that the asymmetric architecture (the second row) degrades the performance of the network (the last row) in terms of both mIoU and Chamfer distance by 2.3 absolute percentage and 0.01, respectively. Moreover, when we apply inter-set mixing, the performance gap further increases in both semantic segmentation and point reconstruction tasks.

Table 5. Ablation study about positional encoding (left), types of mixing (top-right) and token-mixing MLPs (bottom-right). In the bottom-right table, we denote channel-mixing MLPs and token-mixing MLPs as C-MLP and T-MLP, respectively. Note that number of parameters (Param.) and training time (Time) is measured under semantic segmentation task on S3DIS dataset [2].

Preserve (✓) Pos. enc. in			Semantic seg		Point recon	
Intra	Inter	Hier	mIoU	mAcc	CD(↓)	F1(↑)
			64.7	71.8	1.13	53.0
	✓		65.9	72.5	1.13	53.0
✓			64.0	70.5	1.13	53.0
✓	✓		66.1	72.9	1.12	53.6
✓			69.6	76.3	1.12	53.6
✓		✓	70.2	76.8	1.13	52.5
✓	✓		69.9	76.5	1.13	53.5
✓	✓	✓	**71.4**	**77.4**	**1.11**	**53.7**

Preserve (✓)			Semantic seg		Point recon	
Intra	Inter	Hier	mIoU	mAcc	CD(↓)	F1(↑)
✓			69.2	75.8	1.13	53.5
✓	✓		69.1	75.7	1.12	53.5
✓		✓	69.3	76.6	**1.11**	53.5
✓	✓	✓	**71.4**	**77.4**	**1.11**	**53.7**

C-MLP	T-MLP	Softmax	Param.	Time	mIoU	CD(↓)
✓			6.5M	40h	58.3	1.23
✓		✓	6.5M	44h	**71.4**	**1.11**
✓	✓		7.4M	88h	71.1	1.12
✓	✓	✓	7.4M	95h	71.1	**1.11**

5   Conclusion

We propose a MLP-like architecture for point cloud understanding, which focuses on sharing point responses in numerous and diverse point sets through a universal point set operator, *PointMixer*. Regardless of the cardinality of a point set, Point-Mixer layer can "mix" point responses in intra-set, inter-set, and hierarchical-set. Moreover, we present a point-based general architecture that involves symmetric encoder-decoder blocks for propagating information through hierarchical point sets. Extensive experiments validate the efficacy of our PointMixer network with superior or compelling performance compared to Transformer-based studies. Through out this paper, we claim that dense token-wise calculation, such as self-attention layers or token-mixing MLPs, is not an essential choice for point cloud processing. Instead, we emphasize the importance of information sharing toward various point sets.

Acknowledgements. (1) IITP grant funded by the Korea government (MSIT) (No. 2019-0-01906, Artificial Intelligence Graduate School Program (POSTECH)) and (2) Institute of Information and communications Technology Planning and Evaluation (IITP) grant funded by the Korea government (MSIT) (No. 2021-0-02068, Artificial Intelligence Innovation Hub).

References

1. Aanæs, H., Jensen, R.R., Vogiatzis, G., Tola, E., Dahl, A.B.: Large-scale data for multiple-view stereopsis. Int. J. Comput. Vis. (IJCV) **120**(2), 153–168 (2016)
2. Armeni, I., et al.: 3D semantic parsing of large-scale indoor spaces. In: Proceedings of the IEEE International Conference on Computer Vision and Pattern Recognition (2016)
3. Bello, I.: Lambdanetworks: modeling long-range interactions without attention. In: International Conference on Learning Representations (2020)
4. Chen, C.F.R., Fan, Q., Panda, R.: Crossvit: cross-attention multi-scale vision transformer for image classification. In: Proceedings of the IEEE/CVF International Conference on Computer Vision (ICCV), pp. 357–366 (2021)
5. Chen, S., Xie, E., Ge, C., Liang, D., Luo, P.: CycleMLP: a MLP-like architecture for dense prediction. In: International Conference on Learning Representations (ICLR) (2022)
6. Choe, J., Joo, K., Imtiaz, T., Kweon, I.S.: Volumetric propagation network: stereo-lidar fusion for long-range depth estimation. IEEE Robot. Autom. Lett. **6**(3), 4672–4679 (2021)
7. Choe, J., Joung, B., Rameau, F., Park, J., Kweon, I.S.: Deep point cloud reconstruction. In: International Conference on Learning Representations (ICLR) (2022)
8. Choy, C., Gwak, J., Savarese, S.: 4D spatio-temporal convnets: minkowski convolutional neural networks. In: Proceedings of the IEEE/CVF Conference on Computer Vision and Pattern Recognition (CVPR), pp. 3075–3084 (2019)
9. Dai, A., Chang, A.X., Savva, M., Halber, M., Funkhouser, T., Nießner, M.: Scannet: richly-annotated 3D reconstructions of indoor scenes. In: Proceedings of the IEEE/CVF Conference on Computer Vision and Pattern Recognition (CVPR), pp. 5828–5839 (2017)
10. d'Ascoli, S., Touvron, H., Leavitt, M.L., Morcos, A.S., Biroli, G., Sagun, L.: Convit: improving vision transformers with soft convolutional inductive biases. In: International Conference on Machine Learning, pp. 2286–2296. PMLR (2021)
11. Devlin, J., Chang, M.W., Lee, K., Toutanova, K.: Bert: pre-training of deep bidirectional transformers for language understanding. In: Proceedings of the 2019 Conference of the North American Chapter of the Association for Computational Linguistics: Human Language Technologies, Volume 1 (Long and Short Papers), pp. 4171–4186 (2019)
12. Ding, X., Xia, C., Zhang, X., Chu, X., Han, J., Ding, G.: Repmlp: re-parameterizing convolutions into fully-connected layers for image recognition. In: Proceedings of the IEEE/CVF Conference on Computer Vision and Pattern Recognition (CVPR) (2022)
13. Dosovitskiy, A., et al.: An image is worth 16x16 words: transformers for image recognition at scale. arXiv preprint arXiv:2010.11929 (2020)
14. Graham, B., Engelcke, M., van der Maaten, L.: 3D semantic segmentation with submanifold sparse convolutional networks. In: CVPR (2018)

15. Graham, B., van der Maaten, L.: Submanifold sparse convolutional networks. arXiv preprint arXiv:1706.01307 (2017)
16. Guo, J., et al.: Hire-MLP: vision MLP via hierarchical rearrangement. arXiv preprint arXiv:2108.13341 (2021)
17. Guo, M.H., Cai, J.X., Liu, Z.N., Mu, T.J., Martin, R.R., Hu, S.M.: PCT: point cloud transformer. Comput. Vis. Media **7**(2), 187–199 (2021)
18. Guo, Y., Wang, H., Hu, Q., Liu, H., Liu, L., Bennamoun, M.: Deep learning for 3D point clouds: a survey. IEEE Trans. Pattern Anal. Mach. Intell. (PAMI) **43**(12), 4338–4364 (2020)
19. Han, K., Xiao, A., Wu, E., Guo, J., Xu, C., Wang, Y.: Transformer in transformer. arXiv preprint arXiv:2103.00112 (2021)
20. Handa, A., Whelan, T., McDonald, J., Davison, A.J.: A benchmark for RGB-D visual odometry, 3D reconstruction and slam. In: IEEE International Conference on Robotics and Automation (ICRA) (2014)
21. He, K., Zhang, X., Ren, S., Sun, J.: Deep residual learning for image recognition. In: Proceedings of the IEEE/CVF Conference on Computer Vision and Pattern Recognition (CVPR), pp. 770–778 (2016)
22. Hendrycks, D., Gimpel, K.: Gaussian error linear units (GELUs). arXiv preprint arXiv:1606.08415 (2016)
23. Hou, Q., Jiang, Z., Yuan, L., Cheng, M.M., Yan, S., Feng, J.: Vision permutator: a permutable MLP-like architecture for visual recognition. arXiv preprint arXiv:2106.12368 (2021)
24. Hu, H., Zhang, Z., Xie, Z., Lin, S.: Local relation networks for image recognition. In: Proceedings of the IEEE/CVF International Conference on Computer Vision (ICCV), pp. 3464–3473 (2019)
25. Hu, Q., et al.: RandLA-Net: efficient semantic segmentation of large-scale point clouds. In: Proceedings of the IEEE/CVF Conference on Computer Vision and Pattern Recognition (CVPR), pp. 11108–11117 (2020)
26. Huang, Q., Wang, W., Neumann, U.: Recurrent slice networks for 3D segmentation of point clouds. In: Proceedings of the IEEE/CVF Conference on Computer Vision and Pattern Recognition (CVPR) (2018)
27. Jensen, R., Dahl, A., Vogiatzis, G., Tola, E., Aanæs, H.: Large scale multi-view stereopsis evaluation. In: Proceedings of the IEEE/CVF Conference on Computer Vision and Pattern Recognition (CVPR) (2014)
28. Jiang, L., Zhao, H., Liu, S., Shen, X., Fu, C.W., Jia, J.: Hierarchical point-edge interaction network for point cloud semantic segmentation. In: Proceedings of the IEEE/CVF International Conference on Computer Vision (ICCV), pp. 10433–10441 (2019)
29. Johnson, J., Douze, M., Jégou, H.: Billion-scale similarity search with GPUs. IEEE Trans. Big Data **7**(3), 535–547 (2019)
30. Khan, S., Naseer, M., Hayat, M., Zamir, S.W., Khan, F.S., Shah, M.: Transformers in vision: a survey. ACM Comput. Surv. (CSUR) **54**, 1–41 (2021)
31. Klokov, R., Lempitsky, V.: Escape from cells: deep KD-networks for the recognition of 3D point cloud models. In: Proceedings of the IEEE/CVF International Conference on Computer Vision (ICCV) (2017)
32. Knapitsch, A., Park, J., Zhou, Q.Y., Koltun, V.: Tanks and temples: benchmarking large-scale scene reconstruction. ACM Trans. Graph. (ToG) **36**(4), 1–13 (2017)
33. Komarichev, A., Zhong, Z., Hua, J.: A-CNN: annularly convolutional neural networks on point clouds. In: Proceedings of the IEEE/CVF Conference on Computer Vision and Pattern Recognition (CVPR), pp. 7421–7430 (2019)

34. Lee, J., Choy, C., Park, J.: Putting 3D spatially sparse networks on a diet. arXiv preprint arXiv:2112.01316 (2021)
35. Li, J., Hassani, A., Walton, S., Shi, H.: ConvMLP: hierarchical convolutional MLPs for vision. arXiv preprint arXiv:2109.04454 (2021)
36. Li, J., Chen, B.M., Lee, G.H.: So-net: self-organizing network for point cloud analysis. In: Proceedings of the IEEE/CVF Conference on Computer Vision and Pattern Recognition (CVPR) (2018)
37. Li, R., Li, X., Heng, P.A., Fu, C.W.: Point cloud upsampling via disentangled refinement. In: Proceedings of the IEEE/CVF Conference on Computer Vision and Pattern Recognition (CVPR) (2021)
38. Li, Y., Bu, R., Sun, M., Wu, W., Di, X., Chen, B.: PointCNN: convolution on X-transformed points. In: Advances in Neural Information Processing Systems, vol. 31 (2018)
39. Lian, D., Yu, Z., Sun, X., Gao, S.: AS-MLP: an axial shifted MLP architecture for vision. In: International Conference on Learning Representations (2022)
40. Lin, Y., et al.: FPConv: learning local flattening for point convolution. In: Proceedings of the IEEE/CVF Conference on Computer Vision and Pattern Recognition (CVPR), pp. 4293–4302 (2020)
41. Liu, H., Dai, Z., So, D., Le, Q.V.: Pay attention to MLPs. In: Beygelzimer, A., Dauphin, Y., Liang, P., Vaughan, J.W. (eds.) Advances in Neural Information Processing Systems (NeurIPS) (2021)
42. Liu, Y., Fan, B., Meng, G., Lu, J., Xiang, S., Pan, C.: Densepoint: learning densely contextual representation for efficient point cloud processing. In: Proceedings of the IEEE/CVF International Conference on Computer Vision (ICCV), pp. 5239–5248 (2019)
43. Liu, Y., Fan, B., Xiang, S., Pan, C.: Relation-shape convolutional neural network for point cloud analysis. In: Proceedings of the IEEE/CVF Conference on Computer Vision and Pattern Recognition (CVPR), pp. 8895–8904 (2019)
44. Liu, Z., et al.: Swin transformer: hierarchical vision transformer using shifted windows. In: Proceedings of the IEEE/CVF International Conference on Computer Vision (ICCV), pp. 10012–10022 (2021)
45. Liu, Z., Tang, H., Lin, Y., Han, S.: Point-voxel CNN for efficient 3D deep learning. In: Advances in Neural Information Processing Systems (NeurIPS), vol. 32 (2019)
46. Long, J., Shelhamer, E., Darrell, T.: Fully convolutional networks for semantic segmentation. In: Proceedings of the IEEE/CVF Conference on Computer Vision and Pattern Recognition (CVPR), pp. 3431–3440 (2015)
47. Ma, X., Qin, C., You, H., Ran, H., Fu, Y.: Rethinking network design and local geometry in point cloud: a simple residual MLP framework. In: International Conference on Learning Representations (ICLR) (2022)
48. Mao, J., Wang, X., Li, H.: Interpolated convolutional networks for 3D point cloud understanding. In: Proceedings of the IEEE/CVF International Conference on Computer Vision (ICCV), pp. 1578–1587 (2019)
49. Mao, J., et al.: Voxel transformer for 3D object detection. In: Proceedings of the IEEE/CVF International Conference on Computer Vision (ICCV), pp. 3164–3173 (2021)
50. Maturana, D., Scherer, S.: Voxnet: a 3D convolutional neural network for real-time object recognition. In: IEEE/RSJ International Conference on Intelligent Robots and Systems (IROS), pp. 922–928. IEEE (2015)
51. Mazur, K., Lempitsky, V.: Cloud transformers: a universal approach to point cloud processing tasks. In: Proceedings of the IEEE/CVF International Conference on Computer Vision (ICCV), pp. 10715–10724, October 2021

52. Muja, M., Lowe, D.G.: Fast approximate nearest neighbors with automatic algorithm configuration. VISAPP (1) **2**(331–340), 2 (2009)
53. Noh, H., Hong, S., Han, B.: Learning deconvolution network for semantic segmentation. In: Proceedings of the IEEE/CVF International Conference on Computer Vision (ICCV), pp. 1520–1528 (2015)
54. Park, C., Jeong, Y., Cho, M., Park, J.: Fast point transformer. In: Proceedings of the IEEE/CVF Conference on Computer Vision and Pattern Recognition (CVPR), pp. 16949–16958 (2022)
55. Qi, C.R., Su, H., Mo, K., Guibas, L.J.: Pointnet: deep learning on point sets for 3D classification and segmentation. In: Proceedings of the IEEE/CVF Conference on Computer Vision and Pattern Recognition (CVPR), pp. 652–660 (2017)
56. Qi, C.R., Yi, L., Su, H., Guibas, L.J.: Pointnet++: deep hierarchical feature learning on point sets in a metric space. arXiv preprint arXiv:1706.02413 (2017)
57. Qi, X., Liao, R., Jia, J., Fidler, S., Urtasun, R.: 3D graph neural networks for RGBD semantic segmentation. In: Proceedings of the IEEE/CVF International Conference on Computer Vision (ICCV), pp. 5199–5208 (2017)
58. Qian, G., Hammoud, H., Li, G., Thabet, A., Ghanem, B.: Assanet: an anisotropic separable set abstraction for efficient point cloud representation learning. In: Advances in Neural Information Processing Systems (NeurIPS), vol. 34 (2021)
59. Radford, A., Narasimhan, K., Salimans, T., Sutskever, I.: Improving language understanding by generative pre-training (2018)
60. Ramachandran, P., Parmar, N., Vaswani, A., Bello, I., Levskaya, A., Shlens, J.: Stand-alone self-attention in vision models. In: Proceedings of the 33rd International Conference on Neural Information Processing Systems, pp. 68–80 (2019)
61. Simonovsky, M., Komodakis, N.: Dynamic edge-conditioned filters in convolutional neural networks on graphs. In: Proceedings of the IEEE/CVF Conference on Computer Vision and Pattern Recognition (CVPR), pp. 3693–3702 (2017)
62. Simonyan, K., Zisserman, A.: Very deep convolutional networks for large-scale image recognition. arXiv preprint arXiv:1409.1556 (2014)
63. Su, H., et al.: Splatnet: sparse lattice networks for point cloud processing. In: Proceedings of the IEEE/CVF Conference on Computer Vision and Pattern Recognition (CVPR), pp. 2530–2539 (2018)
64. Tang, H., et al.: Searching efficient 3D architectures with sparse point-voxel convolution. In: Vedaldi, A., Bischof, H., Brox, T., Frahm, J.-M. (eds.) ECCV 2020. LNCS, vol. 12373, pp. 685–702. Springer, Cham (2020). https://doi.org/10.1007/978-3-030-58604-1_41
65. Tay, Y., Bahri, D., Metzler, D., Juan, D., Zhao, Z., Zheng, C.: Synthesizer: rethinking self-attention in transformer models. In: ICML (2021)
66. Tay, Y., Dehghani, M., Bahri, D., Metzler, D.: Efficient transformers: a survey. arXiv preprint arXiv:2009.06732 (2020)
67. Thomas, H., Qi, C.R., Deschaud, J.E., Marcotegui, B., Goulette, F., Guibas, L.J.: Kpconv: flexible and deformable convolution for point clouds. In: Proceedings of the IEEE/CVF International Conference on Computer Vision (ICCV), pp. 6411–6420 (2019)
68. Tolstikhin, I.O., et al.: MLP-mixer: an all-MLP architecture for vision. In: Advances in Neural Information Processing Systems (NeurIPS), vol. 34 (2021)
69. Touvron, H., et al.: Resmlp: feedforward networks for image classification with data-efficient training. arXiv preprint arXiv:2105.03404 (2021)
70. Touvron, H., Cord, M., Douze, M., Massa, F., Sablayrolles, A., Jégou, H.: Training data-efficient image transformers & distillation through attention. In: International Conference on Machine Learning, pp. 10347–10357. PMLR (2021)

PointMixer: MLP-Mixer for Point Cloud Understanding 639

71. Trockman, A., Kolter, J.Z.: Patches are all you need? arXiv preprint arXiv:2201.09792 (2022)
72. Vaswani, A., Ramachandran, P., Srinivas, A., Parmar, N., Hechtman, B., Shlens, J.: Scaling local self-attention for parameter efficient visual backbones. In: Proceedings of the IEEE/CVF Conference on Computer Vision and Pattern Recognition (CVPR), pp. 12894–12904 (2021)
73. Vaswani, A., et al.: Attention is all you need. In: Advances in Neural Information Processing Systems (NeurIPS) (2017)
74. Wang, C., Samari, B., Siddiqi, K.: Local spectral graph convolution for point set feature learning. In: Proceedings of the European Conference on Computer Vision (ECCV), pp. 52–66 (2018)
75. Wang, L., Huang, Y., Hou, Y., Zhang, S., Shan, J.: Graph attention convolution for point cloud semantic segmentation. In: Proceedings of the IEEE/CVF Conference on Computer Vision and Pattern Recognition (CVPR), pp. 10296–10305 (2019)
76. Wang, S., Suo, S., Ma, W.C., Pokrovsky, A., Urtasun, R.: Deep parametric continuous convolutional neural networks. In: Proceedings of the IEEE/CVF Conference on Computer Vision and Pattern Recognition (CVPR), pp. 2589–2597 (2018)
77. Wang, W., et al.: Pyramid vision transformer: a versatile backbone for dense prediction without convolutions. In: Proceedings of the IEEE/CVF International Conference on Computer Vision (ICCV), pp. 568–578 (2021)
78. Wang, Y., Sun, Y., Liu, Z., Sarma, S.E., Bronstein, M.M., Solomon, J.M.: Dynamic graph CNN for learning on point clouds. ACM Trans. Graph. (ToG) **38**(5), 1–12 (2019)
79. Wu, W., Qi, Z., Fuxin, L.: Pointconv: deep convolutional networks on 3D point clouds. In: Proceedings of the IEEE/CVF Conference on Computer Vision and Pattern Recognition (CVPR), pp. 9621–9630 (2019)
80. Wu, Z., et al.: 3D shapenets: a deep representation for volumetric shapes. In: Proceedings of the IEEE/CVF Conference on Computer Vision and Pattern Recognition (CVPR), pp. 1912–1920 (2015)
81. Xie, E., Wang, W., Yu, Z., Anandkumar, A., Alvarez, J.M., Luo, P.: Segformer: simple and efficient design for semantic segmentation with transformers. In: Advances in Neural Information Processing Systems (NeurIPS), vol. 34 (2021)
82. Xu, M., Zhou, Z., Qiao, Y.: Geometry sharing network for 3D point cloud classification and segmentation. In: Association for the Advancement of Artificial Intelligence (AAAI) (2020)
83. Xu, M., Ding, R., Zhao, H., Qi, X.: Paconv: position adaptive convolution with dynamic kernel assembling on point clouds. In: Proceedings of the IEEE/CVF Conference on Computer Vision and Pattern Recognition (CVPR), pp. 3173–3182 (2021)
84. Xu, Q., Sun, X., Wu, C.Y., Wang, P., Neumann, U.: Grid-GCN for fast and scalable point cloud learning. In: Proceedings of the IEEE/CVF Conference on Computer Vision and Pattern Recognition (CVPR), pp. 5661–5670 (2020)
85. Yang, Z., Sun, Y., Liu, S., Qi, X., Jia, J.: CN: channel normalization for point cloud recognition. In: Vedaldi, A., Bischof, H., Brox, T., Frahm, J.-M. (eds.) ECCV 2020. LNCS, vol. 12355, pp. 600–616. Springer, Cham (2020). https://doi.org/10.1007/978-3-030-58607-2_35
86. Yao, Y., Luo, Z., Li, S., Fang, T., Quan, L.: Mvsnet: depth inference for unstructured multi-view stereo. In: European Conference on Computer Vision (ECCV) (2018)
87. Yi, L., et al.: A scalable active framework for region annotation in 3D shape collections. ACM Trans. Graph. (ToG) **35**(6), 1–12 (2016)

88. Yu, T., Li, X., Cai, Y., Sun, M., Li, P.: S^2-MLP: spatial-shift MLP architecture for vision. arXiv preprint arXiv:2106.07477 (2021)

89. Yu, T., Li, X., Cai, Y., Sun, M., Li, P.: S^2-MLPV2: improved spatial-shift MLP architecture for vision. In: Proceedings of the IEEE/CVF Winter Conference on Applications of Computer Vision (WACV) (2022)

90. Yu, W., et al.: Metaformer is actually what you need for vision. In: CVPR (2022)

91. Yuan, L., et al.: Tokens-to-token VIT: training vision transformers from scratch on imagenet. In: Proceedings of the IEEE/CVF International Conference on Computer Vision (ICCV), pp. 558–567 (2021)

92. Zhang, D.J., et al.: MorphMLP: a self-attention free, MLP-like backbone for image and video. arXiv preprint arXiv:2111.12527 (2021)

93. Zhang, F., Fang, J., Wah, B., Torr, P.: Deep FusionNet for point cloud semantic segmentation. In: Vedaldi, A., Bischof, H., Brox, T., Frahm, J.-M. (eds.) ECCV 2020. LNCS, vol. 12369, pp. 644–663. Springer, Cham (2020). https://doi.org/10.1007/978-3-030-58586-0_38

94. Zhao, H., Jia, J., Koltun, V.: Exploring self-attention for image recognition. In: Proceedings of the IEEE/CVF Conference on Computer Vision and Pattern Recognition (CVPR), pp. 10076–10085 (2020)

95. Zhao, H., Jiang, L., Fu, C.W., Jia, J.: Pointweb: enhancing local neighborhood features for point cloud processing. In: Proceedings of the IEEE/CVF Conference on Computer Vision and Pattern Recognition (CVPR), pp. 5565–5573 (2019)

96. Zhao, H., Jiang, L., Jia, J., Torr, P.H., Koltun, V.: Point transformer. In: Proceedings of the IEEE/CVF International Conference on Computer Vision (ICCV), pp. 16259–16268 (2021)

97. Zhou, Q.Y., Park, J., Koltun, V.: Open3D: a modern library for 3D data processing. arXiv preprint arXiv:1801.09847 (2018)

98. Zhou, Y., Tuzel, O.: Voxelnet: end-to-end learning for point cloud based 3D object detection. In: Proceedings of the IEEE/CVF Conference on Computer Vision and Pattern Recognition (CVPR), pp. 4490–4499 (2018)

Initialization and Alignment for Adversarial Texture Optimization

Xiaoming Zhao[✉], Zhizhen Zhao, and Alexander G. Schwing

University of Illinois, Urbana-Champaign, Champaign, USA
{xz23,zhizhenz,aschwing}@illinois.edu
https://xiaoming-zhao.github.io/projects/advtex_init_align

Abstract. While recovery of geometry from image and video data has received a lot of attention in computer vision, methods to capture the texture for a given geometry are less mature. Specifically, classical methods for texture generation often assume clean geometry and reasonably well-aligned image data. While very recent methods, *e.g.*, adversarial texture optimization, better handle lower-quality data obtained from hand-held devices, we find them to still struggle frequently. To improve robustness, particularly of recent adversarial texture optimization, we develop an explicit initialization and an alignment procedure. It deals with complex geometry due to a robust mapping of the geometry to the texture map and a hard-assignment-based initialization. It deals with misalignment of geometry and images by integrating fast image-alignment into the texture refinement optimization. We demonstrate efficacy of our texture generation on a dataset of 11 scenes with a total of 2807 frames, observing 7.8% and 11.1% relative improvements regarding perceptual and sharpness measurements.

Keywords: Scene analysis · Texture reconstruction

1 Introduction

Accurate scene reconstruction is one of the major goals in computer vision. Decades of research have been devoted to developing robust methods like 'Structure from Motion,' 'Bundle Adjustment,' and more recently also single view reconstruction techniques. While reconstruction of geometry from image and video data has become increasingly popular and accurate in recent years, recovered 3D models remain often pale because textures aren't considered.

Given a reconstructed 3D model of a scene consisting of triangular faces, and given a sequence of images depicting the scene, texture mapping aims to find for each triangle a suitable texture. The problem of automatic texture mapping has been studied in different areas since late 1990 and early 2000. For instance, in the graphics community [12,29,30], in computer vision [27,43,45], architecture [19]

Supplementary Information The online version contains supplementary material available at https://doi.org/10.1007/978-3-031-19812-0_37.

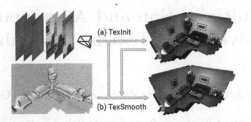

Fig. 1. We study texture generation given RGBD images with associated camera parameters as well as a reconstructed mesh. **(a) TexInit**: we initialize the texture using an assignment-based texture generation framework. **(b) TexSmooth**: a data-driven adversarial loss is utilized to optimize out artifacts incurred in the assignment step.

and photogrammetry [14]. Many of the proposed algorithms work very well in a controlled lab-setting where geometry is known perfectly, or in a setting where accurate 3D models are available from a 3D laser scanner.

However, applying texture mapping techniques to noisy mesh geometry obtained *on the fly* from a recent LiDAR equipped iPad reveals missing robustness because of multiple reasons: 1) images and 3D models are often not perfectly aligned; 2) 3D models are not accurate and the obtained meshes aren't necessarily manifold-connected. Even recent techniques for mesh flattening [41] and texturing [16,24,54] result in surprising artifacts due to streamed geometry and pose inaccuracies as shown later.

To address this robustness issue we find equipping of the recently-proposed adversarial texture optimization technique [24] with classical initialization and alignment techniques to be remarkably effective. Without the added initialization and alignment, we find current methods don't produce high-quality textures. Concretely and as illustrated in Fig. 1, we aim for texture generation which operates on a sequence of images and corresponding depth maps as well as their camera parameters. Moreover, we assume the 3D model to be given and fixed. Importantly, we consider a streaming setup, with all data obtained *on the fly*, and not further processed, *e.g.*, via batch structure-from-motion. The setup is ubiquitous and the form of data can be acquired easily from consumer-grade devices these days, *e.g.*, from a recent iPad or iPhone [1]. We aim to translate this data into texture maps. For this, we first flatten the triangle mesh using recent advances [41]. We then use a Markov Random Field (MRF) to resolve overlaps in flattened meshes for non-manifold-connected data. In a next step we determine the image frame from which to extract the texture of each mesh triangle using a simple optimization. We refer to this as TexInit, which permits to obtain a high-quality initialization for subsequent refinement. Next we address inaccuracies in camera poses and in geometry by automatically shifting images using the result of a fast Fourier transformation (FFT) [6]. The final optimized texture is obtained by integrating this FFT-alignment component into adversarial optimization [24]. We dub this stage TexSmooth. The obtained texture can be used in any 3D engine for downstream applications.

To study efficacy of the proposed framework we acquire 11 complex scenes using a recent iPad. We establish accuracy of the proposed technique to generate and use the texture by showing that the quality of rendered views is superior to prior approaches on these scenes. Quantitatively, our framework improves prior work by 7.8% and 11.1% relatively with respect to perceptual (LPIPS [53]) and sharpness (S_3 [47]) measurements respectively. Besides, our framework improves over baselines on ScanNet [11], demonstrating the ability to generalize.

2 Related Work

We aim for accurate recovery of texture for a reconstructed 3D scene from a sequence of RGBD images. For this, a variety of techniques have been proposed, which can be roughly categorized into four groups: 1) averaging-based; 2) warping-based; 3) learning-based; and 4) assignment-based. Averaging-based methods find all views within which a point is visible and combine the color observations. Warping-based approaches either distort or synthesize source images to handle mesh misalignment or camera drift. Learning-based ones learn the texture representation. Assignment-based methods attempt to find the best view and 'copy' the observation into a texture. We review these groups next:

Averaging-based: Very early work by Marshner [29] estimates the parameters of a bidirectional reflectance distribution function (BRDF) for every point on the texture map. To compute this estimation, all observations from the recorded images where the point is visible are used. Similar techniques have been investigated in subsequent work [9].

Similarly, to compute a texture map, [30] and [12] perform a weighted blending of all recorded images. The weights take visibility and other factors into account. The developed approaches are semi-automatic as they require an initial estimate of the camera orientations which is obtained from interactively selected point correspondences or marked lines. Multi-resolution textures [33], face textures [36] and blending [8,31] have also been studied.

Warping-based: Aganj *et al.* [4] morph each source image to align to the mesh. Furthermore, [23,54] propose to optimize camera poses and image warping parameters jointly. However, this line of vertex-based optimization has stringent requirements on the mesh density and cannot be applied to a sparse mesh. More recently, Bi *et al.* [10] follow patch-synthesis [7,50] to re-synthesize aligned target images for each source view. However, such methods require costly multiscale optimization to avoid a large number of local optima. In contrast, the proposed approach does not require those techniques.

Learning-based: Recently, learning-based methods have been introduced for texture optimization. Some works focus on specific object and scene categories [18,40] while we do not make such assumptions. Moreover, learned representations, *e.g.*, neural textures, have also been developed [5,44,46]. Meanwhile, generative models are developed to synthesize a holistic texture from a single image or pattern [21,32] while we focus on texture reconstruction. AtlasNet [20] and NeuTex [52] focus on learning a 3D-to-2D mapping, which can be utilized in texture editing, while we focus on reconstructing realistic textures from source images. The recently-proposed adversarial texture optimization [24] utilizes adversarial training to reconstruct the texture. However, despite advances, adversarial optimization still struggles with misalignments. We improve this shortcoming via an explicit high-quality initialization and an efficient alignment module.

Assignment-based: Classical assignment-based methods operated within controlled environments [14,15,38,39] or utilized special camera rigs [15,19]. These works suggest computing for each vertex a set of 'valid' images, which are subsequently refined by iterating over each vertex and adjusting the assignment to obtain more consistency. Finally, texture data is 'copied' from the images. In contrast, we aim to create a texture in an uncontrolled setting. Consequently, 3D geometry is not accurate and very noisy. Other early work [13,22,28,39,51] focuses on closed surfaces and small-scale meshes, making them not applicable to our setting. More recently, upon finding the best texture independently for each face using cues like visibility, orientation, resolution, and distortion, refinement techniques like texture coordinate optimization, color adjustments, or scores-based optimization have been discussed [3,34,48].

Related to our approach are methods that formulate texture selection using a Markov Random Field (MRF) [16,27,42]. Shu *et al.* [42] suggest visibility as the data term and employ texture smoothness to reduce transitions. Lempitsky *et al.* [27] study color-continuity which integrates over face seams. Fu

Fig. 2. Noisy geometry. The wall has two layers.

et al. [16] additionally use the projected 2D face area to select a texture assignment for each face. However, noisy geometry like the one shown in Fig. 2, makes it difficult for assignment-based methods to yield high quality results, which we will show later. Therefore, different from these methods, we address texture drift in a data-driven refinement procedure rather than in an assignment stage.

3   Approach

We want to automatically create the texture T from a set of RGBD images $I = \{I_1, \ldots, I_T\}$, for each of which we also know camera parameters $\{p_t\}_{t=1}^{T}$, *i.e.*, extrinsics and intrinsics. We are also given a triangular scene mesh $M = \{Tri_i\}_{i=1}^{|M|}$, where Tri_i denotes the i-th triangle. This form of data is easily accessible from commercially available consumer devices, *e.g.*, a recent iPhone or iPad.

We construct the texture T in two steps that combine advantages of assignment-based and learning-based techniques: 1) TexInit: we generate a texture initialization $T_{init} \in \mathbb{R}^{H \times W \times 3}$ of height H, width W and 3 color channels in an assignment-based manner (Sect. 3.1); 2) TexSmooth: we then refine T_{init}

with an improved data-driven adversarial optimization that integrates an efficient alignment procedure (Sect. 3.2). Formally, the final texture $\mathcal{T}$ is computed via

$$\mathcal{T} = \texttt{TexSmooth}\left(\mathcal{T}_{\text{init}}, \{I_t\}_{t=1}^T, \{p_t\}_{t=1}^T, M\right),$$

$$\text{where } \mathcal{T}_{\text{init}} = \texttt{TexInit}\left(\{I_t\}_{t=1}^T, \{p_t\}_{t=1}^T, M\right). \tag{1}$$

We detail each component next.

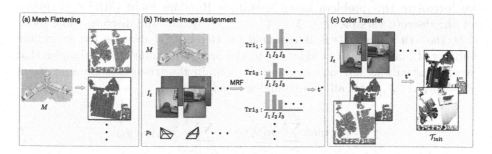

Fig. 3. Texture initialization TexInit (Sect. 3.1). **(a)** Mesh flattening: we flatten a 3D mesh into the 2D plane using overlap detection. **(b)** Triangle-image assignment: we develop a simple formulation to compute the triangle-image assignment $\mathbf{t}^*$ from mesh M, frames I_t and camera parameters p_t. We assign frames to each triangle $\texttt{Tri}_i$ based on $\mathbf{t}^*$. **(c)** Color transfer: based on the flattened mesh in **(a)** and the best assignment $\mathbf{t}^*$ from **(b)**, we generate the texture $\mathcal{T}_{\text{init}}$.

3.1 Texture Initialization (TexInit)

The proposed approach to obtain the texture initialization $\mathcal{T}_{\text{init}}$ is outlined in Fig. 3 and consists of following three steps: 1) We flatten the provided mesh M. For this we detect overlaps within the flattened mesh, which may happen due to the fact that we operate with general meshes that are not guaranteed to have a manifold connectivity. Overlap detection ensures that every triangle is assigned a unique position in the texture. 2) We identify for each triangle the 'best' texture index $\mathbf{t}^*$. Hereby, 'best' is defined using cues like visibility and color consistency. 3) After identifying the index $\mathbf{t}^* = (t_1^*, \ldots, t_{|M|}^*)$ for each triangle, we create the texture $\mathcal{T}_{\text{init}}$ by transferring for all $(u, v) \in [1, \ldots, W] \times [1, \ldots, H]$ locations in the texture, the RGB data from the corresponding location (a, b) in image I_t.
1) Mesh Flattening: In a first step, as illustrated in Fig. 3 (left), we flatten the given mesh M. For this we use the recently proposed boundary first flattening (BFF) technique [41]. The flattening is fully automatic, with distortion mathematically guaranteed to be as low or lower than any other conformal mapping.

However, despite those guarantees, BFF still requires meshes to have a manifold connectivity. While we augment work by [41] using vertex duplication to circumvent this restriction, flattening may still result in overlapping regions as illustrated in Fig. 4. To fix this and uniquely assign a triangle to a position in the texture, we perform overlap detection as discussed next.

Overlap Detection: Overlap detection operates on flattened and possibly overlapping triangle meshes like the one illustrated in Fig. 4a. Our goal is to assign triangles to different planes. Upon re-packing the triangles assigned to different planes, we obtain the non-overlapping triangle mesh illustrated in Fig. 4b.

In order to not break the triangle mesh at a random position and end up with many individual triangles, *i.e.*, in order to maintain large triangle connectivity, we formulate this problem using a Markov Random Field (MRF). Formally, let the discrete variable $y_i \in \mathcal{Y} = \{1, \ldots, |\mathcal{Y}|\}$ denote the discrete plane index that the i-th triangle $\mathtt{Tri}_i$ is assigned to. Hereby, $|\mathcal{Y}|$ denotes the maximum number of planes which is identical to the maximum number of triangles that overlap initially at any one location. We obtain the triangle-plane assignment $y^* = (y_1^*, \ldots, y_{|M|}^*)$ for all $|M|$ triangles by addressing

$$y^* = \arg \max_y \sum_{i=1}^{|M|} \phi_i(y_i) + \sum_{(i,j) \in \mathcal{A} \cup \mathcal{O}} \phi_{i,j}(y_i, y_j), \tag{2}$$

where $\mathcal{A}$ and $\mathcal{O}$ are sets of triangle index pairs which are adjacent and overlapping respectively. Here, $\phi_i(\cdot)$ denotes triangle $\mathtt{Tri}_i$'s priority over $\mathcal{Y}$ when considering only its *local* information, while $\phi_{i,j}(\cdot)$ refers to $\mathtt{Tri}_i$ and $\mathtt{Tri}_j$'s joint preference on their assignments. Equation (2) is solved with belief propagation [17].

Intuitively, by addressing the program given in Eq. (2) we want a different plane index for overlapping triangles, while encouraging mesh M's adjacent triangles to be placed on the same plane. To achieve this we use

$$\phi_i(y_i) = \begin{cases} 1.0, & \text{if } y_i = \min \mathcal{Y}_{i,\text{non-overlap}} \\ 0.0, & \text{otherwise} \end{cases}, \text{ and} \tag{3}$$

$$\phi_{i,j}(y_i, y_j) = \begin{cases} \mathbb{1}\{y_i = y_j\}, & \text{if } (i,j) \in \mathcal{A} \\ \mathbb{1}\{y_i \neq y_j\}, & \text{if } (i,j) \in \mathcal{O} \end{cases}. \tag{4}$$

Here, $\mathbb{1}\{\cdot\}$ denotes the indicator function and $\mathcal{Y}_{i,\text{non-overlap}}$ contains all plane indices where $\mathtt{Tri}_i$ has no overlap with others. Intuitively, Eq. (3) encourages to assign the minimum of such indices to $\mathtt{Tri}_i$.

As fast MRF optimizers remove most overlaps but don't provide guarantees, we add a light post-processing to manually assign the remaining few overlapping triangles to separate planes. This guarantees overlap-free results. As mentioned before, after having identified the plane assignment y^* for each triangle we use a bin packing to uniquely assign each triangle to a position in the texture. Conversely, for every texture coordinate u, v we obtain a unique triangle index

$$i = G(u, v). \tag{5}$$

A qualitative result is illustrated in Fig. 4b. Next, we identify the image which should be used to texture each triangle.

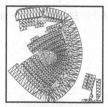

(a) Flattened mesh overlaps.

(b) Overlap-free.

Fig. 4. Flattening. **(a)** Red triangles indicate where overlap happens. **(b)** The proposed method (Sect. 3.1) resolves this issue while keeping connectivity of areas. (Color figure online)

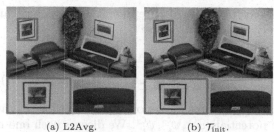

(a) L2Avg.   (b) $\mathcal{T}_{init}$.

Fig. 5. Initialization comparison. **(a)** We use PyTorch3D's rendering pipeline [37] to project each pixel of every RGB image back to the texture. The color of each pixel in the texture is the average of all colors that project to it. This texture minimizes the $\mathcal{L}_2$ loss of the difference between the rendered and the ground truth images. We dub it L2Avg. **(b)** $\mathcal{T}_{init}$ from Sect. 3.1 permits to maintain details. The seam artifacts will be optimized out using TexSmooth (Sect. 3.2). Besides over-smoothness, without taking into account misalignments of geometry and camera poses, L2Avg produces texture that overfits to available views, *e.g.*, the sofa's blue colors are painted onto the wall.

2) Textures from Triangle-Image Assignments: Our goal is to identify a suitable frame I_{t_i}, $t_i \in \{1, \ldots, T + 1\}$, for each triangle Tri_i, $i \in \{1, \ldots, |M|\}$. Note that the $(T + 1)$-th option I_{T+1} refers to an empty texture. We compute the texture assignments $\mathbf{t}^* = (t_1^*, \ldots, t_{|M|}^*)$ using a purely local optimization:

$$\mathbf{t}^* = \underset{\mathbf{t}}{\mathrm{argmax}} \sum_{i=1}^{|M|} \psi_i(t_i). \tag{6}$$

Here ψ_i captures *unary* cues. Note, we also studied *pairwise* cues but did not observe significant improvements. Please see the Appendix for more details. Due to better efficiency, we therefore only consider unary cues. Intuitively, we want the program given in Eq. (6) to encourage triangle-image assignment to be 'best' for each triangle Tri_i. We describe the unary cues to do so next.

Unary Potentials $\psi_i(t_i)$ for each pair of triangle Tri_i and frame I_{t_i} are

$$\psi_i(t_i) = \begin{cases} \psi_i^{\mathsf{C}}(t_i), & \text{if } \psi_i^{\mathsf{V}}(t_i) = 1 \\ -\infty, & \text{otherwise} \end{cases}, \tag{7}$$

where $\psi_i^{\mathsf{V}}(t_i)$ and $\psi_i^{\mathsf{C}}(t_i)$ represent validity check and potentials from cues respectively. Concretely, we use

$$\psi_i^{\mathsf{V}}(t_i) = \mathbb{1}\{I_{t_i} \in \mathcal{S}_i^{\mathsf{V}}\}, \tag{8}$$

$$\psi_i^{\mathsf{C}}(t_i) = \omega_1 \cdot \psi_i^{\mathsf{C}_1}(t_i) + \omega_2 \cdot \psi_i^{\mathsf{C}_2}(t_i) + \omega_3 \cdot \psi_i^{\mathsf{C}_3}(t_i), \tag{9}$$

where $\mathcal{S}_i^{\mathsf{V}}$ denotes the set of valid frames for $\mathtt{Tri}_i$ and $\omega_1, \omega_2, \omega_3$ represent weights for potentials $\psi_i^{\mathsf{C}_1}, \psi_i^{\mathsf{C}_2}, \psi_i^{\mathsf{C}_3}$. We discuss each one next:

- **Validity** (V). To assess whether frame I_{t_i} is valid for $\mathtt{Tri}_i$, we check the visibility of $\mathtt{Tri}_i$ in I_{t_i}. We approximate this by checking visibility of $\mathtt{Tri}_i$'s three vertices as well as its centroid. Concretely, we transform the vertices and centroid from world coordinates to the normalized device coordinates of the t_i-th camera. If all vertices and centroid are visible, *i.e.*, their coordinates are in the interval $[-1, 1]$, we add frame I_{t_i} to the set $\mathcal{S}_i^{\mathsf{V}}$ of valid frames for triangle $\mathtt{Tri}_i$.
- **Triangle area** (C_1). Based on a camera's pose p_{t_i}, a triangle's area changes. The larger the area, the more detailed is the information for $\mathtt{Tri}_i$ in frame I_{t_i}. We encourage to assign $\mathtt{Tri}_i$ to frames I_{t_i} with large area by defining $\psi_i^{\mathsf{C}_1}(t_i) = \mathtt{Area}_{t_i}(\mathtt{Tri}_i)$ and set $\omega_1 > 0$.

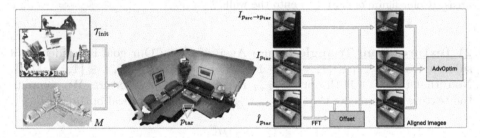

Fig. 6. Texture smoothing TexSmooth (Sect. 3.2). We utilize adversarial optimization (AdvOptim) [24] to refine the texture $\mathcal{T}_{\text{init}}$ from Sect. 3.1. Differently: 1) We initialize with $\mathcal{T}_{\text{init}}$. 2) To resolve the issue of misalignment between rendering and ground truth (GT), we integrate an alignment module based on the fast Fourier transform (FFT).

- **Discrepancy between z-buffer and actual depth** (C_2). For a valid frame $I_{t_i} \in \mathcal{S}_i^{\mathsf{V}}$, a triangle's vertices and its centroid project to valid image coordinates. We compute the discrepancy between: 1) the depth from frame I_{t_i} at the image coordinates of the vertices and centroid; 2) the depth of vertices and centroid in the camera's coordinate system. We set $\psi_i^{\mathsf{C}_2}(t_i)$ to be the sum of absolute value differences between both depth estimates while using $\omega_2 < 0$.

- **Perceptual consistency** (C_3). Due to diverse illumination, triangle Tri_i's appearance changes across frames. Intuitively, we don't want to assign a texture to Tri_i using a frame that contains colors that deviate drastically from other frames. Concretely, we first average all triangle's three vertices color values across all valid frames, *i.e.*, across all $I_{t_i} \in S_i^{\vee}$. We then compare this global average to the local average obtained independently for the three vertices of every valid frame $I_{t_i} \in S_i^{\vee}$ using an absolute value difference. We require $\omega_3 < 0$.

3) Color Transfer: Given the inferred triangle-frame assignments $\mathbf{t}^*$ we complete the texture $\mathcal{T}_{\text{init}}$ by transferring RGB data from image $I_{t_i^*}$ for $\text{Tri}_i, i \in \{1, \dots, |M|\}$. For this we leverage the camera pose $p_{t_i^*}$ which permits to transform the texture coordinates (u, v) of locations within Tri_i to corresponding image coordinates (a, b) in texture $I_{t_i^*}$ via the mapping $F : \mathbb{R}^2 \to \mathbb{R}^2$, *i.e.*,

$$(a, b) = F(u, v, t_i^*, p_{t_i^*}). \tag{10}$$

Intuitively, given the (u, v) coordinates on the texture in a coordinate system which is local to the triangle Tri_i, and given the camera pose $p_{t_i^*}$ used to record image $I_{t_i^*}$, the mapping F retrieves the image coordinates (a, b) corresponding to texture coordinate (u, v). Using this mapping, we obtain the texture $\mathcal{T}_{\text{init}}$ at location (u, v), *i.e.*, $\mathcal{T}_{\text{init}}(u, v)$, from the image data $I_{t_i^*}(a, b) \in \mathbb{R}^3$ via

$$\mathcal{T}_{\text{init}}(u, v) = I_{t_i^*}(F(u, v, t_i^*, p_{t_i^*})). \tag{11}$$

Note, because of the overlap detection, we obtain a unique triangle index $i = G(u, v)$ for every (u, v) coordinate from Eq. (5). Having transferred RGB data for all coordinates within all triangles results in the texture $\mathcal{T}_{\text{init}} \in \mathbb{R}^{H \times W \times 3}$, which we compare to standard L2 averaging initialization in Fig. 5. We next refine this texture via adversarial optimization. We observe that this initialization $\mathcal{T}_{\text{init}}$ is crucial to obtain high-quality textures, which we will show in Sect. 4.

3.2 Texture Smoothing (TexSmooth)

As can be seen in Fig. 5b, the texture $\mathcal{T}_{\text{init}}$ contains seams that affect visual quality. To reconstruct a seamless texture $\mathcal{T}$, we extend recent adversarial optimization (AdvOptim). Different from prior work [24] which initializes with blank (paper) or averaged (code release[1]) textures, we initialize with $\mathcal{T}_{\text{init}}$. Also, we find AdvOptim doesn't handle common camera pose and geometry misalignment well. To resolve this, we develop an efficient alignment module. This is depicted in Fig. 6 and will be detailed next.

---

[1] https://github.com/hjwdzh/AdversarialTexture.

Smoothing with Adversarial Optimization: To optimize the texture, AdvOptim iterates over camera poses. When optimizing for a specific target camera pose p_{tar}, AdvOptim uses three images: 1) the ground truth image $I_{p_{\text{tar}}}$ of the target camera pose p_{tar}; 2) a rendering $\hat{I}_{p_{\text{tar}}}$ for the target camera pose p_{tar} from the texture map $\mathcal{T}$; and 3) a re-projection from another camera pose p_{src}'s ground truth image, which we refer to as $I_{p_{\text{src}} \rightarrow p_{\text{tar}}}$. It then optimizes by minimizing an $\mathcal{L}_1$ plus a conditional adversarial loss. However, we find AdvOptim to struggle with alignment errors due to inaccurate geometry. Therefore, we integrate an efficient alignment operation into AdvOptim. Instead of directly using the input images, we first compute a 2D offset $(\Delta h_{p_{\text{tar}}}, \Delta w_{p_{\text{tar}}})$ between $I_{p_{\text{tar}}}$ and $\hat{I}_{p_{\text{tar}}}$, which we apply to align $I_{p_{\text{tar}}}$ and $\hat{I}_{p_{\text{tar}}}$ as well as $I_{p_{\text{src}} \rightarrow p_{\text{tar}}}$ via

$$I^{\text{A}} \doteq \texttt{Align}(I, (\Delta h, \Delta w)), \tag{12}$$

where I^{A} marks aligned images. We then use the three aligned images as input:

$$\mathcal{L} = \lambda \|I^{\text{A}}_{p_{\text{tar}}} - \hat{I}^{\text{A}}_{p_{\text{tar}}}\|_1 + \mathbb{E}_{I^{\text{A}}_{p_{\text{tar}}}, I^{\text{A}}_{p_{\text{src}} \rightarrow p_{\text{tar}}}} \left[\log D(I^{\text{A}}_{p_{\text{src}} \rightarrow p_{\text{tar}}} | I^{\text{A}}_{p_{\text{tar}}}) \right]$$
$$+ \mathbb{E}_{I^{\text{A}}_{p_{\text{tar}}}, \hat{I}^{\text{A}}_{p_{\text{tar}}}} \left[\log(1 - D(\hat{I}^{\text{A}}_{p_{\text{tar}}} | I^{\text{A}}_{p_{\text{tar}}})) \right]. \tag{13}$$

Here, D is a convolutional deep-net based discriminator. When using the unaligned image I instead of I^{A}, Eq. (13) reduces to the vanilla version in [24]. We now discuss a fast way to align images.

Alignment with Fourier Transformation: To align ground truth $I_{p_{\text{tar}}}$ and rendering $\hat{I}_{p_{\text{tar}}}$, one could use naïve grid-search to find the offset which results in the minimum difference of the shifted images. However, such a grid-search is prohibitively costly during an iterative optimization, especially with high-resolution images (*e.g.*, we use a resolution up to 1920×1440). Instead, we use the fast Fourier transformation (FFT) to complete the job [6]. Specifically, given a misaligned image pair of $I \in \mathbb{R}^{h \times w \times 3}$ and $\hat{I} \in \mathbb{R}^{h \times w \times 3}$, we compute for every channel the maximum correlation via

$$\operatorname*{argmax}_{(i,j)} \texttt{FFT}^{-1} \left(\texttt{FFT}(I) \cdot \overline{\texttt{FFT}(\hat{I})} \right) [i, j]. \tag{14}$$

Here, $\texttt{FFT}(\cdot)$ represents the fast Fourier transformation while $\texttt{FFT}^{-1}(\cdot)$ denotes its inverse and $\overline{\texttt{FFT}(\hat{I})}$ refers to the complex conjugate. After decoding the maximum correlation response and averaging across channels, we obtain the final offset $(\Delta h, \Delta w)$. As can be seen in Fig. 7(d), the offset $(\Delta h, \Delta w)$ is very accurate. Moreover, the computation finishes in around 0.4 s even for 1920×1440-resolution images. Note, we don't need to maintain gradients for $(\Delta h, \Delta w)$, since the offset is only used to shift images and not to backpropagate through it.

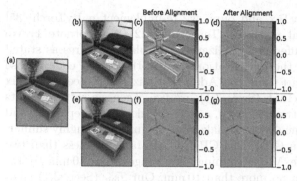

(a)   (b)   (c)

Fig. 8. Alignment is important for evaluation (Sect. 4.1). Clearly, (c) is more desirable than (b). However, before alignment, LPIPS yields 0.3347 and 0.4971 for (a)-(b) and (a)-(c) pairs respectively. This is misleading as lower LPIPS indicates higher quality. After alignment, LPIPS produces 0.3343 and 0.2428 for the same pairs, which provides correct signals for evaluation.

Fig. 7. Alignment with fast Fourier transformation (FFT) (Sect. 3.2). We show results for $\mathcal{T}_{init}$ (Sect. 3.1) and L2Avg (Fig. 5) in top and bottom rows. **(a):** ground-truth (GT); **(b) and (e):** texture rendering with (a)'s corresponding camera; **(c) and (d):** difference between (a) and (b); **(f) and (g):** difference between (a) and (e). The top row: FFT successfully aligns GT image and rendering from $\mathcal{T}_{init}$. Within expectation, there is almost no misalignment for the texture L2Avg as it overfits to available views (Fig. 5).

4 Experiments

4.1 Experimental Setup

Data Acquisition. We use a 2020 iPad Pro and develop an iOS app to acquire the RGBD images I_t, camera pose p_t, and scene mesh M via Apple's ARKit [1].

UofI Texture Scenes. We collect a dataset of 11 scenes: four indoor and seven outdoor scenes. This dataset consists of a total of 2807 frames, of which 91, 2052, and 664 are of resolution 480×360, 960×720, and 1920×1440 respectively. For each scene, we use 90% of its views for optimization and the remainder for evaluation. In total, we have 2521 training frames and 286 test frames. This setting is more challenging than prior work where [24] "select(s) 10 views uniformly distributed from the scanning video" for evaluation while using up to thousands of frames for texture generation. On average, the angular differences between test set view directions and their nearest neighbour in the training sets are 2.05° (min 0.85°/max 13.8°). Angular distances are computed following [25]. Please see Appendix for scene-level statistics.

Implementation. We compare to five baselines for texture generation: L2Avg, ColorMap [54], TexMap [16], MVSTex [48], and AdvTex [24]. For ColorMap, TexMap, and MVSTex, we use their official implementations.[2] For AdvOptim

---

[2] ColorMap: https://github.com/intel-isl/Open3D/pull/339; TexMap: https://github.com/fdp0525/G2LTex; MVSTex: https://github.com/nmoehrle/mvs-texturing.

(Sect. 3.2) used in both AdvTex and ours, we re-implement a PyTorch [35] version based on their official release in TensorFlow [2].(See footnote 1) We evaluate AdvTex with two different initializations: 1) blank textures as stated in the paper (AdvTex-B); 2) the initialization used in the official code release (AdvTex-C). We run AdvOptim using the Adam optimizer [26]. See Appendix for more details. For our TexInit (Sect. 3.1), we use a generic set of weights across all scenes: $\omega_1 = 1e^{-3}$ (triangle area), $\omega_2 = -10$ (depth discrepancy), and $\omega_3 = -1$ (perception consistency), which makes cue magnitudes roughly similar.

On a 3.10 GHz Intel Xeon Gold 6254 CPU, ColorMap takes less than two minutes to complete while TexMap's running time ranges from 40 min to 4 h. MVSTex can be completed in no more than 10 min. Our $\mathcal{T}_{init}$ (Sect. 3.1) completes in two minutes. Additionally, the AdvOptim takes around 20 min for 4000 iterations to complete with an Nvidia RTX A6000 GPU.

Evaluation Metrics. To assess the efficacy of the method, we study the quality of the texture from two perspectives: perceptual quality and sharpness. 1) For perceptual quality, we assess the similarity between rendered and collected ground-truth views using the Structural Similarity Index Measure (SSIM) [49] and the Learned Perceptual Image Patch Similarity (LPIPS) [53]. 2) For sharpness, we consider measurement S_3 [47] and the norm of image gradient (Grad) following [24]. Specifically, for each pixel, we compute its S_3 value, whose difference between the rendered and ground truth (GT) is used for averaging across the whole image. A similar procedure is applied to Grad. For all four metrics, we report the mean and standard deviation across 11 scenes.

Alignment in Evaluation. As can be seen in Fig. 8, evaluation will be misleading if we do not align images during evaluation. Therefore, we propose the following procedure: 1) for each method, we align the rendered image and the GT using an FFT (Sect. 3.2); 2) to avoid various resolutions caused by different methods, we crop out the maximum common area across methods. 3) we then compute metrics on those cropped regions. The resulting comparison is fair as all methods are evaluated on the same number of pixels and aligned content.

4.2 Experimental Evaluation

Quantitative Evaluation. Table 1 reports aggregated results on all 11 scenes. The quality of our texture $\mathcal{T}$ (Row 6) outperforms baselines on LPIPS, S_3 and Grad, confirming the effectiveness of the proposed pipeline. Specifically, we improve LPIPS by 7.8% from 0.335 (2nd-best) to 0.309, indicating high perceptual similarity. Moreover, $\mathcal{T}$ maintains sharpness as we improve S_3 by 11.1% from 0.135 (2nd-best) to 0.120 and Grad from 7.171 (2nd-best) to 6.871. Regarding SSIM, we find it to favor L2Avg in almost all scenes (see Appendix) which aligns with the findings in [53].

Ablation Study. We verify the design choices of TexInit and TexSmooth in Table 2. 1) **TexSmooth is required:** we directly evaluate $\mathcal{T}_{init}$ and 1st vs. 4th row confirms the performance drop: -0.092 (SSIM), +0.033 (LPIPS), +0.021 (S_3), and +1.221 (Grad). 2) $\mathcal{T}_{init}$ **is needed:** we replace $\mathcal{T}_{init}$ with L2Avg as it

Table 1. Aggregated quantitative evaluation on UofI Texture Scenes. We report results in the form of mean±std. Please see Fig. 9 for qualitative texture comparisons and Appendix for scene-level quantitative results.

		SSIM↑	LPIPS↓	S_3 ↓	Grad↓
1	L2Avg	**0.610**±0.191	0.386±0.116	0.173±0.105	7.066±4.575
2	ColorMap	0.553±0.193	0.581±0.132	0.234±0.140	7.969±5.114
3	TexMap	0.376±0.113	0.488±0.097	0.179±0.062	8.918±4.174
4	MVSTex	0.476±0.164	0.335±0.086	0.139±0.047	8.198±3.936
5-1	AdvTex-B	0.495±0.174	0.369±0.092	0.148±0.047	8.229±4.586
5-2	AdvTex-C	0.563±0.191	0.365±0.096	0.135±0.067	7.171±4.272
6	Ours	0.602±0.189	**0.309**±0.086	**0.120**±0.058	**6.871**±4.342

Table 2. Ablation study. We report results in the form of mean±std.

	Adv Optim	FFT Align	T_{init}	SSIM↑	LPIPS↓	S_3 ↓	Grad↓
1			✓	0.510±0.175	0.342±0.060	0.141±0.052	8.092±4.488
2	✓	✓		0.592±0.192	0.332±0.102	0.130±0.066	**6.864**±4.211
3	✓		✓	0.559±0.196	0.346±0.082	0.125±0.057	7.244±4.359
4	✓	✓	✓	**0.602**±0.189	**0.309**±0.086	**0.120**±0.058	6.871±4.342

performs better than ColorMap and TexMap in Table 1 and still incorporate FFT into AdvOptim. We observe inferior performance: -0.010 (SSIM), +0.023 (LPIPS), +0.010 (S_3) in 2nd *vs.* 4th row. **3) Alignment is important:** we use the vanilla AdvOptim but initialize with T_{init}. As shown in Table 2's 3rd *vs.* 4th row, the texture quality drops by -0.043 (SSIM), +0.037 (LPIPS), +0.005 (S_3), and +0.373 (Grad).

Qualitative Evaluation. We present qualitative examples in Fig. 9. Figure 9a and Fig. 9b demonstrate that L2Avg and ColorMap produce overly smooth texture. Meanwhile, due to noise in the geometry, *e.g.*, Fig. 2, TexMap fails to resolve texture seams and cannot produce a complete texture (Fig. 9c). MVSTex results in Fig. 9d are undesirable as geometries are removed. This is because MVSTex requires ray collision checking to remove occluded faces. Due to the misalignment between geometries and cameras, artifacts are introduced. We show results of AdvTex-C in Fig. 9e as it outperforms AdvTex-B from Table 1. Artifacts are highlighted. Our method can largly mitigate such seams, which can be inferred from Fig. 9f. In Fig. 9g, we show renderings, which demonstrate the effectiveness of the proposed method. Please see Appendix for complete qualitative results of scenes in Fig. 10.

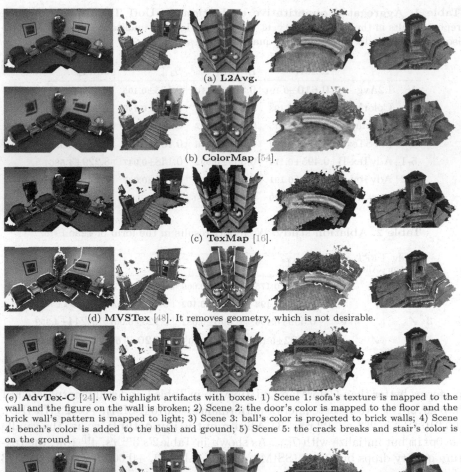

(a) **L2Avg.**

(b) **ColorMap** [54].

(c) **TexMap** [16].

(d) **MVSTex** [48]. It removes geometry, which is not desirable.

(e) **AdvTex-C** [24]. We highlight artifacts with boxes. 1) Scene 1: sofa's texture is mapped to the wall and the figure on the wall is broken; 2) Scene 2: the door's color is mapped to the floor and the brick wall's pattern is mapped to light; 3) Scene 3: ball's color is projected to brick walls; 4) Scene 4: bench's color is added to the bush and ground; 5) Scene 5: the crack breaks and stair's color is on the ground.

(f) **Ours**. Compared to Fig. 9e, our method reduces artifacts.

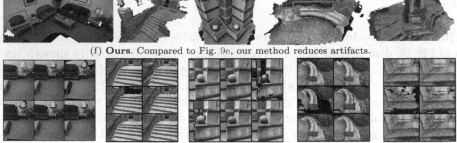

(g) **Highlights**. From left to right and top to bottom, we show ground-truth image and renderings at the same camera pose with texture from ColorMap, TexMap, MVSTex, AdvTex-C, and ours respectively. Compared to AdvTex-C: 1) Scene 1: ours produces much more complete and sharper pattern for the sofa; 2) Scene 2: ours generates sharper cracks on brick walls; 3) Scene 3: our balls are more complete while AdvTex-C maps the top of the ball to the left brick wall; 4) Scene 4: AdvTex-C maps the bench to the bush while ours is much cleaner; 5) Scene 5: the pattern on the ground from ours is much sharper.

Fig. 9. Qualitative results on UofI Texture Scenes. For each method, we show results for Scene 1 to 5 from left to right. Best viewed in color and zoomed-in. (Color figure online)

Table 3. ScanNet results. We report results in the form of mean±std. Note, this can't be directly compared to [23]'s Table 2: while we reserve 10% views for evaluation, [23] reserves only 10/2011 (≈ 0.5%), where 2011 is the number of average views per scene.

		SSIM↑	LPIPS↓	S_3 ↓	Grad↓
1-1	AdvTex-B	0.534± 0.074	0.557± 0.071	0.143± 0.028	3.753± 0.730
1-2	AdvTex-C	0.531± 0.074	0.558± 0.075	0.161± 0.044	4.565± 1.399
2	Ours	**0.571**± 0.069	**0.503**± 0.090	**0.127**± 0.031	**3.324**±0.826

Fig. 10. Remaining six scenes with our textures. See Appendix for all methods' results on these scenes.

Fig. 11. Results on ScanNet. Left to right: AdvTex-B/C and ours. Ours alleviates artifacts: colors from box on the cabinet are mapped to the backpack and wall. (Color figure online)

On ScanNet [11]. Following [24], we study scenes with ID ≤ 20 (Fig. 11, Table 3). We improve upon baselines (AdvTex-B/C) by a margin on SSIM (0.534 → 0.571), LPIPS (0.557 → 0.503), S_3 (0.143 → 0.127), and Grad (3.753 → 3.324).

5 Conclusion

We develop an initialization and an alignment method for fully-automatic texture generation from a given scene mesh, and a given sequence of RGBD images and their camera parameters. We observe the proposed method to yield appealing results, addressing robustness issues due to noisy geometry and misalignment of prior work. Quantitatively we observe improvements on both perceptual similarity (LPIPS from 0.335 to 0.309) and sharpness (S_3 from 0.135 to 0.120).

Acknowledgements. Supported in part by NSF grants 1718221, 2008387, 2045586, 2106825, MRI #1725729, and NIFA award 2020-67021-32799.

References

1. Augmented reality - Apple developer. https://developer.apple.com/augmented-reality/ (2021). Accessed 14 Nov 2021
2. Abadi, M., et al.: TensorFlow: a system for large-scale machine learning. In: OSDI (2016)
3. Abdelhafiz, A., Mostafa, Y.G.: Automatic texture mapping mega-projects. J. Spat. Sci. (2020)
4. Aganj, E., Monasse, P., Keriven, R.: Multi-view texturing of imprecise mesh. In: ACCV (2009)
5. Aliev, K.A., Ulyanov, D., Lempitsky, V.S.: Neural point-based graphics. In: ECCV (2020)
6. Anuta, P.E.: Spatial registration of multispectral and multitemporal digital imagery using FastFourierTransform techniques. Trans. Geosci. Electron. (1970)
7. Barnes, C., Shechtman, E., Finkelstein, A., Goldman, D.B.: PatchMatch: a randomized correspondence algorithm for structural image editing. In: SIGGRAPH (2009)
8. Baumberg, A.: Blending images for texturing 3D models. In: BMVC (2002)
9. Bernardini, F., Martin, I., Rushmeier, H.: High quality texture reconstruction from multiple scans. In: TVCG (2001)
10. Bi, S., Kalantari, N.K., Ramamoorthi, R.: Patch-based optimization for image-based texture mapping. In: TOG (2017)
11. Dai, A., Chang, A.X., Savva, M., Halber, M., Funkhouser, T.A., Nießner, M.: Scannet: richly-annotated 3D reconstructions of indoor scenes. In: CVPR (2017)
12. Debevec, P., Taylor, C., Malik, J.: Modeling and rendering architecture from photographs: a hybrid geometry and image-based approach. In: SIGGRAPH (1996)
13. Duan, Y.: Topology adaptive deformable models for visual computing. Ph.D. thesis, State University of New York (2003)
14. El-Hakim, S., Gonzo, L., Picard, M., Girardi, S., Simoni, A.: Visualization of frescoed surfaces: buonconsiglio castle - aquila tower, "Cycle of the Months". In: IAPRS (2003)
15. Früh, C., Sammon, R., Zakhor, A.: Automated texture mapping of 3D city models with oblique aerial imagery. In: 3DPVT (2004)
16. Fu, Y., Yan, Q., Yang, L., Liao, J., Xiao, C.: Texture mapping for 3D reconstruction with RGB-D sensor. In: CVPR (2018)
17. Globerson, A., Jaakkola, T.: Fixing Max-Product: convergent message passing algorithms for MAP LP-Relaxations. In: NIPS (2007)
18. Goel, S., Kanazawa, A., Malik, J.: Shape and viewpoint without keypoints. In: ECCV (2020)
19. Grammatikopoulos, L., Kalisperakis, I., Karras, G., Petsa, E.: Automatic multi-view texture mapping of 3D surface projections. In: International Workshop 3D-ARCH (2007)
20. Groueix, T., Fisher, M., Kim, V.G., Russell, B.C., Aubry, M.: AtlasNet: a Papier-Mâché approach to learning 3D surface generation. In: CVPR (2018)
21. Henzler, P., Mitra, N.J., Ritschel, T.: Learning a neural 3D Texture space from 2D exemplars. In: CVPR (2020)
22. Hernández-Esteban, C.: Stereo and Silhouette fusion for 3D object modeling from uncalibrated images under circular motion. Ph.D. thesis, École Nationale Supérieure des TéléCommunications (2004)

23. Huang, J., Dai, A., Guibas, L., Nießner, M.: 3DLite: towards commodity 3D scanning for content creation. In: ACM TOG (2017)
24. Huang, J., et al.: Adversarial texture optimization from RGB-D scans. In: CVPR (2020)
25. Huynh, D.: Metrics for 3D rotations: comparison and analysis. J. Math. Imag. Vis. (2009)
26. Kingma, D.P., Ba, J.: Adam: a method for stochastic optimization. ArXiv (2015)
27. Lempitsky, V., Ivanov, D.: Seamless mosaicing of image-based texture maps. In: CVPR (2007)
28. Lensch, H., Heidrich, W., Seidel, H.P.: Automated texture registration and stitching for real world models. In: Graphical Models (2001)
29. Marshner, S.R.: Inverse rendering for computer graphics. Ph.D. thesis, Cornell University (1998)
30. Neugebauer, P.J., Klein, K.: Texturing 3D models of real world objects from multiple unregistered photographic views. Eurographics **18**, 245–256 (1999)
31. Niem, W., Wingbermühle, J.: Automatic reconstruction of 3D objects using a mobile camera. In: IVC (1999)
32. Oechsle, M., Mescheder, L.M., Niemeyer, M., Strauss, T., Geiger, A.: Texture fields: learning texture representations in function space. In: ICCV (2019)
33. Ofek, E., Shilat, E., Rappoport, A., Werman, M.: Multiresolution Textures from image sequences. Comput. Graph. Appl. (1997)
34. Pan, R., Taubin, G.: Color adjustment in image-based texture maps. Graph. Models (2015)
35. Paszke, A., et al.: PyTorch: an imperative style, high-performance deep learning library. ArXiv abs/1912.01703 (2019)
36. Pighin, F., Hecker, J., Lischinski, D., Szeliski, R., Salesin, D.H.: Synthesizing realistic facial expressions from photographs. In: CGIT (1998)
37. Ravi, N., Reizenstein, J., Novotny, D., Gordon, T., Lo, W.Y., Johnson, J., Gkioxari, G.: Accelerating 3D Deep Learning with PyTorch3D. arXiv:2007.08501 (2020)
38. Rocchini, C., Cignoni, P., Montani, C., Scopigno, R.: Multiple textures stitching and blending on 3D objects. Eurograph. Workshop Render. (1999)
39. Rocchini, C., Cignoni, P., Montani, C., Scopigno, R.: Aquiring, stitching and blending diffuse appearance attributes on 3D models. Vis. Comput. (2002)
40. Saito, S., Wei, L., Hu, L., Nagano, K., Li, H.: Photorealistic facial texture inference using deep neural networks. In: CVPR (2017)
41. Sawhney, R., Crane, K.: Boundary first flattening. In: ACM TOG (2018)
42. Shu, J., Liu, Y., Li, J., Xu, Z., Du, S.: Rich and seamless texture mapping to 3D mesh models. In: Tan, T., et al. (eds.) IGTA 2016. CCIS, vol. 634, pp. 69–76. Springer, Singapore (2016). https://doi.org/10.1007/978-981-10-2260-9_9
43. Sinha, S.N., Steedly, D., Szeliski, R., Agrawala, M., Pollefeys, M.: Interactive 3D architectural modeling from unordered photo collections. In: SIGGRAPH 2008 (2008)
44. Sitzmann, V., et al.: DeepVoxels: learning persistent 3D feature embeddings. In: CVPR (2019)
45. Thierry, M., David, F., Gorria, P., Salvi, J.: Automatic texture mapping on real 3D model. In: CVPR (2007)
46. Thies, J., Zollhöfer, M., Nießner, M.: Deferred Neural Rendering. In: ACM TOG (2019)
47. Vu, C.T., Phan, T.D., Chandler, D.M.: S_3: A spectral and spatial measure of local perceived sharpness in natural images. IEEE Trans. Image Process. 21, 934–945 (2012)

48. Waechter, M., Moehrle, N., Goesele, M.: Let there be color! large-scale texturing of 3D Reconstructions. In: ECCV (2014)
49. Wang, Z., Bovik, A., Sheikh, H.R., Simoncelli, E.P.: Image quality assessment: from error visibility to structural similarity. IEEE Trans. Image Process. **13**, 600–6112 (2004)
50. Wexler, Y., Shechtman, E., Irani, M.: Space-time video completion. In: CVPR (2004)
51. Wuhrer, S., Atanassov, R., Shu, C.: Fully automatic texture mapping for image-based modeling. Technical Report, Institute for Information Technology (2006)
52. Xiang, F., Xu, Z., Havsan, M., Hold-Geoffroy, Y., Sunkavalli, K., Su, H.: NeuTex: neural texture mapping for volumetric neural rendering. In: CVPR (2021)
53. Zhang, R., Isola, P., Efros, A.A., Shechtman, E., Wang, O.: The unreasonable effectiveness of deep features as a perceptual metric. In: CVPR (2018)
54. Zhou, Q.Y., Koltun, V.: Color map optimization for 3D reconstruction with consumer depth cameras. In: ACM TOG (2014)

MOTR: End-to-End Multiple-Object Tracking with Transformer

Fangao Zeng[1], Bin Dong[1], Yuang Zhang[2], Tiancai Wang[1(✉)], Xiangyu Zhang[1], and Yichen Wei[1]

[1] MEGVII Technology, Beijing, China
wangtiancai@megvii.com
[2] Shanghai Jiao Tong University, Shanghai, China

Abstract. Temporal modeling of objects is a key challenge in multiple-object tracking (MOT). Existing methods track by associating detections through motion-based and appearance-based similarity heuristics. The post-processing nature of association prevents end-to-end exploitation of temporal variations in video sequence.

In this paper, we propose MOTR, which extends DETR [6] and introduces "track query" to model the tracked instances in the entire video. Track query is transferred and updated frame-by-frame to perform iterative prediction over time. We propose tracklet-aware label assignment to train track queries and newborn object queries. We further propose temporal aggregation network and collective average loss to enhance temporal relation modeling. Experimental results on DanceTrack show that MOTR significantly outperforms state-of-the-art method, ByteTrack [42] by **6.5%** on HOTA metric. On MOT17, MOTR outperforms our concurrent works, TrackFormer [18] and TransTrack [29], on association performance. MOTR can serve as a stronger baseline for future research on temporal modeling and Transformer-based trackers. Code is available at https://github.com/megvii-research/MOTR.

Keywords: Multiple-object tracking · Transformer · End-to-End

1 Introduction

Multiple-object tracking (MOT) predicts the trajectories of instances in continuous image sequences [2,39]. Most of existing methods separate the MOT temporal association into appearance and motion: appearance variance is usually measured by pair-wise Re-ID similarity [37,43] while motion is modeled via IoU [4] or Kalman Filtering [3] heuristic. These methods require similarity-based matching for post-processing, which becomes the bottleneck of temporal information flow across frames. In this paper, we aim to introduce a fully end-to-end MOT framework featuring joint motion and appearance modeling.

F. Zeng, B. Dong and Y. Zhang—Equal contribution.

S. Avidan et al. (Eds.): ECCV 2022, LNCS 13687, pp. 659–675, 2022.
https://doi.org/10.1007/978-3-031-19812-0_38

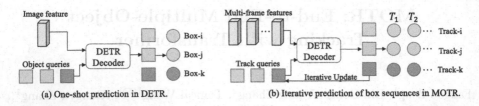

(a) One-shot prediction in DETR.   (b) Iterative prediction of box sequences in MOTR.

Fig. 1. (a) DETR achieves end-to-end detection by interacting object queries with image features and performs one-to-one assignment between the updated queries and objects. (b) MOTR performs set of sequence prediction by updating the track queries. Each track query represents a track. Best viewed in color. (Color figure online)

Recently, DETR [6,45] was proposed for end-to-end object detection. It formulates object detection as a set prediction problem. As shown in Fig. 1(a), object queries, served as a decoupled representation of objects, are fed into the Transformer decoder and interacted with the image feature to update their representation. Bipartite matching is further adopted to achieve one-to-one assignment between the object queries and ground-truths, eliminating post-processes, like NMS. Different from object detection, MOT can be regarded as a sequence prediction problem. The way to perform sequence prediction in the end-to-end DETR system is an open question.

Iterative prediction is popular in machine translation [30,31]. The output context is represented by a hidden state, and sentence features iteratively interact with the hidden state in the decoder to predict the translated words. Inspired by these advances in machine translation, we intuitively regard MOT as a problem of *set of sequence prediction* since MOT requires a set of object sequences. Each sequence corresponds to an object trajectory. Technically, we extend object query in DETR to *track query* for predicting object sequences. Track queries are served as the hidden states of object tracks. The representations of track queries are updated in the Transformer decoder and used to predict the object trajectory iteratively, as shown in Fig. 1(b). Specifically, track queries are updated through self-attention and cross-attention by frame features. The updated track queries are further used to predict the bounding boxes. The track of one object can be obtained from all predictions of one track query in different frames.

To achieve the goal above, we need to solve two problems: 1) track one object by one track query; 2) deal with newborn and terminated objects. To solve the first problem, we introduce tracklet-aware label assignment (TALA). It means that predictions of one track query are supervised by bounding box sequences with the same identity. To solve the second problem, we maintain a track query set of variable lengths. Queries of newborn objects are merged into this set while queries of terminated objects are removed. We name this process the entrance and exit mechanism. In this way, MOTR does not require explicit track associations during inference. Moreover, the iterative update of track queries enables temporal modeling regarding both appearance and motion.

To enhance the temporal modeling, we further propose collective average loss (CAL) and temporal aggregation network (TAN). With the CAL, MOTR takes video clips as input during training. The parameters of MOTR are updated based on the overall loss calculated for the whole video clip. TAN introduces a shortcut for track query to aggregate the historical information from its previous states via the key-query mechanism in Transformer.

MOTR is a simple online tracker. It is easy to develop based on DETR with minor modifications on label assignment. It is a truly end-to-end MOT framework, requiring no post-processes, such as the track NMS or IoU matching employed in our concurrent works, TransTrack [29], and TrackFormer [18]. Experimental results on MOT17 and DanceTrack datasets show that MOTR achieves promising performance. On DanceTrack [28], MOTR outperforms the state-of-the-art ByteTrack [42] by **6.5%** on HOTA metric and **8.1%** on AssA.

To summarize, our contributions are listed as below:

- We present a fully end-to-end MOT framework, named MOTR. MOTR can implicitly learn the appearance and position variances in a joint manner.
- We formulate MOT as a problem of *set of sequence prediction*. We generate track query from previous hidden states for iterative update and prediction.
- We propose tracklet-aware label assignment for one-to-one assignment between track queries and objects. An entrance and exit mechanism is introduced to deal with newborn and terminated tracks.
- We further propose CAL and TAN to enhance the temporal modeling.

2   Related Work

Transformer-Based Architectures. Transformer [31] was first introduced to aggregate information from the entire input sequence for machine translation. It mainly involves self-attention and cross-attention mechanisms. Since that, it was gradually introduced to many fields, such as speech processing [7,13] and computer vision [5,34]. Recently, DETR [6] combined convolutional neural network (CNN), Transformer and bipartite matching to perform end-to-end object detection. To achieve the fast convergence, Deformable DETR [45] introduced deformable attention module into Transformer encoder and Transformer decoder. ViT [9] built a pure Transformer architecture for image classification. Further, Swin Transformer [16] proposed shifted windowing scheme to perform self-attention within local windows, bringing greater efficiency. VisTR [36] employed a direct end-to-end parallel sequence prediction framework to perform video instance segmentation.

Multiple-Object Tracking. Dominant MOT methods mainly followed the tracking-by-detection paradigm [3,12,22,24,39]. These approaches usually first employ object detectors to localize objects in each frame and then perform track association between adjacent frames to generate the tracking results. SORT [3] conducted track association by combining Kalman Filter [38] and Hungarian algorithm [11]. DeepSORT [39] and Tracktor [2] introduced an extra cosine distance and compute the appearance similarity for track association. Track-RCNN

[26], JDE [37] and FairMOT [43] further added a Re-ID branch on top of object detector in a joint training framework, incorporating object detection and Re-ID feature learning. TransMOT [8] builds a spatial-temporal graph transformer for association. Our concurrent works, TransTrack [29] and TrackFormer [18] also develop Transformer-based frameworks for MOT. For direct comparison with them, please refer to Sect. 3.7.

Iterative Sequence Prediction. Predicting sequence via sequence-to-sequence (seq2seq) with encoder-decoder architecture is popular in machine translation [30,31] and text recognition [25]. In seq2seq framework, the encoder network encodes the input into intermediate representation. Then, a hidden state with task-specific context information is introduced and iteratively interacted with the intermediate representation to generate the target sequence through the decoder network. The iterative decode process contains several iterations. In each iteration, hidden state decodes one element of target sequence.

3   Method

3.1   Query in Object Detection

DETR [6] introduced a fixed-length set of object queries to detect objects. Object queries are fed into the Transformer decoder and interacted with image features, extracted from Transformer encoder to update their representation. Bipartite matching is further adopted to achieve one-to-one assignment between the updated object queries and ground-truths. Here, we simply write the object query as "detect query" to specify the query used for object detection.

3.2   Detect Query and Track Query

When adapting DETR from object detection to MOT, two main problems arise: 1) how to track one object by one track query; 2) how to handle newborn and terminated objects. We extend detect queries to track queries in this paper. Track query set is updated dynamically, and the length is variable. As shown in Fig. 2, the track query set is initialized to be empty, and the detect queries in DETR are used to detect newborn objects (object 3 at T_2). Hidden states of detected objects produces track queries for the next frame; track queries assigned to terminated objects are removed from the track query set (object 2 at T_4).

3.3   Tracklet-Aware Label Assignment

In DETR, one detect (object) query may be assigned to any object in the image since the label assignment is determined by performing bipartite matching between all detect queries and ground-truths. While in MOTR, detect queries are only used to detect newborn objects while track queries predict all tracked objects. Here, we introduce the tracklet-aware label assignment (TALA) to solve this problem.

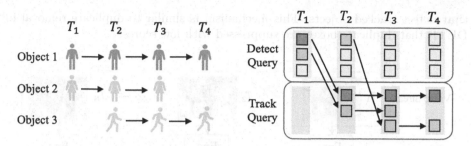

Fig. 2. Update process of detect (object) queries and track queries under some typical MOT cases. Track query set is updated dynamically, and the length is variable. Track query set is initialized to be empty, and the detect queries are used to detect newborn objects. Hidden states of all detected objects are concatenated to produce track queries for the next frame. Track queries assigned to terminated objects are removed from the track query set.

Generally, TALA consists of two strategies. For detect queries, we modify the assignment strategy in DETR as **newborn-only**, where bipartite matching is conducted between the detect queries and the ground-truths of newborn objects. For track queries, we design an **target-consistent** assignment strategy. Track queries follow the same assignment of previous frames and are therefore excluded from the aforementioned bipartite matching.

Formally, we denote the predictions of track queries as $\widehat{Y}_{tr}$ and predictions of detect queries as $\widehat{Y}_{det}$. Y_{new} is the ground-truths of newborn objects. The label assignment results for track queries and detect queries can be written as ω_{tr} and ω_{det}. For frame i, label assignment for detect queries is obtained from bipartite matching among detect queries and newborn objects, i.e.,

$$\omega_{det}^i = \arg\min_{\omega_{det}^i \in \Omega_i} \mathcal{L}(\widehat{Y}_{det}^i|_{\omega_{det}^i}, Y_{new}^i), \tag{1}$$

where $\mathcal{L}$ is the pair-wise matching cost defined in DETR and Ω_i is the space of all bipartite matches among detect queries and newborn objects. For track query assignment, we merge the assignments for newborn objects and tracked objects from the last frame, i.e., for $i > 1$:

$$\omega_{tr}^i = \omega_{tr}^{i-1} \cup \omega_{det}^{i-1}. \tag{2}$$

For the first frame ($i = 1$), track query assignment ω_{tr}^1 is an empty set $\emptyset$ since there are no tracked objects for the first frame. For successive frames ($i > 1$), the track query assignment ω_{tr}^i is the concatenation of previous track query assignment ω_{tr}^{i-1} and newborn object assignment ω_{det}^{i-1}.

In practice, the TALA strategy is simple and effective thanks to the powerful attention mechanism in Transformer. For each frame, detect queries and track queries are concatenated and fed into the Transformer decoder to update their representation. Detect queries will only detect newborn objects since query interaction by self-attention in the Transformer decoder will suppress detect queries that detect tracked objects. This mechanism is similar to duplicate removal in DETR that duplicate boxes are suppressed with low scores.

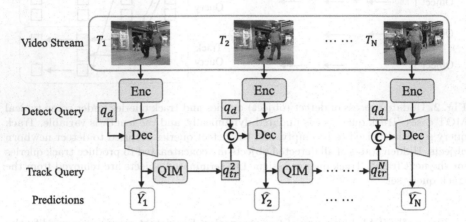

Fig. 3. The overall architecture of MOTR. "Enc" represents a convolutional neural network backbone and the Transformer encoder that extracts image features for each frame. The concatenation of detect queries q_d and track queries q_{tr} is fed into the Deformable DETR decoder (Dec) to produce the hidden states. The hidden states are used to generate the prediction $\widehat{Y}$ of newborn and tracked objects. The query interaction module (QIM) takes the hidden states as input and produces track queries for the next frame.

3.4   MOTR Architecture

The overall architecture of MOTR is shown in Fig. 3. Video sequences are fed into the convolutional neural network (CNN) (e.g. ResNet-50 [10]) and Deformable DETR [45] encoder to extract frame features.

For the first frame, there are no track query and we only feed the fixed-length learnable detect queries (q_d in Fig. 3) into the Deformable DETR [45] decoder. For successive frames, we feed the concatenation of track queries from the previous frame and the learnable detect queries into the decoder. These queries interact with image feature in the decoder to generate the hidden state for bounding box prediction. The hidden state is also fed into the query interaction module (QIM) to generate the track queries for the next frame.

During training phase, the label assignment for each frame is described in Sect. 3.3. All predictions of the video clip are collected into a prediction bank $\{\widehat{Y}_1, \widehat{Y}_2, \ldots, \widehat{Y}_N\}$, and we use the proposed collective average loss (CAL) described in Sect. 3.6 for supervision. During inference time, the video stream can be processed online and generate the prediction for each frame.

3.5 Query Interaction Module

In this section, we describe query interaction module (QIM). QIM includes object entrance and exit mechanism and temporal aggregation network (TAN).

Object Entrance and Exit. As mentioned above, some objects in video sequences may appear or disappear at intermediate frames. Here, we introduce the way we deal with the newborn and terminated objects in our method. For any frame, track queries are concatenated with the detect queries and input to the Transformer decoder, producing the hidden state (see the left side of Fig. 4).

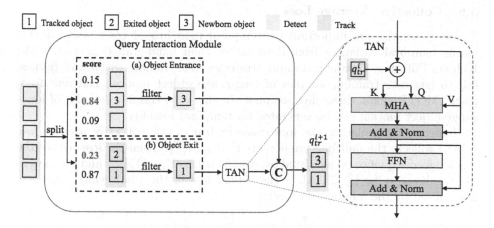

Fig. 4. The structure of query interaction module (QIM). The inputs of QIM are the hidden state produced by Transformer decoder and the corresponding prediction scores. In the inference stage, we keep newborn objects and drop exited objects based on the confidence scores. Temporal aggregation network (TAN) enhances long-range temporal modeling.

During training, hidden states of terminated objects are removed if the matched objects disappeared in ground-truths or the intersection-over-union (IoU) between predicted bounding box and target is below a threshold of 0.5. It means that the corresponding hidden states will be filtered if these objects disappear at current frame while the rest hidden states are reserved. For newborn objects, the corresponding hidden states are kept based on the assignment of newborn object ω_{det}^i defined in Eq. 1.

For inference, we use the predicted classification scores to determine appearance of newborn objects and disappearance of tracked objects, as shown in Fig. 4. For object queries, predictions whose classification scores are higher than the entrance threshold τ_{en} are kept while other hidden states are removed. For track queries, predictions whose classification scores are lower than the exit threshold τ_{ex} for consecutive M frames are removed while other hidden states are kept.

Temporal Aggregation Network. Here, we introduce the temporal aggregation network (TAN) in QIM to enhance temporal relation modeling and provide contextual priors for tracked objects.

As shown in Fig. 4, the input of TAN is the filtered hidden state for tracked objects (object "1"). We also collect the track query q_{tr}^i from the last frame for temporal aggregation. TAN is a modified Transformer decoder layer. The track query from the last frame and the filtered hidden state are summed to be the key and query components of the multi-head self-attention (MHA). The hidden state alone is the value component of MHA. After MHA, we apply a feed-forward network (FFN) and the results are concatenated with the hidden state for newborn objects (object "3") to produce the track query set q_{tr}^{i+1} for the next frame.

3.6   Collective Average Loss

Training samples are important for temporal modeling of track since MOTR learns temporal variances from data rather than hand-crafted heuristics like Kalman Filtering. Common training strategies, like training within two frames, fail to generate training samples of long-range object motion. Different from them, MOTR takes video clips as input. In this way, training samples of long-range object motion can be generated for temporal learning.

Instead of calculating the loss frame-by-frame, our collective average loss (CAL) collects the multiple predictions $\widehat{Y} = \{\widehat{Y}_i\}_{i=1}^N$. Then the loss within the whole video sequence is calculated by ground-truths $Y = \{Y_i\}_{i=1}^N$ and the matching results $\omega = \{\omega_i\}_{i=1}^N$. CAL is the overall loss of the whole video sequence, normalized by the number of objects:

$$\mathcal{L}_o(\widehat{Y}|\omega, Y) = \frac{\sum_{n=1}^N (\mathcal{L}(\widehat{Y}_{tr}^i|\omega_{tr}^i, Y_{tr}^i) + \mathcal{L}(\widehat{Y}_{det}^i|\omega_{det}^i, Y_{det}^i))}{\sum_{n=1}^N (V_i)} \tag{3}$$

where $V_i = V_{tr}^i + V_{det}^i$ denotes the total number of ground-truths objects at frame i. V_{tr}^i and V_{det}^i are the numbers of tracked objects and newborn objects at frame i, respectively. $\mathcal{L}$ is the loss of single frame, which is similar to the detection loss in DETR. The single-frame loss $\mathcal{L}$ can be formulated as:

$$\mathcal{L}(\widehat{Y}_i|\omega_i, Y_i) = \lambda_{cls}\mathcal{L}_{cls} + \lambda_{l_1}\mathcal{L}_{l_1} + \lambda_{giou}\mathcal{L}_{giou} \tag{4}$$

where $\mathcal{L}_{cls}$ is the focal loss [14]. $\mathcal{L}_{l_1}$ denotes the L1 loss and $\mathcal{L}_{giou}$ is the generalized IoU loss [21]. λ_{cls}, λ_{l_1} and λ_{giou} are the corresponding weight coefficients.

3.7   Discussion

Based on DETR, our concurrent works, TransTrack [29] and TrackFormer [18] also develop the Transformer-based frameworks for MOT. However, our method shows large differences compared to them:

TransTrack models a full track as a combination of several independent short tracklets. Similar to the track-by-detection paradigm, TransTrack decouples MOT as two sub-tasks: 1) detect object pairs as short tracklets within

Table 1. Comparison with other MOT methods based on transformer.

Method	IoU match	NMS	ReID
TransTrack [29]	✓		
TrackFormer [18]		✓	✓
MOTR (ours)			

Table 2. Statistics of chosen datasets for evaluation.

Datasets	Class	Frame	Video	ID
DanceTrack [28]	1	106k	100	990
MOT17 [19]	1	11k	14	1342
BDD100K [41]	8	318k	1400	131k

two adjacent frames; 2) associate short tracklets as full tracks by IoU-matching. While for MOTR, we model a full track in an end-to-end manner through the iterative update of track query, requiring no IoU-matching.

TrackFormer shares the idea of track query with us. However, TrackFormer still learns within two adjacent frames. As discussed in Sect. 3.6, learning within short-range will result in relatively weak temporal learning. Therefore, Track-Former employs heuristics, such as Track NMS and Re-ID features, to filter out duplicate tracks. Different from TrackFormer, MOTR learns stronger temporal motion with CAL and TAN, removing the need of those heuristics. For direct comparison with TransTrack and TrackFormer, please refer to the Table 1.

Here, we clarify that we started this work independently long before Track-Former and TransTrack appear on arXiv. Adding that they are not formally published, we treat them as *concurrent and independent* works instead of *previous* works on which our work is built upon.

4 Experiments

4.1 Datasets and Metrics

Datasets. For comprehensive evaluation, we conducted experiments on three datasets: DanceTrack [28], MOT17 [19], and BDD100k [41]. MOT17 [19] contains 7 training sequences and 7 test sequences. DanceTrack [28] is a recent multi-object tracking dataset featuring uniform appearance and diverse motion. It contains more videos for training and evaluation thus providing a better choice to verify the tracking performance. BDD100k [41] is an autonomous driving dataset with an MOT track featuring multiple object classes. For more details, please refer to the statistics of datasets, shown in Table 2.

Evaluation Metrics. We follow the standard evaluation protocols to evaluate our method. The common metrics include Higher Order Metric for Evaluating Multi-object Tracking [17] (HOTA, AssA, DetA), Multiple-Object Tracking Accuracy (MOTA), Identity Switches (IDS) and Identity F1 Score (IDF1).

4.2 Implementation Details

Following the settings in CenterTrack [44], MOTR adopts several data augmentation methods, such as random flip and random crop. The shorter side of the input image is resized to 800 and the maximum size is restricted to 1536. The inference speed on Tesla V100 at this resolution is about 7.5 FPS. We sample keyframes with random intervals to solve the problem of variable frame rates. Besides, we erase the tracked queries with the probability p_{drop} to generate more samples for newborn objects and insert track queries of false positives with the probability p_{insert} to simulate the terminated objects. All the experiments are conducted on PyTorch with 8 NVIDIA Tesla V100 GPUs. We also provide a memory-optimized version that can be trained on NVIDIA 2080 Ti GPUs.

We built MOTR upon Deformable-DETR [45] with ResNet50 [10] for fast convergence. The batch size is set to 1 and each batch contains a video clip of 5 frames. We train our model with the AdamW optimizer with the initial learning rate of $2.0 \cdot 10^{-4}$. For all datasets, we initialize MOTR with the official Deformable DETR [45] weights pre-trained on the COCO [15] dataset. On **MOT17**, we train MOTR for 200 epochs and the learning rate decays by a factor of 10 at the 100th epoch. For state-of-the-art comparison, we train on the joint dataset (MOT17 training set and CrowdHuman [23] val set). For ~5k static images in CrowdHuman val set, we apply random shift as in [44] to generate video clips with pseudo tracks. The initial length of video clip is 2 and we gradually increase it to 3,4,5 at the 50th,90th,150th epochs, respectively. The progressive increment of video clip length improves the training efficiency and stability. For the ablation study, we train MOTR on the MOT17 training set without using the CrowdHuman dataset and validate on the 2DMOT15 training set. On **DanceTrack**, we train for 20 epochs on the train set and learning rate decays at the 10th epoch. We gradually increase the clip length from 2 to 3,4,5 at the 5th,9th,15th epochs. On **BDD100k**, we train for 20 epochs on the train set and learning rate decays at the 16th epoch. We gradually increase the clip length from 2 to 3 and 4 at the 6th and 12th epochs.

4.3   State-of-the-Art Comparison on MOT17

Table 3 compares our approach with state-of-the-art methods on MOT17 test set. We mainly compare MOTR with our concurrent works based on Transformer: TrackFormer [18] and TransTrack [29]. Our method gets higher IDF1 scores, surpassing TransTrack and TrackFormer by 4.5%. The performance of MOTR on the HOTA metric is much higher than TransTrack by 3.1%. For the MOTA metric, our method achieves much better performance than TrackFormer (71.9% vs. 65.0%). Interestingly, we find that the performance of TransTrack is better than our MOTR on MOTA. We suppose the decoupling of detection and tracking branches in TransTrack indeed improves the object detection performance. While in MOTR, detect and track queries are learned through a shared Transformer decoder. Detect queries are suppressed on detecting tracked objects, limiting the detection performance on newborn objects.

If we compare the performance with other state-of-the-art methods, like Byte-Track [42], it shows that MOTR is **frustratingly inferior** to them on the MOT17 dataset. Usually, state-of-the-art performance on the MOT17 dataset is dominated by trackers with good detection performance to cope with various appearance distributions. Also, different trackers tend to employ different detectors for object detection. It is pretty difficult for us to fairly verify the motion performance of various trackers. Therefore, we argue that the MOT17 dataset alone is **not enough** to fully evaluate the tracking performance of MOTR. We further evaluate the tracking performance on DanceTrack [28] dataset with uniform appearance and diverse motion, as described next.

Table 3. Performance comparison between MOTR and existing methods on the MOT17 dataset under the private detection protocols. The number is marked in bold if it is the best among the Transformer-based methods.

Methods	HOTA↑	AssA↑	DetA↑	IDF1↑	MOTA↑	IDS↓
CNN-based:						
Tracktor++ [2]	44.8	45.1	44.9	52.3	53.5	2072
CenterTrack [44]	52.2	51.0	53.8	64.7	67.8	3039
TraDeS [40]	52.7	50.8	55.2	63.9	69.1	3555
QDTrack [20]	53.9	52.7	55.6	66.3	68.7	3378
GSDT [35]	55.5	54.8	56.4	68.7	66.2	3318
FairMOT [43]	59.3	58.0	60.9	72.3	73.7	3303
CorrTracker [32]	60.7	58.9	62.9	73.6	76.5	3369
GRTU [33]	62.0	62.1	62.1	75.0	74.9	1812
MAATrack [27]	62.0	60.2	64.2	75.9	79.4	1452
ByteTrack [42]	63.1	62.0	64.5	77.3	80.3	2196
Transformer-based:						
TrackFormer [18]	/	/	/	63.9	65.0	3528
TransTrack [29]	54.1	47.9	**61.6**	63.9	**74.5**	3663
MOTR (ours)	**57.8**	**55.7**	60.3	**68.6**	73.4	**2439**

4.4 State-of-the-Art Comparison on DanceTrack

Recently, DanceTrack [28], a dataset with uniform appearance and diverse motion, is introduced (see Table 2). It contains much more videos for evaluation and provides a better choice to verify the tracking performance. We further conduct the experiments on the DanceTrack dataset and perform the performance comparison with state-of-the-art methods in Table 4. It shows that MOTR achieves much better performance on DanceTrack dataset. Our method gets a much higher HOTA score, surpassing ByteTrack by 6.5%. For the AssA metric, our method also achieves much better performance than ByteTrack (40.2% *vs.* 32.1%). While for the DetA metric, MOTR is inferior to some state-of-the-art methods. It means that MOTR performs well on temporal motion learning while the detection performance is not that good. The large improvements on HOTA are mainly from the temporal aggregation network and collective average loss.

4.5 Generalization on Multi-class Scene

Re-ID based methods, like FairMOT [43], tend to regard each tracked object (e.g., person) as a class and associate the detection results by the feature similarity. However, the association will be difficult when the number of tracked objects is very large. Different from them, each object is denoted as one track query in MOTR and the track query set is of dynamic length. MOTR can easily deal with the multi-class prediction problem, by simply modifying the class number of the classification branch. To verify the performance of MOTR on multi-class scenes, we further conduct the experiments on the BDD100k dataset (see Table 5). Results on bdd100k validation set show that MOTR performs well on multi-class scenes and achieves promising performance with fewer ID switches.

Table 4. Performance comparison between MOTR and existing methods on the Dance-Track [28] dataset. Results for existing methods are from DanceTrack [28].

Methods	HOTA	AssA	DetA	MOTA	IDF1
CenterTrack [44]	41.8	22.6	**78.1**	86.8	35.7
FairMOT [43]	39.7	23.8	66.7	82.2	40.8
QDTrack [20]	45.7	29.2	72.1	83.0	44.8
TransTrack [29]	45.5	27.5	75.9	88.4	45.2
TraDes [40]	43.3	25.4	74.5	86.2	41.2
ByteTrack [42]	47.7	32.1	71.0	**89.6**	**53.9**
MOTR (ours)	**54.2**	**40.2**	73.5	79.7	51.5

Table 5. Performance comparison between MOTR and existing methods on the BDD100k [41] validation set.

Methods	mMOTA	mIDF1	IDSw
Yu *et al.* [41]	25.9	**44.5**	8315
DeepBlueAI [1]	26.9	/	13366
MOTR (ours)	**32.0**	43.5	**3493**

4.6 Ablation Study

MOTR Components. Table 6a shows the impact of integrating different components. Integrating our components into the baseline can gradually improve overall performance. Using only object query of as original leads to numerous IDs since most objects are treated as entrance objects. With track query introduced, the baseline is able to handle tracking association and improve IDF1 from 1.2 to 49.8. Further, adding TAN to the baseline improves MOTA by 7.8% and IDF1 by 13.6%. When using CAL during training, there are extra 8.3% and 7.1% improvements in MOTA and IDF1, respectively. It demonstrates that TAN combined with CAL can enhance the learning of temporal motion.

Collective Average Loss. Here, we explored the impact of video sequence length on the tracking performance in CAL. As shown in Table 6b, when the length of the video clip gradually increases from 2 to 5, MOTA and IDF1 metrics are improved by 8.3% and 7.1%, respectively. Thus, multi-frame CAL can greatly boost the tracking performance. We explained that multiple frames CAL can help the network to handle some hard cases such as occlusion scenes. We observed that duplicated boxes, ID switches, and object missing in occluded scenes are significantly reduced. To verify it, we provide some visualizations in Fig. 5.

Erasing and Inserting Track Query. In MOT datasets, there are few training samples for two cases: entrance objects and exit objects in video sequences. Therefore, we adopt track query erasing and inserting to simulate these two cases with probability p_{drop} and p_{insert}, respectively. Table 6c reports the performance using different value of p_{drop} during training. MOTR achieves the best performance when p_{drop} is set to 0.1. Similar to the entrance objects, track queries

Table 6. Ablation studies on our proposed MOTR. All experiments use the single-level C5 feature in ResNet50.

(a) The effect of our contributions. TrackQ: track query. TAN: temporal aggregation network. CAL: collective average loss.

TrackQ	TAN	CAL	MOTA↑	IDF1↑	IDS↓
		-		1.2	33198
✓			37.1	49.8	562
✓	✓		44.9	63.4	257
✓		✓	47.5	56.1	417
✓	✓	✓	**53.2**	**70.5**	**155**

(b) The impact of increasing video clip length in Collective Average Loss during training on tracking performance.

Length	MOTA↑	IDF1↑	IDS↓
2	44.9	63.4	257
3	51.6	59.4	424
4	50.6	64.0	314
5	**53.2**	**70.5**	**155**

(c) Analysis on random track query erasing probability p_{drop} during training.

p_{drop}	MOTA↑	IDF1↑	IDS↓
5e-2	49.0	60.4	411
0.1	**53.2**	**70.5**	**155**
0.3	51.1	69.0	180
0.5	48.5	62.0	302

(d) Effect of random false positive inserting probability p_{insert} during training.

p_{insert}	MOTA↑	IDF1↑	IDS↓
0.1	51.2	**71.7**	**148**
0.3	**53.2**	70.5	155
0.5	52.1	62.0	345
0.7	50.7	57.7	444

(e) The exploration of different combinations of τ_{ex} and τ_{en} in QIM network.

τ_{ex}	0.6	0.6	0.6	0.5	0.6	0.7
τ_{en}	0.7	0.8	0.9	0.8	0.8	0.8
MOTA↑	52.7	**53.2**	53.1	**53.5**	53.2	52.8
IDF1↑	69.8	**70.5**	70.1	**70.5**	70.5	68.3
IDS↓	181	155	**142**	153	155	181

(f) The effect of random sampling interval on tracking performance.

Intervals	MOTA↑	IDF1↑	IDS↓
3	53.2	64.8	218
5	50.8	62.8	324
10	**53.2**	**70.5**	**155**
12	53.1	69	158

transferred from the previous frame, whose predictions are false positives, are inserted into the current frame to simulate the case of object exit. In Table 6d, we explore the impact on tracking performance of different p_{insert}. When progressively increasing p_{insert} from 0.1 to 0.7, our MOTR achieves the highest score on MOTA when p_{insert} is set to 0.3 while the IDF1 score is decreasing.

Object Entrance and Exit Threshold. Table 6e investigates the impact of different combination of object entrance threshold τ_{en} and exit threshold τ_{ex} in QIM. As we vary the object entrance threshold τ_{en}, we can see that the performance is not that sensitive to τ_{en} (within 0.5% on MOTA) and using an entrance threshold of 0.8 produces relatively better performance. We also further conduct experiments by varying the object exit threshold τ_{ex}. It is shown that using a threshold of 0.5 results in slightly better performance than that of 0.6. In our practice, τ_{en} with 0.6 shows better performance on the MOT17 test set.

Sampling Interval. In Table 6f, we evaluate the effect of random sampling interval on tracking performance during training. When the sampling interval increases from 2 to 10, the IDS decreases significantly from 209 to 155. During training, the network is easy to fall into a local optimal solution when the frames are sampled in a small interval. Appropriate increment on sampling interval can simulate real scenes. When the random sampling interval is greater than 10, the tracking framework fails to capture such long-range dynamics, leading to relatively worse tracking performance.

(a)   (b)

Fig. 5. The effect of CAL on solving (a) duplicated boxes and (b) ID switch problems. Top and bottom rows are the tracking results without and with CAL, respectively.

5   Limitations

MOTR, an online tracker, achieves end-to-end multiple-object tracking. It implicitly learns the appearance and position variances in a joint manner thanks to the DETR architecture as well as the tracklet-aware label assignment. However, it also has several shortcomings. First, the performance of detecting newborn objects is far from satisfactory (the result on the MOTA metric is not good enough). As we analyzed above, detect queries are suppressed on detecting tracked objects, which may go against the nature of object query and limits the detection performance on newborn objects. Second, the query passing in MOTR is performed frame-by-frame, limiting the efficiency of model learning during training. In our practice, the parallel decoding in VisTR [36] fails to deal with the complex scenarios in MOT. Solving these two problems above will be an important research topic for Transformer-based MOT frameworks.

Acknowledgements. This research was supported by National Key R&D Program of China (No. 2017YFA0700800) and Beijing Academy of Artificial Intelligence (BAAI).

References

1. CodaLab Competition - CVPR 2020 BDD100K multiple object tracking challenge, July 2022. https://competitions.codalab.org/competitions/24910. Accessed 19 Jul 2022
2. Bergmann, P., Meinhardt, T., Leal-Taixe, L.: Tracking without bells and whistles. In: ICCV (2019)
3. Bewley, A., Ge, Z., Ott, L., Ramos, F., Upcroft, B.: Simple online and realtime tracking. In: ICIP (2016)
4. Bochinski, E., Eiselein, V., Sikora, T.: High-speed tracking-by-detection without using image information. In: AVSS (2017)
5. Camgoz, N.C., Koller, O., Hadfield, S., Bowden, R.: Sign language transformers: Joint end-to-end sign language recognition and translation. In: CVPR (2020)
6. Carion, N., Massa, F., Synnaeve, G., Usunier, N., Kirillov, A., Zagoruyko, S.: End-to-end object detection with transformers. In: Vedaldi, A., Bischof, H., Brox, T., Frahm, J.-M. (eds.) ECCV 2020. LNCS, vol. 12346, pp. 213–229. Springer, Cham (2020). https://doi.org/10.1007/978-3-030-58452-8_13
7. Chang, X., Zhang, W., Qian, Y., Le Roux, J., Watanabe, S.: End-to-end multi-speaker speech recognition with transformer. In: ICASSP (2020)
8. Chu, P., Wang, J., You, Q., Ling, H., Liu, Z.: TransMOT: spatial-temporal graph transformer for multiple object tracking. arXiv preprint arXiv:2104.00194 (2021)
9. Dosovitskiy, A., et al.: An image is worth 16 x 16 words: transformers for image recognition at scale. In: ICLR (2021)
10. He, K., Zhang, X., Ren, S., Sun, J.: Deep residual learning for image recognition. In: CVPR (2016)
11. Kuhn, H.W.: The Hungarian method for the assignment problem. Naval Res. Logistics Q. **2**(1–2), 83–97 (1955)
12. Leal-Taixé, L., Canton-Ferrer, C., Schindler, K.: Learning by tracking: Siamese CNN for robust target association. In: CVPRW (2016)
13. Li, N., Liu, S., Liu, Y., Zhao, S., Liu, M.: Neural speech synthesis with transformer network. In: AAAI (2019)
14. Lin, T.Y., Goyal, P., Girshick, R., He, K., Dollár, P.: Focal loss for dense object detection. In: ICCV (2017)
15. Lin, T.Y., et al.: Microsoft coco: common objects in context. In: ECCV (2014)
16. Liu, Z., et al.: Swin transformer: hierarchical vision transformer using shifted windows. arXiv preprint arXiv:2103.14030 (2021)
17. Luiten, J., et al.: HOTA: a higher order metric for evaluating multi-object tracking. Int. J. Comput. Vis. 1–31 (2020). https://doi.org/10.1007/s11263-020-01375-2

18. Meinhardt, T., Kirillov, A., Leal-Taixe, L., Feichtenhofer, C.: TrackFormer: multi-object tracking with transformers. arXiv preprint arXiv:2101.02702 (2021)
19. Milan, A., Leal-Taixé, L., Reid, I., Roth, S., Schindler, K.: Mot16: a benchmark for multi-object tracking. arXiv preprint arXiv:1603.00831 (2016)
20. Pang, J., et al.: Quasi-dense similarity learning for multiple object tracking. In: CVPR (2021)
21. Rezatofighi, H., Tsoi, N., Gwak, J., Sadeghian, A., Reid, I., Savarese, S.: Generalized intersection over union: a metric and a loss for bounding box regression. In: CVPR (2019)
22. Schulter, S., Vernaza, P., Choi, W., Chandraker, M.: Deep network flow for multi-object tracking. In: CVPR (2017)
23. Shao, S., et al.: CrowdHuman: a benchmark for detecting human in a crowd. arXiv preprint arXiv:1805.00123 (2018)
24. Sharma, S., Ansari, J.A., Murthy, J.K., Krishna, K.M.: Beyond pixels: leveraging geometry and shape cues for online multi-object tracking. In: ICRA (2018)
25. Shi, B., Bai, X., Yao, C.: An end-to-end trainable neural network for image-based sequence recognition and its application to scene text recognition. TPAMI **39**(11), 2298–2304 (2016)
26. Shuai, B., Berneshawi, A.G., Modolo, D., Tighe, J.: Multi-object tracking with Siamese track-RCNN. arXiv preprint arXiv:2004.07786 (2020)
27. Stadler, D., Beyerer, J.: Modelling ambiguous assignments for multi-person tracking in crowds. In: Proceedings of the IEEE/CVF Winter Conference on Applications of Computer Vision, pp. 133–142 (2022)
28. Sun, P., et al.: DanceTrack: multi-object tracking in uniform appearance and diverse motion. arXiv preprint arXiv:2111.14690 (2021)
29. Sun, P., et al.: TransTrack: multiple-object tracking with transformer. arXiv preprint arXiv: 2012.15460 (2020)
30. Sutskever, I., Vinyals, O., Le, Q.V.: Sequence to sequence learning with neural networks. In: NeurIPS (2014)
31. Vaswani, A., et al.: Attention is all you need. In: NeurIPS (2017)
32. Wang, Q., Zheng, Y., Pan, P., Xu, Y.: Multiple object tracking with correlation learning. In: Proceedings of the IEEE/CVF Conference on Computer Vision and Pattern Recognition, pp. 3876–3886 (2021)
33. Wang, S., Sheng, H., Zhang, Y., Wu, Y., Xiong, Z.: A general recurrent tracking framework without real data. In: Proceedings of the IEEE/CVF International Conference on Computer Vision, pp. 13219–13228 (2021)
34. Wang, X., Girshick, R., Gupta, A., He, K.: Non-local neural networks. In: CVPR (2018)
35. Wang, Y., Kitani, K., Weng, X.: Joint object detection and multi-object tracking with graph neural networks. In: 2021 IEEE International Conference on Robotics and Automation (ICRA), pp. 13708–13715. IEEE (2021)
36. Wang, Y., et al.: End-to-end video instance segmentation with transformers. In: CVPR (2021)
37. Wang, Z., Zheng, L., Liu, Y., Li, Y., Wang, S.: Towards real-time multi-object tracking. In: ECCV (2020)
38. Welch, G., Bishop, G., et al.: An introduction to the kalman filter (1995)
39. Wojke, N., Bewley, A., Paulus, D.: Simple online and realtime tracking with a deep association metric. In: ICIP (2017)
40. Wu, J., Cao, J., Song, L., Wang, Y., Yang, M., Yuan, J.: Track to detect and segment: an online multi-object tracker. In: CVPR (2021)

41. Yu, F., et al.: Bdd100k: a diverse driving dataset for heterogeneous multitask learning. In: IEEE/CVF Conference on Computer Vision and Pattern Recognition (CVPR), June 2020

42. Zhang, Y., et al.: ByteTrack: multi-object tracking by associating every detection box. arXiv preprint arXiv:2110.06864 (2021)

43. Zhang, Y., Wang, C., Wang, X., Zeng, W., Liu, W.: FairMOT: on the fairness of detection and re-identification in multiple object tracking. Int. J. Comput. Vis. **129**(11), 3069–3087 (2021). https://doi.org/10.1007/s11263-021-01513-4

44. Zhou, X., Koltun, V., Krähenbühl, P.: Tracking objects as points. In: ECCV (2020)

45. Zhu, X., Su, W., Lu, L., Li, B., Wang, X., Dai, J.: Deformable DETR: deformable transformers for end-to-end object detection. In: ICLR (2020)

GALA: Toward Geometry-and-Lighting-Aware Object Search for Compositing

Sijie Zhu[1(✉)], Zhe Lin[2], Scott Cohen[2], Jason Kuen[2], Zhifei Zhang[2], and Chen Chen[1]

[1] Center for Research in Computer Vision, University of Central Florida, Orlando, USA
sizhu@knights.ucf.edu, chen.chen@crcv.ucf.edu
[2] Adobe Research, San Jose, USA
{zlin,scohen,kuen,zzhang}@adobe.com

Abstract. Compositing-aware object search aims to find the most compatible objects for compositing given a background image and a query bounding box. Previous works focus on learning compatibility between the foreground object and background, but fail to learn other important factors from large-scale data, i.e. geometry and lighting. To move a step further, this paper proposes GALA (Geometry-and-Lighting-Aware), a generic foreground object search method with discriminative modeling on geometry and lighting compatibility for open-world image compositing. Remarkably, it achieves state-of-the-art results on the CAIS dataset and generalizes well on large-scale open-world datasets, i.e. Pixabay and Open Images. In addition, our method can effectively handle non-box scenarios, where users only provide background images without any input bounding box. Experiments are conducted on real-world images to showcase applications of the proposed method for compositing-aware search and automatic location/scale prediction for the foreground object.

Keywords: Foreground object retrieval · Image compositing

1 Introduction

Compositing-aware object search/retrieval [26] aims to find suitable source images for compositing [17,24]. Specifically, given a background image and a bounding box indicating the compositing location, the objective is to retrieve compatible foreground objects from a large reference database, so that the composite image appears realistic. Harmonization [2,7,15,22,29] is then applied to

S. Zhu—This work was done during the first author's internship at Adobe Research.

Supplementary Information The online version contains supplementary material available at https://doi.org/10.1007/978-3-031-19812-0_39.

Original Image   Query   Top Retrieved Results

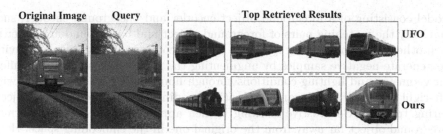

UFO

Ours

Fig. 1. Comparison between state-of-the-art method (UFO [27] in the first row) and the proposed geometry-and-lighting-aware search (second row). The retrieved objects in the first row do not respect the geometry of the background scene, while results of the proposed method have better geometry compatibility.

adjust the color and edge pixels, but it is extremely challenging to automatically adjust the semantics, lighting, or geometry of foreground objects. Although recent relighting method [19] can generate realistic lighting change for human portraits, it does not tackle general object categories and the required 3D reconstruction is not always available. Therefore, the quality of the final composite image highly depends on the performance of foreground retrieval system, and a good system should be aware of semantics, lighting, and geometry of foreground objects.

Early work [26] on foreground retrieval follows a constrained setting, which requires the user to specify the object category for retrieval. Specifying the category sets a limit on the search space, thus preventing the system from recommending diverse sets of objects. Later, UFO [27] proposes an unconstrained search method, i.e. objects from all categories are considered as candidates for retrieval. The unconstrained setting is closer to real-world scenarios, which require a large and diverse foreground object gallery to satisfy different users. However, UFO [27] focuses on finding semantically compatible foreground object and does not explicitly model lighting and geometry, which are critical factors for making object compositing realistic, as shown in Figs. 1 and Sect. 1 in supplementary material.

More recent work [13,23] either explores additional annotation [13] for constrained setting, or only focuses on indoor furniture [23] with fine-grained subcategories. Therefore, how to encourage awareness on geometry and lighting is still unclear for general unconstrained foreground retrieval. One way to consider these factors is to explicitly estimate the 3D geometry and lighting of the scene, but it is extremely challenging to obtain realistic training data with 3D labels to do so. Instead, we aim to build a discriminative model which is sensitive to lighting and geometry mismatches using real-world image datasets, leading to a more generalizable and scalable solution.

In this paper, we propose a novel Geometry-And-Lighting-Aware (GALA) foreground object search system, which aims to retrieve objects that are compatible in terms of semantics, geometry, and lighting. Specifically, we design a model consisting of a foreground object encoder and background encoder, such that only the matching pairs of foreground object and background are closer to each other in the embedding space. To encode geometry and lighting sensitivity, we generate negative samples by augmenting the same objects with very different geometry and lighting conditions through homography transformation with left-right flip and non-linear illumination modification on foreground objects during training. Contrastive learning is then applied to push the transformed foreground object far away from the original one in the embedding space. However, the semantic compatibility of retrieved objects could degrade significantly if we train the foreground network jointly with the background network. Thus, we introduce an alternating training strategy to maintain semantic compatibility, while learning to respect geometry and lighting. GALA can also be extended to handle non-box scenarios, where the users only provide the background image without any bounding box or text input. Our model automatically retrieves foreground objects and predicts the best location and scale for compositing.

Table 1. Comparison between our method and previous works on settings.

	Zhao [26]	UFO [27]	Li [13]	Wu [23]	Ours
One model for all	✓	✓	✓	✗	✓
Unspecified class	✗	✓	✗	✓	✓
Non-box scenarios	✗	✗	✗	✗	✓
Large-scale dataset	✗	✗	✗	✗	✓
Open-world setting	✗	✗	✗	✗	✓

Furthermore, we perform experiments and validate GALA for open-world datasets with an arbitrarily large number of categories, targeting real-world unconstrained applications. Previous works are mostly implemented on medium scale datasets (<100,000 objects) with limited categories, e.g. MSCOCO [16] only has 80 object categories. In contrast, we conduct experiments on large-scale real-world datasets, i.e. Pixabay [1] and Open Images [9], which contain significantly more categories and images with diverse contents. We show comparisons of various settings between the proposed method and previous works in Table 1. Our contributions are summarized as follows:

- A novel compositing-aware search method that discriminatively models geometry and lighting with contrastive training.
- An alternating training strategy to address the challenge of losing semantic compatibility when learning the foreground network in an unconstrained setting.
- Extensive experiments to demonstrate significant improvements over previous works on the CAIS dataset, as well as a new large-scale open-world dataset, i.e. Pixabay.

- An extension of the method for non-box conditioned scenarios which are never considered in previous works.

2 Related Work

Search for Compositing. The idea of searching for foregrounds to insert into a new background is first proposed by Lalonde et al. [10], by explicitly estimating the 3D geometry of foreground objects, and the lighting map of background scenes. Zhao et al. [26] propose a learning-based compositing-aware search method, where the users provide a specific class as text input. The positive samples are augmented based on shape and semantics. UFO [27] assumes that the user does not specify any category, which is the most relevant setting to our work, but it only focuses on the semantic compatibility and ignores lighting and geometry. It trains a discriminator to distinguish real/fake object for a certain background and selects candidate positive samples for each background image. Li et al. [13] manually annotates multiple attributes as additional information to determine "Interpretable Foreground Object" with given categories. Wu et al. [23] propose a teacher-student framework for fine-grained indoor categories, which adopts multiple pre-trained features for foreground objects as teacher and trains the background network with KL-divergence. None of them learn discriminitive features on geometry and lighting for general unconstrained foreground search.

Object Placement. A thread of works [11,14,25] focus on object placement along with adversarial training, which predicts locations and scales to insert an object. Lee et al. [11] train a spatial transformer network to predict the location for placement and a shape mask to guide generation. Zhang et al. [25] train a location-scale prediction model using inpainted pure background images. Li et al. [14] first find candidate locations in indoor scenes, then predict the best human pose for a specific location. These methods either focus on street scenes with limited object categories, e.g. person, car, or indoor scenes with only human pose joints. Our location-scale prediction deals with a more challenging setting with general objects from diverse scenes by directly adopting our retrieval model.

3 Method

In this section, we introduce GALA, Geometry-and-Lighting-Aware foreground object search for compositing. We first formulate the problem and describe training data generation in Sect. 3.1. Then we present the details of contrastive learning with self-transformations and the alternating training strategy in Sect. 3.2 and 3.3. Finally, we show how GALA handles non-box scenarios in Sect. 3.4.

3.1 Problem Statement

Given a background image I_b with a bounding box (l, r, w, h), our objective is to retrieve a set of most compatible foreground object images $\{I_f\}$, so that realistic composite images can be generated with simple harmonization techniques. Our framework aims to learn an embedding space so that compatible images are close to each other in this space and the ranking can be obtained by simply computing the cosine similarity or euclidean distance. Since foreground and background images have very different distributions and appearances, we use two different encoder networks N_b, N_f to generate the embedding features for I_b, I_f, respectively. During training, the only available annotation is semantic segmentation mask for each object. We use the mask to crop out the object as I_f. Then I_b is generated by applying a rectangle mask on the image covering the whole object. Since there is no manual annotation on positive and negative samples, we consider I_b and I_f generated from the same image as a positive sample to each other, while other image pairs are considered as negative samples. With a hard-margin triplet loss [3], the optimization can be formulated as $\arg\min_{N_b, N_f} \mathcal{L}_t$, where

$$\mathcal{L}_t = [S(N_b(I_b), N_f(I_f^-)) - S(N_b(I_b), N_f(I_f^+)) + m]_+. \tag{1}$$

Here S means cosine similarity, and $[.]_+$ denotes the hinge function. m is the margin for triplet loss and I_f^+, I_f^- indicate the positive and negative foreground objects for a given I_b.

3.2 Contrastive Learning with Self-transformation

The standard loss in Eq. 1 only considers the contrastive information between the original foreground object and other objects, which mainly focuses on semantic information. We argue that a Geometry-and-Lighting-aware system should be able to tell the difference if the foreground object has exactly the same semantics with different lighting and geometry conditions. We thus perform transformation on the original positive foreground object so that it can be considered as negative.

As shown in Fig. 2, the transformed foreground objects have very different lighting or geometry conditions, which do not match with the background image anymore. We consider the transformed object image I_f^t as negative and formulate another triplet loss (Fig. 3):

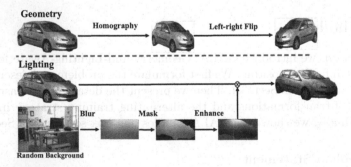

Fig. 2. Pipeline of generating lighting and geometry transformations used in contrastive learning.

$$\mathcal{L}_c = [S(N_b(I_b), N_f(I_f^t)) - S(N_b(I_b), N_f(I_f)) + m]_+. \tag{2}$$

The final loss is given by $\mathcal{L} = \mathcal{L}_t + \mathcal{L}_c$ from Eqs. 1 and 2. In Fig. 2, we show the pipeline of self transformations. For geometry transformation, we first apply random homography transformations, then left-right flip is applied with a 50% probability. For lighting transformation, we first find a random background image and apply Gaussian blur with a large radius, e.g. 100. The blurred map is then resized with interpolation to the size of foreground object, and masked with the segmentation mask. Finally, we enhance the variance of the lighting map with an exponential function so that the largest value of the map is 5. In this way, we get a non-linear illumination map which highlights a random region in the object image, and it is multiplied by the original object image to generate the final transformed image. Although the lighting may not be as realistic as 3D relighting [18], it is enough to be considered as a negative sample with very different illuminations.

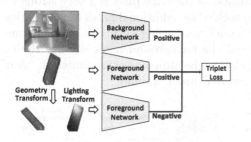

Fig. 3. Contrastive learning with self-transformations.

Table 2. Performance of different training strategies on CAIS.

	mAP
Fix foreground	29.10
Direct training	17.93
Aug	23.45
Aug + Alternating	**31.20**

3.3 Alternating Training

We notice that previous works [23,27] generally use pre-trained weights for foreground network N_f and freeze its parameters during training (denoted as "Fix Foreground"), which means N_f cannot learn from data. Since data augmentation like left-right flip is adopted for pre-training on ImageNet [4], the feature would be invariant to the left-right flip, which could change the geometry and direction of lighting. Therefore, the pre-trained weights are not discriminative to lighting and geometry changes, which will be further demonstrated in Sect. 4.2.

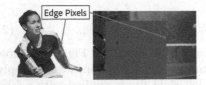

Fig. 4. Imperfect segmentation mask and edge pixel example.

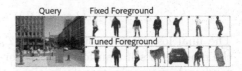

Fig. 5. An example of poor compatibility on semantics when training foreground network.

To learn geometry-and-lighting-aware representation, N_f must be learnable. However, performance drops significantly if N_f and N_b are directly trained with Eq. 1 (denoted as "Direct Training" in Table 2), partly due to the imperfect segmentation mask, as some annotations (MSCOCO) are based on polygon. When cropping with an imperfect mask (Fig. 4), some edge pixels of the object are actually background pixels, which are very likely to be the same as other background edge pixels. Direct training may optimize the model to match the edge pixels without compatibility on semantics, as the edge pixel is a very strong cue for positive pairs. This issue could be tackled by additional mask augmentations (denoted as "Aug") to prevent the model from using such cue. We randomly erode the foreground mask and extend the background mask so that the cue becomes random. Examples are included in the supplementary material. "Aug" significantly improves the performance over direct training.

However, the performance is still much lower than using fixed foreground network. Another issue is that the foreground object images have very different appearances and distributions from regular images. And the "Direct Training" model N_f does not respect semantics very well as compared with using ImageNet pre-trained weights. As shown in Fig. 5, "tuned foreground" retrieves irrelevant categories for a sidewalk query, e.g. bottle, car. Our solution

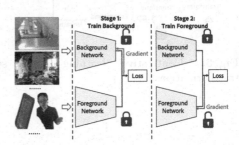

Fig. 6. The proposed alternating training strategy.

is to alternatively train N_b and N_f as shown in Fig. 6. Since there is only one network trained in one stage, the embedding features of the trained network will not have much drift. In this way, our method maintains semantic information in foreground feature, while allowing N_f to learn from data for other factors, i.e. lighting and geometry.

3.4 Extension to Non-box Scenarios

When the user only provides a background image without any bounding box, we adopt the following random seed and greedy search algorithm to retrieve matching foreground objects. We first sample multiple random locations. Each location is assigned with multiple bounding boxes with different aspect ratios and scales. We retrieve foreground objects based on each of the bounding boxes and re-rank all the results based on cosine similarity. We select

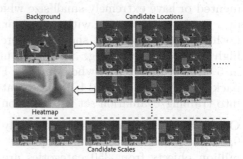

Fig. 7. Example of location/scale prediction.

the best one as the default object, then assign an initial bounding box with the same aspect ratio as the object. The area of the initial box is empirically assigned as $1/25$ of the query image. Then we apply $k \times k$ grid of locations (Fig. 7) with initial bounding box to cover the query image in a sliding window manner. By computing the similarity score between the object and background with all the possible boxes, the box with the highest score is considered as the best location. A location heatmap is generated by interpolating the $k \times k$ score matrix to the size of query image. One can always increase k or apply further refinement with smaller stride to improve the location. The scale is then selected by applying a range of scale ratios on the initial box at the best location, as shown in Fig. 7.

4 Experiment

We first conduct experiment on CAIS [26], which is specifically annotated for compositing-aware search. Then we generate two large-scale datasets based on Pixabay [1] and Open Images [9] to demonstrate our model's generalization ability on open-world setting.

CAIS: The dataset is generated by selecting 8 popular categories from three datasets, i.e. MS-COCO [16], PASCAL VOC 2012 [5], ADE20K [28]. The training set has $86,800$ background images, and the original foreground object in each image is considered as ground-truth. The evaluation set has 80 manually selected background images and query bounding box to insert objects. About 16–140 compatible foreground objects are annotated for each background image.

Pixabay: "pixabay.com" is a stock image website containing tons of high-quality photos which are perfect for composing. The images are highly diverse, free to use, and substantial in number. We first collect about $928,018$ images, then apply object detection [21] and segmentation [12] to generate foreground objects and background images based on masks. In total, we get $5,771,912$ foreground objects and $928,018$ background images. But some objects are not well segmented or have extremely small size which is not likely to be used for composting. Background images with overly large box is also not suitable as there is nothing left to tell what should be here. Therefore we only keep images with high confidence score (e.g. > 0.6) and proper bounding box size (e.g. box area in 5–50% of the area of whole image). Finally, we get $833,964$ foreground and background pairs with 914 non-zero categories. They are then randomly split into training/evaluation set with portion of 90%/10%.

Open Images: Open Images originally contains about 9 million images with $9,605$ trainable classes, thus is perfect for open-world evaluation. Up to 2.8 million objects from 350 categories are annotated with segmentation masks. We originally select $944,024$ images with $2,686,666$ objects, then apply the same filtering procedure as Pixabay based on box size only, as the mask is annotated. In total, we keep $1,374,344$ background and foreground object pairs in our experiments. They are then randomly split into training/evaluation set with portion of 90%/10%. Open Images is only used in ablation study.

Implementation Details. We implement our method based on PyTorch [19] with multiprocessing to support large-scale training and evaluation. The models are trained on 8 T V100 GPUs. Batch size is 40 per card for training. Following [27], we use VGG-19 [20] pre-trained on ImageNet [4] as backbone, as it achieves the best performance among different networks. All foreground objects are padded with white pixels as square images. The original object in background image is covered with rectangle mask with average value. Both foreground and background images are resized to 224×224 and normalized with average value before feed into networks. We use Adam [8] optimizer with learning rate of 0.00008 based on linear scaling rule [6] of multi-card training. The margins of Eq. 1, 2 are set as 0.3, 0.1.

Evaluation Metrics. For retrieval, we use the most widely used metric mAP (mean Average Precision) and R@k (Recall@k). We also report mAP-100 which is the mAP for top 100 retrievals as a fair comparison with constrained methods, because constrained retrieval methods do not rank object in all categories. When there is only one ground-truth (the original object) for each background query, we report R@k as the percentage of background queries whose ground-truth foreground reference appears in top k retrievals. Although other objects may also be compatible, the original one should always have a good rank among all the objects.

4.1   Comparison with Previous Methods

In this section, we compare our method with previous works on CAIS [26] and Pixabay dataset. [13,23] are infeasible for comparison because they both have very different settings, and their codes and datasets are not released. **More qualitative results are included in supplementary materials.**

CAIS: We compare our method with previous state-of-the-art methods and their variants in Table 3. "Shape" [26] ranks all the foreground images by comparing their aspect ratio with the aspect ratio of query bounding box. "RealismCNN" [29] trains a discriminator to distinguish real/fake composite images by copy-paste original and irrelevant objects into a background image. The score of the discriminator measures the realism of each composite, which is used to rank all the objects. "CFO-C Search" [26] and "CFO-D Search" [26] are two constrained search methods evaluated in unconstrained scenarios. "CFO-C Search" first trains a classifier to specify the category, then apply constrained retrieval only from this class. The results will be completely wrong if the classification fails. "CFO-D Search" first apply constrained search to retrieve 100 samples from each category. Then it adopts the discriminator of "RealismCNN" to re-rank all these retrievals by compositing with each background. Note that this is computationally expensive and not scalable if there are hundreds of classes. "UFO Search" [27] applies the discriminator to generate extra positive samples.

In Table 3, we show the mAP-100 per class and the overall performance. The proposed method significantly (+5.33%) outperforms previous state-of-the-art methods on overall performance. It also achieves better performance than UFO [27] on most of the categories. "CFO-C Search" and "CFO-D Search" may performs well on two categories, but they are both not scalable, because it is infeasible to train one model for each category or scan all objects with discriminator for each background on large-scale datasets with hundreds of categories. The results indicate that geometry and lighting awareness can help the retrieval in general unconstrained retrieval.

Table 3. Comparison with previous works on CAIS in terms of mAP-100. "†" denotes constrained methods with multiple models, which are not scalable in practice.

Method	Boat	Bottle	Car	Chair	Dog	Painting	Person	Plant	Overall
Shape [26]	7.47	1.16	10.40	12.25	12.22	3.89	6.37	8.82	7.82
RealismCNN [29]	12.33	7.19	7.55	1.81	7.58	6.45	1.47	12.74	7.14
†CFO-C search [26]	57.48	14.24	18.85	21.61	38.01	27.72	**47.33**	20.20	30.68
†CFO-D search [26]	55.48	8.93	24.10	18.16	**57.82**	21.59	27.66	23.13	29.61
UFO search [27]	59.73	**21.12**	36.63	19.27	36.51	25.84	27.11	31.19	32.17
Ours	**70.58**	19.41	**40.22**	**24.17**	37.81	**28.20**	44.72	**34.91**	**37.50**

Table 4. Retrieval performance of selected classes in terms of Recall@10 (%) on pixabay.

Category	Majority				Medium				Minority
	#samples≈ 5000				#samples≈ 50				#samples< 5
	Person	Flower	Birds	Vehicle	Cell Phone	Mandarin Orange	Christmas Tree	Boiled Egg	Last 50 Classes
UFO [27]	3.84	8.00	6.74	8.41	5.71	36.36	2.94	6.06	8.00
Ours	**19.36**	**28.55**	**21.11**	**26.83**	**20.00**	**63.64**	**20.59**	**30.30**	**24.00**

Pixabay: Since none of the previous works conduct experiments on large-scale open-world setting, we implement the state-of-the-art unconstrained search method (UFO [27]) on Pixabay and provide detailed comparison. Table 4 shows the Recall@10 on selected categories in Pixabay. We select 4

Table 5. Overall retrieval accuracy in terms of Recall@k (%) on pixabay.

Method	R@1	R@5	R@10	R@1%
UFO [27]	2.04	6.66	10.24	61.76
Ours	**7.75**	**20.13**	**28.20**	**85.61**

majority and 4 medium classes, with about 5000 and 50 samples per class in evaluation set (Note that training set is 9 times larger). Then we compute the average Recall@10 on the last 50 long-tail classes. The proposed method significantly outperforms UFO [27] on all the classes. We also show the overall R@k on Pixabay in Table 5. The proposed method significantly outperforms UFO, which means the proposed method generalizes well on large-scale open-world setting.

4.2 Ablation Study

Geometry and Lighting Sensitivity: Since our goal is to gain awareness on geometry and lighting, a good model should be discriminative/sensitive to the change of geometry and lighting on foreground images. We conduct experiment on Pixabay [1] and Open Images [9] to verify this point. We randomly select 2,000 foregrounds along with their corresponding background images. Then for each foreground, we use the geometry and lighting transformations in Sect. 3.2 to generate transformed image. In total, we generate 100 transformed images for each foreground image, 50/50 for geometry/lighting transformation. Then we rank the original one along with the 50 geometry or lighting transformed images to compute the Recall@k in Table 6. We also measure the discriminative ability as the sensitivity to these transformations, i.e. the square euclidean dis-

Table 6. Evaluation of sensitivity (discriminative ability) to lighting and geometry transformation. The "sensitivity" denotes the squared L2 distance between the normalized embedding of original and transformed foreground images.

Ablation	Lighting				Geometry			
	Sensitivity(↑)	R@5	R@10	R@15	Sensitivity(↑)	R@5	R@10	R@15
Pixabay								
UFO [27]	0.27	53.70	67.90	75.50	0.39	58.25	69.90	77.95
Baseline	0.27	53.40	67.30	75.35	0.39	58.10	69.70	77.65
No contrastive	0.51	55.60	70.70	79.70	0.72	61.30	74.30	82.75
Overall	**0.57**	**60.55**	**74.70**	**82.85**	**1.12**	**98.55**	**99.45**	**99.70**
Open images								
Baseline	0.24	51.70	65.45	74.60	0.40	60.10	71.80	78.45
No contrastive	0.53	54.80	71.55	80.10	0.98	71.70	82.60	89.10
Overall	**0.56**	**59.35**	**73.90**	**81.80**	**1.58**	**99.50**	**99.75**	**99.90**

tance between normalized embedding features of the original and transformed foregrounds. With L2 normalization, the square euclidean distance is $d = 2 - 2s$, where s is the cosine similarity. Therefore higher sensitivity value means larger distance between the features of original and transformed objects, thus indicates stronger ability on distinguishing geometry or lighting transformations.

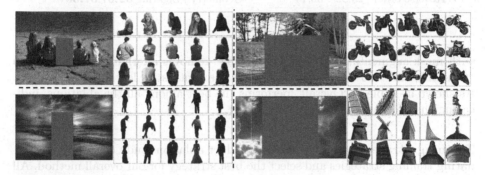

Fig. 8. Qualitative comparison on pixabay and open images. Each of the four examples contains three rows of retrieval results, corresponding to: "Baseline" (1st row), "No Contrastive" (2nd row), "Overall" model (3rd row).

In Table 6, the overall proposed method has much higher sensitivity to both geometry and lighting transformations for both datasets. UFO [27] and "Baseline" both use fixed foreground features, thus have a low sensitivity. "No Contrastive" removes the proposed contrastive transformation but keeps the alternating training, which has a lower sensitivity and retrieval performance than "Overall", but better than "Baseline". The results demonstrate the effectiveness of both alternating training and contrastive learning on improving discriminative ability. We also show qualitative results of our ablations in Fig. 8 with diverse scenes, viewpoints and lighting. Our overall method better respects the geometry and lighting than baseline methods.

Components Ablations: We conduct detailed ablation study on CAIS to show the effectiveness of each component. "Direct Training" mean directly training two networks with loss in Eq. 1. "Aug" denotes direct training along with mask augmentations in Sect. 3.3 to prevent the model from overfitting on edge pixels. "Fix+Aug" is also used as "Baseline"

Table 7. Ablation study on components.

Ablations	mAP	mAP-100
Direct training	17.93	24.02
Aug	23.45	31.78
Fix+Aug	28.65	30.33
No alternating	29.99	32.13
No contrastive	31.20	36.30
Overall	**32.67**	**37.50**

in other tables. It uses a fixed foreground network with mask augmentations. Our "Overall" method adopt both alternating training and contrastive learning

Table 8. Ablation study on different alternating training strategies.

Ablations	mAP	mAP-100
Zero round	28.65	30.33
One round	**31.20**	**36.30**
Two rounds	30.35	36.22
Reverse order	28.82	36.14

Table 9. Ablation study on different transformations.

Ablations	mAP	mAP-100
No Contrastive	31.20	36.30
Geometry	32.11	36.68
Geometry+Color	30.80	35.06
Geometry+Lighting	**32.67**	**37.50**

with mask augmentations. "No Alternating" removes alternating training from "Overall", and "No Contrastive" removes the contrastive learning loss in Eq. 2. As shown in Table 7, "Overall" performs the best among all the ablations, indicating the effectiveness of each component.

Training Strategy Ablations: We conduct ablation study on different alternating training strategies and select the best strategy for our overall method. All these ablations adopt mask augmentations without using contrastive learning. "Zero Round" means no alternating training, which is equivalent to the "Baseline". "One Round" ($\arg\min_{N_b} \mathcal{L}$, then $\arg\min_{N_f} \mathcal{L}$) trains foreground network after the background network is trained. "Two Round" trains the background network for another round based on the "One Round" model. "Reverse Order" ($\arg\min_{N_f} \mathcal{L}$, then $\arg\min_{N_b} \mathcal{L}$) first trains the foreground network, then trains the background network. Table 8 shows that "One Round" strategy performs the best among all the strategies, indicating that training more rounds is not beneficial. We thus use one round for our overall method.

Transformation Ablations: To show the effectiveness of each transformation, we train our method with different transformations in contrastive learning. "No Contrastive" removes contrastive learning loss in Eq. 2. "Geometry" only adopts geometry transformation in Fig. 2, and "Geometry+Lighting" means each foreground is applied with both transformations. "Geometry+Color" uses linear color jittering instead of our non-linear lighting transformation on the top of "Geometry". In Table 9, the "Geometry+Lighting" outperforms other ablations, indicating that both transformations are necessary in our framework, and linear color jittering does not well simulate lighting changes.

4.3 Location and Scale Prediction

Since CAIS has annotated bounding boxes on intact background images, we evaluate our location and scale prediction method based on these boxes for non-box scenarios. We compare the proposed method with random strategy and "Baseline" model. For each background image, we randomly select 5 of its annotated compatible foregrounds for evaluation and compute the average value to report. Qualitative results are included in supplementary material.

Foreground   Background   Random Heapmap   Our Heapmap   Annotated Box

Fig. 9. Example heatmaps for location prediction evaluation.

Table 10. Evaluation on location and scale prediction. NS (normalized similarity) denotes the cosine similarity of the ground truth location normalized by the maximum and minimum similarity of the other sliding window locations.

Method	Location			Scale		
	$NS > 0.99$	$NS > 0.95$	$NS > 0.9$	$IOU > 0.9$	$IOU > 0.75$	$IOU > 0.5$
Random	5.50	9.25	12.25	4.25	14.50	38.25
Baseline	15.25	25.25	38.25	5.75	19.75	48.50
Ours	**22.25**	**31.50**	**39.00**	**6.75**	**24.25**	**51.75**

For location prediction, given a background along with its annotated foreground object, we first apply 10 grid search with sliding window method in Sect. 3.4. To evaluate location and scale separately, the scale here is fixed as the scale of annotated box. Then bilinear interpolation is adopted to generate the heapmap, as shown in Fig. 9. The heapmap value is then normalized with the maximum and minimal value in the grid matrix, so that all values are in $[0, 1]$. Higher value means the model assigns high compatibility on the corresponding location. Note that the annotated box location may not be the only good location, other boxes with zero IOU (Intersection Over Union) can also have compatible locations, e.g. all the non-occluded locations on the wall in Fig. 9. However, the ground-truth location should always have a good compatibility score as compared with scores of other locations. Therefore, we compute the similarity score on the annotated location and normalize it with the same normalization factors as the heatmap. A good location prediction model should give a high normalized similarity (NS) on the annotated locations. For "Random" strategy, the normalized similarity is randomly selected in $[0, 1]$ since the heatmap is random.

For scale prediction, given a background along with its annotated foreground object, all methods use the annotated ground-truth locations as the center of the box. With a fixed initial size with $1/25$ area of the whole background image, we assign 9 different scales by $scale = 1.2^{k-4}, k = 0, 1, ..., 8$. The box size is then multiplied by the scale to get 9 candidate boxes. "Random" strategy selects one scale randomly, while the other two methods use the similarities between the background with boxes and the foreground to rank all the scales. We then compute the IOU between the predicted box and the annotated box.

As shown in Table 10, we report the percentage of correct predictions with different thresholds on two evaluation metrics, i.e. NS and IOU. Our method performs the best on both location and scale prediction, indicating the superiority of the proposed method on non-box scenarios.

5   Limitations and Potential Social Impact

Current framework only uses 2D transform for contrastive learning, which is efficient and scalable, but not as accurate as 3D transform. This limitation could be addressed in the future by adopting 3D transform as better pre-processing w/o changing the proposed learning framework. Another limitation is that the search space is currently bounded by the gallery, and hence there may not be any perfectly compatible object images in the database even with the large-scale open-world database setting we adopt in our work. One solution is to augment the search space by allowing transformation of objects in the database.

Retrieval-based compositing could be indirectly used to generate fake images, but we can make sure all the gallery object images do not have ethical or privacy issues. Also, fake images usually have incompatible geometry or lighting conditions which can be detected using our model.

6   Conclusion

We propose a novel unconstrained foreground search method for compositing (GALA), as the first to learn geometry-and-lighting awareness from large-scale data for real-world scenarios. GALA achieves state-of-the-art results on CAIS and Pixabay dataset. It also tackles non-box scenarios by automatic location-scale prediction, which is not explored by previous works.

References

1. https://pixabay.com/
2. Azadi, S., Pathak, D., Ebrahimi, S., Darrell, T.: Compositional GAN: Learning image-conditional binary composition. Int. J. Comput. Vis. **128**(10), 2570–2585 (2020)
3. Chechik, G., Sharma, V., Shalit, U., Bengio, S.: Large scale online learning of image similarity through ranking. J. Mach. Learn. Res. **11**(3), 1109–1135 (2010)
4. Deng, J., Dong, W., Socher, R., Li, L.J., Li, K., Fei-Fei, L.: ImageNet: a large-scale hierarchical image database. In: 2009 IEEE Conference on Computer Vision and Pattern Recognition, pp. 248–255. IEEE (2009)
5. Everingham, M., Van Gool, L., Williams, C.K., Winn, J., Zisserman, A.: The pascal visual object classes (VOC) challenge. Int. J. Comput. Vis. **88**(2), 303–338 (2010)
6. Goyal, P., et al.: Accurate, large minibatch SGD: Training ImageNet in 1 hour. arXiv preprint arXiv:1706.02677 (2017)

7. Jiang, Y., et al.: SSH: a self-supervised framework for image harmonization. In: Proceedings of the IEEE/CVF International Conference on Computer Vision, pp. 4832–4841 (2021)

8. Kingma, D.P., Ba, J.: Adam: a method for stochastic optimization. arXiv preprint arXiv:1412.6980 (2014)

9. Kuznetsova, A., et al.: The open images dataset v4. Int. J. Comput. Vis. **128**(7), 1956–1981 (2020)

10. Lalonde, J.F., Hoiem, D., Efros, A.A., Rother, C., Winn, J., Criminisi, A.: Photo clip art. ACM Trans. Graph. (TOG) **26**(3), 3-es (2007)

11. Lee, D., Liu, S., Gu, J., Liu, M.Y., Yang, M.H., Kautz, J.: Context-aware synthesis and placement of object instances. arXiv preprint arXiv:1812.02350 (2018)

12. Lee, Y., Park, J.: CenterMask: real-time anchor-free instance segmentation. In: Proceedings of the IEEE/CVF Conference on Computer Vision and Pattern Recognition, pp. 13906–13915 (2020)

13. Li, B., Zhuang, P.-Y., Gu, J., Li, M., Tan, P.: Interpretable foreground object search as knowledge distillation. In: Vedaldi, A., Bischof, H., Brox, T., Frahm, J.-M. (eds.) ECCV 2020. LNCS, vol. 12373, pp. 189–204. Springer, Cham (2020). https://doi.org/10.1007/978-3-030-58604-1_12

14. Li, X., Liu, S., Kim, K., Wang, X., Yang, M.H., Kautz, J.: Putting humans in a scene: Learning affordance in 3d indoor environments. In: Proceedings of the IEEE/CVF Conference on Computer Vision and Pattern Recognition, pp. 12368–12376 (2019)

15. Lin, C.H., Yumer, E., Wang, O., Shechtman, E., Lucey, S.: St-GAN: spatial transformer generative adversarial networks for image compositing. In: Proceedings of the IEEE Conference on Computer Vision and Pattern Recognition, pp. 9455–9464 (2018)

16. Lin, T.-Y., et al.: Microsoft coco: common objects in context. In: Fleet, D., Pajdla, T., Schiele, B., Tuytelaars, T. (eds.) ECCV 2014. LNCS, vol. 8693, pp. 740–755. Springer, Cham (2014). https://doi.org/10.1007/978-3-319-10602-1_48

17. Niu, L., et al.: Making images real again: a comprehensive survey on deep image composition. arXiv preprint arXiv:2106.14490 (2021)

18. Pandey, R., et al.: Total relighting: learning to relight portraits for background replacement. ACM Trans. Graph. (TOG) **40**(4), 1–21 (2021)

19. Paszke, A., et al.: PyTorch: an imperative style, high-performance deep learning library. Adv. Neural Inf. Process. Syst. **32**, 8026–8037 (2019)

20. Simonyan, K., Zisserman, A.: Very deep convolutional networks for large-scale image recognition. arXiv preprint arXiv:1409.1556 (2014)

21. Tian, Z., Shen, C., Chen, H., He, T.: FCOS: fully convolutional one-stage object detection. In: Proceedings of the IEEE/CVF International Conference on Computer Vision, pp. 9627–9636 (2019)

22. Tsai, Y.H., Shen, X., Lin, Z., Sunkavalli, K., Lu, X., Yang, M.H.: Deep image harmonization. In: Proceedings of the IEEE Conference on Computer Vision and Pattern Recognition, pp. 3789–3797 (2017)

23. Wu, Z., Lischinski, D., Shechtman, E.: Fine-grained foreground retrieval via teacher-student learning. In: Proceedings of the IEEE/CVF Winter Conference on Applications of Computer Vision, pp. 3646–3654 (2021)

24. Zhang, H., Zhang, J., Perazzi, F., Lin, Z., Patel, V.M.: Deep image compositing. In: Proceedings of the IEEE/CVF Winter Conference on Applications of Computer Vision, pp. 365–374 (2021)

25. Zhang, L., Wen, T., Min, J., Wang, J., Han, D., Shi, J.: Learning object placement by inpainting for compositional data augmentation. In: Vedaldi, A., Bischof, H., Brox, T., Frahm, J.-M. (eds.) ECCV 2020. LNCS, vol. 12358, pp. 566–581. Springer, Cham (2020). https://doi.org/10.1007/978-3-030-58601-0_34
26. Zhao, H., Shen, X., Lin, Z., Sunkavalli, K., Price, B., Jia, J.: Compositing-aware image search. In: Proceedings of the European Conference on Computer Vision (ECCV), pp. 502–516 (2018)
27. Zhao, Y., Price, B., Cohen, S., Gurari, D.: Unconstrained foreground object search. In: Proceedings of the IEEE/CVF International Conference on Computer Vision, pp. 2030–2039 (2019)
28. Zhou, B., Zhao, H., Puig, X., Fidler, S., Barriuso, A., Torralba, A.: Scene parsing through ade20k dataset. In: Proceedings of the IEEE Conference on Computer Vision and Pattern Recognition, pp. 633–641 (2017)
29. Zhu, J.Y., Krahenbuhl, P., Shechtman, E., Efros, A.A.: Learning a discriminative model for the perception of realism in composite images. In: Proceedings of the IEEE International Conference on Computer Vision, pp. 3943–3951 (2015)

LaLaLoc++: Global Floor Plan Comprehension for Layout Localisation in Unvisited Environments

Henry Howard-Jenkins$^{(\boxtimes)}$ ⓘ and Victor Adrian Prisacariu ⓘ

Active Vision Laboratory, University of Oxford, Oxford, UK
{henryhj,victor}@robots.ox.ac.uk

Abstract. We present LaLaLoc++, a method for floor plan localisation in unvisited environments through latent representations of room layout. We perform localisation by aligning room layout inferred from a panorama image with the floor plan of a scene. To process a floor plan prior, previous methods required that the plan first be used to construct an explicit 3D representation of the scene. This process requires that assumptions be made about the scene geometry and can result in expensive steps becoming necessary, such as rendering. LaLaLoc++ instead introduces a global floor plan comprehension module that is able to efficiently infer structure densely and directly from the 2D plan, removing any need for explicit modelling or rendering. On the Structured3D dataset this module alone improves localisation accuracy by more than 31%, all while increasing throughput by an order of magnitude. Combined with the further addition of a transformer-based panorama embedding module, LaLaLoc++ improves accuracy over earlier methods by more than 37% with dramatically faster inference.

1 Introduction

Floor plans are ubiquitous in the built, indoor environment. For almost any modern building, these structural plans are stored by local government, builders, real estate agents and even as fire-safety maps and other guides to indoor environments. The prevalence of these documents across domains is not an historical fluke, but instead because they have a number of very useful characteristics. *Permanence*, while furniture and objects present within an environment may move or change, the structure represented in a floor plan remains the same, and therefore these documents are able to provide a description of the environment over a period of years and decades. *Expressiveness*, the structure depicted in a floor plan gives the reader a good basis for understanding that particular indoor environment: in a fire safety map, one is able to bridge the gap between their egocentric view and the plan to determine an exit route; when viewing a property online, one is able to imagine living in the space illustrated by the top-down plan. *Convenience*, these blueprints are extremely lightweight format

---

Supplementary Information The online version contains supplementary material available at https://doi.org/10.1007/978-3-031-19812-0_40.

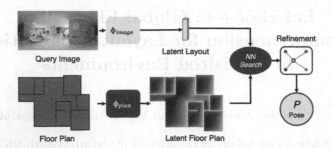

Fig. 1. An overview of our proposed method for floor plan localisation. LaLaLoc++ takes a 2D floor plan and infers 3D structure across the free space of the plan. To localise, an image branch infers layout structure from the query image. Position is predicted by aligning the image's latent structure to the globally inferred structure.

for expressing this structure, allowing them to be easily stored and interpreted across physical and digital formats.

It is for these reasons that, in this paper, we turn our attention to direct interpretation of structural blueprints, specifically in the context of floor plan localisation. Visual relocalisation estimates the pose of a camera given some prior of an environment. Commonly in localisation methods, the prior takes the form of a built 3D structural point-map, *e.g.* [24], a series of stored images, *e.g.* [1,2], or in the weights in a neural network, *e.g.* [4]. Floor plan localisation, however, takes an architectural plan of the indoor environment as prior.

We present LaLaLoc++ to perform floor plan localisation directly from 2D plans. Previous methods for floor plan localisation relied on translation of the architectural floor plan into an explicit 3D geometry, either relying on the assumption of known [15], or manually-estimated [9] ceiling and camera heights to extrude the plan into 3D. LaLaLoc++, however, learns a general prior over 2D floor plans which allows us to implicitly hallucinate 3D structure across the entire plan in a single pass, and without the need for the intermediate conversion into an explicit 3D representation. This is depicted in Fig. 1.

The contributions of this paper can be summarised as follows: (*i*) We present a floor plan comprehension module that learns to implicitly hallucinate 3D visible structure from 2D floor plans. This removes the need for explicit extrusion with an assumed or known camera height. (*ii*) We demonstrate that, when combined with an improved RGB panorama embedding module, this method is a significant advance over previous work, both in terms of accuracy (over 37% and 29% improvement over LaLaLoc on Structured3D [34] and Zillow Indoor Dataset [9], respectively) and speed (35x speed up).

2   Related Work

Camera relocalisation has seen a vast collection of research progress, inspiring a diverse set of problem settings and methods to solve them. Generally, visual localisation seeks to make associations between query image and prior knowledge of the environment in order to predict the capture location. However, the type and construction requirements of this prior offers a variety of design choices. A large portion of methods offer prior construction that is generalisable across scenes. Structure-based methods [19,20,24] establish correspondences by matching points between the query image and an explicit 3D representation built using a method such as SfM [13,26]. Retrieval-based methods [1,2,11,25] primarily estimate pose by matching the query image to its most similar counterpart in a database. On the other hand, other methods require that a new prior be learned for each environment in which localisation is performed, usually learning an implicit representation of the scene within neural network weights. Absolute pose regression methods [8,16,17] train a deep neural network to directly regress the camera pose. Scene-coordinate regression methods [4–6,27,30] densely regress global 3D coordinates across image locations. These generalisable and scene-specific methods share a common attribute, which is that, although the form their prior takes differs, they require a training sequence of images in order to construct or learn it. In this paper, however, we approach the task of floor plan localisation, which takes only a floor plan as its prior. Therefore, the need for a training set of images to enable localisation in a new environment is alleviated.

Like other forms of visual localisation, floor plan-based methods can take many forms. The task has seen particular interest in the context of robotics, where methods operate by forming a room layout observation model between a location in the floor plan and query by extracting layout edges [3,29,32], layout corners [14] or aggregating depth [33] from which an observation likelihood can be estimated. Further, if depth information is available, scan-matching techniques [22] estimate an alignment between the observed depth and the floor plan. These methods are generally not standalone, instead relying on multiple sequential measurements used as hypothesis weightings for a Monte Carlo Localisation [10] frameworks. In this paper, however, we approach the task as defined by LaLaLoc [15]. This localisation formulation, unlike previous works, aims to localise a panorama image within a floor plan without depth information, motion or time-coherency cues, and without assuming a good initialisation. Concurrent to this work, Min et al. [21] also perform floor plan localisation in the same vein. Cruz et al. [9] construct a similar layout-based localisation task for panorama registration, however, they aim to localise with respect to other panoramas, rather than in an unvisited location.

LaLaLoc [15] learns a latent space to capture room layout [18]. Localisation is performed as retrieval between a database of embedded layouts from sparsely sampled poses within the floor plan and the embedding of the panorama image. This is followed by a gradient-based optimisation of pose to minimise the distance between layout and query embeddings, enabled through differentiable rendering. However, the model of the scene used by LaLaLoc had to be created by extruding the floor plan in the z-dimension, assuming a known camera and ceiling height. In addition, LaLaLoc's formulation requiring rendering across the plan for retrieval, and multiple (differentiable) rendering steps for pose refinement is slow. LASER [21] addressed these limitations by rendering embeddings individually using a codebook scheme. In this work, we instead propose dense and global structural comprehension of the 2D plan. In doing so, LaLaLoc++ is able to dramatically improve accuracy and inference speed over LaLaLoc, all while removing the need for height assumptions at inference time.

3   Method

LaLaLoc++ consists of two parallel branches which operate across data modalities. An overview of its architecture is depicted in Fig. 1. The floor plan comprehension module, Φ_{plan}, infers the layout structure that is visible across a 2D floor plan, computing a latent vector at every location in the $x - y$ plane that covers the scene. The image embedding module, Φ_{image}, on the other hand, aims to capture the layout that is visible within a cluttered, RGB panorama image. They map to a shared latent space such that a panorama captured at a location and embedded by Φ_{image} should have the same latent vector as that location sampled from Φ_{plan}'s output. Therefore, LaLaLoc++ performs localisation of a query panorama by finding the location in the floor plan that most accurately matches the visible room layout, with matching cost being computed in the shared layout latent space. In the following, we detail the task, the form that our architecture takes, how it is used to localise, and how it is trained.

3.1   Floor Plan Localisation

We follow the floor plan localisation task as used in LaLaLoc [15]. This is the task of performing localisation of a panorama within a scene which has not been visited previously, given only a floor plan as prior. Specifically, we predict the 2 DoF camera pose to an $x - y$ location in the 2D floor plan assuming a known orientation, an assumption we explore in Sect. 5.6. We also detail some tacit assumptions arising from dataset characteristics in the supplementary material. The floor plan consists of a 2D image which denotes an empty scene consisting of only walls, floors and ceilings.

3.2 Φ_{plan}: Global Latent Floor Plan

Given a 2D floor plan of an environment, we wish to infer the architectural structure of the scene at any given location within it. In order to achieve a similar objective, LaLaLoc [15] formed an explicit representation of the scene in the form of a mesh using a known ceiling height. This explicit geometry was then rendered as a depth image at a given location from which the implicit layout representation could be computed by LaLaLoc's Φ_{layout}. While shown to be effective, this method proves to be slow, requiring multiple rendering steps and forward passes in order to form only a sparse map of layout across the floor plan, and also requires that camera and ceiling heights are known.

Instead, with LaLaLoc++ we propose that the implicit representation of layout can be inferred directly from the floor plan itself. This formulation allows us to walk well-trodden ground in architecture design for fast, efficient, and *dense* inference of layout across the floor plan.

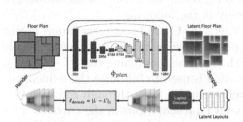

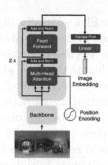

Fig. 2. Φ_{plan}, the floor plan comprehension network and its training routine. The network takes as input a 2D plan of the scene and outputs a dense grid of features which capture the 3D structure visible at their respective locations. Feature maps are depicted with spatial dimensions unrolled for simplicity, and channel dimensions are listed.

Fig. 3. Φ_{image}, the transformer-based image embedding module. A ResNet backbone is used and its output is fed into a transformer encoder architecture. The resulting features are pooled and projected to get the final embedding.

Specifically, Φ_{plan} takes the form of a UNet [23] inspired encoder-decoder structure. It takes as input a 2D structural floor plan and outputs a dense feature map. The vector at each location is a latent representation of the layout visible there. Therefore, in just a single forward pass we are able to build a dense expression of layout within a plan. This structure is depicted at the top of Fig. 2.

3.3 Φ_{image}: Image Embedding with Long-Range Attention

While forming an expressive latent space for layout inferred from a floor plan was shown to be readily achievable to a high degree of effectiveness in LaLaLoc [15], the difficulty of (implicitly) predicting layout from RGB panoramas proved to be a significant source of error. We therefore propose an improved image embedding module based on a transformer encoder [31]. This module allows Φ_{image} to better capture long-range structural patterns present in the query panorama image.

We implement a transformer encoder to refine the feature-map computed by the image branch backbone, which is a ResNet50 network [12]. The features outputted by the backbone are linearly projected from 2048d to 128d. These projected features are then fed into the transformer encoder, with 2 encoder blocks before finally being pooled and projected to form the image embedding for a panorama. The multi-headed self-attention present in the encoder blocks encourages long-range attention. This architecture is visualised in Fig. 3.

3.4 Localisation

At inference time, a dense reference grid of latent layout vectors are computed by passing the 2D floor plan. An initial estimate of position is computed as the location corresponding to the nearest latent layout in this grid. However, since this is still a spatially discretised grid across the scene, we introduce further alignment in the form of pose optimisation allowing for a continuous estimate of position. We describe this more concretely in the following.

We denote the floor plan encoded by Φ_{plan} as $\mathbf{G}$, and the query latent layout computed by Φ_{image} as f. The initial position estimate, p_0, is taken as whole pixel location, $i.e. p_0 = (i_0, j_0) \in \mathbb{Z}^2$, with the lowest matching cost $|f - \mathbf{G}[p_0]|_2$, where $[\cdot]$ is a look-up function. This location is used to initialise the refinement.

We then perform the continuous refinement of pose through interpolation of the local neighbourhood of latent layout representations in the encoded floor plan. Position is initialised at the nearest location in the feature grid. During refinement, the position estimate is relaxed to allow sub-pixel locations, $p_r \in \mathbb{R}^2$, and $[\cdot]$ is extended to use sub-pixel interpolation. The refined pose is iteratively updated to minimise the matching cost in a gradient-based optimisation scheme,

$$\min_{p_r} |f - \mathbf{G}[p_r]|_2. \tag{1}$$

3.5   Training

LaLaLoc++ follows an analogous training philosophy to that proposed in LaLaLoc [15] where the network is trained in two separate stages. In the first stage, we train Φ_{plan} alone. Since Φ_{plan} takes a form of explicit structure as input, its training is used to establish an expressive latent space for capturing the room layout at any given location in the scene. This latent space is then frozen and, in the second stage, Φ_{image} is trained to map images to this fixed representation space.

Φ_{plan} : **Learning the Latent Space.** We train Φ_{plan} with a single loss, where the layout embedding at a given location is passed through a simple layout depth prediction decoder and compared with a rendered layout at the same location:

$$\ell_{decode} = |L' - L|_1, \tag{2}$$

where L' is the predicted layout, and L is the ground-truth rendering at a given location. During training, we use known camera and ceiling heights for the rendering of the target layout, however, the floor plan comprehension module is forced to infer the structure without these parameters. Therefore, it must learn a generalised prior for the hallucination of 3D structure from the top-down 2D input. Illustration of how this loss is computed can be found in Fig. 2.

Φ_{image} : **Mapping to the Latent Space.** The training of Φ_{image} takes the form of a simple strategy, which reflects its role in the localisation method. Given a training batch of panorama images, their respective poses, and a floor plan, the global latent floor plan is computed by Φ_{plan} and sampled at the panorama poses. The panorama images are then embedded by Φ_{image}, and a loss is applied to the difference between the embeddings produced by Φ_{image}, f, and those sampled from Φ_{plan}'s output, g, which is defined as follows:

$$\ell_{L2} = |f - g|_2. \tag{3}$$

4   Implementation Details

Here, we describe the specific nature of the task evaluated in the experiments section of the paper. We start with the datasets, followed by the configuration of our method. Additional details can be found in the supplementary material.

4.1   Datasets

The bulk of evaluation experiments are performed on the Structured3D dataset [34], which consists of 3,500 photorealisticly-rendered synthetic indoor scenes. We follow the split of data used in LaLaLoc [15], which itself follows the dataset's predefined split with some scenes excluded due to corrupted data. This leaves 2979/246/249 scenes for training/validation/testing, respectively. Every scene comprises of multiple rooms, each containing a single panorama image which is used as a query. Since there are no reference images captured from within the same scene, we label each scene as *unvisited*, as there is no RGB data that can be leveraged for training or database building and therefore the method must rely on floor plan data alone. There are three furniture configurations, empty, simple and full, as well as three lighting configurations for each scene, cold, warm and raw. During training, we randomly sample a furniture and lighting configuration at each iteration. At test time, we perform evaluation in the full and warm setting. This is the most difficult furniture configuration as there are the most possible distractors from layout present in the image.

We also explore how this method extends to real data by performing evaluation on the recently released Zillow Indoor Dataset [9]. We processes the dataset to match the problem setting on the Structured3D dataset, namely considering localisation across a single floor and alignment of panorama images. This results in 1957/244/252 scenes for training/validation/testing, respectively. However, the dataset only provides a single lighting and furniture configuration for each panorama. The remaining implementation details apply across both Structured3D and the Zillow Indoor Dataset.

Floor Plans. We represent the 2D floor plans as image. Each pixel location can take three possible values: 1 represents a wall, 0.5 is used to denote free-space within the floor plan, and 0 is assigned to free space outside of the floor plan. To ensure that absolute scale is preserved in the creation of these plans, we use a consistent scale across all scenes in the dataset. It is set such that one image pixel covers 40mm of space in reality. This value was set heuristically as a balance between keeping the overall size of the floor plan manageable, and ensuring that all walls are still discernible. At the most compact representation in Φ_{plan}, the spatial resolution of the feature map is 1/32th of the original height and width, we zero-pad the floor plans so that both height and width are divisible by 32.

4.2   Network Architecture

As depicted in Fig. 2, Φ_{plan} consists of 5 down-sample and 5 up-sample layers. These layers each consist of a convolutional block which contains a 3×3 convolution, a batch-norm and a ReLU activation repeated twice. In the down-sample block, the convolutional block is followed by a 2×2 max-pooling layer. In the up-sample block it is preceded by a 2×2 bilinear up-sampling of the feature map. This up-sampled feature map is then concatenated with the feature map from the corresponding down-block (taken before pooling), to form skip connections. The output of the final up-sampling layer is passed through a final 3×3 linear convolution to form the final latent floor plan. This latent floor plan keeps the same spatial resolution as the original input floor plan with a 128d descriptor for each location which are normalised. The layout decoder used in training takes an identical structure to that used in [15].

Φ_{image}takes the form of a ResNet50 backbone. In its simplest formulation, the feature map outputted by this backbone is pooled to a single vector, then linearly projected to 128d and normalised. However, in our transformer formulation, a transformer encoder forms an intermediate refinement of the image feature map before pooling and projecting. More specifically, a 2D sinusoidal positional encoding [31] is generated for each spatial location in the feature map. The feature map is then flattened, linearly projected to 128d, and fed into a vanilla transformer encoder [31] with two repeated blocks. There are 8 attention heads, and the feed-forward hidden dimension is set to 256 dimensions. We apply the positional encoding at the attention layers, rather than input, following [7]. The encoded features are then pooled and projected once more before being normalised to form the image embedding.

5   Experiments

In this section, we perform experimental evaluation of LaLaLoc++. Initially, we explore the performance of the method as a whole before exploring the constituent components and their impact on the final accuracy. Finally, we perform ablation experiments to validate the design of these components. Unless otherwise stated, experiments are performed on the Structured3D [34] dataset.

Table 1. Localisation performance of LaLaLoc++ compared against three other floor plan localisation methods on Structured3D

Method	Localisation accuracy				
	Median (cm)	<1 cm	<5 cm	<10 cm	<1 m
ICP	21.8	**9.5%**	26.4%	35.6%	68.5%
HorizonNet [28] + Loc	9.1	3.3%	29.3%	53.4%	77.4%
LaLaLoc [15]	8.3	3.6%	32.0%	58.0%	87.5%
LaLaLoc++	**5.2**	5.4%	**48.8%**	**72.3%**	**92.3%**

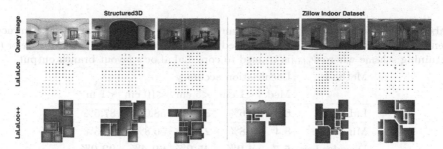

Fig. 4. Qualitative comparison of the floor plan comprehension differences between LaLaLoc++ and LaLaLoc. Visualised as a plot of the latent distance between the query image and embeddings across the floor plan in each of the two methods. While LaLaLoc++'s Φ_{plan} is able to infer layout densely within the scene, LaLaLoc instead just has a sparse sampling (0.5 m in each direction). The difference in the resulting understanding of the environment is stark.

Table 2. Localisation performance of LaLaLoc++ compared to LaLaLoc with real data on the Zillow Indoor Dataset.

Method	Localisation accuracy				
	Med.	<1 cm	<5 cm	<10 cm	<1 m
LaLaLoc	13.1	1.3%	19.9%	40.9%	77.6%
LaLaLoc++	9.3	2.5%	32.1%	51.7%	80.7%

Table 3. Inference time comparison on a single Nvidia Titan RTX GPU. Times are displayed as: Total time (Render time).

Method	Inference time (s)		Total
	Embedding & retrieval	Refinement (Rendering)	
2D-ICP	–	–	20.1
LaLaLoc w/o VDR	0.05	2.33 (0.85)	2.38
LaLaLoc	0.05	4.60 (3.34)	4.65
LaLaLoc++	0.01	0.12	0.13

5.1   Floor Plan Localisation

We first perform localisation on the test split of the Structured3D [34] dataset. We compare the performance of LaLaLoc++ to three other methods, LaLaLoc itself, as well as the 2D-ICP and HorizonNet [28]-based baseline presented in LaLaLoc [15]. Results are listed in Table 1.

As can be seen in Table 1, LaLaLoc++ is able to localise in these unseen environments significantly more accurately than the original LaLaLoc. The median localisation accuracy represents a 37% improvement over LaLaLoc. When considering the accuracy thresholds, it is notable that LaLaLoc++ not only is able to localise more images to the fine-grained accuracy thresholds, but is also able to localise more images to within 1m (87.5% *v.s.* 92.3%). This suggests that LaLaLoc++ reduces the frequency of catastrophic failure to localise. We visualise some failure modes in the supplementary material.

We further investigate how this performance extends beyond synthetic data into the real world captures on the Zillow Indoor Dataset [9]. We report these results in Table 2. Inline with results on Structured3D, LaLaLoc++ offers significantly improved accuracy over LaLaLoc (29% increase). The real world layout distributions appear to pose a harder challenge, with more complex floor plan geometry. However, it does show that the method can extend to real data.

Table 4. Contribution of latent floor plan training to the final localisation accuracy. Identical image branch architecture is used in each scenario. *Mimic* is used to refer to a training scheme where Φ_{plan} is trained to copy LaLaLoc's layout branch output

Method	Localisation accuracy				
	Med.	<1 cm	<5 cm	<10 cm	<1 m
LaLaLoc	8.3	3.6%	32.0%	58.0%	87.5%
Mimic	8.4	1.8%	27.3%	56.8%	88.5%
Decoder loss	**5.7**	**4.9%**	**45.0%**	**69.4%**	**92.0%**

Figure 4 illustrates the contrast in prior-forming between LaLaLoc and LaLaLoc++. The dense prediction of Φ_{plan} is able to far more expressively capture the layout across the floor plan, whereas the sparse strategy to form reference embeddings in LaLaLoc is comparatively low in fidelity. Although LaLaLoc could sample reference poses more densely, inferring at the same level of density with LaLaLoc quickly become intractable.

In Table 3, we compare the time complexities of LaLaLoc++ against LaLaLoc. LaLaLoc++ offers more than a 35x speed up over LaLaLoc. This is predominantly for two reasons. Firstly, LaLaLoc++'s direct inference from 2D plans means that expensive rendering steps can be removed. Notably, this also includes the expensive backwards passes in the differentiable rendering optimisation scheme. Secondly, LaLaLoc required a forward pass through a ResNet18 [12] for each rendered layout. Although this could be performed in batches, depending on the density of sampling the total number of items could reach hundreds. On the other hand, LaLaLoc++ allows dense inference of structure in a single forward pass, which proves to be significantly faster.

5.2 Global Floor Plan Comprehension

To evaluate the contribution of our proposed global floor plan processing, we perform localisation using various configurations of Φ_{plan} all with equivalent image branch architectures. The image branch architecture is chosen to be identical to the one proposed in LaLaLoc. The first comparison is to LaLaLoc's layout branch and its scheme of sparse floor plan rendering and embedding. We then train our proposed global floor plan module as a direct substitution for the layout embedder in LaLaLoc. Therefore, the floor plan network is trained to mimic the output of LaLaLoc's layout branch, and the original image branch is used without any modification or fine-tuning. We call this "Mimic". Finally, we compare to our proposed method, where the Φ_{plan} is trained with the layout decoding loss, is frozen, and then Φ_{image} is trained to map panoramas to the learned space.

Results for these experiments can be found in Table 4. Worth considering first is the results for the "Mimic" configuration. This experimental setup can be considered a test of whether 3D structure can be directly inferred from the 2D layout to a similar degree of expressiveness as the original LaLaLoc's render and

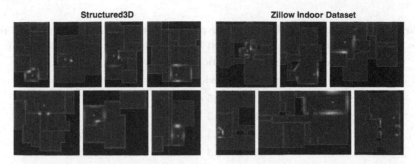

Fig. 5. Investigation into floor plan saliency for inferring layout at a given location from a global floor plan. The query location is marked with a pink cross, and computed saliency is overlaid onto the floor plan. The floor plan comprehension module demonstrably learns to differentiate between visible and invisible structure for the query locations when computing their descriptor. (Color figure online)

embed methodology. The results show that the module is in fact able to nearly match the original performance of the network for which it is substituting. This is particularly notable as the 2D comprehension module is not given height information (neither ceiling nor camera) and instead must learn a generalised 2D to 3D room structure prior which holds for these unseen environments. As such, there is an inherent degree of inaccuracy expected from this formulation as it must replicate a method while dealing with significantly more ambiguity.

When trained to form its own layout latent space in the "Decoder Loss" setting, the performance improvement over LaLaLoc is dramatic. This is likely because the latent space for layouts can be constructed in a way compatible with the structure that can be determined from a 2D floor plan. In the supplementary material, to aid in the intuition of the learned space, we visualise the output of the decoder. In addition, the dense estimation of layout may provide a better setting for pose refinement than the Latent Pose Optimisation proposed in LaLaLoc, which relies on differentiable rendering. We investigate this in Sect. 5.3.

Floor Plan Saliency. In the explicit rendering formulation used in LaLaLoc, the structure rendered at any given point in the scene has the same level of context as the query image with which you wish to compare it to, *i.e.* only the visible structure from that location. However, when processing the entire floor plan, the receptive field of the network for structural inference at any given location quickly moves beyond what is strictly visible from that location. If global information is leveraged to form the layout descriptor from the plan, it is likely that the image branch will not be able to map to the same latent space.

To investigate this, we plot saliency of floor plan structure in computation of the descriptor at any given location. The saliency is computed by masking a sliding window across the floor plan such that any walls in this window are instead assigned as free-space. We compare how a descriptor at a chosen location

Table 5. Exploration of the Latent Floor plan resolution on localisation. *Init.* refers to the median accuracy of the initialisation for refinement, reported in cm

Floor plan subsampling	Localisation accuracy					
	Init.	Med.	<1 cm	<5 cm	<10 cm	<1 m
LaLaLoc LPO	22.5	10.5	2.0%	27.4%	48.4%	87.5%
LaLaLoc	11.0	8.3	3.6%	32.0%	58.0%	87.5%
8x	28.4	6.5	4.7%	41.3%	64.3%	87.2%
4x	15.1	5.3	5.7%	47.7%	71.4%	92.1%
2x	8.8	5.3	5.3%	48.0%	69.9%	92.1%
Full-size	6.1	5.2	5.4%	48.8%	72.3%	92.3%

in the plan changes against the original from an unmasked plan via L2 distance. This distance is assigned to the centre point of the mask to form a saliency map.

Some examples of these saliency maps are plotted in Fig. 5. It is apparent that the floor plan module does not unduly exploit global structure, but instead the structure local to the test point is the most salient regions of the plan.

5.3   Sub-pixel Refinement

In this section, we wish to investigate the performance properties of the proposed sub-pixel floor plan optimisation process. We perform refinement initialised with retrieval results from increasingly sparse representations of the floor plan. In each of these experiments the floor plan is embedded at full-resolution, but the resulting feature maps are sub-sampled by factors of 2. This has the effect of testing the refinement performance with wider baseline initialisation. For each level of sub-sampling, we re-train the image branch. We also include results for LaLaLoc in its operation mode where the latent pose optimisation is the only pose refinement after retrieval, thus skipping the local retrieval normally performed, and in the configuration with local re-sampling and continuous refinement.

The results for this are listed in Table 5. The median error of the refinement initialisation is included for each method and formulation. It can be seen that LaLaLoc++, and specifically its continuous pose refinement through interpolation, is able to recover extremely well from increasingly poor initialisation. Even subsampling the latent floor plan by 8x, LaLaLoc++ still outperforms LaLaLoc by 1.8 cm, despite the initialisation being nearly 3x worse.

5.4   Image Transformer

We show a localisation performance comparison between the image embedding structure consisting of a simple feature backbone, pooling and projection and our proposed transformer formulation. Results are listed in Table 6. As can be seen, the transformer leads to a nearly 9% improvement in localisation accuracy over the baseline. This result suggests that the long-range attentional mechanisms

Table 6. Comparison of the image embedding architecture that is used. ResNet50 denotes a simple backbone followed by average pooling and a linear projection. R50 + Transformer is the proposed formulation where the image feature map is refined with a transformer encoder

Method	Localisation accuracy				
	Med.	<1 cm	<5 cm	<10 cm	<1 m
ResNet50	5.7	4.9%	45.0%	69.4%	92.0%
R50 + Transformer	**5.2**	**5.4%**	**48.8%**	**72.3%**	**92.3%**

Table 7. Localisation with differing numbers of down and up-sampling layers in Φ_{plan}. * denotes the chosen configuration.

Φ_{plan}	Localisation accuracy				
# Layers	Med.	<1 cm	<5 cm	<10 cm	<1 m
3	12.9	2.5%	27.4%	44.8%	70.0%
4	6.0	4.0%	44.0%	65.4%	90.5%
5*	**5.2**	**5.4%**	**48.8%**	**72.3%**	**92.3%**
6	5.3	5.1%	48.0%	70.4%	92.1%

Table 8. Localisation as the number of transformer encoder blocks in Φ_{image} is varied. * denotes the chosen configuration.

Φ_{image}	Localisation accuracy				
# Blocks	Med.	<1 cm	<5 cm	<10 cm	<1 m
1	5.9	3.7%	43.5%	69.2%	**92.3%**
2*	**5.2**	5.4%	**48.8%**	**72.3%**	**92.3%**
3	5.6	**5.7%**	45.2%	68.7%	92.0%
4	5.7	4.8%	45.1%	69.3%	92.2%

introduced by the transformer encoder allow the embedding module to better capture layout from the panorama image.

5.5 Ablation Experiments

We validate LaLaLoc++'s architecture through the ablation experiments discussed here. First, we see how the localisation accuracy is impacted by the number of down and up-sample layers in Φ_{plan}. We then vary the number of encoder blocks used in Φ_{image}. Results for each of these experiments are listed in Tables 7 and 8, respectively. In Table 8 it is notable that, although the chosen configuration performs almost identically to the configuration with 6 down-sample and up-sample layers, the chosen configuration has significantly fewer trainable parameters (24.1M *vs.* 63.3M). Therefore, the configuration with 5 down-sample and up-sample layers is the most appropriate.

5.6 Rotational Ambiguity

In this section, we conduct experiments extending LaLaLoc++ to also predict orientation of the query panorama.

To estimate the unknown orientation of the query panorama, we rectify the image using the prepossessing step as described in [35]. Through vanishing point detection, this estimates a semi-canonical alignment of the panorama. We consider this orientation, as well as 3 other candidates formed by successive 90° rotations. LaLaLoc++'s retrieval stage is performed on each of these candidate

Table 9. Localisation with and without an orientation prior. Methods which assume a known rotation are *italicised*.

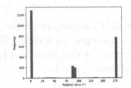

Method	Localisation success		
	<5 cm/2°	<10 cm/5°	<20 cm/10°
LaLaLoc	19.9%	40.9%	61.6%
LaLaLoc++	32.1%	51.7%	67.5%
LaLaLoc++ (Top 1)	16.4%	28.0%	36.0%
LaLaLoc++ (Top 2)	27.9%	45.6%	58.5%

Fig. 6. Histogram of rotation error frequency on the Zillow Indoor Dataset.

rotations. The predicted position and orientation being given by the lowest computed embedding distance across the rotations. These are then used to initialise the sub-pixel refinement stage to further optimise position.

We list results from the Zillow Indoor Dataset in Table 9. Rotation prediction significantly increases the difficulty of the task. However, analysis of the rotational errors (Fig. 6) suggests that the vanishing point alignment is generally accurate, but that there is ambiguity when multiple orientations can be considered, with multiple plausible poses. Therefore, we also consider a strategy where the *Top 1* orientation is computed as before, but the orientation with the second lowest predicted distance is also kept, labelled *Top 2* in Table 9. Localisation is considered successful if either hypothesis is within the tolerated error.

The results show that this generation of multiple pose hypotheses allows LaLaLoc++ to largely recover accuracy. And this setup actually outperforms LaLaLoc [15] for the strict thresholds, despite LaLaLoc using a known orientation. However, disambiguation of these hypotheses would require additional architectural information, such as windows and doors.

6   Discussion

Through experimental evaluation, LaLaLoc++ has been shown to outperform the previous floor plan localisation methods tested. However, floor plan localisation itself has some inherent limitations. For example, it is trivial to imagine buildings with many near structurally identical rooms. Even within the correct room, rotation can cause symmetries which leave two poses plausible, as explored in the previous section. In these scenarios, localisation through layout structure alone will fail due to the level of ambiguity. Despite this, and for the reasons stated in Sect. 1, we believe floor plan localisation is a promising and worthwhile avenue for research. In practical application, localisation methods are seldom used in isolation, and floor plan localisation is particularly useful as a strong prior from which more accurate methods can be initialised or verified, especially as it is designed for indoors where GPS is significantly less reliable.

7   Conclusion

In this paper, we have presented LaLaLoc++, a method for localisation in unseen environments with leveraging a floor plan as its only prior. We have demonstrated that a representative space of 3D layout structure can be inferred directly from 2D floor plans, and that doing so yields significant accuracy and performance improvements over previous methods for this task. We therefore show that localisation can be performed effectively in unseen environments by leveraging data that is near universal in the built world.

References

1. Arandjelovic, R., Gronat, P., Torii, A., Pajdla, T., Sivic, J.: NetVLAD: CNN architecture for weakly supervised place recognition. In: Proceedings of the IEEE Conference on Computer Vision and Pattern Recognition, pp. 5297–5307 (2016)
2. Balntas, V., Li, S., Prisacariu, V.: RelocNet: continuous metric learning relocalisation using neural nets. In: Ferrari, V., Hebert, M., Sminchisescu, C., Weiss, Y. (eds.) Computer Vision – ECCV 2018. LNCS, vol. 11218, pp. 782–799. Springer, Cham (2018). https://doi.org/10.1007/978-3-030-01264-9_46
3. Boniardi, F., Valada, A., Mohan, R., Caselitz, T., Burgard, W.: Robot localization in floor plans using a room layout edge extraction network. arXiv preprint arXiv:1903.01804 (2019)
4. Brachmann, E., et al.: DSAC-differentiable RANSAC for camera localization. In: Proceedings of the IEEE Conference on Computer Vision and Pattern Recognition, pp. 6684–6692 (2017)
5. Brachmann, E., Rother, C.: Learning less is more-6D camera localization via 3D surface regression. In: Proceedings of the IEEE Conference on Computer Vision and Pattern Recognition, pp. 4654–4662 (2018)
6. Brachmann, E., Rother, C.: Expert sample consensus applied to camera relocalization. In: Proceedings of the IEEE/CVF International Conference on Computer Vision, pp. 7525–7534 (2019)
7. Carion, N., Massa, F., Synnaeve, G., Usunier, N., Kirillov, A., Zagoruyko, S.: End-to-end object detection with transformers. In: Vedaldi, A., Bischof, H., Brox, T., Frahm, J.-M. (eds.) ECCV 2020. LNCS, vol. 12346, pp. 213–229. Springer, Cham (2020). https://doi.org/10.1007/978-3-030-58452-8_13
8. Chen, S., Wang, Z., Prisacariu, V.: Direct-PoseNet: absolute pose regression with photometric consistency. arXiv preprint arXiv:2104.04073 (2021)
9. Cruz, S., Hutchcroft, W., Li, Y., Khosravan, N., Boyadzhiev, I., Kang, S.B.: Zillow indoor dataset: annotated floor plans with 360deg panoramas and 3D room layouts. In: Proceedings of the IEEE/CVF Conference on Computer Vision and Pattern Recognition, pp. 2133–2143 (2021)
10. Dellaert, F., Fox, D., Burgard, W., Thrun, S.: Monte carlo localization for mobile robots. In: Proceedings 1999 IEEE International Conference on Robotics and Automation (Cat. No. 99CH36288C), vol. 2, pp. 1322–1328. IEEE (1999)
11. Ding, M., Wang, Z., Sun, J., Shi, J., Luo, P.: CamNet: coarse-to-fine retrieval for camera re-localization. In: Proceedings of the IEEE/CVF International Conference on Computer Vision, pp. 2871–2880 (2019)
12. He, K., Zhang, X., Ren, S., Sun, J.: Deep residual learning for image recognition. In: Proceedings of the IEEE Conference on Computer Vision and Pattern Recognition, pp. 770–778 (2016)
13. Heinly, J., Schonberger, J.L., Dunn, E., Frahm, J.M.: Reconstructing the world* in six days*(as captured by the yahoo 100 million image dataset). In: Proceedings of the IEEE Conference on Computer Vision and Pattern Recognition, pp. 3287–3295 (2015)

14. Hile, H., Borriello, G.: Positioning and orientation in indoor environments using camera phones. IEEE Comput. Graph. Appl. **28**(4), 32–39 (2008)
15. Howard-Jenkins, H., Ruiz-Sarmiento, J.R., Prisacariu, V.A.: LaLaLoc: latent layout localisation in dynamic, unvisited environments. arXiv preprint arXiv:2104.09169 (2021)
16. Kendall, A., Cipolla, R.: Geometric loss functions for camera pose regression with deep learning. In: Proceedings of the IEEE Conference on Computer Vision and Pattern Recognition, pp. 5974–5983 (2017)
17. Kendall, A., Grimes, M., Cipolla, R.: PoseNet: a convolutional network for real-time 6-DOF camera relocalization. In: Proceedings of the IEEE International Conference on Computer Vision, pp. 2938–2946 (2015)
18. Kim, S., Seo, M., Laptev, I., Cho, M., Kwak, S.: Deep metric learning beyond binary supervision. In: Proceedings of the IEEE/CVF Conference on Computer Vision and Pattern Recognition, pp. 2288–2297 (2019)
19. Lim, H., Sinha, S.N., Cohen, M.F., Uyttendaele, M.: Real-time image-based 6-DOF localization in large-scale environments. In: 2012 IEEE Conference on Computer Vision and Pattern Recognition, pp. 1043–1050. IEEE (2012)
20. Liu, L., Li, H., Dai, Y.: Efficient global 2D–3D matching for camera localization in a large-scale 3D map. In: Proceedings of the IEEE International Conference on Computer Vision, pp. 2372–2381 (2017)
21. Min, Z., et al.: Laser: latent space rendering for 2d visual localization. In: Proceedings of the IEEE/CVF Conference on Computer Vision and Pattern Recognition, pp. 11122–11131 (2022)
22. Pomerleau, F., Colas, F., Siegwart, R.: A review of point cloud registration algorithms for mobile robotics. Found. Trends Robot. **4**(1), 1–104 (2015)
23. Ronneberger, O., Fischer, P., Brox, T.: U-Net: convolutional networks for biomedical image segmentation. In: Navab, N., Hornegger, J., Wells, W.M., Frangi, A.F. (eds.) MICCAI 2015. LNCS, vol. 9351, pp. 234–241. Springer, Cham (2015). https://doi.org/10.1007/978-3-319-24574-4_28
24. Sarlin, P.E., Cadena, C., Siegwart, R., Dymczyk, M.: From coarse to fine: robust hierarchical localization at large scale. In: Proceedings of the IEEE/CVF Conference on Computer Vision and Pattern Recognition, pp. 12716–12725 (2019)
25. Schindler, G., Brown, M., Szeliski, R.: City-scale location recognition. In: 2007 IEEE Conference on Computer Vision and Pattern Recognition, pp. 1–7. IEEE (2007)
26. Schonberger, J.L., Frahm, J.M.: Structure-from-motion revisited. In: Proceedings of the IEEE Conference on Computer Vision and Pattern Recognition, pp. 4104–4113 (2016)
27. Shotton, J., Glocker, B., Zach, C., Izadi, S., Criminisi, A., Fitzgibbon, A.: Scene coordinate regression forests for camera relocalization in RGB-D images. In: Proceedings of the IEEE Conference on Computer Vision and Pattern Recognition, pp. 2930–2937 (2013)
28. Sun, C., Hsiao, C.W., Sun, M., Chen, H.T.: HorizonNet: learning room layout with 1D representation and Pano stretch data augmentation. In: Proceedings of the IEEE/CVF Conference on Computer Vision and Pattern Recognition, pp. 1047–1056 (2019)
29. Unicomb, J., Ranasinghe, R., Dantanarayana, L., Dissanayake, G.: A monocular indoor localiser based on an extended kalman filter and edge images from a convolutional neural network. In: 2018 IEEE/RSJ International Conference on Intelligent Robots and Systems (IROS), pp. 1–9. IEEE (2018)

30. Valentin, J., Nießner, M., Shotton, J., Fitzgibbon, A., Izadi, S., Torr, P.H.: Exploiting uncertainty in regression forests for accurate camera relocalization. In: Proceedings of the IEEE Conference on Computer Vision and Pattern Recognition, pp. 4400–4408 (2015)
31. Vaswani, A., et al.: Attention is all you need. In: Advances in Neural Information Processing Systems, pp. 5998–6008 (2017)
32. Wang, S., Fidler, S., Urtasun, R.: Lost shopping! monocular localization in large indoor spaces. In: Proceedings of the IEEE International Conference on Computer Vision, pp. 2695–2703 (2015)
33. Winterhalter, W., Fleckenstein, F., Steder, B., Spinello, L., Burgard, W.: Accurate indoor localization for RGB-D smartphones and tablets given 2D floor plans. In: 2015 IEEE/RSJ International Conference on Intelligent Robots and Systems (IROS), pp. 3138–3143. IEEE (2015)
34. Zheng, J., Zhang, J., Li, J., Tang, R., Gao, S., Zhou, Z.: Structured3D: a large photo-realistic dataset for structured 3D modeling. arXiv preprint arXiv:1908.00222 **2**(7) (2019)
35. Zou, C., Colburn, A., Shan, Q., Hoiem, D.: LayoutNet: reconstructing the 3D room layout from a single RGB image. In: Proceedings of the IEEE Conference on Computer Vision and Pattern Recognition, pp. 2051–2059 (2018)

3D-PL: Domain Adaptive Depth Estimation with 3D-Aware Pseudo-Labeling

Yu-Ting Yen[1,2], Chia-Ni Lu[1], Wei-Chen Chiu[1(✉)] (iD), and Yi-Hsuan Tsai[2]

[1] National Chiao Tung University, Hsinchu, Taiwan
walon@cs.nctu.edu.tw
[2] Phiar Technologies, Redwood City, USA

Abstract. For monocular depth estimation, acquiring ground truths for real data is not easy, and thus domain adaptation methods are commonly adopted using the supervised synthetic data. However, this may still incur a large domain gap due to the lack of supervision from the real data. In this paper, we develop a domain adaptation framework via generating reliable pseudo ground truths of depth from real data to provide direct supervisions. Specifically, we propose two mechanisms for pseudo-labeling: 1) 2D-based pseudo-labels via measuring the consistency of depth predictions when images are with the same content but different styles; 2) 3D-aware pseudo-labels via a point cloud completion network that learns to complete the depth values in the 3D space, thus providing more structural information in a scene to refine and generate more reliable pseudo-labels. In experiments, we show that our pseudo-labeling methods improve depth estimation in various settings, including the usage of stereo pairs during training. Furthermore, the proposed method performs favorably against several state-of-the-art unsupervised domain adaptation approaches in real-world datasets.

Keywords: Domain adaptation · Monocular depth estimation · Pseudo-labeling

1 Introduction

Monocular depth estimation is an ill-posed problem that aims to estimate depth from a single image. Numerous supervised deep learning methods [3,9,11,21,28,47] have made great progress in recent years. However, they need a large amount of data with ground truth depth, while acquiring such depth labels is highly expensive and time-consuming because it requires depth sensors such as LiDAR [14] or Kinect [50]. Therefore, several unsupervised methods [13,15,16,30,42,49] have been proposed, where these approaches estimate

Supplementary Information The online version contains supplementary material available at https://doi.org/10.1007/978-3-031-19812-0_41.

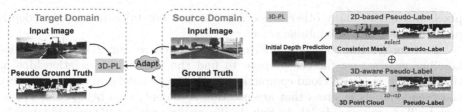

(a) Overview of our proposed method for domain adaptation.

(b) Basic concept behind our 3D-aware Pseudo-Labeling (3D-PL).

Fig. 1. (a) We propose a 3D-aware pseudo-labeling (3D-PL) technique to facilitate source-to-target domain adaptation for monocular depth estimation via pseudo-labeling on the target domain. **(b)** Our 3D-PL technique consists of 2D-based and 3D-aware pseudo-labels, where the former selects the pixels with highly-confident depth prediction (colorized by light blue in the consistent mask), while the latter performs 3D point cloud completion that provides refined pseudo-labels projected from 3D. (Color figure online)

disparity from videos or binocular stereo images without any ground truth depth. Unfortunately, since there is no strong supervision provided, unsupervised methods may not do well under situations such as occlusion or blurring in object motion. To solve this problem, recent works use synthetic datasets since the synthetic image-depth pairs are easier to obtain and have more accurate dense depth information than real-world depth maps. However, there still exists domain shift between synthetic and real datasets, and thus many works use domain adaptation [6,23,29,51,53] to overcome this issue.

In the scenario of domain adaptation, two major techniques are commonly adopted to reduce the domain gap for depth estimation: 1) using adversarial loss [6,23,53] for feature-level distribution alignment, or 2) leveraging style transfer between synthetic/real data to generate real-like images as pixel-level adaptation [51,53]. On the other hand, self-learning via pseudo-labeling the target real data is another powerful technique for domain adaptation [27,43,55], yet less explored in the depth estimation task. One reason is that, unlike tasks such as semantic segmentation that has the probabilistic output for classification to produce pseudo-labels, depth estimation is a regression task which requires specific designs for pseudo-label generation. In this paper, we propose novel pseudo-labeling methods in depth estimation for domain adaptation (see Fig. 1a).

To this end, we propose two mechanisms, 2D-based and 3D-aware methods, for generating pseudo depth labels (see Fig. 1b). For the 2D type, we consider the consistency of depth predictions when the model sees two images with the same content but different styles, i.e., the depth prediction can be more reliable for pixels with higher consistency. Specifically, we apply style transfer [19] to the target real image and generate its synthetic-stylized version, and then find their highly-consistent areas in depth predictions as pseudo-labels. However, this design may not be sufficient as it produces pseudo-labels only in certain confident pixels but ignore many other areas. Also, it does not take the fact that depth prediction is a 3D task into account.

To leverage the confident information obtained in our 2D-based pseudo-labeling process, we further propose to find the neighboring relationships in the 3D space via point cloud completion, so that our model is able to even select the pseudo-labels in areas that are not that confident, thus being complementary to 2D-based pseudo-labels. Specifically, we first project 2D pseudo-labels to point clouds in the 3D space, and then utilize a 3D completion model to generate neighboring point clouds. Due to the help of more confident and accurate 2D pseudo-labels, it also facilitates 3D completion to synthesize better point clouds. Next, we project the completed point clouds back to depth values in the 2D image plane as our 3D-aware pseudo-labels. Since the 3D completion model learns the whole structural information in 3D space, it can produce reliable depth values that correct the original 2D pseudo-labels or expand extra pseudo-labels outside of the 2D ones. We also note that, although pseudo-labeling for depth has been considered in the prior work [29], different from this work that needs a pre-trained panoptic segmentation model and can only generate pseudo-labels for object instances, our method does not have this limitation as we use the point cloud completion model trained on the source domain to infer reliable 3D-aware pseudo-labels on the target image.

We conduct extensive experiments by using the virtual KITTI dataset [12] as the source domain and the KITTI dataset [14] as the real target domain. We show that both of our 2D-based and 3D-aware pseudo-labeling strategies are complementary to each other and improve the depth estimation performance. In addition, following the stereo setting in GASDA [51] where the stereo pairs are provided during training, our method can further improve the baselines and perform favorably against state-of-the-art approaches. Moreover, we directly evaluate our model on other unseen datasets, Make3D [39], and show good generalization ability against existing methods. Here are our main contributions:

- We propose a framework for domain adaptive monocular depth estimation via pseudo-labeling, consisting of 2D-based and 3D-aware strategies that are complementary to each other.
- We utilize the 2D consistency of depth predictions to obtain initial pseudo-labels, and then propose a 3D-aware method that adopts point cloud completion in the structural 3D space to refine and expand pseudo-labels.
- We show that both of our 2D-based and 3D-aware methods have advantages against existing methods on several datasets, and when having stereo pairs during training, the performance can be further improved.

2   Related Work

Monocular Depth Estimation. Monocular depth estimation is to understand 3D depth information from a single 2D image. With the recent renaissance of deep learning techniques, supervised learning methods [3,9,11,21,28,47] have been proposed. Eigen *et al.* [9] first use a two-scale CNN-based network to directly regress on the depth, while Liu *et al.* [28] utilize continuous CRF to improve depth estimation. Furthermore, some methods propose different designs to extend the CNN-based network, such as changing the regression loss to classification [3,11], adding geometric constraints [47], and predicting with semantic segmentation [21,44].

Despite having promising results, the cost of collecting image-depth pairs for supervised learning is expensive. Thus, several unsupervised [13,15,16,30, 42,49] or semi-supervised [1,17,20,24] methods have been proposed to estimate disparity from the stereo pairs or videos. Garg *et al.* [13] warp the right image to reconstruct its corresponding left one (in a stereo pair) through the depth-aware geometry constraints, and take photometric error as the reconstruction penalty. Godard *et al.* [15] predict the left and right disparity separately, and enforce the left-right consistency to enhance the quality of predicted results. There are several follow-up methods to further improve the performance through semi-supervised manner [1,24] and video self-supervision [16,30].

Domain Adaptation for Depth Estimation. Another way to tackle the difficulty of data collection for depth estimation is to leverage the domain adaptation techniques [6,23,29,34,51,53], where the synthetic data can provide full supervisions as the source domain and the real-world unlabeled data is the target domain. Since depth estimation is a regression task, existing methods usually rely on style transfer/image translation for pixel-level adaptation [2], adversarial learning for feature-level adaptation [23], or their combinations [51,53]. For instance, Atapour *et al.* [2] transform the style of testing data from real to synthetic, and use it as the input to their depth prediction model that is only trained on the synthetic data. AdaDepth [23] aligns the distribution between the source and target domain at the latent feature space and the prediction level. T^2net [53] further combines these two techniques, where they adopt both the synthetic-to-real translation network and the task network with feature alignment. They show that, training on the real stylized images brings promising improvement, but aligning features is not effective in the outdoor dataset.

Other follow-up methods [6,51] take the bidirectional translation (real-to-synthetic and synthetic-to-real) and use the depth consistency loss on the prediction between the real and real-to-synthetic images. Moreover, some methods employ additional information to give constraints on the real image. GASDA [51] utilizes stereo pairs and encourages the geometry consistency to align stereo images. With a similar setting and geometry constraint to GASDA, SharinGAN [34] maps both synthetic and real images to a shared image domain for depth estimation. Moreover, DESC [29] adopts instance segmentation to apply pseudo-labeling using instance height and semantic segmentation to encourage the prediction consistency between two domains. Compared to these prior works, our proposed method provides direct supervisions on the real data in a simple and efficient pseudo-labeling way without any extra information.

Pseudo-Labeling for Depth Estimation. In general, pseudo-labeling explores the knowledge learned from labeled data to infer pseudo ground truths for unlabeled data, which is commonly used in classification [4,18,26,38,41] and scene understanding [7,27,32,33,40,52,55,56] problems. Only few depth estimation methods [29,46] adopt the concept of pseudo-labeling. DESC [29] designs a model to predict the instance height and converts the instance height to depth values as the pseudo-label for the depth prediction of the real image. Yang *et al.*[46] generate the pseudo-label from multi-view images and design a few ways to refine pseudo-labels, including fusing point clouds from multi-views. These methods succeed in producing pseudo-labels, but they require to have the instance information [29] or multi-view images [46]. Moreover, as [46] is a multi-stereo task, it is easier to build a complete point cloud from multi views and render the depth map as pseudo-labels. Their task also focuses on the main object instead of the overall scene. In our method, we design the point cloud completion method to generate reliable 3D-aware pseudo-labels based on a single image that contains a real-world outdoor scene.

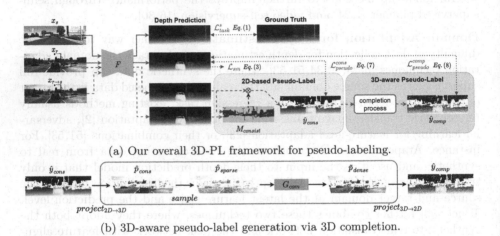

(a) Our overall 3D-PL framework for pseudo-labeling.

(b) 3D-aware pseudo-label generation via 3D completion.

Fig. 2. (a) Illustration of our proposed 3D-PL framework together with the training objectives. F is the depth prediction network, with input of the synthetic image x_s, the real image x_r, and the synthetic-stylized image $x_{r \to s}$. In 3D-PL, we obtain 2D-based pseudo-labels $\hat{y}_{cons}$ through finding the region with consistent depth (light blue color in $M_{consist}$) across the predictions of x_r and $x_{r \to s}$ (see Sect. 3.2), while 3D-aware pseudo-labels $\hat{y}_{comp}$ are obtained via the 3D completion process. Here we denote solid lines as the computation flow where the gradients can be back-propagated, while the dashed lines indicate that pseudo-labels are generated offline based on the preliminary model in Sect. 3.1. (b) We first project the 2D-based pseudo-labels $\hat{y}_{cons}$ to the 3D point cloud $\hat{p}_{cons}$, followed by uniformly sub-sampling $\hat{p}_{cons}$ to sparse $\hat{p}_{sparse}$. Then, the completion network G_{com} densifies $\hat{p}_{sparse}$ to obtain $\tilde{p}_{dense}$, in which we further project $\tilde{p}_{dense}$ back to 2D and produce 3D-aware pseudo-labels $\hat{y}_{comp}$ (see Sect. 3.2). (Color figure online)

3 Proposed Method

Our goal in this paper is to adapt the depth prediction model F to the unlabeled real image x_r as the target domain, where the synthetic image-depth pair (x_s, y_s) in the source domain is provided for supervision. Without domain adaptation, the depth prediction model F can be well trained on the synthetic data (x_s, y_s), but it cannot directly perform well on the real image x_r because of the domain shift. Thus, we propose our pseudo-labeling method to provide direct supervisions on target image x_r, which reduces the domain gap effectively.

Figure 2 illustrates the overall pipeline of our method. To utilize our pseudo-labeling techniques, we first use the synthetic data to train a preliminary depth prediction model F, and then adopt this pretrained model to infer pseudo-labels on real data for self-training. For pseudo-label generation, we propose 2D-based and 3D-aware schemes, where we name them as *consistency label* and *completion label*, respectively. We detail our model designs in the following sections.

3.1 Preliminary Model Objectives

Here, we describe the preliminary objectives during our model pre-training by using the synthetic image-depth pairs (x_s, y_s) and the real image x_r, including depth estimation loss and smoothness loss. Please note that, this is a common step before pseudo-labeling, in order to account for initially noisy predictions.

Depth Estimation Loss. As synthetic image-depth pairs (x_s, y_s) can provide the supervision, we directly minimize the L_1 distance between the predicted depth $\tilde{y}_s = F(x_s)$ of the synthetic image x_s and the ground truth depth y_s.

$$\mathcal{L}_{task}^s(F) = \|\tilde{y}_s - y_s\|_1. \tag{1}$$

In addition to the synthetic images x_s, we follow the similar style translation strategy as [53] to generate real-stylized images $x_{s \to r}$, in which $x_{s \to r}$ maintains the content of x_s but has the style from a randomly chosen real image x_r. Note that, to keep the simplicity of our framework, we adopt the real-time style transfer AdaIN [19] (pretrained model provided by [19]) instead of training another translation network like [53].

$$\mathcal{L}_{task}^{s \to r}(F) = \|\tilde{y}_{s \to r} - y_s\|_1. \tag{2}$$

Smoothness Loss. For the target image x_r, we adopt the smoothness loss as [15,53] to encourage the local depth prediction $\tilde{y}_r$ being smooth and consistent. Since depth values are often discontinuous on the boundaries of objects, we weigh this loss with the edge-aware term:

$$\mathcal{L}_{sm}(F) = e^{-\nabla x_r} \|\nabla \tilde{y}_r\|_1, \tag{3}$$

where ∇ is is the first derivative along spatial directions.

3.2   Pseudo-Label Generation

With the preliminary loss functions introduced in Sect. 3.1 that pre-train the model, we then perform our pseudo-labeling process with two schemes. First, 2D-based consistency label aims to find the highly confident pixels from depth predictions as pseudo-labels. Second, 3D-aware completion label utilizes a 3D completion model G_{com} to refine some prior pseudo-labels and further extend the range of pseudo-labels (see Fig. 2).

2D-Based Consistency Label. A typical way to discover reliable pseudo-labels is to find confident ones, e.g., utilizing the softmax output from tasks like semantic segmentation [27]. However, due to the nature of the regression task in depth estimation, it is not trivial to obtain such 2D-based pseudo-labels from the network output. Therefore, we design a simple yet effective way to construct the confidence map via feeding the model two target images with the same content but different styles. Since pixels in two images have correspondence, our motivation is that, pixels that are more confident should have more consistent depth values across two predictions (i.e., finding pixels that are more domain invariant through the consistency of predictions from real images with different styles).

To achieve this, we first obtain the synthetic-stylized image $x_{r \to s}$ for the real image x_r, which combines the content of x_r and the style of a synthetic image x_s, via AdaIN [19]. Then, we obtain depth predictions of these two images, $\tilde{y}_r = F(x_r)$, $\tilde{y}_{r \to s} = F(x_{r \to s})$, and calculate their difference. If the difference at one pixel is less then a threshold τ, we consider this pixel as a more confident prediction to form the pseudo-label $\hat{y}_{cons}$. The procedure is written as:

$$M_{consist} = |\tilde{y}_r - \tilde{y}_{r \to s}| < \tau,$$
$$\hat{y}_{cons} = M_{consist} \otimes \tilde{y}_r, \tag{4}$$

where $M_{consist}$ is the binary mask for consistency, which records where pixels are consistent. τ is the threshold, set as 0.5 in meter, and $\otimes$ is the element-wise product to filter the prediction $\tilde{y}_r$ of the target image.

3D-Aware Completion Label. Since depth estimation is a 3D problem, we expand the prior 2D-based pseudo-label $\hat{y}_{cons}$ to obtain more pseudo-labels in the 3D space, so that the pseudo-labeling process can benefit from the learned 3D structure. To this end, based on the 2D consistency label $\hat{y}_{cons}$, we propose a 3D completion process to reason neighboring relationships in 3D. As shown in Fig. 2b, the 3D completion process adopts the point cloud completion technique to learn from the 3D structure and generate neighboring points.

First, we project the 2D-based pseudo-label $\hat{y}_{cons}$ to point clouds $\hat{p}_{cons} = project_{2D \to 3D}(\hat{y}_{cons})$ in the 3D space. In the projection procedure, we reconstruct each point (x_i, y_i, z_i) from the image pixel (u_i, v_i) with its depth value d_i based on the standard pinhole camera model (more details and discussions are provided in the supplementary material). Next, we uniformly sample points from $\hat{p}_{cons}$ to have sparse point clouds $\hat{p}_{sparse} = sample(\hat{p}_{cons})$, followed by taking $\hat{p}_{sparse}$ as the input to the 3D completion model G_{com} for synthesizing the missing points. Those generated points from the 3D completion model G_{com} compose new dense point clouds $\tilde{p}_{dense} = G_{com}(\hat{p}_{sparse})$, and then we project each point $(\tilde{x}_i, \tilde{y}_i, \tilde{z}_i)$ back to the original 2D plane as $(\tilde{u}_i, \tilde{v}_i)$ with updated depth value $\tilde{d}_i = \tilde{z}_i$.

Therefore, our 3D-aware pseudo-label $\hat{y}_{comp}$ (i.e., completion label) is formed by the updated depth value $\tilde{d}_i$. Note that, as there could exist some projected points falling outside the image plane and not all the pixels on the image plane are covered by the projected points, we construct a mask M_{valid} which records the pixels on the completion label $\hat{y}_{comp}$ where the projection succeeds, i.e., having valid $(\tilde{u}_i, \tilde{v}_i)$.

$$\hat{y}_{comp} = M_{valid} \otimes project_{3D \rightarrow 2D}(\tilde{p}_{dense}). \tag{5}$$

In Fig. 3, we show that the 3D-aware completion label $\hat{y}_{comp}$ expands the pseudo-labels from the 2D-based consistency label $\hat{y}_{cons}$, i.e., visualizations in $\hat{y}_{comp} - \hat{y}_{cons}$ are additional pseudo-labels from the 3D completion process (please refer to Sect. 4.3 for further analyzing the effectiveness of 3D-aware pseudo-labels).

Input image x_r Ground truth y_r $\hat{y}_{cons}$ $\hat{y}_{comp}$ $\hat{y}_{comp} - \hat{y}_{cons}$

Fig. 3. Examples for our pseudo-labels. The third and fourth columns are pseudo-labels for 2D-based $\hat{y}_{cons}$ and 3D-aware $\hat{y}_{comp}$. The final column represents the complementary pseudo-labels produced by $\hat{y}_{comp}$. Note that ground truth y_r is the reference but not used in our model training.

3D Completion Model. We pre-train the 3D completion model G_{com} using the synthetic ground truth depth y_s in advance and keep it fixed during our completion process. We project the entire y_s to 3D point clouds $\hat{p}^s = project_{2D \rightarrow 3D}(y_s)$ and then perform the same process (i.e., sampling and completion) as in Fig. 2b to obtain the generated dense point clouds $\tilde{p}^s_{dense}$. Since $\hat{p}^s$ is the ground truth point clouds of $\tilde{p}^s_{dense}$, we can directly minimize Chamfer Distance (CD) [10] between these two point clouds to train the 3D completion model G_{com},
$\mathcal{L}_{cd}(G_{com}) = CD(\hat{p}^s, \tilde{p}^s_{dense})$.

3.3   Overall Training Pipeline and Objectives

There are two training stages in our proposed method: the first stage is to train a preliminary depth model F, and the second stage is to apply the proposed pseudo-labeling techniques through this preliminary model. The loss in the first stage consists of the ones introduced in Sect. 3.1:

$$\mathcal{L}_{base} = \lambda_{task}(\mathcal{L}_{task}^{s} + \mathcal{L}_{task}^{s \to r}) + \lambda_{sm}\mathcal{L}_{sm}, \tag{6}$$

where λ_{task} and λ_{sm} are set as 100 and 0.1 respectively, following the similar settings in [53]. Note that in our implementation, for every synthetic image x_s, we augment three corresponding real-stylized images $x_{s \to r}$, where their styles are obtained from three real images randomly drawn from the training set.

Training with Pseudo-Labels. In the second stage, we use our generated 2D-based and 3D-aware pseudo-labels in Eq. (4) and Eq. (5) to provide direct supervisions on the target image x_r. Since the completion label $\hat{y}_{comp}$ is aware of the 3D structural information and can refine the prior 2D-based pseudo-labels $\hat{y}_{cons}$, we choose the completion label $\hat{y}_{comp}$ as the main reference if a pixel has both consistency label $\hat{y}_{cons}$ and completion label $\hat{y}_{comp}$. The 2D and 3D pseudo-label loss functions are respectively defined as:

$$\mathcal{L}_{pseudo}^{cons}(F) = \|M'_{valid} \otimes (M_{consist} \otimes \tilde{y}_r - \hat{y}_{cons})\|_1, \tag{7}$$

$$\mathcal{L}_{pseudo}^{comp}(F) = \|M_{valid} \otimes \tilde{y}_r - \hat{y}_{comp}\|_1, \tag{8}$$

where $M'_{valid} = (1 - M_{valid})$ is the inverse mask of M_{valid}. In addition to the two pseudo-labeling objectives, we also include the supervised synthetic data to maintain the training stability. The total objective of the second stage is:

$$\mathcal{L}_{total} = \alpha(\lambda_{cons}\mathcal{L}_{pseudo}^{cons} + \lambda_{comp}\mathcal{L}_{pseudo}^{comp})$$
$$+(1 - \alpha)\lambda_{task}^{s}\mathcal{L}_{task}^{s} + \lambda_{sm}\mathcal{L}_{sm}, \tag{9}$$

where α set as 0.7 is the proportion ratio between the supervised loss of the synthetic and real image. λ_{task}^{s}, λ_{cons}, λ_{comp}, and λ_{sm} are set as 100, 1, 0.1, and 0.1, respectively. Here we do not include the $\mathcal{L}_{task}^{s \to r}$ loss as in Eq. (6) to make the model training more focused on the real-domain data.

Stereo Setting. The training strategy mentioned above is under the condition that we can only access the monocular single image of the real data x_r. In addition, if the stereo pairs are available during training as the setting in GASDA [51], we can further include the geometry consistency loss $\mathcal{L}_{tgc}$ in [51] to our proposed method (more details are in the supplementary material):

$$\mathcal{L}_{stereo} = \mathcal{L}_{total} + \lambda_{tgc}\mathcal{L}_{tgc}, \tag{10}$$

where $\mathcal{L}_{total}$ is the loss in Eq. (9), and λ_{tgc} is set as 50 following [51].

4   Experimental Results

In summary, we conduct experiments for the synthetic-to-real benchmark when only single images or stereo pairs are available during training. Then we show ablation studies to demonstrate the effectiveness of the proposed pseudo-labeling methods. Moreover, we provide discussion to validate the effectiveness of our 3D-aware pseudo-labeling method. Finally, we directly evaluate our models on two real-world datasets to show the generalization ability. More results and analysis are provided in the supplementary material.

Datasets and Evaluation Metrics. We adopt Virtual KITTI (vKITTI) [12] and real KITTI [14] as our source and target datasets respectively. vKITTI contains 21,260 synthetic image-depth pairs of the urban scene under different weather conditions. Since the maximum depth ground truth values are different in vKITTI and KITTI, we clip the maximum value to 80 m as [53]. For evaluating the generalization ability, we use the KITTI Stereo [31] and Make3D [39] datasets following the prior work [51]. We use the same depth evaluation metrics as [51, 53], including four types of errors and three types of accuracy metrics.

Table 1. Quantitative results on KITTI in the single-image setting, where we denote the best results in bold. For the training data, "K", "CS", and "S" indicate KITTI [14], CityScapes [8], and virtual-KITTI [12] datasets respectively. We highlight the rows in gray for those methods using the domain adaptation (DA) techniques.

Method	Supervised	Dataset	Cap	Error metrics (lower, better)				Accuracy metrics (higher, better)		
				Abs Rel	Sq Rel	RMSE	RMSE log	$\delta < 1.25$	$\delta < 1.25^2$	$\delta < 1.25^3$
Eigen et al. [9]	Yes	K	80 m	0.203	1.548	6.307	0.282	0.702	0.890	0.958
Liu et al. [28]	Yes	K	80 m	0.202	1.614	6.523	0.275	0.678	0.895	0.965
Zhou et al. [54]	No	K	80 m	0.208	1.768	6.856	0.283	0.678	0.885	0.957
Zhou et al. [54]	No	K+CS	80 m	0.198	1.836	6.565	0.275	0.718	0.901	0.960
All synthetic	No	S	80 m	0.253	2.303	6.953	0.328	0.635	0.856	0.937
All real	No	K	80 m	0.158	1.151	5.285	0.238	0.811	0.934	0.970
AdaDepth [23]	No	K+S(DA)	80 m	0.214	1.932	7.157	0.295	0.665	0.882	0.950
T²Net [53]	No	K+S(DA)	80 m	0.182	1.611	6.216	0.265	0.749	0.898	0.959
3D-PL (Ours)	No	K+S(DA)	80 m	**0.169**	**1.371**	**6.037**	**0.256**	**0.759**	**0.904**	**0.961**
Garg et al. [13]	No	K	50 m	0.169	1.080	5.104	0.273	0.740	0.904	0.962
All synthetic	No	S	50 m	0.244	1.771	5.354	0.313	0.647	0.866	0.943
All real	No	K	50 m	0.151	0.856	4.043	0.227	0.824	0.940	0.973
AdaDepth [23]	No	K+S(DA)	50 m	0.203	1.734	6.251	0.284	0.687	0.899	0.958
T²Net [53]	No	K+S(DA)	50 m	0.168	1.199	4.674	0.243	0.772	0.912	0.966
3D-PL (Ours)	No	K+S(DA)	50 m	**0.162**	**1.049**	**4.463**	**0.239**	**0.776**	**0.916**	**0.968**

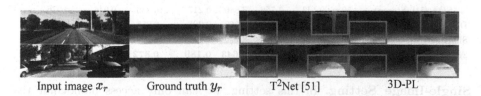

Input image x_r Ground truth y_r T²Net [51]   3D-PL

Fig. 4. Qualitative results on KITTI in the single-image setting. We show that our 3D-PL produces more accurate results for the tree and grass (upper row) and better shapes in the car (bottom row), compared to the T²Net [53] method.

Implementation Details. Our depth prediction model F adopts the same U-net [37] structure as [53]. Following [45], the 3D completion model G_{com} is modified from PCN [48] with PointNet [35]. We implement our model based on the Pytorch framework with NVIDIA Geforce GTX 2080 Ti GPU. All networks are trained with the Adam optimizer. The depth prediction model F and 3D completion model G_{com} are trained from scratch with learning rate 10^{-4} and linear decay after 10 epochs. We train F for 20 epochs in the first stage and 10 epochs in the second stage, and pre-train G_{com} for 20 epochs. The style transfer network AdaIN is pre-trained without any finetuning. Our code and models are available at https://github.com/ccc870206/3D-PL.

4.1   Synthetic-to-Real Benchmark

We follow [53] to use 22,600 KITTI images from 32 scenes as the real training data, and evaluate the performance on the eigen test split [9] of 697 images from other 29 scenes. Following [51], we evaluate the depth prediction results with the ground truth depth less than 80 m or 50 m. There are two real-data training settings in domain adaptation for monocular depth estimation: 1) only single real images are available and we cannot access binocular or semantic information as [53]; 2) stereo pairs are available during training, so that geometry consistency can be leveraged as [51]. Our pseudo-labeling method does not have an assumption of the data requirement, and hence we conduct experiments in these two different data settings as mentioned in Sect. 3.3.

Table 2. Quantitative results on KITTI with having stereo pairs during training.

Method	Cap	Error metrics (lower, better)				Accuracy metrics (higher, better)		
		Abs Rel	Sq Rel	RMSE	RMSE log	$\delta < 1.25$	$\delta < 1.25^2$	$\delta < 1.25^3$
Synthetic + Stereo	80 m	0.151	1.176	5.496	0.237	0.787	0.926	0.972
T^2Net [53] + Stereo	80 m	0.154	1.115	5.504	0.233	0.800	0.929	0.971
GASDA [51] (Stereo)	80 m	0.149	1.003	4.995	0.227	0.824	0.941	0.973
DESC [29] + Stereo	80 m	0.122	0.946	5.019	0.217	0.843	0.942	0.974
SharinGAN [34] (Stereo)	80 m	0.116	0.939	5.068	0.203	0.850	0.948	0.978
3D-PL + Stereo	80 m	**0.113**	**0.903**	**4.902**	**0.201**	**0.859**	**0.952**	**0.979**
Synthetic + Stereo	50 m	0.145	0.909	4.204	0.224	0.800	0.934	0.975
T^2Net [53] + Stereo	50 m	0.148	0.828	4.123	0.219	0.815	0.938	0.975
GASDA [51] (Stereo)	50 m	0.143	0.756	3.846	0.217	0.836	0.946	0.976
DESC [29] + Stereo	50 m	0.116	0.725	3.880	0.206	0.855	0.948	0.976
SharinGAN [34] (Stereo)	50 m	0.109	0.673	3.770	0.190	0.864	0.954	0.981
3D-PL + Stereo	50 m	**0.106**	**0.641**	**3.643**	**0.189**	**0.872**	**0.958**	**0.982**

Single-Image Setting. In this setting, we can only access monocular real images in the whole training process, as the overall objective in Eq. (9). Table 1 shows the quantitative results, where the domain adaptation methods are high-lighted in gray. "All synthetic/All real" are only trained on synthetic/real image-depth pairs, which can be viewed as the lower/upper bound. Our 3D-PL method outperforms T^{2}Net (state-of-the-art) in every metric, especially 13% and 15% improvement in the "Sq Rel" error of 50 m and 80 m. Figure 4 shows the qualitative results, where we compare our 3D-PL with T^{2}Net [53]. In the upper row, 3D-PL produces more accurate results for the tree and grass, while T^{2}Net predicts too far and close respectively. In the lower row, our result has a better shape in the right car and more precise depth for the left two cars.

Stereo-Pair Setting. If stereo pairs are available, we can utilize the geometry constraints to have self-supervised stereo supervisions as [51] using the objective in Eq. (10). Table 2 shows that our 3D-PL achieves the best performance among state-of-the-art methods. In particular, without utilizing any other clues from real-world semantic annotation, 3D-PL outperforms DESC [29] with 12% lower "Sq Rel" error in the stereo scenario. This shows that our pseudo-labeling is able to generate more reliable pseudo-labels over the single-image setting.

Figure 5 shows qualitative results, where we compare our 3D-PL with DESC [29] + Stereo and SharinGAN [34]. 3D-PL produces better results on the overall structure (e.g., tree, wall, and car in the top row). For challenging situations such as closer objects standing alone and hiding in a complicated farther background (e.g., road sign in the middle row, tree in the bottom row), other methods tend to produce similar depth values as the background, while 3D-PL predicts better object shape and distinguish the object from the background even if it is very thin. (e.g., traffic light in the bottom row). This shows the benefits of our 3D-aware pseudo-labeling design, which reasons the 3D structural information.

Table 3. Ablation study on KITTI in the single-image setting.

Method	Error metrics (lower, better)			
	Abs Rel	Sq Rel	RMSE	RMSE log
Only synthetic	0.244	1.771	5.354	0.313
$+\hat{y}_{cons}$ (all pixels)	0.166	1.125	4.557	0.244
$+\hat{y}_{cons}$ (confident)	0.163	1.095	4.555	0.243
$+\hat{y}_{comp}$ (confident)	0.164	1.054	4.473	**0.239**
3D-PL ($\hat{y}_{comp}$ all pixels)	**0.161**	1.070	4.504	0.240
3D-PL ($\hat{y}_{comp}$ confident)	0.162	**1.049**	**4.463**	**0.239**

Input image x_r Ground truth y_r DESC [29]   SharinGAN[33]   3D-PL+Stereo

Fig. 5. Qualitative results on KITTI with having stereo pairs during training. We show that our 3D-PL produces better results on the overall structure (e.g., tree, wall, and car in the top row), closer objects (e.g., road sign in the middle row, tree in the bottom row), and shapes (e.g., traffic light in the bottom row), compared to DESC [29] and SharinGAN [34].

4.2 Ablation Study

We demonstrate the contributions of our model designs in Table 3 using the "50 m Cap" and single-image settings, where "Only synthetic" trains only on the supervised synthetic image-depth pairs.

Importance of Pseudo-Labels. First, we show that either using the 2D-based or 3D-aware pseudo-labels improve the performance, i.e., "$+\hat{y}_{cons}$ (confident)" and "$+\hat{y}_{comp}$ (confident)". Then, our final model in "3D-PL ($\hat{y}_{comp}$ confident)" further improves depth estimation, and shows the complementary properties of using both 2D-based and 3D-aware pseudo-labels.

Importance of Consistency Mask. We show the importance of having the consistency mask in Eq. (4) as the confidence measure. For the 2D-based pseudo-label, we compare the result of using the consistency mask "$+\hat{y}_{cons}$ (confident)" and the one using the entire depth prediction as the pseudo-label, "$+\hat{y}_{cons}$ (all pixels)". With the consistency mask, it has 3% lower in the "Sq Rel" error. Moreover, this consistency mask also improves 3D-aware pseudo-labeling when we project depth values to point clouds for 3D completion. When inputting all the pixels for this process, i.e., "3D-PL ($\hat{y}_{comp}$ all pixels)", this may include less accurate depth values for performing 3D completion, which results in less reliable pseudo-labels compared to our final model using the confident pixels, i.e., "3D-PL ($\hat{y}_{comp}$ confident)".

Table 4. Statistics of pixel proportion in our 2D/3D pseudo-labels. "R" and "E" indicate "refined" and "extended".

Method	2D proportion	3D proportion
2D only ($+\hat{y}_{cons}$)	48.91%	0%
3D-PL	5.28%	43.63% (R) + 3.9% (E)

Table 5. Results of using either the 2D-based $\hat{y}_{cons}$ or the 3D-aware $\hat{y}_{comp}$ pseudo-label as the reference, when there is a duplication on both pseudo-labels.

Main reference	Error metrics (lower, better)			
	Abs Rel	Sq Rel	RMSE	RMSE log
Completion Label $\hat{y}_{comp}$	**0.162**	**1.049**	**4.463**	**0.239**
Consistency Label $\hat{y}_{cons}$	0.164	1.095	4.529	0.243

4.3 Effectiveness of 3D-Aware Pseudo-Labels

To show the impact of 3D-aware pseudo-labels, we compute the proportions of pixels chosen as 2D/3D pseudo-labels in each image and take the average as the final statistics. The effectiveness of 3D-aware pseudo-labels is in two-fold: **refine** and **extend** from 2D-based pseudo-labels. In Table 4, the initial proportion of confident 2D-based pseudo-labels "2D only $(+\hat{y}_{cons})$" is 48.91% among image pixels. As stated in Sect. 3.3, 3D-PL improves original 2D labels, which results in 43.63% refined and 3.9% extended labels. The rightmost subfigure of Fig. 3 visualizes extended labels $\hat{y}_{comp} - \hat{y}_{cons}$, in which it shows that the improved performance is contributed by the larger proportion of 3D-aware pseudo-labels.

Ability of Pseudo-Label Refinement. Since the 2D-based and 3D-aware pseudo-labels may have the duplication on the same pixel, we conduct experiments to use either $\hat{y}_{cons}$ or $\hat{y}_{comp}$ as the reference when such cases happen. In Table 5, choosing $\hat{y}_{comp}$ as the main reference has the better performance, which indicates that updating the pseudo-label of a pixel from original $\hat{y}_{cons}$ to $\hat{y}_{comp}$ brings the positive effect. This validates that $\hat{y}_{comp}$ can refine the prior 2D-based pseudo-labels since it is aware of the 3D structural information.

4.4 Generalization to Real-World Datasets

KITTI Stereo. We evaluate our model on 200 images of KITTI stereo 2015 [31], which is a small subset of KITTI images but has different ways of collecting groundtruth of depth information. Since the ground truth of KITTI stereo has been optimized for the moving objects, it is denser than LiDAR, especially for the vehicles. Note that, this benefits DESC [29] in this evaluation as their method relies on the instance information from the pre-trained segmentation model. Table 6 shows the quantitative results, where our 3D-PL in both single-image and stereo settings performs competitively against existing methods.

Table 6. Quantitative results on KITTI stereo 2015 benchmark [31]. "S°" denotes synthetic data that [2] captures from GTA [36]. "Supervised" represents whether the method is trained on KITTI stereo.

Method	Supervised	Dataset	Error metrics (lower, better)				Accuracy Metrics (higher, better)		
			Abs Rel	Sq Rel	RMSE	RMSE log	$\delta < 1.25$	$\delta < 1.25^2$	$\delta < 1.25^3$
Godard et al. [15]	No	K	0.124	1.388	6.125	0.217	0.841	0.936	0.975
Godard et al. [15]	No	K+CS	0.104	1.070	5.417	0.188	0.875	0.956	0.983
Atapour et al. [2]	No	K+S°(DA)	0.101	1.048	5.308	0.184	0.903	0.988	0.992
T^2Net [53]	No	K+S(DA)	0.155	1.731	6.510	0.237	**0.800**	**0.921**	**0.969**
3D-PL	No	K+S(DA)	**0.147**	**1.352**	**6.157**	**0.233**	**0.800**	0.918	0.967
GASDA [51] (Stereo)	No	K+S(DA)	0.106	0.987	5.215	0.176	0.885	0.963	0.986
DESC [29] + Stereo	No	K+S(DA)	**0.085**	**0.781**	4.490	0.158	0.909	0.967	0.986
SharinGAN [34] (Stereo)	No	K+S(DA)	0.092	0.904	4.614	0.159	0.906	0.969	0.987
3D-PL + Stereo	No	K+S(DA)	**0.085**	0.830	**4.489**	**0.149**	**0.915**	**0.971**	**0.988**

Make3D Dataset. Moreover, we directly evaluate the model on the Make3D dataset [39] without any finetuning. We choose 134 test images with central image crop and clamp the depth value to 70 m, following [15]. Here, since Make3D is a different domain from the KITTI training data, we apply the single-image

Table 7. Quantitative results on Make3D [39]. "Supervised" represents whether the method is trained on Make3D.

Method	Supervised	Error metrics (lower, better)		
		Abs Rel	Sq Rel	RMSE
Karsch *et al.* [22]	Yes	0.398	4.723	7.801
Laina *et al.* [25]	Yes	0.198	1.665	5.461
AdaDepth [23]	Yes	0.452	5.71	9.559
Godard *et al.* [15]	No	0.505	10.172	10.936
AdaDepth [23]	No	0.647	12.341	11.567
T²Net [53]	No	0.508	6.589	8.935
Atapour *et al.* [2]	No	0.423	9.343	9.002
GASDA [51]	No	0.403	6.709	10.424
DESC [29]	No	0.393	4.604	8.126
SharinGAN [34]	No	0.377	4.900	8.388
S2R-DepthNet [5]	No	0.490	10.681	10.892
3D-PL	No	**0.352**	**3.539**	**7.967**

model to reduce the strong domain-related constraints such as the stereo supervisions. In Table 7, 3D-PL achieves the best performance compared to other approaches. It is also worth mentioning that 3D-PL outperforms the domain generalization method [5] and supervised method [22] by 66% and 25% in "Sq Rel", showing the promising generalization capability.

5 Conclusions

In this paper, we introduce a domain adaptation method for monocular depth estimation. We propose 2D-based and 3D-aware pseudo-labeling mechanisms, which utilize knowledge from synthetic domain as well as 3D structural information to generate reliable pseudo depth labels for real data. Extensive experiments show that our pseudo-labeling strategies are able to improve depth estimation in various settings against several state-of-the-art domain adaptation approaches, as well as achieving good performance in unseen datasets for generalization.

Acknowledgement. This project is supported by MOST (Ministry of Science and Technology, Taiwan) 111-2636-E-A49-003 and 111-2628-E-A49-018-MY4.

References

1. Amiri, A.J., Loo, S.Y., Zhang, H.: Semi-supervised monocular depth estimation with left-right consistency using deep neural network. In: IEEE International Conference On Robotics and Biomimetics (ROBIO) (2019)
2. Atapour-Abarghouei, A., Breckon, T.P.: Real-time monocular depth estimation using synthetic data with domain adaptation via image style transfer. In: IEEE Conference on Computer Vision and Pattern Recognition (CVPR) (2018)

3. Cao, Y., Wu, Z., Shen, C.: Estimating depth from monocular images as classification using deep fully convolutional residual networks. IEEE Trans. Circ. Syst. Video Technol. (TCSVT) **28**, 3174–3182 (2017)
4. Chen, C., et al.: Progressive feature alignment for unsupervised domain adaptation. In: IEEE Conference on Computer Vision and Pattern Recognition (CVPR) (2019)
5. Chen, X., Wang, Y., Chen, X., Zeng, W.: S2R-DepthNet: learning a generalizable depth-specific structural representation. In: IEEE Conference on Computer Vision and Pattern Recognition (CVPR) (2021)
6. Chen, Y.C., Lin, Y.Y., Yang, M.H., Huang, J.B.: CrDoCo: pixel-level domain transfer with cross-domain consistency. In: IEEE Conference on Computer Vision and Pattern Recognition (CVPR) (2019)
7. Chen, Z., Zhang, R., Zhang, G., Ma, Z., Lei, T.: Digging into pseudo label: a low-budget approach for semi-supervised semantic segmentation. IEEE Access **8**, 41830–41837 (2020)
8. Cordts, M., et al.: The cityscapes dataset for semantic urban scene understanding. In: IEEE Conference on Computer Vision and Pattern Recognition (CVPR) (2016)
9. Eigen, D., Puhrsch, C., Fergus, R.: Depth map prediction from a single image using a multi-scale deep network. ArXiv:1406.2283 (2014)
10. Fan, H., Su, H., Guibas, L.J.: A point set generation network for 3d object reconstruction from a single image. In: IEEE Conference on Computer Vision and Pattern Recognition (CVPR) (2017)
11. Fu, H., Gong, M., Wang, C., Batmanghelich, K., Tao, D.: Deep ordinal regression network for monocular depth estimation. In: IEEE Conference on Computer Vision and Pattern Recognition (CVPR) (2018)
12. Gaidon, A., Wang, Q., Cabon, Y., Vig, E.: Virtual worlds as proxy for multi-object tracking analysis. In: IEEE Conference on Computer Vision and Pattern Recognition (CVPR) (2016)
13. Garg, R., B.G., V.K., Carneiro, G., Reid, I.: Unsupervised CNN for single view depth estimation: geometry to the rescue. In: Leibe, B., Matas, J., Sebe, N., Welling, M. (eds.) ECCV 2016. LNCS, vol. 9912, pp. 740–756. Springer, Cham (2016). https://doi.org/10.1007/978-3-319-46484-8_45
14. Geiger, A., Lenz, P., Urtasun, R.: Are we ready for autonomous driving? The kitti vision benchmark suite. In: IEEE Conference on Computer Vision and Pattern Recognition (CVPR) (2012)
15. Godard, C., Mac Aodha, O., Brostow, G.J.: Unsupervised monocular depth estimation with left-right consistency. In: IEEE Conference on Computer Vision and Pattern Recognition (CVPR) (2017)
16. Godard, C., Mac Aodha, O., Firman, M., Brostow, G.J.: Digging into self-supervised monocular depth estimation. In: IEEE International Conference on Computer Vision (ICCV) (2019)
17. Guizilini, V., Li, J., Ambrus, R., Pillai, S., Gaidon, A.: Robust semi-supervised monocular depth estimation with reprojected distances. In: Conference on Robot Learning (CoRL) (2020)
18. Hu, Z., Yang, Z., Hu, X., Nevatia, R.: Simple: similar pseudo label exploitation for semi-supervised classification. In: IEEE Conference on Computer Vision and Pattern Recognition (CVPR) (2021)
19. Huang, X., Belongie, S.: Arbitrary style transfer in real-time with adaptive instance normalization. In: IEEE International Conference on Computer Vision (ICCV) (2017)
20. Ji, R., et al.: Semi-supervised adversarial monocular depth estimation. IEEE Trans. Pattern Anal. Mach. Intell. (TPAMI) **42**, 2410–2422 (2019)

21. Jiao, J., Cao, Y., Song, Y., Lau, R.: Look deeper into depth: monocular depth estimation with semantic booster and attention-driven loss. In: Ferrari, V., Hebert, M., Sminchisescu, C., Weiss, Y. (eds.) ECCV 2018. LNCS, vol. 11219, pp. 55–71. Springer, Cham (2018). https://doi.org/10.1007/978-3-030-01267-0_4

22. Karsch, K., Liu, C., Kang, S.B.: Depth transfer: depth extraction from video using non-parametric sampling. IEEE Trans. Pattern Anal. Mach. Intell. (TPAMI) **36**, 2144–2158 (2014)

23. Kundu, J.N., Uppala, P.K., Pahuja, A., Babu, R.V.: AdaDepth: unsupervised content congruent adaptation for depth estimation. In: IEEE Conference on Computer Vision and Pattern Recognition (CVPR) (2018)

24. Kuznietsov, Y., Stuckler, J., Leibe, B.: Semi-supervised deep learning for monocular depth map prediction. In: IEEE Conference on Computer Vision and Pattern Recognition (CVPR) (2017)

25. Laina, I., Rupprecht, C., Belagiannis, V., Tombari, F., Navab, N.: Deeper depth prediction with fully convolutional residual networks. In: International Conference on 3D Vision (3DV) (2016)

26. Lee, D.H., et al.: Pseudo-label: the simple and efficient semi-supervised learning method for deep neural networks. In: International Conference on Machine Learning (ICML) (2013)

27. Li, Y., Yuan, L., Vasconcelos, N.: Bidirectional learning for domain adaptation of semantic segmentation. In: IEEE Conference on Computer Vision and Pattern Recognition (CVPR) (2019)

28. Liu, F., Shen, C., Lin, G., Reid, I.: Learning depth from single monocular images using deep convolutional neural fields. IEEE Trans. Pattern Anal. Mach. Intell. (TPAMI) **38**, 2024–2039 (2015)

29. Lopez-Rodriguez, A., Mikolajczyk, K.: DESC: domain adaptation for depth estimation via semantic consistency. ArXiv:2009.01579 (2020)

30. Mahjourian, R., Wicke, M., Angelova, A.: Unsupervised learning of depth and ego-motion from monocular video using 3d geometric constraints. In: IEEE Conference on Computer Vision and Pattern Recognition (CVPR) (2018)

31. Menze, M., Geiger, A.: Object scene flow for autonomous vehicles. In: IEEE Conference on Computer Vision and Pattern Recognition (CVPR) (2015)

32. Pastore, G., Cermelli, F., Xian, Y., Mancini, M., Akata, Z., Caputo, B.: A closer look at self-training for zero-label semantic segmentation. In: IEEE Conference on Computer Vision and Pattern Recognition (CVPR) (2021)

33. Paul, S., Tsai, Y.-H., Schulter, S., Roy-Chowdhury, A.K., Chandraker, M.: Domain adaptive semantic segmentation using weak labels. In: Vedaldi, A., Bischof, H., Brox, T., Frahm, J.-M. (eds.) ECCV 2020. LNCS, vol. 12354, pp. 571–587. Springer, Cham (2020). https://doi.org/10.1007/978-3-030-58545-7_33

34. PNVR, K., Zhou, H., Jacobs, D.: SharinGAN: combining synthetic and real data for unsupervised geometry estimation. In: IEEE Conference on Computer Vision and Pattern Recognition (CVPR) (2020)

35. Qi, C.R., Su, H., Mo, K., Guibas, L.J.: PointNet: deep learning on point sets for 3d classification and segmentation. In: IEEE Conference on Computer Vision and Pattern Recognition (CVPR) (2017)

36. Richter, S.R., Vineet, V., Roth, S., Koltun, V.: Playing for data: ground truth from computer games. In: Leibe, B., Matas, J., Sebe, N., Welling, M. (eds.) ECCV 2016. LNCS, vol. 9906, pp. 102–118. Springer, Cham (2016). https://doi.org/10.1007/978-3-319-46475-6_7

37. Ronneberger, O., Fischer, P., Brox, T.: U-Net: convolutional networks for biomed-ical image segmentation. In: Navab, N., Hornegger, J., Wells, W.M., Frangi, A.F. (eds.) MICCAI 2015. LNCS, vol. 9351, pp. 234–241. Springer, Cham (2015). https://doi.org/10.1007/978-3-319-24574-4_28

38. Saito, K., Ushiku, Y., Harada, T.: Asymmetric tri-training for unsupervised domain adaptation. In: International Conference on Machine Learning (ICML) (2017)

39. Saxena, A., Sun, M., Ng, A.Y.: Make3d: learning 3d scene structure from a single still image. IEEE Trans. Pattern Anal. Mach. Intell. (TPAMI) **31**, 824–840 (2008)

40. Shin, I., et al.: MM-TTA: multi-modal test-time adaptation for 3d semantic seg-mentation. In: IEEE Conference on Computer Vision and Pattern Recognition (CVPR) (2022)

41. Taherkhani, F., Dabouei, A., Soleymani, S., Dawson, J., Nasrabadi, N.M.: Self-supervised Wasserstein pseudo-labeling for semi-supervised image classification. In: IEEE Conference on Computer Vision and Pattern Recognition (CVPR) (2021)

42. Tosi, F., Aleotti, F., Poggi, M., Mattoccia, S.: Learning monocular depth esti-mation infusing traditional stereo knowledge. In: IEEE Conference on Computer Vision and Pattern Recognition (CVPR) (2019)

43. Vu, T.H., Jain, H., Bucher, M., Cord, M., Pérez, P.: ADVENT: adversarial entropy minimization for domain adaptation in semantic segmentation. In: IEEE Confer-ence on Computer Vision and Pattern Recognition (CVPR) (2019)

44. Wang, P., Shen, X., Lin, Z., Cohen, S., Price, B., Yuille, A.L.: Towards unified depth and semantic prediction from a single image. In: IEEE Conference on Computer Vision and Pattern Recognition (CVPR) (2015)

45. Xiang, R., Zheng, F., Su, H., Zhang, Z.: 3dDepthNet: point cloud guided depth completion network for sparse depth and single color image. ArXiv:2003.09175 (2020)

46. Yang, J., Alvarez, J.M., Liu, M.: Self-supervised learning of depth inference for multi-view stereo. In: IEEE Conference on Computer Vision and Pattern Recog-nition (CVPR) (2021)

47. Yin, W., Liu, Y., Shen, C., Yan, Y.: Enforcing geometric constraints of virtual nor-mal for depth prediction. In: IEEE International Conference on Computer Vision (ICCV) (2019)

48. Yuan, W., Khot, T., Held, D., Mertz, C., Hebert, M.: PCN: point completion network. In: International Conference on 3D Vision (3DV) (2018)

49. Zhan, H., Garg, R., Weerasekera, C.S., Li, K., Agarwal, H., Reid, I.: Unsupervised learning of monocular depth estimation and visual odometry with deep feature reconstruction. In: IEEE Conference on Computer Vision and Pattern Recognition (CVPR) (2018)

50. Zhang, Z.: Microsoft kinect sensor and its effect. IEEE Multimedia **19**, 4–10 (2012)

51. Zhao, S., Fu, H., Gong, M., Tao, D.: Geometry-aware symmetric domain adaptation for monocular depth estimation. In: IEEE Conference on Computer Vision and Pattern Recognition (CVPR) (2019)

52. Zhao, X., Schulter, S., Sharma, G., Tsai, Y.-H., Chandraker, M., Wu, Y.: Object detection with a unified label space from multiple datasets. In: Vedaldi, A., Bischof, H., Brox, T., Frahm, J.-M. (eds.) ECCV 2020. LNCS, vol. 12359, pp. 178–193. Springer, Cham (2020). https://doi.org/10.1007/978-3-030-58568-6_11

53. Zheng, C., Cham, T.-J., Cai, J.: T²Net: synthetic-to-realistic translation for solving single-image depth estimation tasks. In: Ferrari, V., Hebert, M., Sminchisescu, C., Weiss, Y. (eds.) ECCV 2018. LNCS, vol. 11211, pp. 798–814. Springer, Cham (2018). https://doi.org/10.1007/978-3-030-01234-2_47

54. Zhou, T., Brown, M., Snavely, N., Lowe, D.G.: Unsupervised learning of depth and ego-motion from video. In: IEEE Conference on Computer Vision and Pattern Recognition (CVPR) (2017)
55. Zou, Y., Yu, Z., Vijaya Kumar, B.V.K., Wang, J.: Unsupervised domain adaptation for semantic segmentation via class-balanced self-training. In: Ferrari, V., Hebert, M., Sminchisescu, C., Weiss, Y. (eds.) ECCV 2018. LNCS, vol. 11207, pp. 297–313. Springer, Cham (2018). https://doi.org/10.1007/978-3-030-01219-9_18
56. Zou, Y., et al.: PseudoSeg: designing pseudo labels for semantic segmentation. ArXiv:2010.09713 (2020)

Panoptic-PartFormer: Learning a Unified Model for Panoptic Part Segmentation

Xiangtai Li[1], Shilin Xu[1], Yibo Yang[1,3], Guangliang Cheng[2(✉)],
Yunhai Tong[1(✉)], and Dacheng Tao[3]

[1] Key Laboratory of Machine Perception, MOE, School of Artificial Intelligence,
Peking University, Beijing, China
lxtpku@pku.edu.cu, xushilin@stu.pku.edu.cn
[2] SenseTime Research, Hong Kong, China
chengguangliang@sensetime.com
[3] JD Explore Academy, Beijing, China

Abstract. Panoptic Part Segmentation (PPS) aims to unify panoptic segmentation and part segmentation into one task. Previous work mainly utilizes separated approaches to handle thing, stuff, and part predictions individually without performing any shared computation and task association. In this work, we aim to unify these tasks at the architectural level, designing the first end-to-end unified method named Panoptic-PartFormer. In particular, motivated by the recent progress in Vision Transformer, we model things, stuff, and part as object queries and directly learn to optimize the all three predictions as unified mask prediction and classification problem. We design a decoupled decoder to generate part feature and thing/stuff feature respectively. Then we propose to utilize all the queries and corresponding features to perform reasoning jointly and iteratively. The final mask can be obtained via inner product between queries and the corresponding features. The extensive ablation studies and analysis prove the effectiveness of our framework. Our Panoptic-PartFormer achieves the new state-of-the-art results on both Cityscapes PPS and Pascal Context PPS datasets with around 70% GFlops and 50% parameters decrease. Given its effectiveness and conceptual simplicity, we hope the Panoptic-PartFormer can serve as a strong baseline and aid future research in PPS. Our code and models will be available at https://github.com/lxtGH/Panoptic-PartFormer.

Keywords: Panoptic Part Segmentation · Scene understanding · Vision Transformer

Supplementary Information The online version contains supplementary material available at https://doi.org/10.1007/978-3-031-19812-0_42.

1   Introduction

One essential problem in computer vision is to understand a scene at multiple levels of concept. In particular, when people perceive a scene, they can catch each visual entities such as car, bus, or person, and they can also understand the parts of entities, such as person-head and car-wheel, etc. The former is named as scene parsing, while the latter is termed as part parsing. One representative direction of unified scene parsing is Panoptic Segmentation (PS) [22,23]. It predicts a class label and an instance ID for each pixel. The part parsing has a wide range of definitions, such as human part or car part [14,33]. Both directions are independent, while both are equally important for many vision systems, including auto-driving and robot navigation [8].

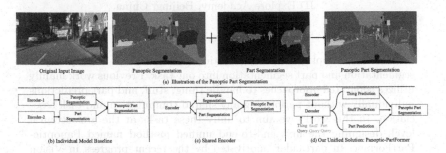

Fig. 1. Illustration of Panoptic Part Segmentation (PPS) and different Approaches for solving such PPS task. (a) An illustration of the Panoptic Part Segmentation task. It combines the Panoptic Segmentation and Part Segmentation in a unified manner that provides the multi-level concept understanding of the scene (b) The baseline method proposed in [15] combines results of panoptic segmentation and part segmentation. (c) Panoptic-FPN-like baseline [22,29,64] adds part segmentation into the current panoptic segmentation frameworks. (d) Our proposed approach represents things, stuff, and part via object queries and performs joint learning. Best view in color. (Color figure online)

Recently, the Panoptic Part Segmentation (PPS, or called Part-aware Panoptic Segmentation) [15] is proposed to unify these multiple levels of abstraction into one single task. As shown in Fig. 1(a), it requires a model to output per-pixel scene-level classification for background stuff, segment things into individual instances and segment each instance into specific parts. Several baselines using combined approaches [18,73,75] were proposed to tackle this task. As shown in Fig. 1(a), they fuse different individual model predictions to obtain PPS results. In particular, they fuse the panoptic segmentation and part segmentation results from the non-shared backbone networks. This makes the entire process exceptionally complex with huge engineering efforts. Also, the shared computation and task association are ignored, which leads to inferior results. Another solution for this task is to make the part segmentation as an extra head with shared backbone as shown in Fig. 1(b). Such design is well explored in PS studies [4,5,22,25,31,47,58,63,64,68]. However, most of them treat PS as separated tasks [64] or sequential tasks with several post processing components [5].

Since Detection Transformer (DETR) [1], there are several works [6,57,72] unifying both thing and stuff learning via *object queries* in PS, which makes the entire pipeline elegant and achieves strong results where the mask classification and prediction can be performed directly. These results show that many complex components including NMS and box detection can be removed. In particular, such design considers the full scene understanding via performing interactions among things, stuff, and part simultaneously. Joint training with things, stuff, and part leads to better part segmentation results since the full scene information renders part representation a more discriminative information such as global context. Motivated by these analysis, we take a further step on the more challenging PPS task and propose the **first unified model** for this task.

In this paper, we present a simple yet effective baseline named Panopic-PartFormer, a unified model for PPS task. As shown in Fig. 1(c), we introduce three different types of queries for modeling thing, stuff, and part prediction, respectively. Then a decoupled decoder is proposed to generate fine-grained features. These features are used to decode thing, stuff, and part mask prediction. The decoupled decoder contains a part decoder and a scene decoder. For part decoder, we design a feature aligned decoder to keep more fine details in part. Rather than directly using the pixel-level self-attention in Transformer, we consider the recent works [52,72] that perform self-attention on query level. To be more specific, we focus on refining queries via their corresponding query features. We define the *query feature* as *grouped features* that are generated from the *corresponding mask* of each query and *decoder features*. The masks are generated via dot product between queries and decoder features. In particular, the initial query features are grouped via the initial mask prediction from the decoupled decoder. Then we perform updating object queries with the query features. This operation is implemented with one dynamic convolution [52,72] and multi-head self-attention layers [56] between query and query features iteratively. The former poses instance-wise information from feature to enhance the query learning where the parameters are generated by the features itself while the latter performs inner reasoning among different types of queries to model the relationship among thing, stuff, and part. Moreover, the entire procedure avoids pixel-level computation in other vision Transformer decoder [1,6]. In this way, since all thing, stuff, and part information is encoded into query, the relation between these queries can be well explored and optimized jointly via pure mask based supervison. Extensive experiments (Sect. 4) show that our approach achieves much better results than the previous design in Fig. 1(b).

Moreover, our Panopic-PartFormer can support both CNN backbones [19] and Transformer backbones [39] for feature extraction. Panopic-PartFormer is also memory and computation efficient, which is mainly benefited by avoiding pixel-level computation of self-attention layers. Panopic-PartFormer can directly output thing, stuff, and part segmentation predictions in box-free and NMS-free manner. It can also be evaluated by sub-task of PPS such as Panoptic Segmentation. In the experiment part, we verify our panoptic segmentation predictions on Cityscaeps datasets [8] and it also achieves better results than the recent works [31]. To sum up, our main contributions are as follows:

- We present a novel, simple and effective baseline named Panopic-PartFormer for the PPS task. To the best of our knowledge, it is the first unified end-to-end model for this task.
- We propose a decoupled decoder and a joint query updating and reasoning framework for the joint feature learning of thing, stuff, and part. Besides, a joint loss function is proposed to supervise the whole model.
- Extensive experiments and analyses indicate the effectiveness and generalization of our model. In particular, with our framework, we find the part segmentation can be improved significantly via joint training. We achieve the new state-of-the-art results on two challenging PPS benchmarks including Pascal Context PPS dataset (about 6–7% PartPQ gain on ResNet101, 10% PartPQ gain using swin Transformer [39]) and Cityscapes PPS dataset (about 1–2% PartPQ gain).

2   Related Work

Part Segmentation. Most previous approaches for both instance and semantic part segmentation mainly focus on human analysis [48,51]. Several works [11, 38,60] design specific methods for semantic part segmentation which are in category-level settings. There are two paradigms for human part segmentation: *top-down* pipelines [21,26,50,65,66] and *bottom-up* pipelines [17,24,74,76]. Meanwhile, there are also several works focusing on task-specific part segmentation [34,42,75]. Compared with these methods, the focus of this paper is to solve the PPS task which naturally contains the part segmentation as a sub-task.

Panoptic Segmentation. Earlier work [23] mainly performs segmentation for things and stuff via separated networks where the original benchmark directly combines predictions of things and stuff from different models. To alleviate the computation cost, recent works [4,22,25,29,47,63,68] are proposed to model both stuff segmentation and thing segmentation in one model with different task heads. Detection based methods [20,22,49,64] usually represent things with the box prediction while several bottom-up models [5,13,58,67] perform grouping instance via pixel-level affinity or center heat maps from semantic segmentation results. The former introduces complex process while the latter suffers from the performance drops in complex scenarios. Recently, several works [6,57,72] propose to directly obtain segmentation masks without box supervision. However, these works do *not* cover the *knowledge of part-level semantics* of images which can provide more comprehensive information for scene understanding.

Panoptic Part Segmentation. To better understand the full scene, the PPS task [15] is proposed. This work annotates two datasets (Cityscape PPS [8] and Pascal Context PPS [10]) and proposes a new metric named PartPQ [15] for evaluation. This work also presents several baseline methods to obtain the final results. However, these methods are all separated networks for instance

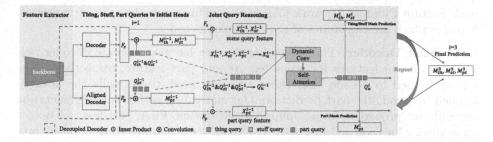

Fig. 2. Our proposed Panoptic-PartFormer. It contains three parts: (1) a backbone to extract features (Red area) (b) a decoupled decoder to generate scene features and part features along with the initial prediction heads to generate initial mask predictions. (Yellow area) (c) a cascaded Transformer decoder to jointly do reasoning between the query and query features. (Green area) Green arrows mean input (come from previous stage) while Red arrows represent current stage output (used for next stage). $i = 3$ is the final mask outputs. (Color figure online)

and semantic segmentation to obtain the panoptic segmentation or use existing panoptic segmentation algorithms with part semantic segmentation as an isolated sub-network (shown in Fig. 1(a) and (b)). For the comparison, our goal is to design a unified and effective network for all the tasks.

Vision Transformer. There are mainly two different usages for Transformer in vision: feature extractor and query modeling. Compared with CNN, vision Transformers [9,39,55] have more advantages in modeling global-range relation among the image patch features. The second design is to use the object query representation. DETR [1] models the object detection task as a set prediction problem with learnable queries. The following works [52,78] explore the locality of the learning process to improve the performance of DETR. Query based learning can also be applied to other fields [12,41]. Our methods are inspired by these works with the goal of unifying and simplifying the PPS task based on query learning.

3   Method

3.1   Basic Architecture

Figure 2 presents an overall illustration of the proposed method. Our method contains three parts: (1) an encoder backbone to extract features; (2) a decoupled decoder to obtain the scene features and part features individually. We denote the scene features are used to generate things, stuff masks while the part features are used to generate part masks; (3) a Transformer decoder which takes three different types of queries and backbone features as inputs and provides thing, stuff, and part mask predictions.

Encoder Network: We first extract image features for each input image. It contains a backbone network (Convolution Network [19] or Vision Transformer [39]) with Feature Pyramid Network [35] as neck. This results in a set of multiscale features which are the inputs of the decoupled decoder.

Decoupled Decoder: The decoupled decoder has two separate decoder networks to obtain features for scene feature and part feature, respectively. The former is used to decode both thing and stuff predictions, while the latter is applied to decode the part prediction. Our motivation is that part segmentation has different properties from panoptic segmentation. First, part features need a more precise location and fine details. Second, scene features focus on mask proposal level prediction while part features pay more attention to the inner parts of mask proposal, which conflicts with each other. We show that the decoupled design leads to better results in the experimental section. (see Sect. 4.2).

For implementation, we adopt semantic FPN design [22] to fuse features in a top-down manner. Thus, we obtain the two features named F_s and F_p. In particular, for part segmentation, we design a light-weight aligned feature decoder for part segmentation. Rather than the naive bilinear upsampling, we propose to learn feature flow [28,76] to warp the low resolution feature to high resolution feature. Then we sum all the predictions into the highest resolution as semantic FPN. Moreover, to preserve more locational information, we add the positional embedding to each stage of the semantic FPN following the previous works [61,62]. In summary, decoupled decoder outputs two separate features: scene features F_s and part features F_p. The former is used to generate thing and stuff masks while the latter is used to generate part masks and both have the same resolution.

3.2 Thing, Stuff, and Part as Queries with Initial Head Prediction

Previous works [6,57,72] show that single mask classification and prediction can achieve the state-of-the-art results on COCO [37]. Motivated by this, our model treats thing, stuff, and part as the input queries to directly obtain the final panoptic part segmentation. Following previous works [52,72], the initial weights of these queries are directly obtained from the first stage weights of the initial decoupled decoder prediction. For mask predictions of thing, stuff, and part, we use three 1×1 convolution layers to obtain the initial outputs of thing, stuff, and part masks. These layers are appended at the end of the decoupled decoder.

All these predictions are directly supervised with corresponding ground truth masks. As shown in [52,72], using such initial heads can avoid heavier Transformer encoder layers for pixel-level computation, since the corresponding query features can be obtained via mask grouping from the initial mask prediction.

In this way, we obtain the three different queries for thing, stuff, and part along with their initial mask prediction. We term them as Q_{th}, Q_{st}, Q_{pt} and M_{th}, M_{st}, M_{pt} with shapes $N_{th} \times d$, $N_{st} \times d$, $N_{pt} \times d$ and shapes $N_{th} \times H \times W$, $N_{st} \times H \times W$, $N_{pt} \times H \times W$. d, W, H are the channel number, width, height of feature F_p and F_s. N_{th}, N_{st}, N_{pt} are numbers of categories for thing, stuff, and part classification.

3.3   Joint Thing, Stuff, and Part Query Reasoning

The cascaded Transformer decoder takes previous mask predictions, previous object queries and decoupled features as inputs and outputs the current refined mask predictions and object queries. The refined mask predictions and object queries along with decoupled features will be the inputs of the next stage. The relationship between queries and query features is jointly learned and reasoned.

Our key insights are: Firstly, joint learning can learn the full correlation between scene features and part features. For example, car parts must be on the road rather than in the sky. Secondly, joint reasoning can avoid several scene noisy cases, such as car parts on the human body or human parts on the car. We find joint learning leads to better results (see Sect. 4.2).

We combine the three queries and the three mask predictions into a unified query Q_u^{i-1} and M_u^{i-1} where $Q_u^{i-1} = concat(Q_{th}, Q_{st}, Q_{pt})$, $Q_u^{i-1} \in R^{(N_{th}+N_{st}+N_{pt}) \times d}$ and $M_u^{i-1} = concat(M_{th}^{i-1}, M_{st}^{i-1}, M_{pt}^{i-1})$, $M_u^{i-1} \in R^{(N_{th}+N_{st}+N_{pt}) \times H \times W}$. i is the stage index of our Transformer decoder. $i = 1$ means the predictions come from the initial heads. Otherwise, it means predictions from the outputs of previous stage. $concat$ is preformed along the first dimension.

In particular, following the previous work [72], we first obtained query features X^i via grouping from previous mask predictions M_u^{i-1} and input features (F_p, F_s) shown in Eq. 1 (dot product in Fig. 2). We present this process in one formulation for simplicity.

$$X^i = \sum_u^W \sum_v^H M^{i-1}(u, v) \cdot F(u, v), \tag{1}$$

where $X^i \in R^{(N_{th}+N_{st}+N_{pt}) \times d}$ is the per-instance extracted feature with the same shape as Q_u, M^{i-1} is the per-instance mask extracted from the previous stage $i - 1$, and F is the input feature extracted for the decoupled decoder head. u, v are the indices of spatial location. i is layer number and starts from 1. As shown in center part of Fig 2, the part mask prediction and scene mask prediction are applied on corresponding features (F_p, F_s) individually where we obtain part query features X_{pt}^i and scene query features X_{th}^i and X_{st}^i. Then we combine these query features through $X_u^i = concat(X_{th}^i, X_{st}^i, X_{pt}^i)$. These inputs are shown in the green arrows in Fig. 2.

Then we perform a dynamic convolution [52,54,72] to refine input queries Q_u^{i-1} with the query features X_u^i which are grouped from their masks.

$$\hat{Q}_u^{i-1} = DynamicConv(X_u^i, Q_u^{i-1}), \tag{2}$$

where the dynamic convolution uses the query features X_u^i to generate parameters to weight input queries Q_u^{i-1}. To be more specific, $DynamicConv$ uses input query features X_u^i to generate gating parameters via MLP and multiply back to the original query input Q_u^{i-1}. Our motivation has two folds: Compared with pixel-wise MHSA [1,6], dynamic convolution introduces less computation and faster convergence for limited computation. Secondly, it poses the instance-wised information to each query dynamically during training and inference, which shows better generalization and has complementary effects with MHSA. More details can be found in Sect. 4.2.

This operation absorbs more fine-grained information to help query look for more precise location.

In particular, we adopt the same design [72] by learning gating functions to update the refined queries. The *DynamicConv* operation is shown as follows:

$$\hat{Q}_u^{i-1} = Gate_x(X_u^i)X_u^i + Gate_q(X_u^i)Q_u^{i-1}, \tag{3}$$

where *Gate* is implemented with a fully connected (FC) layers followed by Layer-Norm (LN), and a sigmoid layer. We adopt two different gate functions including $Gate_x$ and $Gate_q$. The former is to weight the query features, while the latter is to weight corresponding queries.

After that, we adopt one self-attention layer with feed forward layers [56,57] to learn the correspondence among each query and update them accordingly. This operation leads to the full correlation among queries, shown as follows:

$$Q_u^i = FFN(MHSA(\hat{Q}_u^{i-1}) + \hat{Q}_u^{i-1}), \tag{4}$$

where $MHSA$ means Multi Head Self Attention, FFN is the Feed Forward Network that is commonly used in current vision Transformers [1,9]. The output refined query has the same shape as the input, i.e. $Q_u^i \in \mathbf{R}^{(N_{th}+N_{st}+N_{pt}) \times d}$.

Finally, the refined masks are obtained via dot product between the refined queries Q_u^i and the input features F_p, F_s. For mask classification, we adopt several feed forward layers on Q_u^i and directly output the class scores (thing, stuff, and part). For mask prediction, we also adopt several feed forward layers on Q_u^i and then we perform the inner product between learned queries and features (F_s F_p) to generate scene masks (thing and stuff) and part masks of stage i. These masks will be used for the next stage input as shown in the red arrows in Fig. 2. The process of Eqs. 1, 2 and 4 will be repeated for several times. We set the iteration number to 3 by default. The inter mask predictions are also optimized by mask supervision.

Discussion. We admit that we use the dynamic convolution and self-attention among queries that are proposed by [52,72]. However, we **do not claim** this is our contribution for Panoptic-PartFormer. Our main contribution is a system level unified model for this challenging task(PPS) and we are the first work to prove that joint learning of the thing, stuff and part learning benefits PPS tasks than many other designs. More details can be found in supplementary.

3.4 Training and Inference

Training: To train the Panoptic-PartFormer, we need to assign ground truth according to the pre-defined cost since all the outputs are encoded via queries. In particular, we mainly follow the design of [6] to use bipartite matching as a cost by considering both mask and classification results. After the bipartite matching, we apply a loss jointly considering mask prediction and classification for each thing, stuff, and part. In particular, we apply focal loss [36] on both classification and mask prediction. We also adopt dice loss [43] on mask predictions (L_{part}, L_{thing}, L_{stuff}). Such settings are *the same as previous works* [1,6]. The loss for each stage i can be formulated as follows:

$$\mathcal{L}_i = \lambda_{part} \cdot \mathcal{L}_{part} + \lambda_{thing} \cdot \mathcal{L}_{thing} + \lambda_{stuff} \cdot \mathcal{L}_{stuff} + \lambda_{cls} \cdot \mathcal{L}_{cls} \qquad (5)$$

Note that the losses are applied to each stage $\mathcal{L}_{final} = \sum_i^N \mathcal{L}_i$, where N is the total stages applied to the framework. We adopt $N = 3$ and all λs are set to 1 by default.

Table 1. Experiment Results on CPP. Previous works combine results from commonly used (top), and state-of-the-art methods (bottom) for semantic segmentation, instance segmentation, panoptic segmentation and part segmentation. Metrics split into P and NP are evaluated on scene-level classes with and without parts, respectively.

Panoptic seg. method	Part seg. method	PQ			PartPQ		
		All	P	NP	All	P	NP
Cityscapes Panoptic Parts validation set							
UPSNet [64](ResNet50)	DeepLabv3+ [3] (ResNet50)	59.1	57.3	59.7	55.1	42.3	59.7
DeepLabv3+(ResNet50) & Mask R-CNN(ResNet50) [18]	DeepLabv3+ [3] (Xception- 65)	61.0	58.7	61.9	56.9	43.0	61.9
Panoptic-PartFormer (ResNet50)		**61.6**	**60.0**	**62.2**	**57.4**	**43.9**	**62.2**
EfficientPS [45](EfficientNet) [53]	BSANet [75] (ResNet101)	65.0	64.2	65.2	60.2	**46.1**	65.2
HRNet-OCR (HRNetv2-W48) [59,70] & PolyTransform [32]	BSANet [75] (ResNet101)	66.2	64.2	67.0	61.4	45.8	67.0
Panoptic-PartFormer (Swin-base)		**66.6**	**65.1**	**67.2**	**61.9**	45.6	**68.0**

Inference: We directly get the output masks from the corresponding queries according to their sorted scores. To obtain the final panoptic part segmentation, we first obtain the panoptic segmetnation results and then merge part masks into panoptic segmentation results. For panoptic segmentation results, we adopt the method used in Panoptic-FPN [22] to merge panoptic mask. For part merging process, we follow the original PPS task to obtain the final panoptic part segmentation results. For scene-level semantic classes that do not have part classes, we simply copy the predictions from panoptic segmentation. For predicted instances with the part, we extract the part predictions for the pixels corresponding to this segment. Otherwise, if a part prediction contains a part class that does not correspond to the scene-level class, we set it to *void* label. This setting mainly follows the previous work [15].

4   Experiment

Datasets. We mainly carry out experiments on two datasets including Cityscapes Panoptic Parts (CPP) and PASCAL Panoptic Parts (PPP), which are based on the established scene understanding datasets Cityscapes [8] and PASCAL VOC [10], respectively. The CPP extends with part-level semantics the Cityscapes dataset [8] and is annotated with 23 part-level semantic classes. In particular, 5 scene-level semantic classes from the human and vehicle high-level categories are annotated with parts. The CPP contains 2975 training and 500 validation images. PPP extends the PASCAL VOC 2010 benchmark [10] with part-level and scene-level semantics. PPP has 4998 training and 5105 validation images. To perform fair comparison, following previous settings [10,15], we perform experiments 59 scene-level classes (20 things, 39 stuff), and 57 part classes. We further report Cityscapes Panoptic Segmentation validation set [8] results as sub-task comparison.

Experiment Settings. ResNet [19] and Swin Transformer [39] are adopted as the backbone networks and other layers use Xavier initialization [16]. The optimizer is AdamW [40] with weight decay 0.0001. The training batch size is set to 16 and all models are trained with 8 GPUs. For PPP datasets, we first pretrain our model on COCO dataset [37] since most previous baselines [15] are pretrained on COCO. For PPP dataset, we adopt the multiscale training [1] by resizing the input images from the scale 0.5 to scale 2.0. We also apply random crop augmentations during training, where the train images are cropped with probability 0.5. For CPP dataset, we follow the similar setting in Panoptic-Deeplab [5] where we resize the images with scale rang from 0.5 to 2.0 and randomly crop the whole image during training with batch size 16. All the results are obtained via single scale inference.

Metric. We report PartPQ [15] and PQ [23] as the main metrics, since PartPQ is a unified metric that contain both scene-level output and part-level output. Part segmentation results such as mIoU can be found in the appendix file. The PartPQ per scene-level class l is formalized as PartPQ $= \frac{\sum_{(p,g) \in TP} \text{IOU}_p(p,g)}{|TP| + \frac{1}{2}|FP| + \frac{1}{2}|FN|}$. TP is true positive, FP is false positive, and FN is false negative segments, receptively. The definition of these is based on the Intersection Over Union (IOU) between a predicted segment p and a ground-truth segment g for a class l (where $l \in \mathcal{L}$, $\mathcal{L}$ is the label set). A prediction is a TP if it has an overlap with a ground-truth segment with an IOU > 0.5. An FP is a predicted segment that is not matched with the ground-truth, and an FN is a ground-truth segment not matched with a prediction. IOU contains two cases (part and non-part):

$$\text{IOU}_p(p,g) = \begin{cases} \text{mean IOU}_{part}(p,g), & l \in \mathcal{L}^{\text{parts}} \\ \text{IOU}_{inst}(p,g), & l \in \mathcal{L}^{\text{no-parts}} \end{cases}$$

4.1   Main Results

Results on Cityscape Panoptic Part Dataset. In Table 1, we compare our Panoptic-PartFormer with previous baselines. All the models use the single scale inference without test time augmentation. Our method with ResNe50 backbone achieves 57.4% PartPQ which outperforms the previous work using complex pipelines [3,18] with even stronger backbone [7]. For the same backbone, our method results in 2.3% PartPQ gain over the previous baseline. For large model comparison, our method with Swin-Transformer achieves 61.9 %PartPQ. It outperforms previous works that use state-of-the-art individual models [32,59,70,75] by 0.5%. Note that the best model from HRNet [70] is pretrained using Mapillary dataset [46]. We follow the same pipeline for fair comparison. Both settings prove the effectiveness of our approaches.

GFlops and Parameter Comparison. Since our method is one single unified model, our Panoptic-PartFormer has advantages on both GFlops and Parameters. Since the work [32] is not public available, we estimate the lower bound by its baseline model [18]. As shown in Table 2, our model obtain around 60% GFlops drop and 70% parameter drop.

Results on Pascal Panoptic Part Dataset. We further compare our method with previous work on the Pascal Panoptic Part dataset in Table 3. For different settings, our methods achieve state-of-the-art results on both PQ and PartPQ with a very significant gain. For ResNet backbone, our methods achieve **6–7% gains** on PartPQ. Moreover, our resnet101 model can achieve better results than previous work using *larger* backbone [49]. Using Swin Transformer base as backbone [39], our method achieves **47.4% PartPQ** which shows the generalization ability on large model.

Results on Cityscapes Panoptic Segmentation. We also compare our method with several previous works on cityscapes panoptic validation set. As shown in Table 5, our Panoptic-PartFormer also achieves state-of-the-art results compared with previous works [5,31]. This proves the generalization ability of our framework.

Table 2. More detailed comparison on Cityscapes PPS dataset. GFlops are measured with 1200 × 800 input.

Method	PQ	PartPQ	Param(M)	GFlops
UPSNet + DeepLabv3+ (ResNet50)	59.1	55.1	>87	>890
Panoptic-PartFormer (ResNet50)	**61.6**	**57.4**	**37.35**	**185.84**
HRNet(OCR) +PolyTransform + BSANet	66.2	61.4	>181	>1154
Panoptic-PartFormer (Swin-base)	**66.6**	**61.9**	**100.32**	**408.52**

Table 3. Experiment Results on PPP dataset. All the methods use single scale inference.

Panoptic seg. method	Part seg. method	PQ	PartPQ
Pascal Panoptic Parts validation set			
DeepLabv3+ & Mask R-CNN [18](ResNet50)	DeepLabv3+ [3](ResNet50)	35.0	31.4
DLv3-ResNeSt269 [71] & DetectoRS [49]	BSANet [75]	42.0	38.3
Our unified approach			
Panoptic PartFormer (ResNet50)		**47.6**	**37.8**
Panoptic PartFormer (ResNet101)		**49.2**	**39.3**

Table 4. Ablation studies and analysis on Cityscapes Panoptic Part validation set with ResNet50 as backbone. Best view it in color.

DD	DC	SA	I=1	I=3	PQ	PartPQ
✓	✓	✓	-	✓	61.6	57.4
-	✓	✓	-	✓	61.2	55.9
✓	-	✓	-	✓	57.0	52.2
✓	✓	-	-	✓	57.3	53.4
✓	✓	✓	✓	-	58.3	54.2

(a) Effect of each component. DD: Decoupled Decoder. DC: Dynamic Convolution. SA: Self Attention. I: Interaction number.

Setting	PQ	PartPQ
Joint Reasoning	61.6	57.4
Separate Reasoning	61.1	56.8
Sequential Reasoning	60.8	56.3

(b) Ablation on Query Reasoning Design

Method	PQ	PartPQ
Joint Query	61.6	57.4
DP-Based	59.8	55.9
DP-Based w ASPP [2]	59.9	56.1

(c) Dense Prediction or Query Prediction on Part. DP: Dense Prediction. w: with. ASPP: Atrous Spatial Pyramid Pooling [2].

Settings	PQ	PartPQ	P	NP
w Aligned Part Decoder	61.6	57.4	43.9	62.2
w/o Aligned Part Decoder	61.4	56.3	41.2	62.1
Aligned Part Decoder on Both Features	61.4	57.2	43.7	62.0

(d) Effect of Aligned Decoder Design.

Setting	Panoptic-GT	Part-GT	PartPQ	P
baseline	-	-	57.4	43.9
	-	✓	61.6	56.1
	✓	-	88.4	56.4

(e) Upper bound Analysis. GT: Ground Truth

4.2 Ablation Study and Model Design

In this section, we present ablation study and several model designs of our Panoptic-PartFormer.

Effectiveness of Each Component. As shown in Table 4a, we start with the effectiveness of each component of our framework by removing it from the original design. Removing Decoupled Decoder (DD) results in a 1.4 % drop on PartPQ. Removing Dynamic Convolution (DC) or Self Attention (SA) results in a large drop on PQ which means both are important for the interaction between queries and corresponding query features. Decreasing stage number to 1 also leads to a significant drop. Performing more interaction results in more accurate feature location for each query, which is the same as previous works [52,72].

Whether the part query depends more on thing query? With our framework, we can easily analyze the relationship among stuff query, thing query, and part query. We present several ways of reasoning and fusing different queries. From intuitive thought, part information is more related to thing query. We design two different query interaction methods, shown in Tab 4b. For separate reasoning, we adopt DD and SA on two query pairs, including stuff-thing query

Table 5. **Experiment Results on Cityscapes Panoptic validation set.** * indicates using DCN [77].

Method	Backbone	PQ	PQ_{th}	PQ_{st}
Panoptic FPN [22]	ResNet101	58.1	52.0	62.5
UPSNet [64]	ResNet50	59.3	54.6	62.7
SOGNet [68]	ResNet50	60.0	56.7	62.5
Seamless [47]	ResNet50	60.2	55.6	63.6
Unifying [27]	ResNet50	61.4	54.7	66.3
Panoptic-DeepLab [5]	ResNet50	59.7	–	–
Panoptic FCN* [31]	ResNet50	61.4	54.8	66.6
Panoptic FCN++ [30]	Swin-large	64.1	55.6	70.2
Panoptic-PartFormer	ResNet50	61.6	54.9	66.8
Panoptic-PartFormer	Swin-base	66.6	61.7	70.3

Table 6. More analysis using our Panoptic-PartFormer.

Method	PQ	PartPQ
baseline	61.6	57.4
w/o positional encoding	59.0	55.1

(a) Effect on Position Encoding.

Method	PQ	PartPQ
baseline	61.6	57.4
+ boundary loss	61.5	57.2

(b) Effect of adding boundary supervision

Method	PQ	PartPQ
things and stuff only	61.2	-
+ part annotation (ours)	61.6	57.4

(c) Effect on adding part annotations.

and thing-part query. For sequential reasoning, we perform DD and SA with thing-part query first and stuff-thing query second. However, we find the best model is the joint reasoning, which is the default setting described in method part. We argue that better part segmentation needs the whole scene context rather than thing features only.

Choose Joint Query Modeling or Separate Modeling on Part? Following PanopticFPN settings [22], we also adopt semantic-FPN like model for part segmentation. Dense Prediction (DP) is the baseline method shown in Fig. 1(b). We adopt the same merging process for panoptic segmentation and part segmentation. As shown in Table 4c, our joint query based method achieves the better results and outperforms previous dense prediction based approach and its improved version [2]. This indicates that joint learning benefits part segmentation a lot, which proves the effectiveness of our framework.

Aligned Decoder is More Important for Part Segmentation. As shown in Table 4d, using aligned part decoder results in better PartPQ especially for the things with Part (P). Adding both paths with aligned decoder does not bring extra gain. This verifies our motivation: part segmentation needs more detailed information, while thing and stuff predictions do not need it.

Necessity of Positional Encoding on X_p and X_u. In Table 6a, removing positional encoding leads to inferior results on both PQ and PartPQ which indicates the importance of position information [1,62,72].

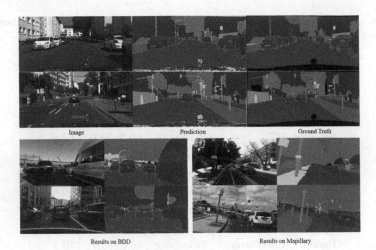

Fig. 3. Visualization of our Panoptic-PartFormer. Top: results on Cityscapes PPS validation set. Bottom left: prediction on BDD dataset [69]. Bottom right: prediction on Mapillary dataset [46]. Best view it on screen.

Will Boundary Supervision Help for Part Segmentation? In Table 6b, we also add boundary supervision for part segmentation where we use the dice loss [44] and binary cross entropy loss. However, we find no gains on this since our mask is generated from aligned decoder since it already contains detailed information.

Will Joint Training Help for Panoptic Segmentation? As shown in Table 6c, joint learning benefits the panoptic segmentation baseline. However, the benefit is *limited* since both thing and stuff prediction does not need much detailed information.

4.3 Analysis and Visualization

Visualization and Generalization. We give several visualization examples using our model on Cityscapes PPS validation set. Moreover, we also visualize several examples on the Mapillary dataset [46] and BDD dataset [69] to show the generalization ability of our method. As shown in the first row of Fig. 3, our method achieves considerable results. Moreover, on the Mapillary [46] and BDD datasets [69] which do not have part annotations, our method can still work well as shown in the last row of the Fig. 3. Moreover, we also visualize the results on PPP datasets. The first two rows show the crowded human scene and outdoor scene. Both cases show that our model can obtain the convincing results. The last row shows the small objects cases. The failure cases are due to tiny objects including their parts.

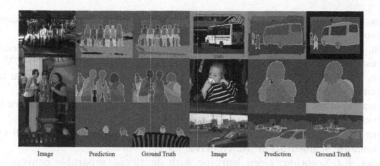

Image   Prediction   Ground Truth   Image   Prediction   Ground Truth

Fig. 4. More visualization results on Pascal Context Panoptic Part validation set. Best viewed in color and by zooming in. Note that stuff classes have the same color, while thing classes are not.

Upper Bound Analysis of Our Model. In Table 4e, we give the upper bound analysis to our model by replacing the panoptic segmentation Ground Truth or part segmentation Ground Truth into our prediction. Replacing panoptic segmentation GT leads to a huge gain on PartPQ while replacing part segmentation only results in a limited gain. That indicates PartPQ is more *sensitive to panoptic segmentationt than part segmentation on CPP dataset*. We conclude that a stronger panoptic segmentation model maybe the key for better PPS results.

5 Conclusion

In this work, we present Panoptic-PartFormer, the first unified end-to-end model for Panoptic Part Segmentation. We present a decoupled decoder with three different queries to generate thing, stuff and part masks at the same time. We propose to jointly learn the three queries with corresponding query features. With this framework, we present detailed analysis of the relationship among things, stuff, and part. As a result, our method achieves the new state-of-the-art results on Cityscapes Panoptic PPS dataset and Pascal Contexct PPS dataset. Panoptic-PartFormer would serve as a unified baseline and benefit multiple level concepts scene understanding by easing the idea development.

Acknowledgement. This research is also supported by the National Key Research and Development Program of China under Grant No. 2020YFB2103402. We thank the computation resource provided by SenseTime Research.

References

1. Carion, N., Massa, F., Synnaeve, G., Usunier, N., Kirillov, A., Zagoruyko, S.: End-to-end object detection with transformers. In: Vedaldi, A., Bischof, H., Brox, T., Frahm, J.-M. (eds.) ECCV 2020. LNCS, vol. 12346, pp. 213–229. Springer, Cham (2020). https://doi.org/10.1007/978-3-030-58452-8_13

2. Chen, L.C., Papandreou, G., Schroff, F., Adam, H.: Rethinking atrous convolution for semantic image segmentation. arXiv:1706.05587 (2017)
3. Chen, L.C., Zhu, Y., Papandreou, G., Schroff, F., Adam, H.: Encoder-decoder with atrous separable convolution for semantic image segmentation. In: ECCV (2018)
4. Chen, Y., et al.: Banet: bidirectional aggregation network with occlusion handling for panoptic segmentation. In: CVPR (2020)
5. Cheng, B., et al.: Panoptic-deeplab: a simple, strong, and fast baseline for bottom-up panoptic segmentation. In: CVPR (2020)
6. Cheng, B., Schwing, A.G., Kirillov, A.: Per-pixel classification is not all you need for semantic segmentation. In: NeurIPS (2021)
7. Chollet, F.: Xception: Deep learning with depthwise separable convolutions. In: CVPR (2017)
8. Cordts, M., et al.: The cityscapes dataset for semantic urban scene understanding. In: CVPR (2016)
9. Dosovitskiy, A., et al.: An image is worth 16 x 16 words: transformers for image recognition at scale. arXiv preprint arXiv:2010.11929 (2020)
10. Everingham, M., Van Gool, L., Williams, C.K., Winn, J., Zisserman, A.: The pascal visual object classes (VOC) challenge. IJCV 88(2), 303–338 (2010)
11. Fang, H.S., et al.: Weakly and semi supervised human body part parsing via pose-guided knowledge transfer. In: CVPR (2018)
12. Fang, Y., et al.: Instances as queries. arXiv preprint arXiv:2105.01928 (2021)
13. Gao, N., et al.: SSAP: single-shot instance segmentation with affinity pyramid. In: ICCV (2019)
14. Geng, Q., et al.: Part-level car parsing and reconstruction in single street view images. IEEE Trans. Pattern Anal. Mach. Intell. 44(8), 4291–4305 (2021)
15. de Geus, D., Meletis, P., Lu, C., Wen, X., Dubbelman, G.: Part-aware panoptic segmentation. In: CVPR (2021)
16. Glorot, X., Bengio, Y.: Understanding the difficulty of training deep feedforward neural networks. In: Proceedings of the Thirteenth International Conference on Artificial Intelligence and Statistics, pp. 249–256. JMLR Workshop and Conference Proceedings (2010)
17. Gong, K., Liang, X., Li, Y., Chen, Y., Yang, M., Lin, L.: Instance-level human parsing via part grouping network. In: ECCV (2018)
18. He, K., Gkioxari, G., Dollár, P., Girshick, R.: Mask R-CNN. In: ICCV (2017)
19. He, K., Zhang, X., Ren, S., Sun, J.: Deep residual learning for image recognition. In: CVPR (2016)
20. Hou, R., et al.: Real-time panoptic segmentation from dense detections. In: CVPR (2020)
21. Ji, R., et al.: Learning semantic neural tree for human parsing. In: ECCV (2020)
22. Kirillov, A., Girshick, R., He, K., Dollár, P.: Panoptic feature pyramid networks. In: CVPR (2019)
23. Kirillov, A., He, K., Girshick, R., Rother, C., Dollár, P.: Panoptic segmentation. In: CVPR (2019)
24. Li, J., et al.: Multiple-human parsing in the wild. arXiv preprint arXiv:1705.07206 (2017)
25. Li, J., Raventos, A., Bhargava, A., Tagawa, T., Gaidon, A.: Learning to fuse things and stuff. arXiv:1812.01192 (2018)
26. Li, Q., Arnab, A., Torr, P.H.: Holistic, instance-level human parsing. arXiv preprint arXiv:1709.03612 (2017)
27. Li, Q., Qi, X., Torr, P.H.: Unifying training and inference for panoptic segmentation. In: CVPR (2020)

28. Li, X., et al.: Semantic flow for fast and accurate scene parsing. In: ECCV (2020)
29. Li, Y., et al.: Attention-guided unified network for panoptic segmentation. In: CVPR (2019)
30. Li, Y., et al.: Fully convolutional networks for panoptic segmentation with point-based supervision. arXiv preprint arXiv:2108.07682 (2021)
31. Li, Y., et al.: Fully convolutional networks for panoptic segmentation. In: CVPR (2021)
32. Liang, J., Homayounfar, N., Ma, W.C., Xiong, Y., Hu, R., Urtasun, R.: PolyTransform: deep polygon transformer for instance segmentation. In: CVPR (2020)
33. Liang, X., et al.: Human parsing with contextualized convolutional neural network. In: ICCV (2015)
34. Lin, J., Yang, H., Chen, D., Zeng, M., Wen, F., Yuan, L.: Face Parsing with RoI Tanh-Warping. In: CVPR (2019)
35. Lin, T.Y., Dollár, P., Girshick, R.B., He, K., Hariharan, B., Belongie, S.J.: Feature pyramid networks for object detection. In: CVPR (2017)
36. Lin, T.Y., Goyal, P., Girshick, R., He, K., Dollár, P.: Focal loss for dense object detection. In: ICCV (2017)
37. Lin, T.Y., et al.: Microsoft coco: Common objects in context. In: ECCV (2014)
38. Liu, S., et al.: Cross-domain human parsing via adversarial feature and label adaptation. In: AAAI (2018)
39. Liu, Z., et al.: Swin transformer: Hierarchical vision transformer using shifted windows. In: ICCV (2021)
40. Loshchilov, I., Hutter, F.: Decoupled weight decay regularization (2017)
41. Meinhardt, T., Kirillov, A., Leal-Taixe, L., Feichtenhofer, C.: TrackFormer: multi-object tracking with transformers. arXiv preprint arXiv:2101.02702 (2021)
42. Michieli, U., Borsato, E., Rossi, L., Zanuttigh, P.: GMNet: graph matching network for large scale part semantic segmentation in the wild. In: ECCV (2020)
43. Milletari, F., Navab, N., Ahmadi, S.: V-Net: fully convolutional neural networks for volumetric medical image segmentation. In: 3DV (2016)
44. Milletari, F., Navab, N., Ahmadi, S.A.: V-net: fully convolutional neural networks for volumetric medical image segmentation. In: 3DV (2016)
45. Mohan, R., Valada, A.: EfficientPS: efficient panoptic segmentation. Int. J. Comput. Vis. **129**(5), 1551–1579 (2021)
46. Neuhold, G., Ollmann, T., Rota Bulo, S., Kontschieder, P.: The mapillary vistas dataset for semantic understanding of street scenes. In: ICCV (2017)
47. Porzi, L., Bulo, S.R., Colovic, A., Kontschieder, P.: Seamless scene segmentation. In: CVPR (2019)
48. Qi, S., Wang, W., Jia, B., Shen, J., Zhu, S.C.: Learning human-object interactions by graph parsing neural networks. In: ECCV (2018)
49. Qiao, S., Chen, L.C., Yuille, A.: Detectors: Detecting objects with recursive feature pyramid and switchable atrous convolution. In: CVPR (2021)
50. Ruan, T., Liu, T., Huang, Z., Wei, Y., Wei, S., Zhao, Y.: Devil in the details: Towards accurate single and multiple human parsing. In: AAAI (2019)
51. Shen, Z., et al.: Human-aware motion deblurring. In: ICCV (2019)
52. Sun, P., et al.: Sparse R-CNN: end-to-end object detection with learnable proposals. In: CVPR (2021)
53. Tan, M., Le, Q.: EfficientNet: rethinking model scaling for convolutional neural networks. In: ICML, pp. 6105–6114. PMLR (2019)
54. Tian, Z., Shen, C., Chen, H.: Conditional convolutions for instance segmentation. arXiv preprint arXiv:2003.05664 (2020)

55. Touvron, H., Cord, M., Douze, M., Massa, F., Sablayrolles, A., Jégou, H.: Training data-efficient image transformers & distillation through attention. In: ICML, PMLR (2021)
56. Vaswani, A., et al.: Attention is all you need. arXiv preprint arXiv:1706.03762 (2017)
57. Wang, H., Zhu, Y., Adam, H., Yuille, A., Chen, L.C.: MaX-DeepLab: end-to-end panoptic segmentation with mask transformers. In: CVPR (2021)
58. Wang, H., Zhu, Y., Green, B., Adam, H., Yuille, A., Chen, L.-C.: Axial-DeepLab: stand-alone axial-attention for panoptic segmentation. In: Vedaldi, A., Bischof, H., Brox, T., Frahm, J.-M. (eds.) ECCV 2020. LNCS, vol. 12349, pp. 108–126. Springer, Cham (2020). https://doi.org/10.1007/978-3-030-58548-8_7
59. Wang, J., et al.: Deep high-resolution representation learning for visual recognition. In: PAMI (2020)
60. Wang, W., Zhang, Z., Qi, S., Shen, J., Pang, Y., Shao, L.: Learning compositional neural information fusion for human parsing. In: ICCV (2019)
61. Wang, X., Kong, T., Shen, C., Jiang, Y., Li, L.: SOLO: segmenting objects by locations. In: Vedaldi, A., Bischof, H., Brox, T., Frahm, J.-M. (eds.) ECCV 2020. LNCS, vol. 12363, pp. 649–665. Springer, Cham (2020). https://doi.org/10.1007/978-3-030-58523-5_38
62. Wang, X., Zhang, R., Kong, T., Li, L., Shen, C.: SOLOv2: dynamic and fast instance segmentation. In: NeurIPS (2020)
63. Wu, Y., Zhang, G., Xu, H., Liang, X., Lin, L.: Auto-panoptic: Cooperative multi-component architecture search for panoptic segmentation. In: NIPS (2020)
64. Xiong, Y., et al.: UPSNet: a unified panoptic segmentation network. In: CVPR (2019)
65. Yang, L., et al.: Renovating parsing R-CNN for accurate multiple human parsing. In: Vedaldi, A., Bischof, H., Brox, T., Frahm, J.-M. (eds.) ECCV 2020. LNCS, vol. 12357, pp. 421–437. Springer, Cham (2020). https://doi.org/10.1007/978-3-030-58610-2_25
66. Yang, L., Song, Q., Wang, Z., Jiang, M.: Parsing R-CNN for instance-level human analysis. In: CVPR (2019)
67. Yang, T.J., et al.: DeeperLab: single-shot image parser. arXiv:1902.05093 (2019)
68. Yang, Y., Li, H., Li, X., Zhao, Q., Wu, J., Lin, Z.: Sognet: Scene overlap graph network for panoptic segmentation. In: AAAI (2020)
69. Yu, F., et al.: Bdd100k: a diverse driving dataset for heterogeneous multitask learning. In: CVPR, pp. 2636–2645 (2020)
70. Yuan, Y., Chen, X., Wang, J.: Object-contextual representations for semantic segmentation. In: Vedaldi, A., Bischof, H., Brox, T., Frahm, J.-M. (eds.) ECCV 2020. LNCS, vol. 12351, pp. 173–190. Springer, Cham (2020). https://doi.org/10.1007/978-3-030-58539-6_11
71. Zhang, H., et al.: ResNeSt: split-attention networks. arXiv preprint arXiv:2004.08955 (2020)
72. Zhang, W., Pang, J., Chen, K., Loy, C.C.: K-net: towards unified image segmentation. In: NeurIPS (2021)
73. Zhao, H., Shi, J., Qi, X., Wang, X., Jia, J.: Pyramid scene parsing network. In: CVPR (2017)
74. Zhao, J., Li, J., Cheng, Y., Sim, T., Yan, S., Feng, J.: Understanding humans in crowded scenes: deep nested adversarial learning and a new benchmark for multi-human parsing. In: MM (2018)
75. Zhao, Y., Li, J., Zhang, Y., Tian, Y.: Multi-class part parsing with joint boundary-semantic awareness. In: ICCV (2019)

76. Zhou, T., Wang, W., Liu, S., Yang, Y., Van Gool, L.: Differentiable multi-granularity human representation learning for instance-aware human semantic parsing. In: CVPR (2021)
77. Zhu, X., Hu, H., Lin, S., Dai, J.: Deformable convnets v2: More deformable, better results. In: CVPR (2019)
78. Zhu, X., Su, W., Lu, L., Li, B., Wang, X., Dai, J.: Deformable DETR: deformable transformers for end-to-end object detection. In: ICLR (2020)

Author Index

Ang, Yi Zhe 178
Arandjelović, Relja 123
Ashok, Arjun 105

Bai, Lei 1
Bai, Xuyang 248
Balasubramanian, Vineeth N. 105
Bian, Yikai 565

Cai, Jianfei 197
Cao, Zhiguo 231
Carreira, João 123
Chang, Shih-Fu 69
Chen, Chen 676
Chen, Jingdong 266
Chen, Pei 340
Chen, Qianyu 409
Chen, Yuedong 197
Cheng, Guangliang 582, 729
Cheng, Yu 69
Chirikjian, Gregory S. 479
Chiu, Wei-Chen 710
Choe, Jaesung 620
Chua, Tat-Seng 409
Codella, Noel 69
Cohen, Scott 676

Dai, Angela 425
Deng, Youming 266
Ding, Changxing 444
Ding, Runyu 284
Dong, Bin 659

Fan, Bin 496
Fang, Guangchi 600
Fischer, Volker 88
Foo, Lin Geng 391
Fu, Hongbo 248
Fu, Hongtao 231

Gaidon, Adrien 549
Gao, Yan 19
Gao, Yang 161
Gu, Jiuxiang 374, 391

Guo, Yulan 600
Guo, Zujin 178

Han, Xiaoguang 340, 425
He, Mu 565
Hénaff, Olivier J. 123
Hou, Zhi 461
Howard-Jenkins, Henry 693
Hu, Qingyong 600
Hu, Zeyu 248
Huang, Shaoli 444
Hui, Le 565

Jaegle, Andrew 123
Ji, Wei 409
Jiang, Li 284
Jiao, Yang 19
Joseph, K. J. 105
Ju, Lili 357

Kitani, Kris M. 549
Koppula, Skanda 123
Kuen, Jason 374, 391, 676
Kweon, In So 620

Lee, Kuan-Hui 549
Leonardis, Aleš 600
Li, Hai 36
Li, Jun 214
Li, Kejie 197
Li, Runfa 322
Li, Xiang 214
Li, Xiangtai 582, 729
Li, Xueqian 144
Li, Yanchao 391
Li, Yansheng 266
Li, Zijian 444
Lim, Ser-Nam 304
Lin, Zhe 676
Liu, Frank 36
Liu, Haolin 340
Liu, Jun 374, 391
Liu, Weixiao 479
Liu, Wenze 231

Liu, Xian   197
Liu, Yingfei   531
Liu, Zhiyuan   409
Liu, Ziwei   178
Lu, Chia-Ni   710
Lu, Hao   231
Lucey, Simon   144

Ma, Jiayi   266
Markham, Andrew   600
McAllister, Rowan   549
Meng, Gaofeng   496
Moskalev, Artem   88

Nan, Junyu   549
Nguyen, Truong   322
Nguyen, Xuan Son   52
Ni, Bolin   496
Nie, Yinyu   425
Nießner, Matthias   425

Ouyang, Wanli   1

Pan, Chunhong   496
Park, Chunghyun   620
Park, Jaesik   620
Prisacariu, Victor Adrian   693

Qi, Lei   161
Qi, Xiaojuan   284
Qu, Haoxuan   374, 391

Ramasinghe, Sameera   144
Rameau, Francois   620
Ren, Jian   565
Rhinehart, Nicholas   549
Ruan, Sipu   479

Schwing, Alexander G.   641
Shelhamer, Evan   123
Shi, Yinghuan   161
Smeulders, Arnold   88
Sosnovik, Ivan   88
Sun, Guangyuan   248
Sun, Jian   531
Sun, Maosong   409
Sun, Yi   19

Tai, Chiew-Lan   248
Tang, Shixiang   1
Tao, Dacheng   461, 582, 729

Tian, Kun   496
Tong, Yunhai   582, 729
Torralba, Antonio   304
Trigoni, Niki   600
Tsai, Yi-Hsuan   710

Vineet, Vibhav   304

Wan, Jin   357
Wang, Chien-chih   19
Wang, Jian   266
Wang, Kun   214
Wang, Song   357
Wang, Tiancai   531, 659
Wang, Xin   248
Wei, Yichen   659
Weng, Xinshuo   549
Womble, David   36
Wu, Qianyi   197
Wu, Xinyi   357
Wu, Yuwei   479
Wu, Zhenyao   357

Xiang, Xiang   266
Xiao, Bin   69
Xie, Jin   565
Xie, Ning   19
Xu, Dan   514
Xu, Li   374
Xu, Mutian   340
Xu, Ruochen   69
Xu, Shilin   729
Xu, Xiaogang   304

Yan, Zhiqiang   214
Yang, Bo   600
Yang, Jian   214, 565
Yang, Jihan   284
Yang, Jingkang   178
Yang, Yibo   582, 729
Yao, Yuan   409
Ye, Hanrong   514
Yeats, Eric   36
Yen, Yu-Ting   710
You, Haoxuan   69
Yu, Baosheng   461
Yuan, Haobo   582
Yuan, Lu   69

Zeng, Fangao   659
Zhang, Ao   409
Zhang, Chenghao   496
Zhang, Jian   161
Zhang, Jing   582
Zhang, Lefei   582
Zhang, Runze   248
Zhang, Wayne   178
Zhang, Xiangyu   531, 659
Zhang, Yongjun   266
Zhang, Yuang   659
Zhang, Zhaoxiang   496
Zhang, Zhenyu   214
Zhang, Zhifei   676

Zhao, Hengshuang   304
Zhao, Rui   1
Zhao, Xiaoming   641
Zhao, Zhizhen   641
Zheng, Chuanxia   197
Zheng, Jianmin   197
Zheng, Jianqiao   144
Zhong, Xubin   444
Zhou, Kaiyang   178
Zhou, Luowei   69
Zhu, Feng   1
Zhu, Sijie   676
Zisserman, Andrew   123
Zoran, Daniel   123